ELECTRONIC COMMERCE 2002
A MANAGERIAL PERSPECTIVE

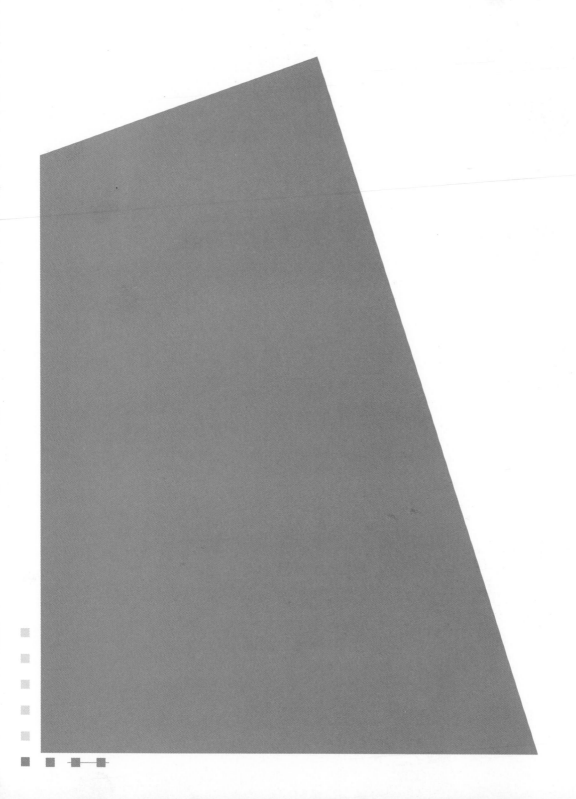

Electronic Commerce 2002

A MANAGERIAL PERSPECTIVE

Efraim Turban

City University of Hong Kong

David King

Comshare Inc.

Jae Lee

Korea Advanced Institute
of Science and Technology

Merrill Warkentin

Mississippi State University

H. Michael Chung

California State University at Long Beach

Prentice
Hall

Upper Saddle River, New Jersey 07458

Library of Congress Cataloging-in-Publication Data

Electronic commerce 2002 / Efraim Turban . . . [et al.].—2nd ed.
   p. cm.
   Rev. ed. of: Electronic commerce. 2000.
   Includes bibliographical references and index.
   ISBN 0-13-065301-2
      1. Electronic commerce.   2. Electronic commerce—Management.   3. Information
technology—Management.   4. Business enterprises—Computer networks.   I. Turban,
Efraim.   II. Electronic commerce.

HF5548.32.E34 2002
658.8′4—dc21

                                                                    2001036829

Executive Editor: Robert Horan
Senior Executive Editor: David Alexander
Publisher: Natalie Anderson
Project Manager: Lori Cerreto
Editorial Assistant: Maat VanUitert
Media Project Manager: Joan Waxman
Senior Marketing Manager: Sharon Turkovich
Marketing Assistant: Scott Patterson
Manager, Production: Gail Steier deAcevedo
Permissions Coordinator: Suzanne Grappi
Associate Director, Manufacturing: Vincent Scelta
Production Manager: April Montana
Manufacturing Buyer: Natacha St. Hill Moore
Design Manager: Pat Smythe
Interior Design: Setting Page
Cover Design: Joan O'Connor
Cover Illustration/Photo: John Bleck
Manager, Print Production: Christy Mahon
Composition: BookMasters, Inc.
Full-Service Project Management: BookMasters, Inc.
Printer/Binder: Courier/Kendallville

Printed in the United States of America
10 9 8 7 6 5 4 3

ISBN 0-13-065301-2

Pearson Education LTD
Pearson Education of Australia Pty. Limited, Sydney
Pearson Education (Singapore)Pte. Ltd.
Pearson Education North Asia Ltd
Pearson Education, Cancada, Ltd
Pearson Educación de Mexico, S.A. de C.V.
Pearson Education—Japan
Pearson Education Malaysia, Pte, Ltd
Pearson Education Upper Saddle River, New Jersey

Dedicated to all those who are interested in learning all about electronic commerce.

Contents in Brief

Contents

Preface

As we enter the third millennium, we experience one of the most important changes in our lives—the move to an Internet-based society. Almost everything is changed at home, in school, at work, in the government—even in our leisure activities. Some changes are already here, and they are spreading around the globe. Others are just beginning. One of the most significant changes is in the manner we conduct business, especially in how we manage the marketplaces and commerce.

Electronic commerce (EC) describes the manner in which transactions take place over networks, mostly the Internet. It is the process of electronically buying and selling goods, services, and information. Certain EC applications, such as buying and selling stocks on the Internet, is growing at a rate of several hundred percent every year. EC could have an impact on a significant portion of the world, on businesses, professions, and, of course, on people.

However, the impact of EC is not just the creation of Web-based corporations. It is the building of a new industrial order. Such a revolution brings a myriad of opportunities as well as risks. Bill Gates is aware of that, as Microsoft is continually developing Internet and EC products and services. Yet, Gates has said that Microsoft is always 2 years away from failure, that somewhere out there is a competitor, unborn and unknown, who will render your business model obsolete. Bill Gates knows that competition today is not among products, but among business models. He knows that irrelevancy is a bigger risk than inefficiency. What is true for Microsoft is true for just about every other company. The hottest and most dangerous new business models out there are on the Web.

The purpose of this book is to describe what EC is; how it is being conducted and managed; and its major opportunities, limitations, issues, and risks. EC is an interdisciplinary topic and, therefore, it should be of interest to managers and professional people in any functional area of the business world.

This new edition, the 2002 edition, is as different from the first edition as EC in 2002 is different from EC in 2000. Today, e-commerce is going through a period of consolidation, where instead of enthusiasm, careful attention is given to proper strategy and implementation. Most of all, people recognize that e-business has two parts, one of which is business, not just technology. These changes are reflected in the second edition.

In addition, people in government, education, health services, and other areas could benefit from learning about EC. This book is structured around the notion that EC applications, such as home banking, e-government, or auctions, require certain technological infrastructures and other support mechanisms. The applications are divided into business-to-consumer, business-to-business, and intrabusiness. The infrastructure is in the areas of hardware, networks, and software. The support services range from secured payment systems to logistics and legal issues.

This book is one of the first texts entirely dedicated to EC. It is written by experienced authors who share academic as well as real-world experiences, including an e-business lawyer. It is a comprehensive text that can be used in one-semester or even two-semester courses, or it can supplement a text on Internet fundamentals, on MIS, or on marketing.

FEATURES OF THIS EDITION

Several features are unique to this book. They include:

- **Managerial Orientation.** EC can be approached from two major aspects: technological and managerial. This text uses the second approach. Most of the presentations are about EC applications and implementation and are geared toward functional and general managers. However, we do recognize the importance of the technology; therefore, we present the essentials of system building and security in Chapters 12 and 13. We also provide some more detailed technology material in the appendices and on the book's Web site: www.prenhall.com/turban.

- **Interdisciplinary Approach.** EC is interdisciplinary and we illustrate this throughout the book. Major related disciplines are accounting, finance, information systems, marketing, management, and human resources management. In addition, some nonbusiness disciplines are related, especially public administration, computer science, engineering, psychology, political science, and the legal field. Finally, economics plays a major role in the understanding of EC.

- **Real-World Orientation.** Extensive, vivid examples from large corporations, small businesses, and government and not-for-profit agencies all over the world make concepts come alive by showing students the capabilities of EC, its cost and justification, and some of the innovative ways real corporations are using EC in their operations.

- **Solid Theoretical Background.** Throughout the book we present the theoretical foundations necessary for understanding EC, ranging from consumer behavior to economic theory of competition. Furthermore, we provide extensive references, Web site addresses, and many exercises to supplement the theoretical presentations.

- **Most Current.** The book presents the most current topics of EC, as evidenced by the many 2000 and 2001 citations. Topics such as e-marketplaces, e-government, e-strategy, Web-based supply chain systems, and EC economics are presented both from the theoretical point of view and from the application side.

- **Economic Justification.** Information technology is mature enough to stand the difficult test of economic justification, a topic ignored by most textbooks. It is our position that investment in EC must be scrutinized like any other investment, despite the difficulties of measuring technology benefits.

- **Integrated Systems**. In contrast with other books that highlight isolated Internet-based systems, we emphasize those systems that support the enterprise and supply chain management. Interorganizational systems are particularly highlighted, including the latest innovations in global EC and in Web-based Electronic Data Interchange (EDI); also, collaborative commerce is highlighted.
- **Global Perspective**. The importance of global competition, partnerships, and trading is increasing rapidly. EC facilitates export and import, managing multi-national companies, and trading electronically around the globe. International examples are provided throughout the book.
- **EC Failures and Lessons Learned**. In addition to success stories, there are stories of EC failures and an analysis of their causes.
- **Comprehensiveness and Ease of Reading**. All major topics of EC are covered. Furthermore, the book is user friendly, easy to understand and follow, and full of interesting real-world examples and "war stories" that keep the reader's interest at a high level.

THE MAJOR DIFFERENCES BETWEEN THE 1ST EDITION AND THIS EDITION

- **Eight New Chapters.** The 2nd edition has eight new chapters covering the following topics: the digital economy (Chapter 2), e-marketplaces (Chapter 7), EC services (Chapter 8), auctions (Chapter 9), e-government, C2C, and intrabusiness EC (Chapter 11), security (Chapter 13), order fulfillment (Chapter 15), and m-commerce (Chapter 19). In addition there is a hands-on, detailed storefront building guide (Appendix 12A).
- **Four Completely Revised Chapters.** Four chapters have been completely revised, these include: Internet marketing (Chapter 3), company-centered B2B (Chapter 6), Web application development (Chapter 12), and strategy (Chapter 16). All other chapters were updated, reorganized, and streamlined. The regulatory chapter (Chapter 17) was updated by a lawyer, Dr. Matthew Lee.
- **New Two-Color Design.** Vivid presentation in a new two-color design that better highlights text pedagogy.
- **Hyperlinks**. Hundreds of hyperlinks that illustrate many of the applications and issues have been added to the text. These will be monitored and updated on the Web site at www.prenhall.com/turban.
- **More Exercises, Including Role Playing**. The number of review questions, exercises, and Internet exercises has been doubled.

ORGANIZATION OF THE BOOK

The book is divided into six parts composed of 19 chapters with five supplemental technology appendices.

PART I—A REAL REVOLUTION

In this part we provide an overview of the entire book as well as the fundamentals of EC and some of its terminology (Chapter 1) and a discussion of the digital economy (Chapter 2).

PART II—B2C EC-INTERNET MARKETING

In this part we describe EC B2C applications in three chapters. Chapters 3 deals with e-tailing, Chapter 4 with Internet consumers and market research, and Chapter 5 deals with EC advertisement, which is mostly related to business-to-consumer EC.

PART III—B2C EC

In this part we cover the one-to-many model (Chapter 6, including auctions), many-to-many model (Chapter 7, including exchanges), and business-to-business services (Chapter 8).

PART IV—OTHER EC MODELS AND APPLICATIONS

This part begins with detailed description of online auctions (Chapter 9), then it moves to service industries online (travel, stocks, banking, etc.) (Chapter 10). In Chapter 11 we cover e-government, intrabusiness applications, and consumer-to-consumer EC.

PART V—BUILDING EC SYSTEMS

This part of the book opens with an overview of EC application development (Chapter 12). This is followed by security (Chapter 13) and payments (Chapter 14). Appendix 12A provides step-by-step instructions on how to build a storefront. Chapter 15 closes this part with order fulfillment and supply chain management coverage.

PART VI—IMPLEMENTING EC

Starting with e-strategy (Chapter 16), this part deals with implementing and deploying EC. The legal environment is the subject of Chapter 17. Chapter 18 gives a glance at electronic communities as well as at several other issues, such as global EC, small businesses and EC, and EC research. This chapter also provides an overview of future EC directions. The text concludes with Chapter 19 on mobile commerce (m-commerce).

LEARNING AIDS

We developed a number of learning aids including:

- **Chapter Outline.** Detailed outlines, "Contents," at the beginning of each chapter provide a quick indication of the major topics covered.
- **Learning Objectives.** Learning objectives at the beginning of each chapter help students focus their efforts and alert them to the important concepts to be discussed. Role playing exercises were added.
- **Opening Vignettes.** Each chapter opens with a real-world example that illustrates the importance of EC to modern corporations. These cases were carefully chosen to call attention to the major topics covered in the chapters.
- **Managerial Issues.** The final section of every chapter explores some of the special concerns managers face as they adapt to doing business in cyberspace.
- **Key Terms.** All boldface terms introduced within the chapter appear in a list at the end of the chapter and are defined in the glossary at the end of the book.

- **Chapter Summary.** The chapter summary is linked one-to-one to the learning objectives introduced at the beginning of each chapter.

- **End-of-Chapter Exercises.** Different types of questions measure students' comprehension and their ability to apply knowledge. Questions for Review ask students to summarize the concepts introduced. Discussion Questions are intended to promote class discussion and develop critical-thinking skills. Exercises are challenging assignments that require students to apply what they have learned, the exercises also include about 200 hands-on exercises send students to interesting Web sites to conduct research, investigate an application, download demos or learn about state-of-the-art technology. The Team Assignments are projects designed to foster teamwork.

- **Application Cases.** In-text cases highlight real-world problems encountered by corporations as they develop and implement EC.

- **Real-World Cases.** Each chapter ends with a somewhat more in-depth Real-World Case. Case questions follow each case study.

SUPPLEMENTARY MATERIALS

The following material is available to support this book:

- **Instructor's Resource CD-ROM.** This convenient Instructor's CD-ROM includes all of the supplements: Instructor's Manual, Test Item File, Windows PH Test Manager, PowerPoint Lecture Notes, and Image Library (text art).

- **Instructor's Manual with Test Item File (Test Bank).** This manual includes answers to all review and discussion questions, exercises, and case questions. The Test Item File includes multiple-choice questions for each chapter. An electronic version of the Test Item File is available in the form of the Windows PH Test Manager.

- **PowerPoint Lecture Notes.** An extensive set of Microsoft PowerPoint lecture notes, oriented toward text learning objectives, is available for each chapter. Lecture Notes can be downloaded from the text's Web site at prenhall.com/turban and can be found on the Instructor's CD-ROM.

- **MyPHLIP Web Site.** The book is supported by a MyPHLIP Web site that includes:
    a. Chapter Updates posted periodically to help both students and instructors stay up to date with what's happening in E-Commerce and E-Business today and how it relates to chapter material.
    b. A password-protected faculty area where instructors can download the PowerPoint Lecture Notes and the Instructor's Manual.
    c. URLs for all the major topics in the book with links to other sources.
    d. Links to a large number of case studies, including customer success stories and academically oriented cases.
    e. Links to many EC vendors' sites.
    f. Longer cases from several countries and links to many cases.
    g. Appendices A–D covering infrastructure for EC, Web page design and creation, Web programming, and intelligent agents.

ACKNOWLEDGEMENTS

Many individuals helped us create this text. Faculty feedback was solicited via reviews and through a focus group. We are grateful to the following faculty for their contributions.

Content Contributors

The following individuals contributed material for the updated and new chapters:

- Matthew Lee, City University of Hong Kong, an Internet lawyer and IS Professor, contributed to Chapter 17.
- Mohamed Khalifa, City University of Hong Kong, contributed to Chapter 12.
- Joe Walls, University of Michigan, contributed to Chapter 12.

Reviewers

DAVID AMBROSINI
Cabrillo College

DEBORAH BALLOU
University of Notre Dame

MARTIN BARRIFF
Illinois Institute of Technology

JOSEPH BROOKS
University of Hawaii

JOHN BUGADO
National University

JACK COOK
State University of New York at Geneseo

LARRY CORMAN
Fort Lewis College

MARY CULNAN
Georgetown University

TED FERRETTI
Northeastern University

KEN GRIGGS
California Polytechnic State University

VARUN GROVER
University of South Carolina

JAMES HENSON
Barry University

JEFFREY JOHNSON
Utah State University

MORGAN JONES
University of North Carolina

DOUGLAS KLINE
Sam Houston State University

BYUNGTAE LEE
University of Illinois at Chicago

LAKSHMI LYER.
University of North Carolina

MICHAEL MCLEOD
East Carolina University

SUSAN MCNAMARA
Northeastern University

MOHAN MENON
University of South Alabama

AJAY MISHRA
SUNY-Binghamton

BUD MISHRA
New York University

WILLIAM NANCE
San Jose State University

CRAIG PETERSON
Utah State University

LINDA SALCHENBERGER
Loyola University of Chicago

GEORGE SCHELL
University of North Carolina at Wilmington

KAN SUGANDH
DeVry Institute of Technology

LINDA VOLONINO
Canisius College

GREGORY WOOD
Canisius College

JAMES ZEMANEK
East Carolina University

Many students at City University of Hong Kong participated in this project in several ways. Some helped us to find materials and others provided feedback. There are too many to name, but thanks goes to all of you.

Several individuals helped us with the administrative work. Special mention goes to Grace Choi of City University of Hong Kong and Judy Lang of Eastern Illinois University, who helped in typing and editing. Several student assistants help in library research, typing, and diagramming. Most of the work was done by Venus Ma. We thank everyone for the dedication and the superb performance shown throughout the project.

The information system department of City University was extremely supportive in providing all the necessary assistance. Many faculty members provided advice and support material. Special thanks go to Matthew Lee, the department chair, and to Doug Vogel and Louis Ma.

We also recognize the various organizations and corporations that provided us with permission to reproduce material.

Finally, thanks goes to the Prentice Hall team who helped us from the inception of the project under the leadership of Executive Editor Bob Horan and Vice President and Publisher Natalie Anderson. The dedicated staff includes Associate Editor Lori Cerreto, Production Manager Gail Steier de Acevedo, Production Editor April Montana, Editorial Assistant Erika Rusnak, Marketing Manager Sharon Turkovich, and Marketing Assistant Jason Smith.

PART 1

1

Overview of Electronic Commerce

LEARNING OBJECTIVES

Upon completion of this chapter, the reader will be able to:

- Define electronic commerce (EC) and describe its various categories.

- Distinguish between electronic markets and interorganizational systems.

- Describe and discuss the content and framework of EC.

- Understand the forces that drive the widespread use of EC.

- Describe the benefits of EC to organizations, consumers, and society.

- Describe the limitations of EC.

- Discuss some major managerial issues regarding EC.

CONTENT

THE PROBLEM

In 1999 and 2000, rising fuel costs placed pressure on the airline industry. Increased fuel prices arrived quickly and without warning. For Qantas Airways, Australia's largest airline, the increase in fuel prices was just one of many problems. The airline faced two new domestic competitors, Impulse and Virgin Blue, as well as higher fees at Sydney International Airport. The airline needed to upgrade its fleet to stay competitive, replacing aging aircraft and purchasing new 500–seat planes. In addition, the Australian economy slowed down in 2000 and the Australian dollar was sinking. Will Qantas, the world's second oldest airline, survive?

■___ THE SOLUTION

In addition to traditional responses such as buying fuel contracts for future dates, Qantas took major steps to implement **electronic commerce** (e-commerce, EC), which involves buying, selling, and exchanging goods, services, information, and payment electronically. Qantas made a number of major initiatives in the business-to-business (B2B) e-commerce arena.

- Joined Airnew Co., a purchasing B2B e-marketplace, that links dozens of major airlines with suppliers of fuel, fuel services, flight maintenance services, catering, and other services and suppliers. The e-marketplace uses electronic catalogs and conducts a variety of auctions.

- Together with 13 other large corporations in Australia, Qantas joined *corprocure.com.au* to purchase general goods and services, such as office supplies, light bulbs, and maintenance services.

Formed a Pan-Pacific marketplace that provides a full spectrum of travel services (airline tickets, hotels, cars, etc.). The Pan-Pacific marketplace provides an opportunity for business partners such as travel agencies to provide special and personalized services to their customers at competitive prices. This e-marketplace will also sell directly to individual consumers. Because of this, it will act both as a business-to-customer (B2C) and business-to-business (B2B) marketplace.

In addition to these major initiatives, Qantas also plans on implementing the following B2B and B2C features:

- Send an e-mail to all 2.4 million Qantas frequent flyers inviting them to book a flight online. As an incentive, customers will be rewarded with bonuses and an opportunity to win AUD10,000. (Online booking has been offered since 1997.)
- Support wireless communications by providing information on arrival and departure times, as well as flight delays, to travelers via mobile phone and other wireless devices.

Qantas also uses e-commerce technologies to interact with its employees and contractors. Additionally, Qantas increases brand visibility through a series of partnerships.

- Qantas provides online training to Qantas travel agents (*gdstrainingQantas.com.au*).

- Qantas College Online assists in the training of Quatas' 30,000 employees in 32 countries. This program is part of Qantas's business-to-employees (B2E) initiative (*qfcollege.edu.au*).
- Another B2E project is online banking. Qantas operates a credit union with 50,000 members worldwide. Members make over 100,000 transactions a month at *qantascu.com.au*. Services are comparable with commercial online banks (see Chapter 10).
- Qantas is involved in several projects with Telstra (Australia's largest telecommunications company) that include cobranding with credit cards and mobile phones.

■___ THE RESULTS

No one ever said leading an old-economy company into e-commerce was going to be easy. It means interfering with existing power structures and fitting new-economy strategies with old-economy ways of thinking. Qantas knows that this is the path it must take. Results are not expected overnight. It will take years and hundreds of millions of dollars to implement the entire EC initiative. Yet, Qantas expects to see an estimated AUD85 million in cost reductions per year by 2003. Also, it will increase annual revenues by AUD700 million from nontravel sales. Many airlines are involved in similar projects including United Airlines (*united.com*) and *CathayPacific.com*.

Sources: Compiled from *Financial Review*, Aug. 11, 2000, from Australia's *Business Review Weekly*, Aug. 25, 2000 and May 5, 2000, and from Qantas's media releases Sep. 14, 1999.

1.2   DEFINITIONS

The opening vignette illustrates a new way of conducting business—electronically, using networks and the Internet. The vignette demonstrates the many ways that businesses can use e-commerce to improve the bottom line. In general, there are two major types of e-commerce: **business-to-consumer (B2C)** and **business-to-business (B2B).** In B2C transactions, online transactions are made between businesses and individual consumers, such as when airlines sell tickets to travelers. In B2B transactions, businesses make online transactions with other businesses, such as when businesses purchase parts, fuel, or services online. The case study also presents **business-to-employee (B2E)** services.

The Qantas case study also points to a number of issues involved in the implementation of e-commerce by businesses. These issues, shown in the following list, are the topic of future chapters.

- The speed of change in the business environment (Chapter 2)
- The diversity of electronic marketplaces (Chapters 6, 7, and 8)
- Customer service and activities within an organization (Chapters 4 and 11)
- The economic impacts of EC, especially on competition (Chapter 2)
- The various models of electronic procurement (Chapters 6, 7, and 8)
- The role of intermediaries (Chapters 3 and 10)
- The operation of online travel businesses (Chapter 10)
- The interaction of EC and supply chain management (Chapters 6, 7, 8, 9, and 15)

EC could become a significant global economic element within 10 to 20 years (*forrester.com*). Networked computing is the infrastructure for EC, and it is rapidly emerging as the standard computing environment for business, home, and government applications. Networked computing connects multiple computers and other electronic devices that are located in several different locations by telecommunications networks, including wireless ones. This allows users to access information stored in several different physical locations and to communicate and collaborate with people separated by great geographic distances. Although some people still use a stand-alone computer exclusively, the vast majority of people use computers connected to a global networked environment known as the **Internet** or to its counterpart within organizations, an intranet. An **intranet** is a corporate or government network that uses Internet tools, such as Web browsers, and Internet protocols. Another computer environment is an **extranet,** a network that uses the Internet to link multiple intranets (see Fingar et al., 2000).

This new breed of computing is enabling large numbers of organizations, both private and public, in manufacturing, agriculture, and services, not only to excel, but also in many cases to survive. An interesting example of the use of EC to turn losses into profits is that of *Egghead.com* (Application Case 1.1).

Why are companies resorting to EC? The reason is simple. Information technology (IT) in general and EC in particular have become the major facilitators of business activities in the world today (Mankin 1996, Gill 1996). E-commerce is also a catalyst of fundamental changes in the structure, operations, and management of organizations (Dertouzos 1997, McLaren and McLarnen 1999).

APPLICATION CASE   **1.1**

Egghead Becomes a Virtual Software Company

Egghead Software was a successful retailer selling PC software in North America. The company grew 20 percent a year until 1995, when sales peaked at $434 million. Since 1995, however, sales have declined about 10 percent per year, with losses growing to $40 million in 1997. The company closed its unprofitable stores, but due to competition from large companies such as CompUSA and Best Buy, losses continued to increase. In 1997, the company started to sell software over the Internet through three Web sites and began to take orders by telephone and mail order. Even after implementing these changes and closing unprofitable retail stores, Egghead was still losing money. By February 1998, the mounting losses forced the company to close all of its stores. The company changed its name to *Egghead.com* and concentrated on EC. Within a week its stock price jumped 60 percent. In late 1998, company revenues increased dramatically when *Egghead.com* started to sell nonsoftware products and conduct online auctions. By 2001 the company had become a major retailer, selling numerous types of products and services in direct competition with EC giants such as *Amazon.com* and revolutionizing the face of e-retailing (see Chapter 3).

Sources: Condensed from *Infoworld*, February 9, 1998, p. 53, *Internet World*, March 9, 1998, p. 78, and *egghead.com* (2001).

Electronic Commerce Terms

ELECTRONIC COMMERCE (EC)

Electronic commerce (EC) is an emerging concept that describes the process of buying, selling, or exchanging products, services, and information via computer networks, including the Internet. Kalakota and Whinston (1997) define EC from these perspectives:

- **From a communications perspective,** EC is the delivery of goods, services, information, or payments over computer networks or by any other electronic means.
- **From a business process perspective,** EC is the application of technology toward the automation of business transactions and work flow.
- **From a service perspective,** EC is a tool that addresses the desire of firms, consumers, and management to cut service costs while improving the quality of goods and increasing the speed of service delivery.
- **From an online perspective,** EC provides the capability of buying and selling products and information on the Internet and other online services.

We add to this:

- **From a collaborations perspective,** EC is the framework for inter- and intraorganizational collaboration.
- **From a community perspective,** EC provides a gathering place for community members, to learn, transact, and collaborate.

E-BUSINESS

The term *commerce* is defined by some as describing transactions conducted between business partners. When this definition of commerce is used, some people find the term *electronic commerce* to be fairly narrow. Thus, many use the term **e-business.** E-business refers to a broader definition of EC, not just the buying and selling of goods and services, but also servicing customers, collaborating with business partners, and conducting electronic transactions within an organization. According to Lou Gerstner, IBM's CEO, "E-business is all about time cycle, speed, globalization, enhanced productivity, reaching new customers and sharing knowledge across institutions for competitive advantage."

In this book we use the broadest meaning of electronic commerce, which is basically equivalent to e-business. The two terms will be used interchangeably throughout the text.

PURE VS. PARTIAL EC

Electronic commerce can take many forms depending on the degree of digitization of (1) the *product* (service) sold, (2) the *process,* and (3) the *delivery agent* (or intermediary). Choi et al. (1997) created a model that explains the possible configurations of these three dimensions (Figure 1-1). A product can be physical or digital, an agent can be physical or digital, and the process can be physical or digital. These create eight (2 × 2 × 2) cubes, each of which has three dimensions. In traditional commerce all dimensions are physical (lower-left cube), and in pure EC all dimensions are digital (upper-right cube). All other cubes include a mix of digital and physical dimensions.

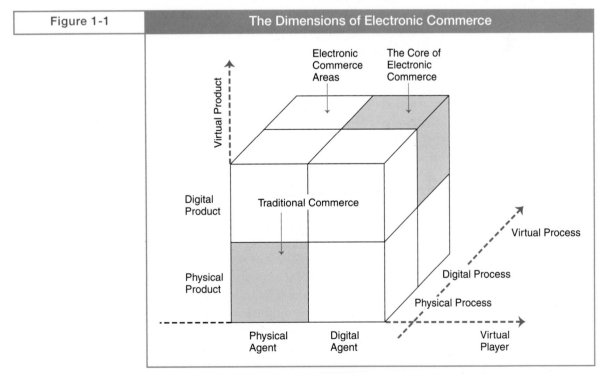

Figure 1-1	The Dimensions of Electronic Commerce

Source: Choi et al. (1997), p.18.

If there is at least one digital dimension, we will consider the situation EC, but not pure EC. For example, buying a book from *Amazon.com* is not pure, because the book is delivered by FedEx. However, buying an e-book from *Amazon.com* or software from *Egghead.com* is pure EC because the delivery, payment, and agent are all digital.

Pure physical organizations (corporations) are referred to as **brick-and-mortar organizations,** whereas pure EC organizations are referred to as **virtual corporations.**

INTERNET VS. NON-INTERNET EC

Most EC is done over the Internet. But EC can be also be conducted on private networks, such as value-added networks (VANs), on local area networks (LANs), and even on a single machine. For example, buying food from a vending machine with a smart card can be viewed as EC.

Click-and-mortar organizations are those that conduct some e-commerce activities, yet their primary business is done in the physical world. Gradually, many old-economy companies are changing to click-and-mortar ones (e.g., Qantas Airways).

Business Models

One of the major characteristics of EC is that it enables the creation of new business models. A **business model** is a method of doing business by which a company can generate revenue to sustain itself. The model spells out how the company is positioned in the value chain. Some models are very simple. For example, Nokia sells cellular phones and generates a profit. On the other hand, a TV station provides free broadcasting. Its survival depends on a complex model involving advertisers and content providers. Internet portals, such as Yahoo, also use a complex business model.

There are many types of EC business models, the following is a list of some of the most common or visible models. Additional business model examples and details can be found throughout this text and in Timmers (1999) and Applegate (2001).

Name your price. Pioneered by *Priceline.com,* this model allows a buyer to set the price he or she is willing to pay for a specific product or service. *Priceline.com* will try to match the customer's request with a supplier willing to sell the product or service at that price. Customers may submit several bids before they get the product. Most of *Priceline.com's* services and products are travel-related (e.g., airline tickets, hotels); however, consumers can also use *Priceline.com* to set their own price for groceries or loan interest rates.

Find the best price. According to this model, a consumer specifies his or her needs and then the company locates the lowest price for that service or product. *Hotwire.com* uses this model. With *hotwire.com,* the consumer names his or her itinerary. *Hotwire.com* matches it against a database, locates the lowest price, and submits it to the consumer. The potential buyer then has 30 minutes to accept or reject the offer. A variation of this is also available for insurance. For example, a consumer can submit a request for insurance to *insweb.com* and receive several quotes. However, in the travel example the consumer buys from the online service, with *insweb.com* the consumer is only referred to an insurance company. Many companies employ similar models to find the lowest price. For example, consumers can use *eloan.com* to find the best rates for auto or home loans.

Dynamic brokering. In the digital age, customers can specify requirements. These are Webcasted to service providers in an automatic invitation to tender. Bids can be automatically offered, amended, and considered, all without any additional input from the consumers. An example of the dynamic brokering model is *GetThere.com* for travel-related services and products.

Affiliate marketing. Affiliate marketing is an arrangement where a marketing partner (business, organization, or even individual) has an arrangement with a company to refer consumers to the company's Web site so that a consumer can purchase a service or product. The marketing partner receives a 3 to 15 percent commission on the purchase price when a customer they refer to the company's Web site makes a purchase there. In other words, a company can create a *virtual commissioned sales force.* Pioneered by CDNow (see Hoffman and Novak 2000), the concept now is employed by thousands of retailers or direct sellers. For example, *Amazon.com* has close to 500,000 affiliates, and even tiny *cattoys.com* offers individuals and organizations the opportunity to put the *cattoys.com* logo and link on a Web site to generate commissions.

Group purchasing. Discounts are usually available for quantity purchasing. Using the concept of group purchasing, a small business, or even an individual, can get a discount. EC has spawned the concept of *electronic aggregation,* where a third party finds the individuals or small, medium enterprises (SMEs), aggregates orders, and then negotiates (or conducts a tender) for the best deal. Some leading aggregators are *aphs.com* and *bazaare.com* (see Rugullis 2000).

Electronic tendering systems. Large buyers, private or public, usually make their purchases through a tendering (bidding) system. Now tendering can be done online, saving time and money. Pioneered by General Electric Corp. (*gegxs.com,* Chapter 7), e-tendering systems are gaining popularity. Several government agencies mandate that all sales to the agency must be through e-tendering.

Online auctions. Of course we have all heard about *eBay.com,* the world's largest online auction site. However, several hundred other companies also conduct online auctions, including *Amazon.com* and *Yahoo.com.*

Customization and personalization. These are not new models, in fact they are as old as commerce itself! What *is* new is the ability to quickly customize and personalize products for consumers at prices not much higher than their noncustomized counterparts. Dell Computers is a good example of a company that customizes and personalizes products for its customers. Many other companies are following Dell's lead, including the automotive industry, which expects to save 10 billion dollars in inventory reduction alone every year by producing cars made to order. In order for companies to implement electronic customization and personalization, they will need to modify their old way of doing business (discussed in Chapters 15–18 and in Wiegram and Koth 2000).

Electronic marketplaces and exchanges. Electronic marketplaces existed in isolated applications for decades (e.g., stock exchanges). But, as of 1999, there are thousands. E-marketplaces introduce efficiencies to the marketplace, and if they are well organized and managed, they can provide benefits to both buyers and sellers. Of special interest are vertical marketplaces (also called vertical portals or vortals), which concentrate on one industry (e.g., *e-steel.com* for the steel industry and *chemconnect.com* for the chemical industry).

Supply chain improvers. One of the major contributions of EC is in the creation of new models that improve supply chain management. An example of such an improvement is provided in Application Case 1.2.

ORBIS Corp. Supply Chain Improvements

ORBIS Corp. is a small, Australian company that provides Internet and EC services. One of their services is called ProductBank (*productbank.com.au*). This service revolutionized the flow of information and products in the B2B advertising field. In order to understand how the service works, let's look at a traditional example of how a retail catalog or brochure is put together. A catalog shows pictures of many products. The pictures in the catalog are obtained from manufacturers such as Sony or Nokia. The traditional process is linear, as shown in the following figure.

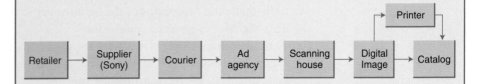

The total transactional cost of preparing one picture for the catalog is about AUD150. The process works like this: when retailers need a photo of a product they contact the manufacturers who send the photo to an ad agency. The ad agency decides which photos to use and how to present them. The ad agency then sends the photos to be scanned and converted into a digital image. The digital image can then be printed in the catalog. The cycle time for each photo is 4 to 6 weeks.

ProductBank simplifies this lengthy process. ProductBank improves the supply chain of not only one picture from one vendor for one catalog, but that of the entire industry, namely, multiple vendors and multiple catalogs. It has centralized the entire transactional process by creating an information exchange, or hub, as shown in the following figure.

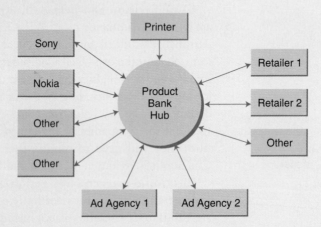

The new process works through the exchange of electronic information. With the new process, manufacturers send photos (usually digitized) to ORBIS. ORBIS enters and organizes the photos into a database. When retailers need a picture, they can view the images in the database and decide which they want to include in the catalog. The retailers communicate

APPLICATION CASE   1.2

(continued)

electronically with the ad agency about what images they want to include in their catalog. The ad agency works on the design of the catalog. Once the design is complete, the catalog can be downloaded by the printer. The transaction cost per picture is 30 to 40 percent lower and the cycle time is 50 to 70 percent shorter than the traditional catalog production method.

The ORBIS case illustrates the following business models' characteristics:

- Digitize as much as you can; eliminate paper and other physical transactions.
- Digitize at the beginning of the transaction process.
- Change the supply chain from a linear model to a hub-based model.
- Aggregate many business partners into one place.
- Savings are in cost, cycle time, quality, and customer service.

Collaborative commerce. The ORBIS case also illustrates that in addition to selling and buying, collaboration is a major EC activity. Michael Rappa (*digitalenterprise.org/mrappa.html*) classifies these and other models into nine categories, as shown in Table 1-1.

Electronic Markets

Electronic markets (e-markets), also referred to as **e-marketplaces** or **marketspaces**, are rapidly emerging as a vehicle for conducting business online. A market is a network of interactions and relationships where information, products, services, and payments are exchanged. When the marketplace is electronic, the business center is not a physical building, but rather a network-based location. As shown in Figure 1-2, buyers and sellers meet in electronic marketplaces, and the market handles all the necessary transactions that occur, including the transfer of money between banks.

TABLE 1-1

E-Commerce Business Models

Type of Business Model	Examples
Brokerage Model	Buy/sell fulfillment, market exchange, business trading community, buyer aggregator, distributor, virtual mail, metamediary, auction broker, reverse auction, classifieds, search agent
Advertising Model	Generalized portal, personalized portal, specialized portal, attention/incentive marketing, free model, bargain discounter
Infomediary Model	Recommender system, registration model
Merchant Model	Virtual merchant, catalog merchant, surf-and-turf, bit vendor
Manufacturer Model	Direct marketing
Affiliate Model	Provide commission for online referrals
Community Model	Voluntary contributor model, knowledge networks
Subscription Model	Access valuable content for fee (sometimes free)
Utility Model	Pay by the byte

Source: Compiled from *digitalenterprise.org/models/models.html* and from Applegate (2001).

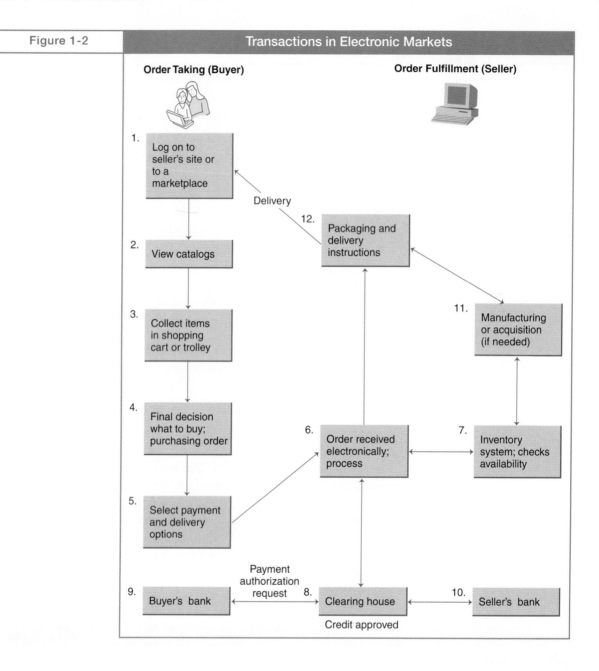

Figure 1-2   Transactions in Electronic Markets

In electronic markets, the principal participants—transaction handlers, buyers, brokers, and sellers—are not only at different locations, but seldom even know one another. The means of interconnection varies among parties and can change from event to event. A special type of e-market is the electronic exchange.

ELECTRONIC EXCHANGES

Prices in markets can be either fixed, such as in a supermarket or other retail stores, or they can vary, depending on real time (or close to it) matching of supply and demand. The latter case is referred to as **dynamic pricing.** A market that conducts the matching is called an **exchange** and in EC it is an **e-exchange.** In its most effi-

TABLE 1-2

Distinctive Features of Interorganizational Systems and Electronic Markets

Interorganizational Systems

Customer/supplier relationship is determined in advance with the anticipation it will be an ongoing relationship based on multiple transactions.

Interorganizational systems may be built around private or publicly accessible networks. When outside communications companies are involved, they are typically value-added carriers (VANs).

Advance arrangements result in agreements on the nature and format of business documents that will be exchanged and payments methods.

Advance arrangements are made so both parties know which communications networks will be integral to the system.

Joint guidelines and expectations of each party are formulated so each knows how the system is to be used and when transactions will be submitted and received by each business partner. Two types of relationships may exist:

- Customer/seller linkage is established at time of transactions and may be for one transaction only (i.e., purchase transaction).
- Customer/seller purchase agreement is established whereby the seller agrees to deliver services or products to customer for a defined period of time (i.e., a subscription transaction).

Electronic Markets

Electronic markets are typically built around publicly accessible networks.

When outside communications companies are involved, they are typically online service providers (which function as market makers).

Sellers determine, in conjunction with the market maker, which business transactions they will provide.

Customers and sellers independently determine which communications networks they will use in participating in the electronic market. The network used may vary from transaction to transaction.

No joint guidelines are drawn in advance.

Source: Distinct Feature of Inter-Organizational System and Electronic Markets from J. A. Senn "Capitalization on Electronic Commerce" *Information System Management* (Summer 1996), p. 17. ©CRC System.

cient form, matching and dynamic pricing occur in real time, such as in a live auction or in a stock exchange.

Interorganizational Information Systems

An **interorganizational information system (IOS)** involves information flow among two or more organizations. Its major objective is efficient transaction processing, such as transmitting orders, bills, and payments, using EDI/Internet or extranets. All relationships are predetermined; there is no negotiation, just execution. In contrast, in electronic markets, sellers and buyers negotiate, submit bids, agree on an order, and finish the transaction online or off-line. The distinction between the two systems is shown in Table 1-2. Interorganizational systems are used exclusively for B2B applications, mostly supply-chain related, whereas electronic markets exist in both the B2B and B2C cases.

1.3   THE EC FIELD

The EC field is a comprehensive one, involving many activities, organizational units, and technologies (see Shaw et al., 2000). Therefore, it may be useful to use a framework to describe its content.

An EC Framework

Many people think EC is just having a Web site or a corporate portal, but EC is much more than that. There are dozens of EC applications, some of which were illustrated in the Qantas case. Other EC applications include shopping in online stores and malls, buying stocks, finding a job, conducting an auction, collaborating electronically on research and development projects, and running global exchanges (see Huff et al., 1999). To execute these applications, companies need the right information, infrastructure, and support systems. Figure 1-3 shows how EC applications are supported by infrastructure. Successful EC implementation is dependent also on five major areas (shown in Figure 1-3 as supporting pillars): people, public policy, marketing and advertisement, business partners, and support services.

- **People.** These are sellers, buyers, intermediaries, IT employees, and any other participants.
- **Public policy.** These are legal and other policy issues, such as privacy protection, that are determined by the government. Public policy includes: technical standards and protocols.
- **Marketing and advertisement.** The Web is huge, so it is necessary to attract customers to the Web site using both traditional and new marketing and advertisement strategies.

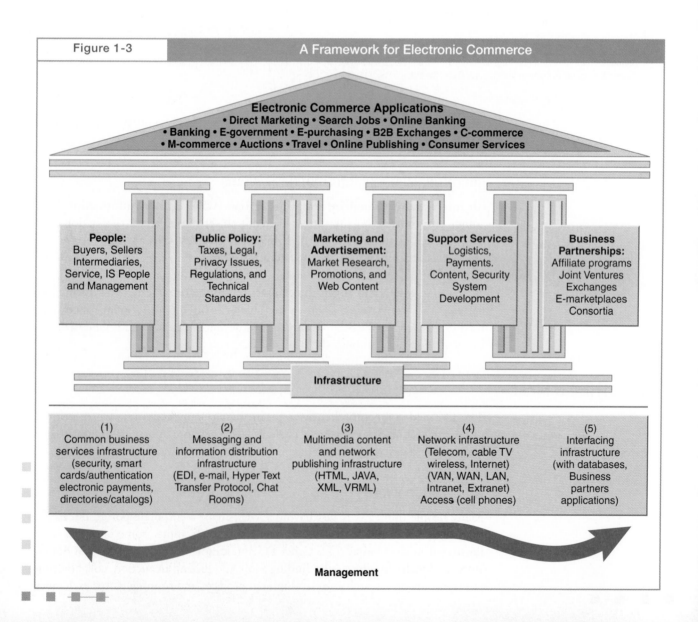

| Figure 1-3 | A Framework for Electronic Commerce |

Electronic Commerce Applications
• Direct Marketing • Search Jobs • Online Banking
• Banking • E-government • E-purchasing • B2B Exchanges • C-commerce
• M-commerce • Auctions • Travel • Online Publishing • Consumer Services

People:	Public Policy:	Marketing and Advertisement:	Support Services	Business Partnerships:
Buyers, Sellers Intermediaries, Service, IS People and Management	Taxes, Legal, Privacy Issues, Regulations, and Technical Standards	Market Research, Promotions, and Web Content	Logistics, Payments. Content, Security System Development	Affiliate programs Joint Ventures Exchanges E-marketplaces Consortia

Infrastructure

(1)	(2)	(3)	(4)	(5)
Common business services infrastructure (security, smart cards/authentication electronic payments, directories/catalogs)	Messaging and information distribution infrastructure (EDI, e-mail, Hyper Text Transfer Protocol, Chat Rooms)	Multimedia content and network publishing infrastructure (HTML, JAVA, XML, VRML)	Network infrastructure (Telecom, cable TV wireless, Internet) (VAN, WAN, LAN, Intranet, Extranet) Access (cell phones)	Interfacing infrastructure (with databases, Business partners applications)

Management

- **Business partners.** E-commerce usually occurs throughout the supply chain between or among business partners.
- **Support services.** Large numbers of support services are needed. Most important are market research (Chapter 4), content creation and other services (Chapter 8), payments (Chapter 14), logistics (Chapter 15), IT support (Chapter 12), and security (Chapter 13).

All of these infrastructure and support components require good management practices. This means that companies need to plan, organize, motivate, devise strategy, and reengineer processes as needed. The need for **management** is shown in Figure 1-2, as well as in Chapters 16–18, and in other places throughout the book.

Figure 1-3 can be viewed as a framework for understanding the relationships among the EC components and for conducting research in the EC field (Zwass 1996; Shaw 1999). In this text we will provide details on most of the topics. However, less attention is devoted to the fast-changing infrastructures.

Classification of the EC Field by the Nature of the Transactions

A common classification of EC is by the nature of the transaction. The following types of transactions are distinguished:

- **Business-to-business (B2B).** All of the participants in this type of EC are businesses or other organizations. Today most EC is B2B (Cunningham, 2001). B2B transactions include the IOS transactions and e-market transactions between and among organizations.
- **Business-to-consumer (B2C).** These transactions include retail transactions with individual shoppers. The typical shopper at *Amazon.com* is a consumer, or customer. This business model is also called **e-tailing.**
- **Consumer-to-consumer (C2C).** In this category, consumers sell directly to other consumers. Examples include individuals selling residential property, cars, and so on in classified ads (e.g., *classifieds2000.com*). The advertisement of personal services over the Internet and the selling of knowledge and expertise online are other examples of C2C. In addition, several auction sites allow individuals to place items up for auction. Finally, many individuals use personal Web pages and portals as well as intranets to advertise items or personal services.
- **People-to-people (P2P).** This type of transaction is a special type of C2C where people exchange CDs, videos, software, and other goods. A well-known organizer of P2P is Napster (*napster.com*).
- **Consumer-to-business (C2B).** This category includes individuals who use the Internet to sell products or services to organizations, as well as individuals who seek sellers, interact with them, and conclude transactions online. *Priceline.com* is a well-known C2B organizer.
- **Intrabusiness (Organizational) EC.** This category includes all internal organizational activities, usually performed on intranets or corporate portals, that involve the exchange of goods, services, or information among various units and individuals in that organization. Activities can range from selling corporate products to employees to online training and collaborative design efforts. These types of transactions are discussed in more detail in Chapter 11 and in the Real-World Case at the end of this chapter.

- **Business-to-employees (B2E).** This is a subset of the intrabusiness category where the organization delivers services, information, or products to individual employees (see Chapter 11 for more detail).
- **Government-to-citizens (G2C) and to others.** In this type of EC, a government entity buys or sells goods, services, or information to businesses or individual citizens. (See Chapter 11 for more detail.)
- **Exchange-to-exchange (E2E).** With the proliferation of exchanges and portals, it is logical for exchanges to connect to one another. E2E is a formal system that connects exchanges.
- **Collaborative commerce.** C-commerce is an application of IOS for electronic collaboration between business partners and between organizational employees.
- **Mobile commerce.** When EC takes place in a wireless environment, it is called **mobile commerce (m-commerce).**

A Brief History of EC

EC applications were first developed in the early 1970s with innovations such as electronic fund transfers (EFT). However, the extent of the applications was limited to large corporations, financial institutions, and a few daring small businesses. Then came electronic data interchange, known as EDI, which expanded from financial transactions to other types of transaction processing, thus enlarging the pool of participating companies from financial institutions to manufacturers, retailers, services, and many other types of businesses. More new EC applications followed, ranging from stock trading to travel reservation systems. Such systems were described as IOS applications, and their strategic value was widely recognized.

As the Internet became more commercialized and users flocked to participate in the World Wide Web in the early 1990s, the term electronic commerce was coined and EC applications rapidly expanded. One reason for the rapid expansion of e-commerce was the development of new networks, protocols, software, and specifications. The other reason was the increase in competition and other business pressures (see Section 1.4).

Since 1995, Internet users have witnessed the development of many innovative applications ranging from interactive advertisements to virtual reality experiences. Almost every medium- and large-sized organization in the world now has a Web site, and most large U.S. corporations have comprehensive portals. Many of these sites contain tens of thousand of pages and links. In 1999, the emphasis of EC shifted from B2C to B2B. Also, consolidation is now taking place following a number of industry failures in the late 1990s (see Useem 2000).

The Interdisciplinary Nature of EC

Because electronic commerce is a new field, it is just now developing its theoretical and scientific foundations. Just from a brief overview of the different EC models and infrastructure, it is clear that EC is based on several different disciplines. The major EC disciplines and some samples of the issues with which they are concerned follows:

- **Marketing.** Many off-line marketing issues are relevant to online EC, for example, cost benefits of advertisements and advertisement strategies. Other issues are unique to EC, such as online marketing strategies and interactive kiosks.
- **Computer sciences.** Many of the issues listed in the infrastructure box of Figure 1-3, such as computer languages, multimedia, and networks, fall into the discipline of computer science. Intelligent agents also play a major role in EC.
- **Consumer behavior and psychology.** Consumer behavior is the key to the success of B2C trades, but so is the behavior of the sellers. The relationship between culture and consumer attitudes in electronic markets is an example of a research issue in this field.
- **Finance.** The financial markets and banks are one of the major participants in EC as payments are part of most online transactions. Issues such as paying for small transactions, smart cards, and fraud in online stock transactions are a sampling of the many finance-related topics.
- **Economics.** EC is influenced by economic forces and has a major impact on both global and national economies. Economists are currently examining the application of microeconomics to EC planning and the economic impact of EC on corporations.
- **Management information systems (MIS).** The information systems department is usually responsible for the deployment of EC. This discipline covers issues ranging from systems analysis to system integration, as well as EC planning and implementation, security, and payment systems.
- **Accounting and auditing.** The back-office operations of electronic transactions are similar to off-line transactions in some respects, but different in others. Auditing electronic transactions presents a challenge for the accounting profession; as does the development of methodologies for cost-benefit justification.
- **Management.** Electronic commerce efforts need to be managed properly, and because of the interdisciplinary nature of EC, its management may require new approaches and theories.
- **Business law and ethics.** Legal and ethical issues are extremely important in EC, especially in the global marketplace. A large number of legislative bills are pending. Many of the ethical issues regarding EC are interrelated with legal ones, such as those involving privacy rights and intellectual property.
- **Others.** Several other disciplines are involved in various aspects of EC to a lesser extent—for example, linguistics (translation in international trades), robotics and sensory systems, operations research/management science, statistics, and public policy and administration. Also, EC is of interest to the engineering, health care, communications, and entertainment fields.

EC Failures

Starting in 1999, a large number of EC companies, especially e-tailing ones, began failing (*startupfailures.com*). At the same time, many EC initiatives in click-and-mortar organizations were discontinued. Reasons for these failures are discussed in Chapters 2, 3, and 16 (also see Useem 2000). Does this mean that EC is just a buzzword and its days are numbered? Absolutely not! The EC field is basically experiencing consolidation as companies test different business models and organizational structures. Most EC companies, including giants such as *Amazon.com,* are not making a profit. They are expanding operations and generating increasing sales. It is believed that by 2002 many of the major EC companies will begin to generate profits.

The Future of EC

In 1996, Forrester Research Institute (*forrester.com*) predicted that B2C would be a $6.6 billion business in 2000, up from $518 million in 1996. They then revised the figure to $20 billion, and the figure kept growing. In 1997, about $10 billion worth of B2B transactions were conducted over the Internet. Today's predictions on the future size of EC vary. For 2004, total online shopping and B2B transactions are estimated to be in the range of $2 to $7 trillion. Some EC applications, such as online auctions and online stock trading, are growing at a rate of 15 to 25 percent per month. The number of Internet users worldwide is predicted to reach 750 million by 2008. Experts predict that as many as 50 percent of all Internet users will shop online.

1.4   BUSINESS PRESSURES, ORGANIZATIONAL RESPONSES, AND E-COMMERCE

To understand the popularity of EC, it is worthwhile to examine today's business environment, the pressures it creates on organizations, the organizational responses to those pressures, and the potential role of EC.

The New World of Business

Market, economic, societal, and technological factors have created a highly competitive business environment in which customers are becoming more powerful. These factors can change quickly, sometimes in an unpredictable manner. For example, James Strong, the CEO of Qantas, once said (*BRW,* 2000), "The lesson we have learned is how quickly things can change. You have to be prepared to move fast when the situation demands." Companies need to react quickly to both the problems and the opportunities resulting from this new business environment (see Drucker 1995). Because the pace of change and the degree of uncertainty in tomorrow's competitive environment are expected to accelerate, organizations will be operating under increasing pressures to produce more products faster and with fewer resources.

Boyett and Boyett (1995) emphasize this dramatic change and maintain that in order to succeed, or even to survive, companies must take not only traditional actions such as lowering cost and closing unprofitable facilities (as in the case of *Egghead.com*), but also innovative actions such as customizing or creating new products or providing superb customer service. We refer to these activities as *critical response activities.*

Critical response activities can take place in some or all organizational processes, from the daily processing of payroll and order entry to strategic activities such as the acquisition of a company. Responses can also occur in what is known as the extended supply chain, that is, the interactions among a company and its suppliers, customers, and other partners, as demonstrated by Qantas Airways. A response can be a reaction to a pressure already in existence, or it can be an initiative that will defend an organization against future pressures. It can also be an activity that exploits an opportunity created by changing conditions. Many response activities can be greatly facilitated by EC. In some cases, EC is the only solution to these business pressures (Tapscott et al. 1998; Callon 1996).

The relationship among business pressures, organizational responses, and EC is shown in Figure 1-4. Organizations respond to the business pressures with activities supported by IT in general and EC in particular. Now, let's examine the three components of this model in more detail.

Business Pressures

To understand the role of EC in today's organizations, it is useful to review the major factors that pressure the business environment. The business environment refers to the social, economic, legal, technological, and political actions that affect business activities. In this text, business pressures are divided into the following categories: market, societal, and technological. These are summarized in Table 1-3.

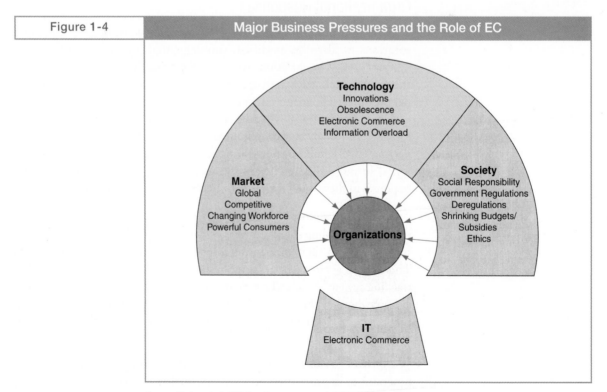

Figure 1-4 — Major Business Pressures and the Role of EC

Source: Turban et al. (2001), p. 6.

TABLE 1-3	**Major Business Pressures**
	Market and Economic Pressures
	• Strong competition • Global economy • Regional trade agreements (e.g., NAFTA) • Extremely low labor cost in some countries • Frequent and significant changes in markets • Increased power of consumers
	Societal and Environmental Pressures
	• Changing nature of workforce • Government deregulation • Shrinking government subsidies • Increased importance of ethical and legal issues • Increased social responsibility of organizations • Rapid political changes
	Technological Pressures
	• Rapid technological obsolescence • Increased innovations and new technologies • Information overload • Rapid decline in technology cost versus performance ratio

Organizational Responses

Because traditional response activities may not work with EC, many of the old solutions need to be modified, supplemented, or discarded (as in the case of *Egghead.com*). Organizations can also take proactive measures to create change in the marketplace. Such activities include exploiting opportunities created by external pressures. The major critical response activities are summarized in Figure 1-5.

Major organizational responses can be divided into four categories: strategic systems for competitive advantage, continuous improvement efforts, business process reengineering (BPR), and business alliances. Several responses are interrelated and can be found in more than one category. As we will discuss later, EC can facilitate the responses in these four categories. Each of the four categories are described here briefly.

Strategic systems. These systems provide organizations with strategic advantages, thus enabling them to increase their market share, better negotiate with their suppliers, or prevent competitors from entering into their territory (Callon 1996). There is are a variety of EC-supported strategic systems. One example is FedEx's tracking system, which allows FedEx to identify the status of every individual package anywhere in the system. Most of FedEx's competitors have already mimicked the FedEx system. In response, FedEx is now introducing new activities (see Application Case 1.3 on p. 20).

Continuous improvement efforts. Many companies continuously conduct programs to improve their productivity, quality, and customer service. Examples of such programs include customer relationship management (CRM) and total qual-

Figure 1-5	Critical Response Activities

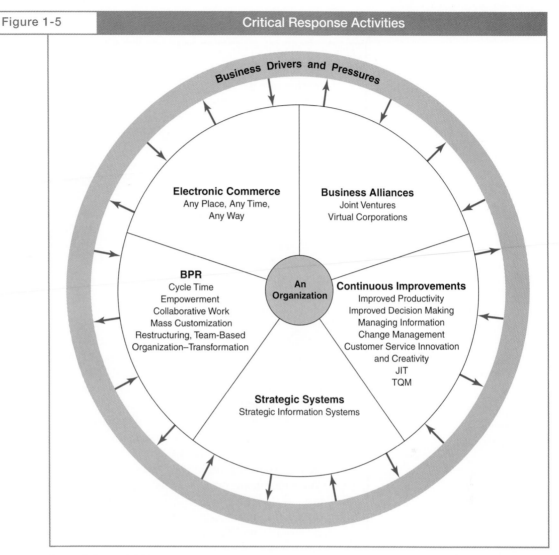

Source: Turban et al. (2001), p. 12.

ity management (TQM). Additional examples are provided in Table 1-4. As an example, Dell Computer takes its orders electronically and immediately moves them via Enterprise Resources Planning (ERP) software into the just-in-time assembly operation. Intel tracks the consumption of its products by 11 of its largest customers using an almost real-time extranet in order to plan production schedules and deliveries. However, continuous improvement programs may not be the best solution for business problems. Strong business pressures may require a radical change. Such an effort is referred to as business process reengineering (BPR).

Business process reengineering (BPR). Business process reengineering occurs when a company makes major innovations in the organization's structure and the way it conducts business. Technological, human, and organizational dimensions of a firm may all be changed in BPR (Hammer and Champy 1993). More than 70 percent of all large U.S. companies claim to be doing reengineering of some sort. EC-BPR relationships are described in Chapter 18.

APPLICATION CASE   1.3

FedEx Solutions

FedEx provides a host of logistics solutions to enterprise customers. These solutions are segmented and based on customers' needs and range from turnkey distribution centers to full-scale logistics services that incorporate expedited delivery. The major services provided to business customers are:

- **FedEx Distribution Centers.** This service uses a worldwide network of warehouses to provide turnkey warehousing services to businesses. This allows for instant expansion of distribution capabilities, especially by small businesses.
- **FedEx Express Distribution Depots.** This service is primarily limited to U.S. businesses and provides a one-stop source of express distribution capabilities. Goods in these depots are available for delivery 24 hours a day. This service is targeted at time-critical businesses.
- **FedEx Returns Management.** FedEx NetReturn is designed to streamline the process of customer returns. FedEx customers can use the Internet-based system to schedule pickup of packages from consumers and obtain time-definite delivery, as well as online status tracking and customized reporting to provide complete inventory control.
- **Virtual Order.** Virtual Order is touted as being "a fully integrated electronic commerce system that offers an effective solution to supply chain management by building an effective online catalog-based delivery system."
- **Other Value-Added Services.** FedEx offers several value-added services. For example, products can be shipped from a FedEx operated warehouse instead of the customer's warehouse. In addition, FedEx sometimes provides a "merge-in-transit" service to customers like Micron Computers that operate on rapid turnaround and delivery. Under the merge-in-transit program, FedEx stores peripherals such as monitors and printers in its Memphis, TN air hub. FedEx then matches those products with the computers en route to a customer. If a customer in Boston, for example, orders a popular PC model online, Micron sends the electronic order to FedEx, which will transport the computer from Micron's warehouse to FedEx's Boston, MA station. At the station, FedEx matches the computer with a standard Micron monitor and printer shipped from a FedEx-managed warehouse in Memphis, TN. The FedEx driver then delivers the computer, monitor, and printer to the customer's home.

Sources: Compiled from Rao et al. (1999) and from FedEx press releases.

Business alliances. Many companies realize that alliances with other companies, even competitors, can be beneficial. For example, General Motors, Ford, and others in the automotive industry created a huge e-marketplace called Covisint (see also Chapter 7). There are several types of business alliances, such as resource-sharing partnerships, permanent supplier-company relationships, and joint research efforts. One of the most interesting types is the temporary joint venture, in which companies form a special organization for a specific, time-limited mission. This is an example of a **virtual corporation,** which could be a common busi-

Continuous Improvement Efforts	
Area/Subject	**Description**
Productivity improvement	Increasing output-to-input ratio
Just-in-time	A comprehensive production and inventory control program
Total quality management (TQM)	Corporate-wide effort to improve quality
Improved decision making	Making better and more timely decisions
Managing information and knowledge	Proper storage, retrieval, and use of information
Innovation and creativity	Encouraging innovation and using creative thinking
Change management	Introducing and properly managing change
Customer service	Planning and providing superb customer service

TABLE 1-4

ness organization model in the future. A more permanent type of business alliance that links manufacturers, suppliers, and finance corporations is known as *keiretsu* (a Japanese term meaning a permanent business alliance). Similarly, supply chain management is facilitated by extranets (see also Chapter 7). This and other types of alliances can be heavily supported by EC technologies ranging from EDI to electronic transmission of maps and drawings.

Electronic markets. Most electronic markets require the cooperation of different companies, including competitors. As will be shown in Chapter 7, there are thousands of vertical e-markets. Vertical markets include companies in the same industry, which usually compete with each other. Now, these companies create consortia, usually for e-purchasing. However, even if the market is organized and managed by a third party, as is the case with Chemdex and Ventro (Application Case 1.4), it is still necessary for companies to cooperate.

IT Support and EC

Information technology in general and EC in particular, have played a major role in organizations' response activities for a long time. For example, EDI facilitates rapid paperless transactions that enable companies to reduce some departments' labor forces by as much as 80 percent (Ford case in Hammer and Champy 1993).

EC solutions can help implement many popular critical support activities, as will be demonstrated throughout this book. Here we provide only some examples.

- **Reducing cycle time and time to market.** Reducing the business process time (cycle time) is extremely important for increasing productivity and competitiveness (Wetherbe 1996). Similarly, reducing the time from the inception of an idea to its implementation (time to market) is important because those who are first on the market with a product or who can provide customers with a service faster than competitors enjoy a distinct competitive advantage. Extranet-based applications can be used to expedite the various steps in the process of product or service development, testing, and implementation. An example of cycle time reduction in bringing new drugs to the market is shown in Application Case 1.5 on p. 23.

The Rise and Fall of Chemdex

Research chemicals are used by over 300,000 laboratory scientists across the United States. Over 250,000 specialty biological science products are produced by more than 2,000 manufacturers, most of which are very small. Overall, more than $1 billion of chemicals are traded every year, and the market is growing rapidly.

Until 1998, the market used paper-based catalogs with Sigma-Aldrich Corp. acting as a central distributor to about 15 percent of the market. Buyers had to search through many paper catalogs, some of which were out of date, and purchase products from distributors who charged up to 40 percent commission. In many cases, buyers frequently missed the best suppliers. Sellers were unable to reach all potential buyers and were subject to the whims of the distributors. The market was very inefficient, with prices often varying 40 percent on similar items from different vendors. Comparison shopping was hard to do, and customers (mostly small companies) were scattered across the country and costly to reach.

Chemdex changed the situation by connecting the buyers and other business partners. The company aggregated the vendors' catalogs into a Web-accessible database and created an e-commerce site where customers could search for chemicals by product and category. Buyers were now able to locate what they needed, compare prices, get detailed product information, and place an order. Chemdex collects a 5 to 12 percent commission from each sale versus the 40 percent commission charged by traditional distributors.

Chemdex completed its beta testing of the e-commerce site in mid-1998, and since then has grown rapidly. By November 2000, Chemdex offered over 1.7 million products from 2,200 vendors.

Buyers were impressed. Ken Kilgore from the Department of Pharmacology at the University of Michigan said, "It's long overdue, it's user friendly, it's a basic system, and my technicians can use the system in minutes instead of searching hours." He also seemed encouraged by the prospect that the consolidation of chemical information might help to standardize an industry in which reagents tend to differ qualitatively.

Small vendors were especially happy. Dako Corp., for example, claims that its products, which sell very well among clinical pathologists, are little known among biotech researchers who use similar products. The company hopes that Chemdex will help increase sales by placing Dako products alongside those of better-known competitors.

In 1999, Chemdex won the best B2B EC site award (*Internet Week*, April 19, 1999). In 2000, Chemdex merged with a company called Ventro (*ventro.com*). Ventro is a marketplace service provider to Chemdex and five other related marketplaces.

However, in December 2000 Chemdex was closed. Competing exchanges slowed its growth and losses accumulated rapidly. Chemdex's contribution to EC is significant since it helped create B2B exchanges (see Chapter 7).

Sources: Complied from *Interactive Week* (January 26, 1998), *The Scientist* (July 6, 1998), and from *chemdex.com*.

APPLICATION CASE   1.5

The Internet and the Intranet Shorten Time-to-Market for New Drugs

The Problem

The Federal Drug Administration (FDA) must be extremely careful in approving new drugs. However, there is public pressure on the FDA to approve new drugs quickly, especially those for cancer and HIV. The problem is that to assure quality, the FDA requires companies to conduct extensive research and clinical testing. The development programs of such research and testing cover 300,000 to 500,000 pages of documentation for each drug. The subsequent results and analyses are reported on 100,000 to 200,000 additional pages. These pages are reviewed by the FDA prior to approval of new drugs. Manual processing of this information significantly slows the work of the FDA, so much so that the total approval process takes 6 to 10 years.

The Solution

Computer-Aided Drug Application Systems (Research Data Corporation, New Jersey) is a software program that uses a network-distributed document-processing system. The pharmaceutical company scans all related documents into a database. The documents are indexed, and full-text search and retrieval software is attached to the system. Using keywords, corporate employees can search the database via their company's intranet. The database is also accessible, via the Internet, to FDA employees, who no longer have to spend hours looking for a specific piece of data. (It takes only 6 to 8 seconds to access an image in the database.) Information can be processed or printed at the user's desktop computer.

This system not only helps the FDA, but also the companies' researchers who now have every piece of required information at their fingertips. Remote corporate and business partners can also access the system. The overall results: The time to market of a new drug is reduced by up to a year. (Each week saved can be translated into the saving of many lives and can also yield up to $1 million profit.) The system also reduces the time it takes to patent a new drug.

An interesting example of this technology is the case of ISIS Pharmaceuticals, Inc. ISIS Pharmaceuticals developed an extranet-based system similar to the one described here. The company uses CD-ROMs to submit reports to the FDA and opens its intranet to FDA personnel. This step alone could save 6 to 12 months from the average 15-month review time. One month is saved by the electronic submission of an FDA report. To cut time even further, SmithKline Beecham Corporation is using electronic publishing and hypertext links to enable quick navigation.

Sources: Compiled from *IMC Journal* (May/June 1993), *INCTechnology* (No. 3, 1997), and *openmarket.com.*

- **Empowerment of employees and collaborative work.** Giving employees the authority to act and make decisions on their own is a strategy used by many organizations as part of their CRM. Empowerment is also related to the concept of self-directed teams (Mankin 1996; Lipnack and Stamps 1997). Management delegates authority to teams who can then execute the work faster and with fewer delays. Information technology allows the decentralization of decision making and authority but simultaneously supports a centralized control. For example, the Internet and intranets enable empowered employees to access the information and knowledge they need to make quick decisions. Empowered salespeople and customer service employees can make customers happy and do it quickly, helping to increase customer loyalty.
- **Supply chain improvements.** EC, as will be shown throughout the book, especially in Chapter 15, can help in reducing supply chain delays and inventories and eliminate other inefficiencies, as shown in the Orbis case.
- **Mass customization.** Today's customers demand customized products and services. The problem is how to do it efficiently. This can be done, in part, by changing manufacturing processes from mass production to mass customization (Pine and Gilmore 1997). In mass production, a company produces a large quantity of identical items. In **mass customization,** items are produced in a large quantity but are customized to fit the desires of each customer. EC is an ideal facilitator of mass customization.
- **Change Management.** The introduction of EC is a major change for most organizations. Change management can be explained through a management framework originally developed by Levitt, later modified by Scott-Morton (Scott-Morton and Allen 1994) and further modified by the

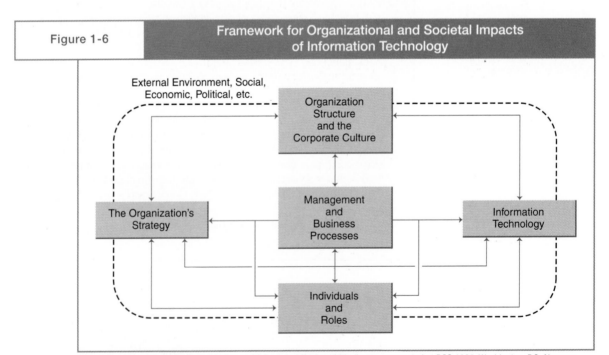

| Figure 1-6 | Framework for Organizational and Societal Impacts of Information Technology |

Sources: Adapted from M. Scott-Morton, "DSS Revisited for the 1990s," paper presented at DSS 1986, Washington, DC. Also see Scott-Morton and Allen (1994).

authors, to reflect the role of IT in general and EC in particular. The framework is depicted in Figure 1-6.

Organizations are composed of five major components, one of which is IT (including EC), and they are surrounded by an environment that also includes EC. The five components are in a stable condition, called *equilibrium,* as long as no significant change occurs in the environment or in any of the components. However, as soon as a significant change occurs, the system becomes unstable and possibly ineffective and/or inefficient. As you can see in Figure 1-6, the internal components are interconnected and interrelated. Therefore, a significant change, for example, in an organization's strategy, may create a major change in the corporate structure. Similarly, the introduction of EC, either in the environment (e.g., by a competitor) or the initiation of EC in the company itself, creates a change. Unstable organizations may be unable to excel or even survive this change; therefore, organizations need to make appropriate adjustments by using critical response activities. If the change introduced by EC is properly managed, a company can expect many benefits.

1.5   BENEFITS AND LIMITATIONS

The Benefits of EC

Few innovations in human history encompass as many potential benefits as EC does. The global nature of the technology, the opportunity to reach hundreds of millions of people, its interactive nature, the variety of possibilities for its use, as well as the resourcefulness and rapid growth of its supporting infrastructures, especially the Web, will result in many potential benefits to organizations, individuals, and society. These benefits are just starting to materialize, but they will increase significantly as EC expands. It is not surprising that some maintain that the EC revolution is just "as profound as the change that came with the industrial revolution" (Clinton and Gore 1997).

BENEFITS TO ORGANIZATIONS

The benefits to organizations are as follows:

- Electronic commerce expands the marketplace to national and international markets. With minimal capital outlay, a company can easily and quickly locate more customers, the best suppliers, and the most suitable business partners worldwide. For example, Boeing Corporation reported a savings of 20 percent after a request for a proposal to manufacture a subsystem was posted on the Internet. A small vendor in Hungary answered the request and won the electronic bid. Not only was the subsystem cheaper, but it was delivered about twice as quickly.
- Electronic commerce decreases the cost of creating, processing, distributing, storing, and retrieving paper-based information. For example, by introducing an electronic procurement system, companies can cut purchasing administrative costs by as much as 85 percent.
- Supply chain inefficiencies, such as excessive inventories and delivery delays, can be minimized with EC. For example, by building autos to order instead of for dealers' showrooms, the automotive industry is expected to save tens of billions of dollars annually just from inventory reduction. This

approach is based on the concept of pull-type production, which begins when an order is placed (Chapter 2).

- Pull-type processing allows for inexpensive customization of products and services and provides a competitive advantage for companies who implement this strategy. A well-known example of pull-type processing is that used by Dell Computer Corp.
- EC allows for many innovative business models that provide strategic advantages and/or increase profits. Group purchasing (Chapter 6) combined with reverse auctions is one example of such an innovative business model.
- EC allows for a high degree of specialization that is not economically feasible in the physical world. For example, a store that sells only dog toys can operate in cyberspace (*dogtoys.com*), but in the physical world such a store would not have enough customers.
- EC reduces the time between the outlay of capital and the receipt of products and services.
- EC supports BPR efforts. By changing processes, the productivity of salespeople, knowledge workers, and administrators can increase by 100 percent or more.
- EC lowers telecommunications costs—the Internet is much cheaper than VANs.
- EC enables efficient e-procurement that can reduce administrative costs by 80 percent or more, reducing purchasing prices by 5 to 15 percent, and reducing cycle time by more than 50 percent.
- EC enables companies to interact more closely with customers, even if through intermediaries. (See Chapter 4 opening vignette for an example.) This promotes better CRM and increases customer loyalty.
- Other benefits include improved corporate image, improved customer service, new business partners, simplified processes, compressed time-to-market, increased productivity, reduced paper and paperwork, increased access to information, reduced transportation costs, and increased flexibility.

Here are some other examples of savings:

- It costs a bank $1.08 to perform a simple teller transaction at a branch. On the Web, the same transaction costs only $.10.
- The cost of issuing an airline ticket on the Web is $1. With a physical system the transaction costs $8.
- It costs $70 to make an average appointment over the phone, but only $10 on the Internet.
- Each transaction costs a bricks-and-mortar retailer $12 to $20. Selling over the Internet reduces it to $2.
- The administrative cost to send a bill is $1.60. This amount can be cut in half if bills are sent electronically.
- It costs the U.S. government $.43 to issue a paper check vs. $.02 to send the same payment electronically.

BENEFITS TO CONSUMERS

The benefits of EC to consumers are as follows:

- EC allows consumers to shop or perform other transactions year round, 24 hours a day, from almost any location.

- EC provides consumers with more choices; they can select from many vendors and from more products.
- EC frequently provides consumers with less expensive products and services by allowing them to shop in many places and conduct quick comparisons.
- In some cases, especially with digitized products, EC allows for quick delivery.
- Consumers can locate relevant and detailed product information in seconds, rather than days or weeks.
- EC makes it possible to participate in virtual auctions. These allow sellers to sell things quickly and buyers to locate collectors' items and bargains.
- EC allows customers to interact with other customers in electronic communities and exchange ideas as well as compare experiences.
- EC facilitates competition, which results in substantially lower prices for consumers.

BENEFITS TO SOCIETY

The benefits of EC to society are as follows:

- More individuals work at home and do less traveling for work or shopping, resulting in less traffic on the roads and reduced air pollution.
- Some merchandise can be sold at lower prices, allowing less affluent people to buy more and increase their standard of living.
- People in Third World countries and rural areas are now able to enjoy products and services that otherwise are unavailable. This includes opportunities to learn skilled professions or earn a college degree.
- Public services, such as health care, education, and distribution of government social services can be delivered at a reduced cost and/or improved quality. For example, EC provides rural doctors access to information and technologies with which they can better treat their patients.

The Limitations of EC

There are both technical and nontechnical limitations of EC, most of these limitations are also discussed elsewhere in this book.

TECHNICAL LIMITATIONS OF EC

The major technical limitations of EC are as follows:

- System security, reliability, standards, and some communication protocols are still evolving (Chapters 13 and 14).
- In many areas, telecommunications bandwidths are insufficient.
- Software development tools are still evolving and changing rapidly (Chapter 12).
- It is difficult to integrate the Internet and EC software with some existing applications and databases (Chapter 12).
- Vendors may need special Web servers, network servers, and other infrastructure developments (Chapter 12).
- Some EC software might not fit with some hardware, or it may be incompatible with certain operating systems or components.

As time passes, these limitations will lessen or will be overcome. Appropriate planning can minimize their impact.

NONTECHNICAL LIMITATIONS

The following are the major limitations that slow the spread of EC.

- The cost of developing EC in-house can be very high and mistakes made due to lack of experience may result in delays. There are many opportunities for outsourcing, but where and how to do it are not simple issues (Chapter 12). Furthermore, to justify the system one must deal with some intangible benefits (such as improved customer service and the value of advertisement), which are difficult to quantify.
- Security and privacy are important in the B2C area, especially security issues, which are perceived to be more serious than they really are (if appropriate controls are used). Privacy protection measures are constantly being improved (Chapter 17). Customers think these issues are very important. The EC industry has a very long and difficult task of convincing customers that online transactions and privacy are, in fact, very secure.
- In many cases, customers do not trust an unknown, faceless seller, paperless transactions, and electronic money. Because of this, switching consumer preferences from physical to virtual stores may be difficult.
- Some customers like to touch items, such as clothes, so they know exactly what they are buying.
- Many legal issues are as yet unresolved, and in many circumstances government regulations and standards are not yet refined enough to deal with the intricacies of EC (Chapter 17).
- As a discipline, EC is still evolving and changing rapidly. Many people are looking for EC to stabilize before they enter into it.
- EC does not have enough support services. For example, copyright clearance centers for EC transactions are just starting to appear and qualified EC tax experts are rare.
- In many areas there is not enough critical mass for EC to be successful. In most applications, there are not yet enough sellers and buyers for profitable EC operations.
- Some fear that as EC reduces face-to-face social interactions, there could be a breakdown in human relationships.
- Internet access is still expensive and/or inconvenient for many potential customers. (With Web TV, kiosks, cell phones and constant media attention, the critical mass will eventually develop.)

Despite these limitations, EC is rapidly expanding. For example, the number of people in the United States who buy and sell stocks electronically increased from 300,000 at the beginning of 1996 to over 17 million by the fall of 2001. In Korea, about 60 percent of all stock market transactions took place over the Internet in the fall of 2001 (versus 2 percent in 1998), and, according to J.P. Morgan, the number of online brokering customers in Europe will reach 17.1 million in 2003 (versus 1.4 million in 1999). As experience accumulates and technology improves, the cost-benefit ratio of EC will increase, resulting in greater rates of EC adoption.

The benefits presented here may not be convincing enough reasons for a business to implement EC. Much more compelling are the business pressures discussed earlier that will force many companies to engage in EC and the characteristics of the digital economy discussed in Chapter 2.

1.6   PUTTING IT ALL TOGETHER

The major concern of many companies today is how to transform themselves in order to take part in the digital economy, where e-business is the norm. If the transformation is successfully completed, many companies will reach the status of our hypothetical company, Toys, Inc., which uses the Internet, intranets, and extranets in an integrated manner to conduct various EC activities (Figure 1-7).

Toys, Inc. conducts all of its internal communications, collaboration, dissemination of information, and database access over an intranet. The company uses an extranet (upper left of Figure 1-7) to cooperate with its large business partners such as suppliers, distributors, noncorporate retail stores, and liquidators. In addition, the company is connected to a toy exchange via an extranet (upper right of Figure 1-7), which includes other manufacturers, professional associations, and large suppliers.

The company is networked to several e-marketspaces and large corporations. For example, some major corporations allow Toys, Inc. to connect to their intranet via their own extranets. Toys, Inc. is also connected with its banks and other financial institutions (loan providers, stock issuers) over a highly secured EDI that runs on a VAN. The company is also using the VAN-based EDI with some of its largest suppliers and other business partners. An Internet-based EDI is used with smaller business partners that are not on the corporate EDI. The company communicates with others via the Internet.

The company's business partners and employees interact with each other and with the company via the corporate portal. A **portal** is a major gateway through which employees, business partners, and the public can access corporate information and communicate and collaborate as needed. Many companies are moving towards a similar network configuration. Today, it is almost impossible to do business without being connected to business partners through the Internet, extranets, or EDI.

1.7   MANAGERIAL ISSUES

Many managerial issues are related to EC and they are discussed throughout the book. The following issues are germane to management:

1. **Is it real?** For those not involved in EC, the first question that comes to the mind is "Is it real?" We do believe that the answer is definitely "yes." Just ask anyone who has experienced home banking, online stock purchasing, or bought a book from Amazon. An interesting tip was given by Randy Mott, Wal-Mart's CIO: "Start EC as soon as possible; it is too dangerous to wait." Jack Welch, CEO of General Electronic, has commented, "The Internet and E-commerce are *as important as breathing*."

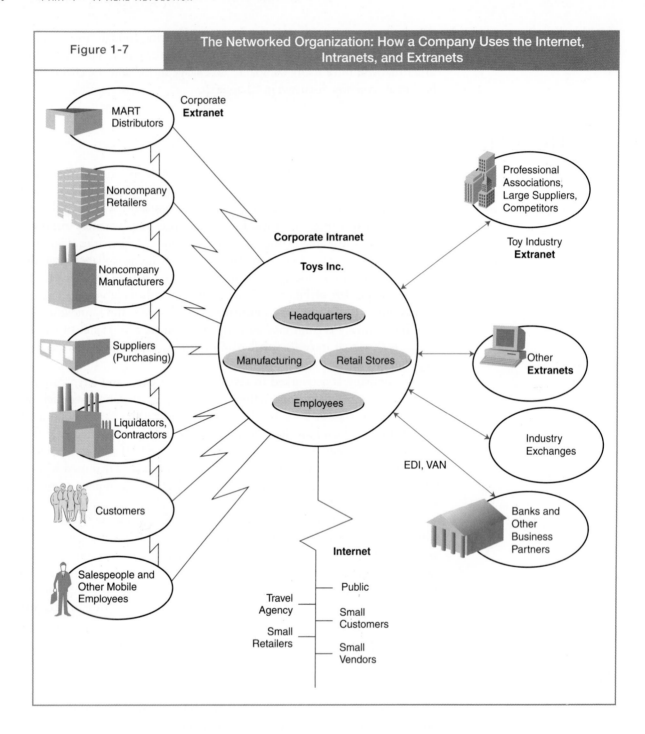

Figure 1-7 — The Networked Organization: How a Company Uses the Internet, Intranets, and Extranets

2. How to evaluate the magnitude of the business pressures. The best approach is to solicit the expertise of research institutions, such as GartnerGroup or Forrester Research, which specialize in EC. Often, by the time you determine what is going on it may be too late. The big certified public accounting companies may be of help too. (PriceWaterhouseCoopers, Andersen Consulting, and many others provide considerable EC information on their Web sites.) It is especially important for management to know what is going on in its industry.

3. **What should be my company's strategy toward EC?** There are three basic strategies: lead, wait, or experiment. This issue is revisited in Chapter 16 together with related issues such as the cost benefits of EC, integration of EC into the business, outsourcing, and how to handle resistance to change. Another strategic issue is the prioritization of the many initiatives and applications available to a company (see Rosen 1999).

4. **Why is the B2B area so attractive?** In contrast with B2C, which has several major problems ranging from channel conflict with existing distributors to lack of a critical mass of buyers, some B2B models are easier to implement. Many companies can start buying or selling electronically in a matter of days by joining existing marketplaces. The problem is knowing which marketplaces to join.

5. **What is the best way to learn EC?** Start with this book. It provides a comprehensive treatment of the EC field and points to many support resources. This book has a companion Web page that has links to major EC resources (*prenhall.com/turban*). You may be astonished to learn how much information already exists on EC (try a search on EC at *google.com*). You may want to consider creating an EC task force within your organization.

6. **What ethical issues exist?** Organizations must deal with ethical issues when dealing with their employees, customers, and suppliers. This may be difficult because what is ethical in one company or country may be unethical in another. Ethical issues are very important because they can damage the image of an organization as well as destroy the morale of its employees. The use of EC raises many ethical issues, ranging from participation in a consortia that uses cookies to trace customers' activities on the Internet in order to target focused ads to customers to the potential invasion of privacy of millions of customers whose data are stored in private and public databases. Because EC is new and rapidly changing, there is little consensus on how to deal with EC-related ethical issues.

7. **There are so many failures, how can one avoid them?** As of early 2000, we have witnessed the failure of many EC projects within companies, as well as the failure of many "Internet companies." Industry consolidation often occurs after a "gold rush." About 100 years ago, hundreds of companies tried to manufacture cars in the United States, only three survived. The important thing is to learn from the failures of others (Useem 2000).

1.8   TEXT OVERVIEW

This book is composed of 19 chapters divided into 6 parts as shown in Figure 1-8.

Part I—A Real Revolution

This section of the book includes the overview of EC presented in Chapter 1. Chapter 2 deals with the economics of the digital revolution and some of its major characteristics and changes.

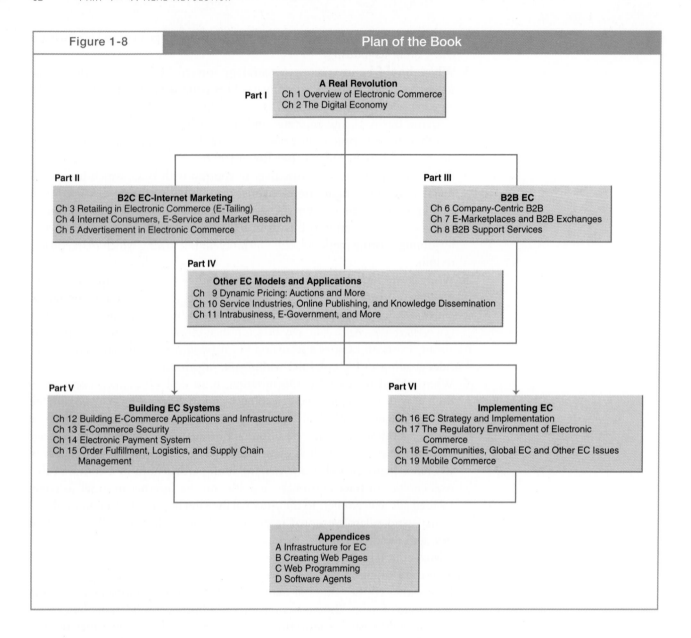

Figure 1-8   Plan of the Book

Part II—B2C EC-Internet Marketing

This section is composed of three chapters. In Chapter 3 we describe e-tailing (B2C), including some of its most innovative applications. Chapter 4 is dedicated to the explanation of consumer behavior in cyberspace, market research, and customer service. Lastly, Chapter 5 discusses Internet advertising.

Part III—B2B EC

This section is composed of three chapters. In Chapter 6 we introduce B2B and describe primarily company-centric models (one buyer-many sellers, one seller-many buyers). Electronic exchanges are the subject of Chapter 7, and in Chapter 8 we describe unique B2B models as well as B2B support services.

Part IV—Other EC Models and Applications

Here we present several different topics. In Chapter 9 we discuss all types of online auctions. Chapter 10 is dedicated to online service industries, ranging from travel to online learning. In Chapter 11 we introduce C2C, G2C, intrabusiness, and corporate portals.

Part V—Building EC Systems

This section deals first with EC development approaches, including outsourcing, which are presented in Chapter 12. Then, we delve into EC security in Chapter 13. EC payment systems are the subject of Chapter 14. Lastly, Chapter 15 is dedicated issues of order fulfillment and logistics.

Part VI—Implementing EC

This final section includes four chapters. Chapter 16 deals with e-strategy and planning, including organization transformation to the digital economy. Chapter 17 presents EC legal and policy issues. Chapter 18 covers multiple topics such as global EC, small businesses in EC, e-communities, and other current issues. We conclude with a discussion of the future of EC. Finally, Chapter 19 deals with mobile commerce.

Appendices

Four appendices are available on the Web (*prenhall.com/turban*):

A. Infrastructure for EC
B. Creating Web Pages
C. Web Programming
D. Software Agents

Summary

In this chapter, you learned about the following EC issues as they relate to the learning objectives:

1. **Define EC and describe its categories.** EC involves conducting transactions electronically. Its major categories are B2B, B2C, C2C, collaborative commerce, and intraorganizational transactions.
2. **Electronic markets and interorganizational systems.** Electronic marketplaces involve the selling and buying of products and services electronically. These can be B2C or B2B. Interorganizational information systems (IOS) refer to the flow of repetitive information among business partners and between organizations (including governments) and customers.
3. **The framework and content of EC.** The applications of EC, and there are many of them, are based on infrastructures and supported by people, public policies, technical standards, advertising, logistics, and business partners—all bonded by management.

4. **The driving forces of EC.** Market (economics), technological, and societal pressures force organizations to respond to business pressures. Traditional responses may not be sufficient because of the magnitude of the pressures and the frequent changes involved. Therefore, organizations frequently must innovate and reengineer their operations. In many cases, EC is the major facilitator of organizational responses.

5. **Benefits to organizations, consumers, and society.** There are numerous benefits of EC. Because these benefits are substantial, it proves that EC is here to stay and can't be ignored.

6. **Limitations of EC.** The many limitations of EC can be categorized as technological and nontechnological. As time passes, the barriers posed by technological limitations diminish, as capacity, security, and accessibility continue to improve through technological innovations. The nontechnical limitations will also diminish with time, but some of them, especially the behavioral ones, may persist for many years in some organizations.

7. **Managerial issues.** Management needs to know that EC is real, which EC strategy to use, how to learn about EC, and how to avoid failures. This book should clarify these issues.

Key Terms

Business model	Electronic exchanges
Business-to-business (B2B)	Electronic markets (e-market)
Business-to-consumers (B2C)	Empowerment
Business-to-employees (B2E)	Exchange-to-exchange (E2E)
Brick-and-mortar organizations	Extranet
Click-and-mortar organizations	Government-to-citizens (G2C)
Collaborative commerce (c-commerce)	Internet
Corporate portals	Interorganizational information systems (IOS)
Customization	Intranet
Cycle time reduction	Marketspace (see electronic markets)
Dynamic pricing	mass customization
E-business	Mobile commerce (m-commerce)
E-tailing	Portal
Electronic commerce (EC)	Supply chain management
Electronic communities	Value-added networks
Electronic data interchange (EDI)	Virtual corporation

Questions for Review

1. Define EC and e-business.
2. List the organizational, consumer, and societal benefits of EC.
3. List the major technological and nontechnological limitations of EC.
4. List the market, technological, and societal pressures on organizations.
5. List the major activities undertaken by organizations to deal with business pressures.
6. Define intranet and extranet.
7. Describe the major components of the EC framework (Figure 1-3).

8. Define a corporate portal.
9. List the major impacts of EC on direct marketing.
10. Define a virtual corporation.
11. Define electronic exchange.
12. Define E2E, C2C, and G2C.
13. Define B2B and B2C.
14. Define collaborative commerce.
15. Define mobile commerce.

Questions for Discussion

1. Distinguish between IOS and electronic markets. Describe the major characteristics of each. Relate IOS to c-commerce.
2. Carefully examine the nontechnological limitations of EC. Which of them are company-dependent and which are generic?
3. Compare brick-and-mortar and click-and-mortar organizations.
4. What are the major benefits of EC to Qantas's customers?
5. Why is it said that EC is a catalyst of fundamental changes in organizations?
6. What drove Qantas to EC?
7. Explain how EC facilitates supply chain management.
8. Explain how EC can reduce cycle time, improve employees' empowerment, and customer support.
9. How can EC facilitate customization of products and services?
10. Why is buying with a smart card from a vending machine considered EC?
11. Find some applications of m-commerce and discuss what is unique about them.
12. Compare EC with mail order from paper catalogs and television.
13. Why is distance learning considered EC?
14. Examine all the EC applications presented in this chapter. Which of them can be classified as electronic markets and which as IOS? Also identify which are B2B, which are B2C, and which are intraorganizational.
15. Read Clinton and Gore's "A Framework for Global Electronic Commerce." Why do they emphasize the importance of global EC?
16. Examine the failure of *living.com*.

Internet Exercises

1. Chevron Corporation's Web site for children (*chevroncars.com*) was selected as the "most innovative site in 1998." Visit the site and try to determine why.
2. Locate recent information on *Amazon.com* and its battle with Barnes & Noble (*bn.com*).
    a. Enter Amazon's site and find the top selling textbooks on EC.
    b. Find a review of one of these textbooks.
    c. Review the services you can get from Amazon and describe all the benefits you can receive.
3. Enter *emarketer.com* and find the latest statistics on EC growth.
4. Go to *fedex.com* (you will need to go to its U.S. operations) and find information about recent EC projects that are related to logistics and supply chain management.

5. Go to *mixonic.com* and create a CD. Then visit *iprint.com* and create your own business card. Finally, enter *jaguar.com* and configure a car. What are the advantages of each activity? The disadvantages?

6. It is time you try to sell or buy on an online auction. You can try *eBay.com, auction.yahoo.com,* or an auction of your choice. You can participate in an auction from almost any country. Prepare a short report describing your experience.

7. Try to save on your next purchase by using group purchasing. Visit *bazaare.com, startupfailures.com,* or *zwirl.com.* Which site do you prefer? Why?

Team Assignments and Role Playing

1. Assign each team member a failed or failing Internet company (e.g., *living.com*). Use *startupfailures.com* to identify companies that are in distress. *Fortune* is also a good source of details for particular business failures. Have each team prepare a report of why the company they examined failed or is failing.

2. Each team will research an EC success story. Members of the group should examine companies that operate solely online and some that utilize a click-and-mortar strategy. Each team is responsible for identifying the critical success factors for their company and presenting a report to the team. (See *prenhall.com/turban* for case studies and relevant URLs.)

REAL-WORLD CASE: E-Commerce Cures Hospitals

Changes in U.S. government regulations and strong competition in the health care industry in the late 1990s caused headaches for many health care institutions. Even Kaiser Permanente, the largest U.S. health maintenance organization (HMO), could not escape the problem, losing $288 million in 1998 alone. Kaiser Permanente serves about 10 million members (patients) with 361 hospitals and clinics, 10,000 doctors, and tens of thousands of support employees. The company realized that the old way of doing business, working with old-fashioned paper records and communicating with telephones, faxes, and letters, was only going to aggravate their financial problems. So in a bold move, Kaiser Permanente decided to move toward EC by investing $2 billion in various Web-based systems. Here are some of the projects:

- An Internet-based communications system was implemented. The system includes customized Web sites for each organization with which Kaiser has a contract. Staff from those organizations can locate particular rates or coverage online, and do not have to call Kaiser's employees for the information.

- Kaiser's portal allows patients to schedule and check their appointments via the Internet and e-mail routine queries to Kaiser employees.

- Kaiser's corporate intranet allows doctors and other employees to electronically order supplies, equipment, and services.

- The corporate intranet has an application that checks the drugs that a doctor suggests for each patient. The computer then suggests cheaper or less dangerous alternatives. The doctor can then decide if the substitution is acceptable.

- As an HMO, Kaiser has to compete with other HMOs for customers, both organizational (with all their employees) and individual. The intranet allows for real-time quotes, so Kaiser's sales force of over 4,000 brokers can provide customers with customized rates within minutes.

- Digital records of patients' tests are kept on the intranet and can be accessed by authorized personnel in seconds. This means that staff no longer have to repeat 10 to 15 percent of patient tests due to lost or misread paper records.

- An e-procurement system expedites shipments, reduces inventories, and cuts cost.

- All medical records are digitized. A doctor can instantly tap into a patient's records from a keyboard and a flat-panel computer screen attached to the wall. The doctor can also add notes to the computer.

Dozens of other EC applications are in the works. All of the EC applications will be part of a huge network that will be completed in 2003.

EC implementation has not been easy. The HMO started phasing in EC in the northwestern states in 1999. During the phase-in, some employees resisted, mistakes were made, and vendors had to be managed. But the results are clear. The Internet is the only medicine for large health care organizations. In the first 2 years, costs in the Internet system were about 60 percent lower than costs in comparable non-Internet systems. Most importantly, the use of EC also improves the quality of the delivery, and this is what really matters.

Questions for the case

1. Review the EC applications listed and classify them as B2C, B2B, c-commerce, etc.

2. What factors drove Kaiser Permanente to implement EC? Read more about patients' demands and political pressures on HMOs.

3. Identify the EC applications related to supply chain management.

4. Many doctors do not like computers to provide them with suggestions. What can management do about this?

5. It is said that placing a large computer screen in an examination room increases the doctor's productivity and improves doctor-patient interaction. Elaborate.

Sources: Compiled from *Business Week E.BIZ*, Feb. 7, 2000, and from Kaiser's 2000 and 2001 press releases.

REFERENCES AND BIBLIOGRAPHY

Applegate, L. M. E-business models. Chap. 3 in *Information Technology for the Future Enterprise: New Models for Managers*, edited by G.W. Dickson and G. DeSanctis. Upper Saddle River, New Jersey: Prentice Hall, 2001.

Boyett, J. H. and J. T. Boyett. *Beyond Workplace 2000: Essential Strategies for the New American Corporation*. New York: Dutton, 1995.

Callon, J. D. *Competitive Advantage Through Information Technology*. New York: McGraw-Hill, 1996.

Choi, S. Y., et al. *The Economics of Electronic Commerce*. Indianapolis: Macmillan Technical Pub., 1997.

Clinton, W. J. and A. Gore, Jr. "A Framework for Global Electronic Commerce." *iitf.nist.gov/eleccomm/ecomm.htm*, 1997.

Cunningham, M. S. *B2B: How to Build a Profitable E-Commerce Strategy*. Cambridge: Perseus Pub., 2001.

Dertouzos, M. *What Will Be: How the New World of Information Will Change Our Lives*. San Francisco: Harper Edge, 1997.

Drucker, D. F. *Managing in a Time of Great Change*. New York: Truman Tally Books, 1995.

Fingar, P., et al. *Enterprise E-Commerce*. Tampa, Florida: Meghan Kiffer Press, 2000.

Gill, K. S., ed. *Information Society*. London: Springer Publishing Co., 1996.

Hammer, M. and J. Champy. *Reengineering the Corporation*. New York: Harper Business, 1993.

Hoffman, D. L. and T. P. Novak. "How to Acquire Customers on the Web." *Harvard Business Review* (May–June 2000), 179–187.

Huff, S. L., et al. *Cases in Electronic Commerce*. Chicago: Irwin Professional Pub., 1999.

Kalakota, R. and A. B. Whinston. *Electronic Commerce: A Manager's Guide*. Reading, Massachusetts: Addison-Wesley, 1997.

Lipnack, J. and J. Stamps. *Virtual Teams—Reaching Across Space, Time, and Organizations with Technology*. New York: John Wiley & Sons, 1997.

Mankin, D. *The Digital Economy*. New York: McGraw-Hill, 1996.

McLaren, B. J. and C. H. McLaren. *E-Commerce: Business on the Internet*. Cincinnati, Ohio: South-Western Pub., 1999.

Pine, B. J. and J. Gilmore. The Four Faces of Mass Customization. *Harvard Business Review* (Jan.–Feb. 1997), 91–101.

Pyle, R. "Electronic Commerce on the Internet," *Communications of the ACM* (special issue June 1996), 22–33.

Rao, B., et al. "Building World-Class Logistics, Distribution, and E-commerce Infrastructure." *Electronic Markets*. Vol. 9, no. 3 (1999).

Rosen, A. *The E-Commerce Q and A Book: A Survival Guide for Business Managers*. New York: AMACOM, 1999.

Rugullis, E. Power to the Buyer with Group Buying Sites. *e-BUSINESS ADVISOR* (Feb. 2000).

Scott-Morton, M. and T. J. Allen, eds. *Information Technology and the Corporation of the 1990's*. New York: Oxford University Press, 1994.

Senn, J. A. "Capitalization on Electronic Commerce," *Information Systems Management* (Summer 1996).

Shaw, M. J. "Electronic Commerce: Review of Critical Research Issues." *Information Systems Frontiers*. Vol. 1, no. 1 (1999).

Shaw, M. J., et al. *Handbook on Electronic Commerce*. Berlin: Springer-Verlag, 2000.

Tapscott, D., et al., eds. *Blueprint to the Digital Economy: Wealth Creation in the Era of E-Business*. New York: McGraw-Hill, 1998.

Timmers, P. *Electronic Commerce*. New York: Wiley, 2001.

Turban, E., et al. *Information Technology for Management*, 2nd ed. New York: John Wiley & Sons, 2000.

Useem, J. "Dot-coms: What Have We Learned." *Fortune* (October 30, 2000).

Wetherbe, J. C. *The World on Time*. Santa Monica, California: Knowledge Exchange, 1996.

Wiegram, G. and H. Koth. *Custom Enterprise.com*. Upper Saddle River, New Jersey: Financial Times/Prentice Hall, 2000.

Zwass, V. Electronic Commerce: Structures and Issues. *International Journal of Electronic Commerce* (Fall 1996).

BUILDING THE SUPPLY CHAIN

A **supply chain** refers to the flow of materials, information, and services, from raw material suppliers through factories and warehouses to the end customers. A supply chain also includes the *organizations* and *processes* that create and deliver these products, information, and services to the end customers.

SUPPLY CHAIN COMPONENTS

The term *supply chain* comes from a picture of how the partnering organizations are linked together. As shown in Figure A1-1, a simple supply chain links a company that manufactures or assembles a product (middle of the chain) with its suppliers (on the left) and distributors and customers (on the right). The upper part of the picture shows a generic supply chain, while the bottom part shows a specific example of making toys.

The arrows in the figure show the flow of material among the various partners. Not shown is the flow of returns, which may be in the reverse direction. The bro-

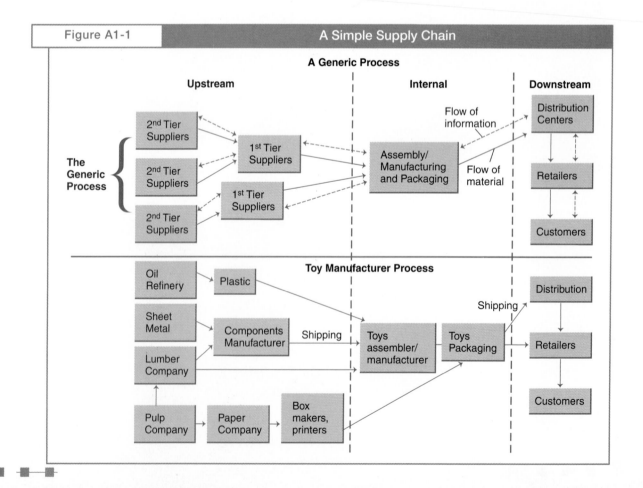

Figure A1-1   A Simple Supply Chain

ken lines, which are shown only in the upper part, indicate the bidirectional flow of information.

The supply chain is composed of three parts:

1. **Upstream.** This part includes the suppliers (which can be manufacturers and/or assemblers) and their suppliers. Such a relationship can be extended, to the left, in several tiers, all the way to the origin of the material (e.g., mining ores, growing crops).

2. **Internal Supply Chain.** This part includes all the processes used in transforming the inputs received from the suppliers to outputs, from the time the inputs enter an organization to the time that the product(s) goes to distribution outside the organization.

3. **Downstream.** This part includes all the activities involved in delivering the product to final customers. (The supply chain actually ends when the product reaches its after use disposal—presumably back to Mother Earth somewhere).

As one can see, a supply chain involves activities during the entire **product life cycle,** from "dirt to dust." However, a supply chain is more than that, since we also deal with a movement of information and money, and with procedures that support the movement of a product or a service. Finally, the organizations and individuals involved are considered a part of the chain as well.

For more information on supply chains and for references, see Chapter 15.

2

The Digital Economy

LEARNING OBJECTIVES

Upon completion of this chapter the reader will be able to:

- Describe the major characteristics of the digital economy.

- Compare marketplaces with marketspaces.

- Describe the nature of competition in marketspaces.

- Describe some economic rules of the digital economy.

- Describe the impacts of the digital economy on trading and intermediaries.

- Describe the impacts of the digital economy on business processes and functional areas in organizations.

- Understand the role of m-commerce in the digital economy.

CONTENT

THE PROBLEM

Rosenbluth International (*rosenbluth.com*) is a major international player in the competitive travel agency industry. The digital revolution introduced the following threats to Rosenbluth and the travel agent industry in general:

- Airlines, hotels, and other service providers are attempting to bypass travel agents by moving aggressively to direct electronic distribution systems (e.g., electronic ticketing via online booking as in the Qantas case [Chapter 1]).

- Commissions caps have been reduced (from $50 to $10) and most major airlines decreased travel agents' commission percentages from 10 percent to 5 percent.

- Large numbers of new online companies (e.g., *expedia.com*) provide diversified travel services at bargain prices in an effort to attract individual travelers. However, these online services are now penetrating the corporate travel market as well.

- Competition among the major players is rebate-based. The travel agencies basically give part of their commission back to their customers by using the commission to subsidize lower prices.

- Innovative business models that were introduced by e-commerce, such as name your own price, auctions, and reverse auctions, have been embraced by many companies in the travel industry (see Qantas case in Chapter 1), adding competitive pressures.

THE SOLUTION

Rosenbluth International responded to theses new pressures with two strategies. First, they decided to get out of the leisure travel business, becoming a pure corporate travel agency. Second, they decided to rebate customers with their *entire* commission. Instead of generating revenues by commission, Rosenbluth now bills customers according to the service provided. For example, fees are assessed for consultations on how to lower corporate travel costs, for the development of in-house travel policies for corporate clients, for negotiating for their clients with travel providers, and for travel-related calls answered by the Rosenbluth staff.

To implement the second strategy, which completely changed the company's business model, Rosenbluth now uses several innovative e-commerce applications. The company uses a comprehensive Web-based business travel management solution that integrates travel planning technology, policy and profile management tools, proprietary travel management applications, and seamless front-line service/support. This browser-based service allows corporate travelers to book reservations anytime, anywhere, within minutes. The specific tools in this system are:

- **DACODA** (Discount Analysis Containing Optimal Decision Algorithms) is a patented yield-management system that optimizes a corporation's travel savings, enabling travel managers to decipher complex airline pricing and identify the most favorable airline contracts.

- **Electronic messaging services** allow clients to manage their travel requests via e-mail. It uses a Web-based template that permits clients to submit reservation requests without picking up the phone. Additionally, a structured itinerary is returned to the traveler via e-mail.

- **E-Ticket tracking** tracks, monitors, reports on, and collects the appropriate refund or exchange for unused e-tickets. As the amount of e-tickets usage grows, so does the amount of unused e-tickets that need to be refunded or exchanged.

- **Res-Monitor,** a patented low-fare search system, tracks a reservation up until departure time and finds additional savings for one out of every four reservations.

- **Global distribution network** electronically links the corporate locations and enables instant access to any traveler's itinerary, personal travel preferences, or corporate travel policy.

- **Custom-Res** is a global electronic reservation system that ensures policy compliance, consistent service, and accurate reservations.

- **IntelliCenters** are advanced reservations centers that use innovative telecommunications technology to manage calls from multiple accounts resulting in cost savings and personal service for corporate clients.

- **Network Operations Center (NOC)** monitors the many factors impacting travel, including weather, current events, and air traffic. This information is disseminated to the company's front-line associates so they can inform their clients of potential changes to their travel plans. The NOC also tracks call volume at all offices and enables the swift rerouting of calls as needed.

■───┘ **THE RESULTS**

In 1979 the company had $40 million in sales, primarily from leisure-oriented travelers in the Philadelphia area. By 1997 that figure had grown to over $3 billion due mainly to several EC and IT innovations. Today, the company operates in 24 countries and has about 4,500 employees. Since the introduction of the Web-based solutions in 1997, sales increased to about $5 billion in 3 years (60 percent increase). The company not only survived the threats of elimination but increased its market share and profitability.

Sources: Compiled from E. K. Clemons and L. H. Hann, "Rosenbluth International: Strategic Transformation," *Journal of MIS* (Fall 1999) and from information at *rosenbluth.com* in May 2001.

2.2 THE DIGITAL ECONOMY—AN OVERVIEW

The opening case is a vivid example of a company that has achieved a competitive advantage in the digital era by using EC. Rosenbluth's experience illustrates the following points:

- It is sometimes necessary to completely change business models and strategies to succeed in the digital economy.
- Web-based IT and EC are the facilitators of survival by providing companies a competitive advantage.
- Global competition is not just about price and quality; it is also about service.
- An extensive networked computing infrastructure is necessary to support a large global system. This may be very costly, as is the cost of building the EC applications.
- Web-based applications are used to provide superb customer service, not just sales or procurement support.
- It is necessary to patent innovative systems to assure competitive advantage.

The most important lesson learned from this case is that EC can threaten an entire industry, yet EC is an extremely important tool that allows innovative companies within that industry to gain a strategic advantage. As a matter of fact, many executives who were cynical about the strategic advantage of IT and EC until 1998, completely reversed their attitudes at that time. Web-based EC opportunities and risks are now attracting universal attention in executive boardrooms.

Web-based EC systems certainly provide some organizations with a competitive advantage. In a study conducted by Lederer et al. (1998), "enhancing competitiveness or creating strategic advantage" was ranked as the number one benefit of Web-based systems. However, EC systems are not the only useful type of IT application. Computer-based information systems of all kinds have enhanced competitiveness and created strategic advantages of their own or in conjunction with EC applications (e.g., see Griffiths et al., 1998 and Galliers et al., 1999).

The Digital Economy Defined

The **digital economy**, also known as the **Internet economy, new economy,** or the **Web economy,** refers to the economy that is based in a large part on digital technologies, including digital communication networks (Internet, intranets, etc.), computers, software, and other related information technologies. Digital networking and communication infrastructures provide a global platform to interact, communicate, collaborate, and search for information. According to Choi and Whinston (2000), this platform includes the following:

- A vast array of products made of digital bits—databases, news and information, books, magazines, TV and radio programming, movies, electronic games, musical CDs, and software—that are delivered over the digital infrastructure anytime, anywhere in the world.
- Consumers and firms conduct financial transactions digitally through digital currencies or financial tokens downloaded and carried on smart cards via networked computers and mobile devices.
- Physical goods such as home appliances and automobiles are embedded with microprocessors and networking capabilities.

The term *digital economy* refers to the convergence of computing and communication technologies through the Internet and the resulting flow of information and technology that is stimulating EC and spurring vast organizational changes. The digital economy has created an economic revolution, which according to the *Emerging Digital Economy II* (ecommerce.gov) is evidenced in the United States by unprecedented economic growth and the longest period of uninterrupted economic expansion in history. According to this report and U.S. released statistics:

- Information technology industries have been growing at more than double the rate of the overall economy, reaching close to *9 percent of GDP in 2000,* up from 4.9 percent in 1985.
- IT industries by themselves have driven on average *over one-quarter of total real economic growth* (not including any indirect effects) in the years 1996 to 2000.
- Without information technology, overall inflation would have been *3.1 percent in 1997,* more than a full percentage point higher than *the 2.0 percent* that it was. Because of information technology, the United States enjoys sustainable growth with almost no inflation.
- Companies throughout the economy are betting on IT to boost productivity. In the 1960s, business spending on IT equipment represented only *3 percent of total business equipment investment.* In the late 1990s, IT's share rose to *45 percent each year.*
- In 1999, over 8.5 million people worked in the IT sector and in IT-related jobs in the U.S. workforce. These workers earned just *under $49,000 per year,* compared to an average of *$29,000* for the private sector as a whole.
- At almost *$60,000 per year*, workers in the software and services industries were the highest wage earners. Salaries have been growing at a rate of 6.6 percent per year, versus 3.8 percent for total private sector employment.

- There were nearly 2.5 million Internet-related jobs in the United States in December 1999, up 36 percent during the year.
- In Silicon Valley, unemployment is the lowest in the world, frequently at a *negative* 3 to 5 percent (more jobs than employees).

These figures indicate that we are indeed experiencing a digital revolution. According to Porter (2001), the Internet technology by itself increases competition and tends to weaken industry profitability. Therefore, it is important to view the Internet as a complement to, not a cannibal of, traditional ways of competing. Companies must distinguish themselves through a strategy facilitated by the Internet, as Rosenbluth did, in order to excel.

In this chapter we will examine the economics of EC, competition in the digital economy, and the impacts of EC on organizations and industries. We will conclude this chapter by describing the emerging area of mobile commerce (m-commerce).

2.3   MARKETSPACES VS. MARKETPLACES

The Rosenbluth case is only one example of some of the changes that EC has introduced into our economic system. The digital economy is characterized by many examples of companies that created new products, services, and business models. One factor behind these developments is the unique economics of EC. Schwartz (1997), who coined the term Webonomics, or Web economy, claimed that Webonomics amounts to new economic rules, new forms of currency, and new consumer behavior.

Before analyzing the economic aspects of EC, it will be useful to review the economic role of markets. Markets, according to Bakos (1998), play a central role in the economy, facilitating the exchange of information, goods, services, and payments. In the process, they create economic value for buyers, sellers, market intermediaries, and for society at large.

Markets (electronic or otherwise) have three main functions: (1) matching buyers and sellers; (2) facilitating the exchange of information, goods, services, and payments associated with market transactions; and (3) providing an institutional infrastructure, such as a legal and regulatory framework, that enables the efficient functioning of the market (Table 2-1).

In recent years, the markets have seen a dramatic increase in the role of IT and EC (Turban et al., 2002). Basically, EC was successful in increasing market efficiencies by expediting or improving the functions listed in Table 2-1. Furthermore, EC was able to significantly decrease the cost of executing these functions.

The emergence of electronic marketplaces, called *marketspaces,* especially Internet-based marketspaces, changed several of the processes used in trading and in supply chains. These changes, which were driven by IT, resulted in even greater economic efficiencies. EC leverages IT with increased effectiveness and lower transaction and distribution costs, leading to more efficient, "friction-free" markets. An example of such efficiency can be seen in the NTE case (Application Case 2.1). Another example is provided in the real world case at the end of this chapter.

Rayport and Sviokla (1994) noted that the process of doing business in the virtual world is completely different from the real world because instead of processing raw materials and distributing them, EC involves gathering, selecting, synthesizing,

TABLE 2-1

Functions of a Market

Matching Buyers and Sellers

- Determination of product offerings
  _ Product features offered by sellers
  _ Aggregation of different products
- Search (of buyers for sellers and of sellers for buyers)
  _ Price and product information
  _ Organizing bids and bartering
  _ Matching seller offerings with buyer preferences
- Price discovery
  _ Process and outcome in determination of prices
  _ Enabling price comparisons

Facilitation of Transactions

- Logistics
  _ Delivery of information, goods, or services to buyers
- Settlement
  _ Transfer of payments to sellers
- Trust
  _ Credit system, reputations, rating agencies like Consumers Reports and BBB. Special escrow and trust online agencies

Institutional Infrastructure

- Legal
  _ Commercial code, contract law, dispute resolution, intellectual property protection
  _ Export and import law
- Regulatory
  _ Rules and regulations, monitoring, enforcement

Source: Based on Bakos (1998), p. 35.

APPLICATION CASE   2.1

National Transportation Exchange (NTE)

The hauling industry is not very efficient. While trucks are likely to be full on outbound journeys, on the way back they are often empty (about 50 percent of the trucks on America's roads at any one time are empty). National Transportation Exchange (NTE) is attempting to solve this problem.

NTE (*nte.com*) uses the Internet to connect shippers who have loads they want to move cheaply with fleet managers who have space to fill. NTE helps create a spot market by setting daily prices based on information from several hundred fleet managers about the destinations of their vehicles and the amount of space they have available. It also gets information from shippers about their needs and flexibility in dates. NTE then works out the best deals for the shippers and the haulers. When a deal is agreed upon, NTE issues the contract and handles payments. The entire process takes only a few minutes. NTE collects a commission based on the value of each deal, the fleet

APPLICATION CASE   2.1

(continued)

manager gets extra revenue that he would otherwise have missed out on, and the shipper gets a bargain price, at the cost of some loss of flexibility.

When NTE was first set up in 1995, it used a proprietary network that was expensive and limited the number of buyers and sellers who could connect through it. By using the Internet, NTE has been able to extend its reach down to the level of individual truck drivers and provide a much wider range of services. Today, drivers can use wireless Internet access devices to connect to the NTE Web site on the road.

In 2000, NTE expanded its services to improve inventory management, scheduling, and vender compliance along the entire supply chain. NTE's software is integrated with their customers' operations and systems. NTE's business is currently limited to ground transportation within the United States. In Hong Kong, *Portsnportals.com* (called Line) provides similar services for port services.

Sources: Compiled from *The Economist* (June 26, 1999), *nte.com* (April 2001), and *portsnportals.com* (April 2001).

and distributing information. Therefore, the economics of EC, starting with supply and demand and ending with pricing and competition, are completely different from traditional economic models. The new order of economics covers many topics, and it cannot be covered in one chapter (for detailed coverage see Choi et al., 1997 and Choi and Whinston, 2000). Therefore only selected topics are discussed here.

2.4   THE COMPONENTS OF DIGITAL ECOSYSTEMS

Similar to a marketplace, in the **marketspace** sellers and buyers exchange goods and services for money (or for other goods and services if bartering is used), but they do it electronically. Exchange of goods and services is a subset of economic activities (Hanappi and Rysavy, 1998). The marketspace includes actions that bring about a new distribution of goods and services. The expected utility of the entities pursuing this trade is rising. The major components and players of a marketspace are digital products (in a pure marketspace), consumers, sellers, infrastructure companies, intermediaries, support services, and content creators. A brief description of each follows.

Digital products. One of the major differences between the marketplace and the marketspace is the possible digitization of products and services. In addition to digitization of software and music, it is possible to digitize dozens of other products and services, as shown in Table 2-2. As will be described later, digital products have different cost curves than those of regular products. In digitization, most of the costs are fixed and the variable cost is very small. Therefore, profit will increase very rapidly as volume increases once the fixed costs are paid for.

TABLE 2-2

Examples of Digital Products

1. Information and entertainment products that are digitized:
   - Paper-based documents: books, newspapers, magazine journals, store coupons, marketing brochures, newsletters, research papers, and training materials
   - Product information: product specifications, catalogs, user manuals, sales training manuals
   - Graphics: photographs, postcards, calendars, maps, posters, x-rays
   - Audio: music recordings, speeches, lectures, industrial voice
   - Video: movies, television programs, video clips
   - Software: programs, games, development tools
2. Symbols, tokens, and concepts:
   - Tickets and reservations: airlines, hotels, concerts, sports events, transportation
   - Financial instruments: checks, electronic currencies, credit cards, securities, letters of credit
3. Processes and services:
   - Government services: forms, benefits, welfare payments, licenses
   - Electronic messaging: letters, faxes, telephone calls
   - Business-value-creation processes: ordering, bookkeeping, inventorying, contracting
   - Auctions, bidding, bartering
   - Remote education, telemedicine and other interactive services
   - Cybercafes, interactive entertainment, virtual communities

Source: Based on Choi et al. (1997), p. 64.

Consumers. The tens of millions of people worldwide that surf the Web are potential buyers of the goods and services offered or advertised on the Internet. The consumers are looking for bargains, customized items, collectors' items, entertainment, and more. They are in the driver's seat. They can search for detailed information, compare, bid, and sometimes negotiate. Organizations are the major consumers, accounting for over 85 percent of EC activities.

Sellers. Hundreds of thousands of storefronts are on the Web, advertising and offering millions of items. Every day it is possible to find new offerings of products and services sellers can sell direct from their Web site or from e-marketplaces.

Intermediaries. Intermediaries of all kinds offer their services on the Web. The role of these intermediaries, as will be seen throughout the text and especially in Chapters 3, 8, and 10, is different from that of regular intermediaries. Intermediaries create and manage the online market (such as in the NTE case). Intermediaries help match buyers and sellers, provide some infrastructure services, and help customers and/or sellers to institute and complete transactions. Most of the intermediaries are computerized systems, referred to as **e-intermediaries,** or **infomediaries.**

Support services. Many different support services are available, ranging from certification and trust services, which ensure security, to knowledge providers (see Chapter 8). These services are created in order to address implementation issues.

Infrastructure companies. Thousands of companies provide the hardware and software necessary to support EC. Many companies that provide software also provide consulting services on how to set up a store on the Internet. Other companies offer hosting services for small sellers (for example, *gegxs.com*).

Content creators. Hundreds of media-type companies create and perpetually update Web pages and sites. They do it for their own Web sites and those of other companies. The quality of Web content is a major critical success factor in EC.

Business partners. In addition to sellers and buyers there are several types of partners that collaborate on the Internet, mostly along the supply chain.

Electronic marketplaces. There are several types of electronic marketplaces. The major types are: *exchanges* (many-to-many) (see Chapter 7), *sell-side* (one seller-many buyers), and *buy-side* (one buyer-many sellers) (see Chapter 6). E-marketplaces can be public, open to all, or private, open to invited trades only (see Real-World Case). A variety of *market mechanisms* are used in e-marketplaces. Most notable are electronic auctions.

2.5   COMPETITION IN MARKETSPACES

Competition is going through a fundamental change as can be seen in the *Amazon.com* versus Barnes & Noble example (Application Case 2.2).

APPLICATION CASE   **2.2**

Amazon.com vs. Barnes & Noble

In the first 3 years of its existence, *Amazon.com's* sales grew very rapidly (800 percent from 1996 to 1997). It took Barnes & Noble, the world's largest physical bookstore, about 18 months to react to *Amazon.com's* initiative by opening a competing online division. By that time *Amazon.com* was in full control of the market and had a strong leadership position. While *Amazon.com* was still losing money in 2000, it controlled over 60 percent of all online book sales, and it established business partnerships with over 400,000 companies. Today, the name *Amazon.com* is much more recognized, worldwide, than that of Barnes & Noble.

To offset *Amazon.com's* control of the B2C market, Barnes & Noble demonstrated initiative by adding a B2B component to its EC model. To increase its competitive edge, Barnes & Noble created a completely separate company to handle all its online activities including B2B. In response, *Amazon.com* acquired several online companies in other countries and diversified its product line by adding CDs and other products.

The competition between these two companies will continue to increase as new innovations and strategies develop. In addition to lowering prices on many books by as much as 40 percent due to the lower distribution cost of online operations, customers now enjoy a huge selection of easy-to-find books, partly because of the competition between these two online giants.

While Barnes and Noble concentrates on books and its recently added music division, *Amazon.com* now offers hundreds of different types of products and competes with many other companies. For example, in CD sales it competes with CDNow. However, despite changes and diversification, *Amazon.com* and Barnes and Noble are still in a very stiff competition.

Sources: Compiled by the authors from a variety of online and offline sources over a period of 2 years.

Competition in the Internet Ecosystem

The **Internet ecosystem** is the business model of the online economy. The prevailing model of competition in the Internet economy is more like a web of interrelationships than the hierarchical, command-and-control model of the industrial economy. Unlike the value chain, which rewarded exclusivity, the Internet economy is inclusive and has low barriers to entry. Just like an ecosystem in nature, activity in the Internet economy is self-organizing. The process of natural selection takes place around company profits and value to customers. As the Internet ecosystem evolves both technologically and in population, it will be even easier and likelier for countries/companies/individuals to participate in the Internet economy. Already, there is $1 trillion in technical infrastructure in place, ready and available for anyone to use at any time—free of charge. That's why new ideas and ways of doing things can come from anywhere at any time in the Internet economy. The old rules no longer apply.

EC competition is very intense for the following reasons:

- **Lower buyers' search cost.** Electronic markets reduce the cost of searching for product information, frequently to zero. This can significantly impact competition (Bakos, 1997). Enabling customers to find cheaper (or better) products forces sellers, in turn, to reduce prices and/or improve customer service. Companies that do just that, can exploit the Internet to gain a considerably larger market share.
- **Speedy comparisons.** Not only can the customers find inexpensive products, they can find them quickly. For example, a customer does not have to go to several bookstores to quickly find the best price for a particular book. Using shopping search engines such as *allbookstores.com* or *bestbookbuys.com,* customers can find what they want and compare prices. Companies that trade online and provide information to search engines will gain a competitive advantage.
- **Differentiation and personalization.** *Amazon.com* provides customers with information that is not available in a physical bookstore, such as communication with authors, almost real-time book reviews, and book recommendations, differentiating itself from other book retailers. In addition, EC provides for personalization or customization of products and services. Personalization refers to the ability to tailor a product, service, or Web content to specific user preferences. For example, *Amazon.com* will notify you by e-mail when new books on your favorite subject or by your favorite author are published.

Consumers like differentiation and personalization and are frequently willing to pay more for them. Differentiation reduces the substitutability between products. Also, price cutting (in differentiated markets) does not impact market shares very much.

- **Lower prices.** *Amazon.com, buy.com,* and other companies can offer low prices due to their low costs of operation (no physical facilities, minimum inventories, and so on). If volume is large enough, prices can be reduced by 40 percent.
- **Customer service.** *Amazon.com* provides superior customer service. As we will see in Chapters 3 and 4, such a service is an extremely important competitive factor.

Other competitive factors to consider are:

- The size of a company may no longer be a significant competitive advantage, as will be shown later.
- Geographical distance from the consumer may play an insignificant role.
- Some language barriers may be easily removed.
- Digital products lack normal wear and tear (see discussion in Choi and Whinston, 2000).

All in all, EC supports efficient markets and could result in almost perfect competition. In such markets, a commodity is produced when the consumer's willingness to pay equals the marginal cost of producing the commodity, and neither sellers nor buyers can influence supply or demand conditions individually.

In order to be in perfect competition it is necessary to:

1. Enable many buyers and sellers to enter the market at no entry cost (no barriers to entry).
2. Not allow large buyers or sellers to individually influence the market.
3. Make certain that the products are homogeneous (no product differentiation).
4. Supply buyers and sellers with comprehensive information about the products and the market participants' demands, supplies, and conditions.

EC could provide, or come close to providing, these conditions. It is interesting to note that the ease of finding information benefits both buyers (finding information about products, vendors, prices, etc.) and sellers (finding information about customer demands, competitors, etc.).

It is said that competition between companies is being replaced by competition between networks. The company with better networks, advertisement capabilities, and relationships with other Web companies (such as Rosenbluth International or *Amazon.com*) has a strategic advantage. It is also said that competition is between business models. With a better business model you will win.

PORTER'S COMPETITIVE ANALYSIS IN AN INDUSTRY

Porter's competitive analysis model in an industry views five major forces of competition that determine the industry's structural attractiveness. These forces, in combination, determine how the economic value created in an industry is divided among the players in the industry. Such industry analysis helps companies to develop their strategy in order to increase their profitability. Since the five forces are affected by the Internet and e-commerce, it is interesting to examine how the Internet influences the industry structure portrayed by Porter's model. Porter (2001) divided the impacts of the Internet into either positive or negative for the industry. As shown in Figure 2-1 most of the impacts are negative (marked by a minus sign). Of course, there are variations and exceptions to the impacts shown in Figure 2-1, depending on the industry, its location and size.

This means that competition will intensify in most industries. The competition is not only between online and offline companies but also among the online newcomers. This competition which is especially strong in commodity-type products (toys, books, CDs), was a major contributor to the collapse of many dotcom companies in 2000-2001. To survive and prosper in such an environment one needs to use innovative strategies, as Rosenbluth did. We will return to this topic in Chapter 16.

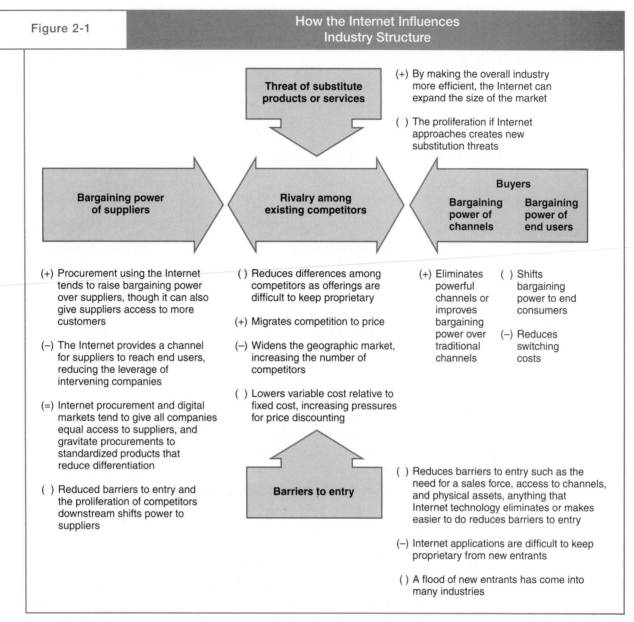

Figure 2-1 — How the Internet Influences Industry Structure

Threat of substitute products or services

(+) By making the overall industry more efficient, the Internet can expand the size of the market

( ) The proliferation if Internet approaches creates new substitution threats

Bargaining power of suppliers

Rivalry among existing competitors

Buyers — Bargaining power of channels / Bargaining power of end users

(+) Procurement using the Internet tends to raise bargaining power over suppliers, though it can also give suppliers access to more customers

(–) The Internet provides a channel for suppliers to reach end users, reducing the leverage of intervening companies

(=) Internet procurement and digital markets tend to give all companies equal access to suppliers, and gravitate procurements to standardized products that reduce differentiation

( ) Reduced barriers to entry and the proliferation of competitors downstream shifts power to suppliers

( ) Reduces differences among competitors as offerings are difficult to keep proprietary

(+) Migrates competition to price

(–) Widens the geographic market, increasing the number of competitors

( ) Lowers variable cost relative to fixed cost, increasing pressures for price discounting

Barriers to entry

(+) Eliminates powerful channels or improves bargaining power over traditional channels

(–) Reduces switching costs

( ) Shifts bargaining power to end consumers

( ) Reduces barriers to entry such as the need for a sales force, access to channels, and physical assets, anything that Internet technology eliminates or makes easier to do reduces barriers to entry

(–) Internet applications are difficult to keep proprietary from new entrants

( ) A flood of new entrants has come into many industries

Source: Porter, M., "Strategy and the Internet," *Harvard Business Review*, March 2001, p.67.

2.6   ISSUES AND SUCCESS FACTORS IN THE DIGITAL ECONOMY

There are several other issues related to the economics of EC. Most of them are discussed by Choi et al. (1997) and Choi and Whinston (2000). Some examples follow.

- **Cost curves.** The total cost curves of many physical products and services are U-shaped (Figure 2-2a). First, as quantity increases the cost declines, but later the cost (average per product) increases due to the growth of both the fixed and the variable costs (especially administrative and marketing costs).
- **Digital products.** With digital products (Figure 2-2b), the variable cost per unit is very low (in most cases) and almost fixed, regardless of the quantity.

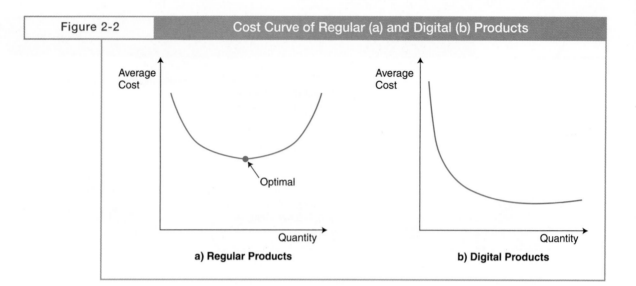

Figure 2-2 — Cost Curve of Regular (a) and Digital (b) Products

Therefore, cost per unit will decline as quantity increases due to the proration of the fixed component of the cost over more units. This results in increasing returns with increased sales.

- **Buying versus renting.** Just like with physical products, in EC one can rent or a group can share products. Availability of such options will influence both demand and prices.
- **Bundling products/services.** Bundling several products or services is especially common in software products that are digitized. Bundling provides for a useful price discrimination method, and it is used extensively by vendors. In EC, there are more opportunities for bundling, and the pricing issue becomes critical.

There are many other related issues. However, due to space limitations we will describe here only three issues that have a major impact on the deployment of EC.

The Need for a Critical Mass of Buyers and Sellers

A critical mass of buyers is needed for an EC company or initiative to survive. As indicated earlier, the fixed cost of deploying EC can be high, sometimes very high. Without a large number of buyers, sellers will not make money. In 2001, the number of Internet users worldwide was estimated by Forrester Research to be at the 350 million to 450 million range. This number is still small compared with an estimated 2 billion television viewers. This situation will change, especially when TV/PC integration becomes widespread and wireless devices become a popular way to access the Internet (Section 2.9).

So, should a business wait a few years before implementing EC? Definitely not. People must not be misled by Internet penetration macrostatistics. Business planners should look at the microlevel segmentation of the market they are trying to reach. For example, if a company's target market segment is not the average consumer but the highly educated ones, the percentage of online surfers may be much higher, therefore affording you a potentially large critical mass factor. The reason, for example, that PCs and PC-related equipment have been popular items for B2C sales, is that most PC users have a much higher rate of Internet access than the rest of the population. On the business side, if we take Intel, IBM, Cisco Systems, and Marshall Industries as prime examples, their primary customers have been Internet users longer than most other B2C customers.

At the global level, a critical mass of EC-enabled countries is required. Canada, for example, has a goal to be recognized as an EC-friendly country in order to attract international investments and business. Hong Kong is developing a multibillion dollar Cyberport, that will facilitate EC development and may position the country as a center for global EC in southeast Asia. Korea supports nine major B2B exchanges that relate to the country's major industries (e.g., semiconductors). Finally in 2001 the U.S. government introduced *BuyUSA.com* to facilitate global trade.

Critical mass of buyers and sellers is also referred to as **liquidity.** One of the major success factors for B2B exchanges is *early liquidity* (see Ramsdell, 2000, and Chapter 7). Finally, in addition to the issue of profitability, critical mass of both buyers and sellers is needed for markets to be truly efficient, so that strong and fair competition can develop.

Quality Uncertainty and Quality Assurance

While price is a major factor for any buyer, quality is extremely important in many situations, especially when buyers cannot see and feel what they purchase. When a consumer buys a brand-name PC from Dell, IBM, or Compaq, he or she is fairly sure about the quality of the product or service purchased. When a consumer buys from a not-so-well-known vendor, however, quality can become a major issue. The issue of quality is related to the issue of trust, as discussed in Chapter 4, and the issue of consumer protection, which is covered in Chapter 17. In both chapters, we discuss the idea of providing quality assurance through a trusted third-party intermediary. For example, TRUSTe and the BBBOnLine provide a testimonial seal for participating vendors. BBBOnLine is known for its quality assurance system and its physical testing of products.

The problem of quality is frequently referred to as the **quality uncertainty.** Customers have a cognitive difficulty accepting products that they have never seen, especially from a strange vendor. The BBBOnLine and TRUSTe seals can convince some customers, but not all. Customers are not sure what they will get. Here are some possible solutions.

- **Provide free samples.** This is a clear signal that the vendor is confident about the quality of its products. However, samples cost money. It is a sunk cost that will need to be recovered from future sales. The cost for digital samples, however, is minimal. Shareware-type software is based on this concept.
- **Return if not satisfied.** This policy is common in several countries and is used by most large retailers and manufacturers. This policy, which provides a guarantee or a full refund for dissatisfied customers, is helpful in facilitating trust in EC. Such a policy, however, might not be feasible for digital products for several reasons.

    The return of digital products has many complications. First, many digital products such as information, knowledge, or educational material are fully consumed when they are viewed by consumers. After they are consumed, therefore, returning the products has little meaning. Unlike physical products, returning a digital product does not prevent the consumer from using the product in the future. Also, the vendor cannot resell the returned product.

Second, returning a product or refunding a purchase price may be impractical due to transaction costs. For example, a microproduct, a small digital product costing a few cents or less, must be transported twice over the network, so the cost of the refund may exceed the price. Microproducts supported by micropayments, therefore, may not be sold with any quality guarantee or a refund. For further discussion of quality uncertainty see Choi et al. (1997) and Choi and Whinston (2000).

For physical products the issue of returns is critical. In some cases returns reach 30 percent, creating a major logistics problem (see Chapter 15).

- **Insurance, escrow, and other services.** Many services are available to ensure quality and prevent fraud. Of special interest are those offered by auction houses, such as *eBay.com,* as shown in Chapter 9.

Pricing on the Internet

Pricing products and services are very important in any economy, including the digital one. Pricing in many cases determines sales volume, market share, and product profitability. Several issues are related to pricing.

According to Bakos (1998), electronic marketplaces enable new types of price discovery to be employed in different markets. For example, some airlines auction last-minute unsold seats to the highest bidders, and Web-based auctions that function like financial markets have created markets for consumer goods. Intermediaries such as *Priceline.com* allow buyers to specify product requirements and the amount they are willing to pay and then make corresponding offers to the participating sellers, reversing the traditional functioning of retail markets. Finally, intelligent agents such as Kasbah (*kasbah.com*) and Tête-à-Tête, can negotiate purchases on behalf of buyers and sellers, and may restructure the price discovery process in e-marketplaces.

The ability to customize products, combined with the ability of sellers to access substantial information about prospective buyers, such as demographics, preferences, and past shopping behavior, is greatly improving sellers' ability to conduct **price discrimination,** that is, to charge different prices to different buyers. Price discrimination is also conducted, especially in B2B markets, by the use of customized catalogs and Web pages.

The new types of price discovery are changing the microstructure of consumer markets, the distribution channels, and the bargaining power of buyers and sellers (depending on the circumstances). In a market with highly differentiated and customized products, prices tend to be determined by buyers' willingness to pay rather than by the cost of production. The market force behind this fact is the market power obtained by **product differentiation.** Thus, pricing is a matter of how valuable a product is to a buyer, not how much it costs to produce it. Suppose that a digital product can be produced at zero variable cost. Even then, prices can be set at the consumer's value. Therefore, its price will not be zero unless the product is truly valueless. Prices based on user values necessitate better information gathering about consumers' tastes and income. The methods of collecting such information are discussed in Chapter 4.

ONLINE VS. OFF-LINE PRICING

Many organizations are becoming click-and-mortar, offering the same products and services both online and off-line. For example, you can buy a book at Barnes & Noble's physical store or buy it at their online store. Your bank will offer you the same services online and off-line, and so will most stockbrokers. The question is how to price the online products and services versus those off-line. This is an important strategic question. Some examples follow.

Most brokerage houses offer almost a 50 percent commission discount per trade if the trade is conducted online. In contrast, most banks do not offer any discounts for going online; some even charge additional (usually minimal) online fixed monthly service fees. Some banks, however, whose strategy is to aggressively go online, provide discounts, as do virtual banks. And what about retailers such as Toys 'R' Us and Wal-mart? What about Disney Online and Tower Records? In most of these cases there is no clear strategy. Some products are offered online at a discount, others are not. Promotions are sometimes conducted online at different times than off-line promotions. Furthermore, some retailers do not provide any online discounts. Shoppers' convenience may play a major role in such a decision. If the vendors believe that the major reason the buyers come to the Web is convenience, they will not provide a discount. An example is online supermarkets. Grocery shoppers frequently pay delivery charges when they buy online (see examples in Chapter 3); such shoppers are looking primarily for convenience. This situation may change when more online grocers and a critical mass of buyers join the marketspace. Some online grocers (for example, *netgrocer.com*) offer discounts, but only for non-perishable items. An issue related to pricing is product design (Bhargava et al., 2000).

Economic Impacts of EC

Another way to view the economic impacts of EC is shown is Figure 2-3. In Part A we show a company's production function. As seen, companies can substitute capital (automation) for labor for the same quantity of production, Q. For example, the lower the labor needed for the quantity Q = 1,000, the higher is the required

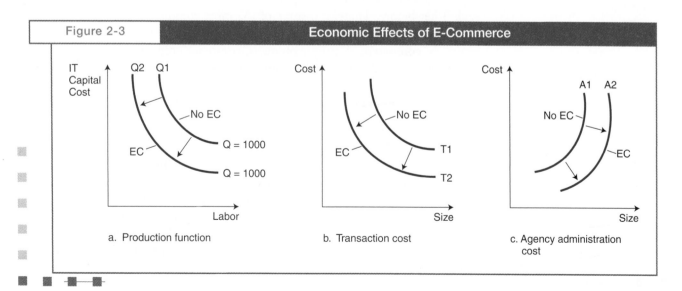

Figure 2-3   Economic Effects of E-Commerce

a. Production function
b. Transaction cost
c. Agency administration cost

investment. What EC does is shift the function inward from Q1 to Q2, lowering the amount of labor and/or capital needed to produce the same Q = 1000.

ECONOMIC EFFECTS OF E-COMMERCE

In Part B we show the effect of EC on transaction cost. Traditionally, firms had to grow in size to reduce cost (curve T1); in the digital economy the transaction cost is shifted inward to position T2. This means that now one can have low transaction costs with smaller firm size, or get much lower transaction costs when firm size increases.

In Part C we show the impact on administrative costs, known as agency cost. In the old economy these costs (A1) used to grow with the size (and complexity) of the firm, preventing companies from growing to a very large size. In the digital economy the curve is shifted to A2, meaning that companies can significantly expand their business without too much increase in the agency cost.

Contributors to Electronic Market Success

Based on an analysis of the EC examples previously discussed, it is apparent that EC will impact some industries more than others. The question is "what are some of the factors that determine this level of impact?" Strader and Shaw (1997) have identified several factors that each fall within one of four categories: product, industry, seller, and consumer characteristics.

PRODUCT CHARACTERISTICS

Digitizable products are particularly suited for electronic markets because they not only take advantage of the digitization of the market mechanism, but also the distribution mechanism, resulting in very low transaction costs. Digitization also allows the order fulfillment cycle time to be minimized.

A product's price may also be an important determinant. The higher the product price, the greater the level of risk involved in the market transaction between buyers and sellers who are geographically separated and may have never dealt with each other before. Therefore, some of the most common items currently sold through electronic markets are low-priced items such as CDs and books.

Finally, computers, electronic products, consumer products, and even cars can be sold electronically because the consumer knows exactly what he or she is buying. The more standards and product information available the better. The use of multimedia for example can dramatically facilitate product description.

INDUSTRY CHARACTERISTICS

Electronic markets are most useful when they are able to directly match buyers and sellers. However, some industries require transaction brokers, so they may be affected less by electronic markets than are industries where no brokers are required. Stockbrokers, insurance agents, and travel agents may provide services that are still needed, but in some cases software may be able to replace the need for these brokers. This is particularly true as more intelligent systems become available to assist consumers.

SELLER CHARACTERISTICS

Electronic markets reduce search costs, allowing consumers to find sellers offering lower prices. In the long run, this may reduce profit margins for sellers that compete in electronic markets, although it may also increase the number of transactions that take place. If sellers are unwilling to participate in this environment, then the impact of electronic markets may be reduced. However, in highly competitive industries with low barriers to entry, sellers may not have a choice. In oligopolistic situations, however, sellers may determine the success of electronic markets if they want to maintain an environment of low-volume, higher-profit-margin transactions.

CONSUMER CHARACTERISTICS

Consumers can be classified as either impulse, patient, or analytical as we will discuss in Chapter 4. Electronic markets may have little impact on industries where a sizable percentage of purchases are made by *impulse buyers.* Because e-markets require a certain degree of effort on the part of the consumer, e-markets are more conducive to consumers who do some comparisons and analyses before buying (the patient or analytical buyers). Analytical buyers can use the Internet to analyze a wide range of information before deciding where to buy. On the other hand, m-commerce is banking on impulse buyers (Chapter 19).

These determinants provide a framework for estimating the impact of electronic markets on current or future industries. The more industry features (including product, industry, seller, and consumer characteristics) associated with electronic markets, the greater the expected impact of electronic markets on that industry.

2.7   IMPACTS ON INDUSTRY STRUCTURE, INTERMEDIARIES, AND OTHERS

It is apparent from the examples provided in this book that the diffusion of electronic markets in an industry has an impact on the structure and process of the value chain involved in supplying the products and/or services to the final consumers. Some of these changes are shown in Figure 2-4, where traditional relationships (Parts a or b) are replaced by an electronic hub or marketplace (Part c). The hub or marketplace is usually managed by an *infomediary,* an electronic intermediary that controls the flow of information. A hub-based supply chain was shown in Chapter 1 (the Orbis case). The e-market changes in some cases, the linear process to an hub process, as will be shown throughout this book.

Industry Structure

Electronic markets also change the industry structure (Strader and Shaw, 1997). The first phase in the transformation of the structure of an industry is the digitization of the market mechanism that reduces the *search costs* (money, time, and effort expended to gather product price, quality, and feature information) for consumers. Searching *reduces the likelihood that sellers will be able to charge significantly higher prices than their competitors* because the consumer is now aware of the competitors' prices. The result is that consumers can buy products at the lowest prices, intermediaries such as wholesalers may be eliminated from the value chain, a new industry that provides access to electronic markets is created, and firms that produce products are able to maintain a profit margin comparable to the traditional markets.

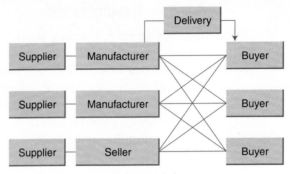

a. Direct Relationship (point-to-point)

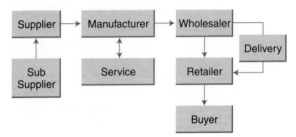

b. Traditional Intermediaries

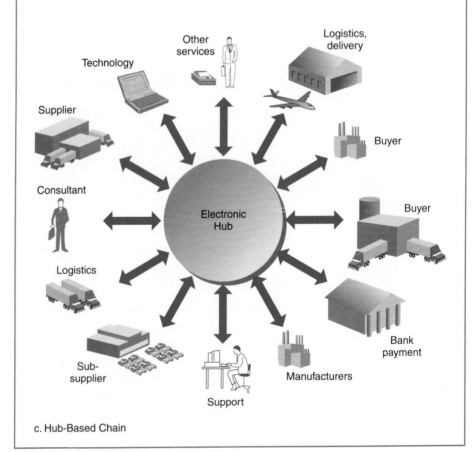

c. Hub-Based Chain

The second phase in the transformation of the structure of an industry is the digitization of the product itself as well as its distribution. Digitized products involve a cost structure with increasing returns and low marginal reproduction costs. Increasing returns to scale accrue when a business incurs large up-front expenditures to develop a new product/service, and the incremental cost of producing each new unit is minimal. Digitization also eliminates the need for sellers to maintain an inventory that must be physically shipped to the consumer.

The electronic market and distribution network enables a wide range of seller and customer activities, including marketing, order processing, distribution, payments, and even product development processes involving several separate firms, to converge into one place. This makes these activities easier and more convenient, while also reducing the costs involved. Beyond cost reduction, cycle time for order fulfillment is minimized, which may result in improved customer satisfaction. Digitized information can be distributed in minutes, whereas shipping a physical product generally takes days (or longer to some parts of the world).

The Roles and Value of Intermediaries in E-Markets

The roles and values of intermediaries were analyzed by Resnick et al. (1998) who postulated that producers and consumers interact directly in a marketplace: Producers provide information to customers, who then select from among the available products. In general, producers set prices, but sometimes prices are negotiated. However, direct negotiations are sometimes undesirable or unfeasible. Intermediaries, whether human or electronic, can address the following five important limitations of privately negotiated transactions.

1. **Search costs.** It may be expensive for providers and consumers to find each other. In the bazaar on the information superhighway, thousands of products are exchanged among millions of people. Brokers can maintain databases of customer preferences and reduce search costs by selectively routing information from providers to consumers and by matching customers with products and/or services. But producers may have trouble accurately gauging consumer demand for new products; many desirable items may never be produced simply because no one recognizes the demand for them. Brokers with access to customer preference data can predict demand. Large numbers of intermediaries already offer such services.
2. **Lack of privacy.** Either the buyer or seller may wish to remain anonymous or at least protect some information relevant to a trade. Brokers can relay messages and make pricing and allocation decisions without revealing the identity of one or both parties.
3. **Incomplete information.** The buyer may need more information than the seller is able or willing to provide, such as information about product quality, competing products, or customer satisfaction. A broker can gather product information from sources other than the product provider, including independent evaluators and other customers. Examples include some online travel agents, stockbrokers, and real estate agencies. Many third-party Web sites provide such information (e.g., *bizrate.com, mysimon.com,* and *consumerguide.com*).

4. **Contracting risk.** A consumer may refuse to pay after receiving a product, or a producer may provide inferior products or give an inadequate post-purchase service. Brokers have a number of tools to reduce risk. First, the broker can disseminate information about the behavior of providers and consumers. The threat of publicizing bad behavior or removing a seal of approval may encourage both producers and consumers to meet the broker's standard for fair dealing. Second, if publicity is insufficient, the broker may accept responsibility for the behavior of parties in transactions it arranges and act as a policeman on its own. Third, the broker can provide insurance against bad behavior. The credit card industry uses all three approaches to reduce providers' and consumers' exposure to risk. In the online auction area, there are companies that act as "escrow agencies," which are described in Chapter 9.

5. **Pricing inefficiencies.** By jockeying to secure a desirable price for a product, providers and consumers may miss opportunities for mutually desirable trades. This is particularly likely in negotiations over unique or custom products, such as houses, and in markets for information products and other public goods where freeloading is a problem. Brokers can use pricing mechanisms that induce just the appropriate trades, for example, dealing with an imbalance of buy and sell orders in stock markets.

Disintermediation and Reintermediation

One of the most interesting EC issues is that of intermediation. Intermediaries provide two types of services: (1) matching and providing information and (2) value added services such as consulting. As seen in the Rosenbluth case, the first type of services can be fully automated, and therefore, it is likely to be assumed by e-marketplaces and portals that provide free services. The second type requires expertise, and it can only be partially automated. Rosenbluth decided to charge only for the second type of service. Intermediaries who provide only (or mainly) the first type of service may be eliminated, a phenomena called **disintermediation.** On the other hand, brokers who provide the second type of service or who manage electronic intermediation, also known as **infomediation,** are not only surviving, but may actually prosper, as Rosenbluth did. This phenomenon is called **reintermediation.**

The Web offers new opportunities for reintermediation. First, brokers are especially valuable when the number of participants is enormous, as with the stock market or when complex information products are exchanged. Second, many brokering services require information processing; electronic versions of these services can offer more sophisticated features at a lower cost than is possible with human labor. Finally, for delicate negotiations, a computer mediator may be more predictable, and hence more trustworthy, than a human. For example, suppose a mediator's role is to inform a buyer and a seller whether a deal can be made, without revealing either side's initial price to the other, since such a revelation would influence subsequent price negotiations. An independent auditor can verify that a software-based mediator will reveal only the information it is supposed to; a human mediator's fairness is less easily verified. The subject of reintermediation and intermediation is discussed further in Chapters 3, 7, and 16.

Syndication

A new EC model is the syndication of goods and services. **Syndication,** per Werbach (2000), involves the sale of the same good to many customers, who then integrate it with other offerings and redistribute it. Syndication is extremely popular in the world of entertainment, but was rare elsewhere until the arrival of the Internet. The digitization of products and services, and the ease with which information flows, makes syndication a popular business model. Let's look at a few examples.

Virtual stock brokers, such as E*Trade, offer considerable information on their portal (financial news, stock quotes, research, etc.). Yahoo! and other portals offer other types of information. These portals buy the information from information creators, such as Reuters. The information creator (or originators) sell the same information to many portals or other users. They sometimes do it directly, but in most cases they use a supply chain of syndicators and distributors to move it to the consumers (see Figure 2-5).

SYNDICATION SUPPLY CHAIN

Syndication of information is critical to the success of EC. Distributors of information (content) try to distinguish themselves from their competitors by providing free (or inexpensive) information to consumers, while at the same time packaging and pricing the information. Content creators, such as Inktomi (see Carr, 2000), make their money by selling the same information to many syndicators and/or distributors. The syndicators act as intermediaries in the chain, and the distributors usually pay the bills.

Syndication is especially popular with software and other digitizable items. For example, companies syndicate EC services such as payments and shopping-cart ordering systems for e-tailers. Logistic, security, and systems integration tools are frequently syndicated. The increasing trend to use application service providers (ASPs), which will be discussed later, is another example of syndication.

Syndication can be done in many ways. Similarly, there are a number of different revenue-sharing models along the supply chain in Figure 2-5. For example, the *affiliate program* discussed in Chapter 1, also see Helmstetter and Metivier (2000), which is used by CDNow, *Amazon.com,* and many other e-tailers, is a variation of syndication. For a discussion on the organizational impacts of syndication, see Werbach (2000) and Carr (2000).

The Internet and the Value Chain

The **value chain** is a framework that identifies the activities that an organization performs in order to create its products or services. These activities are interconnected and sequenced and can be shown graphically for each product/or process. The value chain is used mainly to analyze the activities by looking at the cost of

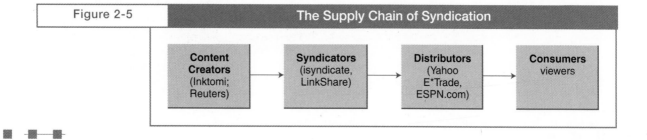

Figure 2-5   **The Supply Chain of Syndication**

these activities as well as the value delivered. The value chain can be drawn for each participant of a supply chain and therefore the value provided to business partners and customers can also be analyzed.

Michael Porter, the creator of the value chain concept, examined the impact of the Internet on the value chain (Porter, 2001). He showed that the Internet can be integrated into every type of activity in the value chain. The magnitude and nature of the integration depends on the specific industry and company. Porter views this impact as a step of an evolutionary process in which information technologies increasingly penetrate the value chain. Currently, the Internet enables the integration of the value chain and entire **value systems,** that is, a set of value chains in an entire industry. This includes the value chains of tiers of suppliers, distribution channels, and customers.

An example of prominent applications of the Internet in the value chain are provided in Figure 2-6.

Figure 2-6	Prominent Applications of the Internet in the Value Chain

Firm Infrastructure
- Web-based, distributed financial and ERP systems
- On-line investor relations (e.g., information dissemination, broadcast conference calls)

Human Resource Management
- Self-service personnel and benefits administration
- Web-based training
- Internet-based sharing and dissemination of company information electronic time and expense reporting

Technology Development
- Collaborative product design across locations and among multiple value-system participants
- Knowledge directories accessible from all parts of the organization
- Real-time access by R&D to on-line sales and service information

Procurement
- Internet-enabled demand planning; real-time available-to-promise/capable-to-promise and fulfillment
- Other linkage of purchase, inventory, and forecasting systems with suppliers
- Automated "requisition to pay"
- Direct and indirect procurement via marketplaces, exchanges, auctions, and buyer-seller matching

Inbound Logistics	Operations	Outbound Logistics	Marketing and Sales	After Sales Service
• Real-time integrated scheduling, shipping, warehouse management, demand management and planning, and advanced planning and scheduling across the company and its suppliers • Dissemination throughout the company of real-time inbound and in-progress inventory data	• Integrated information exchange, scheduling, and decision making in in-house plants, contract asseblers, and components suppliers Real-time available-to-promise and capable-to-promise information available in the sales force and channels	• Real-time transaction of orders whether initiated by an end consumer, a sales person, or a channel partner • Automated customer-specific agreements and contract terms • Customer and channel access to product development and delivery status • Collaborative integration with customer forecasting systems • Integrated channel management including information exchange, warranty claims, and contract management (versioning, process control)	• On-line sales channels including Web sites and marketplaces • Real-time and outside access to customer information, production logs, dynamic pricing, inventory availability, on-line submission of quotes, and order entry • On-line product configurators • Customer-tailored marketing via customer profile • Push advertising • Tailored on-line access • Real-time customer feed-back through Web server opt in/opt-out marketing and promotion response tracking	• On-line support of customer service representatives through e-mail response managment, billing integration, co-browse, chat, "call me now", voice-over-IP, and other uses of video streaming • Customer self service via web sites and itelligent service request processing including updates to billing and shipping profiles • Real-time field service access to customer account review, schematic review, parts availability and ordering, work-order update, and service parts management

← •Web-distributed supply chain management →

Source: Porter, M., "Strategy and the Internet," *Harvard Business Review*, March 2001, p. 75.

The impact of the Internet on the value chain determines, in part, the winners and losers of EC.

Potential Winners and Losers in EC

It is still unclear who will be the final winners and losers in EC. Some predict that many traditional brokers will soon become an "endangered species." Here are some potential winners and losers.

WINNERS

- **Internet access providers.** America Online is clearly a winner, but several other companies will also be winners.
- **Providers of diversified portal services.** Yahoo!, Lycos, and other early search engines now provide diversified services, ranging from targeted advertising to community hosting.
- **EC software companies.** Starting with IBM, Microsoft, and HP, there are scores of other winners in this area, especially in the B2B area (Ariba, Commerce One).
- **Proprietary network owners.** Most EC networks are open systems, not owned by any one company. However, some large manufacturers or resellers (e.g., John Deere in farm equipment, W. W. Grainger in industrial supply distribution, or Baxter Healthcare in medical supplies) may have enough power to sustain proprietary systems for at least several years. Without regulatory action, these types of companies will be able to lower their selling costs, differentiate themselves from competitors without EC networks, attract new customers, and gain a significant strategic advantage.
- **Midsize manufacturers.** Midsize manufacturers are squeezed between the dominance of market leaders and the flexibility of smaller competitors. With an open EC network, midsize manufacturers will have greater access and exposure to customers. Small vendors will also gain access, but buyers will likely be skeptical about smaller vendors' support and financial and delivery capabilities. Exceptions are in niche markets and earlier movers in EC that established a name, such as *Amazon.com.*
- **Technology suppliers.** As EC networks revolutionize the distribution business, the demand for related software, services, and hardware will climb astronomically. Industry leaders such as Cisco and Intel will do very well. The same is true for wireless technology companies that support m-commerce.
- **Advertising and target marketing companies.** Starting with pioneers such as Broadvision and DoubleClick, there are scores of companies that are making their fortune in these rapidly expanding fields.
- **A few large resellers.** With less need for customized support and the personal relationships it fosters, a few large resellers in each industry will use their economies of scale in logistics and automation to gobble up market shares. Some surprising companies may emerge in this large reseller arena. Overnight delivery companies such as FedEx or UPS are examples. Super express delivery services, such as *samedayit.net* may be successful too.

- **Security, special infrastructure, and payment systems providers.** Dozens of companies are assuming leadership positions in the areas of security, special infrastructures (such as VPN), encryption, payments, and special Internet languages (Java, PERL, VRML, etc.). Of special interest is cerfication services such as provided by *verisign.com.*
- **Online-only companies.** Companies such as E*TRADE, eBay, and *Amazon.com* are establishing strong leadership roles in the online market.
- **Conventional retailers that are online.** Starting with Wal-Mart, Dell, and Wells Fargo Bank, there are hundreds of large corporations in manufacturing, retailing, banking, and services that have created successful online divisions, which provide them with a strategic advantage.
- **Market makers.** Companies that organize electronic markets such as GE Information Services (*geis.com*), or *chemconnect.com* will emerge by the dozens and replace traditional brokers and salespeople (see losers).
- **Portals.** Portals were developed from search engines in an effort to provide comprehensive gateways to the Internet. In addition to Yahoo!, there are many other successful portals.
- **Consumers.** As a result of the increased competition and the ease of comparing prices and finding more sellers, consumers are winning by paying less, finding more products and shopping more conveniently.
- **Others.** Dozens of other companies are growing rapidly by providing Internet and/or EC services. These range from *acnielsen.com* to *verisign.com.*

LOSERS

- **Many wholesalers, especially small ones.** There are almost half a million distributors in the United States alone; 98 percent of them have fewer than 100 employees. Technology has already reduced the need for local distributors that can provide rapid delivery and service. EC will accelerate this trend.
- **Brokers.** Brokers of all kinds will lose. Airlines are cutting commissions due to electronic ticketing, and many real estate, stock, insurance, and other brokers will lose their jobs as these industries become increasingly automated.
- **Salespeople.** EC networks will dramatically alter the role of salespeople. Companies will increasingly rely on EC networks at the expense of product-focused salespeople. However, as EC networks provide more pricing, product, and delivery data online, the surviving salespeople will be those that offer real, value-added consulting as shown in the Rosenbluth case. They will help customers interpret, analyze, and prioritize the increased data available through EC networks. They will also help customers restructure their purchasing, stocking, and usage patterns.
- **Nondifferentiated manufacturers.** EC networks will expose to a risk those companies that are neither low cost nor innovative. Over the last few years, increasing customer awareness and increasing availability of products and price information have already squeezed out many marginal suppliers. The ability of EC networks to highlight price and product information will accentuate this trend.

The question of who will win or lose is critical. Charles Darwin said, "It is not the strongest of the species that survives, not the most intelligent, but the one most responsive to change." Flexibility, as shown by Choi and Whinston (2000), becomes a critical issue. For practical suggestions of how to survive in the digital economy see Schwarz (1999).

2.8   IMPACTS ON BUSINESS PROCESSES AND ORGANIZATIONS

The field of EC is relatively new; as such, little statistical data or empirical research are available. Therefore, the discussion in this section is based primarily on experts' opinions, logic, and some actual data. The discussion here is also based in part on the work of Bloch and Segev (1996), who approached the impact of EC from a value-added point of view. Their model (shown in Figure 2-7) divides the impact of EC into three major categories: EC improves direct marketing, EC transforms organizations, and EC redefines organizations.

Improving Direct Marketing

Traditional direct marketing was done by mail order (catalogs) and telephone (tele-marketing). In 1998, $75 billion in sales were estimated in the United States to be done by direct mail, of which only $2 billion was via computers (B2C). This figure

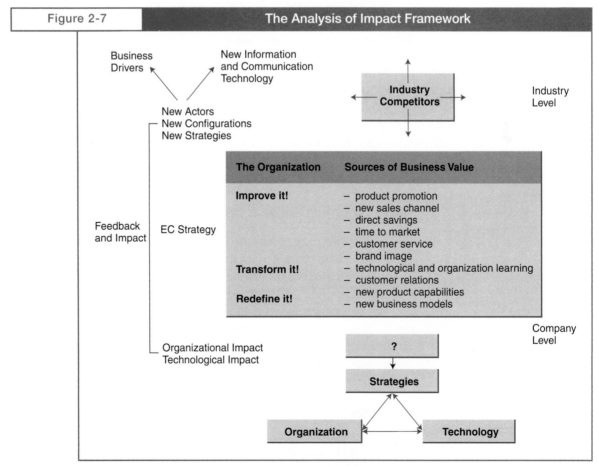

Figure 2-7   The Analysis of Impact Framework

Source: Block and Seger (1998). Reproduced with permission of the authors.

is small, but it is growing rapidly. Therefore, Bloch et al. (1996) suggested the following impacts of B2C direct marketing:

- **Product promotion.** EC enhances promotion of products and services through direct, information-rich, and interactive contact with customers.
- **New sales channels.** EC creates a new distribution channel for existing products, because of its direct reach to customers and the bidirectional nature of communications.
- **Direct savings.** The cost of delivering information to customers over the Internet results in substantial savings to senders (when compared with non-electronic delivery or delivery via VAN systems). Major savings are also realized in delivering digitized products (such as music and software) versus delivery of physical products.
- **Reduced cycle time.** The delivery of digitized products and services can be reduced to seconds. Also, the administrative work related to physical delivery, especially across international borders, can be reduced significantly, cutting the cycle time by more than 90 percent. One example is TradeNet in Singapore, which reduces the administrative time of port-related transactions from days to minutes. Cycle time can be reduced through improvements along the supply chain. In Chapter 10 we will discuss how obtaining a mortgage in Hong Kong has been reduced from about 30 days to less than an hour.
- **Customer service.** Customer service can be greatly enhanced by enabling customers to find detailed information online (for example, FedEx and other shippers allow customers to trace the status of their packages). Also, intelligent agents can answer standard e-mail questions in seconds. Finally, human experts' services can be expedited using help-desk software.
- **Brand or corporate image.** On the Web, newcomers can establish corporate images very quickly. What *Amazon.com* did in 3 years took traditional companies generations to achieve. Corporate image facilitates *trust,* which is necessary for direct sales. Traditional companies such as Intel, Disney, Wal-Mart, Dell, and Cisco use their Web activities to affirm their corporate identity and brand image.

Other Marketing-Related Impacts

CUSTOMIZATION

EC enables customization of products and services; in contrast, buying in a store or ordering from a television usually limits customers to a supply of standard products. Dell Computers, Inc. is a customization success story. Today, you can configure not only computers but also cars, jewelry, gifts, and hundreds of other products and services. If properly done, one can achieve mass customization that provides a competitive advantage as well as increases the overall demand for certain products and services. Customization will change marketing and sales activities both in B2C and in B2B.

ADVERTISING

With direct marketing and customization comes one-to-one or direct advertising, which is much more effective than mass advertising. This creates a fundamental change in the manner in which advertising is conducted, not only for online trades, but also for products and services that are ordered and shipped in traditional ways. As we will see in Chapter 5, the entire concept of advertising is going through a fundamental change due to EC.

ORDERING SYSTEMS

Taking orders from customers can drastically be improved if it is done online, reducing both processing time and mistakes. Electronic orders can be quickly routed to the appropriate order-processing site. This saves time and reduces expenses so that salespeople have more time to sell products. Also, when ordering online, customers can configure orders and compute their costs, saving time for all parties involved.

MARKETS

EC is changing traditional markets. Some physical markets disappear, as does the need to deliver goods to the marketplace. In an electronic marketspace, goods are delivered directly to buyers upon completion of the purchase, making markets much more efficient. Traditional markets can be very inefficient, as illustrated throughout the text.

For digitally based products—software, music, and information—the changes will be dramatic. Already, small but powerful software packages are delivered over the Internet. This affects packaging and greatly reduces the need for specialized distribution models.

New selling models such as shareware, freeware, and pay-as-you-use are emerging to maximize the potential of the Internet. Although these models have emerged within particular sectors, such as the software and publishing industries, they will eventually pervade other sectors. New forms of marketing will also emerge, in addition to affiliate marketing, group purchasing, and electronic auctions, as well as an increased emphasis on relationship (interactive) marketing.

Many other activities can improve marketing, as we will see throughout the text. For example, customer's convenience is greatly enhanced (any place, any time), availability of products and services is much greater (e.g., 10 million books in *Amazon.com's* catalog), and cheaper products are offered via auctions.

All these provide companies with a competitive advantage over the traditional direct sales methods. Furthermore, because the competitive advantage is so large, EC is likely to replace many nondirect marketing channels. Some people predict the "fall of the shopping malls," and many retail stores and brokers of services (stocks, real estate, and insurance) are labeled by some as soon to be endangered species.

As is discussed throughout the text, the role of marketing channels, wholesalers, retailers, intermediaries, and storefronts may be dramatically changed by EC. A summary of these changes is provided in Table 2-3.

Transforming Organizations

TECHNOLOGY AND ORGANIZATIONAL LEARNING

Rapid progress in EC will force companies to adapt quickly to the new technologies and offer them an opportunity to experiment with new products, services, and business models. Companies will have to immediately learn the new technologies. Learning may be followed by strategic and structural changes. These changes may

The Phases of Industry Structure Transformation Enabled by Electronic Markets

TABLE 2-3

	Traditional Market (example: retail store)	Electronic Market (Phase 1)	Electronic Market and Distribution (Phase 2)
Required industry characteristics	Transactions that do not require hierarchical governance	Accepted standards for describing the product through the electronic market	Description standards plus product that is feasibly digitized
Market digitized?	No	Yes	Yes
Product and distribution digitized?	No	No	Yes
Examples of intermediaries removed		Wholesalers and some forms of brokers (ones that simply gather and analyze information for consumers)	Phase 1 intermediaries plus firms in the physical network distribution
Examples of intermediaries added		Firms that provide access to the the electronic market (ISPs or firms that operate electronic markets or electronic auctions) and possibly new forms of brokers (such as online better business bureaus)	Phase 1 intermediaries

Source: Reprinted from *Decision Support Systems,* Vol. 21, No. 3, T. J. Strader and H. J. Shaw "Characteristics of Electronic Markets" pp. 185–198, Copyright 1997, with permission from Elsevier Science.

transform the way in which business is done, such as in the case of Rosenbluth International.

Bloch et al. (1996) believe that if EC will progress rapidly, it will have a large and durable impact on the strategies of most organizations. Therefore, it is critical that organizations quickly become familiar with the technology. The learning curve of mastering such technologies and understanding their power to reshape customer relationships is slow and cannot be achieved overnight. It is often an iterative process, requiring organizations to try new offerings and rearrange them according to customer feedback.

In a similar fashion, new technologies require new organizational approaches. For instance, the structure of the organizational unit dealing with EC might have to be different from the conventional sales and marketing departments. To be more flexible and responsive to the market, new processes must be put in place. This type of corporate change must be planned and managed. Before getting it right, organizations might have to struggle with different experiments.

THE CHANGING NATURE OF WORK

The nature of some work and employment will be transformed in the Digital Age; it is already happening before our eyes. For example, driven by increased competition in the global marketplace, firms are reducing the number of employees down to a core of essential staff and outsourcing whatever work they can to countries where wages are significantly less. The upheaval brought on by these changes is creating new opportunities and new risks and forcing us into new ways of thinking about jobs, careers, and salaries.

Digital Age workers will have to be very flexible. Few will have truly secure jobs in the traditional sense, and many will have to be willing and able to constantly learn, adapt, make decisions, and stand by them. Many will work from home.

The Digital Age company will have to prize its workers as its most valuable asset. It will have to constantly nurture and empower them and provide them with every means possible to expand their knowledge and skill base.

Redefining Organizations

Here are some of the changes that will redefine organizations:

NEW PRODUCT CAPABILITIES

EC allows for new products to be created and/or for existing products to be customized in innovative ways. Such changes may redefine organizations' missions and the manner in which they operate. EC also allows suppliers to gather personalized data on customers. Building customer profiles (see also Chapter 4), as well as collecting data on preferences of customers, can be used as a source of information for improving products or designing new ones.

Mass customization, as described earlier, enables manufacturers to create specific products for each customer, based on his or her exact needs. For example, Motorola gathers customer needs for a pager or a cellular phone, transmits them electronically to the manufacturing plant where they are manufactured, along with the customer's specifications (like color and features), and then sends the product to the customer within a day. Dell Computers and General Motors use the same approach. Using the Web, customers can design or configure products for themselves. For example, customers can use the Web to design their T-shirts, furniture, cars, jewelry, Nike shoes, and even a Swatch watch. Using mass-customization methods, the cost of customized products is at or slightly above the comparable retail price of standard products.

NEW BUSINESS MODELS

EC affects not only individual companies and their products, but entire industries. This will lead to the use of new business models that are based on the wide availability of information and its direct distribution to consumers. Electronic intermediaries are one kind of new model, as shown in the case of Orbis (Chapter 1). Other new business models are described throughout the text.

Impacts on Manufacturing

EC is changing manufacturing systems from mass production lines to demand-driven, just-in-time manufacturing. Furthermore, these new production systems are integrated with finance, marketing, and other functional systems, as well as with business partners and customers. Using Web-based ERP systems (supported by software such as SAP R/3), customer orders can be directed to designers and/or to the production floor within seconds. Production cycle time is cut by 50 percent or more in many cases, especially if production is done in a different country from where the designers and engineers are located.

An interesting concept is that of **virtual manufacturing,** which is the ability to run your global plants as though they were one location. The business controls everything, from the supply of components to shipment, while making it completely transparent to customers and employees. For example, Cisco System works with 34 plants globally, 32 of which are owned by other companies. Even though a product may be manufactured in a different plant, it will look exactly alike, regardless of where it was manufactured. Up-to-the-minute information sharing is critical for the success of this mass production approach (Pine, 1999).

Companies such as IBM, General Motors, General Electric, and Boeing assemble products from components that are manufactured in many different locations, even countries. Subassemblers gather materials and parts from their vendors, and they may use one or more tiers of manufacturers. Communication, collaboration, and coordination are critical in such multitier systems. Using electronic bidding, assemblers get subassemblies 15 to 20 percent cheaper than before and 80 percent faster (e.g., GE case in Chapter 6). Furthermore, such systems are flexible and adaptable, allowing for fast changes with minimum cost. Also, costly inventories that are part of mass-production systems can be minimized.

BUILD-TO-ORDER

The biggest change in manufacturing will be the move to build-to-order systems. Manufacturing or assembly will start only after an order is received. This will change not only the production planning and control, but the entire supply chain, as will be shown in Chapter 15.

Impact on Finance and Accounting

EC requires special finance and accounting systems. Most notable are electronic payment systems. Traditional payment systems are ineffective or inefficient for electronic trade. The use of the new payment systems such as electronic cash is complicated because it involves legal issues and agreements on international standards. Nevertheless, electronic cash is certain to come soon, and it will change the manner in which payments are made.

In many ways, electronic cash, which can be backed by currency or other assets, represents the biggest revolution in currency since gold replaced cowry shells. Its diversity and pluralism is perfectly suited to the Internet. It could change consumers' financial lives and shake the foundations of financial systems and even governments. Payment systems involve security issues, interinstitutional transfer of funds, and much more (Chapter 14).

Executing an electronic order triggers an action in what we call the back office. *Back-office transactions* include buyer's credit checks, product availability checks, confirmation, movements in accounts payable and receivable, billing, and much more. These activities must be efficient, synchronized, and fast so the electronic trade will not be slowed down. An example is online stock trading. In most cases, orders are executed in less than 3 seconds and the trader can find an online confirmation of the trade immediately. Speaking of online trading, it is interesting to note that today individual investors have substantial free information at their fingertips. This information cost tens of thousands of dollars up to the late 1990s. With commissions of less than $10 per trade, many individuals are taking their money from mutual funds and trying to trade on their own. For some, day trading is a huge success.

One of the most innovative concepts in finance/accounting is the *virtual close* project of Cisco Systems (Application Case 2.3.)

Cisco's Virtual Close

Cisco System, Inc., the company that supplies the vast networks that connect computers to the Internet, is developing a new product called *virtual close,* which, by 2002 or 2003, will allow companies to close their financial books with 1 hour notice, instead of doing it once every 3 months. This will be done by connecting an entire company, even one with operations in dozens of countries, via an intranet. Cisco's infrastructure will permit information sharing almost instantly. The advantages of "virtual close" are:

- Companies can become proactive, spotting problems and opportunities at any time, instead of once a quarter.
- It will bring huge productivity gains related to corporate financial reporting.
- Problems that persisted undetected for months will be detected as soon as they start to develop. Thus, their damage will be minimized.
- New opportunities will be detected early, allowing companies to exploit them quickly.
- Virtual Close enables quick "drill down" analysis, which aims at locating the causes of either poor or excellent performance.

Implementing Virtual Close is a lengthy process that may end in a failure due to the project's complexity. However, not implementing it may result in a competitive disadvantage.

Source: *Cisco.com,* several press releases, 2000, 2001.

Several EC activities are fairly complex, involving an intermediary, arranging banking, services, implementing EC software support, and so on. Payment of commissions to all parties for every transaction are part of such systems, and they need to be planned for and made secure.

Impact on Human Resource Management, Training, and Education

EC is changing the manner in which people are recruited, evaluated, promoted, and developed (Chapter 10). Intranets are playing a major role in this transformation (Chapter 11). EC will change the way training and education are offered to employees. Online distance learning is exploding, providing opportunities that never existed before. Companies are cutting training costs by 50 percent or more, and virtual courses, programs, and universities are mushrooming.

New distance learning systems can offer two-way video, on-the-fly interaction, and application sharing. Such systems provide for interactive remote instruction systems, which link sites over a high-speed intranet. For example, at Old Dominion University in Virginia, Telnet systems use broadcast satellite technology with terrestrial audio feedback from students and e-mail to connect the main campus to 23 community colleges, as well as government and industrial sites. At the City University of Hong Kong, an interactive MBA program was on the Web as of 1999 (Chapter 10). At the same time, corporations are finding that distance learning may be their ticket to survival as changing environments, new technologies, and continuously changing procedures make it necessary for employees to be trained and retrained constantly.

2.9   MOBILE COMMERCE

The widespread adoption of wireless and mobile networks, devices, and middleware creates an opportunity not only to transact applications that so far were possible only from a PC, but also to use new applications online. **Mobile commerce (m-commerce)** refers to the conduct of e-commerce via wireless devices. There is a strong interest in this topic because according to the International Data Corporation and GartnerGroup, the number of mobile devices is projected to top 1.3 billion by 2004 (predictions made in March 2001). Furthermore, these devices can be connected to the Internet, allowing users to conduct transactions from anywhere. GartnerGroup estimates that at least 40 percent of all B2C transactions, totaling over $200 billion by 2004, will be initiated from smart wireless devices. Others predict much higher figures because mobile devices (handsets, PDAs, etc.) will soon overtake PCs as the predominant Internet access device, creating a global market of over 500 million subscribers.

Applications of M-Commerce

Here are some representative applications of m-commerce. (For further details see Chapter 19)

- **Online stock trading.** It is done all over the world, from I-MODE in Japan to E*Trade in several countries. Dagens Industri of Sweden allows subscribers to trade on the Stockholm Exchange and receive financial data using a PDA. Stock trading from any location is important for traders and investors alike.
- **Online banking.** Mobile banking is rapidly taking off. The Swedish Postal Bank allows customers to make payments from their headsets, while Marita-Nordabanken, also in Sweden, allows several other transactions. CityBank has mobile banking services in Singapore, Hong Kong, and other countries.
- **Micropayments.** Consumers in Japan can use their mobile phones to pay for purchases in vending machines. In Scandinavia, consumers can use cell phones to pay for parking in unattended parking lots, car washes, gasoline, and even for soft drinks in vending machines. Similar capabilities exist in France (Carte Bancaire) and in several other countries. In Germany, customers pay for transportation, including taxis, from their mobile phones.
- **Online gambling.** Eurobet, a large UK vendor, allows online gambling. In Hong Kong, you can use your cell phone to bet in horse races.
- **Ordering and service.** Barnes and Noble, Inc. created a service for PDAs and cell phones that allows users to listen to personalized music clips by downloading the music to the devices. You can order books as well.
- **Online auctions.** *QXL.com,* a UK online auction company, lets users open accounts on its Web sites and bid for items using their cell phones. e-Bay conducts online auctions as well.
- **Messaging systems.** Mobile Internet e-mail is referred to as Short Messaging Service (SMS). In 2000, it was possible to send or receive up to 160 characters. In Summer 2001, about 17 billion messages were sent worldwide. SMS can be used for advertising. Given that advertisers know something about a user, a segmented or personalized message can be sent to users wherever they are (Chapter 19).

- **B2B.** M-commerce can empower professionals to collect and evaluate data in order to make better decisions faster. Employees in a remote location can handle tasks such as checking inventory or submitting orders while in the field. The Internet becomes a repository of corporate information, serving as a virtual service and goods warehouse.

A SUCCESSFUL VENDOR: I-MODE

To illustrate the potential spread of m-commerce, we will examine I-MODE, the pioneering wireless service that took Japan by storm in 1999 and 2000. With a few clicks on a handset, I-MODE users can conduct a large variety of m-commerce activities ranging from online stock trading and banking to purchasing travel tickets and booking Karaoke rooms. Users can also use I-MODE to send and receive color images. I-MODE, which was launched in February of 1999, had over 15 millions users by the end of 2000. I-MODE went international in late 2000. Here are some interesting applications of I-MODE:

- Receive Tamagotchi's characters, every day, for only $1 a month.
- Train timetables, guides to shopping areas, and automatic notification of train delays are available.
- Receive discount coupons for shopping and restaurants.
- Purchase music online.
- Send or receive photos.
- Purchase airline tickets.
- Locate information about best-selling books and then buy the books.

2.10   MANAGERIAL ISSUES

The following issues are germane to management:

1. **New business models.** The digital economy is characterized by new business models. These models are possible because of the broad reach and low cost of the Internet, the ability to digitize products and services and the creative thinking of individuals worldwide. Any organization should consider some of these models. These models may result in high productivity, low cost and better customer services. The problem of determining which models are most appropriate is deferred to Chapter 12.
2. **Competition in the digital economy.** Although the basic theories of competition are unchanged, the rules are different. Of special interest are the digital products and services whose variable cost is very low. Competition involves both old-economy and new-economy companies. The speed of changes in competitive forces can be rapid, and the impact of new business models can be devastating. As Bill Gates said: Competition is not among companies, but among business models.
3. **How to transform to the digital economy?** Sure it is not simple, and several strategies exist (see Chapter 16). In general doing nothing while waiting can be very dangerous. Some EC planning is needed. Considering that some

EC projects are very expensive, the transformation must be done carefully and with detailed planning.

4. **Disintermediation and reintermediation.** Many EC applications will change the role of intermediation. This may create a conflict between your company and your distributors. It may also create opportunities. In many cases your distributors will need to change their roles. This is a sensitive issue that needs to be planned for during the transformation plan.

5. **Going global.** The digital economy destroys political borders, enabling global competition. This creates tremendous opportunities for many companies, but threats to others. Going global is not easy, nor fast in most cases as will be shown in Chapter 18.

6. **Organizational changes.** Companies should expect organizational changes in all functional areas once e-commerce reaches momentum. At minimum, purchasing will be done differently in many organizations, but introducing models such as name-your-own price and affiliate programs may have a major impact on your business operations.

7. **Alliances.** It is safer, in many cases, to wander in the new frontier together with some one else. As will be shown throughout the book, alliances can take several shapes. They certainly need to be considered when major EC applications are considered.

Summary

In this chapter, you learned about the following EC issues as they relate to the learning objectives:

1. **The characteristics of the digital economy.** The digital economy is characterized by the digitization of many products and services and by the use of the Internet and other networks to support economic activities. Such computerization changes the manner in which business is done and considerably improves economic activities and competition.

2. **Marketspace vs. marketplaces.** A marketspace or e-marketplace is a virtual market that does not suffer from space, time, borders, and other limitations. As such, it can be very effective.

3. **Competition in the marketspace.** Competition is very intense and major changes are occurring, such as lower buyers' search cost, speedy comparisons by consumers, and personalization. In the B2C market, prices are generally lower while customer services improve. Competition is becoming global and digital products and services can be produced and delivered much cheaper and faster. Impacts are along all dimensions of Porter's model.

4. **The new economic rules.** In addition to the changing nature of competition, cost curves are different for digital products. The production function and transaction and administrative costs are much better in e-commerce, and there is no need to be a large organization to achieve economies of scale. Products, industry, and sellers and buyers' characteristics are different in e-commerce.

5. **The impact on intermediation.** The role of intermediation will be changed while some will be eliminated. New value-added services that range from

content creation to consultation are mushrooming (see Chapter 8). An example is syndication of content creation.

6. **The impact on functional areas.** All functional areas are impacted. Direct marketing (manufacturing to customers) and one-to-one marketing and advertisement are becoming a norm. Also, mass customization and personalization are taking off. So production is moving to a pull model, changing the supply chain relationship. Cycle time is reduced, financial planning and budgeting are expedited, and human resources need to be managed differently due to their interaction with machines. Virtual manufacturing is on the rise and so are virtual organizations.

7. **The role of m-commerce.** Mobile commerce is emerging as a phenomenon that can ease the access to the Internet to millions of people. It also creates new applications related to where individuals are at specific times (see Chapter 19).

Key Terms

Build-to-order
Digital economy
Digital products (services)
Disintermediation
E-intermediaries
Infomediaries
Internet economy
Internet ecosystem
Liquidity (in EC)
Marketspace
Micropayments
Mobile commerce (M-commerce)
New economy

Personalization
Price discovery
Price discrimination
Product differentiation
Product life cycle
Quality uncertainty
Reintermediation
Value chain
Value systems
Virtual manufacturing
Web economy
Webonomics

Questions for Review

1. Define marketspace.
2. Describe what digitizable products are and provide a few examples.
3. Define price discovery and relate it to search cost.
4. Define disintermediation and reintermediation.
5. Define syndication.
6. Describe the issue of "quality uncertainty" and outline possible solutions.
7. List three major winners in EC.
8. List three major losers in EC.
9. Define cycle-time reduction.
10. Define mass customization.
11. Define build-to-order.
12. Define micropayments.
13. Define m-commerce.

Questions for Discussion

1. Explain how information technology facilitated Rosenbluth's new business model.
2. Compare marketplaces with marketspaces.
3. Why is the digital economy considered a revolution?
4. What are the major benefits of syndication to the various participants?
5. Below are six statements regarding conditions that are necessary for the success of an electronic market. For each, explain why you agree or disagree:
   a. The market should be fragmented on both the buying and selling sides, with a lot of vendors and a lot of buyers and no overly dominant player on either side.
   b. The market should be technologically sophisticated, with an Internet-savvy customer base.
   c. The online service should be able to fully describe products on the Web so that buyers receive enough information to make purchases.
   d. The products being offered on the Web should not be a pure commodity; for a lively marketplace, vendors should be able to distinguish their offerings.
   e. If a certain market is already efficient, there is no sense moving it online.
   f. Trading stocks online becomes very popular.
6. Compare and contrast competition in the traditional markets with competition in digital markets.
7. Compare a traditional market industry structure with an electronic market structure.
8. Relate price discovery to price discrimination. Provide an example in retailing and an example in services.
9. Liquidity (critical mass) is considered a major success factor in EC. Explain why this is so.
10. Discuss the advantage of m-commerce over e-commerce.
11. Discuss the importance of industry structure in EC.
12. Relate personalization to mass customization.
13. Discuss what is meant by "redefining organizations."
14. Explain how NTE provides real time procurement services (Application Case 2.2).
15. Which type of a marketplace is NTE (Application Case 2.2)? Why?
16. Discuss the advantages of paying from your cell phone vs. paying with a smartcard.

Internet Exercises

1. Use Porter's five-force model to analyze the impact of EC on the bookstore industry and on the airline industry. Find the impact of EC on each force, then analyze the proposed defense strategies.
2. Competition between online companies is rapidly increasing. Prepare a report on the competition among *ticketmaster.com, ticketonline.com, tickets.com,* ticketweb, and others. For each company, identify market niches, strategies, and relationships to off-line operations. Generalize your findings to the entire entertainment ticketing industry.

3. Enter *ecommerce.gov/ede.* Find the latest government reports on the digital revolution (economy).
4. Enter *portsnportals.com* and examine the products and services provided. Which are similar to that of NTE? Examine the Global Cargo exchange and other initiatives. Classify the services according to Chapter 1.
5. Go to *cisco.com, google.com,* and *cio.com* and locate information about the status of 'virtual close.' Write a report based on your findings.
6. Enter *mobile.msn.com* and find the latest services provided by MSN Mobile. Distinguish between messaging services and commercial applications.
7. Enter *packetvideo.com,* check their offerings, and write a report on the potential commercial uses of the technology in m-commerce.
8. Enter *gegxs.com* and examine their products and services.

Team Assignments and Role Playing

1. Have each team member examine an area of fierce online competition, for example, books, computers/computer parts, CDs, toys, auctions, and stock trading. Each team member should identify evidence of competition in the area, with at least one case each of off-line versus online and online versus online competition. Identify common threads in the various industries. Submit a group report of your findings.
2. Read the story about Marshall Industries *marshall.com* at MIS Quarterly, September 1999 (EL-Sawy et al.) or *simnet.org/library/doc/paper1.doc* Prepare a report on all of the economic implications derived from this case. Concentrate on the following issues: changes in the value chains, the competitive strategy, the role of the intermediaries, and the roles of the CEO and CIO.
3. Several competing exchanges operate in the steel industry (*metalsite.net, e-steel.com, isteelasia.com,* etc). Assign one group to each company. Look at their market structure, at the services they offer, and so on. The group then makes a presentation to convince buyers and sellers to use their exchange.
4. As a team, examine a functional area (finance, marketing, etc). Find the latest innovations in these areas that are Web-related. Make a presentation to convince an audience that your functional area is the most wired one.
5. Investigate "price discovery" as a group. There are several ways to compare prices (see Chapter 3). Assign each group to one rater such as *BarPoint.com, mysimon.com* and *Bizrate.com* to identify the customer service and information they provide.

REAL-WORLD CASE: How a Singaporean Hotel Transformed Itself to the Digital Economy

Raffles Hotel, Singapore's colonial-era landmark, (now a national monument) is the flagship of the Raffles Holdings Ltd., which manages 16 luxury hotels worldwide, including 2 in Singapore as well as 36 restaurants. Raffles Hotel (which is a must visit when visiting Singapore) is operating in a very competitive environment. To maintain its worldwide reputation, the hotel spent lavishly on every facet of its operation. For example, the hotel once stocked 12 different kinds of butter at a high cost.

All this changed in 2001, when Raffles moved its purchasing and sales to the Web by creating a private online marketplace. Here is how it works:

To do business with Raffles, each of 5,000 potential vendors must log on to Raffle's private exchange. As for the purchasing, Raffles conducts reverse auctions among qualified suppliers. This way the number of suppliers is reduced while the quantity purchased from each is increasing, enabling lower purchasing prices. For example, butter is purchased now from only two suppliers. Also, negotiations can take place online. In contrast to a public exchange where it is difficult to develop buyer-seller relationships, it is easier to do so in a private exchange.

The marketplace was built by *BeXcom.com* of Singapore, in which Raffles holds 10 percent equity. This way the site is tailored to Raffles' needs. The private exchange is strategically advantageous to Raffles in forcing suppliers to disclose their prices on the exchange, thus increasing competition among suppliers. The suppliers like the private exchange because they do not have to show their prices publicly. A major problem was to convince the purchasing agents at Raffles that their job was secure, so they collaborate on the system. The company is saving about $1 million a year on procurement of eight high volume supplies (toilet paper, butter, etc.) alone.

The exchange is also used as a sell-side, allowing other hotels to buy Raffles-branded products like tiny shampoo bottles and bathrobes. Competitors buy Raffles-branded products because they are inexpensive, so money can be saved. Also, the luxury products make the hotel purchasing the products look upscale.

Questions for the case

1. What was the logic of combining e-procurement and selling in one marketplace?

2. It is said that both Raffles and BeXcom benefited from the business partnership. Explain.

3. Several public exchanges exist for hotels to buy and sell (e.g., *avendra.com*). Raffles could have used any of them and saved the IT investment. What are the benefits of the private exchange? The disadvantages?

Source: Compiled from I. Greenberg, *Asian Wall Street Journal*, May 21, 2001, pg. T1. Also available at *bexcom.com*

REFERENCES AND BIBLIOGRAPHY

Applegate, L. M. "E-Business Models: Making Sense of the Internet Business Landscape." In *Information Technology for the Future Enterprise: New Models for Managers*, edited by G.W. Dickson and G. DeSanctis. Upper Saddle River, New Jersey: Prentice Hall, 2001.

Bakos, Y. "The Emerging Role of Electronic Marketplaces on the Internet," *Communications of the ACM* (August 1998).

Bakos, Y. "Reducing Buyers' Search Costs: Implications for Electronic Marketplaces." *Management Sciences* (December 1997).

Bhargava, H. K., et al. "Pricing and Product Design: Intermediary Strategies in Electronic Markets," *Int. Jour. of Elect. Comm.* (Fall 2000).

Bloch, M. and A. Segev. "Leveraging Electronic Commerce for Competitive Advantage: A Business Value Framework." Proceedings of the Ninth International Conference on EDI-IOS (Bled, Slovenia, June 1996).

Carr, N. G. "On The Edge," *Harvard Business Review* (May-June 2000).

Choi, S. Y. and A. B. Whinston. *The Internet Economy: Technology and Practice*. Austin, Texas: Smartecon.com, 2000.

Choi, S. Y., et al. *The Economics of Electronic Commerce*. Indianapolis, Indiana: Macmillan Technical Publications, 1997.

Dickson, G. W. and G. DeSanctis. *Information Technology and the Future Enterprise: New Models for Managers*. Upper Saddle River, New Jersey: Prentice Hall, 2001.

Evans, P. B. and T. S. Wurster. *Blown to Bits: How the New Economics of Information Transforms Strategy*. Boston: Harvard Business School Press, 1999.

Galliers, D. E., et al. *Strategic Information Systems*. Woburn, Massachusetts: Butterworth-Heinemann, 1999.

Golman, M. C. "Brave New Economy," *cnnfn.com/output/pfv/2000/05/22* (May 22, 2000).

Griffiths, P. M., et al. (eds). *Information Management in Competitive Success*. New York: Pergamon Press, 1998.

Gupta, A., ed. "The Economics of Electronic Commerce." *Decision Support Systems* Special issue, (Spring 1998).

Hagel, J., III and M. Singer. *Net Worth: Sharing Markets When Customers Make the Rules*. Boston: Harvard Business School Press, 1999.

Hamel, G. *Leading the Revolution*. Boston: Harvard Business School Press, 2000.

Hanappi, G. and E. Rysavy. "Economic Foundations of Electronic Commerce," *Proceedings International Conference on Electronic Commerce* (Seoul, Korea, April 1998), *www.icec.net*.

Helmstetter, G. and P. Metivier. *Affiliate Selling: Building Revenue on the Web*. New York: John Wiley & Sons, 2000.

Jerume, M. "The Internet Is Crushing Whole Industries . . . Is Your Company Next?" *PC Computing* (a commentary on the digital economy) (February 2000).

Kampas, P. J. "Road Map to the E-Revolution" *Information Systems Management*. (Spring 2000).

Kelly, K. *New Rules for New Economy*. New York: Penguin USA, 1999.

Kiani, R. "Marketing Opportunities in the Digital World." *Internet Research: Electronic Networking Applications & Policy* 8, no. 2 (1998).

Komenar, M. *Electronic Marketing*. New York: John Wiley & Sons, 1997.

Kosiur, D. R. *Understanding Electronic Commerce*. Seattle: Microsoft Press, 1997.

Lane, N. "Advancing the Digital Economy into the Twenty-First Century," *Information Systems Frontiers* 1, no. 3 (1999).

Lederer, A. L., et al. "Using Web-based Information Systems to Enhance Competitiveness," *Communications of the ACM* (July 1998).

Lee, G. E. "Do Electronic Marketplaces Lower the Price of Goods?" *Communication of the ACM* (January 2000).

Lewis, M. "Boom or Bust? The New Economy Hasn't Just Changed Business. It Has Fundamentally Altered. *Business 2.0* (April 1, 2000).

Lim, E. P. and K. Siau. "Mobil Commerce," *Journal of Database Management* (April 2001).

Lisse, W. C. "The Economics of Information and the Internet," *Competitive Intelligence Review* (April 1998).

Martin, J. *Cybercorp: The New Business Revolution*. New York: Amacom, American Management Association, 1996.

McGonagle, J., Jr. and C. Vella. *The Internet Age of Competitive Intelligence*. Westport, Connecticut: Quorum Books, 1999.

Michaels, J. "How New Is the New Economy?" *Forbes* (December 13, 1999).

Mougayear, W. *Opening Digital Markets: Advanced Strategies for Internet Driven Commerce*. New York: McGraw-Hill, 1998.

Pine, J. II. *Mass Customization*. Boston: Harvard Business School Press, 1999.

Pine, J. II and J. H. Gilmore. *The Experience Economy*. Boston: Harvard Business School Press, 1999.

Porter M. E., "Strategy and the Internet," *Harvard Business Review* (March 2001).

Ramsdell, M. "The Real Business of B2B," *The Mckinsey Quarterly* (Third quarter 2000).

Ranadive, V. *The Power of Now*. New York: McGraw-Hill, 1999.

Rayport, J. F. and J. J. Sviokla. "Managing in the Marketspaces," *Harvard Business Review* (November/December 1994).

Redman, P. "Mobile E-commerce Evolves," *e-Business Advisor* (July 2000).

Resnick, P., et al. "Roles for Electronic Brokers," *ccs.mit.edu/ccswp179.html* (1998).

Schwartz, E. I. *Digital Darwinism: Seven Breakthrough Business Strategies for Surviving in the Cutthroat Web Economy*. New York: Broadway Books, 1999.

Schwarz, E. I. *Webonomics*. New York: Broadway Books, 1997.

Schwartz, K. M. "It's a Tool, Not a Toy," *Mobile Computing and Communication* (May 2000).

"Shopping Around the Web," *The Economist*, special issue (February 26, 2000).

Strader, T. J. and H. J. Shaw. "Characteristics of Electronic Markets," *Decision Support Systems* no. 21 (1997).

Swass, V. "Structure and Macro-Level Impacts of Electronic Commerce." In *Emerging Information Technologies*, ed. K. E. Kendall. Thousand Oaks, CA: Sage Publishing, 1999.

Tapscott, D., editor. *Creating Value in the Network Economy*. Boston: Harvard Business School Press, 1999.

Tapscott, D., et al., editors. *Blueprint of the Digital Economy: Creating Wealth in the Era of E-Business*. New York: McGraw-Hill, 1998.

Tapscott, D., et al. *Digital Capital*. Boston: Harvard Business Review Press, 2000.

Turban, E., et al. *Information Technology for Management*, 3rd ed. New York: John Wiley & Sons, 2002.

Varshney, U. and R. Vetter. "Mobil Commerce," *Journal on Mobile Networks and Applications* (Summer 2001).

Ware, J., et al. *The Search for Digital Excellence*. New York: McGraw-Hill with CommerceNet Press, 1998.

Werbach, K. "Syndication—The Emerging Model for Business in the Internet Era," *Harvard Business Review* (May/June 2000).

U.S. Department of Commerce Report: The Emerging Digital Economy II, *ecommerce.gov/ede* June 1999.

PART 2

3

Retailing in Electronic Commerce (E-Tailing)

CONTENT

LEARNING OBJECTIVES

Upon completion of this chapter the reader will be able to:

- Define and describe the primary business models of electronic retailing ("e-tailing").

- Discuss various e-tail consumer aids, including comparison-shopping aids.

- Discuss various e-tail markets, such as groceries, music, cars, and others.

- Identify the critical success factors of direct marketing and e-tailing, along with mistakes to avoid.

- Identify the principles of "click-and-mortar" strategies for traditional retailers

- Describe the issue of disintermediation, reintermediation, and channel conflicts in e-tailing.

- Identify various managerial issues of concern to e-tailers.

Competition among online sellers of books and music is keen. Books and music are commodities—all copies of a single book title (or CD) are identical. Because of this, consumers look primarily for the lowest price, and to a lesser extent for fast shipment, good return policies, and helpful customer service. Let's look at one of the best known e-commerce sites, the online bookseller *Amazon.com* (*amazon.com*). In this chapter, we will investigate the competitive structure of the electronic marketspace for books and music by comparing the strengths and weaknesses of *Amazon.com* with its competitors, not just in the book sector, but also in the sale of music, toys, and cars. Most of Amazon's customers are individual buyers. Thus it is an example of the B2C business model.

LARGEST BOOKSTORE IN THE WORLD

Amazon.com is the largest online bookstore in the world, and leads the market in online book sales. *Amazon.com* bills itself as having "Earth's Biggest Selection." It serves over 17 million customers in over 150 countries, and offers millions of items for sale in categories such as books, music, DVDs, videos, toys, electronics, software, video games, and home improvement products. By clicking on "International" on the *Amazon.com* home page, visitors can visit *Amazon.com's* newest Web site, a site targeted at non-U.S. consumers. In an effort to internationalize their market, *Amazon.com* now offers over one million Japanese-language

titles, a growing list of German and Spanish-language products, videotapes in the European PAL format, and many books, CDs, DVDs, and videos for sale in France.

Amazon.com started business in July 1995, and it had $15.7 million in sales in 1996. Sales climbed to $600 million in 1998, and by 2000, its annual sales exceeded $1.8 billion. *Amazon.com* listed more than 5 million titles in its electronic catalog in spring 1999, and by 2000 it offered an aggregate of over 13 million book, music, and DVD/video titles. It has continually enhanced its bookstore by expanding product selection and improving the customer experience. It now offers new specialty stores, such as its professional and technical store. *Amazon.com* has also expanded its editorial content through partnerships with experts in certain fields and increased product selection with the addition of millions of used and out-of-print titles.

Auctions. Amazon also offers marketplace services such as Amazon Auctions and zShops, which are operated from Amazon's Web site. Amazon Auctions hosts and operates auctions on behalf of individuals and small businesses throughout the world, using a model that differs from eBay's. (See Chapter 9 for more on Internet auctions.) The zShops service, coupled with the Amazon marketplace and Amazon payment processing, offers small businesses the opportunity to have custom storefronts supported by the richness of Amazon's back-end order fulfillment processing.

Features. Key features of the *Amazon.com* superstore are easy browsing and searching, useful product information, reviews, recommendations and personalization, broad

selection, low prices, 1-Click order technology, (e-wallet, see Chapter 14) secure payment systems, wide selection, and efficient order fulfillment. The *Amazon.com* Web site provides other functionalites to make online shopping more enjoyable. Its "Gift Ideas" sections feature seasonally appropriate gift ideas and services. In its "Community" section, it provides a gathering place where customers can share product information and recommendations. Through its e-cards section, customers can send free animated electronic greeting cards to friends and family.

CUSTOMER RELATIONSHIP MANAGEMENT

Amazon is recognized as an online leader in creating sales through customer intimacy and customer relationship management (CRM) by creating effective and informative marketing front-ends, supported by highly automated, efficient back-end systems. Its expertise also extends to online order fulfillment efficiency, which offers extensive information to the customer (e.g., order tracking). *Amazon.com* also provides visitors with unique links to lists such as *Top Sellers,* which lists some of their most popular products, and *Back to Basics,* which provides lists of classic literature.

When a customer makes a return visit to *Amazon.com*, a cookie file (Chapter 17) identifies the user and says, for example, "Welcome back, Merrill Warkentin," and proceeds to recommend new books from the same genre of former customer purchases. When a customer browses a specific book or music selection, the underlying Web-enabled database provides customer reviews and tells the customer that "Customers who bought titles by this author also bought titles by these authors . . ." Visitors can also register online, create a user profile, and submit a wish list. Customers can personalize their account and manage orders online at Amazon with its patented "1-Click Settings" feature.

Among other things, this personalized service allows customers to:

- View their order status.
- Cancel or combine orders that have not entered the shipping process.
- Edit the shipping options and addresses on unshipped orders.
- Modify the payment method for unshipped orders.
- Update the Personal Notification Services subscriptions.

Amazon.com tracks customer purchase histories and sends purchase recommendations via e-mail in order to cultivate repeat buyers. *Amazon.com* also provides detailed product descriptions and product ratings in order to help consumers make informed purchase decisions. These efforts usually result in satisfactory shopping experiences and encourage customers to return to the site. *Amazon.com* frequently cites their high percentage of repeat business from loyal customers.

■___| FINANCIAL PERFORMANCE

In late 2000, CEO Jeff Bezos announced that *Amazon.com's* oldest business, the U.S.-based stores for books, music, and DVD/video titles, was profitable. Yet their overall losses continued to mount and their stock price tumbled. In late 2000, Downside's Deathwatch (*downside.com/ deathwatch.html*) forecasted that, based solely on company financial statements filed with the U.S. Securities and Exchange Commission (SEC), *Amazon.com* would run out of cash during July of 2001. (This was not the case).

A primary managerial concern is *Amazon.com's* ability to move into new areas of business, while simultaneously controlling costs and moving toward overall profitability. Most observers agree that *Amazon.com* has certainly excelled at providing a high level of customer service and has achieved a high degree of customer loyalty. The challenge now is to translate that loyalty and market position into real long-term value for its shareholders. One analyst estimates that it will take Amazon almost 2 years, on average, to leverage each loyal customer into a profitable customer. How can *Amazon.com* concentrate on profitable customers and not spend resources on profitable ones? What are the critical success

factors for capturing market share and for reaching profitability?

Diversification. Recently, *Amazon.com* has also undertaken alliances with "trusted partners" that provide knowledgeable entry into new markets. Their alliance with *GreenLight.com* allows them to sell cars online, clicking "health and beauty" takes the visitor to the site they jointly operate with *drugstore.com*, and clicking on "wireless phones" will suggest a service plan from their partner in that market. One of *Amazon.com's* unsuccessful ventures was its alliance with *Living.com*, an online furniture company that went bankrupt. Like other co-branded projects, this alliance involved a "referral fee" arrangement, in which *Living.com* would pay *Amazon.com* millions of dollars for referring customers to the living.com Web site. *Amazon.com* had the "eyeballs" (visitors), and the furniture seller needed customers. This customer acquisition problem is common to all e-tailers. (It has been estimated that the customer acquisition costs for online stock brokers averages almost $500 per customer.) However, because of the bankruptcy, *Living.com* was unable to pay Amazon these fees, adversely affecting *Amazon.com's* bottom line. Later in this chapter, we discuss the successful alliance between Amazon and Toys R Us.

3.2   ELECTRONIC RETAILING (E-TAILING) AND B2C MARKET GROWTH

The opening vignette has demonstrates some of the features and managerial issues related to electronic retailers, also known as **e-tailers.** The goal of this chapter is to understand the methods for achieving success as an e-tailer, by looking at several key e-tail sectors. As indicated in Chapter 1, EC can be classified as

Business-to-Consumer EC (B2C) or *Business-to-Business EC (B2B).* This chapter focuses on B2C, although B2B and B2C share many features. *Amazon.com* sells books to corporate acquisition departments as well as to individual consumers. *Amazon.com's* chief rival, Barnes & Noble, has a special division that caters to business customers. *Walmart.com* sells to both individuals and businesses (via Sam's Club). Dell sells their computers to both consumers and businesses, and travel sites sell to both groups as well.

However, B2B operations typically require greater accountability and formal relationships than B2C transactions, and B2B transactions are often accompanied by related business services, such as logistical support or financing. The distinctive features of B2B e-commerce are covered in Chapters 6–8. In this chapter we focus on B2C marketing, focusing primarily on those companies that sell so-called *hard goods* that are shipped to a customer, as opposed to *soft goods* or **digital goods,** such as news and information, which can be easily downloaded via the Internet. Certain digital goods can be distributed in physical form by Web sites or by traditional retail stores, or they may be sold directly to consumers and downloaded over the Internet. In section 3.7, we will discuss the sale of digital goods by e-tailers.

One of the most significant characteristic of B2C commerce is the ability to create a direct relationship with the consumer without the involvement of intermediaries, such as distributors, wholesalers, or dealers. Manufacturers with established brands, such as Dell, are able to execute a successful direct marketing strategy if they pay attention to the basic rules of successful direct marketing and efficiently deliver quality merchandise to the customer. Dell sells over $17 million dollars in computers per day directly to businesses and individuals, and their widely recognized corporate motto is "Be Direct." In section 3.5, we will explore how Dell has achieved its phenomenal success in online PC sales over the past few years.

In the early days of e-tailing, established retailers (department stores and discount stores) were not major players in the online B2C market. Their Web sites were typically used as *brochureware* and lacked interactivity. The Web site's primary purpose was to drive customers to the physical store. Traditional e-tailers are now implementing successful strategies for combining an online presence with their *physical retail stores* ("**brick-and-mortar**" stores). This strategy of having both an off-line and online presence is called a "**click-and-mortar**" model, or sometimes "**brick-and-click**," and it may represent the future of retailing. The direct marketing and the physical marketing channels, along with the telephone catalog sales channel, must be jointly managed to deliver value to customers while at the same time maximizing sales and profits.

The B2C Market. What is the volume of direct marketing transactions and how much will it grow? The statistics for the volume of past and current B2C EC sales, as well as forecasts for future sales, come from many sources, with substantial variations in the way the numbers are derived. This stems from the use of different definitions of EC—when tallying the financial data, some analysts include the investment cost in Internet infrastructure, whereas others merely include the pure transactions conducted via the Internet. Another issue is the categories of items sold. Since the Internet's inception, the major items sold over the Internet have included apparel, gifts, books, food, and computers. Increasingly significant are digitized goods and services such as software, music, video subscriptions, online games, and consumer finance and insurance services.

During 2001, it was estimated that about 75 million individual Internet users participated in some form of online shopping (*emarketer.com,* July 2001). Worldwide B2C revenues, according to eMarketer report (May 2001) ranged from 53 to 238 billion (depending on the source) in 2000 and are forecasted in the range of $428 to $2,134 billion in 2004. The optimistic predictions were made by Goldman Sachs. Men are more likely to purchase consumer electronics and computer hardware and software, while women are more likely to purchase apparel items.

Retail and e-tail success fundamentally comes from offering quality merchandise at good prices, coupled with excellent service. In that sense, the direct and traditional channels are not very different. But online retail stores have the ability to offer expanded consumer services not offered by traditional retailers. These consumer services will be discussed later in this chapter. But with all else being equal in the online environment, merchandise that has the following characteristics are expected to facilitate sale in higher volumes.

Characteristics of Goods Leading to Higher Online Sales Volumes

1. High brand recognition.
2. A guarantee is provided by highly reliable or well-known vendors.
3. Digitized goods, such as books, music, software and videos.
4. Relatively inexpensive items.
5. Frequently purchased items (e.g., groceries, prescription drugs).
6. Commodities that have standard specifications, making physical inspection unimportant.
7. Well-known packaged items that cannot be opened even in a traditional store.

So how do online consumers decide what to buy and where? What is their decision-making process and how can e-tailers influence consumer purchasing decisions? The following section offers some insights into the purchase decision and the role of marketing.

3.3   CONSUMER PURCHASE PROCESS AND THE MARKETING PLAN

In this section, we will describe the consumer purchase process and the role of marketing. Note that many of the perspectives and business models described here can also be applied to the B2B EC that is described in Chapter 6.

To understand the managerial process of successfully selling merchandise directly to consumers, we must first look at the process that consumers follow when they shop and purchase items. Of course, this process is not the same for all items—consumers usually give far more thought to the decision of purchasing a car than to buying a carton of milk. But the underlying purchase decision process is essentially the same for both items.

The process starts with *prepurchase steps,* followed by the *actual purchase,* and finally by *postpurchase steps* (Figure 3-1). Consumers begin with an awareness that they need to make a purchase and identify the basic need or want. Consumers then establish the decision criteria and refine it. Again, in the case of certain purchases, this is very brief (e.g., "I want to buy a cup of hot coffee"). Consumers may seek recommendations at this stage from individuals or from information sources, such

Figure 3-1	The Consumer Purchase Decision Process

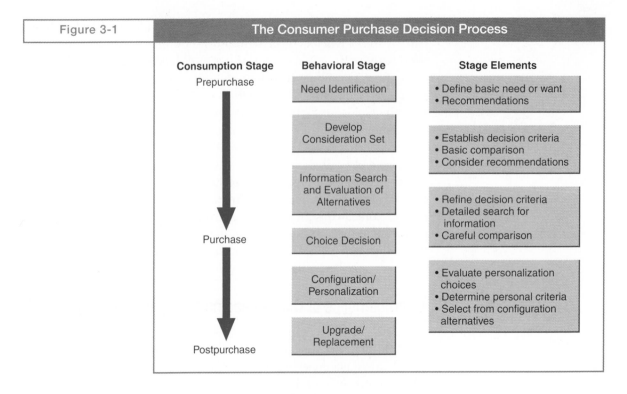

as a manufacturer's Web site, comparison Web sites, or from intelligent agents that collect data according to their criteria and present them with recommendations. Once consumers have established their search criteria and determined how they will make their purchase decision, the consumer is then free to collect germane information from all available sources. This is the "Information Search and Evaluation of Alternatives" stage. Recall that price is often the overriding consideration, especially for products that are *pure commodities* (no real differentiation between various items for sale).

We will return to this process in Chapter 4 and relate it there to market research. Here we focus on the Internet marketing aspects.

A consumer's decision is based partly on the value, quality, or price of the underlying product or service, and partly on the policies and procedures of the traditional retailer or online e-tailer. In other words, at times the retailer's service policy, return policy, or shipping policy is more important than the quality or price of the actual item.

It is more difficult to compare features of notebook computers or cars than it is to compare features of standard items, such as a gallon of whole milk or a specific best-selling book. Every copy of a particular book is identical, except for its price, and retailer's policies may vary. Air travel from one city to another is a commodity unless consumers have a brand preference for one airline over another for reasons related to service, safety, reliability, or loyalty based on frequent flier programs. Complex decisions may require more time, more information, and more assistance than simple decisions, regardless of whether the purchase is made from a traditional seller or from an online seller.

Once a consumer has purchased an item, he or she is often presented with options regarding item configuration or personalization. These decisions can often be made directly on the Web site. Consumers may also need assistance with product installation and setup. For example, a consumer may need to know how to hook up a new DVD player, troubleshoot a new dishwasher, customize unfamiliar software, or configure drivers for a new computer. With physical stores, this is often accomplished through telephone assistance or return visits to the physical store, both of which are very expensive customer support functions for the retailer. E-tailers often provide online help desks that assist customers at near zero marginal cost. With a visit to *Maytag.com*, a customer can learn not only how to correctly use his or her new dishwasher, but also learn tips on removing stains from clothing and find out about other Maytag appliances.

Types of Online Shoppers

Consumers have not universally embraced the broad choices and convenience offered by the Internet. Some gravitate toward the idea of spending only a few minutes online and then having items shipped to their homes, whereas others relish the online shopping experience. Harris Interactive (2000), the Consumer Direct Cooperative (Orler, 1998), and others have identified several unique categories of online shoppers, differentiated by buying motivation and spending behavior as follows.

1) *Time-starved consumers,* often found in two-income homes, will be willing to pay higher prices or extra fees to save time on shopping, whether or not they enjoy the online shopping experience.

2) *Shopping avoiders* dislike shopping, and may use the Internet just to avoid people, lines, or traffic.

3) *New technologists,* often young and comfortable with technology in general, may just shop online "because it's cool."

4) *Time-sensitive materialists,* or *click-and-mortar consumers,* only use the Internet to look for products; they prefer to make their purchases from traditional stores because of security concerns or other reasons.

5) *Traditionals* just prefer stores, and may never adopt online shopping behaviors.

6) *Hunter-gatherers* (about 20 percent of all online shoppers) enjoy the process of price comparison and the search for good values.

7) *Brand loyalists,* consumers who shop online for a particular brand, probably account for the greatest per-person profit levels.

8) *Single* shoppers (about 16 percent of online shoppers) prefer the Internet not only for shopping, but also for banking, communications, game playing, news, and other activities.

So what are the criteria that individual shoppers use when deciding which item to purchase and from which source to buy it? What tools and aids do consumers employ to assist in the research and purchase decision? The following sections evaluate some of these criteria and decision aids.

Decision Criteria

Some of the primary criteria that consumers use when making a purchase decision are presented here. These factors drive success for retailers and e-tailers alike.

Value proposition. What a retailer offers may be unique and valuable to the consumer—customer service, better prices, or higher quality. Price is often the most important criteria, but not always. Customers are willing to pay more for special services or friendly policies.

Personal service. Firms that treat each customer as a unique individual (not "just a number") will outsell firms that do not do it. E-tailers can customize information and interactive features for each user by using cookies to identify an individual user when he or she returns to a Web site or by asking users about their preferences. The e-tailer can then use that person's profile to determine the features to display or procedures to be followed. An example is the ability to arrange information on the screen according to each consumer's personal tastes, to default to various values (such as window seats for airline flights or next-day delivery for cigars), and to "remember" various information, such as shipping addresses and credit card information.

Convenience. Time is a valuable commodity. Busy consumers look for ways to save time and add convenience. Again, the Web offers many ways to make shopping more convenient. Creating effective, easy user interfaces for Web sites can enhance the convenience of shopping. (Think about Web sites you have visited that were confusing and those you recall as easy to navigate.) Another way to add value through convenience is to create shopping sites that are self-contained, that is, serving all the customer's needs at one location in one transaction. Today, many consumers expect to interact with businesses via wireless technologies, touch-tone phones, or Web sites anytime from anywhere. Consumers sometimes prefer self-service options over human customer service representatives, but they also expect to be able to speak with a human representative if necessary.

Other criteria. Service after the sale may be more important for certain purchases, such as cars, computers, or software, if the consumer believes that there may be difficulties in installation. Consumers may prefer an e-tailer that has a Web site with powerful online help features or 24/7 telephone support. In other cases, if a consumer thinks that a product return may be likely, as with apparel purchases, they may prefer an e-tailer with generous return policies, even if the prices are slightly higher. The overall reputation of the e-tailer also has value for many consumers. Some consumers may be unwilling to spend hundreds of dollars on a product from an unfamiliar travel site, and will gladly pay higher prices to deal with an e-tailer they trust. The available forms of payment are another common criteria, as are shipping options.

Many Web sites offer customers assistance in order to facilitate the online shopping experience during all phases of the consumer purchase decision. Some sites are operated by neutral third parties with no financial interest in the sale of any particular product or the sales of any particular e-tailer. Others take affiliate fees and may encourage sales of one product over another or from one e-tailer over another. Some of these aids are presented in section 3.4.

A Marketing Plan

Several other factors may influence a consumer's decision, and an e-tailer must identify all possible ways to influence that decision process. This is the primary task of marketing research and management. **Marketing management** is the process of making it attractive and easy for consumers to buy a firm's ideas, goods, or services.

This is done by influencing (1) the portfolio of items available for sale (*"product"*), (2) the *prices* of those products, (3) the *promotion* of the products through advertising and other communications, and (4) the *packaging* and delivery (*"physical distribution"*) of the products, also thought of as *place* or placement. These four elements of the market plan are sometimes called the "**four Ps**" or the *"marketing mix."* The Internet clearly has or can have an impact on the execution of each element of the market plan.

3.4   ONLINE PURCHASE DECISION AIDS

Many sites and tools are available to help online consumers with purchasing decisions. Consumers must decide which product or service to purchase, which site to use for the purchase (which may be a manufacturer site, a general purpose e-tailer, a niche digital intermediary, or some other site), and what other services to employ. Some sites offer price comparisons as their primary tool, while others evaluate services, trust, quality, and other factors. There are *shopping portals, shopping robots ("shopbots"), business ratings* sites, *trust verification* sites, and *other shopping aids* as discussed in this section.

Shopping Portals

Several consumer shopping portals offer advice and ratings of products or e-tailers. Some offer interactive tools to create a custom comparison based on the visitor's selection criteria. Others simply provide standard static tables and links, which the visitor can select and consider.

Shopping portals may be comprehensive or niche-oriented. Comprehensive or general-purpose portals have links to many different sellers that evaluate a broad range of products. Comprehensive portals include Gomez Advisors (*gomez.com*) and *activebuyersguide.com*. Many search engines and directories also offer general shopping comparison sites, such as *shopping.altavista.com*, *shopping.yahoo.com*, *eshop.msn.com*, and *webcenter.shop.aol.com/main.adp*. These are all clear links from the main page of the search engine and generate revenues by directing consumers to their affiliates' sites. Some of these portals even offer comparison tools to help identify the best price for a particular item. Several of these evaluation companies have purchased shopbots or other smaller shopping aids and incorporated them into their portals.

Shopping portals may also offer specialized niche aids, offering information and links for purchasers of automobiles, toys, computers, travel, or some other narrow area. Examples include *bsilly.com* for kid's products and *zdnet.com/computershopper* or *shopper.cnet.com* for computer equipment. The advantage of niche shopping portals is their ability to specialize in a certain line of products and carefully track consumer tastes within a specific market segment. Some of these portals seek only to collect the referral fee from their affiliation with sites they recommend. Others have no formal relationship with the sellers—they sell banner ad space to advertisers who wish to reach the communities who regularly visit these specialized sites. In other cases, shopping portals act as intermediaries by selling directly to consumers, though this may harm their reputation for independence and objectivity.

Shopbots and Agents

Savvy Internet shoppers may already have their favorite shopping sites, but how can they find other stores with good service and policies that sell similar items at lower prices? **Shopping robots** ("**Shopping agents**" or "**shopbots**") are tools that scout the Web for consumers that specify search criteria. Different shopbots use different search methods. For example, *Mysimon.com* searches the Web to find the best prices for thousands of popular items. This task is not simple. The shopbot may have to evaluate dozens of different SKU (Stock Keeping Unit) numbers for the same item, since each e-tailer may have a different SKU rather than using a standardized data-representation code. (See Chapter 8 for a discussion about of the role of XML in facilitating such comparisons.) Mysimon and comparison tools like it are comprehensive shopping support sites. Other portals specialize in certain product categories or niches. For example, *AutoBytel.com*, *Autovantage.com*, and *Carpoint.com* help consumers shop for cars. *Zdnet.com/computershopper* searches for information on computers, software and peripherals. The agent in *office.com* helps consumers find the best price for office supplies. In addition, agents such as *pricegrabber.com* are able to identify customers' preferences. *dealtime.com* provides a "shopping bar" that allows consumers to compare over 1,000 different merchant sites, and keeps seeking lower prices on your behalf. Hagglesome.com even negotiation agents and agents that assist auction bidders by automating the bid process using the bidders wishes. These are discussed in Chapter 4 and 9.

Business Ratings Sites

Bizrate.com and *Gomez.com* (Gomez Advisors) are two of many sites that purport to rate various e-tailers and online products, based on multiple criteria. At *Gomez.com*, the consumer can actually specify the relative importance of different criteria when comparing online banks, toy sellers, or e-grocers. *Bizrate.com* has a network of shoppers that report on various sellers, and uses the compiled results in its evaluations.

Trust Verification Sites

There are a number of companies that purport to evaluate and verify the trustworthiness of various e-tailers. The TRUSTe seal (they call it a "trustmark") appears at the bottom of an e-tailers Web site. E-tailers pay TRUSTe for use of the seal. Its 1,300-plus members hope that consumers will use the TRUSTe seal as an assurance and as a proxy for actual research into their privacy policy, credit card security, fulfillment process integrity, etc. With so many choices, many consumers are not sure who they should trust. However, TRUSTe is not foolproof. TRUSTe has been criticized for its lax verification processes, and a number of high-profile privacy violations and other problems with TRUSTe members has led one author to publish the TRUSTe "Hall of Shame" (Rafter, 2000).

Other sources of trust verification or similar services include BBBOnLine and Secure Assure, which charge yearly license fees based on a company's annual revenue. In addition, Ernst and Young, the global public accounting firm, has created it own service for auditing e-tailers in order to offer some guarantee of the integrity of their business practices. See Chapters 4 and 17 for further discussion on trust verification sites.

Other Shopper Aiding Tools

There are other digital intermediaries who fill a role assisting buyers or sellers or both with the research and purchase process. An example would be escrow services. Since buyers and sellers do not see and know each other, there is frequently a need for a trusted third party to assure the proper exchange of money and goods (see Chapter 9). Similar to portals, these sites may offer research information or they may provide other services (Chapters 8 and 9). These sites may also provide payment-processing support. In traditional retail, most customers pay for a purchase with cash, a credit card (or debit card), or a personal check. Cash cannot be used for online purchases, and many consumers worry about giving their credit card or debit card numbers over the Internet. A number of technologies have evolved to facilitate online payment. Among these are various forms of electronic cash, streamlined credit card authorization methods, digital wallet technology, and various third-party payment systems. These payment-processing sites are discussed further in Chapters 8 and 14.

Other decision aids include communities of consumers who offer advice and opinions on products and e-tailers. One such site is *Epinions.com*, which has searchable recommendations on thousands of products. *PriceSCAN.com* is a price comparison engine and *PriceGrabber.com* is a comparison shopping tool that covers over one million products. *DealTime.com* specializes in electronics products, while *eTour.com* specializes in apparel, health and beauty, and other categories. Other software agents and comparison sites are presented in Table 3-1.

3.5   E-TAILING BUSINESS MODELS

A business model as defined in Chapter 1 embodies a plan for offering a value proposition to customers, a source of revenues, an identification of costs, and a detailed set of processes for execution. In B2C, *business models* are often categorized by the way that revenues are generated, for example, *subscription models, transaction-fee models, advertising-supported models,* or *various sponsorship models.*

- *Subscription models:* Charge a monthly or annual subscription fee for the service
- *Transaction fee models:* Charge a service fee based on the level of transactions offered
- *Advertizing-supported models:* Instead of charging to users, charge to the advertising companies. But the revenue by advertising service can be applied with the subscription and/or transaction fee models.
- *Sponsorship models:* The companies who can benefit or who are willing to donate beyond financial reasons may sponsor the business. This model is usually a supplementary source of income.

Another angle of classifying e-tailing business models is the type of sites that sell directly to consumers:

(1) **Direct marketing** sites from manufacturers such as Dell, Nike or Sony site.

(2) **Pure-play e-tailers** (no physical stores), such as *Amazon.com.*

(3) **Traditional retailers with Web sites** which are called click-and-mortar retailers, such as Wal-Mart or Home Depot.

TABLE 3-1	Representative Comparison Software Agents			
	Agent Classification	**Product**	**Description**	**URL**
	Learning Agents	Empirical	Surveys users' reading interests and then uses machine learning to find new Web pages and news articles using neural-network-based collaborative filtering technology.	Empirical.com
	Comparison Shopping Agents	Jango	Adapted to Excite's shopping guide.	Dealtime.com
			Constructs a lot of shopping guides such as Yahoo!, Visa, Compaq, Hot Bot, and so on.	
		MySimon	Using VLA (Virtual Learning Agent) technology, Simon can shop at merchants in hundreds of product categories on the web. Simon shops with a real-time interface for the best price.	Mysimon.com
		CompareNet	An interactive buyer's guide that educates shoppers and allows them to make direct comparisons between brands and products.	Compare.net
			Provides shopping guide by linking to other sites.	
	AI/Logic-supported Approaches	cnetshopper	Price comparison.	Shopper.cnet.com
	Computer-related Shopping Guide	Netbuyer	Supplies sales and marketing solutions to technology companies, by delivering actionable, fact-based information on computer and communications industry trends, products developments, and buyer activity.	Netbuyer.com
	Car-related Shopping Guide	Auto-by-Tel	A low-cost, no-haggle car-buying system of choice for leading search engines and online programs such as Excite, Netscape's NetCenter, Lycos, and AT&T WorldNet Services.	Autobytel.com
		Autovantage	Provides the Web's premier savings site for great deals on auto, travel, shopping, dining, and other services.	Cendant.com
		CarPoint	Makes the auto site a one-stop shopping place for searching and purchasing automobiles.	Carpoint.msn.com
	Microsoft-related Agent Technology	Agentmart	Introduces and reviews Microsoft's agent. Provides agent infospace and agent directory. First Web site on animated conversational characters such as Genie, Merlin, and so on.	Agentmart.com
	Aggregator Portal	Pricing Central	Aggregates information from other shopping agents and search engines.	Pricingcentral.com
			Comparison shopping is done in real time (latest pricing information).	
	Real-Time Agents	Gold digger	Find the lowest price automatically when you visit a store (takes few minutes, very comprehensive).	Mygolddigger.com
		EdgeGain	Compare prices.	Edgegain.com

The e-tailing businesses can also be classified by the scope of handling items (*general purpose* versus *specialty* or *niche e-tailing*) and scope of covering region (*global* versus *regional*).

Direct Marketing

Formerly, the term **direct marketing** referred to mail order catalog sales, supported by telephone interaction with the customer. Direct marketers bypassed the traditional retail store and took orders directly from consumers. The direct marketer may have purchased the products directly from the manufacturer, bypassing traditional wholesale distribution. The Web offers another mechanism for interaction between the direct marketer and the customer, and firms with established, mature mail-order businesses have a distinct advantage in online sales given their existing payment processing, inventory management, and order fulfillment operations as shown in Application Case 3.1.

Lands' End: How a Mail Order Company Moved Online

Some of the most successful B2C e-tailers are mail order companies that used paper catalogs or TV before. One reason for this success is the logistic system they had in place and the experience in virtual stores. Here we look at Lands' End, a successful direct marketing company that served over 6.2 million customers in 2000. The company is well known for its quality products, styled casual clothing and gifts, and customer service. Internet sales in 2000 were 10 percent of the 1.3 billion total, doubling the 5 percent Internet sales of 1999. Projected Internet sales are 20 percent in 2003. *Landsend.com* offers all catalog products (in 1995, it offered only 100). The Web site allows women to build and store a 3-D model of themselves (Personal Model). The model then recommends outfits that flatter body profiles and suggest sizes based upon customers' measurements. Using its "Oxford Express," customers can sort through hundreds of fabrics, styles, collar and cuff options, and sizes within seconds, to find just the dress shirt that fits them. Personalized shopping accounts are also available on the Web site. In addition, customers can track their order status online and request catalogs using the Internet. The company has an affiliate network that pays 5 percent commission for every sale that comes from a referral. Also, Land's End Live allows online customers to shop with the assistance of a "real" personal shopper. By using the Internet, Land's End extends its presence globally by having localized sites in Japan, Germany, and the United Kingdom.

Because 88 percent of the company's customers are college graduates, mostly with computers, the company expects its online business to continue to grow rapidly during the next few years.

Note: Lands' End operates also 16 physical outlets in the United States and 3 in the United Kingdom. Shipments in the United States are received within 2 days after ordering. A B2B store is available at *landsend.com/corpsales*.

Source: Compiled from *landsend.com*.

By using the Internet, manufacturers can sell directly to customers and provide customer support online. In this sense, the traditional intermediaries are eliminated. **Disintermediation** refers to the removal of organizations or business process layers responsible for certain intermediary steps in a given value chain. In the traditional distribution channel, there are intermediating layers between the manufacturer and consumer, such as wholesalers, distributors, and retailers, as shown in Figure 3-2. In some countries, such as Japan, one may find inefficient distribution networks that are comprised of as many as 10 layers of intermediaries that can add a 500 percent markup to a product.

When manufacturers connect directly with consumers and shorten the distribution chain, inefficiencies can be eliminated, product delivery time can be decreased, and manufacturers can build a closer relationship with the consumers. When the Internet can serve as a replacement for the information channel from consumers back to the manufacturers, so that demand can be gauged and orders can be placed, and when the Internet can also provide the opportunity for manufacturers to directly contact consumers to provide product information or information about orders, the need for the traditional intermediaries is reduced or eliminated.

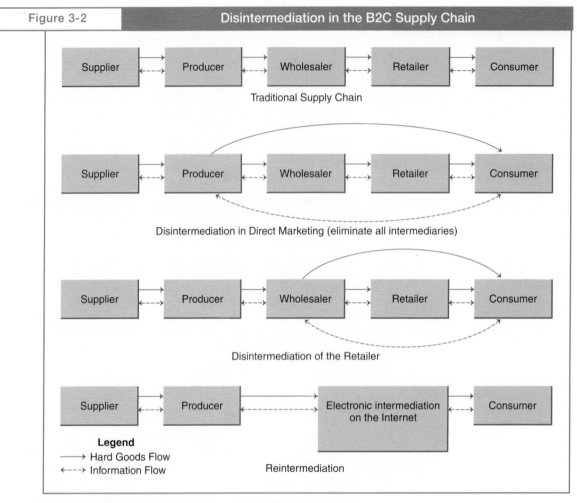

Figure 3-2   Disintermediation in the B2C Supply Chain

Source: M. Warkentin, et al. (2000). Used with permission of Dr. Merrill Warkentin.

Dell has established itself as one of the world's most successful e-tailers by profitably selling computers directly to millions of consumers over the Internet. Besides the cost advantages, the parties have a greater opportunity to influence each other—sellers better understand their markets because of the direct connection to consumers, and consumers gain greater information about the products through their direct connection to the manufacturer.

Direct Marketing Between Manufacturers and Customers. Direct sales by manufacturers are gaining popularity and it is done by thousands of manufacturers worldwide (e.g., see *lego.com*, *samsung.com*, *ge.com*, etc.). It is mainly done as an **additional** marketing channel. This is the most common type of click-and-mortar. Direct marketing can more effectively support the consumer's build-to-order request (See Application Case 3.2: Buying Cars Online).

In the world of online new and used car sales, there are many new digital intermediaries that assist buyers and/or sellers. There are also new reintermediaries who

| APPLICATION CASE | 3.2 |

Buying Cars Online: Build to Order

The world's automobile manufacturers are very complex enterprises with thousands of suppliers and large numbers of customers. Their traditional channel for distributing cars has been the automobile dealer, who orders cars and then sells them to consumers from the lot. When a customer wants a particular feature or color, the dealer may have to wait until the "pipeline" of vehicles has that particular car in a delivery. The manufacturers conduct market research in order to estimate which features and options will sell well, and then make the cars they wish to sell. In some cases, certain cars are ultimately sold from stock at a loss when the market exhibits insufficient demand for a particular vehicle. The carmakers have operated under this "build-to-stock" environment, where they built cars that were carried as inventory during the outbound logistics process (ships, trucks, trains, and dealers' lots). General Motors estimates that they hold as much as $40 billion worth of parts and unsold vehicles in their entire distribution channels. Other automakers hold similar amounts.

Ford and GM, along with many other carmakers around the world, have announced plans to implement a "build-to-order" program much like the Dell approach to building computers. These auto giants intend to transform themselves from build-to-stock companies to build-to-order companies, thereby cutting inventory requirements in half (Simison, 2000), while at the same time giving customers exactly what they want. (See more about customization in Chapter 4.)

As an example of this trend toward build-to-order mass customization in the new car market, Jaguar car buyers can build their dream car online. Using the Web site, they are able to custom configure their car's features and components, see it online, price it, and have it delivered to a nearby dealer. Using a virtual car on the Web site, customers can view more than 1,250 possible exterior combinations in real time, rotate the image 360 degrees, and see the price updated automatically with each selection of trim or accessories. After storing the car in a virtual garage, the customer can decide on their purchase and select a dealer at which to pick up the completed car. (Conflicts with the established dealer network channel are avoided.) The site primarily helps with the research process—it is not a fully transactional site. The configuration, however, is transmitted to the production floor, thereby reducing delivery time and contributing to increased customer satisfaction.

sell cars to consumers without the involvement of traditional car dealers. Some of these sites include Kelly Blue Book (*kbb.com*), which offers pricing information for consumers, *Edmunds.com*, which gives consumers information about the dealer's true costs, *Carfax.com*, which will research a specific used car and tell you if it has ever been in an accident or had an odometer roll-back, and *Carclub.com*, which gives members discounts on insurance, gas, and repairs. Additionally, there are "lead services" that direct buyers to member dealers and, in some cases, also offer direct sales of new cars. The leading site in this category is *AutoBytel.com*; others include *GreenLight.com* (*Amazon.com* partner) and *Cars.com*.

Pure-Play E-Tailers

Pure-play e-tailers are firms that sell directly to consumers over the Internet without maintaining a physical sales channel. *Amazon.com* is an example of a pure-play e-tailer. Pure-play e-tailers have the advantage of low overhead costs and streamlined processes. The pure-play e-tailers can be categorized by general and special e-tailers.

General purpose e-tailers sell a broad range of products to a large number of consumers. They leverage their expertise in order fulfillment or personalization to reach great numbers of customers so they can maximize revenues. *Amazon.com*, which started as a book and music e-tailer, now sells many other types of products, either directly or through their alliances with other firms (discussed elsewhere in this chapter).

Specialty or niche e-tailers sell to a specific market segment. They leverage their expertise in one specific product area in order to assemble the items in greatest demand and use the most effective practices to appeal to their potential customers. Some examples of market segments for which there are specialty e-tailers include books, CDs, flowers, consumer electronic products, computer hardware and software, automobiles, and clothing. Read the *CatToys.com* example in Application Case 3.3. In addition, there are several successful online services in the financial services niche, such as online stockbrokers and online banks as described in Chapter 10.

APPLICATION CASE   **3.3**

CatToys.com, a Specialized E-tailer

CatToys.com is a specialized e-tail site for selling toys to cat owners for their pet cats. The Web site is designed to be visually appealing to cat enthusiasts, with cat images everywhere. It has no banner ads, is easy to navigate, is updated weekly, and displays products in clear categories. The fonts are informal to put the buyer at ease. Buyers can receive discounts by donating cat toys to animal shelters. Their retail prices are comparable to pet stores, and are kept low through aggressive cost control. They have weekly specials and wholesale prices for qualified businesses. Marketing is limited and mostly accomplished through search engines and an affiliate program. They have no membership or personalization in viewing the products; they use cookies only for the shopping cart process. *CatToys.com* hosts their site on Yahoo!, which allows *CatToys.com* to use sophisticated technology (cookies and payment security), while having access to a large audience. This enables *CatToys.com* to concentrate on their core competency, selecting the right cat toys and marketing them effectively. *CatToys.com* is an example of a low-volume specialized store that attracts people with specific needs.

Traditional Retailers with Web Sites

Another type of online retailer is the traditional brick-and-mortar retailer with a mature transactional Web site. Traditional marketing (retailing) frequently involves a single channel of communication and distribution to the customer—the physical store. In some cases, traditional sellers may also operate a mail-order business or a catalog telephone sales division. Today, there are firms that sell through stores, over the Internet through interactive Web sites, with touch-tone phones, through voice phone calls to human operators, and by mobile devices. A firm that operates both physical stores and an online e-tail site is said to be a **multichannel store.** (Later we will discuss related click-and-mortar strategies and channel conflicts.) There may be practical advantages to being a pure-play seller, such as lower overhead costs, but most experts suggest that the ultimate winners in many market segments will be the companies that are able to leverage the best of both worlds using sophisticated click-and-mortar strategies.

3.6   ON-DEMAND DELIVERY SERVICES: GROCERY MARKET CASE

Most e-tailers use common carriers to handle their outbound logistics or distribution function. They may use the postal system within their country or they may use private shippers, such as Airborne Express, Tiger, FedEx, UPS, or others. Delivery can be within days or overnight if the customer is willing to pay for the expedited delivery.

However, there is a segment of direct consumer marketing that owns or controls its own fleet of delivery vehicles and incorporates the delivery function into its business plan in order to provide greater value to the consumer. These firms will either provide regular deliveries on a weekly schedule or will deliver items within very short periods of time, usually 1 hour. They may also provide additional services to extend the value proposition for the buyer. The online grocer or e-grocer is a typical example of businesses in this category. Another example is the category of firms that promise virtually instantaneous delivery of third-party goods to consumers. See Figure 3-3 for the model.

On-demand Delivery Service (ODDS) Model

The U.S. grocery market is valued at over $300 billion annually. Online grocery sales will exceed $5 billion in 2000 and Andersen Consulting projects the market to top at $85 billion by 2007, capturing about 15 percent of U.S. households (Taylor, 1998). The grocery e-tail market is very competitive. *StreamLine.com* and *ShopLink.com* folded in 2000 and *WebVan.com* and *HomeGrocer.com* folded in 2001. Other e-Grocers worth noting are *Peapod.com* and *NetGrocer.com*. All offer consumers the ability to order items online and have them delivered to their house. Some offer regular "unattended" weekly delivery (for example, to your garage) based on a monthly subscription model. Others offer on-demand deliveries (if you

Figure 3-3	The On-Demand Delivery Services Model

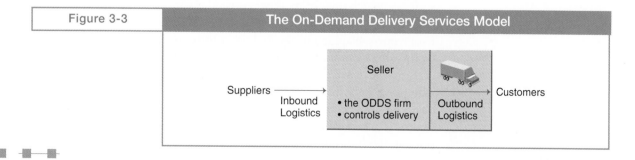

are home) with a surcharge on the grocery bill and sometimes an additional delivery charge. Many offer additional services, such as dry cleaning pickup and delivery. One e-tail grocer sells only nonperishable items shipped via common carrier. Other unique features include "don't run out" automatic reordering of office supplies, fresh flower delivery, movie rental and pickup, shoe shines, meal planning, recipe tips, multimedia features, and nutritional information.

An extensive survey conducted by the Consumer Direct Cooperative (Orler, 1998) (which included Peapod, Coca-Cola, Harvard Business School, and others), pointed to six major groups of potential online grocery shoppers, some of whom are more likely to use online grocers than others. These include:

1. Shopping avoiders who dislike grocery shopping
2. Necessity users who are limited in their ability to shop
3. New technologists who are young and comfortable with technology
4. Time-starved consumers who will pay to free up time in their schedules
5. Responsibles, consumers who gain a sense of self-worth from shopping
6. Traditionals, who are older individuals who enjoy shopping in stores

Online grocery customers are generally repeat customers who order week after week in a tight ongoing relationship with the grocer. The user interaction with the Web site is much more substantial than with other B2C Web sites, and user feedback is also more prevalent than for most Web sites. "It's a very sophisticated purchase versus if you're going to Amazon you might be buying one to three to four items—our average order has 54 different items in it cutting across five temperature zones" (Kruger, 2000).

Around the world, other e-tailers are targeting the busy consumer with the promise of home delivery of groceries. Parknshop is one of the two largest supermarket chains in Hong Kong. It offers home delivery of grocery items from its Web site, which offers a "personal shopping list" that helps customers easily order repetitive items, each visit. The Web site also has advertising, giving the company two sources of revenue. The Safeway chain in the United Kingdom (*tesco.com*) is another successful example. So far, online sales are not as profitable as selling in grocery stores due to the delivery costs. However, this additional channel allows Parknshop to increase their sales volume and serve customers who are unable to visit their physical stores. In addition, they can increase their publicity by maintaining an Internet presence. (Also see the *Woolworths.com* of Australia discussion in Chapter 15.)

3.7   DIGITAL DELIVERY: MUSIC, SOFTWARE, NEWS, AND MORE

As described previously, some consumer goods are physical goods ("hard goods"), such as apparel, toys, or food, whereas others are digital goods ("soft goods"). This latter group includes music, movies, videos, software, newspapers, magazines, journals, reports, graphic images, and other forms of digital content. These goods may be distributed in a physical form, such as CD-ROM, DVD, and newsprint, or they may be delivered in digital format over the Internet. For example, a consumer may purchase a shrink-wrapped CD-ROM containing software (along with the owner's manual and a warranty card), or a consumer may instead pay for the software at a Web site and immediately download it onto his or her computer (usually through File Transfer Protocol [FTP], a fast way to download large files).

Digital Goods		
Digital Good Category	**Physical Distribution**	**Digital Distribution**
Software	Boxed, shrink-wrapped	FTP, direct download, e-mailed
Newspapers, Magazines	Home delivery, post (mail)	Display on Web, "e-zines"
Greeting Cards	Retail stores	E-mail, URL link to recipient
Images—Clipart, Graphics	CD-ROM, magazines	Web site display, downloadable
Movies	DVD, VHS, NTSB, PAL	MPEG3, Streaming Video: RealNetwork, AVI, QuickTime, etc.
Music	CD, cassette tape	MP3, WAV, RealAudio downloads

TABLE 3-2

Table 3-2 shows some digital goods that may be distributed either way. There are advantages and disadvantages to each method for both sellers and buyers. Customers, for example, may prefer the formats available through physical distribution. They perceive value in holding a physical CD-ROM or music CD as opposed to a downloaded file. In addition, the related packaging of a physical product may be significant. Current technology makes a standard music CD more versatile for use in cars and portable devices than a downloaded MP3 file. In some cases, customers enjoy the "liner notes" that accompany a music CD. Paper-based software user manuals and other materials also have value, and may be preferred over online help features. On the other hand, customers may have to wait days for physical delivery.

For sellers, the costs associated with manufacture, storage, and distribution of physical products (DVDs, CD-ROMs, paper magazines, etc.) can be enormous. Inventory management becomes a critical cost issue. The need for retail intermediaries requires the establishment of relationships with channel partners and revenue sharing plans. Direct sales of digital content through digital download, however, allow a producer of digital content to bypass the traditional retail channel, thereby reducing overall costs and capturing greater profits. But a retailer often accounts for much of the demand creation through in-store displays, advertising, and human sales efforts, all of which are lost when the producer "disintermediates" the traditional channel.

Napster Experience

Because compression algorithms have improved dramatically and because the adoption in 2000 of Internet technologies exceeds 50 percent in many Western countries (and is over 90 percent among certain segments of the population, such as college students), the possibility exists for widespread distribution of digital content from individual to individual (consumer to consumer). The rise in importance of Napster, a person-to-person file-sharing tool, coincided with the near universality of computer availability on college campuses and the widespread adoption of MP3 as a music file compression standard. MP3 files are much smaller than earlier file alternatives, and allow individuals to download a standard song in far less time. The Napster network does not require the use of a standard Web browser, such as Netscape or Internet Explorer. Nor does the user's client machine actually download the MP3 files from Napster's servers. Rather, Napster only shares "libraries," or lists of songs, and then enables a "peer-to-peer" file-sharing environment in which the individual users literally download the music from each others' machines. In this way, Napster never actually publishes music that may be "pirated" or copied illegally in violation of internationally recognized copyright and licensing laws. However, the court ruled that as a manager of file exchanges, it must observe copyright laws (see Chapter 17).

The growth of the "Napster community" (with over 50 million registered users by the end of 2000 and as many as 1.3 million using the service at the same time) has been nothing short of phenomenal. It is said to have grown faster than any other community in history. Because of the potential challenge to their revenue sources, the Recording Industry Association of America and five major record labels have engaged in a legal battle with Napster, suing it for copyright infringement.

Napster surprised everyone when it entered into an agreement with Bertelsmann AG, the large global music label based in Germany. As part of the deal, Bertelsmann's BMG music unit, which is participating in the lawsuit against Napster, has agreed to withdraw from the complaint. The latest version of Napster's file-swapping software features a "buy button" that links to CDNow, a Bertelsmann-owned Web site that sells traditional, physical music CDs. The future of this consumer environment is clearly in doubt, though it is clear that technological developments will probably continue to outpace the ability of the market and legal structures to react and adapt. Meanwhile, other peer-to-peer tools have emerged, including Freenet, Gnutella, and P2P.

Some analysts believe that peer-to-peer file sharing will be beneficial to overall music sales as more individuals are able to easily sample and experience a much broader range of music. In fact, CD sales increased more than 10 percent during the time that Napster grew from an obscure college project to about 50 million registered users.

New Developments

An interesting development in music distribution is the availability of custom-publishing music CD sites (e.g., see *angelfire.com* and *grabware.com*). These sites enable a consumer to collect his or her favorite songs from various artists and master a "personal favorites" compilation CD, which is then shipped to the consumer. The CD mastering sites pay royalties to the various artists through established channels.

Another trend is the disintermediation of traditional print media. Several journals and magazines ceased publishing "dead paper" versions and have become strictly online distributors of digital content, generating revenues through advertising or by online subscriptions. (Some of these transformations have subsequently been reversed.) Other prominent publications, including the *Wall Street Journal*, now offer either a paper-only subscription, an online-only subscription (at a lower subscription price), and a dual-mode subscription for consumers who might access their business news through both methods.

Similarly, Egghead closed all of its brick-and-mortar stores and became a pure-play software store called *Egghead.com*. In doing so, they dramatically cut operating costs and streamlined their inventory requirements, but lost certain advantages offered by their physical presence. Time will tell if digital delivery replaces or enhances traditional delivery methods for all types of digital content. The dual mode of delivery is similar to the click-and-mortar strategies presented in the next section.

3.8   SUCCESSFUL CLICK-AND-MORTAR STRATEGIES

Although thousands of companies have evolved their online strategies into mature value propositions with extensive use of interactive features that add value to the consumer's purchase process, many sites remain simple "brochureware" sites with limited interactivity. Many traditional companies are in a transitional stage. Only a minority of large and small companies is equipped to handle online transactions, provide online information to customers, and provide e-services. By 2003, according to International Data Corp., only 32 percent of companies who have Web sites will support interactive online transactions.

Maturing to full transactional systems means more than just tacking on a piece of software or writing a few lines of HTML code. It involves implementing systems for payment processing, order fulfillment, logistics, inventory management, and a host of other tasks. In most cases, a company must replicate each of its business processes and design many more that can only be performed online. Today's environment includes sophisticated access to order information, shipping information, product information, and more through Web pages, touch-tone phones, Web-enabled cellular phones, and PDAs over wireless networks. The challenges to implementing EC can be daunting.

The real gains for traditional retailers will come from leveraging the benefits of their physical presence (brick-and-mortar stores) and the benefits of their online presence (Web site). Web sites frequently offer better prices and selection, whereas physical stores offer a trustworthy staff and the ability to evaluate items before purchasing. (Physical evaluation is critical for clothing and ergonomic devices, for example, but not for commodities, music, or software.) Large efficient established retailers, such as Wal-Mart (with *Walmart.com*), Kmart (with *bluelight.com*), and Takashimaya (with takashimaya.co.jp) are able to create the optimum value proposition for the consumer by providing a complete offering of services.

A traditional brick-and-mortar store with a mature Web site uses a click-and-mortar hybrid strategy in the following ways.

Speak with one voice. First, a firm can link all of its back-end systems to create an integrated customer experience. Whether the customer accesses information or services through face-to-face encounters with store personnel, touch-tone phone, Web pages, telephone customer service representatives or sales staff, or by other methods such as wireless devices or kiosks, the information received and service provided should be consistent. This is often accomplished with the use of so-called "middleware" software that links all the back-end databases with a single "customer-facing system" (Seybold, 1998).

Empower the customer. By utilizing various technologies to ensure that customers are empowered with information and by giving the customers the opportunity to use online technologies to perform various functions interactively, the seller creates a powerful 24/7 channel for service and information. *Staples.com* and *OfficeMax.com*, like many sites, have store locators that help consumers find the nearest store and even provide point-to-point driving directions and maps. The Web is used to help bring customers to the store. Many sites allow the customer to check product selection or inventory levels before driving to the store. The *CircuitCity.com* site allows customers to receive rich product comparisons between various models of consumer electronics products before driving to the store.

Servicing personal account information can be facilitated by Web-enabled data-bases that were once unavailable to the customer.

Leverage the channels. Third, the innovative retailer will offer the advantages of each marketing channel to customers from all channels. Whether the purchase is made online or at the store, the customer should benefit from the presence of both. For example, customers who purchase from the Web site are often allowed to return items to the physical store, as with L.L.Bean or Eddie Bauer. In addition, combining both channels can enhance the inventory of available items. (Established mail-order direct marketers such as Eddie Bauer have a distinct advan-tage due to the ready availability of order processing systems, payment processing systems, supply management expertise, etc. See Chapter 15.) Many physical stores, such as BestBuy, now have terminals in the store to order items from the Web site if they are not available in the store. And many companies will allow the customer to have those items shipped to the customer's home or to the store to evaluate before purchasing. Needless to say, prices should be consistent to avoid "channel conflict" (discussed later). In some cases, the physical store offers a customer more convenience (for returns, for example), while in other cases, the Web site offers greater flexibility and convenience. Again, allowing the customer to choose the method of interfacing with the store gives the customer the greatest value and increases overall sales. Let's look at a few examples of this strategy in practice.

Transform to Click-and-Mortal Retailer: Circuit City Case

Circuit City is the number two U.S. retailer of consumer electronics (behind BestBuy, which has fewer stores but higher sales). Circuit City's more than 630 stores located across the United States are mostly superstores that sell items such as audio and video equipment and computers. The company is remodeling its super-stores and has stopped selling appliances in favor of more profitable items, includ-ing home office products. Prior to the summer of 1999, Circuit City and BestBuy had largely brochureware sites, capable only of selling gift certificates. When Circuit City launched the new *CircuitCity.com*, it already had some of the needed EC sys-tems in place—it had credit card authorization and inventory-management systems at its national brick-and-mortar stores. But linking the company's brick-and-mortar systems with the EC system was neither cheap nor easy. "It's safe to say that millions of dollars need to be spent to have a Fortune 500 kind of presence on the Web in a transactional way," indicated George Barr, Circuit City's director of Web develop-ment. "It's just not something you could do for $100,000" (Calem, 2000).

A few features of the *CircuitCity.com* site deserve special attention. First, the site educates customers about the various features and capabilities of different prod-ucts, cutting through the jargon to help the customer understand why these features may be desirable and what the trade-offs are. In this personal and non-threatening way, customers can gain valuable knowledge to assist them in the pur-chase decision. Some consumers find shopping in the traditional brick-and-mortar Circuit City store to be intimidating because they don't understand the terms and product features discussed by store personnel. Second, on *CircuitCity.com* cus-tomers can perform powerful searches on a product database to help find the appropriate models to consider. Third, the site offers an extensive amount of infor-mation about electronics and other products, organized in a very flexible way. This assists buyers as they gather information before a purchase is made, whether or not they eventually buy from *CircuitCity.com*. Visitors can select several models and compare them by viewing a dynamically created table of purchase criteria, displayed side-by-side along with drill-down details if necessary.

Of course, the purchase itself (if one chooses to buy online) is smooth, secure, and seamless. Poor process design will scare off many customers. It has been reported that only 17 percent of all purchase processes are completed—customers will abandon the purchase because of confusion and complexity, surprises (such as shipping costs), concerns about security, concerns about personal information that is requested, system errors, slow transmission speeds, and other factors. Simplified online purchase systems that are fast, secure, and respectful of personal information are more likely to be successful than those that are not. Finally, the "order fulfillment" method is flexible at *CircuitCity.com*. The customer is given the choice of receiving the purchase via common carrier (shipper) with no sales tax, but with a small shipping charge for 3-day delivery via express shipper or a larger shipping charge if the consumer needs overnight delivery, or by driving to the nearby brick-and-mortar store and paying sales tax, but no shipping, and having the item almost immediately. In one recent purchase, the Web site provided a confirmation page that the consumer printed out and displayed at the front desk of the store, along with a picture ID, and the consumer was able to pick up the new purchase, a DVD player, in under two minutes. The store had already brought the item to the front of the store and released it to the customer with the confirmation page since payment had already been made online. The brick-and-mortar store would also provide an easy point of contact for service or a product return.

Alliance of Pure-Player with Traditional Retailer: Amazon and Toys R Us Case

In online toy retailing, eToys was the pioneering forerunner. As electronic orders, particularly during peak season increased, eToys could not meet the delivery requirements due to its limited logistics capability. Eventually, eToys was closed, (sold to *kbkids.com*) and traditional toy retailers like Toys R Us are coming online in alliance with a pure online company like *Amazon.com*. As described earlier, *Amazon.com* is known as a premier site for creating customer loyalty and for driving sales through its execution of CRM with efficient back-office order fulfillment systems. Toys R Us, backed by 40 years of experience, is known for its broad product design and offering. It also has a knowledge of the toy industry, including a deep understanding of the market, tastes, and suppliers. It has strong B2B supplier relationships and has a well-developed inventory system. Recently, Toys R Us formed an alliance with *Amazon.com* to sell toys online. Before the deal, *Amazon.com* had failed in the toy business because it lacked the strong B2B supplier relationships with toy manufacturers—it could not get the best toys and did not know how to manage inventory against the demand (Karpinski, 2000).

ToysRUs.com also had problems. It could not figure out how to effectively manage a direct-to-consumer distribution center or how to balance its retail stores business with its online business (Karpinski, 2000). During the 1999 Christmas season, both *Amazon.com* (pure-play e-tailer) and Toys R Us (traditional retailer with a new Web site) failed to profitably deliver toys on time to families for Christmas.

Amazon.com miscalculated inventory requirements, and was left with millions of toys it had to write off. *ToysRUs.com* badly bungled the operations side by creating a Web site that was unable to handle large amounts of traffic and shipping orders. *ToysRUs.com* couldn't execute their Web business effectively due to a lack of experience with both the front-end design and the back-end order fulfillment processes. As a result, 1 in 20 children failed to get presents in time for Christmas from Toys R Us.

After bad press, lost business, and fines, these two companies decided to combine efforts for this year's season. They have pooled their expertise to form a single online toy store. The alliance will allow these two partners to leverage each other's core strengths (Schwartz, 2000). Under the 10-year agreement, *ToysRUs.com* will identify, purchase, and manage inventory, using their parent's clout to get the best lineup of toys. Since *Amazon.com* has a distribution network with plenty of excess capacity and a solid infrastructure, it is responsible for order fulfillment and will handle customer service. *Amazon.com* will apply its expertise in front-end site design offering a powerful customer-support environment. Revenues will be split between the two companies and the risks are also equally shared.

This is an innovative model, but there is much work to be done. The two companies must coordinate disparate systems—operational, technological, and financial—as they merge their corporate cultures. If they succeed and execute this strategy successfully, this kind of partnership could be a prime model for the future of e-tailing.

3.9 DISTINTERMEDIATION, REINTERMEDIARY, CHANNEL CONFLICT, AND PERSONALIZATION

Disintermediation and Reintermediaries

The issue of disintermediation was explained in direct marketing with Figure 3-2 (see section 3.5). In direct marketing, the manufacturer bypassed the wholesalers and retailers directly selling to consumers. This phenomenon is called **disintermediation.** However, consumers need to select among a large number of manufacturers online, which is not an easy task at all. So new online assistance is emerging, which replaces the role of traditional intermediaries. They are known as **reintermediaries**; they fill new intermediary roles in the digital environment. For the intermediary, the Internet offers new ways to reach new customers, new ways to bring value to customers, and perhaps new ways to generate revenues. Some reintermediaries are rivals to traditional retail stores, while others are operations established by the traditional retailers. Other reintermediaries cooperate with manufacturers or retailers to provide a needed service to the seller or distributor in the online environment. Other reintermediaries are pure-play e-tailers who fill a unique niche. Intermediaries such as online retailers (*Walmart.com*), shopping portals, directories, and comparison-shopping agents can also act as reintermediaries.

Channel Conflict

As discussed earlier in this chapter, many traditional retailers are establishing a new marketing channel as they develop their Web sites into fully transactional EC sites. Some of these retailers previously operated not only brick-and-mortar stores, but also telephone catalog sales departments. In some cases, retailers now operate three or more separate marketing channels. Similarly, some manufacturers have instituted direct marketing strategies that parallel their established channels of distribution, such as retailers or dealers. A classic example is an automobile manufacturer that sells through its dealer network, through new digital intermediaries, and also direct to consumers. In all these cases, channel conflict can occur. **Channel conflict** refers to any situation in which the channel members are antagonistic due to real or perceived differences in incentives, rewards, policies, or support. (Conversely, **channel cooperation** describes a situation in which the strategies and functions of two or more channel members are consistent and harmoniously linked.) For more on channel conflict, see Chapter 16.

Personalization

One significant characteristic of many of the online marketing business models is the ability of the seller to create an element of personalization for each individual consumer. As described in the discussion of *Amazon.com*, e-tailers can utilize cookie files and other technologies to track the specific browsing and buying behavior of each consumer, and can create a marketing plan tailored to that consumer's pattern by showing items of interest, offering incentives that appeal to that consumer's sense of value, or providing certain services that will attract that consumer back to the Web site. The phenomenon of mass customization is observable in a variety of physical and digital goods and services sold over the Internet. Procter & Gamble launched *Reflect.com* with the notion of giving consumers a personal online beauty boutique where individuals can create their own makeup, skin care, and hair care products. They promise, "We are passionate about helping you look and feel beautiful with customized beauty products made just for you." (This site is available.) A similar initiative has been launched by *Chipshot.com* for custom golf equipment. Chapter 4 explores the issue of mass customization, or one-to-one marketing, where e-tailers market to each individual consumer.

3.10   PROBLEMS WITH E-TAILING AND LESSONS LEARNED

E-tailing is no panacea—it offers some serious challenges and tremendous risks for those who fail to provide value to the consumer, who fail to establish a profitable business model, or who fail to execute the model they establish. The road to e-tail success is littered with dead companies that could not deliver on their promise. The shakeout in mid to late 2000 caused many companies to fail, but others learned and adapted. Some enduring principles have been distilled from the failures, and these "lessons learned" are now discussed.

Profitability. One fundamental lesson is that each marginal sale should lead to marginal profits. It has been said that "if it doesn't make cents, it doesn't make sense." The trouble with most pure-play e-tailers is that they lose money on every sale as they try to grow to profitable size and scale. *Amazon.com* may generate about $5 per book order, but they still lose about $7 per sale on non-book sales. Some e-tailers will have to adjust prices or refocus their market targets in order to concentrate on profitable sales.

Branding. Branding has always been considered to be a key to the success of e-tailers, but the drive to establish brand often leads to excessive spending. In one case, an upstart e-tailer spent over 50 percent of its venture capital funding on one 30-second television advertisement during the Superbowl game. In other cases, Web sites offered extravagant promotions and loss-leader offers to drive traffic to their sites, where they lost money in huge volumes. The lesson from success stories is that most customers (and especially long-term customers) come to a Web site from affiliate links, search engines, or personal recommendations—not from Superbowl ads.

Performance. Today's savvy Internet shoppers expect Web sites to offer superior technical performance—fast page loads, quick database searches, streamlined graphics, etc. Web sites that delay or frustrate consumers will not experience a high sales volume due to the high percentage of abandoned purchases.

Static design. Web sites without dynamic content will bore returning visitors. Today, most e-tailers offer valuable tips and information for consumers, who often come back just for that content and may purchase something in the process. L.L.Bean, for example, offers a rich database of information about parks and recreational facilities as well as buying guides. Visitors who visit the site to find a campground or a weekend event may also purchase a tent or raincoat.

3.11   MANAGERIAL ISSUES

The following issues are germane to management:

1. **Managerial decision making in the B2C section.** There are many issues that B2C enterprise managers should consider. The pitfalls described in the previous section require careful attention; all e-tail managers must be able to adapt and learn from their mistakes and the mistakes of others. New challenges will be posed by the rise of mobile commerce, globalization of EC, the end of the sales tax moratorium, as well as other future events. Managers must be alert to changes in technology, the regulatory environment, and the market environment. The market considerations include general economic conditions, demographics, and consumer tastes and preferences. Fundamental issues, such as cost control, pricing strategies, and product offerings are critical. A more complex set of issues includes the selection of appropriate outsourcing partners for logistics, order fulfillment, payment processing, advertising, customer service, and other business-critical services. Decisions about advertising strategies and participation in various affiliate programs are important also.

    Just as with traditional retail, e-tailers' profit margins are generally very small, and the underlying revenues and costs must be managed very carefully. Economies of scale are critical in this environment in order to achieve sufficient volume to make the small margins profitable. This is why so many e-tailers have forsaken profits in the short run in order to grow to sufficient size to be profitable in the long run. But sooner or later, the short run becomes the long run, and the race for profitability is forced on an e-tailer who runs out of investor funding.

2. **First-mover advantage or wait and learn?** It has often been suggested that the first firm to enter a new marketspace and sell products online in that category will be able to dominate that niche by establishing their brand and becoming the recognized seller. This is known as the "first-mover advantage,"

and it seems to be true in certain categories. For example, *Amazon.com* was the first major online bookseller, and despite competition from Barnes & Noble, their Web site remains the largest and most recognized Web site for online consumer purchases of books. However, in many cases, the "first-to-market" firms make many mistakes, and if they are not agile enough to adapt to the market or other conditions, they may fail, leaving room for the "second-to-market" firms to rush in and attract the online customers who leave the first mover.

In many cases, the second-mover firm or firms can learn from the initial company's mistakes and avoid the expense and losses associated with building the wrong technology, stocking the wrong inventory, establishing the wrong image, making the wrong alliances, setting the wrong prices, or executing the wrong tactics and strategy. If the first mover makes a strategic mistake that upsets buyers, such as failure to ship items in a timely way or violation of personal information privacy, the buyers will actively look for another e-tailer.

3. **Strategic positioning.** The most important decision for retailers and e-tailers is the overall strategic position they establish within their market. What niche will they fill? What business functions will they execute internally and which functions will be outsourced? What partners will they use? How will they integrate "brick and mortar" facilities (retail stores, warehouses, etc.) with their online presence? What are their revenue sources in the short and long term, and what are their fixed and marginal costs? An e-business is still a business and must establish solid business practices in the long run in order to ensure profitability and viability.

4. **Trust.** As discussed earlier in this chapter, e-commerce managers are concerned about the level of trust that customers and potential customers have in their ability to deliver goods and services efficiently without misusing the personal information provided by the consumer or collected by cookie files. It is imperative that e-tailers establish a privacy policy and ensure that it is strictly followed. The loss of public trust from even one publicized violation of personal information confidentiality could be disastrous. E-tailers may want to join a program that certifies their trustworthiness, since a small portion of the consumers will look for such affirmation. See Chapter 4 for more information about consumer trust and trust verification sites.

5. **New risk exposure.** The Internet creates new connectivity with customers and offers the opportunity to expand markets. However, it also has the potential to expose a retailer to more sources of risk. Local companies have to contend with local customers and local regulations, while national firms have more constituents with which to interact. Global firms have to contend with numerous cultural perspectives and many separate legal structures. Will they offend potential customers because of a lack of awareness of other cultures? Global Internet firms have to manage their exposure to risk from the mosaic of international laws and regulations. Can they be sued under these jurisdictions for their business practices?

Groups of disgruntled employees or customers can band together to contact the news media, file a class action lawsuit, or launch their own Web site to publicize their concerns. One example is the *walmartsucks.com* site, which was created by a customer who felt he was mistreated at one Wal-Mart store. He has created a repository combining all the negative news stories he can find about Wal-Mart and anecdotal accounts from fired employees and unhappy customers. (Wal-Mart has unsuccessfully offered to buy his Web site from him to shut it down, but he refuses!) When such an individual used to tell his 50 to 100 friends and co-workers about his frustration, it may have resulted in a few lost sales, but with the Internet, he can now reach thousands or even millions of potential customers.

After a disgruntled New York bank customer started a site to complain about errors on his Chase Manhattan checking account statements, Chase quickly secured the rights to chasesucks, chasestinks, and ihatechase. But you may not always be able to anticipate what these domain names might be. When two customers felt abused by their experience with a rental truck that constantly broke down, they launched the "U-Hell Website."

6. **Financial viability.** Many pure-play e-tailers were initially funded by venture capital firms that provided enough financing to get the e-tailers started and growing. However, in many cases, the funding ran out before the e-tailer achieved sufficient size and maturity to break even and become self-sufficient. In some cases, their underlying cost and revenue models were not sound—the firms would never be profitable without major changes in their sources and volumes of costs and revenues. What is required is financial viability.

The events of the collapse of the "dot com bubble" as of April 2000 provided a wake-up call to many e-tailers. A return to fundamentals was pursued by some, while others sought to redefine their business plan in terms of click-and-mortar strategies or alliances with traditional retailers (as *Amazon.com* did with Toys R Us). Because most easy sources of funding have dried up and revenue models are being scrutinized, many e-tailers are also pursuing new partners, and consolidation will continue until there is greater stability within the e-tail segment. Ultimately, there will likely be a smaller number of larger sellers, resulting in fewer comprehensive sites and many smaller niche Web sites that specialize in various market segments. Some analysts feel that *Amazon.com* will eventually be the comprehensive site for buying anything and everything, while others state that it will need to entrench and focus on its core business of book and music sales in order to succeed in the long run. Only time will tell, but changes in this industry are inevitable.

Earlier in this chapter, we addressed the demise of *Living.com* and its impact on *Amazon.com*. Let's now explore the failure of *Garden.com*, and see what lessons can be learned from their experience. *Garden.com* was a Web site that provided rich, dynamic content (how to plant bulbs, tips on gardening, "ask the expert," etc.) and a powerful landscape design tool, which allowed a visitor to lay out an entire garden and then purchase all the necessary materials with one click. *Garden.com* also hosted various "community" features with discussions about various types of gardening-related topics. Gardeners are often passionate about their hobby and like to learn more about new plants and gardening techniques. The site failed due to the inability to raise venture capital that was necessary to cover losses until enough business volume was reached.

7. **Successes.** While there were many failures, mostly of pure e-tailers, but some of click-and-mortar companies, there were many success stories as well. Some are described in Chapter 16 with the appropriate analysis. A successful case is presented in Application Case 3.4

APPLICATION CASE   **3.4**

Ambassador.com.hk

Jody Yan had been running a steady floral business in the busy downtown district of Wanchai in Hong Kong since 1987. In 1997, an online auction site asked Jody to sponsor gifts for auctions and she agreed. Intrigued by the potential of the Internet, she herself set up an online store named *Ambassador.com.hk* in 1998. When many orders started to flow in, Jody decided to expand the business by adding functions such as online payments. In the first year of operation, the online store accounted for about 10 percent of the total revenue of the firm. Online sales have since doubled every year and accounted for 30 percent of the firm's total revenue of around HK$ 5mn (US$ 640,000) in 2000.

The Business Model: Ambassador sells customized designer flower baskets, flower bouquets, cakes, and fruit and gourmet gift baskets, all attractively packaged, at an average price of US$100 each. Colorful pictures of all products are displayed on the online storefront. The firm runs a warehouse on the south side of Hong Kong. In addition to sourcing from local wholesalers, fresh flowers are air-shipped from Holland and New Zealand.

By 2001 the company closed its physical retail shop. The remaining sales channel comprises mail order catalogs and the online store. Local telephone purchase orders are also accepted. Customers receive through email a detailed picture of the actual product at the time of delivery, for example. Both an in-house team and an outsourced company are used to support local deliveries helping Ambassador to cope up with seasonal fluctuations. Courier companies carry out all international deliveries. This multi-channel business model for floral gift products works very well.

Innovations

Jody reckoned that most of her competitors had no clue about how to use IT effectively to leverage their business. The exception was *wickerexpress.com*, which also operates a substantial online floral gift shop. Jody realized that it would be very difficult to develop and maintain an in-house software to address the flexible requirements of an online store. She therefore hired an IT consulting firm to develop the online store from scratch and also retained them for maintenance, hosting, employee training and operational support. "There is absolutely no need to build an in-house IT function when you can outsource it to reliable experts," says Jody.

To stay ahead of competitors, Jody emphasized product design by a good product design team. Another strength was her loyal staff, most of them having been with her for over six years.

APPLICATION CASE   3.4

(continued)

Other Success Factors:

1. Principal's extensive experience in the floral gift products business.
2. Backend operations for the online floral gift shop were already in place, hence additional costs were marginal.
3. Principal's analysis that floral gift products are suitable for Internet selling.
4. Identification of the online store as part of a multi-channel retailing strategy.
5. Initial pilot implementation that resulted in sales orders.
6. Prepared plans and budgets for experimentation.
7. Outsourced the implementation from scratch; hosting, maintenance and training to one vendor.
8. Provided online store functions and integrated it with other business models and IT systems.

Source: This case was written by Matthew K. O. Lee, City University of Hong Kong, 2001. An expanded version of the case with review questions is available at the book's Web site.

Summary

In this chapter, you learned about the following EC issues as they relate to the learning objectives:

1. **Consumer purchase process.** The consumer purchase process includes the following steps: identify basic need or want; establish decision criteria; collect information; seek recommendations; perform comparisons; select seller; make purchase; configure, install, or set up the product; and receive service as needed.
2. **Aiding consumer purchase decision.** To aid the consumer purchase decision, one must study the consumer's purchasing process and decision criteria. The available purchase decision aids are shopping portals, shopbots and agents, business rating sites, trust verification sites, and so on.
3. **E-tailing business models.** The e-tailing business models can be classified as pure-play e-tailing or as click-and-mortars that use online channels to complement traditional channels.
4. **Disintermediation and reintermediation.** Direct marketing by manufacturers results in disintermediation by removing wholesalers and retailers. However, online reintermediaries appear to help consumers make selections among multiple manufacturers. Traditional retailers may pressure the manufacturers not to sell online at cheaper prices, causing channel conflict.
5. **Typically successful products.** Successful products include books, software, hardware, CDs, video, travel reservations, electronics, apparel, banking, stock brokerage services, and flowers.
6. **Critical success factors.** Critical success factors for online sales to consumers are product selection, price competitiveness, mass customization, customer intimacy, global reach, customer's single contact point, and delivery-tracking services, among others.
7. **On-demand delivery service.** On-demand delivery service e-tailers succeed when the items are perishable goods and delivery costs are high.

Key Terms

Brick-and-click strategy	Four Ps
Brick-and-mortar strategy	Marketing management
Channel conflict	Pure-play e-tailer
Click-and-mortar strategy	Reintermediation
Digital goods	Shopping agent
Direct marketing	Shopping robot (Shopbot)
Disintermediation	Shopping portal
E-tailers/E-tailing	

Questions for Review

1. What are the current and prospective sizes of the markets for online sales? Describe your answer in terms of B2C versus B2B electronic sales. What are successful sectors?
2. What are the success factors of *Amazon.com*? Should *Amazon.com* limit their sales to books, music, and movies, or is their broader selection of items a good direct marketing strategy? Do you think they will dilute their brand or extend the value proposition to their customers?
3. Discuss the major business models of online retailing or e-tailing.
4. Will direct marketing of automobiles be a successful strategy? How should the dealers' inventory and the automakers' inventory and manufacturing scheduling be coordinated to meet a specific order with a due date? How should the manufacturers avoid channel conflict?
5. Why do some consumers prefer to shop online and others are resistant? For consumers, what are the most appealing aspects of online shopping—choices, flexibility, convenience, prices, or other factors? What about the role of trust in the growth of e-tail? Discuss your answer using books, travel, cars, or another consumer product as an example.

Questions for Discussion

1. Discuss the advantages of established click-and-mortar companies, such as Wal-Mart Online, over pure e-tailers, such as Amazon.
2. Why is *Amazon.com* diversifying?
3. Discuss the advantages of a partnership such as Amazon and Toy R Us. Are there any disadvantages?
4. Discuss the issue of channel conflict and find some strategies used by companies to solve it.
5. Discuss the advantages of shopping aids to the consumer. Should a vendor provide a comparison tool on its site? Why or why not?
6. Discuss the advantages of a specialized e-tailer, such as *dogtoys.com*. Can such a store survive in the physical world? Why or why not?
7. Discuss the benefits of build-to-order to buyers and sellers. Are there any disadvantages?
8. Discuss how the four Ps can be facilitated on the Internet.

Internet Exercises

1. Visit both *Peapod.com* and *Epions.com*. Compare the products and services offered by the two companies and evaluate their chances for success. Why did the "unattended delivery" e-grocers like *ShopLink.com* fail?

2. There are many consumer portals that offer advice and ratings of products or e-tailers. Some are comprehensive portals and others are specialized, offering information and links for purchasers of automobiles, toys, computers, travel, etc. Some offer interactive features that generate customized information to help consumers with specific purchases, while others provide standardized tables for consumers to evaluate. Identify and examine two separate general consumer portals that look at other sites and compare prices or other purchase criteria. Try to find and compare prices for a hat, a microwave oven, and an MP3 player. Summarize your experience. Comment on the strong and weak points of such shopping tools.

3. Almost all car manufacturers allow you to configure your car online. Visit three major automakers' Web sites and configure a car of your choice. Also visit one electronic intermediary. After you decide what you want, examine the payment options and monthly payments. Print your results. How does this process compare to visiting an auto dealer? Do you think you found a better price? Would you consider buying a car this way? Are you happy with the policies for service if you purchase online?

4. Choose a general merchandise retailer and an apparel retailer located in your area. Find their Web sites and evaluate their use of click-and-mortar strategies. Are the product offerings different? Can you use the Web site to locate the nearest retail store? Will they provide a map or directions? Can you search their inventory to see if an item is in stock at the store? Identify their purchase options if you can—does the Web site give you the option of picking up the item at the store or returning an item to the store? What other click-and-mortar strategy elements can you identify? Ask the store personnel about the Web site. Are they knowledgeable and helpful about their Web site? Do they suggest using the Web site or make suggestions on how to use it?

5. Visit *Amazon.com* and identify at least three specific elements of their personalization and individual customization features. Browse some specific books on one particular subject and then leave their site. Now go back and revisit the site, what do you see? Are these features likely to encourage you to purchase more books in the future from *Amazon.com*? List the features and discuss how they may lead to increased sales. Now visit Amazon zShops to identify and compare three sellers of food and beverages. Can you find items not normally available in your local grocery store?

6. Use your favorite search engine and look for recent statistics about the growth of Internet-based consumer-oriented EC in your country and in three other countries. Where is the greatest growth occurring? Which countries have the largest total e-tail sales and which countries have the highest per-capita participation (called "penetration rate")? What are the forecasts for continued growth in the coming years?

7. Visit *nike.com* and submit a customized order for a shoe just for your right and left feet. What is the process? Do you think this will result in a better fitting

shoe? Do you think this personalization feature will lead to greater sales volume for Nike?

8. Find three places to buy a computer and compare the three sites on their ability to inform you.

Team Assignments and Role Playing

1. Investigate the topic of online car sales. Assign each member one of the categories listed below. When each member has finished, bring your research together and discuss your findings.
   a. Buy new cars through an intermediary (*autobytel.com*, *greenlight.com*, or *amazon.com*)
   b. Buy used cars (*autotrader.com*)
   c. Buy used cars from dealers (*manheim.com*)
   d. Support for used car dealers (*dealers.autotrader.com*)
   e. Automobile ratings sites (*carsdirect.com*, *autoinvoices.com*, and *fueleconomy.gov*)
   f. Investigate the car buying portal sites
   g. Investigate sites where antique cars can be purchased.
2. Create a group report on innovative click-and-mortar strategies. Each team member should identify one traditional brick-and-mortar store with a transactional Web site and one pure-play e-tailer with a new physical presence or traditional partner and write a one-page report, complete with references. Then assemble a group report summarizing the findings, identifying new trends, common strategies, and interesting comparisons. Include the individual reports.

REAL-WORLD CASE: *Walmart.com*

Wal-Mart is the largest retailer in the United States with over 2,500 stores. Wal-Mart also has more than 700 stores outside the United States. Their standard company cheer ends with "Who's number one? The customer." They have established themselves as a master of the retail process by streamlining their supply chain process and undercutting competitors with low prices. But one problem with their strategy for growing their online sales is the demographics of their primary customer base. The target demographic is the household with a $25,000 annual income, while the Internet consumer median income is perhaps $60,000.

Despite these demographics, online sales (primarily in music, travel, and electronics) already account for about 10 percent of Wal-Mart's U.S. sales. One way in which their chief rival, Kmart, Inc., attracted their demographic audience to their Web site (*bluelight.com*) was to offer free Internet access. This appealed to the cost conscious, lower-income constituency they serve, and also provided the opportunity for them to access the site to conduct purchases! Wal-Mart also has concerns about cannibalizing their in-store sales. Their recent alliance with AOL to provide co-branded Internet access to rural dwellers might lure in a new market segment and cancel the effect of cannibalization. And

ultimately, a hybrid e-tailer that can offer a combination of huge selection with the click-and-mortar advantages of nearby stores may prove to be the 800-pound gorilla of online consumer sales.

Questions for the case

1. Will Wal-Mart become the dominant e-tailer in the world? What factors would contribute to their success in the online marketplace? What factors would detract from their ability to dominate online sales the way they have been able to dominate physical retail sales in many markets?

2. Perform a strategic analysis of *Walmart.com*. Who are their competitors, customers, and suppliers? What is their relative strength or power in each of these relationships? What is their distinctive competence? What environmental factors influence their success? How much of their strength is borrowed from their physical store knowledge?

3. Visit *walmart.com*, *bluelight.com*, and *sears.com*. Identify the common features of their online marketing and at least one unique feature evident at each site. Do these sites have to distinguish themselves primarily in terms of price, product selection, or Web site features?

REFERENCES AND BIBLIOGRAPHY

Allen, C., et al. *Internet World Guide to One-to-One Marketing* (Internet World Series). New York: John Wiley & Sons, 1998.

Calem, R. E. "Deal Clinchers: How to Get from Brochureware to Online Business," *Industry Standard* (February 14, 2000).

Green, H. "Q & As with Two Top E-Tailing Venture Capitalists," *Business Week* (May 4, 2000).

Hanson, W. *Internet Marketing.* Cincinnati, Ohio: South-Western College Publishing, 2000.

Harris Interactive. "Six Types of eShoppers," *NUA Internet Surveys,* vol. 5, no. 22 (December 6, 2000).

Helperin, J. R. "Something Old, Something New," *Business 2.0* (December 12, 2000).

Kare-Silver, M. D. *E-Shock: The Electronic Shopping Revolution: Strategies for Retailers and Manufacturers.* New York: AMACOM, 1999.

Karpinski, R. "E-Business Risk Worth Taking on Path to Success." *B to B,* vol. 85 (August 28, 2000).

Kleindl, B. A. *Strategic Internet Marketing: Managing E-Business.* Cincinnati, Ohio: South-Western College Publishing, 2001.

Kruger, J. Structured Interview of E-Grocer Executive by Merrill Warkentin (Fall 2000).

Leebaert, D. *The Future of the Electronic Marketplace.* Boston: MIT Press, 1998.

Maes, P., et al. "Agents That Buy and Sell: Transforming Commerce as We Know It," *Communications of the ACM* (March 1999).

Orler, V. *Early Learnings From the Consumer Direct Cooperative,* Anderson Consulting (1998).

Quick, R. "The Attack of the Robots: Comparison-Shopping Technology Is Here—Whether Retailers Like It or Not," *The Wall Street Journal* (December 7, 1998).

Rafter, M. V. "Trust or Bust?" *Industry Standard* (March 6, 2000).

Raisglid, R., et al. *Buying and Leasing Cars on the Internet.* Los Angeles, California: Renaissance Books, 1998.

Richardson, P. *Internet Marketing: Readings and Online Resources.* New York: McGraw Hill/Irwin, 2001.

Schwartz, E. "Amazon, Toys R Us in E-Commerce Tie-Up." *InfoWorld,* vol. 22 (August 14, 2000).

Seybold, P. *Customers.com.* New York: Times Business Books, 1998.

Simison, R. L. "GM Retools to Sell Custom Cars Online," *Wall Street Journal* (February 22, 2000).

Strauss, J. and R. Frost. *E-Marketing,* 2nd ed. Upper Saddle River, New Jersey: Prentice Hall, 2001.

Taylor, R. "On-Line Grocery Shopping on Track for Rapid Growth," *Anderson Consulting News* (December 1, 1998).

Turban E., et al. *Information Technology for Management,* 2nd ed. New York: John Wiley & Sons, 1999.

Warkentin, M. "Protect Your Name!—Web Strategy Tip," *Tech New England, thebostonchannel.com/ bos/technology/technewenglandarticles/stories (20000907-085013.html),* 1999.

Warkentin, M., et al. "The Role of Mass Customization in Enhancing Supply Chain Relationships in B2C E-Commerce Markets," *Journal of Electronic Commerce Research,* vol. 1, no. 2, p. 1–17 (2000).

Warkentin, M. and A. Bajaj. "The On-Demand Delivery Services Model for E-Commerce," In A. Gangopadhay, ed., *Managing Business with Electronic Commerce: Issues and Trends.* Hershey, Pennsylvania: Idea Group Publishing, 2001.

4

Internet Consumers, E-Service, and Market Research

C O N T E N T

LEARNING OBJECTIVES

Upon completion of this chapter the reader will be able to:

- Describe the essentials of consumer behavior.

- Describe the characteristics of Internet surfers and EC purchasers.

- Understand the decision-making process of consumer purchasing.

- Describe the way companies are building relationships with customers.

- Explain the implementation of customer service and its relationship with CRM.

- Describe consumer market research in EC.

- Understand the role of intelligent agents in consumer applications.

- Describe the organizational buyer behavior model.

4.1 BUILDING CUSTOMER RELATIONSHIPS: RITCHEY DESIGN, INC.

Ritchey Design, Inc. of Redwood City, California, is a relatively small ($15 million sales per year) designer and manufacturer of mountain-bike components. The company sells its products to distributors and/or retailers, that then sell them to individual consumers. The company opened a Web site in 1995, (*ritcheylogic.com*), but like so many companies' Web sites, Ritchey's was more a status symbol than a business tool. Most of the site's visitors came to get the dirt on Team Ritchey (now Ritchey Yahoo! Team), the company's world-class mountain-bike team, or to find out where Ritchey products were sold. But that's where the site's usefulness ended. It didn't give customers all the information they wanted or enable the company to gain insight into their customers' wants and needs.

■⌐⌐ Obtaining useful marketing and customer information had become one of the company's biggest problems. The company was getting information from informal conversations with distributors and retailers, but formal market research was too expensive for the small company.

In late 1995, Philip Ellinwood, Ritchey's chief operating officer and IS director, decided to rework the Web site so that the company could hear from its customers directly. He searched for a software package that allows businesses to sell products and services over the Internet and collect information from consumers. Ellinwood found a product called Web Trader (from SBT Corp.), but it was too expensive for Ritchey Corp. to purchase. Therefore, Ellinwood struck a deal with SBT—a lower price on the software in exchange for Ritchey's willingness to test the package and put SBT's logo on the company Web site. It took 1 year and only $7,500 to turn the static Web site into an interactive marketing tool.

Ellinwood set up customer surveys on the Web site. To induce visitors to participate, the company offers visitors who answer the surveys a chance to win free Ritchey products. Visitors are asked to enter their names and addresses and then to answer questions about the company's products. Web Trader automatically organizes and saves the answers in a database. The information is later used to help make marketing and advertising decisions. Ellinwood can easily change the questions to learn customers' opinions about any of about 15 new products Ritchey develops each year. In the past, the company knew little about how consumers might react to a new product until it was in the stores. Ellinwood says, "The process could save us as much as $100,000 a year on product development."

To educate retailers and consumers about the technological advantages of Ritchey's high-end components over competitors' parts, Ellinwood created an electronic catalog. Visitors can browse through the product catalog, which includes detailed descriptions and graphics of Ritchey's products.

As of this writing, Ritchey does not yet sell directly to individuals online, because the company wants to maintain its existing distribution system. However, dealers can place orders on the site, and they can learn about new products quickly, so they no longer push only those products about which they know the most.

Source: ritcheylogic.com

■ ■

4.2 CONSUMER BEHAVIOR ONLINE

The opening vignette illustrates the benefits a company can derive from changing its Web site from passive to interactive. Ritchey, Inc. can now hear from its customers directly, even though it uses intermediaries for its sales. The new interactive Web site allows the company to learn more about its customers, while educating customers at the same time. Why is a relatively small company making these efforts?

As you may recall from Chapter 1, companies today operate under increasing business environment pressures. The major pressures are labeled the 3C's: competition, customers, and change. Companies treat customers like royalty as they try to lure them to buy their goods and services. Finding and retaining customers is a major critical success factor for most businesses.

The presence of the 3C's is not new. Companies have been "fighting" for customers for decades. What is new is the intensity of the competition, the strength of the customers, and the magnitude of the changes. All of this boils down to a strategy: You need to control the 3C's to succeed, or even to survive.

EC can be viewed as a new distribution channel that competes against conventional ones. Furthermore, as soon as a company succeeds in its EC in a certain area, many competitors will try to follow suit, as in the case of *Amazon.com*. Thus, the task of attracting customers to an online company, *customer acquisition,* can be difficult and expensive, because it is necessary to first convince customers to shop online and then to choose that company over its online competitors. Then, a company must work to build loyalty with new and existing customers.

In this chapter, we describe the new relationships that companies such as Ritchey Design are attempting to build with their customers. The key to building such relationships is understanding consumer behavior. We also deal with the conduct of market research for learning about customers, products, and competition. Finally, this chapter examines customer service to individual customers.

Consumer Behavior

For decades market researchers have tried to understand consumer behavior (e.g., East 1997). Their findings are summarized in models of consumer behavior. We adjusted one popular model for the EC environment.

A MODEL OF EC CONSUMER BEHAVIOR

According to our model of EC consumer behavior, shown in Figure 4-1, the purchasing decision process is triggered by a customer's reaction to stimuli (on the left). The process is then influenced by the buyer's characteristics, the environment, the technology, the EC logistic, and other factors. Figure 4-1 identifies some of the variables in each category and also shows the chapter in this book (in parentheses) in which the topic is further discussed. For example, the issue of marketing stimuli in EC is discussed in Chapter 5 (advertisement and promotions). In Chapters 2 and 3, the pricing decision is elaborated upon. In this chapter we deal mainly with the following issues—personal characteristics, the decision process, relationship building, and customer service. Discussion of other issues can be found in Internet marketing books, such as Sterne (2000).

Before we explore the details of the EC model, we need to describe who EC consumers are, what they buy online, and what the differences are between customer relations in direct sales versus intermediary-based markets.

Consumer Types

Online consumers can be divided into two types: individual consumers, who get much of the media attention, and organizational buyers, who do most of the actual shopping in cyberspace. Organizational buyers include governments, private corporations, resellers, and public organizations. Organizational buyers' purchases are

Figure 4-1	EC Consumer Behavior Model

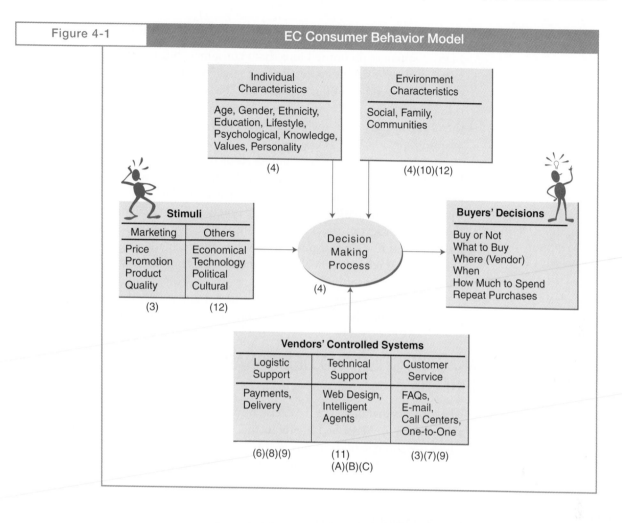

not intended for personal consumption. Rather, purchased products or services are generally used to create other products (services) by adding value to the products. Also, products may be purchased for resale without any further modifications.

Consumer behavior, which has a profound impact on the way B2C online systems are developed, can be viewed in terms of two questions: (1) Why is the consumer shopping? and (2) What benefit does the consumer get from shopping online?

PURCHASING TYPES AND EXPERIENCES

Market researchers have categorized shopping experiences into two dimensions: *utilitarian,* carrying out a shopping activity "to achieve a goal" or "complete a task"; and *hedonic,* carrying out a shopping activity because "It is fun and I love it." An understanding of hedonic and utilitarian shopping can provide insight into many EC consumer behaviors that are frequently not taken into account in the design and layout of electronic marketplaces.

Consumers can also be categorized into three other categories: *Impulsive buyers,* who purchase products quickly; *patient buyers,* who purchase products after making some comparisons; and *analytical buyers,* who do substantial research before making the decision to purchase products or services. Also, there are window shoppers, who simply browse for pleasure.

Direct Sales, Intermediation, and Customer Relations

Many companies do not sell directly to consumers but to intermediaries—whole-salers, dealers, distributors, retailers, or resellers. Even if a company does not sell directly to the end user of its product, it still has an interest in creating a better relationship with that end user, as shown in the opening vignette. It is the end user—the ultimate consumer—who supports everyone in a network of value-creating relationships.

Ford Motor Company sells almost all of its cars to dealers, not to consumers, but it does recognize, nevertheless, that the ultimate drivers of Ford vehicles think of themselves as having a relationship with Ford. Hewlett-Packard sells testing equipment to purchasing agents at large microchip-manufacturing companies, but the ultimate users of these products are the bench engineers who develop new products and test current ones. In developing EC marketing and advertisement strategies, it is critical to first define who the target customers are—the end users, the intermediaries, or both.

Now, let us return to the model of Figure 4-1 and look at the environmental and personal variables that may influence consumer buying decisions.

4.3   PERSONAL CHARACTERISTICS AND DEMOGRAPHICS OF INTERNET SURFERS

The variables that influence the decision-making process include environmental variables, which are described briefly in this section; personal characteristic variables, which are also described in this section; and vendor-controlled variables, which are discussed in subsequent sections of this chapter and in other chapters. Knowing about these variables can help vendors design marketing and advertisement plans.

Environmental Variables

Environmental variables can be grouped into the following categories:

- **Social variables.** Social variables play an important role in EC purchasing. People are influenced by family members, friends, coworkers, and "what's in fashion this year." Of special importance in EC are *Internet communities* (Chapter 18) and *discussion groups,* which communicate via chat rooms, electronic bulletin boards, and newsgroups. These topics are discussed in various places in the text.
- **Cultural variables.** It makes a big difference if a consumer lives near Silicon Valley in California or in the mountains in Nepal. The interested reader is referred to Hasan and Ditsa (1999), who provide some insights regarding the impact of culture on IT adoption.
- **Psychological variables.** These variables are briefly mentioned in several places throughout the text. The reader who is interested in the details of psychological variables should see East (1997).
- **Other environmental variables.** These include the available information, government regulations, legal constraints, and situational factors. Also, notice that environmental variables are included in the "other stimuli" of Figure 4-1.

Personal Characteristics and Personal Differences

Several variables are unique to individual customers. These include consumer resources, age, knowledge, gender, educational level, attitudes, motivation, marital status, personality, values, lifestyle, and more. Also important for EC are Internet usage and users' profiles. Only some of these data as they relate to EC are available. More data are available, however, on Internet consumer demographics.

Several consumer demographics provide information on customer buying habits. The major demographics presented here include gender, age, marital status, educational level, ethnicity, occupation, and household income. Sufficient data for EC consumer demographics were not available at the time this book was written. Therefore, most of the data presented here are related to Internet surfers (potential buyers) and are not about actual buyers. However, it is logical to assume that there is a close association between Internet users and EC buyers.

Until 1998, the major source of Internet use data was the Graphic, Visualization, and Usability (GVU) Center at Georgia Tech University. Today, many organizations provide Internet data. Table 4-1 summarizes data sources and types.

The analysis of demographic data is important as illustrated in Application Case 4.1.

It is interesting to note that the more experience people have with the Internet, the more likely they are to spend money online, as shown in Figure 4-2. From Internet statistics we can learn not only what people buy, but also why they do not buy.

The two most cited reasons for not making purchases on the Web are security (30 percent) and the difficulty in judging the quality of the product (20 percent). Some users, about 9.3 percent, do not make purchases because they've heard that buying on the Web is not reliable, trustworthy, or secure, but only 1.9 percent of online consumers have actually had an unfavorable experience. In fact, having a negative experience was the least-cited reason for not making more purchases on the Web. An additional 4.5 percent of users do not purchase online because they consider the process complicated.

TABLE 4-1

Sources and Types of Internet and EC Statistics

Data Source	Type of Data
Allnetresearch.com	Gender
bizrate.com	Age
Commencement Research Center	Marital status
cyberdialogue.com	Educational level
Ernst and Young (shopping survey)	Internet usage occupation
forrester.com	Ethnicity
gartnergroup.com	Household income
lionbridge.com	Country of residence
ldc.com	
jup.com	
mediametrix.com	Internet access options
nua.com/surveys	Length and frequency of use
statmarket.com	Buying patterns (items, price)
zonaresearch.com	

Purchasing and Baby Boomers

Honda Motorcycle was selling a million bikes a year in the mid-1980s. But by the early 1990s, sales numbers dropped by half. Honda was puzzled and anxious for an explanation.

The firm discovered that the immense Baby Boom generation of 76 million consumers had now been replaced in the youth market by the "Baby Bust" generation of consumers—a generation only half the size of the Baby Boom generation. "Simply put, we're missing some 38 million consuming Americans in the Baby Bust generation," Bill Gronbach, a manager in a marketing research firm, said. It was not that teenagers stopped liking motorcycles, but there simply were not as many of them to keep the market strong.

Levi Strauss experienced the same problem. In November 1998, the manufacturer announced that it would lay off 7,000 workers—a third of its North American manufacturing workforce—because of a drop in demand for its blue jeans. "They thought that the five-pocket jeans would sell in perpetuity," Gronbach said. The numbers indicate that jeans are still popular, particularly with 20-year-olds—but there are fewer of them around. There were 3.3 million babies born in 1977—1 million fewer babies than were born 20 years earlier at the height of the Baby Boom. These people are now 22 years old, completing college, and starting to shop around.

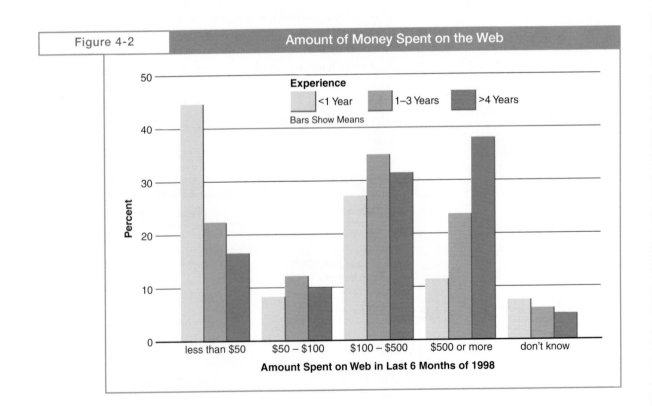

Figure 4-2   Amount of Money Spent on the Web

One area that is extremely important to EC, but is outside the boundaries of this text, is the adoption of Internet technology in general and EC adoption in particular. For barriers to Internet adoption see Nambisan and Wang (1999).

4.4   CONSUMER PURCHASING DECISION MAKING

We return again to Figure 4-1. Specifically, the central part of the figure where consumers' make purchasing decisions. Before we discuss this topic, it is necessary to clarify the role people play in the decision-making process. The major roles are as follows (Kotler and Armstrong 1999):

- **Initiator.** The person who first suggests or thinks of the idea of buying a particular product or service.
- **Influencer.** A person whose advice or views carry some weight in making a final purchasing decision.
- **Decider.** The person who ultimately makes a buying decision or any part of it—whether to buy, what to buy, how to buy, or where to buy.
- **Buyer.** The person who makes an actual purchase.
- **User.** The person who consumes or uses a product or service.

Advertising and marketing strategies become very difficult when more than one individual plays these roles. How marketers deal with such an issue is beyond the scope of this book.

Several models have been developed in an effort to describe the details of the purchase decision-making process. These models provide a framework for learning about the process in an attempt to predict, improve, or influence consumer decisions. The models are also used as guidelines for research purposes. We will introduce only two models here.

The Purchasing Decision-Making Model

A general purchasing decision-making model consists of five major phases. In each phase we can distinguish several activities and, in some of them, one or more decisions. The five phases are (1) need identification, (2) information search, (3) alternatives evaluation, (4) purchase and delivery, and (5) after-purchase evaluation. Although these stages offer a general guide to the consumer decision-making process, do not assume that consumers' decision making will necessarily proceed in this order. In fact, the consumer may revert back to a previous phase or end the process at any time.

The first phase, *need identification,* occurs when a consumer is faced with an imbalance between actual and desired states of a need. A marketer's goal is to get the consumer to recognize such imbalance and then convince this consumer that the product or service the seller offers will certainly fill in the gap between the two states.

After identifying the need, the consumer *searches for information* (stage 2) on the various alternatives available to satisfy the need. Here, we differentiate between a decision of what product to buy, **product brokering**, and from whom to buy it, **merchant brokering**. These two decisions can be separate or interrelated. This stage is basically an information search. An information search can occur internally, externally, or both. The internal information search is the process of recalling information stored in the memory. In contrast, an external information search seeks information in the outside environment, typically in Internet databases. In the external search, catalogs, advertising, promotions, and reference groups will influence consumer decision making. Product search engines, such as *compare.com*, can be very beneficial at this phase. The consumer's information search will eventually generate a smaller set of preferred alternatives. From this set, the buyer will further *evaluate the alternatives* (phase 3) and, if possible, will negotiate terms (this can be a complex task). In this phase, a consumer will use the information stored in memory and obtained from outside sources to develop a set of criteria. These criteria will help the consumer evaluate and compare alternatives. In phase 4 the consumer will *make the purchasing decision,* arrange payment and delivery, buy warranties, and so on.

Finally, there is a postpurchase stage (fifth phase) of *customer service* (e.g., maintenance) and evaluation of the usefulness of the product. This process can also be seen as a life cycle in which, at the end, the product is disposed of.

The Customer Decision Model in Web Purchasing

The above purchasing model was used by O'Keefe and McEachern (1998) to build a framework, called the Consumer Decision Support System (CDSS). According to their framework, shown in Table 4-2, each of the phases of the purchasing model can be supported by both CDSS facilities and generic Internet and Web facilities. The CDSS facilities support the specific decisions in the process, whereas e-commerce technologies provide information and enhance communication. This framework can help companies in using Internet technologies to improve, influence, and control the decision process. Specific implementation of this framework is demonstrated throughout the text.

A Model of Internet Consumer Satisfaction

Consumer behavior on the Internet may be more complex due to the involvement of Web technology. A comprehensive framework for such a situation was developed by Lee (2001). His model, shown in Figure 4-3, is based on the assumption

TABLE 4-2

Purchase Decision-Making Process and Support System

Decision Process Steps	CDSS Support Facilities	Generic Internet and Web Support Facilities
Need recognition ↓	Agents and event notification	Banner advertising on order Web sites URL on physical material Discussions in newsgroups
Information search (what, from whom?) ↓	Virtual catalogs Structured interaction and question/answer sessions Links to (and guidance on) external sources	Web directories and classifiers Internal search on Web site External search engines Focused directories and information brokers
Evaluation, negotiation, selection	FAQs and other summaries Samples and trials Provisions of evaluative models Pointers to (and information) about existing customers	Discussions in newsgroups Cross-site comparisons Generic models
Purchase, payment, and delivery ↓	Product or service ordering Arrangement of delivery	Electronic cash and virtual banking Logistics providers and package tracking
After-purchase service and evaluation ↓	Customer support via e-mail and newsgroups E-mail communication	Discussions in news groups

Source: O'Keefe and McEachern, 1998.

Figure 4-3	A Comprehensive Model of Internet Consumer Satisfaction

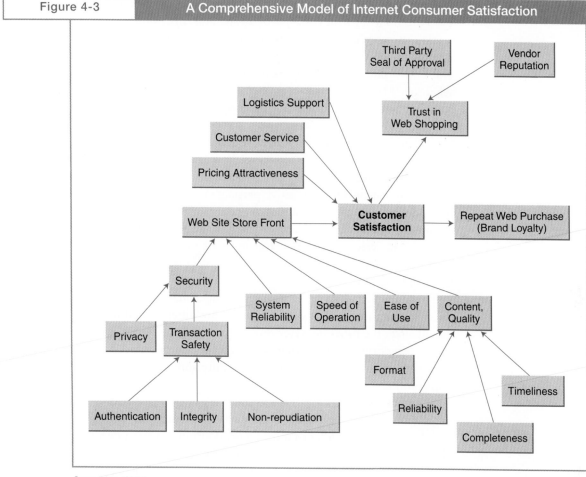

Source: Lee (2001)

that a repeat Web purchase is mainly determined by customer satisfaction. Understanding this and similar models is essential for the appropriate development of consumer relationships and for increasing customers' satisfaction, as is discussed later in this chapter.

4.5 MATCHING PRODUCTS WITH CUSTOMERS: PERSONALIZATION

One of the greatest benefits of EC is to match products and services with individual consumers. Such matching can be economically done by software agents, as will be explained later. But, let's first understand why one-to-one matching is valuable.

One-to-One Marketing: An Overview

THE BASIC IDEA

One-to-one marketing is a type of relationship marketing. Relationship marketing, according to Mowen and Minors (1998), is the "overt attempt of exchange partners to build a long-term association, characterized by purposeful cooperation and mutual dependence on the development of social, as well as structural, bonds" (p. 540). It includes the concepts of loyalty and trust, which we discuss later in this section. But not everything that could be called relationship marketing is in fact one-to-one marketing. To be a genuine one-to-one marketer, a company must be able and willing to change its behavior toward an individual customer based on what they know about that customer. So, one-to-one marketing is really a simple idea: "Treat different customers differently." It is based on the fact that no two customers are alike.

One-to-one marketing involves much more than just sales and marketing, because a firm must be able to change how its products are configured or its services are delivered based on the needs of individual customers. Smart companies have always encouraged the active participation of customers in the development of products, services, and solutions. For the most part, however, being customer oriented has always meant being oriented to the needs of the *typical customer* in the market—the average customer. But in order to build enduring one-to-one relationships, a company must continuously interact with customers and address their needs individually.

The actual, detailed mechanics of building a one-to-one relationship depend on understanding the various ways customers are different and how these differences should affect the firm's behavior toward particular, individual customers. One reason so many firms are beginning to focus on one-to-one marketing is that this kind of marketing can create high customer loyalty and, as a part of the process, help a firm's profitability.

A company increases loyalty in its own customers—one customer at a time—by establishing a learning relationship with each customer, starting with the *most valuable customers.* Think of a learning relationship as a relationship that gets better with every new interaction. A customer tells a company of some need (or they learn about it otherwise), and the company customizes its product or service to meet this need. With each interaction and recustomization, the company better fits its product to this particular customer. Thus, the company makes the product more valuable to this customer. Then the customer is more likely to remain loyal to the company.

HOW ONE-TO-ONE RELATIONSHIPS ARE PRACTICED

One of the benefits of doing business over the Internet is that it enables companies to better understand their customers' needs and buying habits, which in turn enables them to improve and frequently customize their future marketing efforts. For example, Prodigy offers its subscribers a personal librarian service in the form of a search engine capable of prioritizing information by topics of interest, and *Amazon.com* can e-mail customers announcements of new books published in a customer's area of interest.

Although some companies have had programs similar to one-to-one marketing for years, it may be much more beneficial to institute a corporate-wide policy of building one-to-one relationships around the Web. There are several ways to do this (e.g., Peppers et al. 1999). The GartnerGroup, an IT consulting company, proposed what they call The New Marketing Cycle of Relationship Building. Their proposal, illustrated in Figure 4-4, views relationships as a two-way street in which customer

Figure 4-4	The New Marketing Model

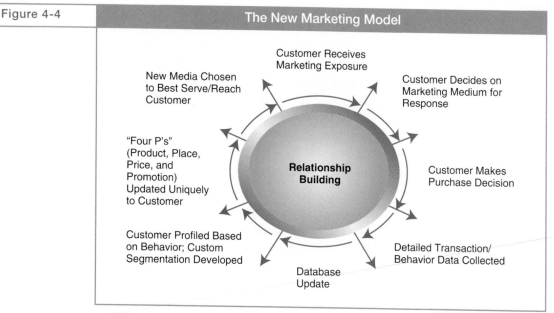

Source: GartnerGroup

information is collected and placed in a database. Then, a customer's profile is developed and the so-called four marketing P's (product, place, price, and promotion) are updated on a one-to-one basis. Based on this, appropriate advertisements are prepared that will hopefully lead to a purchase by the customer. The detailed transaction is then added to the database and the cycle is repeated.

Issues in EC-Based One-to-One Marketing

Of the many issues related to implementing EC-based one-to-one marketing, we will address only *loyalty, trust,* and *referrals.* For details and other topics see Allen and Yaeckel (1998) and Peppers et al. (1999).

CUSTOMER LOYALTY

Customer loyalty is the degree to which a customer will stay with a specific vendor or brand. It is an important element in consumer purchasing behavior (e.g., see Reichheld 1996). Customer loyalty is one of the most significant contributors to profitability. By keeping customers loyal, a company can increase its profits because customers will buy more and over time sales will grow. Also, it costs about five to eight times more to acquire a new customer than to keep an existing one. Customer loyalty strengthens a company's market position because loyal customers are kept away from the competition. A company becomes less sensitive to price competition when it assumes that customers will not be too sensitive to minor differences in price. Furthermore, increased loyalty can bring cost savings to a company in many ways: lower marketing costs, lower transaction costs (such as contract negotiation and order processing), customer turnover expenses, lower failure costs such as warranty claims, and so on.

Loyal customers have a specific opinion about what to buy and from whom. Loyal customers buy regularly over a cross-section of specific products or services and often are immune to competitors' efforts. Also, loyal customers refer other customers to a site. During the past decade, customer loyalty in general has been decreasing. The introduction of EC accelerated this trend because customers' ability to shop, compare, and switch to different business vendors has become extremely easy, fast, and inexpensive given the aid of search engines, mall directories, and intelligent agents (Section 4.8). Customer loyalty can be increased by increasing customers' satisfaction. This can be done in several ways, including the provision of one-to-one marketing and meeting the customer's cognitive needs.

MEETING CUSTOMERS' COGNITIVE NEEDS

Gaining information about current and potential customers' needs and converting those needs into demand is more feasible in EC than in any other marketing channel. For those products that require more sophisticated service or information before and after purchase, addressing the cognitive needs of the customers is an advantage. On the other hand, addressing the customer's cognition and perceptual process may be a hurdle in EC, because EC experiences cannot be compared with a direct sales experience in a grocery or department store. Because shopping is an interpersonal activity, customer service in EC should not ignore the cognitive aspect of a vendor and customer interaction.

To take into account perceptual processes among different buyers, Zellweger (1997) points out the knowledge differences among different consumers. The main difference among buyers is in their understanding of a specific product or service. Customers may have novice, intermediate, or expert skill levels. Internet-based customer service should be organized in a way that helps a novice buyer select the most general topics and progress toward more specific details until a product matches their need; customers with a more advanced knowledge base should have the option of using shorter, more direct routes.

E-LOYALTY

E-loyalty refers to customers' loyalty to an e-tailer. E-loyalty is very important because of the ease in which customers can turn to another e-tailer. Customer acquisition is a critical success factor in e-tailing. The expense of acquiring a new customer can be over $100, and even at *Amazon.com* it is more than $15. In contrast, the cost of maintaining an existing customer at *Amazon.com* is $2 to $4.

Companies can foster e-loyalty by learning about their customers' needs, interacting with customers, and providing superb customer service. A major source of information on e-loyalty is *e-loyalty.com*. One of their major services is an online journal, the *Journal of Customer Loyalty*, which offers numerous articles describing the relationships among e-loyalty, customer service, personalization, CRM, and Web-based tools (e.g., Fluss et al. 2000). A comprehensive review of the use of the Web and the Internet to foster e-loyalty is provided by Reichheld (2001) and Reichheld and Schefter (2000).

Loyal customers buy more on the Web. This is also true for B2B relationships. For example, *Grainger.com*, a large industrial-supply company, found that loyal customers increased their purchases substantially when they began using Grainger's Web site.

TRUST IN EC

Trust is the psychological status of involved parties who are willing to pursue further interactions to achieve a planned goal. A trading party makes itself vulnerable to the other party's behavior. In other words, both parties in a transaction assume risk. In the marketspace, sellers and buyers do not meet face to face. The buyer can see a picture of the product but not the product itself. Promises of quality and delivery can be easily made—but will they be kept? To deal with these issues, a high degree of trust must exist between buyers and sellers. It is critical for EC vendors to establish high levels of trust with current and potential customers. Trust is particularly important in global EC transactions due to the difficulty in taking legal action in cases of a fraud and the potential for conflicts caused by differences in culture and business environments.

In addition to trust between the buyers and sellers, it is necessary to have trust in the EC infrastructure and in the EC environment. Shapiro et al.'s (1992) trust model describes three forms of trust:

1. Deterrence-based trust is related to the threat of punishment. The threat of punishment is likely to be a more significant motivator than the promise of reward.
2. Knowledge-based trust is grounded in the knowledge of the other trading partner (trustee), which allows the trustor to understand and predict the behavior of the trustee. The key factor in this trust is the information derived out of a relationship over time that permits a trustor to predict the behavior of a trustee or vice versa; also, brand recognition is very important in EC. For example, when a consumer buys online from Disney or Wal-Mart, the consumer probably will have a great deal of trust. Obviously, the consumer needs to be assured that Disney is the actual seller.
3. Identification-based trust is based on empathy and common values with the other trading partner's desire and intentions, to the point that one trading partner is able to act as an agent for the other.

How does one establish the necessary level of trust for EC? The desired level of trust is determined by the following factors (Shapiro et al. 1992): the degree of initial success that each party experienced with EC and with each other; well-defined roles and procedures for all parties involved; and realistic expectations as to outcomes from EC. On the other hand, trust can be decreased by any user uncertainty regarding the technology, by lack of initial face-to-face interactions, and by lack of enthusiasm among the parties. In fact, it is extremely difficult to measure the level of trust because it involves multiple parties, far apart both in time and location, as well as difficulties in measuring the nature of the mental process involved. Some theoretical and practical extensions of Shapiro's were made by Lewicki and Bunker (1996).

Therefore, EC security mechanisms and technology can also help solidify trust. Security issues are discussed in detail in Chapter 14. In addition to relying on security techniques, it is necessary for EC vendors to disclose and update their latest business status and practices for potential customers and build transaction integrity into the system, as well as to guarantee information protection through various communication channels. Moreover, as discussed in Chapter 17, there is a considerable amount of fraud on the Internet. This fraud is leading to mistrust, especially when unknown parties are involved. In Chapter 17 we describe measures that are being taken to reduce fraud and increase trust. For comprehensive treatment of EC trust, see Ratnasingham (1998) and Keen et al. (2000).

EC TRUST MODEL

Lee and Turban (2001) examined the various aspects of EC trust and developed the model shown in Figure 4-5. According to this model the level of trust is determined by several factors. The figure illustrates the complexity of trust relationships, especially in B2C EC.

THE VALUE OF EC REFERRALS

A few years ago as part of a beta test to evaluate a new online shipping service, FedEx sent an e-mail message to select customers inviting them to try the new service. To their surprise, FedEx found that a large, unexpected number of customers who were not on the FedEx e-mail list began to use the service. This demonstrates how powerful the Internet referral network can be. Many of the FedEx customers who use the online shipping service reported that they learned of it when they received a package that had been sent using the new Web service. Thus, for companies like 1-800-Flowers and FedEx, the word-of-mouth potential is multiplied because every transaction initiated by one person or company is completed through delivery to another. According to Reichheld and Schefter (2000), more

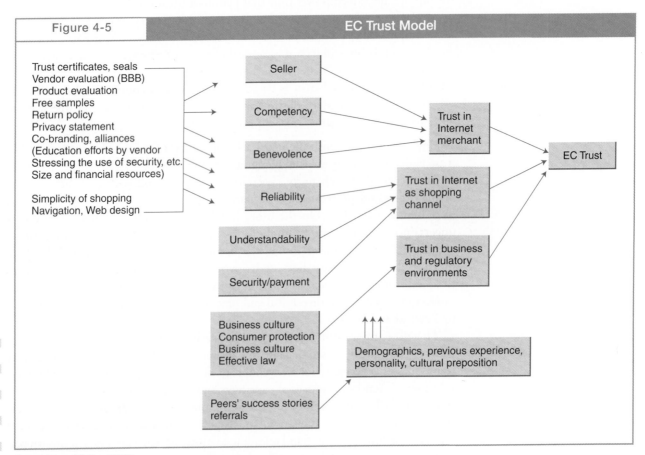

Figure 4-5   **EC Trust Model**

Source: Lee and Turban (2001)

than half of eBay's users are referrals from loyal customers. Referrals are the basis for *viral marketing,* a topic that will be discussed in Chapter 5.

Personalization

Personalization refers to the process of matching content, services, or products to individuals. The matching process is based on what a company knows about the individual user; this information is usually referred to as a **user profile**. The user profile defines customer preferences, behaviors, and demographics.

There are several ways to build user profiles, and the profiles are updated on a regular basis. The major strategies used to compile user profiles include (see also Section 4.7):

- Solicit information directly from the user by asking the user to fill in a questionnaire or simply state what information he or she would like to receive.
- Use cookies or other methods to observe what people are doing online.
- Perform data mining or Web mining.

Once a profile is constructed, a company matches the profile to a product, service, or content. The actual matching process is usually done by software agents, as will be described later. Manual matching is too time consuming and expensive.

Personalization can be applied through several different methods. Some of the most well-known methods include the following.

Rule-based filtering. A company asks the consumers a series of yes/no or multiple-choice questions. The questions may range from personal information to the specific information the customer is looking for on the Web site. Certain behavioral patterns are predicted using the collected information. This is basically an expert system approach. A derived behavior rule may look like this: If customer age > 35, and customer age < 40, and customer income > $100,000, then show Jeep Cherokee, else show Mazda Protégé.

Content-based filtering. With this technique, vendors ask users to specify certain favorite products. Based on these user preferences, the vendor's system will recommend additional products to the user. This technique is fairly complex because mapping among different product categories must be completed in advance.

Constraint-based filtering. Similar to content-based filtering, this technique requires users to provide information about preferred products. However, instead of asking many questions regarding specifications of products, this method takes as input a sequence of demographic and other constraints to represent a user's preferences.

Learning-agent technology. This is a very nonintrusive type of personalization. With this method, users do not answer any questions because their preferences are collected by cookies or other technologies while they surf the Web. Such profiling can even be done anonymously. Some important personal indicators can be collected from learning-agent technologies, such as browsing duration, time spent online, and browsing sequences.

COLLABORATIVE FILTERING

Once a company knows a consumer's preferences (e.g., what music they like), it would be useful if a company could predict, without asking, what other products or services a new or existing customer might enjoy. One way to do this is through *collaborative filtering.* With collaborative filtering, the prediction is based on vector-based similarity calculations, correlation coefficients, or statistical Baysian methods (see *sins.berkeley.edu/resources.collab/* for details). One of the pioneer filtering systems was Firefly (now part of Microsoft Network). Many personalization systems are based on collaborative filtering. Here are some examples:

- *backflip.com* will recommend a restaurant based on information from the user. (The more input entered, the more accurate the recommendation.)
- *c5solutions.com* (of Hong Kong) sends one-to-one messages to users via cell phones. The personalized messages are based on the user's current location and user profile.
- *The London Times* will send the latest news in a user's area of interest to the user's PC or wireless device.
- *Predictivenetworks.com* assists users in making purchasing decisions based on personal information provided by the user.

There are several different ways to implement collaborative filtering. For example, one popular approach, called *group filtering,* asks users to rank certain products to establish personal profiles. The individual profiles are then compared against the general preferences of a population, and a subgroup of users with similar interests is identified. The subgroup's other preferences then become recommendations to the user.

For more about personalization and filtering see *lycos.com* and *cio.com*.

LEGAL AND ETHICAL ISSUES

Information is frequently collected from users without their knowledge or permission. This raises several ethical and legal questions, including privacy issues, which are discussed in Chapters 5 and 17. Several vendors offer *permission-based* personalization tools (e.g., see *youpowered.com/personalization*).

4.6   DELIVERING CUSTOMER SERVICE IN CYBERSPACE AND CRM

When customers engage in the purchasing process described in Table 4-2, they may sometimes require assistance. For example, in the need-recognition phase customers sometimes need help in determining what they need. Then, they may need assistance in finding out what item they should buy to satisfy the need. Customers often have questions about a product's characteristics before they make a purchase, as well as questions on proper maintenance and repair after the sale. Sellers must be able to assist customers in any and all of the phases. Such assistance is a major objective of customer service.

Customer service is a series of activities designed to enhance customer satisfaction, that is, the feeling that a product or service has met the customer's expectations. Customer service is responsible for resolving problems customers encounter in any phase of the purchase decision-making process (Table 4-2) or the product life cycle (to be described soon). Whereas traditional customer service places the burden on the customer to direct a problem or inquiry to the right place and receive information, EC delivers improved customer service by improving communication, automating the process, and speeding the resolution of customer problems.

In the early years of EC, online consumers did not demand high levels of customer service, so the first generation of customer service was fairly simple. However, next-generation customer service requires the best, most powerful systems and software in order to satisfy the increased customer expectations. If customer service options and solutions do not maintain the same level of excitement and interaction as that shown in advertising and sales presentations, the level of intensity declines and the vendor runs the risk of losing customers. Therefore, EC marketers must respond to increasing consumer demands.

As part of the demand for higher levels of customer service, customers may want to receive "entertainment" values on the Internet. Customers invest money in hardware, software, and Internet access fees to get to a Web site. They take time to learn systems and are ready to commit to a purchase. Such a commitment can be stronger when customers are happy. EC entertainment is discussed in Chapter 5.

E-Service

When customer services is supplied over the Internet, sometimes automatically, it is referred to as *e-service* (*searchhp.com*). E-service often provides online help for online transactions. In addition, even if a product is purchased off-line, customer service may be offered online. For example, if a consumer purchases a product off-line and needs expert advice on how to use it, he or she may find detailed instructions online (e.g., *livemanuals.com*). It is also important that companies provide customer service throughout the product's life cycle. According to Voss (2000), most companies in the United Kingdom and the United States are fairly limited in the e-services they offer. Voss distinguishes three levels of service:

1. **Foundation of service.** This includes the minimum necessary services such as site responsibleness (for example, how quickly and accurately the service is provided), site effectiveness, and order fulfillment.
2. **Customer-centered services.** These are services that make the difference. They include order tracing, configuration and customization, and security/trust.
3. **Value-added services.** These are extra services such as dynamic brokering, online auctions, or online training and education.

Product Life Cycle and Customer Service

With EC, customer service is critical, because customers and merchants do not meet face to face (Sterne 2000). According to McKeown and Watson (1998), customer service should be provided during the entire product life cycle, which is composed of the following four phases:

1. **Requirements.** Assisting the customer to determine his or her needs (e.g., photographs of a product, video presentations, textual descriptions, articles or reviews, sound bites on a CD, and downloadable demonstration files). All of these can be provided electronically.
2. **Acquisition.** Helping the customer to acquire a specific product or service (e.g., online order entry, negotiations, closing of sale, downloadable software, and delivery).

3. **Ownership.** Supporting the customer on an ongoing basis (e.g., interactive online user groups, online technical support, frequently asked questions and answers, resource libraries, newsletters, and online renewal of subscriptions).
4. **Retirement.** Helping the client to dispose of a service or product when the product is no longer of use to the customer (e.g., online resale, classified ads).

Many of the activities conducted in each of these phases are shown throughout the text.

Customer Relationship Management (CRM)

Customer service is part of an approach known as **customer relationship management,** or **CRM.** CRM is an approach that recognizes that customers are the core of the business, and that a company's success depends on effectively managing their relationship with them (see Brown 2000). CRM is about building long-term and sustainable customer relationships that add value both to the customer and the company (Kalakota and Robinson, 1999). For more on CRM see *CRM-forum.com* and *crmassist.com.*

CRM IN ACTION

According to Seybold and Marshak (1998) there are five steps in building a customer-focused EC. These are:

1. Make it easy for customers to do business.
2. Focus on the end customer.
3. Redesign the customer-facing business processes from the end customer's point-of-view.
4. Wire the company for profit—design a comprehensive, evolving EC architecture.
5. Foster customer loyalty, the key to profitability in EC.

To make these steps successful, it is necessary to take the following actions:

- Deliver personalized services (e.g., *dowjones.com*)
- Target the right customers (e.g., *aa.com, nsc.com*)
- Help the customers do their jobs (e.g., *Boeing.com*)
- Let customers help themselves (e.g., *iprint.com*)
- Streamline business processes that impact the customers (e.g., *ups.com, amazon.com*)
- Own the customer's total experience (e.g., *amazon.com, hertz.com*)
- Provide a 360-degree view of the customer relationship (e.g., *wellsfargo.com, verizon.com*)

Some of the previous steps and actions are valid both for B2C and for B2B.

Customer Service Functions

Customer service on the Web can take many forms, such as answering customer inquiries, providing search and comparison capabilities, providing technical information to customers, allowing customers to track order status, and allowing customers to place an online order. The following describes different kinds of customer service in more detail.

PROVIDING SEARCH AND COMPARISON CAPABILITIES

One of the major problems consumers have with EC is locating specific items. With hundreds of thousands of online stores and with new ones being added daily, customers often find it difficult to locate a particular item. Consumers may also have difficulties finding an item on large e-tail Web sites. Many large e-tailers (e.g., *Amazon.com*) and independent comparison sites (e.g., *mysimon.com, compare.com*) provide search and comparison capabilities.

PROVIDING FREE PRODUCTS AND SERVICES

One approach companies use to differentiate themselves from others is to give consumers something for free. For example, *compubank.com* provides free bill payment and ATM services. For additional discussion of this topic, see Chapter 5 and P. Keen in Dickson and DeSanctis (2001).

PROVIDING SPECIALIZED INFORMATION AND SERVICES

Consumers place great importance on the ability to get free information on demand. Innovative use of links and keywords should be the norm when building Web sites that keep the consumer coming back for more. For example, on the 1-800-Flowers Web site (*1-800-Flowers.com*), customers can access useful information from experts or enter online contests. This added value motivates them to choose 1-800-Flowers as their floral delivery service. To make this process more efficient, a company can use intelligent agents to provide customized information to customers (Section 4.8).

Companies can inspire loyalty by providing customers with information and services that would be difficult to obtain off-line. For example, General Electric's Web site (*ge.com*) provides detailed technical and maintenance information for its products, and it sells replacement parts for discontinued models to those who need to fix outdated home appliances. Such information and parts are quite difficult to find off-line. Another example is *Goodyear.com*, which provides extensive information about tires and their use.

As is shown in Chapter 10, online travel is a huge industry. Airlines and hotels offer consumers the advantage of direct booking. However, this is not enough. Travel sites enhance their customer service by providing maps, price comparisons, push technology that sends customers e-mail information about cheap tickets to their favorite destinations, weather reports, travelers' experiences, news, and so on.

Many car manufacturers now offer "build-to-order" cars. Manufacturers enhance their customer service by providing customers who have bought build-to-order cars with tracking tools, some of which are provided by UPS or FedEx, so that the customer can find the exact status of their new car in the factory or elsewhere in the supply chain.

ALLOWING CUSTOMERS TO ORDER CUSTOMIZED PRODUCTS AND SERVICES

Dell Computer has revolutionized how computers are purchased by letting customers design their own computers and then delivering the computers to customers' homes. This customization process is now used by hundreds of vendors for products ranging from cars to shoes and is frequently referred to as *mass customization*. With the mass customization model, consumers are shown prepackaged "specials" and are then given the option of "custom-building" their own product.

Web sites such as *hamaracd.com* or *homecraft.com* allow consumers to handpick individual music titles from an online library and create a custom CD, a service that is not offered by traditional music stores. The *gap.com* allows customers to "mix and match" their entire wardrobe. Customer information such as clothing sizes, color and style preferences, and dates for gift shipments can be manipulated to increase sales and the probability of repeat business. Finally, JCPenney and Levi's combine old and new economies by enabling customers to be physically measured at stores, and then send electronic orders for the customized clothing to the production lines.

ENABLING CUSTOMERS TO TRACK ACCOUNTS OR ORDER STATUS

Many companies allow users to check their accounts or order status online. For example, customers can use the Web to check their account balances at financial institutions, the value of their stock portfolio, or the status of a loan application. Customers can also check the shipping status of merchandise they have ordered. FedEx and other shippers allow customers to track their packages once they have shipped from an e-tailer. When a customer orders books from *Amazon.com*, he or she can find, online, the anticipated arrival date. *Amazon.com* even goes one step further; it notifies a customer by e-mail once an order is accepted and provides the anticipated delivery date, and once the package has shipped, it e-mails the customer an actual delivery date. Many companies have adopted the *Amazon.com* model and provide similar services.

Customer Service Tools

There are many innovative Web-related tools that can be used to enhance customer service. Some of the major tools include personalized Web pages, FAQ pages, tracking tools, chat rooms, e-mail and automated responses, and Web-based help desks and call centers.

PERSONALIZED WEB PAGES

Many companies provide customers with tools to create their own individual Web pages. These Web pages can then be used to record customer purchases and preferences. Using personalized Web sites, customized information, such as product information and warranty information, can be efficiently delivered to the customer when the customer logs on to the personalized page. Not only can a customer pull information from the vendor's site, but the vendor can also push information to the consumer.

Vendors can use customer information collected from customized Web sites to facilitate customer service and enhance sales. Information that previously may have been provided to the customer 1 to 3 months after a transaction was completed is now provided in real or almost real-time, and it can be traced and analyzed for an immediate response or action. Companies now use customer information to help market additional products by matching valuable information about product performance and consumer behavior. American Airlines is an example of one company that uses personalized Web sites to help increase the bottom line (see Application Case 4.2).

APPLICATION CASE   **4.2**

> ### American Airlines Offers Personalized Web Sites for One-to-One Interactions
>
> In late 1998, American Airlines (AA) unveiled a number of features on its new Web site (*aa.com*) that some thought made *im.aa.com* the most advanced site for personalized, one-to-one interactions and transactions on the Web. The most innovative feature of this site is its ability to generate personalized Web pages for each of about 1,000,000 American Airlines registered, travel-planning customers (as of 2000). How can AA handle such a large amount of information and provide real-time customized Web pages for each customer? The answer—intelligent agents.
>
> The AA site was developed by Broadvision (*broadvision.com*), a major developer of one-to-one marketing applications, using a system called One-to-One Application. One-to-One is a complex software application for the development and real-time operation of Internet business applications. Many components are needed to generate personalized Web pages. One of the core components is intelligent agents, which dynamically match customer profiles (built on information supplied by the customer, observed by the system, or derived from existing customer databases) to the database of contents. The output of the matching process triggers the creation of a real-time customized Web page, which in the case of AA can contain information on the consumer's home airport and preferred destinations.
>
> By using intelligent-agent technology, American Airlines is building a considerable edge over its competitors. Personalizing Web pages is becoming more important because of its potential in increasing customer loyalty and cementing relationships with customers.

FAQs

The frequently asked questions (FAQs) feature is a simple and inexpensive tool that can be used to handle repetitive customer questions. Because customers use this tool by themselves, the delivery costs are minimal. However, FAQs cannot answer all customer questions. Nonstandard questions should probably be sent and responded to via e-mail. It is also important to note that FAQs are usually not customized, and therefore do not contribute to personalizing the vendor-consumer relationship. (In the future a system will be created that can access a user's profile and provide a customized FAQ.)

TRACKING TOOLS

Companies can supply customers with tracking tools so that customers can track their own orders, saving the company time and money. Customers generally like tracking tools as it gives them a quick and easy way to check on the status of an order or delivery. FedEx initiated the concept of online order tracking and has saved millions of dollars from its implementation. Customer inquiries that once went to a FedEx call center now are answered automatically using the *FedEx.com* Web site.

A CHAT ROOM

Another tool that provides customer service, attracts new customers, and increases customer loyalty is a chat room. For example, at Virtual Vineyard's chat room, (*wine.com*), visitors can discuss wines with both company experts and other wine lovers.

E-MAIL AND AUTOMATED RESPONSE

The most popular online customer service tool is e-mail. Inexpensive and fast, e-mail is used to disseminate information (e.g., confirmations), to send product information, and to conduct correspondence regarding many topics, but mostly responses to customer inquiries.

The ease of sending e-mail messages has resulted in a flood of customer e-mail. Some companies receive tens of thousands of e-mails a week or even a day. Answering these e-mails manually is expensive and time-consuming. Customers want quick answers, usually within 24 hours (a policy of many organizations). Several vendors offer automated e-mail reply systems, priced at about $50,000 (in 2000), that can provide answers to commonly asked questions (see *eGain.com*, *brightware.com*, *quark.com*, and *aptex.com*).

The eGain system, for example, looks for certain phrases or words such as "complaint" or "information on a product" and then taps into a knowledge base to generate a response. For messages that require human attention, the query is assigned an ID number and passed along to a customer agent for a reply. The eGain automated response tool is just one feature in eGain's Web-based call center initiative (*see eGain.com*).

Many companies do not provide actual answers in their automatic responses, but only acknowledgement that a query has been received. Customer queries are classified in a decision-support repository until a human agent logs in and responds. This is usually part of a call center.

HELP DESKS AND CALL CENTERS

One of the most important customer service tools is the *help desk*. Customers can drop in at a physical site or communicate by telephone, fax, or e-mail. Because the communication was initially conducted by telephone, the remote help desk is often called the call center.

Today's **call center** is a comprehensive customer service entity in which EC vendors take care of customer service issues communicated through various contact channels. New products are extending the functionality of the conventional call center to e-mail and to Web interaction, integrating them into one product. For example, eFrontOffice (*e.epicor.com/efrontoffice/conductor*) combines Web channels, such as automated e-mail reply, Web knowledge bases, and portal-like self-service, with call center agents or field service personnel. Such centers are sometimes called **telewebs**. An example of how a Web-based call center (or teleweb) works is provided in Application Case 4.3.

APPLICATION CASE   4.3

Canadian Tire Provides Superb Customer Service via an Integrated Call Center

Canadian Tire Acceptance, Ltd. (CTAL), the financial services division of the $4 billion Canadian Tire Corp., Ltd., serves 4 million of Canadian Tire's credit card holders. In 1998, CTAL became the company's primary call center in an effort to increase sales and enhance customer retention by eliminating annoying and time-consuming call transfers and ensuring that customers were treated on an individual basis.

"The call center is a strategic asset," says Mary Turner, vice president of customer services at CTAL. "This is our main point of contact with the customer. We have to maximize it."

Canadian Tire operates 10 call centers, each dealing with a different business area (general information and retail, wholesale, service, and so on) or geographical zone. The demands are heavy. CTAL's 10 call centers operate 24 hours a day 7 days a week and respond to more than 16 million calls a year. Call center representatives are expected to provide personalized service while handling a diverse set of customer needs—responding to more than 200 types of customer requests. CTAL's new system ensures that any representative can resolve any customer need without handoffs to other departments.

CTAL has several key business objectives:

- greater customer loyalty to Canadian Tire as a result of enhanced service;
- personalized customer attention and reduced transfers;
- rapid introduction of new products or changes to existing business services;
- reduced training requirements for customer service representatives; and
- integration of all customer touch points via a single system capable of handling Web, e-mail, and call center interactions.

The primary goal is to create a customer service environment that provides a complete set of customer-focused services in which the company understands customer behavior and needs and offers timely introduction of new services valued by the customers.

"When we began the project, we took a look at our operations and saw too many independent call centers," says Turner. "It seemed that every time we introduced a new product or service, we set up a new call center. We decided to streamline operations to make it possible for customers to reach the right representative whenever they call." CTAL's new call center technology integrates data from multiple sources and media.

The call center integrates telephone, fax, e-mail, and the Web. One of its major capabilities is to build customer profiles and act on them when needed, providing one-to-one relationships. The call center can be viewed as an interaction center that immediately recognizes the individual customer and integrates data that reflects on the relationship. Although the Web-based call center is still new, it is expected to pay for itself quickly. (For further details, see Peppers et al. 1999.)

For both consumers and businesses, the Internet is a medium of instant gratification. Delays can easily send customers or potential customers elsewhere. More and more Internet users demand not only prompt replies, but proactive alerts. For example, the travel Web site Travelocity sends an e-mail to the customer with updated gate and time information if a customer's flight is delayed. An online mortgage lender, *loanshop.com*, focuses on the teleweb center for sales and support using a natural language-based application. To use the system, customers submit structured e-mail questionnaires in which they answer a number of questions related to their problem. A comprehensive description of Web-based call centers, including information on leading vendors, is available at Orzech (1998).

Some of the hurdles a call center must address include the deployment of technologies such as e-mail management software, the creation of knowledge bases for FAQs, the integration of telephone, fax, and e-mail into a single center, the training of customer service representatives who can function in the call-center environment, and how to handle non-English-speaking customers.

Providing well-trained customer service representatives who have access to data such as customer history, purchases, and previous contacts with call center agents is another way to improve customer service. This enables a customer service representative to maintain a personal connection with the online customer. An example of a well managed and integrated call center is that of Bell Advanced Communication in Canada, whose subscribers can submit customer service queries over the Web. From the Bell Advanced Web site, a customer can fill out an e-mail form with drop-down menus that help pinpoint the customer's problem. The e-mail is then picked up by the call center, which either answers the question immediately or tries to respond within 1 hour. "From a customer service perspective, it provides good context. It keeps the personal aspect alive," says Maggi Williams, director of business development. This form of online "managed comprehensive contact" also gives Bell insight into what kind of information customers are interested in, which may, in turn, generate selling or marketing opportunities.

Today, call centers are multimedia, Web-enabled contact facilities that can arrange quick contact with humans, mobile device connections, and more (see *eGain.com*).

TROUBLESHOOTING TOOLS

Companies and customers can save large amounts of time if customers can solve their problems by themselves. Many vendors provide Web-based troubleshooting software to assist customers in this task (e.g., *prismnet.com* and *woodfinishsupply.com*). This enables vendors to reduce dramatically their customer support.

Justifying Customer Service and CRM Programs

Customer service programs can be expensive, and many companies require justification for their use. Two major problems arise when justifying customer service and CRM programs. The first problem is the fact that most of the benefits are intangible, and the second is that substantial benefits can be reaped only from loyal customers. This, of course, is true for both off-line and online organizations. In a study published in *Harvard Business Review* (1990) titled, "Zero Defections: Quality Comes to Services," the researchers demonstrated that the high costs of acquiring customers renders many customer relationship programs unprofitable during their early years. Only in later years, when the cost of retaining loyal customers falls and the volume of their purchases rises, do CRMs generate big returns (Reichheld and Scheffer, 2000). Therefore, companies are very careful in determining how much customer service to provide (see Petersen 1999).

Metrics.   One way to determine how much service to provide is to compare a company against a set of standards known as **metrics.** Here are some Web-related metrics a company can use to determine the appropriate level of customer support:

- **Response time.** Many companies have a target response time of 24 to 48 hours. If a company uses intelligent agents, response time can be in real-time and can at least provide an acknowledgement that the customer's message has been received.
- **Site availability.** Customers should be able to reach the company Web site at any time (24 hours a day). This means that downtime should be as close to zero as possible.
- **Download time.** Users will usually not tolerate downloads that last more than 20 to 30 seconds.
- **Up-to-date.** Information on the company site must be up-to-date.
- **Security and privacy.** Web sites must provide privacy statements and an explanation of security measures.
- **Fulfillment.** Order fulfillment must be fast and when promised to the customer.
- **Return policy.** In the United States and a few other countries, return policies are a standard service. Having a return policy increases customer trust and loyalty.
- **Navigability.** A Web site must be easy to navigate in order to please customers.

For more on EC metrics, see Chapter 16.

Examples of Superb Customer Service

How do companies increase customer satisfaction? And what role does the Internet play in the process? Some examples of how companies use the Internet to increase customer service are provided in Application Case 4.4.

4.7   MARKET RESEARCH FOR EC

Market research is aimed at finding information and knowledge that describes the relationship between consumers, products, marketing methods, and marketers in order to discover marketing opportunities and issues, to establish marketing plans, to better understand the purchasing process, and to evaluate marketing performance. Market research includes gathering information about topics such as the economy, industry, firms, products, pricing, distribution, competition, promotion, and consumer purchasing behavior.

APPLICATION CASE 4.4

Representative Examples of Superb Customer Service

On the 1-800-Flowers Web site customers have three ways to buy: telephone, retail shop, and online. By offering three purchase options, 1-800-Flowers provides consumers flexibility and attempts to attract new, first-time customers who were previously unaware of its services. Special online marketing programs leverage brand marketing, and off-line promotions, including direct mail, television, and printed media, call attention to its online services. 1-800-Flowers uses e-mail for order confirmation and customer communication. This is quite effective because customers appreciate the fact that someone has received their order and quickly responded to it. Contests and incentives such as discounts for early holiday buying also promote repeat orders. Several value-added programs featuring frequent flier miles or other tie-in rewards also work to increase customer satisfaction.

Blackstar (*blackstar.co.uk*) is a music retailer that thanks customers for their e-mail, lets them know how many e-mails are in front of them in a queue, and tells them how many hours they will have to wait for a response. Blackstar also provides a toll-free telephone number for urgent calls and a tracking system so that customers can find the status of their order.

For *Amazon.com*, convenience, selection, value, and special services contribute to very high customer loyalty. More book buyers buy from *Amazon.com* (as described in Chapter 3) than from any other online bookstore. More than one-third of *Amazon.com*'s customers have bought from *Amazon.com* two or more times. What changed customer buying patterns in this case is the convenience of buying over the Internet. Customers have access to a large assortment of books that they often cannot get anywhere else at discounted prices. In addition, Amazon uses e-mail as a low-cost vehicle for order confirmation and to personalize its services. For example, the company records each customer's topic and author preferences in a database and regularly sends out e-mail communications whenever a new book arrives that may appeal to that customer. Online editorials also keep customers coming back to the site to get reviews about books they are considering. This interactive function has been effective in building faithful followers for *Amazon.com*. Finally, there is a high level of trust in the brand. The name *Amazon.com* is well known worldwide despite the fact that the company was established only in 1995.

Federal Express (FedEx) views the Internet as a front door to its service offerings. The company initially created a Web site to enable customers to track their packages, and then it found that more than 30,000 customers used the service in its first week of operation. Giving customers an alternate method of tracking packages took pressure off its customer service representatives and gave customers an incentive to choose its service over competitors. Based on the popularity of its tracking program, FedEx later added shipping-administration capabilities that allow customers to visit the FedEx Web site, calculate delivery costs, fill in a shipping form, arrange for courier pickup, or find a local drop-off point. When customers use the FedEx Web site, they are delighted to find that something in the real world occurs as a result of what they did in the cyberworld. This has led to a high percentage of repeat visitors to the Web site, including customers who use the online services daily. The use of e-mail is also improving FedEx's customer communications by giving customers direct access to customer service professionals and not just telephone operators.

Sources: 1-800-flowers.com, amazon.com, and *fedex.com*; miscellaneous press releases 1999 through 2001.

The generic marketing research process is shown in Figure 4-6. It includes four major phases. The first phase defines the problem to be investigated (e.g., why grocery shopping online is expanding more slowly than selling books online) and the research objective (e.g., find the major reasons, rank them by importance). The second phase involves a research methodology (e.g., a sample survey) and data collection plan. In the third phase, data are collected. In the fourth phase, data are analyzed and integrated.

Various tools are used by businesses, educational institutions, and governments to conduct market research. For example, business representatives with questionnaires in shopping malls collect information from people on clothing, consumer products, or Internet usage. Surveyors may appear at supermarkets, at the front door of your house, at churches, airport terminals, or theaters. These places have high traffic, and replicating the surveys in various cities can give fairly generalized results. Another conventional way of conducting market research is by telephone surveys, where an interviewer calls prospective clients, current customers, or a randomly selected sample of customers regarding a specific product or service. Questionnaires may also be sent to specific individuals in a company or household.

In addition, focus groups and other primary research methods can be useful in identifying differences in attributes, benefits, and values of various potential markets. Analyzing these differences among groups of consumers is important when companies seek new target markets.

In the next section, we focus on conducting market research online. Internet marketing research is primarily aimed at supporting one-to-one EC. However, because EC also has to identify an appropriate customer group for specific products and services, it is important first to understand how groups of consumers are classified. This classification is called segmentation.

Market Segmentation

Market segmentation is the process of dividing a consumer market into logical groups for conducting marketing research, advertising, and sales. A consumer market can be segmented in several ways, for example, by geography, demographics, psychographics, and benefits sought. Segmentation is performed in order to formulate effective marketing strategies that appeal to specific consumer groups (e.g., see Vellido et al., 1999).

The process of segmenting the consumer market involves several different classifications, as shown in Table 4-3.

An important task involved in market segmentation is analyzing consumer-product relationships. Marketers need to investigate the product concept and

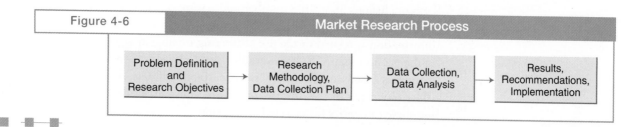

Figure 4-6   Market Research Process

Problem Definition and Research Objectives → Research Methodology, Data Collection Plan → Data Collection, Data Analysis → Results, Recommendations, Implementation

Consumer Market Segmentation in the United States (Partial List)	
Segmentation	**Bases/Descriptors**
Geographic	Region
	Size of city, county, or Standard Metropolitan Statistical Area (SMSA)
	Population density
	Climate
Demographic	Age
	Occupation
	Sex
	Education
	Family size
	Religion
	Family life cycle
	Race
	Income
	Nationality
Psychosocial	Social class
	Lifestyles
	Personality
Cognitive, Affective, Behavioral	Attitudes
	Benefits sought
	Loyalty status
	Readiness stage
	Usage rate
	Perceived risk
	User status
	Innovativeness
	Usage situation
	Involvement

TABLE 4-3

consider what types of consumers are likely to purchase and use a product and how they differ from those less likely to purchase and use a product. In EC, however, geographic segmentation is somewhat less meaningful.

When conducting segmentation, relationships must be checked carefully. For example, consumer lifestyles shape **psychographic segmentation.** That is, consumers are first asked a variety of questions about their lifestyles and then are grouped on the basis of the similarity of their responses. Lifestyles are typically measured by having consumers answer questions about activities such as work and family, interests such as hobbies and community work, preferences, and opinions.

Psychographic segmentation surveys usually generate rich information about consumers (Appendix 4A). Although psychographic segmentation assumes that the more a company knows and understands consumers, the more effectively the company can address its marketing needs, psychographic studies often reach different conclusions about the number and nature of lifestyle categories. For this reason, the validity of psychographic segmentation is sometimes questioned. This information is related to the use of filtering intelligent agents, which are described in the Section 4.8. AOL, for example, is sorting its millions of subscribers into 200 categories based on where they live, their buying habits, demographic profiles, etc. (they buy some of this information from commercial databases). AOL will then use these categories for targeted advertising.

WHY SEGMENTATION?

For years companies used direct mail to contact customers. However, they did it regardless of whether the products or services were appropriate for the individuals on the company's mailing list. The cost of the direct mailings was about $1 per customer, and only 1 to 3 percent responded. This meant that the cost per responding customer was between $33 and $100. Obviously, this type of direct marketing was not cost effective.

In segmentation, the company breaks thousands of customers into smaller segments and tailors its campaigns to each of those segments. Segmentation is done with the aid of tools such as data modeling, warehousing, and mining (e.g., see Levinson 2000 and Berry and Linoff 2000). Using data mining and Web mining, businesses can look at consumer buying patterns to slice segments ever finer. Unfortunately, this is not an easy process, and it requires considerable resources and computer support. Most of the segmentation success stories involve large companies. For example, Royal Bank of Canada segments their 10 million customers at least once a month to determine credit risk, profitability, and so on. Their segmentation is very successful. The response to Royal Bank of Canada advertising campaigns has increased from 3 to 30 percent. Segmentation is less expensive than one-to-one personalization. It is also easier to obtain and maintain the necessary data. Segmentation is important when the Internet goes to localization (e.g., see Chapter 19), for advertisement (e.g., Internet/radio), and in certain languages and countries.

Market research, including EC market research, can be conducted by conventional methods (e.g., Burns and Bush, 1998, and Churchill, 1999), or it can be done with the assistance of the Internet, as discussed next.

Conducting Online Market Research

The Internet is a powerful and cost-effective tool for conducting market research regarding consumer behavior, identifying new markets, and testing consumer interest in new products. Although telephone or shopping mall surveys will continue, interest in interactive Internet research methods is on the rise. Market research that utilizes the Internet is frequently more efficient, faster, and cheaper, and allows the researcher to access a more geographically diverse audience than those found in offline surveys. Furthermore, the size of a market research sample is a key determinant of research design. The larger the sample size, the larger the accuracy and the predictive capabilities of the results. On the Web, market researchers can conduct a very large study much more cheaply than with other methods (20 to 80 percent less). Telephone surveys can cost as much as $50 dollars per respondent. This may be too expensive for a small company that needs several hundred respondents. An online survey will cost a fraction of a similarly sized telephone survey. An overview of Internet market research is provided in Application Case 4.5.

Internet-based market research is often done in an interactive manner by allowing personal contacts with customers, and it provides marketing organizations with greater ability to understand the customer, market, and the competition. For example, it can identify early shifts in products and customer trends, enabling marketers to identify products and marketing opportunities and to develop those products that customers really want to buy. It also tells management when a

Marketing Research on the Internet

Like the Internet itself, performing market research over the Internet is still in its infancy. But as the use of the World Wide Web and online services becomes more habit than hype for a small but desirable fraction of U.S. consumers, online research is becoming a quick, easy, and inexpensive way to tap into their opinions.

Online researchers don't pretend that Web surfers are representative of the U.S. population. Online users tend to be better educated, more affluent, and younger than the average consumer, and a higher proportion are male. However, these are highly important consumers to companies offering products and services online. They are also some of the hardest to reach when conducting a research study. Online surveys and chat sessions (or online focus groups) often prove effective in getting elusive teen, single, affluent, and well-educated audiences to participate.

Online research isn't right for every company or product. For example, mass marketers who need to survey a representative cross-section of the population will find online research methodologies less useful. According to Greenfield Online, an online research company, if the target for the product or service you are testing is inconsistent with the Internet user profile, then it is not the medium to use. For example, you would not test consumer reaction to Campbell's Chunky Soup, but you would test consumer reaction to Campbell's Web site.

When appropriate, online research offers marketers two distinct advantages over traditional surveys and focus groups: speed and cost-effectiveness. Online researchers routinely field quantitative studies and fill response quotas in only a matter of days. Online focus groups require some advance scheduling, but results are practically instantaneous.

Research on the Internet is also relatively inexpensive. Participants can dial in for a focus group from anywhere in the world, eliminating travel, lodging, and facility costs, making online chats cheaper than traditional focus groups. For surveys, the Internet eliminates most of the postage, phone, labor, and printing costs associated with other survey approaches.

However, using the Internet to conduct marketing research does have some drawbacks. One major problem is knowing who's in the sample. Tom Greenbaum, president of Groups Plus, recalls a cartoon in *The New Yorker* in which two dogs are seated at a computer, and one says to the other, "On the Internet, nobody knows you are a dog." "If you can't see a person with whom you are communicating, how do you know who they really are?" Greenbaum says. Moreover, trying to draw conclusions from a "self-selected" sample of online users, those who clicked through to a questionnaire or accidentally landed in a chat room, can be troublesome. "Using a convenient sample is a way to do research quickly, but when you're done, you kind of scratch your head and ask what it means."

To overcome such sample and response problems, NPD Group and many other firms that offer online services construct panels of qualified Web regulars to respond to surveys and participate in online focus groups. NPD's panel consists of 15,000 consumers recruited online and verified by telephone; Greenfield Online picks users from its own database, then calls them periodically to verify that they are who they say they are. Another online research firm, Research Connections, recruits in advance by telephone, taking time to help new users connect to the Internet, if necessary.

APPLICATION CASE   4.5

(continued)

Even when using qualified respondents, focus group responses can lose something in the translation. "You're missing all of the key things that make a focus group a viable method," says Greenbaum. "You may get people online to talk to each other and play off each other, but it's very different to watch people get excited about a concept." Eye contact and body language are two direct, personal interactions of traditional focus group research that are lost in the online world. Although researchers can offer seasoned moderators, the Internet format—running, typed commentary and online "emoticons" (punctuation marks that express emotion, such as :-) to signify happiness)— greatly restrict respondent expressiveness. Similarly, technology limits researchers' capability to show visual cues to research subjects. But just as it hinders the two-way assessment of visual cues, Web research can actually permit some participants the anonymity necessary to elicit an unguarded response. "There are reduced social effects online," Jacobson says. "People are much more honest in this medium."

Some researchers are wildly optimistic about the prospects for market research on the Internet; others are more cautious. One expert predicts that in the next few years, 50 percent of all research will be done on the Internet. "Ten years from now, national telephone surveys will be the subject of research methodology folklore," he proclaims. "That's a little too soon," cautions another expert. "But in 20 years, yes."

Sources: Kotler and Armstrong (1999, p. 115). Portions adapted from Ian P. Murphy, "Interactive Research," *Marketing News*, January 20, 1997, pp. 1, 17. Selected quotes from "NFO Executive Sees Most Research Going to Internet," *Advertising Age*, May 19, 1997, p. 50. Also see Brad Edmondson, "The Wired Bunch," *American Demographics*, June 1997, pp. 10–15, and Charlie Hamlin, "Market Research and the Wired Consumer," *Marketing News*, June 9, 1997, p. 6.

product or a service is no longer popular. To learn more on market research on the Web see the tutorials at *Webmonkey.com*. The following discussion describes online market research methods.

Online Market Research Methods

The Internet provides an efficient channel for fast, cheap, and reliable collection and processing of marketing information, even in a multimedia format. Online research methods range from one-to-one communication with specific customers, usually by e-mail, to moderated focus groups conducted in chat rooms to surveys placed on Web sites. A typical Internet-based market research process is shown in Table 4-4.

Companies can encourage interaction with customers on the Web site by attracting customers with games, prizes (see opening vignette), quizzes, or sweepstakes. Using questionnaires, information is collected from customers before they are allowed to play games, win prizes, or download free software. However, according to the eighth GVU Survey (1998), more than 40 percent of the information people place on questionnaires is inaccurate or incorrect. Therefore, appropriate design of Web questionnaires and incentives for true completion are critical for the

TABLE 4-4

Online Market Research Process and Results

Steps in Collecting Market Research Data	1. Define the research issue and the target market. 2. Identify news groups and Internet communities to study. 3. Identify specific topics for discussion. 4. Subscribe to the pertinent groups; register in communities. 5. Search discussion group topic and content lists to find the target market. 6. Search e-mail discussion group lists. 7. Subscribe to filtering services that monitor groups. 8. Read FAQs and other instructions. 9. Enter chat rooms, whenever possible.
Content of the Research Instrument	1. Post strategic queries to groups. 2. Post surveys on your Web site. Offer rewards for participation. 3. Post strategic queries on your Web site. 4. Post relevant content to groups with a pointer to your Web site survey. 5. Post a detailed survey in special e-mail questionnaires. 6. Create a chat room and try to build a community of consumers.
Target Audience of the Study	1. Compare your audience with the target population. 2. Determine your editorial focus. 3. Determine your content. 4. Determine what Web services to create for each type of audience.

Source: Based on Vassos (1996), pp. 66–68.

validity of the results. Professional pollsters and marketing research companies frequently conduct online voting polls (e.g., see *cnn.com*).

Online market researchers have to address numerous issues. For example, customers may refuse to answer certain questions. Also, the analysis of questionnaires can be lengthy and costly. Furthermore, researchers risk losing people who do not complete online questionnaires because the respondents may not have the latest, fastest computers or a fast Internet connection. For example, long download times and slow processing of Web-based questionnaires lead only to frustration on the part of the customers; it can convince them not to return to a site, leading to lost respondents and future sales.

Web surveys can incorporate radio buttons, data-entry fields, and check boxes, which keep respondents from selecting more than one choice or adding comments where none was intended. Questions are skipped automatically based on respondents' previous answers rather than by written instructions to the respondent. Responses can be validated as they are entered, and other elements can be added to the questionnaire, such as graphics, logos, and links to other Web pages. Also, data re-entry errors are eliminated and statistical analyses can be done in minutes. Data from prospective participants can also be collected across international borders. In addition, the participants have the flexibility of responding at any time, at their own convenience. Real-time information and reporting can also be accomplished.

Conducting Web-Based Surveys.   Web-based surveys are becoming popular among companies and researchers. For example, Mazda North America used a Web-based survey to help design its Miata line. For an introduction on how to conduct Web-based surveys see Lazar and Preece (1999). Free software to create forms and analyze results is available at *zoomerang.com*. For more information and software tools see *websurveyor.com*, *clearlearning.com*, and *tucows.com/webForms*. For hands-on-experiences see Compton (1999).

TRACKING CUSTOMER MOVEMENTS ON THE INTERNET

To avoid some of the problems cited earlier with regards to online surveys, especially the provision of false information, it is advisable to learn about customers by *observing their behavior* rather than by interacting with them and asking them questions. Many marketers keep track of consumers' Web movements using cookie files attached to a user's browser to help track a Web surfer's movements online, whether consumers are aware of it or not. For example, Internet Profile Corporation (IPC) will collect data from a company's client/server logs and provide the company with periodic reports that include demographic data such as where customers come from or how many customers have gone straight from the home page to placing an order. IPC also translates Internet domain names into real company names and includes general and financial corporate information in their reports. Tracking customers' activities without their knowledge or permission may be unethical or even illegal. For a discussion about cookies and tracking see Chapter 17.

Limitations of Online Research

Concerns have been expressed over the potential lack of representativeness in samples composed of online users. Online shoppers tend to be primarily "baby busters" and "baby boomers"—wealthy, employed, and well educated. Although this is good for some markets, the research results may not extendable to other markets. Another important issue concerns the lack of clear understanding of the online communication process and how online respondents think and interact in cyberspace.

Online research is not suitable for every customer or product. Although the Web user demographic is rapidly diversifying, it is still skewed toward certain population groups, such as those with Internet access. If a company manufactures a consumer product such as laundry detergent, Internet research may not be an ideal research tool, because it may not reach enough of the company's target market.

Depending on the demographic or target audience a company wants, it is important that the company verify who the target audience is so it can go after the right kind of sampling. Web-based surveys typically have a lower response rate than e-mail surveys, and there is no respondent control for public surveys. If your target respondents are allowed to be anonymous, it may encourage them to be more truthful in their opinions. The same attribute, however, may prevent researchers from knowing whether the respondent is projecting a false online image. It is not clear yet what kind of effect the electronic medium has on respondents' thinking and attentiveness—whether it is a stimulation or an impediment. Finally, there are still concerns about securing the transmission of information, which may also have an impact on the truthfulness of the respondents.

Data Mining

Customer data accumulates daily in an ever increasing quantity. Large companies such as retailers, telecommunication companies, PC makers, and car manufacturers build large data warehouses to store such information (e.g., see Gray and Watson, 1998). To sift through the large amounts of data (e.g., in order to analyze buying habits), marketers use data mining tools.

Data mining derives its name from the similarities between searching for valuable business information in a large database and mining a mountain for a vein of valuable ore. Both processes require either sifting through an immense amount of material or intelligently probing it to find exactly where the value resides. Given databases of sufficient size and quality, data mining technology can generate new business opportunities by providing these capabilities:

- **Automated prediction of trends and behaviors.** Data mining automates the process of finding predictive information in large databases. Questions that traditionally required extensive hands-on analysis can now be answered directly and quickly from the data. A typical example of a predictive problem is targeted marketing. Data mining can use data on past promotional mailings to identify the targets most likely to respond favorably to future mailings. See Application Case 4.6.
- **Automated discovery of previously unknown patterns.** Data mining tools identify previously hidden patterns. An example of pattern discovery is the analysis of retail sales data to identify seemingly unrelated products that are often purchased together, such as baby diapers and beer. Other pattern discovery targets include detecting fraudulent credit card transactions and identifying anomalous data that may represent data entry keying errors.

APPLICATION CASE   4.6

British Telecom Uses Data Mining

British Telecom is a large telecommunications company in the United Kingdom. Its 1.5 million business users make about 90 million calls a day. The company provides 4,500 products and services. The company was looking for the best way to reach out and touch individual customers. The solution was a customer data warehouse. The company was using neural computing technology known as MPP (massively parallel processing). The data warehouse contained initially 3 GB of RAM. The company uses the system to analyze customer buying habits in order to better understand customer needs and target marketing opportunities. Using the system, the company identified purchasing profiles for individual products, packages of products, and customers. One area is to identify customers that could be at risk of capture by the competition. Data mining is especially useful for identifying trends in products that have a high sales value, such as intranets. This improves the relationship between marketing and sales. Now the sales force is guided on where to put their resources. Prior to data mining, marketing involved analyzing data that were 6 months to 1 year old. Now sales people can trust marketing information because they have almost real-time marketing information.

The following are other characteristics and objectives of data mining:

1. Relevant data are often difficult to locate in very large databases.
2. In some cases, the data are consolidated in data warehouses and data marts; in others they are kept in databases or in Internet and intranet servers. Data mining tools help remove the information "ore" buried in corporate files or archived in public records.

3. The "miner" is often an end user empowered by "data drills" and other power query tools to ask ad hoc questions and get answers quickly, with little or no programming skills.
4. "Striking it rich" often involves finding unexpected, valuable results.
5. Data mining tools are easily combined with spreadsheets and other end-user software development tools; therefore, the mined data can be analyzed and processed quickly and easily.
6. Data mining yields five types of information: (a) association, (b) sequences, (c) classifications, (d) clusters, and (e) forecasting.

Data miners can use several tools and techniques. The most well-known tools of data mining are:

- **Neural computing.** Neural computing is a machine learning approach by which historical data can be examined for patterns. Users equipped with neural computing tools can go through huge databases and, for example, identify potential customers for a new product or search for companies whose profiles suggest that they are headed for bankruptcy.
- **Intelligent agents.** One of the most promising approaches to retrieving information from the Internet or from intranet-based databases is through the use of intelligent agents.
- **Association analysis.** This approach uses a specialized set of algorithms that sorts through large data sets and expresses statistical rules among items.

It is estimated (e.g., *gartnergroup.com*) that at least half of all the *Fortune* 1000 companies worldwide use data mining technologies. Data mining can be very helpful as shown by the examples in Table 4-5.

WEB MINING

Data mining can also be used to analyze Web sites. **Web mining** is the application of data mining techniques to discover actionable and meaningful patterns, profiles, and trends from Web resources. The term Web mining is being used in two different ways. The first, *Web content mining,* is very similar to text mining. It is the process of information discovery from millions of Web documents. The second, *Web usage mining,* is the process of analyzing Web access logs (or other information connected to user browsing and access patterns) on one or more Web localities.

TABLE 4-5

Data Mining Applications

Industry	Applications
Retailing and sales distribution	Predicting sales, determining inventory levels and schedules.
Banking	Forecasting levels of bad loans and fraudulent credit card use, predicting credit card spending by new customers; predicting customer response to offers.
Airlines	Capturing data on where customers are flying and the ultimate destination of passengers who change carriers in midflight; thus, airlines can identify popular locations that they do not service and check the feasibility of adding routes to capture lost business.
Broadcasting	Predicting what is best to air during prime time and how to maximize returns by interjecting advertisements.
Marketing	Classifying customer demographics that can be used to predict which customers will respond to a mailing or buy a particular product.

Web mining is used in the following areas:

- Information filtering (e-mail, magazines, newspapers)
- Surveillance (Internet competitors, patents)
- Mining Web access logs
- Assisted browsing
- Services fighting crime on the Internet

Web mining is critical for EC due to the large number of visitors to EC sites (about 2 billion during the Christmas 2000 season). For additional discussion of Web mining see Parsa (1999) and *sas.com*.

4.8   INTELLIGENT AGENTS IN CUSTOMER-RELATED APPLICATIONS

As the number of customers, products, vendors, and information increases, it becomes uneconomical, or even impossible, to manually match customers and products and consider all relevant information. The practical solution to handle the information overload is to use intelligent and software agents. In Chapter 3, we demonstrated how intelligent agents help in finding and comparing products. Intelligent agents, and their subset software agents (Appendix D), are computer programs that help users conduct routine tasks, search and retrieve information, support decision making, and act as domain experts. Agents sense the environment and act autonomously without human intervention. This results in a significant saving of time (up to 99 percent) to users. There are various types of agents, ranging from those with no intelligence (software agents) to learning agents, which exhibit some intelligent behavior. (see special issue of *International Journal of Electronic Commerce*, Spring 2000)

Agents are used to support many EC tasks. For example, Wang (1999) describes eight types of agents that assist B2B EC. Maes et al. (1999) provides an overview of EC agents, some of which are described in this section. One of the primary reasons for using such agents is to overcome the tremendous amount of information overload. When going through the purchasing decision process described earlier, for example, a customer must examine large numbers of alternatives, each of which is surrounded by considerable amounts of information.

In this section we will concentrate on intelligent agents that assist customers. However, before we do delve into the topic, it will be beneficial to distinguish between search engines, which can be classified as software agents, and the more intelligent types of agents.

A search engine is a computer program that can automatically contact other network resources on the Internet, search for specific information or keywords, and report the results. For example, people tend to ask for information (e.g., requests for product information or pricing) in the same general manner. This type of request is repetitive, and answering such requests is costly when done by a human. Search engines deliver answers economically and efficiently by matching questions with FAQ templates, which include standard questions and "canned" answers to them.

Unlike search engines, an intelligent agent can do more than just "search and match." For example, it can monitor movement on a Web site to check whether a customer seems lost or ventures into areas that may not fit his or her profile, and the agent can notify the customer and provide assistance. Depending on their level of intelligence, agents can do many other things, some of which are demonstrated here. Of the many agent applications, we cover only several representative ones.

A Framework for Classifying EC Agents

A logical way to classify EC agents is by relating them to the consumer purchasing decision-making process (Figure 4-3). This process has been modified slightly as shown in Figure 4-7.

Figure 4-7	The Purchasing Decision-Making Process: Agent Classification

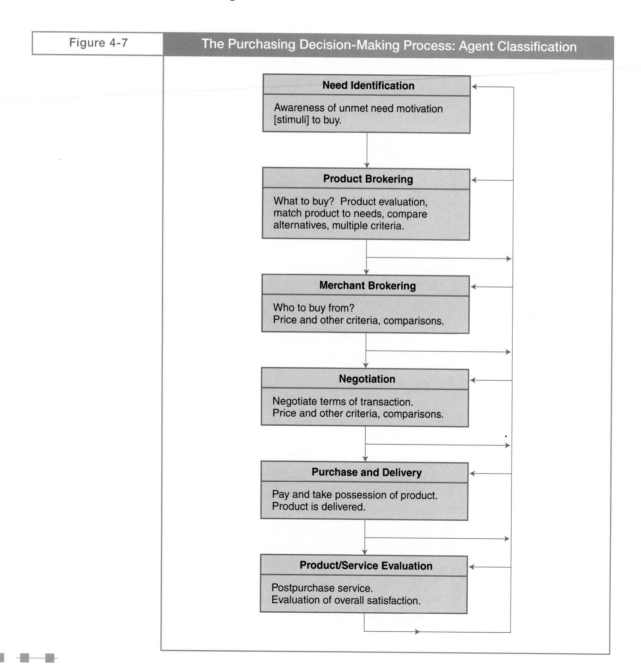

Need Identification

Awareness of unmet need motivation [stimuli] to buy.

Product Brokering

What to buy? Product evaluation, match product to needs, compare alternatives, multiple criteria.

Merchant Brokering

Who to buy from?
Price and other criteria, comparisons.

Negotiation

Negotiate terms of transaction.
Price and other criteria, comparisons.

Purchase and Delivery

Pay and take possession of product.
Product is delivered.

Product/Service Evaluation

Postpurchase service.
Evaluation of overall satisfaction.

Need Identification

Agents can assist the buyer with need identification by providing product information and stimuli. For example, *Amazon.com* provides its customers with an agent that continuously monitors sets of data (such as the arrival of new books) and notifies customers when a book in their area of interest arrives. Similar agents watch for stocks to go below or above a certain price level, sending the customer an e-mail when that level is reached. *Expedia.com* notifies customers about low airfares to a customer's desired destination whenever they become available. *AuctionRover.com* watches auctions. Need identification is frequently combined with product brokering, since some agents that find products also compare prices.

Several commercial agents can facilitate need recognition directly or indirectly. Here are several examples:

- *Salesmountain.com* helps people who are looking for certain items when they are put "on sale." If a customer specifies what he or she wants, *salesmountain.com* will send notification. General browsing is also available to boost need recognition.
- Likemind at *discogs.com* helps people decide what music is available to sample and buy.
- *Findgift.com* asks customers questions about the person they are buying a gift for and helps the customer hunt down the perfect present.
- *Querybot.com/shopping* not only looks for deals, but also finds related information such as newsgroup discussions about the type of product for which the consumer is searching.

Product Brokering

Once a need is established, customers search for a product (or service) that will satisfy this need. Several agents are available to assist customers with this task.

The pioneering agent in this category was Firefly. This agent, which was purchased by Microsoft and is no longer available independently, initially helped users find music they were likely to enjoy. Firefly (and similar agents) use a **collaborative filtering** process to build profiles of people who visit a Web site. Firefly provided users with a "passport" that identified them when they visited sites participating in the Firefly program and recommended products/services to them. Based on people's likes (favorite movies, music, interests), Firefly helped marketers predict what customers were likely to want next. This allowed marketers to reach out to consumers with a customized pitch that was cheaper and more effective than mass advertising. A similar agent from AOL is Personalogic. It made product recommendations based on the prioritization of attributes such as price and delivery time by users (see Internet Exercise 10).

Personalogic and similar agents can provide benefits to individuals who are not sure what to buy. For example, they can listen to recommended CD sound samples and then buy the CDs while they are still online. Furthermore, some agents can even match people that have similar interest profiles. Even more ambitious agents try to predict which brands of computers, cars, and other goods will appeal to customers, based on preferences in entirely different product categories such as wine, music, or breakfast cereal.

Webdoggie (from MIT Media Laboratory) recommends Web documents and NewsWeeder (from *cs.cmu.edu*) finds news articles based on monitored users' reading interests and/or rating of past articles on a 1 to 5 scale provided by users. Both are examples of agents of product brokering.

Merchant Brokering

Once a customer knows what product he or she wants, the customer needs to find *where* to buy it. BargainFinder (from Andersen Consulting) was the pioneering agent in this category. The agent, used in online CD shopping, queried the price of a specific CD from a number of online vendors and returned a list of prices. However, this system has encountered problems because vendors who do not want to compete on price only have managed to block out the agent's requests. Today's version is at *cdrom-guide.com/bargainfinder.htm*.

The blocking problem has been solved by Jango (*jango.excite.com*) and other new agents. Jango originates the requests from the user's site instead of from Jango's. This way vendors have no way of determining whether the request is from a real customer or from the agent. Jango is also more complete than BargainFinder, because it includes more categories of products. Furthermore, Jango provides product reviews. Several other agents compete with Jango. They include Inktomi Shopping Agent, My Simon (*mysimon.com*), and Junglee (of *Amazon.com*).

PRODUCT (SERVICES) COMPARISON AGENTS

Large numbers of agents enable consumers to perform all kinds of comparisons. Here are some examples:

- *Allbookstores.com* and *bestbookbuys.com* are two of several agents that help consumers find the lowest prices of books available online.
- *Bottomdollar.com*, *compare.net*, *pricewonders.com*, *shopper.com*, *smarts.com* and *bargainvillage.com* are examples (out of several dozen) of agents that suggest brands and compare prices once consumers specify what they want to buy.
- *Buyerzone.com* is a B2B portal at which businesses can find the best prices of many products and services.
- *Pricescan.com* guides consumers to the best prices on thousands of computer hardware and software products.

A special agent-based mediator worth mentioning is Kasbah (from the MIT Media Lab.). With Kasbah, users who want to buy or sell a product assign the task to an agent, who is then sent out to proactively seek buyers or sellers. In creating the agent, users must specify constraints including the desired price, highest (or lowest) acceptable price, and a date by which the transaction should be completed. The agent's goal is to complete an acceptable transaction based on these parameters. This agent can also negotiate on the part of the buyers, as will be discussed next.

Negotiation

The concept of "market" implies negotiation, mostly about prices. While many retail stores engage in fixed-price selling, many small retail stores and most markets (especially in developing countries) use negotiations extensively. In B2B transactions, negotiation is very common. The benefit of dynamically negotiating a price is that the decision is shifted from the seller to the marketplace. In a fixed-price situation, if the seller fixes a price that is too high, sales will suffer. If the price is set too low, profits will be lower.

Negotiations, however, are time consuming and often disliked by individual customers who cannot negotiate properly because they lack information about the marketplace and prices. Many vendors do not like to negotiate either. Therefore, electronic support of negotiation can be extremely useful (for examples see Beer et al. 1999).

Kasbah, an experimental program, also used intelligent agents in the negotiation process. Kasbah agents negotiated with each other following specific strategies assigned by their creators. However, this agent's usefulness was limited by the fact that price was the only parameter considered. A more capable agent called Tete-@-tete was developed by the creators of Kasbah.

Tete-@-tete was unique compared to other online negotiation systems because Tete-@-tete agents negotiated a number of different parameters: price, warranty, delivery time, service contracts, return policy, loan options, and other value-added services. Another innovative feature of this system was that, unlike the Kasbah where negotiation was conducted along the lines of simple increase or decrease functions, negotiation by Tete-@-tete agents was argumentative. This system integrated five stages of the decision purchasing model shown in Table 4-2. This integrative approach made Tete-@-tete the most advanced agent-based environment available in 2001.

Agents can negotiate in pairs, or one agent can negotiate for a buyer with several sellers' agents. In such a case, the contact is done with each seller's agent individually, but the buyer's agent can conduct comparisons (Yan et al. 2000).

Purchase and Delivery

Agents are used extensively during the actual purchase, including arranging payment and delivery with the customer. For example, if a customer makes a mistake when completing an electronic order form, an agent will point it out immediately. When a customer buys stocks, for example, the agent will tell the customer when a stock he or she wants to buy on margin is not marginable, or when the customer does not have sufficient funds. Delivery options at *Amazon.com*, for example, are posted by agents and the total cost is calculated in real-time.

After Sale Service and Evaluation

Agents can be used to facilitate after sale service. For example, automatic answering agents that send e-mail responses are usually productive in answering customer queries. Agents can also monitor automobile usage and notify customers when it is time to take a car in for periodic maintenance. Agents that facilitate feedback from customers are also useful.

Some agents support several of the decision steps seen in Figure 4-7. For example, Answer Agent and Advice Agent (*firepond.com*) deal with e-mail from customers, providing replay to queries and advice. Other EC agents are described next.

Other EC Agents

A large number of agents support many EC activities ranging from advertising to payment systems. For lists of EC agents see *botspot.com* and *agents.umbc.edu* (look at Agents 101 Tutorial). For a comprehensive guide to EC agents see Peter Finger's paper "A CEO's Guide to EC Using Intelligent Agents" available at *verizon.com*. Here are just few examples:

- BullsEye2 (from *intelliseek.com*) is an intelligent desktop portal. This is a free service that delivers personalized content to users. A similar agent is Portico (see demo at *genmagic.com*).
- VReps (from *neuromedia.com*) provides tools for companies to create virtual online sales and customer service representatives who dynamically interact with customers in real-time, natural-language dialog for EC support (try to converse with their demo agent, Red).
- *Webassured.com* offers a service that is designed to dramatically increase the level of trust, reliability, and brand recognition between buyers and sellers.
- *Resumix.com* (now part of TMP worldwide) is an application that wanders the Web looking for Web pages containing résumé information. If it identifies a page as being a résumé, it attempts to extract pertinent information from the page, such as the e-mail address, phone number, skill descriptions, and location. The resulting database is used to connect job seekers with recruiters.

AUCTION SUPPORT AGENTS

Several agents support auction participants. The most common support is through *auction aggregators,* such as *auctionrover.com*, *rubylane.com*, *auctionwatch*, and *auction-octopus*. These sites tell consumers where and when certain items will be auctioned. Some aggregators provide real-time access to auctions.

Auctions are one of the most popular activities on the Web because they easily overcome the problem of being physically dispersed. However, almost all auctions require users to personally execute the bidding. This is not the case with AuctionBot, which allows users to create intelligent agents that will take care of the bidding process. With AuctionBot, users create auction agents by specifying a number of parameters that vary depending on the type of the auction selected. After that, it is up to the agent to manage the auction until a final price is met or the deadline of the offer is reached.

FRAUD PROTECTION AGENTS

Fraud is a big problem in EC since buyers cannot see the products or the sellers. Several vendors offer agent-based fraud detection systems. One such system is eFalcon from *hnc.com*. It is based on pattern recognition driven by neural computing.

CHARACTER-BASED INTERACTIVE AGENTS

Several intelligent agents enhance customer service by interacting with customers via characters. Animation characters are software agents with personalities. These agents are not intelligent; rather they are versatile and employ friendly front ends to communicate with the users. These animated agents are called **avatars**. Avatars are computer representations of users in a computer-generated 3-D world. Advanced avatars can "speak" and exhibit behaviors such as gestures and facial expressions. They can be fully automated to act like robots. The purpose of avatars is to introduce believable emotions, so that the agents can gain credibility with users. Avatars are considered a part of **social computing**, an approach aimed at making the human–computer interface more natural. Studies conducted at *extempo.com* showed that interactive characters can improve customer satisfaction and retention by offering personalized, one-to-one service. They can also help companies to get to know their customers.

"Virtual pets" are an interesting subcategory of animated agents. Virtual pet owners are required to feed and clean up after their virtual pets. The handheld computer toy, "Tamagotchi, the cute little egg," is probably the best known virtual pet system. Another example is "Dogz and Catsz" (from PF Magic Inc.), which installs a virtual pet on a PC.

Many Web sites use characters to interact with customers. Here are some examples:

- The Personal Job Search Agent (at *monster.com*) helps users find a job, for free.
- Digit is an interactive agent that can speak and move around at BankOne online services (*bankone.com*). Digit interacts with site visitors, assisting them as they explore the site.
- Max is a virtual guide who helps visitors who wish to learn more about products and tools available at *extempo.com* (a vendor specializing in avatars).
- Merlin guides visitors who want to visit Web sites of shops, restaurants, and other enterprises on San Francisco's Haight Street (see *extempo.com*).
- *Zoesis.com* created an interactive, animated theme park. The characters in the park have autonomy and can respond to actions.

For additional information on interactive characters see Hayes-Roth et al. (1999).

LEARNING AGENTS

A learning agent (also called a remembrance) is capable of learning individuals' preferences and making suggestions (see Huang, 1999). An example learning agent is IBM's Memory Agent. Memory Agent uses a neural network technique called associative memory, which learns by creating a knowledge base of attributes of cases.

A similar agent is Learn Sesame (from Open Sesame). This agent uses learning theory by monitoring customers' interactions. It learns customers' interests, preferences, and behavior and delivers customized services to them accordingly. Groaphens, from Netperceptions, personalizes content and creates customer loyalty programs with learning agent technology. Finally, Plangent (from Toshiba) is an agent that "moves around and thinks." It is classified as a "knowledge" agent because it performs tasks relying on a knowledge base of "actions."

ORGANIZATIONAL BUYER BEHAVIOR

To end the discussion of consumer behavior and market research, let's look at an organization and a customer. Organizations may buy the same products or services that individuals do. For example, both may buy the same book, camera, or computer. Although the number of organizational buyers is much smaller than the

Major Characteristics of Retail Buyers Versus Organizational Buyers		
Characteristic	**Retail Buyers**	**Organizational Buyers**
Demand	Individual	Organizational
Purchase volume	Smaller	Larger
Number of customers	Many	Fewer
Location of buyers	Dispersed	Geographically concentrated
Distribution structure	More indirect	More direct
Nature of buying	More personal	More professional
Nature of buying influence	Single	Multiple
Type of negotiations	Simple	More complex
Use of reciprocity	No	Yes
Use of leasing	Lesser	Greater
Primary promotional method	Advertising	Personal selling

TABLE 4-6

Source: From *Marketing*, 4th Edition by C. Lamb, J. F. Hair, and C. McDaniel © 1998. Reprinted with permission of South-Western College Publishing, a division of Thomson Learning. Fax 800-730-2215.

number of individual buyers, their transaction volumes are far larger, and the terms of negotiations and purchasing are more complex. In addition, the purchasing process itself, as seen in Chapter 6, may be more important than the purchasing process of an individual customer. Also, the organization's buyer may be a group. Factors that affect individual consumer behavior and organizational buying behavior are quite different, as seen in Table 4-6.

A BEHAVIORAL MODEL OF ORGANIZATIONAL BUYERS

The behavior of an organizational buyer can be described by a model similar to that of an individual buyer, which was shown in Figure 4-1. However, some influencing variables differ (e.g., the family and Internet communities may have no influence). What is added to this model (see Figure 4-8) is an organizational module that includes the organization purchasing guidelines and constraints (e.g., contracts) and the system used. Also, interpersonal influences such as authority are added. Finally, the possibility of group decision making must be considered. For a detailed discussion of organizational buyers see Chapter 6 of Kotler and Armstrong (1999).

Management Issues

The following issues are germane to management:

1. **Understanding consumers.** Understanding the customers, specifically what customer needs are and responding to those needs, is the most critical part of consumer-centered marketing. To excel, companies need to satisfy and retain customers, and management must monitor the whole process of marketing, sales, maintenance, and follow-up service. It is difficult to justify the expense of such an approach, since the benefits are mostly intangible.
2. **Consumers and technology.** Complex lives and lifestyles, a more diverse and fragmented population, and the power of technology all contribute to changing consumer needs and expectations in the digital age. Moreover, consumers today want more control over their time. In certain societies, EC has become more and more popular because it saves *time,* not because it saves

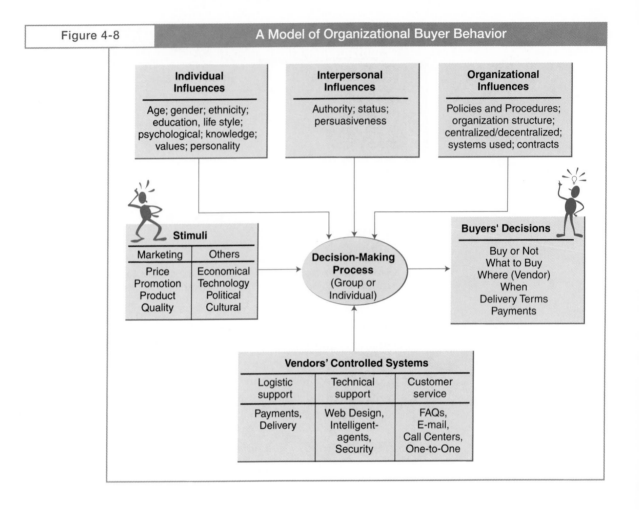

Figure 4-8 — A Model of Organizational Buyer Behavior

money. Technology provides consumers the ability to get customized products quickly. Vendors should understand these relationships and utilize them
in their marketing efforts.

3. **Response time.** Acceptable standards for response in customer service must
be set. For example, customers want acknowledgment of their query within
24 to 48 hours. Most companies want to provide this response time and do it
at a minimum cost. Offering services online allows companies to meet customers' needs and cut costs. The investment in technology may be offset by a
reduction in the number of customer service representatives needed and,
more important, in savings resulting from customer retention.

4. **Intelligent agents.** Any company engaged in EC must examine the possibility of using intelligent agents to enhance customer service, and possibly to
support market research. Commercial agents are available on the market at a
reasonable cost. For heavy usage, companies may develop customized agents.

5. **Market research.** B2C requires extensive market research. This research is
not easy to do, nor it is inexpensive. Deciding whether to outsource or have
a market research staff is a major management issue. Customer acquisition
is a major success factor in B2C. Without a large number of customers, an
EC business will not survive.

6. **CRM and EC integration.** Management must consider the integration of EC and CRM. Market research and service is done online as well as offline. If properly integrated, a beneficial synergy will occur. Otherwise, conflicts may arise.

7. **Measuring customers' satisfaction from a Web site.** This is a key issue and it can be done in many ways. Many vendors can assist you; some provide free software. For discussion see *epulse.com* and *e-satisfy.com*.

Summary

In this chapter, you learned about the following EC issues as they relate to the learning objectives:

1. **Essentials of consumer behavior.** Consumer behavior in EC is similar to that of any consumer behavior. It describes a stimuli-based process-purchasing decision model. However, it also includes a significant vendor-controlled component that deals with logistics, technology, and customer service.

2. **Characteristics of customers.** Customers are the most critical factor for the success of EC. Knowing who the customers are, what they need, and how to address those needs is important. Although most of the available data relates to Internet surfing in general rather than specifically to EC, we can make EC inferences from general Internet usage data.

3. **Consumer decision-making process.** Understanding the process of consumers buying decision making online, and formulating an appropriate strategy to influence their behavior, is the essence of marketing efforts. For each step in the process, sellers can develop appropriate strategies. Also, it is possible to use intelligent agents to automate some activities in these steps. Various models are available to describe or explain this process.

4. **Building one-to-one relationships with customers.** In EC there is an opportunity to build one-to-one relationships that do not exist in other marketing systems. Of special interest are the approaches to boost loyalty and increase trust. Product customization, personalized service, and getting the customer involved (e.g., in feedback, order tracking, and so on) are all practical in cyberspace.

5. **Implementing customer service.** Retaining customers by satisfying their needs is in the core of customer service. Customer service on the Web is provided by e-mail, on the corporate Web site, in customized Web pages, in integrated call centers, and by intelligent agents. Online customer service is media rich, effective, and less expensive than the services offered offline.

6. **EC market research.** Understanding market segmentation and grouping consumers into different categories is a necessity of effective EC market research. Several methods of Internet market research are available. They provide for fast, economical, and accurate research due to the large samples involved. The two major approaches for data collection are to get information voluntarily or to use cookies to track customers' movements on the Internet. Finally, Internet-based market research has several limitations, including data accuracy.

7. **Intelligent agents.** Gathering and interpreting data about consumer purchasing behavior can be done with intelligent software agents. Intelligent agents can also generate automatic e-mail replays, analyze customers' movements on

the Internet, and support customer service and market research. Advanced agents can even learn about customer behavior and needs.

8. **Organizational buyer behavior model.** Venders need to understand how organizational buyers make purchasing decisions. Organizational policies and constraints and interpersonal variables, such as authority and status, may affect the decision.

Key Terms

Avatars	Market research
Call centers	Merchant brokering
Collaborative filtering	Metrics
Consumer behavior	One-to-one marketing
Consumer decision making	Online market research
Customer loyalty	Product brokering
Customer Relationship Management (CRM)	Social computing
Data mining	Relationship marketing
E-loyalty	Segmentation
E-service	Software agents
Filtering process	Telewebs
Intelligent agents	Trust
Learning agents	User profile

Questions for Review

1. Describe the typical Internet user profile.
2. List the typical characteristics of individual retail buyers.
3. Describe the online purchasing decision-making process.
4. Explain the concept of e-loyalty.
5. Describe trust in EC and how to increase it.
6. Explain how a call center is enhanced with Internet technology.
7. List typical examples of intelligent agents for consumers and their benefits.
8. Define market segmentation and provide examples.
9. Explain the goals of market research.
10. List the major methods of Internet-based market research.
11. Provide an example of an online market research tool.
12. Define data mining and describe its use for market research.

Questions for Discussion

1. What would you do to maintain customer loyalty in the highly competitive online retail clothing industry?
2. When would a consumer deviate from the standard decision-making process? Provide specific examples and explain what you would do as a marketer in each case.
3. Explain how to control, if possible, ever-increasing customer expectations for EC services. Provide some examples.
4. What are potential limitations of online market research? Can they be overcome? How?

5. What would you tell an executive officer of a bank about several critical success factors for increasing customer loyalty by using the Internet?
6. What can a vendor do to increase the trust level of online customers?
7. Why is data mining becoming an important element in EC? How is it used to learn about consumer behavior? How can it be used to facilitate customer service?
8. Compare organizational purchasing decisions to those of an individual.
9. CRM was initially created for off-line operations. Explain why it is wise to integrate it with EC.
10. Distinguish between one-to-one marketing and CRM.
11. Explain the need for intelligent agents in EC.

Internet Exercises

1. Compare the following two online grocery stores to see how they stack up against their brick-and-mortar competitors in terms of cost of service and overall quality: *netgrocer.com* and *mypcgrocer.com*.
2. Go to *priceline.com*. Review the strategies used to attract and retain customers. What additional efforts could *priceline.com* exercise to retain its customers?
3. Find recent Web-based call center and automatic response products. Start with *amdocs.com* (customers' success stories), and *eGain.com*.
4. Survey two department store Web sites, such as JCPenney (*jcpenney.com*) or Sears (*sears.com*). Write a report that highlights the different ways they provide customer service online.
5. Surf the Home Depot Web site (*homedepot.com*) and check whether (and how) the company provides service to customers with different skill levels.
6. Investigate whether a brand name plays a major role in maintaining online customer loyalty compared with traditional shopping in the coffee and tea markets. Check *starbucks.com* as an example.
7. Enter *Amazon.com* and *ups.com* and identify all of the free customer services each provides.
8. Examine a market research Web site such as *acnielsen.com* and discuss what might motivate a consumer to provide answers to market research questions.
9. Surf *e-land.com* and list the types of consumer information you can collect from the site.
10. Enter *mysimon.com* and share your experiences about how the information you provide might be used by the company for marketing in a specific industry (e.g., the clothing market).
11. Get a guest pass from *jup.com* and cruise the site. Examine the types of data they gather. Are there any implications for privacy?
12. When would market research data not be quite valid? Consider a global EC case by looking at World Market Watch (*wmw.com*).
13. Enter *netdialog.com* and review the services they provided. Sign up for their gold paper: online customer management. Prepare a summary of the paper.
14. Go to *Reflect.com*. Examine how this company provides a personalized service.
15. Examine *ecommerceandmarketing.com* and *lycos.com* and identify new developments in product and service personalization.

Team Assignments and Role Playing

1. Each team member should select an overnight delivery service company (FedEx, DHL, UPS, and so on) and identify all of the online customer service features it offers. Write a report on common and unique services in the industry.

2. Have each team member apply demographic and psychosocial grouping to three different geographical areas of population. Where would you find such data? If no data are available, how would you apply Internet technology to collect data?

3. Find five companies whose business is to enhance trust (start with *broadvision.com*, *iescrow.com*, and *etrust.com*). Each team member should examine one or two companies and identify the services they offer. Prepare a report that describes how trust can be built using third-party solutions. Each group will demonstrate that their company is the best.

4. Go to *webmonkey.com* and find the market research tutorial. Each team member should explore two different tools. As a group, compare the tools and prepare a written report.

REAL-WORLD CASE: Kansas City Power & Light

Due to recent deregulation and competition, power companies can rapidly lose market share. A critical issue for their survival is to provide better and more competitive customer service. Kansas City Power & Light (KCPL) is no exception. The company has built a Web site (*kcpl.com*) that lets more than 400,000 customers check their own power usage, pay their bills, learn how to keep electric costs down, and much more. Douglas Morgan, vice president of information technologies, says, "We have competitors with offices in our city, and they are trying to lure our customers. We believe the Net is going to be a very positive force in expanding our products and services. It's still far too soon to tell if KCPL's Web initiative will help the century-old utility hang on to customers. . . ."

At first, no one at KCPL understood the difference between publishing in hard copy and publishing online. So they just took printed brochures and put them on the Web site. They soon found that the static Web site was ineffective. So they added a place for press releases. Then the company started to learn a great deal about what works online and what does not. For example, they placed links on the lower left-hand side (it is better to place them on the right). They realized they must communicate directly with customers and try to learn what kind of value-added services might be made available through the Web. What began as a relatively modest effort to get something up online — and perhaps sell some additional products and services — expanded as the company learned what customers wanted.

"The customers started to drive the Web site development toward being able to pay their bills online. Another thing that came out of those discussions was that the customers were aware of what deregulation meant. The customers were looking to KCPL to provide them with information to help them decide what to do." Morgan realized that when it came to giving customers immediate feedback on their use of electric power, KCPL can have an advantage over virtually all other power companies. In 1994 the company had invested heavily in the installation of a wireless, automatic meter-reading system that gave utility employees sitting in front of computers at corporate headquarters real-time access to meter readings for more than 400,000 businesses and homes. Unlike most automatic meter-reading systems, which check power usage only once a month, KCPL's system could check any meter anytime. By hooking that data into the Web site, the utility company could give customers with Internet access the ability to monitor their power usage in real-time. The site provides formulas to figure out the average cost per hour needed to operate appliances and suggestions for saving energy. Customers can determine if their bill is higher than it should be. This application, called AccountLink, was phased in to residential and commercial customers in 1998.

When there is a problem or a disruption in service, KCPL also turns to the Web. The automated meter-reading system can tell KCPL repair units if a problem is in the customer's house or in the wires leading to the house. Each meter is equipped with a "last gasp" alarm, which alerts customer representatives when the flow of power stops. The wireless system saves the company about 105,000 field service trips a year.

The site also posts some marketing and sales information that had previously been available only in hard copy. There is a section for information of special interest to senior citizens and special needs customers, and there are explanations about the cold-weather program, which helps protect customers from electric power termination during the winter months. By mid-1998, the KCPL site had signed up more than 1,800 residential users and 800 commercial users for AccountLink.

Questions for the case

1. Carefully review the actions KCPL has taken to address customer service issues and relate them to the set of guidelines presented in the customer service section of the chapter. Are there any additional actions KCPL can implement to enhance the level of customer service?

2. Examine the KCPL Web site (*kcpl.com*) and discuss how effective and customer friendly it is. Can you suggest any improvements?

3. Compare this case with the opening vignette and comment.

4. How is KCPL developing one-to-one relationships with its consumers?

5. Should the Web site be integrated with the company's telephone-based call center? Would the costs be justified?

Sources: Condensed from *cioMagazine*, July 1, 1998 and from *kcpl.com*, January 2001.

REFERENCES AND BIBLIOGRAPHY

Allen, C. D. and B. Yaeckel. *Internet World Guide to One-to-One Marketing* (Internet World Series). New York: John Wiley & Sons, 1998.

Bayne, K. M. "Humanize Your Web Customer Service," *e-Business Advisor* (August 2000).

Beer, M., et al. "Negotiation in Multi-agents Systems," *Knowledge Engineering Review,* vol. 14, no. 3.

Benassi, P. "TRUSTe: An Online Privacy Seal Program," *Communications of the ACM,* vol. 42, no. 2 (1999).

Berry, J. A. and G. Linoff. *Data Mining Techniques for Marketing, Sales and Customer Support,* 2nd edition. New York: Wiley, 2000.

Blankenship A. B., et al. *State of the Art of Marketing Research.* Lincolnwood, Illinois: NTC Business Books, 1998.

Bradshaw, J. *Software Agents.* Boston, MA: MIT Press, 1997.

Brown, S. A. *Customer Relationship Management: Linking People, Process, and Technology.* New York: Wiley, 2000.

Burns, A. C. and R. F. Bush. *Marketing Research*, 2nd edition. Upper Saddle River, New Jersey: Prentice Hall, 1998.

Butler, P. and J. Peppard. "Consumer Purchasing on the Internet: Processes and Prospects," *European Management Journal* (October 1998).

Churchill, G. *Marketing Research*, 7th edition. Fort Worth, Texas: The Dryden Press, 1999.

Compton, J. "Instant Customer Feedback," *PC Computing* (December 1999).

Dalgleish, J. *Customer-Effective Web Sites.* Upper Saddle River, New Jersey: Pearson, 2000.

DePalma, D. "Meet Your Customers' Need Through Cultural Marketing," *e-Business Advisor* (October 2000).

Dickson, G. W. and G. DeSanctis, editors. *Information Technology and the Future Enterprise: New Models for Management.* Upper Saddle River, New Jersey: Prentice Hall, 2001.

East, R. *Consumer Behavior.* London: Prentice Hall, 1997.

Eemke, R., et al. *E-service: 24 Ways to Keep Your Customers When the Competition Is Just a Click Away.* New York: AMACOM, 2000.

Fluss, D., et al. "Internet-Based Customer Service: Miracle or Mirage," *Journal of Customer Loyalty,* Issue 14 (2000).

Fram, E. and E. Grady. "Internet Shoppers: Is There a Surfer Gender Gap?" *Direct Marketing* (January 1997).

Gilmor, J. and B. J. Pine, editors. *Markets of One: Creating Customer-Unique Value Through Mass Customization.* Cambridge, Massachusetts: Harvard Business School Press, 2000.

Graphics, Visualization, & Usability (GVU) Center in Georgia Institute of Technology, Tenth Survey, 1998 (*gvu.gatech.edu*).

Gray, P. and H. J. Watson. *Decision Support in the Data Warehouse.* Upper Saddle River, New Jersey: Prentice Hall, 1998.

Guttman, R. H., et al. "Agent-Mediated Electronic Commerce: A Survey," *Knowledge Engineering Review* (June 1998).

Hasan, H. and G. Ditsa. "The Impact of Culture on the Adoption of IT: An Interpretive Study," *Journal of Global Information Management* (January/February 1999).

Hayes-Roth, B., et al. "Web Guides," *IEEE Intelligent Systems* (March/April 1999).

Ho, C. F. and W. H. Wu. "Antecedents of Customer Satisfaction on the Internet: An Empirical Study of Online Shopping," *Proceedings of the 32nd HICSS* (January 1999).

Hofacker, C. F. *Internet Marketing, 3rd ed.* New York: John Wiley & Sons, 2000.

Hoffman, D. L. and T. P. Novak. "How to Acquire Customers on the Web," *Harvard Business Review* (May–June 2000).

Huang, K. T. "Intelligent Diagnose Learning Agents," *Journal of Computer Information Systems* (Fall 1999).

Josefek, R. and R. Kaufman. "Dark Pockets and Decision Support: The Information Technology Value Cycle in Efficient Markets," *Journal of Electronic Markets* (1997) (*electronicmarkets.org*).

Kalakota, R. and M. Robinson. *e-Business: Roadmap for Success.* Reading, Massachusetts: Addison-Wesley (1999).

Kalakota, R. and A. Whinston. *Electronic Commerce—A Manager's Guide.* Reading, Massachusetts: Addison Wesley, 1997.

Kalakota, R. and A. Whinston, editors. *Readings in Electronic Commerce.* Reading, Massachusetts: Addison Wesley, 1997.

Keen, P., et al. *Electronic Commerce Relationships: Trust by Design.* Upper Saddle River, New Jersey: Prentice Hall, 2000.

Keen, P. and M. McDonald. *e-Process Edge: Creating Customer Value and Business Wealth in the Internet Era.* New York: McGraw-Hill, 2000.

Komenar, M. *Electronic Marketing.* New York: John Wiley & Sons, 1997.

Kotler, P. and G. Armstrong, *Principles of Marketing,* 8th edition. Upper Saddle River, New Jersey: Prentice Hall, 1999.

Kraff, K. "Examining the Alternatives for eCRM Solutions," *Journal of Customer Loyalty*, Issue 14 (2000).

Lamb, C., et al. *Marketing,* 4th edition. Cincinnati, Ohio: South-Western College Publishing, 1998.

Lamb, C., J. Hair, Jr., and C. McDaniel. *Marketing,* 4th edition. Cincinnati, Ohio: South-Western Publishing, 1998.

Lazar, J. and J. Preece. "Designing and Implementing Web-Based Surveys," *Journal of Computer Information Systems* (April 1999).

Lee, M. K. O. "Comprehensive Model of Internet Consumer Satisfaction," unpublished working paper, City University of Hong Kong, 2001.

Lee, M. K. O. and E. Turban. "A Framework for a Trust Model in E-Commerce," unpublished working paper, March 2001.

Lee, M. K. O. and E. Turban. "A Comprehensive Electronic Trust Model," unpublished working paper, City University of Hong Kong, 2001.

Leebaert, D. *The Future of the Electronic Marketplace.* Boston, Massachusetts: MIT Press, 1998.

Levinson, M. "Customer Segmentation: Slices of Lives," *CIO Magazine* (August 15, 2000).

Lewicki, R. J. and B. Bunker. "Developing and Maintaining Trust in Work Relationships," In R. M. Kramer and T. R. Tyler, editors. *Trust in Organizations.* Thousand Oaks, California: Sage, 1996.

Liang, T. P. and H. S. Doong. "Effect of Bargaining on Electronic Commerce," *Int. Jour. of Electronic Commerce* (Spring 2000).

Lohse, G. L. and P. Spiller. "Electronic Shopping," *Communications of the ACM,* vol. 41 (July 1998).

Maes, P., et al. "Agents that Buy and Sell," *Communication of the ACM* (March 1999).

McKeown, P. G. and R. T. Watson. *Metamorphosis— A Guide to the www and Electronic Commerce.* New York: John Wiley & Sons, 1998.

Moon, B. K., J. K. Lee, and K. J. Lee. "A Next Generation Multimedia Call Center on the Internet: IMC," *Proceedings of the International Conference on Electronic Commerce,* Seoul, Korea, 1998.

Morley, P. *Handbook of Customer Service.* Brookfield, Vermont: Gower Publishing, 1997.

Moukas, A., et al. "Agent-Mediated Electronic Commerce: An MIT Media Laboratory Perspective," *Int. Journal of Electronic Commerce* (Spring 2000).

Mowen, J. C. and M. Minors. *Consumer Behavior,* 5th edition. Upper Saddle River, New Jersey: Prentice Hall, 1998.

Murch, R. and T. Johnson. *Intelligent Software Agents.* Upper Saddle River, New Jersey: Prentice Hall, 1999.

Nambisan, S. and Y. M. Wang. "Roadblocks to Web Technology Option?," *Communications of the ACM* (January 1999).

O'Keefe, R. M. and T. McEachern. "Web-Based Customer Decision Support System," *Communications of the ACM* (March 1998).

Orzech, D. "Call Centers Take to the Web," *Datamation* (June 1998).

Parsa, I. "Web Mining Crucial to E-Commerce Success," *DM News* (December 7, 1999).

Peppers, D., et al. *The One-to-One Fieldbook*. New York: Currency and Doubleday, 1999.

Petersen, G. S. *Customer Relationship Management Systems: ROI and Results Measurement*. New York: Strategic Sales Performance, 1999.

Porter, M. E. *Competitive Advantage: Creating and Sustaining Superior Performance*. New York: Free Press 1985.

Ratnasingham, P. "The Importance of Trust in Electronic Commerce," *Internet Research,* vol. 8, no. 4 (1998).

Reichheld, F. *The Loyalty Effect*. Boston, Massachusetts: Harvard Business Press, 1996.

Reichheld, F. *Building Loyalty in the Age of the Internet*. Boston, Massachusetts: Harvard Business School Press, 2001.

Reichheld, F. and P. Schefter. "E-Loyalty—Your Secret Weapon on the Web," *Harvard Business Review* (July–August 2000).

Seybold, P. B. and R. Marshak. *Customer.com: How to Create a Profitable Business Strategy for the Internet and Beyond*. New York: Times Books, 1998.

Shapiro, D., et al. "Business on a Handshake," *The Negotiation Journal* (October 1992).

Siebel, T. M., et al. *Cyber Rules: Strategies for Excelling at E-Business*. New York: Doubleday, 1999.

Sterne, J. *Customer Service on the Internet: Building Relationships, Increasing Loyalty, and Staying Competitive,* 2nd edition. New York: Wiley, 2000.

Strauss, J. and R. Frost. *Internet Marketing,* 2nd ed. Upper Saddle River, New Jersey: Prentice Hall, 2001.

Turban, E., et al. *Information Technology for Management*, 3rd edition. New York: John Wiley & Sons, 2002.

Vassos, J. *Strategic Internet Marketing*. Indianapolis, Indiana: QUE Publishing, 1996.

Vellido, A., et al. "Segmentation of the Online Shopping Market Using Neural Networks," *Expert Systems with Applications*, vol. 17 (1999).

Voss, C. "Developing an eService Strategy," *Business Strategy Review*, vol. 11, no. 11 (2000).

Wang, S. "Analyzing Agents for Electronic Commerce," *Information Systems Management* (Winter 1999).

Ware, J. *The Search for Digital Excellence*. New York: McGraw-Hill, 1998.

Wiegram, G. and H. Koth. *CustomerEnterprise.com*. Upper Saddle River, New Jersey: Financial Times/Prentice Hall, 2000.

Wiersema, F. *Customer Service: Cases of Excellence*. New York: Harper Business, 1998.

Yan, Y., et al. "A Multi-Agent Based Negotiated Support System," *Proceedings 33rd HICSS* (January 2000).

Zellweger, P. "Web-Based Sales: Defining the Cognitive Buyer," *Journal of Electronic Markets,* vol. 7, no. 3 (1997), (*electronicmarkets.org*).

EXAMPLE OF AN ONLINE MARKET RESEARCH TOOL FOR SEGMENTATION

A well-known psychographic segmentation was developed by SRI International in California. The original segmentation divided consumers in the United States into nine groups and is called VALS™, which stands for values and lifestyles. It helps businesses identify who to target market, uncover what the target group buys, locate where concentrations of the target group live, identify how best to communicate with the target group, and gain insight into why the target group acts the way it does. VALS has been applied in a variety of areas: new product/service design, marketing and communications, targeting, product positioning, focus-group screening, promotion planning, advertising, and media planning.

With VALS, consumers are asked whether they agree or disagree with statements such as, "My idea of fun at a national park would be to stay at an expensive lodge and dress up for dinner" or "I could stand to skin a dead animal." Consumers are then clustered into different groups based on their answers.

VALS™ is an advanced version of the "original" VALS (see Figure A4-1). VALS consumer groups are organized along two dimensions. The vertical dimension

Figure A4-1   VALS™ Questionnaire

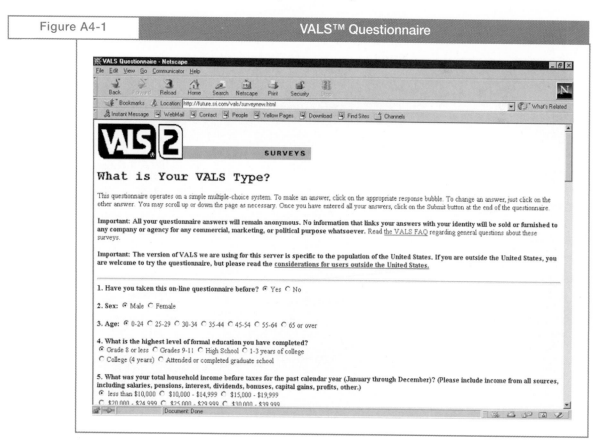

Source: sri.com/VALS/VALSindex.html

represents resources, which include income, education, self-confidence, health, eagerness to buy, and energy level. The horizontal dimension represents self-orientation and includes three different types: principle-oriented consumers, who take an intellectual approach to life and are guided by their views of how the world is or should be; status-oriented consumers, who are guided by the opinions of others in respected peer groups; and action-oriented consumers, who are guided by a desire for social or physical activity, variety, and risk taking. Each of the VALS groups represents from 9 to 17 percent of the U.S. adult population. Marketers can buy VALS product services and media data from custom VALS surveys and from linkages VALS has with other consumer database companies such as Simmons Market Research and Scarborough Research.

5

Advertisement in Electronic Commerce

LEARNING OBJECTIVES

Upon completion of this chapter, the reader will be able to:

- Describe the objectives of Web advertisement, its types, and characteristics.

- Describe the major advertisement methods used on the Web.

- Describe various Web advertisement strategies.

- Describe various types of promotions on the Web.

- Discuss the benefits of push technology and intelligent agents.

- Understand the major economic issues related to Web advertisement.

- Describe the issues involved in measuring the success of Web advertisement as it relates to different pricing methods.

- Compare paper and electronic catalogs and describe customized catalogs.

- Describe Web advertisement implementation issues.

5.1 ADVERTISEMENT IN THE DIGITAL ECONOMY: ILLUSTRATIVE EXAMPLES

With the increasing use of the Web, the nature of advertising is changing to take advantage of the Internet as shown in the following examples.

Each year, almost 500,000 brides-to-be use *theknot.com* to plan their wedding. A "Knox Box" with insert folders is sent to users by regular mail. Each insert is linked to a corresponding page on the *theknot.com* Web site. Advertisers underwrite the mail campaign. The Web site provides brides with information and help in planning the wedding and selecting vendors. Orders can be placed by phone or online (not all products can be ordered online). *Bridalguide411.com* is a similar service, but operates primarily online. Both *Bridalguide411.com* and *theknot.com* include promotions and ads from vendors.

Promosinmotion.com and others painted Volkswagen Bugs with advertisers logos, tag lines, or ad messages. The painted cars were displayed on Web sites and even driven on the streets, attracting considerable attention.

An old economy seller of hard-to-find light bulbs changed its name to *topbulb.com*; created an online catalog, named the bulbguy; and sells bulbs online at a discount. The Web site is advertised both online and offline. Business is booming!

To promote its sport utility, the 4Runner, Toyota wanted to reach as many Internet users as possible. In an effort to do so Toyota displayed Toyota banners on the search engine AltaVista (*altavista.com*).

Whenever a user used AltaVista to search for anything automotive related, the user would see the Toyota banner. Also, Kelly Blue Book's new car pricing catalog (*kbb.com*) has links to Toyota's car. In the first 2 months of the campaign, over 10,000 potential car buyers clicked on the banner ads, looking for more detailed information about the Toyota 4Runner.

To promote its recruiting visits on U.S. college campuses, IBM created over 75,000 college-specific banners such as: "There is life after Boston College: click to see why." The students clicked on the banners at a very high rate (5 to 30 percent). As a result, IBM restructured their traditional media plans using the "Club Cyberblue" scheme.

5.2 WEB ADVERTISEMENT

An Overview

The opening examples demonstrate the use of banners, promotions, and other forms of Internet advertising. Using the Internet, advertisers can focus on special interest groups (segmentation) and even on individuals, which is useful in direct marketing. Such activities and many more are part of the new approach to advertising in the new economy, which is the subject of this chapter.

Advertisement is an attempt to disseminate information in order to affect a buyer–seller transaction. In the traditional sense, advertisement was impersonal, one-way mass communication, which was paid for by sponsors. Telemarketing and direct mail were attempts to personalize advertisement in order to make it more effective. These direct marketing approaches worked fairly well but were expensive and slow. For example, a direct mail campaign costs about $1 per person. However, the response rate is only 1 to 3 percent. This makes the cost per responding person $33 to $100. Such an expense can be justified only for high-ticket items.

One of the problems with direct mail advertising was that the advertisers knew very little about the recipients. Segmentation (Chapter 4) helped a bit, but did not solve the problem. The Internet redefined the meaning of advertisement. The

Internet has enabled advertisers to learn about customers and to *interact* directly with them. In interactive marketing, a consumer can click on an ad for more information or send an e-mail to ask a question. The Internet has provided sponsors with two-way communication and e-mail capabilities, as well as allowing them to target specific groups on which they want to spend their advertising dollars. Finally, the Internet enables a truly one-to-one advertisement. A comparison of these concepts is shown in Table 5-1.

Brick-and-mortar companies use Internet advertisments as one of their advertisement channels; at the same time virtual (online) companies may use TV, newspapers, or other resources as advertisement channels. In this chapter we deal with Internet advertisement in general, regardless of who uses it.

In the previous chapters we discussed the importance of interactive marketing and the reasons why consumers prefer it. In this chapter we will show how the advertisement part of interactive marketing is implemented online. Most of the discussion in this chapter is relevant for B2C only. However, some methods and strategies can be used in B2B as well. We will return to B2B advertisement in Chapter 8. For resources on Internet advertisement see *adage.com*, *hotwired.com/webmonkey*, and the Internet advertisement and marketing books listed in the bibliography. But first, let's start by providing some essential advertising terminology.

Internet Advertising Terminology

There is some confusion regarding Web advertising terminology. Hence, the following glossary may by of help:

Ad views. Also known as page views or impressions, ad views are the number of times users call up a page with a banner during a specific time (e.g., "ad views per day"). The actual number of times the ad is *seen* by users may differ because of "caching" (which increases the real number of ad views) and browsers that view documents but ignore the ads (which decreases this number).

Banner. A banner is a graphic display on a Web page that is used for advertising. The size of the banner is usually 5 to 6.250 inches in length, .5 to 1 inch wide, and is measured in pixels. A banner ad is linked to an advertiser's Web page. When a user "clicks" on the banner, he or she will be transferred to the advertiser's site.

TABLE 5-1

From Mass Advertisement to Interactive Advertisement

	Mass Marketing	Direct Marketing	Interactive Marketing
Best Outcome	Volume sales	Customer data	Customer relationships
Consumer Behavior	Passive	Passive	Active
Leading Products	Food, personal care products, beer, autos	Credit cards, travel, autos	Upscale apparel, travel, financial services, autos
Market	High volume	Targeted goods	Targeted individual
Nerve Center	Madison Ave	Postal distribution centers	Cyberspace
Preferred Media Vehicle	Television, magazines	Mailing lists	Online services
Preferred Technology	Storyboards	Databases	Servers, on-screen navigators, the Web
Worst Outcome	Channel surfing	Recycling bins	Log off

Source: Based on *InformationWeek* (October 3, 1994), p. 26.

Button. A button is a small banner that is linked to a Web site. It may contain downloadable software.

Click. A click (or ad click or click-through), is counted each time a visitor clicks on an advertising banner to access the advertiser's Web site.

Click ratio. A ratio indicating the success of an advertising banner in attracting visitors to click on the ad. For example, if a page received 1,000 views and there are 100 "clicks" on a banner, the click ratio is 10 percent.

Cookie. A cookie is a program that is stored on the user's hard drive, frequently without disclosure or the user's consent. Sent by a Web server over the Internet, the information stored will surface when the user's browser again crosses the specific Web server (see *cookiecentral.com* and Chapter 17).

CPM. The CPM is the cost-per-thousand impressions. This is the fee the advertiser pays when 1,000 people view the page a banner ad is on.

Hit. Web term for any request for data from a Web page or file, often used to compare popularity/traffic of a site in the context of getting so many "hits" during a given period. One hit represents one file retrieved from the server. Every access to a Web server counts as a hit. A *qualified hit* is one that successfully retrieves content from the server. A single page view may be recorded as several hits, and depending on the browser, the page size, and other factors, the number of hits per page can vary widely.

Impressions. See ad views. This is also referred to as the *exposure* to an ad.

Interactive advertisement. An interactive advertisement is any ad that requires or allows the viewer/consumer to take some action. In the broadest sense, even clicking on a banner is an interaction. However, usually action is defined as sending a query or looking for detailed information.

Page. A page is an HTML document that may contain text, images, and other online elements, such as Java applets and multimedia files. It may be statically or dynamically generated.

Reach. This is the number of people or households exposed to an ad at least once over a specified period of time.

Visit. A visitor may make a sequence of requests during one visit to a site. Once a visitor stops making requests from a site for a given period of time called a time-out (usually 15 or 30 minutes), the next hit by this visitor is considered a new visit. In a *unique visit,* one can identify the visitor by asking the user to register or by placing a cookie on the user's computer.

Why Internet Advertisement?

There are several reasons why companies advertise on the Internet. To begin with, television viewers are migrating to the Internet. The media follows, acknowledging that the goal of any advertiser is to reach its target audience effectively and efficiently. Advertisers recognize that they have to adapt their marketing plans to account for the ever-growing number of people spending increasing amounts of time online.

Numerous studies have found that over three-quarters of PC users are giving up some television time to spend more time on their computers. Add to this the fact that many Internet users are well educated and have high incomes, it is only logical to conclude that Internet surfers are a desired target for advertisers.

Other reasons why Web advertising is growing rapidly include:

- Ads can be updated at any time with minimal cost; therefore, they are always timely.
- Ads can reach very large numbers of potential buyers, both locally and globally.
- Online ads are sometimes cheaper than television, newspaper, or even radio ads, all of which are expensive since they are determined by space occupied, how many days (times) they are shown, and on how many national and local television stations and newspapers they are posted.
- Web ads can effectively use the convergence of text, audio, graphics, and animation.
- Games, entertainment, and promotions can easily be combined in online advertisements.
- Web TV and Internet radio bring more people to the Internet.
- The use of the Internet itself is growing very rapidly.
- Web ads can be interactive and targeted to specific interest groups and/or individuals.

As of 1998, these factors began to convince large, consumer-products companies to shift an increasing amount of advertising dollars away from traditional media to Web advertisements. Toyota is a prime example of the power of Internet advertising. Saatchi and Saatchi, a major ad agency, developed Toyota's Web site (*toyota.com*) and placed Toyota's traffic-luring banner ads on other popular Web sites such as *espn.com*. Within a year, the site overtook Toyota's 800 number as its best source of sale leads.

The Internet Versus Traditional Methods

The major traditional advertisement media are television (about 36 percent), newspapers (about 35 percent), magazines (about 14 percent), and radio (about 10 percent). Although Internet advertisement is a small percentage of the $120 billion-a-year industry (in 2001), it is growing rapidly. For example, in 1995 Internet advertising expenditures were about $43 million, this amount grew to over $1 billion in 1998 (*iab.net*) and close to $3 billion in 1999. The estimate for 2005 is $15 billion.

The Internet can be viewed as just another advertisement media with its own advantages and limitations. Table 5-2 compares the Internet advertising media against the traditional media.

Combining Advertising Media

There is a trend to combine Internet advertisements with other media. For example, you view an advertisement on TV, but get additional product details and make an order on the Internet. For details see *crq.com* and *microcast.com*.

THE INTERNET IS THE FASTEST GROWING MEDIUM IN HISTORY

In 1997, a study entitled "The Internet Advertising Report" (Meeker, 1997) examined the rate of Internet adoption against three traditional media: radio, network television, and cable television. Meeker examined the length of time it took

TABLE 5-2	Advantages and Limitations of Internet Advertisement as Compared to Traditional Media		
Medium	**Pros for Generating Advertising Revenue**		**Cons for Generating Advertising Revenue**
TV	• Intrusive impact—high awareness getter. • Ability to demonstrate product and feature "slice of life" situations. • Very "merchandisable" with media buyers.		• Ratings fragmenting, rising costs, "clutter." • Heavy "downscale" audience skew. • Time is sold in multiprogram packages. Networks often require major up-front commitments. Both limit the advertiser's flexibility.
Radio	• Highly selective by station format. • Allows advertisers to employ time-of-day or time-of-week to exploit timing factors. • Copy can rely on the listener's mood or imagination.		• Audience surveys are limited in scope, do not provide socioeconomic demographics. • Difficult to buy with so many stations to consider. • Copy testing is difficult, few statistical guidelines.
Magazines	• Offer unique opportunities to segment markets, demographically and psychographically. • Ads can be studied, reviewed at leisure. High impact can be attained with good graphics and literate, informative copy.		• Reader controls ad exposure, can ignore campaign, especially for new products. • Difficult to exploit "timing" aspects.
Newspapers	• High single-day reach opportunity to exploit immediacy, especially on key shopping days. • Reader often shops for specific information when ready to buy. • Portable format		• Lack of demographic selectivity, despite increased zoning—many markets have only one paper. • High cost for large-size units. • Presumes lack of creative opportunities for "emotional" selling campaigns. • Low-quality reproduction, lack of color.
Internet	• Internet advertisements are accessed on demand 24 hours a day, 365 days a year, and costs are the same regardless of audience location. • Accessed primarily because of interest in the content, so market segmentation opportunity is large. • Opportunity to create one-to-one direct marketing relationship with consumer. • Multimedia will increasingly create more attractive and compelling ads. • Distribution costs are low (just technology costs), so the millions of consumers reached cost the same as one. • Advertising and content can be updated, supplemented, or changed at any time, and are therefore always up-to-date. Response (click-through rate) and results (page views) of advertising are immediately measurable. • Ease of logical navigation—you click when and where you want, and spend as much time as desired there.		• No clear standard or language of measurement. • Immature measurement tools and metrics. • Although the variety of ad content format and style that the Internet allows can be considered a positive in some respects, it also makes apples-to-apples comparisons difficult for media buyers. • Difficult to measure size of market, therefore difficult to estimate rating, share, or reach and frequency. • Audience is still small.

Source: Based on Meeker (1997), pp. 1–10.

for each ad media to reach 50 million U.S. users. Meeker found that the length of time it took for the Internet to reach 50 million users was about 5 years, which is remarkable considering that it took radio 38 years, television 13 years, and cable television 10 years. Figure 5-1 extends the study to 2000, at which time more than 300 million people used the Internet. According to these statistics, the Internet is by far the fastest growing communication medium.

Objectives and Growth of Internet Advertisement

The objectives of advertising on the Internet are the same as those of any other type of advertising, namely, to persuade customers to buy a certain product or service. Thus, it is seen as an alternative (or complementary) medium to traditional advertising media. Customers' awareness of this alternative is growing rapidly.

The largest U.S. advertiser, Proctor & Gamble, announced in 1998 that the company would shift a substantial amount of its advertisement budget to the Internet. According to the Internet Advertising Bureau (IAB) (*iab.net*), the top categories for Web ad spending in 2000 were computers (25 percent), consumer

| Figure 5-1 | Adoption Curves for Various Media |

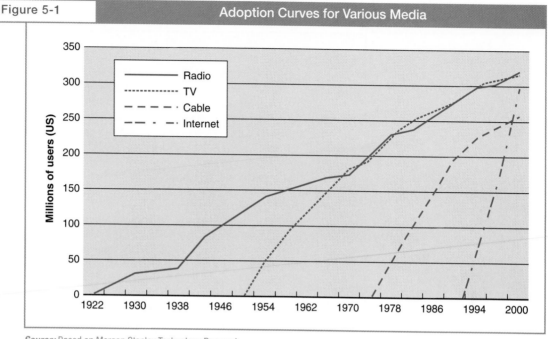

Source: Based on Morgan Stanley Technology Research.

products (25 percent), financial services (13 percent), telecom (14 percent), and news media (10 percent).

Targeted (One-to-One) Advertisements

As stated earlier, one of the major advantages of Internet advertising is the ability to customize ads to fit individual viewers. One company that pioneered such advertising is DoubleClick (Application Case 5.1).

APPLICATION CASE   5.1

Targeted Advertisements: The DoubleClick Approach

One-to-one targeted advertisements can take many forms. Assume that 3M Corp. wants to advertise its $10,000 multimedia projectors. It knows that potential buyers are people who work in advertising agencies or in IS departments of large corporations or companies that use Unix as their operating system. 3M approaches DoubleClick, Inc. and asks the firm to identify such potential customers. How does DoubleClick find them? The answer is clever and simple.

As of 1997, DoubleClick (*doubleclick.net*) monitors people browsing the Web sites of several hundred cooperating companies such as Quicken (*quicken.com*) and Travelocity (*travelocity.com*). By inspecting the Internet addresses of the visitors to these companies' Web sites and matching them against a database with about 100,000 Internet domain names that include a line-of-business code, DoubleClick can find those people working for advertising agencies. By checking the browsers, it can also find out which

(continued)

visitors are using the Unix system. While DoubleClick cannot find out your name, it can build a dossier on you, attached to an ID number that was assigned to you during your first visit to any of the cooperating sites. As you continue to visit the sites, an intelligent software agent builds a relatively complete dossier on you, your spending, and your computing habits. This process is done with a device known as a cookie, a file created at the request of a Web server and stored on the user's hard drive, so the Web site can "remember" your past behavior on the Internet.

DoubleClick then prepares an ad about 3M projectors. The ad is targeted to people whose profiles match the criteria listed earlier. If you are a Unix user or an advertising agency, on your next browsing trip in any of the participating Web sites, you will be surprised to find exactly what you wanted: information about the multimedia project. How is all this financed? DoubleClick charges 3M for the ad. The fee is then split with the Web sites that carry the 3M ads, based on how many times the ad is matched with visitors.

In 1998, DoubleClick expanded the service, called Dynamic Advertising Reporting and Targeting (DART), to the leading online publishers in the advertising industry. Furthermore, the company expanded the service from pinpoint target and ad design to advertisement control, ad frequency determination, and providing verifiable measures of success. DoubleClick brings the right advertisement, to the right person, at the right time. Its clients are ad agencies and media companies. Thus, it is a B2B company. DART works with 22 criteria that it tries to find on each consumer (e.g., location, time of day, etc.). Using cookies, a profile is built for the advertisers.

In June 1999, DoubleClick announced the purchase of Abacus Direct, whose database contains the buying habits of 88 million U.S. households DoubleClick wanted to tie its online-consumer data with that of Abacus to establish industry guidelines for the collection of personal information online. This way names and addresses will be in DoubleClick's database. Privacy protection groups opposed the merger, asking the FTC to open an investigation. Under the pressure, DoubleClick agreed to limit the connection.

Sources: Compiled from Rothenberg (2000) and from *doubleclick.com.*

One-to-one targeted advertising and marketing can be expensive. However, it can be very rewarding. For example, according to Taylor (1997), successful targeted ads were proven very effective for Lexus cars (at a cost of $169 per car sold). Targeting ads to groups (based on segmentation) rather than to individuals can also be very cost effective.

5.3   ADVERTISEMENT METHODS

Banners

Banner advertising is the most commonly used form of advertising on the Internet. As you surf your way through the Web, banners are everywhere. Typically, a banner contains a short text or graphical message to promote a product. Advertisers go to great lengths to design a banner that catches consumers' attention. Banners with video clips and sound are also common. Banners contain links that, when clicked on, transfer the customer to the advertiser's home page or another page the advertising wishes to target.

An important factor an advertiser needs to scrutinize is the size of the banner. Advertisers need to make sure that the image size the Web site uses is appropriate for the intended location and that the file size and animation limits are correct. The file size of the image should be about 7kb to 10kb. An image with a large file size or unlimited animation looping may require several minutes of downloading time. This could prevent the remainder of the Web page from being displayed until the image is finished, resulting in impatient visitors who leave the site before the Web page is shown.

There are two types of banners: **keyword banners** and **random banners.** Keyword banners appear when a predetermined word is queried from a search engine. They are effective for companies who want to narrow their target audience. Random banners appear randomly. Companies that want to introduce new products (e.g., a new movie or CD) use random banners.

If an advertiser knows something about a visitor, such as the visitor's user profile, it is possible to match a specific banner to that customer. Obviously such targeted, personalized banners are the most effective.

A 1998 study by AOL showed that 9 out of 10 people responded favorably to banner advertisements and about 50 percent of the viewers were able to recall ads immediately after seeing them (*adage.com*, March 15, 1998).

BENEFITS AND LIMITATIONS

The major benefit of banner ads is that by clicking on them users are transferred to an advertiser's site. Another advantage of using banners is the ability to customize them to the target audience. At a minimum, an advertiser can decide which market segments to focus on. Also, "forced advertising" marketing strategy is utilized with banners, which means customers are forced to see banner ads before they can get free information or entertainment they like to see.

The major disadvantage of banners is its potentially high cost. If a company demands a successful marketing campaign, it will need to allocate a large percentage of the advertisement budget to acquire a high volume of CPM. Another drawback of using banners is that a limited amount of information can be placed on the banner. Hence, advertisers need to think of a creative but short message to attract viewers.

Another limitation of banners has been the declining click ratio over time. It looks as though many viewers have developed an *immune system.* They simply do not notice banners. Therefore, it is important to decide where to place banners. For example, a study of Web ads done by the University of Michigan for Athenia Associates showed that ads placed in the lower right-hand corner of the screen, next to the scrollbar, generate 228 percent higher click-through than ads at the top of the page. The study also found that ads placed one-third of the way down the page increased click-through 77 percent over ads at the top of the page, where ads are usually positioned. Andrew Kind, Athenia's Webmaster, attributed the higher click-through to the ads' positioning in the "click zone," where a user's mouse is naturally drawn. Information about the study is available at *webreference.com/dev/banners*.

Banners are generally more effective when they are placed on popular sites. But this can be an expensive option for companies with small advertising budgets. Less expensive options are discussed in the following sections.

BANNER SWAPPING

Banner swapping means that company A agrees to display a banner of company B in exchange for company B displaying company A's ad. This is probably the least expensive form of banner advertising to establish and maintain, but it is also difficult to arrange. A company must locate a site that could generate a sufficient amount of quality traffic. Then, the company must contact the owner/Webmaster of the site and inquire if they would be interested in a reciprocal banner swap. Since individual matching may be difficult, many companies use banner exchanges.

BANNER EXCHANGES

When several Web sites are interested in banner swapping, a multicompany match may be easier to arrange. For example, out of three companies, A can display B's banner, but B cannot display A's banner optimally. However, B can display C's banner, and C can display A's banner. Such *bartering* may involve many companies. Banner exchange organizers arrange for trading among three or more partners. It works similarly to an off-line bartering exchange. A firm, which is willing to display others' banners, joins the exchange. Each time a participant displays a banner for one of the other exchange's members, it receives a credit. After a participant has "earned" enough credits, its own banner is displayed on another member's desired site. Most exchanges offer members the opportunity to purchase additional display credits. Some exchanges also permit the participants to specify what type of site the banner should be displayed on; thus allowing the advertisers to target what type of audience will see the banner ad.

Most exchanges offer a credit ratio of approximately 2:1. This means for every two banners displayed on a company's site, that company's banner will be displayed once on an equivalent site. You may wonder why the ratio is not 1:1. The banner exchange company must generate revenue to cover its operating expenses and to offer additional services, so they take the credit of about 50 percent of all banners and sell it. For example, one banner exchange, net (*net.com*), offers help with banner design, provides membership in newsgroups, delivers HTML tutorials, and even runs contests. *Bcentral.com*, via its Link Exchange, acts as a banner ad clearinghouse for several hundred thousand small Web sites. The site is organized into more than 1,600 categories. Bcentral monitors the content of the ads of all its members.

Some banner exchanges will not allow certain types of banners; hence, the decision of whether or not to participate is important. Another problem is the tax implications of banner bartering. Overall, banner exchanging can be very valuable and should be considered by advertisers.

Standard and Classified Ads

On February 26, 2001, the Internet Advertising Bureau, the industry trade group, adopted five standard advertising sizes for the Internet. These ads are larger and more noticeable than banner ads. Therefore, in preliminary tests, it was found that users read these ads four times as frequently than banners (Tedeschi, 2001). Some of these ads are interactive; users can click on a link inside the ad for more information. These ads, which are also called **micro-site ads,** are read on the same page that was originally clicked. Publishers, like the *New York Times* online, (*nytimes.com*) and *snowball.com*, publish these ads, sometimes four on one Web page. These ads look like the ads in a newspaper or magazine, so viewers and advertisers like them. The ads appear in columns. A full column deep ad is popular and called a **skyscraper ad.** They appear also as boxes.

Another type that resembles a newspaper ad is the **classified ad.** There are special sites for such ads, like *classifieds2000.com*, and they also appear in newspapers online, exchanges, portals, and so on. In many cases, posting regular ads is free, but placing them in a larger size or with some noticeable features is done for a fee.

E-Mail

A popular way to advertise on the Internet is to send company information to people or companies listed in mailing lists. E-mail messages may be combined with brief audio or video clips promoting a product with on-screen links that users can click on to buy (see *aceconcept.com*). The advantages of the e-mail approach are its low cost and the ability to reach a wide variety of targeted audiences. Most companies have a database of customers to which they can then send e-mail messages. However, using e-mail to send ads may be considered spamming (see Chapter 17).

E-mail is emerging as a marketing channel that affords cost-effective implementation and better, quicker response rates than other advertising channels. Therefore, marketers are embracing this medium. Furthermore, it is an interactive medium and it can combine advertising and customer service. What happens, though, when every marketer starts inundating prospects and customers with e-mail? How much e-mail will result? How will consumers deal with it? What areas must marketers focus on to ensure e-mail marketing success?

Undoubtedly, the quantity of e-mail that consumers receive is exploding. According to a study by Jupiter Communications, the annual number of messages per consumer will increase from 1,166 in 1998 to 1,606 by 2002. In light of this, marketers employing e-mail must take a long-term view and work toward the goal of motivating consumers to continue to open and read messages they receive. This is especially important as even now nearly one-third of consumers read e-mail only from senders with whom they have a relationship. As the volume of e-mail increases, consumers' tendency to screen messages will rise as well. Several e-mail services permit users to block, forever, messages from specific sources (e.g., see *hotmail.com*)

When considering who they should target, marketers must supplement existing database information with data relevant to e-mail campaigns (e.g., see Kinnard, 2000). When deciding what to include in an e-mail, marketers must integrate inbound customer service e-mail solutions with their outbound marketing efforts. Finally, with regard to the "how," or the execution, of the message, marketers must develop e-mail-specific copy writing skills and the ability to deliver multimedia-rich e-mail.

A list of e-mail addresses can be a very powerful tool because a company can then target a group of people it knows something about. For information on how to create a mailing list consult *onelist.com* (the service is free) or *topica.com*. E-mail advertisement is considered a success by many (e.g., see Roberts 2000), and

Forrester Research estimates its volume to reach 200 billion messages and $5 billion by 2004. E-mail can also be sent to PDA devices (e.g., Palm) or to mobile phones.

Mobile Phones

Mobile phones offer advertisers a real chance to advertise interactively and on a one-to-one basis with consumers. In the future, ads will be targeted not only to individuals based on their user profiles, but also based on their physical location at a particular point in time, such as where an individual is located or what the weather is in a certain area. See Chapter 19 for examples of this new concept.

Splash Screen

A **splash screen,** also known as **e-mercial** or *interstitial,* is an initial Web site page or a portion of it that is used to capture the user's attention for a short time, as a promotion or lead-in to the site home page or to tell the user what kind of browser and other software they need to view the site. It pops onto the PC screen much like a TV commercial.

The major advantage of a interstitials over any other online advertising method is that advertisers can create innovative multimedia effects or provide sufficient information for a delivery in one visit. The splash screen can be interactive. The viewers can delete splash screens in many cases.

Spot Leasing

Popular portals often provide space (spot) on their home or other Web pages for any individual business to lease. The duration of the lease depends upon the contract agreement between the Web site host and the lessee. Unlike banners, which show up at various times, the ad place on the spot will always be there. The disadvantage of spot leasing is that the size of the ad is often small, causing some viewers to miss the ads. Also, the cost of spot ads can be very high.

URL (Universal Resource Locators)

Most search engine companies have a page for companies to submit their Internet addresses, (URLs) for free. When submitting a URL to a search engine, the search engine spider can crawl through the submitted site, following and indexing all related content and links. Because the spider usually indexes the full text of the pages, there is no need to submit a list of keywords. Nor does one need to give the search engine summaries or descriptions; they are generated automatically.

The major advantage of using URLs as an advertising tool is that it is free. Anyone can submit a URL to a search engine and be listed. Also, by using URLs, it is more likely that searchers of the topics will come to the Web site, rather than finding it by accident. On the other hand, the URL method has several drawbacks. The major limitation is that the chance that a specific site will be placed by a search engine at the top of the list it presents to users (say places 1 through 10) is very slim. Furthermore, even if a certain URL makes it to the top, others can quickly displace that URL from the top slot. Second, different search engines index their listings differently. Therefore, it is difficult to make the top of several lists. One may have the correct keywords, but if the search engine indexed its listing using the "title" or "content description" in the meta tag, then the effort could be fruitless. There are several thousand search engines, and advertisers should register URLs with as many of them as possible.

IMPROVING A COMPANY'S RANKING ON THE SEARCH ENGINES' LISTS

By simply adding, removing, or changing a few sentences, a Web designer may alter the way a search engine's spider ranks its findings. For this reason, when designing or redesigning a Web site, a designer needs to think about the queries people use when they try to find the site. Then, the designer creates a site that will be most responsive to those queries (see Nobles and O'Neil, 2000).

For example, say a user is searching for "Hawaiian Bed and Breakfast." The user will receive a list of 20 top locations. The problem is how to be included in the top 20 and then how to attract users to the site. To do so, a Web designer must not describe the way the ocean looks from a bedroom window, but emphasize key terms, such as bed, breakfast, and Hawaii. Once the user is on the site, he or she can see the picture with the ocean views. Several companies have services that optimize Web content so that a site has a better chance of being discovered by a search engine (e.g., *keywordcount.com*).

Chat Rooms

Electronic chat refers to an arrangement where multiple participants exchange messages over the Internet in real-time. The software industry estimates that several hundred thousand Web sites have millions of chat rooms.

A chat room is a virtual meeting ground where groups of regulars come to gab (see Chapter 12 for technical explanation). The chat rooms can be used to build a community, to promote a political or environmental cause, to support people with medical problems, or to let hobbyists share their interest. And since customer–supplier relationships need to be sustained without face-to-face meetings, online communities are increasingly being used to serve business interests, including advertising (see Chapter 18, *roguemarket.com*, and Bressler and Grantham, 2000).

Vendors frequently sponsor chat rooms. Chat capabilities may be added to a business site for free by letting software chat vendors host a session on the site. The sponsoring vendor simply places a chat link on its site and the chat vendor does the rest, including the advertising that pays for the session. The advertisement in a chat room merges with the activity in the room and the user is conscious of what is being presented.

The main difference between an advertisement that appears on a static Web page and one that comes through a chat room is that the latter allows advertisers to cycle through messages and target the chatters again and again. Also, advertising can become more thematic. An advertiser can start with one message and build upon it to a climax, just as an author does with a good story. Chatters are used to seeing multiple ads on their screens, so they are bound to take notice. For example, imagine you are a toy maker and you have a chat room dedicated to electronic toys. You can use the chat room to pose a query such as: "Can anyone tell me about the new Electoy R3D3?" When chatters respond, perhaps telling you that the product is not working well, you can ask "Why is this so?" Of course you can do the same in your competitors' chat room.

It is estimated that in 2001, Internet chats generated over 10 billion hours of online use, leading to about $1 billion in advertising revenue worldwide. Chat rooms are also used as one-to-one connections between a company and their customers. For example, Mattel sells about one-third of its Barbies to collectors. These collectors use the chat room frequently to make comments or ask questions that are then answered by Mattel's staff.

Other Forms of Advertisement

Online advertisement can be done in several other ways ranging from advertisements in newsgroups to the use of kiosks (O'Keefe 1997). Advertisement on Internet radio is just beginning, and soon advertising on Internet television will commence. **Advertorial** is material that looks like editorial, or general information, but it is really an advertisement. Of special interest is advertisement to Internet communities' members (Chapter 18). Community sites, such as *geocities.com*, offer direct advertisement opportunities, and members can usually buy the advertised products at a discount. There are also ads that link users to other sites that might be of interest to a type of community member. Targeted ads can also go to the members' portals. Finally, the domain name itself can be used for brand recognition. This is why some companies are willing to pay millions of dollars for certain domain names (see *alldomains.com*).

5.4   ADVERTISEMENT STRATEGIES

Several advertisement strategies can be used over the Internet. Before we describe them, it will be useful to present some important considerations in Internet-based ad design.

Considerations in Internet-Based Ad Design

Some commonly accepted rules of advertising on the Internet are advocated by Choi et al. (1997) and by others. Representative rules include the following:

- Advertisements should be visually appealing. In mass media, advertisements should be colorful to catch the reader's attention. On the Internet, adopting interactive and moving Web content can capture attention.
- Advertisements must be targeted to specific groups or to individual consumers. Ads should be customized and speak on a personal level.
- Ad content should be valuable to consumers. Web pages should provide valuable information, avoiding useless and large files that slow downloading time.
- Advertisements must emphasize brands and a firm's image. Ads should emphasize how a firm and its products and services differ from the competition.
- Advertisements must be part of an overall marketing strategy. Firms should actively participate in all types of Internet activities, such as newsgroups, mailing lists, and bulletin boards. All activities constitute a strategy. Also, online advertisements should be coordinated with off-line advertisements.

- Advertisements should be seamlessly linked with the ordering process. When a customer has become interested after viewing an ad, the advertised items should be able to be ordered and paid for conveniently, preferably online with as few clicks as possible.

Successful Web site design is an art as well as a science. In many cases it is best to solicit the help of an expert or consultant to design Internet ads. Turban and Gehrke (2000) identified 50 variables that may increase (or decrease) shoppers' satisfaction with a Web page and their willingness to read ads. The 50 variables were divided into five categories. The authors conducted experiments to find the relative importance of each variable. Several of the most important variables in each category are listed below:

- **Page-loading speed.** Graphics and tables should be simple and meaningful and they should match standard monitors. Thumbnail (icon graphs) are useful in reducing page-loading speed.
- **Business content.** The text should be clear and concise. A compelling page title and header text is also useful. The amount of requested information for registration should be minimal.
- **Navigation efficiency.** Well-labeled, accurate, meaningful links are a must.
- **Compatibility.** Sites must be compatible with multiple browsers, software, etc.
- **Security and privacy.** Customers must be able to reject cookies.
- **Marketing customer focus.** The ad should provide clear terms and conditions of the purchases, including delivery information, return policy, etc. A confirmation page after a purchase is needed.

When the designed ads are in line with the above commandments and design principals, advertisers can effectively implement Internet-based advertisements using one or a combination of the following strategies.

Pull (Passive) Strategy

Usually, customers will look for and visit a site only if it provides helpful and attractive content. The strategy of waiting for a customer's passive access is referred to as **pull (passive) strategy.** The pull strategy is effective and economical when advertising to open, unidentified potential customers worldwide. However, since there are so many Web sites open to all customers, directories are needed that can guide customers to targeted sites. Directories are available on many portals for shopping and business opportunities (e.g., *yahoo.com*).

A site may be either a pure advertisement site, which means it does not offer order taking or payment capabilities, or it may be a complete retail storefront. The ads in the latter case can be directly linked to sales. Another option is an e-mall, where customers can use the e-mall's own directory and search engines to locate desired products and services.

Push (Active) Strategy

If customers do not visit the merchants' sites voluntarily, merchants need to actively advertise to the targeted customers. This kind of strategy, which includes sending e-mails or SMS's or using banners, etc., is called push (active) strategy. In addition, some companies use extensive off-line advertisement, especially when the vendor is not well known.

Associated Ad Display Strategy

Sometimes it is possible to associate the content of a Web page with a related ad. *Amazon.com* and *barnesandnoble.com* do it frequently. Suppose you are interested in finding material on e-loyalty. If you use Yahoo!, it will bring you a list of sources and a banner ad that will say, "Search Books!, Barnes and Noble, E-Loyalty." The same banner ad will appear when you click on the top sites that deal with e-loyalty. This is called **associated ad display strategy** or **text links**. For example, when using MapQuest (*mapquest.com*), which supports hotel reservations, the user may select an indexed category such as "lodging" within a city. Then, a Radisson ad may be displayed. Another example of associated ad display can be found at *Amazon.com*. When a customer reads about a book, a list of books under the title "Customers who bought this book also bought . . . " is displayed. To support this kind of service, *Amazon.com*'s system must have data mining capabilities. Keyword banners are also a kind of associated ad. The associated ad strategy can be regarded as a just-in-time strategy. Associated ads can be paid for by commission, such as with *Amazon.com*, whereas other companies are implementing the strategy through their affiliates programs (e.g., see Helmstetter and Metivier, 2000). If a CPM payment (see Section 5.6) is used, the rate will be about 50 percent higher than normal.

Ads as a Commodity

With the ads-as-a-commodity strategy, the time of viewing an ad is sold as a product. This approach is used by CyberGold (*cybergold.com*) and others. With CyberGold, interested consumers read ads in exchange for payment made by the advertisers. Consumers fill out data on personal interests, then CyberGold distributes targeted banners based on the personal profiles. Each banner is labeled with the amount of payment that will be paid if the consumer reads the ad. If interested, the consumer clicks the banner to read it and, passing some tests as to its contents, is paid for the effort. Readers can sort and choose what they read, and the advertisers can vary the payment level reflecting the frequency and desirability of readers. Payments can be cash (e.g., 50¢ per banner) or discounts on the products sold.

A screen from *MyPoints.com* is shown in Figure 5-2. Cybergold is part of MyPoints, a diversified promotion site. The screen explains some of the site's activities. Take the tour to learn about the free rewards and more.

For details regarding CyberGold's strategy, see Ware et al. (1998).

Viral Marketing

Viral marketing refers to word-of-mouth marketing, which has been used for generations, except that now its *speed* and *reach* are multiplied many fold by the Internet. This ad model can be used to build brand awareness at a minimal cost (Helm, 2000). It has long been a favorite strategy of online advertisers pushing youth-oriented products.

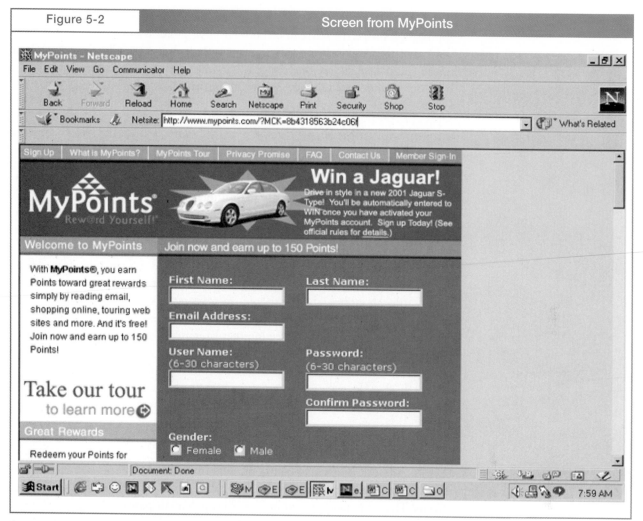

| Figure 5-2 | Screen from MyPoints |

The idea is to have people forward messages to friends, asking them, for example, to "check this idea out." Advertisers can distribute a small game program, which is embedded with a sponsor's e-mail, that is easy to forward. By releasing a few thousand copies of the game, vendors hope to reach hundreds of thousands of consumers. For example, *Coshopper.com*, a Singapore auction site, allows users to type in friends' e-mail addresses; Coshopper then e-mails those friends with details about its service. In the 2000 U.S. presidential election, the Bush campaign Web site urged supporters to bring in new backers via e-mail. The person in each state that recruited the most supporters won an autographed picture of Governor Bush and a commemorative Bush–Cheney 2000 jacket. In July 2000, the promoters of Lee Jeans posted fictitious home pages of three dorky people on its site, hoping that people would forward the funny pictures to others. Then, the company began to use the same characters in its printed ads. This approach was used by the founder of Hotmail, a free e-mail service, which grew from zero to 12 million subscribers in just 18 months. Each e-mail sent via Hotmail carried an invitation for free Hotmail service. Known also as "**advocacy marketing**" this innovative approach, if properly used, can be both effective and efficient.

One of the downsides of this strategy is that several e-mail hoaxes have been spread this way. Also, another danger of a viral advertisement is that a destructive virus can be added to an innocent advertisement-related game or message.

Implementing the Strategy

CUSTOMIZING ADS (PERSONALIZATION)

There is too much information on the Internet for customers to view. Filtering irrelevant information by providing consumers with customized ads can reduce this information overload. BroadVision (*broadvision.com*) provides a customized ad service platform. Their One-to-One product allows the rapid creation and alteration of secure and robust visitor-centric Web sites. The heart of One-to-One is a customer database, which includes registration data and information gleaned from site visits. Marketing staff can use One-to-One on their own desktops to set up or modify rules about how the site should react. Using this feature, a marketing manager can customize display ads based on users' profiles. For an example of how *micromass.com* customizes ads, see Internet Exercise 11 at the end of the chapter.

Another model of personalization can be found in **webcasting**, a free Internet news service that broadcasts personalized news and information (Section 5.5). A user establishes the webcasting system and selects the information he or she would like to receive, such as sports, news, headlines, stock quotes, etc.

INTERACTIVE AD STRATEGIES

Internet ads can be passive or interactive. Interaction may be executed online through the use of chat and call center services or asynchronously using Web screens. These interactions can be used to supplement passive Web pages. One of the major advantages of the Web is its ability to provide various types of interactive options at a reasonable cost. There are several methods of interaction ranging from animated characters to online quizzes.

USING COMPARISONS AS A MEDIUM FOR ADVERTISEMENT

Customers need to be able to compare alternative products and services. Suppose a consumer wants to buy a TV and has found a specific model and brand in a Web catalog or in an e-mail. Then, the consumer would like to find the least expensive place to buy that TV. Instead of going to several sites, the consumer goes to one of the many comparison sites discussed in Chapter 3. The comparison site offers a list of vendors that offer that product along with price (Figure 5-3). Any vendor listed gets some publicity. At issue here is who provides the information for the comparisons. One possible policy is to let the e-mall managers provide such information as a free service for all the brands listed in a mall. The other policy is to generate the comparisons only for those companies willing to pay to be included. The Meta-Malls Architecture (Lee et al. 1998) comparison service has been implemented not only in one mall, but also over multiple independent e-malls, using the architecture shown in Figure 5-4.

Figure 5-3	An Illustrative Screen for Product Comparison

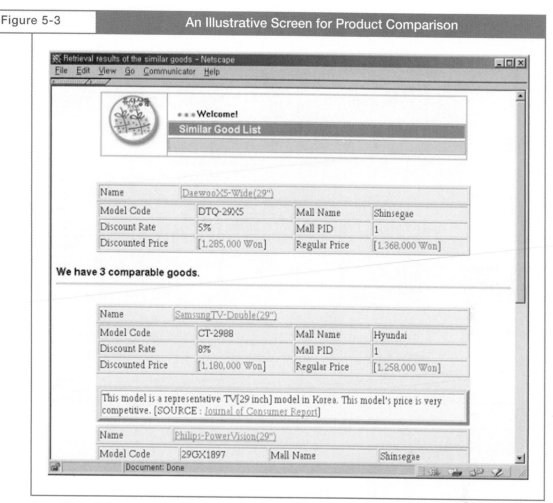

Source: Korean Search Engine (no longer in business).

Online Events, Promotions, and Attractions

It was the winter of 1994, the term EC was barely known, and people were just starting to discover the Internet. Yet, one company demonstrated that there was a new way of doing business—on the Internet. DealerNet, which was selling new and used cars in physical lots, started a virtual showroom. It let people "visit" dozens of dealerships and compare prices and features. At that time it was a revolutionary way of selling cars. To get people's attention, DealerNet gave away a car, and it gave it away over the Internet.

This promotion was unique at that time and it was a total success, receiving a lot of off-line media attention. Today, such promotions are regular events on thousands of Web sites. Contents, quizzes, coupons, and *giveaways,* designed to attract visitors, are integral to EC as much as, or even more than, off-line commerce (e.g., see Giannoni, 2000, and Wong, 2000). Application Case 5.2 provides some innovative examples.

Bargain hunters can find lots of bargains on the Internet. Special sales, auctions, and coupons, are frequently combined with ads. Of special interest are sites such as *coolsavings.com*, *hotcoupons.com*, *supercoups.com*, *primarewards.com*, *mypoints.com*, *cybergold.com*, and *windough.com*. A popular lottery site is *world-widelotto.com*.

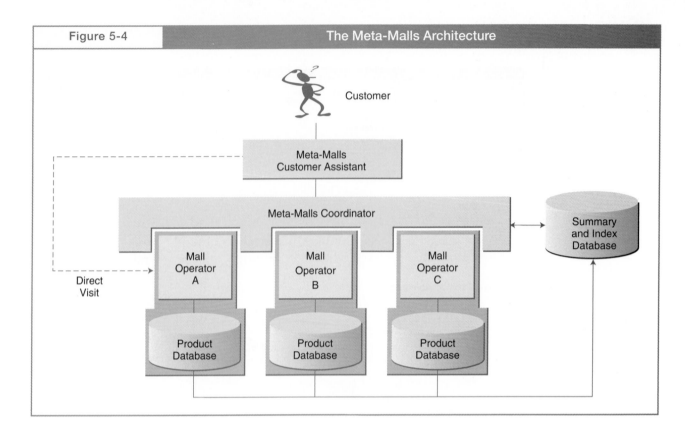

Figure 5-4   **The Meta-Malls Architecture**

How to Entice Web Surfers to Read Internet Ads

There are dozens of innovative ways that advertisers lure consumers into viewing online ads. The following are only a sample.

- Yoyodyne, Inc. (*yoyo.com*) conducts giveaway games, discount contests, and sweepstakes. Entrants agree to read product information from advertisers ranging from Major League Baseball to Sprint Communications. For example, Yoyodyne organized a contest in 1997 in which H&R Block paid $20,000 toward the winner's federal income taxes (H&R Block helps in tax preparation). Yoyodyne also offers multisponsor games.
- Netzero and others offer free Internet access in exchange for viewing ads.
- At *egghead.com*, you can arrange for live people to chat with you in real time. At *lucent.com*, live people talk to you over the phone "pushing" material and ads to your computer.
- Retailers can provide shoppers with special offers while they are purchasing or "checking out" online. If a shoppers' profile or shopping history is known, the ads can be targeted. See *@pos.com*.
- Riddler (*riddler.com*) provides users an opportunity to play games in realtime and win prizes. People also play games for no prizes at all.

APPLICATION CASE   **5.2**

(continued)

- In contrast with other contests, Netstakes runs sweepstakes that require no skills. Users register only once and can randomly win prizes (*webstakes.com*). Prizes are given away in different categories. The site is divided into channels and each channel has several sponsors. The sponsors pay Netstakes to send them traffic. Netstakes runs online ads, both on the Web and through e-mail lists that people subscribe to.
- *Cydoor.com* places ads, news etc. on software applications (see their Ads On Software product). Consumers who download the software receive incentives each time they use the software.
- "Try-before-you buy" gives consumers confidence in what they are buying. *Freesamples.com* began to offer free samples in June 2000.
- Use cursors that are shaped like a corporate logo, or cursors that turn into banner ads when they rest on the desktop. These types of cursors can be placed at public places like Kinko's rented computers. So, when users rent the computers, the ads are displayed by the cursors.

If you like to help the Red Cross, try *pluslotto.com*. Several sites compile current contents by theme, prize, entry deadlines, and so on. They also provide search engines for finding sweepstakes.

Running promotions on the Internet is similar to running off-line promotions. According to Chase (1998) and O'Keefe (1997), some of the major considerations when implementing an online ad campaign are:

- The target audience needs to be clearly understood.
- The target audience needs to be online surfers.
- The traffic to the site should be estimated, and a powerful enough server must be prepared to handle the increased traffic.
- Assuming the promotion is successful, what will the result be? This assessment is needed for evaluating the budget and promotion strategy.
- Consider co-branding. Many promotions succeed because they bring together two or more powerful partners.

5.5   PUSH TECHNOLOGY AND INTELLIGENT AGENTS

Push Technology

The explosion of the Internet has led to a growing acceptance of electronic messaging and news transmission. In response to this trend, several new vehicles for information transmission have appeared. Prominent among them is the concept of **push technology**, which allows for the direct delivery of information to an individual's computer desktop or cell phone. In contrast, the typical Internet format involves a pull format; users must seek out information through a search engine or other delivery system and then pull out the information. Push technology allows for the direct delivery of desired content to an end user. The term "push" comes from "server push," a term used to describe the streaming of Web page contents from a Web server to a Web browser.

The benefits to the subscriber of push technology is that instead of spending hours searching the Web, they can have the information they are interested in delivered automatically to their desktop. The computer **pointcasts** (as opposed to broadcast) information of interest directly to the user. Let's look at an analogy. In the past, manufacturers mass-produced products, today they are mass customizing them to suit customers' needs. The same is true here. Broadcasting is analogous to mass-production and pointcasting is analogous to mass customization. Only the information that is most relevant to the user is transmitted directly to him or her (see Szuprowich, 1998, and Smith, 1997).

To have information pointcasted to a user's personal computer, the user must take part in three steps: *creation of a prespecified profile, selection of appropriate content,* and *downloading the selection.* The prespecification of a user profile occurs when users register for a push delivery service. Sometimes users may need to download client software on their computer that can be customized to deliver only certain channels or categories such as international news, sports, financial data, and so on. In this step, the transmission of information is tailored to the individual user's preferences. A user can even specify how often this information should be transmitted to his or her PC. After a profile is submitted to the push delivery service and stored in a database, special software programs monitor Web sites for the pertinent and relevant information that is requested by the user.

Upon finding information of interest to the user, the push program downloads the information to the push client. The push client then notifies the user by e-mail, playing a sound, displaying an icon on the desktop, sending full articles or Web pages, or by displaying headlines on a screen saver that new information is available.

This process is designed for convenience and efficiency. Often the service is free to the user. It is the advertisers that "foot the bill" for organizations that offer push technology. One example of a leading push delivery service is *webcast.com*.

There are four types of push technology. The first one, self-service delivery, gives Web surfers the tools to download pages for later viewing. Another type, aggregated delivery, acts like a television network or commercial online service in that it provides users with a wide variety of content and advertising choices packaged in a single offering. A third popular push technology, mediated delivery, lets Internet users control what information they receive from participating marketers and publishers by selecting from a menu of choices on the mediator's Web site. The last model is direct delivery, in which the PC desktop interface pulls information from the Internet itself.

A major drawback of push technology is its high bandwidth requirements. Since information is being constantly downloaded, it puts a tremendous stress on system resources. Several experts predict that the technology will never fly. Others see a trend for specialized applications (e.g., see *tibco.com* and *backweb.com*).

Intelligent Agents

In previous chapters we have described how companies collect information about consumers. The purpose of such collections is to create a customer's profile. If the company knows a user's profile, the company can tailor an ad to the customer or ask the customer if he or she would like to receive specific product information. We referred to this as *product brokering* in Chapter 4. It alerts the users of new releases or recommends products based on past selections or constraints specified by the buyer. Examples would be the intelligent agents used by *Amazon.com*, Fastparts (*fastparts.com*), and *classifieds2000.com*. Vendors such as Net Perceptions, Predictivenetworks, BroadVision, and Vignette build such agent systems. An example of how intelligent agents are used in advertising is provided in Application Case 5.3.

APPLICATION CASE   **5.3**

Fujitsu Uses Agents for Targeted Advertising in Japan

At the end of 1996, Fujitsu started using an agent-based technology called Interactive Marketing Interface (iMi) that allows advertisers to interact directly with targeted customers and provide valuable services and information. The system enhances the customers' Internet experiences.

Interactive Marketing Interface allows advertisers to interact directly with specific segments of the consumer market through the use of software agents, while ensuring that consumers remain anonymous to advertisers. Consumers submit a personal profile to iMi, indicating such characteristics as product categories of interests, hobbies, travel habits, and the maximum number of e-mail messages per week that they are willing to receive. In turn, customers receive product announcements, advertisements, and marketing surveys by e-mail from advertisers based on their personal profile information. By answering the marketing surveys or acknowledging receipt of advertisements, consumers earn iMi points, redeemable for gift certificates and phone cards.

Another agent application exists in the area of interactive smart catalogs. This type of experimental application was developed by Stanford University, Hewlett-Packard, and CommerceNet. The goal was to demonstrate the efficiencies and added capabilities afforded by making catalogs accessible on the Web in a form that allows potential customers to locate products according to descriptions of their specifications and for data in the catalogs to include descriptions of function as well as structure. The setup lets users focus quickly on their area of need and obtain a "personalized" view of it. By linking information about a product and its attributes throughout the entire distribution chain, buyers can view "virtual" catalogs in real-time as new products become available. Consumers need truly interactive personalized smart catalogs to enhance the shopping experience. Future advances in personalized interactive catalogs will make it easier to locate products and their attributes throughout the value chain.

5.6   EFFECTIVENESS AND PRICING OF ADVERTISEMENT

Justifying Internet advertisement is more difficult than doing so for conventional advertisements. One of the major reasons for this is the difficulty in measuring the effectiveness of online advertising and disagreements on pricing strategies. Several methods are available for measuring advertisement effectiveness, conducting cost-benefit analyses, and for pricing ads. Four representative methods are discussed here.

Exposure Models That Are Based on Ad Views

Traditional ad pricing has been based on exposure or circulation. So far, this model has been the standard advertising rate-pricing tool for Web sites as well, usually using ad views to measure circulation. While exposure charges on the Web vary widely, on average they have been at higher levels than they are in most other media because of the small supply of highly trafficked Web sites.

Since advertisers pay an agreed upon multiple of the number of "guaranteed" ad views, it is very important that ad views are measured accurately in the context of the advertising business model. This limits the site's responsibility for ad delivery, and the ad revenue generated to the space seller is simply the product of the traffic volume times a multiple, which is generally priced in terms of CPM, which can range from $10 to $700 (in 2001). The price charged is different for some portals and other popular sites. For example, in 2000 *Excite.com* charged $68 per CPM and *Lycos.com* charged $50 to $60 per CPM. Generally, CPMs seem to average on the order of $40, resulting in a cost of $0.040 per impression viewed.

The wide price spread suggests that the Web can function both as a mass medium and a direct-marketing vehicle and that context, audience, technology, and anticipated results all play a part in determining what price an advertiser will pay. A few well-branded portals in a very broad range of categories (such as news, entertainment, and sports) will dominate, and these portals will be able to charge a premium for ad space.

Some companies, such as USA Today, charge their clients according to the number of hits (about 3 cents per hit in 2001). As explained earlier, there may be several hits in one ad view.

Click-Through

Ad pricing based upon click-through is an attempt to develop a more accountable way of charging for Web advertising. The payment for a banner ad is based on the number of times visitors actually click on it. However, a relatively small proportion of those exposed to a banner ad actually click on the banner, about 1 to 3 percent of viewers. Thus, payment based upon click-through guarantees not only that the visitor was exposed to the banner ad, but also actively decided to click on the banner and become exposed to the target ad (Hoffman and Novak 2000). Space providers usually object to this method, claiming that viewing an ad itself may lead to a purchase later or to an off-line purchase, much as newspaper or TV ads do. On the other hand, advertisers do not like to pay for ad views and prefer the click-through method. Only large advertisers such as Procter and Gamble can pressure space sellers to accept click-through payment methods, or even better—interactivity.

Interactivity

This measure was initially proposed by Hoffman and Novak (2000). While a payment based upon click-through guarantees exposure to target ads, it does not guarantee that the visitor liked the ad or even spent any substantial time viewing it. The interactivity model suggests basing ad pricing on how the visitor interacts with the target ad. Such an interactivity measure could be based upon the duration of time spent viewing the ad, the number of pages of the target ad accessed, the number of additional clicks generated, or the number of repeat visits to the target ad. Obviously, this method is more complex to administer than the previous methods.

Back in 1996, Modern Media, an interactive advertising agency, had developed a pricing model in which its clients paid not for exposures or click-throughs, but only for activity at the client's Web site. This has raised a controversy surrounding Web media. Web publishers argued that the problem with activity-based measures like click-through or interactivity is that the Web publishers cannot be held responsible for activity related to an advertisement. They also argued that traditional media, such as newspapers or television, charge for ads whether or not they lead to sales. So why should the interactive condition be applied on the Net?

Advertisers and their agencies, on the other hand, argued that since the Web medium allows for accountability, models can and should be developed that measure actual consumer activities. A standard solution may eventually be developed in the future or different approaches will be used by different companies.

Actual Purchase

Marketers are interested in outcomes, and the ultimate outcome is a purchase. It is obvious that 1,000 people visiting a site is worth something, but a site that only five people visit can be worth much more if they are actually shopping there. It is also important to know how an advertisement influences the amount of money customers actually spend.

In an outcome-based approach to pricing, Web advertisers start by specifying exactly what the marketer would like the target ad to do. Examples of typical outcomes include influencing attitudes, motivating the consumers to provide information about themselves, or leading the consumer to an actual purchase. For example, if a customer purchased a book at *Amazon.com* after he or she saw *Amazon.com*'s ad at AOL's Web site, then AOL receives a referral fee of say 5 percent of the purchase price of the book. Many merchants ask consumers to place their logo on their Web sites. The companies promise to pay the affiliate a commission of 5 to 15 percent if customers click on their logo on the affiliate's Web site and eventually move to the merchant site to make a purchase (e.g., see *cattoys.com*). The referral fee is the basis for the affiliates program used by *Amazon.com* and many other retailers. Unfortunately, this method is valid only at sites where actual purchases are made. At *cocacola.com*, you only get information and brand awareness, so this method is inappropriate.

Other Methods

Other methods can be used to pay for ads. For example, some space providers charge a fixed monthly fee to host a banner, regardless of the traffic. Others use a hybrid approach, a combination of some of the previous methods.

5.7   USING ONLINE CATALOGS FOR ADVERTISEMENT

An important factor in EC is the manner in which products or services are presented to the users. This is frequently done via online catalogs and can be considered as advertisement.

Evolution of Online Catalogs

Catalogs have been printed on paper for a long time. However, recently electronic catalogs on CD-ROM and the Internet have gained popularity. For merchants, the objective of online catalogs is to advertise and promote products and services, whereas the purpose of catalogs to the customer is to provide a source of information on products and services. Electronic catalogs can be searched quickly with the help of search engines. For a comprehensive discussion of online catalogs see Chapter 9 in Kosiur (1997) and Danish and Gannon (1998).

Electronic catalogs consist of a product database, directory and search capabilities, and a presentation function. In Web-based e-malls, Web browsers, along with Java and sometimes virtual reality, play the role of presenting static and dynamic information.

The majority of early online catalogs were replications of text and pictures from the printed catalogs. However, online catalogs have evolved to become more dynamic, customized, and integrated with selling and buying procedures. As the online catalog is integrated with shopping carts, order taking, and payment, the tools for building online catalogs are being integrated with merchant sites (see *store.yahoo.com*).

Electronic catalogs can be classified according to three dimensions:

1. The dynamics of the information presentation.
   - Static catalogs. The catalog is presented in textual description and static pictures.
   - Dynamic catalogs: The catalog is presented in motion pictures or animation, possibly with supplemental sound.
2. The degree of customization.
   - Ready-made catalogs: Merchants offer the same catalog to any customer.
   - Customized catalogs: Deliver customized content, pricing and display depending upon the characteristics of customers.
3. The degree of integration of catalogs with the following business processes or features.
   - Order taking and fulfillment.
   - Electronic payment systems.
   - Intranet workflow software and systems.
   - Inventory and accounting systems.
   - Suppliers' or customers' extranet.
   - Paper catalogs.

Comparison of Online Catalogs with Paper Catalogs

The advantages and disadvantages of online catalogs are contrasted with those of paper catalogs in Table 5-3. Although there are significant advantages of online catalogs, such as ease of updating, ability to integrate with the purchasing process, and coverage of a wide spectrum of products with a strong search capability, there are still disadvantages and limitations. To begin with, customers need computers and the Internet to access online catalogs. However, since computers and Internet access are spreading rapidly, we can expect a large portion of paper catalogs to be replaced by or at least supplemented by electronic catalogs. On the other hand, considering the fact that printed newspapers and magazines have not diminished

Comparison of Online Catalogs with Paper Catalogs		
Type	**Advantages**	**Disadvantages**
Paper Catalogs	• Easy to create without high technology • Reader is able to look at the catalog without computer system • More portable than electronic catalog	• Difficult to update changed product information promptly • Only a limited number of products can be displayed • Limited information through photographs and textual description is available • No possibility for advanced multimedia such as animation and voice
Online Catalogs	• Easy to update product information • Able to integrate with the purchasing process • Good search and comparison capabilities • Able to provide timely, up-to-date product information • Provision for globally broad range of product information • Possibility of adding on voice and animated pictures • Long-term cost savings • Easy to customize • More comparative shopping • Ease of connecting order processing, inventory processing, and payment processing to the system	• Difficult to develop catalogs, large fixed cost • There is a need for customer skill to deal with computers and browsers

TABLE 5-3

due to the online ones, we can guess that the paper catalogs will not disappear in spite of the popularity of online catalogs. There seems to be room for both media, at least in the near future. However, in B2B, paper catalogs may disappear more quickly, as shown in Application Case 5.4.

APPLICATION CASE   5.4

Electronic Catalogs at Boise Cascade

Boise Cascade Office Products is a $3 billion office products wholesaler whose customer base includes over 100,000 large corporate customers and 1 million small ones. The company's 900-page paper catalog is mailed to customers once each year. Throughout the year, minicatalogs are sent to customers tailored to their individual needs based on past buying habits and purchase patterns. The company sells over 200,000 different items.

In 1996, the company placed its catalogs online. Customers view the catalog at *bcop.com* and can order straight from the site or they can e-mail in orders. The orders are shipped the next day. Customers are then billed. In 1997, the company generated 20 percent of its sales through the Web site. In early 1999, the figure was above 30 percent. The company acknowledges that its Internet business is the fastest growing segment of its business and that it expects the Internet business to generate 70 percent of its total sales in just a few years.

The company prepares thousands of customers' customized catalogs. It used to take about 6 weeks to produce a single customer paper catalog, primarily because of the time involved in pulling together all the data. Now the process of producing a Web catalog takes 1 week. One major advantage of customized catalogs is pricing. With paper catalogs that everyone shares, you cannot show the customized price for each buyer, which is based on the type of the contract signed and the volume of goods being purchased.

APPLICATION CASE   **5.4**

(continued)

The company estimates that electronic orders cost approximately 55 percent less to process than paper-based orders. The application figure illustrates the process of working with the electronic catalogs. Some catalogs on Web sites provide text and pictures without linking them to order taking. For instance, Coca-Cola's Web site (*cocacola.com*) is not appropriate for taking Coke's orders online. It just reminds people about the taste of Coca-Cola. However, you can buy Coke's collectors' items and more at the online store.

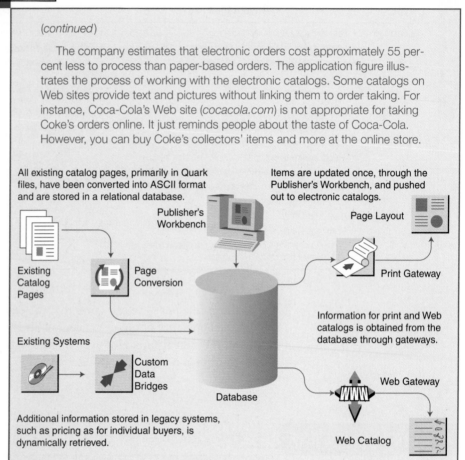

All existing catalog pages, primarily in Quark files, have been converted into ASCII format and are stored in a relational database.

Items are updated once, through the Publisher's Workbench, and pushed out to electronic catalogs.

Information for print and Web catalogs is obtained from the database through gateways.

Additional information stored in legacy systems, such as pricing as for individual buyers, is dynamically retrieved.

Source: home.netscape.com/solutions/business/profiles/boisecoscale.html. Also see *bcop.com/about/ecommerce.shtml* (2001).

Representative tools for building online catalogs are Boise's Marketing Service (Boise), IBM's Net.commerce (IBM), and Oracle's ICS (Oracle). See Chapter 12 for details.

Customized Catalogs

A customized catalog is a catalog assembled specifically for a company, usually a customer of the catalog owner. It can also be tailored to individual shoppers. There are two approaches to customized catalogs.

The first approach is to let the customers identify the interesting parts out of the total catalog as is done by products such as One-to-One from *broadvision.com*. Then, customers do not have to deal with irrelevant topics.

Customized catalog-creation software allows the creation of catalogs with branded value-added capabilities that make it easy for customers to find the products they want to purchase, locate the information they need, and quickly compose their order. Product offerings can be specialized for each customer's organization or for individuals with specific needs. Every customer company can view a custom catalog with individualized prices, products, and display formats. An e-mall manager who uses the software can control a complete range of information that the customer sees and link the online catalog with related computing resources. Several software packages feature a specialized catalog language that offers complete control over the look and feel of catalogs. This combination of power and flexibility allows a catalog to be quickly and easily modified to meet the evolving needs of customers.

The second approach is to let the system automatically identify the characteristics of customers based on their transaction records. To collect the necessary data, cookies can be used to trace transactions. However, to generalize the relationship between the customer and items of interest, data mining technology and support by intelligent systems, such as a neural network, is necessary. This second approach can be effectively combined with the first one.

As an example of the second approach, let us review a scenario of using a tool by Oracle Corp. called Internet Commerce Server (ICS) in a customized catalog:

Example: Joe logs on to the Acme Shopping site, where he has the option to register as an account customer and record his preferences in terms of address details, preferred method of payment, and interest areas. Acme Shopping offers a wide range of products, including electronics, clothing, books, and sporting goods. Joe is only interested in clothing and electronics. He is not a sportsman or a great book lover. Joe also has some very distinct hobby areas—one is photography.

Example: After Joe has recorded his preferences, the first page of the electronic store will show him only the clothing and electronics departments. Furthermore, when Joe goes into the electronics department, he only sees products related to photography—cameras and accessories. But some of the products are way out of Joe's price range, so Joe further refines his preferences to reflect that he is only interested in electronics that relate to photography and cost $300 or less.

Such personalization gives consumers a value-added experience and adds to the compelling reasons for revisiting the site, building brand loyalty to that Internet store. Against the backdrop of intense competition for Web airtime, personalization provides a valuable way to get the consumer matched to the products and information they are most interested in as quickly and painlessly as possible. An example of how corporations customize their catalogs for corporate clients is provided in Application Case 5.4.

5.8   SPECIAL ADVERTISEMENT TOPICS

How Much to Advertise

Like any other advertisement, Internet advertisement needs to justify itself; otherwise a company may spend more than it really needs. It is important that companies know what their advertisement objectives are. The rationale is straightforward. A lack of objective evaluation about the Web may lead to problems of image and information overkill. Also, if what is expected from Web advertising cannot be articulated in broad terms and systematically evaluated in terms of deliverability by the medium, there may be no point in using the Web. Once it has been determined that using the Web as an advertising vehicle could indeed benefit a company in achieving its objectives, management's attention should turn to learning about the Web. They need to understand what the Web is and how it works, and they must realize the need for long-term commitment to the medium and short-term dynamics in information display. Only then can they decide how much to spend on Internet advertisement.

Transplanting TV ad objectives into Web objectives does not seem to suffice. Web ads are dictated by different dynamics. Television, radio, newspapers, and magazines rely on in-your-face advertising and intrusions into a person's consciousness. Web advertisement may impact people differently because of the interactivity. Firms need to assess whether they have the commitment—manpower, time, and financial resources—needed to stay on course once they have decided to adopt the Web. Lack of commitment is likely to result in typical Web sites that disappointingly lead nowhere or constantly inform the visitor that they are under construction. Web sites are never truly finished; they require constant and dynamic changes to attract visitors.

For individuals and businesses, it may be wise to utilize the services of an established ad agency knowledgeable in the specialized medium of Internet advertising. Such an agency may have a much better idea of what type of ads will actually influence the viewers, thereby generating the desired traffic to your Web site.

Permission Advertisement

One of the major issues of advertisement done on a one-to-one basis is the flooding of users with unwanted junk mail. One of the authors of this book experienced a flood of X-rated ads. Each time an e-mail comes, it is blocked. This helps for a day or two; then the same ad comes from another e-mail address. Some people place software agents to delete such junk mail. Another problem is that of **spamming**, where users are flooded by e-mails from members of a newsgroup that may not like what the user said. In either case the user is upset and this may keep any type of advertisement from reaching them. To overcome the problem, advertisers use permission advertisement (marketing) in which users register and agree to accept advertisements. The authors of this book receive large numbers of e-commerce newsletters that include ads. This way we can keep abreast of what is happening in the field. We also agree to accept e-mail from research companies, newspapers, travel agencies, and more. They push very valuable information to us with some accompanying ads.

Measuring, Auditing, and Analyzing Web Traffic

Before a company decides to advertise on someone's Web site, it is important that the company knows that the number of hits, clicks-through, or other data it was told about are legitimate, because the potential for manipulation of data is large. A site audit is critical; it validates the number of ad views and hits claimed by the site, assuring advertisers that they are getting their money's worth. An impartial, external analysis and review is crucial to advertisers to verify the accuracy of the page impression counted by the site.

A longtime friend of advertisers is the Audit Bureau of Circulation (ABC), established in 1914 as a not-for-profit association by advertisers, advertising agencies, and publishers who came together to establish advertisement standards and rules. They created ABC (see *abc.org.uk*) to verify circulation reports by auditing circulation figures and, as a result, to provide credible and objective information to the buyers and sellers of print advertising.

As part of its services:

- ABC provides a forum for buyers and publishers and ad space sellers to come together to determine information critical to the buying and selling process.

- ABC provides circulation audits. An ABC audit is an in-depth examination of space seller's Web records to assure buyers that circulation claims are accurate.
- ABC disseminates circulation data, both in print and in electronic format, for ABC members' use.
- ABC continually improves its products and services so they remain relevant to buyer and publisher members.

The ABC has adapted itself to Web advertisement. Several other independent third-party Internet auditing companies are in operation, including PCMeter, BPA, and Audit. An example of auditing is provided in Application Case 5.5.

APPLICATION CASE   5.5

Sample of an Audit Report

The following is a summary of an audit quarterly report issued by BPA Audit (*bpai.com*) for *Adage.com* for the period ending March 31, 2001.

Purpose

This BPA International Interactive Audit Report provides an independently verified summary of a census of activity recorded at *Adage.com*. This audit report includes verification of all traffic and general traffic users. All verified counts are based on a census, not a sample, of activity at this site. Activity by general traffic users has been audited for counts only as reported separately herein.

Site Content

Adage.com features daily advertising, marketing and media news, and daily news feeds covering interactive and international marketing for an audience of marketing professionals, ad agency personnel and media executives. In addition to daily news, the site includes features from *Advertising Age* magazine, special reports, agency and marketer data, and more.

Independent Auditors' Opinion

BPA International required and has examined the complete and entire access log files of this Web site for the period covered by this report. Sample or extracts of log files are not accepted.

BPA's examination of site usage and accurate tracking by log files was made in accordance with generally accepted auditing standards and accordingly included tests and confirmations of actual access by site's users. BPA International used multiple software analysis tools for this Web site audit.

Based on such examination, it is BPA International's opinion that the statements set forth in this report present fairly and accurately the access of this Web site in conformance with generally accepted auditing principles.

Report Highlights

- Total Quarterly Page Requests 3,324,800
- Average Daily Page Requests 29,923
- January, 1.1 million; February, .95 million; March, 1.1 million
- Weekly Demand by Day: Range from 11,000 (Saturday) to 44,000 (Monday)
- Hourly Usage: Low usage 2 A.M.–7 A.M. about 430/hour to about 2,160/hour during 9 A.M.–5 P.M.

Related to auditing is the rating of sites. This is done by companies such as Accure, Accipiter, Ipro, Netcount, Interse, Hotstats, and CNet. Rating is done by looking at multiple criteria such as content, attractiveness, ease of navigation, and privacy protection.

SELF-MONITORING OF TRAFFIC

Several vendors sell softwares that allow Webmasters to monitor traffic advertisements on their own Web sites. Examples are *Webconnect.com*, *Webtrends.com*, *siteguage.com*, and *netratings.com*. Additionally, Webmasters can measure who is coming to a site (e.g., *leadspinner.com*).

Internet Ad Standards

With so many creative ways to advertise on the Web, it would seem that the last thing anyone would want to do is make it more standardized and regulated. But, paradoxically, that's the way much of the Web ad industry is heading.

One proposed standard deals with cookies. The standard encourages browser vendors to make the utilization of cookies and its prevention more apparent to users. The standard seeks to take control of the cookie away from online publishers and marketers to protect consumer privacy.

Localization

Localization is the process of converting media products developed in one country to a form culturally and linguistically acceptable in countries outside the original target market. It is usually done by a set of guidelines called internationalization. Web-page translation (Chapter 18) is only one aspect of internationalization. There are several more. For example, a jewelry manufacturer that displays its products on a white background was astonished to find that this might offend customers in other countries that want a blue background. If a company aims at the global market (there are millions of potential customers out there), it must make an effort to localize its Web pages. This may not be a simple task because of the following factors:

- Many countries use English, yet they differ in terminology, culture, and even spelling (e.g., United States vs. United Kingdom vs. Australia).
- Some languages use accented characters. If text includes an accented character, it will disappear when converted into English.
- Hard-coded text and fonts cannot be changed, so they remain in their original format in the translated material.
- Graphics and icons look different to viewers in different countries. For example, a U.S. mailbox looks like a trash can in Europe.
- When translating into Asian languages, significant cultural issues must be addressed.
- Dates that are written mm/dd/yy (e.g., June 6, 2001) in the United States are written dd/mm/yy (e.g., 6 June 2001) in many other countries.
- Consistent translation over several documents is difficult.

For free translations to six languages see *freetranslation.com*. To help with localization, a company may want to hire a consultant (for example, see *islg.com*).

USING INTERNET RADIO FOR LOCALIZATION

Internet radio is especially interested in local communities. For example, *kiisfmi.com* is a Los Angeles site that features music from up-and-coming bands, live concerts, interviews with movie stars, etc. About 40 percent of the site's traffic comes from listeners in California. The big advantage of Internet radio is that there are no limits on the type of or number of offerings it can offer, as compared to traditional radio stations. The company that powers *kiisfmi.com* also operates sites with country music, Latin music, etc. Advertisers can reach fairly narrow segments this way.

The Major Web Ad Players

Meeker (1997) has identified the following five major categories of Web advertisement players (besides the companies that create and operate Internet sites that are funded, in whole or in part, by advertising dollars):

1. **Advertising agencies and Web site developers.** Includes companies involved in the generation of Internet advertising campaigns, from campaign planning to media buying, as well as developers of sites that allow companies to promote their brands and develop an online consumer presence.
2. **Market research providers.** In such a new field, advertisers, publishers, investors, and other interested parties are all looking for real data about what is happening, how big it is, and where it is going. These are companies that are tracking the evolution of Internet technology with a focus on its impact on business and certain industries, including the Web advertising arena.
3. **Traffic measurement and analysis companies.** To validate advertising media buys on the Internet, advertisers need to be able to justify and verify the investments they make. Traffic analysis companies fill that need by offering software and services to aid publishers in tracking and executing advertising delivery on their Web sites.
4. **Networks/rep firms.** These companies provide value-added services for Web advertisers and publishers alike by brokering the distribution of advertisements and overseeing their delivery.
5. **Order processing and support.** These are companies that provide outsourcing services to Internet publishers and service providers.

5.9   MANAGERIAL ISSUES

The following issues are germane to management:

1. **Make vs. buy.** Web advertisement is a complex undertaking. Therefore, outsourcing should be seriously considered (see O'Keefe, 1997, and the list of sources there). Companies should examine *adobe.com* for its index of Web sites, their advertising rates, and reported traffic counts before selecting a site on which to advertise. Companies should also consult third-party audits.
2. **Finding the most visited sites.** One way a company can determine where to advertise is to check a prospective site's traffic. Several places report the traffic on popular Web sites such as Yahoo! or AOL. One good source for such lists

is *100hot.com*. Advertisers can also access *arbitron.com* to find survey results, by metropolitan areas, about Internet advertisements.

3. **Company research.** Companies should research the Web thoroughly before meeting with an Internet marketing/advertising service. With so many services available, they should be researched, too. In addition, currently most ad networks provide little or no control to the advertiser regarding the execution of an ad campaign. An ad network should provide a convenient way for Web publishers to manage a portfolio of Web pages or sites.

4. **Commitment to Web advertising and coordination with traditional advertisement.** Once a company is totally committed to advertising on the Web, it must remember that a successful program is multifaceted. It requires input and vision from marketing, cooperation from the legal department, and strong technical leadership from the corporate information systems (IS) department. A successful ad Web program also requires top management support.

5. **Integrated marketing campaigns.** Many companies are integrating TV and computer campaigns. For example, the TV or the newspaper ads direct the viewers to the Web site where short videos and sound ads, known as **rich media** are used. With click-through ratios of banner ads down to less than 0.5 percent, innovations are certainly needed.

6. **Ethical issues.** Several ethical issues relate to advertisement online. One issue that receives a great deal of attention is spamming, which is now subject to legislation (Chapter 17). Another issue is the selling of mailing lists and customer information. Some people believe that not only does a company need the consent of the customers before selling a list, but that the company should share with them the profits derived from the sale. Using cookies without individual consent is another ethical issue.

7. **Integrating advertisement with ordering and other business processes.** This is an important requirement. If a user goes to *Amazon.com*'s site, the user is directed to the shopping cart, then to the catalog, then to ordering and paying. Such integration should be seamless.

8. **Content is critical.** The content of the ads is critical, so companies need to make sure that content is produced by experts, internally or externally. While there is plenty of expert help available, it may not be cheap. Also, incorrect content may lead to unethical, or even illegal, situations.

Summary

In this chapter, you learned about the following EC issues as they relate to the learning objectives:

1. **Objectives and characteristics of Web advertisement.** Web advertisement attempts to attract surfers to advertiser's sites where they can receive lots of information, interact with the sellers, and in many cases place an order. Distinctive features are customized ads to fit groups of people with similar interests and even individuals. Also, the ads offer dynamic presentation by rich multimedia.

2. **Major online advertisement methods.** While banners are the most popular ad method, other methods are frequently used. Notable are those involving

e-mail, (including to mobile phones), registration of the URL with search engines, splash screens, newsgroups, and spot leasing.

3. **Various advertisement strategies.** The major strategies are:
   - Pull (passive) approach that lets customers find ads by themselves.
   - Push (active) approach such as sending e-mail to customers.
   - Ads associated with search results. (text links)
   - Pay or offer incentives for customers to view ads.
   - Ads can be customized on a one-to-one basis.

4. **Types of promotions on the Web.** Web promotions are similar to off-line promotions. They include giveaways, contests, quizzes, entertainment, coupons, and so on. Customization and interactivity distinguishes the Internet promotions from conventional promotions.

5. **Push technology and intelligent agents.** Push technology allows the collection and delivery of desired information and the sending it to customers, including advertisement on demand. The customization of information saves time and energy for users. When information is sent for free, it is usually supplemented by banner ads. Intelligent agents are used to identify customer profiles and to tailor ads to these customers.

6. **Major economic issues related to Web advertisement.** The major issue is justification, and it is related to pricing mechanisms. Also, the allocation of money among the various Web alternatives (e.g., banners vs. e-mail) is important.

7. **Measuring the success of advertisement and pricing ads.** The traditional concept of paying for exposure (by CPM) is used on the Internet, but it is being challenged. Space sellers like the CPM approach. Advertisers like to pay for act-ins such as click-through. Paying commissions for electronic referrals is becoming a popular method.

8. **Comparing paper and electronic catalogs and describe customized catalogs.** The major advantages of electronic catalogs over paper ones are the lower cost, high speed of preparing customized catalogs, and the possible inclusion of animation, videos, and audio. Online catalogs are also easy to update and can be integrated with ordering, inventory, and payment processing. Finally, creating customized catalogs becomes economically feasible. Customized catalogs are used mainly in B2B because different customers pay different prices and may get customized products as well.

9. **Implementation issues.** The major issues are finding the appropriate advertisement level, auditing Web traffic, using ad agencies, using advertisement standards, localization of content, and dealing with spamming.

Key Terms

Advertisement	Click-through (or ad click)
Advertorial	CPM (cost per thousand impressions)
Advocacy marketing	Cookie
Associated ad display strategy (text links)	E-mercial
Ad views	Electronic catalog
Banner	Hit
Banner exchange	Impressions
Click ratio	Integrated marketing campaigns

Interactive advertisement

Interactive marketing

Internet radio

Keyword banner

Localization

Micro-site ads

Online catalogs

Permission advertisement (marketing)

Personalization

Pointcasts

Pull technology

Push technology

Random banner

Reach

Rich media

Spamming

Splash screen

Text links

Visit (or unique visit)

Viral marketing

Webcasting

Questions for Review

1. Define Internet advertisement.
2. List the advantages of Internet advertisement.
3. What is a banner ad?
4. List the major methods of Internet advertisement.
5. Describe the role of intelligent agents in advertisement.
6. List the advantages of electronic catalogs over paper catalogs.
7. Describe push technology and its benefits.
8. List the major measures of advertisement success (and basis for payments).
9. Explain banner swapping and banner exchanges.
10. Define viral marketing.
11. Why is the pull technology a passive strategy?
12. Where can a company obtain e-mail lists of consumers?
13. How can we escape from the flood of junk e-mails?
14. What is the associated ad display strategy?
15. How can an ad be sold as a commodity?
16. What is the typical model of customized ad strategy?
17. How can the product comparison process be used as an opportunity for advertisement?

Questions for Discussion

1. Compare banner swapping to a banner exchange.
2. Compare and contrast "pulling" information with "pushing" it.
3. In what ways does push technology resemble mass customization?
4. Explain the need to audit Internet traffic.
5. Discuss why banners are so popular in Internet advertisement.
6. Compare and contrast Internet and television advertisements.
7. Discuss the advantages and limitations of listing your URL with search engines.
8. How is the chat room used for advertisement?
9. What is the purpose of entertainment in EC?
10. Describe the steps of push technology and relate pointcasting to advertisement.
11. Why might the use of CPM to charge advertisers be inappropriate for the Internet?

12. Compare the use of "click-through" with more interactive approaches as a basis for ad rates.
13. Is it ethical for a vendor to enter a chat room of its competitor and pose queries under an assumed name?
14. Should all online catalogs be tightly linked with order taking and payments?
15. Do catalog personalizations based on past transaction records truly reflect the customer's preferences?
16. How can push and pull advertisements work together?
17. Some say that companies such as bCentral constitute a threat to ad agencies. Others disagree. Examine the services of bCentral and compare it to the services of an Internet agency. Write a report on your conclusions.

Internet Exercises

1. Visit the chat room of Lotus Development Company (*lotus.com*), called Domino Chat, and describe its capabilities. Analyze the advertisement on this site. Also, check the chat room of 1-800-FLOWERS. Compare the two sites. Finally, find general information about chat rooms (for example, *cws.internet.com*). Prepare a report based on your findings.

2. Locate information about banner ads on the following sites and identify all of the benefits and issues related to Internet banner advertising. Prepare a report of your findings.
   - *bcentral.com*
   - *coder.com*
   - *sharat.co.il/services/services.html*
   - *doubleclick.net*

3. Enter the Web site of *ipro.com* and find what Internet traffic management, Web results, and auditing services are provided. What are the benefits of each service? Find at least one competitor in each category (such as *netratings.com*, observe their "demo"). Compare the services provided and prices.

4. Examine the status of the growth of Web advertisement. Surf the sites of *iab.net*, *jup.com*, *forrester.com*, and *adage.com*. Prepare a report and project the growth of Web advertising for the next 5 years.

5. Investigate the services provided in chat rooms. Start with *talkcity.com* and list its services. Why do some vendors provide free chat rooms? Examine *yack.com*. Why are their chat listings so popular?

6. Investigate the tools available for monitoring Web sites. What are the major capabilities provided? Start with *Webarrange.com*, *Webtrends.com*, and *doubleclick.com*.

7. Investigate the status of push technology by visiting companies such as *backweb.com*, *marimba.com*, *netdelivery.com*, *verity.com*, *myyahoo.com*, and *myway.com*.

8. Consult *saqqara.com* for their Product/Server e-catalog Management. List the major capabilities.

9. For a chance to win $25,000, or at least have fun, register with *windough.com*. Prepare a report on the success of the site in attracting the attention of surfers.

10. Enter *hotwired.com* and try to identify all the advertising methods used. Can you find those planned for targeted advertisement?

11. Enter *micromass.com/mmctv/default.htm*. Go to the auto online demo. Fill in the questionnaire and examine the customized ad generated by the "IntelliWeb." How well was the fit for you as a consumer? Also check the ad coder and healthcare demos.

12. Sign up with *hvaa.com/guessthe.htm*. Try to win a $50 U.S. savings bond by estimating the damage to a pictured car on the site. Use the hints provided.

13. Plan a contest and other promotions for your company or for a company with which you are familiar. Start with *Webmagnet.com* (be sure to read "Ideas For You").

14. Generate a banner for your company. Several vendors provide free banner generation software. Your mission is to create a banner using a vendor of your choice, such as *coder.com* or *bcentral.com* (click on instant banner and on banner creation). A good overview is provided at *coder.com*'s "documentation" pages. Make use of the many options provided. Report on your experiences.

15. Enter *myprospects.com*. Go to *messageblaster.com* and use "try it" to send a message to yourself. You can use the tool to poll responses and for tracking.

Team Assignments and Role Playing

1. It is said that the number of Web ads is mushrooming due to the following trends:
   - E-mail gains respect
   - Women's sites launched
   - Ad servicing broadens
   - Measurement of ads' success improves
   - EC is growing rapidly
   - Web expands its reach

   Find evidence that supports these trends, such as new companies, statistics, and experts' testimonials. Prepare a report.

2. Measuring Web traffic and verifying how many ad impressions are delivered is critical to the success of Web ads. Visit the following companies, find their products and services and comment on them: *NetRatings.com* (plan), *RelevantKnowledge.com*, *MediaMetrix.com*, *ABCInteractiveaudits.com*, BPA Interactive (*bpa.com*), and *ipro.com*. Also evaluate Matchlogic (True Count Service *gane.com/ads/whoiscoming.htm*).

3. The use of classifieds ads is on the rise. The problem is how to find what you need or where to place the ads. Companies such as *classifind.com* and *classifieds2000.com* may assist you. Investigate the issue of classified ads, including the role of Yahoo! and AOL in the classified ad market. Examine the issue of local advertising.

4. Examine all the advertisement options offered by BSF (Application Case 5.2) to vendors. Which are unique to m-commerce? Investigate similar m-commerce companies (start with I-MODE in Japan). Find information at *Nokia.com*,

Motorola.com, and *Ericsson.com*. Also check *adage.com* and other sources. Prepare a report of your findings.

5. Select one area of advertisement and conduct an in-depth investigation of the major players there. For example, direct mail is relatively inexpensive. Visit *the-dma.org* to learn about direct mail. Then visit: *bulletmail.com*, *e-target.com*, *permissiondirect.com* and *venturedirect.com*. Review the services provided for direct mail and write a report.

REAL-WORLD CASE: Chevron's World of Car Characters

To have its brand more easily recognized, especially among children, Chevron Corp., a major oil and gas company, ran an animated toy car promotional campaign that was centered around the Web site *chevroncars.com*. It built one of the freshest, most innovative corporate Web sites. Within 3 months, traffic at the site increased from about 1,500 hits per day to over 150,000 hits per day (over 10,000 percent). The site won the 1997 Best of the Internet (BOTI) Award and generated about 100 suggestions per day from viewers, mostly children, ranging from ideas for new claymation characters to having the consumer actually design "the goods they want to consume."

Among the highlights of *Chevroncars.com* are a question and answer section (FAQ), the ability to customize cars and put them in "My Garage," free stuff (e.g., screen saver), and a knowledge base about cars. A squirrel points out commercial messages and tasks for which children may need adult permission. Kidshop is a place where users can grab a cart and buy a plastic version of Chevron's animated vehicles or other Chevron items. Finally a playground with games such as crossword puzzles, connect the dots, and concentration-style-matching games is available.

The game allowing users to check how they did against players nationwide seems to be the hands-down favorite. If you get the wrong answer, the site provides an empathetic "bummer" response.

The site has a definite commercial and branding message: to show that Chevron is a responsible, necessary, and even fun type of business; to demonstrate that Chevron is ecologically aware and doing things like protecting baby owls nesting in pumps; and to let users find out how a company like Chevron operates.

The Road Adventure game is ever expanding, and the company is thinking of ways to use the site to promote Chevron's math and science awards and to help teachers locate videos and other educational materials.

So what's the most popular part of the site? Shopping for the toy cars, of course. The largest buying group tends to be the parents of children between 3 and 9; then come 18- to 21-year-olds, followed by "kids" 35 years and older.

For a national gasoline company in just 26 markets, however, the real success of Chevron's site comes in the brand recognition it affords for both existing and future customers. And the fun message also reflects the changing nature of the gasoline business—pumps give way to complexes including commercial markets, car washes, fast-food chains, and even hotels. The company feels that the site's success has more to do with listening to what people want than any master plan.

Questions for the case

1. Explain the logic of using claymation cars to advertise the sale of gasoline.

2. The company also used the claymation cars in their television ads. Visit chevroncars and examine the advantages of the Web site over the television ad (if you have not seen it, try to find information about it).

3. Why is Chevron targeting 5- to 12-year-olds? They certainly do not buy gasoline, and by the time they drive cars, we will see many changes in gasoline sales.

4. From what you have learned in this chapter, what do you think are the factors that contribute to the site's success?

5. Investigate the role of animated characters in advertisement. Try: *agentmart.com* and *extempo.com*.

REFERENCES AND BIBLIOGRAPHY

Abrams, M., editor. *World Wide Web: Beyond the Basics*. Upper Saddle River, New Jersey: Prentice Hall, 1998.

Banning, K. L. and H. Gregg. "Webmasters' Secret Internet Marketing and Search Engine Positioning Strategies," *American Multimedia Publisher* (October 1999).

Bresster, S. E. and C. Grantham. *Communities of Commerce: Building Internet Business Communities*. New York: McGraw-Hill, 2000.

Chau, P. Y. K., et al. "Impact of Information Presentation Modes on Online Shopping," *Journal of Org. Computing and e-Commerce* (Spring 2000).

CommerceNet. "Catalog Interoperability Study: Issues, Practices, and Recommendations." (February 27, 1998).

Chase, L. *Essential Business Tactics on the Net*. New York: John Wiley & Sons, 1998.

Choi, S., et al. *The Economics of Electronic Commerce*. Indianapolis, Indiana: Macmillan Technical Publishing, 1997.

Carpenter, P. *eBrand: Building an Internet Business at Breakneck Speed*. Boston: Harvard Business School Press, 2000.

Danish, S. and P. Gannon. *Building Database-Driven Catalogs*. New York: Computing McGraw-Hill, 1998.

Giannoni, G. *E-promotions: The Value of E-mail Marketing*. New York: Inter-American Development Bank, 2000.

Gray, D. and D. Gray. *The Complete Guide to Associate and Affiliate Programs on the Net*. New York: McGraw Hill Professional Publishing, 1999.

Gurian, P. *E-mail Business Strategies and Dozens of Other Great Ways to Take Advantage of the Internet*. Spokane, Washington: Grand National Press, 2000.

Helm, S. "Viral Marketing," *Electronic Markets*, vol. 10, no. 3 (2000).

Helmsteller, G. and P. Metivier. *Affiliate Selling: Building Revenue on the Web*. New York: John Wiley & Sons, 2000.

Hoffman, D. L. and T. P. Novak. "Advertising Pricing Models for the Web." In *Internet Publishing and Beyond*, edited by D. Hurley et al. Cambridge, Massachusetts: MIT Press, 2000.

Hoffman, D. L. and T. P. Novak. "Marketing in Hypermedia Computer Mediated Environments: Conceptual Foundations," *Journal of Marketing* (July 1996).

Jeffers, M. and E. Schibsted. "The Sizzle: What's New and Now in E-commerce and E-business Marketing and Advertisement," *Business 2.0* (August 22, 2000).

Kalakota, R. and A. B. Whinston, editors. *Readings in Electronic Commerce*. Reading, Massachusetts: Addison-Wesley, 1997.

Kassay, W. "Global Advertising and the World Wide Web," *Business Horizons* (May/June 1997).

Keller, A. M. "Smart Catalogs and Virtual Catalogs." In *Readings in Electronic Commerce*, R. Kalakota and Andrew Whinston, editors. Reading, Massachusetts: Addison-Wesley, 1997.

Kinnard, S. *Marketing with E-mail*. Gulf Breeze, Florida: Maximum Press, 2000.

Kosiur, D. *Understanding Electronic Commerce*. Seattle, Washington: Microsoft Press, 1997.

Lee, J. K., et al. "A Comparison Shopping Architecture Over Multiple Malls: The Meta-Malls Architecture," *Proceedings of the International Conference on Electronic Commerce '98*, Seoul, Korea, pp. 149–54 (1998).

Leonard, D. "Madison Avenue Fights Back," *Fortune*, (February 5, 2001).

Meeker, N. *The Internet Advertising Report*. New York: Morgan Stanley Corporation, 1997.

Nobles, R. and S. O'Neil. *Streetwise Maximize Web Site Traffic: Build Web Site Traffic Fast and Free by Optimizing Search Engine Placement*. Holbrook, Massachusetts: Adams Media Corporation, 2000.

O'Keefe, S. *Publicity on the Internet*. New York: John Wiley & Sons, 1997.

Oracle. ICS White Paper. *oracle.com/products/ics/ html/ics_wp.htm*. (1998).

Peppers, D., et al. *The One-to-One Fieldbook*. New York: Currency/Doubleday, 1999.

Rewick, J. "Beyond Banners," *The Wall Street Journal* (October 23, 2000).

Roberts, S. *Internet Direct Mail: A Complete Guide to Successful E-Mail Marketing Campaigns*, Ntc Business Book, 2000.

Ruthenberg, R. "An Advertising Power, but Just What Does DoubleClick do?" *New York Times* (September 22, 2000).

Smith, B. E. *Push Technology for Dummies*. Foster City, California: IDG Books Worldwide, 1997.

Sweeney, S. *101 Ways to Promote Your Web Site*. Gulf Breeze, Florida: Maximum Press, 2000.

Szuprowich, B. O. *Webcasting and Push Technology Strategies*. New York: Computer Technology Research Corp., 1998.

Taylor, C. P. "Is One-to-One the Way to Market?" *Interactive Week* (May 12, 1997).

Tedeschi, B. "E-Commerce Report: New Alternatives to Banner Ads," *New York Times* (February 20, 2001).

Turban, E. and D. Gehrke. "Success Determinants of E-commerce Web Site Design," *Human Systems Management* (Summer 2000).

Ware, J., et al. *The Search for Digital Excellence*. New York: McGraw-Hill, 1998.

Williamson, H. "The Pull of Push," *Webmaster* (July 1997).

Wong, T. *101 Ways to Boost Your Web Traffic*. New York: Intesync, 2000.

Yuan, Y., et al. "The Relationship between Advertising and Content Provisions on the Internet," *European Journal of Marketing* (July/August 1998).

Zeff, R. L. and B. Aronson. *Advertising on the Internet*, 2nd ed. New York: Wiley, 1999.

PART 3

6

Company-Centric B2B

LEARNING OBJECTIVES

Upon completion of this chapter, the reader will be able to:

- Describe the B2B field.

- Describe the major types of B2B models.

- Describe the characteristics of the sell-side marketplace.

- Describe the sell-side intermediaries models.

- Describe the characteristics of the buy-side marketplace and e-procurement.

- Explain how forward and backward auctions work in B2B.

- Describe B2B aggregation and group purchasing models.

- Describe collaborative e-commerce.

- Understand issues concerning the implementation of company-centric B2B.

- Distinguish Internet-based EDI from traditional EDI.

General Motors (GM) is the world's largest vehicle manufacturer. The company sells cars in 190 counties and has manufacturing plants in about 50. The automotive industry is very competitive; therefore, GM is always looking for ways to improve its effectiveness. In 1999 and 2000, GM embarked on several EC initiatives. The most publicized is its futuristic build-to-custom project. GM expects to custom make the majority of its cars by 2005. This way, the company can save billions of dollars by reducing its inventory of finished cars. In 1999, GM initiated two interesting projects that are described here.

■ SELLING CAPITAL ASSETS

GM owns huge amounts of capital assets such as machines for manufacturing. Capital assets depreciate over time, and when they are no longer sufficiently productive they must be replaced. GM used to sell these assets, usually through intermediaries that auctioned the assets. The problem was that the auctions took weeks, even months. Furthermore, the auction prices seemed to be too low, and a 20 percent commission had to be deducted for the intermediary.

To solve this problem, GM implemented its own electronic market called TradeXchange to conduct **forward auctions.** In a forward auction (Chapter 9), items are put up for sale on an online auction and buyers bid on them from their PCs until the items are sold to the highest bidder. The first items put up for bid on *TradeXchange.com* in early 2000

were eight 75-ton stamping presses. GM invited 140 precertified bidders to view the pictures and service records of the presses online. On January 27, after only 1 week of preparation, the auction went live online. In just 89 minutes, the eight presses were sold for $1.8 million. With the off-line method, a similar item would have sold for less than half of its online price and the process would have taken 4 to 6 weeks. In 2000, GM conducted over 150 auctions on TradeXchange. Other sellers were encouraged to put their items up for sale as well, paying a commission on the final sales price to GM.

■ BUYING COMMODITY PRODUCTS

GM spends close to *$100 billion* annually for commodity products, which can be either *direct materials* going into the cars or *indirect materials* such as light bulbs or office supplies. GM buys about 200,000 different products from 20,000 suppliers. Because GM purchases in large quantities, GM uses a bidding (tendering) process to negotiate with potential suppliers. In the past, such a process was done manually. The specifications of the needed materials were sent by mail to potential suppliers in a process known as a **request for quote** (RFQ). The suppliers would submit a bid, and GM would select a winner if a supplier offered a low enough price. If all the bids were too high, second and third rounds of bids were conducted. In some cases the process took weeks, even months, before GM was confident that the best deal, from a price and quality standpoint, had been achieved. The preparation costs

involved in this process prohibited some bidders from submitting bids, so less than optimal numbers of suppliers participated.

To improve the process, GM automated the bidding, creating online **reverse auctions** (Chapter 9) on the TradeXchange site. In a reverse auction, qualified suppliers use the Internet to bid on each item GM needs to purchase in an "open bid," where all bidders can see the bids of their competitors.

In a reverse auction a buyer is able to accept bids from many suppliers concurrently. The job is awarded quickly to the most suitable bidder based on predetermined criteria, such as price, delivery date, and payment terms. In the first online reverse auction on TradeXchange, GM purchased a large volume of rubber sealing packages for vehicle production. The price GM paid was *significantly lower* than the price GM used to pay for the same items when negotiated by manual tendering. Now, many similar bids are conducted on the site every week. The administrative costs per order have been reduced by 40 percent or more.

■ EVOLUTION TO CONSORTIUM—COVISINT

In both cases, TradeXchange significantly streamlined trading operations. Actual monetary savings were also recorded. By opening its site to other buyers and sellers, GM can generate commission income making TradeXchange more profitable. In 2001, GM began trading at *Covisint.com* and eventually may transfer TradeXchange business to Covisint. (see Section 7.1)

6.2   CONCEPTS AND CHARACTERISTICS OF B2B EC

The GM case demonstrates how a large company engaged in two EC activities: (1) selling used equipment to customers via electronic auctions, and (2) conducting purchasing or procurement via an electronic bidding (tendering) system in a process called a reverse auction.

Both activities are part of B2B EC. They belong to what we call a **company-centric EC**, where there is either one seller and many buyers or one buyer and many sellers. When conducting such trades, a company can employ auctions, such as GM did, or it can use other methods, as will be shown later.

B2B Basic Concepts

Business-to-business (B2B) EC, also known as **eB2B** *(electronic B2B)* or just *B2B,* is a transaction conducted electronically between businesses over the Internet, extranets, intranets, or private networks. Such transactions may be conducted between a business and its supply chain members, as well as between a business and any other business. A business refers to any organization, private or public, for profit or nonprofit.

The major characteristic of B2B is that companies attempt to *automate* the trading process in order to improve it. Therefore, it will be beneficial to look at the trading process in more detail.

MARKET SIZE AND CONTENT

B2B EC is expected to grow to at least ten trillion dollars by 2005 and will continue to be the major component of the EC market (Freeman, 1998; Retter and Calyniuk, 1998; Forrester Research, 2001). Market forecasters estimate that by 2003 the global B2B market will be in the range $1.1 to $4 trillion. The percentage of Internet-based B2B EC compared to total B2B commerce increased from 0.2 percent in 1997 to 2.1 percent in 2000 and is expected by some to grow to 10 percent in 2005. Chemicals, computing electronics, utilities, agriculture, shipping and warehousing, motor vehicles, petrochemicals, paper and office products, and food are the leading items in B2B (see *gs.com* [special report, February 15, 2001]).

It is interesting to note different B2B market forecasters use different definitions and methodologies. Because of this, there are often frequent changes in predictions and numerous contradictions in predictions and other statistical data. Therefore, we will not provide any data here. Data sources are listed in Team Assignment #1.

PRIVATE AND PUBLIC E-MARKETPLACE

Conducting EC in *one-to-many* mode is sometimes referred to as a **private e-marketplace.** This is in contrast to a *many-to-many* marketplace, which is called a **public e-marketplace** or **exchange.** Public e-marketplaces are discussed in Chapter 7.

HOW IS B2B CONDUCTED?

B2B commerce can be conducted directly between a buyer and a seller or via an **online intermediary.** The intermediary can be an organization, a person, or an electronic system.

The common B2B activities are usually conducted along the supply chain of a manufacturing or assembling company, as shown in Figure 6-1. As will be shown later, B2B can make supply chains more efficient and effective by making small changes, or change it completely, eliminating one or more intermediaries.

Figure 6-1 can be viewed as a definition of B2B. Notice that in contrast with a typical supply chain, here the end consumer is not an individual, but a business. Notice that traditional B2B was conducted over the telephone, fax, or EDI, whereas eB2B is conducted over an electronic network, usually the Internet. Also note that B2B may take place along the entire supply chain or between any of its segments.

The introduction of B2B may eliminate the distributor and/or the retailer. In previous chapters we referred to such a phenomena as **disintermediation**. Alternatively, EC can change the role of an intermediary in what is called **reintermediation.** For a case of reintermediation see Section 6.7.

TYPES OF TRANSACTIONS

There are two basic types of B2B transactions: spot buying and strategic sourcing. **Spot buying** refers to the purchasing of goods and services at market prices, which are determined by supply and demand in a dynamic manner. The buyers and the sellers usually do not know each other. Stock exchanges and commodity exchanges (oil, sugar, corn, etc.) are examples of spot buying. In contrast, **strategic sourcing** involves long-term contracts that are usually based on negotiation between the sellers and buyers. Spot buying can be more economically supported by the third-party exchanges, while the strategic purchase can be supported more effectively and efficiently through a streamlined supply chain.

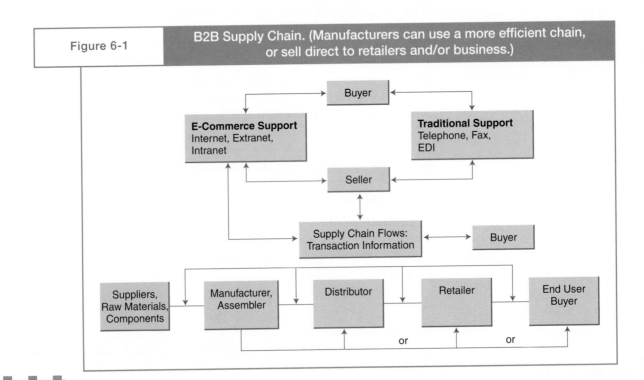

| Figure 6-1 | B2B Supply Chain. (Manufacturers can use a more efficient chain, or sell direct to retailers and/or business.) |

Supply Chain Relationships

Even though there are many B2B applications, the relationships between businesses are best understood in the supply chain context. As shown in Appendix A.1 (Chapter 1), the supply chain process consists of a number of interrelated subprocesses and roles, all the way from the acquisition of materials from suppliers to the processing of a product or service, to packaging it and moving it to distributors and retailers, ending with its eventual purchase by end consumers.

Historically, many of the segments and processes in the supply chain, especially the upstream and downstream activities, have been managed through paper transactions (e.g., purchase orders, invoices, and so forth). This is where B2B applications come into play. B2B applications can serve as supply chain enablers that can offer distinct competitive advantages. Supply chain management encompasses the coordination of order generation, order taking, and order fulfillment/distribution of products, services, and information (see Chapter 15 for more).

Entities of B2B

The key entities in B2B and their concerns are the following:

- **Selling companies**—with individual company's marketing management perspective
- **Buying companies**—with individual company's procurement management perspective
- **Electronic intermediaries**—a third-party service provider like exchanges and supply chain service eHubs (the scope of service may be extended to include order fulfillment).
- **Trading platforms**—pricing and negotiation protocol like auctions, reverse auctions, and more
- **Payment services**—provide the mechanism for transferring money to sellers
- **Logistics providers**—Packaging, storage, deliveries, and other logistics needed for completion of transactions
- **Network platforms**—Internet, intranets, extranets, or value-added networks
- **Protocols of communication**—EDI or XML
- **Other services**—directory services, matching buyers and sellers, security, escrow
- **Back-end integration**—connecting to ERP systems, databases, intranet, and functional applications

Information Processed in B2B

As Handfield and Nichols (1999) suggest, B2B applications offer enterprises access to the following sorts of information:

- **Product**—specifications, prices, sales history
- **Customer**—sales history and forecasts
- **Supplier**—product line and lead times, sales terms and conditions
- **Product process**—capacities, commitments, product plans
- **Transportation**—carriers, lead times, costs

- **Inventory**—inventory levels, carrying costs, locations
- **Supply chain**—key contacts, partners' roles and responsibilities, schedules
- **Competitor**—benchmarking, competitive product offerings, market share
- **Sales and marketing**—point of sale (POS), promotions
- **Supply chain process and performance**—process descriptions, performance measures, quality, delivery time, customer satisfaction

Electronic Intermediaries in B2B

The electronic intermediaries for consumers mentioned in Chapter 3 can also be referenced for B2B by replacing the individual consumers with business customers. Both individual consumers and businesses purchase items such as books, stationery, and personal computers. In this case, consumers and business buyers can share the intermediary. However, certain items, such as industrial equipment and parts, are purchased only by businesses. For instance, the parts for jumbo jets are purchased only by businesses. An example in which Boeing plays the role of intermediary between airline customers and 300 parts suppliers is described in Section 6.7.

Benefits of B2B Models

The benefits of B2B models depend on the model used. Generally, businesses can use B2B to eliminate paper-based systems, expedite cycle time, reduce errors, increase employee productivity, reduce costs, and increase customer service and partnership relationship management.

6.3 B2B MODELS

B2B activities and initiatives can take several forms. In this book we divide them into three classes: company-centric models, many-to-many marketplaces, and other models.

Company-Centric Models (One-to-Many, Many-to-One)

In company-centric models, one company does either all of the selling, which is known as a **sell-side marketplace** (one-to-many), and/or one company does all of the buying, which is known as a **buy-side marketplace** (one-from-many). The company has complete control over the supportive information systems. Several selling and buying methods are used. Company-centric models are the subject of this chapter.

Many-to-Many Marketplaces—the Exchange

These are **electronic marketplaces** (e-marketplaces) where many buyers and sellers meet electronically for the purpose of trading electronically with each other. There are different types of e-marketplaces, which are also known as **trading communities, trading exchanges,** or **exchanges.** We will use the term exchanges in this book. These are described in Chapter 7.

Other B2B Models and Services

Businesses deal with businesses for purposes other than just selling or buying. One example is that of collaborative commerce described in Section 6.12. Several types of services and relationships such as value-chain integrators, value-chain service providers, and information brokers are the subject of Chapter 8.

Vertical Versus Horizontal Marketplaces

Marketplaces, including exchanges, can be classified as either horizontal or vertical. **Vertical marketplaces** are those that deal with one industry or industry segment. Examples include electronics, cars, steel, chemicals, and so forth. **Horizontal marketplaces** are those that concentrate on a service or a product that is used in all types of industries. Examples are office supplies, PCs, or travel services.

Virtual Service Industries in B2B

In addition to trading products between businesses, there is also the provision of services. Service industries such as banking, insurance, real estate, job matching, and stock trading can be conducted electronically both for businesses and for individuals and are described in Chapters 8 and 10.

The major services are:

- **Travel and tourism services.** Many large corporations arrange special travel discounts through travel agents. To further reduce costs, companies can make special arrangements that enable employees to plan and book their own trips online. For instance, Rosenbluth International (Chapter 2) provides an agentless service to corporate clients.
- **Real estate.** Commercial real estate transactions can be very large and complex. Therefore, the Web may not be able to completely replace existing human agents. Instead, the Web can help businesses find the right properties, compare properties, and assist in negotiations. Some auctions on foreclosed real estate sold by the government are open only to dealers and are conducted online.
- **Electronic payments.** Internet banking is an economical way of making business payments, transferring funds, or performing other transactions. For example, electronic fund transfer (EFT) through financial EDI is popular with businesses. Transaction fees over the Internet are less costly than any other alternative method.
- **Online stock trading.** Corporations are important stock investors. Because fees for online trading are very low (as low as $5.00 per transaction) and flat, regardless of the trading amount, online trading services are very attractive to institutional investors.
- **Online financing.** Business loans can be solicited online from lenders. Bank of America, for example, offers IntraLoan's matching service, which uses an extranet to match business loan applicants with potential lending corporations. Several sites, such as *garage.com*, provide information about venture capital.
- **Other online services.** Consulting services, law firms, health organizations, and others sell knowledge online. Many other online services, such as purchasing electronic stamps, are described in Chapter 10.

6.4   SELL-SIDE MARKETPLACES: ONE-TO-MANY

In Chapter 3, we introduced the direct-selling model where a manufacturer or a retailer sells directly to consumers. An analogy to this is the case of selling to business buyers. The **sell-side marketplace** delivers a Web-based, private-trading sales channel, frequently over an extranet, to business customers. Smaller buyers usually use the Internet with some encryptions. The seller can be a manufacturer selling to a wholesaler, to a retailer, or to a large business. The seller can also be a distributor selling to wholesalers, to retailers, or to businesses. Either way we deal with *one seller* and *many potential buyers.* In this model, both individual consumers and business buyers may use the same sell-side marketplace, as shown in Figure 6-2.

The architecture for this B2B model is similar as that for B2C EC, and the purchasing process is similar. The major differences are in the process. For example, in B2B, large customers may get customized catalogs and prices. Usually, companies will separate B2C orders from B2B orders. One reason for the separation is the different order fulfillment process (see Chapter 15). There are three major methods for the direct sale one-to-many model: selling from electronic catalogs; selling via forward auctions, just as GM does with its old equipment; and one-to-one selling, usually under a long-term contract. We describe the first method in this section and describe the others in Section 6.5.

Virtual Sellers

As indicated earlier, sellers may be manufacturers or intermediaries, usually distributors or wholesalers. While manufacturers must be real, intermediaries may be virtual, as in the case of *bigboxx.com.hk* (Application Case 6.1).

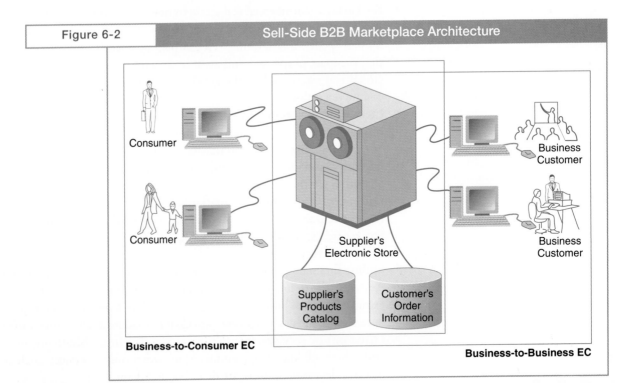

Figure 6-2	Sell-Side B2B Marketplace Architecture

Consumer

Consumer

Supplier's
Electronic Store

Business
Customer

Business
Customer

Supplier's
Products
Catalog

Customer's
Order
Information

Business-to-Consumer EC

Business-to-Business EC

APPLICATION CASE   6.1

Bigboxx.com.hk of Hong Kong

Bigboxx.com.hk is a Hong Kong-based virtual B2B office supply retailer. The company has three types of customers: large corporate clients, medium corporate clients, and small offices (SOHO). The company offers more than 10,000 items from 300 suppliers. *Bigboxx.com*'s goal is to sell its products in various countries in southeast Asia. The company began operations in Spring 2000. By Fall 2000, it had over 5,000 registered customers.

The company's portal is attractive and easy to use. The company also has a tutorial to instruct users on how to use the Web site. Once a user registers, the user starts shopping using the online shopping cart. Users can look for items by browsing through the online catalogs or they can locate items with a search engine.

Users can pay by cash or by check (upon delivery), by automatic payments from a bank account, by credit card, or by purchasing card (see Chapter 14). Soon users will be able to pay by Internet-based direct debit, by electronic bill presentation, or by Internet banking.

Using its own trucks and warehouses, deliveries are made within 24 hours or even on the same day. Delivery is scheduled online. The ordering system is integrated with a SAP-based back-office system.

As a value-added customer service, several functionalities are provided. They are:

- Customers can track the status of each item in their order.
- Customers can check item availability in real-time.
- Offers promotions and suggests items based on customers' user profiles.
- Customized prices, for every product, for every customer.
- For customers with multibranching (e.g., banks), a group account by branch is set, and comparative management reports are provided.
- Related to multibranching, a control and a central approval feature is provided.
- A standing order for repeat purchasing at desired time intervals can be automatically activated.
- A large number of Excel reports and data are also available.

Customer Service

Online sellers can add sophisticated customer services (see Chapter 4) and even save money. For example, General Electric (GE) receives 20 million calls a year regarding appliances. While most of these calls come from individuals, many come from businesses. By using the Internet and automatic response software agents, the cost of calls can be reduced from $5/call by phone to $0.20/call by automatic responce.

Another example of B2B customer service is that of Milacron, Inc., which produces industrial consumable products for metalworking. The company launched an award-winning EC site that provides more than 100,000 small and medium enterprises (SMEs) an easy-to-use and secure way of selecting, purchasing, and applying Milacron's 55,000 products. From this site, the SMEs are provided with a level of technical service beyond that supplied previously to even Milacron's largest customers (see *milacron.com*).

Direct Sales from Catalogs

Companies can use the Internet to sell directly from online catalogs. There may be one catalog for all customers or a customized catalog for each customer. In Chapter 5 we presented the advantages of e-catalogs over paper catalogs and showed how Boise Cascade Corp. uses e-catalogs for B2B sales. Without enhancements, this model may not be convenient for large and repetitive business buyers, because the buyers' order information is stored in the suppliers' servers and is not easily integrated with the buyer's corporate information system. In order to facilitate the B2B direct sale, the seller provides the buyer with a *buyer-customized shopping cart,* which can store order information that can be integrated with the buyer's information system. This is particularly important when buyers have to visit several sites in one or several shopping malls. Many sellers provide separate pages and catalogs to their major buyers. For example, *Staples.com,* an office supply vendor, offers its business customers personalized catalogs and pricing at *StaplesLink.com* that can use several vendors' e-procurement systems (e.g., Ariba, Oracle).

CONFIGURATION AND CUSTOMIZATION

Similar to B2C, here too, direct sales offer an opportunity for efficient customization. As we will see in the case of Cisco, manufacturers provide online tools for self-configuration. Business customers can customize products, get a price quote, and submit the order for production, all online.

Successful Cases and Benefits

Successful examples of the direct sales model include Dell, Intel, IBM, and Cisco (discussed later in Section 6.6). Thousands of companies use this model. Companies that use this model may be successful as long as the vendor has a superb reputation in the market and a large enough group of loyal customers. One of the major issues facing smaller sellers is how to find buyers. This issue is discussed in Chapter 8.

The major benefits of direct sales are:

- Reduces order processing costs and paperwork
- Speeds the ordering cycle
- Reduces errors in ordering and product configuration
- Reduces buyers' search costs (find sellers, compare prices)
- Reduces sellers' search costs (advertise to buyers)
- Reduces logistics costs
- Ability to customize products
- Ability to offer different prices to different customers (personalization, customization)

Limitations

As with B2C, B2B sellers may experience channel conflicts with existing distribution systems. Another limitation is that if traditional EDI is used, the cost to the customers can be high (as will be discussed later). Finally, the number of business partners online must be large enough to justify the system.

6.5   SELLING SIDE: AUCTIONS AND OTHER MODELS

Auctions are comprehensively covered in Chapter 9. As you may recall, GM used auctions to sell capital assets. In a **forward auction,** items are displayed on an auction site for quick disposal. Forward auctions offer a number of benefits to sellers:

- **Revenue generation.** The new sales channel supports and expands online sales. For example, Weirton Steel Corp. doubled its customer base when it started auctions (Fickel, 1999). Forward auctions offer businesses a new venue for disposing of excess, obsolete, and returned products quickly and easily.
- **Increased page views.** Forward auctions give Web sites **stickiness,** meaning that auction users spend more time on a site and generate more page views than other users.
- **Member acquisition and retention.** All bidding transactions result in additional registered members.

There are several types of forward auctions. GM conducts its forward auctions from its own Web site (*TradeXchange.com* along with Covisint). Alternatively, a company can sell from an intermediary auction site, such as eBay or *freemarkets.com*. Let's examine these options.

Selling from Own Site

For large and well-known companies that conduct auctions frequently, such as GM, it makes lots of sense to build an auction mechanism on its site. Why should a company pay a commission to an intermediary if the intermediary cannot provide the company with much added value? Of course, a company will have to pay for infrastructure and operate and maintain the auction site. But, if a company already has an electronic marketplace for selling from catalogs, the additional cost for conducting auctions may not be too high.

Using Intermediaries for e-Auctions

Large numbers of intermediaries offer B2B auction sites. Even eBay has a special "business exchange" for small companies. Here are some generic benefits, per *fairmarket.com*, which hosts corporate auctions:

1. No Resources Required
   - No additional hardware, bandwidth, engineering resources, or IT personnel.
   - No opportunity costs associated with the redeployment of the necessary resources or hiring costs.
2. Own and Control Auction Information
   - No intermediary branding, looks like the merchant site.
   - Control the valuable Web traffic, page views, and member registration data.
   - Set all auction parameters: transaction fee structure, user interface, and reports.
   - Easy integration within the merchant site for cohesive auction functionality.
3. Fast Time to Market
   - Have a robust, customized auction up and running immediately.

Other services provided by intermediaries that facilitate both buyer and seller functionalities are:

Searching and Reporting

A complete set of tools is available to merchants using auction software that enables them to search and report on virtually every relevant auction activity conducted on their auction site. For example, a summary called an "At a Glance" report, a comprehensive set of standard reports, and additional ways to analyze more complex information are provided through the administrative module. Reports can be exported to Excel or other programs.

Billing and Collection

Using auction software, merchant-specific shipping weights and charges can be input for automatic calculation of shipping charges of auctioned items. Another service is payment; end user credit-card data may be required to place a bid. Therefore, all credit card data are encrypted for secure transmission and storage. Similarly, all billing information can be easily downloaded for integration with existing systems.

Sell-side marketplaces for B2B EC can be successful if the supplier has a sufficient number of loyal business customers, if its products are well known, and if price is not the major purchasing criteria. Cisco's marketplace belongs in this category.

6.6   SELL-SIDE CASE: CISCO CONNECTION ONLINE (CCO)

Cisco Systems is the world's leading producer of routers, switches, and network interconnect services. Cisco's portal has evolved over several years, beginning with technical support for customers and developing into one of the world's largest EC sites. Today, Cisco offers nearly a dozen Internet-based applications to both end-user businesses and reseller partners.

Customer Service

Cisco began providing electronic support in 1991 using value-added networks (VANs). Software downloads, defect tracking, and technical advice were the first applications offered. In spring 1994, Cisco placed its system on the Web and named its site Cisco Connection Online (CCO). By 2001, Cisco's customers and reseller partners were logging onto Cisco's Web site about 1.3 million times a month to receive technical assistance, place and check orders, or download software. The online service has been so well received that nearly 85 percent of all customer service inquiries and 95 percent of software updates are delivered online. It is delivered globally in 14 languages. The CCO is consider a model for B2B success and several books have been written about it (e.g., Bunnel and Brate, 2000; Stauffer, 2000).

Online Ordering

Cisco builds virtually all its products made-to-order, so it has very few off-the-shelf products. Before the CCO, ordering a product could have been a lengthy, complicated, and error-prone process, because it was done by fax or snail mail. Cisco began deploying Web-based commerce tools in July 1995, and as of July 1996, the Internet Product Center allows users to purchase any Cisco product over the Web. Today, a customer's engineer can sit down at a PC, configure a product, find out immediately if there are any errors in the configuration (some feedback is even given by intelligent agents), and route the order to its procurement department, which submits the order electronically to Cisco.

By providing online pricing and configuration tools to customers, almost all orders (about 98 percent) are now placed through CCO, saving time for both Cisco and their customers. In the first 5 months of its operation in 1996, Cisco booked over $100 million in online sales. This figure grew to $4 billion in 1998 and to over $7 billion in 2000.

Order Status

Each month Cisco used to receive over 150,000 order status inquiries such as: "When will my order be ready? How should the order be classified for customs? Is the product eligible for NAFTA agreement? What export control issues apply?" Cisco provides customers with tracking and FAQ tools so that customers can find the answers to their questions by themselves. In addition, the company's primary domestic and international freight forwarders update Cisco's database electronically about the status of each shipment. CCO can record the shipping date, the method of shipment, and the current location of each product. All new information is made available to customers immediately. As soon as an order ships, Cisco sends the customer a notification by e-mail.

Benefits to Cisco

Cisco reaps many benefits from the CCO system. The most important benefits as of 1998 are:

- **Reduced operating costs for order taking.** By automating its order process online in 1998, Cisco has saved $363 million per year, or approximately 17.5 percent of its total operating costs. This is due primarily to increased productivity of the employees who take and fulfill orders.
- **Enhanced technical support and customer service.** With more than 85 percent of its technical support and customer service calls handled online, Cisco's technical support productivity has increased by 250 percent per year.
- **Reduced technical support staff cost.** The online technical support reduced technical support staff costs by roughly $125 million in 1998 alone.
- **Reduced software distribution costs.** Customers download new software releases directly from Cisco's site, saving the company $180 million in distribution, packaging, and duplicating costs each year. Having product and pricing information on the Web and Web-based CD-ROMs saves Cisco an additional $50 million annually in printing and distributing catalogs and marketing materials to customers.
- **Lead times were reduced from 4 to 10 days to 2 to 3 days.**

Benefits to Customers

The new system also benefits customers. Cisco customers can configure orders more quickly, immediately determine costs, and collaborate much more rapidly and effectively with Cisco's staff. Also technical support is faster. [*Sources:* Compiled from *cisco.com* (press releases, 2000), and from *The Economist,* June 26, 1999s.]

6.7   SELL-SIDE INTERMEDIARIES: MARSHALL INDUSTRIES AND BOEING PART

In this section we will present two examples of sell-side intermediaries: Marshall Industries, a major multinational distributor of electronic components, and Boeing, a major supplier of airline parts.

Marshall Industries

Marshall Industries (*marshall.com*), now part of Avnet Marshall, is a large distributor of electronic components. Prior to its merger with Avnet in 1999, Marshall posted $1.7 billion in sales in fiscal 1999, and served over 30,000 business customers, many of which are small in size. Marshall distributed over 130,000 different products worldwide. Avnet was a competitor. Now, together, they sell close to $10 billion a year.

The electronics industry is very competitive. Distributors compete against direct marketing by the manufacturers and are threatened by disintermediation. Thus, providing value-added services is key to a distributor's survival. Marshall adds value through IT support. The company is known for its innovative use of information technologies and the Web (e.g., see Wilson, 1998). The company won a first prize in the 1997 SIM International paper awards competition (*simnet.org*). In 1999, the company was the first ever to use the XML-based interoperable solution for B2B integration (from WebMethods, Inc.).

In order to fully appreciate Marshall's accomplishment, please take a moment and try to answer the true-or-false quiz presented here. To properly answer the quiz you need to read the full story of Marshall at *simnet.com* (SIM 1997 International paper winners) or at EL-Sawy et al. (1999). See Questions for Discussion 11.

1. In the digital economy, the middleman disappears and is disintermediated by information technology.
2. In the digital economy, the movement of information replaces movement of physical goods.
3. In the digital economy, the value-chain model is good for thinking about an extended enterprise.
4. Ubiquitous access to product information and self-service transactions through the Internet will make the difference between regular and excellent performers.
5. Web-enabling IS applications are tasks that can be outsourced easily.
6. Do not deploy an IS application until it is thoroughly tested.
7. It is better to develop integrated-architecture solutions for EC rather than continuous incremental functionality.
8. In building an IT architecture, decide on one standard platform and use software products that conform to it.

In addition to the physical distribution of components, distributors have increasingly taken on value-added tasks such as technical support, processing payments and accounts receivable, offering credit, logistics and more. The semiconductor industry, for example, is cyclical, causing major delivery and inventory problems. Large customers are global, requiring global sourcing. Time-to-market competition and customization at the customer end require a fast and flexible response from distributors. Just-in-time and supplier-managed inventories are increasingly required from distributors. These demands require tight integration of information and provision of value-added services along the value chain. Let's see how this is done at Marshall.

PRODUCTS AND SERVICES

Marshall has been pioneering the use of the Internet and IT applications, with a view to reengineering its business and creating new competitive strengths. Its major Web-based initiatives, which are interconnected, are listed in Table 6-1.

SURVIVAL STRATEGY

Marshall's use of e-commerce was combined with other innovations and with BPR. For example:

- Providing continuous improvement programs and innovations together with business partners.
- Using team-based organization, flat hierarchy, and decentralization of decision making.
- The salesperson's compensation was changed from commission-based to profit sharing.
- Use of the customer-centric approach (CRM) is highly promoted.
- Providing new Web-based services to continuously create value between suppliers and customers.
- Changing the internal organizational structure and procedures to fully support e-commerce initiatives.

TABLE 6-1

Marshall Industries EC Initiatives

Initiative	Description
MarshallNet	An intranet supporting sales people in the field via wireless devices and portable PCs. Real-time access to corporate database, DSS applications, workflow, and collaboration.
Marshall on the Internet (portal)	A B2B portal for customers offering information, ordering, and tracking (using UPS software) capabilities. Discussion, chat, connection to call centers. Special pages for value-added resellers. Troubleshooting capabilities.
Strategic European Internet	A strategic partner in Europe, offering MarshallNet in 17 languages, plus additional local information.
Electronic Design Center	Includes an online configuration tool. Provides technical specs. A simulation capability for making virtual components. Marshall can produce sample products designed by customers.
PartnerNet	Customized Web pages for major customers and suppliers. Accessibility to Marshall's intranet. Electronic payments. Historical data and records. Planning tools online.
NetSeminar	Training online; bringing together suppliers and customers for live interactions.
Education and News Portal	Education news and entertainment services, including consulting, sales training, and interactive public product announcements.

Marshall was very successful and profitable. Its EC initiatives are now practiced at Avnet-Marshall as well. For further information see Timmers (1999) and EL-Sawy et al. (1999).

Boeing's PART (Part analysis and Requirement Tracking)

Boeing's PART case demonstrates the intermediary-oriented B2B marketplace. Boeing plays the role of intermediary in supplying maintenance parts to airlines. Unlike other online intermediaries like ProcureNet and *Industry.net*, revenue as an intermediary may be a minor concern to Boeing, since the company makes most of its revenue from selling airplanes. Supporting customers' maintenance needs appears to be the major goal.

The purpose of Boeing's electronic intermediary, PART, is to link airlines that need maintenance parts with suppliers who are producing the parts for Boeing's aircraft (Teasdale, 1997). Boeing's online strategy is to provide a single point of online access through which airlines (the buyers of Boeing's aircraft) and maintenance providers can access data about the parts needed to maintain and operate aircraft, regardless of whether the data is from the airframe builder, component supplier, engine manufacturer, or the airline itself. Thus, Boeing is acting as an intermediary between the airlines and the parts suppliers. With data from 300 key suppliers of Boeing's airplane parts, Boeing's goal is to provide its customers with one-stop shopping with online maintenance information and ordering capability.

SPARE PARTS BUSINESS USING TRADITIONAL EDI

Ordering spare parts has been a multistep process for many of Boeing's customers. For example, an airline's mechanic informs the purchasing department when a part is needed. Purchasing approves the purchase order and sends it to Boeing by phone or fax. At this point, the mechanic does not need to know who produced the part, because the aircraft was purchased from Boeing as one body. However, Boeing has to find out who produced the part and then ask the producer to deliver the part (unless Boeing happens to keep an inventory of the part). The largest airlines began to streamline the ordering process nearly 20 years ago. Because of the volume and regularity of their orders, the largest airlines established EDI connections with Boeing over VANs. Not all airlines were quick to follow suit, however. It took until 1992 to induce 10 percent of the largest customers, representing 60 percent of the volume, to order through EDI. The numbers have not changed much since then due to the cost and complexity of VAN-based EDI.

DEBUT OF PART ON THE INTERNET

Boeing views the Internet as an opportunity to encourage more of its customers to order parts electronically. With the initial investment limited to a standard PC and basic Internet access, even its smallest customers can now participate. Because of its interactive capabilities, many customer service functions that were handled over the telephone are now handled over the Internet.

In November 1996, Boeing debuted its PART page on the Internet, giving its customers around the world the ability to check part availability and pricing, order parts, and track order status, all online. Less than a year later, about 50 percent of

Boeing's customers used it for parts orders and customer service inquiries. In its first year of operation, the Boeing PART page handled over half a million inquiries and transactions from customers around the world.

BENEFITS OF PART ONLINE

Boeing's primary objective for PART online is to improve customer service. Boeing also expects to realize significant operating savings as more of its customers use the Internet. In addition, PART online may lead to new sales opportunities. Boeing's spare parts business processed about 20 percent more shipments per month in 1997 than it did in 1996 with the same number of data entry people. In addition, as many as 600 phone calls a day to telephone service staff have been eliminated because customers access information about pricing, availability, and order status online. Over time, Boeing anticipates that PART online will result in fewer parts being returned due to administrative errors. Furthermore, airlines may buy Boeing aircraft the next time they make an aircraft purchase.

PORTABLE ACCESS TO TECHNICAL DRAWINGS/SUPPORT

Airline maintenance is spread out over a wide geographical area. It takes place everywhere in the world an aircraft flies. At an airport, maintenance activities may take place at the gate, in the line-maintenance department, or at the maintenance operations center. Mechanics are traditionally forced to make repeated, time-consuming trips to the office to consult paper or microfilm reference materials. A single manual may contain as many as 30,000 pages.

For this reason, in April 1996 Boeing On Line Data (BOLD) went into operation, incorporating not only engineering drawings but also manuals, catalogs, and other technical information. As of October 1997, BOLD had 7,500 users from 40 different airlines and another 60 airline customers in the pipeline. In addition, Portable Maintenance Aid (PMA), which solves the issue of portable access, was developed. Because of BOLD and PMA, mechanics or technicians are able to access all the information they need to make decisions about necessary repairs at the time and place they need the information.

BENEFITS TO BOEING'S CUSTOMERS

Because they are such recent developments, little data is available on the full impact of BOLD and PMA. However, early users report benefits such as:

- **Increased productivity.** Spending less time searching for information freed up engineers and maintenance technicians to focus on more productive activities. One U.S. airline saved $1 million a year when it gave 400 users access to Boeing's BOLD program. Seeing the results of the initial implementation, the airline expanded the service to 2,000 users. A European airline estimated that it will save $1.5 million from BOLD in the first year, due to a nearly 4 percent boost in production and engineering staff productivity.
- **Reduced costs.** With information available online at the gate through PMA, rather than in the crew office, delays at the gate resulting from missing information can be reduced. The European airline mentioned earlier estimates that PMA will reduce flight delays by 5 to 10 percent.

- **Increased revenues.** Every 3,000 hours, an airline does a schedule C maintenance check that can keep an airline grounded for up to a week. Idle aircraft costs tens of thousands of dollars a day. Not having information readily available can lengthen the process. The longer the maintenance check, the less revenue opportunity. Through BOLD and PMA, the European airline estimates it will save 1 to 2 days per year for each aircraft, resulting in a $43 million in increased revenue.

6.8   BUY SIDE: ONE-FROM-MANY, E-PROCUREMENT

A unique feature of B2B that does not exist in B2C, is the buy-side marketplace and its use for procurement. Purchasing in organizations is done by *purchasing agents,* also known as *buyers.* There are two types of purchasing: *direct* and *indirect.* As shown in the GM case, **direct materials**, also called production materials, go directly to the manufacture or assembly of a product or the creation of a service. The characteristics of direct materials are: their use is scheduled, they are usually not shelf items, and they are usually purchased in large volume and after negotiation and contracting. **Indirect materials** are usually used in **maintenance, repairs, and operations** activities and are known collectively as **MROs** or *nonproduction materials.*

Inefficiencies in Procurement Management of Indirect Materials

Procurement management refers to the coordination of all the activities pertaining to purchasing goods and services necessary to accomplish the mission of an enterprise. Approximately 80 percent of an organization's purchased items, mostly MROs, constitute 20 percent of the total purchase value. Furthermore, a large portion of corporate buyers' time is spent on non-value-added activities such as data entry, correcting errors in paperwork, expediting delivery, or solving quality problems. As a result, buyers do not have sufficient time to pay full attention to properly deal with the purchasing of high-value or high-volume direct materials. For the 20 percent of high value items, purchasing personnel need to spend a lot of time and effort on upstream procurement activities such as qualifying suppliers, negotiating prices and terms, building rapport with strategic suppliers, and carrying out supplier evaluation and certification. If the buyers are busy with the details of the smaller items, usually the MROs, they do not have enough time to devote to the high-value items. Organizations try to address this imbalance by implementing new purchasing models.

There are many other potential inefficiencies in procurement, and not only for MROs. These range from delays to paying too much for rush orders. The major reason is that the traditional process shown in Figure 6-3 is inefficient (discussed more fully in Chapter 15). To correct the situation, companies reengineer their procurement systems using innovative management.

Innovative Procurement Management

Purchasing and supply management (P&SM) professionals, such as buyers, inventory managers, and material management staff, now advocate innovative purchasing as a strategic approach to increasing profit margins. Many organizations are discover-

Figure 6-3	A Traditional Purchasing Process Flow

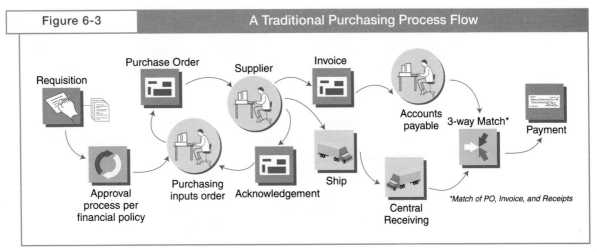

Source: ariba.com, February 2001.

ing that every dollar saved in P&SM contributes directly to the bottom line. Some of the tactics facilitated by the Web include electronic tendering, volume purchasing, buying from approved suppliers, aggregating suppliers catalogs at the buyer's site, selecting the right supplier, group purchasing, awarding business based on performance, improving quality of existing suppliers, doing contract negotiation, forming partnerships with suppliers, and reducing paperwork and administrative costs.

The Goals of Procurement Reengineering

Reengineering of procurement has been attempted for decades, usually by using some information technologies. But the real opportunity lies in the use of e-procurement. By automating and streamlining the laborious routines of the purchasing function, purchasing professionals can focus on more strategic purchases, achieving the following goals:

- Increasing purchasing agent productivity
- Authorizing requisitioners to perform purchases from their desktops bypassing the procurement department
- Lowering purchase prices through product standardization and consolidation of buys
- Improving information flow and management (e.g., supplier's information and pricing information)
- Minimizing the purchases made from non-contract vendors, a practice known as **maverick buying**.
- Improving the payment process
- Streamlining the purchasing process making it simple and fast
- Reducing the administrative processing cost per order by as much as 90 percent. (In many cases, GM achieved a reduction from $100 to $10.)
- Finding new suppliers and vendors which can provide goods and services faster and/or cheaper
- Integrating the procurement process with budgetary control in an efficient and effective way
- Minimizing human errors in the buying or shipping process.

E-procurement is relatively easy to implement. There are no channel conflicts and the resistance to change is minimal. Also, a wide selection of software packages and other infrastructure are available at a reasonable cost.

As indicated earlier, the procurement of MROs is a major problem for many organizations. An immediate benefit that e-procurement can bring about is in the purchase of MRO items. But, improvement can be made for direct materials as well. All existing manual processes of requisition creation, requests for quotation, invitation to tender, purchase order issuance, receiving goods, and payment can be streamlined and automated. However, to implement such automated support, the people involved in procurement need to use not only internal workflow, group-ware, and the internal marketplace, but also must collaborate with the suppliers' Web sites. In this sense, the seamless support of procurement management using intranets (for internal marketplace) and extranets (for bid sites) is recommended.

Buy-Side Marketplaces

When a buyer goes to a sell-side marketplace, such as Cisco's, the buyer's acquisition department has to manually enter the order information into its own corporate information system. Furthermore, searching e-stores and e-malls to find and compare suppliers and products can be very slow and costly. Therefore, large buyers can open their own marketplace, which we call the **buy-side marketplace**, as depicted in Figure 6-4. Under this model, a buyer opens an electronic market on its own server and invites potential suppliers to bid on the items the buyer needs. This model is also called the reverse auction, tendering, or bidding model.

Thousands of companies use the reverse auction model. For example, *shoppoint.co.kr* invites suppliers to bid on parts on the Web. As the number of such

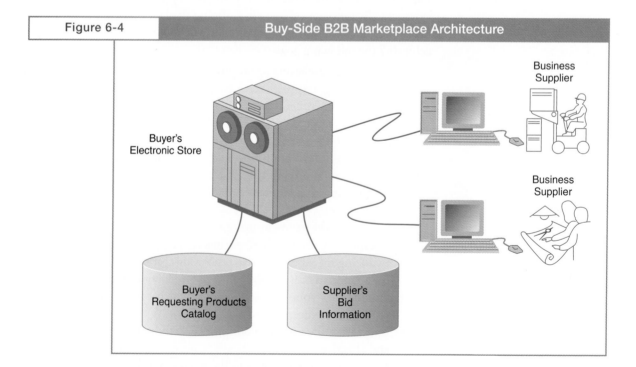

Figure 6-4   **Buy-Side B2B Marketplace Architecture**

sites increases, suppliers will not be able to manually monitor all such tendering sites. This situation is improved with the introduction of online directories that list open RFQs. Another way to solve this problem is the use of software search and match agents, which can also reduce RFQ search efforts. Other software agents can reduce the human burden in the bidding process. In addition to reverse auctions, e-purchasing may include other models such as:

- Aggregation of suppliers' catalogs at the buyer's site
- Joining a group purchasing plan
- Bartering

Direct Versus Indirect Sourcing

The earliest and biggest trend in e-procurement adoption to date is the use of tools to automate processes related to the purchasing of indirect goods. Tools that support procurement of such non-mission-critical items are available from dozens of vendors such as Ariba, Oracle, and Clarus.

Slower to be adopted so far are technologies that support e-procurement of direct goods and mission-critical supplies. The importance of these supplies relates directly to their potential benefit. Because the dollar value of direct materials may account for 80 percent of some manufactures' expenses, the savings derived from implementing e-procurement systems can be compelling. But unlike indirect procurement, where the focus is on getting standard goods at the lowest possible price, direct procurement requires a relationship—usually long term—with a vendor who will deliver a known quality of goods. With mission-critical buying, "you can't just buy from anyone." With these materials, people are betting their careers on the buy. If an order for supplies goes unfulfilled, the missing goods can shut down a production line or an entire factory. So for direct sourcing, tight integration with major suppliers along the supply chain is a must. This is in contrast to using public exchanges for indirect sourcing. (See Chapter 15 for discussion on the supply chain.) Next we look at some e-procurement models.

6.9   BUY SIDE: REVERSE AUCTIONS

The most common model for large purchases is the reverse auction. Many bidding and tendering systems, a common method for purchasing, use reverse auctions. Governments and large corporations frequently mandate this approach which may provide considerable savings. To understand why this is so, let us review the reverse auction process first (See Chapter 9).

The Pre-Internet Reverse Auction Process

Before the Internet, companies used the following tendering process:

1. The buyer prepares a description of the product (project) that needs to be produced. The description includes specifications, blue prints, quality standards, delivery date, and required payment method.
2. The buyer announces the project via newspaper ads, direct mail, fax, or telephone.

3. Vendors (suppliers) that express interest receive detailed information (sometimes for a fee), usually sent by mail or a courier.
4. Vendors prepare proposals. They may call the company for additional information. Sometimes changes are made that must be disseminated to all interested bidders.
5. Bidders submit document proposals, usually several copies of the same documents.
6. Proposals are evaluated, usually by several departments at the buyer organization. Communication and clarification may take place by letters or phone/fax.

The Web-Based Reverse Auction Process

With the development of the Internet, many businesses now use a Web-based reverse auction process to procure supplies. The common steps in this process are:

1. Buyers prepare bidding project information.
2. Buyers post the projects for bid on their secured portal.
3. Buyers identify potential suppliers.
4. Buyers invite suppliers to bid on projects.
5. Suppliers download the project information from the Web.
6. Suppliers submit electronic bids for projects.
7. The reverse auction can be in real-time, like GM's, or it can take a few days, until a predetermined closing date.
8. Buyers evaluate the suppliers' bids and may negotiate electronically to achieve the "best deal."
9. Buyers award a contract to the bidders that best meet their requirements.

The electronic process is faster and administratively much less expensive. It can also result in locating the cheapest possible products or projects.

CONDUCTING REVERSE AUCTIONS

Reverse auctions may be administered from a company's Web site, as with GM in the opening case. Alternatively, a third-party intermediary may run the electronic bidding, as well as forward auctions. General Electric's TPN (Section 6.10) opened its own bidding site to other buyers so that they can post their requests for quotations. The TPN site, therefore, can be regarded as an intermediary-oriented marketplace. Auction sites like A-Z Used Computers (*marex.com/solutions/ecommerce.jsp.htm*) and FairMarkets belong to this category.

Managed Interactive Bidding

The bidding process conducted by companies such as GE lasts a day or more and may be managed by the companies themselves. In some cases the bidders bid only once. In other cases the bidders can view the lowest bid and change theirs. Bidding can also be managed by an intermediary as shown in Application Case 6.2.

APPLICATION CASE   **6.2**

Bidding Through the Third-Party Auctioneer: FreeMarkets

Imagine this scenario: United Technologies Corp. needs suppliers to make $24 million worth of circuit boards. Twenty-five hundred suppliers were identified as possible contractors. These were found in electronic registries and directories. The list was submitted to FreeMarkets OnLine Inc. (*freemarkets.com*). FreeMarkets experts reduced the list to 1,000, based on considerations ranging from plant location to the size of the supplier. After further analysis of plant capacity and customer feedback, the list was reduced to 100. A detailed evaluation of the potential suppliers resulted in 50 qualified suppliers who were invited to bid. The suppliers received a password to review the circuit board specifications.

Three hours of online competitive bidding was conducted. FreeMarkets divided the job into 12 lots, each of which was put up for bid. At 8:00 A.M., the first lot valued at $2.25 million was placed online. The first bid was $2.25 million, which was seen by all bidders. Minutes later, another bidder placed a $2.0 million bid. Using the reverse auction approach, the bidders further reduced the bids. Minutes before the bid closed, at 8:45 A.M., the 42nd bid of $1.1 million was received. No other bids were received. When it all ended, the bids for all 12 lots totaled $18 million (about a 35 percent savings to United Technologies).

To finalize the process, FreeMarkets conducted a very comprehensive analysis on several of the lowest bidders of each lot, attempting to look at other criteria in addition to cost. FreeMarkets then recommended the winners and collected its fees.

Sources: A. Jahnke, complied from "How Bazaar," *CIO Magazine,* August 1, 1998, and *freemarkets.com.*

6.10   PROCUREMENT REVOLUTION AT GENERAL ELECTRIC

General Electric's material costs increased 16 percent between 1982 and 1992. During those same years GE's products' prices remained flat and for some products they even declined. In response to these cost increases, GE began an all-out effort to improve its purchasing system. The company analyzed its procurement process and discovered that its purchasing was inefficient, involved too many transactions, and did not leverage GE's large volumes to get the best price. In addition, more than one-quarter of its 1.25 million invoices per year had to be reworked because the purchase orders, receipts, and invoices did not match.

TPN at GE Lighting Division

General Electric has taken a number of steps to improve its procurement, and the most recent one involves the Internet. One of the first initiatives was an electronic tendering system for GE's Lighting Division.

Factories at GE Lighting used to send hundreds of RFQs to the corporate sourcing department each day, many for low-value machine parts. For each requisition, the accompanying blueprints had to be requested from storage, retrieved from the vault, transported to the processing site, photocopied, folded, attached to paper requisition forms with quote sheets, stuffed into envelopes, and mailed out to bidders. This process took at least seven days and was so complex and time-consuming that the sourcing department normally sent out bid packages for each part only to two or three suppliers (see *The Economist* June 26, 1999).

In 1996, GE Lighting piloted the company's first online procurement system, the Trading Process Network (TPN) Post (*gegxs.com*). Now, the sourcing department receives the requisitions electronically from its internal customers and can send off a bid package to suppliers around the world via the Internet. The system automatically pulls the correct drawings and attaches them to the electronic requisition forms. Within 2 hours from the time the sourcing department starts the process, suppliers are notified of incoming RFQs by e-mail, fax, or EDI and are given 7 days to prepare a bid and send it back over the extranet to GE Lighting. The bid is transferred over the intranet to the appropriate evaluators and a contract can be awarded that same day. In 2000, GE purchased $1.2 billion in goods using TPN.

Benefits of TPN

As a result of implementing TPN, GE has realized a number of benefits:

- Labor involved in the procurement process declined by 30 percent. At the same time, material costs declined 5 to 50 percent due to the procurement department's ability to reach a wider base of competing suppliers online.
- Of all the staff involved in the procurement process, 60 percent have been redeployed. The sourcing department has at least 6 to 8 free days a month to concentrate on strategic activities rather than on the paperwork, photocopying, and envelope stuffing.
- It used to take 18 to 23 days to identify suppliers, prepare a request for bid, negotiate a price, and award the contract to a supplier. It now takes 9 to 11 days.
- With the transaction handled electronically from beginning to end, invoices are automatically reconciled with purchase orders, reflecting any modifications that happen along the way.
- GE procurement departments around the world now share information about their best suppliers. In February 1997 alone, GE Lighting found seven new suppliers through the Internet, including one that charged 20 percent less than the second-lowest bid.

Benefits to Buyers

GE's TPN Post system can improve the productivity of the buyer's sourcing process and allow buyers to access quality goods and services from around the world. This larger pool of suppliers fosters competition and enables the buyers to spend more time negotiating the best deals and less time on administrative procedures. The benefits to GE's purchasing departments are:

- Identifying and building partnerships with new suppliers worldwide
- Strengthening relationships and streamlining sourcing processes with current business partners
- Rapidly distributing information and specifications to business partners

- Transmitting electronic drawings to multiple suppliers simultaneously
- Cutting sourcing cycle times and reducing costs for sourced goods
- Quickly receiving and comparing bids from a large number of suppliers so as to negotiate better prices

By 2001, most of GE's divisions were using TPN for some of their procurement needs. The company bought over $1 billion worth of goods and supplies over the Internet during 1997; by 2000, 12 of its divisions were purchasing their nonproduction and MRO materials over the Internet, for an annual total of $5 billion. General Electric estimates that streamlining these purchases alone can save the company $500 to $700 million annually.

Benefits to Suppliers

Suppliers in the GE TPN system can gain instant access to a global buyer with billions of dollars in purchasing power. In addition, they may dramatically improve the productivity of their own bidding and sales activities. Other benefits are:

- Increased sales volume
- Expanded market reach, finding new buyers
- Lowered administration costs for sales and marketing activities
- Shortened requisition cycle time
- Improved sales staff productivity
- Streamlined bidding process

General Electric reports that TPN benefits extend beyond its own walls. A computer reseller, Hartford Computer Group, reports that since joining TPN, it has increased its exposure to different GE business units so that its business with GE has grown by over 250 percent. In addition, TPN has introduced Hartford Computer Group to other potential customers.

Deployment Strategies

The GE case also demonstrates two deployment strategies: Start EC in one division (GE started in its lighting division) and slowly go to all divisions; and use the site also as a public bidding marketplace generating commission income for GE. In 1998, GE opened *tpn.com* to public bidding and started with 2,500 registered suppliers in December 1998 (see Blankenhorn, 1997 for more details). The site is powered by TPN Register, a service that facilitates trading communities (see Chapter 8). TPN Register was acquired in 2001 by GE Global Exchange Services (*gegxs.com*).

6.11   AGGREGATING CATALOGS, GROUP PURCHASING, AND BARTERING

Three additional e-purchasing methods are used by companies: *aggregating catalogs, group purchasing,* and *bartering.*

Aggregating Suppliers' Catalogs: An Internal Marketplace

Large organizations have many buyers or purchasing agents, usually located in different places. These buyers buy from a large number of suppliers. The problem is that even if these are all approved suppliers, it is difficult to plan and control procurement. In many cases, in order to save time, buyers purchase from the most convenient supplier and pay a premium (this kind of buying behavior is called **maverick buying**). In addition, an organization needs to control the purchasing budget. This situation is especially serious in government agencies and multinational entities where many buyers and large numbers of purchases are involved. For example, Bristol-Myers Squibb Corporation has over 30,000 corporate buyers all over the world.

The solution to this problem is to aggregate the items of all approved suppliers (all relevant suppliers' catalogs) in one place, at the corporate headquarters. Prices can be negotiated in advance (or items are placed for RFQ), so that the buyers do not have to negotiate. By aggregating the suppliers' catalogs on the organization's server, it is possible to *centralize* all control and procurement.

REDUCED NUMBER OF SUPPLIERS

Using a search engine, buyers can find what they want, check availability and delivery times, and complete an electronic requisition form. Another advantage of such aggregation is that the company can reduce the number of suppliers. For example, Caltex, a multinational oil company, reduced the number of its suppliers from over 3,000 to 800. The reason for this reduction is that the central catalog enables buyers at multiple corporate locations to buy from remote but fewer sellers, thus the quantities are increased and the price is lower. Finally, such internal marketplaces allow for easy financial controls. As buyers make purchases, their account balances are displayed. Once the budget is depleted, the system will not allow the purchase order to go through. Therefore, this model is popular in public institutions and governments. An example of a successful implementation of aggregation is that of MasterCard International (see Application Case 6.3).

The introduction of this model with financial controls enables organizational changes. For example, Korean Institute of Science and Technology (KIST), a major research institution in Seoul, installed this model as early as 1998. As a result, the desktop purchasing for small items like PCs are allowed online, and the purchasing cycle time was reduced from 20 days to 1 day! Recently, Microsoft deployed the desktop purchasing strategy too.

Group Purchasing

An increased number of companies are moving to group purchasing. With **group purchasing** the orders from several buyers are aggregated, so better prices can be negotiated. Two models are in use: *internal aggregation* and *third-party (external) aggregation*.

Internal aggregation. Large companies, such as GE (see *Forbes Global,* July 24, 2000), buy billions of dollars of MROs every year. Company-wide orders are aggregated, using the Web, and are replenished automatically. Besides economies of scale, namely lower prices on many items, GE saves on the administrative cost of the transactions reducing transaction costs from $50–$100 per transaction to $5–$10. With four million transactions, annually, this is a substantial savings.

External aggregations. Many SMEs would like to enjoy quantity discounts, but cannot find others to join them to increase the procurement volume. Such a matching can be accomplished by a third party, such as *simplexity.com*. The company's idea is to provide SMEs with better prices, selection, and services by aggre-

APPLICATION CASE   6.3|

MasterCard's Procurement Case

Pleased with the progress of a 6-month pilot program, MasterCard International expanded the use of its online buying program throughout the company. Over 9 months in 1998, purchasing agents placed thousands of transactions with the company's preferred suppliers using Elekom Corp.'s procurement system (*elekom.com*). The system allows corporate buyers to select goods and services from MasterCard's own electronic catalog that aggregates more than 10,000 items. Then, buyers place orders electronically with suppliers. Payments are made with MasterCard's corporate procurement card. The software, initially pilot tested by more than 250 buyers, was rolled out to 2,300 users in 1998 and used by more than 2,500 buyers in 2001.

The goal of this project is to consolidate buying activities from multiple corporate sites, improve process costs, and reduce the supplier base. In conjunction with the expanded deployment, MasterCard is continuously adding suppliers and catalog content to the system.

The Procurement Process

The procurement department in the buyer's internal marketplace defines the scope of products or projects to buy and invites vendors to bid or negotiate prices. The agreed-upon prices (contract prices) are stored in the buyer's internal electronic catalog. The final buyer (not the procurement department) can compare the available alternatives in the electronic catalogs, and an organizational purchasing decision can be tightly coupled with an internal workflow management system. The internal electronic catalog can be updated manually or by using software agents.

gating demand online. Taking into consideration that even in the United States, 90 percent of all businesses have less than 100 employees, yet they account for over 35 percent of all MRO business volume, one can appreciate the importance of this market. *Miso21.com* aggregates demand, and then either negotiates with suppliers or conducts reverse auctions. The process is shown in Figure 6-5.

Several big companies including large CPA firms, EDS, and Ariba are providing similar services, mainly to their regular customers. Yahoo! and AOL offer such services too. Many start-ups such as *shop2gether.com* are competing with *miso21.com*. A key to the success of these companies is a critical mass of buyers. An interesting straegy is to not offer aggregation on your Web site, but to outsource it. For example, *purchasepooling.com* provides group buying for community site partners such as *about.com*.

Group purchasing, which started with commodity items such as MROs and consumer electronic devices, has now moved to services ranging from travel to payroll processing and Web hosting. Some aggregators use Priceline's "name-your-price" approach. Others try to find the lowest possible price. Similar approaches are used in B2C and several vendors serve both markets.

Electronic Bartering

Bartering is the exchange of goods and/or services without the use of money. The basic idea is for a company to exchange its surplus for something that it needs. Companies can advertise their surpluses in a classified area and may find an exchange partner, but usually a

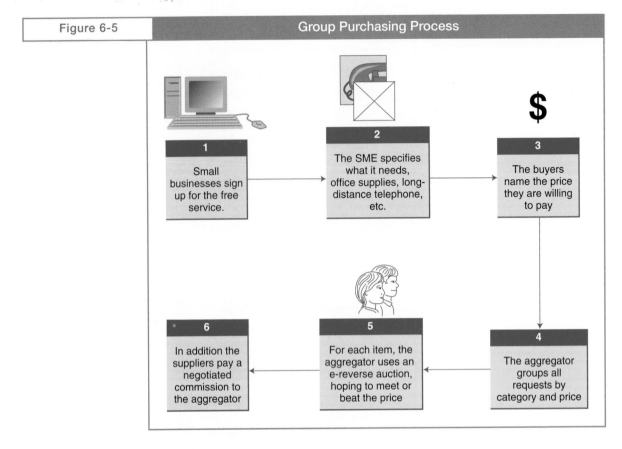

Figure 6-5   **Group Purchasing Process**

company will have little success in finding an exact match. Therefore, companies ask an intermediary to help. The intermediary can use a manual search-and-match approach or create an electronic **bartering exchange**. With a bartering exchange, a company submits its surplus to the exchange and receives points of credit. Then, these points can be used to buy the items that the company needs. Popular bartering items are office space, idle facilities and labor, products, and even banner ads (see Chapter 5). In Chapter 9 we will explain how this process works electronically and provide the names of some electronic bartering exchanges.

6.12   COLLABORATIVE COMMERCE (C-COMMERCE)

In the previous section we introduced the reader to B2B activities related to selling and buying. However, as demonstrated in Chapter 1, e-commerce can be used for other applications. A major area of application is **collaborative commerce (c-commerce)** where a Web-based system is used for communication, design, planning, information sharing, and information discovery. These activities are usually conducted between and among supply chain partners. In Chapter 2 we provided an example of Orbis, a small Australian company that uses a hub to get all its business partners together. A similar model is used by Webcor Builders, as shown in Application Case 6.4.

There are many varieties of c-commerce ranging from joint design to forecasting. Collaboration can be done both between and within organizations. For example, a collaborative platform can help in communication and collaboration between headquarters and subsidiaries or franchisers and franchisees by providing e-mail, message

Webcor Construction Goes Online with Its Partners

Webcor Builders (*Webcor.com*) builds apartment buildings, hotels, and office parks for about $500 million a year. For years the company suffered from poor communication with its partners (architects, designers, building owners, subcontractors), as well as dealing with too much paperwork. Reams of documents were sent back and forth through snail mail. In a very competitive industry, inefficiencies can be costly. So Webcor decided to go c-commerce, meaning collaborating with its partners.

Webcor decided to turn its computer-aided design (CAD) drawings, memos, and other information into shared digital information. To enable the collaboration, Webcor is using an ASP (BlueLine Online) that hosts Webcor's projects, using ProjectNet software. (ProjectNet from BlueLine Online is managed by *Cephren. com*, now part of *citadon.com*.) ProjectNet runs on a secured extranet.

The partners can post, send, or edit complex CAD drawings, digital photos, memos, status reports, and project histories. Everyone involved in a project is more accountable, because there is a digital trail; partners now get instant access to new building drawings, instead of having to wait for them to be printed and delivered. ProjectNet provides a central meeting place where

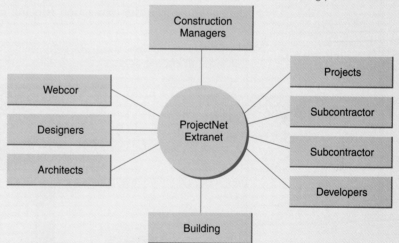

users can download information and transmit information to all parties, all with a PC. The major problem was getting everyone to accept ProjectNet. The software is complex, and some user training is necessary. In the near future, the company will not partner with anyone unless they use ProjectNet.

One of the major benefits of the project is that people now spend more time managing their work and less time on administrative paperwork. Several clerical workers were laid off. The salary saved is covering the software rental fees. (Note that *bidcom.com* [now part of *citadon.com*] provides similar software and services; see Cone, 2000).

Sources: Compiled from *Webcor.com* and *PC Computing* (December 1999).

boards and chat rooms, and online corporate data access around the globe no matter what the time zone. Such a platform helps a franchiser create global brand marketing and management for franchisees. On-demand training programs can also be shared by franchisees. Advanced extranets can link headquarters to franchisees and approved suppliers, making it easier for them to do business and reduce overhead and duplication. Advanced extranets can also improve functionalities of EDI when a retailer collaborates with its supplier.

Retailer-Supplier Collaboration: Dayton Hudson Case

Hudson Dayton is a large retail conglomerate (Target, Marshall Field's, Mervyn's, Dayton's, Hudson's) that needs to conduct EC activities with about 20,000 trading partners. The initial EC initiative started in 1998 by establishing an extranet-based system for those partners that were not connected to its VAN-based EDI. The extranet enabled Hudson Dayton not only to reach many more partners, but also to use many applications not available on the traditional EDI. The system enabled the company to streamline its communications and collaboration with suppliers. The system is based on GE's InterBusiness Partner Extranet platform (*geis.com*). The system also allows Hudson's customers to create personalized Web pages and it is accessible via either the Internet or GE's private VAN (see Figure 6-6).

The system is extending its capabilities from communication and collaboration to other e-commerce initiatives. Note that the extranet enhances the capabilities of EDI to support e-commerce activities. For example, the extranet improves communication before a transaction is initiated, and then serves as a tool for improving data alignment as the transaction is being processed. Finally, the extranet can be

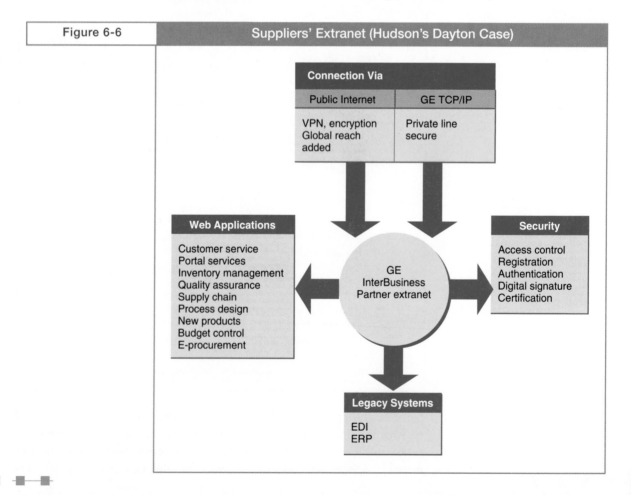

Figure 6-6 — Suppliers' Extranet (Hudson's Dayton Case)

Connection Via

Public Internet	GE TCP/IP
VPN, encryption Global reach added	Private line secure

Web Applications
Customer service
Portal services
Inventory management
Quality assurance
Supply chain
Process design
New products
Budget control
E-procurement

GE InterBusiness Partner extranet

Security
Access control
Registration
Authentication
Digital signature
Certification

Legacy Systems
EDI
ERP

used to inspect a transaction before it is put into the system. More examples of collaborative commerce, such as joint forecasting between retailers and their suppliers, are provided in Chapter 15.

Reduce Design Cycle Time by Connecting Suppliers: Adaptec, Inc.

Adaptec, Inc. is a large microchip manufacturer supplying critical components to electronic equipment makers. The company outsources manufacturing tasks, concentrating on product research and development. Outsourcing production, however, puts the company at a disadvantage with competitors that have their own manufacturing facilities and can optimize their delivery schedules. Before it implemented the extranet, Adaptec required up to 15 weeks to deliver products to customers; competitors were able to deliver similar chips in only 8 weeks.

The longer delivery time was mainly caused by the need to coordinate design activities between Adaptec headquarters in California and its three principal fabrication factories in Hong Kong, Japan, and Taiwan. The company reduced its chip production cycle times by shortening order-to-product-delivery time from 15 weeks to between 10 and 12 weeks. The solutions to Adaptec's problem were an extranet and enterprise-level supply chain integration software, which incorporates automated workflow and EC tools.

One initial benefit included the reduced time required to generate, transmit, and confirm purchase orders. This was done by using e-mail to communicate with manufacturers across several time zones, thereby automatically starting the flow of raw materials, which in turn reduced invoicing and shipping times. In addition to business transaction documents, Adaptec can send chip design diagrams over the extranet, enabling the manufacturers to prepare for product changes and new designs. This faster communication method required Adaptec to adjust its decision-making processes that were based on the old assumption that at least 2 weeks were needed to put an order into production.

Reduce Product Development Time by Connecting Suppliers: Caterpillar, Inc.

Caterpillar, Inc., a multinational heavy machinery manufacturer, was an early extranet adopter. The company operated an intranet that was accessible to customers who wanted to make changes to customized vehicles. In the traditional mode of operation, such changes increased cycle time because the process involved paper document transfers among managers, salespeople, and technical staff.

Using an extranet, the company demonstrated in 1998 how a request for a customized tractor component was received through a dealer from a farm company and handled by designers and suppliers, all in a very short time. Suppliers produced and delivered the final product directly to the customers. Caterpillar uses extranet applications as competitive tools to shorten product development cycles. During 1998, the company connected its engineering and manufacturing divisions with its active suppliers, distributors, overseas factories, and customers, all in a global extranet.

Caterpillar customers, for example, can use the extranet to retrieve and modify detailed order information while the vehicle remains on the assembly line. This ability to collaborate remotely between customer and product developers decreases cycle time delays resulting from additional rework time. The system is also used for expediting maintenance and repairs.

Other Examples of C-Commerce

Leading businesses are moving quickly to realize the benefits of c-commerce. For example:

- Tricon Restaurant International, which operates 10,000 KFC, Pizza Hut, and Taco Bell restaurants in 83 countries, uses c-commerce platforms in global brand marketing and management.
- The real estate franchiser RE/MAX uses a c-commerce platform to improve communications and collaboration among its nationwide network of independently owned real estate franchisees, sales associates, and suppliers.
- Marriott International, the world's largest hospitality company, started with an online brochure and then developed an advanced EC initiative aimed at linking corporations, franchisees, partners, and suppliers, as well as customers, located around the world. (See Intel 1999a and 1999b for details.)
- Nygard of Canada developed a collaborative system along the entire supply chain as shown in Application Case 6.5.

APPLICATION CASE   6.5

Interorganizational Collaboration at Nygard of Canada

The apparel industry is one of the most competitive industries, and global manufacturers are willing to operate with razor thin margins. The only way to survive is to use IT. Nygard International of Winnipeg, Canada (*Nygard.com*) is a leader in adopting IT and e-commerce in the apparel industry. Here is what the company did:

- Developed an ERP and supply chain management that controls all internal operations, purchasing, product development, accounting, production planning, and sales.
- Developed tight integration with its trading partners. For example, the moment that a customer buys a pair of pants at a retail store, the information moves from the POS terminal to automatically generate a reorder. The SCM not only matches orders with the right fabrics, but it searches the market pool for the most efficient combinations for use with those fabrics.
- When sales trigger orders, Nygard's manufacturing automatically triggers records on all raw materials, such as fabrics, zippers, and buttons. The moment that raw material is used, an automatic order is generated. This allows just-in-time production and delivery of orders the same day that they are received. If not delivered as promised, the company pays a delay penalty. This happens very rarely.
- A Web-based control system enables the company to conduct detailed profitability studies, so every proposal and decision is evaluated by its impact on the bottom line. Decision Support Systems (DSS) models are used for this purpose.

APPLICATION CASE   **6.5**

(continued)

- In the apparel industry, it is most important to use EC tools on the procurement side. To ensure just-in-time delivery, Nygard must have the ability to have visibility, not only into their suppliers' systems, but also into their suppliers' suppliers. This way they can make commitments that they can fulfill.
- One of the major issues in the apparel industry is the transfer of manufacturing operations to countries where labor is inexpensive. Nygard decided not to do this because it may double the cycle time as well as the inventory levels. So to stay in Canada, the company *must* use EC to control its labor and manufacturing costs.

Sources: Compiled from *Apparel Industry Magazine* (March 1999) and from *nygard.com*

6.13   INFRASTRUCTURE, INTEGRATION, EDI, AND B2B AGENTS

B2B company-centric marketplaces can be developed by different approaches and methods. Large numbers of vendors, including Ariba (see Application Case 6.6), Oracle, and IBM, offer all the necessary tools. The major infrastructure needed for B2B marketplaces are:

- Server(s) for hosting the databases and the applications
- Software for executing the sell-side activities, including catalogs
- Software for conducting auctions and reverse auctions
- Software for e-procurement (buy side)
- Software for CRM, possibly related to a call centers
- Security for hardware and software
- Software for building a storefront
- Other software
- Telecommunications networks and protocols, including EDI and EML.

For the alternative approaches to developing EC systems using these and other components, see Chapter 12 and Hoque (2000). Chapter 12 also provides criteria for software and vendor selection. Most companies use vendors to build their applications, as shown in the Real-World Case at the end of this chapter. The vendor sells or leases all the necessary software to create the marketplace at the single buyer or single seller premises. One of the major vendors is Ariba as shown in Application Case 6.6.

Extranet and EDI

In order for business partners to communicate online, companies must implement some type of secure interorganizational network like an extranet and a common protocol like EDI. Traditional EDI systems were implemented in VAN, limiting the accessibility of small companies. Internet-based EDI can offer wide accessibility to most companies in the world. Internet-based EDI can replace traditional EDI or supplement it for SMEs. Internet-based EDI provides several capabilities that are not available in traditional EDI. For the evolution of traditional EDI to Internet-based EDI, see the comprehensively material described in Appendix 6.1.

Ariba's ORMS

Ariba Corp. (*ariba.com*) is one of the most well-known B2B vendors that provides sell-side and buy-side solutions named ORMS (Operating Resource Management System), as well as solutions for exchanges described in Chapter 7. In addition, the company offers auction mechanisms and B2B support services. Here are the major products offered in spring 2001.

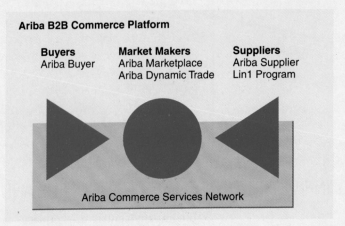

Ariba Buyer

Ariba Buyer is Ariba's answer to the procurement needs of today's global enterprises. Leading companies use Ariba Buyer as their single solution to buy both direct and indirect goods, acquire services, track travel costs and other expenses, and analyze strategic spending. The application totally redefines the buying process, reducing costs, eliminating inefficiencies, and speeding up the transaction flow from end to end.

Ariba Marketplace

Ariba Marketplace is a flexible, rapid-deployment solution for market makers of all kinds. Suitable for all types of B2B exchanges—from horizontal procurement marketplaces to highly specialized vertical marketplaces and commodity exchanges—the application bridges the gap between traditional buy-side and sell-side solutions.

Ariba Dynamic Trade

Ariba Dynamic Trade is Ariba's highly configurable, fully integrated auction and exchange application. The solution delivers the full range of dynamic pricing mechanisms—auction, bid/ask exchange, and reverse auction—in a flexible architecture. Ariba Dynamic Trade manages approved vendor lists, price and bidder confidentiality, time sensitivity, and differing quality or support levels.

Ariba Commerce Services Network

Tightly integrated with the Ariba B2B Commerce Platform, the Ariba Commerce Services Network provides sourcing, liquidation, supplier content and directory services, secure transaction routing, multiprotocol exchange of transaction information, payment services, and logistics. Ariba's set of network-based commerce services helps businesses streamline their supply chain and seize new revenue opportunities. Offered both directly and through partnerships with other leading service providers, these services allow businesses to take maximum advantage of online B2B trade.

Source: Ariba.com Web site (January 2001).

The extranet concept and its core technology, Virtual Private Networks (VPNs), is explained in Appendix 7.1 in Chapter 7 (see also Chapter 13).

Integration with Existing Information Systems

Marketplaces of any kind need to be connected to the existing information systems of both buyers and sellers. All major EC software vendors, such as Ariba, IBM, Oracle, Commerce One, and SAP, provide for such integration. This integration includes:

- ERP software
- Customers, suppliers, and other databases
- Legacy systems and their applications
- Catalog (product) information
- Inventory systems
- Sales statistics
- Supply Chain Management (SCM) and DSS applications

System integrators and middleware vendors (such as *tibco.com*) provide many alternative solutions for such an integration. Details are provided in Chapter 12.

ISSUES IN INTEGRATING WITH BACK-END INFORMATION SYSTEMS

Back-end information systems may be implemented using intranet-based work-flow, database management systems (DBMS), application packages, and ERP. In the sell-side marketplace setting, the integration of EC with suppliers' back-end information systems is relatively easy because the suppliers keep the platform for both EC and their back-end systems in their servers. However, it is not easy for the buyers to trace their transactions once they are placed on several suppliers' servers. By the same token, in the buyer-side marketplace setting, business buyers, but not suppliers, can integrate EC with their back-end information systems easily. In the intermediary-oriented marketplace setting, neither buyers nor sellers can organize their transactions easily. This difficulty is a challenge to the participating buyers and sellers in B2B EC, but is a good opportunity for solution providers.

Integration with Business Partners

EC can be integrated easily with the one-company-centric side but not with the other side (any buyers or sellers). For instance, in the sell-side marketplace, it is not easy for buying companies to organize ordering information, because the information is scattered over various sellers' servers. Therefore, a buyer-owned shopping cart (Lim and Lee 2000), which can interface with back-end information systems, may be necessary.

The Role of Software Agents for B2B EC

Agents play multiple roles in B2B. Here are some examples.

AGENT'S ROLE IN THE SELL-SIDE MARKETPLACE

In Chapter 3, we discussed how software agents are used to aid the comparison-shopping process. The major role of software agents in that case is collecting data from multiple commercial sites, mainly sell-sides. Similarly, in B2B, agents will collect information from sellers' sites for the benefit of the buyers.

| Figure 6-7 | Intelligent-Agent-Based Commerce: A Prototypical Scenario |

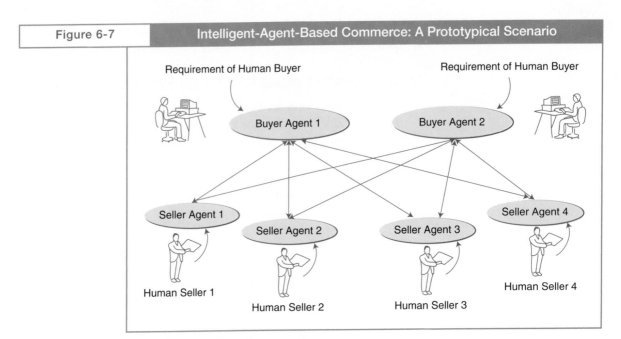

Source: J. K. Lee and W. Lee (1997).

AGENT'S ROLE IN THE BUY-SIDE MARKETPLACE

Suppose that a large number of customers need to request quotes from multiple potential suppliers in the buy-side marketplace. Doing so manually will become physically impossible or uneconomical. Therefore, software agents are needed to assist both buyers and sellers. To make agent-based commerce possible, intelligent buyer agents and seller agents can be developed in the same platform, as depicted in Figure 6-7.

Agents need to have meta-problem-solving skills (the ability to understand how to react to the received message and what specifically to answer) and communication controller capabilities (to interpret the other agent's message and synthesize messages understandable to the other agents). UNIK-AGENT adopted this architecture (Lee and Lee, 1997). A special issue on agents was published by *Communications of the ACM* (March 1999), and includes a review of agents that buy and sell (Maes et al., 1999).

6.14 IMPLEMENTATION ISSUES

Several implementation issues may be encountered when a company is implementing B2B e-commerce.

Justification and Prioritization

Because there are several B2B models, each of which can be implemented in different ways, it becomes critical to conduct a cost-benefit analysis of the proposed projects. Such an analysis should include organizational impacts, such as possible channel conflicts and dealing with resistance to change due to the required process reengineering. Such cost-benefit analysis is related to the issues of finding B2B opportunities and prioritizing the potential initiatives. These are described in Chapters 12 and 16.

Vendor Selection

Vendors normally develop B2B projects. Two basic approaches to vendor selection exist:

1. Select a primary vendor such as IBM, Ariba, or Oracle. This vendor will use its software and procedures and will add partners as needed.
2. Use an integrator that will mix and match existing products and vendors to create "the best of breed" for your needs (see Chapter 12).

Affiliate Programs

Like any EC activity, acquiring customers and their business is a major problem. A popular B2C program used by CDNow and *Amazon.com* is a referral program called an **affiliate program.** This approach is especially useful for B2B intermediaries. For example, *shop2gether.com*, a group purchasing aggregator, has a comprehensive affiliate program (*shop2gether.com/affiliates/AffInfo.asp*).

Implementing E-Procurement

Putting the buying department on the Internet may be the easy part of e-procurement. The difficult part is dealing with the following issues:

- Fitting e-procurement into the company EC strategy.
- Reviewing and changing the procurement process itself. For example, how many purchasing agents exist, where are they located, and how purchases are being approved. Also important is the degree of purchasing centralization.
- It is important to determine if there is ERP or SCM (see Chapter 15) in place. If yes, it is necessary to integrate e-procurement with them. If not, it may beneficial to do some business process reengineering (BPR) prior to the installation of e-procurement.
- It is necessary to coordinate the buyer's information system with that of the sellers. But sellers have many potential buyers. For this reason, some major suppliers such as SKF (a European automotive parts maker, *skf.com*), developed an integration-oriented procurement system for their buyers. For example, the SKF information system is designed to make it easier for the procurement systems of others, notably the distributors in other countries which buy the company's bearings and seals, to interface with the SKF system. The SKF system allows distributors to gain real-time technical information on the products, as well as details on product availability, delivery times, and commercial terms and conditions.

6.15   MANAGERIAL ISSUES

The following issues are germane to management:

1. **B2B marketing.** Sell-side marketplaces may require advertisement and incentives. Unless a company is a Cisco, Dell, or IBM, it is likely that a company will need to promote its site. (See Chapters 5 and 8).
2. **Which models to use and when.** The availability of so many B2B models means that companies need selection strategies and prioritization (see Chapter 16). In addition to the company-centric models, there are several types of exchanges to consider (Chapter 7).

3. **Purchase process reengineering.** To reengineer the purchasing process, a company should establish a buy-side marketplace on its server if volume is big enough to attract the attention of major vendors. Otherwise, a company should join the third-party intermediary-oriented marketplace (Chapter 7).

4. **Integration.** Trading in e-marketplaces is interrelated with logistics. While this is particularly true in many-to-many exchanges (Chapter 7), it is beneficial to consider integration with logistics and other support services in the company-centric marketplace (Chapter 15).

5. **Business ethics.** Since B2B EC counts on the sharing of mutual information, business ethics are a must. Accessing unauthorized areas in the trading system should not be allowed, and privacy of partners should be protected both technically and legally.

6. **Auctions.** Both forward and reverse auctions must be considered. The benefits are substantial and the implementation is relatively simple (see Chapter 9). There is considerable flexibility in how to do it.

Many organizations fail to understand that a fundamental change in their internal processes must be implemented to realize the full benefits of e-procurement. The two critical success factors that many organizations overlook are the need to cut down the number of routine tasks and to reduce the overall procurement cycle through the use of appropriate information technologies such as workflow, groupware, and ERP software, as well as the B2B models.

Summary

In this chapter, you learned about the following EC issues as they relate to the learning objectives:

1. **The B2B field.** The B2B field includes e-commerce activities between businesses, such as manufacturers, intermediaries, business customers, and governments. B2B activities account for 85 percent of all EC, and they are growing rapidly.

2. **The major B2B models.** The B2B field is very diversified. It can be divided into the following segments: sell-side marketplaces, buy-side marketplaces, auctions and reverse auctions, trading exchanges, and B2B services.

3. **The characteristics of sell-side marketplaces.** Direct sale by manufacturers or intermediaries that are conducted online are defined as sell-side EC. The major technology used is electronic catalogs, but forward auctions are becoming more popular, especially for selling surpluses. Sell-side activities include extensive customer service.

4. **Sell-side intermediaries.** Intermediaries use B2B primarily to provide value-added services to manufacturers and business customers. They can also install electronic ordering and e-procurement systems.

5. **The characteristics of buy-side marketplaces.** Today, companies are moving to e-procurement to expedite purchasing, save on item and administrative costs, and get better control of the purchasing process. A popular e-procurement model is the reverse auction (also known as tendering or bidding). Other models are company internal marketplaces and group purchasing.

6. **Forward and reverse auctions.** Auctions play a major role in B2B. Forward auctions are used by sellers either as a new marketing channel or to liquidate

surpluses and old equipment. A reverse auction is a tendering system used by buyers to collect bids electronically from suppliers.

7. **B2B aggregation and group purchasing.** Increasing the exposure and/or the bargaining power of companies can be done by aggregating either the sellers or the buyers. Buyer aggregation is very popular since it allows businesses to get better prices on their purchases.

8. **Collaborative EC.** Collaborative EC is conducted among supply chain partners. A common model is changing the linear communications chain to a hub accessible by all partners. This model helps to speed communication and collaboration and eliminate errors made in paper-based systems.

9. **Implementing B2B EC.** Several issues are encountered in implementing company-centric B2B. These may include integration with existing information systems, transformation of business processes, appropriate selection of applications, and vendor selection and management.

10. **Characteristics of Internet-based EDI.** Traditional EDI systems were implemented in VAN, limiting the accessibility of small companies. Internet-based EDI can offer wide accessibility to most companies in the world. Internet-based EDI can replace traditional EDI or supplement it for SMEs. Internet-based EDI provides several capabilities not available in traditional EDI.

Key Terms

Bartering exchange	Intermediary-oriented marketplace
Business-to-business electronic commerce (B2B EC)	Internet-based EDI
Buy-side marketplace	Maintenance, repairs, and operations (MROs)
Collaborative commerce (c-commerce)	Maverick buying
Company-centric EC	Online intermediary
Direct materials	Private e-marketplace
Disintermediation	Procurement management
eB2B	Public e-marketplace
E-bartering	Request for quote (RFQ)
E-procurement	Sell-side marketplace
Electronic catalogs	Spot buying
Electronic data interchange (EDI)	Stickiness
Enterprise resource planning (ERP)	Strategic sourcing
Exchange	Supply chain management
Group purchasing	Trading exchanges (or communities)
Horizontal marketplace	Value-added networks (VANS)
Indirect materials	Vertical marketplace

Questions for Review

1. Describe the relationships between B2B and the supply chain.
2. Define company-centric B2B.
3. List the major business models of B2B.
4. Define the benefits of sell-side marketplaces.
5. Describe sell-side B2B models.

6. Define forward and reverse auctions.
7. List the benefits of e-procurement.
8. Describe collaborative commerce.
9. Define group purchasing and explain its benefits.

Questions for Discussion

1. Explain how a catalog-based sell-side marketplace works and discuss its benefits.
2. Can both consumers and businesses use the sell-side marketplace, and if so, under what circumstances?
3. Distinguish sell-side from buy-side marketplaces.
4. Can both consumers and businesses use the buy-side marketplace?
5. How can companies buying from a sell-side marketplace integrate order information with their corporation's procurement systems?
6. GE has opened its TPN for public tendering.
   - Can other big corporations follow the same strategy? Why or why not?
   - Can small businesses follow the same strategy as well? If not, what should their strategy be?
   - What could be the response of vendors to the proliferation of buyer-oriented marketplaces?
7. How do companies eliminate the potential limitations and risks associated with Internet-based EDI? (Read the appendix to the chapter.)
8. How can software agents work for multiple sellers and buyers?
9. Discuss and compare all the mechanisms that aggregators of group purchasing can use.
10. Discuss the advantage of Internet-based EDI over traditional EDI.
11. Review the eight questions at Marshall Industries Case (Section 6.7) and answer the quiz. Explain the logic of your answers.

Internet Exercises

1. Visit *milacron.com* and examine the site from the business buyer's perspective. Find out how to order on the sell-side marketplaces. Design a way to integrate the electronic marketplace with the ERP system of the buying company.
2. Enter *atcost.com* and review the bidding process. Describe the preparations your company should make in order to bid.
3. Enter *CommerceOne.com* and review the capabilities of BuySite and MarketSite. Find out how Commerce One supports the integration of many sellers' electronic catalogs for a specific buyer.
4. Visit *allsystem.com* to review All-System Aerospace International, Inc., a company that handles aircraft parts from several vendors. From an aircraft repairman's point-of-view, evaluate whether this site can compete with Boeing's PART system.
5. Visit sites such as *zwirl.com*, *shop2gether.com*, and *miso21.com*. Compare the services offered by these businesses.
6. Examine the sites *fastparts.com*, *ariba.com*, *nonstop.compaq.com*, *trilogy.com*, *freemarkets.com*, *electricnet.com*, *harbinger.com*, and *ecweb.com*. Match a B2B business model with each site.

7. Visit *supplyworks.com* and examine how they streamline the purchase process. How does it differ from *ariba.com*?

8. Enter *soho.org* and *onlinesoho.com* and locate EC applications for small offices and home offices (SOHO). Also, check the business services provided by *officedepot.com*.

9. Visit *ebay.com* and identify all activities related to their small business auctions (business eXchange). What services are provided by eBay?

10. Review the GE TPN Application Case and answer the following questions.
    a. Describe the motivations for developing TPN Post.
    b. Describe the benefits of TPN in terms of procurement processing time, labor costs, and purchasing price.
    c. List the benefits of linking with suppliers.
    d. Visit *gegyx.com* and find the services offered to companies that are invited to place RFQs on the public site.
    e. What is the TPN Post business model?
    f. What motivates suppliers to join the TPN?
    g. What are the pros and cons of opening the TPN to other buyers?

11. Visit *avnet.com* and find how the supply chain is structured. Draw the chain, showing Avnet's role. (Hint: look at Timmers, 1999 and Kalakota and Robinson, 2000)

12. Read the Cisco Connection Online (CCO) case.
    a. What is the CCO business model?
    b. Where are the success factors of CCO?
    c. What kinds of inquiries are supported when customers check their order status?
    d. What are the major benefits of CCO to Cisco and its customers?

Team Assignments and Role Playing

1. Predictions about the magnitude of B2B and statistics on its actual volumn in various countries and by product/application keep changing. The team's mission is to find current predictions. Teams can be assigned to world regions (Asia, Europe, North America), or B2B applications (e.g., industry type, company-centric vs. exchanges, etc). Then the team will search for the predicted B2B volume ($) in that region from at least five sources, for the next five years. Some sources of data are: Datamonitor, Gomez Research, Giga Research, AMR Research, Forrester Research, GartnerGroup, Morgan Stanley, Duracher Research, Ltd., Goldman Sachs (*gs.com*), *Aberdeen.com*, Gomez Research, etc.

2. Your goal in this assignment is to investigate the major B2B vendors. A good place to start is with the B2B e-commerce report of *durlacher.com*. Each team should investigate a major vendor (e.g., Ariba, Commerce One, Oracle, or IBM), or an application type (buy-side, sell-side, or auction). Find the major products and services offered and examine customer success stories. Write a report of your findings.

REAL-WORLD CASE: Eastman Chemical Makes Procurement a Strategic Advantage

A multibillion dollar, multinational corporation, Eastman Chemical (ECM) is operating in an extremely competitive environment. In response to pressures, management identified the improvement of the procurement of the nonproductive (MRO) supply chain as a strategic initiative. To do so, the company embarked on two interrelated activities: integrating the supply chain (a channel supply) and introducing e-procurement. The objectives of the project, which started in late 1999, were:

1. Increase compliance with purchasing policies (reduce maverick buying).

2. Support frontline employees while maintaining existing rules.

3. Reduce procurement transaction cost via elimination of non-value-added and redundant processes.

4. Leverage corporate spending to negotiate favored trading terms with channel supply partners.

The Problem with the Old Process

The company purchased over $900 million in MROs from over 3,500 suppliers. The company used a SAP R/3 ERP system which provided good control, but at a cost of $115 per order when a purchasing card was used. (see Chapter 8). The ERP helped in reducing the work load on accounts payable personnel and procurement approvers. However, purchasing from noncontracted suppliers increased (it was easy to do it with the card). This reduced purchase volumes with the primary suppliers, reducing the company's negotiation leverage. Thus, the costs were high.

The Solutions

ECM established channel partnership relationships with its largest MRO suppliers. This increased ECM's buying leverage and reduced costs and delays. Inventories and service levels were improved. In addition, ECM introduced two EC applications: Commerce One's BuySite e-procurement software for dealing with the suppliers and MarketSite for transaction management and value-added services.

Using BuySite, ECM has created an internal catalog of all MRO products located in Eastman's storerooms. The e-commerce software checks availability and prevents redundant purchases. The software also supplies catalog management features that assure that all vendors' changes and updates are entered into the internal catalog.

The MarketSite application supported the creation of a portal that enables:

- Use of a common Web browser by 16,000 employees

- Use of the system by different types of employees without training

- Support for Windows NT platform, which was already in use

- Ability to integrate SAP R/3 with EC and the procurement card

- Effective and efficient catalog management strategy

- Maintenance of the existing systems infrastructure

- Simplification of business processes

- Flexibility and empowerment of frontline employees

Questions for the case

1. Enter *CommerceOne.com* and find information about the capabilities of BuySite and MarketSite. What are the differences between the two applications?

2. Why did ECM concentrate on e-procurement and not on the sell-side? You may want to visit *Eastman.com* to learn more.

3. In July 2000, ECM introduced an EC project that enables buyers to participate in Eastman's private online price negotiations using LiveExchange from Moai (*moai.com*). Explain how the software works and why it is referred to as "dynamic commerce."

4. Which of the problems cited in this case can be solved by other EC applications? Relate your answer to Commerce One products.

REFERENCES AND BIBLIOGRAPHY

Blankenhorn, D. "GE's E-Commerce Network Opens Up to Other Marketers," *NetMarketing* (May 1997) (*netb2b.com*).

Bunnell, D. and A. Brate. *Making the Cisco Connection*. New York: Wiley & Sons. 2000.

Cone, E. "Building a Stronger Economy," *Interactivework* (January 24, 2000).

Cunningham, M.J. *B2B: How to Build a Profitable E-Commerce Strategy*. Cambridge, Massachusetts: Perseus Book Group, 2000.

E-Supply Chain and Logistics: Special Vendors' Section, *Fortune* (*Fortune.com/fortune/sections/esupply*) (2000).

EL-Sawy, O., et al. "Intensive Value Innovation in the Electronic Economy: Insight from Marshall Industry," *MIS Quarterly* (September 1999).

Fabris, P. "EC Riders (GE's TPN)" *CIO Magazine* (July 15, 1997).

Fickel, L. "Online Auctions: Bid Business," *CIO Web Business Magazine* (June 1, 1999).

Forrester Research, "Estimates of the B2B Market," *Forrester.com* (March 7, 2001).

Freeman, L. "Net Drives B-to-B to New Highs Worldwide," *NetMarketing* (January 1998).

Frook, J. E. "Web Links with Back-End Systems Pay Off," *Internet Week* (July 13, 1998).

Gugullis, E. "Power to the Buyer with Group Buying Sites," *e-Business Adviser* (February 2000).

Handfield, R. and E. Nicols. *Supply Chain Management*. Upper Saddle River, New Jersey: Prentice Hall, 1999.

Hoque F., *E-Enterprise,* Cambridge, UK: Cambridge University Press, 2000.

Intel Corp. "Franchising Meets the Internet," (*Intel.com/ebusiness/* then go to Industry solutions) (March 4, 1999a).

Intel Corp. "Marriott International Checks In," (*Intel.com/ebusiness/* then go to Industry solutions) (March 4, 1999b)

Kalakota, R. and M. Robinson. *E-Business 2.0.* Reading, Massachusetts: Addison-Wesley, 2000.

Lawrence, E., et al. *Internet Commerce. Digital Models for Business*. New York: John Wiley & Sons, 1998.

Lee, J. K. and W. Lee. "An Intelligent Agent Based Contract Process in Electronic Commerce: UNIK-AGENT Approach," *Proceedings of 13th Hawaii International Conference on System Sciences* (1997).

Lim, G. and J. K. Lee. "Buyer-Carts for B2B EC: The B-Cart Approach," *Proceedings of the Second ICEC, Seoul Korea* (August 2000).

Maes, P., et al. "Agents That Buy and Sell," *Communications of ACM* (March 3, 1999).

McGagg, B. *The Essential Guide to Selling Surplus Assets*. Valhalla, New York: *Tradeoeut.com*, 1999.

O'Connell, B. *B2B.com: Cashing in on the B2B EC Bonanza*. Holbrook, Massachusetts: Adams Media Corp., 2000.

Retter, T. and M. Calyniuk. *Technology Forecast: 1998*. Menlo Park, California: Price Waterhouse (March 1998).

Senn, J. A. "B2B E-Commerce," *Information Systems Management* (Spring 2000).

Silverstein, B. *Business-to-Business Internet Marketing*. Gulf Breeze, Florida: Maximum Press, 1999.

Stauffer, D. *Nothing But the Net: Business the Cisco Way*. Oxford, UK: Capstone Ltd., 2000.

Sullivan, D. "Extending E-Business to ERP," *e-business Advisor* (January 1999).

Teasdale, S. "Boeing Extranet Speeds Ordering Process for Spare-parts Buyers," *Net Marketing* (June 1997).

The Economist, special issue on Electronic Commerce (Large Collection) (June 26, 1999).

Timmers, P. *Electronic Commerce: Strategies and Models for B2B Trading*. Chichester, UK: John Wiley & Sons, Ltd., 1999.

Trading Process Network. "Extending the Enterprise: TPN Post Case Study—GE Lighting," (*gegxs.com*) (1999).

Turban, E., et al. *Information Technology for Management*, 3rd ed. New York: John Wiley & Sons, 2002.

Warkentin, M. and E. Turban. *B2B Electronic Commerce.* Upper Saddle River, New Jersey: Prentice Hall, 2002.

Wilson, T. "Marshall Industries: Wholesale Shift to the Web," *InternetWeek* (July 20, 1998).

A P P E N D I X   6A

FROM TRADITIONAL TO INTERNET-BASED EDI

The majority of B2B transactions are supported by **electronic data interchange (EDI)** and/or extranets. In this appendix, EDI and its transition to the Internet platform are described. The extranet is covered in Chapter 7.

TRADITIONAL EDI

EDI can be defined as the electronic movement of specially formatted standard business documents, such as orders, bills, and confirmations sent between business partners. An EDI implementation is a process in which two or more organizations determine how to work together more effectively. EDI often serves as a catalyst and a stimulus to improve the business processes that flow between organizations. For others, it is an internal decision spurred by the desire for competitive advantage. Like e-mail, EDI allows sending and receiving of messages between computers connected by a communication link. However, EDI has the following special characteristics

- **Business transactions messages.** EDI is used primarily to electronically transfer *repetitive* business transactions. These include purchase orders, invoices, approvals of credit, shipping notices, confirmations, and so on.
- **Data formatting standards.** Since EDI messages are repetitive, it is sensible to use some formatting (coding) standards. Standards can shorten the length of the messages and eliminate data entry errors, since data entry occurs only once. In the United States and Canada, data are formatted according to the ANSI X.12 standard. An international standard developed by the United Nations is called EDIFACT.
- **EDI translators.** An EDI translator does the conversion of data into standard format.

EDI and Standards

EDI has been around for almost 30 years in the non-Internet environment. It is a system that standardizes the process of trading and tracking routine business documents, such as purchase orders, invoices, payments, shipping manifests, and delivery schedules. EDI translates these documents into a globally understood business language and transmits them between trading partners using secure telecommunications links (Figure A6-1). To distinguish it from Internet-based EDI, we call EDI on the non-Internet platform *traditional EDI*.

Figure A6-1	Traditional and Web-Based EDI

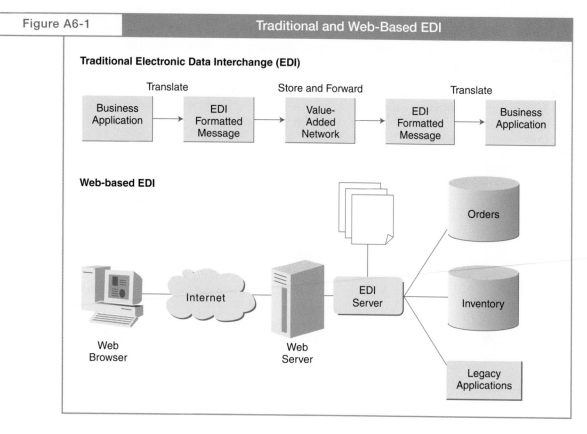

Traditional Electronic Data Interchange (EDI)

Translate → Store and Forward → Translate

Business Application → EDI Formatted Message → Value-Added Network → EDI Formatted Message → Business Application

Web-based EDI

Web Browser → Internet → Web Server → EDI Server → Orders / Inventory / Legacy Applications

Applications of EDI

Traditional EDI has changed the landscape of business, triggering new definitions of entire industries. Well-known retailers, such as The Home Depot, Toys R Us, and Wal-Mart, would operate very differently today without EDI, since it is an integral and essential element of their business strategy. Thousands of global manufacturers, including Proctor and Gamble, Levi Strauss, Toyota, and Unilever, have used EDI to redefine relationships with their customers through such practices as quick-response retailing and just-in-time (JIT) manufacturing. These highly visible, high-impact applications of EDI by large companies have been extremely successful. The benefits of EDI are listed in Table A6-1.

Limitations of Traditional EDI

However, despite the tremendous impact of traditional EDI among industry leaders, the set of adopters represented only a small fraction of potential EDI users. In the United States, where several million businesses participate in commerce every day, fewer than 100,000 companies have adopted traditional EDI. Furthermore, most of the companies have had only a small number of their business partners on EDI, mainly due to its high cost. Therefore, in reality, many businesses have not benefited from EDI, the major factors being:

- Significant initial investment is needed
- Restructuring business processes is necessary to fit EDI requirements
- A long start-up time is needed

	The Benefits of EDI
TABLE A6-1	• EDI enables companies to send and receive large amounts of routine transaction information quickly around the globe. • There are very few errors in the transferred data as a result of computer-to-computer data transfer. • Information can flow among several trading partners consistently and freely. • Companies can access partners' databases to retrieve and store standard transactions. • EDI fosters true (and strategic) partnership relationships since it involves a commitment to a long-term investment and the refinement of the system over time. • EDI creates a complete paperless TPS environment, saving money and increasing efficiency. • Payment collection can be shortened by several weeks. • Data may be entered offline, in a batch mode, without tying up ports to the mainframe. • When an EDI document is received, the data may be used immediately. • Sales information is delivered to manufacturers, shippers, and warehouses almost in real time. • EDI can save a considerable amount of money.

- Use of expensive, private VANs are necessary
- High operating cost of EDI
- There are multiple EDI standards, so one company may have to use several standards
- The system is complex to use
- A converter is required to translate business transactions to EDI code

These factors suggest that traditional EDI—relying on formal transaction sets, translation software, and VANs—is not suitable as a long-term solution for most corporations, because it does not meet the following requirements:

- Enables more firms to use EDI
- Encourages full integration of EDI into trading partners' business processes
- Simplifies EDI implementation
- Expands the capabilities of online information exchange

Therefore, a better infrastructure is needed; Internet-based EDI is such an infrastructure.

INTERNET-BASED EDI

Why Internet-Based EDI?

When considered as a channel for EDI, the Internet appears to be the most feasible alternative for putting online B2B trading within reach of virtually any organization, large or small. There are several reasons for firms to create EDI ability over the Internet:

- The Internet is a publicly accessible network with few geographical constraints. Its largest attribute, large-scale connectivity (without the need for any special company networking architecture), is a seedbed for growth of a vast range of business applications.
- The Internet global internetwork connections offer the potential to reach the widest possible number of trading partners of any viable alternative currently available.
- Using the Internet can cut communication costs by over 50 percent.

- Using the Internet to exchange EDI transactions is consistent with the growing interest of business in delivering an ever-increasing variety of products and services electronically, particularly through the Web.
- Internet-based EDI can complement or replace many current EDI applications.
- Internet tools such as browsers and search engines are very user-friendly, and most users today know how to use them.
- Internet-based EDI has several functionalities not provided by traditional EDI, which include collaboration, workflow, and search engines.

Types of Internet-Based EDI

The Internet can support EDI in a variety of ways:

- Internet e-mail can be used as the EDI message transport in place of a VAN. To this end, standards for encapsulating the messages within Secure Internet Mail Extension (S/MIME) were established.
- A company can create an extranet that enables its trading partners to enter information in Web form whose fields correspond to the fields in an EDI message or document.
- Companies can utilize the services of a Web-based EDI hosting service in much the same way that companies rely on third parties to host their commerce sites. Netscape Enterprise is illustrative of the type of Web-based EDI software that enables a company to provide their own EDI services over the Internet, while Harbinger Express is illustrative of those companies that provide third-party hosting services.

The Prospects of Internet-Based EDI

Companies that used traditional EDI have had a positive response to Internet-based EDI. A Forrester Research, Inc. sample survey of 50 Fortune 1,000 companies showed that nearly half of them plan to use EDI over the Internet by 2000. The companies polled said that an average of 16 percent of their traffic will move from VAN and leased lines to the Internet by 2000. In traditional EDI, they also have to pay for network transport, translation, and routing of EDI messages into their legacy processing systems. Frequently, companies combine traditional EDI with the Internet by having their Internet-based orders transmitted to a VAN or service provider that translates the data into an EDI format and sends it to their host computers. The Internet simply serves as an alternative transport mechanism to a more expensive lease line. The combination of the Web, XML, and Java makes EDI worthwhile even for small, infrequent transactions. Whereas EDI is not interactive, the Web and Java were designed specifically for interactivity as well as ease of use.

Here are some examples of the transformation to or initiation of Internet-based EDI:

- Compucom systems was averaging 5,000 transactions per month with traditional EDI, and now averages 35,000 transactions in just a short time after the transition. The system helped the company to grow rapidly.
- Tradelink of Hong Kong was successful in recruiting only several hundred of the potential 70,000 companies that used the system to communicate with government agencies regarding export/import transactions. In 2000, the

Internet-based system had thousands of companies registered and hundreds were being added monthly.

- Atkins Carlyle Corp., which buys from 6,000 suppliers and has 12,000 customers in Australia, is a wholesaler of industrial, electrical, and automotive parts. The large suppliers were using three different EDI platforms. By moving to an Internet-based EDI called Intercommerce, the company is conducting collaboration with many more business partners, reducing the transaction cost by about $2 per message.
- Procter & Gamble replaced a traditional EDI system with 4,000 business partners to an Internet-based system with tens of thousands suppliers.

7

E-Marketplaces and B2B Exchanges

LEARNING OBJECTIVES

Upon completion of this chapter, the reader will be able to:

- Define e-marketplaces and exchanges.

- List all types of e-marketplaces.

- Describe B2B portals.

- Describe third-party exchanges.

- Explain dynamic pricing and describe its trading mechanisms.

- Distinguish between e-procurement and e-selling consortia.

- Describe the various ownership and revenue models.

- Describe networks of exchanges and exchange management.

- Describe the critical success factors of exchanges.

- Discuss implementation and development issues of e–marketplaces and exchanges.

- Describe the extranet and its role in supporting marketplaces and exchanges.

CONTENT

7.1 CHEMCONNECT AND COVISINT

THE WORLD CHEMICAL EXCHANGE— CHEMCONNECT

Today, buyers and sellers of chemicals and plastics can meet electronically in a large Internet marketplace called *ChemConnect.com*. Global industry leaders, such as British Petroleum, Dow Chemical, BASF, Hyundai, Sumitomo, and many more, make transactions here every day in real-time. They save on transaction costs, reduce cycle time, and find new markets and trading partners around the globe.

ChemConnect provides a trading marketplace and an information portal for 12,000 members in 125 countries (membership is free). In 2001, over 60,000 products were traded in this public e-marketplace, which was founded in 1995. This is an unbiased third-party marketplace that offers three trading places:

- A public exchange floor where members can post items for sale or bid anonymously for all types of products at market prices.
- The commodities floor allows more than 200 top producers, intermediaries, and end users, to buy, sell, and exchange commodity products online in real-time through regional trading hubs.
- Corporate trading rooms are private online auction places where members save time and increase profits by negotiating contracts and spot deals in timed events managed by ChemConnect.

All three trading locations provide up-to-the-minute market information that can be translated into 30 different languages. Members pay transaction fees only for successfully completed transactions. Business partners provide several support services. For example, Citigroup and ChemConnect offer several financial services for exchange members.

A large electronic catalog of "offers to sell" and "requests to buy," which includes starting prices and shipping terms, is organized by category. Buyers can bid by changing the starting prices. The *private trading room* allows a company to host private auction events for simultaneously negotiating online with several suppliers or buyers. ChemConnect can bring new potential partners into the trading rooms. The trading room allows companies to save up to 15 percent in just 30 minutes, instead of weeks or months, which was the case with manual methods. For example, a company that placed an RFQ for 100 metric tons of acid to be delivered in Uruguay with a starting price of $1.10 per kilogram reduced the price to $0.95 in six consecutive bids, offered in 30 minutes. A demo for such a reverse auction is available on the site (see Corporate Trading Rooms, CTR Demo).

ChemConnect is an independent intermediary, so it works with certain rules and guidelines that assure an unbiased approach to trades. There is full disclosure of all legal requirements, payments, trading rules, etc. (click on "Legal and privacy issues" on the site). ChemConnect is growing rapidly, adding members and increasing trading volume.

Source: Compiled from *chemconnect.com*, February 2001.

COVISINT: THE E-MARKET OF THE AUTOMOTIVE INDUSTRY

On February 25, 2000, General Motors Corporation, Ford Motor Company, and DaimlerChrysler launched a B2B integrated buy-side marketplace, Covisint. The goal was to eliminate redundancies and burdens from suppliers through integration and collaboration with promises of lower costs, easier business practices, and marked increases in efficiencies for the entire industry. The name Covisint (pronounced KO-vis-int) is a combination of the primary concepts of why the exchange was formed. The letters "Co" represent *connectivity, collaboration,* and *communication.* "Vis" represents the *visibility* that the Internet provides and the vision of the future of supply chain management. "Int" represents the *integrated* solutions the venture provides as well as the *international* scope of the exchange. *Connectivity* is about integrating buyers and sellers into a single network. *Visibility* means real-time information presented in a way that speeds decision making and enables communication through every level of a company's supply chain, anywhere in the world. By using the Web, a manufacturer's production schedule and any subsequent changes can be sent simultaneously and instantly throughout its entire supply chain. The result is less need for costly inventory at all levels of the supply chain and an increased ability to respond quickly to market changes.

To better understand the Covisint concept, let's look at Figure 7-1. On the left side we show how one automaker works with one supplier. The supplier, in turn, works with its suppliers, and so on. Note that in this traditional linear supply chain the automaker communicates only with its top-tier (Tier 1) suppliers.

Now, try to imagine that the auto manufacturer has hundreds of similar supply chains, one for each supplier, and that many of the suppliers in all tiers produce for several manufacturers. The flow of information, which is shown by the connecting lines on the left side, will be very complex. This introduces inefficiencies in communication and difficulties for the suppliers in planning their production schedules to meet demand, resulting in supply chain problems (see Chapter 15).

The solution on the right shows how the supply chain communication is accomplished with Covisint. Note that in the center are the auto companies. In 2001 there were six of them, the three U.S. companies, Renault (France), Peugeot Citroen (France) and Nissan (Japan). Covisint created a hub whereby anyone can communicate directly with anyone. But, instead of an array of unorganized communication lines, it is all organized in one place.

FIGURE 7-1   The Covisint Supply Chain Revolution

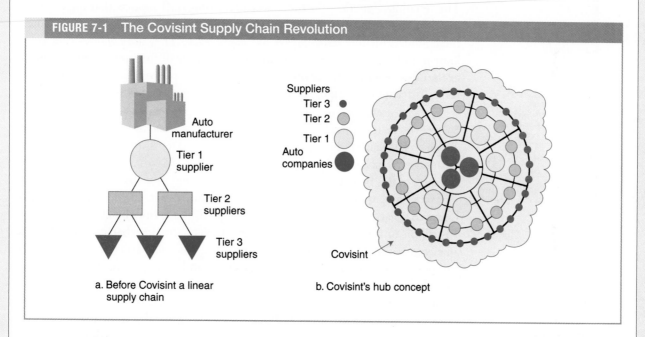

a. Before Covisint a linear supply chain

b. Covisint's hub concept

COLLABORATIVE COMMERCE

One of the major objectives of the exchange is to facilitate product design. (see Question for Discussion #18). Covisint offers its customers best-of-breed functionality from multiple technical providers that integrate and provide visibility across the supply chain, create a unique environment for collaborative design and development, e-enable the procurement process, and provide a broad marketplace of buyers and suppliers. It brings a wealth of supply chain expertise and experi-ence, ranging from procurement to product development. Covisint's potential membership is about 30,000 suppliers.

Note that despite all its advantages, Covisint will not be the only exchange for the automotive industry. Volkswagen, BMW, Honda, and Toyota are not joining, so a competing exchange is likely (see Section 7.11).

The Covisint case demonstrates an e-marketplace with a few large buyers in one industry and many sellers (the suppliers to the industry). This type of a marketplace is called *a vertical consortia trading exchange* and is probably the most popular type of the many-to-many e-markets. Notice that Covisint is not only a trading place, but also is a facilitator of supply chain organizational changes. This type of marketplace is described in Section 7.5.

Also note that in this case the marketplace is owned by a few large buyers. In contrast, the ChemConnect market is owned and operated by an intermediary. As will be seen later, ownership has some major implications for B2B marketplaces.

Sources: Compiled from *covisint.com* (miscellaneous press releases 2000, 2001).

7.2   B2B E-MARKETPLACES AND EXCHANGES—AN OVERVIEW

The opening vignettes illustrate two interesting B2B models that are used in e-marketplaces. In contrast with the company-centric models presented in Chapter 6, these models include *many buyers* and *many sellers*. They are *public e-marketplaces,* known under a variety of names, and with a variety of functions: **e-marketplaces, exchanges, e-markets, trading communities, trading exchanges, exchange hubs, Internet exchanges, B2B portals**, as well as several others.

The term *exchange* is used very frequently to describe many-to-many e-marketplaces. So, we will use it in this chapter. According to *The New Shorter Oxford English Dictionary,* an exchange is a building, office, or other area used for the transaction of business or for monetary exchange. On the Web the exchanges are virtual. We will use the term exchange in this book to describe certain types of many-to-many e-marketplaces.

Exchanges appear in several forms and are expected, according to AMR Research, to account for over 50 percent of all B2B activities by 2004 and host over $3 trillion of transactions. All exchanges share one major characteristic: They are an electronic trading community meeting place for many sellers and many buyers, and possibly other business partners, as shown in Figure 7-2. In the center there is a **market maker**, the organizer of the e-marketplace.

In an exchange, just like a traditional open-air marketplace, buyers and sellers can interact, negotiate prices and quantities, and generally allow free-market economics to rule the community of trade, just as ChemConnect is doing.

According to Forrester Research, there were 2,500 exchanges worldwide—at several stages of operation—in the spring of 2001. The companies that use these exchanges, both as sellers and buyers, are generally happy and plan to increase the number of exchanges they are dealing with from 1.7 to 4.1 in 2 years. These companies expect to more than double the value of transactions that they do through the exchanges. Although companies are racing to marketplaces, they are aware of the risks. This issue is also discussed in Chapter 8. During 2001, many exchanges were closed (e.g., *chedex.com* and *metalsite.com*).

Classification of Exchanges

There are several ways of classifying exchanges. We will use the approach suggested by Kaplan and Sawhney (2000) and by Durlacher (2000). According to this classification, an exchange can be classified into one of four cells in a matrix. The matrix is

Figure 7-2	Trading Communities: Information Flow and Access to Information

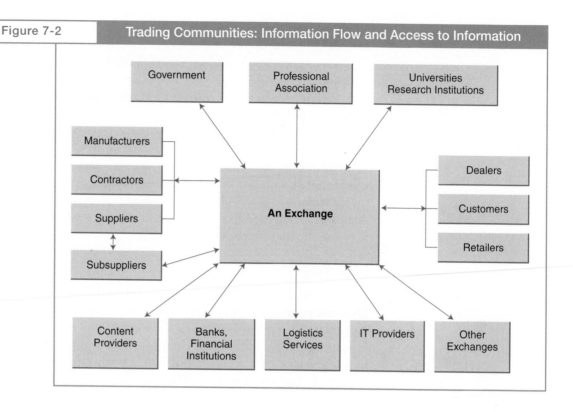

shown in Table 7-1 and it is composed of two dimensions. On the top, we distinguish two types of materials traded, either direct or indirect (MRO), as defined in Chapter 6. On the left, we see two possible sourcing strategies, either **systematic sourcing** that deals with long-range supplier-buyer relationships, or **spot sourcing** is used where purchasing is made as the need arises.

Note that direct materials are purchased in **vertical exchanges**, while the indirect materials are purchased in horizontal exchanges. In spot sourcing the prices are dynamic, based on supply and demand at any given time. An example is a stock exchange. Another example is *e-steel.com* (see Real-World Case of this chapter), which also conducts auctions and bids online. Also, the trading rooms of ChemConnect belong to this category. The *market makers* in this case match supply and demand in their exchange. On the other hand, if systematic sourcing is used, the market maker basically aggregates the buyers and/or the sellers and provides the framework for negotiated prices and terms. Then prices are basically fixed. An example of this type of exchange is *interplastic.com*. *Interplastic.com* is an exchange for the plastics

TABLE 7-1	Classification of B2B Marketplaces		
	Direct Material (Services)	**Indirect MROs**
Systematic Sourcing	Vertical Distributors (Catalog hubs) *Interplastic.com* *Paperexchange.com* *Methods:* Aggregation, fixed/negotiated prices	Horizontal Distributors *MRO.com* *Methods:* Aggregation, fixed/negotiated prices
Spot Sourcing (buying)	Vertical Exchanges *e-Steel.com ChemConnect.com* *Methods:* Matching, dynamic pricing	Functional Exchanges (yield managers) *EmployEase.com* *Methods:* Matching, dynamic pricing

industry. Using the speed, access, and ease of the Internet, it simplifies and streamlines the process of buying and selling at substantially reduced costs.

Commerxplasticsnet.com, which folded in 2001, focused on content and community. Since 1999, the site has continually increased its product offerings and supplier base, featuring (in its prime) more than 31,000 product SKUs (stock keeping units) from major global companies.

With MROs, the market maker basically aggregates the sellers' catalogs, like *MRO.com* does.

MRO.com provides tools and technology in a hosted environment that enables manufacturers and distributors of industrial parts—the "supply" of the industrial supply chain—to participate in e-commerce quickly and affordably. Then, they create one catalog, connect to one system to process orders, and have one solution to connect to many types of buyers.

Dynamic Pricing

The previous classification lists *dynamic pricing* as the major element of spot sourcing. **Dynamic pricing** refers to a rapid movement of prices over time and possibly across customers. Such prices are based on market information available to traders. The Internet and certain market mechanisms (such as auctions) provide a large amount of such information, sometimes in real time. Dynamic pricing means that exactly the same product or service is sold at different prices, to different customers. The Internet facilitates many of the dynamic pricing models for both B2B and B2C. For example, *priceline.com* uses a reverse auction that results in dynamic pricing. In Chapter 6 we described group purchasing and auctions, which also employ dynamic pricing. Stock exchanges, which can be considered as spot sourcing, are typical examples of dynamic pricing. When dynamic pricing is used in such methods as auctions and exchanges, the process is referred to as **dynamic trading**. For example, IBM's WebSphere commerce suite includes a dynamic trading module (reverse auctions, exchanges, contracts).

The process used in most exchanges is:

1. Company lists a bid to buy a product or an offer to sell one.
2. Buyers and sellers can see the bids and offers, but may not always see who is doing the buying or selling. Anonymity is often a key.
3. Buyers and sellers interact in real time with their own bids and offers. Sometimes buyers join together to obtain a volume discount price.
4. A deal is struck when there is an exact match between a buyer and a seller on price, volume, and other variables such as location or quality.
5. The deal is consummated, and payment and delivery are arranged.
6. Third-party companies outside the exchange provide supporting services such as credit verification, quality assurance, insurance, and order fulfillment. They ensure that the buyer has the money and that the product is in good condition. They also make the delivery. These services are discussed in Chapter 8.

Ownership of Exchanges

There are three basic ownership models for Internet exchanges, and each raises its own set of issues:

1. **An industry giant.** One manufacturer, distributor, or broker sets up the exchange and runs it. But will the giant's competitors use it? An example is

IBM. IBM established an exchange for the purpose of selling patents (*delphian.com*). IBM placed 25,000 of its own patents up for sale and invited others to sell their patents as well. This model is an extension of the sell-side model described in Chapter 6. General Electric's TPN is an example of a buy-side exchange controlled by an industry giant. In the past, Samsung of Korea manually brokered various commodities. Now it has several electronic exchanges, including one for fish.

2. **A neutral entrepreneur.** A third-party intermediary sets up an exchange and promises to run an efficient and unbiased exchange, like ChemConnect does. But will anyone come? These exchanges are discussed in Section 7.4.

3. **The consortia or co-op.** Several industry players get together and decide that no one will dominate the exchange, so all can benefit. Covisint is an example of such as exchange. But who is the boss? These exchanges are discussed in Section 7.5.

An interesting approach to exchange ownership is to determine equity shares for the founding members based on the volume of transactions they generate. This provides incentives for using the exchange, guaranteeing its survival.

Gains and Risks of B2B Exchange Participation

The potential gains and risks of B2B exchanges for buyers and for sellers are summarized in Table 7-2. To summarize the major many-to-many models, we created Table 7-3. The table includes the major characteristics and types of models.

Governance

Exchanges are governed by guidelines and rules, some of which are required by law. These must be very specific regarding how the exchange operates, what the requirements are to join the exchange, what fees are involved, and what rules need to be followed. Furthermore, the governance document needs to specify security and privacy arrangements, what happens in cases of disputes, etc. The contract terms

TABLE 7-2

Gains and Risks in B2B Exchanges

	Potential Gains	Potential Risks
For Buyers	• One-stop shopping, huge variety • Search and comparison shopping • Volume discounts • 24/7 ordering from any location • Make one order from several suppliers • Unlimited, detailed information • Access to new suppliers • Status review and easy reordering • Speedy delivery is likely • Less maverick buying	• Unknown vendors; may not be reliable • Loss of customer service quality (inability to compare all services)
For Sellers	• New channel for selling • No physical store is needed • Reduce ordering errors • Sell 24/7 • Reach new customers at little extra cost • Promote your business via the exchange • An outlet for surplus inventory • Can go global easier	• Loss of direct CRM, and customers' experiences and practices • Price wars, to gain attention • Competition for value-added services • Pay transaction fees (including on your existing customers) • Possible loss of customers to your competitors

TABLE 7-3

Comparing the Major B2B Many-to-Many Models		
Name	**Major Characteristic**	**Types**
B2B Catalog-Based Exchanges	A place for selling and buying Fixed prices (updated as needed)	Vertical, Horizontal • Shopping directory • Usually with hyperlinks (only) • Shopping carts with services (payment, etc.)
B2B Portals	Community services Communication tools Classified ads Employment market May sell, buy Fixed prices May do auctions	Vertical (vortals), Horizontal • Shopping directory usually with hyperlinks • Shopping carts with services (payment, etc.)
B2B Dynamic Exchanges	Match buyer/sellers orders at dynamic prices, auctions Provide trading-related information and services (payment, logistics) Highly regulated May provide general information, news, etc. May provide for negotiations	Vertical, Horizontal

between an exchange and buyers/sellers are also critical, as well as indications that the exchange is fair.

Organization of Exchanges

Regardless of their structure, exchanges may include the following elements:

Membership. Membership refers to the community in the exchange. It may be free, as many exchanges are (*Alibaba.com*, *ChemConnect.com*), and then collect transaction and other fees. Some exchanges charge registration fees and annual membership fees. Members may be either *observing members,* who can only view what's going on, or *trading members,* who can make offers and bid, pay, and arrange deliveries. Trading members usually need to go through a qualification process with the market maker. In some cases a cash deposit is required. Some exchanges set limits on how much each member can trade.

Site access and security. Exchanges must be secured. Members' activities can be very strategic, and information should be carefully protected since competitors frequently congregate in the same exchange. In addition to the regular EC security measures (Chapter 13), special attention should be made to prevent illegal offers and bids. Several exchanges have a list of individuals that are authorized to represent the participating companies.

Services. Exchanges provide many services to buyers and sellers. These depend on the nature of the exchange. For example, a stock exchange will provide completely different services from a steel or food exchange. An intellectual property or patent exchange will provide some unique services. However, there are some services that most vertical exchanges provide. These are shown in Figure 7-3.

7.3   INFORMATION PORTALS

As the reader may recall, selling in B2C can be conducted in various types of public Web sites. Some of these are basically information portals such as Yahoo!, which also contain a collection of catalogs. In some portals you can place an order; in oth-

Figure 7-3	Services in Exchanges

The Exchange

Sellers
A
B
C
D
•
•
•

- Buyer-seller registration, qualification, coordination
- Catalog management
- conversion, integration, maintenance
- Communication / protocol translation
- EDI, XML, CORBA
- Sourcing—RFQ, bid coordination
- product configuration, negotiation
- Security, anonymity
- Software: groupware, workflow
- Integration with members' back-office systems
- Auction management
- News, Information, industry analysis
- Support services
- financing, payment, insurance, logistics, tax, escrow, order tracking
- Administration—profiles, statistics, etc.

Buyers
X
Y
Z
•
•
•

ers the buyer is transferred to a seller's storefront to complete the transaction. Other portals or e-malls provide extensive order taking and order fulfillment services. Similar situations exist in B2B. Some exchanges act as pure information portals. Buyers can then hyperlink to sellers' sites for completing trades. Information portals have a difficult time generating revenues, and therefore, they are starting to offer for fee additional services that support trading. This brings them close to being trading communities or exchanges. Let's look at two examples:

Thomas Register

Thomas Register of America publishes a directory of millions of manufacturing companies. In 1998, it teamed up with GE's TPN (see Chapter 6) to create the *TPN Register,* a portal that facilitates the business transactions of MROs. *TPN Register* works with buyers and sellers to build electronic trading communities. Sellers can distribute information on what they have, buyers can find what they need and purchase over a comprehensive and secure procurement channel that helps them reduce costs, shrink cycle times, and improve productivity. There are no transactions on this portal.

Let's look now at another example of an intermediary that started as a pure information portal and is moving toward becoming a trading exchange. This is the story of *alibaba.com.*

Alibaba.com

Launched in 1999, *Alibaba.com* is a horizontal portal that concentrates on China, but actually serves traders from over 200 countries. It includes a large, robust community of international buyers and sellers who are interested in direct trade without an intermediary. Initially, the site was a huge classified posting place, due to its incredible database. To understand the power of *alibaba.com* you need to explore its *marketplace,* which is a collection of classified ads organized in a database.

The database. The center of *alibaba.com* is its huge database. The database is organized by product category. In 2001, there were 27 major categories, which included agriculture, apparel and fashion, automobiles, and toys. In each product category, one can find subcategories. For example, the toy category includes items such as dolls, electrical pets, and wooden toys. Each subcategory includes classified ads, organized into four groups: sellers, buyers, agents, and cooperation. Each group may include many companies. The ads are fairly short as shown in Figure 7-4. Note that in all cases you can click for details. All ads are posted free (Spring 2001). In some categories there are thousands of postings; therefore, a search engine is provided. The search engine works by country, type of advertisers, and how old the postings are.

The portal's features. In Spring 2001, the following features were provided: free e-mail, free e-mail alerts, a China club membership, news (basically related to import and export), legal information, arbitration, and forums or discussion groups. Finally, a member can create a company's Web page, as well as a "sample house" (for showing products).

Reverse auctions. The site allows buyers to post an RFQ. (Go to "My trade activity" and take the tours, initiate a negotiation, and issue a purchase order.) The sellers can then send bids to the buyer, conduct negotiations, or accept the purchase order. In June 2001, the process was not automated (no auction engine exists).

Services. Certain services are available for a fee. In the future, this category will be expanded to make the company profitable.

Languages. In 2001, the site offered its services in English, Chinese, and Korean.

Revenue model. By Spring 2001, the site provided many free services. Its revenue stream was limited to advertisement and fees for special services. *Alibaba.com* competes with several global exchanges that provide similar services (e.g., *meetworldtrade.com*, *chinatradeworld.com*, and *globalsources.com*). The advantage of *alibaba.com* is its low operational cost. Therefore, it can sustain losses much longer than its competitors. Some day in the future, *alibaba.com* may be in a position that will enable it to make a great deal of money. Possible sources of future revenue are:

Figure 7-4	B2B Classified Ads

- **Electronic Pets** (October 21, 2000) [SELLER]
  UMC group [China]
  We offer you electronic pets that can either be sound activated or remote controlled. These hot selling toys are welcomed all over the world. They come in different sizes. *(Click for details . . .)*

- **Electronic, Intelligent Pet** (October 23, 2000) [BUYER]
  Scheer Wholesale [United States]
  We are looking for electronic, intelligent pets like: Tekno, T-cat 2000, Clever dog 2000. Please forward your info for purchasing large quantities of these robot dogs. *(Click for details . . .)*

- **Toys/Electrical Pets Representation in India** (November 24, 2000) [AGENT]
  Penguin Exports [India]
  We are a marketing organization having a network of eight offices in India with representatives in most of the major cities and towns of India. We seek to represent manufacturers of toys/electrical pets. *(Click for details . . .)*

- **Looking for Partner of Rep-Ornament of 100 Percent Handmade** (January 06, 1999) [COOPERATION]
  Jogift Enterprise Corporation [Taiwan]
  Jogift Enterprise, we specialize in manufacturing delicate hand-crafted ornaments of the most characterized dolls in detailed leather. Our factory is located in the city of Shanghai in China. *(Click for details . . .)*

Note that in all cases you can click on details. All ads are posted free (Spring 2001).

one time registration fees, annual maintenance fees, transaction fees, and fees for services. Will *alibaba.com* be strong enough to sustain losses until that day? There is a good chance, according to experts (see discussion in Section 7.9).

More on Information Portals

An interesting information portal for the international trading community is *trading.wmw.com*. It provides access to a large amount of information, mostly free, or for a monthly fee. It also provides buying, selling, and auction services as a third-party market maker.

Information portals can be horizontal or vertical. The vertical portals are referred to as **vortals**. Notice that some use the word portal as an equivalent for an exchange. The reason is that B2B portals are adding capabilities that make them look like a full exchange. Also, many exchanges include their own portal.

7.4   THIRD-PARTY (TRADING) EXCHANGES

The opening vignette introduced us to a B2B exchange in which a *neutral, public third-party market* maker, ChemConnect, created an electronic market for the plastics and chemical industry from scratch. ChemConnect's initial success was well publicized and dozens of similar third-party exchanges, mostly in specific industries, were developed. These exchanges are characterized by two contradicting properties. On one side they are neutral, not favoring either sellers or buyers. On the other hand, they have a problem attracting enough buyers and/or sellers to make them financially viable. Therefore, these exchanges try to team up with partners, like ChemConnect did. Chemdex, a pioneering exchange that was closed in late 2000, aligned itself with VWR Scientific Products, a large brick-and-mortar intermediary, in order to increase liquidity. **Liquidity** refers to the ability to recruit large numbers of buyers and sellers (see Section 7.9). In the case of Chemdex, the liquidity was not large enough.

Third-party exchange makers are electronic intermediaries. They create a unique type of e-marketplace. In contrast with a portal structure, such as *alibaba.com*, the intermediary not only presents catalogs, but also tries to match buyers and sellers and push them to make transactions. Let's see how this is done by looking at two models: *supplier aggregation* and *buyer aggregation*.

Supplier Aggregation Model

In this model, virtual distributors standardize, index, and aggregate suppliers' catalogs or content and make these available to buyers in a centralized location. The hosting can be done by an ISP or by a large telecommunications company such as NTT, Deutsche Telecom, or MCI. An example is Commerce One's catalog of MRO suppliers. Commerce One acts as the aggregator in this case. The system is shown in Figure 7-5. Once catalogs are aggregated, they are presented to potential buyers (This is similar to the sell-side e-marketplace in Chapter 6). The diagram shows two types of buyers: large and small. Large buyers need software support in the purchasing approval process (for example, using workflow software), budgeting, and the tracking of purchases across the buying organization. This requires system integration with existing regulations, contracts, pricing, etc. Such integration is

Figure 7-5	Suppliers Aggregation Model

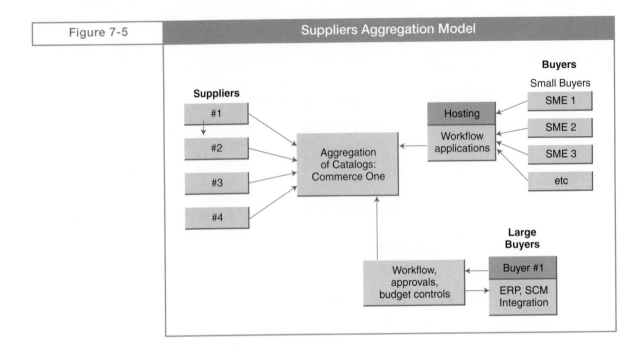

provided by an ERP. As you may recall, in Chapter 6, *bigboxx.com* provided such a service to its large buyers, using SAP software (see Application Case 6.1). Also, *e-steel.com* (See the Real-World case at the end of this chapter) is using integration as its major strategy. For more on ERP integration see Norris et al. (2000).

For smaller buyers, hosted workflow and applications are available from ASPs, which team up with aggregators such as Ariba and Commerce One. The major problems encountered in this model are the recruiting of suppliers and the pushing of the system to buyers.

Buyer Aggregation Model

In this case, buyer's RFQs are aggregated and then linked to a pool of suppliers that are automatically notified of the RFQs (this is similar to buy-side e-marketplace in Chapter 6). The suppliers can then make bids. The buyers (usually small businesses) benefit from volume discounts. The sellers benefit from the new source of pooled buyers. See Figure 7-6 for the process.

Aggregation models work best with MROs and services that are well defined and have stable prices, and where the supplier or buyer base is fragmented. Buyers save on search and transaction costs and are exposed to more sellers. Sellers benefit from lower transaction costs as well as an increase in their customer base. As in other types of e-marketplaces, the key to success is the critical mass of buyers and sellers (the liquidity problem).

Suitability of Third-Party Markets

Three basic types of participant involvement in markets exist.

- **Fragmented markets.** These markets have large numbers of both buyers and sellers. Examples include the life sciences and food industries. Third-

Figure 7-6	Buyers Aggregation Model

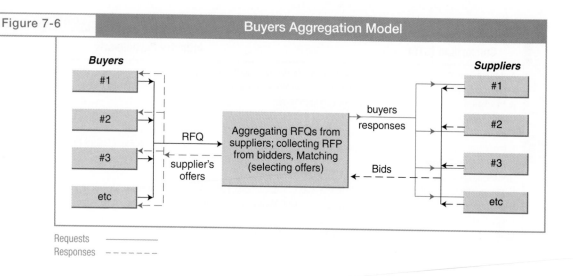

Requests ——————
Responses - - - - - - -

party managed markets are mainly suitable to MROs, where a large percentage of the market is fragmented.

- **Buyer-concentrated markets.** In this type of market, several large companies do most of the buying from a large number of suppliers. Examples are the automotive industry, the airline industry, and the electronics industry. Here consortia may be most appropriate.
- **Seller-concentrated markets.** In this type of market, several large companies sell to a very large number of buyers. Examples are plastics and transportation. Here consortia may be most appropriate.

7.5   CONSORTIUM TRADING EXCHANGES

A subset of third-party exchanges is a **consortium trading exchange** (CTE) formed by a group of major companies. The major declared goal of CTEs is to provide industry-wide transaction services that support buying and selling, including links to the participant's back-end processing systems, as well as collaborative planning and design services. During 2000, hundreds of CTEs appeared all over the world. Some are limited to one country, but many are international. Examples are given in Table 7-4.

There are four types of CTEs:

1. Vertical, purchasing-oriented
2. Horizontal, purchasing-oriented
3. Vertical, selling-oriented
4. Horizontal, selling-oriented

First, we describe the characteristics of these four types and then look at several examples and issues of concern.

E-Procurement Consortia (Purchasing Oriented)

This is by far the most popular B2B consortia model. The basic idea is that a group of companies join together in order to streamline the purchasing processes, and as some claim, to pressure the suppliers to cut prices. This model can be either vertical or horizontal.

TABLE 7-4

Representative Vertical Consortia

Consortium (CTE)	Industry Participants
Aerospace Consortium	Boeing, Lockheed Martin, BAE Systems, Raytheon
Airlines Consortium	Air France, American Airlines, British Airways, Continental, Delta, United Airlines
AutoExchange	GM, Ford, DaimlerChrysler
CoNext (For MROs)	Ariba, EDS
Consumer Products Consortium	General Mills, Heinz, Kellogg's, Nestle, Proctor & Gamble, Sara Lee
Energy Consortium	Royal/Dutch Shell, BP Amoco, Conoco, Equilon, Occidental Petroleum, Phillips Petroleum, Repsol, Statoil, Tosco, Unocal
Global Transport Exchange	Hutchinson Port (Hong Kong)
GlobalNetXchange (retailers)	Sears, Carrefour (France)
Health Care Distributors Consortium	AmeriSource Health, Cardinal Health, Fisher Scientific International, McKesson, HBOC, Owens Minor
Health Care Insurance	Johnson & Johnson, GE Medical Systems, Baxter International, Abbott Laboratories, Medtronic
Hospitality Consortium	Hyatt, Marriott
Medical Equipment	Samsung (Korea), hospitals (carecamp)
Mining Consortium	Alcoa, Anglo American, Rio Tinto
Natural Gas & Electricity Consortium	American Electric Power, Aquila Energy, Duke Energy, El Paso Energy, Reliant Energy, Southern Company
Paper Consortium	International Paper, Georgia-Pacific, Weyerhaeuser
Petrocosm (*upstreaminfo.com*)	Chevron, Texaco
PC Components (*E2open.com*)	IBM, Nortel, LG Electronics, Matsushita
PC Makers	HP, Compaq, Gateway, NEC, Samsung, Hitachi
Plastics Consortium	DuPont, Dow Chemical, BASF, Bayer, Ticona
Real Estate/Project Constellation	Chase, Equity Office, Hick Muse, Jones Lang Lasalle, Kaufman & Broad, Simon Properties, Spieker, Trammell Crow
Rooster.com	Cargill, DuPont, Cenex Harvest Cooperative
Rubbernetwork.com	Goodyear Tire & Rubber, Continental AG, Cooper Tire & Rubber, Groupe Michelin, Pirelli SpA, Sumitomo Rubber Industries
Star Alliance (airlines)	Air Canada, Lufthansa, Singapore Airlines, SAS, and others
TransPlace	Carriers, Hunt, Swift, US Xpress, Werner

Vertical, purchasing-oriented CTEs. Most of the CTEs are vertical, meaning all the players are in the same industry, such as in the case of Covisint (see Baker and Baker, 2000). While the declared objective is to support buying and selling, it is very obvious that in a market owned and operated by large buyers, the orientation is towards purchasing. Many of the exchanges in Table 7-4 belong to this type (for example: aerospace, airlines, hospitality, mining, retailers). Each exchange may have tens of thousands of suppliers.

Horizontal, purchasing-oriented CTEs. In this type of CTE, the owner-operators are large companies from different industries that unite for the purpose of improving the supply chain of MROs used by most industries. To illustrate this kind of CTE, we can look at Corprocure in Australia. Fourteen of the largest companies in Australia (Qantas, Telstra Communications, the Post Office, ANZ Banking Group, Coles Myer, Coca-Cola, etc.) created an exchange to buy MROs (*corprocure.com*).

Selling-Oriented Consortia

Selling-oriented consortia are less popular than buying ones. Most selling-oriented consortia are vertical. Participating sellers have thousands of potential buyers. Here are some examples of selling-oriented consortia:

- Cargill, a producer of basic food ingredients, has a wide range of buyers and has ownership in an exchange.

- There are several international airlines consortia that act like large travel agencies, selling tickets or travel packages.
- Health care suppliers and health care distributors.
- Plastics consortia.

Legal Challenges for B2B Consortia

B2B exchanges and other e-marketplaces typically introduce some level of collaboration among both competitors and business partners. In both cases, antitrust and other competition laws must be considered. The concept of consortia itself may lead to antitrust scrutiny by governments, especially for oligopolistic industries, either monopolies or monopsonies. This could happen in many countries, especially in European countries, the United States, Australia, Japan, Korea, Hong Kong, and Canada.

One example is *adhesives.com*, which is an exchange for industrial sealants. GE Toshiba Silicone initiated this exchange and started discussions with other leading industrial sealant makers such as Dow Corning, Wacker Chemical, and Shin-Etsu Chemical, about joining the marketplace. The initial participants control over 80 percent of the world market. The potential exists for the participants to informally deal with some sensitive business issues such as industry pricing policies, price levels, price changes, and price differentials in some meeting of the exchange. These contacts may violate antitrust laws. Similarly, many fear that buyers' consortia will "squeeze" the small suppliers in an unfair manner. Antitrust investigations may slow the creation of CTEs, especially global ones. For example, the Covisint venture required approval in the United Kingdom, the United States, and Germany. The German antitrust investigation was very slow and delayed the project by several months.

SIGNALS THAT MAY PROMPT LEGAL SCRUTINY

Goldman and Sachs (2000) (*gs.com/hightech/research/b2b*) have identified a handful of signals from an exchange that would trigger suspicion by investigators. Examples of such areas of concern might include:

- Price increases for end-users—this would suggest counter-competitive behavior
- Reduced quality for end-users—this would suggest counter-competitive behavior
- Unfair pressure on suppliers to reduce prices
- Selective denial of qualified parties

According to the same Goldman Sachs report (2000), in order to reduce legal challenges a consortium needs to:

- Reduce information transparency so as to inhibit participants' access to others' competitive information.
- Make participation in the exchange broadly available and non-exclusionary in order to guard against legal problems.
- Create an independent entity with autonomous management and an independent board to achieve neutrality.

The Critical Success Factors of Consortia

In addition to critical success factors for exchanges, which are discussed in Section 7.9, there are also critical success factors for consortia. According to Goldman Sachs (2000), the following are critical success factors for consortia:

Size of the industry. The larger the size of the industry, the larger the addressable market, which in turn means a greater volume of transactions on the site. This leads to greater potential cost savings to the exchange participants and ultimately more profitability for the exchange itself. The danger here is the appearance of several competing consortia, which has already happened in the banking, mining, and airline industries.

Ability to drive user adoption. Consortia must have the ability to provide immediate *liquidity* to an exchange. The more oligopolistic the consortium is, the more accelerated the adoption will be.

Elasticity. A critical factor for any exchange is the degree of elasticity the exchange fosters. Elasticity is the measure of the incremental spending by buyers as a result of the savings generated.

Standardization of commodity-like products. The breadth of the suppliers brought in to transact with the buyers will help standardize near-commodity products due to content management and product attribute description needs of online marketplaces.

Management of intensive information Flow. An exchange has the ability to be a repository for the huge amounts of data that flow through supply chains in a given industry. It can also enable information-intensive collaboration between participants, including product collaboration, planning, scheduling, and forecasting.

Smoothing of inefficiencies in the supply chain. It is important for the consortium-led exchange to help smooth inefficiencies in the supply chain such as fulfillment, logistics, and credit-related services.

7.6   DYNAMIC TRADING: AUCTIONS AND MATCHING

One of the major features of exchanges is **dynamic trading**. In dynamic trading, prices are determined by supply and demand, and therefore change continuously. Two major mechanisms are used in exchanges: auctions and matching.

Auctions

As seen in the ChemConnect case, exchanges offer members the ability to conduct auctions or reverse auctions in *private trading rooms*. When this takes place, the one-to-many model is activated, as described in Chapter 6, with the hosting done by the exchange. The advantage of running an auction in an exchange is the ability to attract many buyers to a forward auction and many suppliers to a reverse auction. In contrast, as demonstrated in Chapter 6, auctions are conducted by a large single company that is well known to others, so there is less of a problem in finding participants. For small or medium-sized companies, finding participants is a major problem. By going to an exchange this problem may be solved.

There are several arrangements for auctions. These may include the following:

- An exchange offers auction services as just one of its activities like ChemConnect does. Most vertical exchanges offer this option.
- An exchange is fully dedicated to auctions. Examples include Smart Consumer Services (*atcost.com*), eBay for Businesses, and Ariba's Dynamic Trading.

An exchange can conduct many-to-many auctions, known also as **double auctions** (Chapter 9). These are public auctions with many buyers and sellers.

Auctions may be vertical or horizontal and can run on the Internet or on private lines. Examples of auctions conducted on private lines are Aucnet in Japan, which is for selling used cars to dealers, and TFA, the Dutch flower market auction (described in Application Case 7.1).

APPLICATION CASE   7.1

New Entrants to the Dutch Flower Market: TFA

The Dutch flower market auction is the largest in the world, attracting 11,000 sellers from dozens of countries such as Thailand, Israel, and East Africa; 3,500 varieties of flowers are sold in 120 auction groups to about 5,000 buyers. The auctions used to be semi automated. Buyers and sellers had to come to one location, where the flowers were then shown to the buyers. The auctioneer of each flower variety used a clock with a large hand, which he or she started at a high price and dropped until a bidder stopped the clock by pushing an ordering button. Using an intercom, the quantity ordered was clarified; then, the clock hands were reset at the starting price level for the next batch of flowers. The process continued until all of the flowers were sold.

In September 1994, the Dutch growers (DFA), who own the auction organization, decided to ban foreign growers from participating in the auction during the summer months in order to protect the Dutch growers against low prices from abroad. By March 1995, some foreign growers, together with some local buyers, created a competing auction place called the TeleFlower Auction (TFA), an electronic auction that enables its initiators to penetrate the Dutch flower market.

In the TFA, buyers can bid on flowers via their PCs at designated times, from any location connected to the private network. The process is similar to the traditional Dutch auction, and the auction clock is shown on the PC screen (see Figure 9.4 in Chapter 9). The buyers can stop the clock by pushing the space bar. The auctioneer then converses with the buyers by telephone and a sale is conducted. After the sale, the clock on the PC is reset. The flowers are not physically visible to the buyers; however, a large amount of relevant information is available online. For example, the buyers are alerted to a specific auction, in real-time, when their item of interest is auctioned.

Initial results indicated that buyers and growers were enthusiastic. While prices were about the same as in the regular auctions, the process is much quicker and the after-sale delivery is much faster than in other markets (less

(continued)

than half an hour). A major issue can be the quality of the flowers, since the buyers cannot see them. But the quality of the flowers is actually better since there is less handling (no need to bring the flowers to an auction site), and the growers stand behind their products. As a result, there is enough trust so that everyone is happy.

The TFA has gained considerable market share at the expense of existing organizations and is a real new-entrant success story. Using IT, the new entrant quickly built a competitive advantage. This advantage impressed the DFA, but it took more than a year to cancel the import restrictions and implement their own electronic clearinghouse for flowers. However, the TFA continues its own auctions.

Sources: Condensed from E. van Heck et al., "New Entrants and the Role of IT—Case Study: The TeleFlower Auction in the Netherlands," Proceedings of the 30th Hawaiian International Conference on Systems Sciences, Hawaii, January 1997. See also A. Kambil and E. van Heck, "Reengineer the Dutch Flower Auctions," *Information Systems Research* (March 1998) and van Heck and Ribbers in "Experiences with Electronic Auctions in the Dutch Flower Industry," vol. 7, no. 4, *Electronic Markets* (1997).

Matching

An example of matching supply and demand is the stock market. While buyers place their bids and sellers list their asking prices, the market makers are conducting the matching, sometimes by buying or selling stocks from their own accounts. The matching may be more complex than regular auctions due to the need to match both prices and quantities. In other cases, times and locations need to be matched as well. Today, matching in stock exchanges is fully computerized.

7.7   BUILDING AND INTEGRATING MARKETPLACES AND EXCHANGES

Building e-marketplaces and exchanges is a complex process and it is usually performed by a major B2B software company such as Commerce One, Ariba, Oracle, or IBM. In large exchanges, a management consulting company such as Andersen Consulting (now Accenture), PriceWaterhouseCoopers, GartnerGroup, or McKinsey usually participates. Also, technology companies such as IBM, Oracle, EDS, i2, and SAP have major roles in building large exchanges. Most exchanges are built jointly by several vendors.

Most large B2B software vendors have e-marketplace packages. For example, Commerce One has a set of e-marketplace solutions (MarketSite, MarketSet, (compliant with SAP) and Net Market Maker). Ariba offers its Marketmaker, and so on. The selection of vendors and their management will be discussed in Chapter 12. Here we present a brief description of the development process that a market maker goes through, regardless of who the partnering vendors are.

A Possible Process for Building a Vertical E-Marketplace

The following is a typical process used:

STEP 1: THINK AHEAD

In this step, the builder should think through how the e-market can make a change in the target industry, and what the monetary contribution for the players will be. Therefore, it is important for a builder to have in-depth knowledge of the market environment. Here are some activities to consider when developing such an e-business strategy:

- Align the e-business with existing brick-and-mortar operations of companies in the industry. Then, clearly identify potential cost savings and revenue enhancement opportunities for both sellers and buyers. After that find out if there is a competitor or a planned competitor in that industry. Finally, outline the mission of the exchange.

STEP 2: PLANNING

In this step, the builder should think through the vertical exchange's business scope, specifically how the exchange will operate in the target industry, and what kind of capabilities and benefits it will have for the players. Then, the builder should identify strategic objectives for the exchange, such as financial returns, target number of participants in the virtual market, and so on. The scope must include sharing industry information and trading direct parts and materials. This is where the participants expect big savings.

The exchange should also improve communication among companies and their customers and business partners. It should also be able to automate the bidding and offering processes. In addition, during this step, the builder should estimate the market potential, number of participants/players, and the trading volume generated at different times. The builder should also plan the details of how to build and implement the virtual exchange (see Chapter 12), addressing such issues as financing, human resources, marketing, operations, etc., as well as payments, logistics and how they will interface with the exchange.

STEP 3: SYSTEM ANALYSIS AND DESIGN

Based on the scope, objectives, desired capabilities, and the estimation of the trading volume in different time periods, the builder should start to design the exchange's technological platform, such as hosting, hardware and software architecture, and databases. Most important is the issue of networking and integration of all exchange members. Then, a *development strategy* needs to be formulated. Some exchanges will use a technology partner. Many builders will need to outsource the construction of various components of the exchange (see Chapter 12).

STEP 4: BUILDING THE EXCHANGE

At this step, it is possible to build, test, and implement the exchange's platform. A good project management tool may be useful here. The market maker must think about connecting the exchange members to the exchange and the possibility of integrating members' systems (see the *e-steel.com* case at the end of this chapter).

The exchange may be hosted on the market maker's server or on a Web hosting vendor. A combination of the two is also possible as demonstrated in Application Case 7.2.

How *PaperExchange.com* Handles Infrastructure (now Paperspace.com)

PaperExchange.com, an e-marketplace for the pulp and paper industry, decided not to use third-party Web hosting, but rather build its own infrastructure. In just 18 months, the exchange grew from 250 members to over 7,000, so *PaperExchange.com* knew that a flexible, scalable infrastructure was a must. Web hosting is only part of a much broader effort by *PaperExchange.com* to deliver fast, secure services to buyers and sellers. Therefore, PaperExchange decided not to separate Web hosting from its other services. Also, unlike most B2B sites, which handle more browsers than buyers, *PaperExchange.com* supports even amounts of HTML browser traffic and SSL transaction traffic. The latter requires more processing power because of the encryption, and more reliability because there are dollars on the line.

However, the company uses a vendor's Web hosting to *supplement* its own infrastructure. For example, they use hosting services from Exodus Communications, a popular Web hosting B2B company.

The Web hosting is performed in collaboration with corporate staff for internal application monitoring and testing efforts conducted by the exchange staff. The area of cooperation with Exodus is the large databases (from Oracle). The monitoring and testing is done for *data integrity,* one of the major areas of concern for B2B exchanges.

Source: paperexchange.com (daily news)

STEP 5: TESTING, INSTALLATION, AND OPERATION

At this stage, tests must be conducted, improvements made, members connected, and the system perfected. Once testing is complete, the exchange is ready for business.

STEP 6: SYSTEM EVALUATION AND IMPROVEMENT

As with any information system, the system must be monitored and evaluated continuously. Continuous improvements are common in most exchanges.

In each of these steps, the builder should think through how the exchange can change the target industry and how it will generate revenue. Therefore, it is important for the builder to have in-depth knowledge of the market environment.

Integration

Seamless integration is needed between the third-party exchange and back-office systems of the participants through interfacing with applications and protocols and building on XML and EDI technologies. In addition, there is a need for integration across multiple, frequently incompatible exchanges, each with its own XML scheme. *Tibco.com* is the major infrastructure service provider for vertical exchanges.

The four most common elements of B2B integration solutions, which are discussed in the following sections, are *external communications, process and information coordination, system and information management,* and a *shopping cart.* A brief discussion of each follows.

EXTERNAL COMMUNICATIONS

Web/client access. Businesses can use a Web browser, such as Internet Explorer, to interact with a Web server application hosted by other businesses.

Data exchange. Information is extracted from an application, converted into a neutral data format, and sent to other businesses. Examples of this include EDI over VANs and FTP- or HTTP/XML-based approaches.

Direct application integration. Application integration often requires middleware technologies, such as distributed object technologies, message queuing, and publish/subscribe brokers, to coordinate information exchange between applications (see *tibco.com* and *extricity.com*).

Share process. Businesses can agree to use the same procedures for some processes. For example, a supplier and a buyer may agree to use the same order management process.

PROCESS AND INFORMATION COORDINATION

Process and information coordination concerns how to coordinate external communications with internal information systems. The coordination includes external processes, internal processes, data transformation, and exception handling. For example, an online sales transaction, through process and information coordination, must be processed directly to an internal accounting system.

SYSTEM AND INFORMATION MANAGEMENT

System and information management involves the management of software, hardware, and several information components, including partner-profile information, data and process definitions, communications and security settings, and users' information. Furthermore, because hardware and software change rapidly (i.e., upgrades or releases of new versions), the management of these changes is an essential element of B2B integration.

SHOPPING CARTS

An interesting approach to integration is the creation of a customer B2B shopping cart that enables customers to shop at any participating vendor. In the B2B environment, a buyer needs to maintain order information on its own site in order to integrate it with its internal e-procurement system. However, sell-side e-marketplaces cannot support such a capability, resulting in the order information being scattered among the multiple sellers' sites. This can be a nightmare for procurement management.

To overcome this problem, a b-cart approach was proposed by Lim and Lee (2002) (Figure 7-7). A b-cart is a buyer's shopping cart that resides on the buyer's PC rather than on the seller's (intermediary's) site. A significant benefit of the b-cart approach is the interoperable interface between heterogeneous e-marketplaces

Figure 7-7	The B-Cart

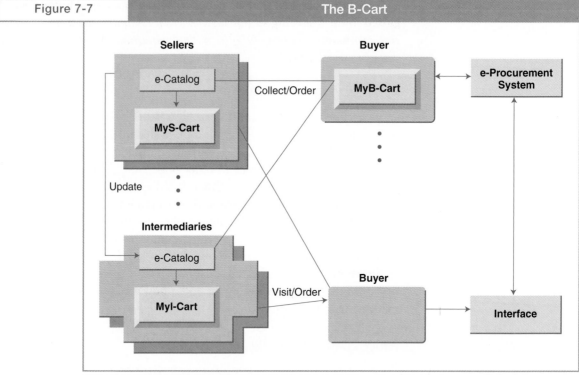

Source: Lim and Lee (2001). Used with permission of Joe K. Lee, Chairman, International Conference on Electronic Commerce.

and e-procurement systems. By developing a standard interface between the b-cart and e-marketplaces and between the b-cart and e-procurement systems, the heterogeneous e-marketplaces and e-procurement systems can be interoperable.

In the proposed architecture, sellers support both a seller's cart and a b-cart. Buyers may pick either type of cart. Once a b-cart is selected, the buyer's information will be added to the electronic cart in the buyer's PC. The b-cart is equipped with the following capabilities: product information collection, recording data, trashing data, ordering and order process tracking, identification of buyers, electronic payment interface, organizational e-procurement process support, and transmission of order information to e-procurement systems in XML file format. The b-cart approach can be an effective framework for integrating e-marketplaces with e-procurement systems, including ERP systems.

7.8   MANAGING EXCHANGES

The scope of managing exchanges is very broad. Only the major issues will be described here (for details see Schully and Woods, 2000).

Revenue Models

Exchanges are electronic intermediaries and they require revenue to survive. The following are potential sources of revenue.

- **Transaction fees.** These fees are basically a commission paid by sellers for each transaction they make. Several methods exist for setting fees. The most popular are fees based on a percentage of the total value of the sale, such as in real estate, and a flat fee per trade, such as in discount stock brokering. Combinations of these two methods are also used. Sellers may object to transaction fees, especially when their regular customers are involved. An exchange must charge low transaction fees per order in order to attract sellers. Therefore, the exchange must generate enough volume to cover its expenses.

- **Fee for service.** As seen in Chapter 2, Rosenbluth International, a large travel agency, successfully changed its revenue model from commission to "fee for service." Buyers are more willing to pay for value-added services than pay commissions.
- **Membership fees.** A membership fee is usually a fixed annual or a monthly fee. It usually entitles the member to get some services free or at a discount. In some countries, such as China, the government may ask members to pay annual membership fees, and then provides the businesses with free services and no transaction fees. This encourages members to use the exchange. The problem is that low membership fees result in losses to the exchange, while high membership fees discourage participants from joining.
- **Advertisement fees.** Exchanges can also derive income from fees for advertising on the portal. For example, some sellers may want to increase their exposure and will pay for advertisements on the portal (like boxed ads in the yellow pages of telephone books).

Networks of Exchanges

With the increased number of vertical and horizontal exchanges, it is logical to think about connecting them. Large corporations work with several exchanges, and they like to see these exchanges connected in a seamless fashion. Today, most exchanges have different logon procedures, separate sets of rules for fulfilling orders, and different business models for charging for their services.

At present, exchanges are created quickly, so they can be first movers. The primary objective of these newly created exchanges is the acquisition of buyers and sellers. Integration with other companies or with another exchange is a low priority.

Commerce One and Ariba have developed a marketplace strategy that allows them to plug a broad range of horizontal exchanges into their main networks, such as the British Telecommunications' MarketSite, as well as an increasing number of vertical marketplaces, such as ChemConnect (see Figure 7-8). Commerce One MarketSite and The Ariba Network are merging.

Corporations can plug into Ariba or Commerce One networks and reach thousands of suppliers. Each time a new customer signs up with Ariba or Commerce One, the customer can bring its business partners into the network. These business partners are then connected to any other company that plugs into the network.

The network is expanding rapidly, and Ariba and Commerce One are launching horizontal exchanges in several countries. These exchanges range from a marketplace for governmental and educational institutions (*buysense.com*) to a New Zealand marketplace for business (*supplynet.co.nz*). Ariba and Commerce One are also partnering with vertical exchanges such as ChemConnect. The network allows any customer to buy from any supplier connected to the network. Other large vendors, such as Oracle and SAP, may join the networks some day. For further details see Duvall (2000).

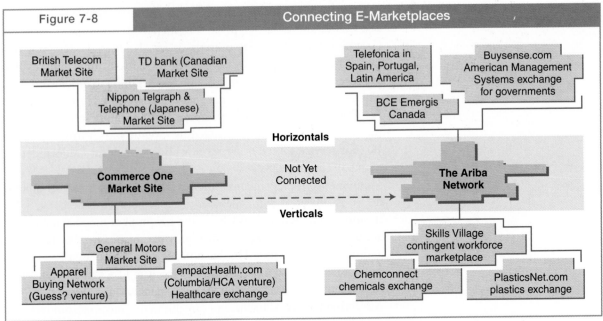

Figure 7-8   Connecting E-Marketplaces

Centralized Management

Managing exchanges and providing services to them on an individual basis can be expensive. Therefore, it makes sense to have "families" of exchanges managed jointly. This way, one market builder can build and operate several exchanges from a unified, centralized place. It offers all the exchanges catalogs, auction places, discussion forums, and so on. Centralizing accounting, finance, human resources, and IT services. Furthermore, dealing with third-party vendors that provide logistic services and payment systems may be more efficient if the vendor is supplying services for many exchanges instead of just one. Two such "families" of exchanges are those of Vertical Net and Ventro (see Application Case 7.3).

Finding a CEO and Independent Management Team

With the development of large numbers of new exchanges, many of which are large and complex, the demand for CEOs is increasing dramatically. Obviously, there are no experienced CEOs available in this new field, but every exchange would like to have one. A company would at least want a CEO who understands both the exchange concept and the target industry. To attract CEOs, exchanges offered in 2000, annual salaries between $500,000 and $1,000,000, plus 5 to 10 percent equity in the exchange (in 2001, with the collapse of many exchanges, salaries decreased) were offered.

Some exchanges tap into existing sources for a CEO. The GlobalNetXchange, a B2B retail marketplace set up by Sears Roebuck, Carrefour (of France), and others, selected a 35-year-old Sears senior vice president of finance who is known for his IT skills. A similar approach was used by *Transora.com*, an online supplier exchange created by Coca-Cola, Proctor & Gamble, Sara Lee, and dozens of suppliers. This exchange chose a senior vice president from Sara Lee.

VerticalNet and *Ventro.com*

VerticalNet

VerticalNet owns and provides centralized management services to 58 vertical exchanges. Specifically, it:

- Provides a unique combination of content, community, and commerce, acting as an essential, comprehensive source of information, interaction, and transaction for each specific vertical market.
- Provides hosted e-commerce capabilities to help businesses of all sizes increase sales reach and improve efficiency of marketing efforts.

  The VerticalNet exchanges themselves share the following characteristics:

- Focus on direct material, providing open and spot markets for traditional offline businesses moving online.
- Leverage exchange capabilities and scalable skills in supply chain, fulfillment, risk management, and globalization to create a platform that meets the demands of growing businesses.

VerticalNet delivers comprehensive digital marketplace solutions for industry alliances, Global 2000 enterprises, and Internet market makers. VerticalNet provides services to all 58 exchanges. For example, a Buyer's Guide helps companies find products, services, and vendors in the exchange. Product showcases provide the ability to evaluate industry expert viewpoints on new products, and the RFQ functionality enables both buyers and suppliers to create, track, and manage RFQ requests and responses online. Other services found in all 58 exchanges are discussion forums, free software libraries, and career job centers.

The Ventro Family of Exchanges

Ventro.com operates four exchanges in the life science industry. (Initially, there were six companies, including *Chemdex.com*, a B2B pioneer, but Chemdex was closed.) Ventro can be viewed as an *e-marketplace service provider*, a company that delivers the services necessary for operating exchanges; it unites buyers, sellers, and enterprises in its four marketplaces (as of 2001) and in other exchanges. Ventro's goal is to streamline the exchange member's business processes, enhance exchange productivity, and reduce costs.

Customers also benefit from Ventro's Complete Marketplace Solution. Ventro marketplaces offer customers extensive online catalogs, e-procurement capabilities, integration tools required to interface with third-party and back-office systems, and comprehensive services and support.

Source: Complied from *ventro.com*

But not all exchanges fill the job with an insider. Some consortia are looking for unaffiliated CEOs, and of course third-party exchanges do not have insiders. Some consortia, such as World Wide Retail (Kmart, Royal World) and the Oil Exchange (Amoco, BP, Shell, Unocal, Conoco) decided that the CEO should be a neutral outsider. This issue is related to another one, namely "Can competing members truly cooperate and allow an independent management team to lead a joint exchange?" Some exchanges hire major consulting firms such as Andersen Consulting (Accenture Ltd.) to oversee negotiations during the start-up phase.

7.9   CRITICAL SUCCESS FACTORS

By 2001 there were thousands of announced B2B exchanges. As in the B2C area, many, maybe 90 percent, will fail. There were dozens of failures in 2000, including *Chemdex.com*. The question on everyone's mind is what are the necessary factors for exchanges to survive. Before we present some critical success factors, let's restate what we said in Chapter 3: In certain areas or countries there are already too many competing exchanges. For example, there is probably no room for three toy exchanges in Hong Kong. Therefore, there will be failures and consolidation in B2B exchanges.

According to Ramsdell (2000) of McKinsey & Company, a major management consulting company, the following five factors will influence the outcome of what he believes will be a B2B shakeout:

1. **Early liquidity.** Liquidity refers to the volume of business conducted. The earlier a business achieves the necessary liquidity level, the better its chances are for survival. The more buyers that trade on an exchange, the more suppliers will come, which will lead to low spread or transaction fees, which in turn will increase the liquidity even more. In both B2B and B2C, customer acquisition is critical.

2. **The right owners.** One way to increase liquidity is to partner with companies that can bring liquidity to the exchange. We have seen that Covisint was founded by the big automakers that are committed to buying via the exchange. This is why many vertical exchanges are of the consortia type. In a situation where both the sellers and buyers are fragmented, such as in the bioscience industry, the best owner may be an intermediary who can increase liquidity by pushing both the sellers and the buyers.

3. **The right governance.** Good management (see Section 7.8) and fair and effective operations and rules are critical success factors. The governance provides the rules for the exchange, minimizes conflicts, and supports decision making. Furthermore, good management will try to induce the necessary liquidity. Also, good governance will minimize conflicts among the owners and the participants. Owners may try to favor some of their trading partners, a situation that may hurt the exchange. Good exchanges ***must*** be neutral. Finally, good management of operations, resources, and people is mandatory for success.

4. **Openness.** Exchanges must be open to all, both from organizational and technological points of view. Commitment to open standards is required, but there should be a universal agreement on these standards. Using the wrong standards may hurt the exchange.

5. **A full range of services.** While prices are important, buyers and sellers are interested in cutting their total costs. Therefore, exchanges that help cut inventory costs, spoilage, maverick buying, and so on, will attract participants. Many exchanges team up with banks, logistic services, and IT companies to provide support services (see Chapter 8). Furthermore, exchanges must be integrated with the information systems of their members, and this is not a simple task (see the Real-World Case at the end of this chapter).

In addition to the five factors cited by Ramsdell (2000), there are a number of other factors that are critical to the success of exchanges.

Importance of domain expertise. Market makers need to have an in-depth understanding of the given industry, as well as a detailed understanding of the business processes inherent in a specific industry. In order to meaningfully aggregate buyers and sellers in a community and subsequently enable transactions among them, operators should have knowledge of the industry structure, the nature of buyer and seller behavior in the industry, and government and policy stipulations that impact the sector.

Targeting inefficient industry processes. The traditional business processes in most industries have many points of inefficiencies. These contribute to increased costs, time and delays in businesses interacting and transacting with one another, and create significant opportunities for vertical exchanges to add value.

Targeting the right industries. The most attractive verticals typically are characterized by:

- a large base of transactions;
- many fragmented buyers and sellers;
- difficulties in bringing buyers and sellers together;
- high vendor and product search/comparison costs; information-intensive products with complex configurations and nonstandard specifications;
- high process costs associated with manual processes based on paper catalogs, manual requisitioning, telephone or fax-based ordering, as well as for credit verification, and order tracking;
- strong pressure to cut expenses, and;
- a climate of technological innovation.

Brand building is critical. The low switching costs inherent in exchanges will make branding of paramount importance to the long-term viability of exchanges. For this reason, exchange operators should find ways to increase switching costs. Adding valuable features and functionality is one way to increase switching costs. Exchange operators must first invest in gaining brand awareness and getting businesses to use their exchange and then focus on customer retention. For example, in Hong Kong, *bigboxx.com* even advertises on buses.

Exploiting economies of scope. Many think that exchanges must do more than simply establish a mechanism to facilitate transactions in order to survive in the longer term. Once a critical mass is reached, the exchange operators must expand the services they provide to users. Value-added services such as industry news, expert advice, or detailed product specification sheets, and so on, can make an exchange even more compelling. Expanding the range of services may also increase switching costs.

Better-developed exchanges are now offering complimentary services including systems integration, hosting, financial services (e.g., payment processing, receivables management, credit analysis), and logistics services (e.g., shipping, warehousing, and inspection), as well as risk mitigation services. In other words, adjacent trading services are bundled into the hub to provide a logical trading package addressing all of the service attributes associated with trading in physical products (See Chapter 8).

Adjacent services are springing up next to B2B exchanges. For example, banks and financial information providers such as Dun & Bradstreet are assisting businesses in confirming the identities and solvency of trading partners over the

Internet. Identification is being supported by sophisticated digital certificate architecture.

In addition, revenue models, content, and channel conflict management may also affect the success of exchanges.

Choice of business/revenue models. Exchange operators should garner diverse and multiple revenue streams. Companies have the potential to generate multiple revenue steams, including software licensing, advertising, and sponsorship, and recurring revenues from transaction fees, subscription fees, software subscription revenues, and other value-added services. As exchanges aggregate a critical mass of users, these companies will be able to garner additional value-added service revenues from auction services and financial services, as well as value-added applications such as business reporting and data mining services.

Blending content, community, and commerce. Exchanges differ in their approaches—some originate from a content/community perspective and others have an EC transaction perspective. While content and community features have the advantage of stimulating traffic, it is believed that the ability to conduct EC transactions is likely to create a higher level of customer "stickiness" and hence, greater value for the exchanges. A successful exchange should combine rich content and community with the ability to conduct EC transactions.

Managing channel conflict. The movement of buyers to interact directly with sellers and the consequent disintermediation of the supply chain is invariably a hostile phase. Impacts on short-term revenues of both buyers and sellers may result from a backlash from existing fulfillment channels, resulting in price erosion that may affect a company's medium-term profitability.

In order to achieve these critical success factors, market makers must carefully select the vendors that design and build the exchanges (see Chapter 12).

7.10   B2B NETWORKS AND EXTRANETS

In Chapter 6, we pointed out the need for computer networks to support communication and collaboration among B2B business partners. We also described EDI and its supporting role in facilitating B2B communication and collaboration.

The major network structure used in e-marketplaces and exchanges is an **extranet**. An extranet adds value to the Internet by increasing its security and expanding the available bandwidth. In order better understand how an extranet interfaces with the Internet and intranets, let's turn our attention to the basic concepts of the Internet, intranets, and extranets.

The Internet

The **Internet** (see Appendix A) is a public, global communications network that provides direct connectivity to anyone over a local area network (LAN) via an Internet Service Provider (ISP) or directly via an ISP. The Internet is a public network that is connected and routed over gateways. The ISPs are connected to Internet access providers, to network access providers, and eventually to the Internet backbone. Since access to the Internet is open to all, there is a minimum level of control and security.

Intranets: Intra-Business Delivery Systems

An **intranet** is a corporate LAN or wide area network (WAN) that uses Internet technology and is secured behind a company's firewalls (see Chapter 13). An intranet links various servers, clients, databases, and application programs, such as ERP. Although intranets are based on the same TCP/IP protocol as the Internet, they operate as a private network with limited access. Only authorized employees are able to use them. Intranets are limited to information pertinent to the company and contain exclusive and often proprietary and sensitive information. The intranet can be used to enhance communication and collaboration among authorized employees, customers, suppliers, and other business partners (see Appendix 7A). Since an intranet allows access through the Internet, it does not require any additional implementation of leased networks. This open and flexible connectivity is a major capability and advantage of intranets.

Extranets

An extranet, or "extended intranet," uses the TCP/IP protocol networks of the Internet to link intranets in different locations (as shown in Figure 7-9). Extranet transmissions are usually conducted over the Internet, which offers little privacy or transmission security. Therefore, when using an extranet, it is necessary to improve the security of the connecting portions of the Internet. This is done by creating tunnels of secured data flows, using cryptography and authorization algorithms. An extranet with tunneling technology is known as a virtual private network (VPN) (see Chapter 13).

Extranets provide secured connectivity between a corporation's intranets and the intranets of its business partners, materials suppliers, financial services, government, and customers. Access to extranets is usually limited by agreements of the collaborating

Figure 7-9	An Extranet

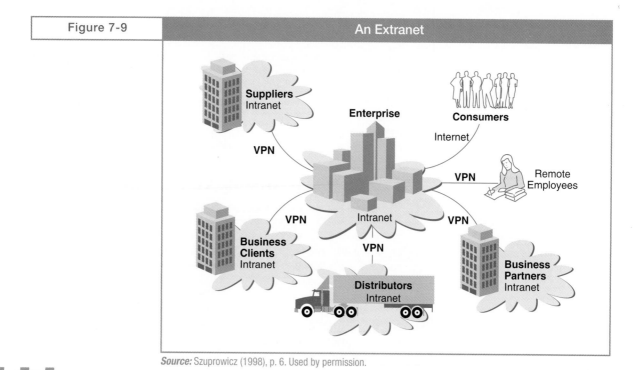

Source: Szuprowicz (1998), p. 6. Used by permission.

parties, is strictly controlled, and is only available to authorized personnel. The protected environment of an extranet allows groups to collaborate, share information, and perform these functions securely.

Since an extranet allows connectivity between businesses through the Internet, it is an open and flexible platform suitable for supply chain management. To increase security, many companies replicate the portions in the databases that they are willing to share with their business partners and separate them physically from their regular intranets. However, even separated data needs to be well-protected (See Chapter 13).

To illustrate how the extranet functions, let's look at the example illustrated in Application Case 7.4.

APPLICATION CASE   7.4

The ANX

In September 1997, the "big three" U.S. auto manufacturers and two dozen other auto industry companies piloted what is probably the world's largest extranet, the Automotive Network Exchange (ANX). The ANX is an infrastructure for B2B applications, particularly Covisint, that promises to cut costs by billions of dollars and change the way the auto supply chain does business (Davis et al., 1997). Backed by General Motors, Ford, and Chrysler, ANX allowed companies in the automotive market to swap supply and manufacturing data. The commercial network would ultimately involve tens of thousands of companies and their counterparts globally.

Benefits of ANX

ANX applications include one-to-one and one-to-many connections, such as procurement, CAD/CAM file transfers, EDI, e-mail, and groupware. The ANX organizers believe that the network's EDI element alone slices $71 from the cost of designing and building a car. That translates into an industry wide savings of $1 billion a year. Each of the "big three" expects to save many millions by consolidating communications links onto the ANX. Not only will the companies pay for fewer T1 lines and satellite connections, but standardizing the protocol reduces support costs.

The extranet helps auto suppliers reduce order turn-around time. The faster the parts and subassemblies come in, the faster the cars leave the assembly line. Ford Motor Co., for example, hopes to compress some work-order communications from 3 weeks to 5 minutes. "We may well convert our entire WAN to ANX," says Rick Collins, a senior IS consultant at Paccar Inc., a maker of custom semi-trailer trucks.

Virtually Private Network (VPN) for ANX

The ANX is the most visible B2B implementation of virtual private networks (VPNs), networks that run over the Internet across the country and the globe (see Chapter 13 for VPN). As for security, all participants must have tools compliant with Internet Protocol (IP) security standards, which cover encryption, authentication, and encryption key management. Each packet that travels over the ANX is encrypted and authenticated. The ANX was initiated on November 1, 1998, and is now operational as a start-up company ANXeBusiness (*anxo.com*), meeting participants' expectations overall. Similar networks exist in Europe, South America, and other parts of the world.

Source: Compiled from Dalton and Davis (1998), Davis et al. (1997), and *anxo.com*.

Benefits of Extranets

According to Szuprowicz (1998), there are five categories of extranet benefits. They are:

1. Enhanced communications
   - Improved internal communications
   - Improved business partnership channels
   - Effective marketing, sales, and customer support
   - Collaborative activities support
2. Productivity enhancements
   - Just-in-time information delivery
   - Reduction of information overload
   - Productive collaboration between work groups
   - Training on demand
3. Business enhancements
   - Faster time to market
   - Simultaneous engineering potential
   - Lower design and production costs
   - Improved client relationships
   - New business opportunities
4. Cost reduction
   - Fewer errors
   - Improved comparison shopping
   - Reduced travel and meetings
   - Reduced administrative and operational costs
   - Elimination of paper-publishing costs
5. Information delivery
   - Low-cost publishing
   - Leveraging of legacy systems
   - Standard delivery systems
   - Ease of maintenance and implementation
   - Elimination of paper-publishing and mailing costs

7.11   IMPLEMENTATION ISSUES

Exchanges, especially global or very large ones, may have several implementation issues. Let's look at some of these now.

Problems with Exchanges

The super exchanges are supposed to bring together entire industry sectors, creating supply chain efficiencies and cost reductions for buyers and sellers alike. However, despite the fact that more than 1,500 exchanges were created between January 1999 and December 2000, only a few hundred were active by winter of 2001, and less than half of these were conducting a high volume of transactions.

PRIVATE VERSUS PUBLIC EXCHANGES

As described earlier, exchanges may be owned by a third party and as such they are referred to as **public exchanges.** Private exchanges on the other hand are owned and operated by an industry giant or a consortia. Both types of exchanges have implementation and viability problems.

PROBLEMS WITH PUBLIC EXCHANGES

Exchanges need to attract sellers and buyers. Attracting sellers, especially large businesses to *public exchanges,* is difficult for the following reasons.

- **Transaction fees.** One of the major reasons that large and successful suppliers refuse to join third-party exchanges is that they are required to pay transaction fees even when engaging in transactions with their existing customers.
- **Sharing information.** Many companies do not like to join public exchanges because they have to share key business data with their competitors.
- **Cost savings.** Many of the first-generation exchanges were horizontal, concentrating on MROs. These are low-valued items. While administrative costs can be reduced, the cost of the products to the buyers usually remains the same. So the monetary savings may not be attractive enough to SME buyers.
- **Recruiting suppliers.** One of the major difficulties facing public exchanges is the recruitment of large suppliers. For example, GE Plastics, a major vendor of plastic materials, said that the company was asked to join *plastic-net.com*, but that it does not see any benefit in doing so. There is simply no business case for it. GE Plastics is working very hard to develop e-purchasing capabilities for its customers, and it is working quite well. The company likes the direct contact with its customers. Some suppliers just want to wait and see how exchanges will fare. They are afraid to join the public exchanges now and will join only if the exchanges succeed.
- **Too many exchanges.** When an exchange receives the publicity of being the ***first mover,*** like *Chemdex.com* did, it is sure to attract some competition. People believe that they can do better than the first mover or that they have "deeper pockets" to sustain losses and survive. For example, in Hong Kong there were three competing toy exchanges in late 2000. Similarly, two exchanges competed against Chemdex, which closed in 2000. (For competition among exchanges see the *e-steel.com* case at the end of this chapter.)
- **Supply chain improvements.** Public exchanges prepare the entire infrastructure and ask suppliers to just plug in and start selling. However, companies are interested in streamlining their supply chains, which requires integration with internal operations, and not just plugging in. This is why companies like i2 and Aspect, leaders in supply chain management (SCM), are partnering with some exchanges.

Problems in private exchanges. Private exchanges may not be trusted, and as discussed earlier, they may face legal and liquidity problems. In 2001, major manufacturers adopt private exchanges for the main supply chain, so the combined use of private and public exchanges is a new issue for manufacturers to consider.

Software Agents in B2B Exchanges

The use of B2B exchanges has fostered a need within the B2B community for an efficient infrastructure to provide real-time, tighter integration between buyers and sellers, and to facilitate management of multiple trading partners and their transactions across multiple virtual industry exchanges. Such capabilities can be provided by software agents like AgentWare's Syndicator. This software provides a scalable solution that enables customized syndication of content and services from multiple sources on the Internet to any device connected to the Internet. The software allows access to real-time information on the exchange. For further details, see *agentware.net*. Another software agent, *xchain.com*, monitors traffic on a B2B exchange and takes appropriate actions when needed. Some of the shopping agents in Table 3.1 (Chapter 3) can also be used for B2B purposes.

Disintermediation

Exchanges, especially consortia-type, could replace many traditional B2B intermediaries to complete third-party exchanges. Let's look at some examples.

- In September 2000, eight metal companies created *metalspectrum.com*. The consortium offers a market for specialty metals and business services to the industry. The exchange may eliminate traditional wholesalers and retailers. The participating companies tend to prefer the consortia sites over third-party exchanges like e-steel.
- Sun Microsystems, after publicly announcing that there was no need for third-party exchanges because they waste time, joined a consortium headed by IBM that develops and smooths lines in the computer maker's supply chain. This exchange competes with a similar exchange created by Compaq, HP, AMD, and NEC.
- Marriott and Hyatt, large competing hoteliers, created an MRO exchange that could eliminate wholesalers in that industry.

Evaluating Exchanges

With the increased number of competing exchanges, companies need to carefully evaluate which ones work best for them. According to *works.com*, the following are some useful suggestions for evaluating exchanges.

- Analyze how much the company will really save and/or gain.
- Determine the viability of the exchange, and check its ownership and management team.
- Look out for contracts and technology that locks a company into a long-term relationship.
- Look at the membership; discover who sits on the board.
- Find out who provides payment, logistics, and other services.

According to the GartnerGroup, buyers need to ask:

- Does the B2B exchange have a critical mass of buyers and suppliers?
- Can buyers and sellers hide their identities (anonymity feature)?
- What kinds of secretive information does my company have? Would it be uncovered?

- How much will it cost to be online and to use the e-marketplace?
- Can past trading records be traced?

Similarly, sellers need to ask:

- Could I acquire more buyers?
- Could I sell independently in the future?
- What is the transaction fee?
- How much does it cost to participate in e-trading?
- What kind of information do I have? Would it be uncovered and exposed to others?
- How would it affect the price of my goods?
- How severe is the competition in the exchange itself?

7.12   MANAGERIAL ISSUES

The following issues are germane to management:

1. **Planning.** Plan the most secure and economical choice for exchange implementation. Consult the technical staff inside and outside of each partnering company.
2. **Use the Internet.** Review the current proprietary or leased network and determine if it can be replaced by intranets and extranets. Doing so may reduce costs and widen connectivity for customers and suppliers.
3. **Which exchange?** One of the major concerns of management is the selection of exchanges in which to participate. At the moment, exchanges are not integrated, so there is a major start-up effort and cost for joining the exchanges. This is a multicriteria decision and should be carefully analyzed.
4. **Restructuring.** Joining an exchange may require a BPR of the internal supply chain. This may be expensive and time consuming. Therefore, this must be taken into consideration when deciding whether or not to join an exchange.
5. **Channel conflicts.** Channel conflicts may arise when a company joins an exchange. This issue must be considered and an examination for its impact must be carried out.
6. **Benefit and risk analysis.** Companies must take the issues in Table 7-2 very seriously. The risks of joining an exchange must be carefully considered.

Summary

In this chapter, you learned about the following EC issues as they relate to the learning objectives:

1. **E-marketplaces and exchanges defined.** Exchanges are e-marketplaces that provide a trading platform for conducting business to many buyers, many sellers, and other business partners. Other names used are portals or e-hubs.
2. **The major types of e-marketplaces.** E-marketplaces include information portals, trading exchanges (exchanges for short), and dynamic trading floors (for auctions and matching). They can be vertical (industry-oriented) or horizontal. They can target systematic buying (long-term relationships) or spot buying for fulfilling an immediate need.

3. **B2B portals.** These portals are similar to B2C portals such as Yahoo!. B2B portals are gateways to community-related information. They are usually of a vertical structure; therefore they are referred to as vortals. Some information portals offer product and vendor information and even possibilities for conducting trades.

4. **Third-party exchanges.** These are owned by an independent company and usually operate in highly fragmented markets. They try to maintain neutral relations with both buyers and sellers. Their major problem is customer acquisition.

5. **Dynamic pricing and trading.** Dynamic pricing occurs when prices are determined by supply and demand at any given moment. The two major dynamic pricing mechanisms are auctions (forward and reverse) and matching supply and demand (such as in stock markets). Dynamic trading refers to trading where prices are changing.

6. **E-procurement and e-selling consortia.** An e-procurement consortium is an exchange that is established by several large buyers (e.g., automakers). Their major objective is to smooth the purchasing process. An e-selling consortium is owned and operated by several large sellers, usually in the same industry (e.g., plastics). Their major objective is to increase sales and smooth the supply chain to their customers.

7. **Ownership and revenue models.** Exchanges may be owned by an intermediary (a third party), a large group of buyers or sellers (a consortium), or one large company. The major revenue models are: annual fees, transaction fees (flat or percentage), fees for added-value services, and advertisement income.

8. **Exchange networks and management of exchanges.** It is advisable to connect many exchanges for the benefit of customers. Such integration is complex and will take years to complete. Managing exchanges individually can be expensive; therefore, we see the emergence of "families" of exchanges like VerticalNet.

9. **Critical success factors of exchanges.** Some of the major critical success factors are: early liquidity, proper ownership, proper management, openness (technological and organizational), a full range of services, and the right governance.

10. **E-marketplaces and exchange implementation and development issues.** E-marketplaces and exchanges are usually developed and implemented by vendors. Therefore, vendor selection and management is a critical issue.

11. **Extranets.** An extranet connects the intranets of business partners in an effective and efficient manner. Several extranets can be combined, even globally. Using a VPN provides security so the Internet can be used rather than private lines. Extranets support both company-centric e-marketplaces and exchanges.

Key Terms

B2B portals	E-marketplace service provider
Consortium trading exchange (CTE)	E-markets
Dynamic pricing	Exchange hubs
Dynamic trading	Exchanges
E-marketplaces	Extranet

Internet
Internet exchanges
Intranet
Liquidity
Market maker
Portals
Private exchanges
Public e-marketplaces (exchanges)
Spot buying

Spot sourcing
Systematic purchasing
Systematic sourcing
Trading communities
Trading exchanges
Vertical marketplaces (exchanges)
Virtual Private Network (VPN)
Vortal (vertical portal)

Questions for Review

1. Define e-marketplaces and exchanges.
2. Define dynamic pricing and dynamic trading.
3. List the major types of e-markets.
4. Define a vortal.
5. Define B2B information portals.
6. List the major application purposes of extranets.
7. Describe the major components of an extranet.
8. Define VPN.
9. List the major services provided to buyers and sellers in exchanges.
10. Define systematic buying and spot buying.
11. Define a B2B consortium and list four different types.
12. Describe the revenue model of exchanges.
13. List the major five critical success factors for exchanges.

Questions for Discussion

1. How does dynamic pricing differ from fixed pricing?
2. How can external users like customers and suppliers access company-centric e-markets?
3. Can extranets eventually replace the role of leased-line-based WANs?
4. Suppose a manufacturer counts on an outside shipping company. How can the manufacturer use an exchange to arrange for the best possible shipping? How can status be tracked?
5. How are exchanges governed?
6. Explain the legal concerns regarding consortia.
7. Which exchanges are most suitable to third-party ownership and why?
8. Compare and contrast the supplier aggregation model with the buyer aggregation model.
9. Describe the various mechanisms for dynamic pricing.
10. Describe the various issues of integration related to B2B exchanges.
11. Explain the logic of a network of exchanges.
12. Discuss the logic of companies such as VerticalNet.
13. Explain the importance of early liquidity and describe methods to achieve it.
14. Explain the relationships between ANX and Covisint (see Appendix).
15. How do exchanges affect disintermediation?
16. Explain how buyers and sellers should evaluate exchanges.
17. Compare the viability of private vs. public exchanges.

18. Enter *covisint.com* and go to product development. View the product development overview chart and explain how collaborative commerce can facilitate it.

Internet Exercises

1. Visit *ariba.com* and *commerceone.com* and find the software tools they have for e-markets. Check the capabilities provided by each and comment on their differences.

2. Go to *alibaba.com* and sign-up (free) as a member. Go to the site map and find the "sample house." Create a product and place it in the sample house. Tell your instructor how to view this product.

3. Compare the services offered by *globalsources.com* with those offered by *alibaba.com*, and *meetworldtrade.com*.

4. Suppose you are a supplier for automakers. How will you react to the Covisint project? How can you achieve a competitively advantageous position in this situation?

5. Enter *chemconnect.com* and view the demos for different trading alternatives. Evaluate the services from both the buyer and seller points of view. Also, examine policies and legal guidelines. Are they fair? Compare *chemconnect.com* to *eglobalchem.com*.

6. Most of the major exchanges use an ERP/SCM partner. Enter *i2.com* and view their solutions, such as TradeMatrix. What are the benefits of these solutions?

7. Enter *FastParts.com* and review all the services offered there. Write a report based on your findings.

8. Investigate the various auctions offered by *FreeMarkets.com*. Comment on the services provided.

9. Enter *isteelasia.com*, *gsx.com*, and *e-steel.com* and compare their operations and services. These exchanges compete in global markets. Examine the trading platforms, portal capabilities, and support services (e.g., logistics, payments, etc.). In what areas do these companies compete? In what areas do they not compete? What are the advantages of *isteelasia.com* in dealing with Asian companies? Do we need regional exchanges? If it is good for Asia to have a regional exchange, why not have a Western European exchange, an Eastern European exchange, a Central American exchange, and so on. If we need these regional exchanges, can they work together? How? If there are too many, which will survive? Research this topic and prepare a report.

10. Air Cargo is a rapidly growing business that is heavily dependent on information technology. Indeed, in the last 20 years there have been many attempts to provide appropriate information services to industry partners. Some were successful and others failed. For example, one of the most diversified services is that provided by Traxon (Asia Ltd., Europe Ltd., and World Ltd.).

    Your mission is to design an information portal for the air cargo industry, specifically one that will support the following 16-step process.

    STEP 1. Consignee places an order with the shipper and he confirms receipt of the order.

STEP 2. Shipper places a transport order with the forwarder and then confirms receipt of the order.

STEP 3. Shipper passes on shipping instructions to the forwarder.

STEP 4. Forwarder reserves and books freight capacity with the road transporter and confirms the reservation and booking.

STEP 5. Forwarder reserves and books freight capacity with the airline company and confirms the reservation and booking.

STEP 6. Forwarder makes up the bill of lading for road transporter and this document goes with the freight during the road transport.

STEP 7. Forwarder makes up an Air Waybill and this document goes with the air freight from one airport to the other.

STEP 8. Forwarder gives an assignment to the forwarder at the airport of destination to reserve and book freight capacity with the road transporter and confirms receipt of this assignment.

STEP 9. Foreign forwarder reserves and books freight capacity at the road transporter and confirms the reservation and booking.

STEP 10. Forwarder supplies information about the air freight it is sending through customs, and customs provides the forwarder with the necessary documents.

STEP 11. Airline company provides the agent with a booking list for a specific flight to customs and customs gives confirmation to the agent.

STEP 12. Agent gives information about the load on a specific flight to customs and customs gives confirmation to the agent.

STEP 13. Airline company provides the agent with a booking list for a specific flight at the airport of destination.

STEP 14. Agent at the airport of destination gives details about the load on a specific flight to customs and customs gives confirmation back.

STEP 15. Forwarder at the airport of destination provides local customs with details about the load and gets information about this from customs in return.

STEP 16. Forwarder at the airport of destination makes up a bill of lading for road transporter there and this document goes with the freight during the road transport.

The process is shown in Figure 7-10

11. Some people compare a portal with a TV. And, indeed, for years Caterpillar Corp. has used a telecommunications system called "CAT TV" as a link to its dealers that includes audio and video capabilities. Investigate the role of portals in B2B. Describe the advantages and disadvantages of portals over CAT TV and other similar corporate projects.

Team Assignments and Role Playing

1. Form two teams (A and B) of five or more members. On each team, Person 1 plays the role of an assembly company that produces television monitors. Persons 2 and 3 are domestic parts suppliers to the assembling company, and Persons 4 and 5 play foreign parts suppliers. Now, the television monitor company wants to sell televisions directly to consumers. Let each team design the

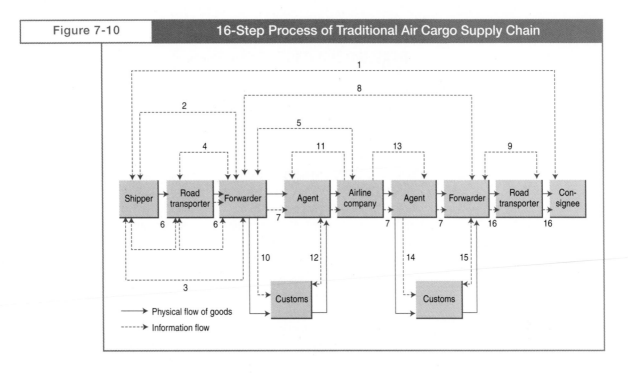

| Figure 7-10 | 16-Step Process of Traditional Air Cargo Supply Chain |

network environment for this situation and present their results. The other groups will evaluate each team's result.

2. Investigate the status of Covisint, both in the United States and in Europe. What are the relationships between Covisint and the company-centered marketplaces of the large automakers? Relate Covisint with the European-based ENX and the U.S.-based ANX. Have another team find similar industry-wide exchanges and compare them to Covisint.

REAL-WORLD CASE: E-Steel.com

The steel industry is well known for its cumbersome, paper-based supply chain. This is one of the reasons why the industry is unprofitable. *E-steel.com* decided to change this situation. Founded in 1998, *e-steel.com* initially wanted to bring buyers and sellers together to trade in an efficient manner over the Internet. Also, the company wanted to connect with "difficult to reach" buyers and sellers. The site allows the various industry players, from steel mills to service centers, to submit RFQs for all types of steel products, compare prices and packages across multiple suppliers, negotiate prices, and complete transactions, all in a secure, global marketplace.

As discussed earlier in this chapter, there are two purchasing strategies: systematic sourcing and spot sourcing. E-steel decided to support systematic sourcing, where transactions are negotiated among known parties. This is in contrast with the strategy of its primary rival, *MetalSite.com* (which folded in Spring 2001), supported auctions for spot purchasing. For *e-steel.com* to support systematic sourcing, it had to deal with the issue of *integration,* the process of linking participating companies' back-end financial, order entry, inventory, and manufacturing control to the *e-steel.com* exchange. *E-steel.com*'s goal is to create a highly automated online supply chain that delivers such efficiencies at reduced transaction costs, with less inventory in the pipeline, improved collaboration, and forecasting and scheduling among suppliers, suppliers' suppliers, and so on.

Integration is not simple to achieve, especially in light of the fact that one company may be a member of several (four to five) exchanges (recall the Qantas case in Chapter 1). The difficulties of integration are not only technical. One problem with implementing integration is that most exchanges are more concerned with liquidity, so integration is not a prime concern. This is true not only of the steel industry, but of most industries. Also, with B2B EC, companies need to rethink the global supply chain practices and institute a massive change—a BPR. Companies must review their existing processes and their interaction with the supply chains in which they are involved. This may be difficult if one company has several supply chains. Thus, companies need to make bold decisions about changes.

Companies need to connect the exchanges to the ERP, otherwise the exchanges just automate paper transactions, which may not be sufficient incentive to attract members, particularly when they are asked to pay transaction fees (see Norris et al., 2000).

In contrast with other exchanges, *e-steel.com* approached integration as a high-priority initiative. The company built an IT unit specializing in integration (with the help of Computer Sciences Corp.). The company selected several software companies and products, as well as consultants who are experts in providing integration services to steel companies. Then, there was a need to consider standards such as XML and EDI. To help automate the process of loading inventory information into a marketplace, *e-steel.com* created DataJet—a free data mapping and uploading tool that helps customers upload made-to-order inventory and product catalog information to the site without data format conversions. Also, *e-steel.com* helped the steel industry develop a Steel Markup Language, a set of extensions to XML. E-steel partnered with *webmethods.com*, a company that makes special hub and spoke software for integration, taking it to a higher level. All in all, *e-steel.com*'s preparation for delivering integration solutions will take 12 to 18 months.

E-steel has 3,500 members, including U.S. Steel Corp., which owns a minor part of *e-steel.com* and helps *e-steel.com* experiment with the new systems (*MetalSite.com* works with Bethlehem Steel Corp. in a similar fashion). One of the challenges, for example, is integration after a negotiation is completed. One illustration of this is when U.S. Steel needs to flow the results of an agreed-upon deal through its Oracle-based applications that handle invoicing, billing, and production planning (using an MRP software). Finally, to maximize efficiencies, there is a need to help U.S. Steel integrate itself with its own customers, such as Ford Motors, so that U.S. Steel's partners can seamlessly upload their purchasing requirements to the *e-steel.com* exchange. To do all of this, U.S. Steel had to redesign its databases and data collection procedures. To complete the integration, *e-steel.com* partnered with Ford Motors, offering the automaker its ValueTrack program. The strategic alliance covers Ford's steel supply program, and includes Ford's Tier 1 suppliers. The joint program is aimed at eliminating manual processes and giving the complete supply chain access to the same database of inventory, ordering, and pricing information.

Questions for the Case

1. Visit *e-steel.com* and *isteelasia..com* and compare the services they offer to their members.

2. A variety of smaller or niche exchanges compete with *e-steel.com* and *isteelasia..com*. These include *materialnet.com*. Investigate the nature of such competition.

3. *E-steel.com*'s exchange deals with sellers, such as U.S. Steel, and buyers, such as Ford Motors. But *e-steel.com* also reaches Ford's other Tier 1 suppliers. At the same time, Ford, through Covisint, can reach not only U.S. Steel, but U.S. Steel's suppliers and subsuppliers. This creates a confusion; why not just merge *e-steel.com* into Covisint?

4. *E-steel.com* expects to generate revenue by building and selling specialized software applications for its exchange for a specific buyers' industry (such as automotive). How can they do this?

5. What value-added services can *e-steel.com* provide to sellers in the exchange?

Sources: Compiled from *CIO Magazine* (October 15, 2000), *InteractiveWeek* (January 17, 2000), *steel-net.com*, and *worldsteel.org*.

REFERENCES AND BIBLIOGRAPHY

Baker, S. and K. Baker. "Going Up!, Vertical Marketing on the Web," *Journal of Business Strategy* (May/June 2000).

Bayles, D. *Extranets: Building the Business-to-Business Web*. Upper Saddle River, New Jersey: Prentice Hall, 1998.

Chan, S. and T. R. V. Davis. "Partnering on Extranets for Strategic Advantage," *Information Systems Management* (Winter 2000).

Cunningham, M. J. *B2B: How to Build a Profitable E-Commerce Strategy*. Cambridge, Massachusetts: Perseus Book Group, 2000.

Dalton, G. and B. Davis. "ANX Gets Certified Network Providers," *InformationWeek* (August 31, 1998).

Davis, B. G., et al., "Automotive Extranet Set for Test Drive," *InformationWeek* (September 1, 1997).

Durlacher Research Ltd. *Business to Business E-Commerce*. Research Report (*durlacher.com*) (2000).

Duvall, M. "E-Marketplaces Getting Connected," *Interactive Week* (January 10, 2000).

Gill, J. "What Most Big B2B Exchanges are Missing: A CEO," *Business Week* (July 14, 2000).

Grimes B., "The Rise and Fall (and Rise?) of E-Markets," *PC World* (June 2001).

Johnson, E. "Money for Nothing," *CIO Magazine* (September 15, 2000).

Jones, K. "Extranet Eliminates Loan Paperwork," *Interactive Week* (September 27, 1997).

Kaplan, S. and M. Sawhney. "E-Hubs: The New B2B Market Places," *Harvard Business Review*. (May/June 2000).

Kobielus, J. G. *Biz Talk: Implementing B2B E-Commerce*. Upper Saddle River, New Jersey: Prentice Hall, 2001.

Lehman Brothers, *Guide to Industry Consortia* (May 24, 2000).

Leitzes, A. and J. Solan. "Best of the Web," *Forbes Global* (July 24, 2000).

Lim, G. G. and J. K. Lee. "Buyer-Carts for B2B EC: The B-Cart Approach," *Organizational Computing and Electronic Commerce* (2002).

Loshin, P. *Extranet Design and Implementation*. Berkeley, California: Sybex, 1997.

Miner, R. C. *Dynamic Trading*. Tucson, Arizona: Dynamic Trading Group, 2000.

Norris, G., et al. *E-Business and ERP*. New York: Wiley & Sons, 2000.

O'Connell, B. *B2B.com: Cashing-In on the B2B E-Commerce Bonanza*. Avon, Massachusetts: Adams Media Pub. Co., 2000.

Pfaffenberger, B. *Building a Strategic Extranet*. New York: IDG Books Worldwide, 1998.

Price, D. A. "Exchange Trustbusters," *Business 2.0* (August 22, 2000).

Radeke, M. "Understanding B2B Online Exchanges," *Workz.com* Corp. (*workz.com/content/1694.asp*) (January 2001).

Ramsdell, G. "The Real Business of B2B," *BRW* (July 2000) (also in *McKinsey Quarterly* vol. 2, 2000).

Reid, K. "Invasion of the Vortals," *National Petroleum News* (July 2000).

Riggins, F. J. and H. S. Rhee. "Toward a Unified View of E-Commerce." *Communications of the ACM* (October 2000).

Riggins R. and H. Rhee, "Developing the Learning Network Using Extranets," (riggins-mgt.iac. gatech.edu/papers/learning.html) (1997).

Sachs, G. *Internet: B2B E-Commerce* (*www.gs.com*) (May 8, 2000).

Sara, E. "E-Marketplaces: Opportunity or Threat?" *e-Business Advisor* (July 2000).

Schully, A. B. and W. W. Woods. *B2B Exchanges*. New York: ISI Publications, 2000.

Silverstein, B. *Business-to-Business Internet Marketing*. Gulf Breeze, Florida: Maximum Press, 1999.

Stackpole, B. "Apps of Steel," *CIO Magazine*, October 15, 2000.

Szuprowicz, B. *Extranet and Intranet: E-Commerce Business Strategies for the Future*. Charleston, South Carolina: Computer Technology Research Corp., 1998.

Timmers, P. *Electronic Commerce: Strategies and Models for B2B Trading*. Chichester: John Wiley & Sons, Ltd., 1999.

Turban, E., et al. *Information Technology for Management*, 3rd ed. New York: John Wiley & Sons, 2002.

Watson, J. K., Jr., et al. "Free Trade Zone," *Doculabs Report* (July 1999).

Wilson, T. "B2B Exchanges Prepare for the Deluge," *InternetWeek* (September 25, 2000).

Yager, T. "Building the Perfect Exchange," *InfoWorld* (June 5, 2000).

A P P E N D I X   7A

THE EXTRANET

PLANNING EXTRANETS: COORDINATION AND SECURITY

Although extranets are easy to use, implementing an efficient extranet requires extensive coordination between the company and its business partners. Legacy systems, databases, and other corporate resources must be interconnected for outside access and protected from unauthorized intruders. Companies must approach extranet design and development with a needs analysis to identify the best business opportunities.

The success of the extranet depends on the security measures implemented for the system. The extranet is useless without the ability to securely transmit sensitive data between the intranet and authorized partners. Although 100 percent security is impossible, discerning actual threats from perceived threats, and then selecting appropriate measures will help secure the communication environment. Is selecting the strongest possible security for the entire extranet and associated intranets the best strategy? Not necessarily, because the stronger the security measures, the more hardware and software resources are required to maintain an acceptable performance level. A balance between security levels and return on investment analysis is an important component of an initial investigation to conduct extranet development.

Once a thorough needs analysis is completed, the feasibility of outsourcing must be checked. For most companies, the best strategy is to acquire a complete extranet package from a vendor such as Nortel Communication, Microsoft, or Netscape Communications. Select an ISP that provides high performance, low-latency connectivity, dial-in availability, and written service-level guarantees.

ELEMENTS OF EXTRANETS

Extranets are comprised of a wide variety of components and participants, and there are several possible configurations. The components include *intranets, Web servers, firewalls, ISPs, tunneling technology, interface software,* and *business applications.* The tunneling principle is the basic concept that makes the extranet possible. Tunneling means that data transmissions across the Internet can be made secure by authenticating and encrypting all IP packets. Several tunneling protocols are available, but IP security sponsored by IETF (Internet Engineering Task Force) is one of the more popular protocols.

Extranets are configured by two basic methods:

1. They can be implemented using a direct leased line with full control over it, linking all intranets.
2. A secure link (tunnel) can be created across the Internet, which can be used by the participating companies as a VPN, usually at a much lower cost. See Chapter 13 for details.

Besides the security issue, the effectiveness of an extranet depends on the degree to which it is integrated with legacy systems and databases. In many instances, integrating with legacy systems involves integrating a System Network Architecture (SNA)—the backbone of legacy systems in many corporations—with TCP/IP, the Web backbone. The technical differences between the two systems are often sources of conflicts.

EXAMPLES OF EXTRANET APPLICATIONS

Connect Business Customers to Sell Parts: AMP

AMP of Harrisburg, Pennsylvania, is a large electric-connectors distribution company with annual sales of over $5 billion, conducting business in 50 countries. The company sells nearly 80,000 different products, including fiber-optic connectors, printed wiring boards, splices, and switches. In 1996, AMP launched an extranet called AMP Connect, which is based on electronic catalogs with product descriptions, three-dimensional models, and comparative charts and tables of all its products. The company operates one of the most advanced portals. The information is available in eight languages and the site receives 100,000 hits daily from approximately 15,000 business customers worldwide.

This application is an example of connecting a company with its customers through an extranet. AMP Connect is used to place orders and has given the company a forum for communicating with wholesalers, distributors, resellers, and customers, which is necessary for the creation of an exchange.

Connect Dealers by Kiosk: General Motors

General Motors wanted to change the way automobiles are marketed by using an extranet accessed in kiosks and through personal digital assistants (PDAs). The interactive kiosks are installed in dealerships and shopping malls. The extranet uses the GM-access network, which connects 8,600 North American dealers with GM factories. GM-access is implemented worldwide using the Pulsar satellite system, which is operated by Hughes Network Systems.

The goal is to link the interactive kiosks to GM's legacy infrastructure. Ideally, these are instantly updated whenever GM changes the configuration or price of a car.

Connect with Suppliers for Procurement: VHA, Inc.

VHA, Inc., the Irving, Texas, alliance of 18 hospitals and 1,400 health-care organizations, developed an extranet that supports collaboration and allows access to an electronic catalog of products for approximately 22,000 dial-up users. VHA members purchase more than $8 billion in products annually under contracts from 350 suppliers.

Initial use of *VHA.com* was for access to VHA healthcare organizations and the Internet. Since 2000, VHA members can buy and sell merchandise and offer a wide range of medical, legal, and pharmaceutical research capabilities. The extranet allows all VHA members to purchase directly from suppliers.

VHA.com allows all VHA members to exchange information through a ubiquitous, secure environment. VHA chose IBM as its ISP because of its experience with data networking. Security is a particularly important issue because of the sensitive nature of clinical information. Hospitals, clinics, home health companies, and managed care facilities in numerous locations are involved, and patient information must remain private.

Tracking Shipping Status: CSX Technology

In 1996, a railroad company, CSX Technology, developed a highly publicized intranet for tracking cross-country train shipments from point to point. The company expanded this intranet to an extranet, named TWSNet Premium, which links more than 200 freight shippers and forwarders. The extranet allows CSX customers to track shipments, initiate work orders, and view pricing data over the Internet. TWSNet includes large suppliers of transportation services such as railroads, trucks, container ships, and barges.

The TWSNet Premium is also open to non-CSX customers who require Web-based solutions for managing inbound shipping or outbound delivery information as part of their supply-chain management. The extranet allows tracking of shipments to the line-item level, simplifying identification of bottlenecks or problems. A global reporting system analyzes carrier performance and trends. It also allows users to perform precise demand forecasting, while a special programming interface enables integration with legacy systems.

For additional applications, see Riggins and Rhee (1998).

8

B2B Support Services

LEARNING OBJECTIVES

Upon completion of this chapter, the reader will be able to:

- Identify the major types of B2B services usually provided by specialized e-service providers.

- Understand why EC services are frequently outsourced.

- Describe the role and types of e-strategy consultants.

- Understand the e-infrastructure process and the role of Web hosting and integration.

- Describe various financial services in B2B.

- Explain the various B2B logistics services and order fulfillment services.

- Differentiate B2C from B2B with respect to marketing, advertisement, and sales, and describe some B2B initiatives.

- Describe content creation, syndication, delivery, and management.

- Describe the role of directory services in B2B.

- Describe how CRM is done in B2B and its relationships with e-communities.

In December 2000, Hewlett-Packard (HP) launched a B2B e-payment solution that enables financial institutions to provide their customers with a seamless electronic payment, each time a B2B EC transaction takes place. By allowing payments to be processed, completed, and recorded online at the time of the transaction, this technology eliminates the paper-based payment inefficiencies of B2B exchanges—dramatically improving the speed and accuracy of transactions and reducing costs by as much as 80 percent.

The HP e-payment solution can be integrated with e-marketplaces, online exchanges, e-procurement hubs, and sell/buy Web sites, to guarantee immediate status updates for corporations transacting electronically. Foreign currency payments can be integrated with user accounting systems to ensure accounts receivable and accounts payable reflect up-to-date values as business is conducted online. The solution also increases efficiencies by decentralizing the initiation of payments across all parties and locations and by allowing for centralized control over workflow rules and transactions.

The HP B2B e-payment solution consists of two components that are preintegrated with the complete HP Enterprise Commerce solution suite, and together provide end-to-end payment automation. The B2B e-payment handler offers embedded payment options that establish business rules to facilitate direct debit payment options. These options allow companies to set up buyer accounts, purchasing limits, corporate discounting, and other payment-related authentication and alert mechanisms. The solution securely connects customers' e-commerce sites enabled with the HP B2B e-payment handler to their online financial institutions. Combined, these components are robust enough to even handle the most complex cross-border transactions quickly and securely.

In the new digital world, companies look for values they have come to expect from financial services, such as low-cost real-time transactions performed by trusted partners. With this solution, HP connects the financial world to the new economy, bringing those values to the Web environment. The HP solution closes the payment gap in the B2B Internet value chain, while driving companies' business growth and profitability by offering customers the best value, end-to-end online purchasing experience.

HP has integrated its B2B e-payment solution with BroadVision's Business Commerce application to create comprehensive B2B e-commerce systems that feature seamless payment processing. The integrated system also reduces the cost of order processing, contract administration, and customer service, and captures and analyzes information that allows companies to provide unique purchasing experiences for each customer, partner, and employee.

8.2 EC SERVICES: OVERVIEW AND STRATEGIC OUTSOURCING

The opening vignette illustrates an important support service provided by a vendor—an electronic payment system that supports B2B transactions. Implementing most EC applications requires the use of support services. The most obvious support services are payments (Chapter 14), security (Chapter 13), logistics (Chapter 15), and infrastructure and technology (Chapter 12). Most of the services described in these later chapters are relevant for both B2C and B2B. In this chapter, we concentrate on services for B2B. However, some of these are also valid for B2C. The major B2B services described in these chapters are summarized in Figure 8-1.

Figure 8-1 organizes B2B services into the following categories suggested by the Delphi Group (*delphigroup.com*).

- e-infrastructure
- e-process

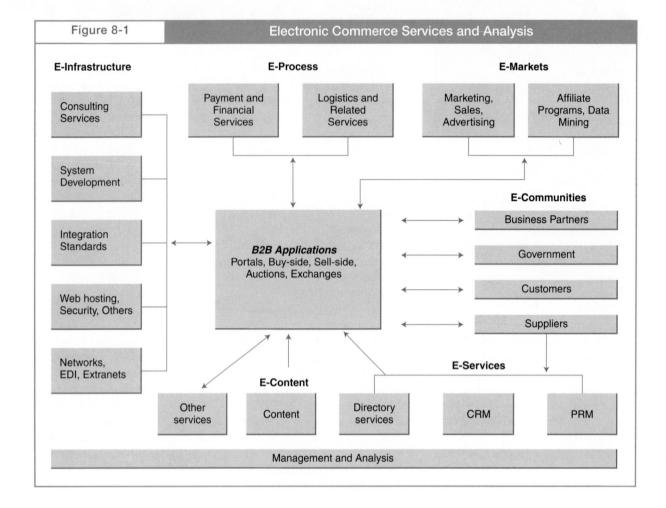

Figure 8-1 | Electronic Commerce Services and Analysis

- e-markets
- e-content
- e-communities
- e-services

The figure shows the major topics in each category.

Most companies do not provide the support services by themselves. Instead, they use outsourcing services.

Why Outsource B2B Services?

When EC emerged, it became obvious that it would be necessary to outsource many of the support services involved in its deployment. The major reasons why most companies prefer to do this are:

- A desire to concentrate on core business
- The need to have services up and running rapidly
- Lack of expertise (experience and resources) for many of the required support services

- The inability to have the economy of scale enjoyed by outsourcers often results in high costs for in-house options
- Inability to keep up with rapidly fluctuating demands if an in-house option is used
- There are simply too many required services for one company to handle

To illustrate the importance of outsourcing, we will look at the typical process of developing and managing EC applications (the e-infrastructure), a topic we address in detail in Chapter 12.

The process includes the following major steps:

STEP 1: EC strategy formulation
STEP 2: Application design
STEP 3: Building (or buying) the application
STEP 4: Hosting, operating, and maintaining the EC

Each of these steps may be comprised of several activities, as shown in Figure 8-2. A firm may execute all the activities of this process internally, or it may outsource some or all of them. In addition to the technical systems design and maintenance, there are many business system design issues and business functions related to using a Web site that must also be addressed. For example, a firm doing EC must design and operate its order fulfillment system and outbound logistics (delivery) functions, or it must provide dynamic content on the site. It must also provide services to its customers and partners. These and other business functions will also be addressed in this chapter.

Strategic Outsourcing

Historically, early businesses were vertically integrated—they owned or controlled their own sources of materials, manufactured components, performed final assembly, and managed the distribution and sale of their products to consumers. Later,

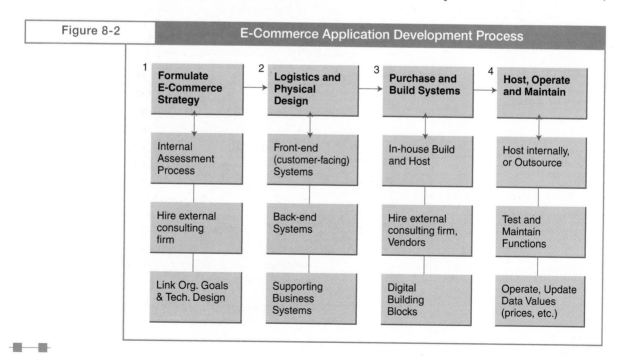

Figure 8-2   E-Commerce Application Development Process

nearly all firms began to contract with other firms to execute various activities along the supply chain, from manufacturing to distribution and sale, in order to concentrate their activities in their core competency. This practice is known as "outsourcing."

Of all business outsourcing, IT outsourcing is done more often than in any other area. Most enterprises engaged in EC, and practice a very large degree of outsourcing. While concentrating on core competencies, they develop strategic alliances with partner firms in order to provide activities such as payment processing, order fulfillment, outbound logistics, Web site hosting, and customer service. This phenomena is especially evident in exchanges.

Most exchanges are going through an evolutionary process that is shown in Figure 8-3. As illustrated by Figure 8-3, exchanges start by concentrating on matching buyers and sellers (Phase I). In Phase II they move to support services

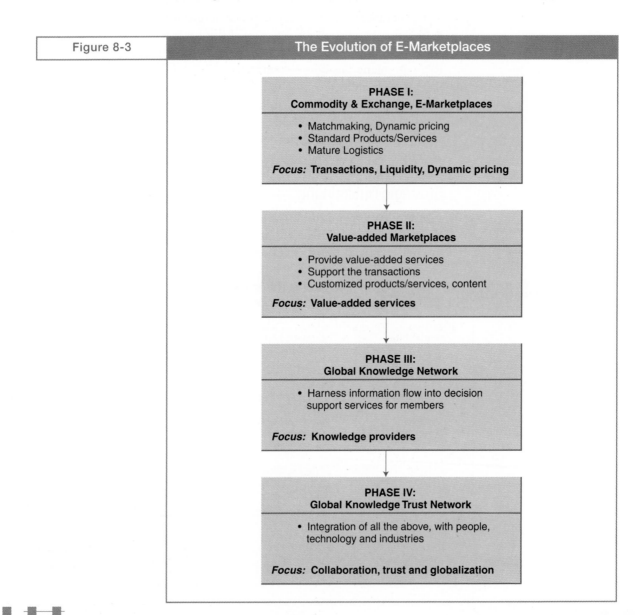

Figure 8-3	The Evolution of E-Marketplaces

PHASE I:
Commodity & Exchange, E-Marketplaces

- Matchmaking, Dynamic pricing
- Standard Products/Services
- Mature Logistics

Focus: **Transactions, Liquidity, Dynamic pricing**

PHASE II:
Value-added Marketplaces

- Provide value-added services
- Support the transactions
- Customized products/services, content

Focus: **Value-added services**

PHASE III:
Global Knowledge Network

- Harness information flow into decision support services for members

Focus: **Knowledge providers**

PHASE IV:
Global Knowledge Trust Network

- Integration of all the above, with people, technology and industries

Focus: **Collaboration, trust and globalization**

that provide added value and are the topic of this chapter. Once the services are in place, companies can move to global knowledge networks (Phase III) and finally to global value trust networks (Phase IV). For details see Raisch (2001).

8.3   CONSULTING SERVICES

Consulting services are used for many purposes in B2B. The major areas where such consulting services are used are:

E-strategy. Consultants help determine the general EC strategy and which specific EC applications to implement. This is done as the first step of e-infrastructure development.

Technology. Consultants advise companies on technology, ranging from EC architecture to security.

Whether a firm is a pure-play Internet firm or a brick-and-mortar firm building its online initiative, it needs to identify an overall strategy and determine what its *value proposition* will be. A firm must determine if it will conduct online transactions, and if so, what it will sell and buy and how. A firm must decide if it will engage in online relationships with supply chain partners and with other partners and allies. It must establish procedures and guidelines to govern its electronic interaction and collaboration with both internal and external constituents. Simply stated, the firm needs an EC (or e-business) strategy, as will be described in Chapter 16.

How do firms make these very important decisions before they begin developing technical solutions and implementing operational procedures for online activities? One is reminded of the popular TV ad that shows a team watching their new Web site come online. As the first 10 sales are made, then hundreds, and then hundreds of thousands, their jubilation turns to terror when they realize they will have to fulfill orders at a level far higher than they anticipated! Firms must plan for the most probable set of outcomes, but they must also establish contingency plans for other scenarios. They must also decide how to turn their overall strategies for EC into actual business functions and operations. They must build a Web site, link it to their legacy back-end systems, create countless new job functions, build an interconnectedness between departments and divisions, and much more.

How does a firm know how to do something it has never done before? Many firms, both start-ups and established companies, are turning to consultants that have established themselves as experts in guiding their clients through the maze of legal, technical, strategic, and operational problems and decisions that must be addressed in order to ensure success in this new business environment. Some of these firms have established a reputation in one area of expertise, whereas others are generalists. Some consultants even take equity positions in the firms they advise. Some consultants will build, test, and deliver a working Web site, and may even host it and maintain it for their clients. There are four broad categories of consulting firms.

The first type of firm includes those that provide expertise in the area of EC, but not in traditional business. Some of the consultants in this category are *Agency.com*, Answerthink, Breakaway, Cysive, Digital Lighthouse, Digitas, IXL, Inforte, Lante, Luminant, Organic, Primix, Razorfish, Scient, Sapient, Verity, WebTrends, and Webmethods. See Application Case 8.1 for an overview of Sapient's services.

APPLICATION CASE   **8.1**

Consulting Services at Sapient

To illustrate the perspective of a firm specializing in providing Internet strategy consulting services, the following excerpt has been extracted from the Sapient Web site.

"The pace of change we're seeing in the marketplace is unprecedented," comments Jack Dickerson, Sapient's Vice President who leads the company's strategy practice. "The idea of 'e-business' as a distinct identity is going by the wayside, as players either find ways to make the Internet central to their business plans or risk losing relevance in today's competitive environment."

Sapient's strategy consultants—who have both business and technology backgrounds—have a demonstrated knack for guiding clients through complex industry and technology landscapes to create entirely new business models. Sapient helps its clients create workable digital solutions that address specific target audiences across the value chain—and support the company's long-term business goals.

The company's strategy program works as part of an overall multidisciplinary approach. Unlike many strategy consulting firms, the firm focuses on digital, networked technology and its implications for business models, brands, organizations, technology systems, and the end user's experience. As a result, the company is able to rapidly identify and interpret the issues facing clients, then create and implement a strategy that covers all facets of the client's business objective.

The services provided include:

- business strategy research, development, and articulation;
- rapid business assessment and business solution workshops;
- process innovation;
- competitive analysis and research; and
- business plan development.

Source: Compiled from *sapient.com/expertise/strategy.asp*

The second type of consulting firm is a traditional consulting company who maintain divisions that focus on EC. These include the so-called "Big 5" U.S. accounting firms and the large established U.S. national consulting firms. These firms leverage their existing relationship with their corporate clients and offer EC value-added services. Representative companies are Accenture (formerly Andersen Consulting); Computer Services Corp.; Cambridge Technology Partners; Boston Consulting Group; Booz-Allen & Hamilton; Deloitte & Touche; Ernst and Young; EDS; KPMG; McKinsey; and PriceWaterhouseCoopers.

The third type of consulting firm includes thousands of smaller consulting firms that specialize in EC. Some of these fill a unique niche in the growing field. Matching these consultants with clients can be done via service companies such as *EXP.com*, *eLance.com*, and *SoloGig.com*. These sites find consultants for the visitor, but the sites are not focused on B2B or even EC strategy. One site that locates firms specializing in Web site design is *DesignShops.com*. This site has two services, The New Architect, a weekly newsletter focusing on business strategy for Web services firms, and FirmFinder. The New Architect features a rotating series of authors, all of whom are renowned experts in the field of interactive design and development. FirmFinder features a robust search system, enabling firms to showcase their services to prospective clients.

The fourth category of consulting firms is EC hardware and software vendors that provide consulting services. These include *mysap.com*, *ibm.com*, *oracle.com*, *sun.com/service*, and many more.

Consultants often specialize in one or more design methodologies or implementation technologies. For example, they may specialize in developing Web-enabled interactive databases using Allaire's ColdFusion environment, or they may specialize in graphic design processes based on the Macromedia design platform (Flash, etc.). (Macromedia and Allaire merged in 2001.)

It is imperative that any firm seeking help in devising a successful online strategy select not only an experienced and competent consulting firm, but also one with sufficient synergies with the client firm. For a discussion of vendor selection and management see Chapter 12.

Once an EC strategy has been formulated, it must be implemented. Some firms may have in-house expertise in Web site design and hosting. As indicated above, many consulting firms will also design solutions on behalf of their clients. In other cases, firms seek to hire design vendors to build and implement their applications for them. Sections 8.4 and 8.5 are dedicated to these topics, as well as Chapter 12, which goes into execution details.

8.4   APPLICATION-BUILDING SERVICES AND REQUIRED STANDARDS

As will be seen in Chapter 12, once the EC strategy is completed and specific applications have been selected and prioritized, the application infrastructure needs to be constructed.

While Chapter 12 focuses on the process of building, this chapter will describe some of the services that can be used to support B2B applications. In some cases, these services are utilized by in-house design teams who want to put together a system that incorporates the best-of-breed EC components (building blocks) that are available; in other cases, vendors and system integrators will do the job. Some EC components are very special-purpose niche tools, such as tax-calculation software, while others are broad EC packages that facilitate nearly all aspects of running a successful transaction online.

Some of these building blocks are licensed and incorporated into the system hosted on the client's own servers, whereas others reside on the service provider's site, and the real-time service is provided over the Internet via an ASP (see Chapter 12). Some of these externally hosted "digital building blocks" are used according to a subscription pricing model, where the company that uses the e-service pays the vendor a standard monthly fee for the right to use the service. In other cases, the service is actually free! Some of these service providers offer different service levels at different prices. The details of building component-based applications are provided in Chapter 12.

When building B2B applications and other EC solutions, one must pay attention to various protocols and standards that are necessary for the integration of components and the connection of applications and business partners.

Industry Standards—XML, XSL, and Support Organizations

For B2B companies of all kinds to interact with each other easily and effectively, they must be able to connect their servers, applications, and databases. For this to happen, standard protocols and data representation schemes are needed. The Web is based on the standard communication protocols of TCP/IP and HTTP. Further, Web pages are written in the universally recognized standard notation of HTML. However, this standard environment is only useful for displaying static visual Web pages. To further extend the functionality of EC sites one can utilize JavaScript and other Java and ActiveX programs. These tools allow for human interaction, but they do not address the need to interconnect back-end database systems and applications. For that purpose, the industry is pursuing several alternatives for standardized data representation.

One of the most promising standards is **XML** (eXtensible Markup Language) and its variants. XML is used to improve compatibility between the disparate systems of business partners by defining the meaning of data in business documents (see Appendix B for details; see also *webmethods.com*). An example of an XML variant is voice XML, which is used to increase interactivity and accessibility with speech recognition systems. For an example of how XML works see Application Case 8.2.

APPLICATION CASE   **8.2**

XML Unifies Air Cargo Tracking System

TradeVan Information Services of Taiwan provides information services about the cargo flights of different airlines. As such, it can be classified as a B2B infomediary. Since different airlines have different information systems, the query results all look completely different. XML, as shown in Appendix B, can facilitate data exchange between heterogeneous databases. A special application was developed by Li and Shue (2001) to unify different document presentations for cargo status information in Taiwan. Furthermore, the information can be presented on wireless application protocol (WAP) based cell phones. (see Chapter 19).

The system offers a uniform GUI cargo status inquiry and returns with a consistent and personalized presentation for different airlines. This benefits customs brokers, who can reduce the cycle time by preparing declarations of imports faster. Buyers and other supply chain partners can schedule production lines with precision and in advance. Finally, the quality of door-to-door delivery companies such as FedEx and UPS can be improved. At present, the answers to queries are generated in carriers' databases, including those of China Air and Eva Air.

The system integrates XML with Java Servlet and Wireless technology. A fast delivery of unified information helps to improve the supply chain by reducing simultaneously delivery lead times and inventory levels. Shippers and receivers can use the system to track the status of deliveries. Prior to the installation of the system, an air cargo shipment spent 80 percent of its transport time waiting and only 8 percent in the air. The new system is expected to reduce delays significantly to the benefit of all members of the supply chain.

Since XML and related standards such as XSL (see Appendix B) require national and international agreements and cooperation, there are several organizations that concentrate on this topic. Some important organizations include:

- The UN body for Facilitation of Electronic Commerce (UN/CEFACT) see *messageq.com* and *ebxml.org*
- The W3C (*w3.org*) deals with XML and other EC standards
- RosettaNet (*RosettaNet.org*) concentrates on supply chain topics in the computer/electronic industries
- The OBI consortium (*openbuy.org*) is concerned with standards for purchasing MROs
- UDDI standard for registration of products (*uddi.org*)
- **ebxml** is a set of specifications that together enable a modular EC framework. It is an enabler of global trade.

8.5   WEB HOSTING AND OTHER SERVICES

There are several options for acquiring the hardware and software necessary to operate a Web server. Some of these tools are proprietary (such as a system from Sun Microsystems), whereas others are in the public domain, such as Linux and Apache. Many Web sites require additional data storage equipment, database servers, security firewalls, multimedia servers, and other related hardware and software associated with robust Web sites. Owning a Web server can be very costly and requires technical expertise that may not be available in-house.

Therefore, rather than building and operating a Web site in-house, many organizations choose to use **Web hosting**. Firms that host Web sites for their clients provide space on a Web server and frequently offer an entire suite of services to remove the technical burdens and allow the client to focus on their own core competency. Verio is one such company, as shown in Application Case 8.3.

APPLICATION CASE   8.3

Verio

Verio hosts Web sites at various service levels, each priced higher than the previous level. In each case, Verio offers state-of-the-art servers, a Tier-1 network, and a team of experts to assist in the process. It also promises the following features: availability (get started quickly), reliability (99.9 percent uptime), confidentiality (secure files), data integrity (they perform daily backups to protect files from loss or corruption), throughput (pages come up quickly), scalability (upgrade account as client grows), support (24/7 access), control (easily changed Web design), and information (Web site traffic statistics, etc.). Clients can acquire self-service accounts for simple transactional functionality or they may work closely with Verio to design and build robust systems to be hosted by Verio. For an additional charge, clients may also purchase payment processing functionality to ease some of the security concerns in a transactional Web site.

APPLICATION CASE   8.3

(continued)

Verio also offers other value-added services related to Web site design and hosting. It offers NetAnnounce Premiere, a professional Web site promotional service to help Web sites get noticed. Besides registering its clients' sites with over 250 search engines, it also offers several proprietary techniques to help a site get listed prominently, including optimized word relevancy advice and optimized meta tags. It also offers load balancing, server monitoring, security, and system administration services. Some of their clients share servers with other clients (essentially renting space on a Web server alongside other "tenants"), while others pay higher fees to have their own dedicated servers. Clients can also utilize additional technology applications such as Active Server Pages (ASP) and ColdFusion. While most of these services are B2C-orientated, Verio hosts B2B sites as well.

Source: Compiled from *verio.com*

Business hosting. Hosting is popular for SMEs, but for large businesses, more advanced services are needed such as dedicated servers and co-location (physical location of the server). A **dedicated server** is assigned to a specific purpose or customer. One example is *dellhost.com*. Others are *globalcrossing.com*, *exodus.com*, *loudcloud.com*, *hostopia.com*, and *digex.com*.

Other major companies providing similar quality Web hosting solutions, include Network Solutions and Rackspace.

Network Solutions, the company that registers domain names, was acquired by VeriSign. Network Solutions' goal is to capture customers when they register their domain name with Network Services, and then become their provider for an entire set of services related to Web hosting, including security, payment processing, affiliation provision, and so forth.

Rackspace provides dedicated servers, each leased to a single customer. The server hardware, routing equipment, and network connectivity are monitored and maintained by the service provider (Rackspace Managed Hosting), while the server software is remotely maintained by the customer. Rackspace has also developed its "Enterprise Hosting Program" to provide the highest level of service for mission-critical applications. Rackspace promises 99.999 percent uptime, dedicated 24/7 telephone support specialists, and advanced database administration services.

Free Web hosting is an attractive option for small start-ups. The companies providing free Web space typically insert a banner ad at the top of the pages they host, so this may not be an option for large business sites, but it may provide a starting point for a company that seeks to minimize its initial starting costs. Some of the companies providing free Web hosting services include *Angelfire.com*, *Tripod.com* (owned by Lycos), *GeoCities.com* (owned by Yahoo!), *Dreamwater.com*, *Netfirms.com*, *free.prohosting.com*, and *Homestead.com*. Of special interest are Yahoo! Store, (Chapter 12) *FreeMerchant.com*, and *bigstep.com*.

There are hundreds of Web hosting companies. Companies can learn more about Web hosting services from the following resources.

Sources of Information about Web Hosting

There are several sources of information about Web hosting services, including ones that tell you how to select a free Web host based on various criteria. A good place to start is with the *Web Host Review* at *hostreview.com*. It offers a Web hosting glossary and a guide to Web hosting. It also provides reviews submitted by other users. In addition, it recommends specific hosts and distributes a monthly newsletter about the Web hosting industry.

Another comprehensive source for Web hosting information is *Host Search* (*hostsearch.com*)—"Helping you find a home for your Web site." Using multiple criteria, including monthly cost, disk space requirements, monthly transfer volume, features, programming requirements, and platform requirements (NT, Unix, or Mac), their search engine will recommend the best host. Host Search also provides power search options. Visitors to this site can offer their own reviews of various hosts. There is a Q&A area, a list of articles about hosts, and the latest news and press releases. This site also showcases the leading hosts in several categories, such as dedicated servers or the lowest cost hosts.

WebHosting Magazine (*whmag.com*) is primarily a source of information for members of the Web hosting industry, but it also offers comprehensive information for firms seeking to outsource their Web hosting and related services.

Management Service Provider (MSP)

Another emerging business model is the **management service provider (MSP)** model. MSPs deliver IT infrastructure management services to multiple customers over networks on a subscription basis. The concept is similar to ASPs (application service providers) (see Chapter 12), but unlike ASPs, which deliver business applications to end users, MSPs deliver systems management services to IT departments who manage their own technology assets. For further discussion and a demonstration see *mspassociation.org*. MSPs specialize in e-business and in enterprise solutions. *Crosscommerce.com* billed itself as the first "Merchandising Service Provider," but is no longer in business. For an example of MSPs see *merchandisingavenue.com*. For more information check *line56.com*.

End-to-End Solutions

An **end-to-end business solution provider** builds Web sites and EC applications from conceptual design to deployment (see Chapter 12). In addition to e-infrastructure, such companies can supply payment systems, delivery management, site monitoring, and other services. Some vendors that provide such services are *bcentral.com* (from Microsoft), *WebVision.com*, *ibm.com* (WebSphere), and more. The advantages and disadvantages of such an approach are discussed in Chapter 12.

8.6   FINANCIAL B2B SERVICES

Several financial-related services are needed for B2B. The most obvious one is payments.

Payments

The opening vignette illustrates how HP provides B2B customers with an integrated payment system. The essentials of EC payments are covered in Chapter 14. Here we discuss some of the methods and issues related to B2B payments.

Payments in EC are similar to payments in the physical world. However, there are some instruments that can make B2B payments fast and secure. One such instrument is a **purchasing card**.

PURCHASING CARDS

Purchasing cards are gaining popularity for B2B transactions. They are special purpose, nonrevolving payment cards that are issued to employees for purchasing MROs and paying for travel expenses. They are very popular in government agencies, where up to 80 percent of all purchases are for MROs. The purchasing cards' benefits and limitations are described in Chapter 14. The participants and their role in using such cards are shown in Figure 8-4. Usually, cards have a limit of $1,000 to $2,000 per purchase.

As mentioned earlier, purchasing cards are extremely popular with government agencies. Here is how the State of New Jersey (*state.nj.us/treasury*) describes the win-win benefits of the card.

Figure 8-4	The Participants and the Process of Using a Purchasing Card

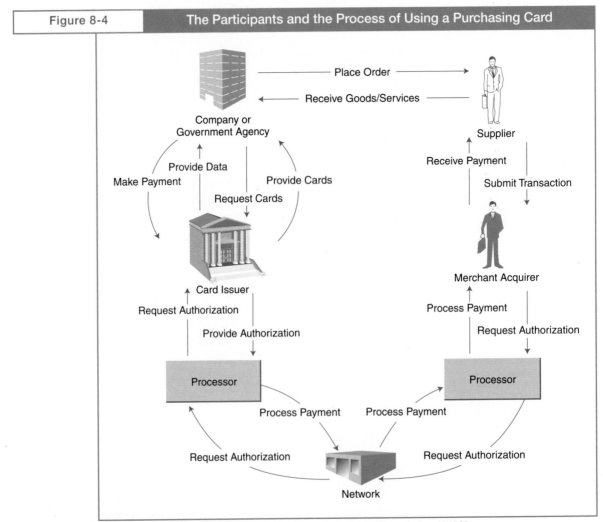

Source: napcp.org/napcp/napcp.nsf/Cardparticipants!OpenPage. Used with permission of NAPCP.

Benefits for the cardholder are:

- Purchasing convenience
- Empowered to make purchases without an invoice or having a check issued
- Expedites delivery of goods and services

Benefits for the agency are:

- Efficient purchasing and payment process (reduced cost from $100 to $10 per order)
- Effective, software-based management reporting
- Software-based, electronic billing capability
- Eliminates unnecessary work
- Enhances accountability
- Provides information to management

Benefits for the merchant are:

- Expedites payment
- Reduces paperwork
- Promotes state and local business relationships

To learn more about purchasing cards, see the National Association of Purchasing Card Professionals (*napcp.org*), *visa.com*, and *ge.com/capital.cardservices/factsheet.htm*. Such cards are used by most state governments (e.g., *purchasingcard.state.fl.us*) and by many public universities.

Purchasing cards are used within countries; for global trade one can use electronic letters of credit.

ELECTRONIC LETTERS OF CREDIT

A Letter of Credit (LC) is a written undertaking by a bank to pay the beneficiary (seller) on account of the applicant (buyer) a sum of money upon presentation of stipulated documents that comply with the terms and conditions of the credit. The LC gives precise instructions concerning the documents that must be produced by the beneficiary for payment or acceptance by the LC expiration date.

The benefits of LCs to the seller are:

- Credit risk is reduced as payment is now accessed via the creditworthiness of the issuing bank instead of the buyer.
- Payment is highly assured if all the terms and conditions stipulated in the LC are complied with.
- Political/country risk is reduced if the LC is confirmed by a bank in the seller's country.

The benefits of LCs to the buyer are:

- An LC may allow the buyer to negotiate for a lower purchase price, as credit risk is reduced.
- Buyer may expand its source of supply since certain sellers are only willing to supply goods under LC arrangements.
- Seller will only receive payment after the documents have been inspected by the issuing bank.

There are five steps related to LC arrangements: LC issuance, LC credit advising, LC confirmation, LC transfer, and LC negotiation. These five steps may be conducted online, much faster than they can be off-line, as done at ANZ Online (*anz.com.au*).

ANZ Online provides comprehensive set of electronic banking. For example, in the area of international and personal trade it offers:

- Baur's confirmed documentary credit instrument.
- ANZ Export Book for documentation preparation (80 percent time reduction).
- ANZ eGate is an Internet-based payment gateway.
- ANZ ebiz is an Internet comprehensive procurement service.
- MerchantConnect-Fraud Prevention helps in identifying fraudulent credit cards.
- ANZ Foreign Currency Accounts allows netting of foreign currency transactions.

Royal Bank of Canada (RBC) issues electronic LCs from its International Business Centre (*Royalbank.com/trade/lettersofcredit.html*). Advantages are available to both sellers and buyers as follow:

Benefits of RBC LCs for importers:

- Credit application is submitted online
- Electronic LC is issued in less than 24 hours
- Templates increase productivity and reduce errors
- An ID number that can be used immediately is provided when the importer applies
- Monitoring and control reports are generated

Benefits of RBC LCs for exporters:

- Receive the LC electronically in their PCs (no more faxes)
- Information is easily imported from the LC into common formats (fewer errors, speeding processes)
- Templates of common documents are available (invoices, certificates of origin, packing lists, weight lists, etc.)
- Reporting information is available

Electronic LCs are also used in auctions such as at *eBay.com*. Payments are guaranteed in minutes. One problem with e-LCs is that their cost is too high for many SMEs. For these, MasterCard provides the following solution.

PAYMENTS IN B2B GLOBAL TRADING

Payments in B2B global trading are usually done with a letter of credit, which involves one or more banks and an expense that may be too high for an SME. An alternative solution introduced by MasterCard-TradeCard payment allows businesses to seamlessly complete B2B e-commerce transactions through a single mechanism. Using TradeCard's patented compliance and transaction workflow technology, and MasterCard's trusted brand, purchasing card platform, and global reach, the companies offer an online payment solution that enables businesses to complete transactions whether large or small, domestic or cross-border, in multiple currencies.

The service can be integrated with B2B exchanges and marketplaces, which currently (summer 2001) have no similar comprehensive online payment solution for handling different sizes and types of transactions. Businesses can pay for spot transactions, or track larger, more complicated corporate purchase orders through their transaction cycle and then pay for them when the contract terms have been satisfied. Companies are able to receive integrated payment information, including transaction-level detail, via secure Web access.

For more information, see *tradecard.com* (see the Global Trading Program; A video of "World Business Review" dealing with the program is available on *tradecard.com*). Also, see a detailed case study on TradeCard by Marissa McCuley at *business.hku.hk/ research.centers*.

Venture Capital to Fund E-Commerce Initiatives

The building of EC initiatives is often a costly undertaking that usually requires large amounts of capital over several years. This funding is frequently provided by outsiders. "Angel investors" and **venture capital (VC)** firms provide financial resources to Internet start-ups in exchange for a significant equity position (ownership). Angel investors are usually wealthy individuals who wish to pursue high-risk, high-potential-payoff investment opportunities. Angel investors are usually the initial funders of a new EC initiative. VC firms specialize in various funding stages, providing early seed money, bridge money to keep a start-up in operation until the IPO, or mezzanine-level funding immediately before the IPO. The process of funding a new EC project is summarized in Table 8-1.

Angel investors and VC firms take huge risks on unproven, potentially unprofitable business plans in order to achieve "the big payoff" from the one true winner in a bunch. Most of their investments are "burned" rapidly; several companies may reach the initial public offering (IPO), but only few will earn the angel or VC firm a lot of money.

INTERNET INCUBATORS

Internet incubators are companies that specialize in the development of EC initiatives. They provide some funding, serve on the board of directors, work with the EC development team, and more. They take a stake in the business, sometimes 50 percent or more. Once the business is running, the incubator team moves on to another company, leaving behind a small staff for management purposes.

TABLE 8-1

Stages of Growth and Financing for Business Start-Ups

Stage	Amount of Money and Purpose	Sources of Capital
Start-Up	Amount: Seed investments (less than $250K) Purpose: Initial business plan, identify sources of revenue and costs	• Family and friends • Angel investors • SBIC, SBIRs, etc.
First Round	Amount: Under $3 million Purpose: Initial management team, product line development	• Angel investors • Venture capital firms • Selected corporate investors • Initial revenues (as strategic investment)
Second Round	Amount: $3 to $10 million Purpose: Supporting infrastructure; sales, distribution, support, partners	• Venture capital firms • Corporations (technology focused)
Third Round or IPO	Amount: $25 million to hundreds of millions	• Largest venture capital firms • Corporations • Investment Banks (for IPO)

Source: Adapted from Marc Meyer's "Stages and Growth and Financing," *www.cba.neu.edu/~mmeyer/courses/ent3965/financing.htm*

Representative EC incubators are *raremedium.com*, *ecorporation.com*, *idealab.com*, and *ehatchery.com*. For B2B, one should look at CMGI Corp. (*cmgi.com*) and Internet Capital Group (*internetcapital.com*). Incubators have encountered numerous problems due to the failure of many EC start-ups (see Duvall and Guglielmo, 2000).

For more information about the venture capital business, consult the National Venture Capital Association at *nvca.org* or the Venture Capital Database at *infon.com*. Another resource for information about the venture capital industry and the funding process is the Venture Economics Division of Thomson Financial Securities Data (*ventureeconomics.com*). This site has valuable resources, including the *European Venture Capital Journal* (*evcj.com*), *Private Equity Week* (*privateequityweek.com*), and the *Venture Capital Journal* (*venturecapitaljournal.net*).

Tax Calculation Services

E-tailers face a bewildering patchwork of tax rules both nationally and internationally. In the United States alone, there are over 30,000 taxing jurisdictions. In some cases, food and clothing are exempt from sales taxes. In others, one or the other or both are taxed or are taxed only up to some level. In Massachusetts, for example, articles of clothing are free from sales tax up to the first $175, but the value over $175 is taxed at 5 percent. In many states, there is a statewide sales tax plus local (city and/or county) sales tax levies that range dramatically from one jurisdiction to another. Total sales taxes in the Denver area vary from under 4 percent to over 8 percent. Global EC sales add significantly to the sales tax confusion. There is a temporary sales tax moratorium on Internet sales within the United States, but it only applies if the seller has no physical presence (a store, a factory, or a distribution center) in the state of the buyer. Noncompliance with sales tax collection regulations can lead to fines and penalties. To further complicate matters, the tax rules are dynamic and most companies are not equipped to keep up with the hundreds of changes that can happen monthly.

In B2B, one must differentiate between a tax on final products and a tax on raw materials or semifinished products. In many countries such a distinction is made with a VAT (value added tax). To ease the problem of calculating taxes, both in B2B and in B2C, one can use tax services. Here are some example services:

- **DPC.** This company (at *Salestax.com*) licenses software that makes it simple to collect and report sales taxes. DPC promises that its software, which is updated monthly, reduces errors and puts its clients in compliance with the law. The company provides assistance with the integration of its databases into its client's systems, if necessary.
- **HotSamba.** This company is a B2B service provider that offers its customers (e-tailers and mail order catalog companies) CyberSource Payment Services and Tax Services. This software enables real-time credit card processing and sales tax calculations online.
- **Sales tax clearinghouse (STC).** The STC has a free online sales tax calculator for the United States and Canada at *thestc.com/RateCalc.stm*. Their licensed software module allows a merchant's NT- or Unix-based business system to connect to their server to calculate sales taxes and post transactions in real-time, online.

- **Taxware International.** This company (*taxware.com*) produces software that operates seamlessly with leading financial and accounting packages on multiple hardware platforms to accurately automate tax compliance. Its SALES/USE Tax System has a fully populated Product Taxability Matrix to ensure accurate tax calculation for all products sold on the Internet in all U.S. and Canadian tax jurisdictions. It also calculates European VAT and other tax rates around the world. This software can be integrated with the VERAZIP system, which matches state, zip code, city, and county information to assure that an address is correct so that the SALES/USE Tax System will be able to locate the correct taxing jurisdiction and tax rate.

IMPLEMENTING TAX COLLECTION IN THE UNITED STATES

In 2001, four U.S. states (Kansas, Michigan, North Carolina, and Wisconsin) tested an Internet-based tax calculation and remission system using software and services from several vendors as a cost-effective way to manage the complexities of the evolving tax code. The Streamlined Sales Tax Project (SSTP) is designed to create uniformity in the way states administer sales and use taxes. The SSTP project involves tax collection and management software from *Taxware.com*, *Vertex.com*, and *esalestax.com* that is being integrated by Pitney Bowes, Inc. and Hewlett-Packard. Merchants will send live sales transaction data in real-time, using the Internet, to one of four systems in the pilot. The system works as follows.

After a consumer initiates an online purchase, the e-business uses the Internet to access a trusted third-party tax service provider that calculates the tax on the purchase based on the locations of the buyer and the seller, as well as applicable state and local tax laws. The third party provides custom links, typically with XML, between its system and a commonly used ERP or EC platform, making it easier for retailers to connect to the system through the Internet.

For each client, the third party will make a single monthly or quarterly tax payment to a government tax authority. The tax authority would then securely access a database, managed by the third party over the Web, to examine the transaction data for tax compliance. The multistate approach—in which one or more third parties gets certified to manage tax compliance for businesses that choose to use the service rather than handle tax compliance alone—ultimately makes sense. Online merchants would also save money because the service provider would monitor changes in tax rules and change its compliance database accordingly. For further details see Tillett (2001) and Chapter 17.

Other Financial Services

Here are some examples:

- **Credit reporting firms.** Companies like Equifax have long served as independent sources of unbiased financial data. In the Internet economy, these firms deliver their data in machine-readable XML formats and tie them directly to digital certificates, as Dun & Bradstreet is doing with its *eccelerate.com* subsidiary.
- **New credit intermediaries broker credit risks.** With many B2B transactions including a credit component, firms such as *eCredit.com* play a key

role in the real-time selection of short-term financing. Using up-to-the-second data streams from information brokers, these new credit intermediaries connect sellers to institutions that will guarantee against financial loss.

- **Assurance firms guarantee quality.** For bulky goods or goods that are shipped long distances, buyers need to know the quality of goods before shipment. Underwriters use quality assurance firms like *segue.com* with its global network of testing laboratories, to vouch for the quality of goods and stand behind them with a guarantee.
- **Exchanges strike insurance deals.** In any given vertical industry, only a few exchanges are likely to survive. To increase liquidity and help ensure their own survival, leading exchanges are beginning to offer complete transaction guarantees to their members by purchasing insurance from underwriters and absorbing the costs in their transaction fees.
- **E-credit services.** *Ecredit.com* offers a variety of services to business, including verification checks of customer data, automated credit analysis, automated collections management, and more.

Transaction-Based Financing at *eRevenue.com*

One company, eRevenue (*eRevenue.com*), is providing a key service at a critical point in the procurement process—a transaction-based finance (TBF) solution for e-marketplaces. This solution enables sellers to make the decision to receive payment at the time of the transaction, without having to convince buyers to alter their payment cycles.

eRevenue focuses on the value proposition of B2B that is centered around shortening cycle times in procuring goods and services. Financial incentives exist for buyers to leverage the increased efficiencies of shorter cycle times, except in the

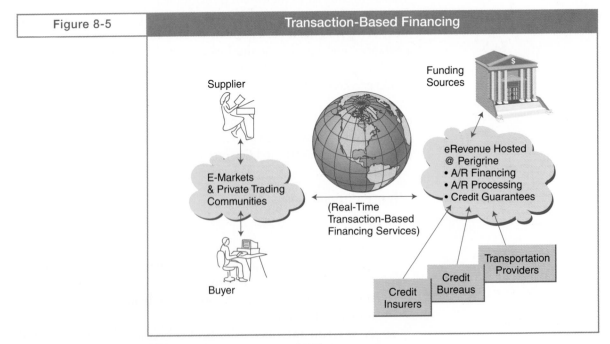

Figure 8-5   **Transaction-Based Financing**

Source: Aberdeen Group, Inc. November 2000

payment cycle where buyers benefit from the float. eRevenue enables sellers to overcome this dynamic without alienating their customers.

The company combines both front-and back-office operations with credit administration delivered as a hosted service by ASPs. eRevenue offers an integrated and customizable online transaction-based receivables financing solution for suppliers that has the potential to significantly enhance the traditional batched-invoice financing model. In turn, eRevenue enables suppliers to exchange their invoices for funds at the time an online transaction occurs, as well as support transactions that occur off-line. eRevenue's model also integrates both the technology enablers that create and supply EC platforms and the funding partners that are responsible for financing the invoices. As a result, eRevenue's solution integrates financing for accounts receivable directly into the buy/sell transaction process. For details see Aberdeen (2000).

8.7   ORDER FULFILLMENT, LOGISTICS, AND SUPPLY CHAIN SERVICES

In the early days of EC, many entrepreneurs put all their energies into the design of the front end, or what is termed the "customer-facing" system. The "pick and pack and ship" function was viewed as a necessary, but uninteresting business process. However, it is now clear that the back-end systems, from sophisticated customer database functions to the mundane jobs of putting products into boxes and shipping them, are critical to the overall success of EC. Some firms, such as *Amazon.com*, handle order fulfillment internally but outsource the job of outbound logistics (delivery services) to common carriers, such as UPS, FedEx, and other shippers.

Order fulfillment is related to other logistics services as well as to the supply chain. These topics are described in Chapter 15, mostly from a B2C point of view. Here we present the topic from a B2B perspective. To understand the complexity of B2B fulfillment, let's look at the services provided by the UPS Logistics Group as shown in Application Case 8.4.

APPLICATION CASE   8.4

UPS Logistics Group

UPS Logistics Group offers a full spectrum of supply chain solutions. The group can design, re-engineer, and manage all parts of a supply chain. Solutions teams include industrial engineers, software systems integrators and developers, facility designers, operations managers, high-tech repair technicians, logisticians, and transportation, financial, EC, and international trade experts. Services include:

- **Supply chain management.** Provides for the re-engineering and managing of complex supply chains—from supplier through manufacturer, distributor, dealer, and/or direct to the consumer.
- **Transportation services.** Manages complex transportation networks, dedicated fleets, carriers, and multimodel shipments.

APPLICATION CASE **8.4**

(continued)

- **Parts distribution.** Provides comprehensive return-and-repair and parts distribution operations for a wide variety of industries.
- **Logistics technologies.** Provides for the integration of logistics information systems and services to provide supply chain visibility.
- **EC solutions.** Offers logistics services to Web-based businesses worldwide.
- **Global services.** Provides logistics facilities, staffing, and expertise to pave the way for global commerce.
- **Call center services.** Provides customer care and communications from call center services to EC capabilities.
- **Financial services.** Through UPS Capital, UPS offers a full range of financial services to complement logistics, transportation, and additional business needs. In addition, a variety of customized services are provided.

    UPS Logistics offers a number of solutions for EC initiatives, including:

    - Tracking systems
    - Product return systems
    - Shipping solutions
    - Electronic document exchange
    - Customization of EC software in conjunction with EC software providers

For more information on B2B logistics visit any of the following sites.

- *Biz2biztransportation.com/marketplace*
- *Lawdistribution.co.uk*
- *V-line.com*, (procurement)
- *Usps.com*, (look at news releases)
- *FedEx.com*, (look at vendor services)

8.8 MARKETING AND ADVERTISEMENT

B2B marketing is completely different from B2C marketing, which we introduced in Chapters 3 through 5. In Chapter 4 we also discussed the corporate purchaser's decision making. Major differences also exist between B2B and B2C with respect to the nature of the demand and the trading process (see Coupey, 2001 for details).

Off-line marketers use the following advertisement methods:

- Vertical trade shows to exhibit products
- Advertisements in industry magazines
- E-mail and paper catalogs to advertise products/services.
- Salespeople call on existing customers and potential buyers.

In the digital world, these approaches may not be effective, feasible, or economical. Some of the B2C marketing and advertisement tools and approaches are applicable to B2B, but most of them are not. Organizations are using a variety of other online methods, many of which are presented in this section.

When a B2C niche e-tailer tries to attract its audience of skiers or musicians or cosmetic customers, it may often advertise in traditional media targeted to those audiences, such as magazines or television shows. But when a B2B service provider wants to grow by adding new customers, it may not have a reliable, known advertising channel. How will it reach its potential customers? A B2B company, whether an operator of a trading exchange or a provider of digital real-time services, can contact all of its targeted customers individually when they are part of a well-defined group. For example, to attract companies to an exchange for auto supplies, one might use information from industry trade association records or industry magazines to identify potential customers.

Another method of bringing new customers to a B2B site is through an *affiliation service* (see Section 8.9), which operates just as a B2C affiliate programs does. A company pays a small commission every time the affiliation company "drives traffic" to its site. For more on online B2B marketing see Coupey (2001) and *b2business.net*.

An important part of any marketing effort is advertisement. Several of the methods presented in Chapter 5 are applicable to B2B. An additional advertisement tool available for B2B is an ad server network provider.

Ad Server Network Provider

An important technical and business function often outsourced to a specialist is ad serving. An **adserver** (also spelled Ad server) **network provider** is a company that brokers banner ad sales, bringing together online advertisers and providers of online advertising space, while targeting the ads to consumers who are presumed to be interested in categories of advertisements based on technology-based profiling. Ad server networks provide a powerful service to both parties that exceeds the simple economic brokerage function.

DoubleClick is the premier ad server network provider. DoubleClick servers post banner ads millions of times per day (see Rothenberg, 1999). In Chapter 5 we provided an example of how DoubleClick arranged for a 3M ad to reach business buyers by profiling certain users and then directing one-to-one ads to them. Other ad servers are Accepter, Ad Force, Ad Juggler, Banager, Bondsmith, Central Ad, NetGravity, and OrbitCycle. Doubleclick's method works for both B2B and for B2C. The architecture of ad servers in general is illustrated in Figure 8-6.

Electronic Wholesalers

One of the interesting new B2B ventures is the e-wholesaler. This kind of intermediary sells directly to businesses. An example is *bigboxx.com* described in Chapter 7.

8.9   AFFILIATE PROGRAMS, INFOMEDIARIES, AND DATA MINING

Affiliate Programs

The concept of B2C affiliation services was introduced in Chapters 1 through 3. There are several types of **affiliate programs**. In the simplest one, which is used extensively in B2C, affiliates are invited to put a banner of a vendor such as

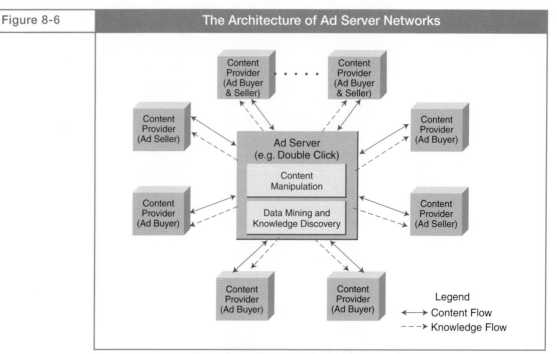

Figure 8-6 — The Architecture of Ad Server Networks

Source: Warkentin, Merrill, Vijayan Sugumaran, and Ravi Bapna. "eKnowledge Networks for Inter-Organizational Collaborative eBusiness," *Logistics Information Management,* Vol. 14, No. 1/2, March 2001, pp. 149–162. Used with permission of MCB University Press.

Amazon.com or CDNow on their sites. Whenever a consumer clicks on the vendor's banner, the consumer brings up that company's EC site. A commission is paid to the affiliate if the customer makes a purchase. The same method works for B2B. However, with B2B, there are other types of affiliate programs.

SchaefferResearch.com offers a content alliance program to financial institutions. In Chapter 5, we described banner exchanges among businesses. Such exchanges can dramatically increase exposure (e.g., see linkexchange at *bcentral.com*). An interesting affiliate program is also offered by Commerce One (see Real-World Case at the end of this chapter). Other programs are offered by *linkshare.com*. For more on affiliate programs see Gary and Gary (1999). Note that not all affiliate programs are successful. For some unsuccessful ones see Cross (2000).

Infomediaries and Online Data Mining Services

Marketing managers need to understand their customers and potential customers. They need to evaluate customers' shopping behavior in order to understand how to advertise or approach customers in the future. Traditional B2C retailers evaluate point-of-sale (POS) data (e.g., grocery scanner data) and other available data (e.g., grocery membership club information) in order to generate valuable marketing information. In today's online environment, there is more relevant information than ever before, but the potential of the information can only be realized if the **clickstream data**, data collected by monitoring what people do online (see Chapter 12 for Web usage), can be analyzed and mined to produce useful knowledge that can be used to improve services and marketing efforts. A new intermediary is emerging to provide such services to Web site owners who do not have the specialized knowledge and systems to perform such data mining on their own. These B2C and B2B service providers are called infomediaries.

An **infomediary** is a business that collects data about consumer behavior, analyzes and repackages it, and sells the resulting information for marketing and profiling purposes. Infomediaries are also in the business of buying and selling customer information, mostly for the purpose of increasing customer loyalty. Infomediaries start by manipulating existing information until new, useful information is extracted from it. This new information is sold to B2B customers or exchanged for more information, which is manipulated yet again, until even more valuable information can be extracted.

Vendors use the information from infomediaries to identify likely buyers with much greater precision than ever before—leading to increased sales and drastically reduced marketing expenses.

Some infomediaries are involved in consumer intelligence gathering—consumers agree to use a software agent that will evaluate their clickstream data (for profiling purposes) in exchange for receiving some service. Other infomediaries capture the data from a server with the knowledge or permission of the customer, and act as a provider of real-time data mining services, which can then be used to target banner ads, determine what products to display, or to personalize each individual's Web page. These services are available mainly for B2C, but can be used for B2B as well. One of the first infomediaries was NetPerceptions, which provides its services to retailers and others. By using infomediary technology and information, a retailer can create demand, improve merchandising programs, and optimize marketing strategies.

Infomediaries provide several B2B services, and firms can use these services to extend their ability to execute their EC strategy successfully. Representative infomediaries and data mining specialists are *sas.com*, NetTracker, WebTrends, NetIntellect, HitList, and SurfReport. For an example of data mining see Application Case 8.5. See Chapter 4 for more information on data mining.

APPLICATION CASE   8.5

How Free Trade Zone Mines Data

Free Trade Zone (FTZ, *freetradezone.com*) uses data mining technology to locate hard-to-find electronic components, and then brokers them to needy manufacturers in what is known as spot marketing. The company uses PartMiners technology for this task. Using standard browsers, buyers can post RFQs on the site, then conduct reverse auctions to find bidders with the lowest price. The software also includes order entry and tracking, shipping scheduling, data exchange, and invoicing. FTZ provides for auctions and price negotiations using XML and Java. Data are easily exchanged with back-end systems that contain inventory and other procurement information.

(continued)

The following table from PartMiner shows how FTZ is changing business and procurement processes in the electronics industry.

Process	Before	After
RFQs and responses	RFQs mailed/faxed to likely suppliers; responses mailed/faxed back	RFQs posted to the Web for all suppliers to view; responses posted electronically
Purchasing	Suppliers chosen based on bids; orders faxed or re-entered into purchasing system	Reverse auction lets buyer find low bid quickly and place orders online
Purchase orders, shipping invoicing	Traditional EDI value-added network	Real-time or EDI documents shared via Web
Data exchange between customer, supplier	Interconnection of disparate applications	Web-hosted application service requires no special software

The service combines an electronic marketplace, content aggregation, and hosting application services.

Source: Compiled from *freetradezone.com*.

Other Marketing Services

Several other marketing services exist. Here are just three examples:

- **Digitalcement.com.** This service provides corporate marketing portals that help corporations build stronger relationships with their business customers. Digital Cement portals help companies put their products into the context of business management solutions. As a result, 10 percent of the material viewed is client content and product information. In essence, what this company does is provide content tailored to the client's customer base for a fee. The company has posted several papers on its site that advocate utilizing a *private label* content approach versus partnering with a branded dot.com that will give you content for free, but also may take away your customers.
- **BusinessTown.com.** This company provides information and services to small businesses including start ups. It includes a directory of businesses in over 20 industries, information on functional areas (accounting, finance, legal, marketing), and business planning advice. Although much of the offering deals with intrabusiness and B2C, there are several directories and information sources relevant to B2B.
- **Freepolls.com.** This vendor offers free tools that help increase traffic to a company's Web site. These tools range from horoscopes to guest books.

8.10   CONTENT GENERATION, SYNDICATION, DELIVERY, AND MANAGEMENT

Providing content to EC sites may be a complex job because of the variety and quantity of sources from which content is acquired, and the fact that the content must frequently be updated (see Chapter 10 in Coupey, 2001). The latter requirement is referred to as **dynamic content**. Also, B2B content, especially catalogs, must include pictures, diagrams, and even sound. The major content categories are:

- Information about the company, products, services, customers, investor relations, press releases, and so on.
- Information provided to the B2B community, such as industry news. This is especially important in exchanges.
- Detailed product information provided in electronic catalogs, which are sometimes personalized for major customers.
- Customers' personalized Web pages
- Other content

For each type of content, companies may use a different approach for content creation and delivery. Let's look at the life cycle of content (Figure 8-7) and discuss some of its elements.

Syndication

In Chapter 2 we introduced the concept of **syndication**. The basic idea is that knowledge creators can use syndicators to distribute the creator's content to a large number of delivery companies who then provide it to the end customer (see *isyndicate.com*). The financial industry often uses syndicated content. The syndication approach is appropriate for the second type of content listed earlier (community-type content).

The concept of syndication can be used in marketing and sales as well (see Real-World Case at end of chapter). In the Real-World Case, **reverse syndication** was feasible. B2B exchanges were syndicating information for the syndicator, Commerce One.

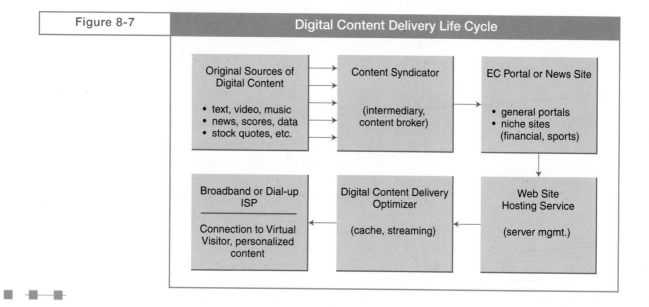

| Figure 8-7 | Digital Content Delivery Life Cycle |

Original Sources of Digital Content
- text, video, music
- news, scores, data
- stock quotes, etc.

Content Syndicator
(intermediary, content broker)

EC Portal or News Site
- general portals
- niche sites (financial, sports)

Web Site Hosting Service
(server mgmt.)

Digital Content Delivery Optimizer
(cache, streaming)

Broadband or Dial-up ISP
Connection to Virtual Visitor, personalized content

Thousands of consumer-oriented Web sites provide free dynamic content to their visitors. This content may be daily news, sports, weather, or stock quotes, or it may be specialized information, such as the snow reports from various ski resorts. The content may be text, graphics, or sound, such as music or streaming audio. It may also be in the public domain or proprietary in nature. The sites may be general-purpose consumer portals, such as Yahoo! or Lycos. Or they may be specialized portals designed to appeal to a specific audience, such as *ESPN.com* or *Ski.com*. Up-to-the-minute dynamic content is what attracts new and returning customers ("eyeballs") and makes them stay longer ("stickiness"); therefore, dynamic content contributes to customer loyalty. For banner-ad-supported Web sites, the dynamic content may be the primary draw for a site. For transactional sites (one selling ski equipment, for example), the dynamic content may be the distinguishing factor bringing certain customers back repeatedly.

In addition to generic content, Web sites may have proprietary content, such as information about the company and its products and services.

Content-Delivery Networks (CDNs)

Content delivery is a service that is sometimes offered by hosting companies to help their customers manage their content. Using content delivery networks (CDNs), companies can update content, improve the quality of the site, increase consistency, control content, and decrease the time needed to create or maintain a site. CDNs are provided by *allaire.com*, *mediasurface.com*, and Akamai. The case of Akamai is discussed later in this section.

In B2B, the information contained in electronic catalogs is of extreme importance. Companies create and maintain the content or they can use services to do it. Let's see how the process works.

Catalog Content

Much of the content in B2B and B2C sites is catalog-based content. In Chapter 5 we discussed the benefits of electronic catalogs. Although there are many positive aspects of electronic catalogs, poorly organized catalogs may deter buyers. Companies need to make sure that their catalog content is well managed. For buyers who aggregate suppliers' catalogs on their own Web site, **content management** begins with engaging suppliers and then collecting, standardizing, classifying, hosting, and continually updating their catalog data. That's no small task, considering that most large buying organizations have hundreds of suppliers, each using different data formats and nomenclature to describe their catalog items. Specifically, catalog content management is costly and complex for the following reasons:

- Existing catalog content is often paper-based; or even if it's in electronic form, the content is usually not ready for dynamic EC.
- Content is in different and often incompatible formats.
- There is very little standardization in the way products are described, even for the same commodity or by the same supplier.
- Product information is rarely categorized or classified.
- Frequent changes can be expected.
- Description information must be combined with contract-critical information, such as negotiated pricing, for each buying organization.

CONTENT MANAGEMENT OPTIONS

Companies have five basic options to manage catalog content:

1. **Do it yourself.** This option is satisfactory for small buyers with few suppliers or large buyers that buy from few suppliers. The per line item is about $30. The cost for a catalog containing a large number of products can easily be $1 million or more for the first year.

2. **Let the suppliers do it.** Most suppliers do not like to modify their catalogs to meet the buyers' format. A few suppliers may agree to meet the buyer's format, but not all of them. This solution is not feasible when many suppliers are involved.

3. **Buy the content from an aggregator.** Some companies standardize and aggregate content across industries. The result may be in a standard format that large buyers want. The buyers then host the content on their servers. For smaller companies that can host and manage content, this is a viable option. The problem is that the content is not customized to the buyer's needs. Furthermore, the buyer is expected to keep the catalogs up-to-date. Also, updating through aggregators can be expensive.

4. **Subscribe to a vertical exchange.** Vertical exchanges can be an excellent solution for occasional spot buys and for one or few commodities. The problem here is that one buyer may need to visit many exchanges to find everything it needs. Finally, most vertical exchanges do not usually offer customized views or negotiated prices, nor do they enable integration with a buying organization's e-procurement applications.

5. **Outsource to a full-service Internet exchange.** A full-service exchange connects many suppliers with many buyers and offers comprehensive catalog services such as:

- Supplier engagement and data hosting
- Cleansed, standardized, and categorized supplier catalog content
- Online content maintenance and update tools
- Classification of data using a common classification system (e.g., that of Thomas Register)
- Easy creation and management of trading partner contracts
- Robust search capabilities, including quick searches, category browsing, and advanced parametric (attribute-based) searches
- Buyer specific "virtual private catalogs" with negotiated pricing information
- Access to an extensive sourcing marketplace for strategic unplanned buying
- Seamless integration with ERP and other Internet procurement systems or Web portals using a single sign-on

This option may be expensive and it may be difficult to find an exchange that will meet all the special needs of every buyer. One exchange to consider is *atcost.com*.

So far we have discussed the role of intermediaries and other third-party B2B providers in channeling digital content to the sites that display that content to consumers. Now, we will address the next step in the content delivery chain, the task of optimizing and delivering digital content to customers.

Content Maximization and Streaming Services

Many companies provide media rich content, such as video clips, music, or flash media, in an effort to reach their target audience with an appealing marketing message. For example, automakers want to provide a virtual driving experience as seen from the car's interior, realtors want to provide 360 degree views of their properties, and music sellers want to provide easily downloadable samples of their songs. Public portals and others are using considerable amounts of media rich information as well. Finally, B2B e-catalogs may include thousands of photos. These and other content providers are concerned about the download time from the user's perspective. Fickle Web surfers may click "Stop" even before the multimedia has had a chance to be fully downloaded. Remember that B2C and B2B customers not only want their news stories, music, video clips, reference information, financial information, and sports scores delivered to them over the Web, they want them to be delivered fast and effortlessly. Therefore, it is important that content providers and marketers use technical delivery solutions that will not cause "traffic jams" during the download process. Several technical solutions are available from vendors who are referred to as content maximizers and/or streaming services. One such vendor is Akamai (see Application Case 8.6).

APPLICATION CASE 8.6

Akamai Corporation

An Internet company decided to name itself after the Hawaiian word meaning "intelligent, clever, or cool"—Akamai (ah-kuh-my). And indeed, the company has created a clever product. Let's explain.

As user interest in high-speed Internet connections grows, demand for bandwidth-heavy applications and media has also begun to surge. It is estimated that revenues from streaming media services will total $1.2 billion by 2002 and $12 billion by 2008. In addition, the interactive broadcast video market will reach $4.2 billion by 2005. Finally, streaming video is estimated to grow to over $1 billion by 2005.

But user connection speeds are only part of the streaming media picture. How will the networks themselves handle the influx of bandwidth-chewing material? With a growing number of users and an abundance of rich media, the Internet is becoming extremely congested. So now there is a need for network traffic control. Akamai and its competitors (Digital Island, Ibeam, Mirror Image) are managing Internet traffic.

Akamai products act as Internet traffic cops by using complicated mathematical algorithms to speed Web pages from the closest Akamai-owned server to a customer's location—thereby passing through fewer router hops. This process also helps to eliminate Internet gridlock. Today, caching and content distribution are the only practical way to reduce network delay.

How does it work? To provide the service, Akamai maintains a global network of thousands of servers and leases space on them to giant portals as such as Yahoo! and CNN. These sites use the servers to store graphic-rich information closer to Internet users' computers and circumvent Web traffic jams. Akamai allows customer data to move to and from big Web sites through its global network for a fee (in 2001 it was $2,500 for setup and

(continued)

$5,500/month per data center). Savings are in reducing delivery time by 20 to 30 percent. For example, when a user visits a Web site, all its multimedia objects must be downloaded from a Web server. If a company's Web server is located in Germany and a user in the United States visits the Web site, the multimedia content of the site have to be transmitted halfway around the globe. Akamai's *FreeFlow* technology speeds the delivery of images, multimedia, and other Web content by placing that content on servers worldwide. Using the FreeFlow Launcher, Web site designers "Akamaize" their site by marking content to be delivered using the Akamai network. FreeFlow takes this content and stores it on Akamai Web servers around the world. When a user visits a Web site that has been "Akamaized," the images and multimedia content are downloaded from an Akamai server near the user for faster content delivery.

Unfortunately, the service is not 100 percent reliable.

The speed for the end user depends upon how many people are using the local area network at any given point in time, and also on the speed of the server downloading any given Web site. There are competing technologies that try to provide the same solutions and only a limited number of large companies that use lots of rich media are willing to pay for the service. Akamai and its competitors were losing money in early 2001, but their revenues were increasing rapidly.

8.11   DIRECTORY SERVICES, SEARCH ENGINES, AND NEWSLETTERS

The B2B landscape is huge, with hundreds of thousands of companies online. How can a buyer find all suitable sellers? How can a seller find all suitable buyers? Vertical exchanges can help, but they include only a limited number of potential partners, usually located in one country. Several solutions to this problem are available. The most notable are directory services.

Directory Services

There are several types of directory services. Some just list companies by categories, others provide links to companies. In many cases the data are classified in several different ways for easy search purposes. In others, special search engines are provided. Finally, value-added services such as matching buyers and sellers are available. Here are some popular directories.

- **B2Business.net.** This site is a major resource for B2B professionals. It includes listings of business resources in about 30 functional areas, company research resources (e.g., credit checks, customs research, financial reviews), information on start-ups (business plans, domain names, recruiting, patents, incubators, and even a graveyard), general EC information (e.g., books, articles, reports, events, research, e-marketplace listings (e.g., enablers and builders, services, support services, major markets), and infrastructure resources (e.g., security, connectivity, catalogues, content, portal builders, and ASPs).
- **B2BToday.com.** This directory contains listings of B2B services organized by type of service (e.g., Web site creation, B2B marketing, and B2B

software) and product category (e.g., automotive, books). Each part of the directory highlights several companies at the start of the list that pay extra fees to be listed on the top; after the premium slots, the directory is organized in alphabetical order. The directory listings are hyperlinked to the companies' Web sites. Many of the sites are involved in B2C.

- **Communityb2b.com.** This site offers many B2B community services, such as news, a library, events calendar, job market, resource directory, and more.
- **A2zofb2b.com.** This is a directory of B2B companies organized in alphabetical order or industry order. It specifies the type and nature of the company, the VC sponsor, and the stock market ticker (if it is an IPO).
- **I-stores.co.uk.** This is a UK-based directory that targets online stores. The company provides validation of secure Web sites.
- **Websteronline.com.** This is a large business directory organized by location, SIC/NAICS codes, and by product or service. In addition, it provides listings by industry and subindustry (according to SIC code).
- **Thomasregister.com.** This site provides a directory of more than 150,000 manufacturers of industrial products and services.
- **Bocal.com.** This is a comprehensive B2B guide for marketers, market places, directories, news, auctions, and much more.
- **b2b.yahoo.com.** B2BYahoo! provides business directories and has over 250,000 listed companies (in 2001).

Search Engines and News Aggregators

Several search engines can be used to discover information about B2B. Some of these are embedded in the directories. Let's look at some examples.

- **Moreover.com.** This search engine not only locates information for you, but it aggregates B2B (and other business) news.
- **Google.com.** This search engine offers a directory of components for B2B and B2C Web sites. These range from currency exchange calculators to server performance monitors (see *directory.google.com*).
- **Ientry.com.** This site provides B2B search engines, targeted "niche engines," and several industry-focused newsletters. iEntry operates a network of Web sites and e-mail newsletters that reaches over 2,000,000 unique opt-in subscribers. There are multiple newsletters available in each of the following categories: Web Developers, Advice, Technology, Professional, Sports & Entertainment, Leisure & Lifestyles, and Web Entrepreneurs. Click on a newsletter to get a brief description and a sample of content.

Newsletters

There are many B2B newsletters to choose from. Several can be e-mailed to individuals free of charge. Examples of B2B newsletters are *emarketer.com/newsletters* (look for B2B Weekly) and *line56.com*. For information about the ASP businesses (Chapter 12) see *ASPNews.com*. This site has news and resources for the ASP industry. Many companies issue corporate newsletters and e-mail them to people who ask to receive them (e.g., Ariba, Intel). Also, companies can use *biz2bizpress.com* to send online press releases to thousands of editors.

8.12   E-COMMUNITIES AND PARTNER RELATIONSHIP MANAGEMENT

E-Communities

B2B applications involve many participants: buyers and sellers, service providers, industry associations, and others. Thus, in many cases the B2B application creates a community, such as in exchanges. Moreover, even in the case of a company-centric market, communities are likely to be formed. In such cases, the B2B application needs to provide community services such as chat rooms, bulletin boards, and possibly personalized Web pages. A detailed list of such services is provided in Chapter 18.

According to the Delphi Group (*Delphigroup.com*), **e-communities** are connecting personnel, partners, customers, and any combination of the three. The facilitation of e-communities offers a powerful resource for e-businesses to leverage online discussions and interaction to maximize innovation and responsiveness. It is therefore beneficial to study the tools, methods, and best practices of building and managing e-communities.

Although the technological support of B2B e-communities is basically the same as for any other online community (for a list and discussion see Chapter 18), the nature of the community itself, and the information provided by the community, is different.

B2B e-communities are basically *communities of transactions,* and as such, the major interest of the members is trading. Most of the communities are associated with vertical exchanges; therefore, their needs may be fairly specific. However, it is common to find generic services such as classified ads, job vacancies, announcements, industry news, and so on. Service providers are also available for the design of exchange portals and their community services.

Partner Relationship Management (PRM)

Successful e-businesses carefully manage partners, prospects, and customer touch-points across the entire value chain, most often in a 24/7 environment. Therefore, one should examine the role of e-service solutions and technology in creating an integrated online environment for engaging e-business customers and partners. These activities appear under two names: CRM and PRM.

In Chapter 4 we introduced the concept of CRM in the B2C environment. Here our interest shifts to a situation where the customer is a business. Many of the customer service features of B2C are also used in B2B. For example, it may be beneficial to provide customers with a chat room and a discussion board. A Web-based call center may also be useful.

Corporate customers may require additional services. For example, customers need to have access to the supplier's inventory status report so they know what items can be delivered fast. Customers may want to see their historical purchasing records, and they may need private show and trade rooms. Large numbers of vendors are available for designing and building appropriate B2B CRM solutions. This type of e-service is sometimes called **partner relationship management** (PRM).

Customers are only one category of business partners. Suppliers, partners in joint ventures, service providers, and others are also part of the B2B community in an exchange or company-centric B2B initiative.

Implementing PRM is different from implementing CRM with individual customers. Behavioral and psychological aspects of the relationships are less important in B2B, but trust, commitment, quality of services, and continuity are more important. For details see Coupey (2001) and Cannon and Perreault (1999).

A STRATEGY FOR E-SERVICE

PRM requires a significant investment and offers intangible returns. Therefore, companies need a strategy to determine how much to invest in e-services and what services to provide. Voss (2000) researched this area mainly with regard to B2C. However, the methodology suggested, and some of the results, are applicable to B2B. For some interesting insights see Chapter 16, Sections 16.5 and 16.8.

8.13 OTHER B2B SERVICES

Many other B2B service providers support e-commerce in different ways. Each service provider adds a unique value-added service. Therefore, the economic models of these companies vary considerably, as does the maturity and formality of their interaction. This section describes representative examples.

- **Trust services.** Chapter 4 introduced the role of trust in B2C. Trust is also important in B2B since one cannot touch the products sold, and since buyers may not be known to sellers. Some of the trust-support services that are used in B2C but can also be used in B2B are trust ratings services such as TRUSTe, BBBOnline, and Ernst & Young's trust service.
- **Trademark and domain names.** A number of domain name services are available to B2B companies. Some companies offering these services are *register-internet-domain.com.com*, *register.com*, *easyspace.com*, and *virtualavenue.com*.
- **Digital photos.** Companies such as *ipix.com* provide innovative pictures for Web sites.
- **Global business communities.** The eCommerce Portal from *wiznet.net* is a global, Web-based "business community" that supports the unique requirements of buying organizations, including cross-catalogue searches, RFQ development and distribution, and decision support, while simultaneously enabling suppliers to dictate the content and presentation of their own product catalogues.
- **Client matching.** *Techrepublic.com* matches clients with firms that provide a wide variety of information technology services. It works like a match-making service. Clients define what it is they want and *Techrepublic.com* performs the searching and screening, checking against some general parameters and criteria. This reduces the risk of making bad decisions. Buyers also save time and have greater exposure to a larger number of IT service providers.
- **E-business rating sites.** A number of services are available for businesses to research rankings of potential partners and suppliers. *Bizrate.com*, *forrester.com*, *Gomez.com*, and ShopNow all provide business ratings.
- **Promotion programs.** Some promotion programs of interest to B2B include NetCentives, ClickRewards, AirMiles, eCentives, and MyPoints.

Other B2B Services

TABLE 8-2

Category	Description	Examples
Marketplace Concentrator (aggregator)	Aggregates information about products and services from multiple providers at one central point. Purchasers can search, compare, shop, and sometimes complete the sales transaction.	InternetMall, DealerNet, InsureMarket, Industrial Marketplace
Information Brokers (infomediaries)	Provide product, pricing, and availability information. Some facilitate transactions, but their main value is the information they provide.	PartNet, Travelocity, Auto-by-Tel
Transaction Brokers	Buyers can view rates and terms, but the primary business activity is to complete the transaction.	E*Trade, Ameritrade
Digital Product Delivery	Sells and delivers software, multimedia, and other digital products over the Internet.	Build-a-Card, PhotoDisc, SonicNet
Content Provider	Creates revenue by providing content. The customer may pay to access the content, or revenue may be generated by selling advertising space of by having advertisers pay for placement in an organized listing in a searchable database.	*Wall Street Journal*, Interactive, *Quote.com*, Tripod
Online Service Provider	Provides service and support for hardware and software users.	Cyber Media, *TuneUp.com*

- **Encryption sites.** VeriSign provides valuable encryption tools for B2B and B2C organizations.
- **Web research services.** There are a number of Web research providers that can help companies learn more about technologies, trends, and potential business partners and suppliers. Some of these are MMXI, WebTrack, IDG, ZDNet, and Forrester.
- **Coupon-generating sites.** A number of companies can provide online coupons. Some of these are *Q-pon.com*, *CentsOff.com*, LifeMinders, and *TheFreeSite.com*.

Additional services available for B2B operations are given in Table 8-2. In Appendix 8A we list some representative companies and other services described in this chapter. (Appendix 8A is on the book's Web site).

8.14   INTEGRATION AND HYPERMEDIATION

We conclude this chapter with two interesting issues: integration of service provision and hypermediation.

Integration in E-Marketplaces and Exchanges

In this chapter we presented several value-added services. In other chapters we provide some more. These services need to interact with each other. In exchanges the integration of such services becomes very important.

One model of such integration is shown in Figure 8-8. It was proposed by *keenanvision.com* (April 24, 2000 report). According to this model, **B2X** hubs connect all the Internet business services, the e-merchant services, the exchange infrastructure, buying and selling, member enterprises, and other B2X exchanges. Commerce One and Global World Trade can be viewed as types of B2X hubs. (see Real-World Case at the end of this chapter).

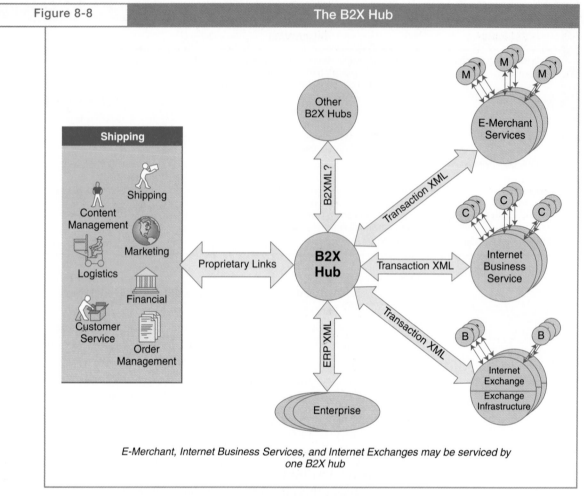

Source: Compiled from "B2B Exchanges," Internet Exchange 2000 at *Keenanvision.com*, April 24, 2000.

Hypermediation

Initially, many thought that the Internet would do away with the middleman. The presumption was that the producers of goods and services would use their Web sites to connect directly with consumers, bypassing wholesalers and retailers altogether. This presumption has proved to be incorrect in most cases. With few exceptions, manufacturers have not been able to do much direct selling over the Web. In the virtual world, as in the physical world, people want a broad selection of goods when they go shopping; they don't want to be limited to a single product line. Therefore, transactions over the Web, even very small ones, routinely involve all sorts of intermediaries—not just the familiar wholesalers and retailers, but content providers, affiliate sites, search engines, portals, ISPs, software makers, and many other entities that haven't been named yet. This phenomenon has been labeled by Carr (2000a) as **hypermediation**. The middlemen who manage the hypermediation will be in a position to capture most of the profits.

So what does hypermediation mean for the future of EC? Some argue that the lion's share of the profits in EC will likely flow to two very different types of intermediaries: content providers and deliverers and e-infrastructure providers.

8.15   MANAGERIAL ISSUES

The following issues are germane to management:

1. **Which services and to what level?** The large number of B2B services and the levels and options offered by each of them creates a complex decision situation for management. While the use of metrics can help, in most cases they may not be available in a particular industry. Companies should look at what the competition is doing. Talking to vendors can also provide some useful direction. Reading white papers, consultant publications, and trade magazines can be most helpful. If all else fails, a company should call a reputable EC management consultant.

2. **Selecting service providers.** This is a difficult task, especially when there are so many service providers to choose from. Selecting the "big" names can add safety, but may be expensive and even ineffective when a company's situation is very specialized. Public ratings and rankings of different service providers against different criteria is done by several magazines, and some are available online. Managers should talk to others in the industry, examine the growth rate of the business of the provider (especially if it is a public company), or just try the vendor by giving it a small project first.

3. **E-infrastructure.** A company will spend a large part of its outsourcing funds on e-infrastructure. Chapter 12 provides details on vendor selection and management.

4. **Joint ventures.** A company should look for potential partnerships with a service provider, especially in e-infrastructure and e-process. By relinquishing some equity, a company may get a devoted partner. Also, vendors are frequently looking for sites where they can beta test products and services. A company may have a chance to create a delivery company together with a vendor and provide services for others in the business community.

5. **End-to-end outsourcing vs. best-of-breed.** Some service providers offer complete, end-to-end service. A company going this route will deal with only one vendor. The problem in this case is that some of the services are not the best or the company uses unreliable partners. Using different vendors in the best-of-breed approach may create coordination and connectivity problems, as well as maintenance problems. The costs of the best-of-breed approach may also be high. Deciding between the two methods is difficult.

Summary

In this chapter, you learned about the following EC issues as they relate to the learning objectives:

1. **The major B2B services.** These services include: e-infrastructure (consultants, system developers, standards developers); Web hosting, security and network services; e-process (payments, financial services, logistics, supply chain integrators); e-markets (sales, advertisement, marketing programs); e-content (syndicators and catalog management); e-service (CRM, PRM, and directory services); e-community (designers, builders); and e-management and analysis.

2. **Outsourced services.** The major reasons services are outsourced is because of a lack of in-house expertise, the need for fast implementation, an inability to

keep up with fast moving technologies, the need to meet the unpredictable, and fast changing demands and costs.

3. **The role and types of e-strategy consultants.** Consultants help a company to create the EC mission, goals, and plans, and their alignment with the business's strategy. The large CPA and management consultant firms provide such services as do thousands of small management and IT consultants. Finally, there are consultants who specialize only in EC strategy and implementation.

4. **Understand the infrastructure-building process.** Building EC applications can be lengthy and complex when done in-house. Frequently, several vendors are needed to implement different parts of the initiative. Web hosting is a viable option, even for large companies. Finally, integration is a major issue as well as development of standards, primarily XML.

5. **Payments and financial services.** Fast and convenient payment systems are needed, especially with buyers that the sellers are unfamiliar with. In addition to purchasing cards and e-letters of credit (LCs), there are payment mechanisms that are tightly integrated with the EC process, such as the services offered by HP and MasterCard.

6. **Order fulfillment and logistics.** While off-line B2B relationships have well-established order fulfillment mechanisms, this is not the case in online B2B. Yet, orders must be filled fast and according to agreements. Outsourcing is a viable alternative, but in certain cases companies prefer to do it themselves.

7. **B2B vs. B2C marketing, advertising, and sales.** In B2B, organizational buyers make decisions differently than individual customers. Therefore, the nature and methods used to market products and services are different. Information about products and services must reach all potential buyers. This is done through directory services, matching services, and community services in exchanges. Using affiliate programs, data mining, and special CRM services may also help.

8. **Content delivery in B2B.** General content, economic and financial news, investor's corners and the like are delivered on B2B sites. Information that is general enough and used on many sites is usually purchased from content creators via syndication. More specialized information can be purchased from content services that are customizing content. Catalog management is especially important for buyers who aggregate many suppliers' catalogs on their site.

9. **Directory services.** These services direct companies to suppliers in hundreds of different areas. Using a hierarchy of menus and search engines, online information discovery is easy, fast, and cheap.

10. **CRM, PRM, and communities.** These are all interrelated. The key to PRM is quick and accurate responses and finding and meeting partners' needs at a reasonable price. Communities can facilitate EC and increase collaboration.

Key Terms

Affiliate programs
Ad server network provider
B2B e-services
B2X networks
Clickstream data
Customer Relationship Management (CRM)

Dynamic content
E-communities
E-service
End-to-end service
Hypermediation
Internet incubator

Infomediary
Management service provider (MSP)
Partner relationship management (PRM)
Purchasing card
Reverse syndication

Syndication
Venture capital (VC)
XML
Web hosting

Questions for Review

1. Define a B2B service and provide an example.
2. List the major EC service areas (consult Figure 8-1).
3. List the major factors driving the outsourcing of B2B services.
4. Describe the four steps of the EC development process (consult Figure 8-2).
5. List the four phases in the life cycle of exchanges (Figure 8-3) and identify the places in which services are needed.
6. List the major categories of consultants for B2B strategic issues.
7. Describe the process of content delivery to B2B sites.
8. Define infomediary.
9. Describe a purchasing card.
10. Define syndication and dynamic content.
11. List the benefits of e-letters of credit.
12. Define Internet incubator and venture capital.
13. Describe the services provided by Web hosts.
14. Define PRM.

Questions for Discussion

1. Under what situations might the outsourcing of B2B services not be desirable?
2. Why does it make sense to use a consultant to develop an e-strategy?
3. Discuss the services that can be provided by using Web hosting.
4. Discuss the advantages of B2B content syndication.
5. Compare and discuss the option of content creation and management in a company-centric e-procurement.
6. Why is XML so important to B2B?
7. Explain why some hosting services offer content management.
8. Discuss the benefits of e-letters of credit.
9. Relate hypermediation to affiliate programs.
10. UPS and other logistic companies also provide financial services. Discuss the logic of this.
11. Differentiate B2C affiliate programs from B2B affiliate programs.

Internet Exercises

1. Visit *onlinestore.ups.com*. Enter the store and simulate a purchase. Explain how the tools provided add value to customer transactions.
2. Visit *EXP.com*, *eLance.com*, and *SoloGig.com*. Identify at least three consultants at each site who specialize in e-strategy, three who specialize in general EC systems design, and three who specialize in designing some specialized

component of an EC system, such as graphics, billing systems, or inventory systems. For each of these categories, list the three consultants' names, URL or e-mail, and a two-sentence overview of the major services provided.

3. Visit three separate Adult Verification sites. Who is this service primarily targeting (which category of B2C Web sites)? Who pays for the service and who benefits? What distinguishes the various services, and which one seems to offer the greatest value? Are there other methods of verifying the age of a visitor? List three of these sites along with a synopsis of each business.

4. Visit *ecredit.com* and review the services provided both to businesses and to financial institutions.

5. Check out *hp.com*. Find out more about the B2B e-payment system described in the opening case. Look for customer success stories and for business partners.

6. Enter *b2byellowpages.com*, *a2zofb2b.com*, and *b2bbusiness.net* and compare the information provided on each site. What features do all three sites share? How do the sites differ?

7. Visit *b2btoday.com*. Go to the B2B Communities area and identify the major vendors there. Then select three vendors and examine the services they provide to the B2B community. Also enter *communityb2b.com* and examine the information provided and the usefulness of joining the site.

8. Enter *emarket.com*, *google.com*, and *cnnfn.com* and find recent information about Akamai. Summarize recent information on Akamai.

9. Surf the Internet and find three companies that offer B2B affiliate programs that are not cited in this chapter. Comment on the similarities and differences of the three sites.

10. Find XML-related projects by visiting *ebXML.org*, *w3.org*, and *rosettanet.org*. Prepare a report based on your research.

11. Visit *dellhost.com* and review all the B2B services that it provides.

12. Enter *mspassociation.org*. Go to the buyers' guide and take the demonstration tour. What are the potential advantages of using an MSP?

13. Enter *LinkShare.com* and examine their LinkSynergy program. Compare the concept to that of LinkExchange at *bcentral.com*.

Team Assignments and Role Playing

1. As a team, build a new Web site and host it on one of the free Web hosting firms (see Appendix 12A). Your site should contain at least six separate pages of information on a topic of your choice. In addition to outsourcing your hosting, you should use at least three of the following tools that you will acquire from other sites: a counter, site map, internal search engine, banner ad, dynamic text content, local weather, images, chat rooms, message boards, instant messaging, guestbook, and polls or surveys. To get started, visit *homestead.com* and take their tutorial.

2. Each team member should identify two venture capital firms and describe their stated investment objectives, if any. List their successful projects. Have they brought any start-ups successfully to the IPO stage? After the information has been collected, pool that information together with that of the other group

members. As a team, evaluate all of the venture capital firms and select the best three overall. Make the case for the success of these three firms over the next 2 years. Are these venture capital firms backing winners?

3. Each team will examine one of the following payment companies: Visa, MasterCard, Mondex, or Europay. Find what instruments they offer for B2B payments. Do any of these companies support international payments? Convince an audience that your company is the best.

4. Examine several exchanges, for example *e-steel.com*, *chemconnect.com*, or another globally orientated exchange in the same industry. For each exchange, each team should examine the following areas: logistics, payments, and community services. The teams should try to show why their exchange is the best.

5. Each team will role play a different fulfillment/logistics firm. Have the teams represent UPS, FedEx, and the U.S. Postal Service. Each team should review the services provided by each company and then suggest how the company they represent can do a better job than the competition. Start your research by reading *Money Magazine* (February 2000, pp. 34–38).

REAL-WORLD CASE: Commerce One and B2B Services

Commerce One (*commerceone.com*) is a major B2B player with activities in the following areas:

- Provides software solutions to e-marketplaces and exchanges.

- Provides software solutions to individual enterprises of all sizes.

- Operates a horizontal exchange for MROs for SMEs and e-marketplaces (*commerceone.net*).

- Is the leading force behind the Global Trading Web (GTW), the world's largest B2B global trading community. (See Chapter 18 for a description.)

- Provides business services for e-marketplaces, including financial, auctions, catalog content, logistics, CRM, HRM, planning, and more. These are provided directly by Commerce One or through the affiliate program for business services providers.

Commerce One.net Affiliate Program

The *CommerceOne.net* is the B2B e-marketplace of Commerce One. Its affiliate program is an opportunity for business service providers, market makers, and suppliers to get their brand, products, and services in front of a targeted audience of EC business decision makers. Through the program, affiliates are able to establish a presence through a direct channel to new customers and prospects across the Global Trading Web (GTW), which is connected to over 7,000 buying organizations and more than 50 exchanges. Affiliates also have the ability to build relationships with their targeted market.

By joining the program, a company can expose its products or services, as well as its brand, to the other affiliate members, as well as to the partners of GTW, who in turn will expose the affiliate's products and services to their established communities, ultimately providing participants with a new, global sales channel. Becoming an affiliate also gives companies the opportunity for direct discussions with key management regarding expanding the relationship to a strategic partnership with *CommerceOne.net*.

The affiliate program allows participants to promote their brand with activities such as a yearly storefront for selling products and services, an ad banner targeted at the vertical markets of the participant's choice, and the ability to provide editorial content that supports branding and positioning. And, depending on the affiliate level selected, participants can receive a dedicated Commerce One account manager to help leverage the company's brand across the GTW through joint marketing initiatives, including participation in eLink events, "Webinars," case studies, and speaking opportunities. Participants also have access to a large number of B2B services available at *commerceone.com/solutions*. They also can become providers of these services.

There are four membership levels: bronze, silver, gold, and platinum. Each level is entitled to different services and the fees for each level are different.

Trade Zone Services

CommerceOne.net Trade Zones describe the vertical communities at *CommerceOne.net*. There are 15 vertical communities that span many industries, including Aerospace, Financial Services, Life Sciences, and Telecommunications. Each vertical community is comprised of news, events, industry information, and the program members' banner advertisements.

Gold members of *CommerceOne.net* have the opportunity to advertise their brand in two targeted vertical communities of their choice. Platinum Members are given exposure in all 15 vertical communities. This exposure to the *CommerceOne.net* Trade Zones allows companies to target their products and services to a specific audience.

Syndication

Syndication that is used in content distribution (Section 8.10) can also be used in other services. Here *syndication* refers to the sale of the same good or service to many customers, who then repackage it with other offerings and redistribute it. Syndication at *CommerceOne.net* is the process of aggregating services at the company's site and redistributing those services to other exchanges throughout the GTW. Reverse syndication is also possible, where services are syndicated to *CommerceOne.net* from

exchanges throughout the GTW. Through syndication, business service providers, market makers, and suppliers are able to access a new, global channel to resell their services, and exchanges are able to offer a wide variety of services to their trading communities.

Questions for the case

1. Enter *commerceone.com* and check their current business services. Which ones are not discussed in this chapter?

2. Enter *commerceone.com* and find supplier services. Distinguish these from business services.

3. Examine the following services as they relate to similar services discussed in this chapter:

   - Strategy consulting
   - Creative design
   - Interactive marketing
   - Technology consulting and integration
   - Customer operations

4. If two or more members provide basically the same services, should they join the same affiliate program? Why or why not?

REFERENCES AND BIBLIOGRAPHY

Aberdeen Group. "The Case for Supplier Financing E-Services," A Research Report, Boston: Aberdeen Group (November 2000).

Cannon, J. P. and W. D. Perreault. "Buyer-Seller Relationships in Business Markets," *Journal of Marketing Research* vol. 36 (1999).

Carr, N. G. "The Future of Commerce—Hypermediation: Commerce as Clickstream," *Harvard Business Review* (January/February 2000a).

Carr, N. G. "On the Edge: An Interview with Akamai's George Conrades," *Harvard Business Review* (May/June 2000b).

Coupey, E. *Marketing and the Internet.* Upper Saddle River, New Jersey: Prentice Hall, 2001.

Cross, K. "The Ultimate Enablers: Business Partners," *Business 2.0* (February 2000).

Duvall, M. and C. Guglielmo. "Incubators Face Mountains of Hurt," *Interactive Week* (August 2000).

Gary, D. and D. Gary. *The Complete Guide to Associate and Affiliate Programs on the Net.* New York: McGraw-Hill, 1999.

Hoffman, D. L. and T. P. Novak. "How to Acquire Customers on the Web," *Harvard Business Review* (May/June 2000).

Karpinshi, R. "The Logistics of E-Business," *Internet Week* (May 1999).

Karpinshi, R. "E-Business Risk Worth Taking on Path to Success," *B to B* (August 28, 2000).

Keenan Vision, Inc. "B2B Exchanges," Internet Exchange 2000, *keenanvision.com*, April 24, 2000.

King, J. "Shipping Firms Exploit IT to Deliver E-Commerce Goods," *Computerworld* (August 1999).

Lee, H. L. "Creating Value Through Supply Chain Integration," *Supply Chain Management Review*. (September/October 2000).

Li, S. T. and L. Y. Shue. "Towards XML-Enabling E-Commerce Infomediary—A Case Study in Cargo Tracking," *Proceedings 34th HICSS* (Jaunary 2001).

Mougaya, W. "Aggregation Nation," *Business 2.0* (March 21, 2000).

Pickering, C. "Outsourcing the Store," *Business 2.0* (October 10, 2000).

Raisch, W. *The eMarketplace: Strategies for Success in B2B eCommerce*. New York: McGraw-Hill, 2001.

Rothenberg R., "An Advertising Power, But Just What Does Doubleclick Do?" *New York Times* (September 22, 1999).

Rutstein, C., et al. *Managing eMarketplace Risks*. Cambridge, Massachusetts: Forrester Research, Inc. (December 1999).

Schwartz, E. "Amazon, Toys R Us in E-Commerce Tie-Up," *InfoWorld* (August 14, 2000).

Strauss, J. and R. Frost. *Marketing on the Internet*, 2nd ed. Upper Saddle River, New Jersey: Prentice Hall 2001.

Tillett, L. C. "States Test Systems for E-Commerce Taxation," *Internetweek* (January 16, 2001).

Voss, C. "Developing an eService Strategy," *Business Strategy Review* (Spring 2000)

Warkentin, M., ed. "Dynamic Digital Process Integration in Business-to-Business Networks," *Business-to-Business Electronic Commerce: Challenges and Solutions*. Hershey, Pennsylvania: Idea Group Publishers, 2002.

William, J. "Why Online Distributors—Once Written Off—May Thrive in the Evolving World of E-Tailing," *ecompany.com* (September 1999).

PART 4

9

Dynamic Pricing: Auctions and More

LEARNING OBJECTIVES

Upon completion of this chapter, the reader will be able to:

- Define the various types of auctions and list their characteristics.

- Describe the processes of conducting forward and reverse auctions.

- Describe the benefits and limitations of auctions.

- Describe the various services that support auctions.

- Describe the hazards of e-auction fraud and countermeasures.

- Describe bartering and negotiating.

- Analyze future directions and the role of m-commerce.

CONTENT

9.1 ELECTRONIC AUCTIONS IN ACTION

You may recall the opening case in Chapter 6, in which GM conducted two types of electronic auctions: *forward auctions,* for liquidating old equipment, and *reverse auctions* for conducting bids for e-procurement of parts for GM cars. These were B2B auctions. The following subsections present examples of other auction types.

■ C2B REVERSE AUCTIONS: DM & S

DM & S is a small trucking company with $1.8 million in annual sales. During 1999, truckers were very busy, but in early 2000 the economy in the United States started to slow down while fuel prices increased.

DM & S started to lose money, together with other small movers.

A major problem in trucking is that trucks need to move at certain times, and they may not be full then. Furthermore, on return trips, trucks are usually not completely full. Bert Lampers, owner and CEO of DM & S, had an idea: Create a service in which small moving companies bid on jobs of moving individuals. Customers who have flexibility with moving dates can benefit the most. This is basically a **reverse auction** process.

Once customers place their job on *dickerabid.com*, the auction site Bert Lampers created for a cost of $15,000, the truckers can start to bid. For a trucker with a destination and travel date to match the customers' requirement, hauling anything is

better than going with empty space. Simultaneously, customers can get huge discounts while winning truckers can cover at least their fuel expenses. Starting with four truckers and growing to twenty, the site increased DM & S revenue by $14,000 during the first few months of operation. Additional revenue is generated by advertisers that cater to moving people, such as furniture and window blind companies. The Web site won *Inc.* magazine's third place in Web innovations in 2000.

In this example, DM & S is a third-party auction maker, as well as a mover (trucker). Larger truckers (movers) have their own Web site, *truckstop.com*, which provides a considerable amount of information.

Source: Compiled from *Inc. Tech,* no. 4, 2000, and from *dickerabid.com.*

■ B2C AND C2C FORWARD AUCTIONS: DELL COMPUTERS

If you want to buy or sell a used or obsolete Dell product, go to *dellauction.com*. Whether you are a buyer or a seller, you will find lots of information about the items you are interested in. For example, you can find out if the seller is Dell (B2C) or an individual (C2C), and you will be able to check many product details, such as item warranty and condition (see

Figure 9-1). The same goes for general services, such as escrow. Everything is organized for you, from your own personalized shopping cart and account to payments and shipping.

■ C2C FORWARD AUCTIONS: ALL OF US AT eBAY

A visit to *eBay.com* is a must. EBay is the world's largest auction site with a community of more than 20 million

registered users as of spring 2001. The site basically serves individuals, but it caters to small businesses as well. In 2000 it transacted $5 billion in sales, concentrating on collectibles, but other auctions (such as surpluses) also were conducted. In 2001 eBay started to auction fine art in collaboration with *icollector.com* of the United Kingdom. The site also provides for fixed-price trading. EBay operates globally, permitting international trades to take place. Country-specific

---

FIGURE 9-1   A Dell's Product in an Auction

Seller Information		
Seller Username	COMPAMERICA**(0)**	View Comments on this Seller
Seller Type	Private Party	View All Listings from this seller
		Email Seller
Seller Location	Cranford, NJ, United States	

sites are located in the United States, Canada, France, the United Kingdom, Australia, and Japan. Buyers from more than 150 other countries participate. EBay also offers a business exchange in which small and medium-sized enterprises can buy and sell new and used merchandise in B2B or B2C modes.

EBay has 53 local sites in the United States that allow users to easily find items located near them and to browse through items of local interest. In addition, specialty sites, such as eBay Motors, concentrate on specialty items.

Trading can be done from anywhere, anytime. Wireless trading is also possible (see *ebay.com*). The best way to appreciate eBay is to sell or buy an item in eBay's trading community.

9.2   FUNDAMENTALS OF DYNAMIC PRICING AND AUCTIONS

The opening vignettes illustrate a variety of dynamic pricing auction mechanisms, which are the topics of this chapter.

Definition, Types, and Characteristics

An **auction** is a market mechanism by which buyers make bids and sellers place offers. Auctions are characterized by the competitive nature by which the final price is reached. A wide variety of online markets qualify as auctions using this definition. Auctions, an established method of commerce for generations, deal with products and services for which conventional marketing channels are ineffective or inefficient. Auctions can expedite the disposal of items that need liquidation or a quick sale. They offer trading opportunities for both buyers and sellers that are not available in the conventional channels, and they ensure prudent execution of contracts.

The Internet provides an infrastructure for executing auctions at lower cost, and with many more involved sellers and buyers. Individual consumers and corporations alike can participate in this rapidly growing and very convenient form of electronic commerce. The Internet auction industry is projected to reach $52 billion in sales by 2002.

There are several types of auctions, each with its motives and procedures. Klein (1997) classified them into four major categories as shown in Table 9-1. These can be done online or offline.

TRADITIONAL AUCTIONS

Traditional auctions, regardless of their type, have several limitations. For example, they generally last only a few minutes, or even seconds, for each item sold. This rapid process may give potential buyers little time to make a decision, so they may decide not to bid; therefore, sellers may not get the highest possible price, and bidders may not get what they really want or they pay too much. Also, in many cases, the bidders do not have much time to examine the goods. Since bidders must usually be physically present at auctions, the many potential bidders are excluded.

TABLE 9-1

Motives of the Participants in Different Auction Types

Auction Type	Coordination Mechanism	Price Discovery	Allocation Mechanism	Distribution Mechanism
Buyer role	Short-term acquisition of resources, e.g., for demand peaks, auction as a mechanism to achieve equilibrium	Often experts/professional collectors trying to acquire rare items at a reasonable price	Bargain hunting, gambling motive	Bargain hunting, gambling motive; possible side motive: charity
Supplier role	Short-term allocation of resources, load balance	Exposing items for sale to a sufficient breadth of demand, hope for a high price	Clearance of inventory	Attention, direct sales channel, public relations; possible side motive: charity
Auctioneer/Intermediary role	Often electronic auction without auctioneer	Achieve high breadth and depth of auctions, high trading volume results in high returns, competitive advantage over other auctions	Achieve high breadth and depth of auctions, high trading volume results in high returns, competitive advantage over other auctions	Limited role because of supplier-buyer relationship; possible function as service provider for the supplier side

Source: Klein (1997), p. 4. Used by permission.

Similarly, it may be complicated for sellers to move goods to the auction. Commissions are fairly high, since a place needs to be rented, the auction needs to be advertised, and an auctioneer and other employees need to be paid. Electronic auctioning removes these deficiencies.

ELECTRONIC AUCTIONS

Electronic auctions (**e-auctions**) have been in existence for several years on local area networks (see Section 9.6), and were started on the Internet in 1995. They are similar to offline auctions, except that they are done on a computer. Host sites on the Internet act like brokers, offering services for sellers to post their goods for sale and allowing buyers to bid on those items. Many sites have certain etiquette rules that must be adhered to in order to conduct fair business (see *eBay.com* and *auctionaddict.com*). The *usaweb.com* site provides an Internet auction list and a search engine. *Bidfind.com* is an auction aggregator that enters hundreds of auction sites and lets you know which items are auctioned at which sites.

Major online auctions offer consumer products, electronic parts, artwork, vacation packages, airline tickets, and collectibles, as well as excess supplies and inventories being auctioned off by B2B markets. Another type of B2B online auction is increasingly used to trade new types of commodities, such as electricity transmission capacities, and gas and energy options. Furthermore, conventional business practices that traditionally have relied on contracts and fixed prices are increasingly being converted into auctions with bidding for online procurements.

Although it is true that the majority of consumer goods—except those just discussed—are not suitable for auctions, and that for these items conventional selling—such as posted price retailing—will be more than adequate, the flexibility offered by online auction trading may offer innovative market processes. For example, instead of searching for products and vendors by visiting sellers' Web sites, a buyer may solicit offers from all potential sellers. Such a buying mechanism is so innovative that it has the potential to be used in almost all types of consumer goods, as will be shown later when the concept of "name-your-own-price" is discussed.

Dynamic Pricing and Types of Auctions

The major characteristic of an auction is that it is based on dynamic pricing.

Dynamic pricing refers to a commerce transaction in which prices are not fixed. In contrast, catalog prices are fixed and so are prices in department stores, supermarkets, and many storefronts.

Dynamic pricing appears in several forms. Perhaps the oldest one is *negotiation and bargaining,* which has been practiced for many generations in open-air markets. It is customary to classify dynamic pricing into four major categories depending on how many buyers and sellers are involved, as shown in Figure 9-2.

As can be seen in Figure 9-2, four possible configurations exist.

ONE BUYER, ONE SELLER

In the first configuration one can use negotiation, bargaining, or bartering. The resulting price will be determined by bargaining power, supply and demand in the item's market, and possibly business environment factors.

ONE SELLER, MANY POTENTIAL BUYERS (forward auctions)

In the second configuration the seller uses forward auctions, or just auctions. There are four major types of forward auctions: **English auction**, **Yankee auction**, **Dutch auction**, and **Free-fall auction**.

English Auction   In an English auction, buyers bid sequentially on one item at a time. A minimum bid that specifies the smallest amount that can be entered is usually part of an English auction. The auction will continue until no more bids are rendered, or until the auction time is over. The winner is the one with the highest bid, if price is the only criteria. If other criteria—such as payment arrangement or how quickly the buyer can take the item—are considered, the winner is selected from those who submitted high bids. English auctions can take days on the Internet, but online auctions can be in real time (live) and may take only minutes. English auctions are used in C2C, B2C, B2B, and G2B markets. The process is shown in Figure 9-3.

Yankee Auctions   In a Yankee auction, a seller offers multiple identical items usually with a minimum bid. Bidders can bid for any amount above the minimum. A

Figure 9-2	Types of Dynamic Pricing

Figure 9-3	English Auction, Ascending Price

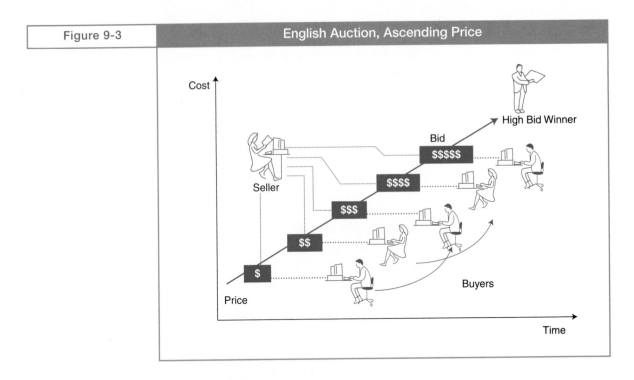

winner pays the exact price of his winning bid (the highest bid). The auction can be run as a reverse auction, too.

Dutch Auction   Prices start at a very high level, as has been done for many decades in the international flower market in the Netherlands. The price is slowly reduced and the bidders specify the quantity they want to buy at the posted price. Dutch auctions are designed for multiple identical items. Before the Internet, the process in the Netherlands was done manually using a big clock whose hands showed the price. Now the clock is computerized (see Figure 9-4). Once a bidder is willing to pay the price indicated by the auctioneer, the quantity available is adjusted until the entire quantity is sold. Dutch auctions happen very fast, even when conducted on the Internet. In contrast, English auctions may take days. There are variations of this method.

The following describes how a Dutch auction is conducted at eBay:

- Sellers list a starting price for one item, and the number of items for sale.
- If no bids are made, the starting price is reduced.
- Bidders specify both a bid price and the quantity they want to buy.
- All winning bidders pay the **same** price per item, which is the lowest successful bid. This might be less than what you bid!
- If there are more buyers than items, the earliest successful bids get the goods.
- Higher bidders are more likely to get the quantities they've requested.
- Proxy bidding is not used in Dutch auctions.
- Bidders can refuse partial quantities. For example, if you place a bid for ten items and only eight are available after the auction, you don't have to buy any of them.

Figure 9-4	Computerized Auction Clock for Dutch Flower Auctions

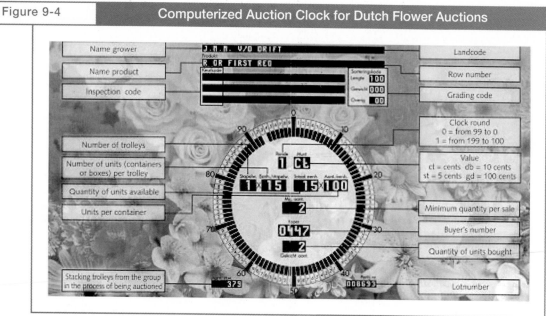

Source: Used with permission of *aquarius-flora.com.*

Free-Fall (Declining Price) Auction   This is a variation of the Dutch auction in which only one item is auctioned at a time. The price starts at a very high level, and then it is reduced at fixed time intervals until a bid is offered and becomes the winning bid. This type of auction is used with popular items, where many bidders are expected; the free-fall auction moves very fast in such a case.

ONE BUYER, MANY POTENTIAL SELLERS

In this third configuration, one uses a **reverse auction** approach, also known as a *bidding* or **tendering system** (see examples of GE and GM in Chapter 6). In a reverse auction, an item the buyer needs is placed on an RFQ. Potential sellers bid on the job, reducing the price sequentially (see Figure 9-5). In electronic bidding, several rounds of bidding take place until the bidders do not reduce the price. The winner is the one with the lowest bid, if only price is considered. Because this is primarily a B2B or G2B mechanism, other criteria are considered and the winner is selected from a group of, say, the five lower bids.

   Sealed-bid first-price auction. You bid only once in this type of auction. It is a silent auction and the bidders do not know who is placing bids or what the prices are. The item is awarded to the highest bidder.

   Sealed-bid second-price auction (Vickrey auction). The item is awarded to the highest bidder, but at the second-highest bid. This is done to alleviate bidders' fears of significantly exceeding the true market value.

   Again, we assume that each bidder submits one bid without knowing the other bids. This method is not used much on the Internet. The reason is that most Internet auctions are not sealed. Actually, Web technology facilitates disclosure of prices, as in the English model. For further details and discussion, including bidding strategies, see Vakrat and Seidmann (2000).

Figure 9-5	The Process of Reverse Auctions

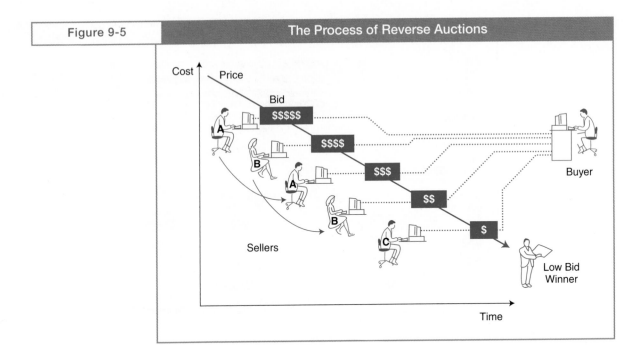

MANY SELLERS, MANY BUYERS

In final configuration (see also Chapter 7), *buyers and their bidding prices* and *sellers and their asking prices* are matched, considering the quantities on both sides. Stocks and commodities markets are typical examples. Buyers and sellers can be individuals or businesses. Such auctions are called **double auctions**.

Reverse auctions can be open where bidding prices are known to all bidders, or they can be sealed.

9.3   BENEFITS, LIMITATIONS, AND ECONOMIC IMPACTS

Electronic auctions are becoming important selling and buying channels for many companies and individuals. E-auctions enable buyers to access goods and services anywhere auctions are conducted. Moreover, almost perfect market information is available about prices, products, current supply and demand, and so on. These characteristics provide benefits to all.

Benefits to Sellers

- Increase revenues by broadening customer base and shortening cycle time. With e-auctions, sellers can reach the most motivated buyers in the most efficient way and sell at a price equal to buyer valuation of the product. This eliminates the need to predict demand and the risk of pricing items too high or too low.
- Optimal price setting. Sellers can make use of the information collected about price sensitivity to set prices in similar fixed-price markets.
- Disintermediation. Sellers can gain more customer dollars by offering items directly, rather than going through an expensive intermediary or by using an expensive physical auction.

- Better customer relationships. Buyers and sellers have more chances and time to interact with each other, thus creating a sense of community and loyalty. Additionally, by making use of the information gathered on customer interests, sellers can improve the overall e-commerce experiences of buyers and can deliver more personalized content to buyers, thus enhancing customer relationships.
- Liquidation. Sellers can liquidate large quantities of obsolete items very quickly.

Benefits to Buyers

- Opportunities to find unique items and collectibles.
- Chance to bargain. Instead of buying at a fixed price, the bidding mechanism allows buyers to bargain with sellers at their desired prices.
- Entertainment. Participating in e-auctions can be entertaining and exciting. The interaction between buyers and sellers may create goodwill and positive feelings, and buyers can interact as little or as much as they like.
- Anonymity. With the help of a third party, buyers can remain anonymous.
- Convenience. Buyers can trade from anywhere, even with a cell phone.

Benefits to E-Auctioneers

- Higher repeat purchases. Jupiter Communications conducted a study in 1998 that shows comparative repeat-purchase rates across some of the top e-commerce sites. The findings indicate that auction sites such as eBay and uBid tend to garner higher repeat-purchase rates than the top e-commerce B2C sites, such as *Amazon.com*.
- A stickier Web site. "**Stickiness**" refers to the tendency of customers to stay at (auction) Web sites longer and come back more. Auction sites are frequently "stickier" than fixed-priced sites. With sticky sites, more advertising revenue can be generated because of more impressions and longer viewing times.
- Expansion of the auction business. An example of how auctioneers can expand their business can be seen in the example of Manheim Auctions (Mckeown and Watson, 1999). Manheim Auctions, the world's largest auction house, created Manheim Online (MOL) in 1999 to sell program cars (cars that have been previously leased or hired) in response to Japanese company Aucnet's efforts to penetrate the U.S. car auction business. This Internet-based electronic sales system has tremendous potential to change the car auction business. There are over 80,000 used car dealers in the United States, and Manheim auctions some 6 million cars for them each year. Trying to leverage its knowledge of the automobile market to provide services to its customers, Manheim developed two other products, Manheim Market Report and AutoConnect. It is also expanding its auction business in Europe. Manheim wants to continue to add value to Manheim Online as a way of discouraging competition and of extending sales through the Internet without cannibalizing Manheim's core business.

Limitations

E-auctions have several limitations, including the following:

- **Possibility of fraud.** Auction items are in many cases unique, used, or antique. Because one cannot see the item, one may get a defective product. Also, buyers can commit fraud; thus, the fraud rate is very high. (For specific fraud techniques and how to prevent them, see Section 9.8.)
- **Limited participation.** Some auctions are by invitation only, while others are open to dealers only, so they are not open to all.
- **Security.** Some of the C2C auctions conducted on the Internet are not secure. On the other hand, some B2B auctions are conducted on highly secure private lines.
- **Software.** Unfortunately, there are only a few "complete" or "off-the-shelf" market-enabling solutions that can support the dynamic commerce functionality required for optimizing pricing strategies *and* that can be easily customized to the unique requirements of a company or industry. In short, dynamic commerce "best practices" are still being defined within industries and will continue to evolve as new business processes emerge online.

Strategic Uses of Auctions and Pricing Mechanisms

By utilizing dynamic pricing, buyers and suppliers are able to optimize product inventory levels and adjust pricing strategies very quickly. For example, by using Web-based auctions and exchanges, suppliers can quickly flush excess inventory and liquidate idle assets. Buyers may end up with the power to procure goods and services at the prices they desire. The endgame is to accurately assess and exploit market supply and demand requirements faster and more efficiently than the competition.

Aberdeen Group (2000) showed that market-makers leveraging auction exchange models are reaching "liquidity" ("critical mass," see Chapter 7) more rapidly than those utilizing only catalog-order-based trading environments. However, businesses are still struggling to understand how to truly implement dynamic pricing models to augment existing business practices.

One suggestion of how to do it was provided by Westland (2000), who observed that e-auctions place much more power in the hands of the consumer than e-tailing. He suggested that the following 10 lessons can be learned from stock exchanges for e-tailing auctions:

LESSON 1: Customers are attracted to e-auction markets because they provide greater liquidity than traditional markets; ceteris paribus, this greater liquidity results directly from the greater geographical reach provided to commercial transactions by electronic networks.

LESSON 2: Electronic auction markets can more efficiently discover the best price at which to trade in a product.

LESSON 3: Electronic auction markets can, at low cost, provide exceptional levels of transparency of both market operations and product quality.

LESSON 4: Electronic auction markets are more efficient than traditional markets. This efficiency allows e-auctions to better provide information required to correctly price assets traded in the marketplace.

LESSON 5: Electronic auctions can provide a market that, ceteris paribus, offers services at a lower transaction cost.

LESSON 6: Customers will abandon a market that is not perceived as fair, even though they may initially profit from "unfair" transactions in that market. By distancing customers from the traders in a market, they can provide a false sense of legitimacy to a market that allows unfair and opaque trading practices.

LESSON 7: Electronic auction systems must manage all aspects of trading activity, from initiation to settlement and delivery. Markets that fail to integrate both price discovery and order completion (settlement) into their operations can encourage unfair trading behavior and opaque trading practices.

LESSON 8: Because the delay in price response may result in significantly faster completion and posting times, there is greater potential for feedback loops and instabilities that are a threat to orderly trading, and to fair and efficient pricing of assets traded.

LESSON 9: Electronic auctions may fuel unfair trading practices through different relative speeds of service through different parts of their networks linking trading to customers.

LESSON 10: Order-driven e-auction markets demand that markets clearly define when a sale has been made.

Impacts

Because the trade objects and contexts for auctions are very diverse, the economic rationale behind auctions and the motives of the different participants for setting up auctions are quite different. Representative impacts include the following:

Auctions as a coordination mechanism. Auctions are increasingly used as an efficient coordination mechanism for establishing an equilibrium in price. An example is auctions for the allocation of telecommunication bandwidth. In these auctions there is little or no human intervention during the trading process.

Auctions as a social mechanism to determine a price. For objects not being traded in traditional markets, such as unique or rare items, or for items that may be offered randomly or at long intervals, an auction creates a marketplace that attracts potential buyers, and often experts. By offering many of these special items at a single time, and by attracting considerable attention, auctions provide the requisite exposure of purchase and sale orders and hence liquidity of the market in which a price can be determined. Typical examples are auctions of fine arts or rare items, as well as auctions of communication frequencies, Web banners, and advertising space. For example, *winebid.com* is a global auction site for wine collectors.

Auctions as a highly visible distribution mechanism. Another type of auction is similar to the previous one, but it deals with special offers. In this case, the setup of the auction is different: Typically, one supplier auctions off a limited amount of items, using the auction primarily as a mechanism to gain attention and to attract those customers who are bargain hunters or have a preference for the gambling dimension of the auction process. The airline-seat auctions by Cathy Pacific, American Airlines, and Lufthansa fall into this category.

Auctions as a component in e-commerce. Auctions can stand alone, or they can be combined with other e-commerce activities. An example is combining group purchasing with reverse auctions (see Application Case 9.1).

Some of the impacts of electronic auctions are presented in Figure 9-6. The figure shows the components of the auctions, the participants, and the process. The impacts are summarized in Table 9-2.

APPLICATION CASE 9.1

Reverse Mortgage Auctions in Singapore

Homebuyers like to get the lowest possible mortgage rates. In the United States, *Priceline.com* will try to find you a mortgage if you "name your own price." However, a better deal may be available to homebuyers in Singapore, where reverse auctions are combined with "group purchasing," saving about $20,000 over the life of a mortgage for each homeowner, plus $1,200 in waived legal fees.

Dollardex.com offers the service in Singpore, Hong Kong, and other countries. In addition to mortgages the site offers, as of Spring 2000, car loans, insurance policies, and other financial services. Here is how the site arranged its first project.

The site invited potential buyers in three residential properties in Singapore to join the service. Applications were made on a secure Web site, including financial credentials. Then, seven lending banks were invited to bid on the loans.

In a secure electronic room, borrowers and lenders negotiated. After 2 days of negotiations of interest rates and special conditions, the borrowers voted on one bank. In the first project, 18 borrowers agreed to give the job to UOB, paying about .5% less than the regular rates. The borrowers negotiated the waiver of the legal fee as well. UOB generated $10 million of business. Today, customers can participate in an individual reverse auction if they do not want to join a group.

The banks can see the offers made by competitors. Flexibility is high, in addition to interest rates, down payment size, and switching from a fixed to variable rate options is also negotiated. On the average, there are 2.6 bank bids per customer.

The site offers matching services for travel and insurance. It also allows comparisons of mutual funds that agreed to give lower front-end fees.

Sources: Compiled from the *Asian Wall Street Journal*, March 14–15, 2000, and from *dollardex.com*.

Figure 9-6	The Components of Auctions

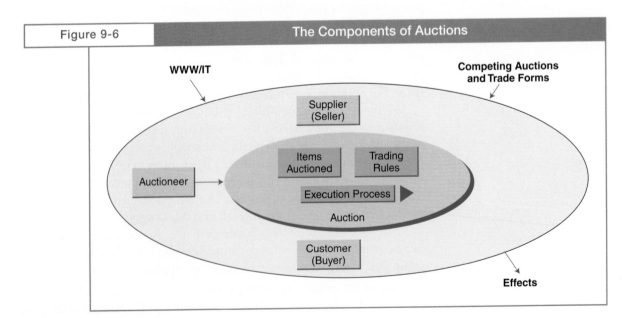

Source: Modified from Klein (1997), p. 4.

	Summary of Impact Areas	
Parameter	**Impact of the Web**	
Auctioneer	Lower entry barriers; opportunity for direct sales.	
Access rules	Customizable; theoretically millions of potential customers can be reached.	
Items auctioned	Focused product segments can be auctioned off; the technology extends the complexity of the product description.	
Trading rules	The trading rules reflect the lack of a guaranteed service.	
Execution process	For digital products, the entire trading cycle can be handled on the Web; for physical products the trading process and the physical logistics of the traded objects can be separated, leading to a reduction of costs.	

TABLE 9-2

Source: Modified from Klein (1997), p. 5.

9.4   THE "NAME-YOUR-OWN-PRICE" C2B MODEL

One of the most interesting models of e-commerce is known as the "**name-your-own-price**" **model**. This model appears in several variations and is associated with *Priceline.com*.

The Priceline Model

Priceline.com pioneered the "name-your-own-price" Internet pricing system that enables consumers to achieve significant savings by naming their own price for goods and services. Therefore, it is basically a consumer-to-business (C2B) model. *Priceline.com* either presents consumer requests to sellers who can fill as much of that guaranteed demand as they wish at "price points" requested by buyers, or searches a *Priceline.com* database that contains vendors' minimum prices and tries to match supply against requests. In short, *Priceline.com*'s "virtual" business model allows for rapid scaling, using the Internet for collecting consumer demand and trying to fill it. The approach is based on the fundamental concept of the downward-sloping demand curve in which prices vary based on demand. For example, airlines have about 500,000 empty seats every day, and Priceline helps to fill them.

The company is currently selling multiple products and services, mainly across the following product categories: a travel service that offers leisure airline tickets, hotel rooms and rented cars, a personal finance service that offers home refinancing and home equity loans, and an automotive service that offers new cars. New services that were added in 2000 include credit cards and long-distance calling. In 2000 the company teamed up with Hutchison Whampoa Limited, one of Asia's largest owners of telecommunications and Internet infrastructure, to offer a range of services in Asia, including China and Hong Kong, India, Taiwan, Indonesia, Singapore, Thailand, Korea, Malaysia, the Philippines, and Vietnam. *Priceline.com* also has offices in many other countries.

According to the market research firm Opinion Research Corporation International of Princeton, New Jersey, *Priceline.com* is the Internet's second most-recognized e-commerce brand behind *Amazon.com*. Two-thirds of all adults in the United States have heard of *Priceline.com* and its "name-your-own-price" commercial formula.

Basically, the concept is that of a C2B *reverse auction*, in which vendors submit offers and the lowest-priced vendor gets the job; however, if database matching is done, the activity may not qualify to be called an auction since the vendors are not placing bids directly in response to a customer request.

Priceline.com asks customers to guarantee acceptance of the offer if it is at or below the requested price. This is guaranteed by giving a credit card number. In 2000, *Priceline.com* suspended the delivery of food, gasoline, and groceries due to accumulated losses.

In 2000, *Priceline.com* initiated a new service for helping people get rid of old things. It is similar to an auction site with heavy emphasis on secondhand goods. However, the auction process is different. The new site, named Perfect YardSale, lets a user make an offer below the seller's asking price for an item, a system that's similar to the haggling that goes on at garage and yard sales. Also, the buyer and seller are expected to meet face-to-face. *Priceline.com* argues that its method leads to bargains for buyers that are better than at auctions, where the highest bidder wins. Buyers and sellers can swap goods in person, eliminating the expense of shipping. Perfect YardSale transactions are limited to local metropolitan areas.

Jay Walker, vice chairman and founder of *Priceline.com*, said he expects Perfect YardSale to attract a different type of merchant: the individual seller seeking to get rid of unwanted possessions on the cheap. In contrast, he argues, much of the trade on Internet auction sites is conducted by dealers selling the hottest new toys, antiques, and other collectibles. These items are not available on Perfect YardSale.

The system works like this: A buyer hunting for a digital camera, for example, selects the features he or she wants on Perfect YardSale, the price he or she is willing to pay, and how long he or she wants the site to search for a seller who meets his or her demands. The buyer will then be required to submit a credit card number to demonstrate that his bid is serious.

Once Perfect YardSale finds a willing seller, the two parties arrange to meet so the buyer can inspect the merchandise. If the buyer is satisfied with the condition of the item, he'll give the seller a secret pass-code. The seller can then enter the pass-code into the Perfect YardSale site to receive payment for the item directly from Priceline and the buyer can take the purchased item.

Unfortunately, Perfect YardSale terminated its services in October 2000 due to a cash shortage at *Priceline.com*.

Other Models

Several similar models are offered by competitors. For example, *Savvio.com* offers a model for travelers that combines a real-time declining-price auction and full disclosure of itinerary details on discounted international and domestic air travel and cruise tickets. Unlike "name-your-own-price" travel sites, *Savvio.com* allows consumers to view the airline, flight number, aircraft type, exact departure and arrival times, and ticket availability before purchasing tickets. However, the company suspended services in 2001.

AsiatravelBids.com allows travelers to place an RFQ, then *atreservation.com* asks vendors to bid on it. The site is similar to *Priceline.com*, except that it uses only auctions.

9.5   THE AUCTION PROCESS AND SOFTWARE SUPPORT

A number of software or intelligent tools are available to help buyers and sellers to find an auction or complete a transaction. The sellers and buyers usually go through a four-phase process: searching and comparing, getting started for an auction, actual bidding, and post-auction activities (see Figure 9-7).

There are several support tools for each phase. Let's explore them, by the auction phase where they are used.

Phase 1: Searching and Comparing

Auctions are conducted on hundreds of sites worldwide. Therefore, sellers and buyers need to execute extensive searches and comparisons to select desirable auction locations. The following support tools may be of interest to them:

MEGA-SEARCHING AND COMPARISONS

Many Web sites offer links to hundreds of auction sites, or they provide search tools for specific sites. The mega-searching utility not only helps sellers find suitable locations to list their items, but it also enables buyers to browse available

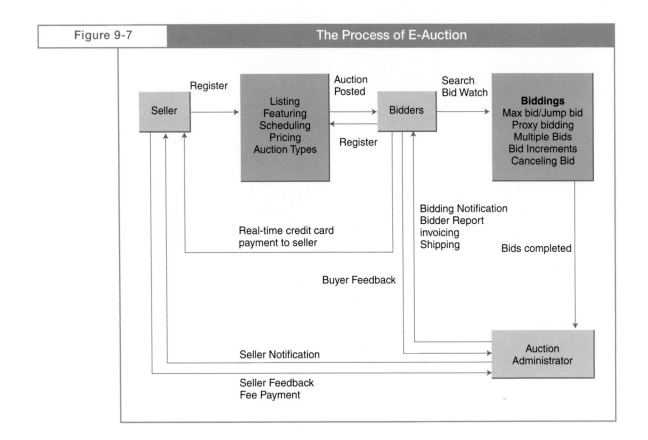

Figure 9-7   The Process of E-Auction

APPLICATION CASE   9.2

Finding When and Where an Item Is Auctioned

This is the process the author (Efraim Turban) went through:

1. Enter *biddersedge.com*
2. Request "Pool Table" on the keyword option

This search engine claims that it searches at more than 200 auction sites. The search found 63 auctions, which are organized as shown here (a sample):

Toys & Beanies> Plush>Other	Auction Site = Trusted	Price (approx.)	Close (ETS) Change zone	Buy Type
Hardvard 8′ Oakwood I Slatron Poo Table w/Ball Return & FREE SHIPPING!	EGGHEAD.com	$745.99	03/05, 05:52PM	Retailer
Voit Competition Table Soccer (New)	EGGHEAD.com	$79.99	04/11, 01:00PM	Retailer
Executive-Size Pool Table/Billiards Set	BidBay	$95.00	02/01, 09:06PM	P2P
Peters Sellers~Pool~Pool Table~16″ × 20″ Poster	Amazon	$18.95	02/05, 12:44AM	P2P

I was able to sort the auctions by:

Type of seller ("Buy Type"), retailer, person to person (P2P), fixed price, and so on. I noticed that eBay was not on the list, probably because of the reasons cited in Application Case 9.3. Next, I went to matching categories. I decided to match the pool table with "jewelry." I found several matches in which people were selling a pool table and some jewelry together. Then I noticed that I could try the same search at eBay. So, I went there and found 15 items such as pool tables, charms, and rings. Some of the items were new and at a fixed price. At that time I had an option to add the search to my personal shopper page.

Next I looked for a "Boeing 777." I found an auction for a Herpa Wings, Emirates Boeing 777-200, for $18. This was, of course, not a real plane. So, I registered with the auction tracker that promise to track the airplane for me, and with "ping me," a free service that promised to send me a notification alert. There was no pricing history on the Boeing 777, nor on a pool table. But I found lots of price history on Barbie Dolls, including price ranges at different times during the last 12 months. Finally the site had a notice about the company relationship with eBay, including the legal situation (see Application Case 9.3).

auction sites efficiently (see Application Case 9.2). Popular searching tools include the following:

- **Auction Watch** (*AuctionWatch.com*) contains a directory of auction sites organized by categories, as well as auction news, message boards, and more.
- **The Internet Auction List** (*Internetauctionlist.com*) is packed with news about e-auctions worldwide and features access to innumerable specialty auctions.

- **Yahoo!'s auction list** (*auctions.yahoo.com*) contains a list of over 400 auction-related links.
- **Bidder's Edge** (*Biddersedge.com*) conducts searches across multiple auction houses for specific auction products and pricing information. It provides detailed historical information on items that have appeared for sale before.
- **Itrack** (*davecentral.com*) searches eBay, Yahoo, and Amazon for specific items that users designate.
- **Turbobid** (*etusa.com*) provides a mega-search service that helps local bidders look for items they want from a pool of e-auction sites.

AUTOMATED SEARCH SERVICES

Automated search services notify buyers when items they are interested in are available at one or more auction sites. Buyers need to complete a simple form specifying the item, then search for assistance tools such as AuctionWatch, *cool-seek.com auction_search*, and Itrack to keep tabs on auction sites and notify buyers by e-mail. The Notify Me When PersonalShopper assists bidders only at eBay.

Automated search engines at auction site entrances are beneficial to users but may not be appreciated by the auction site (see Application Case 9.3).

APPLICATION CASE   **9.3**

Issue in Auction Aggregation

In September 1999, eBay initiated a drastic policy against third-party "predatory" search agents. These agents enter the major online auction sites and search items consumers are looking for, notifying consumers when an auction is being held and where. The policy prohibits the third-party search sites from collecting and sharing information found on eBay's site. The problem, as reported by eBay, was that the search agents were frequently accessing eBay, sifting through auction offers, harvesting the information, and placing it on alternate Web sites, such as *davecentral.com*, *AuctionWatch.com*, *AuctionRover.com*, and Ruby Lane. EBay claimed that these search agents were harmful in many ways. First they slowed down eBay's transaction processing systems, thus reducing performance for all other eBay visitors. Second, outside search agents might not show the most up-to-date information and thus reduce auction users' purchases. Executives from the third-party companies were quick to point out that their systems were actually benevolent in that they served as "repeaters" or mirrors of eBay information, thus actually lowering the load. Furthermore, they stressed that actual purchases were, after all, carried out at eBay's site, so that business was not really taken away from the company, and that they, in fact, brought more bidders to eBay.

The culprits in this situation were mobile intelligent agents that can interact with host computers other than the one they originate on, move from host to host, and extract and store data in the process. In the eBay scenario, they were "harvesting" information and were sending it to their company's computer, which collected, analyzed, and redistributed that information.

Are agents truly culprits or predators as suggested? EBay's response clearly suggests they are predators, as do several readers' comments following the

APPLICATION CASE   **9.3**

(continued)

policy announcement. Yet, Murch and Johnson (1999) are claiming just the opposite, stating "It is in the interest of all companies that wish to sell over the Internet. . . . that their information is formatted and available in such a way that it can be easily accessed by . . . these agents." In other words, agents are viewed by some as having positive characteristics. This incident created a debate in chat rooms and newsgroups (e.g., see "talkback post" at *znet.com*). Most customers critized eBay. In early 2000, eBay licensed Channel Advisor to aggregate auctions from eBay. Channel Advisor had similar agreements with dozens of other auction sites.

Source: Compiled from Wanger, C. and E. Turban (2002).

BROWSING SITE CATEGORIES

Almost all auction-site home pages contain a directory of categories. Buyers can browse the category and its subcategories to narrow the search. Some sites also enable users to sort items according to the time a specific auction is conducted.

BASIC AND ADVANCED SEARCHING

Buyers can use search engines to look for a single term, multiple terms, or key words. To conduct an advanced search, buyers can fill in a search form to specify search titles, item descriptions, sellers' IDs, auction item numbers, price ranges, locations, closing dates, completed auctions, and so forth.

Phase 2: Getting Started at an Auction

To participate in an auction, one needs to register at the selected site. After registration, sellers can list, feature, schedule, and price their items on the site. Buyers can check sellers' profiles and other details—such as the minimum bid amount, the auction policy, and the payment method allowed—then place their bids.

REGISTRATION AND PROFILING

Sellers and buyers must register their names, user IDs, and passwords before they can start participating at a specific auction. The user's page header and the auction listing will display a basic description of sellers and their listings. Before submitting a bid, buyers can check a seller's profile, including information such as membership IDs and previous transaction records. If the auction site provides voluntary verified-user programs such as BidSafe (*auctions.cnet.com*), buyers can check whether sellers are qualified auction community members as verified by the third-party security source.

LISTING AND PROMOTING

Several software programs can help sellers to list and promote their items.

- **Advertisement Wizard** (see *illumix.com*). Helps users in creating attractive advertisements and auction postings. With a simple-to-use, fill-in-the-blank interface, users can create great-looking advertisements for e-auctions.

- **Auction Assistant** (see *tucows.com*). This tool and Ad Studio (*adstudio.net*) help in creating auction listings, changing a font, adding a background, selecting a theme, and including standard details, such as shipping policy and payment terms. The tools also can be used to track sales, payments, and shipping.
- **Auction ePoster2000** (see *auctionposter.com*). This program makes it simple to add pictures, and it interacts directly with eBay. It helps in adding backgrounds, photos, etc., without design or programming skills. The program can create up to 100 ads at a time, and it supports bulk listing.
- **Auction Wizard** (see *davecentral.com*). This program can upload up to 100 items simultaneously. It is an auction-posting tool that saves cutting and pasting. Auction Wizard also enters user ID, password, auction title, location, opening bid, category, and auction duration.
- **Mister Lister** on eBay (see *ebay.com/services/buyandsell*). Sellers can upload many items at one time.
- **Bulk Loader** (see Yahoo Auctions). Seller can load several auctions into a spreadsheet program like Microsoft Excel.

PRICING

To post an item for bid, sellers have to decide the minimum bid amount, the bid increment, and any ***reserve price*** (the lowest price for which a seller is willing to sell an item). Sellers can search for *comparable guides* with Web search engines like *BidFind.com*, *freemerchant.com*, *PriceScan.com*, and *AuctionWatch.com*. If an auction site allows searching for auctions closed in the past, the transacted prices of similar items can provide a benchmark for a buyer's bidding strategy or a minimum acceptable price for a seller.

Phase 3: The Actual Bidding

In the bidding phase, buyers can submit bids themselves or make use of software tools that place bids on their behalf. They can also use tools to view the bidding status and to place bids across different sites in real time.

BID WATCHING AND MULTIPLE BIDDINGS

Buyers can visit the user page of an e-auction Web site at any time and keep track of the status of active auctions. They can review bids and auctions they are currently winning or losing or have recently won. Tools provided in the United States by BidWatch (*egghead.com*), Bid Monitor (*bruceclay.com*), and EasyScreen Layout (*auctionbroker.com*) allow bidders to view their bids across different auction sites in an organized way. Bidders can also place their bids at multiple auction sites using a single screen without switching from one window to another.

AUTO-SNIPPING

Snipping is the act of entering a bid during the very last seconds of an auction and outbidding the highest bidder.

E PROXY BIDDINGS

A software system can operate as a proxy to place bids on behalf of buyers. In such **proxy bidding** a buyer should determine his or her *maximum bid,* then place the first bid manually. The proxy will then execute the bids, trying to keep the bids as low as possible. When someone enters a new bid, the proxy automatically will raise the bid to the next level until it reaches the predetermined maximum price. This function is not applicable in a Dutch auction in which prices are decreasing.

Phase 4: Post-Auction Follow-Up

When auctions are completed, post-auction activities take place. These include e-mail notifications and arrangements for payment and shipping. A typical post-auction tool is Easy! Auction (*saveeasy.com*).

POST-AUCTION NOTIFICATIONS

- **Bidding notifications.** Buyers receive e-mail messages or beeper messages notifying them while the bidding is going on (English bidding), each time they are outbid or winning an auction.
- **End-of-auction notices.** When an auction closes, sellers receive e-mail messages naming the highest bidder. End-of-auction e-mails provide seller and buyer IDs, seller and winner e-mail addresses, a link to the auction ad, auction title or item name, final price, auction ending date and time, total number of bids, and the starting and highest bid amounts.
- **Seller notices.** After an auction ends, the seller generally contacts the buyer. Seller notices typically provide auction number and item name, total purchase price (winning bid plus shipping), payment preferences, mailing address, etc.
- **Postcards and thank-you notes.** *AuctionWatch.com* helps sellers create a customized close-of-auction or thank-you note for winning bidders.

USER COMMUNICATION

User-to-user online communication appears in a number of forms:

- **Chat groups.** Areas on e-auction sites and auction-related sites, where people can post messages in real time to get quick feedback from others.
- **Mailing lists.** A group of people talking about a chosen topic via e-mail messages.
- **Message boards.** Areas on e-auction sites and auction-related sites where people can post messages that other users can read at their convenience. Other message board participants can post replies for all to read.

FEEDBACK AND RATING

Most e-auction sites provide a feedback and rating feature that enables auction community members to monitor each other. This feature enables users to rank sellers or bidders and add short comments about sellers, bidders, and transactions.

INVOICING AND BILLING

An invoicing utility tool can e-mail and print one or all invoices, search and arrange invoices in a number of ways, edit invoices, and delete invoices. This utility automatically calculates shipping charges and sales tax. It can also automatically calculate and charge the seller with the listing fees and/or a percentage of the sale as commission.

PAYMENT METHODS

Sellers and winning bidders can arrange payment to be made by such methods as cashier's check, C.O.D. (cash on delivery), credit card, electronic transfer, and an escrow service (see Chapter 14). A number of online services are available for electronic transfer, escrow services, and credit-card payment, such as the following:

- **Electronic transfer service.** Buyers can pay electronically via *PayByWeb.com*, *Paypal.com*, or *BidPay.com*
- **Escrow service.** An independent third party holds a bidder's payment in trust until the buyer receives and accepts the auction item from the seller. This service charges a fee and is usually reserved for high-end transactions. An example of an escrow service provider is *escrow.com*.
- **Credit-card payment.** *Billpoint.com* or *CCNow.com* services facilitate person-to-person credit-card transactions. Billpoint's payment processing system offers many of the same protections as escrow, such as payment processing, shipment tracking, and fraud protection.

SHIPPING AND POSTAGE

- **Internet shippers.** Shipping providers such as *Iship.com*, *Smartship.com*, and *AuctionShip.com* help sellers by providing a one-stop integrated service for processing, shipping, and packing e-commerce goods.
- **Internet postage.** Postage service providers such as *Stamps.com* allow users to download postage, print "stamped" envelopes and labels, and arrange shipments via the U.S. Postal Service. These providers charge sellers both fixed and transaction fees for services.

Additional Terms and Rules

Each auction house has its own rules and guides. The following are some examples:

Reserve price auction This is the lowest price for which a seller is willing to sell an item.

Vertical auction A specialized auctions, sometimes referred to as "auction vortals." They are particularly useful in B2B. At eBay anything goes, but many auction sites specialize in one area. For example, TechSmart Inc. specializes in selling used or outdated PCs in B2B auctions.

Bid retraction Refers to cancellation of a bid by a bidder, and it is used only in special circumstances. Usually a bid is considered to be a binding contract.

Featured auctions These get extra exposure when they are listed on Web sites. Sellers pay extra for this service.

9.6   AUCTIONS ON PRIVATE NETWORKS

Electronic auctions that run on private networks have been in use for about 15 years. Chapter 7 introduced the flower market in the Netherlands as a B2B example. The following are B2B examples.

Pigs in Singapore and Taiwan. Pig auctioning in Singapore (see Neo, 1992) and Taiwan has been conducted on private networks for more than 10 years. Growers bring the pigs to one area, where they are washed, weighed, and prepared for display. The pigs are auctioned (forward auction) one at a time, while all the data about them is displayed to about 40 approved bidders who bid on a displayed price. If bids are submitted, the price is increased by 20 cents per kilogram. The process continues until no one bids. The bidders' financial capability is monitored by a computer (in other words, the computer verifies that the bidder has available funds in the prepaid account that was opened for the auction). The process is illustrated in Figure 9-8.

Cars in Japan—Aucnet. Started in Japan, Aucnet began auctioning used cars to dealers on television in the mid-1980s. In 1992 it opened Aucnet USA Inc. and started auctioning cars in the United States. In 1996 Aucnet moved to a private network, and in 1998 it moved to the Internet, expanding to flowers, antiques, and more. In 1998 Aucnet USA was closed. Today, Aucnet also auctions computer hardware and software and provides services such as insurance and leasing in Japan. (For further details, see *aucnet.co.jp/english*.)

Livestock in Australia. ComputerAided Livestock Marketing (CALM) is an electronic online system for trading cattle and sheep. It has been in operation since 1986, and in contrast with the pig-auctioning system in Singapore, livestock does not have to travel to CALM, which lowers stress in the animals and reduces costs. The buyers use PCs or Vt100 terminals. The system also handles payments to farmers. (For further details, see *anu.edu.au/people/Roger.Clarke/EC/CALM*.)

9.7   DOUBLE AUCTIONS, BUNDLE TRADING, AND PRICING ISSUES

Double Auctions

Auctions can be **single auctions**, where either an item is offered for sale and the market consists of multiple buyers making bids to buy, or an item is wanted and the market consists of multiple sellers, making offers to sell. In either case, one side of the market consists of a single entity. On the other hand, multiple buyers and sellers may be making bids and offers simultaneously in a **double auction**. An example of a double auction is stock trading.

Although most online auctions are single, double auctions are important for certain types of transactions. Their procedures and market-clearing price levels are unique.

In double auctions, multiple units of a product may be auctioned off at the same time. The situation gets complicated when the quantity offered is more than one and buyers and sellers bid on varying quantities.

In a given trading period, any seller may make an offer while any buyer makes a bid. Either a seller or a buyer may accept the offer or bid at any time. The difference between cost and price paid is the seller's profit; the difference between price

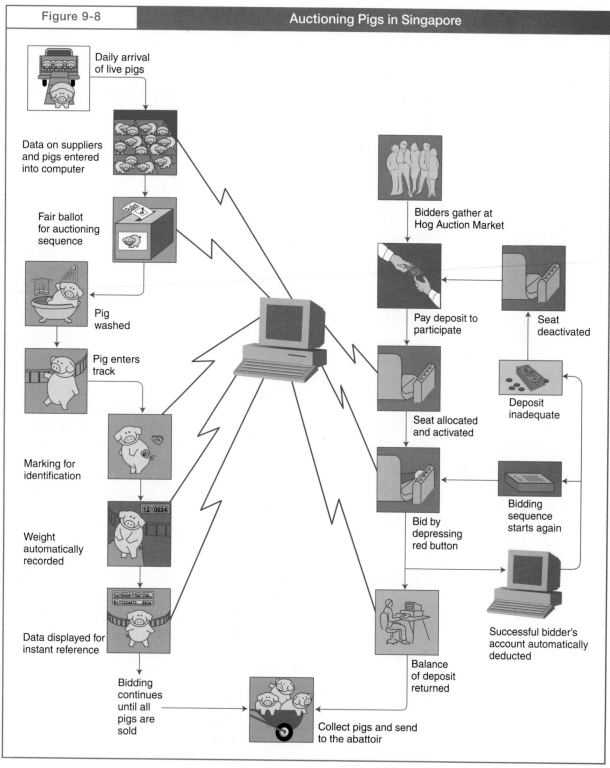

Figure 9-8	Auctioning Pigs in Singapore

Daily arrival of live pigs

Data on suppliers and pigs entered into computer

Fair ballot for auctioning sequence

Pig washed

Pig enters track

Marking for identification

12 0034

Weight automatically recorded

12 0034 60 758
91 7324472 $834

Data displayed for instant reference

Bidding continues until all pigs are sold

Bidders gather at Hog Auction Market

Pay deposit to participate

Seat allocated and activated

Bid by depressing red button

Balance of deposit returned

Collect pigs and send to the abattoir

Successful bidder's account automatically deducted

Bidding sequence starts again

Deposit inadequate

Seat deactivated

paid and valuation is the buyer's surplus. If the quantities vary, as in a stock market, a market maker needs to match quantities as well.

PRICES IN DOUBLE AUCTIONS

According to Choi and Whinston (2000), double auction markets tend to generate competitive outcomes. Simply put, a double auction is an interactive form of market in which both buyers and sellers are competitive. In contrast, in a single auction, contract prices may be much higher or much lower than in a competitive format. This conclusion will have a significant effect on the future use of double auctions in the digital economy.

Ideally, any effort to promote competitiveness should include expanding double auctions and similar market mechanisms as they offer an opportunity to raise economic efficiencies unsurpassed by any physical market organization. For auctioneers, however, single auctions generate substantially more revenue than double auctions.

Bundle Trading

One of the major characteristics of the digital economy is the personalization and customization of products and services (see Chapter 2). This often means a collection of complementary goods and services. A combination of airline tickets, hotel rooms, a rental car, meals, and amusement park admission tickets can be bundled as a packaged leisure product. Some products that are vertically related (e.g., a computer operating system and a Web browser) may be provided by different vendors, requiring buyers to deal with multiple sellers. While a purchase that involves multiple sellers may be carried out through a series of transactions or auctions, bundle trading offers a simplified and efficient alternative solution.

The management and operation of a bundle market is complex, and it differs considerably from those of single or double auction markets. For a discussion see Choi and Whinston (2000).

Prices in Auctions: Higher or Lower?

Compared to competitive markets, prices in auctions tend to be higher, reaching monopoly level when there is only one seller (Choi and Whinston, 2000). In general, the auctioneer is in a better position to maximize revenues. When the auctioneer is selling a product among multiple bidders, the expected price is often higher than the competitive level. Conversely, when the auctioneer is buying from multiple offers, he or she may choose the lowest offer, which is usually lower than the competitive market price. This result is largely due to the simple fact that there is competition among bidders.

However, in many instances prices in auctions are lower. This may happen in cases of liquidation, where the seller's objective is to sell as quickly as possible. Alternatively, buyers go to global markets where they can get products more cheaply than if imported by intermediaries. In general, buyers expect online prices to be lower. For example, truckers or airlines selling unused capacity at the last minute usually do so at a lower price. Also, considering the fact that most C2C auctions are for used merchandise, and surplus B2B auctions may include used or obsolete products, bargain prices are likely to prevail.

Finally, a more fundamental reason for lower online auction prices is that an online auction is usually an alternative selling channel, instead of being an exclusive selling arrangement. Therefore, buyers can always revert to physical markets if bids exceed posted prices. In short, no one is willing to pay what they are expected to pay in physical markets. If products are sold exclusively through online auctions, the average price will certainly increase.

PRICING STRATEGIES IN ONLINE AUCTIONS

Both sellers and buyers may develop strategies for auctioning. Sellers have the option to use different mechanisms, such as English, Dutch, sealed-bid first price, and sealed-bid second price. Buyers need to develop a strategy regarding how much to increase a bid and when to stop bidding. These topics are relevant to offline auctions as well and will not be dealt with here.

9.8   FRAUD IN AUCTIONS AND ITS PREVENTION

According to Internet Fraud Watch (*fraud.org/internet/intstat.htm*), among all e-commerce activities conducted over the Internet, fraud is most serious in e-auctions. It accounted for 87 percent of the e-commerce fraud that occurred in 1999. According to the National Consumer League's National Fraud Information Center, 9 out of 10 registered Internet-related complaints are concerned with auction fraud. The average auction loss is $248 per complaint, and roughly $1.1 million was lost due to fraudulent activity in 1999.

In October 2000, *Amazon.com* cancelled the auctions of World Series tickets because of extensive speculation that violated the New York State law that prohibits selling tickets for $5 or 10 percent more than face value.

Types of E-Auction Fraud

Fraud may be conducted by sellers or by buyers. The following are some examples:

Bid shielding. Bid shielding is the use of phantom bidders to bid at a very high price when an auction begins. The phantom bidders pull out at the last minute, and the bidder who bids with a very low price wins. The bogus bidders were the shields, protecting the low bid of the third bidder in the stack. By bid shielding, a ring of dishonest bidders can target an item and inflate the bid value to scare off other real bidders.

Shilling. Sellers arrange to have fake bids placed on their items (either by associates or by using multiple user IDs) to artificially jack up high bids. If they see a legitimate high bid that doesn't meet their expectations as the end of an auction draws near, they might pop in to manipulate the price.

Fake photos and misleading descriptions. In reaching for bidders' attention, some sellers distort what they can truly sell. Borrowed images, ambiguous descriptions, and falsified facts are some of the tactics that sellers might employ.

Improper grading techniques. Grading items is often the most hotly debated issue among buyers and sellers. The seller might describe an item as 90 percent new while the bidder, after receiving the item and paying the full amount, feels it is only 70 percent new. Condition is often in the eye of the beholder. Although many grading systems have been devised and put to use, condition is still subject to interpretation.

Selling reproductions. A seller sells something that he claims is original, but it turns out to be a reproduction.

High shipping costs and handling fees. Some sellers just want to get a little more cash out of bidders. Postage and handling rates vary from seller to seller. Some charge extra to cover "handling" costs and other overhead intangibles, while others charge to cover the cost of packaging supplies, even though such supplies are often available for free.

Failure to ship merchandise. It's the old collect-and-run routine. Money was paid out but the merchandise never arrived.

Loss and damage claims. Buyers claim they never received an item or received it in damaged condition and then ask for a refund. They might be trying to get a freebie. The seller sometimes can't prove whether the item ever arrived or whether it was in perfect condition when shipped.

Switch and return. The seller has successfully auctioned an item, but when the buyer receives it, he or she is not satisfied. The seller offers a cheerful refund. However, what he or she gets back is a mess that doesn't much resemble the item he or she has shipped. Some buyers might attempt to swap out their junk for someone else's jewels.

Protecting Against E-Auction Fraud

The largest Internet auctioneer, eBay, has introduced several measures in an effort to reduce fraud. Some are free and some are not. The company has succeeded in its goal: only 27 out of every 1,000,000 transactions at eBay were fraudulent in 2000. Following are the measures they take:

User identity verification. EBay uses the services of Equifax to verify user identities for a $5 fee. Verified eBay User, the voluntary program, encourages users to supply eBay with information for online verification. By offering their social security number, driver's license number, and date of birth, users can qualify for the highest level of verification on eBay.

Authentication service. Product authentication is a way of determining whether an item is genuine and described appropriately. Authentication is very difficult to perform because it relies on the expertise of the authenticators. Because of their training and experience, experts can often detect counterfeits based on subtle details (for a fee). However, two expert authenticators may have different opinions about the authenticity of the same item.

Grading services. Grading is a way of determining the physical condition of an item, such as "poor quality" or "mint condition." The actual grading system depends on the type of item being graded. Different items have different grading systems—for example, trading cards are graded from A1 to F1, while coins are graded from poor to perfect uncirculated.

Feedback Forum. The eBay Feedback Forum allows registered buyers and sellers to build up their online trading reputations. It provides users with the ability to comment on their experiences with other individuals.

Insurance policy. EBay offers insurance underwritten by Lloyd's of London. Users are covered up to $200, with a $25 deductible. The program is provided at no cost to eBay users.

Escrow services. For items valued at more than $200, or when either a buyer or seller feels the need for additional security, eBay recommends escrow services (for a fee). With an easy to access link to a third-party escrow service, both partners in a deal are protected.

The buyer mails the payment to the escrow service, which verifies the payment and alerts the seller when everything checks out. At that point, the seller ships the goods to the buyer. After an agreed-upon inspection period, the buyer notifies the service, which sends a check to the seller. (An example of a provider of online escrow services is *tradenable.com*.)

Non-payment punishment. EBay implemented a policy against those who do not honor their winning bids. To help protect sellers, a first-time nonpayment results in a friendly warning. A sterner warning is issued for a second-time offense, with a 30-day suspension for a third offense, and indefinite suspension for a fourth offense.

Appraisal services. Appraisers use a variety of methods to appraise items, including expert assessment of authenticity and condition, and reviewing what comparable items have sold for in the marketplace in recent months. An appraised value is usually accurate at the time of appraisal but may change over time as an item becomes more or less popular in the marketplace.

Verification. Verification is a way of confirming the identity and evaluating the condition of an item. Third parties will evaluate and identify an item through a variety of means. For example, some collectors have their item "DNA tagged" for identification purposes. This provides a way of tracking an item if it changes ownership in the future.

In addition, one can use the general EC fraud protection measures suggested in Chapter 17.

9.9   BARTERING ONLINE

Bartering is the oldest method of trade. It is an exchange of goods and services, and today it is usually done between organizations. The problem in bartering is that it is difficult to find partners. Therefore, **bartering exchanges** were created, in which an intermediary arranges the transactions. The process works like this:

1. You tell the intermediary what you offer.
2. The intermediary assesses the value of your surplus products or services and offers you certain "points" (or "bartering dollars").
3. You use the "points" to buy the things you need.

The problem with manual matching done by a third party is that the commission is very high (30 percent or more), and it may take a long time to complete a transaction.

Electronic bartering (**e-bartering**) can improve the matching process by attracting more customers to the exchange. Also, the matching can be done faster. As a result, better matches can be found and the commission is much lower (5 to 10 percent).

Items that are frequently bartered include office space, storage, factory space, idle facilities and labor, products, and banner ads.

Businesses and individuals may use e-classified ads to advertise what they need and what they offer. However, exchanges can be much more effective. E-bartering may have tax implications that need to be considered. Some of the bartering Web sites are *Bigvine.com*, *Bartertrust.com*, *ubarter.com*, and *whosbartering.com* (see Lorek, 2000).

Bartering sites must be financially secure. Otherwise users may not have a chance to use the points they accumulate. (For further details, see *fsb.com*, and search for "virtual bartering 101".)

As an alternative to bartering, you can auction your surplus and then use the money collected to buy what you need. Several auction sites specialize in surplus sales (e.g., *dovebid.com*).

9.10   NEGOTIATING AND BARGAINING ONLINE

Dynamic prices can also be determined by negotiation, especially for expensive or specialized products. It is a well-known process in the offline world, in real estate, automobiles, and agricultural products.

Much like in auctions, negotiated prices result from interactions and bargaining among sellers and buyers. However, in contrast with auctions, negotiations also deal with nonpricing terms, such as payment method and credit.

According to Choi and Whinston (2000), negotiating in the electronic environment is easier than in the physical environment. Also, due to customization and bundling of products and services, it is necessary to negotiate prices and terms. E-markets allow negotiations to be used for virtually all products and services. Three factors may facilitate negotiated prices:

1. Intelligent agents that perform searches and comparisons, thereby providing quality customer service and a base from which prices can be negotiated.
2. Computer technology that facilitates the negotiation process.
3. Products and services that are bundled and customized.

One price does not fit all consumers, which sometimes makes price comparisons provided by MySimon and other online comparison-shopping services difficult to execute, if not impossible. In personal services or insurance markets, because goods and services differ from individual to individual, we observe no posted prices that are easily identified. To the extent that there is no standard product to speak of at a standard price, digital products and services can be personalized as well as "integrated" as a smart service. Preferences for these bundled services differ among consumers, and thus they are combinations of services and corresponding prices.

Technologies for Bargaining

According to Choi and Whinston (2000), negotiations and bargaining involve a bilateral interaction between a seller and a buyer who are engaged in the following five-step process that is necessary to complete a transaction:

- **Search.** Gathering information about products and services, and locating potential vendors or customers.
- **Selection.** Processing and filtering information in order to select a product and a trading partner.

- **Negotiation.** Interactions with bids and offers, agreement, and contract.
- **Continuing selection and negotiation.** Repeated sequentially, if necessary, until an agreement is reached.
- **Transaction completion.** Payment and delivery.

SEARCH

Bargaining starts with collecting all relevant information about products and sellers or buyers. Computer-mediated markets excel in raising the search efficiency. Once information has been gathered, the next step is to process it into a usable data set that is employed for decision making. (Search tools are described in Chapter 4.)

SELECTION

Selection filters retrieve screened information that helps determine what to buy (sell) and from whom to buy (sell). This encompasses the evaluation of product and seller alternatives based on consumer-provided criteria such as price, warranty, availability, delivery time, and reputation. The selection process results in a set of names of products and partners to negotiate with in the next step. Software agents, such as Pricemix (*pricemix.com*), and other tools can facilitate the selection (see Chapter 4).

NEGOTIATION

The negotiation stage focuses on how to establish the terms of the transaction, such as price, product characteristics, delivery, and payment terms. Negotiation varies in duration and complexity depending on the market. In online markets, all stages of negotiation can be carried out by automated programs or software agents.

Negotiation agents are software programs that make independent decisions to accept or reject offers or make bids within predetermined constraints. There might be negotiation rules or protocols by which agents of sellers and buyers interact. For example, price negotiation may start with a seller's list price as a starting point or in a free form starting with any bid or offer depending on the rule. (For an overview of electronic negotiation and comparison, see Beam et al., 1999.)

The following are the major benefits of electronic negotiations:

1. Buyers and sellers do not need to determine prices beforehand, and thereby do not have to engage in the difficult process of collecting relevant information. Negotiating prices transfers the burden of determining prices (i.e., market valuation) to the market itself. Insofar as the market process is efficient, the resulting negotiated prices will be fair and efficient.
2. Intelligent agents can negotiate both price and non-price attributes such as delivery time, return policy, and other value-added transactions. Intelligent agents can deal with multiple partners (see Appendix D at *prenhall.com/turban*). An example of such an application is several freight dispatch centers of different companies negotiating a solution to their vehicle routing problems. Other applications include a factory floor-scheduling domain, where different companies in a subcontracting web negotiate over a joint scheduling problem, as well as an airport resource management domain, where negotiations take place for the servicing of airplanes between flights. (For further discussion, see Esmahi and Bernard, 2000.)

TRANSACTION COMPLETION

After product, vendor, and price are determined, the final step is to complete the transaction. This involves online payment and product delivery in accordance with the terms determined in the negotiation phase. Other characteristics, such as customer service, warranty, and refunds, may also be implemented.

9.11   MOBILE AUCTIONS AND THE FUTURE OF AUCTIONS

Research institutions have estimated that there will be 1.4 billion mobile phone users in the world by 2003, 50 percent of which will be Internet and Wireless Application Protocol (WAP) enabled. The mobile phone and other wireless devices are going to be the principal way for many people to come to the Internet, resulting in large volume m-commerce (Mobile Commerce). This opportunity is moving to auctions as well.

In the United States, eBay went wireless Internet in October 1999, and uBid and FairMarket started in 2000. Yahoo and other auction sites have been scrambling to go wireless. In the United Kingdom, *bluecycle.com*, which conducts auctions on used cars for dealers, allows dealers to bid from anywhere by using their cell phones.

There are some benefits and limitations of WAP phones for online auctions. Benefits include the following:

- **Convenience and ubiquity.** People can do auction business on the go and from any location via mobile phone.
- **Privacy.** The WAP phone is more private than a PC and will always be within range. One can auction anything from anywhere and search for information in the middle of a discussion around the café table. Bids can be checked on the run. All this can transpire in a secure and private environment.
- **Simpler and faster.** Because online auctions require a limited amount of information, it is relatively easy to adapt WAP-enabled phones, even if they can only handle limited bandwidth and data.

Limitations include the following:

- **Visual quality.** The WAP screen is very small. One cannot read through the same amount of information as on a computer. Also, the screen quality is not as good as on a PC monitor. One can send pictures of desired products to bidders via WAP, but if images are too complicated they will appear as blurs. It is also much harder to send information about products via the phone than via a PC.
- **Memory capacity.** WAP phones have little memory capacity. In the near future, the development of new WAP services will probably press hardware producers to come up with better memory systems for mobile terminals.
- **Security.** The security issues particular to WAP are being tackled through new security standards, such as SIM Toolkit and wireless transport layer security.

For more on these and other benefits and limitations see Chapter 19.

Global Auctions

Many auction companies sell products and services on the Web and are extending their reach. One way of doing that is by going global. However, such companies may face all the regular problems of selling online in foreign countries (see Chapter 18).

Selling Art Online in Real-Time Auctions

Since January 2001, collectors in the United Kingdom can bid online in live show-room auctions using an application of eBay and *icollector.com*. Icollector provides real-time access to 300 independent auction houses, such as London's Phillips. The largest art auction houses, Sotheby's and Christie's, have online sites, but they do not allow (as of spring 2001) online bidding for live showroom auctions. In the United States, *Butterfields.com* allows for real-time auction bidding and partners with eBay (see *New York Times*, January 22, 2001).

Strategic Alliances

Auctions may have a major impact on competition and on industry structure. In addition, auctions may be used as a strategic tool by Internet-based and other com-panies. An example of such a strategy is provided in Application Case 9.4. It seems

APPLICATION CASE   9.4

SOLD of Australia

SOLD (*sold.com.au*) is a pioneer in the online marketplace, where classified advertising and sales merge with the auction process to create a dynamic, fast growing e-commerce community. It is Australia's biggest online auction site. SOLD is a partnership between two leaders in the Internet industry—Fairfax Interactive Network (*fxj.com.au*) and Auctions Universal (*auctions.com*).

On September 13, 1999, SOLD and CitySearch (*citysearch.com.au*) the most popular Australia online leisure and lifestyle guide, launched a B2C program that provides small to medium-sized businesses (SMEs) with a web-based sales channel. This program enables SMEs to use Australia's leading auction site as an outlet to sell general stock lines, excess stock and dis-counted items.

Auction Shop, a division of SOLD, is offering brand-new computer prod-ucts from leading manufacturers, and top quality equipment and household appliances. The offer gives online consumers the chance to snare heavily dis-counted prices with warranties for a greater range of new products including both excess stock and special price promotions.

SOLD had over 75,000 registered members by the end of 2000 and has had 40,000 sales for merchandise worth over $6 million dollars in its first six months of operation. By late 2000 there were 140,000 auction items on the site in over 170 categories, such as collectibles and memorabilia, business goods, sporting equipment, household items, travel and/or accom-modations, millennium event tickets and venues, computer products and Olympic pins.

In late 2000 the listing was free. The commission fee was 3.5% of the final selling price.

SOLD's B2C service offers users Merchant Manager—an inventory man-agement and bulk-loading software which greatly reduces item listing time, assists in inventory management and profit analysis, and provides additional invaluable post-auction services. Merchant Manager allows up to 4,000 items to be listed on the site in 30 minutes.

this type of strategic alliance will be very popular in the future due to its win-win possibilities.

9.12   MANAGERIAL ISSUES

The following issues are germane to management:

1. **Your own auction site vs. a third-party site.** This is a strategic issue, and there are pluses and minuses to each alternative. However, if you decide to auction from your site, you will need to advertise and attract visitors, which may be expensive. Also, you will need to install fraud-prevention mechanisms and provide services. Either way, you may need to consider connectivity to your back-office and logistics system. The following are several issues that need to be handled by management.

2. **Cost-benefit analysis.** A major strategic issue is whether you need to do auctions or not. Auctions do have risks, and in forward auctions you may create conflicts with your other distribution channels.

3. **Auction strategies.** Selecting an auction mechanism, pricing, and bidding strategy can be very complex for sellers. These strategies determine the success of the auction and the ability to attract and retain visitors on the site.

4. **Support services.** Auctions require support services. Decisions about how to provide them and to what extent to use business partners are critical to the success of repeated high-volume auctions. (Chapter 8 describes some support services used in B2B.)

5. **Payment.** An efficient payment mechanism is important for auctions, especially when the buyers or sellers are individuals. Some innovative methods can solve the payment problem (see Chapter 14).

6. **Controlling what is auctioned.** Both individuals and companies would like to auction everything. However, is it ethical or even legal to do it? Ask eBay, which is trying, for example, to clean up pornographic auctions by banning some items and directing some items into a "mature audiences" area. Another issue is pirated software, which is offered on about 2,000 auction sites worldwide. As a matter of fact, eBay was sued in 2000 by video-game manufacturers Nintendo, Sega, and Electronic Arts. (For further discussion, see Beato, 2000.)

7. **Change agent.** Auctions may change the manner in which companies sell their products. They may change the nature of competition in certain industries, as well as price and margin levels.

8. **Building auction applications.** Quite a few vendors offer auction software (e.g., see *fairmarket.com*). (See Chapter 12 for a discussion of what is available, what is needed, and how applications are selected.)

9. **Bartering.** Bartering can be an interesting strategy, especially for companies that need cash and have some surpluses. However, the valuation of what is bought or sold may be different, and the tax implications in some countries are not clear.

10. **Building auction sites.** The process of building auction applications is complex for two reasons:

   a. The number of features can be very large (see Section 9.5 and Figure 9-9).

   b. There may be a need to integrate auctions in the B2B case, with the office and legacy systems of participating companies (see Figure 9-10 and Chapters 8 and 12).

Figure 9-9 — Components of a Comprehensive Auction Site

Online Auctions

Help	Services	Basics	Buyers Guide	Sellers Guide	Rules	Safety and Protection
How to Bid	Online Communities	Registration	How to Buy	How to Sell	User Agreement	Feedback Forum
How to Sell	Tutorials	General Inquiries	Auction Types	Auction Types	Privacy Policy	Insurance
What is Allowed	Charity	Glossary of Terms	Tips for Buyers	Tips for Sellers	GST Policy	Safe Harbor
Authentication	Suggestion Box	Bidding Basics	Proxy Bidding	Packaging and Shipping	Board Usage	Escrow
Grading	Chats	Security, Privacy	Retracting a bid	Retracting a Sale	Trade Offenses	Defamation
	Library		Contacting Others	Closing the Deal	Selling Offenses	Fraud Prevention
	International Traders		Closing a Deal	International Trading	Identity Offenses	Authentication
	Buying and Selling Tools		Buying Abroad	Power Trading	Grading	Grading
	Reverse Auctions		My E-auction		Netiquette	Appraising
	Payments					
	Notification					
	Historical Prices					

Figure 9-10 — Integrated Auction Business Model

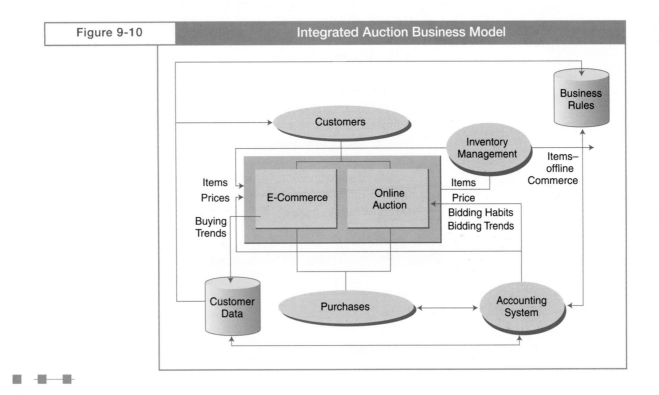

Summary

In this chapter, you learned about the following EC issues as they relate to the learning objectives:

1. **Define the various types of auctions and list their characteristics.** In *forward auctions,* bids from buyers are placed sequentially, either increasing (English mode) or decreasing (Dutch mode). In *reverse auctions* buyers place an RFQ and suppliers (providers) submit offers, in one or several rounds. In "name-your-own-price" auctions, buyers specify how much they are willing to pay for a product or service and an intermediary tries to find a supplier to fulfill the request.

2. **Describe the processes of conducting forward and reverse auctions.** In a forward auction, the seller places the item to be sold on the auction site, with a starting price and closing time. Potential buyers bid from their PCs. The highest bids are constantly shown. At the close, the highest bidder wins. In a reverse auction, a buyer requests quotes for a product or service. These usually come in sequentially and the lowest bids are constantly shown. Reverse auctions are usually fast. The lowest-price bidder wins.

3. **Describe the benefits and limitations of auctions.** The major benefits for sellers are the ability to reach many buyers and to sell quickly. Also, sellers save the commissions they might otherwise pay to intermediaries. Buyers have a chance to obtain collectibles while shopping from their homes, and they can find bargains. The major limitation is the possibility of fraud.

4. **Describe the various services that support auctions.** Services exist along the entire process and include tools for (a) searching and comparing auctions for specific items, (b) registering, promoting, pricing, etc., (c) bid watching, making multiple bids, and proxy bidding, and (d) notification, payment, and shipping.

5. **Describe the hazards of e-auction fraud and countermeasures.** Fraud can be committed either by sellers or by buyers. Good auction sites provide protection that includes voluntary identity verification, monitoring of rules violation, escrow services, and insurance.

6. **Describe bartering and negotiating.** Electronic bartering can greatly facilitate the swapping of goods and services among organizations, thanks to improved search and matching capabilities.

7. **Analyze future directions and the role of m-commerce.** B2B, C2C, G2B, and B2C auctions are all expanding rapidly. Future directions include an increase in global trading, use of wireless devices to monitor and trade at auctions, an increase in the use of intelligent agents in all auction processes, and a merger of various types of auctions to allow traders more flexibility and choices.

Key Terms

Auction	Consumer-to-business (C2B) model
Auction aggregations	Double auction
Auction vortals (vertical auctions)	Dutch auction
Bartering	Dynamic pricing
Bartering exchanges	E-auctions
Bounded auction	E-bartering

English auction	Reserve price auction
Exchanges (dynamic)	Reverse auction
Forward auction	Single auction
Free-fall auction	Snipping
Market maker	Stickiness
Maximum bid	Tendering system
"Name-your-own-price" model	Vertical auction
Negotiation online	Yankee auction
Proxy bidding	

Questions for Review

1. Define dynamic pricing and list its four parts.
2. Distinguish between forward and reverse auctions.
3. Define English auctions and Dutch auctions.
4. Describe the *Priceline.com* approach.
5. Define proxy bidding and describe its purpose.
6. What is meant by "snipping"?
7. List the advantages of e-bartering.
8. Define a double auction.
9. What are the benefits of e-auctions to the auction market makers?
10. Define a reserve price auction.
11. Describe the use of wireless technology in auctions.

Questions for Discussion

1. The "name-your-own-price" method is considered to be a reverse auction. There is no RFQ or consecutive bidding, so why is it called a reverse auction?
2. Discuss the advantages of dynamic pricing over fixed pricing. What are the potential disadvantages?
3. Find some material on why individuals like C2C auctions so much. Write a report.
4. Compare the "name-your-own-price" and RFQ approaches. Under what circumstances is each advantageous?
5. Identify three fraud practices in which a seller might engage. How can buyers protect themselves?
6. Identify three fraud practices in which a buyer might engage. How can sellers protect themselves?
7. It is said that Manheim Auction is trying to sell more online without cannibalizing its core business. Discuss this situation.
8. Discuss the need for software agents in auctions. Start by analyzing proxy bidding and auction aggregators.

Exercises

1. For each of the following situations, which (if any) dynamic pricing approach would you use and why?
   a. breeding and selling horses for racing
   b. buying flour for a bakery

    c. buying a horse for horse racing

    d. selling your used sports car, which is in high demand

    e. selling your old, obsolete PC system

    f. selling the stocks your grandfather left you as a gift

2. Enter *dellauction.com* and click on "site terms." Examine the policies, security and encryption statement, privacy protection statement, escrow services, payment options, and other features. Register (for free), then bid on a computer of interest to you. If you are not interested, bid very low, so you will not get it.

    Alternatively, try to sell a computer. If you do not have one to sell, place an asking price so high that you will not get any bids. Read the FAQs. Which of the following mechanisms are used on the Dell site: English, Dutch (declining), reverse, etc. Why?

    Write a report on your experiences and describe all the features available at this site.

    Note: If you are outside the United States, use an auction site accessible where you are.

3. Compare *dovebid.com* and Yahoo! Auctions for selling surpluses. Use criteria such as fees paid by users, ease of use, execution, and mission. For more ideas about comparing sites, refer to *Interactiveweek*, September 13, 1999.

4. Imagine that you want to start forward auctions for a company with which you are familiar. Consider doing it in-house vs. using a third-party site. Write a comparative report.

Internet Exercises

1. Visit *eBay.com* and examine all the quality assurance measures available either for a fee or for free. Prepare a list.

2. Visit *AuctionWatch.com* and report on the various services offered at the site. What are the site's revenue models?

3. Enter *Bidfind.com* and report on the various services provided. What is the site's revenue model?

4. Enter *mmm.eBay.com* and investigate the use of "anywhere wireless." Review the wireless devices and find out how they work.

5. Enter *imandi.com* and review the process in which buyers can send RFQs to merchants of their choice. Also, evaluate the services provided in the areas of marketing, staffing, and travel. Write a report.

6. Examine the process used by *office.com* regarding auctions. Review its reverse auction arrangement with *BigBuyer.com*. Write a report.

7. Enter *commerceone.com/auctions* and view all the different types of auction software and auction hosting available. Find what they have for a company-centric auction and learn about exchanges.

8. Enter *escrow.com* and view the tutorial on how escrow services work for both buyers and sellers in electronic commerce.

9. Enter *biddersedge.com* and find historical prices on an item of your choice. How may this information be of help to you as a seller? As a buyer?

10. Enter *respond.com* and send a request for a product or a service. Once you receive replies, select the best deal. You have no obligation to buy. Write a short report on your experience.

11. Enter *icollector.com* and review the process used to auction art. Find support services, such as currency conversion and shipping. Take the tour of the site. Prepare a report on online buying as a collector.
12. Enter *ubid.com* and examine the "auction exchange." What is unique about it? Compare the auction there to those conducted on *yahoo.com*. What are the major differences?

Team Assignments and Role Playing

1. Each team is assigned to an auction method (English, Dutch, etc.). Each team should convince a company that wants to liquidate items, that their method is the best. Items to be liquidated:
   a. Five IBM top-of-the-line mainframe systems valued at about $500,000 each
   b. 750 PCs valued at about $1,000 each
   c. A real estate property valued at about $10 million.
   Present arguments for each type of item.
2. Assign teams to major auction sites from your country and from two other countries. Each team should present the major functionalities of the sites and the fraud protection measures they use.

REAL-WORLD CASE: *FreeMarkets.com*

FreeMarkets.com began in 1995 with an idea: By conducting auctions online, procurement professionals could raise the quality of the direct materials and services they buy while substantially lowering the prices they pay for them.

FreeMarkets is a leader in creating B2B online auctions for buyers of industrial parts, raw materials, commodities, and services around the globe. The company has created auctions for goods and services in more than 70 industrial product categories. In 1999, FreeMarkets auctioned more than $2.7 billion worth of purchase orders and saved buyers an estimated 2 to 25 percent.

FreeMarkets has helped customers source billions of dollars worth of goods and services in hundreds of product and service categories through its B2B Global Marketplace. FreeMarkets has also helped companies improve their asset recovery results by getting timely market prices for surplus assets through the FreeMarkets Asset Exchange.

FreeMarkets Asset Exchange creates a robust asset recovery solution that addresses even the most complex transactions. It bridges the gaps in information, geography, and industry that make traditional surplus-asset markets so inefficient.

FreeMarkets Asset Exchange provides a reliable, flexible trading platform that includes an online marketplace, online markets, and onsite auctions. With a combination of online and onsite sales venues, FreeMarkets Asset Exchange has the following solutions to help companies meet their asset recovery goals:

- **FreeMarkets online markets.** An effective method for asset disposal that delivers timely, market-based pricing.

- **FreeMarkets online marketplace.** A self-service venue where sellers post available assets. Useful when getting the right price is more important than a quick sale.

- **FreeMarkets onsite auctions.** Live auction events that are ideal for clearing a facility, time-critical sales, or selling a mix of high- and low-value assets.

When the commercial situation demands, the company also combines onsite auctions and online markets into a single asset disposal solution.

FreeMarkets Onsite Auctions provide the following:

- **Asset disposal analysis.** Market makers work with sellers to determine the best strategy to meet asset recovery goals.

- **Detailed sales offering.** The company collects and consolidates asset information into a printed or online sales offering for buyers.

- **Targeted market outreach.** FreeMarkets conducts targeted marketing to a global database of 500,000 buyers and suppliers.

- **Event coordination.** The company prepares the site, provides qualified personnel, and enforces auction rules.

- **Sales implementation.** FreeMarkets summarizes auction results and assists in closing sales.

Following is a customer's success story:

Emerson Corp., a global diversified manufacturing firm, faced the difficult challenge of consolidating millions of dollars of printed circuit board (PCB) purchases across 14 global divisions. The company wanted to consolidate its supply base and standardize data to understand future buying patterns. It turned to FreeMarkets for assistance.

Using an RFQ, Emerson received 755 bids and achieved the following:

- Obtained buy-in from 14 divisions to participate in a corporate-wide event.

- Standardized data on more than 1,000 PCB designs across 19 divisions.

- Introduced several qualified suppliers from Asian countries.

- Consolidated its supplier's base from 58 to 9.

The company saved more than $10 million in 1 year.

Questions for the case

1. Enter *FreeMarkets.com* and explore the current activities of the company.

2. Look at five customer success stories. What common elements can you find?

3. Identify additional services provided by the company.

4. If you work in a company, register and examine the process as a buyer and as a seller.

5. Compare the use of *FreeMarkets.com* to the option of building your own auction site.

6. What is the logic of concentrating on asset recovery?

7. How does surplus asset recovery become more efficient with FreeMarket?

REFERENCES AND BIBLIOGRAPHY

Aberdeen Group. "The Moment: Providing Pricing Flexibility for eMarkets" (*aberdeen.com*), (July 27, 2000).

Beam, C., et al. "On Negotiations and Deal Making in Electronic Markets," *Information Systems Frontiers*, vol. 1:3, 1999.

Beato, G. "Online Piracy's Mother Ship," (*Business2.com*) (December 12, 2000).

Boileau, R. *The ABCs of Collecting Online*, 3rd ed. (Grantsville, Michigan: Hobby House Press, 2000).

Choi, S. Y. and A. B. Whinston. *The Internet Economy: Technology and Practice*, Austin, Texas: SmarteconPub., 2000.

Elliot, A. C. *Getting Started in Internet Auctions,* New York: John Wiley & Sons, 2000.

Esmahi, L. and J. C. Bernard. "MIAMAP: A Virtual Marketplace for Intelligent Agents," Proceedings of the 33rd HICSS, Maui, Hawaii, January 2000.

Fickel, L. "Bid Business," *CIO WebBusiness Magazine* (June 1, 1999).

Keenanvision.com. *The Keenan Report #1* San Francisco: Keenan Vision Inc., 1998.

Klein, S. "Introduction to Electronic Auctions," *Electronic Markets* vol. 7, no. 4 (1997).

Lorek, L. "Trade ya? E-Barter Thrives," *InteractiveWeek* (August 14, 2000).

Mckeown, P. G. and R. T. Watson. "Manheim Auctions," *Communications of the Association for Information Systems* (June 1999).

Millen-Portor, A. "E-Auction Model Morphs to Meet Buyers' Need," *Purchasing* (June 15, 2000).

Miner, R. *Dynamic Trading*. Tucson: Dynamic Trading Group, 1999.

Murch, R. and T. Johnson. *Intelligent Software Systems*. Upper Saddle River, NJ: Prentice Hall, 1999.

Neo, B. S. "The Implementation of an Electronic Market for Pig Trading in Singapore," *Journal of Strategic Information Systems* (December 1992).

Prince, D. L. *Auction This!: Your Complete Guide to the World of Online Auctions,* Roseville, California: Prima Publishing, 1999.

Strobel, M. "On Auctions as the Negotiation Paradigm of Electronic Markets," *Electronic Markets*, vol. 10, no. 1 (2000).

Taylor D. and S. M. Cooney. *The e-Auction Insider* (Berkeley, Calif.: Osborne-McGraw Hill, 2000).

Vakrat, Y. and A. Seidman. "Implications of Bidders' Arrival Process on the Design of Online Auctions," Proceedings of the 33rd HICSS, Maui, Hawaii, January 2000.

Wagner, C. and E. Turban. "Intelligent Electronic Commerce Agents: Partners or Predators?," *Communications of the ACM.* Forthcoming, 2002.

Westland, J. C. "Ten Lessons that Internet Auction Markets Can Learn from Securities Market Automation," *Journal of Global Management* (January–March 2000).

Wharton University School of Business at Univ. of Penn. "Dynamic Pricing: What Does It Mean?" *ebizchronicle.com/wharton/19-digitalfuture* (October 18, 2000).

Wurman, P. R., et al. "Flexible Double Auctions for E-Commerce: Theory and Implementation," *Decision Support Systems* vol. 24 (1998).

10

Service Industries, Online Publishing, and Knowledge Dissemination

LEARNING OBJECTIVES

Upon completion of this chapter, the reader will be able to:

- Understand how broker-based services are performed online.

- Describe online travel tourism services and their benefits.

- Discuss the impact of EC on the travel industry.

- Describe the online job market, its drivers, and benefits.

- Describe the electronic real estate and online insurance markets.

- Understand how stock trading and global exchanges work online and their benefits.

- Discuss cyberbanking, its drivers, and capabilities.

- Discuss implementation and other important issues of online financial services and its future.

- Describe online publishing.

- Describe online knowledge dissemination and distance learning.

- Discuss disintermediation and reintermediation.

10.1 ORDERING JOURNALS ELECTRONICALLY AT THE UNIVERSITY OF CALIFORNIA

Universities and many other organizations order periodicals for their libraries constantly. New periodicals appear every day, people change their preferences, and the librarians are busy. Typically, a university will contact an agent to place orders. The agent, who is in contact with thousands of publishers, consolidates orders from several universities and then places orders with the publishers. This process is both slow and expensive for the library, which pays a 3 percent commission and loses a 5 percent discount that the publisher passes on to the agent.

In 1996, the University of California at Berkeley pioneered an electronic ordering system, which enabled the university to save about $365,000 per year. Furthermore, the ordering cycle time was cut by as much as 80 percent, providing subscribers with the magazines 1 to 3 months faster.

RoweCom, Inc. (*rowe.com*) manages the electronic ordering. Its software system, Subscribe, enables a university to electronically submit its encrypted orders and a secure payment authorization to a central computer by EDI. The program verifies the order and the authorization, transfers the order by EDI to the publishers, and sends the payment authorization to the automated EFT clearinghouse from the buyer's bank to the seller's bank. This process is shown in Figure 10-1.

The cost to the university is $5 per order. For an average periodical with an annual subscription fee of $400, the cost of online ordering is more than 80 percent lower than ordering with a human agent ($5 vs. $32). The system includes BANC ONE managing software (*boca.bankone.com*) and EC back-office software called OM Transact from Open Market, Inc. (*openmarket.com*).

In 2000, the company offered over 43,000 magazines from more than 13,000 publishers. In addition, more than 5 million books can be ordered through a RoweCom service called kStore. Because RoweCom serves mostly organizations, this is a B2B e-procurement service. Some of the benefits of online periodical ordering are lower costs, time savings, electronic renewals, better subscription management, and easier interfaces. RoweCom is an Internet IPO that survived the stock market dip in the industry.

FIGURE 10-1 Electronic Commerce in Magazine Subscription

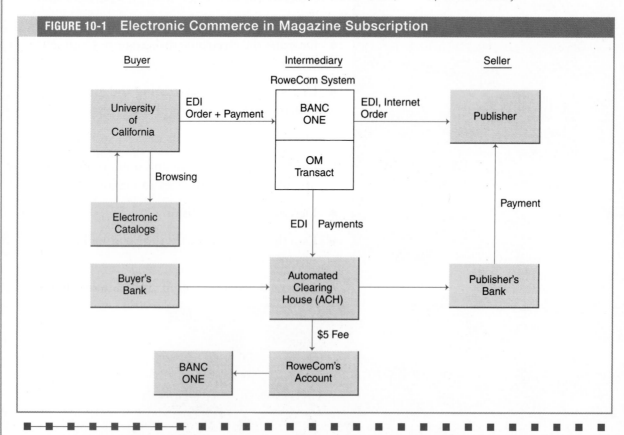

10.2   BROKER-BASED SERVICES

The opening vignette demonstrates the use of an electronic broker (or agent) and some of the potential benefits that EC may introduce in existing business processes. The electronic broker in this case acts as a consolidator, or aggregator, of purchase orders in a market where transactions occur, but no negotiations take place. However, electronic brokers, like human brokers, can play several roles, some of which, as in real estate, may involve negotiations.

Brokers usually work for a commission, acting as intermediaries between buyers and sellers of services or goods. The buyers can be individuals or organizations. Some of the most notable services are travel agencies, job placement agencies, real estate agencies, insurance agencies, and stock market brokerages. Agents basically make the markets, bringing together buyers and sellers. Some of the markets, such as stocks and travel, may involve nonnegotiable prices and/or commissions. Employment agencies basically match jobs with candidates, and real estate agents are involved in matching, negotiating, and contracting. The opening vignette showed a market for magazines that are offered at a fixed price.

Brokers provide many services. For example, travel agents are *information brokers* who pass information from product suppliers to customers. They also take and process orders, collect money, provide travel assistance (such as obtaining visas), and assist with insurance, and may even provide health and safety suggestions for travelers.

Service Industries Versus Manufacturing and Product Retailing

In Chapter 2 we presented a model that classified EC along three dimensions (Figure 2-2). As you may recall, we defined pure EC as a case where the product, the agent, and the process are all digital. When products are traded, we can have pure EC only if the products can be digitized, as with software or music. When we deal with pure EC, the potential advantages are the greatest, since automating the entire process (including delivery) can result in a substantial cost reduction. In most cases, products that are traded must be physically delivered to the buyer, making pure EC impossible. However, with the service industry, pure EC can be used in most cases, since the industry deals with documents that can be digitized easily. Therefore, the potential savings are much larger in service industries than those industries selling physical products.

Companies in the service industries, such as banks and brokerage houses, started to operate online years before the Internet. The major reason for this was the possible digitization of the entire process along the supply chain. In the beginning, vendors such as banks provided users with a disk containing software. The software, which the users installed on their PCs, provided access to the vendor's database over private lines, and later over the Internet. Later on, companies allowed their customers to download the software directly instead of sending them a disk. Today, there is usually no need for software, since the Web browser is used to fulfill all the functions necessary for providing the service or for a trade.

In both B2C and B2B, EC allows customers direct access to service providers. Thus, most of the value-added tasks of the agents or brokers are automated. As more and more people use EC, different types of human agencies may become endangered organizations, as the tasks they perform are increasingly seen as being replaceable by technology. In this chapter we cover some of the major agent-based electronic services. The chapter continues with a presentation of topics related to electronic services. Specifically, we look at online publishing and knowledge dissemination. We also provide examples of some other online services. Finally, we discuss the future of intermediaries.

10.3   TRAVEL AND TOURISM SERVICES

The travel industry is expanding rapidly. Any experienced traveler knows that good planning and shopping around can save a considerable amount of money. The Internet is an ideal place to plan, explore, and arrange almost any trip. Potential savings are available through special sales and the elimination of travel agents by buying directly from service providers.

Some major travel-related Web sites are: *expedia.com* (affiliated with Microsoft), *Travelocity.com*, *asiatravel.com*, *ebookit.com*, *itn.net*, *thetrip.com*, *travelweb.com*, *priceline.com*, and *lonelyplanet.com*. Online travel services are also provided by all major airlines, vacation services, large conventional travel agencies, car rental agencies, hotels, and tour companies. Publishers of travel guides such as *fodors.com* and *lonelyplant.com* provide considerable amounts of travel-related information on their Web sites.

Services Provided

If you visit the AOL or Yahoo Web pages, you will find "travel" on the main menu. By clicking on travel you will get some idea of the various services provided. The home page of a virtual travel agency such as *Expedia.com* shows you the diversity of the services it provides. Note that several of the services can be customized per the consumer's request.

Virtual travel agencies offer almost all the services provided by conventional travel agencies. Virtual travel agency services range from providing general information to reserving and purchasing tickets, accommodations, and entertainment. In addition to regular services, they often provide services that most conventional travel agencies do not offer, such as travel tips provided by people who have experienced certain situations (e.g., a visa problem), electronic travel magazines, fare comparisons, currency conversion calculators, fare tracking (free e-mail alerts on low fares to your favorite destinations), worldwide business and place locators, an outlet for travel accessories and books, experts' opinions, major international and travel news, detailed driving maps and directions for the United States and several other countries (see *biztravel.com*), chat rooms and bulletin boards, and frequent flier deals. In addition, some offer several other innovative services, such as online travel auctions.

Most regular online services do not offer real travel bargains. For special bargain fares consumers need to go to special sites.

Auctions, Bids, and Special Sales

Several airlines conduct online auctions where passengers bid for tickets. American Airlines (*aa.com*) auctions tickets to certain destinations during low-volume seasons. Cathay Pacific (*cathaypacific.com*) auctions tickets on competitive routes, showing current bids on its Web site. A limited amount of tickets sell for as much as half price. Aer Lingus (*aerlingus.ie*) auctions tickets that are set to expire in a week or two. Special discount sales are available at all times. Several airlines offer last-minute discounts.

Priceline.com (*priceline.com*) asks consumers to specify the price they are willing to pay for airfare and/or accommodations. The consumer guarantees that he or she will buy the ticket or package if *Priceline.com* finds one at or below the consumer's set price. Other companies allow consumers to bid on certain types of tickets.

Special Services

In addition to auctions, travel services offer many other online services to travelers. For example, *Lastminute.com* offers very low airfares and accommodation prices. It is one of several sites that offer last-minute bargains. Last-minute trips can also be booked on *americanexpress.com*, sometimes at a steep discount. Also of interest are sites that offer medical advice and services for travelers. This type of information is available from the World Health Organization (*who.int*), governments (e.g., *cdc.gov/travel*), and private organizations (e.g., *tripprep.com*, *medicalert.com*, *cyberdocs.com*).

WIRELESS SERVICES

Several airlines (e.g., Cathay Pacific, Qantas Airways) allow customers with WAP cell phones to check their flight status, update frequent flyer miles, and book flights with their cell phones.

DIRECT MARKETING

Airlines try to sell electronic tickets over the Internet. Using direct marketing techniques, airlines are able to build customer profiles and target specific customers with tailored offers. Many airlines offer "specials" or "cyber offers" on their Web sites (e.g., see *cathaypacific.com*).

ALLIANCES AND CONSORTIA

Airlines and other companies are creating alliances to increase their sales or to reduce purchasing cost (see the Qantas case in Chapter 1). Several alliances exist in Europe, the United States, and Asia. For example, some consortiums aggregate all participants' Internet-only fares.

OTHER SERVICES

Best Western offers interactive kiosks in their hotels that guests can use to access information on local community services. Some hotels offer free or for-fee high-speed Internet access, sometimes even in each hotel room (e.g., see *Sheraton.com* for details). Special vacation places can be found at *Priceline.com*, *rent-a-holiday.com*, and *greatrentals.com*.

Benefits and Limitations

The benefits of online travel services to travelers are enormous. The amount of free information is tremendous and it is accessible anytime from any place. Substantial discounts can be found, especially for those who have time and patience. In the future, consumers will be able to take virtual reality fantasy trips.

Limitations. Online travel services do have their limitations. First, many people do not use the Internet. Second, the goal of a company Web site is to sell a product, not to provide information. Therefore, the amount of time and the difficulty of using virtual travel agencies are not inconsequential. Finally, complex trips require specialized knowledge and arrangements, which must be done by a knowledgeable, human travel agent. Therefore, the need for travel agents as intermediaries is assured, at least for the immediate future. However, as we will show later, intelligent agents may lessen some of these limitations, reducing the reliance on travel agents.

Corporate Travel

Corporations can use all of the services just mentioned. However, many large corporations receive additional services from large travel agencies. To reduce corporate travel costs, companies can make arrangements that enable employees to plan and book their own trips. Using optimization tools provided online by travel companies (like those offered by Rosenbluth, Inc. in Chapter 2), companies can try to reduce travel costs even further. Travel authorization software that checks fund availability and compliance with corporate guidelines is usually provided by companies such as Rosenbluth.

The corporate travel market is growing very rapidly. One service is Oracle's e-Travel, which provides software to automate and manage online booking. American Express has teamed with Microsoft and MCI to provide an interactive corporate travel reservation system called AXI, which displays airline seat charts, maps showing hotels, information about nearby health clubs, and weather information. While trying to reduce costs to the corporate client, AXI creates a profile for each traveler and his or her preferences and, thus, tries to satisfy both travelers and corporate travel managers. American Express, Rosenbluth, Inc., and Carlson compete with the airlines and their travel companies. For example, Sabre Group Holding (of American Airlines) provides considerable discounts to corporations.

The Impact of EC on the Travel Industry (Both Online and Offline)

EC, as demonstrated in earlier chapters, can have major effects on individual companies. These impacts can be extended to an entire industry. Bloch and Segev (1997) analyzed the impact of EC on the travel industry using Porter's framework of competitive advantage (1985). According to Porter's model there are five forces that impact competition in any industry: new entrants, substitute products (or services), the bargaining power of buyers, the bargaining power of suppliers, and the rivalry of the competing companies in the industry. Bloch and Segev constructed an analysis framework that pertains to the travel industry. They first focus on the environment, then on competitive responses, and finally on one firm's strategy. A description of this model and the impact of the Internet on it was provided in Chapter 2.

Such an analysis could fit other industries, but it is especially applicable to the travel industry. (For a competitive analysis of the airline industry see Callon, 1996.) As a matter of fact, the introduction of electronic tickets resulted in a significant commission cut in 1998. And, since 1995, there is a clear trend toward fewer travel agencies. The business pressures described in Chapter 1 are impacting the travel industry, and it is one of the largest industries affected. The industry has clearly been transformed by IT. The computerized airline reservation system is the world's largest nonmilitary information system, and this system is now accessible by customers directly via the Internet, taking away some functions traditionally performed by travel agents.

Bloch and Segev's analysis views the travel industry from a supply chain point of view (Figure 10-2). Four major actors are involved. Each of them can be classified into subcategories depending on the purpose of the travel (e.g., leisure or business) or the nature of the arrangement (e.g., tours, individuals, or groups).

Reviewing some of the applications described earlier, such as buying a ticket online or receiving information on low-cost tickets by push technology, Bloch and Segev (1997) identified several impacts on the travel industry:

- Offering of lower-cost trips
- Providing a more personalized service
- Helping customers understand the products by using multimedia
- Saving money in a paperless environment
- Increasing the convenience of getting information at home
- Supporting a customer-focused strategy (such as targeted advertisement and integration of products)

These impacts may create opportunities for new business models and/or vendors. Examples are new online-only travel agencies like *Expedia.com*. The business model adopted by Rosenbluth, Inc. is another example of such a change (Clemons and Hann, 1999). Other impacts related to intermediaries in general are discussed later in this chapter.

Finally, Bloch and Segev (1997) classify the EC impacts on an individual company in the travel industry into 10 categories ranging from product promotion to new products and new business models. They predict that travel agencies as we know them today will disappear. Only their value-added activities will not be automated, and these will be performed by a new type of organization. For example, these new organizations will serve certain targeted markets and customers (see Van der Heijden, 1996). Travel superstores, which will provide many products, services, and entertainment, may enter the industry, as well as innovative individuals who will operate from their homes. See Application Case 10.1 for an example of how a small tour company utilizes EC.

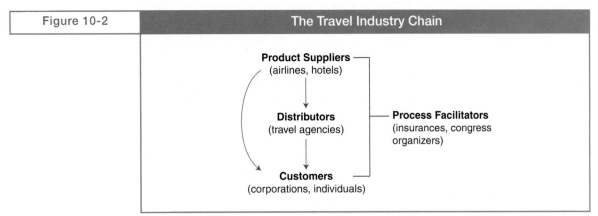

Figure 10-2	The Travel Industry Chain

Product Suppliers
(airlines, hotels)

Distributors
(travel agencies)   **Process Facilitators**
                        (insurances, congress
                        organizers)

Customers
(corporations, individuals)

Source: Block and Segev "The Impact of Electronic Commerce on the Travel Industry" Proceedings, HICSS 31, Hawaii © 1997 IEEE.

APPLICATION CASE   10.1

Zeus Tours and Yacht Cruises, Inc. Uses EC

Zeus Tours and Yacht Cruises, Inc. is a relatively small, private travel company ($30 million annual sales) specializing in tours and cruises. The company uses the Internet both as a marketing tool and as an interoffice bulletin board.

Zeus has been using IT for years. For example, early on it used a multimedia CD-ROM to distribute cruise information to customers. Now it uses both the CD-ROM and the Internet to supplement traditional communication methods. Here is what the company is doing on the Web (*e-travellinks.com/zeus_tours.htm*).

- Sends Web-generated sales leads to 18,000 travel agents
- Continuously offers specials to individuals (honeymoon specials, seniors, two for the price of one, and so on)
- Places press releases on the Web site
- Makes bookings available online
- Provides communication via e-mail
- Makes extensive information available by country
- Publishes customer comments about the company
- Provides push-based information services

Source: Condensed from Rogers (1997).

SURVIVAL STRATEGY

Standing and Vasudavan (2000) proposed a strategy for travel agency survival. It has three elements: (1) minor improvements due to process changes, (2) BPR with significant improvements, and (3) organizational transformation (most risky, highest potential improvements).

Intelligent Agents

There is no doubt that EC will play an even greater role in the travel industry. One area that is very promising is the use of intelligent agents.

An example of potential collaborating agents is provided by Bose (1996), who proposed a framework for automating the execution of collaborative organizational processes performed by multiple organizational members. The agents emulate the work and behavior of human agents. Each of them is capable of acting autonomously, cooperatively, and collectively to achieve the collective goal. The system increases organizational productivity by carrying out several tedious watchdog activities, thereby freeing humans to work on more challenging and creative tasks. Bose (1996) provides an example of a travel authorization process that can be divided into subtasks delegated to intelligent agents.

Intelligent agents could be involved in buyer-seller negotiations as shown in the following scenario: You want to take a vacation in Hawaii. You called a regular travel agent who was too busy; finally, he gave you a plan and a price that you do not like. A friend told you to use an intelligent agent. Here is how the process works:

STEP 1. You turn on your PC and enter your desired destination, dates, available budget, special requirements, and desired entertainment.

STEP 2. Your computer dispatches an intelligent agent that "shops around," entering the Internet and communicating electronically with the databases of airlines, hotels, and other vendors.

STEP 3. Your agent attempts to match your requirements against what is available, negotiating with the vendors' agents. These agents may activate other agents to make special arrangements, cooperate with each other, activate multimedia presentations, or make special inquiries.

STEP 4. Your agent returns to you within minutes with suitable alternatives. You have a few questions and you want modifications. No problem. Within a few minutes, it's a done deal. No waiting for busy telephone operators and no human errors. Once you approve the deal, the intelligent agent will make the reservations, arrange for payments, and even report to you about any unforeseen delays in your departure.

How do you communicate with your agent? By voice, of course. This scenario is not as far off as it may seem. You will probably be able to do just that by 2004.

10.4   EMPLOYMENT PLACEMENT AND THE JOB MARKET

The online job market is one of the largest markets in the world, connecting employers looking for employees with specific skills and individuals looking for a job. In a simplistic way, we can view employees as selling their skills to organizations, frequently at a negotiated price. The job market is very volatile, and supply and demand are frequently unbalanced. Job matching is done in several ways, ranging from ads in classified sections of newspapers to the use of corporate recruiters, commercial employment agencies, and headhunting companies.

Since the inception of the Internet, the job market has moved online. Now there are thousands of employment agencies that try to match employers and employees, hundreds of thousands of employers that advertise jobs on their home pages, and several million job seekers who place their resumes on home pages and databases.

Driving Forces of the Electronic Job Market

The following are some of the deficiencies of the traditional job market, in which most activity is conducted through newspaper ads.

- **Cost.** Newspaper ads are expensive.
- **Life cycle.** Unless renewed at an additional cost, the life of the ads is only days or weeks.
- **Place.** Most ads are local. Nationwide ads are very expensive. International ads are even more expensive.
- **Minimum information.** Because of the high costs of newspaper ads, the information provided is minimal and may not attract the attention of some job seekers.
- **Search.** It is very time consuming to find all relevant available jobs or applicants. It is especially difficult to find information on jobs out of town.
- **Finding applicants.** In the pre-Internet era, most job seekers did not place ads about their availability. Some job seekers sent unsolicited letters with

resumes. This situation made it difficult for companies to find employees with special skills. Companies had to use employment agencies and pay them high commissions.

- **Matching.** It was difficult to match candidates to open jobs and to match supply and demand of labor. Usually, it was done within a city or a country.
- **Lost and dated material.** Some applications or letters of response arrived late or were lost. The applications received would soon be outdated.
- **Speed.** Communication by mail is slow, as is the processing of a large number of applications. Frequently, employers lost good employees, since by the time the application was processed, the applicant had taken another job. Similarly, applicants accepted less desirable jobs because they were afraid to wait too long.
- **Comparisons.** It is difficult, sometimes impossible, for job seekers to compare the monetary value of available positions.

As a result of these deficiencies, the traditional job market was inefficient.

The Internet Job Market

The Internet offers a perfect environment for job seekers and companies searching for hard-to-find employees. The job market is especially effective for technology-oriented companies and jobs; however, there are thousands of other companies that advertise available positions, accept resumes, and take applications over the Internet. The Internet job market is used by the following parties:

- **Job seekers.** Job seekers can reply to employment ads. Alternatively, they can take the initiative and place their resumes on their own home pages or on others' Web sites, send messages to members of newsgroups asking for referrals, and use recruiting firms such as *headhunter.com*, *asiajob.search.org*, *dice.com*, *hotjobs.com*, and *monster.com*. For entry-level jobs and internships for newly minted graduates, job seekers can use *jobdirect.com*. *VaultReports.com* offers information about 1,000 employers and 40 industries in New York City. It also offers a free matching service.
- **Job openings.** Many organizations advertise openings on their Web sites. Others advertise job openings on popular Web sites, online services, bulletin boards, and with recruiting firms. Employers can conduct interviews and administer tests on the Web.
- **Recruiting firms.** Thousands of job placement brokers are active on the Web. They use their own Web pages to post available job descriptions and advertise their services in e-malls and other Web sites. Recruiters use newsgroups, online forums, bulletin boards, Internet commercial resume services, and portals such as Yahoo! and AOL (see their E-Span service at *espan.com*).
- **Government agencies and institutions.** Many government agencies advertise openings for government positions on their Web sites and on other sites. In addition, some government agencies use the Internet to help job seekers find jobs elsewhere, as is done in Hong Kong and the Philippines (Application Case 10.2).

APPLICATION CASE   10.2

Web Site Matches Workers with Jobs in the Philippines

The Philippines is a country with many skilled employees but with few open jobs. In January 1999, the government created a special Web site that matches people with jobs. The site is part of the Department of Labor computerized project, and it is a free service. For those people who do not have computers or Internet access, the government created hundreds of kiosks located throughout the country. The system is also connected with Philippine embassies, especially in countries where there are many overseas Filipino workers, so they can find a job and return home.

Government employees help those applicants who do not know how to use the system. This system gives job seekers a chance to find a job that would best suit their qualifications. At the heart of the system are its matchmaking capabilities.

For the matchmaking process, a database stores all the job vacancies submitted by different employers. Another database stores the job applications fed into the system. The system matches qualified applicants with companies. The system also automatically does a ranking based on the matches. This job-matching feature differentiates this site from other online job sites. Everything is done electronically, so job seekers can see the match results in seconds.

Source: Based on *Computerworld Hong Kong* (January 14, 1999).

WHERE ARE THE ADVERTISEMENTS?

Companies advertise job openings everywhere on the Internet. Companies advertise on all the major portals, newspapers (e.g., *chicago.tribune.com*), industry-specific portals, professional associations, job agencies, government portals, and more.

The Advantage of the Electronic Job Market

The Internet facilitates solutions to the 10 market inefficiencies described earlier.
   The major advantages for *job seekers* are:

- Ability to find information on a large number of jobs worldwide
- Ability to communicate quickly with potential employers
- Ability to write and post resumes for large-volume distribution
- Ability to search for jobs quickly from any place at any time
- Ability to obtain several support services at no cost
- Ability to assess their own market value (*e.g., wageweb.com* and *jobsmart.org*; look for salary surveys)
- Ability to learn how to use your voice in an interview (*greatvoice.com*)

The major advantages for *employers* are:

- Ability to advertise to a large numbers of job seekers
- Ability to save on advertisement costs
- Ability to lower the cost of processing applications (using electronic application forms)
- Ability to provide greater equal opportunity for job seekers
- Ability to find highly skilled employees

The Limitations of Electronic Job Markets

Probably the biggest limitation of the online job market is the fact that many people do not use the Internet. This limitation is even more serious with nontechnology-oriented jobs. To overcome this problem, companies may use both traditional advertising approaches and the Internet. However, the trend is clear—over time, more and more of the job market will be on the Internet. One solution to this problem is the use of kiosks (see Application Case 10.2).

Security and privacy may be another limitation. As we discussed in Chapter 1, this limitation is diminishing with security improvements. The electronic job market may also accelerate employees' movement to better jobs, creating high turnover costs for employers. (To see what employers can do about this, refer to Discussion Question #14). Finally, finding candidates online is more complicated than most people think, mostly due to the large number of resumes available online. Some sites offer prescreening of candidates (e.g., *jobtrak.com*), which may alleviate this problem.

Examples of Online Job Services

The following are some of the interesting job services available to job seekers:

- **Locating jobs.** Most sites offer lists of available jobs by location, by classification, or by other criteria. Many sites also offer a search engine. Once a job is found, an electronic application form can be filled out and a resume can be attached and e-mailed.
- **Writing and posting resumes.** Several sites can help job seekers write a resume and post it on the Web (e.g., *resume-link.com*, *careerbuilder.com*, and *jobweb.com*).
- **Career planning.** Career advice is also available on the Internet. Although personalized guidance by counselors (for a fee) is just starting to emerge, there are several Web sites that provide substantial information at no cost. For example, *hotjobs.com* and *monster.com* provide links to many sources for further research, for accessing job listings, and for finding for-fee counselors. Using a personality test, *discoverme.com* matches candidates with jobs and helps in career planning.
- **Newsgroups.** Large numbers of newsgroups are dedicated to finding jobs (and keeping them). Some examples are listed in Table 10-1.

Examples of Career Services on the Internet

Comprehensive Job Sites

Comprehensive job sites include: *careerpath.com* (combined with *careerbuilder.com*), which covers classified jobs from dozens of newspapers, and *monster.com*.

A Example: *The Internet Professional Association* IPA, (now part of *veriotexas.net*) provides many online services:

- **Recruiters online network.** A virtual association of recruiters, employment agencies, search firms, and employment professionals worldwide.
- **StaffNET.** A virtual association of firms and individuals engaged in contract (or interim) work, a fast-growing field.

TABLE 10-1

Job-Related Newsgroups	
Newsgroup	**Service**
ba.jobs.contract	Issues involving contract employment
misc.job.misc	Discussion about employment, workplaces, careers
misc.jobs.offered	Announcements of available positions
misc.jobs.offered.entry	Job listings only for entry-level positions
misc.jobs.resumes	Postings of resumes and "situation wanted" articles
ba.jobs.misc	Discussions about the job market in the Bay Area
biz.jobs.offered	Position announcements
bionet.jobs.wanted	Requests for employment in the biological sciences
ba.jobs.resumes	Resume postings for Bay Area jobs
la.jobs	Los Angeles area job postings
aboutwork	A chat room and discussion group

- **Global employment network.** An association of search professionals engaged in international job search and placement.
- **Employment opportunities.** A listing for both individuals and organizations. Free to individuals posting resumes and to members of IPA.
- **Intranet job market.** Many companies conduct an internal electronic job market. Openings are posted for employees to look at, and search engines enable managers to identify talents, even if the people are not looking actively for a job change.

Intelligent Agents

The large number of available jobs and resumes online makes it difficult both for employers and employees to search the Internet. Intelligent agents are used to solve this problem by matching openings and jobs (see Figure 10-3).

INTELLIGENT AGENTS FOR JOB SEEKERS

A free service that searches the Internet's top job sites and databases for job postings based on users' profiles is offered at *jobsleuth.com*. Users can create as many as five different profiles based on more than 100 different job categories, geographic region, and key words. Users receive a daily e-mail containing job opportunities from over a dozen top job sites around the Internet (e.g., Career Mosaic), that match their career interests. This saves the users a tremendous amount of time.

INTELLIGENT AGENTS FOR EMPLOYERS

A special search engine helps employers to find resumes that match specific job descriptions. The search is done by intelligent agents such as *resumix.com*. Here is how *resumix.com* describes its product on its Web site:

> *From the time a position becomes available or a resume is received, Resumix gives you the control while dispersing the work. Hiring managers can open jobs; operators can scan resumes; and you can search for a candidate or identify employees for training programs, redeployment opportunities, or new initiatives.*

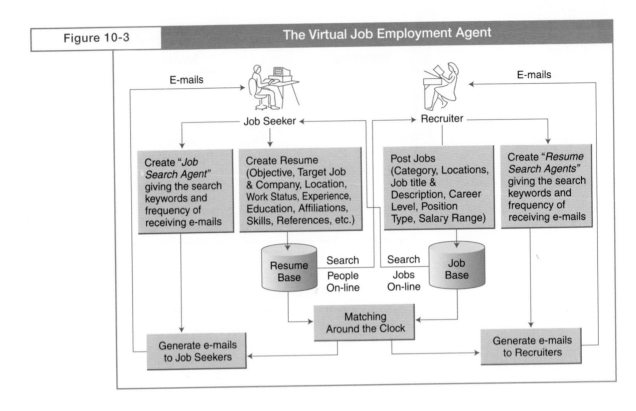

Figure 10-3 | The Virtual Job Employment Agent

The core of this powerful system is Resumix's Knowledge Base. As an expert system, it goes beyond simply matching words. The Knowledge Base works for you to interpret a candidate's resume, determining their skills based on context, and matching those skills to the position criteria. For example, you might be looking for a Product Manager. Being a member of the AMA (American Marketing Association) might be one of the desirable properties for the job. However, with a basic keyword search, you might get candidates who have listed AMA, but are really members of the American Medical Association or American Meatpackers Association. Those are not very relevant to your search. Resumix Knowledge Base would select only the candidates with relevant skills.

10.5   REAL ESTATE AND INSURANCE ONLINE

Real estate transactions are an ideal area for EC for the following reasons. First, potential home buyers can view many properties on the screen, saving time for the buyer and for the broker. Second, potential home buyers can sort and organize properties according to specific criteria and preview the exterior and interior design of the properties, shortening the search process. Finally, potential home buyers can find detailed information about the properties and frequently get even more detailed real estate listings than brokers will provide. In some locations, brokers allow the use of databases available only on private networks from their offices, but in many cities such information is available to potential buyers from their personal Internet connections. For example, *realtor.com* allows buyers to search a database of over 1 million homes located all over the United States. The database is composed of local multiple listings of all available properties and properties just sold in hundreds of locations. Cushman and Wakefield of New York (*cushwake.com*) also uses the Internet to sell commercial property.

Builders now use virtual reality technology on their Web sites to demonstrate three-dimensional floor plans to home buyers; "virtual models" enable buyers to "walk through" three-dimensional mock-ups of homes.

Real Estate Applications

The real estate industry is just starting to discover EC. Here are some services with their representative Web addresses:

- International Real Estate Directory and News (*ired.com*) is a comprehensive real estate Web site.
- A national listing of real estate properties can be found at *cyberhomes.com*.
- A commercial real estate directory is available at *comspace.com*.
- *assist2sell.com* offers consumers assistance in buying or selling a home.
- Mortgage comparisons and calculations and other financing information are available from *eloan.com* and *quicken.com*.
- Listings of residential real estate in multiple databases can be viewed at *homescout.com* and *realestate.yahoo.com*.
- Maps are available on *mapquest.com* and *realestate.yahoo.com*.
- To automate the closing of real estate transactions, which are notorious for the paperwork involved, see *datatrac.net*.
- The National Association of Realtors, *realtor.com*, has links to house listings in all major cities.
- Mortgage brokers can pass loan applications over the Internet and receive bids from lenders who want to issue mortgages.
- The following sites list current mortgage rates: *bankrate.com*, *eloan.com*, and *quickenmortgage.com*.
- Rental properties are listed on *homestore.net*. Several services are available including a virtual walk-through of some listings.
- Online lenders such as *arcsystems.com* can approve loans online.

EC is useful not only to large companies, but also to small ones as shown in Application Case 10.3.

APPLICATION CASE 10.3

How One Deal More Than Paid for the Colliers Arnold Web Site

Colliers Arnold was a commercial realtor in Florida. To improve relationships with existing clients, the company established a Web site in 1995, posting demographic studies, press releases, and photos of available properties. The company was surprised to find out that it was immediately receiving 2,000 hits per day, but, like direct mail, only five inquiries were worth pursuing. Any inquiry may result in a substantial profit due to the large commission that can

APPLICATION CASE **10.3**

(continued)

be generated even from one sale, as was the case of the query from Rockwell Corporation. Interested in leasing a property listed on the Web site, Rockwell sent an e-mail inquiry. Soon, a 5-year lease was signed, bringing Colliers a commission of $16,000, more than enough to pay back the $10,000 investment in the Web site.

Although the real estate industry was slow to use the Web, the situation is changing rapidly. Colliers is expanding its Web site, which includes information about a specific area's business climate, labor pool, consumer market, and transportation infrastructure. Most of the information is available free from local economic development agencies on Florida's southwest coast, where Colliers operates. Colliers closed several deals in addition to Rockwell, yet the company believes that the major benefit it derives is from providing customer service.

Note: The company merged with another real estate company in Southwest Florida in 1999.

Source: Condensed from B. Klein, "Florida Commercial Realtor Siphons Five Web Leads a Day," *NETmarketing* (March 1997) and *netb2b.com* (1997).

In general, online real estate is supporting rather than replacing existing agents. Due to the complexity of the process, real estate agents are still charging high commissions. However, several Web sites have started to offer services at lower commissions (e.g., see *assist2sell.com*).

Real Estate Mortgages

Large numbers of companies compete in the residential mortgage market. Several online companies are active in this area (e.g., *lendingtree.com*, *eloan.com*). Many sites offer loan calculators. *Priceline.com* offers its "name your price" model for residential loans. In another case, a Singaporean company aggregates loan seekers and then places the package for bid on the Internet (see Chapter 9). Some institutions approve loans online in 10 minutes and settle in 5 days (e.g., *homeside.com.au*).

Insurance

An increasing number of companies use the Internet to offer standard insurance policies such as auto, home, life, or health at a substantial discount. Furthermore, third-party aggregators offer free comparisons of available policies. Several large insurance and risk management companies offer comprehensive insurance contracts online. While many people do not trust the faceless insurance agent, others are eager to take advantage of the reduced premiums. For example, a visit to *insurerate.com* will show a variety of different policies. *Order.com* allows customers and businesses to compare car insurance offerings and then make a purchase online. Some popular insurance sites include *Quotesmith.com*, *insweb.com*, *insurance.com*, *ebix.com*, and *quicken.com*. Many insurance companies use a dual strategy (see MacSweeney, 2000), keeping human agents but also selling online.

10.6   INVESTING AND TRADING STOCKS ONLINE

One of the fastest growing EC areas is online trading and investing. By 2001 this activity had become perhaps the most popular area of B2C.

Online Stock Trading

Although U.S. stock traders were among the first to embrace the Internet, traders in Korea really love it. By 2001, more than 60 percent of all stock trades in Korea were transacted online (vs. about 30 percent in the United States). Why is this so? Because it makes a lot of dollars and sense (Schonfeld, 1998).

An online trade commission costs between $5 and $29, compared to an average fee of $100 from a full-service broker and $35 from a discount broker. There is no waiting on busy telephone lines, and the chance of making mistakes is small since there is no oral communication in a frequently very noisy environment. Orders can be placed from anywhere, any time, day or night, and there is no biased broker to push a sale. Furthermore, investors can find a considerable amount of free information about specific companies or mutual funds.

Several discount brokerage houses initiated extensive online stock trading, notably Charles Schwab, (see Chapter 16) in 1995. Full-service brokerage companies such as Merrill Lynch followed in 1998/1999. By 1999, there were more than 120 brokerage firms offering online trading. In the United States alone, the volume of trading has increased significantly in the last 3 years, but the brokerage firms now need fewer employees.

How does online trading work? Let's say an investor has an account with Schwab. The investor accesses Schwab's Web site (*schwab.com*), enters his or her account number and password, and clicks on stock trading. Using a menu, the investor enters the details of the order (buy, sell, margin or cash, price limit, or market order). The computer tells the investor the current "ask" and "bid" prices, much as your broker would do over the telephone, and the investor can approve or reject the transaction. The flow chart of this process is shown in Figure 10-4 for execution on the floor of the New York Stock Exchange. However, companies like Schwab are now licensed as *exchanges*. This allows them to match the selling and buying orders of their own customers for many securities in about 1 to 2 seconds.

Some well-known companies that offer online trading are E*TRADE, Ameritrade, TD Waterhouse, Datek Online, Suretrade, Discover, and Lombard. E*TRADE offers many related services and also challenges investors to participate in a simulated investment game. For further details on brokers and services provided online see Gilbert et al. (2000).

Of the many brokers online, of special interest are *Datek.com*, which provides extremely fast executions, and *Webstreet.com* charged no commissions on trades of 1,000 shares or more on NASDAQ but is no longer in business. However, the most innovative service is that of E*TRADE. Note that in 1999, E*TRADE started its own mutual funds online. E*TRADE is expanding rapidly in several countries, enabling global stock trading.

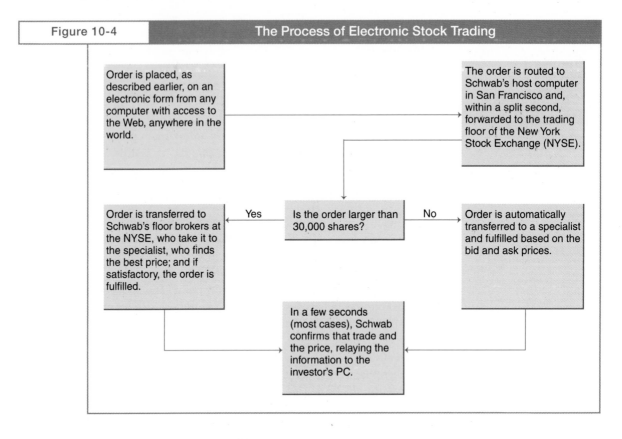

Figure 10-4   The Process of Electronic Stock Trading

Investment Information

There is an almost unlimited amount of information available online, mostly free (usually in exchange for a registration). Here are some examples:

- Current financial news is available at CNN Financial (*cnnfn.com*). This portal also has large amounts of company information, all free. Similar information is available at Hoover's (*Hoovers.com*) and *Bloomberg.com*.
- Municipal bond prices are available at *bloomberg.com*.
- A good source of overall market information and many links is *cyberinvest.com*.
- Free "Guru" advice is available from *upside.com*.
- Stock screening and evaluation tools are available at *multexinvestor.com* and *cnnfn.com*.
- Articles from the *Journal of the American Association of Individual Investors* can be read on *aaii.com*.
- Reports and the latest in IPO funding and pricing is available at *hoovers.com/ipo* and *ipodata.com*.
- Chart lovers will enjoy *bigcharts.com*. Charts are also offered by most other sites.
- Mutual fund evaluation tools and other interesting investment information are available from *morningstar.com*.
- Earnings estimates and much more are found on *firstcall.com*.
- Almost anything that anyone would need to know about finance and stocks can be found at *yahoo.com*.

Most of these services are free. Many other services regarding global investing, portfolio tracking, investor education are also available. An example of finding free information on a mutual fund is shown in Application Case 10.4.

APPLICATION CASE 10.4

How Can the Web Simplify the Picking of a Mutual Fund?

A number of free Web sites let you scan mutual-fund offerings to find a suitable investment sector, country to invest in, and risk profile. Here are some examples:

• *Morningstar.com*. This site not only rates mutual funds, but also provides a search engine to help you narrow your search. Use the "Fund selector" option and go to "Morningstar category." For example, if you like to invest in Southeast Asia, you can find funds operating not only in the United States, but also in Hong Kong, Singapore, or Malaysia. Once you have picked your market, you can segment it by the size of the fund, by return on investment during the last 5 or 10 years, etc. You can consider the risk level and even fund-manager tenure. It has news and chat rooms for each fund. It also lets you look at the top 10 holdings of most funds.

   Other sites also rank funds by volatility. You can get details and a chart against a relevant index for each fund.

• Lipper, a unit of Reuters (*Lipperweb.com*), is a global mutual fund evaluator (Asia, Europe, USA). Services are provided both to individual investors and to institations.

Initial Public Offerings (IPOs) and the Internet

The first successful Internet IPO was that of a beer-making company called Spring Street Brewing. The owner created a special company, Wit Capital Corporation (now traded on the NASDAQ), to offer initial and secondary securities trading over the Internet. Several other successful offerings followed. For example, Internet Venture, Inc. raised $5 million in the spring of 1998 (*perki.net* and *ivn.net*). Virtual Wall Street brings together investors and companies interested in raising capital via direct public offering (DPO), rather than using an underwriting syndicate. Auctions on IPOs are conducted by *openipo.com*. For additional information see *ipo.com*.

Global Stock Exchanges

Using information technology, stock exchanges are moving toward around-the-clock global trading. The NASDAQ exchange teamed up with the London and Frankfurt exchanges to create a global exchange, NASDAQ Europe, specializing in high-growth stocks. Investors in the United States and Europe trade stocks on all three exchanges. A competing exchange involving the New York Stock Exchange and nine other exchanges (Tokyo, Paris, Toronto, Hong Kong, etc.) is the Global Equity Market (GEM). Along with NASDAQ Japan, there is a move to a broader global exchange. These exchanges will eventually operate around-the-clock.

Related Markets

In addition to stocks, online trading is expanding to include financial derivatives, commodities, mutual funds, and more. Futures exchanges around the world are moving to electronic trading. For example, the Chicago Board of Trade, the world's largest futures exchange, is offering full-range electronic trading.

Individual Investors and Day Trading

EC may have a major impact on both individual investors and day traders (professional investors who buy stocks and sells them the same day).

EC provides tools that enable individuals to perform as well as or even better than financial institutions. For possible impacts see Lim (1997).

Electronic Trading of Interest Rate Derivatives

Interest rate derivatives, among the most complicated transactions conducted in the financial world, are used by leading companies to protect themselves against substantial movements in interest rates. These derivatives are called swaps. The average outstanding value of swaps worldwide was estimated at $52 trillion in 1999, a 40.5 percent increase compared with 1998.

SwapsWire, a B2B exchange, (*swapswire.com*) was created in fall 2000 by the six biggest players in the interest rate derivatives market—Chase Manhattan, Citigroup, Deutsche Bank, JP Morgan, Morgan Stanley Dean Witter, and Warburg Dillon Read. Initially, SwapsWire allowed the exchange members to communicate with each other as well as to trade interest rate derivatives electronically. SwapWire is now experimenting with electronic trading for which participating exchanges will pay a fee.

For more information on the top investment and financial Web sites see *Money*, December 1999 and *Forbes.com*, September 4, 2000.

10.7 CYBERBANKING AND PERSONAL FINANCE

Electronic banking, also known as **cyberbanking**, e-banking, virtual banking, home banking, and online banking, includes various banking activities conducted from home, business, or on the road instead of at a physical bank location. Electronic banking has capabilities ranging from paying bills to securing a loan electronically. Today, many traditional banks around the world offer diversified e-banking services (e.g., see *main.hangseng.com*).

Electronic banking saves time and money for users. For banks, it offers an inexpensive alternative to branch banking and a chance to enlist remote customers. Many physical banks are beginning to offer home banking services, and some use EC as a major competitive strategy. One such bank is Wells Fargo, whose use of EC is described in Application Case 10.5. Overall, 7 million online bank accounts were active in 1999 in the United States (20 million are projected by 2002).

APPLICATION CASE   10.5

Cyberbanking at Wells Fargo

Wells Fargo is a large California-based bank (over 1,700 branches). The bank has been known for generations for its financial services, dating back to the days of the wild, wild West. Wells Fargo's declared competitive strategy is cyberbanking. They plan to move millions of customers to the Internet and close hundreds of branches. A visit to the Wells Fargo Web site (*wellsfargo.com*) indicates the richness of services available.

The services are divided into five major categories: online (personal) banking, personal finance services, small business, commercial banking, and international trade. In addition, there are employment opportunities and even shopping. The bank offers many services in all categories. Most interesting are the services that cover all the needs of small businesses. These services are extremely user friendly and can run even on an old PC. The bank also saves money for the customer by offering lower rates.

Some of the capabilities of home banking are:

- **Get current account balances at any time.** Consumers can easily check the status of their checking, savings, credit card, and money market accounts.
- **Obtain charge and credit card statements.** Users can even set up their account to pay off cards automatically every month.
- **Pay bills.** Electronic payments from accounts are normally credited the same day or the next. The cost of paying bills electronically may be less than the postage involved in sending out a large number of payments each month.
- **Download account transactions.** Account transactions can easily be imported into money management software such as Quicken.
- **Transfer money between accounts.** No more waiting lines, deposit slips, and running to the ATM.
- **Balancing accounts.** If you are the kind of person who forgets to record ATM withdrawals, online banking may help you get organized. Just download the transactions and import them into your register.
- **Send e-mail to the bank.** Got a problem with an account? Users can send a quick note to their online bank representative.
- **A new meaning for "banker's hours."** Consumers can manage their money and bills on their own schedule.
- **Handle finances when traveling.** Consumers can access accounts when they are on the road and even arrange for bill payments to be made in their absence.
- **Additional services.** Customers of some banks receive free phone banking with their online banking service, all for a $5 to $7 monthly fee. Union Bank of California throws in free checking, ATM withdrawals, and bill paying (for one year). Several banks, including Bank of America, waive regular checking charges if consumers sign up for online banking.

Electronic banking offers several of the benefits listed in Chapter 1, both to the bank and to its customers, such as expanding the customer base and saving on the cost of paper transactions Gosling (2000). In addition to regular banks that are adding online services, there has been the emergence of virtual banks, solely dedicated to

Internet transactions. The Security First Network Bank (SFNB) was the first such bank offering secure banking transactions on the Web (*centuracom/snfb/snfb_welcome.ctm*). The bank offers savings and checking accounts, certificates of deposit, money market accounts, joint accounts, check imaging, and other services. To attract customers, SFNB offers very high-interest yields for CDs and money market accounts and allows access to information from various locations. If you have an account with your parents, for example, and you are away from home, both you and your parents can view the account and add or withdraw funds. You can transfer money between accounts, review past statements and credit card transactions, pay bills, check balances in all your accounts and credit cards, and calculate the interest to be paid on loans and credit cards. In March 1998, SFNB sold its online banking operations to Royal Bank of Canada. The Canadian bank needs the online services to serve its customers while they are vacationing in the United States. SFNB created a software company that is marketing the online banking software to many banks. Before sending money to any cyberbank, especially those that promise high interest rates for your deposits, make sure that the bank is a legitimate one. Several cases of fraud have already occurred.

Other representative virtual banks in the United States are *netbank.com* and First Internet Bank (*fibank.com*). Virtual banks exist in many other countries. It is interesting to note that in some countries banks are involved in stock trading (for example, see *bank.com*) and stockbrokers are doing banking (e.g., see E*TRADE.com).

International and Multiple-Currency Banking

International banking and the ability to handle trades in multiple currencies is critical for international trading. Although some international retail purchasing can be done by providing a credit card number, other transactions may require international banking support. Two examples of such cross-border support follow.

1. Hong Kong Bank has developed a special system called HEXAGON to provide electronic banking in Asia. Using this system, the bank has leveraged its reputation and infrastructure in the developing economies of Asia to become a major international bank rapidly, without developing an extensive new branch network. For details of this system see Peffers and Tunnainen (1998). Also see the Hexagon case on the Chapter 10 Web site (*prenhall.com/turban*).

2. Mark Twain Bank in the United States is using electronic cash to support trading in 20 foreign currencies. The bank attracts international traders. For details see *marktwain.com*.

Bank of America and most other major banks offer international capital raising, cash management, trades and services, foreign exchange, risk management investments, merchant services, and special services for international traders. Of special interest is NextCard (*nextcard.com*). Consumers can apply online for a credit card, and in one minute they find out if they qualify, and 30 seconds after that they get a card number. Furthermore, NextCard can show you the balances on your other credit cards—automatically, once you have been approved.

FXall.com is a multidealer foreign exchange service that enables faster and cheaper foreign exchange transactions. Special services are being established for stock market traders who need to pay for foreign stocks (e.g., Charles Schwab).

Implementation Issues in E-Banking and Online Stock Trading

The implementation of online banking and online trading are interrelated, and in many instances we can see that one financial institution offers both services. The following are some implementation issues.

SECURING FINANCIAL TRANSACTIONS

Financial transactions such as home banking and online trading must be highly secured. In Chapter 14 we discuss the details of securing EC payment systems. In Application Case 10.6 we provide an example of how Bank of America provides security and privacy to their customers.

APPLICATION CASE **10.6**

Security at Bank of America Online

Bank of America (B of A) provides extensive security to its customers. Here are some of the safeguards provided by the bank:

- Customers accessing the system from the outside must go through encryption provided by SSL and digital certification verification (Chapter 14). The certification process assures you that each time you sign on you are indeed connected to the Bank of America. Then the message goes through an external firewall. Once the logon screen is reached, a user ID and a password are required. This information flows through a direct Web server, then goes through an internal firewall to the application server.
- The bank keeps the information accurate; corrections are made quickly.
- Information is shared only for legitimate business purposes among the company's family of partners. Sharing information with outside companies is done with extreme care.
- The bank does not capture information provided by customers, conducting "what-if" scenarios using the bank's planning tools.
- The company uses "cookies" to learn about its customers. However, customers can control both the collection and use of the information.
- The bank provides suggestions on how to increase security (e.g., "Use a browser with 128-bit encryption").

Bank of America Security System

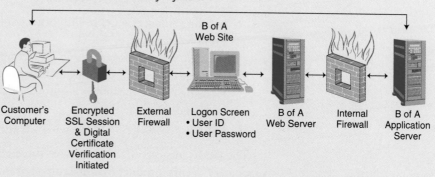

Source: Compiled from press releases and information on security from Bank of America online (*bofa.com*).

USING THE EXTRANET

Many banks provide their large business customers with a personalized service by allowing them access to the bank's intranet. For example, Bank of America, allows its customers access to accounts, historical transactions, and any other related data, including intranet-based decision-support applications, which may be of interest to customers. Bank of America also allows its small-business customers to apply for loans through its Web site.

IMAGING SYSTEMS

Several financial institutions (Bank of America, for example) allow customers to view images of all incoming checks, invoices, and other related online correspondence. Image access can be simplified with the help of a search engine.

PRICING ONLINE VERSUS OFF-LINE SERVICES

Computer-based banking services are offered free by some banks, while others charge $5 to $10 a month. Also, there are problems with respect to pricing individual transactions (such as fee per check, per transfer, and so on). For a discussion of this topic see Kingson (1997).

RISKS

Online banks, as well as click-and-mortar banks, may carry some risks and problems, especially in international banking. Regulators are grappling with the safeguards that need to be imposed on e-banking. Some believe that virtual banks carry liquidity risks and could be more susceptible to panic withdrawals.

The Future of Online Banking

A 1998 study by the Boston Consulting Group (BCG), entitled "The Information Superhighway and Retail Banking," painted a challenging picture for the banking industry. Rapid obsolescence will be the norm in the immediate future, since online transaction costs can be as low as 1 percent of the cost of an off-line transaction. Therefore, it is necessary to have a successful online banking strategy. This strategy depends on factors such as:

- building alliances quickly with other banks, software vendors, and information providers.
- effective outsourcing without neglecting to build in-house skills, particularly with respect to customer information systems;
- focusing on the profitable customer to provide broad channels for services and products;
- keeping a central role in the payment environment.

The study suggests that banks have three core strategies to pursue. These are customers' agents, product manufacturers, or integrated players.

1. Customers agents. There will be a number of banks that will see themselves as unable to achieve economies of scale due to disadvantages in product manufacturing and processing. In many cases they may choose to leave that part of the business. Consistent with this option would be a strategy to offer customers the widest possible choice, including products from multiple sources, and to provide the customer with information-integrated services.

2. **Product manufacturers.** Conversely, some banks will see themselves as able to achieve economies of scale in product development, manufacturing, and processing and may choose to position themselves as either a branded or unbranded wholesaler of product and processing services. According to Bobby Mehta, Vice President of the Boston Consulting Group, "The onset of online banking will strengthen a trend that can already be seen in a number of product segments (residential mortgages and credit card issuance) and in core processing services for small and medium-sized institutions."

3. **Integrated players.** Remaining as integrated players will be an option only for banks with a strong brand as well as a strong position from manufacturing to delivery. The BCG study states that "the banks may determine that if they sold third-party products to increase choices for their customers, sales would not increase sufficiently to offset lost margins. An example of such a player from outside banking is Fidelity Investments, although even such a strong player is bowing to customer demand for choice through its Funds Network offering." In the medium term, say the authors, many banks will adopt a hybrid strategy, but every player needs to make crucial decisions about which areas are strategically too risky to outsource and which capabilities need to be strengthened in-house.

Personal Finance Online

Banking can be beneficial to both businesses and individuals. Individuals often combine home banking with portfolio management and personal finance. Also, brokerage firms such as Schwab offer personal finance services such as retirement planning. However, specialized personal finance vendors offer more diversified services (Tyson, 2000). For example, both Quicken (from Intuit) and Microsoft's Money offer the following capabilities:

- Bill paying and electronic check writing
- Tracking bank accounts, expenditures, and credit cards
- Portfolio management, including reports and capital gains (losses) computations
- Investment tracking and monitoring of securities
- Quotes and past and current prices
- Budget organization
- Record keeping of cash flow and profit and loss computations
- Tax computations and preparations (e.g., try *riahome.com* and *taxlogic.com*)
- Retirement goals, planning, and budgeting

Although Quicken is the most popular personal finance software, there are more sophisticated packages such as Prosper (from Ernst & Young) and CAP-TOOL (*captool.com*). All of these products are available as independent software programs for the Internet or are coupled with other services such as those offered by AOL.

Online Billing

In August 1998, 90 percent of people surveyed in the Bay Area in California indicated a desire to pay their bills on the Internet. People prefer to pay monthly bills, such as telephone, utilities, credit cards, cable television, and so on, online. The recipients of such payments are even more eager than the payers to receive money online, since they can reduce processing costs significantly.

The following are the major existing payment systems:

- **Automatic transfer of mortgage payments.** This method has existed since the late 1980s. The payee authorizes its bank to pay the mortgage directly from the payee's account, including escrow for tax payments.
- **Automatic transfer of funds to pay monthly utility bills.** Since fall 1998, the city of Long Beach has allowed its customers to pay their gas and water bills automatically from their bank accounts. Many other utilities worldwide provide such an option.
- **Paying bills from online banking accounts.** Such payments can be made into any bank account. Many people pay their monthly rent and other bills directly into the payee's bank accounts.
- **A merchant-to-customer direct billing.** Under this model, a merchant such as American Express posts bills on its Web site, where customers can view and pay them. This means that customers have to go to many Web sites to pay all their bills. Several utilities in Los Angeles allow customers to pay bills on the utilities' Web sites, charging customers 20 cents per transaction, which is less than the price of a stamp.
- **Using an intermediary.** According to this model, a third party like MSFDS (Microsoft and First Data Corporation) consolidates all bills related to each customer in one site and in a standard format. Collecting a certain commission, the intermediary makes it convenient both to the payee and payer to complete transactions. This latest model is of interest to many vendors, including E*TRADE and Intuit.
- **ISP services.** As of 2000, ISPs are trying to sell customized solutions to their customers. However, ISPs do not have adequate billing platforms, especially online ones. *Moneymain.com* consolidates the resources of about 30 ISPs into one billing system.
- **Person-to-person direct payment.** An example of this is *paypal.com* (see Chapter 14).

Billing paying can be classified into B2C, B2B, or C2C. B2B services can save businesses about 50 percent of billing costs. In Hong Kong, for example, CitiCorp links suppliers, buyers, and banks on one platform, enabling automatic payment. B2C services help consumers to save time and payees to save on processing costs.

10.8   ONLINE PUBLISHING

Many other services are available on the Internet. In this section we briefly discuss one—online publishing.

Online publishing is the electronic delivery of newspapers, magazines, books, news, music, videos, and other digitizable information over the Internet. It is often related to advertisement since in most cases it is provided free to attract people to certain sites where advertisement is conducted.

Initiated in the late 1960s, online publishing was designed to provide online bibliographies and to sell knowledge that was stored in online databases. Publicly funded online publishing was established for the purpose of disseminating medical, educational, and aerospace research information. Today, online publishing has additional purposes. It is related to worldwide dissemination of knowledge and to advertisement. The potential of new interactive technologies and other Internet applications has aided the growth of online publishing.

Online Publishing Today and Tomorrow

One of the oldest examples of disseminating information through online publishing is the publishing of scholarly works for peer review. Today, online publishing is used mainly for disseminating information, conducting sales transactions interactively, providing customer service, or for public service purposes. Magazine and newspaper publishers such as *Ad Week, PC Magazine, The Wall Street Journal*, and *The Los Angeles Times* all use online publishing to disseminate information online. For example, *chicagotribune.com* (the online version of the *Chicago Tribune*) provides not only its hard copy issue online for free, but also posts additional news details. It also helps people find jobs and housing, and it provides many community services online (see Exercise 13). As of 2001, online publishing includes customized material that a reader either receives free or for a fee.

Publishing Modes and Methods

Several online publishing methods are in use. They include the online-archive approach, new-medium approach, publishing-intermediation approach, and dynamic or just-in-time approach.

The online-archive approach to online publishing is a digital archive such as library catalogs or bibliographic databases. It basically makes paper publications available online.

The new-medium approach is used by publishers that view the Web as a medium for creating new material or adding content and multimedia to paper publication. This form of publishing adds extra analysis and additional information on any issue or topic, and offers more information than a traditional magazine can offer. One way that the new-medium approach does this is by offering integrated hypertext links that offer related stories, topics, and graphics. It also can be easily customized or personalized. Taylor and Francis placed more than 500 of its journals online. The company provides research services, hypertext links, summaries, and more to subscribers. The new-medium approach also offers up-to-date material including breaking news. Examples include HotWired (*hotwired.lycos.com*), which complements a paper version of *Wired Magazine*, and *chicagotribune.com*.

The publishing-intermediation approach can be thought of as an online directory for news services. Publishing intermediation is an attempt to help people locate goods, services, and products online. Netscape and other portals provide services that are an example of this approach.

The dynamic (also referred to as just-in-time or point casting) approach is another method of online publishing. With this approach, content can be personalized in real-time and transmitted on the fly in the format best suited to the user's location, tastes, and preferences.

Content Providers and Distributors

Online publishing is related to content providers and distributors. These services are offered by several companies in this field (e.g., *akamai.com*, *digisle.com*, *edgix.com*). Content providers face major challenges when moving into areas with less-developed infrastructures due to the difficulty of presenting multimedia. Also, the issue of intellectual property payments is critical to the success of content distribution.

Of special interest in this area is *digimarc.com*, which provides a tool for linking print publications with the Web. The model of content delivery is shown in Figure 10-5.

Publishing Music, Videos, and Games

The Internet is an ideal media for publishing music, videos, electronic games, and related entertainment. A major issue here is the payment of intellectual property fees.

One of the most interesting new models is the **people-to-people (P2P) publishing model**. According to this model, people swap files that include digitized information, such as music. When such a swapping is managed by a third party, the organizer of the exchange program, for example Napster, may be in violation of copyright law. See Chapters 11 and 17 for details.

Figure 10-5	A New Content Delivery Business Model

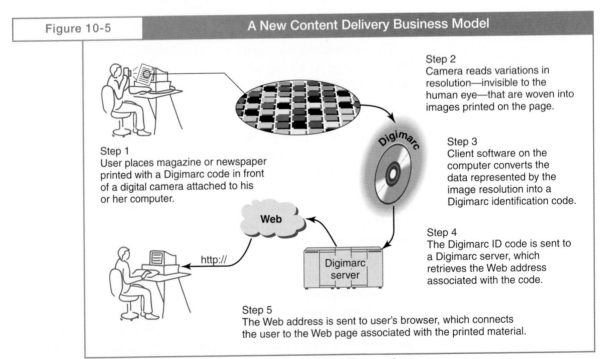

Step 1
User places magazine or newspaper printed with a Digimarc code in front of a digital camera attached to his or her computer.

Step 2
Camera reads variations in resolution—invisible to the human eye—that are woven into images printed on the page.

Step 3
Client software on the computer converts the data represented by the image resolution into a Digimarc identification code.

Step 4
The Digimarc ID code is sent to a Digimarc server, which retrieves the Web address associated with the code.

Step 5
The Web address is sent to user's browser, which connects the user to the Web page associated with the printed material.

Source: Originally published in *Interactive Week*, March 27, 2000, p. 46, *www.xplane.com*

Digital Delivery of Documents

A number of businesses offer delivery of digital documents in a secure environment, including the U.S. Postal Service, United Parcel Service (UPS), and small companies such as e-Parcel (*eparcel.com*). For example, UPS offers computer-to-computer secure document delivery using 128-bit encryption and software for digital signature, authentication, and notarization and nonrepudiation (*exchange.ups.com*). Another UPS product, Courier, is less secure and can move documents between any two computers. In effect, UPS is a third-party trusted service.

Edutainment

Online publishing has also moved into other areas with concepts such as edutainment and push technology. **Edutainment** is a combination of education, entertainment, and games. One of the main goals of edutainment is to encourage students to become active learners, rather than passive learners. With active learning, a student is more involved in the experience of learning and, therefore, it makes the learning experience richer and the knowledge gained more memorable. The idea behind edutainment is that it is a type of embedded learning. It helps students to learn without them knowing it. Edutainment covers various subjects for the active learner, such as mathematics, reading, writing, history, and geography. Edutainment is targeted to varying age groups ranging from three-year-olds to adults, and it is also used in corporate training over intranets. Software Toolworks is a vendor of edutainment products.

There are managerial issues to consider with edutainment in online publishing. Educational games are delivered mostly as CD-ROMs. However, since 1998 increasing numbers of companies offer online edutainment in a distance-learning format.

Printing Online

Several companies serve as one-stop online print shops. An example is *iprint.com*, which offers diversified printing services by working with several business partners. *Iprint.com* automates and aggregates customer orders, allowing it to reduce costs and prices. An example of one of their major clients is the Dallas Mavericks of the National Basketball Association.

Electronic Books

Several publishers offer books, even textbooks, online. Known as **electronic books**, regular books are available in electronic form. The books are portable and 70 of them can be loaded on one disk. They can be updated frequently, contain up-to-the-minute information, and are easy to search. They are also convenience to carry. However, readers need a special eBook reader to view the books. A number of online publishers produce e-books. One electronic book publisher, *wizap.com*. offers selected e-textbooks. For more information on e-books see *ebookconnections.com*, and *netlibrary.com*.

A major event in electronic publishing occurred on March 24, 2000, when Stephen King's book, *Riding the Bullet*, was published exclusively online. For $2.50 readers could purchase the e-book at *ebooks.barnesandnoble.com* and other e-book providers.

Several hundred thousand copies were sold in a few days. However, the publishing event did not go off without some problems. Hackers breached the security system and distributed free copies of the book. Electronic technical documents are available from the eMatter division of Fatbrain (now a *Barnes&Noble.com* company).

10.9 KNOWLEDGE DISSEMINATION, DISTANCE LEARNING, AND OTHER ONLINE SERVICES

Online publishing is closely related to the concept of knowledge dissemination. In this section we briefly look at only two knowledge dissemination applications: virtual teaching and online consulting. We also describe other online services.

Virtual Teaching and Online Universities

The concept of **distance learning**, or learning at home, is not new. Educational institutions have been offering correspondence degrees for decades. Lately, IT in general and the Web in particular have expanded the opportunities for distance learning. The concept of online universities, or **virtual universities**, is expanding rapidly, and hundreds of thousands of students in dozens of countries from Great Britain to Israel to Thailand are studying in such institutions. Large numbers of existing universities, including Stanford University and other top tier institutions, offer online education. Some universities, such as California State University at Dominguez Hills, offer hundreds of courses and dozens of degrees to students worldwide, all online. Other universities offer limited online courses and degrees but use innovative teaching methods and multimedia support in the traditional classroom (Application Case 10.7).

The virtual university allows universities to offer classes worldwide. Moreover, we may soon see integrated degrees, where students customize a degree that will best fit their needs and take courses at different universities.

APPLICATION CASE 10.7

Interactive MBA at City University of Hong Kong

As of May 1999, students in Hong Kong can study for their MBA any time, anywhere, and at any pace. This unique program started by integrating two technologies—the Web and interactive television. The objective of the program is to provide participants with a hi-tech, innovative, and interactive learning experience to improve their managerial and professional competence. The program is composed of 17 standard courses: 8 core courses, 6 advanced, and 3 integrated. Each course includes 45 lecture hours delivered on an interactive television (iTV or TV on demand). The students choose what lecture to watch and when they want to watch it. In addition to the lectures, all support material, exercises, and so on are provided on the Web. The students can interact electronically with the instructors and with each other, using e-mail and chat rooms. The program is supported by Hong Kong Telecom, which provides broadband access service at 1.5 Mbps download speed (about 30 times the speed of a fast regular modem). For details about the program and the technology, check *imba.cityu.edu.hk*.

Several new start-up schools include: *eSchool-World.com* and *trainingzone.co.uk*. The concept of online learning is shown in Figure 10-6. Notice the diversified forces that create the need for online learning.

Online training. A large number of organizations are using online training on a large scale. For example, IBM Taiwan Corp. is using Web-based "electronic training" for new employees. KPMG offers e-learning to the company's customers. Some vendors of online training and educational materials are *digitalthink.com*, *click2learn.com*, and *zdnet.com/smartplanet/*.

Online Advice and Consulting

The online advice and consulting field is growing rapidly as tens of thousands of experts of all kinds sell their expertise on the Internet, for a relatively low price. Here are some examples:

- **Medical advice.** Companies such as *Kasamba.com*, *Keen.com* health advice online provide consultations for the public with top medical experts. You can ask specific questions and get an answer from a specialist in a few days.
- **Management consulting.** Many consultants are selling their accumulated expertise from knowledge bases. A pioneer in this area was Andersen

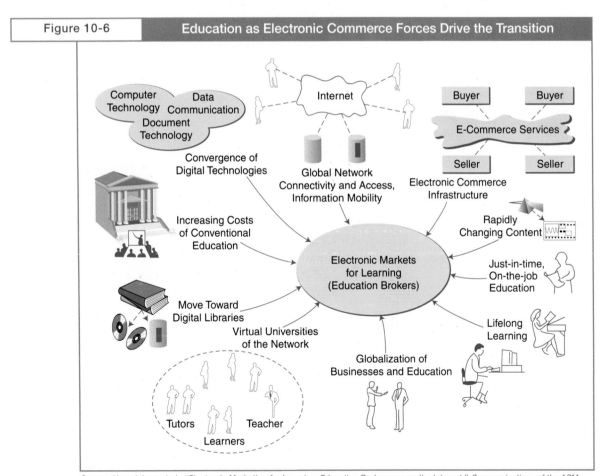

Figure 10-6   Education as Electronic Commerce Forces Drive the Transition

Source: Hamalainen et al., "Electronic Marketing for Learning: Education Brokerages on the Internet," *Communications of the ACM,* June 1996. Hamalainen et al. © 1996 ACM, Inc. Reprinted with permission.

Consulting (with their knowledgespace; Exercise 7). Another one is *Aberdeen.com*. Such services are used mainly by corporations due to the high service fees.

- **Legal advice.** Delivery of legal advice to individuals and businesses by consultation services has considerable prospects. For example, Atlanta-based law firm Alston & Bird coordinates legal counseling with 12 law firms for a large health-care company and for many other clients. The company created a knowledge base that contains information from some of the best law firms in the country. This information is then made available to all law firms. Many lawyers offer inexpensive consulting services online. Linklaters, a leading UK law firm, created a separate company to sell its legal services online (*blueflag.com*). The company offers several products and also sells support technology to other law firms.

- **Gurus.** Several sites provide diversified expert services, some for free. One example is *guru.com* which is a job board for experts on legal, financial, tax, technical, lifestyle, and other issues. It aggregates over 200,000 professional "gurus." Expertise is sold at *allexpert.com* where one can post a required service, so experts can bid on it. Of special interest is Scientific America from the experts at *sciam.com*.

- **Financial advice.** Many companies offer extensive financial advice. For example, Merrill Lynch Online (*askmerrill.ml.com*) provides free access to the firms research reports and analyses.

Other Services Online

There are hundreds of other services online. Some illustrative examples follow.

HEALTH CARE

Many health care services are provided online, for example, *officemed.com* provides information regarding insurance eligibility and patient referral transaction services. Using these services, providers are able to perform secure, interactive health-care transactions with insurance payers.

Healtheon Corp (*now* part of *WebMD.com*) created a virtual healthcare network linking health-care information systems and supporting enrollment, eligibility, referrals, and authorized laboratory and diagnostic test ordering, clinical retrieval, and claims processing. Medtel (*medtel.com*) offers a variety of services in the telemedicine field.

MATCHMAKING

Many of the previous services can be classified as agent-based, where agents play the role of matchmaker. Some more examples follow.

Several Web sites provide venture capital or information about sources of funding. The site *garage.com* matches potential investors with entrepreneurs. Other sites, such as College Edge Match Maker (*excite.collegeedge.com*), match potential students with colleges and universities. It provides all the information, including application forms. *Match.com* (*match.com*) is an online matchmaking service for the singles community with chat rooms, bulletin boards, and more. Finally, *guestfinder.com* helps people in the media find guests and interview sources.

STAMPS ONLINE

Companies that use the "snail mail" to send large numbers of letters and promotional materials can save time by using *stamps.com* to automate the process. Addresses are printed directly from Microsoft Word or a similar word processing program onto envelopes. Then a built-in postage calculator measures the weight of the mail and calculates the postage, and prints the correct postage on the envelope. Customers pay for the stamps through an online account. In addition to postage costs, customers pay a 10 to 15 percent premium, plus a monthly service charge. A special plan exists for SMEs and for individuals. The users/companies save time, and for this they are willing to pay a small premium. Authorized by the U.S. Postal Service, these companies provide a kit that allows customers to securely download and store up to $500 in postage. Users store the postage on their PCs and print out the equivalent of stamps in any denomination on envelopes or packages. Payment is made by credit card. This service competes with mechanical postage meters.

Another company that sells e-stamps is Pitney Bowes Inc., which controls the traditional postage meter market. The U.S. Postal Service favors electronic stamps, since they include better antifraud safeguards. Compaq Computer Corp. delivers the required technology on some of their PCs. For further details see *usps.com/ibip* and a special report at *keenanvision.com*.

10.10   DISINTERMEDIATION AND REINTERMEDIATION

Intermediaries traditionally provided trading infrastructure (such as a sales network), and they manage the complexity of matching buyers' and sellers' needs. The introduction of EC resulted in the automation of many tasks provided by intermediaries. Does this mean that travel agents, real estate brokers, job agency employees, insurance agents, and other such jobs will disappear? In Chapter 3 we referred to the process of cutting out intermediaries as **disintermediation**. Is disintermediation coming to brokers as well? Possibly. In the opening vignette of this chapter we saw that the traditional purchasing agent may have no role in the new system. On the other hand, only large customers will be able to participate in a magazine purchasing system like the one implemented by the University of California; smaller buyers will need the traditional agent or an aggregation agent for group purchasing.

Another example is that of Rosenbluth International (Chapter 2). The travel company completely changed its business model by providing value-added services to its business customers. While many agents will lose their jobs, others may survive, or even prosper. Bloch et al. (1996) think that the agent's role will be changed to emphasize value-added services such as:

- Assisting customers in comparison shopping from multiple sources.
- Providing total solutions by combining services from several vendors.
- Providing certifications and trusted third-party control and evaluation systems.

In this way, the agent's role is changed in a process referred to as **reintermediation**. Such value-added services require an integrated approach. Integration is the ability to sell a package of products to customers based on a very fine understanding of their needs, similar to the purchasing of a basket of stocks. For example, a travel agent that will take care of the complete trip, including booking the golf course and buying tickets for the show is using the integration approach. A bank will offer a basket of financial services, and job placement will be supplemented by resume writing, advice on tax implications, and the necessary transfer rights of pensions and insurance. This may result in new entrants to an industry, those who are information integrators, information aggregators, and **information brokers**. Some issues that could impact the future of intermediaries are:

- The success of intelligent agents. In addition to travel intelligent agents, there are agents to support job matching, to interpret resumes, and so on. The more intelligent the software agents, the less we will need human agents.
- Consumer attitudes and behavior are important. If consumers have good experiences with online insurance, stock purchasing, or travel, why would they ever return to using a human agent?

There will be lots of changes in the role of agencies. Take SABRE as an example. SABRE provided an infrastructure to hundreds of thousands of travel agents. In the future there will be fewer agents, so the infrastructure may become less important, but the *content* that SABRE sells is becoming their business cornerstone. Intermediaries will move from *providing transactions* to *providing knowledge.* Knowledge dissemination is one of the major applications of EC.

Some companies try to cut off disintermediation. For example, Merrill Lynch is trying to augment relationships between advisors and clients, which regular online trading companies cannot provide. For this reason, many of the company's clients continue their trusted relationship and do not move to the less expensive online brokers. This approach is another example of reintermediation.

The issue of intermediaries in an agent-based transaction is part of a broader issue of the role Internet intermediaries will play. There are two roles for electronic marketing intermediaries. The first role is to extend what we are familiar with in the physical markets into the virtual world. For example, search services and e-malls are virtual counterparts of directory services, yellow pages, and buying guides. Certification authorities play roles similar to notaries identification-issuing agencies, insurers, and so on. Electronic cash banks and digital credit card services extend payment clearing functions to the Internet.

The other type of intermediation is evolving from the unique capabilities or needs of online markets. This may involve breaking down the value-creating chain of the physical market into separate entities or combining them into a different type of service. For example, retailers have functions other than distribution. A Web intermediary may sell quality information and nothing else. A toy retailer not only distributes but also presents lines of products toy buyers are interested in examining and comparing. Thus, an intermediary is needed if we are to avoid visiting each and every manufacturer of a toy item.

A retailer sells products as well as a reputation for quality. Sometimes, that reputation is one of the more important function of that business. For example, we assume a superb quality of news if it appears on CNN or in the *New York Times*. But will we accept news from those on the Internet we've never heard of? CNN and the

New York Times are in reality just intermediaries who collect, repackage, and distribute news and information. In the information age, they cannot (or should not) wish to dominate the market. Online versions of CNN and the *New York Times* may emerge as the trusted source of digital information, but their value-creation processes are influenced by the needs of the physical market: the cost of gathering information, being selective due to the constraints of time and space, the idiosyncrasies of broadcast and print media, predominant ad-supported business models, and so on. However, as the news business changes, the greatest asset of CNN and the *New York Times* is their reputation for quality, by which they can become the ultimate information intermediary in the digital economy.

Disintermediation in B2B

The emergence of exchanges in the B2B area would eliminate the need for many of the calls that corporate sales representatives make to purchasing managers. The lone-ranger salesperson is slowly getting rarer in the B2B area, meaning that companies must reengineer their marketing and sales organizations (see Rackham, 1999).

Cybermediation

In addition to reintermediation, there is a completely new role in EC called **cybermediation**, or **electronic intermediary**, such as *rowe.com* in the opening case. Cybermediators can perform many roles in EC. To illustrate the diversity of such roles, Giaglis et al. (1999) used the market functions described in Chapter 2, together with the impacts of EC. As shown in Table 10-2, cybermediation can affect most of the market functions and more. For example, intelligent agents can find when and where an item that a consumer wants will be auctioned. The matching services described in this chapter are done by cybermediator agents. Cybermediator agents also conduct price comparisons of insurance policies, long

TABLE 10-2

Opportunities and Threats to Intermediaries in Electronic Markets

Market Function	Electronic Market Influence	Likely Effects on Intermediation
Determination of Product Offerings	• Personalization of Products • Aggregation • Disaggregation	• Disintermediation (especially in digital products) • Cybermediation (aggregators) • Disintermediation (pay-per-use)
Searching	• Lower Search Costs • More Complex Search Requirements • Lower Barriers to Entry	• Disintermediation • Cybermediation • Cybermediation/Reintermediation
Price Discovery	• Redistribution of Mechanisms • New Markets	• Cybermediation/Reintermediation • Cybermediation
Logistics	• Lower Logistical Costs • Economies of Scale	• Disintermediation • Reintermediation
Settlement	• New Cost Structures • New Payment Mechanisms	• Reintermediation • Cybermediation/Reintermediation
Trust	• Increased Protection Requirements	• Cybermediation/Reintermediation
Legal and Regulatory	• Institutional Support for Electronic Markets	• Reintermediation

Source: Giaglis et al. (1999), p. 401. Used with permission of De. George Giaglis.

distance calls, and other services. Cybermediation services are spreading rapidly around the globe (e.g., see Vandermerwe, 1999; and Berghel, 2000). For further discussion of the changing role of information intermediaries in services see Kauffman et al. (2000).

Hypermediation

In certain cases it was observed that certain EC transactions require extensive human and electronic intermediation. Content providers, affiliate sites, search engines, portals, ISPs, software makers, and more are needed in many cases of EC. According to Carr (2000), this phenomenon, called **hypermediation**, is running opposite to disintermediation, providing intermediaries with a chance to profit greatly from EC.

10.11 MANAGERIAL ISSUES

The following issues are germane to management:

1. **Out-of-town recruitment.** This can be an important source of skilled workers. Using video teleconferencing, recruiters can interview potential employees from a distance. For many jobs, companies can use telecommuters. This strategy could be a major one in the twenty-first century. However, companies may find themselves with too many irrelevant resumes and waste too much time checking them when online recruiting takes place.

2. **Privacy.** As applicant information travels over the Internet, security and privacy become even more important. It is management's job to secure applicant information.

3. **International legal issues.** Recruiting people online from other countries may not be simple. The validity of contracts signed in different countries needs to be checked with legal experts. The same applies for travel arrangements involving foreign countries and to real estate transactions made from a distance.

4. **Ethics.** Ethical issues are extremely important in an agentless system. In traditional systems, human agents play an important role in assuring ethical behavior of buyers and sellers. Will the rules of etiquette be sufficient on the Internet? Only time will tell.

5. **The intermediaries.** It will take a few years before the new roles of Internet intermediaries will be stabilized, as well as their fees. Also, the emergence of support services, such as escrow services in global EC, will have an impact on the intermediaries and their role.

6. **Alliances.** Alliances for online initiatives are spreading rapidly. For example, in Hong Kong, four banks created a joint online e-bank (to save on capital cost and share the risk). The venture has been opened to others. Online trading brokers are teaming with banks. Banks are teaming up with telecommunications companies, software companies, and even airlines. Finally, eBay and Wells Fargo Bank have an alliance for C2C payment transactions and auctions.

Summary

In this chapter, you learned about the following EC issues as they relate to the learning objectives:

1. **How broker-based services are performed online.** With broker-based services, customers communicate their wishes online. In some cases there is an automatic match of customer needs and the services offered. The human-broker role is being changed to that of market maker and a provider of added values that are not available on the Web. Failure to do so will result in the loss of that job. Commissions for human agents are reduced drastically since the electronic markets are more efficient. Customers may have direct access to providers of services and can even negotiate deals electronically.

2. **How online travel/tourism services operate.** Most services available through a physical travel agency are also available online. In addition, customers get much more information much more quickly through online resources. Customers logon to a virtual agency, prepare their desired trip, compare what is available, and can even receive bids from providers. Travelers can set a maximum price they are willing to pay for transportation, accommodations, events, and more. Finally, travelers can compare prices, participate in auctions and chat rooms, and view videos and maps.

3. **The impact of EC on the travel industry.** EC creates much stronger competition among travel agencies and providers of services, resulting in lower prices and lower commissions. The industry is being transformed into a direct marketing operation. The role of travel agents is changing, and many will disappear. The survivors will be those who offer value-added services. More automation is anticipated due to intelligent agents, active bidding, auctions, and negotiations.

4. **The online job market, its drivers, and benefits.** The online job market is growing rapidly with millions of jobs matched annually with job seekers. The major drivers of online job markets are the ability to reach a large number of job seekers at low cost, to provide detailed information online, to take applications, and even to conduct tests. Also, using intelligent agents, resumes can be checked and matches made quickly. Benefits exist for employers, job seekers, government agencies, and successful employment agencies.

5. **The electronic real estate market.** The online real estate market is basically supporting rather than replacing existing agents. However, time and effort of both buyers and sellers can be saved. Buyers can purchase distant properties much more easily and in some places have access to less expensive services. Eventually, commissions on regular transactions will decline.

6. **Online stocks, bonds, and commodities trading.** One of the fastest growing online businesses is online trading. It is inexpensive, convenient, and supported by a tremendous amount of financial and advisory information. Trading is very fast and efficient, almost fully automated, and it is moving toward 24/7 global trading. Day trading is rising rapidly and the traditional brokers are slowly disappearing. Also, IPOs are moving to the Net.

7. **Cyberbanking and its benefits.** Branch banking is on the decline due to less expensive, more convenient online banking. The world is moving toward online banking; today most routine services can be done from home. Banks

are pressuring customers to move online and can reach customers in remote places; customers can bank with faraway institutions. This makes the financial markets more efficient.

8. **Implementing online financial services.** Financial services are moving online, frequently in an integrated fashion: stocks, banking, personal finance, real estate and insurance, all in one stop. Strong growth is seen in all financial services, especially in automatic billing and securities trading.

9. **Innovative service industries applications.** Hundreds of other services are coming online. Notable services include online publishing, knowledge dissemination, distance learning and training, insurance, document management, electronic stamps, matchmaking, astrology online, and many, many more.

10. **The changing roles of intermediaries.** In most cases, the conventional intermediation will disappear or change. Direct marketing will eliminate many types of intermediaries. The survivors will basically be providers of value-added services, market makers, and knowledge disseminators.

Key Terms

Cyberbanking
Cybermediation
Distance learning
Disintermediation
Edutainment
Electronic books (e-book)
Electronic banking (e-banking)
Electronic intermediary

Hypermediation
Intermediaries (intermediation)
Information brokers
Online banking (e-banking)
People-to-people (P2P) publishing model
Reintermediation
Virtual universities

Questions for Review

1. Define edutainment.
2. Define information brokers.
3. List the major services provided by an online travel service.
4. List the limitations of online travel services.
5. List the driving forces of the electronic job market.
6. What are the major advantages of electronic job seeking to the candidate? To the employers?
7. List the major benefits of trading online.
8. List the various options of paying bills electronically.
9. List the various types of online publishing.
10. Define disintermediation, reintermediation, and cybermediation.
11. Define e-books and list their advantages.

Questions for Discussion

1. Why are online travel services such a popular Internet application?
2. What are the major motivations for an airline to sell electronic tickets?
3. Why are so many Web sites providing free travel information?

4. Discuss the potential impact of a virtual travel agency on a traditional one.
5. What are the implications of a virtual travelers' community?
6. Distinguish between corporate and individual travel as conducted on the Internet.
7. What role could intelligent agents play in online travel and why?
8. What strategic advantage is provided to airlines that offer online auctions of tickets?
9. Compare online stock trading with off-line trading.
10. Examine the section about the "future of banking." Select a large bank in your area. Which of the three strategies is this bank most likely to follow. Why?
11. Analyze Bloch and Segev's impact model. Give examples that will show its validity.
12. What role could intelligent agents play in online travel and why?
13. What other services are similar to job placement services? Can they be provided online? Why or why not?
14. Why do Internet job placement services provide free advice on how to write a resume?
15. Intelligent agents are reading resumes and forwarding them to potential employers. What are the benefits of this use of intelligent agents?
16. Online employment services make it easy to change jobs; therefore, turnover rates may increase. This could result in total higher costs because of increased costs for recruiting and training new employees and paying higher salaries and wages. What can companies do to ease the problem?
17. Review the ten deficiencies of a traditional job market as listed in Section 10.4. For each deficiency, explain how it is going to disappear or at least be minimized if the Internet is used.
18. How can companies offer very low commissions for online stock purchases (as low as $5 per trade—some even offering no commission for certain trades)? Why would they choose to offer such low commissions? Over the long run do you expect commissions to increase or continue to decrease?
19. It is said that some banks are going online because they are forced to do so. Others banks are very happy to lead the way. Why do banks use different online strategies?
20. Why does Colliers Arnold (Application Case 10.3), believe that the major value of their Web site is customer service and not additional sales?
21. Compare real estate agents with stock market agents in EC.
22. Why is knowledge dissemination on the Internet growing so rapidly?
23. Explain what is meant by this statement: Intermediaries will become knowledge providers rather than transaction providers.
24. Will e-books eventually eliminate paper books? Why or why not?
25. Examine Table 10-2 and find real-world applications of cybermediation in the area of market functions. Add some other applications to the list.

Internet Exercises

1. Access *sourcer.com*. Find information about software support for recruitment. Try the demos available at the site.

2. Enter *phoenix.placement.oakland.edu* and find the "Internet career guide." You will find more than 100 references to career-oriented sites, organized alphabetically. Use the reference list to find:
   - A summer internship
   - Job openings in Bethlehem, Pennsylvania
   - A computer analyst's job in Hong Kong
   - Related software (Oak repository)
   - Information about job fairs in your city or state (*careermag.com*)

3. Make your resume accessible to millions of people. Ask *careerbuilder.com* for help in rewriting your resume. Consult *jobweb.org* in planning your career. Get prepared for a job interview (*hotjobs.com*).

4. Determine your career vision by exploring *monster.com* and *careerbuilder.com*. Also, use *wageweb.com* to figure what salary you can get in the city of your choice in the United States.

5. Use the Internet to perform the following tasks:
   - Sign up with Expedia and tell them you want to travel from your city to Hawaii. Wait a few days to receive low-price flight suggestions on your e-mail. Check their free travel advisory services. Write a report based on your experience.
   - Track a flight in real time (*thetrip.com*), by flight number, by airline, and by city.
   - Find the lowest possible fare for a trip from Los Angeles to Paris, France, leaving on a weekday, staying 10 days, and returning on a weekday.
   - Use Expedia's Hotel Wizard to find a hotel in London. Use the currency converter to determine your nightly cost in U.S. dollars.
   - Evaluate online medical advice.
   - Find a map of Jerusalem, Israel, a list of attractions, and an entertainment guide.

6. Visit *homeowners.com*, *decisionaide.com*, or a similar site and compute the mortgage payment on a 30-year loan at 7.5 percent fixed interest. Also check current rates. Estimate your closing costs on a $200,000 loan. Compare the monthly payments of the fixed rate with that of an adjustable rate for the first year. Finally, compute your total payments if you take the loan for 15 years at the going rate. Compare it to a 30-year mortgage. Comment on the difference.

7. *Enter* the knowledgespace communities at *Andersen.com* and go to eBusiness. Go to the Hot Issues Archive. Find information about exchanges.

8. Access *virtualtrader.co.uk* and register for their Internet stock game. You will be bankrolled with £100,000 in a trading account every month. Also, identify all the services offered by E*TRADE and comment on them. You can also play a simulation investment game with *investorsleague.com*, E*TRADE (stocks, options), and *marketplayer.com*.

9. Enter *wellsfargo.com* and examine their global and B2B services. For each service that is being offered, comment on the advantages of online versus offline options.

10. Examine the progress of consolidated billing. Start with *e-billingonline.com*, *alysis.com*, (go to money), and *intuit.com*. Identify other contenders in the field. What are the standard capabilities that they all offer? What are some unique capabilities?

11. Enter *etrade.com* and *boom.com* and find how you can trade stocks in countries other than the one you live in. Prepare a report.
12. How about building a Web site for your mortgage company? Try *glyphix.com* or *masresults.com*. Look at demo sites and sample sites.
13. Enter *chicagotribune.com*, *wsj.com*, and *fortune.com*. Find what information is available to customers. Compare the *Tribune's* offering with that of *yahoo.com*. What are the differences?

Team Assignments and Role Playing

1. Each team will represent a broker-based area (e.g., real estate, insurance, stocks, job finding). Each team will find a new development that has occurred in the assigned area over the last 3 months. Look for the vendor's announcement and search for more information on the development with Yahoo!, *google.com*, or another search engine. Examine the business news at *cnnfn.com*. After completing your research, as a team prepare a report on disintermediation in the assigned areas.
2. Airline consortiums are competing with Travelocity, Expedia, and other online travel agents. Research several of these consortiums (each team examines one) and analyze the competitive advantage of the airlines versus online agents. Prepare a report based on your findings. Make a presentation that will predict a winner: Airline sites, travel agencies, or online general sites such as Expedia.
3. Explore the status and issues of e-books. Have each team member examine one of the following issues: required infrastructure, legal and policy issues, and alliances and models. Visit *netlibrary.com*, *gemstar-ebook.com*, *ebooks.bn.com*, *Microsoft.com*, and *Gemstar.co.uk* for information. Debate: will e-books fly?
4. As a team, investigate the online experts business. Have each team register as expert providers and advice seekers at *askanexpert.com*, and *allexperts.com*. Compare the quality of advice rendered (use free sites). Write a report.

REAL-WORLD CASE: Web Takes Banking to Sea

The U.S. Navy Federal Credit Union serves 1.7 million customers. Many of these customers are on active duty, serving on hundreds of ships, and are sometimes at sea for months at a time. Others are dispersed in military bases all over the world.

Using satellites and other technologies, the U.S. Navy created a sophisticated communications system that allows its customers online banking from any place at any time. The network is connected to 150,000 ATMs worldwide, including ATMs on all Navy vessels.

Users can view their accounts, transfer money, pay bills, and apply for loans on the Internet. The system is integrated with an intranet so that the 3,700 employees of the credit union can communicate with headquarters, regardless of their location. Also, the intranet is used for training and facilitating the loan application process.

These secured services are provided through a wireless Internet link connected to the Department of Defense satellite system. This gives the credit union members the ability to access their bank accounts and take care of household finances from the various ships.

The system provides superb customer service, and at the same time, the cost of the new client/server-based system is significantly lower than that of the old mainframe-based system. However, the new system still uses the old legacy system. The contacts are made through a Web interface, making the legacy system accessible through browsers. The intranet consolidates the administrative and member services in an easy-to-read Graphical User Interface, regardless of the back-end application systems to which it may be tied (like payroll and accounts payable).

Questions for the case

1. How can the cost benefit analysis of such a system be measured?

2. The system is linked to global systems such as the U.S. Armed Forces Financial Network as well as to Plus Systems, Inc. (a public network). Why?

3. What is the role of the intranet in this case?

4. What type of EC is this?

5. Find the similarities of this case with the Qantas case in Chapter 1.

REFERENCES AND BIBLIOGRAPHY

Alexander, S. "The Search Is Online," *Careers* (Fall 1997).

Baghai, R. and B. E. Cobert. "The Virtual Reality of Mortgages," *McKinsey Quarterly* (Summer 2000).

Bailey, J. P. "The Emergence of Electronic Market Intermediaries," Proceedings. HICSS, Hawaii (1998).

Bayne, K. M. "Recruiting Via Internet on the Rise," *Advertising Age* (October 1997).

Berghel, H. "Predatory Disintermediation," *Communication of the ACM* (May 2000).

Birch, D. and M. A. Yound. "Financial Services and the Internet—What Does Cyberspace Mean for Financial Services Industry?" *Internet Research: Electronic Networking Applications and Policy,* vol. 7, no. 2. (1997).

Bloch, M., et al. "Leveraging Electronic Commerce for Competitive Advantage: a Business Value

Framework," Proceedings of the Ninth International Conference on EDI-IOS, Bled, Slovenia. (June 1996),

Bloch, M. and A. Segev. "The Impact of Electronic Commerce on the Travel Industry," Proceedings, HICSS, Hawaii (1997).

Bose, K. "Intelligent Agents Framework for Developing Knowledge-based DSS for Collaborative Organizational Processes," *Expert Systems with Applications,* vol. 11, no. 3 (1996).

Boss, S., et al. "Will the Banks Centralize Online Banking"? *McKinsey Quarterly* (Summer 2000).

Callon, J. D. *Competitive Advantage Through Information Technology.* New York: McGraw-Hill, 1996.

Carr, N. G. "Hypermediation: Commerce as Clickstream," *Harvard Business Review* (January/February 2000).

Champy, J., et al. "Creating the Electronic Community," *Information Week* (June 10, 1996).

Chou, D. C. and A. Y. Chou. "A Guide to the Internet Revolution in Banking," *Info. System Manager* (Spring 2000).

Clemons E. K. and H. Hann, "Rosenbluth International: Strategic Transformation," *Jour. of MIS* Fall 1999.

Dahle, C. "Going Places," *Webmaster Magazine* (August 1997).

Davis, J. "E*TRADE's Portal Play," *Business 2.0* (Fall 1998).

Fitch, M. "Cruise the Web to Land the Job of Your Dreams," *Money* (May 1997).

Giaglis, G. M., et al. "Disintermediation, Reintermediation or Cybermediation," *Proceedings 12th International Bled EC Conference*, Bled, Slovenia (June 7–9, 1999).

Gilbert J., et al., *Online Investment Bible,* Berkeley CA: Hungry Minds Inc. (December 2000).

Gosling, P. *Changing Money: How the Digital Age Is Transforming Financial Services.* Dulles, Virginia: Capital Books Inc., 2000.

Hagel, J. III, and M. Singer. *Net Worth: Shaping Markets When Customers Make the Rules.* Cambridge, Massachusetts: Harvard Business School Press, 1999.

Hamalainen, M., et al. "Electronic Marketing for Learning: Education Brokerages on the Internet," *Communications of the ACM* (June 1996).

Helton, R. "Using the Internet and the Web in Your Job Search: A Complete Guide," *Database* (August/September 1997).

Heyworth, A. "Stand by for an E-Mortgage Boom," *JASSA* (Winter 2000).

Jacobs, P. "American Express Travel and Wal-Mart: Breaking Digital Ground," *InfoWorld* (July 28, 1997).

Jandt, F. E. and M. B. Nemnich, eds. *Using the Internet and the Web in Your Job Search*, 2nd ed. Indianapolis, Indiana: Jistwork, 1999.

Kauffman, R., et. al. "Analyzing Information Intermediaries in Electronic Brokerage," Proceedings, 33rd HICSS, Hawaii (January 2000).

King, J. "Web Site Offers Job Lists, Search Services for Free," *ComputerWorld* (January 13, 1997).

Kingston, B. J. "Pricing Home Banking Services: A Puzzle for Vacillating Bankers," *American Banker* (December 1997).

Koonce, R. "Using the Internet as a Career Planning Tool," *Training and Development* (September 1997).

Lim, S. "The Impact of the Web on Individual Investors and Electronic Stock Market Trading" at *employees.org* (go to slim) (1997).

MacSweeney, G. "Dual Strategy," *Insurance and Technology* (July 2000).

Mahan, J. S. "Electronic Commerce and the Future of Banking," *The Bankers Magazine* (March/April 1996).

Mandel, M. J. and T. Gutner. "Your Next Job," *Business Week* (October 13, 1997).

McIlvaine, A. "Cyber Scholars," *Human Resource Executive* (October 6, 1997).

Nelson, W., et al. "Electronic Stock Trading and the Role of the Day-Trader," Proceedings, 33rd HICSS, Hawaii (2000).

Neo, B. S. "The Implementation of an Electronic Market for Pig Trading in Singapore," *Journal of Strategic Information Systems* (December 1992).

Opton, D. B. "Jobs Will Follow 'Net Networking,'" *CommunicationWeek* (March 10, 1997).

Peffers, K. and V. K. Tunnainen. "Expectations and Impacts of a Global Information System: The Case of a Global Bank from Hong Kong," *Jour. Of Global Information Technology Management*, vol. 1, no. 4 (1998).

Porter, M. E. *Competitive Strategy, Techniques for Analyzing Industries and Competitors.* New York: The Free Press, 1985.

Rackham, N. *Rethinking the Sales Force.* New York: McGraw-Hill, 1999.

Rogers, A. "Travel Gods Smile on Zeus," *Information Week* (September 1, 1997).

Sarkar, M., et al. "Intermediaries and Cybermediaries: A Continuing Role for Mediating Players in the Electronic Marketplace," *Journal of Computer-Mediated Communication,* vol. 1, no. 3 (1995).

Schonfeld, E. "Schwab—Put It All Online," *Fortune* (December 7, 1998).

Smetannikov, M. "Billing Systems Become Strategic," *Interactive Week* (December 13, 1999).

Standing, C. and Vasudavan, T. "Effective Internet Commerce Business Models On the Travel

Agency Sector," Proceedings PACIS, Hong Kong (June 2000).

Timewel, S. "Shopping for Money," *Banker* (August 1996).

Tyson, E. *Personal Finance for Dummies,* 3rd ed. San Francisco, California: Hungry Mind, 2000.

Van der Heijden, J. G. M. "The Changing Value of Travel Agents in Tourism Networks: Towards a Network Design Perspective." *Information and Communication Technologies in Tourism,* edited by

Stefan Klein et al. New York: Springer-Verlag, 1996, pp. 151–59.

Vandermerwe, S. "The Electronic 'Go-Between Service Provider': A New Middle Role Taking Center," *European Management Journal* (December 1999).

Vinzant, C. "Electronic Books Are Coming at Last," *Fortune* (July 6, 1998).

Wadsworth, K. H. "Cyber Malling: A Retail Death Sentence?" *Journal of Property Management* (March/April 1997).

11

Intrabusiness, E-Government, and More

LEARNING OBJECTIVE

Upon completion of this chapter the reader will be able to:

- Define intrabusiness e-commerce.

- Describe the intranet and its use in organizations.

- Understand the relationship between corporate portals and the intranets.

- Describe e-government to citizens (G2C) and to business (G2B).

- Describe other e-government initiatives.

- Understand how peer-to-peer technology works in intrabusiness, in B2B, and in C2C e-commerce.

11.1 BUSINESS INTELLIGENCE PORTAL SPEEDS PRODUCT RESEARCH AND DEVELOPMENT (R&D) AT AMWAY

Amway Inc. sells through thousands of independent agents all over the world more than 450 home, nutrition and wellness, and personal products. To be effective, the R&D department at Amway must develop new products in a streamlined and cost-efficient manner. The R&D department consists of 550 engineers, scientists, and quality assurance staff working on more than 1,000 projects at a time.

Fast and easy access to information about current products such as product specifications, formulas, design criteria, production schedules, costs, and sales trends is required for supporting the design activity. This was difficult in the past because the required data sometimes resided in 15 to 20 disparate repositories, such as in a data warehouse, and supply chain and accounting systems were in different departments. When scientists needed production or financial data, for instance, they had to request paper reports from each department, which could take days to be processed.

Amway developed a business intelligence and knowledge management portal, called Artemis, tailored to the R&D division. Artemis is a browser-based intranet application that enables R&D staff to quickly find the required information. It also includes features such as collaboration tools and a database for locating company experts. Using the Lotus search agent and full-text search engine technology, Artemis enables employees to pull data from disparate corporate sources and generate dynamic reports in response to user queries.

Artemis started with the goal of saving each R&D employee 1 hour per week. Structured product data from legacy systems is abstracted by Artemis and used for creating dynamic reports in response to users' search criteria. Time required to access information dropped from days to minutes or seconds, enabling fast what-if investigations needed by product developers.

Amway's development partner, MarchFIRST, suggested that Lotus Domino would best leverage existing resources such as the intranet and data warehouse. Domino's strong security features, easy integration with legacy systems, built-in intelligent agents, and a fast search engine, along with powerful knowledge management capabilities, were instrumental in making Artemis a success.

With a budget of less than $250,000, Amway's IT support group users worked with MarchFIRST to complete Artemis over three phases of 8 to 12 weeks each, and went live in January 2000. The portal runs on Domino 5.0 (in 2000), on a fast, dedicated Windows NT server. Each night, Domino sends intelligent agents out to a Sybase data warehouse and builds or updates an information document for each Amway product stored in a Domino database. R&D staff do full-text searches against this database to locate products of interest, then Domino queries the data warehouse for details. The only non-Domino part of Artemis is an $800 Java utility, called PopChart Live, used to create the trend and pie charts within the final document the user sees.

Collaborative features of Artemis include a time accounting function for the R&D staff. Used to help calculate R&D tax credits, this system has a gated section in which managers can analyze big-picture R&D trends. The Artemis event-reporting database also tracks project content and status, which helps staff to locate colleagues with specific expertise. Domino's strong messaging alerts staffers via e-mail when their projects are updated.

After a staged rollout, all 550 R&D staffers now have access to the system. Initial user surveys indicated that 60 percent are saving 30 minutes or more per week. This is expected to rise as links to more information sources are added and users gain comfort with the system.

Sources: Compiled from Abbott, C., "At Amway, BI Portal Speeds Product R&D," *DM Review*, October 2000, and from *amway.com*.

11.2   INTRABUSINESS AND BUSINESS-TO-EMPLOYEE (B2E) E-COMMERCE

The opening case demonstrates the importance of the corporate intranet in providing an infrastructure for knowledge sharing, and the role of the corporate portal as the gateway to this knowledge. The system enables fast access to information, provides security, and was constructed at a reasonable cost. The system will save about an hour a week, per employee, which is roughly equivalent to 13 employees out of the 550, paying for the system in less than 6 months. The intranet/portal application is an example of intrabusiness e-commerce.

As indicated in Chapter 1, e-commerce is not only done between business partners, but also within an organization. Such activity is referred to as **intrabusiness EC**, or in short, intrabusiness. Intrabusiness can be done between the following:

- a business and its employees (B2E)
- among units within the business (usually done as c-commerce)
- among employees in the same business (usually done as c-commerce)

Business to Its Employees (B2E)

Later in this chapter we will show several examples of B2E. Here are some representative ones:

- Employees electronically order supplies and material needed for their work.
- Many companies have corporate stores that sell a company's products to its employees, usually at a discount. The employees place orders on the intranet, and the store will pack and deliver the items to the employees, at work or at home. Payment is then deducted from payroll.
- Businesses disseminate information on the intranet (Section 11.4).
- Employees can buy discounted insurance, travel packages, and tickets to events on the corporate intranet.
- Businesses allow employees to manage their fringe benefits, take classes, and much more, all electronically (Sections 11.3, 11.4).

Between and Among Units Within the Business

Large corporations frequently consist of independent units, called business units (SBUs), which "sell" or "buy" materials, products, and services from each other. Transactions of this type can be easily automated and performed over the intranet. An SBU can be considered as either a seller or a buyer.

Large corporations also have a net of dealerships that are usually wholly or partially owned by the corporation. In such cases, a special network is constructed to support communication, collaboration, and execution of transactions. Such intrabusiness commerce is conducted by auto dealers, equipment manufacturers (e.g., Caterpiller), and most other large manufacturers, including those dealing with consumer products such as in the case of Toshiba America (see Application Case 11.1).

Intrabusiness E-Commerce at Toshiba America

The Problem. Toshiba America has an intranet that doubles as a dealer extranet. Toshiba works with 300 dealers. Dealers who needed parts quickly had to place a telephone or fax order by 2:00 P.M. for next-day delivery. To handle the shipment, Toshiba's Electronic Imaging Division (EID) (fax machines and copiers) spent $1.3 million on communications and charged $25 per shipment to the dealers. In addition, dealers had to pay the overnight shipping fee. A cumbersome order-entry system was created in 1993, but no significant improvement was achieved.

The Solution. In August 1997, Toshiba created a Web-based order-entry system using an extranet/intranet. Dealers now can place orders for parts until 5:00 P.M. for next-day delivery. The company placed the physical warehouse in Memphis, Tennessee, near FedEx headquarters to ensure quick delivery. Dealers can also check accounts receivable balances, and pricing arrangements, and read service bulletins, press releases, and so on. Once orders are submitted, a computer checks for the part's availability. If a part is available, the order is sent to Toshiba's warehouse in Memphis. Once at the warehouse site, the order pops up on a handheld radio frequency (RF) monitor. Within a few hours the part is packed, verified, and packaged for FedEx. See Figure 11-1.

Toshiba's Customer Service Process

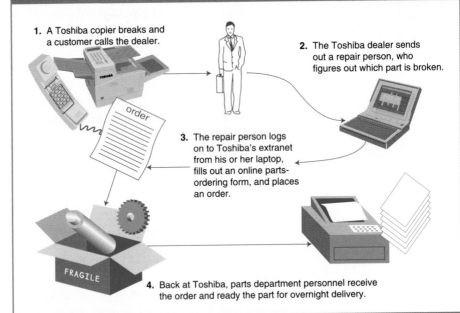

1. A Toshiba copier breaks and a customer calls the dealer.

2. The Toshiba dealer sends out a repair person, who figures out which part is broken.

3. The repair person logs on to Toshiba's extranet from his or her laptop, fills out an online parts-ordering form, and places an order.

4. Back at Toshiba, parts department personnel receive the order and ready the part for overnight delivery.

Figure 11-1
Source: Compiled from Jones (1998). Used by permission.

The intranet also allows sales reps to interact more effectively with dealers. The dealers can be up-to-date and manage their volume discount quotes up to the minute.

APPLICATION CASE   11.1

(continued)

The Results. Using the system, the cost per order has declined to about $10. The networking cost of EID has been reduced by more than 50 percent (to $600,000/year). The low shipping cost results in 98 percent overnight delivery, which increases customer satisfaction. The site processes more than 85 percent of all dealers' orders.

For further details, see McCreary, L. "Intranet Winners 1999," *CIO Web Magazine*, July 1, 1999.

Between and Among Corporate Employees

Many large organizations have classified ads on the intranet through which employees can buy and sell products and services from each other. This service is especially popular in universities where it was conducted even before the commercialization of the Internet. (Note that in some cases several universities interconnect their intranets to increase the exposure, as is the case of universities in Singapore.)

In addition, employees collaborate and communicate using EC technologies.

The most popular infrastructure for intrabusiness is the intranet.

11.3   INTRANETS

An **intranet**, or an internal Web, is a network architecture designed to serve the internal informational needs of a company using Web concepts and tools. It provides Internet capabilities, such as easy and effective browsing, search engines, and tools for communication and collaboration. Using a Web browser, a manager can see resumes of employees, business plans, and corporate regulations and procedures; retrieve sales data; review any desired document; and call a meeting. Employees can check availability of software for particular tasks and test the software from their workstations. Intranets are frequently connected to the Internet, enabling the company to conduct e-commerce activities, such as cooperating with suppliers and customers or checking a customer's inventory level before making shipments. Such activities are facilitated by *extranets*, as described in Chapter 7. Using screen sharing and other groupware tools, the intranets can be used to facilitate the work of groups. Companies also publish newsletters and deliver news to their employees on intranets and conduct online training. Some applications of intranet commerce are discussed later.

The cost of converting an existing client-server network to an internal Web is relatively low, especially when a company is already using the Internet. Many computing facilities can be shared by both the Internet and intranets. An example is a client-server-based electronic conferencing software module (from Picture Talk, Inc., *picturetalk.com*) that allows users to share documents, graphics, and video in real time. This capability can be combined with an electronic voice arrangement.

According to a Meta Group study (Stellin, 2001), nearly 90 percent of all U.S. corporations have some type of intranet, and over 25 percent are using corporate portals—sites that perform functions well beyond publishing material on the intranet.

Intranets, which received a lot of publicity in the 1990s, are back in the limelight as a growing number of organizations are now putting new energy into them.

Intranets are fairly safe, operating within the company's firewalls (see Chapter 13). Employees can venture out onto the Internet, but unauthorized users cannot come in. This arrangement lets companies speed information and software safely to their own employees and business partners.

Intranets change organizational structures and procedures and help reengineer corporations. Application Case 11.2 illustrates the example of a wireless local area network (LAN) and its benefits in accessing a hospital intranet and other applications.

APPLICATION CASE 11.2

Wireless LANs Speed Hospital Insurance Payments

The Bridgeton, is a U.S. holding company that operates four hospitals in New Jersey. The company is using wireless LANs to process insurance documentation so that the number of claims denied by insurers can be reduced. Nurses log on to the network using notebook computers to access the hospital's intranet, pharmacy, and labs and use e-mail.

The network environment broadcasts data over a distance of about 120 feet located above nursing workstations. Nurses can move from the station into patient rooms while maintaining a network connection. As a nurse takes a notebook computer from one nursing station to another, the radio card in the notebook computer goes into a roaming mode similar to a cellular phone. The company is getting a good return on investment, savings in six-figure dollar amounts, for a moderate cost of setting up the network (about $200 for each notebook computer radio card and $750 for each of 28 wireless access points).

Source: Compiled from Cope, J. "Wireless LANS Speed Hospital Insurance Payments," *Computerworld,* April 10, 2000.

Other examples include:

- In 2000, Financial Times (FT) Electronic Publishing implemented its online news and information service, FT Discovery, for 10,000 intranet users at KPMG. FT Discovery is integrated into the KPMG corporate intranet to provide immediate access to critical business intelligence from over 4,000 information sources. For example, corporate Navigator from Story Street Partners is integrated into the intranet to provide in-depth advice on where to go for information on the issues and companies of interest to KPMG.
  (*Source: idm.internet.com/articles/200007/ic_07_26_00e.html*, July 2000.)
- All the Hawaiian islands are linked by a state educational, medical, and other public services network (*htdc.org*). This ambitious intranet provides quality services to residents of all islands.
  (*Source: htdc.org.*)
- Employees at IBM ranked the intranet as the most useful and credible source of information. They use the intranet to order supplies, sign up for

fringe benefits, take classes, track projects, and manage their retirement plans. IBM considers its intranet an extremely valuable source of information that helps increase productivity. For example, managers can post and read information about projects in progress without bothering people, making calls, or sending e-mails. IBM employees who telecommute can log onto the intranet from home and conduct work. In May 2001, IBM asked its employees to contribute ideas for solving current problems. More than 6,000 suggestions were collected over the intranet in 3 days.
(*Source:* Compiled from Stellin, S. "Intranets Nurture Companies from the Inside," *New York Times*, January 29, 2001.)

- At Charles Schwab, 25,000 employees use the intranet (Sch Web) regularly. It helps employees provide better customer service, because it is much easier to respond to customers' inquiries. Using superb search engines employees can find the answers, by themselves, quickly and without asking other employees. It is part of the culture now to look at the intranet first, in order to find answers. Schwab estimates tens of millions of dollars in savings due to the intranet.
(*Source:* Condensed from Stellin, S. "Intranets Nurture Companies from the Inside," *New York Times*, January 29, 2001.)

To build an intranet, we need Web servers, browsers, Web publishing tools, back-end databases, TCP/IP networks (LAN or WAN), and firewalls, as shown in Figure 11-2. A firewall is software and/or hardware that allows only those external users with specific characteristics to access a protected network (Chapter 13). Additional software may be necessary to support the Web-based workflow, groupware, and enterprise resource planning (ERP), depending upon the individual company's need. The security schemes for the intranet, which are basically the same as the ones for the Internet, are described in Chapter 13.

Figure 11-2	Architecture of Intranet

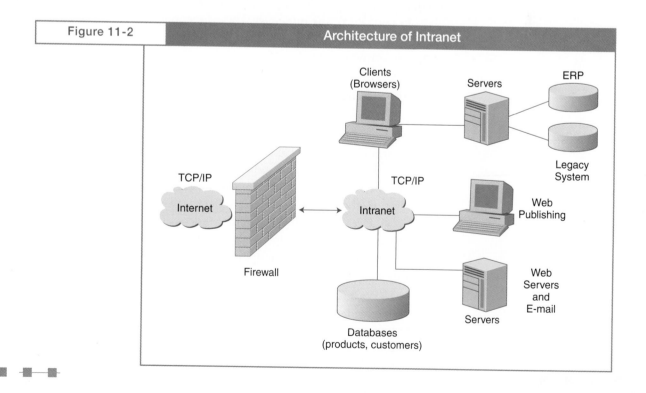

A company may have one intranet composed of many LANs. Alternatively, a company may have several interconnected intranets, each composed of only a few LANs. The decision of how to structure the intranet depends on how dispersed the LANs are, and what technologies are involved.

11.4 INTRANET FUNCTIONALITIES AND APPLICATIONS

In this section we review some intranet applications, but let's first look at the major functionalities of an intranet, which can include corporate, department, and individual Web pages.

Intranet Functionalities

Intranets have some or all of the following:

- Web-based database access for ease of use
- Search engines, indexing engines, and directories that assist in keyword-based searches
- Interactive communication such as chatting, audio support, and video-conferencing
- Document distribution and workflow including Web-based downloading and routing of documents
- Groupware including enhanced e-mail, bulletin boards, screen sharing, and other group support tools
- Conduit for the computer-based telephony system

In addition, intranets usually have the ability to integrate with EC; interface with Internet-based electronic purchasing, payment, and delivery; and be part of extranets (geographically dispersed branches, customers, and suppliers can access certain portions of the intranets). These functions provide for numerous applications that increase productivity, reduce cost, reduce waste and cycle time, and improve customer service.

Intranet Application Areas and Benefits

According to a survey conducted by *InformationWeek* with 988 responding managers (Chabrow, 1998), information that is most frequently included in intranets is in the form of product catalogs (49 percent of all companies), corporate policies and procedures (35 percent), purchase ordering (42 percent), document sharing (39 percent), corporate phone directories (40 percent), human resource forms (35 percent), training programs, customer databases, data warehouse and decision support access, image archives, purchase orders, enterprise suits, and travel reservation services. These figures are much higher today, since intranets are maturing.

In addition to the many activities listed, intranets also provide the following benefits:

- **Electronic commerce:** Intrabusiness marketing can be done online; selling to outsiders is done via the extranet, and it involves portions of the intranet.
- **Customer service:** UPS, FedEx, and other companies have proved that information about product shipments and availability make customers happier. Again, the intranet-extranet combination is used.

- **Search and access to documents:** The intranet provides access to any information that can increase productivity and facilitate teamwork.
- **Personalized information:** The intranet can deliver personalized information, via personalized Web pages and e-mail.
- **Enhanced knowledge sharing:** The Web-based intranet can enhance knowledge sharing.
- **Enhanced group decisions and business processes:** Web-based groupware and workflow are becoming part of the standard intranet platform. These can be part of the internal supply chain operation.
- **Empowerment:** More employees can be empowered because they can easily access the right information and online expertise to make decisions.
- **Virtual organizations:** Web technology used by business partners removes the barrier of incompatible technology between businesses.
- **Software distribution:** Using the intranet server as the application warehouse helps to avoid many maintenance and support problems.
- **Document management:** Employees can access pictures, photos, charts, maps, and other documents regardless of where they are stored, and where the employees' work bases are located.
- **Project management:** Most project management activities are conducted over intranets.
- **Training:** The Web page is a valuable source of knowledge for novices.
- **Enhanced transaction processing:** Data can be entered efficiently through the intranet and only once, thus eliminating errors and increasing internal control.
- **Paperless information delivery:** Elimination of paper by disseminating information on the intranet can result in lower cost, easier accessibility, greater efficiency in maintenance, and better security.
- **Improved administrative processes:** The internal management of production, inventory, procurement, shipping, and distribution can be effectively supported by linking these functions in a single threaded environment— the intranet—and these functions can also be seamlessly integrated with interorganizational extranets.

Industry-Specific Intranet Solutions

Intranet solutions are frequently classified by industry instead of technology, because the technology is no longer a bottleneck for implementation. The development of business models has become a critical concern for the managerial success of intranets. According to the classification of *Information Week Online*, the top 100 intranet and extranet solutions can be classified by industry as follows (Solution Series, 1998):

financial services (banking, brokerages and other financial services, and insurance),

information technology,

manufacturing (chemicals and oil, consumer goods, food and beverage, general manufacturing, and pharmaceuticals),

retail, and

services (construction/engineering, education, environmental, health care, media, entertainment, telecommunications, transportation, and utilities).

Internet applications are very diversified, as can be seen in the list of six industry-specific intranets in the online Appendix 11.1. (See *prenhall.com/turban*.)

Now, let us look at some typical applications in more depth, including their return on investment (ROI).

Intranet Case Studies

International Data Corporation (*idc.com*) compiled a collection of successful intranet case applications by world-class companies such as Amdahl Corporation; Booz, Allen & Hamilton; Cadence Design Systems Inc.; Deere & Company; Lockheed Martin Corporation; Silicon Graphics, Inc.; and Southern California Gas Company. New cases are being added periodically. Each case includes the background of the company, business challenges, before-intranet technology, intranet cost, intranet strategy, after-intranet technology, subjective benefits (optional), lessons learned, and an analysis of ROI. Older cases are available at *netscape.com*. The Cadence Design Systems Inc. case is summarized in the Real-World Case at the end of this chapter. Other representative cases include the following.

MOEN—CONNECTED ERP

Moen Corp. (North Olmstead, Ohio) launched an intranet called CinfoNet in 1997. Moen needed to share information quickly and easily, especially with a huge SAP R/3 system that was implemented at that time. The development team included three employees and several consultants. A favorite user application was the product database. Initially, 70 percent of Moen's 2,500 employees had access to the intranet. When R/3 was implemented, 100 percent were on the intranet. To make CinfoNet a complete success, existing electronic documents were converted to the new system.

COMPAQ COMPUTER CORP.—INVESTMENT ASSISTANT

Compaq's employees use the intranet to connect with the company and to communicate from anywhere, but it has another unique feature. Staff members can also access the human resources database for information such as their retirement accounts. Employees can then choose to reallocate the investments they have in the account; they have a great deal of latitude and control over their retirement plans and how they perform. This enables them to choose where their money goes and gives them individual responsiblility for the performance and growth of their funds. In addition, they can choose benefits, learn about training programs, and much more. Many other companies put such benefit programs on the intranet.

SILICON GRAPHICS, INC.—SHARE HUGE INTERNAL WEB SITES

Silicon Graphics makes high-end graphics workstations. Their intranet system, called Silicon Junction, is accessed by over 7,000 employees. It includes 800 specialized internal Web sites containing more than 144,000 pages of technical information. There is also access to all corporate databases, which was previously not possible. Information that once took days to access can now be obtained in a few minutes, simply by using links, pointing, and clicking.

COOPERS & LYBRAND—SHARE KNOWLEDGE AMONG CORPORATE EMPLOYEES

Coopers & Lybrand, one of the five largest CPA, taxation, and consulting firms, developed a special **knowledge curve intranet**. It originated as a service for company consultants and corporate tax professionals who handle taxes for *Fortune* 1,000 corporations. It was shifted to the Web in 1997. The knowledge curve is now integrated with the Tax News Network (TNN), an extranet for tax consultants for whom Coopers & Lybrand created a one-stop interactive information source on the constantly changing tax laws and regulations. The network contains tax information from numerous sources, integrating internal, external, and even competing resources. In addition, it includes the full text of various tax analyses, legislative tax codes, and major business newspapers. It is available to 75,000 employees and consultants of Coopers & Lybrand worldwide who use Lotus Notes Domino as a standard communications and collaboration system.

The company combined a series of automated Lotus Notes and third-party applications, to replicate internal documents that are published on TNN, across company Notes servers. Company researchers can post their tax findings within Notes bulletin boards and set up database replication systems in Notes, which can be transformed into separate Notes databases on the extranet. The TNN extranet requires potential members to register and receive a password. The extranet runs on three servers located at the Information Access Company data center in Medford, Massachusetts, where backbone communications facilities are particularly suitable for efficient worldwide transmission. This is an example of a corporate knowledge base deliverable on an intranet and extranet. A similar system is available at Arthur Andersen for their *knowledgespace.com*. (For knowledge base application, see Internet Exercise 7 at the end of this chapter.)

Corporate intranets are infrastructures that enable many Web-based applications and they are usually accessed via the corporate portal.

11.5   ENTERPRISE (CORPORATE) PORTALS

With the growing use of intranets and the Internet, many organizations encounter difficulties in dealing with information overload at different levels. Information is scattered across numerous documents, e-mail messages, and databases at different locations and systems. Finding relevant and accurate information is often time consuming and requires access to multiple systems.

As a consequence, organizations lose a lot of productive employee time. One solution is to use portals. Kounadis (2000) defines a **corporate (enterprise) portal** as a personalized, single point of access through a Web browser to critical business information located inside and outside of an organization. A portal is a gateway and a corporate portal is a gateway to corporate information. It attempts to address information overload through an intranet-based environment to search and access relevant information from disparate IT systems and the Internet, using advanced search and indexing techniques.

Portals appear under many descriptions and shapes. One way to distinguish among them is to look at their content, which can vary from narrow to broad, and their community, or audience, which can also vary widely. When combined, one

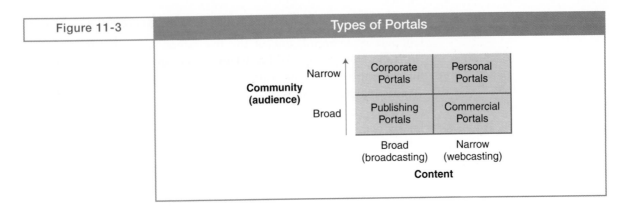

Figure 11-3   Types of Portals

can create a matrix of portals as shown in Figure 11-3. According to this matrix we distinguish four types of portals:

1. *Publishing portals* are intended for large and diverse communities with diverse interests. These portals involve relatively little customization of content except online search and some interactive capabilities, which would be typical for the Web. (Examples are *techweb.com* or *zdnet.com*.)

2. *Commercial portals* offer narrow content for diverse communities, and are the most popular portals today for online communities. Although they offer customization of the user interface, they are still intended for broad audiences and offer fairly simple content (a stock ticker, news on a few preselected items). Examples are My Yahoo! and Excite.

3. *Personal portals* target specific filtered information for individuals. As with commercial portals, they offer relatively narrow content but are typically much more personalized with an effective audience of one.

4. *Corporate portals* coordinate rich content within a relatively narrow community. They are also known as enterprise portals, or enterprise information portals. These are portals built with large enterprise intranet applications. The portal content is much broader than that of a commercial portal, because of the greater diversity of information used to make decisions in an organization. Specifically, a corporate portal offers a single point of entry, which brings together the employees, business partners, and consumers at one virtual place. Through the portal, these people can create a structured and personalized access to information across large, multiple, and disparate enterprise information systems, as well as the Internet. A schematic view of a corporate portal is provided in Figure 11-4.

In contrast with publishing and commercial portals such as Yahoo!, which are only gateways to the Internet, corporate portals provide single-point access to information and applications available on the Internet, intranets, and extranets. Corporate portals are an extended form of intranets that offer employees and customers an organized focal point for their interactions with the firm.

Many large organizations are already implementing portals to cut costs, free up time for busy executives and managers, and add to the bottom line (*Informationweek.com*, May 2000). Corporate portals are popular in large corporations, as shown in Application Case 11.3.

| Figure 11-4 | Corporate Portal as Gateway to Information |

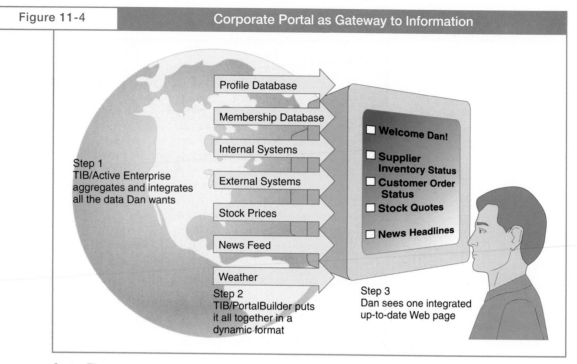

Source: Tibco.com

APPLICATION CASE 11.3

Corporate Portals at Procter & Gamble, DuPont, and Staples

Procter & Gamble's IT division developed a system for sharing documents and information over the company's intranet. The scope of this system has expanded into a global knowledge catalogue to support the information needs of all 97,000 of P&G employees worldwide. Although the system helped in providing required information, it also led to information overload. To solve this problem, P&G developed a corporate portal that provides personalized information to each employee that can be accessed through a Web browser without the need to navigate through 14 different Web sites. P&G's corporate portal, implemented by Plumtree (*plumtree.com*), provides P&G's employees with marketing, product and strategic information, and industry-news documents numbering over one million Web pages, in thousands of Lotus Notes databases. Employees can gain access to the required information through customized preset views of various information sources and links to other up-to-date information.

DuPont & Co. began implementing an internal portal to organize millions of pages of scientific information stored in information systems throughout the company. The initial version of the portal was intended for daily use by over 550 employees to record product orders, retrieve progress reports for research products, and access customer-tracking information. DuPont plans

APPLICATION CASE 11.3

(continued)

to extend the portal to between 20,000 to 60,000 employees in 30 business units in various countries.

Staples' corporate portal, launched in February 2000, is used by 3,000 executives, knowledge workers, and store managers. Staples is expecting that the portal will grow to support 10,000 of the 46,000 employees and serve as the interface to business processes and applications. The portal is used by top management, as well as by managers of contracts, procurement, sales and marketing, human resources, and retail stores. It is also used for internal business by Staples' three business-to-business Web sites. The portal offers e-mail, scheduling, headlines on the competition, new product information, internal news, job postings, and newsletters.

Sources: Compiled from Sonicki, S. "The New Desktop: Powerful Portals," *Informationweek.com*, May 1, 2000, and from *staples.com*

According to a Delphi Group survey (see *Datamation*, July 1999), over 55 percent of the 800 respondents have already begun corporate portal projects with about 42 percent of these conducting the projects at the enterprise level. The top portal applications, in decreasing order of importance, found from their survey are as follows:

- Knowledge bases and learning tools
- Business process support
- Customer-facing sales, marketing, and services
- Collaboration and project support
- Access to data from disparate corporate systems
- Personalized pages for users
- Effective search and indexing tools
- Internal company information
- High level of security
- Policies and procedures
- Best practices and lessons learned
- Human resources and benefits
- Directories and bulletin boards
- Identification of experts
- News and Internet

The Delphi Group also found that poor organization of information and lack of navigation and retrieval tools contribute to over 50 percent of the problems for corporate portal users. For further details see *delphigroup.com/pubs/corporate-portal-excerpt.htm*.

Figure 11-5 depicts a corporate portal framework based on Aneja et al. (2000) and Kounadis (2000). This framework illustrates the features and capabilities required to support various organizational activities using internal and external information sources. For guidelines to define corporate portal strategy, see Table 11-1.

Figure 11-5	Corporate Portal Framework

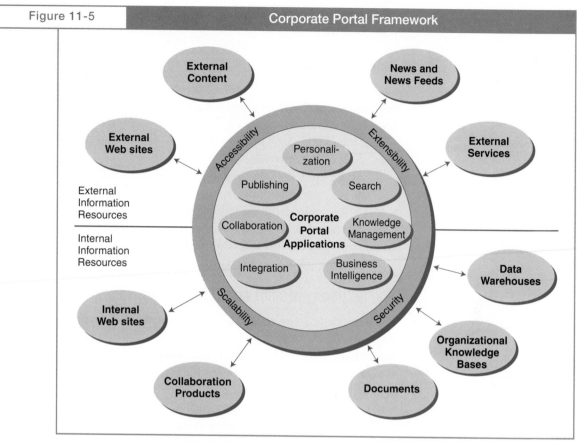

Source: Compiled by N. Bolloju, City University of Hong Kong, from Aneja et al. (2000) and from Kounadis (2000)

Key Steps to Corporate Portal Strategy

TABLE 11-1

Identify the content that is or will be available, and identify where this content resides.
Leverage existing systems, resources, and repositories.
Include both structured and unstructured information.
Organize content into categories that can be browsed and searched.
Integrate search functionality across multiple information repositories.
Build a platform for publishing and subscribing to content.
Deliver personalized content and services to users based on their responsibilities and roles.
Develop the corporate portal in phases.
Create online communities to connect people and enable collaborative work.
Develop an extensible architecture that allows for extended functionality.
Sustain a collaborative portal by institutionalizing it within daily business operations and weaving it into long-term strategies.
Purchase an integrated portal product rather than building custom portal functionality.

Source: Compiled from Aneja et al. "Corporate Portal Framework for Transforming Content Chaos on Intranets," *Intel Technology Journal,* 1st Qtr., 2000.

11.6   EXAMPLE OF INTRANET AND A PORTAL: CADENCE DESIGN SYSTEMS

Cadence Design Systems Inc. is a leading supplier of electronic design automation (EDA) software tools and professional services for managing and accelerating the design of semiconductors, computer systems, networking and telecommunications equipment, consumer electronics, and other electronic-based products. The

San Jose-based company employs more than 3,000 people in offices worldwide to support the development requirements of the world's leading electronic manufacturers.

Business Challenge

Early in 1995, Cadence recognized that the business model for EDA products was beginning to evolve from a tools orientation to one where the value placed on software and consulting services held the potential for the greatest revenue growth. Rather than sell a single product, Cadence wanted to support the customer's entire product development cycle.

To understand and address this changing model, Cadence identified two areas of customer interaction: sales and delivery. The new sales strategy required the sales force to have an in-depth understanding of Cadence's product line of almost 1,000 products and services. With two separate organizations interacting with customers, coordination and communication were needed to ensure an effective and consistent relationship built on a real understanding of the customer's issues.

The Solution: Intranet and Portal Technology

For almost a year, Cadence worked with a consulting firm to create a corporate portal—a Web-based single point of information—for supporting the sales organization. This system, called OnTrack, uses a home page with links to other pages, information sources, and custom applications to map each phase of the sales process with supporting materials and reference information. By adopting OnTrack, Cadence achieved the high return on investment of 1,766 percent.

With OnTrack, the sales rep now has a single unified tool that provides all information and data needed to go through the sales process from prospecting to closing a deal and account management. In addition, global account teams have their own home page where they can collaborate and share information. However, OnTrack is more than a static road map. A sales rep can initiate workflow automatically, eliminating the hurdle of needing to know who to call. Information on a customer or competitor is now available instantly through access to an outside provider of custom news. The sales rep can simply search, using a company name, to get everything from financial information to recent news articles and press releases.

All creators of information in the company, from sales reps to marketing and management personnel, are responsible for maintaining the information contained in OnTrack. With a wide range of people entering data, a simple-to-use information submission process was needed. To avoid the need to understand HTML, forms were created to allow submission or modification of any part of the information in the OnTrack system. Anyone with appropriate access can now add a new message to the daily alerts, modify a step in the sales process, or update a customer presentation by using these custom tools. Feedback is also a key part of OnTrack. Reports highlight frequently accessed pages and documents, and reviews of frequent searches look to include new information and make critical information easier to access.

Lessons Learned

Those who adopted OnTrack learned several lessons. First, balancing the cost of training against return is a difficult task. Although the use of a browser and the navigation of a Web page required minimal training, the application of the OnTrack system to the daily activities of a sales rep was not easy. OnTrack supported a reengineering of the sales process, and Cadence believed that demonstrating the use of OnTrack in supporting the sales rep might have accelerated the use of the system.

Second, for Cadence, the key to success was the holistic approach taken to unifying the technology with the process. Rather than mandate a new process, or install a new software system, the combination of an easy-to-use technology, a refined process, and the appropriate personnel and support systems created a single coherent system that could support the new sales paradigm.

Cadence also worked to design a process and infrastructure that could satisfy 80 percent rather than 100 percent of the sales situations. This strategy helped the company in two ways: (1) It is often more effective to refine a system after gaining experience than to attempt to design the perfect system from the beginning, and (2) a process that can address all possible exceptions is often an exercise in futility. One reason Cadence has achieved such a high return on investment is its focus on supporting the bulk of work process rather than the entire process.

A relatively low cost was needed to implement OnTrack. Cadence leveraged its existing infrastructure and wisely hired outside experts to create the application rather than devoting internal resources. This choice allowed the company to focus its efforts on defining the process and tools needed to support the sales force rather than designing software.

Finally, the greatest impact has been the result of the shortened training time for new sales reps. A new salesperson stated that he had learned in 2 days from OnTrack what it took months to learn at a previous company. With 40 new reps hired in the first year, and 40 planned for each of the next 2 years, reducing the training time for new sales personnel had a substantial impact on additional profits for Cadence.

COLLABORATIVE COMMERCE

Collaborative commerce (c-commerce) is when employees from different organizations design, plan, communicate, and implement projects together on the Web. The same applies to intrabusiness collaboration, where employees of different units collaborate using the intranets and corporate portals.

11.7   E-GOVERNMENT: AN OVERVIEW

Scope and Definitions

As e-commerce matures and its tools and applications improve, greater attention is given to its use to improve the business of public institutions and governments (country, state, county, city, etc.). Several international conferences were organized in 2000 and 2001 to explore the potential of what is called e-government. **E-government** is the use of information technology in general, and e-commerce in particular, to provide citizens and organizations with more convenient access to government information and services; and to provide delivery of public services to citizens, business partners and suppliers, and those working in the public sector. It is also an efficient and effective way of conducting business transactions with citizens and other businesses and within the governments themselves.

DEFINITIONS

- E-government is an opportunity to improve the efficiency and effectiveness of the executive functions of government including the delivery of public services. It also enables governments to be more transparent to citizens and businesses by providing access to more of the information generated by government.
- E-government facilitates fundamental changes in the relationships between the citizens and the state, and between nation states, with implications for the democratic process and structures of government (UK government).
- E-government is a way for governments to use Internet technologies to provide people with more convenient access to government information and services, to improve the quality of the services, and to provide greater opportunities to participate in our democratic institutions and processes (New Zealand government).
- E-government in the United States was especially driven by the 1998 Government Paperwork Elimination Act and by President Clinton's December 17, 1999, Memorandum on E-Government, which ordered the top 500 forms used by citizens to be placed online by December 2000. The memorandum also directed agencies to construct a secure e-government infrastructure.
- E-government is the application of information technology to the processes of government. It has been defined as digital information and online transaction services for citizens. Others use the term as an extension of e-commerce to government procurement and see it only in the realm of B2G (business to government) transactions (*Source:* International Trade Center-Executive Forum 2000, *intracen.org/execforum/docs/ef2000/eb200010.htm*).
- E-government is the birth of a new market and the advent of a new form of government—a form of government that is a powerful force in the Internet economy, bringing together citizens and businesses in a network of information, knowledge, and commerce.

11.8   MAJOR CATEGORIES OF APPLICATIONS OF E-GOVERNMENT

Government-to-Citizens

In the **government-to-citizen (G2C)** category, we include all the interactions between a government and its citizens. As shown in this chapter's Real-World Case in Hong Kong, G2C involves dozens of different initiatives. The basic idea is to allow citizens to interact with the government from their homes. Citizens can find all the information they need on the Web, can ask questions and receive answers, pay tax and bills, receive payments and documents, and so forth. Governments disseminate information on the Web, conduct training, help in finding employment, and more. In California, for example, drivers' education classes are offered online, and can be taken at any time, from anywhere. As a matter of fact, government agencies and departments in many cities, counties, and countries are planning more and more diverse e-services. For example, many governments are now seriously considering electronic voting. In some countries, voters actually see their choice on the computer screen and are asked to confirm their vote, much as is done when purchasing a book from Amazon, transferring funds, or selling stocks (see Schwartz, 2000 for further discussion on this topic).

For an example of diversified application in Switzerland, see Schubert and Hausler (2001).

ELECTRONIC BENEFITS TRANSFER (EBT)

The United States government transfers more than $500 billion in benefits annually to its citizens. More than 20 percent of these transfers go to citizens who do not have bank accounts. In 1993, the U.S. government launched an initiative to develop a nationwide electronic benefits transfer (EBT) system to deliver government benefits electronically. This approach relies on the use of a single smart card to access cash and food benefits at automated teller machines and point-of-sale locations, just like other bank card users do with their smart cards (see Chapter 14). EBT brings users convenience and dignity, dramatically reducing theft, fraud, and abuse of benefits. Also, the cost of dispensing benefits electronically is much lower.

The federal EC program is implementing a nationwide EBT system. Agencies at the federal, state, and local levels are expanding EBT programs into new areas, including health, nutrition, employment, and education. Over 30 states operate EBT systems and others are under consideration.

The basic idea is that recipients will either get electronic transfers to their bank accounts, or be able to download money to their smart cards. The benefit is not only the reduction of the processing cost from 50 cents per check to 2 cents, but also the reduction of fraud. With biometrics (Chapter 13) coming to smart cards and PCs, officials expect fraud to be reduced substantially. For more information see *financenet.gov*.

Governments not only use EBT, but also smart cards as purchasing media for procurement.

Government-to-Business and Business-to-Government

Governments attempt to automate their interactions with businesses (**government-to-business, G2B**). Two areas that receive a lot of attention are e-procurement and auctioning government surpluses.

E-PROCUREMENT

Governments buy large amounts of MROs and material direct from many suppliers. In many cases, an RFQ or tendering system is mandated by law. These requisitions were done manually for years; now they are moving online. In principle, the systems are basically *reverse auction* systems, such as those described in Chapter 6 (buy-side systems). An example is briefly described in the Hong Kong system (the chapter's Real-World Case, and *ets.gov.hk*). For information about such reverse auctions, see *buyers.gov*. Governments provide all the support for such tendering systems, as shown in Application Case 11.4.

E-AUCTIONS

Governments auction surpluses ranging from vehicles to foreclosed real estate all over the world. Such auctions used to be done manually, then were moved to private networks, and now they are being moved online. Governments can use third-party auction sites such as eBay, *Bid4assets.com*, or *freemarkets.com* for this purpose. The General Services Administration in the United States launched, in January 2001, a property auction site online (*auctionrp.com*), where real-time auctions for

Contract Management in Australia

The development of contracting asset management solutions for the public sector in the online environment is the focus of the Western Australian (WA) government agency Contract and Management Services (CAMS). CAMS Online allows government agencies to search existing contracts to discover how to access the commonly used contracts across government, and assists suppliers wanting to sell to the government. Suppliers can view the current tenders on the Western Australia Government Contracting Information Bulletin Board, and download tender documents from this site.

CAMS Online provides government departments and agencies with unbiased expert advice on e-commerce, Internet, and satellite services, and how-to's on building a bridge between the technological needs of the public sector and the expertise of the private sector. The center is divided into three sections—e-commerce, Internet services, and satellite services.

E-Commerce

Government buying: Government clients can purchase goods and services on the CAMS Internet Marketplace—from sending a purchase order to receiving an invoice and paying for an item.

WA government electronic market: This procurement market provides online supplier catalogs for common use contracts and other contract arrangements, electronic purchase orders and goods receipting electronic invoicing, EFT, and check and credit card payments.

ProcureLink: An established CAMS service that sends electronic purchase orders to suppliers for electronic data interchange (EDI), EDI Post, facsimile, and the Internet.

DataLink: Enables the transfer of data using a secure and controlled environment for message management. DataLink is an ideal solution for government agencies needing to exchange large volumes of operational information.

SalesNet: The government secures credit card payment solutions for the sale of government goods and services across the Internet.

Internet Services

ServiceNet: A government-controlled computer network that operates within a secure and firewall-protected environment, offering Internet access in general and access to ProcureLink, SalesNet, WA FastPay, and online buying through the WA Government Electronic Market using desktop browser technologies.

Satellite Services

Westlink: A service delivering adult training and educational programs to remote areas and schools, including rural and regional communities.

Videoconferencing: This service offers two-way video and audio links enabling people to see and hear each other at up to eight sites at any one time. Access to the Online Services Center is via the CAMS Web site at *wa.gov.au/business*.

surpluses and seized goods are conducted. Some of these auctions are restricted to dealers; others are open to the public (see *Govexec.com*, January 18, 2001).

Government-to-Government

The **government-to-government (G2G)** category includes all intragovernmental activities, primarily among different government units, as well as nonbusiness dealings with other governments. Some examples of G2G in the United States include:

- **Intelink.** Intelink is an intranet based on classified networks that have created a new spirit of sharing information among the numerous intelligence agencies.
- *Buyers.gov* **of the general services administration.** This Web site (*buyers.gov*) is seeking to make the most of newly developed Web-based procurement methods. *Buyers.gov* is an experiment in technologies such as demand aggregation and reverse auctions.
- **Federal case registry (department of health and human services).** This service, which is available at *acf.dhhs.gov/programs/cse/newhire/fcr/fcr.htm*, helps state governments locate information about child support, including data on paternity and enforcement.
- **Procurement marketing and access network (small business administration).** This service (*pro-net.sba.gov*) presents PRO-Net, a searchable database that contracting officers can use to find products and services sold by small, disadvantaged, and women-owned businesses.

For more examples, see this chapter's Real-World Case, and *govexec/com*.

Government-to-Employees

Governments employ large numbers of people. Therefore, governments provide e-services (G2E) to their employees in a manner similar to that of private organizations. One example is the Lifeline services provided by the U.S. government to Navy employees and their families (see Application Case 11.5).

APPLICATION CASE **11.5**

G2E in the U.S. Navy

The U.S. Navy is using e-government techniques to improve the flow of information to sailors and their families. Because long shipboard deployments cause strains on navy families, the Navy in 1995 began seeking ways to ensure that quality-of-life information reaches navy personnel and their loved ones all over the world. Examples of quality-of-life information include self-help, deployment support, stress management, parenting advice, and relocation assistance.

Lifelines (*lifelines2000.org*) uses the Internet, simulcasting, cable television, satellite broadcasting, teleconferencing, dish TV, and the EchoStar system for overseas broadcasting. The Navy has found that certain media channels are more appropriate for certain types of information.

Lifelines regularly features live broadcasts, giving forward-deployed sailors and their families welcome information and, in some cases, a taste of home. On the Web, an average of 2,000 people access the Lifelines site each day.

APPLICATION CASE ‎ **11.5**

(continued)

The government provides several other services to Navy personnel. Notable are online banking, personal finance services, and insurance. Education and training is also provided online.

11.9 IMPLEMENTING E-GOVERNMENT

As in any other organization, one can also find large numbers of EC applications in government organizations. And like any other organization, governments want to move into the digital era. This lengthy *transformation* is divided in a Deloitte and Touch's report (see Wong, 2000) into the following six stages, as shown in Figure 11-6.

Deloitte's Transformation Process

STAGE 1: INFORMATION PUBLISHING/DISSEMINATION. Individual government departments set up their own Web sites that provide the public with information about them, the range of services available, and contacts for further assistance. At this stage, governments establish an electronic encyclopedia to reduce the number of phone calls customers need to make to reach the appropriate employee who can fulfill their service requests. Also, paperwork and help-line employees can be reduced.

Figure 11-6	The Stages in E-Government

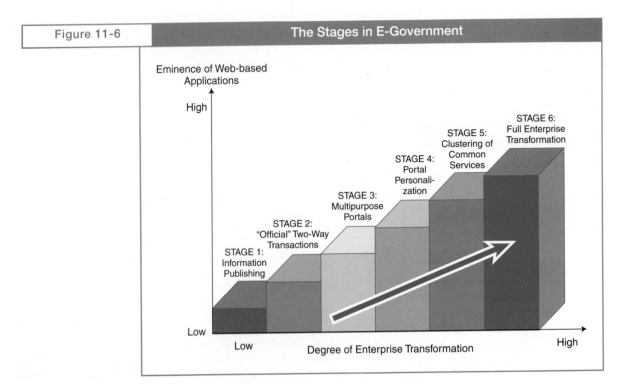

Source: Deloitte Research (see Wong, 2001).

STAGE 2: "OFFICIAL" TWO-WAY TRANSACTIONS. With the help of legally valid digital signatures and secure Web sites, customers are able to submit personal information to—and conduct monetary transactions with—individual departments. At this stage, customers must be convinced of the department's ability to keep their information private and free from piracy. For example, the local government of Lewisham, United Kingdom, lets citizens claim income support and housing benefits using an electronic form. In Singapore, payments to citizens and from citizens to various government agencies can be performed online.

STAGE 3: MULTIPURPOSE PORTALS. At this point, customer-centric governments make a big breakthrough in service delivery. Based on the fact that customer needs can cut across department boundaries, a portal allows customers to use a single point of entry to send and receive information and to process monetary transactions across multiple departments. For example, in addition to acting as a gateway to its agencies and related governments, the government of South Australia's portal (*sa.gov.au*) features a link for citizens to pay bills (utilities, automotive), manage bank accounts and conduct personal stock brokering (see Application Case 11.6).

STAGE 4: PORTAL PERSONALIZATION. Through stage 3, customers can access a variety of services at a single Web site. In stage 4, government puts even more power into customers' hands by allowing them to customize portals with their desired features. To accomplish this, governments will need much more sophisticated Web programming that allows interfaces to be user-manipulated. The added benefit of portal personalization is that governments will get a more accurate read on customer preference for electronic versus non-electronic service options. Like in industry, this will allow for a true CRM in government. In March 2001, such a portal was in a planning stages in several state and country governments.

STAGE 5: CLUSTERING OF COMMON SERVICES. Stage 5 is where real transformation of government structure takes shape. As customers now view once-disparate services as a unified package through the portal, their perception of departments as distinct entities will begin to blur. They will recognize groups of transactions rather than groups of agencies. To make this happen, governments will cluster services along common lines to accelerate the delivery of shared services. In other words, a business restructuring will take place.

STAGE 6: FULL INTEGRATION AND ENTERPRISE TRANSFORMATION. What started as a digital encyclopedia is now a full-service center, personalized to each customer's needs and preferences. At this stage, old walls defining silos of services have been torn down, and technology is integrated across the new government structure to bridge the shortened gap between the front and back offices. In some countries, new departments will have formed from the remains of predecessors. Others will have the same names, but their interiors will look nothing like they did before e-government.

TRANSFORMATION SPEED

The speed at which a government moves from stage 1 to stage 6 varies, but usually it is very slow. Some of the determining factors are the degree of resistance to change by government employees, the adoption rate of applications by citizens, the available budget, and the legal environment. Deloitte Research found that in 2000, most governments were still in stage 1.

APPLICATION CASE 11.6

E-Government in the State of Victoria, Australia

Titled Maxi, the e-government initiative went live online on December 9, 1997, with more than 30 government-related services available, including registering vehicles, obtaining driver licenses, ordering birth certificates, notifying the government about changes of address, and paying utility bills and fines. *Maxi.com.au* is designed around the concept of "life events," similar to the Hong Kong initiative (see this chapter's Real-World Case). It embraces not only the government's relationship with citizens and the business sector, but also the different tiers of government.

The site provides services 24 hours a day, every day of the year. This project is part of the "Victorian Government's Vic 21 strategy" that aims to modernize government-to-citizen services.

The Internet portal features four service areas: (1) general information about Maxi, (2) bill payment and services by agencies, (3) life events (change of address, getting married, turning 18), and (4) a business channel. The business channel offers a range of services to help existing firms expand their practices and start up new businesses.

Maxi kiosks are located in shopping centers, libraries, government offices, and other public locations around Victoria. The kiosks includes a touch screen, bar code scanner, A4 printer, thermal receipt printer, and full EFTPOS (electronic funds transfer at point-of-sale) capability for paying with debit or credit cards. Maxi employs SecureNet Certificates to provide customers with digital certificates of authenticity and public keys for digital signatures.

To encourage better acceptance, Maxi offered a lucky draw to users from July 1 to December 31, 2000. Any one of Maxi usage entitled the user to participate in the lucky draw. The more transactions on Maxi, the better the chance for a citizen to become a winner.

Customer adoption of Maxi has exceeded the government's expectations. One year after Maxi first went live, more than 24,000 transactions were conducted monthly over the network, tripling the initial target of 8,000 a month. Maxi has also given citizens new levels of convenience, with 40 percent of all transactions occurring outside normal 9-to-5 business hours.

They propose an eight-point plan to expedite the transformation progress:

- Define a vision—and a v-business case—for e-government.
- Build customer trust with privacy, security, and confidentiality.
- Plan technology for growth and customer-friendliness.
- Manage access channels to optimize value.
- Weigh insourcing versus outsourcing.
- Establish investment plans that work without funding cycles.
- Understand the impact of fees for transactions.
- Include a strong change management program.

Implementing G2B

Implementation of G2B is easier. In some countries, such as Hong Kong, the implementation is outsourced to a private company who pays all the expenses in an exchange for getting transaction fees at a later time.

Security Issues

Governments are concerned about maintaining the security and privacy of citizens' data. One area is that of health care. From a medical point of view, it is necessary to have quick access to people's data, and the Internet and smart cards provide such capabilities; however, the protection of such data is very expensive (see Chapter 13). Many local and central governments are working on this topic.

Developing Portals

Many vendors offer tools for building government and corporate portals, as well as hosting services. Representative vendors are *tibco.com* (Portal Builder), Computer Associates at *ca.com* (Jasmine ii Portal), and *Plumtree.com*.

Non-Internet E-Government

Today, e-government is associated with the Internet. However, governments have been using other networks, especially internally, to improve government operations for over 15 years. For example, on January 17, 1994, there was a major earthquake in Southern California. About 114,000 buildings were damaged and more than 500,000 victims turned to the Federal Emergency Management Agency for help. Initially, tired and dazed citizens stood hours in line to register and have in-person interviews. To expedite the process, an e-government application was installed to expedite the issuance of checks to citizens. Citizens called an 800 number and the operators entered the information collected directly into online electronic forms. Then the data traveled electronically to the mobile disaster inspectors. Once checked, data went electronically to financial management and finally to check-writing. The data never touched paper, and the cycle time was reduced by more than 50 percent. Non-Internet e-government initiatives will probably be converted sooner or later to Internet-based ones.

11.10   CUSTOMER-TO-CUSTOMER AND PEER-TO-PEER APPLICATIONS

Customer-to-Customer E-Commerce

Auctions are an example of **customer-to-customer (C2C)** e-commerce. Millions of individuals are buying and selling on eBay and hundreds of other Web sites worldwide. In addition to auctions, C2C activities include the following.

CLASSIFIED ADS

People sell to people by using classified ads. Internet-based classified ads have several advantages over newspaper classified ads.

- Ads include national, rather than local selection. This greatly increases the supply. For example, *classifieds2000.com* contains a list of about 500,000 cars.
- A search engine helps to narrow the search.
- Photos are available in many cases.
- Ads are free for private parties.
- Ads can be edited easily.

- Placing an ad in one Web site (e.g. *classifieds2000.com*) brings it automatically into the classified sections of numerous partners. This increases the exposure, at no cost.
- Special features that expedite search are available on some sites. Free personalized services are available.

The major categories of classified ads are similar to those found in the newspaper, including vehicles, real estate, employment, general merchandise, collectibles, computers, pets, tickets, and travel. Classified ads are available through most ISPs (AOL, etc.), in some search engines (Excite, etc.), and from telephone companies, Internet directories, newspapers, and more. Once users find an ad and can get the details, they can e-mail or call the other party.

PERSONAL SERVICES

Numerous personal services are available on the Internet. Some are in the classified ads, but others are in specialized Web sites and directories. See Chapter 10 for examples (advisors, tutors).

C2C BARTER EXCHANGES

Several exchanges for consumer-to-consumer bartering are available (e.g., *switchhouse.com*). For a complete list, see *ecompany.com*.

CONSUMER EXCHANGES

Many exchanges are available for transactions between individuals. A list of exchanges by category is available at *ecompany.com*.

Peer-to-Peer Networks and Applications

Peer-to-peer (P2P) computer architecture is a type of network in which each workstation (or PC) has similar capabilities. This is in contrast with client-server architecture in which some computers serve other computers. As peers, the computers share data, processing, and devices with each other. In P2P the computers communicate directly with each other, rather than through a central server.

The main benefit of P2P is that it can enormously expand the universe of information accessible from a personal computer—users are not confined to just Web pages. Additionally, some proponents claim that a well-designed P2P system can offer better security, reliability, and availability of content than the client-server model, on which the Web is based. The acronym P2P also stands for People-to-People, Person-to-Person, or Point-to-Point.

CHARACTERISTICS OF P2P SYSTEMS

Peer-to-peer systems involve the following seven key characteristics:

- User interfaces load outside of a Web browser.
- User computers can act as both clients and servers.
- The overall system is easy to use and is well integrated.
- The system includes tools to support users wanting to create content or add functionality.

- The system provides connections with other users.
- The system does something new or exciting.
- The system supports "cross-networking" protocols such as SOAP or XML-RPC.

The characteristics of P2P computing show that devices can join the network from anywhere with little effort. Instead of dedicated LANs, the Internet itself becomes the network of choice. Easier configuration and control over the applications allows people without network savvy to join the user community. In fact, P2P signifies a shift in emphasis in peer networking from hardware to applications.

Peer-to-peer networking is connecting people *directly* to other people. It provides an easy setup system for sharing, publishing, and interacting that requires no system administration knowledge. The system wraps everything up into a user-friendly interface and lets people share or communicate with each other.

An example of a P2P network is graphically illustrated in Figure 11-7. The workstations shown in the graph perform a computer-to-computer communication directly through their operating systems.

P2P Applications in C2C

NAPSTER—THE FILE-SHARING UTILITY

In Chapter 3 we introduced the case of Napster as an example of C2C, where people can enter files of other people, to share music and games by logging into the Napster system. The network also allows users to search other members' hard drives for a particular file, including data files created by users or copied from elsewhere. Napster had more than 25 million members by the end of 2001.

The Napster server functions as a directory, which indicates the list of files being shared by other users. Once logged in to the server, users can search the songs they like and locate the file owner. They can directly access the owner's computer and download the songs they have chosen. Napster also includes chat rooms to connect its millions of users.

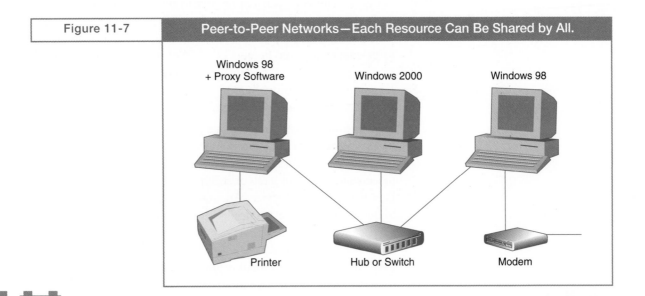

| Figure 11-7 | Peer-to-Peer Networks—Each Resource Can Be Shared by All. |

OTHER FILE SHARING EXAMPLES

An even purer version of P2P is Gnutella, a P2P program that dispenses with the central database altogether (see Chapter 17). For games, try *heat.net* and *battle.net*. As a matter of fact, ICQ (the instant messenger-type chat room) can be considered as a hybrid P2P technology.

Commercial Applications in Business C2C

With P2P, users can sell digital goods directly from their computers rather than going through centralized servers. If users want to sell on eBay, they are required to put an item on eBay's site and upload a photo. If an auction site uses file sharing, it can direct customers to the seller is PC where buyers can find plenty of information, photos, and even videos about the items being sold.

COMPUTER RESOURCES AND DATA FILE SHARING

Sharing of disk drives and printers across a network is quite common in modern office settings. Moreover, data files or other types of information sharing in the local area network (LAN), and the sharing of program files between computers through Windows NT, actually can be regarded as a type of P2P networking.

INTRABUSINESS APPLICATIONS

Several companies are using P2P to facilitate internal collaboration. For example, in 1990, Intel wrote a file transfer program called NetBatch, which allows chip designers to utilize the additional processing power of colleagues' computers across sites in California, Arizona, and even foreign countries such as Israel. Intel saved more than $500 million between 1992 and 2001.

BUSINESS-TO-BUSINESS

P2P could be a technology panacea for system innovators building B2B exchanges. The reason is that Lotus Notes and other business-process automation packages are cumbersome. With P2P, people can share information, but they are not required to send it to an unknown server. Because of a lack of trust in corporate boundaries with exchanges, companies can keep documents in-house instead of on an unknown server.

Several companies are using the P2P architecture as a base for speeding up business transactions. The following are some examples:

- Hilgraeve of Monroe, Michigan, has a technology called DropChute that establishes a point-to-point connection between two computers and allows users to transfer files. The company has won a U.S. patent for its P2P communication process and touts four levels of encryption and virus-scanning protection.
- Fort Knox Escrow Service, Atlanta, leverages DropChute to enable clients to deliver material electronically. "Instead of having to wait for an overnight package, we can do it all over the Internet," says Jeanna Israel, Fort Knox's director of operations.
- *Certapay.com* is a P2P e-mail payment platform that enables e-banking customers to send and receive money using only an e-mail address.

According to *worldstreet.com*, the real winners within the B2B segment will be companies that deliver rich, extensible, balanced, two-way collaborative interactions that are:

- dynamic (supporting extensible, interactive communications between people, applications, systems, and devices),
- real-time (providing delivery of rich, personalized, on-demand information),
- collaborative (delivering a venue for secure interactions between any number of participants, some of whom could not previously find each other),
- structured (spoken in an industry-specific dialect that facilitates communication and transactions),
- relevant (focused on the participants' topics of interest at that time),
- service-based (integrating existing workflows, systems, devices, and applications to provide an optimum method for determining what information is exchanged and how it is delivered),
- cost effective (reducing the costs of establishing and maintaining online business relationships),
- client-focused (enabling the exchange of new kinds of information—or previously inaccessible information—and delivering the highest quality, and most personalized service possible).

Peer networks effectively address the Web's B2B deficiencies. The model is a natural fit for the needs of business, since business relationships are intrinsically peer to peer. Peer networks allow businesses to communicate, interact, and transact with each other as never before by making the business relationships interactive, dynamic, real-time, and balanced—within and between enterprises.

The success of P2P in B2B is not clear. It depends in part on the ability of the technology to address security and scalability issues. For further information, see McAffee (2000).

BUSINESS-TO-CONSUMER

There are several potential applications in marketing and advertisement. For example, *fandango.com* is combining P2P with collaborative filtering (Chapter 4). Its product will work as follows. Assume a user conducts a search for a product:

STEP 1: A user enters a search keyword.
STEP 2: The keyword is sent to 100 peers, which search local indices of the Web pages they have visited.
STEP 3: Those computers also relay the query to 100 of their peers, and that group submits it to 100 of theirs, yielding, in theory, up to one million computers queried.
STEP 4: The resulting URLs are returned to the user, weighted in favor of most recently visited pages and peers with similar interests.

11.11   MANAGERIAL ISSUES

The following issues are germane to management:

1. **Intranet content management.** The content delivered on the intranet is created by many individuals. Two potential risks exist. First, proprietary corporate information may not be protected enough, so unauthorized people may

have access to it. Second, appropriate intranet Netiquette must be maintained, otherwise unethical or even illegal behavior may develop. Therefore, managing intranet content is a must, including its frequent updates.

2. **Designing corporate portals.** Corporate portals are the gateways to corporate information and knowledge. Appropriate portal design is a must not only for easy and efficient navigation, but also for recognizing that portals portray the corporate image to employees and to business partners who are allowed access to it. This issue is related to content management.

3. **Selling the intranet.** In some companies there is a problem of selling the intranet. If paper documents are replaced, then employees must check the intranet frequently. Depending on the organizational culture, in many cases employees often are not using intranets to their fullest capacity. Some companies are making formal presentations to employees including online and offline training. Others provide incentives to users; some penalize nonusers. One approach is the creation of an Intranet Day (see *Internetweek*, May 3, 1999, p. 27).

4. **Accessing the intranet from the outside.** The more applications a company places on the intranet, the more important the need to allow employees to access it while they are outside the organization. This may create security problems, especially when employees try to do it via a modem (see Chapter 13).

5. **Connectivity.** Intranets need to be connected to the Internet and in many cases to extranets for B2B applications. Because many partners may be involved, along with several communication and network protocols, careful planning is needed.

6. **Finding intranet applications.** Intranet technology is mature enough and its applications are fairly standard. Look at vendors' case studies for ideas. Also look at *idm.internet.com/casestudies* and at *google.com* (intranet case studies). The material in this book's Web site (Chapter 11) and *cio.com/research/intranet/intranet_sites.html* are also places to investigate.

7. **Your organization and e-government.** If your organization is doing business with the government, you will eventually do it online. You may find new online business opportunities with the government, because governments are getting serious about going online. Some even mandate it as the only way to conduct B2G and G2B.

8. **P2P applications.** Watch for new developments in tools and applications. Some experts say a major revolution is coming for faster and cheaper online communication and collaboration. As with any other new innovation, it will take time to mature.

Summary

In this chapter, you learned about the following EC issues as they relate to the learning objectives:

- **Defining intrabusiness EC.** Intrabusiness EC refers to all EC initiatives conducted within one organization. These can be activities between an organization and its employees, between SBUs in the organization, and among the organization's employees.

- **The intranet and its use in organizations.** The intranet is the corporate internal network that is constructed with Internet protocols and tools, such as search engines and browsers. It is used for internal communication, collaboration, and discovery of information in various internal databases. It is protected by firewalls against unauthorized access.
- **The relationship between the corporate portal and the intranet.** The corporate portal is the gateway through which users access the various applications conducted over the intranet, such as training, accessing databases, or receiving customized news.
- **E-government to citizens.** Governments worldwide are providing a large variety of services to citizens over the Internet. Such initiatives increase citizens' satisfaction (more responsive government, less waiting time) and decrease government expenses in providing customer service applications.
- **Other e-government activities.** Governments, like any other organization, can use EC applications for great savings. Notable are e-procurement using reverse auctions, payments to and from citizens and businesses, auction of surpluses, and using electronic travel and expense management systems.
- **Applications of peer-to-peer technology.** Peer-to-peer technology allows direct communication for sharing files and for collaboration. While Napster gets a lot of publicity for its support of music and game sharing among millions of its members, the same technology is used in both B2B and in intrabusiness.

Key Terms

Business-to-employees (B2E)	Government-to-citizen (G2C)
Business-to-government (B2G)	Government-to-government (G2G)
Collaborative commerce (c-commerce)	Internet portal
Corporate (enterprise) portal	Intrabusiness EC
Customer-to-customer (C2C)	Intranet
E-government	Knowledge curve intranet
Enterprise portal	Peer-to-peer (P2P)
Government-to-business (G2B)	

Questions for Review

1. Define intrabusiness and list its major categories.
2. Define a corporate portal.
3. Define an intranet.
4. Describe peer-to-peer technology.
5. List the major types of e-government.
6. List the major types of portals.
7. List the major content components of a portal.
8. What is included in G2C?
9. What is B2E? Provide an example.
10. Define C2C and provide an example.

Questions for Discussion

1. Discuss the relationship between a corporate portal and an intranet.
2. Compare and contrast an Internet portal (such as Yahoo!) and a corporate portal.
3. Which e-government EC activities are intrabusiness? Why?
4. Discuss the relationship between knowledge management and a portal.
5. Discuss some of the potential ethical and legal implications of people using P2P to download music, games, and so forth.
6. The interest in intranets is coming back. Discuss the reasons why.
7. Identify the benefits of G2C to citizens and to governments.
8. Discuss the relationship between B2E and portals.
9. Some say that B2G is just B2B. Discuss.
10. Discuss the major properties of P2P.

Exercises

1. Concerning Amway Inc. (Section 11.1):
   a. Describe how information access problems affected the R&D department in developing new products.
   b. Describe the role of business intelligence and the knowledge portal in R&D at Amway.
   c. Enter *amway.com* and examine its corporate structure. What kind of groupware can help the salespeople?
   d. Find a couple of business intelligence and knowledge management portals and compare them with Artemis.
   e. Enter *marchfirst.com* and find out how they work with clients such as Amway.
2. Concerning the Cadence Design Systems, Inc. example (Section 11.6):
   a. What was the purpose of adopting an intranet for Cadence?
   b. What are the functions available in the OnTrack system?
   c. What are the benefits realized by adopting OnTrack?
   d. Describe the outsourcing strategy of Cadence.
   e. Describe the training requirements for OnTrack.

Internet Exercises

1. Enter *whitehouse.gov/government/index* and review the "Gateway to Government." Rate it on the Deloitte Research scale (what stage?). Review the available tours. Make suggestions for the government to improve this portal.
2. Read the issue paper, "E-mail Communication Between Government and Citizens," at *rand.org*. What are the major conclusions and recommendations of this study?
3. Enter *oecd.org/Puma/citizens* and identify the studies conducted by the Organisation for Economic Co-operation and Development (OECD) in Europe on the topic of e-government. What are the major concerns?
4. Enter *fcw.com* and read the latest news on e-government. Identify initiatives not covered in this chapter. Check the B2G corner.

5. Enter *ca.com/products* and register, then take the jasmineii_portal/test_drive. (Flash Player from Macromedia is required).

6. Enter *xdegrees.com*, *centrata.com*, and *Pointera.com* and evaluate some of the solutions offered. Also, enter *aberdeen.com* to learn more about P2P operations. How can they expedite a search for a song at *gnutella.co.uk*?

7. Enter *knowledgespace.com*. This knowledge base resides on Andersen's intranet. Sign up for the service (if still available free for a trial period). Why is such a system better when utilized on the intranet? Why not use a CD-ROM-based technology?

8. Enter *govexec.com/egov* and explore the latest developments in G2C, G2B (and B2G), and G2G.

9. Enter *groove.net* and go to "products." Identify all potential B2B applications, and prepare a report about them.

10. Enter *procurement.com* and *govexec.com*, identify recent e-procurement initiatives, and summarize their unique aspects.

11. Locate IQ Magazine at *cisco.com* and find information about employee portals and P2P/B2B. Prepare a report about them.

Team Exercises and Role Playing

1. Enter *oecd.org/puma/citizens* and examine available country reports. Also, use *google.com* and *govexec.com/features*, to find information about G2C. Compare initiatives in several countries and identify ways to strengthen government-citizen connections. Write a report.

2. Create four teams each representing one of the following: G2C, G2B, G2E, and G2G. Each team will prepare a plan of its major activities in a small country such as Denmark, Finland, or Singapore. A fifth team will deal with the coordination and collaboration of all e-government activities in each country.

REAL-WORLD CASE: E-Government Initiatives in Hong Kong

The Hong Kong SAR government in China (HK), initiated several e-government projects under the Digital 21 IT strategy (*info.gov.hk/digital21*). The major projects described here are

- the electronic service delivery scheme (ESD),
- the interactive government services directory (IGSD),
- the electronic tendering system (ETS),
- the HKSAR Government Information Center, and
- the HK post office certification service (Post e-Cert).

The highlights of these initiatives are provided here. Further information can be found at the specific URLs presented at *info.gov.hk*.

The Electronic Service Delivery Scheme (ESD).

This project provides a major infrastructure through which the public can transact business electronically with 38 different public services provided by 11 government agencies. Examples are:

1) **Transport Department:** Applications for driving and vehicle licenses, appointments for vehicle examinations and road tests, reporting change of address, and so forth.

2) **Immigration:** Application for birth/death/marriage certificates, making appointments for ID card issuance, application for foreign domestic helpers, communication on any other issue concerning immigration.

3) **HK Tourist Association:** Tourist information, maps, answers to queries.

4) **Labour Department:** Register job openings, search for jobs, search for applicants, FAQs regarding legal issues, employee's compensation plans, and so forth.

5) **Social Welfare Department:** Applications for senior citizen cards and card-scheme participation, welfare information, registration for volunteer scheme, request for charitable fund-raising permits, and so forth.

6) **Inland Revenue Department (Taxation):** Filing tax returns electronically, electronic payment program, change of address, interactive tax Q&A, applications for sole proprietor certificate, application for business registrations, purchase tax reserve certificates, and so forth.

7) **Registration and Electoral Office:** Application for voter registration, change of address, interactive Q&A.

8) **Trade and Industry Department:** Business license information and application, SME information center online.

9) **Treasury Department:** Electronic bill payment.

10) **Rating and Valuation Department:** Changes of rates and/or government rent payers' particulars, interactive Q&A.

11) **Innovation and Technology Commission:** Information on technology funding schemes. Electronic application for funding.

These services are provided in Chinese and English under the ESD life title. The project is managed by ESD Services Limited (*esdlife.com*). For additional information, see *esd.gov.hk/esdlife*.

In addition to these services, the Web site includes eight ESD clubs or communities. The public can sign up for a club, get information, share experiences, or just chat. The eight clubs are: **ESDbaby** (for new parents, family planning, etc.); **ESDkids** (how to raise kids); **ESDteens** (a meeting point for the teens on music, culture, learning, etc.); **ESD1822** (lifestyle, education, jobs, etc., for 18 to 22 year olds); **EDScouples** (information on getting married and building a family); **ESDprime** (jobs, education, entertainment, investment, travel, etc., for adults); **ESDsenior** (health care, fitness, education, lifestyle); and **ESDhospice** (complete services for the end of life).

The Interactive Government Services Directory

The interactive government services directory (IGSD) is an interactive service that enables the public to get information and services not included in the ESD. For example, it includes:

- Telephone and Web site directory of public services with information and links to hundreds of services.

- Interactive investment guide of industry department (investing in Hong Kong)

- Interactive employment services

- Interactive road traffic information

The Electronic Tendering System (ETS)

The electronic tendering system (ETS) is a G2B Web site that manages the reverse auctions conducted by the government supplies department. It includes supplier registration, notification of tenders, downloading of tendering documents, interactive Q&A, submission of tender offers and more. The HKSAR government conducts more than 5,000 tenders a year. The benefits of such a system are described in Chapters 6 and 9. For further information, see *ets.com.hk*.

The HKSAR Government Information Center

This is the official government Web site (*info.gov.hk*), which enables the public to obtain news, government notices, guides to major government services, leisure and cultural activities, and more.

The HK Post E-Cert

This site is the home of the Hong Kong public certification authority (*hongkong post.com*). The Hong Kong Post created a PKI system (see Chapter 14), and is issuing digital certificates (Post E-cert) to individuals and to organizations. It also maintains a certificate repository and directory of all certificates issued, so that the public can verify the validity of the certificates. The Post E-cert also issues certificates to servers and to security systems.

Note: Accessibility to the e-government portal is available not only from PCs, but also from hundreds of kiosks placed in many public places in Hong Kong.

Questions for the case

1. Which of the five initiatives is a G2C, G2B, C2G, and G2E?

2. Visit *info.gov.hk/digital21* and identify the goals of the e-government initiatives.

3. How will the role of the HKSAR government change when the initiatives mature and fully utilized?

4. Enter *esdlife.com* and compare the services with those offered in Singapore (*ecitizen.gov.sg*). What are the major differences? Also see *tnbt.com*, Dec. 8, 2000, News.

5. What applications could be added in the future by the HKSAR government?

REFERENCES AND BIBLIOGRAPHY

Aneja, A. et al. 2000. "Corporate Portal Framework for Transforming Content Chaos on Intranets," *Intel Technology Journal* Q1.

Bacon, K. et al. *E-Government: The Blue Print*. New York: John Wiley & Sons, 2001.

Bernard, R. *The Corporate Intranet*. New York: John Wiley & Sons, 1997.

Bort, J. and B. Felix. *Building an Extranet: Connect Your Intranet with Vendors and Customers*. New York: John Wiley & Sons, 1997.

Cashin, J. *Intranet Strategies and Technologies for Building Effective Enterprisewide Intranet Systems*. Charleston, South Carolina: Computer Technology Research Corp., 1998.

Chabrow, E. "Instruments of Growth," *Information Week* (October 5, 1998).

Chaffee, D. *Groupware, Workflow and Intranets: Reengineering the Enterprise with Collaborative Software*. Boston: Digital Press, 1998.

Choi, S. Y. and Whinston, A. B. *The Internet Economy: Technology and Practice*, Austin, TX: SmartEcon Publishing, 2000.

Cope, J. "Wireless LANs Speed Hospital Insurance Payments," *Computerworld* (April 10, 2000).

Damore, K. and M. Savage. "Peer-to-Peer Pressure." *Computer Reseller News*, August 28, 2000.

"Experts Offer 5 Keys to Successful Portals," *F/S Analyzer Case Studies* (February 2000).

"The Feds Play Their Card Hands," *Credit Card Management* (January 1999).

Gonzalez, J. S. *The 21st Century Intranet*. Upper Saddle River, New Jersey: Prentice Hall, 1998.

Griswold, S. *Corporate Intranet Development*. Rocklin, CA: Prima Publishing, 1997.

Hart-Teeter. *E-Government: The Next American Revolution*, 2000.

Hopkins, B. *How to Design and Post Information on a Corporate Intranet*. Hampshire, United Kingdom: Gower Pub. Co., 1997.

Jones, K. "Copier Strategy as Yet Unduplicated," *Interactive Week* (February 9, 1998).

Kounadis, T. "How to Pick the Best Portal." *e-Business Advisor* (August 2000).

Koulopoulos, T. M. "Corporate Portals: Make Knowledge Accessible to All." *Information Week* (April 26, 1999).

Laalo, A. "Intranets and Competitive Intelligence: Creating Access to Knowledge," *Competitive Intelligence Review*, vol. 9, no. 4 (1998).

Lister, T. "Ten Commandments for Converting Your Intranet into a Secure Extranet." *UNIX Review's Performance Computing* (July 1999).

McAffee, A. "The Napsterization of B2B," *Harvard Business Review* (November–December 2000).

Miller, M. et al. *Managing the Corporate Intranet*. New York: John Wiley & Sons, 1998.

Palmer, N. "Transform Your Business into a B2B Portal." *e-Business Advisor* (April 2000).

Richardson, A. *The Intranet: Opportunities within the Corporate Environment*. Elsevier Science Online, 1997.

Robinson, B. "Shopping for the Right B2G Model." *Federal Computer Week* (August 28, 2000).

Schwartz, J. "E voting: Its Day Has Not Come Just Yet," *New York Times* (November 27, 2000).

Schubert, P. and U. Hausler. "E-Government Meets E-Business: A Portal Site for Startup Companies in Switzerland," *Proceedings, HICSS,* Hawaii (January 2001).

Solution Series, "Intranet/Extranet 100," *Information Week* (October 5, 1998).

Sonicki, St. "The New Desktop: Powerful Portals," *Information Week* (May 1, 2000).

Stellin, S. "Intranets Nurture Companies From the Inside." *New York Times* (January 29, 2001).

Tapscott, D. *Digital Capital: Harnessing the Power of Business Webs*. Boston: Harvard Business School Press, 2000.

Wagner, R. L. and E. Englemann. *Building and Managing the Corporate Intranet*. New York: McGraw-Hill, 1997.

Watson, J. and J. Fenner. "Understanding Portals." *Information Management Journal* (July 2000).

Wong, W. Y. *At the Dawn of E-government*. New York: Deloitte Research, Deloitte & Touche, 2000.

PART 5

12

Building E-Commerce Applications and Infrastructure*

---

* Contributions to this chapter were made by M. Khalifa of City University of Hong Kong and J. Walls of the University of Michigan, Ann Arbor.

LEARNING OBJECTIVES

Upon completion of this chapter, the reader will be able to:

- Describe the landscape and framework of EC application development.

- Describe the major EC applications and list their major functionalities.

- Describe the EC architecture development process.

- List the major EC application development options and the approaches for option selection.

- Describe the major activities in system analysis and design.

- Describe the role of ASPs.

- Describe catalogs, Web servers, carts, chatting, and telephony for EC.

- Understand the issue of connecting EC applications to databases, other applications, and networks, and to business partners.

- Describe site usability and management.

- Describe the process of storefront development.

- Build a simple storefront using templates.

VIRTUAL VINEYARDS: WHERE CONTENT IS THE KEY

One of the earliest B2C Web sites was Virtual Vineyards (*wine.com*), established in January 1995 and still in operation today. As its name implies, the site specializes in selling wines from small producers with limited distribution capabilities. In addition to wine, the site also sells gourmet foods from around the world, many of which are made by hand in small batches. The combined number of wines and foods carried by the site varies but was about 1,000 items in Spring 2001. Each item is selected personally by the owners.

If you visit *evineyard.com* you will see that while the "look and feel" of the site is modified frequently to match holidays and accommodate special events, the basic content is fairly stable. Like other successful online sales sites, this site provides:

- Simple, straightforward navigation from one page to the next.
- An electronic catalog of products for sale that can be searched by a variety of parameters.
- A virtual shopping cart where a customer can place items until he or she is ready for checkout.
- Live "get an answer to your question in a real-time" feature.
- Secure payment either by credit card or CyberCash.

What distinguishes Virtual Vineyards from other sales sites is its focus on content and customer convenience. These characteristics are reflected in the following features:

- Personal profiles that enable customers to view records of their purchases and to make notes about the purchases they make.
- Search engine for finding products and prices on the site.
- Monthly programs in which customers receive a selection of wines based on the color they select—white, red, or mixed—and the number of bottles they wish to receive—two, four, or six.
- Shipment arrangement feature.
- Virtual sampler sets to help customers explore different types of wines they might not otherwise try.
- Tasting charts that provide a graphic representation of the flavor profile of each wine. These charts are created by one of the owners whose moniker is the "Cork Dork."
- Other services for the wine lover community, including experts' advice.

From a technical standpoint, it is important to note that all of the distinguishing features are built on basic Web standards. The pages at the Virtual Vineyard site are constructed from simple Web objects—text, forms, and graphics. On the server side of the equation, Virtual Vineyards employs a standard Web server configuration and straightforward database connections (see Appendix C on this book's Web site. Section 12.11 details Web-based database access). The technology is not as important as Virtual Vineyards' attention to customers.

In 1998, Virtual Vineyards became a member of ShopperConnection along with CDNow, Cyberian Outpost, eToys, PreviewTravel, PC Flowers, Datek Online, and others (Davis 1999). ShopperConnection is a network of retail sellers with Web linkages among the member sites. It was designed to increase brand awareness by associating member sites with other powerful brands. However, this initiative was unsuccessful (see Cross, 2000).

When Virtual Vineyards started, there were no EC development vendors or commercial software that could have been purchased, so that site was built in-house by one of its founders who happened to be a technology expert. Today, such a small storefront would be developed quite differently. Virtual Vineyards is a subsidiary of *evineyard.com*.

UNITED PARCEL SERVICE (UPS) SERVICES THE MASSES

United Parcel Service (UPS) has been in the package distribution business since 1907. They are the world's largest package distribution company, transporting over 3 billion parcels and documents per year. For some time UPS has provided the means for customers to track their shipments to determine the status and whereabouts of a particular package. In the past, this was done primarily over the telephone. Servicing these calls was an expensive proposition (estimated at $2 per call). In 1995, UPS put up a Web site. Initially, it was a simple site running on a single Web server and consisting of a small collection of hard-coded, static Web pages. Then in 1996–97 they created a new Web site to service customers.

Besides general marketing information, this site provides customers with the means to access online tracking, to determine the cost and transit time for delivery of a package, to schedule a package for pickup, and to locate the nearest drop-off facility. If a customer clicks on

"Tracking," he or she is taken to an online form where the customer simply enters the tracking number, hits the "Track" button, and receives status information about the designated package.

Although the front end is simple enough, the back-end processing used to handle a tracking request is a little more complicated. When a request first reaches the UPS site, it is handed off to one of a handful of Web servers. The particular server that is selected depends on a variety of factors such as the current load on the various machines. Next, the selected server passes the request to the appropriate application server. In this case, the application is a tracking. From there, the application server passes the request to an IBM AS/400 computer, which is attached to the UPS tracking database. Actually, this database is one of the largest transaction databases in the world, containing over 20 terabytes of data. The mainframe actually does the database search for the status information associated with the tracking number. Once the information is found, it is passed back up the line through the various servers to the customer's browser. Figure 12-1 provides a schematic of the whole operation.

The UPS Web site is designed to handle a substantial amount of network traffic. For the logistics activities of UPS see Chapter 8 (Application Case 8.4).

■ **GENERAL MOTOR'S TRADEXCHANGE**

In Chapter 6 we introduced GM's TradeXchange and in Chapter 18 we will discuss Commerce One's Global Trading Web (Chapters 7 and 18), of

FIGURE 12-1   Architecture of the UPS Web Site

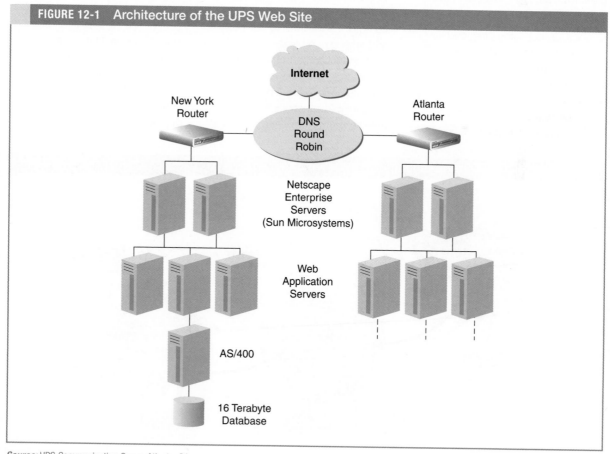

Source: UPS Communication Group: Atlanta, GA

which TradeXchange is a participant. Building this exchange was not a simple task since it was necessary to connect not only thousands of GM corporate buyers with thousands of suppliers, but also to connect TradeXchange with other exchanges as shown in Figure 12-2.

Under Commerce One leadership, the development process started in 1999 and took about a year to complete (Commerce One operates and maintains the exchange as well). In addition to Commerce One software, it was necessary to integrate many other components from different vendors. Here are just a few examples:

- For improving supply chain operations, i2 Technology, Inc. and its products and expertise were added. TradeXchange offers components of i2's RHYTHM suite as a hosted service to all 30,000 suppliers worldwide. The i2 solutions help trading partners collab-

orate more efficiently and also improve responsiveness to their own customers. The suppliers are expected to decrease supply chain costs, reduce inventories, and increase manufacturing efficiencies. The connection to TradeXchange will, therefore, be more efficient, enabling flexibility for improved order-to-delivery.

- The standard for data transfer is XML (see Appendix C on the Web site). Commerce One purchased a VEO system, a hotbed of XML development expertise. This way Commerce One also contributes to the development of XML. XML allows application-to-application communication within a company and among companies.
- For the auction part of the site, Commerce One purchased *CommerceBid.com*, a builder of complex B2B auctions and reverse auction solutions. The

acquisition enabled Commerce One to build generic auction software as well as customize applications, such as those needed for TradeXchange.

- To help small suppliers owned by minorities to connect to the exchange, GM created a partnership with The Empowerment Foundation and Direct Sourcing Solutions, Inc. to help its minority suppliers excel in the B2B marketplace. The partnership helps in providing the suppliers with infrastructure, electronic catalogs, and access to TradeXchange (see *empowermentfoundation.org*).
- PriceWaterhouseCoopers was selected as the lead integrator for TradeXchange. In this role, PriceWaterhouseCoopers is responsible for providing EC services ranging from strategy through technology deployment, across the GM

FIGURE 12-2   GM's TradeXchange

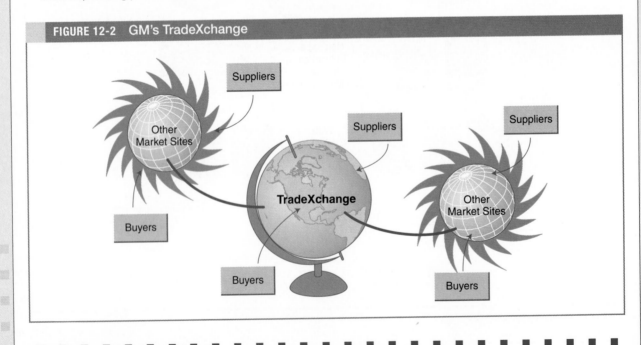

CHAPTER-OPENING CASE

12.1 BUILDING EC APPLICATIONS: SOME EXAMPLES (*CONTINUED*)

supply chain. For further details on PriceWaterhouseCoopers, which is the world's largest professional service organization, see *pwcglobal.com*. The

PriceWaterhouseCoopers' Management Consulting Service helped to plan, design, and improve many aspects of TradeXchange.

- Cisco and other vendors provide secure network management.
- Components from dozens of other vendors, including Oracle, Microsoft, and Intel were incorporated.

12.2   THE LANDSCAPE AND FRAMEWORK OF EC APPLICATION DEVELOPMENT

The examples in the opening vignettes, as well your knowledge about EC applications (or solutions) acquired so far, indicate the following:

- There is a large variety of EC applications.
- EC applications keep changing over time.
- There are several options for developing EC applications.
- Building complex applications from components is a viable strategy.
- One EC application may have many components from several different vendors.
- EC applications may involve several business partners, including a consultant.
- The Web sites and applications can be developed in-house, outsourced, or a combination of the two.

The diversity of EC business models and applications, which vary in size from a small store to a global exchange, requires a variety of development methodologies and approaches. Small storefronts can be developed with HTML, Java, or other programming languages. They can also be quickly implemented with commercial packages or leased from application service providers (ASP) for a small monthly fee. Some packages are available for a free trial period ranging from 30 to 90 days. Larger applications can be outsourced or developed in-house. Building medium to large applications requires extensive integration with existing information systems such as corporate databases, intranets, enterprise resource planning (ERP), and other application programs.

In this chapter, the EC application development process is described, alternative development methods are compared, important development issues are discussed, and the development of a storefront is illustrated through a Yahoo! Store application.

The Development Process

The development of a typical EC application is outlined in Figure 12-3. The activities at the top of the diagram (strategy) are described in Chapter 16. One of the major outputs of this strategy is the set of recommended applications, or an **application portfolio**. The objective of EC application development is to create the applications and implement them. The development process has five major steps, as shown in Figure 12-3.

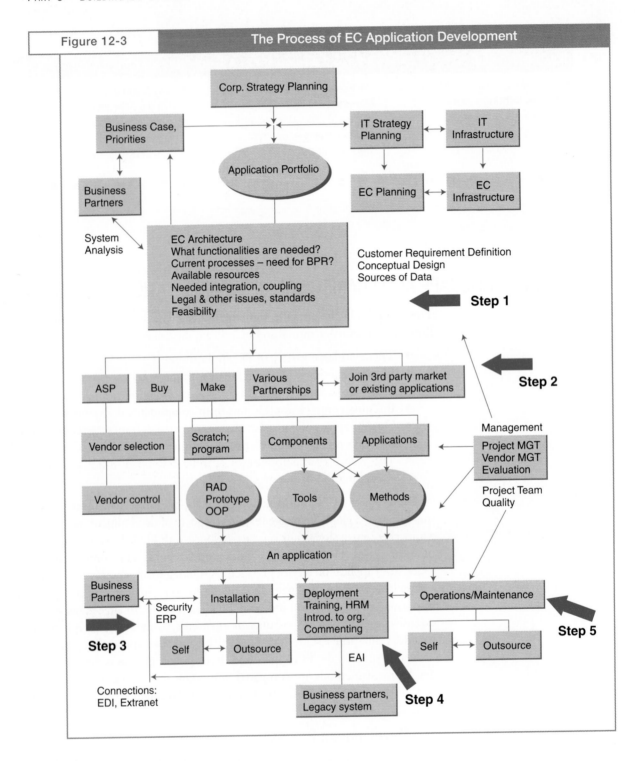

Figure 12-3   The Process of EC Application Development

STEP 1: EC ARCHITECTURE CREATION—A SYSTEMS ANALYSIS APPROACH

The major objective of the first step is to create the EC architecture. A detailed description of this step is provided in Section 12.4. This analysis can be supported by a set of tools and methodologies, some of which are generic to other IT applications (e.g., see Kendall and Kendall, 1999). Of special interest is the Joint Application Development (JAD), a collaborative methodology for identifying system requirements.

The results formulated during this step are routed to the strategic planning level (e.g., to a steering committee). As a result, the application portfolio may be changed. For example, risky applications may be deferred or scaled down. This step can be done in-house or outsourced to consultants.

STEP 2: SELECT A DEVELOPMENT OPTION

EC applications can be developed through several approaches that will be described in detail later. The major development approaches are:

- Use an Application Service Provider (ASP) to do the entire job.
- Buy an application and then install it (turnkey option).
- Build the system in-house.
- Join a third-party e-marketplace, such as an auction site, a bidding (reverse auction) site, or an exchange that provides applications to participants.
- Enter into some kind of partnership or alliance that will enable the company to use someone else's site.
- Use a combination of the approaches listed.

If **insourcing** (building the application in-house) is selected, a company will need to go through systems analysis and design and consider several methodologies and support tools. The considerations for the various methodologies are presented in Section 12.5.

At the end of this step, an application is built (or purchased) and ready to be installed.

STEP 3: INSTALLING, CONNECTING, AND MORE

EC applications need to be connected to the corporate intranet and/or extranets. Connection to databases, other applications, business partners, or exchanges may be required. Details of the connection process are supplied in Section 12.11. This step can be done in-house or outsourced. During this step the applications are tested, user reactions are examined, and more.

STEP 4: DEPLOYMENT

Once the applications pass all of the tests, they can be deployed. Here one may deal with issues such as conversion strategies, training, and resistance to change. This step can be done in-house and/or outsourced. The procedures are similar to those conducted for any IT application (see Whitten et al., 2000).

STEP 5: OPERATION AND MAINTENANCE

Like in any other IT application, operation and maintenance can be done in-house and/or outsourced (Kendall and Kendall, 1999). EC operations can be very complex in EC exchanges with many regulations. Maintenance can be a big problem due to rapid changes in the EC technology field.

Project Management

The development process can be fairly complex and it must be managed properly. A project team is usually created to manage the process and the vendors. Collaboration with business partners is critical. As we will discuss in Chapter 16, some EC failures are the result of delays and lack of cooperation by business partners. You can install a superb e-procurement system, but if your vendors will not use it, the system will collapse.

As with any large-scale development, appropriate management includes periodic evaluations of system performance. Standard project management techniques and tools are sufficient for e-commerce.

12.3   THE MAJOR EC APPLICATIONS AND THEIR FUNCTIONALITIES

As we have seen throughout this book, there are many EC applications, ranging from B2C direct sale to vertical exchanges. When deciding on an EC strategy and plan, which will be discussed in Chapter 16, we specify what applications to build and in what order. However, before we can start planning and organizing for specific applications, it is necessary to describe the desired functionality (or capability) of the applications. In this section we will describe the major EC systems: storefront (sell-side), e-procurement (buy-side), auctions, and an enterprise portal. For each system we will list the major characteristics and the functionalities.

Storefronts

A **storefront** is built on the seller's server. It can be a B2C application and/or a B2B application.

B2C STOREFRONTS

An electronic storefront must support the same steps and tasks that a physical store must support. In particular, an electronic storefront needs to offer a buyer the ability to:

- Discover, search for, and compare products for purchase using e-catalogs.
- Select a product to be purchased and negotiate or determine its total price using search and comparison agents.
- Evaluate products and services.
- Place an order for desired products using a shopping cart.
- Pay for the ordered products, usually through some form of credit.
- Have their order confirmed, ensuring that the desired product is available (confirmation facility).

The seller needs to:

- Sign a guest book for visitors to make comments or request to be on a mailing list.
- Verify their credit and approve their purchase through a credit verification system.
- Get answers to customer questions, or contact a Web-based call center.
- Have their orders processed (back-end services).
- Arrange for delivery with a tracking system.

- View a personalized page with a record of past purchases.
- Verify that the product has been shipped using a tracking system.
- Request postsale support or provide feedback to the seller through a communication system.
- View all of the listed features in a secure user-friendly environment.
- Create an auction mechanism.
- Provide content update; combine content and product information.
- Create the capability for cross-sell and up-sell.
- Provide language translation if needed.
- Connect to inventory management modules.

In order to provide these capabilities, an electronic storefront must contain at least three interrelated subsystems (DeWire, 1998):

1. A merchant system or storefront that provides the merchant's catalog with products, prices, and promotions. A shopping cart is usually included.
2. A transaction system for processing orders, payments, and other aspects of the transaction.
3. A payment gateway that routes payments through existing financial systems primarily for the purpose of credit card authorization and settlement.

The seller should be able to measure traffic, sales, and more. See Section 12.13 and the functionalities of the Yahoo! Store in Appendix 12A.

SUPPLIERS' SELL-SIDE IN B2B

A B2B sell-side is similar to a B2C storefront, but it includes several additional features. Notable ones are:

- Personalized catalogs and Web pages for all major buyers
- A B2B payment gate
- A site map
- Electronic contract negotiation features
- Product configuration (e.g., see Cisco, Dell) by customers
- Order tracking status facility (e.g., such as that provided by UPS)
- Web-based call center
- Automated business process workflow
- Ability for customers to use m-commerce tools (e.g., see *bea.com/products/weblogic/mcommerce/index.shtml*)
- Security and privacy systems
- Information about the company, products, customers (success stories), etc.
- Links and the ability to interact with business partners
- Ability to negotiate online
- Affiliate program capabilities
- Integration with corporate back-end systems
- Business alerts (e.g., about special sales)

SELL-SIDE AUCTIONS

Auctions require a large number of features, especially for B2B, including software agents for providing customer service. Also, fraud protection is important and can be provided through several features. A list of desired auction capabilities is provided in Chapter 9. In addition, auction ratings for marketing purposes are also available.

E-Procurement and Reverse Auctions

There are several variations of e-procurement systems and their required capabilities differ.

REVERSE AUCTIONS (TENDERING SYSTEM)

In such a system one expects to find:

- Catalog of items to be tendered and their content management
- Search engine (if there are many items)
- Personalized pages for potential large bidders
- Reverse auction mechanism, sometimes in real-time
- Facility to help prepare, issue, manage, and respond to RFQs
- Ability to bid dynamically
- Automatic vendor approval and workflow (e.g., SmartMatch's supplier identification technology)
- Electronic collaboration with trading partners
- Standardization of RFQ writing
- A site map
- A mechanism for selecting suppliers to participate
- Automatic matching of suppliers with RFQs
- Automatic business process workflow
- Ability for bidders to use m-commerce for bidding
- Automated language translation

INTERNALIZED AGGREGATION OF CATALOGS

With e-procurement, catalog content (Chapter 8) is of prime concern. Catalog requirements include:

- Search engine
- Comparison engine for alternative vendors
- Ordering mechanism
- Budget and authorization feature
- Usage comparisons (among various departments)
- Payment mechanism (e.g., use of a purchasing card, see Chapters 8 and 14)

Enterprise Portals

Some of the standard features of enterprise portals are:

- **Personalized pages.** Users can choose topics to be included in their page.
- **Searching and indexing.** Search and index features are a must in large portals. This capability allows users to conveniently extract relevant information.
- **Security and privacy protection.** This covers a number of features, including a privacy statement. Personalization may require additional levels of security protection.

- **Integration capabilities.** This is an extremely important part of any portal (see Chapter 11).
- **Modularity.** A modular standard-based approach is necessary to enhance application integration. It should be easy to add new applications.
- **Performance caching.** Personalization may expose each application to more frequent usage and broader audiences. The portal (or Web) server needs to cache data from the applications to improve the portal's performance.
- **Openness.** The success of a portal architecture depends on how easily new modules can be developed by others.
- **Polls and evaluations.** Allows instant feedback from site visitors.
- **E-mail service.** It should be superb.
- **Servers.** According to *plumtree.com*, portals have three server components: Web server, job server, and gadget server. You may need one or more of them.
- **Others.** E-mail, search engines, payment gateway, etc.

Exchanges

Exchanges should have the capabilities of buy-side and e-procurement systems, portals and auctions. They should also have:

- Collaboration services (including multichannel)
- Community services (per Chapter 18)
- Web-automated workflow
- Integrated business process solutions
- Central coordination of global logistics for members, including warehousing and shipping services
- Integration services: systems/process integration into e-marketplace, trading partners, and service providers
- Data mining, customized analysis and reporting, real-time transactions, trend and customer behavior tracking
- Transaction flow managers
- Negotiation mechanisms
- Language translation
- Comprehensive links to related resources

12.4   DEVELOPING AN EC ARCHITECTURE

An EC architecture is a conceptual framework for the organization of the EC infrastructure and applications. It is a plan for the structure and integration of EC resources and applications in the organization. Once the corporate strategy team or steering committee decides on potential applications, an architecture must be developed. Koontz (2000) suggested a six-step process for developing an EC architecture. The steps are:

STEP 1: Define business goals and vision. This preliminary step is explained in Chapter 16.

STEP 2: Define the information architecture. In this step one defines the information necessary to fulfill the objectives and build the EC applications. One should examine each goal, identify the information available, and determine if any of the information is digitized. One tool you can use is Microsoft's Distributed Internet Architecture (DNA). Make sure that all potential users are involved. This step is done on a high level of abstraction.

STEP 3: Define data architecture. Once you know what information must be processed by an EC application, you need to determine exactly what data and information you want to get from customers, including **clickstream data** (Chapter 8). Of special interest is the investigation of all information that flows within the organization and to and from your business partners.

The result of your investigation will probably show that data are everywhere, from data warehouses to mainframe files to Excel files on user's PCs. Of special interest is the anticipated clickstream data. You need to conduct an analysis of the data, understanding its use, and examine the need for new data. All this needs to be done with an eye toward security and privacy. This is when you need to think about how to process this data and what tools to use. If large amounts of data are used, tools such as Microsoft Transaction Server, Tuxedo, or CICS for mainframe data should be considered. Also, think about data mining and the tools the system will need to do it.

STEP 4: Define your application architecture. During this step, you need to think about some of the information requirements, such as security, scalability, and reliability. At this point, you should define the components or modules of the application that will interface with the required data defined in Step 3. During this step you will build the conceptual framework of the application, but not the infrastructure that will support it. An example is shown in Figure 12-4.

Many vendors including IBM, Oracle, and Microsoft offer sophisticated EC application platforms that can significantly reduce the amount of code your programmers need to write. These application platforms also explain how the application should be structured. In this step, you can decide on a specific vendor-defined application architecture, such as Microsoft DNA. However,

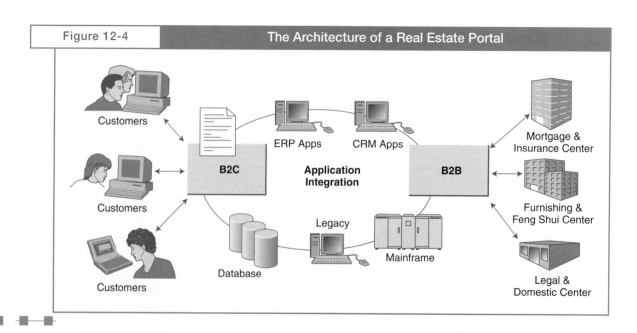

Figure 12-4   **The Architecture of a Real Estate Portal**

for complex applications, DNA and similar ready-made architectures may not be sufficient. One tempting solution is using tools such as DNA to increase programmers' productivity, but the resulting system may not fit.

Other factors that must be considered are scalability, security, the number and size of servers, and the networks. The need to interface with legacy systems and read real-time data is also important. In addition, interfacing with sales, ERP, accounting, and human resources data must be considered.

The major output of this step is to define the components that meet the data requirements. For example, to deal with updated, real-time information, one may consider IBM's MQSeries or Microsoft MSMQ. The software selection process is described in Section 12.12.

STEP 5: Define the EC technical architecture. During the previous steps, the designers informally considered the technical requirements. In this step, one must formally examine the specific hardware and software required to support the analysis in the previous steps. An inventory of the existing information resources is made and an evaluation of the necessary upgrades and acquisitions is performed.

At this stage, developers must examine the middleware needed for the application. EC applications require a considerable amount of transaction processing software. Again, many vendors, ranging from IBM to TIBCO, have products to offer. The more scalability and availability required, the more you need to invest in additional application servers and other hardware and software.

When selecting a programming language, Java, Visual Basic, C++, CGI, and even COBOL may be considered, depending on the application. Also in this step, the operating systems, transaction processors, and networking devices required to support the applications must be decided upon. Obviously, you want to leverage your existing IT resources, but this may not be the optimal approach.

STEP 6: Define the organizational architecture. An organizational architecture deals with the human resources and procedures required by Steps 1 through 5. At this time, the legal, administrative, and financial constraints should be examined. For example, a lack of certain IT skills on your team may require hiring or retraining. Do you have the time and the money to do it? Partial outsourcing may be a useful way to deal with some of deficiencies.

In the worst-case scenario, you outsource the entire job, but you can give the architecture to the vendor as a starting point. Also, vendor selection can be improved if the architecture is considered.

Conclusion

Creating EC architecture may be a lengthy process, but it is necessary to go through it. You may want to develop metrics to help you to track the effectiveness of your EC architecture, and you certainly need to document the process and output of each step. After all, according to GartnerGroup, (*gartnergroup.com*, press release, July 2000) the average cost of developing an EC site is more than $1.5 million, of which approximately 80 percent is related to labor and system integration.

Once the EC architecture has been decided upon, a development strategy can be formulated.

12.5   DEVELOPMENT STRATEGIES FOR EC APPLICATIONS: AVAILABLE OPTIONS AND SELECTION METHODOLOGY

There are several options for developing EC applications. The major options are: buy, lease, and in-house development. Each of these is described in this section, together with selection considerations.

Buy the Applications (Turnkey Approach)

Standard features required by EC applications can be found in commercial packages. Buying an existing package can be a cost-effective and timesaving strategy compared with in-house application development. The "buy" option should be carefully considered and planned for to ensure that all critical features for current and future needs are included in the selected package. Otherwise such packages may quickly become obsolete. In addition, organizational needs are rarely fully satisfied by one software package. It is, therefore, sometimes necessary to acquire multiple packages to fulfill different needs. These packages may then need to be integrated with each other as well as with the existing software. A number of commercial packages for B2C and B2B applications are currently available (see Appendix 12B).

The major advantages of the buy option are:

- Many different types of off-the-shelf software are available
- Saves time
- Often cheaper than in-house solutions
- Requires fewer dedicated personnel
- Company knows what it is getting before it invests in the product
- Company is not the first and only user

The major disadvantages are:

- Software may not exactly meet the company's needs
- Software may be difficult or impossible to modify or it may require huge process changes
- Loss of control over improvements and new versions
- Can be difficult to integrate with existing systems
- Vendors may drop a product or go out of business

The buy option is especially attractive if the software vendor allows for modifications. However, the option may not be attractive in cases of high obsolescence rates or high software cost. In such cases, one should consider leasing.

Lease

Compared with the buy option and the in-house option (to be discussed soon), the "lease" option can result in substantial cost and time savings. Although leased packages may not always exactly fit the application requirements (the same is true with the buy option), many common features that are needed by most organizations are usually included in these packages. In those cases where extensive maintenance is required or where the cost of buying is very high, leasing is more advantageous. Leasing can be especially attractive to SMEs that cannot afford major investments in EC. Large companies may also prefer to lease packages in order to test potential EC solutions before committing to heavy IT investments. Also, because there is a shortage of IT personnel with appropriate skills for developing novel EC applications, many companies choose to lease instead of develop software in-house. Even those companies that have in-house expertise may not be able to afford the long wait for strategic applications to be developed in-house and, therefore, buy or lease applications from external resources to establish a quicker presence in the market.

TYPES OF LEASING VENDORS

Leasing can be done in one of two ways. The first way is to lease the application from an outsourcer and install it on the company's premises. The vendor can help with the installation and frequently will offer to contract the operation and maintenance of the system. Many conventional applications are leased this way. The second way, using an **application system provider (ASP)**, is becoming more popular. ASPs are explored in Section 12.6. Vendors that lease EC applications are sometimes referred to as **commerce system providers (CSP)**.

In-House Development: Insourcing

The third development strategy is to build applications in-house. Although this approach is usually more time-consuming and may be more costly than the other two (buying or leasing), it often leads to a better fit with the specific organizational requirements. Companies that have the resources and time to develop their own EC application in-house may follow this approach to differentiate themselves from the competition, which may be using standard applications that are bought or leased. The in-house development of EC applications, however, is a challenging task, as most applications are novel, have users from outside the organization, and involve multiple organizations.

DEVELOPMENT APPROACHES

There are two major approaches to in-house development: building from scratch or building from components.

Build from scratch. This option is rarely used and should be considered only for specialized applications for which components are not available. It is an expensive and slow process, but it will provide the best fit.

Build from components. Companies with experienced IT staff can use standard components (e.g., a secure Web server), some software languages (e.g., C++, Visual Basic, or Perl), and third-party APIs and subroutines to create and maintain an electronic storefront and other EC applications on their own. Alternatively, companies can outsource the entire development process and ask an integrator to assemble components. From a software standpoint, this alternative offers the greatest flexibility and can be the least expensive option in the long run. However, it can also result in a number of false starts and wasted experimentations. For this reason, even those companies with experienced staff are probably better off customizing one of the packaged solutions as part of the buy option. For details about using components see Section 12.7.

An in-house approach to EC development typically uses a prototyping methodology.

PROTOTYPING METHODOLOGY

With a prototyping methodology, an initial list of basic system requirements is defined and used to build a prototype, which is then improved in several iterations based on users' feedback. This approach can be very rapid. Many companies have used this approach to develop their EC applications for mainly two reasons: (1) time is important, and they want to be the first to market and (2) it is necessary to involve the users (employees, suppliers, and customers) in the design of the applications. By quickly building a prototype instead of a full-fledged application, a company can establish an online presence more quickly than its competitors. The initial prototype is then improved and developed further based on the users' feedback.

The prototyping approach, however, is not without drawbacks and limitations. There is a risk of getting into an endless loop of prototype revisions, as users may never be fully satisfied. Such a risk should be planned for because of the rapid changes in EC technology and business models. Another limitation of prototyping is the risk of idiosyncratic design, where the prototype is revised based on the feedback of only a small group of users that is not necessarily representative of the entire user population. Such a risk can be alleviated by embedding a systematic feedback mechanism in the application itself, such as click trails and online feedback forms to elicit input from as many users as possible.

Other Development Options

A number of other development options are available to EC developers.

Join an e-marketplace or an exchange. With this option, the company plugs itself in into an e-marketplace. For example, a company can place its catalogs in Yahoo's marketplace. Visitors to Yahoo's store will find the company's products and will be able to buy them. The company pays Yahoo! a monthly fee for the catalog space. In Appendix 12A you will learn how to build a storefront in Yahoo!'s marketplace. In such a case, Yahoo! is a hosting service. As far as development goes, you will use *templates* to build your store, and you can start to sell after a few hours. Joining B2B exchanges is more complex, as explained in Chapter 7.

Join a third-party auction or reverse auction. As with the previous case, a company can plug into a third-party site fairly quickly. Many companies use this option for certain e-procurement activities. Finally, a company can join an exchange that offers auctions as described in Chapter 7.

Joint ventures. There are several different partnership arrangements that may facilitate EC application development. For example, four banks in Hong Kong have developed a joint e-banking system. In some cases, companies can team up with a company that already has an application in place.

Join a consortia. This option is similar to the previous one, except that in this case the company will be one of a small number of e-market owners. Thus, the company may have more say regarding the market architecture and operation and it may save on transaction fees.

Hybrid approach. A hybrid approach combines the best of what the company does internally with an outsourced strategy. Hybrid models work best when the outsourced partner offers higher security levels, faster time-to-market, and service level agreements. An example of the hybrid approach is shown in Application Case 12.1.

APPLICATION CASE 12.1

Snap-On's Approach to Developing EC Sites

The 'Buy' Approach

Brad Lewis, EC manager for Snap-On, a tool and equipment maker in Washington, hired Application Service Provider (ASP) OnLink Technologies to implement a catalog for the company's EC site. Lewis wanted his industrial customers to easily navigate through the 17,000 products listed in Snap-On's paper catalog, as well as integrate the site with Snap-On's ERP system. "If we developed this application in-house, we would have spent 6 to 9 months just designing and implementing it," he said. By using an ASP, Snap-On was able to get the entire catalog up and running in 4 months.

The 'Build' Approach

What was unusual is that Lewis integrated his staff with OnLink's to help transfer those catalog-building skills. Lewis himself spent several days a week during the 4-month development period at OnLink's headquarters, where he had his own office. He concentrated on developing application features and integration with back-end systems. "By spending so much time at OnLink, I became a member of their engineering group, and other members of my staff became temporary members of their professional services catalog group," Lewis says.

The Result

The result was that Lewis created an in-house ASP consulting service for Snap-On, providing guidance to other departments and subsidiaries that wanted to put up catalogs on their own Web sites. "One of the first questions we pondered before we outsourced was whether we could later bring that expertise in-house," Lewis says. "We didn't want to do it any other way." "When EC solutions become a mission-critical application, companies can become uncomfortable outsourcing them. If the outsourcer's site goes down, the company's business goes down," says Leah Knight, an analyst of the Gartner Group. Thus, the build versus buy decision changes along the life span of the Web site.

Sources: Compiled from Mullich (2000) and from *snap-on.com* (2001).

12.6   OUTSOURCING AND APPLICATION SERVICE PROVIDERS

Using the lease approach implies the use of outside vendors. This is usually done via some kind of outsourcing or by using an ASP.

Outsourcing

Small or medium-sized companies with few IT staff and smaller budgets are best served by outside contractors. Outside contractors have also proven to be a good selection for large companies wanting to experiment with EC without a great deal of up-front investment, to protect their own internal networks, or to rely on experts to establish sites over which they will later assume control. Some of the best-known B2C sites on the Web (e.g., Eddie Bauer and 1-800-FLOWERS) are run by third-party vendors.

There are several types of providers who offer services for creating and operating electronic storefronts:

- **Internet malls.** There are several thousand malls on the Web. Like a real-world mall, an Internet mall consists of a single entry displaying a collection of electronic storefronts. In contrast to earlier cybermalls, today's malls have a common look and feel. A well-run mall offers cross-selling from one store to another and provides a common payment structure where buyers can use a single credit card purchase to buy products from multiple stores. Theoretically, a mall has wider marketing reach than a stand-alone site and, as a consequence, generates more traffic. The downside is that income must be shared with the mall owner. For additional details see Chapter 3.
- **ISPs.** In addition to providing Internet access to companies and individual users, a large number of ISPs offer hosting services for EC. For the most part, ISPs are focused on operating a secure transaction environment and not on store content. This means that merchants using the services of an ISP must still design their own pages. Of course this task can be outsourced to a third party. A listing of top site designers can be found at *internetworld.com*. In 2000, some of the national ISPs like UUNet have begun offering a wide range of EC solutions.
- **Telecommunication companies.** Increasingly, the large telecommunications companies are expanding their hosting services to include the full range of EC solutions. MCI, for example, offers Web Commerce for a fee of $500 per month. Web Commerce runs on Open Market and Microsoft Commerce Server technologies. Similarly, AT&T provides of number of EC services, including the AT&T eCommerce Suite for $695 per month.
- **Software houses.** Many software companies, starting with IBM and ending with Ariba, offer a range of outsourcing services for developing, operating, and maintaining EC applications.
- **Outsourcers and others.** IT outsourcers, such as EDS, offer a variety of EC services. Also, the large CPA companies and management consultants offer such services.

One of the most interesting types of EC outsourcing is the use of ASPs.

Application Service Providers

An **application server provider (ASP)** is an agent or vendor who assembles the functions needed by enterprises and packages them with outsourced development, operation, maintenance, and other services (see Kern and Kreijger, 2001). The essential difference between an ASP and an outsourcer is that an ASP will manage application servers in a centrally controlled location, rather than on a customer's site. Applications are accessed via the Internet or VANs through a standard Web browser interface. In such an arrangement, applications can be scaled, upgrades and maintenance can be centralized, physical security over the applications and servers can be guaranteed, and the necessary critical mass of human resources can be efficiently utilized. In general, monthly fees, which include fees for the application software, hardware, service and support, maintenance, and upgrades, are paid by the end-user businesses. The fee can be fixed or based on utilization. According to Scott McNealy, Sun Microsystems CEO, by 2005, "if you're a CIO with a head for business, you won't buy software or computers anymore. You'll rent all your resources from a service provider." (Interview by *CIO* magazine November 2000.)

ASPs are especially active in enterprise computing and EC applications, which may be too complex to build and too cumbersome to modify and maintain (e.g., see Ward, 2000). Therefore, the major providers of ERP software, such as SAP and Oracle, are offering ASP options. An example can be seen at *mysap.com*, which is discussed in Chapter 15. IBM, Microsoft, and Computer Associates also offer ASP services. Similarly, major EC vendors, such as Ariba, offer ASP services.

BENEFITS TO THE ASP VENDOR

ASPs come from the ranks of ISPs, systems integrators, managed data center providers, carriers, etc. The benefits presented by the model are many. For example, in the carrier and ISP market, revenues are squeezed, so these companies are looking to generate revenues from sources other than connectivity and transport. Beyond lucrative Web site hosting and Web design consulting, hosted applications coupled with access charges create value and reasons to migrate toward use of an ASP.

BENEFITS TO THE LEASING COMPANIES

Leasing from an ASPs is a particularly desirable option for SME businesses, for which in-house development and operation of EC applications can be time-consuming and expensive. Leasing from ASPs not only saves various expenses (such as labor costs) in the initial development stage, it also helps reduce the software maintenance and upgrading and user training costs in the long run. A company can always select another software from the ASP to meet its changing needs and does not have to invest further in upgrading the existing one. In this way, overall business competitiveness can be strengthened through reducing the time-to-market and enhancing the ability to adapt to changing market conditions. This is particularly true of EC applications for which timing and flexibility are crucial. A detailed list of benefits and risks are provided in Table 12-1.

Leasing from ASPs does have its disadvantages. Many companies are concerned with the adequacy of protection offered by the ASP against hackers, theft of confidential information, and virus attacks. Also, leased software often does not provide the perfect fit for the desired application.

It is also important to ensure that the speed of the Internet connection is compatible with that of the application to avoid distortions in its performance. For example, it is not advisable to run heavy-duty applications on a modem link below a T1 line or a high-speed DSL.

An interesting institution is the ASP Industry Consortium, whose founding members include: AT&T, Cisco, Citrix Systems, Compaq, Ernst & Young, Exodus, Verizon, IBM, Marimba, Sharp Electronic, Sun Microsystems, UUNET, and Verio.

TABLE 12-1

Benefits and Risks of Using an ASP

Type	Benefits	Potential Risks
Business	Reduces the need to attract and retain skilled IT professionals	Loss of control and high level of dependence on ASP
	Enables company to concentrate on strategic use of IT	Inability of ASP to deliver quality of service; lack of skills and experience
	Enables small and medium-sized companies to use Tier 1 applications (e.g., ERP, SCM, and CRM)	
	Application scalability enables rapid growth of companies	
Technical	Fast and easy application deployment	Level of customization and legacy application integration offered by ASP is insufficient
	Higher degree of application standardization	Low reliability and speed of delivery due to bandwidth limitations
	Access to wide range of applications	Low capability of ASP to deal with security and confidentiality issues
	Application maintenance simplified and performed by ASP	
	Simplified user support and training	
Economic	Low total cost of ownership	Pricing changes by ASP unpredictable for application updates and services
	Low up-front investments in hardware and software	
	Improved cost control as result of predictable subscription costs	

Source: Kern and Kreijger, "An Exploration of the ASP Outsourcing Option," *Proceedings,* HICSS 31 Hawaii, 1997 © 2001 IEEE.

12.7 CRITERIA FOR SELECTING A DEVELOPMENT APPROACH

The following is a list of *criteria* that can be used to facilitate the selection of the development approach.

The functionalities of development packages and criteria of choice. In Section 12.3 we listed typical requirements of some applications. The first step is to make sure that the software meets the EC applications' requirements. Often, commercial packages need to be modified or adapted to the specific requirements of an application. It is therefore important to evaluate the extent to which a package can be adapted and the willingness of the vendor to perform or support the adaptation.

Information requirements. The selected package should satisfy the information requirements of the EC application. Information collection, storage, and retrieval capabilities and the database structure should be examined carefully.

User friendliness. User friendliness is especially important for B2C, G2C, and some B2B EC applications, as the users (e.g., customers and suppliers) are from outside the organization. Lack of user friendliness may affect the bottom line, since it could lead to lost business. This consequence may be far more serious in B2C and B2B EC applications than in intrabusiness EC applications, where only productivity or efficiency may be impaired.

Hardware and software resources. The computer type and the operating system required by the package must be compatible with the existing platform. The CPU and storage requirements are also important considerations.

Installation. The installation effort required to implement the package should also be taken into account. Some packages are complex and their installation requires extensive consultation. The installation process may also take a considerable amount of time.

Maintenance services. Because EC application requirements are constantly changing, continuous maintenance is required. It is important to consider how often the package needs to be upgraded and whether the vendor provides assistance for its maintenance.

Security. Data and information flow in EC as well as stored data may include private and/or proprietary information. Thus, a selected package must meet strict security requirements.

Vendor quality and track record. It is less risky to acquire an EC package from a vendor that has a good reputation and track record than from one with a less-than-stellar reputation. The quality of the vendor can be indicated by their related experience in the particular application, their sales and financial records, as well as their responsiveness to clients' requests. A number of novel EC applications are provided by dot.coms that do not have a long track record. It is sometimes difficult to assess such vendors. Some of them may even go out of business—leaving their clients without support. Vendor support may include online help, customer relationship management (CRM) programs, as well as partner relationship management (PRM) tools. To minimize risk, minor applications should be leased first.

Estimating costs. The costs of EC projects are usually difficult to assess and often underestimated because of the novelty of the solutions (no benchmarks) and the involvement of multiple organizations. In addition to the obvious costs associated with EC development, it is important not to forget the installation, integration, and maintenance costs, which are typically high for EC projects. Often, the customization and integration of components acquired from different vendors is necessary for the implementation of an EC solution.

Measuring benefits. It is often difficult to accurately predict the benefits of EC applications, because such applications are usually novel and may have no precedent for comparisons. Furthermore, most EC applications are interorganizational and are thus influenced by the environment of the organization. Such effects are usually intangible and difficult to isolate and quantify.

Personnel. Staffing requirements should be planned for in advance to ensure the organization has the appropriate human resources for systems development (in the case of in-house development), implementation, operation, and maintenance. Currently, it is difficult to recruit and retain IT personnel with appropriate knowledge and experience in EC application development. Special expertise can be acquired from external consultants, usually at a very high cost.

Forecasting and planning for technological evolution. Planning ahead for technological evolution facilitates the upgrade of EC applications and enables the organization to adopt innovations more quickly than the competition. It is therefore very important to allow for flexibility in the application design so the chosen options do not impose major limitations on future choices. Given the rapid pace of IT evolution, it is sometimes preferable to develop EC applications incrementally in order to take advantage of the latest developments in the technology.

Scaling. System scalability refers to how big a system can grow in various dimensions to provide more service. There are several possible measures of scalability. They include the total number of users, the number of simultaneous users, and the transaction volume. These dimensions are not independent, as scaling up the size of the system in one dimension can affect the other dimensions. The growth of scale is facilitated or constrained by the system architecture.

Sizing. The required size and performance are also difficult to predict, since the growth of the user population of certain EC applications is hard to anticipate. Overloading the application decreases performance. For regular IT applications, deterioration in performance may affect productivity and user satisfaction; for EC applications it could result in a major loss of business.

Performance. System performance is a critical factor for business success, particularly if the system is used for EC. In addition to convenience, good performance also brings customers and competitive advantages. Performance is measured by two main metrics: latency and throughput. **Latency** measures the time required to complete an operation such as downloading a Web page. It is an indicator of the user experience with the system. **Throughput** measures the number of operations completed in a given period of time. It indicates the capacity or number of users that a system can handle. Throughput and latency are interrelated. An increase in either measure will lead to an increase in the other.

Reliability. Reliability is an essential requirement for a successful system. Its importance is very significant for EC applications, where system failures may lead to public embarrassment. For off-line businesses, it is always possible to handle system failure by, say, doing the work manually. When an EC application fails, business is interrupted and the company loses customers. System reliability can be enhanced through redundancy (i.e., back-up systems).

Security. Security is one of the most important factors for the adoption and diffusion of EC. Systems, communication, and data security must be addressed early in the design of EC applications and not after their implementation. In addition to technological solutions such as firewalls and encryption, physical and procedural security measures must also be enforced.

Additional Criteria for Selecting an ASP Vendor

In selecting an ASP vendor, one should look at the following in addition to the general outsourcing consideration discussed earlier.

Database format and portability. The schema and physical structure of ASP application databases should be compatible with the client company's existing applications in order to facilitate the integration of the rented application with the existing ones.

Application and data storage. The client company should inquire how the application and its data are stored. Using dedicated servers may be more costly than sharing them with others, but this reduces the security risk.

Scope of service. Terms of fundamental services such as routine maintenance, availability of redundant servers, as well as default file back-ups should be clearly defined and agreed upon.

Support services. User training is a very important support service, especially for complex applications. Other support services include phone, Web, and e-mail help hotlines or sometimes a combination of these. However, not all of these services are always free of charge. It is also important to ascertain whether the services are actually rendered by the ASP itself or subcontracted to other companies.

Integration. Integration is particularly important for applications such as enterprise resource planning (ERP), accounting, and customer relationship management (CRM). It is necessary to integrate these applications with each other and with the EC applications. The effort required for integration and the assistance provided by the ASP for achieving the integration are critical selection factors.

Several other criteria, which are generic to all IT vendors, are described in Section 12.12.

12.8   SYSTEM ANALYSIS ACTIVITIES AND TOOLS: WHAT MANAGERS NEED TO KNOW

In this section we will elaborate briefly on some system analysis activities.

Requirements Analysis

Regardless of which development method (buy, lease, or develop in-house) is selected, system requirements must be clearly defined as part of the EC architecture described earlier. This may not be an easy task since in some cases users may be outside the organization or may not know their own needs. It is difficult to elicit a comprehensive list of requirements. An initial set of requirements can be generated by conducting focus groups involving users' representatives off-line as well as online. The initial set of requirements can serve as the basis for the development of a larger survey to determine the user preferences and priorities.

METHODS FOR DETERMINING REQUIREMENTS

One of the purposes of the prototyping method presented earlier is to identify the users' requirements quickly. By viewing a prototype, users can judge if the system meets their needs or not. By requesting more functionalities, they make their requirements known to the system developer.

Another method is **joint application development (JAD)**. This is basically a participative process, usually done with a facilitator, in which key users, managers, EC users, and business partners meet to contribute their system requirements. The method can be conducted either off-line or online (e.g., see Marakas, 2001, and Valacich et al., 2001). The requirements are solicited via brainstorming and a consensus is attempted. Once a list of requirements is agreed upon, it is used for the initial prototyping. The solicitation is relatively fast, and because of the consensus process, the prototyping requires fewer iterations.

Modeling

Requirements documents need to be dynamic to keep pace with change, this is a part of system modeling. There are different types of models and modeling approaches, such as those based on:

- Data
- Activity/Process
- Use Case/Object-Oriented
- Interprocess

Different models focus on different aspects of a system.

Component-Based Development

Many EC software applications are assembled from a set of components rather then being constructed from scratch. Components have evolved from objects of object-oriented methodology. (An object is the most primitive element in object technology. Objects contain data that describe themselves, as well as the instructions for operating on that data.) Components are much larger than objects, and now serve as plug-and-play building blocks that help in developing large complex systems, such as ERP or EC applications.

COMPONENTS DEFINED

There are several definitions of components. For example, Allen and Frost (1998, p. 4) define them as follows:

> *A component is an executable unit of code that provides physical black-box encapsulation of related services or functions, which can be accessed only through a consistent, published interface that includes an interaction standard. A component must be capable of being connected to other components to form an application.*

Examples of components are user interface icons, word processors (a complete software product), a GUI, an online ordering tool (a business component), inventory reordering systems (a business component), etc. Intranet components include search engines, firewalls, Web servers, browsers, page displays, and telecommunications protocols.

The major reasons for using component-based development are:

- Code reusability, which makes programming faster with fewer errors.
- Support for heterogeneous computing infrastructure and platforms.
- Rapid assembly of new business applications.
- Scalability of applications.

Component-based EC development is gaining momentum. It is supported by Microsoft and the Object Management Group (OMG). These groups have put in place many of the standards needed to make component-based development a reality. The enabling technology for component connection and reuse is a special type of **middleware.**

Components used in distributed computing need to possess several key characteristics to work correctly. The two main traits are borrowed from the world of object-oriented technology: *encapsulation* and *data hiding*. Components encapsulate the routines or programs that perform discrete functions. In a component-based program, one can define components with various published interfaces. One of these interfaces might be, for example, a date comparison function. This function compares two date objects and returns the results. All manipulations of dates are required to use the interfaces defined by the date object, so the complete function is encapsulated in this object, which has a distinct interface with the world. If the function has to be changed, only the program code that defines the object must be changed, and the behavior of the date comparison routine is updated immediately, a feature known as **encapsulation.**

Data hiding addresses a different problem. **Data hiding** places data needed by a component object's functions within the component, where it can be accessed only by specifically designated functions in the component itself. Data hiding is a critical trait of distributed components. The fact that only designated functions can access certain data items, and that outside requestors have to query the component, makes maintenance of component-oriented programs simpler.

The execution of component-based development requires special training and skill. One of the tools used is Perspective (Allen and Frost, 1998). Perspective is a collection of industry best-practice modeling techniques that are applied and adopted using process templates within an architectural framework across a wide range of developments in a component-based setting.

Figure 12-5 shows how components are used to create applications that solve business problems.

Enterprise Application Integration

Enterprise Application Integration (EAI) aims to integrate applications, including internal applications, that have been developed by different organizations. In some systems, the source code is unavailable, so altering the applications themselves is not possible; thus, EAI must be the glue between these applications. EAI is especially useful in connecting EC applications to ERP and EDI.

In principle, entire applications can be seen as very large components. Enterprise applications integration is normally executed across networked machines and is deployed in several distinct units. EAI middleware focuses on the integration of large systems.

Middleware is especially important to B2B EC applications. EAI helps both in internal application-to-application integration and in external business-to-business integration. The major middleware vendors are TIBCO, Extricity, Vitria, and WebMethods. Also, IBM's Biztalk and Microsoft's MQSeries support integration.

When breaking an application into smaller components, other types of middleware besides EAI may be appropriate for the communication between such smaller components. It is likely that this two-level approach, using different communication paradigms at the two levels, will prevail for some time. Different levels of integration are provided by EAI, from vendors such as IBM, GEIS, EDS, and Microsoft. Three levels of integration: data, object, and process are possible, as shown in Figure 12-6. Figure 12-6 also shows the corresponding functionality of a typical EAI system.

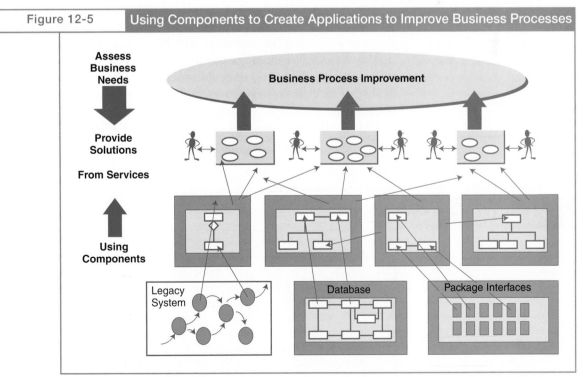

Figure 12-5   Using Components to Create Applications to Improve Business Processes

Source: Allen and Frost (1998), p. 24.

Figure 12-6	Levels of Enterprise Integration		
Process Integration			
Development services	**Process management services** • Transformation coordination services		**Run time services**
Object Integration			
• Process modeling • Transformation specification • Interface development	**Transformation services** • Identification and validation services • Synchronization services • Routing services • Transaction processing services		• Distribution services • Scalability services • Monitoring services
Data Integration			
	Connectivity services • Communication services • Addressing and delivery services • Security services	**Interface services** • Interface translation services • Metadata representation services	

Source: Puschmann and Alt, "Enterprise Application Integration—The Case of Robert Bosch Group," *Proceedings,* HICSS 34 Hawaii © 2001 IEEE.

EAI will undoubtedly remain a high priority and a major challenge for IT managers and software vendors. It has been estimated that 35 percent of the cost of an Enterprise Resource Planning (ERP) implementation is the integration with existing and new applications.

This is why a new breed of servers is gaining popularity. **Integration servers** provide platform-to-host mapping between different schemas and bridge between different messaging technologies. Web-based servers such as those provided by *webMethods.com* are examples of integration servers. **Application servers**, on the other hand, provide integration across services such as transaction processing. It is likely that application servers and integration servers will continue their evolution toward tight, mutual integration.

EAI enables the economical and rapid integration of EC, ERP, SCM, and CRM applications, as shown in Application Case 12.2.

APPLICATION CASE 12.2

Robert Bosch Group

The Robert Bosch Group of Germany is a multinational company operating in 132 countries. It has 250 subsidiaries in 48 countries and 142 manufacturing plants outside Germany. The company manufactures automotive products, tools, communication devices, and more.

European IT activities are centralized and managed by a unit called QI. This unit attempted to integrated new technologies such as ERP, SCM, CRM, and EC into a complete heterogeneous infrastructure. To reduce integration

APPLICATION CASE 12.2

(*continued*)

problems, QI used an EAI approach. The objective was to implement a standardized integration architecture called "business bus." Notice that the "bus" is the backbone of the system and that the major software that is connected is R/3 from SAP, a major ERP vendor (Chapter 15).

Such a large company is implementing a variety of EC applications, including B2C in various of its subsidiaries, intrabusiness in most of them, and B2B among its companies and between its companies and other corporations (both buy-side and sell-side).

12.9 ELECTRONIC CATALOGS, SHOPPING CARTS, WEB CHATTING, WEBCASTING, AND INTERNET TELEPHONY

The following components are common in many EC applications.

Electronic Catalogs, Shopping Carts, and Merchant Servers

An electronic catalog is hosted on a merchant server in a form of stored data and its database management system (DBMS), and includes all the necessary information to conclude a transaction. An **electronic shopping cart** is an order-processing technology that allows customers to accumulate items they wish to buy while continuing to shop. The **merchant server** may include a file with customer information.

Electronic catalogs are the virtual equivalents of traditional product catalogs. Like its paper counterpart, an electronic catalog contains written descriptions and photos of products along with information about various promotions, discounts, payment methods, and methods of delivery. Electronic catalogs and merchant server software include features that make it simple and relatively inexpensive (usually less than $10,000) to set up a catalog operation that has a straightforward pricing and product configuration. Among the features commonly included with this category of software are:

- Templates or wizards for creating a storefront and catalog pages with pictures describing products for sale.
- Electronic shopping carts that enable consumers to gather items of interest until they are ready for checkout.
- Web-based order forms for making secure purchases (either through an SSL or a SET).
- A database for maintaining product descriptions, pricing, and customer orders.
- Integration with third-party software for calculating taxes and shipping costs and for handling distribution and fulfillment.

Figure 12-7 outlines the major components in an electronic catalog or merchant server system. As shown in Figure 12-7, a single server is used to handle product presentation, order processing, and payment processing (Treese and Stewart, 1998). Likewise, in these systems a single database is used to store the catalog (i.e., product descriptions) and to handle the details of customer orders. The pages of the

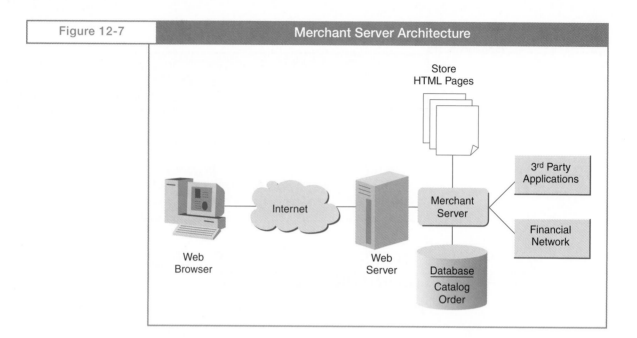

Figure 12-7

Merchant Server Architecture

electronic catalog are created dynamically from the product descriptions contained in the catalog database. For those merchants with only a few products for sale, there is no need to store the product descriptions in a database. Instead, the pages of the Web catalog can be created ahead of time.

Web Chatting

For the most part, businesses have ignored the potential economic payoff from online communications. Except for e-mail, the Internet and the Web have been treated as a broadcast or narrowcast medium with information flowing in only one direction (either pulled by or pushed to the end user). However, in 1999 businesses began to recognize that the Internet and Web offer the ability to engage customers in a dialogue and to create virtual communities where customers can also communicate with one another. After all, the Internet is primarily about establishing and reinforcing connections between people.

Online forums and chat groups are now being used for a variety of purposes in EC. **Online forums** are equivalent to Usenet newsgroups (but with a better interface), and **chat groups** are similar to Internet Relay Chat (IRC). Elderbrock and Borwanker (1996) categorize the various uses of these forums and chat groups in the following way:

- **Communication centers.** Businesses use forums and chat groups as a virtual meeting place where communications can take place among the participants. Revenue is generated either through subscription fees or advertising revenues. One example is *Match.com*, which is an online matchmaking service for professional single adults.
- **Customer service.** A number of companies now offer online support where customers can converse with help-line staff and other customers (see Chapter 4). Much of the discussion revolves around product questions,

problems, and advice. Most online support centers are organized as forums rather than chat groups. There are some exceptions. Mercant (*mercant.com*), a software vendor supplying database and programming utilities, not only provides online forums but also "live cyber discussions" where customers can chat with product managers and outside experts.

- **Community discussion.** Several EC sites provide forums and chat services with a marketing eye toward developing a community of loyal users, followers, and advocates (Chapter 18). Good examples of this strategy are the forums provided by many of the online financial investment firms (e.g., *fool.com*). Other examples are the sports chat rooms and forums provided by sport news sites such as ESPNnet (*espn.com*).
- **Video chat.** This is the next generation of online chat. For information see *visitalk.com*.

For more about Web chatting see Chapter 4.

Webcasting

In the early and mid-1990s, executives envisioned the Information Superhighway being delivered to the homes of consumers by cable connections in the form of "500 cable channels" providing media content and information on demand. During this time period, a number of cable television companies conducted experimental programs by wiring selected communities with cable on demand. Their aim was to gauge consumer willingness to pay for these additional interactive services. Virtually all of these experimental programs were resounding flops. One impact of this was a shake-up of the cable industry. By 1999, the cable industry began to turn its attention away from delivering more television programming into homes and toward offering an infrastructure for delivering a combination of audio, video, Web browsing, and Internet telephone services. This has resulted in a flurry of mergers, acquisitions, and investments among cable, telephone, computer, and Web companies, as the various conglomerates raced to gain control of the wire into the consumer's home.

Rather than wait for a victor in the battle between these conglomerates, several Web companies such as Real Networks (*real.com*) and *Broadcast.yahoo.com* (*broadcast.yahoo.com*) are already delivering real-time Webcasts. **Webcasting** is a term used to describe Internet-based broadcasting of audio and video content. Webcasting is distinguished from standard Web content delivery because it provides a constant stream of information, can be presented live in addition to allowing on-demand listening and viewing, and offers the potential for two-way communication between the broadcaster and the listener or viewer. Webcasting encompasses a variety of content. Novak and Markiewicz (1998) provide a complete listing of the various types of Webcasts, which is summarized below:

- **Text streams.** These are text-only wordcasts and datacasts that are streamed to the end user's desktop in the form of banner ads or chat windows. Text streams are used, for example, to deliver constant news and stock price updates.
- **Ambient webcasts.** Video content is captured from a Webcam and delivered as single-frame updates that are transmitted at periodic intervals (e.g., every

few minutes). EarthCam (*earthcam.com*) provides a directory of Webcam sites. There are literally thousands of these sites throughout the world.

- **Streaming audio.** This is the Web equivalent of radio. The quality of the audio that is delivered ranges from voice quality to AM radio quality to FM radio quality to broadcast quality to near-CD quality. The leader in streaming audio technology is Real Networks with its RealAudio technology. Among the content leaders is *Broadcast.yahoo.com*, which provides an extensive listing of live audio Webcasts.

Internet Telephony

Internet phones come in three versions—PC-to-PC, PC-to-Phone, and Phone-to-Phone. With PC-to-PC Internet phone calls, the caller and recipient are both required to have the same Internet phone software on their computers. Each computer must be equipped with a (full duplex) sound card, speakers, a microphone, and an Internet connection. The Internet phone software runs outside the browser and usually appears as a telephone. When a call is placed, the audio is broken into digital packets and transmitted over the Internet to the recipient's computer (which can be identified by the user's e-mail address) where the packets are transformed back into audio.

PC-to-Phone systems only require the caller to have the Internet phone software. The recipient answers the call with a regular telephone. In this case, the vendor providing the phone software has special Internet gateway computers located throughout the world. When the Internet phone user places a call, the software compresses the audio and turns it into packets that are shipped to the gateway computer closest to the recipient's location. When the packets reach the gateway computer, they are reassembled into a voice signal that is transmitted through the public switch telephone network to the recipient. In this way, the call is basically a local call rather than long distance.

The last Internet phone configuration is Phone-to-Phone. Here, the caller and the recipient use a regular telephone. When the call is placed, the voice signal travels to a gateway computer located near the caller. Again, the gateway computer compresses the signal and converts it into packets. The packets are transmitted to another gateway computer located near the recipient. At this point, the packets are converted back into a voice signal, which is sent over regular telephone lines to the recipient.

Three vendors dominate the Internet telephone marketplace. VocalTec (*vocaltec.com*), *net2phone.com*, and *deltathree.com*. Internet telephone has been under considerable scrutiny by national governments and opposed by existing local and long-distance telephone carriers. The latter are concerned because, even though the Internet relies on the worldwide telephone infrastructure, Internet phone calls avoid the long-distance fees associated with regular telephone calls.

12.10 EC SUITES

Tools for EC can be combined into suites. EC suites offer builders and users greater flexibility, specialization, customization, and integration in supporting complete front- and back-office functionality. In an EC suite, store functionality is distributed across a number of servers and databases instead of relying on a single server and database, as is done in electronic catalog and merchant server systems. The architecture of

Open Market's Transact system, shown in Figure 12-8, is indicative of the manner in which store operations are distributed in these high-end suites (Treese and Stewart, 1998). The capabilities of Transact, which is part of the eBusiness suite, are improving constantly (see the demonstration at *openmarket.com*).

The discussion that follows describes the offerings of three EC suites—Interworld (*interworld.com*), Open Market (*openmarket.com*) and IBM's WebSphere. A similar product from Ariba is described in Chapter 6. For other suites see Appendix 12B (on the book's Web site).

The main product from InterWorld is Commerce Suite, which offers a comprehensive set of sell-side capabilities (see Figure 12-9). The company works with *Webmethods.com* on e-marketplaces as well is an object-oriented, Java-enabled, open, scalable architecture that supports four primary functions:

- **Catalog/product merchandising.** Interactive catalog modules that support extensive personalization facilities, including personalized product presentations; dynamic product pricing and personalized discounts and coupons; up-selling and cross-selling pointing customers to alternative, complementary, or substitute products; product comparisons, alternatives, and recommendations based on buyer characteristics or past purchases; and buyer assistance for making product selections.
- **Order management.** Order management modules that support capturing the information required to place an order (order entry); finalizing the

Figure 12-8	Open Market EC Server Architecture

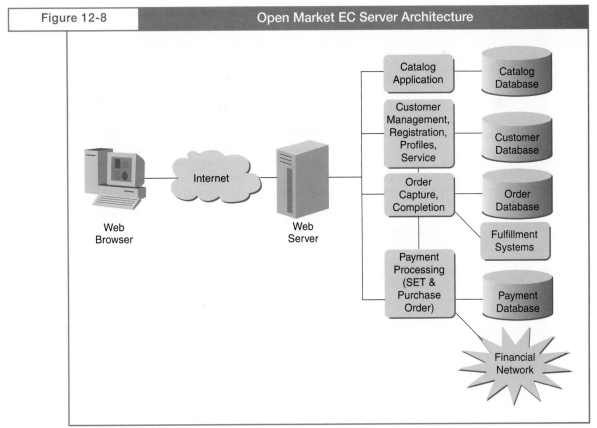

Source: openmarket.com

Figure 12-9	Interworld's Commerce Suite

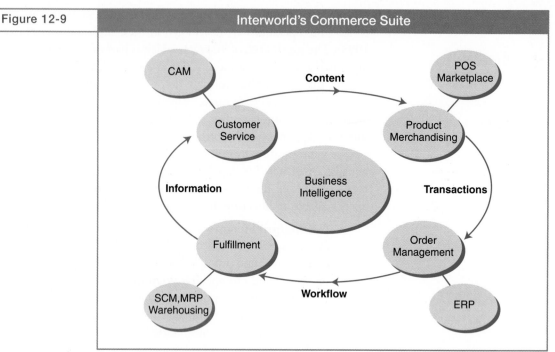

Source: *interworld.com/solutions*

details of the order including the payment, shipping, inventory, and taxation (order processing); billing and account management including definition of preferences such as billing addresses, ship-to addresses, credit card information, credit limits, and credit card verification (payment).

- **Fulfillment.** Interfaces with multiple shipment and fulfillment solutions. Additionally, provides specific "Business Adapters" for shipping with either TanData or FedEx. The FedEx adapter offers customers access to FedEx shipment, ship estimation, ship alert, and tracking systems.
- **Customer service.** Functions that offer customers the ability to verify, edit, and change their profiles; review their orders; and review their payment history.

Open Market is a provider of EC suites. Their focus is on EC sites with high transaction volumes. Their flagship product is OM-Transact, the architecture of which is depicted in Figure 12-8. OM-Transact provides a complete set of end-to-end transaction services including:

- **Analysis and profiling.** Analyzes sales, buyer behavior, and buyer profiles in order to determine the effectiveness of advertisements, special offers, and other promotions.
- **Demand generation.** Delivers digital offers and digital coupons to attract target customer groups.
- **Order management.** Captures orders, validates payment and address information, and controls processing of shipments, credits, and orders.
- **Fulfillment.** Delivers physical goods, digital goods, and subscriptions with automated customer notification by enterprise systems, faxes, e-mail, or secure Web pages.

IBM WebSphere Commerce Suite

Building a successful e-marketplace demands a solution with tight commerce and supply chain integration, streamlined purchasing processes, and real-time information-sharing across a variety of business systems and computing environments. IBM's Commerce Suite provides a fast, flexible, and fearless e-commerce solution that addresses these challenges–and more. Go to *ibm.com/software* and click on Websphere.

The suite is composed of several tools. Its major components are:

1. Web server for catalog management
2. Application server for secure reverse auctions, exchanges, and contracts
3. EC suite server for auctions and sell-side ordering
4. Database server
5. An HTTP interface with buyers, sellers, and corporate administration

The highlights of the system are:

- Delivers an open, standards-based solution platform with integrated components to build your e-marketplace.
- Facilitates operational efficiency and high return on investment with browser-based tools, preconfigured options, and built-in features.
- Uses Java and XML technologies to aggregate seller catalogs into a centralized catalog available to all trading components.
- Provides optimal customization and flexibility to manage membership and access control, approval workflows, reporting, and negotiation processes.
- Incorporates e-marketplace functionality, including exchange, extensible searching, pervasive RFQ/RFP, and real-time contracts.

Figure 12-10	Web to Database Connection

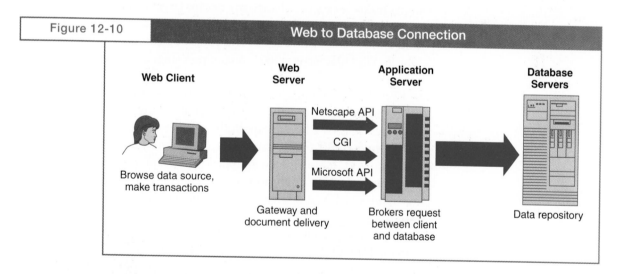

12.11 CONNECTING TO DATABASES, LEGACY SYSTEMS, AND BUSINESS PARTNERS

EC applications must be connected to internal information systems, infrastructure, ERP, etc. They also must be connected to such items as the partners' systems or exchanges. Such connections are referred to as integration and are the subject of this section.

Connecting to Databases and Other Integration Issues

Many EC applications need to be connected to a database. For example, if you order a product, it is nice if the system can immediately find out if the item is in stock. So you need to connect your ordering system (application 'A'), to your inventory systems (application 'B'). Several possibilities exist regarding such a connection, one of which is shown in Figure 12-10. The technology shown in the figure enables customers with a Web browser to access catalogs in the seller's database, request specific data, and receive an instant response. Here the application server manages the client's requests. The application server also acts as the front-end to complex databases.

As indicated earlier, it will often be necessary for a customer (or supplier for that matter) to be able to access data that already exists in a company's legacy databases. There are two basic approaches to achieving this—duplicating the data in databases "owned" by the EC application or enabling communication between the EC and legacy applications. In general, the latter is the preferred option. There are many reasons for this, including the fact that this approach ensures the latest data is available to both applications, there is consistency in the data, and the amount of required disk storage space is reduced. Also, you do not need an extra database to create and maintain.

The current trend is to build applications, including EC applications, in what is termed a three-tier (or multitier) client-server architecture. In this approach, the browser tier is responsible for presentation of information to the user, an application server tier executes business rules (e.g., user authorization), and a database server tier contains the company's data (e.g., product pricing). This separation of duties makes it easier to change any tier (or layer) without impacting the other layers. Thus, an application server can be designed to interface or communicate with a wide variety of databases and database management systems (DBMS) (e.g., Oracle, MS SQL Server, DB2). A common language is used to communicate with the DBMS.

BEA, Inc.'s WebLogic Commerce Server is typical of modern EC development platforms in that it provides a variety of alternatives for connecting to company databases. It is based on an application server that can connect to external databases using JDBC (Java DataBase Connectivity) and ODBC (Open DataBase Connectivity). It also comes equipped with adapter software specifically designed to connect to other applications and services. It also provides the standard EC capabilities such as shopping carts and catalogs. IBM's WebSphere provides similar capabilities.

Another approach to sharing data between applications is to use a messaging system. TIBCO, for example, has a patented technology called The Information Bus (TIB) that enables communication between applications. Microsoft's Active Server Pages (ASP, not to be confused with Application Service Provider) provides the ability to use ODBC to create dynamic Web pages from the content of a variety of DBMSs.

It is often necessary to integrate with the systems of customers and suppliers as well as with internal applications. Several vendors also provide the ability to exchange data with trading partners. BEA's WebLogic Collaborate is a platform for "developing, deploying, managing, and integrating business transactions required by online exchanges, enterprise supply chains, and other complex collaboration environments." XML is emerging as a common language for such exchanges, and will probably replace traditional EDI approaches in many organizations, in the not-too-distant future.

As mentioned is Section 12.8, there is a large number of vendors that provide application-to-application and business-to-business integration. They are referred to as EAIs. For a vendor list see Appendix 12B on the book's Web site.

Connecting to Business Partners

Connecting to business partners is critical to the success of EC, especially for B2B (see Real-World Case, Chapter 7). As described earlier, such connection is done via EDI, EDI/Internet, and extranets (see appendices to Chapters 6 and 7).

In addition to the networking problem, one must deal with issues of connectivity, compatibility, security, scalability, and more. In Appendix 12B we present some of the vendors that provide these services (EAIs and others) and describe some of the products that enable the connection.

12.12   VENDOR AND SOFTWARE SELECTION

Dealing with outside vendors is a veritable necessity when building EC applications or infrastructure. Vendors will supply the hardware, software, hosting services, and often the development expertise that are required to build such applications. Few organizations, especially small to medium enterprises (SMEs), have the time, financial resources, or technical expertise required to develop today's complex e-business systems. Besides, much of the functionality needed to get started in this area (e.g., catalogs, personalization software, shopping carts) has already been built into existing software platforms (e.g., WebLogic Commerce Server or MS Commerce Server). Buying off-the-shelf software, even when it does not exactly meet the needs of a business, is both faster and less expensive than in-house development. In any event, many of these packages generally offer the user the ability to customize the functionality of the package by writing code in Java, C, C++, or Visual Basic (some can even be programmed in Cobol!) or by selecting from a component library.

Therefore, a major aspect of developing an EC application revolves around selecting and managing the vendors who will provide the various pieces of the system that you either can't or choose not to develop within your organization. The approach described next can be used for a buy or lease of application and/or components required for in-house development.

Martin et al. (2000) identified the following steps in selecting a software package.

STEP 1: Identification of suitable packages
STEP 2: Determination of detailed evaluation criteria
STEP 3: Evaluation of the candidate packages
STEP 4: Choosing a package
STEP 5: Negotiating the contract

The following discussion is based largely on their approach. The team should include representatives from areas the system will serve, IS department analysts, EC users, and, if needed, business partners. Some details of the criteria mentioned here and additional criteria were described in Section 12.7.

For a major system, the process usually focuses on the development of a request for proposal (RFP), which is sent to potential vendors inviting them to submit a proposal describing their software package and how it would meet the company's needs. The RFP provides the vendors with information about the objectives and requirements of the system, the environment in which the system will be used, the general criteria that will be used to evaluate the proposals, and the conditions for submitting proposals. It may also request a list of current users of the package who may be contacted, describe in detail the form of response that is desired, and require that the package be demonstrated at the company's facilities using specified inputs and data files.

Identification of Suitable Packages

Helpful software catalogs are published by companies such as Datapro, Auerbach, and International Computer Programs. Hardware vendors often have lists of software they sell or recommend, and their user groups have similar lists, as do many trade and professional associations. Software vendors advertise in technical and trade publications, and consultants who are experienced with an application area or an industry may be helpful. Also, one may hear of good packages being used by friends and competitors.

Usually these sources yield so many packages that one must use some preliminary evaluation criteria to eliminate all but a few of the most promising ones from further consideration. For example, one can eliminate vendors that are too small or that have no track record or a questionable reputation. Also, packages may be eliminated if they do not have the required features or will not work with available hardware, operating system, communications network, or database management software.

Determination of Evaluation Criteria

The most difficult and crucial task in evaluating packaged systems is to determine in detail what one must know about the packages in order to choose the best one and the importance of each criteria. Some areas in which detailed criteria should be developed are characteristics of the vendor, functional requirements of the system, technical requirements the software must satisfy, amount and quality of documentation provided, and vendor support of the package.

The RFP should request information about the vendor, including how long the vendor has been in the EC software business, the number of employees, financial reports over the past five years, its principle products, its yearly software sales revenue, and the location of its sales and support offices. The RFP might also request the date the software system being considered was first released, the date of its last revision, and a list of companies using the software that can be contacted references.

The project team must develop the essential functional requirements (EC architecture, Section 12.4) that the system must satisfy so they can be included in the

RFP. These requirements can be categorized as mandatory requirements (must have) and desired features (nice to have), and are stated as questions about the characteristics of the packages. The ease with which the software can be tailored to fit company needs or enhanced for future needs should also be considered.

This collected information allows one to evaluate how well the package will conform to corporate standards, such as programming languages supported, operating systems, communications software, and database management systems supported.

The types, amount, and quality of the software supporting documentation provided should also be evaluated. The amount of vendor support, including training and consulting provided as part of the purchase price, should be determined. If additional training and consulting can also be obtained, then their costs must be specified. The responsibility of the vendor for maintaining the system and the cost of this service must also be established.

Evaluation of Candidate Packages

The RFP is sent to the short list of qualified vendors. Their responses generate massive volumes of information that must be evaluated to determine the gaps between the company's needs (as specified by the requirements) and the capabilities of the proposed application packages.

One way to organize the information collected is to set up a table with the criteria listed on the left and a column for each candidate package (see Table 12-2). Each package can then be evaluated relative to each criterion, using either numbers (say 1 through 10) or words (outstanding, good, average, poor, bad). If numbers are used, each criterion can also be assigned an importance weight, and a weighted score can be computed for each package. These scores may not determine the decision, but they provide useful input to the decision makers creating a short list.

Choosing the Package

Once a short list has been prepared, negotiations can begin with vendors to determine how their packages might be modified to remove any discrepancies with the company's desired EC application. Thus, one of the most important factors in the

TABLE 12-2

Part of a Form for Evaluating a Vendor				
Criteria	**Weights**	**System A**	**System B**	**System C**
Support for Java standards				
XML				
SSL				
Shopping cart				
Catalogs				
Taxation				
Personalization				
. . .				

decision is the additional development effort that may be required to tailor the system to the company's needs or to integrate it into the company's environment. If modification of the code is required, who will do it and what will it cost? If the system is modified, who is responsible for maintenance?

The decision to purchase a system is more than a choice of the best of the available systems. The use of packaged software is likely to require more compromises than a custom system. Thus, people are likely to have to adapt to the software—there will often be significant changes in how they do their jobs. Unless there is a commitment to making the necessary changes, the system will likely fail. Before completing the decision, the project team should verify that:

1. the users of the system support the decision to buy the selected package and agree that they will make it work, and
2. the IS people who will support the system agree that the system will work in their environment and that they can support it satisfactorily.

Contract Negotiation

The contract with the software vendor is very important. Not only does it specify the price of the software, but it determines the type and amount of support to be provided by the vendor. The contract will be the only recourse if the system or the vendor does not perform as specified. Furthermore, if the vendor is modifying the software to tailor it to the company's needs, the contract must include detailed specifications (essentially the requirements) of the modifications. Also, the contract should describe in detail the acceptance tests the software package must pass.

Contract negotiations should be an integral part of the purchase process. When negotiating with the vendors to determine how to reduce the discrepancies between the company's needs and the capabilities of the packages, one is effectively negotiating a contract with the successful vendor. Although most people view negotiating a contract as a process of reaching an understanding, it is very important to identify misunderstandings so they can be dealt with in the contract, or they may cause serious problems later.

Power is an important aspect of negotiating, and a company's major power source is the ability to purchase another vendor's package. Thus, any concessions from the vendor must be negotiated before making a final decision on which package to buy. The company's bargaining power evaporates when the vendor finds out that his package has been chosen.

Contracts are legal documents, and they can be quite tricky—experienced contract negotiators and legal assistance may be needed. Many organizations have software purchasing specialists who assist in negotiations and write or approve the contract. They should be involved in the selection process from the start. If an RFP is used, these purchasing specialists may be very helpful in determining its form and in providing boilerplate sections of the RFP.

The EC manager is responsible for defining the requirements for the system and for communicating them to the potential vendors through the RFP. The IS department is usually responsible for assuring that the technical quality of the selected system is satisfactory. The selection of the best package, including the evaluation of responses to the RFP and negotiation with selected vendors to reduce the discrepancies between the needs of the company and the capabilities of the packages, is a joint responsibility of the manager and the IS department.

Modification of the package, if required, is usually done by the vendor, but in some cases the IS department assumes this responsibility. Hopefully, major modifications will not be required, and those that are can be done by the vendor.

Contract negotiations are primarily the responsibility of the EC manager and/or the IS department.

Service Level Agreements

Service level agreements (SLAs) are formal agreements regarding the division of work between a company and its vendors. Such divisions are based on a set of agreed upon milestones, quality checks, "what-if" situations, how checks will be made, and what is to be done in cases of disputes. If the vendor is to meet its objectives of installing EC applications, it must develop and deliver support services to meet these objectives. An effective approach to managing SLAs must achieve both facilitation and coordination. Service level agreements do this by (1) defining the partners' responsibilities, (2) providing a framework for designing support services, and (3) allowing the company to retain as much control as possible over their own systems.

An approach based on SLA offers several advantages. First, it reduces "finger pointing" by clearly specifying responsibilities. When an EC project malfunctions, everyone knows who is responsible for fixing it. Second, it provides a structure for the design and delivery of support services by the vendor (e.g., training).

Establishing SLA requires four steps:

1. Defining levels.
2. Dividing computing responsibility at each level.
3. Designing the details of the service levels.
4. Implementing service levels.

The process of establishing and implementing SLA may be applied to each vendor and each of the *major* computing resources: hardware, software, people, data, networks, and procedures—in each project handled by vendors.

Conclusion

The preceding approach was discussed in the context of acquiring a software package, usually for medium to large EC projects. However, the same general methods can employed when choosing a systems integrator to help put together your EC application (e.g., KPMG, CSC, Accenture, etc.), a hardware platform (e.g., Sun, HP, IBM, etc.), and/or choosing an ASP to host your system.

12.13   SITE MANAGEMENT AND USAGE ANALYSIS

Both B2C and B2B Web sites require a thorough understanding of the usage patterns of their sites—the who, what, where, when, and how. Fortunately, every time a user accesses a Web server, the server logs the transaction in a special access **log file. Access logs** are text files. Each line of the file details an individual access. Regardless of the type of Web server, access logs use a common log file format. A typical entry appears as *somewhere.com*-[18/Aug/2001:12:00:0010000] "GET/a.htm HTTP/1.0" 200 15000 where:

- *somewhere.com* is the name of the system making the request
- -[18/Aug/2001:12:00:0010000] is the time of the request
- GET is the type of request and a.htm is the page requested
- 200 is a return code indicating an accepted request
- 15000 is the size of the file in bytes

Access logs can tell you which pages are most popular, which times are most popular, which geographical regions make the most requests, and other interesting tidbits that help site administrators maintain and refine their sites.

Because log files can become quite voluminous, it is hard to analyze the accesses by hand. For this reason, most Web server vendors provide "free" software for analyzing access log files. There are also commercial products that provide more sophisticated log analyses. Included are products such as:

- net.Analysis from net.Genesis (*netgen.com*)
- Insight from Accrue (*accrue.com*)
- WebTrends Log Analyzer from Web Trends Corporation (*webtrends.com*)

Let's see how usage pattern information is used.

Implementation of Evaluation Devices

Long before the emergence of Internet technology, direct marketers have been keeping tracks of their potential customers. For instance, they put unique source codes on almost everything, including coupons, catalogs, and postcards they send out to their customers. When those coupons are presented at the point of purchase, the company can keep track of which placement yields customer interest. Similar marketing strategies are applicable on the Internet as well.

Effectiveness of different marketing strategies also needs to be evaluated promptly. For instance, a direct mail campaign may reach a large number of customers but generate few sales. Putting an advertising banner on other Web sites may draw many customers, but few of them place actual orders. In addition, a specific code can be incorporated in the advertising banner to track the Web sites from where customers were referred. An example of the use of ad banners can be found at *onlinegifts.com*.

Collecting and Analyzing Statistics

Understanding what information is available for further analysis is an important issue in marketing research. The data for tracking customer behavior is actually limited and some of it may not be reliable. Here are some statistical measures.

HITS AND PAGEVIEWS

A **hit** is a request for a file received by the server. This includes anything that appears on a page, such as images and sound files, etc. By using a hit counter, it is easy to find out the number of hits on a certain site. On the other hand, **pageviews** offer higher accuracy and count an entire page as a whole instead of every single part on a page separately. Therefore, pageview counts are more informative than that of hits.

What Can You Get from Pageviews?   There are different types of pageviews, namely, pageviews by time bucket, by customers' logging-in status, by visitor's hardware platform, and visitor's host. Different pageviews provide different statistics. Let's look at some.

- **Pageviews by time bucket.** This type of pageview allows frequent review of the number of site accesses. Group pageviews by time bucket also enables the company to ascertain the time slots, such as morning, afternoon, or evening, during which the site is visited by customers.
- **Pageviews by customers' logging-in status.** This information helps determine whether requiring customers to log in is worthwhile or not. For instance, if the number of pageviews of customers who log in is substantially greater than those who do not, the company may find the log-in requirement effective and worthwhile.
- **Pageviews by referrers.** Some customers are drawn or referred to the site by clicking on banners or links in other Web sites. Knowing the source of such referrers is useful for assessing the effectiveness of the location of banners, and customers' interest can also be determined from the nature of the Web site with those banners.
- **Pageviews by visitor's hardware platform, operating system, browser, and/or browser version.** These types of pageviews allow the company to obtain customer information on the hardware platform used (e.g., Macs or PCs) and their browser type (e.g., Internet Explorer or Netscape).
- **Pageviews by visitor's host.** This type of pageview provides information on the customers' host. The site can be reached via hosts such as AOL or other online services.

These and similar measurements can be used for analyzing and improving various marketing and advertisement strategies, as shown in Table 12-3.

Usability

Usability is the measure of the quality of a user's experience when interacting with a product or system—whether a Web site, a software application, mobile technology, or any user-operated device.

Usability is a combination of factors that affects the user's experience with the product or system, including:

Ease of learning	How fast can a user who has never seen the user interface learn it sufficiently well to accomplish basic tasks?
Efficiency of use	Once an experienced user has learned to use the system, how fast can he or she accomplish tasks?
Memorability	If a user has used the system before, can he or she remember enough to use it effectively the next time or does the user have to start over again learning everything?
Error frequency and severity	How often do users make errors while using the system, how serious are these errors, and how do users recover from these errors?
Subjective satisfaction	How much does the user *like* using the system?

TABLE 12-3

Areas of Usage Analysis and Sample Business Questions for Online Stores

Area of Analysis	Business Questions
Overall Store Performance	• What is the sales value for a specific period of time, say, 1 week? • What is the number of customer visits for the day? • What is the store conversion rate of the week? • What is the sales value index for the week?
Advertising	• Which banner ads are pulling in the most traffic? • How many sales are driven by each banner ad? • What products do shoppers select from a particular banner? • What is the conversion rate for each banner ad?
External Referrals (from others to your site)	• Which portal sites are pulling in the most traffic? • Which are generating the most sales? • How many sales are generated by each referral site/ search engine? • What products do shoppers from a particular portal site purchase?
Shopper Segmentation	• How many visitors are from a specific domain? • What is the distribution of first-time vs. repeat shoppers? • What characterizes shoppers of a particular set of products? • What characterizes shoppers who abandon shopping baskets?
Product Grouping	• How much do cross-sells/up-sells contribute to gross revenue? • What are the best performing cross-sell pairs? Worst? • What is the overall conversion rate for cross-sells/up-sells?
Promotions and Recommendations	• How much do promotions contribute to gross revenue? • Which promotions are generating the most sales? • What is the overall conversion rate for promotions? • What is the overall conversion rate for recommendations? • At what levels in site hierarchy are the best promotions located?
Shopping Metaphor	• What generates the most sales value: searching or browsing? • How much does searching contribute to gross revenue? • What is the conversion rate for searching?
Design Features	• What are the features of links customers most frequently click? • What are the features of links customers most frequently buy from? • What parts of pages do customers most frequently buy from? • Do products sell better in the upper-left corner?
Product Assortment	• What are the top sellers for the week? • What is the conversion rate for a particular department? • How is a product purchased: purchase frequency and quantity? • What characterizes the products that end up being abandoned? • How much of the sales of each product are driven by searching?

These and other measures can help in appropriate site design. For more on strategic usability see *esri.com/software/usability and usability.com/umi_what.htm*.

Usability tests include a variety of approaches as shown in the list of performance testing services and vendors (Table 12-4).

Performance Testing	
Service	**Vendor**
Site Performance Testing	Keynote System Service Metrics
Simulated User-Experience Testing	*WebCriteria.com*
Usability Consultants	Creative Good User Interface Engineering
Usability Testing with Surfer Panel	*Vividence.com*

TABLE 12-4

E-Commerce Management Tools

Managing the performance of a Web site is important. Several vendors offer suites of products or individual packages. For example, BMC Corp. (*bmc.com*) offers the following products:

- **Patrol for e-business management.** Includes Patrol for Internet Services for measuring Web response time; Patrol for Firewalls for firewall administration; and Patrol for Microsoft, Open Market, or Netscape application servers.
- **MainView for e-business management.** Includes MainView for WebSphere for managing mainframe-based EC applications; MainView for Network Management for monitoring mainframe network connections; and MainView for Systems Management for systems administration.
- **Service assurance center for e-business.** Includes a combination of methodology, products, and services designed to optimize the performance and availability of business applications.

12.14   THE PROCESS OF STOREFRONT DEVELOPMENT

A storefront strategy needs to be defined before starting the development process. Issues such as the value proposition to customers, differentiation from competition, planned growth, branding, and image are important decisions that affect storefront design activities.

Several solutions for storefront development are now available. For example, Yahoo! Store (*store.yahoo.com*) serves as a good starting point for small/medium size businesses to create their own stores. It offers a fast way to get a storefront up and running quickly at minimal cost and without requiring any hardware or software investments (see Appendix 12A for details). Furthermore, not only does the company get a storefront, but the service fee includes hosting on Yahoo!'s server. A second example is *Bigstep.com* (*bigstep.com*). It renders Web-based storefront-building services similar to that of Yahoo! Store. The distinction is that users are allowed to set up their storefronts at no cost. Fees are charged only for additional features such as a establishing a merchant account. The drawback of such tools is the possible lack of uniqueness and flexibility in the storefront design.

Alternatively, an organization may also develop its own storefront using off-the-shelf software on its own server. This approach allows for adapting the application design to the specific needs of the business and for differentiating the storefront from those of the competitors. This approach, however, is usually more costly, may take longer, and requires some in-house technical expertise not just for installing the required hardware and software, but also for operation and maintenance. An example of this type of solution is Microsoft's Site Server Commerce Edition, which has a built-in wizard that helps users model their own online business processes graphically.

Before choosing the appropriate solution, a number of issues need to be considered in order to generate a list of requirements. The following is a list of questions that need to be addressed in defining requirements.

- **Customers.** Who are the target customers? What are their needs? What kind of marketing tactics should be used to promote the store and attract customers? How can customer loyalty be enhanced?
- **Merchandising.** What kind of products or services will be sold online? Are soft (digitizable) goods or hard goods being sold? Are soft goods downloadable?
- **Sales Service.** Can customers order online? Can they pay online? Can they check the status of their order online? How are customers' inquiries handled? Are warranties, service agreements, and guarantees available for the products? What are the refunding procedures?
- **Promotion.** How are the products and services promoted? How will you attract sales? Are coupons, manufacturer's rebates, or quantity discounts offered? Is cross-selling marketing possible?
- **Transaction processing.** Is transaction processing in real-time? How are taxes, shipping and handling fees, and payments processed? Are all items taxable? What kinds of shipping methods are being offered? What kinds of payment methods, such as checks, credit cards, or cyber cash are accepted? How will order fulfillment be handled?
- **Marketing data and analysis.** What information, such as sales, customer data, and advertising trends, will be collected? How would such information be utilized for future marketing?
- **Branding.** What image should the storefront reinforce? How is the storefront different from those of the competition?

The initial list of requirements should be as comprehensive as possible. It is preferable to validate the identified requirements though focus-group discussions or surveys with potential customers. The requirements can then be prioritized based on the customers' preferences. The final list of prioritized requirements serves as the basis for selecting/customizing the appropriate package or designing a storefront from scratch.

Design Guidelines

The following is a list of some design guidelines.

- **Availability and fast loading.** One of the major advantages of a virtual store is that it allows consumers to shop from anywhere at any time. Such convenience can be undermined if the storefront is not always up and running or it is too slow. Although the number of consumers with broadband Internet connections is increasing, speed remains an important issue, as storefront applications grow hungrier for resources. Simplicity of Web page design is important and unnecessary multimedia should be eliminated.

- **Simplicity of site structure.** Customers should not be provided with too many choices. Research has found that people are normally distracted by an excessive number of choices. The number of options should be limited to around seven or less.
- **Use of a shopping cart.** A shopping cart in a virtual store is similar to the cart in the supermarket. It lets customers get a clear idea of what products they have selected before they check out.
- **Good navigation.** Navigation efficiency is another important issue. Customers should be able to complete the purchase process within three clicks. There should also be clear links among single pages of the site.
- **Globalization.** The World Wide Web, as its name suggests, is internationally available. Customers may come from any corner of the globe. Therefore, it is important for the company to include details on shipping and handling for nonlocal customers. Different language options should also be provided (see Chapter 18).
- **Maximizing ways to order and ways to pay.** Offering a wide range of ordering and payment methods helps increase sales. Ordering options can include online forms, e-mail, fax, phone, or even snail mail. Acceptable payment methods should include credit cards, digital cash, electronic checking, or COD. For B2B there are additional methods (Chapter 8). Security of payments is a must (see Chapter 14 and *visa.com/_gds_mod/fb/merchants/gds/main.html*).
- **Establishing credibility.** It is important to establish customer trust toward the online store. There are a lot of rip-offs and frauds reported about Internet businesses, and they increase rapidly every year.
- **Offering a personalized service.** Personalization can strengthen relationships with customers. It allows the customer to have his or her individual online presence with information that meets his or her specific interests. Other ways of personalization include sending electronic coupons to frequent shoppers and sending customized newsletters. However, these types of services are costly and are therefore usually offered only by big companies.
- **Pre- and postsale support.** Both pre- and postsale support are important customer services (see Chapter 4).
- **Realistic pricing.** Most customers expect online products to have lower prices or at least about the same price as that offered by physical stores. Competitiveness would be weakened if prices were too high.

Now you are ready to go to Appendix 12A and build your own storefront.

12.15   MANAGERIAL ISSUES

The following issues are germane to management:

1. **It is the business issues that count.** When one thinks of the Web, one immediately thinks of the technology. Some of the most successful sites on the Web

rely on basic technologies—freeware Web servers, simple Web page design, and few bells and whistles. What makes them successful is not the technology, but their understanding of how to meet the needs of their online customers.

2. **In-house or outsource?** Many large-scale enterprises are capable of running their own publicly accessible Web sites for advertisement purposes. However, Web sites for online selling may involve complex integration, security, and performance issues. For those companies venturing into such Web-based selling, a key issue is whether the site should be built in-house, thus providing more direct control, or outsourced to a more experienced provider. Outsourcing services, which allow companies to start small and evolve to full-featured functions, are available through many ISPs, telecommunication companies, Internet malls, and software vendors who offer merchant server and EC applications.

3. **Consider an ASP.** The use of ASPs is a must for SMEs and should be considered by many large companies as well. However, care must be used in selecting a vendor due to the newness of the concept.

4. **Do a detailed EC architecture study.** Some companies rush this process, and this can be a big mistake. If the high-level conceptual planning is wrong, the entire project is at great risk.

5. **Security and ethics.** During the application development process, close attention must be paid to security. It is likely that vendors and business partners will be involved. Protecting customers' privacy is a must and the issue of what and how to use clickstream data is essential.

6. **Choosing a vendor/software.** Management should take the time and expense to obtain the appropriate components and/or applications. Do not compromise quality and be ready to spend time. EC applications can be ruined quickly if the wrong application is developed. All it may take is one bad component to cause a major disaster.

Summary

In this chapter, you learned about the following EC issues as they relate to the learning objectives:

1. **The landscape of EC application development.** The landscape is very diversified. One starts with the EC architecture before the development process is selected. The decision on how to develop the application is lengthy and complex. Once the application is developed, it needs to be tested, integrated, and deployed. Difficulties arise due to the need to work with many business partners.

2. **The functional requirements for online trading.** Just like their physical counterparts, online stores must provide the means to search for and compare products, to select products, to place and confirm orders, to pay for products, to verify credit, to process orders, to verify shipments, and to provide postsale support. Electronic catalog and merchant server software allow businesses to create simple, straightforward electronic storefronts. For every EC there is a large list of necessary functionalities.

3. **EC architecture.** A six-step process may seem lengthy, but it is essential. It helps to evaluate the EC strategy and the selection of development approach, vendors, and software.

4. **Application strategy options.** Several major options exist: buy, lease, use a third-party product, go into partnership, or use a combination of these. Each approach has pluses and minuses. A large number of criteria must be considered.

5. **The major activities in system analysis and design.** Basically, these include the execution of the EC architecture, performing a requirement analysis, evaluating feasibility, and assessing resources and integration issues.

6. **Role of ASPs.** ASPs play a major role in SMEs that cannot do the job by themselves or cannot afford to purchase expensive systems. ASPs may be risky due to the possibility of the ASP going out of business or because of their use of subcontractors.

7. **Web catalogs and other components.** Many development efforts use components, so it is important to understand the basic ones, starting with catalogs. These components are usually produced by different vendors and need to be integrated.

8. **Connecting EC applications.** Applications must be connected inside the company as well as with business partners. This can be done with EAI middleware.

9. **Web site usability and management.** A number of tools are available that allow administrators to measure what is going on a Web site and monitor how it is being used. Web usability is also evaluated in order to improve marketing, advertising, and trading.

10. **Storefront development process.** A simple site can be developed quickly using the hosting vendor's software, but it is necessary to follow many steps. Even simple software can be fairly powerful.

Key Terms

Access log	Enterprise Application Integration (EAI)
Application portfolio	Hit
Application servers	Insourcing
Application service provider (ASP)	Integration servers
Architecture	Internet telephony
Components	Joint application development (JAD)
Chat group	Latency
Chat rooms	Log file
Clickstream data	Merchant server
Commerce system providers (CSP)	Online forums
Component-based development	Pageviews
Data hiding	Service level agreement (SLA)
EC architecture	Storefront
Electronic catalogs	Throughput
Electronic Shopping Carts	Usability (of a Web site)
Encapsulation	Webcasting

Questions for Review

1. Define application development.
2. List the EC development options.
3. Describe an ASP.
4. List the primary functions of a storefront.
5. List the functional requirements of e-procurement.
6. Define EC architecture and list the six-step development process.
7. Define EC component-based development approach.
8. Define JAD and list its objectives.
9. Define Web usability.

Questions for Discussion

1. Discuss the advantages of a lease option over a buy option.
2. Relate component-based development to enterprise application integration (EAI).
3. Why is simplicity the key to the success of an online store?
4. A large company with a number of products wants to start selling on the Web. Should they use a merchant server or an electronic suite? Assuming they elect to establish an electronic storefront, how would you determine whether the company should outsource the site or run it themselves?
5. A computer hardware company that sells to other high-tech companies wants to jazz up their electronic catalog with Webcasting. What sorts of streaming audio and video might they try? In general, would this make sense for the company?
6. Discuss the role of developing an architecture for EC systems.
7. How can companies use chat groups to support and improve customer service?
8. In what ways do you think a Web site's log files violate your privacy? Explain.
9. Compare EC architecture with infrastructure.
10. Discuss why software selection is a multidimensional process and how a unified solution can be achieved.

Internet Exercises

1. Netcraft (*netcraft.com*) conducts regular surveys of the types of Web servers on the Internet. Access Netcraft's Web site and examine their services.
   - Use their Explore facility to determine what type of server is being used either by your school or place of work.
   - How is their survey conducted and what are some of the problems they encounter in doing the survey?
   - They also conduct a survey of SSL servers. What types of information does this survey provide and who might use the survey results?
2. Access the Choice Mall Web site (*choicemall.com*). Visit some of the online stores in the mall.
   - What are the functionalities of the mall?
   - What are some of the benefits of online malls to the participating vendor? To shoppers?

- Do you think a shopper is better off using a mall or using a search site like AltaVista to locate a store providing a product of interest?
- In what ways could Choice Mall improve the chances that buyers will make return visits?

3. Visit a large online storefront of your choice. What functions does it provide to shoppers? In what ways does it make shopping easy? In what ways does it make shopping more enjoyable? What support services does it provide?

4. Open Market (*openmarket.com*) is a vendor of EC software. At their site they provide demonstrations illustrating the types of storefronts they can create for shoppers. They also provide demonstrations of how their software is used to create a store.
- Run either the Shopsite Merchant or Shopsite Pro demonstration to see how these tools help build a storefront.
- What sorts of features are provided by Shopsite?
- Does Shopsite support larger or smaller stores?
- What other products does Open Market offer for creating online stores? What types of stores do these products support?

5. Log files provide a number of details about visitors to a Web site. Select a commercial product (such as net.Analysis) that offers log file analysis. What types of information does the product provide, and how can this information be used to improve a Web site?

6. Visit *tibco.com* and find out how they provide B2B connectivity.

7. Visit *Microsoft.com* and find BizConnect. What kind of software is this? How can it be a component in a EC application?

8. Enter *hotwired.lycos.com/webmonkey* and find the tracking tutorials. Write a summary of the three tutorials (gathering data, using databases, and using pageviews.)

9. Enter *dKg.net* and choose shopping cart, and *bigstep.com* and examine their store-building software. Compare its capabilities to that of *store.yahoo*.

10. Visit *ichat.com* and review their chat rooms and pager. Download the support software (it is free), try it, and describe your experiences.

11. Enter *ecommerce.internet.com*. Find the product review area. Read reviews of three payment solutions. Assess them as possible components.

12. Enter *intershop.com*. Locate information about their products. Is this an EC suite? Why or why not? If it is not a suite, what is it?

13. Enter *ibm.com/software*. Find their WebSphere product. Read recent customers' success stories. What makes this software so popular?

Team Assignments and Role Playing

1. Select a series of Web sites catering to the same type of buyer. For instance, several Web sites that offer CDs or computer hardware. Divide the sites among teams and ask them to prepare an analysis of the different sorts of functions provided by the sites along with a comparison of the strong and weak points of each site from the buyer's perspective.

2. Several vendors offer products for creating online stores. The Web sites of these vendors usually list those online stores using their software (customer stories).

Assign vendors to each team. Have the teams prepare reports comparing the similarities and differences among the sites and evaluating the customers' success stories. Do the customers take advantage of the functionality provided by the various products?

3. Create teams to explore desired capabilities of various EC applications (B2B, B2C, auctions, portals G2C, etc.). Ask each team to expand on the functionalities listed in Section 12.3.

REAL-WORLD CASE: Whirlpool's Trading Portal

Whirlpool (*whirlpool.com*) is a world leader in manufacturing and marketing of major home appliances. Competing in a $75 billion annual, global market the company considers its distributors and partners to be critical players in its continual quest to maintain industry leadership. This being the case, it is in Whirlpool's best interests to operate with utmost efficiency while providing top-notch service to members of its selling chain.

Until recently, providing outstanding service was no problem. But Whirlpool's other processing methods, particularly for its middle-tier trade partners—which comprise 25 percent of its total partner base—were inefficient and costly in time and money. These are the sellers who generate 10 percent of the company's revenue, but aren't large enough to have dedicated, system-to-system connections with Whirlpool, so they typically submitted orders by phone or fax.

Wanting to infuse greater efficiency into this process, Whirlpool turned to EC, developing a B2B trading partner portal that enables these sellers to order online. To make the portal work, the company needed to integrate it with its SAP R/3 inventory system and Tivoli systems management tools. Whirlpool conducted a vendor and product analysis and decided to use IBM.

Following the guidelines of the IBM Application Framework for e-business, Whirlpool built its portal with the IBM WebSphere Application Server, Advanced Edition, IBM *Net.commerce* (new part of the IBM WebSphere Commerce Suite family), IBM HTTP Server, IBM VisualAge for Java, and IBM Commerce Integrator with IBM MQSeries.

Working in concert, these tools have enabled a fast, easy Web self-service ordering process that has cut the cost per order to under $5—a saving of at least 80 percent. Whirlpool has also gained an unexpected benefit—an extendable EC platform that it leveraged for other applications.

IBM e-business solutions run on several different platforms that scale from the very small to the very large. When you have that level of scalability as well as flexibility, you get a powerful system.

Exceeding expectations. Through the portal, called Whirlpool Web World, several thousand middle-tier trade partners select the goods they want to order by checking off the appropriate SKUs and indicating quantities. Aside from appliance ordering, they can also log on to the password-protected site to track the status of their orders.

By going with a B2B portal, Web-based ordering become easier for both trading partners. Before, it was very cumbersome, costly, and time-consuming to service this level of trading partners.

Whirlpool's B2B portal is actually in its second generation (summer 2001). The first-generation portal was developed with low-level products, giving the company a chance to test the Web waters. However, it took off faster than the company had expected. In its first three months, the amount of revenue that flowed through the portal was what they planned for the first 12 months. The investment paid for itself in eight months.

A platform for now and the future

With the success of its first-generation trading partner portal, Whirlpool was ready to migrate the solution to a bigger, more scalable and easier-to-manage platform. At the same time, the company was also implementing SAP R/3 for order entry. So, it was important for its second-generation portal to integrate with SAP R/3.

The company wanted to partner with a vendor that would be around a while, so they checked out IBM and a few others. IBM was the choice because IBM has worked with Whirlpool on joint product development as well as with Whirlpool's ERP system design and architecture. And, when Whirlpool talked to financial analysts, they found that an overwhelming number of Fortune 100 companies use IBM e-business solutions. Finally, Whirlpool saw that IBM is on top of industry Web standards like Java and XML, which provide the development flexibility that enables growth in this space.

After committing to IBM, Whirlpool also decided to develop its e-business platform following the Application Framework for e-business, taking advantage of its rapid development

cycles and associated cost reductions. There are features that come out of the box in the current suite of IBM tools that, a year an a half earlier, Whirlpool tried to build by themselves. This enabled Whirlpool to bring applications to market much faster.

Questions for the case

1. Why can Whirlpool bring their application to market faster now?

2. From a Whirlpool point of view, what kind of a B2B application is this: e-procurement, sell-side, collaborative commerce, or other? Justify your answer.

3. What segments of the supply chain are influenced directly by this system and how?

4. Enter *ibm.com/software* and find more about the latest capabilities of WebSphere that are relevant to this case.

5. How is the back office connected to the front office in this case?

6. How can Whirlpool leverage this application with others?

REFERENCES AND BIBLIOGRAPHY

Allen, P. and S. Frost. *Component-Based Development for Enterprise Systems.* Cambridge, United Kingdom: Cambridge University Press, 1998.

Bass, S. "Internet Phones Take on Ma Bell," *PC World Online* (June 1997).

Brohan, M. "Code Red: Why System Overloads and Crashes Have CIOs Scrambling," *EC Technology News* (May 2000).

Cannataro, M. and D. Pascuzzi. "A Component-Based Architecture for Development and Deployment the WAP-Compliant Transactional Services," *Proceedings, 34th HICSS,* Hawaii (January 2001).

Cohan, P. S. *E-Profit: High-Payoff Strategies for Capturing E-Commerce Edge.* (Part III:

Building E-Commerce Infrastructure). New York: Amacom, 2000.

Cross, K. "The Ultimate Enablers: Business Partners," *Business 2.0* (January 2000).

Danish, S. and P. Gannon. *Database Driven Web Catalogs.* New York: McGraw-Hill, 1998.

Data Base. "Developing E-Commerce Systems: Current Practices and State of Art," *Data Base,* Special issue (December 2001).

Davis, J. "Mall Rats," *Business 2.0* (January 1999).

DeWire, D. *Thin Clients: Delivery Information over the Web,* New York: McGraw Hill, 1998.

Duvall, M. "Integrators Make B2B Exchanges Easier," *Interactive Week* (March 27, 2000).

Elderbrock, D. and N. Borwanker. *Building Successful Internet Business*. Foster City; CA: IDG Books, 1996.

Gordijn, J., et al. "Scenario Methods for Viewpoint Integration in E-Business Requirements Integration," *Proceedings, 34th HICSS,* Hawaii (January 2000).

Jell, T., ed. *Component-Based Software Engineering* (Managing Object Technology Series, No 10), Cambridge, Massachusetts: SIGS Books/Cambridge Press, 1998.

Jestfeld, M. and A. de Moor. "Concept Integration Proceeds Enterprise Integration," *Proceedings, 34th HICSS,* Hawaii (January 2001).

Juul, N. and C. Loebbecke. "Commercial E-Commerce Servers and Enterprise Application Integration: A Case-Base Comparison of Net Commerce and Site Serve Commerce," *Proceedings, 34th HICSS,* Hawaii (January 2001).

Kendall, K. E. and J. E. Kendall. *Systems Analysis and Design*, 4th ed. Upper Saddle River, New Jersey: Prentice Hall, 1999.

Kern, T. and J. Kreijger. "An Exploration of the ASP Outsourcing Option," *Proceedings, 34th HICSS,* Hawaii (January 2001).

Kirtland, M. *Designing Component-Based Applications*. Redmond, Washington: Microsoft Press, 1998.

Koontz, C. "Develop a Solid E-Commerce Architecture," *e-Business Advisor* (January 2000).

Kreijger, T. K. "An Exploration of the ASP Outsourcing Option," *Proceedings, 34th HICSS,* Hawaii (January 2001).

Linthicum, D. S. *B2B Application Integration: e-Business-Enable Your Enterprise*. Reading, Massachusetts: Addison Wesley, December 2000.

Loshin, P. *Extranet Design and Implementation*. San Francisco, California: Sybex Network Press, 1997.

Maddox, K. *Web Commerce*. New York: John Wiley & Sons, 1998.

Marakas, G. *System Analysis and Design: An Active Approach*. Upper Saddle River, New Jersey: Prentice Hall, 2001.

Martin, E. W., et al. *Managing Information Technology*. Upper Saddle River, New Jersey: Prentice Hall, 2000.

McKeen, J. D. and H. A. Smith. "Managing External Relationships in IS," *Proceedings, 34th HICSS,* Hawaii (January 2001).

Minoli, D. and E. Minoli. *Web Commerce Technology Handbook*. New York: McGraw-Hill, 1998.

Mullich, J. "Web Site Development: Back Home," *Internetweek* (January 10, 2000).

Niederst, J. *Learning Web Design*, Cambridge, MA: O'Reilly and Associates, 2001.

Novak, J. and P. Markiewicz. *Guide to Producing Live Webcasts*, New York: Wiley, 1998.

Pffafenberger, B. *Building a Strategic Internet*. Foster City, California: IDG Books, 1998.

Puschmann, T. and R. Alt. "Enterprise Application Integration—The Case of Robert Bosch Group," *Proceedings, 34th HICSS,* Hawaii (January 2001).

Reynolds, J. *The Complete E-Commerce Book: Design, Build and Maintain Web-Based Business*. Gilroy, California: CMP Books, 2000.

Scharl, A. *Evolutionary Web Development*. London: Springer, 2000.

Schwarz, E. "V-Commerce: The Next Frontier," *InfoWorld* (December 14, 1998).

Scoresby, K. "Get the Best Usability Expertise," *e-Business Advisor* (July 2000).

Sharman, V. and R. Sharma. *Developing E-Commerce Sites: An Integrated Approach*. Boston, Massachusetts: Addison-Wesley, 2000.

Sliwa, C. "Plot Your B2B Integration," *Computerworld* (January 1, 2001).

Szuprowicz, B. *Extranet and Intranet: E-Commerce Business Strategies for the Future*. Computer Technology Research Corp., *itworks.be/reports* (1998).

Treese, G. W. and L. C. Stewart. *Designing Systems for Internet Commerce*. Reading, Massachusetts: Addison-Wesley, 1998.

Valacich, J., et al. *Essentials of Systems Analysis and Design*, 2nd ed. Upper Saddle River, New Jersey: Prentice Hall, 2001.

Ward, L. "How ASPs Can Accelerate Your E-Business," *e-Business Advisor* (March 2000).

Weir, J. "A Web/Business Intelligence Solution," *Information Systems Management* (Winter 2000).

Whitten, J., et al. *Systems Analysis and Design Methods*, 5th ed. New York: Irwin/McGraw-Hill, 2000.

BUILDING AN APPLICATION WITH YAHOO! STORE*

HOW TO SET UP A VIRTUAL STORE WITH YAHOO!

Yahoo! Store (*store.yahoo.com*), provided by Yahoo!, is one of the most inexpensive storefront services currently available. It is a good choice for small to medium businesses as users can easily set up their storefronts in a few hours with several predesigned templates provided by Yahoo! Store. The software is free for 10 days. Furthermore, a store created with Yahoo! Store will immediately be launched as part of the Yahoo! Shopping site and subscribed to its search engine once the business is ready to open.

The monthly charge for a Yahoo! Store is $100 for 50 items or less and $300 for up to 1,000 items. No setup fee is required in either case (prices valid as of December 2000).

DIFFERENT FEATURES OF YAHOO! STORE

The table below lists the features that Yahoo! Store supported as of December 2000. Each feature will be discussed in greater detail later in this section.

FEATURES	YAHOO! STORE
Maximum number of products	18,000 in largest site
Own domain name	Available
External product search	Available (on Yahoo! Shopping)
Store products search engine	Available
Database upload	Available
Graphic upload	Available (automatic thumbnails)
Product display flexibility	Available
Soft goods	Available (downloadable feature)
Product options (e.g., size, color, etc.)	Available
Web pages	Static
Computation of invoice pricing	Available
Setting products as specials	Available
Quantity pricing	Automatic

* This appendix was developed by Carmen Wong, City University of Hong Kong.

FEATURES	YAHOO! STORE
Cross-selling	Available
Tax calculation	Auto calculation by state from table. Real-time CGI available.
Computation of shipping charges	Auto calculation from price or weight tables, from UPS calculator, or real-time CGI.
Order tracking by customer and merchant	Available (to store manager only)
Merchant order notification	Available (by e-mail or fax)
Inventory management	Not available (only able to display availability status on site)
Traffic and sales reports	Available (to store manager only)
Merchant credit card account required	Available
Payment gateway	Included
Initial set-up costs	None
Hosting fees	—$100 per month for up to 50 products; —$300 per month for up to 1,000 products. An additional $100/month is charged for each additional 1,000 products.
Transaction fees	None

FEATURES OF THE YAHOO! STORE

Creating Your Own Store

There are three prerequisites for creating an online store with Yahoo! Store.

1. A computer with a Web browser and Internet access.
2. A Yahoo! identification number. Application for this ID can be done at *store.yahoo.com* (refer to Figure 12A-1).
3. A merchant account for processing credit card payments. This can be applied for through Bank One via Yahoo!. Such an account is only necessary for business start-up and is not essential during the stage of creating a store.

STEP 1: Log In or Register for a Yahoo! Account
To build a site, go to the Yahoo! Store home page (*store.yahoo.com*) and log in. If you already have a Yahoo! Store account, type your identification number and password in the boxes on the left-hand side (see Figure 12A-1). If you do not have a Yahoo! account, you may obtain one by clicking on the link "*Sign Up Here.*"

STEP 2: Create a Store
Once you are in, click on the link "*Create a Store*" (see Figure 12A-2) and fill in the name and ID for your store. The ID will act as the site address for your virtual store and, therefore, it must be a unique one. For instance, if you choose *hotfashion* as your ID, then your future store address will look like this: *store.yahoo.com/hotfashion*.

Figure 12A-1	Logging In and Registering for a Yahoo! Account

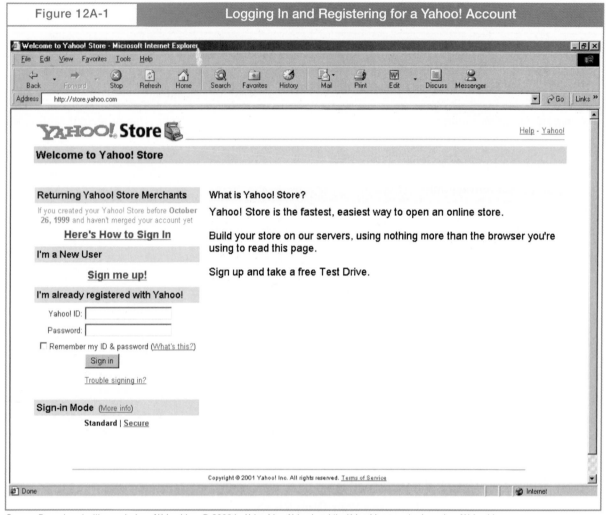

You may create more than one Yahoo! Store with the same user ID and password as long as you give a different store ID to each Yahoo! Store you create. The store will be valid for 10 days.

STEP 3: Take a Short Guided Tour

Next, Yahoo! Store will take you through a short guided tour (Figure 12A-3) to introduce you to the different essential steps to set up the store. The tour will take only a few minutes. Remember, do not click on the Back or Reload buttons during the tour.

Front Page Design

Once you get into your store, you will reach the front page and see four items (refer to Figure 12A-4). The name of your store will appear in the left-hand corner of the screen. There will also be a button bar on the left side; these buttons are called *navigation buttons.* Additional buttons at the bottom of the screen are known as the *edit buttons.*

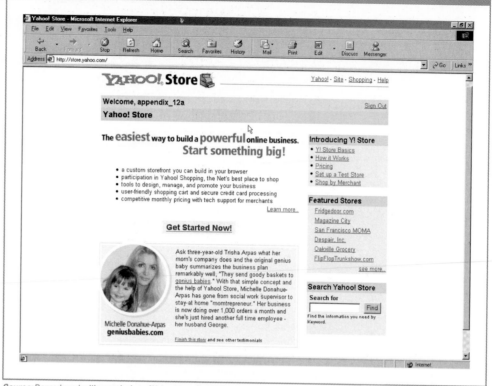

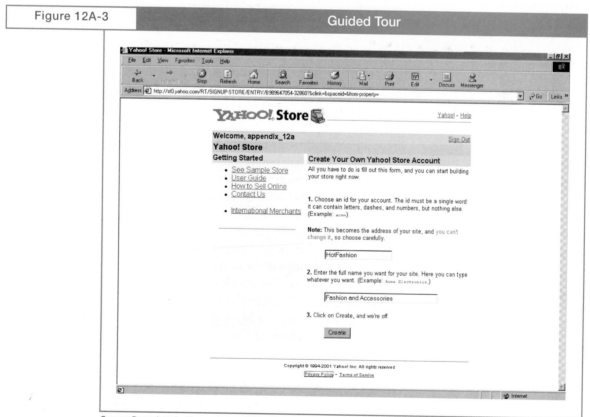

Figure 12A-4	Store Front Page

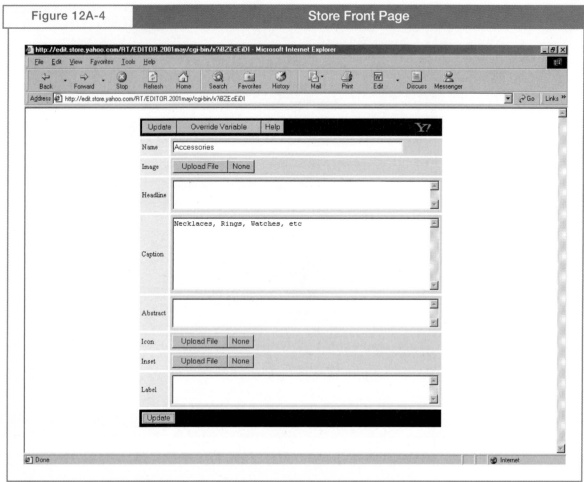

Sections and Items

There are three different types of pages within the simple interface: the *front page, section page,* and *item page.*

Items are the individual products available for sale, whereas sections are categories of similar items. For instance, our online store sells clothes and accessories and we want to add a Disney necklace as one of the items. First, we will need to set up a section called *Accessories* and include several items under it, such as *necklace, bracelet,* and *earrings.* It should be noted that an item page looks different from the section page. In the item page, an enlarged image of the item can be found with a detailed description as well as an order button for placing an online order. A section page contains a series of links to different items, and the size of the item image is also diminished.

The *help button* shows a list of definitions for the edit buttons.

STEP 4: Create a Section

To create a section, you should click on *new section* on the edit button row at the bottom of the front page. You will then see a page containing two fields: Name and Caption. Into the Name field, enter a name such as Accessories for the section you want to create. Additional descriptions of the section can be entered in the caption field (see Figure 12A-5). These changes can be saved by clicking on the *Update* but-

Figure 12A-5	Creating a Section

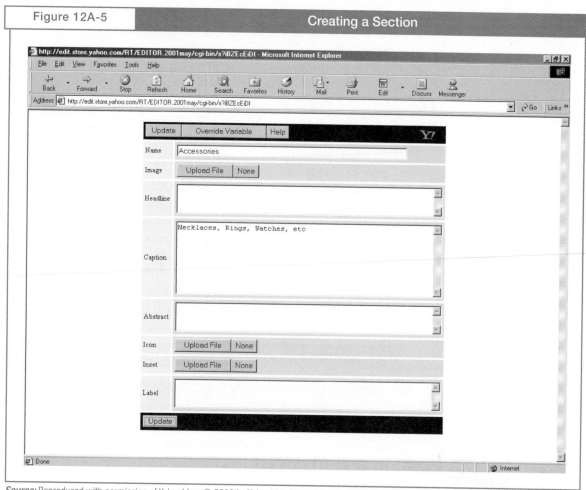

ton in the top left-hand corner. You will now see your new section named as Accessories directly below the name of the store.

STEP 5: Add an Item

Next, we will add an item under this section. Click on *New Item;* you will see a total of four fields on this page: *Name, Code, Price,* and *Caption.* The name of the item such as "necklace," is entered into the name field. The code field is where you fill in your item's SKU, stock number, ISBN, or any other code (such as CA123) to identify the particular product. The selling price is entered in the price field. Although filling in the dollar sign is optional, it is recommended that you state clearly the currency in the caption field. This allows you to put in descriptive text for the item. Similarly, these changes are saved by clicking on *Update.* There is no upper limit for the number of items to be included under one section.

STEP 6: Upload an Image

A product image or picture can be uploaded to the store by going to an item page and clicking on the Image button. Such uploading can only be done with Netscape 2.0 (or higher versions) or Microsoft Internet Explorer 3.0 or higher.

To select the image file to be uploaded, click on the Browse button to locate the file in your local disk drive through the pop-up window. Larger image files require more time. When the target file is found, click on the Send button to upload it to the store. Accordingly an image can be seen on the related item page (refer to Figure 12A-6).

STEP 7: Publish Your Store

The most crucial step of setting up an online store is to make it visible to your customers. Such visibility can be achieved by clicking on the Publish button on the front page.

Go to the front page of your Yahoo! Store. On the list of edit buttons, click the last button, the Publish button. The button changes to "published" to confirm that the store can be visited via the Internet. The URL for this illustration is *store.yahoo.com/hotfashion*.

STEP 8: Place a Test Order

Orders can be placed by clicking on the Order button on each item page unless there is a corporate firewall that prevents you from ordering. All items selected would be taken to a shopping cart that functions in the same way as a supermarket cart. There is no limit on the number of items placed into the shopping cart and you can always pick additional items by clicking on the Keep Shopping button.

When shopping is completed, you may click on *Check Out* to proceed with filling in the order form. Essential information to input includes name, shipping and billing addresses, and credit card numbers if payment method is set to be credit

Figure 12A-6   Item Page

cards. An order number (starting with the number 485 by default) is assigned to a valid and complete order form.

STEP 9: Retrieve an Order

There are several ways for the site manager to retrieve an order. The manager may export the orders to external database software, such as Microsoft Access or Excel, or may have Yahoo! fax the orders (note this feature is only available to companies located in North America). Alternatively, orders can also be reviewed on the Internet.

To view orders online, you must log in as a *store manager* (Figure 12A-7); an editing page will be displayed with functions and settings that can be modified. By default, Yahoo! Store will automatically put an asterisk next to *Order* when there are unread orders. Order status can be reviewed by clicking on the order link.

You may choose to save the order to your hard disk or print a hard copy. Orders received previously will be stored in the server for several months. However, the credit card numbers on the orders should be deleted for security purposes after they have been on Yahoo!'s server for 10 days.

STEP 10: Add Introductory Text

Many stores have an introductory paragraph about the site. This paragraph can be added by clicking on the Edit button on the front page. The Message field

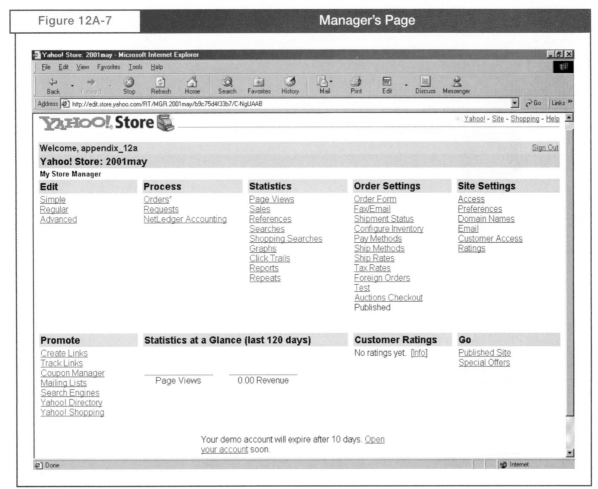

Figure 12A-7   Manager's Page

allows you to enter the introduction and multiple paragraphs can be set by separating each of them with blank lines. These changes can be saved by clicking on the Update button.

STEP 11: Create a Special Item

More attention can be attracted if special items are put on the front page and seen by every visitor to the site. This can be done by clicking on the Special button at the bottom of the item page.

> **STEP 11A:** Go to the item page and click on the sixth edit button from the left (list the Special button). You will see a thumbnail version of the image (if any), together with the name and price of the item (refer to Figure 12A-8) on the front page.
>
> **STEP 11B:** To remove the special item, go back to the item page and click on the sixth button on the edit button list (not the Special button). To keep customers coming back to the site, it is recommended that the items on special be changed regularly, or frequently, if possible.

Follow Step 11A again if you want to put up any other specials for your online store.

STEP 12: Edit Variables

The overall properties of your site can be edited by clicking on *Variables,* an option available on every page. Once changes are made under Variables, every single page

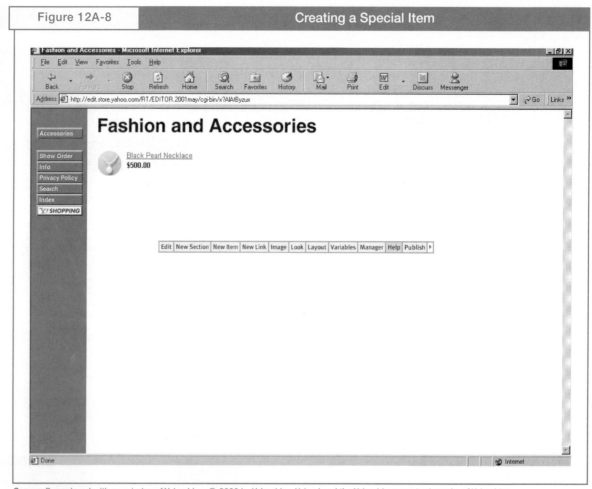

Figure 12A-8   Creating a Special Item

in the site will be changed accordingly. However, unique properties can be created if you have chosen to override the variables on individual pages.

STEP 13: Customize Shipping and Payment Methods

Payment and shipping methods can be customized by first logging onto the account as a store manager and then clicking on Pay Methods under the Order Setting Column. You may select the desired payment method such as Visa and MasterCard by clicking on Yes next to the method. Other forms of payment can also be specified at the bottom such as your store charge card. These changes can be saved by clicking on the Update button (Figure 12A-9).

Customizing shipping methods is also possible by clicking on the type of shipping methods preferred; procedures are similar to those just described.

STEP 14: Use the Regular and Advanced Interface

More features can be added through the Regular interface by clicking on *Regular* under the Edit column.

There are more features, fields, and variables in the Regular interface. Clicking on the small red triangle at the end of the edit button row switches the mode to the Advanced interface, where even more buttons can be found. However, the Advanced interface is suitable for experienced programmers only, because all security

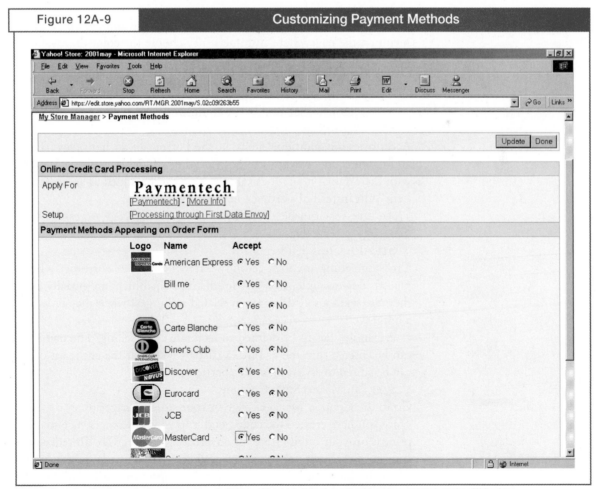

| Figure 12A-9 | **Customizing Payment Methods** |

devices are turned off here. Generally speaking, the Regular interface is adequate for development of most online stores.

STEP 15: Set Discounted Prices and Quantity Pricing

Discounts can be offered by clicking Edit on the item page. There are a number of subfields under the Price field. The marked price, for instance, 100, can be entered in the Price field while the net price after discounts (say, 80) can be entered in the Sales Price field. These changes can be saved by clicking on the Update button.

Quantity discounts can also be set by entering the details into the related field. For example, if a particular item is sold at $10 for one, two for $18, and ten for $90, and so forth, the following numbers should be filled in the Price field:

10 2 18 10 90

STEP 16: Determine Orderable Items

Stock availability can be shown under the Sales Price field by clicking on Yes (for available items) or No (for unavailable items), respectively.

STEP 17: Set the Options Feature

Specification of different colors or sizes can be entered into the Options field. For instance, different colors, such as black, navy blue, or violet, and different sizes, such as XS, S, M, and L can be entered in the following format:

Color: black, navy blue, violet

Size: XS, S, M, L

Each set of options is separated by a blank line and presented as a drop-down menu on the page where customers may choose the color they want (refer to Figure 12A-10).

STEP 17A: Go to the item page, click on the second button on the edit button list (Edit). Under the Options column, type in this format to create two sets of options. Click on Update to finish.

STEP 18: Add an Accessory to an Item

Accessories are additional items at the bottom of an item page. The purpose of adding an accessory is to promote another related item that is closely associated with the original item. For example, a tie can be added as an accessory under the item Shirt instead of starting a new item page for it.

An accessory can be added by clicking on the New Accessory button on any item page (refer to Figure 12A-11).

STEP 19: Cross-Sell Items

Crossing-selling involves selling related items to a customer when orders are placed. For example, in a fast-food shop, customers are usually asked whether they also want a soft drink (item related to burger) when they order and purchase a burger.

A "family" has to be defined to facilitate cross-selling. The name of the family can be entered into the Families variables such that the entire set of related items can be edited to assign them to a particular family.

STEP 20: Make a Store Coupon

Go to the Coupon Manager page in your store manager to create a coupon code. Once you have created the code, send it to your customers via e-mail, display it or print it on your online store, or advertise it on the Web. To redeem the coupon, your customer will only need to input the coupon code on the order form page when checking out. The discount you have specified earlier will be calculated and displayed on the second page of the order form.

Figure 12A-10	Color Choices

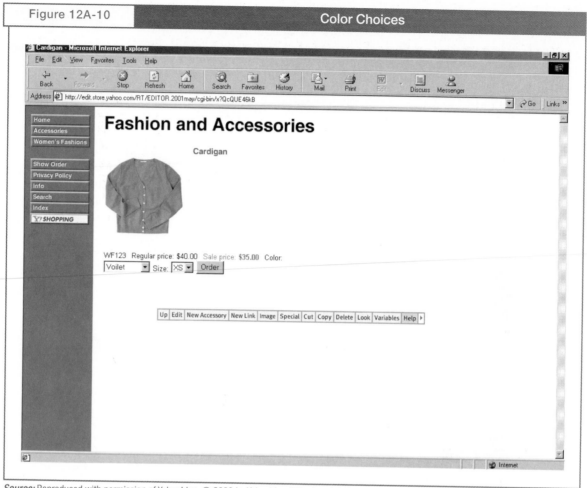

STEP 21: Keep Statistics

Statistics are also available in the Coupon Manager. This allows you to track the effectiveness of your coupon promotions. You may see how many times each coupon is used, and how much revenue is generated from the specific coupons. This information can help you understand what kind of promotion works best for your online store.

STEP 22: Set Shipping and Tax Rates

A shipping and tax wizard is available to help set the shipping and tax rates. The shipping rate can be set by clicking on the Ship Rates link under the Order Setting column and then the Auto Setup Wizard link on the top left of the page. The base country of the store has to be selected before entering the shipping table and the surcharge for international delivery.

Tax rates can be set by following similar procedures with the Auto Setup Wizard under the Tax Rates link and selecting the appropriate tax rates.

STEP 23: Analyze the Statistics

Yahoo! Store offers extensive tracking tools that update statistics once a day. There are different tracking tools including the following:

STEP 23A: Per Page. The Per Page tool shows the page views and income generated for each page. You'll see a thumbnail graph that shows the trend over a

Figure 12A-11	Adding Accessories to an Item

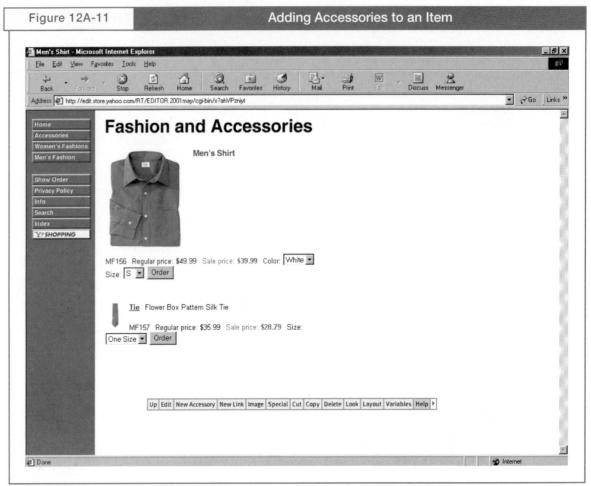

particular period on each line. These graphs are useful in ascertaining which individual page becomes outdated and no longer attractive to visitors.

STEP 23B: Reference. The Reference tool indicates the sites from which customers were referred or linked and how much money they spent on the virtual store.

The actual search keywords entered by visitors and the amount of money they spent using each keyword are available in the Details link under the search engine.

STEP 23C: Search. The Search tool shows the searches done by visitors. It can highlight parts of the site that draw customer interest; parts they expected to be there, but were missing; and parts that were difficult to locate on the site.

STEP 23D: Graphs. The Graphs tool generates graphs of overall trends in the site based on a number of measures such as pageviews, income, and a range of time periods. These graphs are all in .gif format and can be saved to the local disk and imported into applications such as Microsoft Word.

STEP 23E: Click Trails. Paths taken by individual visitors through the site are shown under the Click Trails tool. It indicates the browsing paths of visitors who have placed items in a shopping cart. Note that the statistics saved under this tool last for 60 days only.

STEP 23F: Reports. The Reports tool generates a table that summarizes trends within the site. This report may be exported directly to any database application such as Microsoft Excel.

STEP 23G: Repeat. The Repeat tool tracks customers who revisit the site, sorted by the number of orders. It matches each order with the name of the customer, his/her credit card numbers, and e-mail address.

STEP 24: Determine Other Ways to Retrieve Orders

There are alternative ways to retrieve orders apart from those discussed in the previous section. Orders can be sent to you by fax or e-mail in real time, or exported to database applications such as Quickbooks. Advanced users can have their orders sent to their secure Web server in real time.

STEP 25: Export Orders to Microsoft Access

All tables in the site can be downloaded as a TAR (tape archive) file. In Unix systems, the TAR command can be used to unpack the archive. In Windows, Win Zip can be employed to do so. The number of files exported is limited to 500.

STEP 26: Fax Orders

Yahoo! Store allows up to two fax numbers to send the orders. This service is free if the recipients are within the United States and Canada.

Orders can be faxed without a cover page to the designated numbers daily (8 A.M. and 6 P.M. EST), hourly, or immediately. Each fax has a header such as the following:

Yahoo! Store order hotfashion-675 for HotFashion Company

Yahoo! Store will try dialing up to 50 times at approximate 15-minutes intervals in case the receiving fax machine is out of paper or switched off.

STEP 27: Print Orders

Orders can be printed in only two formats: Postscript and PDF. The printing option is available upon retrieval of orders.

STEP 28: Perform Real-Time Delivery of Orders to Your Secure Web Server

To have real-time delivery of orders, a URL and a format must be specified. It is advisable to use the Yahoo! format, which is a simple CGI script. However, the system also supports the OBI (Open Buying on the Internet) standard for transferring orders.

The Yahoo! format consists of key-value pairs delivered in HTTP POST request to the specified URL. Example keys are Ship-Name, Card-Number, and Item-Description-1. On the other hand, the OBI/1.1 protocol is documented by Open Buying Consortium Orders, and catalog requests are delivered as "OBI Orders" to the URLs specified.

STEP 29: Promote Softgoods

Some storefronts may carry downloadable items for sale on their sites. An example of a downloadable item is software. Yahoo! Store offers a feature that allows a storefront to securely sell downloadable items.

To sell downloadable items, go to the item edit page and upload a file to the Download field specifying a file name for the good to be downloaded.

After ordering a softgood item, the customer can use the Download button on the Order Confirmation page to download the item. Alternatively, the customer can always connect to the Order Status page using the URL from the Order Confirmation e-mail and start to download the product. This can also be done from another computer other than the one where the transaction is conducted.

For free downloadable items, enter the advanced interface and upload your file to the File pages, then create a link to the file by using HTML or the New Link button.

STEP 30: Make a Unique and Outstanding Site

There are a few ways to make a site more outstanding and unique than those created with design templates. Ways to achieve this include modifying the navigation buttons (the section buttons) on the left of the page, customizing appearances of buttons, and displaying specials as thumbnails.

STEP 31: Rearrange the Navigation Buttons

By default, the navigation buttons are listed on the left of the page. Their location can be rearranged by switching the pageformat from sidebuttons to, say, topbuttons.

STEP 32: Conduct Yahoo! Auctions

Yahoo! Auctions is a feature that Yahoo! launched in March 2000 and is free to both buyers and sellers. It allows owners of Yahoo! Stores to participate in the auction platform. Both hot items and hard-to-sell products can be put on sale. This is also a good way to expose products to different customers without the extra costs of marketing or new technology.

STEP 33: Utilize Yahoo! Auction

Products can be linked directly from the Yahoo! Store to Yahoo! Auction by clicking on the Edit button on an item page. When the auction closes, the winning bidder can click directly into the store to check out and complete the transaction.

Multiple items can also be put on auction by using the Yahoo! Auction Bulk Loader option. And now you can build your own store!

Note that there are several other features available. You can view them, and actually build a store, during the guided tour.

13

E-Commerce Security

LEARNING OBJECTIVES

Upon completion of this chapter, the reader will be able to:

- Document the rapid rise in computer and network security attacks.

- Understand the factors contributing to the rise in EC security breaches.

- Explain the basic types of network security attacks.

- Discuss the major steps in developing a security risk management system.

- Describe the major types of attacks against EC systems.

- Discuss some of the major technologies for securing EC.

CONTENT

13.1 BRINGING DOWN AN EC SITE: MERE CHILD'S PLAY

Smurf, Fraggle, Boink, and Teardrop. Kids toys? What about Trinoo, Shaft, mStream and Stacheldraht? Got any ideas? Actually, these are some of the tools that "script kiddies" have used to bring down some of the better-known EC sites. It all began back in February 2000. From February 6 to February 7, *Amazon.com*, *Buy.com*, *CNN.com*, eBay, E*TRADE, Yahoo!, and ZDNet were inundated with so many Internet requests, that legitimate traffic was virtually halted (Kabay and Walsh, 2000) The

combined attacks cost businesses an estimated $1.7 billion. Similar sorts of attacks occurred throughout the year. In January 2001, a number of Microsoft's Web sites—including MSN, MSNBC, Expedia, Hotmail, Carpoint, Homeadvisor, and the Windowsmedia entertainment guide—experienced the same type of outages. Interestingly, that same month a Canadian teenager with the moniker of "Mafiaboy" pled guilty to committing the February attacks (Harrison, 2000).

Technically speaking, all of these sites were the victims of **distributed denial-of-service (DDoS) attacks**. In a **denial-of-service (DoS) attack**, an attacker uses software to send a flood of data packets to the target computer with the aim of overloading its resources. With DDoS, the attacker gains illegal administrative access to as many computers on the Internet as possible. Once an attacker has access to a large number of computers, he or she loads their DDoS software onto these computers. The software lays in wait, listening for a command to begin the attack. When the command is given, this distributed network of computers begins

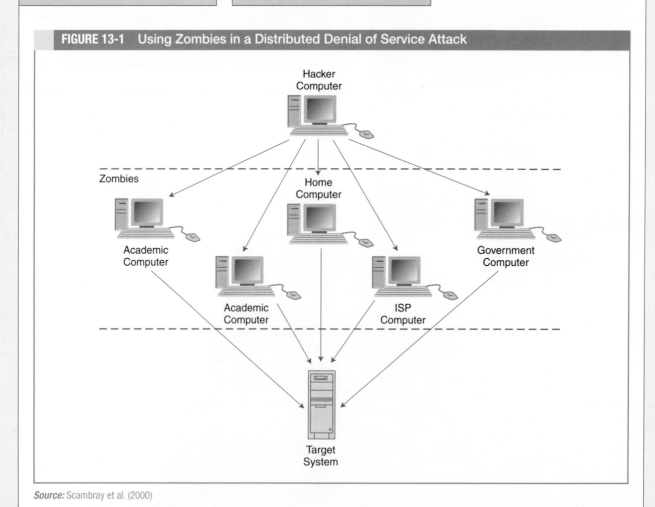

FIGURE 13-1   Using Zombies in a Distributed Denial of Service Attack

Source: Scambray et al. (2000)

13.1 BRINGING DOWN AN EC SITE: MERE CHILD'S PLAY (*CONTINUED*)

sending out requests. There are different types of DDoS attacks. In the simplest case, it is the magnitude of the requests that brings the target computer to a halt.

The machines on which the DDoS software is loaded are known as **zombies** (Heim and Ackerman, 2001). Zombies are often located at university and government sites (Figure 13-1). Increasingly, with the rise of cable modems and DSL modems, home computers that are connected to the Internet and left on all the time have become good zombie candidates. More and more, business Web servers located outside the firewall are also being used in this manner.

DoS attacks are not new. In 1996, a New York ISP had service disrupted for over a week by a DoS attack, denying service to over 6,000 users

and 1,000 companies. At the time, the attacker was considered something of an expert with enough systems knowledge to "spoof" his or her Internet address, making it impossible to determine his or her identify. Today, the intruder population has changed. Due to the widespread availability of free intrusion tools and scripts, virtually anyone—often it's a teenager—with minimal computer experience can mount a DDoS attack. As Figure 13-2 indicates, the same is true of virtually any kind of network attack. As evidenced by the current DDoS attacks, the severity and scope of the various methods of attack are increasing. Yet, even though experienced intruders are getting smarter, the knowledge required by novice intruders to copy and execute known methods of attack is decreasing.

In the past, intruders had to manually enter commands on their PCs. This limited their access to tens or hundreds of systems. It was relatively easy to determine if an intrusion had occurred and what had been done to the system. Today, given the connectivity on the Internet and the availability of automated tools, intruders can access thousands of systems. By disabling commonly used services and reinstalling their own versions, intruders can hide their presence and erase their tracks in audit and log files. In the past, DoS and other attacks were infrequent and considered a minor annoyance. Today, a successful DoS attack can literally threaten the survival of an EC site, especially for small to medium-sized organizations. Unfortunately, as the data indicate, attacks of all sorts are on the rise.

FIGURE 13-2

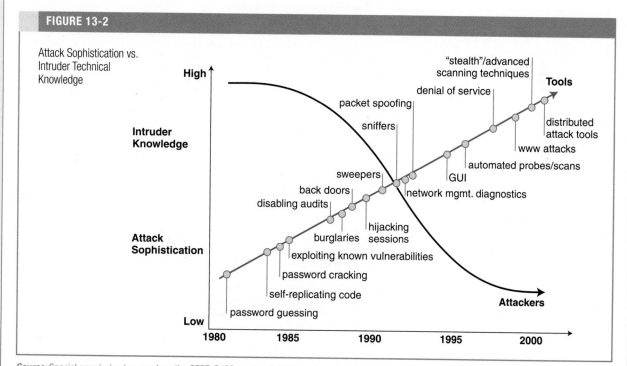

Attack Sophistication vs. Intruder Technical Knowledge

Source: Special permission to reproduce the CERT ©/CC graphic © 2000 by Carnegie Melon University, in Electronic Commerce 2002 in Allen et al. (2000).

13.2 THE NEED FOR SECURITY

In 1988, Robert Morris released a "worm" on the Internet that disrupted service on a number of networks for several days. Back then it was a newsworthy event, but it impacted the lives of very few nontechnical people. For over 10 years, there were no significant viruses or worms released on the Internet. Then in 1999, the security dam broke when the Melissa virus appeared on the scene. Since that time rarely a month has gone by without the announcement of some new kind of cyber attack. Table 13-1 chronicles some of the more infamous attacks. Unlike Morris' worm, these attacks have disrupted the lives of millions of nontechnical people, have resulted in millions of dollars worth of damage, and are taken seriously by organizations of all sorts throughout the world.

TABLE 13-1 — Significant Cyber Attacks 1999–2000

Date	Attack	Description
March 1999	Melissa	The Melissa was a Microsoft World macro virus that was spread as an e-mail attachment. It arrived with the words, "Here is the document you asked for . . . don't show it to anyone else;)." The virus was first posted to the alt.sex newsgroup. When opened it would e-mail itself to the first 50 addresses in the recipient's address book. Melissa was significant because it was the first time in the 10 years since the Morris worm that a virus had infected a significant portion of the Internet.
May 1999	FBI vs. Hackers	After investigating several U.S. hacker groups and seizing the computer of a teenager, a DoS attack was launched against the FBI's Web site. As a result, the site was closed down for a week.
June 1999	Explorer.Zip	Similar to the Melissa virus, this virus was spread through e-mail that, when opened, automatically mailed itself out. The virus could also be spread without human intervention through various network-sharing vulnerabilities. Explorer.Zip created substantial problems for the e-mail systems at Microsoft, Intel, and NBC.
September 1999	Hotmail.hole	A Hotmail security hole was discovered by a Bulgarian hacker named Georgi Guninski that allows a JavaScript program to be injected into the user's systems via an e-mail message. The script could be used to display a fake login screen that steals the user's password. In this way the attacker could read the user's e-mail and send messages of any sort under the user's name.
November 1999	BubbleBoy	This e-mail virus differed from its predecessors because it only required the recipient to preview the message, not open it, in order to infect other computers.
January 2000	CDNow Attacked	A Russian cracker named Maxum stole 300,000 credit-card records from the CD Universe Web site, demanding $100,000 ransom for their return. When CD Universe refused, he started publishing the numbers one-by-one. Maxum's ISP shut him down when they learned about his criminal activity. Both Discover Card and American Express issued new cards to any of their cardholders shopping at CDNow.
February 2000	DDoS Attacks	See the opening case in Section 13.1.
Spring 2000	Credit Card Postings	A hacker named Raphael Gray (net name Curador) broke into EC sites in five countries—United States, Canada, Thailand, Japan, and the United Kingdom—and effortlessly obtained customer credit card numbers—26,000 in all. His stated objective was to bring the security vulnerabilities to the attention of the Webmasters at the sites, which he did by posting the numbers on the Internet.
May 2000	ILOVEYOU	The VBS.LoveLetter.A virus originated in the Philippines, struck Hong King on May 4, and within hours had attacked computers worldwide. By the time it had run its course, it had infected 1.2 million computers in North America and caused an estimated $80 million in damage. The virus was propagated virulently as an e-mail attachment that e-mailed itself to the contacts in the recipient's address book when opened.
August 2000	Brown Orifice	A computer consultant named Dan Brumleve announced that he had found two security flaws in the Netscape browser implementation of Java. The flaws enabled the distributor of a Java applet to view the file.
October 2000	Microsoft Source Code compromised	A cracker gained access to Microsoft's networks, enabling him or her to view the source code of applications under development. The cracker was able to penetrate the network through some "semi-retired" Web servers that hadn't been fixed to correct a vulnerability in Microsoft's Internet Information Server (i.e., Microsoft's commercial Web server product). Some security experts speculated that the hacker used the QAZ Trojan to spy on Microsoft's R&D division.

Source: Mell and Wack (2000).

Empirical evidence leaves no doubt that the rise in attacks against computers and networks has mirrored the growth of the Web. Since 1996, the **Computer Security Institute (CSI)** and the FBI Computer Intrusion Squad have conducted a survey of computer security practitioners in U.S. corporations and government agencies. The findings of their most recent survey (Computer Security Institute and Federal Bureau of Investigation, 2000), based on the responses of 643 practitioners, indicated that:

- **Cyber attacks are on the increase.** In 2000, 70 percent of respondents indicated that their systems had experienced unauthorized use. This is up from 42 percent in 1996.
- **Internet connections are increasingly a point of attack.** The number of respondents indicating that their Internet connection is a frequent point of attack increased from 37 percent in 1996 to 59 percent in 2000.
- **The variety of attacks is on the rise.** Eleven percent detected financial fraud, 17 percent sabotage of data or networks, 20 percent theft of proprietary information, 25 percent penetration from the outside, 27 percent denial of service, 71 percent unauthorized access by insiders, 79 percent employee abuse of Internet access privileges, 85 percent viruses.
- **The reporting of serious crimes to law enforcement has declined.** In 1999, 32 percent of the organizations that had serious attacks reported them to law enforcement. In 2000, it was 25 percent. In 2000, when practitioners were asked why they hadn't reported, 52 percent cited negative publicity, 39 percent said competitors would use it against them, 13 percent didn't know they could report it, and 55 percent said a civil remedy was best. The percent citing negative publicity and competitive disadvantage has actually declined substantially over the years.

The increase in computer attacks is also substantiated by data collected by the **Computer Emergency Response Team (CERT)** at Carnegie Mellon University. According to their statistics, the number of incidents reported to CERT increased from around 2,600 in 1996 to 10,000 in 1999, and then to approximately 22,000 in 2000. Similarly, the number of vulnerabilities that were reported increased by over 100 percent from close to 350 in 1996 to about 775 in 2000 (CERT 2000).

Since 1997, the CSI/FBI survey has also assessed the financial losses associated with these security breaches. For 3 out of the last 4 years, over 70 percent of the respondents said that their organizations had suffered financial losses. In 2000, however, losses totaled $265 million versus an average of $120 million for the previous 3 years. As in the previous years, the most serious financial losses involved the theft of proprietary information ($66 million), financial fraud ($56 million), and viruses ($29 million).

TABLE 13-2

Incidents and Vulnerabilities Reported to CERT					
	1996	1997	1998	1999	2000
Incidents	2,573	2,134	3,734	9,859	21,756
Vulnerabilities	345	311	262	417	774

Source: CERT (2000).

In a similar sort of survey, Omni Consulting Group (Geralds 2001) asked 3,000 businesses worldwide to assess their dollar losses resulting from lapses in security. They put the figure around 6 cents for every dollar of sales. Based on these figures, Omni estimated that security breaches cost European business $4.3 billion in lost revenue in 2000.

Overall, the anecdotal and survey data indicate that security is a major issue for any EC Web site (B2C or B2B) and for consumers as well. This chapter provides an overview of the security risks facing these sites and their users and examines some of the solutions available for reducing these risks. Chapter 14 also addresses some of the issues and solutions but focuses primarily on the security issues surrounding e-payments, especially the importance of the public key infrastructure and encryption. Because security is a multifaceted and highly technical problem, there is no way to address the complexities in a single chapter. For those readers interested in more comprehensive discussions see (Loshin 1998; Merkow and Breithaupt 2000; Scambray et al. 2000; Howard 2000).

13.3   WHY NOW?

Years ago, a well-known bank robber named Willy Sutton was asked, "Why do you rob banks?" His response: "Because that's where the money is." Today if you asked a hacker why he or she attacks the Internet or Web, the hacker might offer a similar response: "Because that's were the money and information is." Prior to the Web, the Internet was a research network. Most of the information was circulated through e-mail or file transfer protocol (FTP) from one researcher to another. Although there was certainly sensitive and proprietary information that could be compromised by a malicious hacker, much of the information was academic in nature and of little interest to the outside world. With the rapid growth of EC, things have changed. Consumers use their credit cards to purchase goods and services online, millions of individuals use their e-mail accounts to conduct business, B2B sites make sensitive business data available to trading partners, and at a minimum, virtually every major business in the world has a marketing site that is open to the public at large. The sheer growth in EC has certainly made the Internet an enticing playground for hackers and crackers. But, there are a large number of other factors contributing to the rise in cyber attacks including (Marchany 2000):

- **Security systems are only as strong as their weakest points.** An EC system consists of a number of components, including security defenses like firewalls, authentication schemes, and encryption. Yet, all an intruder needs is a single weakness in order to attack a system. Consider, for example, the trials and tribulations of a security firm asked to perform a security audit of customer's computer systems (Scambray et al., 2000). "In one particular case, despite a week of work, we had not gained any significant access to their internal LAN. You never want to go into a project update meeting without significant results, as it can shatter the confidence of any client . . . We turned to the only real progress we had made, one dial-in modem, a list of e-mail addresses, and a Windows 95 share allowing us to read the e-mail of one user. We decided to read each e-mail again. Low and behold we came across a message from IT to all employees stating that their initial password was set to their last name and that they should change their passwords immediately. This was the tip we needed. We started dialing in on the modem, trying every username and associated last name as the password. Within an hour we were in, gaining administrative access to the internal LAN." The **Common Vulnerabilities and Exposures Board** (*cve.mitre.org*) has documented over 1,000 security vulnerabilities. Given the complexity of these systems, this means that security must be an ongoing process that evolves as the tools and techniques of the intruders evolve.

- **Security and ease of use (or implementation) are antithetical to one another.** The old adage says that if you want a really secure system, then shut the system off. Obviously this is ludicrous advice, but it does highlight the idea that security and usability tend to be inversely related. Take the case of passwords. If you're assigned a password like "#$8^-96-32," it's hard to remember and hard to use. In all likelihood, you'll write it down somewhere. If you have a password like "johnsmith" it's easy to remember, but not very hard to guess. The same thing is true with other security measures. E-payments (see Chapter 14), digital certificates, electronic wallets, and other specialized security components make it harder for outsiders to compromise a B2C EC site. On the other hand, these components make it much harder for merchants to implement a payment system and customers to actually make purchases. The solution to finding the right balance between security and usability rests on the business requirements of a site.

- **Security takes a back seat to market pressures.** Most EC sites are built from components supplied by third-party vendors. Because of market pressures and rapidly evolving technologies, these vendors have often focused on time-to-market, paying little attention to security features. The software developers creating these components often retrofit the security features at the end of the development cycle or rely on the underlying infrastructure—the Web server and operating system on which the components run—to provide security. Even with subsequent releases of the components, there seems to be little effort to shore up security holes. As noted above, the CERT Coordination Center routinely receives reports of new vulnerabilities. We continue to see the same types of vulnerabilities in newer versions of products that we saw in earlier versions.

- **Security of an EC site depends on the security of the Internet as a whole.** The number of schools, libraries, homes, and small business sites directly connected to the Web continues to increase. While larger companies and ISPs invest a substantial amount of time and effort securing their EC sites, the administration of these other sites often falls upon people with little or no training in network security. Of course, the same can be said about some of the larger companies who, in a rush to bring their sites online, have expended little effort to audit system security and, because of a tight labor market, have relied on less experienced staff with little training in security. Poorly configured or outdated operating systems, e-mail programs, and Web sites result in vulnerabilities that hackers can exploit. Unfortunately, because the Internet is so interconnected, the security of one site often depends on the security of the others. Attackers can often take advantage of a weak site to compromise the security at a stronger site. The DDoS attacks and the distribution of e-mail viruses are strong evidence of this fact.

APPLICATION CASE 13.1

Edgar Search

All publicly traded companies are required by law to file forms with the U.S. Securities and Exchange Commission (SEC). Electronic filings are made to EDGAR, the *Electronic Data Gathering, Analysis and Retrieval* system. The primary purpose of EDGAR is to "increase the efficiency and fairness of the securities market for the benefit of investors, corporations, and the economy by accelerating the receipt, acceptance, dissemination, and analysis of time-sensitive corporate information filed with the agency."

From the hacker's point of view, the 10-Q is one of the best. It provides a quarterly update of company activities including the purchase and sale of other companies. The hacker can use EDGAR to search for terms like "subsidiary" and "subsequent events" to locate companies involved in mergers and acquisitions. When companies acquire other companies, the IT organizations often have problems managing the networks of the acquired entities. In the scramble to connect networks security is often compromised. Security weaknesses can arise in the network of the acquired entity, providing an entree into the network of the parent company.

Source: Scambray et al. (2000).

- **Security vulnerabilities are increasing faster than they can be combated.** As Mark Fabro, chief scientist at a vendor of security systems notes, "The hacker community is huge and very close knit. They share their findings and post them 'in the wild,' where anyone can access them—and build on them (see, for example, *project.honeypot.org*). The recent attacks are the result of hackers exploiting flaws that we have known about for years. There are thousands of viruses, worms, and attacks in the works at any given time, and people are generally unaware of this fact. It's actually very frightening." (Watson 2000). At the same time, the skill required to attack a system has decreased.
- **Security compromised by common applications.** Over the past few years, Microsoft has come to dominate not only the worlds of document processing (Word) and spreadsheets (Excel), but also the worlds of e-mail (Outlook), Web browsers (Internet Explorer), and presentations (PowerPoint). For most organizations, this set of common applications has eliminated a number of administrative costs and headaches and made it easier for people to share documents both inside and outside the organization. The problem is that once a hacker finds a hole in any of these products, the whole world is at risk. For example, the Melissa and ILOVEYOU macro worms were able to spread rapidly because of the widespread usage of Microsoft Outlook (Mell and Wack, 2000).

13.4   BASIC SECURITY ISSUES

Major EC sites such as eBay, Yahoo!, and MSN are constantly on the alert for cyber attacks of all sorts, and rightfully so. The overall costs of the February 2000 DDoS attacks were estimated at $1.7 billion. The estimate was based not only on the person-hours required to restore service, but also on the dollar value of the number of purchases that weren't made and the number of ads that weren't seen. Based on a study by International Data Corporation (IDC), large organizations spent $6.2 billion on security consulting in 1999 and will better than double that amount to $14.8 by 2003 (Neito et al. 2001).

Larger B2C and B2B sites are not the only ones that need to be concerned with security issues. This also applies to smaller business sites, as well as individual users. Consider, for example, the situation in which a user connects to a Web server at a marketing site in order to obtain some product literature (Loshin 1998). In return, the user is asked to fill out a Web form providing some demographic and other personal information in order to receive the literature. In this situation, what kinds of security questions arise?

From the user's perspective:

- How can the user be sure that the Web server is owned and operated by a legitimate company?
- How does the user know that the Web page and form don't contain some malicious or dangerous code or content?
- How does the user know that the Web server won't distribute the information to some other party the user provides?

From the company's perspective:

- How does the company know the user won't attempt to break into the Web server or alter the pages and content at the site?
- How does the company know that the user won't try to disrupt the server so that it isn't available to others?

From both parties' perspectives:

- How do they know that the network connection is free from eavesdropping by a third party listening on the line?
- How do they know that the information sent back and forth between the server and the user's browser hasn't been altered?

These questions are illustrative of the types of security issues that can arise in an EC transaction. For other sorts of transactions, such as those involving e-payments, other types of security issues must be confronted. The following list summarizes some of the major security issues that can occur in EC:

- **Authentication.** When you view a Web page from a Web site, how can you be sure that the site isn't fraudulent? If you file a tax return electronically, how do you know that you've sent it to the taxing authority? If you receive an e-mail, how can you be sure that the sender is who he or she claims to be? The process by which one entity verifies that another entity is who they claim to be is called authentication. Authentication requires evidence in the form of credentials, which can take a variety of forms including: something known (e.g., a password); something possessed (e.g., a smartcard); or something unique (e.g., a signature).
- **Authorization.** Does a person or program have the right to access particular data, programs, or system resources (e.g., files, registries, directories, etc.) once he, she, or it is authenticated? Authorization is usually determined by comparing information about the person or program with access control information associated with the resource being accessed.
- **Auditing.** If a person or program accesses a Web site, various pieces of information are noted in a log file. If a person or program queries a database,

the action is also noted in a log file. The process of collecting information about accessing particular resources, using particular privileges, or performing other security actions (either successfully or unsuccessfully) is known as auditing. Audits provide the means to reconstruct the specific actions that were taken and often the ability to uniquely identify the person or program that performed the actions.

- **Confidentiality or privacy.** Information that is private or sensitive should not be disclosed to unauthorized individuals, entities, or computer software processes. Some examples of things that should be confidential are trade secrets, business plans, health records, credit card numbers, and even the fact that a person visited a particular Web site. Confidentiality is usually ensured by encryption.

- **Integrity.** The ability to protect data from being altered or destroyed in an unauthorized or accidental manner is called integrity. Data can be altered or destroyed while it is in transit or after it is stored. Financial transactions are one example of data whose integrity needs to be secured. Again, encryption is one way of ensuring integrity of data while it is in transit.

- **Availability.** If you're trying to execute a stock trade through an online service, then the service needs to be available in near real-time. An online site is available if a person or program can gain access to the pages, data, or services provided by the site when they are needed. Technologies like load-balancing hardware and software are aimed at ensuring availability.

- **Non-repudiation.** If you order an item through a mail order catalog and pay by check, then it's difficult to dispute the veracity of the order. If you order the same item through the cataloger's "1-800" number and pay by credit card, then there's always room for dispute, although "caller id" can be used to identify the phone from which the order was placed. Similarly, if you use the cataloger's Web site and pay by credit card, then you can always claim that it wasn't you that placed the order. Non-repudiation is the ability to limit parties from refuting that a legitimate transaction took place. One of the keys to non-repudiation is a "signature" that makes it difficult to dispute that you were involved in an exchange.

Figure 13-3 depicts some of the major components involved in most EC applications and indicates where the above security issues come into play. It is safe to say that virtually every component in an EC application is subject to some sort of security threat.

13.5   SECURITY RISK MANAGEMENT

In addressing the above security issues, there is no such thing as a generic set of safeguards. Even among similar types of EC sites (e.g., B2C), the safeguards that should be employed will depend on a number of factors including the specific services being offered, the types of data being handled and stored, and the types of software and hardware being used. Although the specific safeguards will vary, those organizations with sound security practices rely on comprehensive risk-management to determine their specific security needs (King 2001; Power 2000).

Figure 13-3	General Security Issues at EC Sites

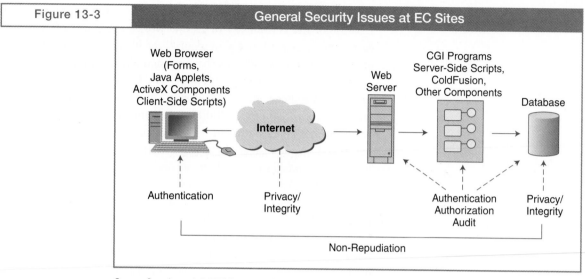

Source: Scambray et al. (2000).

Risk management consists of four phases—assessment, planning, implementation, and monitoring. To understand these phases, a few definitions are in order:

- **Assets.** This is anything of value that is worth securing. Assets can include tangible goods such as computer and network hardware, as well as intangible assets such as business plans, customer data, passwords, digital signatures, brand identity, company reputation, and the like.
- **Threat.** A threat is any eventuality that represents a danger to an asset. All of the issues described above, like the possibility that financial transactions will be altered, are threats.
- **Vulnerability.** A vulnerability is a weakness in a safeguard. For example, the Web forms used for data entry in many EC applications need to check for valid input. If the input isn't validated, there is the possibility that a hacker can enter malicious code that will be inadvertently executed by the computer program processing the form. Validating input data on Web forms is the safeguard, while failure to validate input data is the vulnerability.

In the assessment phase of risk management, organizations evaluate their security risks by determining their assets, threats, and vulnerabilities. This evaluation usually proceeds in the following manner:

1. **Determine organizational objectives.** Risk management is an extension of an organization's objectives. Because it is impossible to safeguard against every eventuality, safeguards should be selected on the basis of an organization's objectives and requirements. For instance, if a company relies on their Web site to service customer complaints, a top priority will be to ensure that service is not disrupted.
2. **Inventory assets.** An inventory of assets should itemize all of the critical tangible and intangible assets on the network. The relative value and criticality of these assets also needs to be determined.
3. **Delineate threats.** Potential risks can come from any person or thing that can use the network to harm an organization's assets, including hackers,

viruses, disgruntled employees, human error, system failures, and the like. Because of the complexity of EC networks, the range of possible threats is extremely diverse. One way to identify the likely threats is to examine the general types of attacks—threats that have actually occurred—that have been perpetrated against EC sites in the past. The CSI/FBI survey cited earlier is one example. Another is the recent survey conducted by *Information Security* and reported in the September 2000 issue (Briney 2000). The survey examines 16 basic types of attacks, nine of which are classified as internal and seven external. Based on the results of the survey (which are reproduced in Table 13-3), EC sites are more susceptible to security breaches than those sites that don't conduct EC. Additionally, EC sites are much more susceptible to external attacks. Section 13.6 describes a number of these external attacks in detail.

4. **Identify vulnerabilities.** The list of vulnerabilities maintained by the Common Vulnerabilities and Exposures Board (CVE) documents the potential weaknesses in any network. Various non-obtrusive tools and methods can be used to inventory the specific weaknesses in a particular network.

5. **Quantify the value of each risk.** In **quantitative risk analysis**, an equation is used to assign a numerical value to a risk. The calculated values of the various risks are used to prioritize those risks that need safeguarding. Various equations are employed for this purpose. One equation is: Risk = Asset × Threat × Vulnerability (Symantec 2000), where estimated numerical values between some predetermined range are assigned to each of the features. For instance, an organization might use a range of 1–10 to estimate the value of an Asset, the probability of a Threat, and the level of Vulnerability, which means that the computed Risk will range from 1 to 1,000. Another equation (Howard 2000) that can be used is Risk = Criticality/Effort, where Criticality is a value between 1 (least critical) and 10 (most critical) and Effort also

TABLE 13-3

Security Risks for EC and Other Internet Sites		
Type of Breach	Conduct EC	Don't Conduct EC
Installation/Use of Unauthorized Software	77%	74%
Infection of Company Equipment via Viruses/Malicious Code/Executables (deliberate or accidental)	75%	66%
Use of Company Computing Resources for Illegal or Illicit Communications or Activities (porn surfing, e-mail harassment)	70%	56%
Abuse of Computer Access Controls	64%	51%
Installation/Use of Unauthorized Hardware/Peripherals	50%	59%
Use of Company Computing Resources for Personal Profit (gambling, spam, managing personal EC site, online investing)	55%	45%
Physical Theft, Sabotage or Intentional Destruction of Computing Equipment	50%	34%
Electronic Theft, Sabotage or Intentional Destruction/Disclosure of Proprietary Data or Information	29%	18%
Fraud	18%	8%
Viruses/Trojans/Worms	82%	76%
DoS/DDoS attacks	42%	31%
Exploits Related to Active Program Scripting/Mobile Code (ActiveX, Java, JavaScript, VBS)	40%	34%
Attacks Related to Protocol Weaknesses	29%	23%
Attacks Related to Insecure Passwords	30%	20%
Buffer Overflows	29%	20%
Attacks on Bugs in Web Servers (e.g., CGI script-related attacks)	33%	16%

Source: Briney (2000). Used with permission of Information Security.

runs between 1 (easiest to mount) and 10 (most difficult to mount). Finally, risk can be evaluated with the equation (Scambray et al. 2000): Risk = (Popularity + Simplicity + Impact)/3 where Popularity is the frequency of use (with 1 being infrequent and 10 most frequent), Simplicity is degree of skill needed to execute the threat (with 1 being easiest and 10 hardest), and Impact is the potential damage (with 1 being least severe and 10 most severe). Regardless of the equation that is used, the basic idea is to arrive at a set of numbers that can be used to set priorities.

The second phase of risk management is planning. The primary goal of this phase is to arrive at a set of security policies defining which threats are tolerable and which are not. A threat is tolerable if the cost of safeguard is too high or the risk is low. The policies also specify the general measures to be taken against those that are intolerable or a high priority. Like the assessment phase, this phase involves a series of steps (King, 2001):

1. **Define specific policies.** Each policy needs to detail how a particular safeguard will be instituted, why the safeguard is being implemented, when it will be enforced, and who will be responsible for the safeguard.

2. **Establish processes for audit and review.** Security is an ongoing activity that needs to be adapted to changes in an organization's objectives, assets, threats, and vulnerabilities. This requires regular reviews in order to determine the effectiveness of particular policies. Best practices dictate that a review be performed at least every 6 months. The review process requires someone to conduct the review, methods for carrying out the review, and someone to determine the required changes.

3. **Establish an incident response team and contingency plan.** In all likelihood a site will be subject to attack. Whether they are successful or unsuccessful, all attacks require a response. This is the job of the **incident response team.** Part of the response should include reporting major incidents to an organization like CERT (the Computer Emergency Response Team at Carnegie Mellon University). Besides responding to direct attacks, it's also the responsibility of this team to monitor public announcements of attacks at other sites and to respond to those. Any response that is taken should be outlined in a contingency plan.

The third phase of risk management is implementation. During implementation, particular technologies are chosen to counter high-priority threats. The selection of particular technologies is based on the general guidelines established in the planning phase. As a first step in the implementation phase, generic types of technology should be selected for each of the high priority threats. Given the generic types, particular software from particular vendors can then be selected. The **Information Protection Assessment Kit (IPAK)** from the CSI Hotline provides a list of generic security controls that might be used by an EC site. The list is reproduced in Table 13-4 (Power 2000).

The last phase of risk management is monitoring. Monitoring is an ongoing process that is used to determine which measures are successful, which measures are unsuccessful and need modification, whether there are any new types of threats, whether there have been advances or changes in technology, and whether there are any new business requirements that need securing.

TABLE 13-4

Internet Commerce Controls

1. A detailed and up-to-date contingency plan for storefront computer outages has been developed.
2. A contingency plan for storefront computer outages is tested on a regular basis with exercises more detailed than tabletop scenarios.
3. A computer emergency response team (internal CERT) has been designated, trained, and periodically drilled to deal with problems like hacker intrusions.
4. An uninterruptible power system (UPS) is employed to provide necessary power in case of a power outage that lasts several hours or longer.
5. Communications with the telephone company are supported by lines to two or more central offices.
6. A mirror site provides geographical diversity for contingency planning purposes as well as increased performance.
7. Redundant computer equipment such as RAID (redundant array of inexpensive disks) ensures that a single hardware fault will not bring the commerce system down.
8. Internet commerce systems are physically isolated from other computers in a data center machine room via locked wire cages, separate locked rooms, etc.
9. Internet commerce systems are protected from hackers with respected firewall (and the most recent version of the firewall is installed).
10. Access controls are used to limit what individual internal users can read, write, or execute based on actual business needs.
11. Card numbers sent over communications lines are encrypted using SSL or a stronger encryption process.
12. Backup tapes are encrypted and stored off-site in a locked container or room.
13. A fraud detection system is used to catch suspicious credit card orders before the order is filled.
14. A publicly accessible digital certificate is provided for all customers to verify that they have reached a legitimate server.
15. All communications between internal machines that make up the Internet commerce suite are encrypted and supported by digital certificates.
16. An intrusion detection system provides instant notification of hacker attacks and related problems.
17. A network management system provides real-time information about system load, response time, system downtime, and other performance issues.
18. A vulnerability identification system identifies configuration and setup problems before hackers can exploit them.
19. Staff with access to Internet commerce systems are given special in-depth background checks.
20. A specific individual is defined as the manager who "owns" the Internet commerce system (and who by extension is responsible for security thereon).

Source: Tangled Web by R. Power (Indianapolis: Que Publishing © 2000).

13.6   TYPES OF THREATS AND ATTACKS

Security experts distinguish between two types of attacks—**nontechnical** and **technical**. Nontechnical attacks are also called **social engineering**. In social engineering attacks, a perpetrator uses chicanery or other forms of persuasion to trick people into revealing sensitive information and performing actions that can be used to compromise the security of a network. For instance, a perpetrator might call a victim, posing as a system administrator or help desk technician who needs some sensitive information (e.g., user id or password) in order to fix a problem. Wanting to help, the victim willingly provides the information. The tables can also be turned. Posing as the IT director traveling on business, the perpetrator could call the help desk and ask for the remote dial-in number or other secure information. Again, wanting to assist, the help desk personnel might willingly provide the information. Technically, neither situation constitutes hacking, but they still serve the same purpose. In the past, the medium of choice for social engineering was the phone. More recently, e-mail has been used to accomplish the task. Several utilities exist for sending fake e-mail that appears to come from one address, while in reality it comes from the perpetrator's e-mail. The victim is fooled into thinking that he or she is responding to the sender, while the response is actually sent to the perpetrator. Figure 13-4 displays one of these utilities. E-mail of this sort has been used to lure AOL users to reveal their account names and passwords (MSNBC Staff 2001).

In contrast to a nontechnical attack, software and systems expertise are used to perpetrate technical attacks. In conducting a technical attack, an expert hacker often uses a methodical approach consisting of the following steps (Merkow and Breihaupt, 2000):

STEP 1: Discovering the key elements of the network.
STEP 2: Scanning for vulnerabilities.

Figure 13-4	Utility for Sending E-mail from Fake Addresses

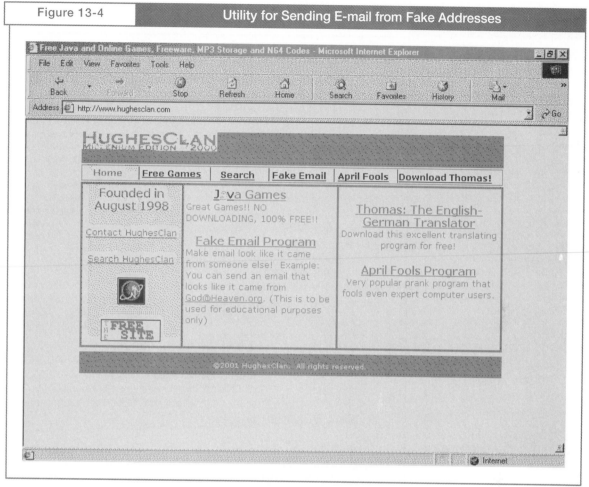

Source: hughesclan.com

STEP 3: Hacking the system to gain root or administrator privileges.

STEP 4: Disabling auditing and removing traces from log files.

STEP 5: Stealing files, modifying data, and stealing source code or other valuable information.

STEP 6: Installing back doors and Trojan horses that permit undetectable reentry.

STEP 7: Returning at will to inflict more damage.

The first step is carried out using a variety of queries, searches, and tools that are readily available on the Internet. These enable the hacker to determine the target's network typology, the types of operating systems and Web servers being run, potential gateways and firewalls, the paths that communication packets travel, which Internet services are currently running, and the like. The hacker uses this information to pinpoint potential vulnerabilities in the system. Detailed information about actual vulnerabilities can be obtained with a network scanning tool, such as Digital Security's (*saintcorporation.com/saint*) open source System Administrator's Integrated Network Tool (SAINT), which provides information about network typologies, network services that are running, the types of hardware and software being used, and security vulnerabilities—usually in the form of incorrectly

APPLICATION CASE 13.2

The Players: Attackers, Hackers, and Crackers

Any time the media reports about a large security attack, there is a great deal of speculation about who perpetrated the attack and why. By now, most people have heard the term "hacker" bandied about in the media. Often attacks are blamed on these so-called hackers. Who or what are hackers? What role do they play in Internet security and what motivates them to do what they do?

Hackers

Originally, the term "hacker" referred to a shared culture of expert programmers and networking wizards that worked on the first time-sharing minicomputers and the earliest ARPANET experiments. This culture created the Unix operating system and helped build the Internet, Usenet, and the World Wide Web. Over time, the term came to be applied to rogue programmers or network wizards who illegally broke into computers and networks. Many hackers employ these skills to test the strength and integrity of computer systems for a wide variety of reasons: to prove their own ability, to satisfy their curiosity about how different programs work, or to improve their own programming skills by exploring the programming of others. The term hacker has been adopted by the mass media to refer to all people who break into computer systems, regardless of motivation; however, in the media the term hacker is often associated with people who hack illegally for criminal purposes. Many in the Internet security community strongly disagree with this use of the term. Sometimes the terms "white-hat" hackers and "black-hat" hackers are used to distinguish the two types of hackers.

Crackers

People within the Internet community tend to refer to people who engage in unlawful or damaging hacking as "crackers," short for "criminal hackers." The term cracker generally connotes a hacker who uses his or her skills to commit unlawful acts or to deliberately create mischief. Unlike hackers, whose motivations may be professional or community enhancement, the motivation of crackers is generally to cause mischief, create damage, or to pursue illegal activities, such as data theft or vandalism.

Script Kiddies

Some of the most highly publicized Internet security breaches, such as the February DoS attacks discussed earlier in this chapter, are committed by middle-class teenagers, who seem to perpetrate mischief in order to make a name for themselves. Security experts often refer to these individuals as "script kiddies." Script kiddies are generally ego-driven, unskilled crackers who use information and software—or scripts—that they download from the Internet to inflict damage on targeted sites. Script kiddies are generally looked upon with disdain by members of the hacking community and by law enforcement authorities because they are generally unskilled individuals with a lot of time on their hands who wreak havoc primarily to impress their friends.

Although there are differences among the various players, the term hacker is used throughout the chapter to denote someone who attacks a site, regardless of his or her motivations.

Source: Sager (2000).

configured network services, well-known bugs in system or network utilities, or poor or ignorant policy decisions. Once the vulnerabilities are known, the hacker can go about the business of compromising the target system.

In 1999, Mitre Corporation and 15 other security-related organizations (*cve.mitre.org*) began to enumerate all publicly known common vulnerabilities and exposures (CVE). One of the goals was to assign standard and unique names to each of the known problems so that information could be collected and shared with the security community throughout the world. To date there are over 1,100 known vulnerabilities. Obviously, there is no way to address all of these in this discussion. Instead, we focus on six categories of vulnerabilities or attacks including DoS attacks, buffer overflows, input validation attacks, intercepted transmissions, malicious code, and malicious mobile code. For those readers who are interested in a detailed description of a wide range of vulnerabilities, as well as the tactics and tools used to exploit these vulnerabilities, see Scambray et al. (2000), Russell and Cunningham (2000), and the Net Security Web site (*net-security.org*).

System and Software Bugs and Misconfigurations

Hackers have been able to exploit various bugs and flaws in operating systems, Web servers, database servers, and storefront and shopping cart software on which EC sites are built. For example, Microsoft's Internet Information Server (IIS), the second most widely used Web server, has proven to be vulnerable to security breaches caused by bugs in the system. In mid-October 2000, for instance, hackers were able to take advantage of the way IIS handled UNICODE and gain access to any file on the hardware where the server was running (this has been labeled the UNICODE Directory Traversal Vulnerability). Microsoft and the other hardware and software vendors supplying EC systems and components are extremely diligent about fixing (also called patching) these security holes as soon as they are found. In spite of the fixes, many companies running EC sites fail to apply the patches as soon as they are available, thus leaving themselves open to attack.

In the same vein, when software and systems are first installed, they come with a number of default settings, sample programs, and templates that have likewise proven vulnerable to attack. For example, shopping cart software comes with a set of templates that can be customized to meet the needs of a particular site. Sample software of this type usually isn't designed with security in mind. Often a site will rely on these default settings or fail to disable or remove the sample software from their servers, again leaving themselves open to attack.

Denial-of-Service (DoS) Attacks

B2C EC is based on the idea of open communications. This means that any consumer can use a browser to communicate with any public Web site. Most of the time, consumers follow the rules. Unfortunately, the open nature of the Internet also makes these sites vulnerable to DoS attacks where one or more hackers can take advantage of the Internet's openness to overwhelm a victim's site with seemingly legitimate communications. For example, if you want to find out whether a particular computer on the Internet is active, you can use the "ping" command. A ping command is issued by simply typing in the word "ping" followed by the

IP address of the computer (see the discussion about "Ping of death" attacks for more details). There's nothing illegal about this. However, there are ways to send a multitude of "pings" so that the computer on the other end is overwhelmed and can no longer service other requests. For smaller B2C sites that rely solely on Web sales, a sustained DoS attack can literally put them out of business.

Given the number of DoS attacks in recent years, it is clearly easier for a hacker to disrupt service than to gain illegal access to a site. The sorts of DoS attacks that have been perpetrated can be divided into two broad categories. First, there are the "bandwidth consumption attacks." Here, one or more attackers consume the communication bandwidth linking a particular site to the Internet. This is easy to do if the victim's Web site is connected to the Internet by a slower network link (e.g., an ISDN line) and the attackers are connected with a high-speed line (e.g., a T1 line). It's also easy to do if an attacker can enlist the support (directly or indirectly) of a number of sites to flood a victim's network connection. Second, there are the "resource consumption" attacks. In this instance, an attacker relies on the fact that a computer has a finite number of resources to handle certain kinds of requests. In some cases if a computer receives a number of these requests in a short time frame, the computer will hang or crash. Some of the better known DoS attacks are described below:

- **IP fragmentation (teardrop, bonk, boink, nestea, and others).** On the Internet, the messages sent from one computer to another are broken into smaller segments called **packets**. The packets are reassembled by the computer receiving the message. Although each packet can be up to 64 kilobytes, most computers can't handle packets that large. To overcome this problem, these larger packets can be divided into segments that are also reassembled by the receiving computer. In order to accomplish this task, special header information is attached to each of the segments. In this sort of attack, the hacker sends packets with incorrect header information. The incorrect information causes some computers to hang, crash, or perform slowly.

- **DNS spoofing.** On the Internet, computers are identified by their domain names (e.g., *abc.com*). Behind every domain name is an associated Internet protocol (IP) address (e.g., 123.123.0.1). When one computer on the Internet wants to communicate with another computer, it first contacts a special computer called the domain name server (DNS) to get the underlying protocol address. The message is then broken into smaller segments called packets. These packets traverse the Internet under the control of other specialized computers called routers. These routers have maps that determine the path the packets will follow enroute to the computer denoted by the selected protocol address.

  Rather than eavesdropping on a communication channel, it may be easier for a hacker to modify the DNS address tables or the router maps and reroute the communications somewhere else (akin to moving a road sign). For instance, a hacker might copy all of the pages of an EC Web site and put the pages on his or her fraudulent Web site. With today's technologies this takes a few minutes at the most. Then the hacker could reroute the traffic from the actual Web site to the fraudulent site. Any information entered by the unsuspecting user at the other site (e.g., credit card number) would be available to the hacker.

APPLICATION CASE 13.3

Critical Internet Software Found Vulnerable

PGP Security recently discovered a high-risk flaw in the most commonly used software for Domain Name Servers (DNS). The name of the program is BIND, which stands for "Berkley Internet Name Domain." Whenever one computer sends a message to another computer, it first asks a DNS to translate the name of the destination computer (say *reuters.com*) into its numeric address. The flaw discovered by PGP enables hackers to gain control of these DNSs. Once in control, hackers could conceivably change and reroute the numeric IP addresses. A change in mapping could be devastating to all Internet traffic, including Web access, e-mail, and file transfers. All of this traffic could be redirected to an Internet site chosen by the hacker. The flaw could also be used to disable access to or from their victim's network, in essence cutting them off from the Internet.

Administrators can address the flaw by upgrading their version of BIND and applying the most recent patch, which is supposedly invulnerable. Technical information and advice on upgrading is available at *cert.org/advisories/CA-2001-02.html*. The Internet Software Consortium, the authors of BIND, have posted new versions of the software on their Web site at *isc.org*.

Source: Wolf (2000).

- **Ping of death.** The **ping** command is used to determine whether a particular computer (i.e., a computer with a particular Internet address) is online. The command determines whether a specific computer is online by sending a special message called an ICMP echo packet to the designated address. If the receiving computer is online, it will send a response in return. By default, an ICMP echo packet is small (64 bytes). They can be larger, under 65,536 bytes. Unfortunately, not all computers can handle large ICMP echo packets. An attacker perpetrates a "ping of death" by sending one of these larger ping messages to one of the susceptible computers. Fortunately, most of the susceptible computers have been fixed to handle this sort of attack.

- **Smurf attack.** It is possible to "broadcast" a ping to a range of Internet addresses to see which computers are online without having to ping each address individually. Administrators use broadcast pings to diagnose network problems. This sort of ping is sent from a special-purpose broadcast address. In contrast, a hacker can utilize the same command to overwhelm another computer. The hacker pings the broadcast address. However, he or she makes it look (through spoofing) as if the command were actually sent by the victim's computer. All of the computers on the broadcast network will then send a response to the victim's computer. Thus, the size of the original command will be amplified significantly by all of the responding computers. By sending enough of these commands, the hacker can easily consume all of the communication bandwidth available to the victim's computer.

- **SYNFlood.** In order for two computers to communicate, they must synchronize. Each computer has to understand who started the communication, who is listening, and in what time sequence. This is done when one computer (say A) sends an "SYN" packet to another computer (say B).

At this point computer B is said to be in a SYN_RECV state. Now, computer B sends a SYN/ACK packet back to computer A. If everything goes well, computer A will send an ACK packet to computer B, and a communication session will be established. Although host computers on the Internet are designed to handle large numbers of communication sessions, they only have limited resources for establishing the communications in the first place.

In a SYNFlood attack, a hacker will send an ACK message from computer A to computer B; however, he or she will substitute (spoof) a fictitious address for computer A. When computer B sends its SYN/ACK response to the fictitious computer, it will wait for an extended period of time for the ACK response, but the response will never come. During this time, one of the resources used by computer B to establish connections will be occupied. Now, the hacker sends another ACK message, and then another, and another. Eventually, computer B will run out of resources until it is eventually disabled.

- **Buffer overflows.** Knowledge about how to exploit buffer overflows has been around for quite some time. While these sorts of attacks date to 1988 with the Morris Worm incident, useful details about buffer overflows were missing until the publication of two classic papers in the area—"How to Write Buffer Overflows" (Mudge 1995) and "Smashing the Stack for Fun and Profit" (Aleph One 1996).

   Buffer overflows are fairly complex. To understand how they work, you need to know what a buffer is. A **buffer** is a temporary region in memory that is usually set to a specific size by the computer program that needs it. For instance, a shopping cart program might allocate a buffer of 10K bytes in memory to hold the purchase data and other customer data entered on a Web form before writing it to a database or using it for other processes. If the program is well written, it will ensure that the user can't enter more than 10K bytes of data on the form. But, what if it isn't well written and allows more? When the program tries to store the data in memory, the buffer will be overwritten. In the best of circumstances, this can cause lost or corrupt data or it can cause the program or computer to crash. It is also a vulnerability that can be used to execute a DoS attack against the computer running the program. More importantly, in the worst of circumstances, a hacker can exploit this problem to gain access to the computer. The hacker does this by overwriting the buffer with their own code in such a way that when the overflow occurs, their code will be executed. Buffer overflows are extremely dangerous and have resulted in a number of security breaches.

Input Validation Attacks

At most EC sites, the Web pages are not static. Instead, programs or scripts dynamically generate the pages in response to user requests. For example, a number of EC sites provide online catalogs displaying products and prices. It doesn't make much sense to create the pages ahead of time. First, there are too many of them; second, there is no way to anticipate the needs of every user. Instead, product information is stored in a database. Web forms are used to determine what the user wants to see. When the user submits the form, a program or script uses the information in the form to query the database for the product information of interest.

Then the program or script takes the results of the query and dynamically generates the Web page that is returned to the user. The types of programs or scripts that are often used to accomplish this task include CGI programs, Microsoft's Active Server Page (ASP) scripts, PHP scripts, and commercial products like ColdFusion.

Although these programs and scripting languages have simplified the task of creating Web sites of all sorts, they have proven vulnerable to a wide range of attacks. Many of these have taken the form of **input validation attacks**. In building input forms and writing programs or scripts to process these forms, the person creating the forms and programs or scripts often forgets to ensure that the user has input valid data. Unfortunately, over the years hackers have discovered that they can attack these programs and scripts in a variety of ways by inputting invalid data. Usually, the hacker types the invalid data directly into the browser's address line rather than using the form.

In one case hackers discovered that they could get CGI programs to run arbitrary commands by surrounding the commands with special characters and entering them as parameters to the CGI programs. For instance, by sending the following command from the browser's address line—*abc.com/cgi-bin/catalog.cgi? product=%0Acat%20/etc/passwd*—a hacker might be able to get the CGI program (*catalog.cgi*) residing on the Unix Web server (*abc.com*) to list the contents of the password file (*cat/etc/passwd*), unless certain security precautions had been taken.

Similarly, hackers discovered with earlier versions of ASP that they could view the script behind an ASP page by putting a "period" at the end of the page request. For example, if the following command were sent to a Web server— *abcnews.go.com/catalog* —then the page produced by the script contained in "catalog.asp" would be displayed in the browser. On the other hand, if a period were added to the end of the request—*abc.com/catalog.asp.*—then the script would be displayed in the browser instead of the page. Normally, there is no way to display the script. The significance is that ASP scripts often contain information such as user ids, passwords, and other sensitive information. When this flaw was discovered, Microsoft immediately fixed the program. Unfortunately, hackers discovered that if they used the hexadecimal representation of a period character rather than the character itself (i.e., they requested *abc.com/catalog.asp%2easp*), they could accomplish the same result. Again, Microsoft was forced to patch their code.

Intercepted Transmissions

When two computers on the Internet communicate with one another, the messages between them are sent as a sequence of smaller segments called packets. In the header of these packets is the Internet address of the computer that is supposed to receive the packets. It's the job of the computer on the receiving end to reassemble them in the appropriate order. If you were able to attach your computer to the network and intercept a copy of the communications between the two computers, you would see that the messages were being sent in plain text.

The problem with eavesdropping is that any computer on the network that has a different Internet address than the one contained in the message packets will ignore them. There is one exception to this. A computer (or at least its network card) can run in something called **promiscuous mode** that allows it to monitor all the packets on the network regardless of which computer they are addressed to. A hacker could write a program that would place his or her computer in promiscuous mode, but there's no need to. There are dozens of network eavesdropping programs that can accomplish the task. One of these is a program called Sniffer Pro from Network Associates (*nai.com*). The term **sniffing,** which was popularized by this program, is often used to describe this type of passive attack and the type of program used to monitor the communications. Programs like Sniffer Pro record the network traffic in a log file, in a window, or some other way that makes it amenable to browsing and analysis.

One method to combat eavesdropping is to encrypt messages between the computers. In this way, if the messages are sniffed, it will take the eavesdropper a long time to decipher them even with the aid of a very high-speed computer (see Chapter 14 for a discussion of encryption).

Malicious Code: Viruses, Worms, and Trojan Horses

Sometimes referred to as **malware** (for malicious software), malicious code is classified by the way in which it is propagated. Some malicious code is rather benign, but it all has the potential to do damage. New variants of malicious code appear with amazing frequency. For example, the Computer Security Association's computer virus prevalence survey showed the number of different viruses doubling every year from 1997 to 1999. In the same vein, virtually every organization with e-mail has been the victim of a virus or worm. In the CSI survey described earlier (Section 13.2), 85 percent of the respondents said that their organizations were the victims of viruses.

Malicious code takes a variety of forms—both pure and hybrid. Their names are taken from the real world pathogens they resemble. Viruses are the best known. A whole industry has grown up around computer viruses. Companies like Network Associates exist for the sole purpose of fighting viruses. The antivirus industry is extensive and profitable. Today, they have expanded beyond viruses and now also follow and catalog worms, macro viruses and macro worms, and Trojan horses.

- **Viruses.** This is the best known of the malicious code categories. While there are many definitions of a computer virus, the Request for Comment (RFC) 1135 definition is widely used: "A virus is a piece of code that inserts itself into a host, including the operating systems, to propagate. It cannot run independently. It requires that its host program be run to activate it."

  Viruses have two components. First, it has a propagation mechanism by which it spreads. Second, it has a payload that refers to what the virus does once it is executed. Sometimes the execution is triggered by a particular event. The Michelangelo virus, for instance, was triggered by Michelangelo's birth date. Some viruses simply infect and spread. Others do substantial damage (like deleting files or corrupting the hard disk).

- **Worms.** The major difference between a worm and a virus is that a worm propagates between systems (usually through a network), whereas a virus propagates locally. RFC 1135 defines a worm in this way: "A worm is a program that can run independently, will consume the resources of its host from within in order to maintain itself, and can propagate a complete working version of itself onto another machine."

- **Macro viruses and macro worms.** A macro virus or macro worm is usually executed when the application object (e.g., spreadsheet, word processing document, e-mail message) containing the macro is opened or a particular procedure is executed (e.g., a file is saved). Melissa and ILOVEYOU were both examples of macro worms that were propagated through Microsoft Outlook e-mail and whose payloads were delivered as a VBA program attached to e-mail messages. When the unsuspecting recipient opened the e-mail, the VBA program looked up the entries in the recipient's Outlook address book and sent copies of itself to the contacts in the address book. If you think this is a difficult task, note that the ILOVEYOU macro was about 40 lines of code.

- **Trojan horses.** "A Trojan horse is a program that appears to have a useful function but also contains a hidden and unintended function that presents a security risk." (Norton and Stockman 2000). The name is derived from the Trojan horse in Greek mythology. Legend has it that the Trojans were presented, during the Troy War, with a large wooden horse as a gift to the goddess Athena. The Trojans hauled the horse into the city gates. During the night, Greek soldiers, who were hiding in the hollow horse, opened the city gates and let in the Greek army. The army was able to take the city and win the war.

    Two of the better-known Trojans are "Back Orifice" and "NetBus." Both Trojans are self-contained and self-installing utilities that can be used to remotely control and monitor the victim's computer over a network. "Whack-A-Mole" is a popular delivery vehicle for NetBus. Whack-A-Mole is actually a game that is delivered as a self-extracting "zip file" (for a non-malicious version of the game see *tomorrowfund.org/swgame09.html*). When a rogue version of the game is installed, so is NetBus.

APPLICATION CASE 13.4

Trojan Horse Attack on BugTraq List

BugTraq is "a full disclosure moderated mailing list for the detailed discussion and announcement of computer security vulnerabilities: what they are, how to exploit them, and how to fix "them." (Lemos 2000). The list has 37,000 subscribers and is moderated by security experts working at *SecurityFocus.com*, a leading provider of security information services for business. Well, it seems like even the experts get fooled sometimes. On February 1, 2000, someone sent them a program designed to identify four flaws in the Berkley Internet Domain Name (BIND) software. *SecurityFocus.com* had Network Associates (a security software maker) check out the code. They gave it their seal of approval.

Unfortunately, hidden in the code was a Trojan horse. The program was actually designed to use any computer on which it runs to send a simple form of Internet data to a single domain name server in an attempt to overwhelm the computer with information (a standard DDoS attack). In this case, the computer to which the data was to be sent was Network Associates' server. When *SecurityFocus.com* sent the code to its 37,000 subscribers, Network Associates soon found themselves under attack. Fortunately, for Network Associates, it only took them 90 minutes to get back online.

SecurityFocus defended the list's posting procedure and said that despite the incident, the way the list is moderated won't change. According to a vice president at the firm, "The BugTraq moderation has never been in place to verify every single piece of information or exploits that go through the list. There is no way we could have a lab or staff to do that. As always, we tell people to wait for other people to test the exploits before installing them themselves."

Source: Lemos (2000).

Malicious Mobile Code

The advent of mobile code was instrumental in evolving the Web from a collection of static pages to a set of interactive network applications. Mobile code is a program or object that is downloaded across the Internet and executed on a user's machine. Most mobile code comes in the form of ActiveX controls or Java applets that are run inside a Web browser.

ActiveX controls are Microsoft's version of mobile code. These controls only run in Microsoft's Web browser—Internet Explorer (IE). A simple example of an ActiveX control is the Ad Rotator that can be used to rotate through a series of advertising banners on a Web page, which, when clicked, will take the user to an associated Web page. The way an ActiveX control works in a browser is relatively straightforward. When a user accesses a page that references an ActiveX control (i.e., has an HTML <OBJECT> tag in the page), the browser first checks to see if the control is already registered on the user's machine. If so, it loads the object in memory and executes the control code. If it isn't registered, it downloads it across the Internet, installs it, and then executes it.

From a security perspective, one of the major problems with ActiveX controls is that a hacker can create a control that can do virtually anything on the user's machine. The only barrier between the unsuspecting user and a malicious ActiveX control is a series of security settings in Microsoft's IE browser and their Authenticode paradigm. The IE browser enables users to select what they want to happen when an ActiveX object is contained in a page. As Figure 13-5 shows, the options are: "disable"—don't run them; "enable"—run them; and "prompt"—ask me before you run them. These selections can be made for both "signed" and "unsigned" controls. This is where Authenticode comes in. Authenticode enables a programmer to digitally sign his or her code (see Chapter 14) and to have the digital signature verified by a trusted, third-party certificate authority. Theoretically, the certificate authority has verified the credentials of the programmers who developed the signed control. Of course, no system is foolproof. Additionally, hackers have developed ways to bypass these security measures.

Unlike ActiveX, Java applets can run in any browser that has a feature called a Java Virtual Machine. Java applets work in much the same way that an ActiveX control does. When a browser downloads a page with an HTML <APPLET> tag in it, it first checks to see whether the applet has been temporarily stored on the computer (in the computer's cache), if so, it loads and executes it. If not, it downloads it across the Internet and then executes it.

By design, Java applets are supposed to be more secure than ActiveX controls. In comparison to ActiveX, a Java applet cannot access memory addresses, restrains programmers from inadvertently creating buffer overflows in their code, has a built-in security manager that limits access to various aspects of the user's machine without the user's consent, and supports digital signatures (similar to Authenticode). Taken together, these security features are called the Java "sandbox." Of course, theory and reality are different things. These security mechanisms have been broken several times. For a listing of the breakdowns see *cs.princeton.edu/sip/history/index.php3.*

Figure 13-5	ActiveX Security Settings

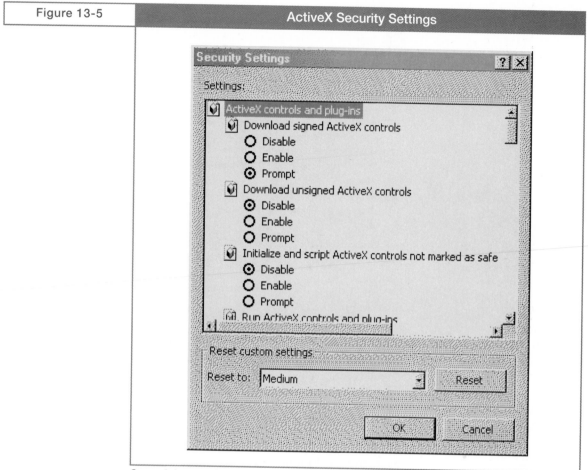

Source: *halcyon.com/mclain/ActiveX.*at *nwnexux.com.*

13.7   SECURITY TECHNOLOGIES

Internet and EC security is a thriving business. International Data Corporation (IDC) estimates that the security software market will increase from $2 billion to $7 billion in 2003 and that the security hardware business will grow from $500 million to $1.9 billion in 2003. The recent CSI/FBI survey and Information Security survey give some indication of where the money is being spent. The CSI/FBI survey combined respondents from both EC and non-EC sites. The results indicated that high on the list of security solutions were: antivirus software (100 percent of the sites); access control—basically user IDs and passwords (92 percent); physical security—controlling physical access to servers (90 percent); firewalls (78 percent); encrypted files (62 percent); encrypted logins (50 percent); and intrusion detection (50 percent). In contrast, the Information Security survey focused specifically on EC sites and grouped the responses by type of site (B2C vs. B2B). The results from the survey are reproduced in Table 13-5. One of the major differences between B2C and B2B sites is that B2B sites use a more layered approach to their security, with 70 percent employing more than four overlapping security technologies to secure communications and commerce. The main reason

EC Security Controls		
Tool	**B2C**	**B2B**
User IDs/Passwords	86%	85%
Firewalls/Packet Filtering	N/A	79%
Transactional Encryption (SSL/SET/SHTTP)	67%	60%
Server Segregation (DMZ)	50%	51%
Application-Specific Controls	44%	N/A
Authentication Servers (Kerberos, RADIUS, RAS)	40%	46%
Digital Certificate-Based Authentication/PKI	39%	45%
Point-to-Point Encryption (VPNs)	38%	56%
Dedicated Circuits	20%	36%
Authentication Tokens (hard or soft, including smart cards)	20%	29%
Other	3%	3%
None	3%	1%

TABLE 13-5

Source: Briney (2000). Used with permission of Information Security.

for this is that B2B is more mature and more money is currently being spent on this form of EC.

In the remainder of this section we'll discuss three of the technologies used to secure EC sites, including firewalls, Virtual Private Networks (VPNs), and intrusion detection systems. The chapter that follows delves into areas of encryption, digital certificates, and secure transmissions.

Firewalls and Access Control

One of the major impediments to EC has been concern about the security of internal networks. A number of companies have sidestepped the issue by letting outside companies host their Web sites. In this way they eliminate the possibility of a hacker breaking into their internal systems, although hackers can still play havoc with the contents of the Web site. For those companies hosting their own sites, one of the immediate concerns is controlling access to network services, both inside and outside the company. Companies need to ensure that intruders cannot gain access to critical applications by tunneling through the Web site to exploit weaknesses in the internal network operating system, application software, and databases.

For most applications the primary means of access control is password protection. Passwords are notoriously susceptible to compromise. Users have a habit of sharing their passwords with others, writing them down where others can see them, and choosing passwords that are easily guessed. On top of these problems, when the Web requests the user to enter a password to access protected documents or applications, the browser transmits the passwords in a form that is easily intercepted and decoded. One way to combat this problem is to make sure that even if the passwords are compromised, the intruder has restricted access to the rest of the network. This is one of the roles of a firewall.

A **firewall** is a network node consisting of both hardware and software that isolates a private network from a public network. Hazari (2000) provides a simple analogy to understand the general operation of a firewall: "We can think of firewalls as being similar to a bouncer in a nightclub. Like a bouncer in a nightclub, firewalls have a set of rules, similar to a guest list or a dress code, that determine if the data should be allowed entry. Just as the bouncer places himself at the door of the club, the firewall is located at the point of entry where data attempts to enter the computer from the Internet. But, just as different nightclubs might have different rules for entry, different firewalls have different methods of inspecting data for acceptance or rejection."

In order to understand how a firewall works, you need to understand the notions of packets, IP addresses, and ports. Packets and IP addresses were described earlier in the discussion about DoS attacks (Section 13.6). Just as a refresher, when two computers communicate with one another over the Internet, the computer sending the message breaks it into smaller segments called packets. The packets are sent over the Internet to the IP address of the receiving computer. The IP address of the sending and receiving computers are contained in the "header" of each packet. After receiving all the packets in a message, the destination computer reassembles them. How does it know what to do with the message? Computers are connected to the Internet via **ports**. Each port has a different number and represents a different service. For example, Web communications are usually carried out via port 80. File transfer requests made with the Internet's file transfer protocol (FTP) are handled on port 21. Like the IP addresses, the port number is contained in the packet header.

There are basically two types of firewalls—**packet-filtering routers** and **application-level proxies**. These can be combined to provide added security. The simplest is the packet-filtering router. **Packet filters** are rules that can accept or reject incoming packets based on source and destination IP addresses, source and destination port numbers, and packet type (i.e., information contained in the packet header). Some examples of simple types of rules include the following:

- "Only allow packets destined for port 80." This would only allow Web connections and block all others.
- "Block all packets sent from a given IP address." Companies sometimes use this to block requests from computers owned by competitors.
- "Block any packet coming from the outside that has the address of a computer on the inside." This eliminates IP spoofing (see Section 13.6).

Packet-filtering firewalls provide low-level control and are difficult to get around. However, they do have their disadvantages. In setting up the rules, an administrator might miss some important rules or incorrectly specify a rule, thus leaving a hole in the firewall. Additionally, the ports open for particular services can sometimes be used by other transports (Norton and Stockman 2000). Finally, because the content of a packet is irrelevant to a packet filter, once a packet is let through the firewall, the inside network is open to data-driven attacks. That is, the data may contain hidden instructions that cause the receiving computer to modify access control or security-related files.

A variant of the packet-filtering firewall is the **stateful packet inspection firewall**. A packet-filtering firewall is called stateless because it only looks at the state of the packet when it is received. It has no information about what occurred before the packet arrived or after the packet was passed through the firewall. Stateful packet inspection is a form of enhanced packet filtering. Not only is the header examined but so are the contents of the packet. The contents can be used to determine the state of the communications. For example, if a computer inside the firewall requests data from a computer with a specific IP address outside the firewall, then a stateful packet inspection firewall can check the IP address of incoming packets to match them against the previous request. This type of firewall can also be used to eliminate network traffic that contains certain content like Java applets, ActiveX controls, or e-mail with executable programs.

The second type of firewall is the **application-level proxy**. This type of firewall often involves a special server called a (dual-homed) **bastion gateway**. The gateway server has two network cards so that data packets reaching one card are not relayed to the other card (see Figure 13-6). Instead, special software programs called proxies run on the gateway server and pass repackaged packets from one network to the other. There is a proxy for each Internet service that an organization wishes to support. For instance, there is a Web (i.e., HTTP) proxy, an FTP proxy, and so on. If a request is made for an unsupported proxy service, then it is blocked by the firewall. In addition to controlling inbound traffic, the firewall and proxies control outbound traffic. All outbound traffic requests are first sent to the proxy server and then forwarded by the proxy on behalf of the computers behind the firewall. This makes all the requests look as if they were coming from a single computer rather than multiple computers. In this way, the IP addresses of the internal computers are hidden to the outside.

The main disadvantage of an application-level proxy firewall is that the users on the internal network must configure their machines or browsers to send their Internet requests via the proxy server.

Packet-filtering firewalls and application-level proxy firewalls can be combined to enhance the security of a network. For example, in a **screened host firewall** (see Figure 13-7) a packet-filtering router firewall is used to control access to the bastion gateway. This ensures that all inbound traffic must pass through the bastion

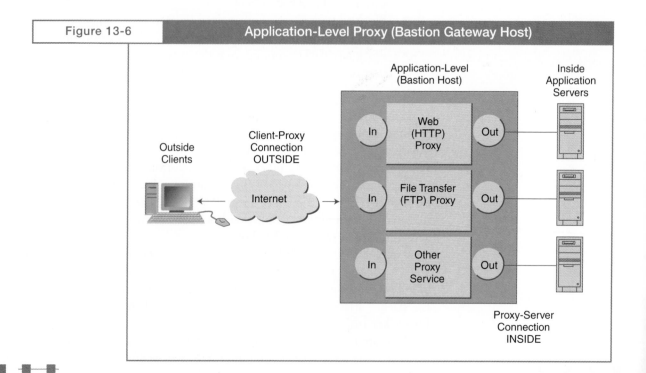

Figure 13-6   Application-Level Proxy (Bastion Gateway Host)

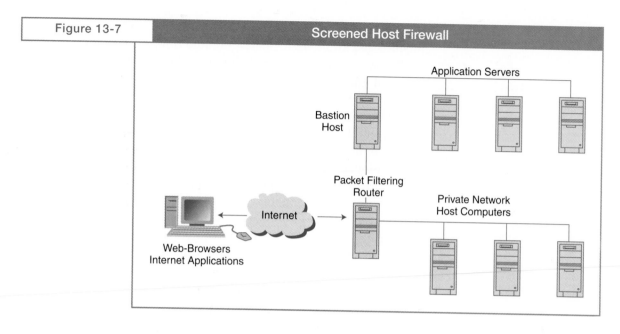

Figure 13-7

Screened Host Firewall

gateway. Another variant of a screened host gateway is the **screened subnet gateway**, in which the bastion gateway offers access to a small segment of the internal network. The open subnet is known as the **demilitarized zone (DMZ)**. Figure 13-8 shows one of the possibilities for a screened subnet configuration. The idea behind the screened subnet is that there is no way for outside traffic to gain access to any of the other hosts on the internal network.

Firewall systems can be created from scratch. However, most companies rely on commercial firewall systems. The CSI Firewall Product Search Center

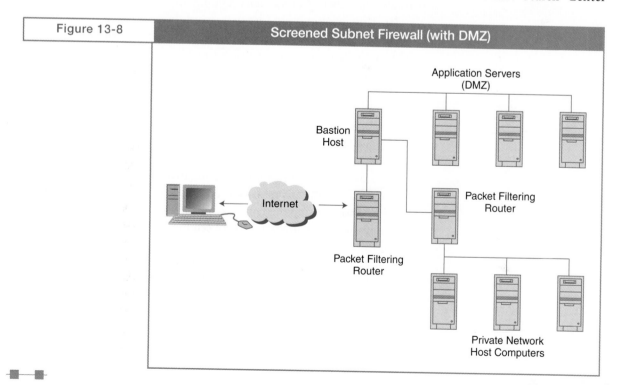

Figure 13-8

Screened Subnet Firewall (with DMZ)

(*spirit.com/CSI/firewalls.html*) provides a listing of a variety of commercial firewall products and the means to do head-to-head comparisons among the systems based on 30 characteristics including hardware and software configurations, vendor support, and price. More than 20 products are included on the list. Among the products are Axent's VelociRaptor, Cyberguard's Firewall, NetGuard's Guardian Firewall, and PGP Security's Gauntlet Firewall.

In recent years, the number of individuals with high-speed broadband—cable modem or digital subscriber lines (DSL)—Internet connections to their homes or small businesses has increased. These "always-on" connections are much more vulnerable to attack than simple dial-up connections. With these connections, the homeowner or small business owner runs the risk of information being stolen or destroyed or sensitive information (e.g., personal or business financial information) being accessed, and of his or her computer being used in a DoS attack on others. **Personal firewalls** are designed to protect these desktop systems by monitoring all the traffic that passes through the computer's network interface card. They operate in one of two ways. On the one hand, the owner can create filtering rules (much like a packet-filtering or a stateful packet inspection firewall) that are used by the firewall to permit or delete packets. On the other hand, the firewall can learn by prompting the user to ask how particular traffic ought to be handled. There are a number of personal firewall products on the market, like Black Ice Defender from Network Ice (*networkice.com*). For a detailed comparison of a number of these products see *firewallguide.com/software.htm*.

Virtual Private Networks (VPNs)

Suppose a company wants to establish a B2B application, providing suppliers, partners, and others access to data residing not only on their internal Web site, but also data contained in other files (e.g., word documents) or in legacy systems (e.g., large relational databases). Traditionally, communications with the company would have taken place over a private leased line or through a dial-up line to a bank of modems or a remote access server (RAS) that provided direct connections to the company's local area network (LAN). With a private line, the chances of a hacker eavesdropping on the communications between the companies would be nil, but it is an expensive way to do business. A less expensive alternative would be to use a **virtual private network (VPN)**. A VPN uses the public Internet to carry information but remains private by using a combination of encryption to scramble the communications, authentication to ensure that the information has not been tampered with and comes from a legitimate source, and access control to verify the identity of anyone using the network. In addition, a VPN can also be used to support site-to-site communications between branch offices and corporate headquarters and the communications between mobile workers and their workplace. In all these cases, communication costs are drastically reduced. The estimate of cost savings for site-to-site networks is 20 to 40 percent for sites in the same country and much more if they are in different countries. The savings for mobile and remote workers is estimated at 60 to 80 percent.

The main technical challenge of a VPN is to ensure the confidentiality and integrity of the data transmitted over the Internet. This is where **protocol tunnel-**

ing comes into the picture. In protocol tunneling, data packets are first encrypted and then encapsulated into IP packets that can be transmitted across the Internet. The IP packets are decrypted at the destination address by a special host or router. Protocol tunneling also supports **multiprotocol networking**. Local area networks (LANs) usually rely on protocols like Netware's IPX protocol. To access a LAN via the Internet, the packets needed for LAN communications (say, IPX packets) need to be encapsulated into IP packets before being transmitted across the Internet. In this way, LAN packets can be delivered across the Internet in such a way that it appears to end users as if they were directly connected to the LAN. Protocol tunneling provides this form of encapsulation.

Various protocols can be used to carry out protocol tunneling (i.e., to encrypt and encapsulate the data being transmitted). Among the protocols, two are more prevalent:

- **Point-to-point tunneling (PTP) protocol.** The main PTP implementation was done by Microsoft and is supported by Windows NT and Windows 2000. This protocol is an extension of the PTP protocol used by ISPs to provide dial-up Internet access and mainly supports client-to-LAN connections instead of LAN-to-LAN connections. It was proposed as a standard, but has lost support as Microsoft has turned its attention to other technologies. Security experts have criticized PTP quite heavily.
- **Layer 2 tunneling protocol (L2TP).** L2TP is rapidly becoming the industry standard. It supports multiprotocol tunneling and provides interoperability between VPN products from different vendors. This protocol is often combined with IPSec, a standard developed by the Internet Engineering Task Force (IETF) for secure IP communications.

Three technologies can be used to create a VPN. First, many of the firewall packages—hardware and software—support VPN functionality. Second, routers cannot only function as firewalls, but they can also function as VPN servers. Finally, there are software solutions that can be used to handle VPN connections. The VPN Consortium (*vpnc.org/features-chart.html*) provides a comparison of a number of commercial VPN products.

Many telecom carriers and larger ISPs offer VPN services for Internet-based dial-up and site-to-site communications. These carriers use their own private network backbones to which they have added security features, intranet connectivity, and new dial-up capabilities for remote services. Some of the carriers providing these services include:

- AT&T (*att.com/emea/vpn*)
- Cable & Wireless (*cwusa.net/internet_ipvpn.htm*)
- MCI WorldCom (*worldcom.com/products*)
- PSINet (*psinet.com/security/datasheets/managedservicesintranet.html*)

Intrusion Detection Systems (IDS)

Even if an organization has a well-formulated security policy and a number of security technologies in place, it is still vulnerable to attack. For example, in 2000, 100 percent of the respondents to the CSI/FBI survey had antivirus software, yet

85 percent reported incidents of virus contamination. This is why an organization must continually watch for attempted, as well as actual, security breaches.

In the past, audit logs, produced by a variety of system components and applications, were manually reviewed for excessive failed logon attempts, failed file and database access attempts, and other application and system violations. Obviously, this manual procedure had its flaws. For example, if intrusion attempts were spread out over a long period of time, they could be easily missed. Today, there is a special category of software that can monitor activity across a network or on a host computer, watch for suspicious activity, and take automated action based on what it sees. This category of software is called **Intrusion Detection System (IDSs)**.

There are two types of IDSs—host-based and network-based (Ott 2001; Norton and Stockman 2000). A **host-based IDS** resides on the server or other host system that is being monitored. Host-based systems are particularly good at detecting whether critical or security-related files have been tampered with or whether a user has attempted to access files that he or she is not authorized to use. The host-based system does this by computing a special signature or check-sum for each file. The IDS checks files on a regular basis to see if the current signatures match the previous signatures. If the signatures don't match, security personnel are immediately notified. Some examples of commercial host-based systems are Axent's Intruder Alert (*axent.com*), Tripwire Security's Tripwire (*tripwiresecurity.com*), and Network Associates CyberCop Monitor (*nai.com*).

A **network-based IDS** uses rules to analyze suspicious activity at the perimeter of a network or at key locations in the network. It usually consists of a monitor—a software package that scans your network—and software agents that reside on various host computers and feed information back to the monitor. This type of IDS examines network traffic (i.e., packets) for known patterns of attack (e.g., IP Spoofing, IP Fragmentation, SYNFlood, etc.) and automatically notifies security personnel when specific events or event thresholds occur. A network-based IDS can also perform certain actions when an attack occurs. For instance, it can terminate network connections or reconfigure network devices, such as firewalls and routers, based on security policies. Cisco Systems' NetRanger (*cisco.com*) and Computer Associates' Session Wall-3 (*abirnet.com*) are both examples of commercially available network-based IDSs.

13.8   MANAGERIAL ISSUES

The following issues are germane to management:

A sizeable percentage of the *Fortune* and Global 500 corporations have EC sites. If you asked the senior management of these organizations whether they take network security seriously, they would certainly answer with a resounding, "Yes." Yet, in spite of this answer, most of these organizations only spend a small percentage of their budgets on network security, have fairly small staffs working on network security issues, and generally relegate network security matters to personnel on lower rungs on the organizational ladder. Because the consequences of poor network security can be severe, it is imperative that senior management have a basic understanding of best practices in network risk management.

1. **Recognize the business consequences of poor security.** According to a 1998 Government Accounting Office (GAO) study (Merkow and Breihaupt, 2000), the single most important factor in establishing an effective network security program is the general recognition and understanding among senior management of the enormous risks to business operations associated with relying on automated and highly interconnected computer systems. In a nutshell, ineffective security opens the door to computer and network attacks that can result in: damage to technical and information assets; theft of information and information services; temporary loss of a Web site and Internet access; loss of income; litigation brought on by dissatisfied organizational stakeholders; loss of customer confidence; and damaged reputation and credibility. In some cases, attacks can literally put a company out of business, especially if EC is their sole source of revenue.

2. **Security through obscurity doesn't work.** Suppose you decide to set up a B2B site in order to service your suppliers and partners. Because it isn't a public site, the only ones who are likely to know of its existence are you, your suppliers, and your partners. There is no need to institute strong security measures. Wrong! Because of the prevalence of automated scanning tools, it will only be a matter of days before hackers discover your site. Once discovered, it will only be a matter of hours or minutes before the hackers have compromised your site and taken control if your system has known vulnerabilities. The moral of the story is that regardless of how obscure, uninteresting, or unadvertised a site is, no EC site can afford to take security for granted. All sites should thoroughly review their security requirements and institute stringent measures to guard against high priority threats.

3. **It's the business that counts, not the technology.** Most discussions about security focus on technology. You hear statements like "firewalls are mandatory" or "all transmissions should be encrypted." While firewalls and encryption can be important technologies, no security solution is useful unless it solves a business problem. Determining your business requirements is the most important step in creating a security solution. Business requirements in turn determine your information requirements. Once your information requirements are known, you can begin to understand the value of those assets and the steps that should be taken to secure those that are most valuable and vulnerable.

4. **Security is an ongoing, closed-loop process.** Security risk management is an ongoing process involving four phases: assessment, planning, implementation, and monitoring. By actively monitoring our existing security policies and measures, we can determine which are successful or unsuccessful and, in turn, which should be modified or eliminated. However, it's also important to monitor changes in business requirements, changes in technology and the way it is used, and changes in the way people can attack our systems and networks. In this way, an organization can evolve its security policies and measures, ensuring that they continue to support the critical needs of the business.

5. **Even for EC sites, internal breaches are more prevalent than external breaches.** As the Internet Security survey showed, EC sites are more likely than non-EC sites to encounter security breaches, both inside and outside the organization. Except for the prevalence of viruses and worms, breaches perpetrated by insiders are much more frequent than those perpetrated by outsiders. This is true for both types of sites. The moral of this story is that security policies and measures for EC sites need to address these insider threats.

Summary

In this chapter, you learned about the following EC issues as they relate to the learning objectives:

1. **Computer and network security attacks are on the rise.** From a network security standpoint, the 11 years between the appearance of the Morris Worm in 1988 to the Melissa Virus in 1999 were relatively calm. In 1999 cyber attacks began to escalate dramatically. Data collected from the Computer Emergency Response Team (CERT) showed that cyber attacks more than doubled from 1998 to 1999 and doubled again in 2000 to approximately 22,000 reported attacks. Survey data reported by the Computer Security Institute and the FBI (CSI/FBI) indicated that better than 70 percent of those organizations surveyed experienced one or more attacks in 2000 and lost approximately $260 million dollars. Both figures were substantially higher than their 1996 levels. In the same vein, survey data from Internet Security demonstrated that e-commerce sites were much more likely to be the victim of attacks than other sites, reaffirming the notion that the rise in cyber attacks on the Internet is a direct result of the rise of e-commerce.

2. **The rise in security attacks is the result of a number of factors.** EC sites have proven to be particularly vulnerable to cyber attack. EC systems are built from a number of complex components and applications. Many of these components and applications are supplied by third-party vendors, some of whom treat security as an afterthought and, even when they find security holes in their systems, expend little effort to correct them. At many sites, the people responsible for building and administering the sites have little training in network security. Even when they are trained, they often opt for minimal security settings because this makes it easier (for consumers and partners alike) to do business with the site. Unfortunately, all it takes is a vulnerability in one component or application to compromise the security of the whole system. Automated tools make it possible for hackers—of practically any skill level—to discover and exploit these vulnerabilities in relatively short order. Even if they can't find a vulnerability at a particular site of interest, they can always perform a flanking maneuver. Because of the interconnectedness of the Internet, its always possible to use a vulnerable site to launch an attack against a secure site.

3. **Basic types of network security issues.** EC sites need to be concerned with a variety of security issues including: authentication—verifying the identity of the participants in a transaction; authorization—ensuring that a person or process has access rights to particular systems or data; auditing—being able to determine whether particular actions have been taken and by whom; confidentiality—ensuring that information is not disclosed to unauthorized individuals, systems, or processes; integrity—protecting data from being altered or destroyed; availability—ensuring that data and services are available when needed; nonrepudiation—ability to limit parties from refuting that a legitimate transaction took place.

4. **Steps in developing a security risk management system.** Security risk management is an ongoing process that consists of four interrelated phases—assessment, planning, implementation, and monitoring. In the assessment phase, an organization inventories its information assets, the threats against

those assets, and the vulnerabilities of the systems on which the assets reside. This phase is also used to calculate a quantitative risk for each asset in order to determine which assets should be safeguarded and which threats need to be minimized. In the planning phase, an organization arrives at a set of security policies defining which threats are tolerable and which are not. The third phase is implementation. During this phase, particular technologies are chosen to address the high priority threats. Finally, in the monitoring phase, an organization determines which policies and technologies have been successful or unsuccessful and what types of new threats are appearing on the horizon. With this information in hand, the process is repeated.

5. **Major types of attacks against EC systems.** EC sites are exposed to a wide range of attacks. Among the more frequent and major forms of attack are: those permitted by holes in operating systems, Web servers, and database servers; through storefront and shopping cart software where attacks are facilitated by system and software bugs and misconfigurations; DoS attacks where a hacker brings the operation of a site to a halt by flooding a site with so many requests that all the bandwidth at the site is consumed or by issuing specific requests that consume all of a particular computing resource at the site; buffer overflow attacks where the hacker sends enough data to a server to overwrite its memory buffer in such a way that the server executes a rogue request contained in the data; input validation attacks where a hacker submits invalid data that results in a server executing a rogue request contained in the data or that exploits a known bug in system software; attacks that enable a hacker to eavesdrop on the communications between two computers on the Internet; malicious code attacks involving viruses, worms, or some combination of both, often propagated by e-mail; and malicious mobile code attacks where ActiveX components or Java applets are used to compromise an end user's desktop.

6. **Major technologies for securing EC.** Virtually all sites—EC or not—rely on antivirus software, user IDs and passwords, physical security, firewalls, encrypted files and transmissions, and intrusion detection to secure their sites. At EC sites, firewalls, VPNs, and IDSs have proven extremely useful. A firewall is a combination of hardware and software that isolates a private network from a public network. Firewalls are of two general types—packet-filtering routers or application-level proxies. A packet-filtering router uses a set of rules to determine which communication packets can move from the outside network to the inside network. In contrast, an application-level proxy is a firewall that accepts requests from the outside for particular services (say a request for a Web page) and repackages the request before sending it to the inside network, thus ensuring the security of the request. VPNs enable secure transmissions across the Internet. They are generally used to support site-to-site transmissions across the Internet between B2B partners or communications between a mobile and remote worker and a LAN at a central office. The Internet transmissions are secured by a combination of encryption, authentication, and access control, creating a "protocol tunnel" between the nodes on the network. Finally, IDSs are used to monitor activity across a network or on a host, watching for suspicious activity, and taking automated actions whenever a security breach or attack occurs.

Key Terms

Application-level proxy firewall	Multiprotocol networking
Asset	Network-based Intrusion Detection System
Attack	Nonrepudiation
Auditing	Nontechnical attack
Authentication	Packet filter
Authorization	Packet-filtering router firewall
Availability	Personal firewall
Bastion gateway	Ping of death
Buffer	Point-to-point tunneling protocol (P2P)
Buffer overflow	Port
Common Vulnerabilities and Exposures Board	Privacy
Computer Emergency Response Team (CERT)	Promiscuous mode
Computer Security Institute (CSI)	Protocol tunneling
Confidentiality	Quantitative risk analysis
Demilitarized zone (DMZ)	Risk management
Denial-of-service (DoS) attack	Screened host firewall
Distributed denial-of-service (DDoS) attack	Screened subnet gateway
DNS spoofing	Smurf attack
Firewall	Sniffer
Host-based Intrusion Detection System	Social engineering
Incident response team	Spoofing
Information Protection Assessment Kit (IPAK)	Stateful packet inspection firewall
Input validation attack	SYNFlood
Integrity	Technical attack
Intrusion Detection System (IDS)	Threat
IP Fragmentation	Trojan horse
Layer 2 tunneling protocol (L2TP)	Virtual private network (VPN)
Macro virus	Virus
Macro worm	Vulnerability
Malicious code	Worm
Malicious mobile code	Zombie
Malware	

Questions for Review

1. Describe the role that a zombie plays in a DDoS attack.
2. What is a script kiddie?
3. What empirical evidence is there that cyber attacks are on the rise?
4. List the basic security issues in EC.
5. Who is CERT?
6. What is an information asset? Threat? Vulnerability? Attack?
7. List the major steps in security risk management. Briefly describe each.
8. What types of network security attacks are EC sites most vulnerable to?
9. Who is the CVE board?
10. What is IPAK?
11. List some of the generic security controls for EC.

12. Describe social engineering.
13. How can SAINT be used by a hacker?
14. Describe the role that software bugs can play in network security.
15. What are some of the major types of DoS/DDoS attacks? Briefly describe each.
16. What is a buffer? How are buffers used to attack EC sites?
17. Describe an input validation attack.
18. What is sniffing?
19. Distinguish viruses from worms.
20. What is a Trojan horse attack?
21. Describe the basic types of malicious mobile code attacks.
22. Which type of EC site—B2C or B2B—is more concerned with security? Explain.
23. List the basic types of firewalls and briefly describe each.
24. How does a virtual private network (VPN) work?
25. Briefly describe the major types of intrusion detection systems (IDSs).

Questions for Discussion

1. Cyber attacks are on the rise. Discuss the factors that have contributed to the increase. Do you expect the situation to get worse or better? Explain.
2. A homeowner has just installed a cable modem at his or her home. The homeowner feels that there is no need to worry about security because no one will ever know about his or her home computer. Why should the homeowner be worried about attacks by hackers? What are some of the steps the homeowner should take to secure his or her home computer?
3. A large number of B2C EC sites have experienced DDoS attacks. Why are these attacks so hard to safeguard against? What are some of the things a site can do to mitigate the attacks?
4. All EC sites share common security threats and vulnerabilities. Discuss these threats and vulnerabilities and some of the security policies that can be implemented to mitigate them. Are there any differences in the types of threats and vulnerabilities faced by B2C and B2C sites? Explain.
5. You've just put up a B2C EC site. The Web pages on your site will have the usual Web forms for selecting and purchasing products. You've also decided to make your site very interactive and will be using a Java applet to display animated pictures of your products. What types of security threats and vulnerabilities do the forms and applet present?
6. What type of security attack is most prevalent on the Internet? Discuss some of the major reasons for its prevalence.
7. All EC sites employ one or more security safeguards. Yet, there are differences between B2C and B2B sites in the safeguards they use. Discuss the similarities and differences between the two types of sites.
8. A business wants to establish and run its own Web site for advertising and marketing. Some of the marketing materials will come from databases located on their LAN. What types of security components could be used to ensure that outsiders don't have direct access to those databases? What type of network configuration (e.g., screened host) will provide the most security?

9. Two businesses want to use the Internet to handle purchase orders, payments, and deliveries. They are afraid that hackers will eavesdrop on the Internet communications between them. What type of security technology could they use to safeguard against this threat?

10. You are responsible for the security at a B2C EC site and need to do an audit of your network's vulnerabilities. What type of software tool should you use to conduct the audit? What types of information will the tool provide? Once you've identified various vulnerabilities and corrected them, can you be sure your site is safe? Explain.

Exercises

1. Visit the hacked pages archive at *www.2600.com* (*www.2600.com/hacked_pages/index.html*). Construct a list of some of the more famous sites that have been the object of hacker attacks.

2. The Computer Vulnerabilities and Exposures Board maintains a list of common network security vulnerabilities. Review the list. How many vulnerabilities are there? Based on that list, which system components appear to be most vulnerable to attack? What impact do these vulnerable components have on EC?

3. A number of B2C sites rely on hidden fields in their Web forms to pass information back and forth between a consumer's browser and their Web servers. Go to AltaVista and search for the following string: <INPUT TYPE=hidden NAME="price". What types of EC forms use this type of hidden field? Give some examples. What sort of security threat does a hidden field of this sort represent?

4. Your B2C site has just been hacked. You'd like to report the incident to the Computer Emergency Response Team (*cert.org*) at Carnegie Mellon University so they can alert other sites. How do you do this and what types of information do you have to provide?

5. Go to Network Associates virus library (*vil.nai.com/vil/default.asp*). What are the general characteristics of a virus? How are risks of viruses assessed (see *mcafeeb2b.com/avert/virus-alerts/avert-risk-assessment.asp*)?

6. The World Wide Web consortium maintains a security FAQ (list of frequently asked questions). Based on this FAQ (*w3.org/Security/Faq/www-security-faq.html#contents*), what sorts of security threats do CGI programs pose and how can they be managed?

7. The Computer Security Institute provides a comparison of various commercial firewall products (*spirit.com/csi/firewalls.html*). Select three of the products and do a comparison of their features. Based on your comparison, which product would you select?

8. You have just installed a DSL line in your home so you will have faster Internet access. You have heard that this makes your computer susceptible to DDoS attacks and you want to install a personal firewall to guard against this threat. What sorts of commercial products are available? Which one would you choose?

Team Assignments and Role Playing

1. The Honeynet Project (*project.honeynet.org*) is a group of 30 security professionals dedicated to learning the tools, tactics, and motives of the black-hat community and sharing those lessons learned. As part of their "Know Your Enemy" series, they did an extensive study of script kiddie attacks (*project.honeynet.org/papers/enemy/*). Based on this study, provide an in-depth discussion of the methods employed by script kiddies to compromise a site and how a site can detect these attacks.

2. Security experts have been especially critical of the security vulnerabilities of Microsoft's software and systems. Using the Web, collect a body of empirical evidence—survey data, reports in journals, the CVE, etc.—to support or refute this claim. Why are Microsoft's software and systems any more or less vulnerable than other software and systems?

3. Select a B2C or B2B site on the Web. Discuss the site's assets, threats, and vulnerabilities. Prepare a brief risk management plan for the site.

REAL-WORLD CASE: The Rise of Security Standards

As Rob Clyde, vice president and CTO at security vendor Symantec Corp., recently said, "On a scale of 1 to 10, in terms of security in the Internet infrastructure, we are probably about 3 or 4." (Lewis 2001) A key factor contributing to this low score is the absence of a set of practical, non-proprietary, widely accepted Internet security guidelines, detailing how systems ought to be configured and what sorts of safeguards should be present. You could think of these guidelines as similar to the preflight maintenance checks used by airlines to ensure the safety of their aircraft before flight (Paller et al. 2000). Without standard guidelines, organizations, especially smaller businesses, will continue to build and maintain EC sites with little knowledge of the security hazards that await them.

On the B2C front, Visa is leading the charge for better security standards. In July 2000, they issued a set of guidelines that each merchant partner must meet if it wants to keep the Visa logo. Included in the list of guidelines are the following:

1. Establish a hiring policy for staff and contractors.

2. Restrict access to data on a need-to-know basis.

3. Assign each person a unique identity to be validated when accessing data.

4. Track access to data, including read access, by each person.

5. Install and maintain a network firewall if data can be accessed via the Internet.

6. Encrypt data maintained on databases or files accessible from the Internet.

7. Encrypt data sent across networks.

8. Protect systems and data from viruses.

9. Keep security patches for software up-to-date.

10. Don't use vendor-supplied defaults for system passwords and other security parameters.

11. Don't leave papers/diskettes/computers with data unsecured.

12. Securely destroy data when it's no longer needed for business reasons.

13. Regularly test security systems and procedures.

14. Immediately investigate and report to Visa any suspected loss of account or transaction information.

15. Use only service providers that meet these security standards.

In a pilot test, Visa will work with members to monitor compliance and will use Information Security Systems (*iss.net*), a supplier of intrusion-detection software and provider of managed security services, to perform monthly vulnerability scans of merchant sites and to fix holes if they emerge. Eventually, enforcement of the standards could involve fines, restricting the dollar amount of sales that individual merchants could process through the network, or terminating their Visa membership.

To encourage widespread acceptance throughout the EC world, representatives from federal, state, and local government agencies are working with academics and corporations (led by representatives of Visa and Merrill Lynch) to convert the Visa effort into one global set of standards. Their not-for-profit organization is called the Center for Internet Security (*cisecurity.org*). These global standards will be aimed not only at B2C sites but also B2B sites.

Currently, spending on B2B Internet security software is estimated by IDC to be $3.5 billion. This is expected to rise to $8.9 billion in 2004. While most B2B firms are confident about safeguarding data residing on corporate premises, they are still very leery about exchanging in-process designs, demand forecasts, inventory management, logistics updates, and a host of other important information across the Internet. They are even more leery about doing contract negotiations across the Internet. These negotiations, which can involve billions of dollars, are still done over the phone or in person. In an effort to address a broad range of B2B security (at least in the electronics industry), Cisco Systems, IBM, Intel, Nortel Networks, and Symantec formed the Information Technology Information Sharing and Analysis Center (IT-ISAC) in January 2000. The aim of the center is to promote best practices in network security

and, in turn, encourage the growth of B2B commerce.

Questions for the case

1. The standards proposed by Visa look like common sense. What types of businesses do you think the standards are aimed at? How do these standards compare to those proposed by IPAK? Based on this comparison, what other standards should Visa impose?

2. Visa is only one credit card vendor among many. Does the success of Visa's program rest on the adoption of these or similar standards by Visa's competitors? Explain.

3. If you were a member of IT-ISAC, what standards would you propose for the transmission of sensitive business information among B2B sites?

4. Given the breadth of vulnerabilities and Internet Security survey statistics, what sort of impact will any set of security standards have on the rise in cyber attacks?

REFERENCES AND BIBLIOGRAPHY

Aleph One. "Smashing the Stack for Fun and Profit," *Phrack Magazine*, vol. 49 (1996).

Allen, J., C. Alberts, S. Behrens, B. Laswell, and Wilson. "Improving the Security of Networked Systems," Pittsburgh, Pennsylvania: Networked Systems Survivability Program, Software Engineering Institute, Carnegie Mellon University, 2000.

Briney, A. "Security Focused: Survey 2000," *Information Security* (September 2000).

CERT Coordination Center. "CERT/CC Statistics 1988–2001," *cert.org/stats/cert_stats.html* (2000).

Compatible Systems. "VPN: The Executive Perspective on Virtual Private Networking," *compatible.com* (2000).

Computer Science Institute. "Firewall Product Comparison," *spirit.com/CSI/firewalls.html* (November 2000).

Computer Science Institute and Federal Bureau of Investigation, "Computer Crime and Security Survey," *gocsi.com* (2000).

Geralds, J., "Hackers Cost Firms Billions of Dollars," *vnunet.com/News/1117559* (February 2001).

Harrison, A. "Update: Mafiaboy Not the Big Fish in DoS Attacks," *ComputerWorld* (April 20, 2000).

Hazari, S. "Firewalls for Beginners," *online.securityfocus.com/infocus/1182* (November 6, 2000).

Heim, K. and E. Ackerman. "'Zombie' Attacks Blamed in New Online Outages," *Mercury News* (January 26, 2001).

Honeynet Project. "Know Your Enemy," *project.honeynet.org* (March 2000).

Howard, M. *Designing Secure Web-Based Applications for Microsoft Windows 2000*. Redmond, Washington: Microsoft Press, 2000.

Jansen, W. and T. Kargiannis. "Security Implications of Active Content," *ITT Bulletin* (March 2000).

Jenkins, J. "Internet Security and Your Business—Knowing the Risks," *securityfocus.com* (November 2000).

Kabay, M. and L. Walsh. "The Year in Computer Crime," *Information Security Magazine* (December 2000).

King, C. "Protect Your Assets with This Enterprise Risk-Management Guide," *Internet Security Advisor* (February 2001).

Lemos, R. "Security Patches Aren't Being Used: What Good Is a Band-Aid If You Don't Use It?" *msnbc.com* (January 2001).

Lemos, R. "Hackers Infiltrate BugTraq List—Experts Send Malicious Code to 37,000 Users," *ZDnet*, (February 1, 2000).

Lewis, N. "Beyond the Firewall: Data Sharing Stirs Privacy Fears," *EBN* (February 12, 2001).

Loshin, P. *Extranet Design and Implementation*, San Francisco: Sybex Network Press, 1998.

Marchany, R. "The Top 10 Internet Security Vulnerabilities Primer," *sans.org/topten.htm* (December 2000).

McMahon, D. *Cyber Threat*. New York: Wiley, 2000.

Mell, P. and J. Wack. "Mitigating Emerging Hacker Trends," *ITT Bulletin* (June 2000).

Merkow, M. and J. Breithaupt. *Internet Security: The Complete Guide*. New York: Amacom, 2000.

MSNBC Staff. "Password-Stealing Virus Hits AOL: Year-Old Bug Making Rounds Again, McAfee Says," *msnbc.com/tools/nm/nm0.asp?c=N6* (February 2001).

Mudge, Dr. "How to Write Buffer Overflows," *sniper.or/tech/mudge_buffer_overflow_tutorial.htm*
insecure.org/stf/mudge_buffer_overflow_tutorial.html
(1995).

Nieto, T., H. Deitel, and P. Deitel. *e-Business and e-commerce How to Program*. Upper Saddle River, New Jersey: Prentice Hall, 2001.

Norton, P. and M. Stockman. *Network Security Fundamentals*. Indianapolis, Indiana: SAMS, 2000.

Orgata, J., E. Orgata, and J. Shirley. "An Overview of Internet Security," *antibozo.net/ogata/security/overview* (2000).

Ott, J. "Intrusion Detection Systems Overview," *Internet Security Advisor* (February 2001).

Paller, A., R. Pethia, and G. Spafford. "Consensus Roadmap for Defeating Distributed Denial of Service Attacks," *sans.org/ddos_roadmap.htm* (February 23, 2000).

Power, R. *Tangled Web*. Indianapolis, Indiana: Que, 2000.

Radcliff, D. "The Info Warrior," *ComputerWorld* (January 22, 2001)

Rosencrance, L. "March Trial Date Set for Alleged Teen Hacker," *ComputerWorld* (December 20, 2000).

Russell, R. and S. Cunningham. *Hack Proofing Your Network*. Rockland, Massachusetts: Syngress Media, 2000.

Sager, I. "The Players," *Business Week* (February 21, 2000).

Scambray, J., S. McClure, and G. Kurtz. *Hacking Exposed*, 2nd ed. New York: McGraw-Hill, 2000.

Stein, L. *Web Security: A Step-by-Step Reference Guide*. New York: Addison-Wesley, 1998.

Symantec Corporation. "Assets, Threats and Vulnerabilities: Discovery and Analysis," *symantec.com* (2000).

Vijayan, J. "Group Pushes for B2B Security Standards," *ComputerWorld* (September 25, 2000).

Visa. "Visa Account Information Security Standards," *visa.com/nt/gds/standards.html* (2000).

Watson, J. "E-security: E-defense Against Hackers, Crackers, and Other Cyber-Thieves," *Fortune* (Special Technology Section) (July 10, 2000).

Wolf, J. "Critical Internet Software Found Vulnerable," *Reuters* (January 29, 2000).

14

Electronic Payment Systems

LEARNING OBJECTIVES

Upon completion of this chapter, the reader will be able to:

■ Understand the crucial factors determining the success of e-payment methods.

■ Describe the key elements in securing an e-payment.

■ Discuss the players and processes involved in using credit cards online.

■ Describe the uses and benefits of purchase cards.

■ Discuss different categories, methods of programming, and potential uses of smart cards.

■ Discuss various online alternatives to credit card payments and identify under what circumstances they are best used.

■ Describe the processes and parties involved in e-checks.

■ Discuss the operation and benefits of e-billing.

LensDoc (*lensdoc.com*) in Hilton Head, South Carolina, is an online retailer of contact lenses, sun and magnifying glasses, and dental care and personal care products. Like most B2C retailers, there's only one way for a customer to pay for a purchase—with a credit card (see the choices in Figure 14-1). Over 80 percent of the purchases made on the Web are done with credit cards. In the United States it is estimated that over 90 percent of all Web purchases are made with credit cards.

Although LensDoc relies on credit cards, they present a troubling dilemma for the retailer (Carr 2000). Credit cards make it easy for customers from all over the world to purchase items from their online store. They also make it easy for a customer to return an item and receive credit for the return. Yet, LensDoc has been the victim of a number of fraudulent charges from customers in Eastern Europe who have used other people's credit cards to buy expensive sunglasses. They also have a problem with the return of contact

lenses. People try them on and return them if they are not satisfied. The difficulty is that U.S. regulations prohibit the return of contact lenses that have been used, but the credit card companies are predisposed at the moment to allow the returns.

LensDoc is not alone. According to Alvin Cameron, credit/loss prevention manager for the online fulfillment house Digital River, "An estimated 20 to 40 percent of online purchases are fraud attempts. Merchants who cannot control the flood of fraudulent purchase attempts will soon be out of

FIGURE 14-1   LensDoc Payment

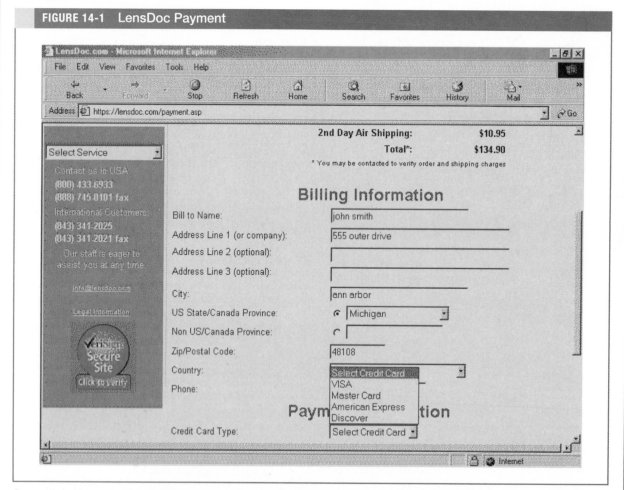

CHAPTER-OPENING CASE

14.1   LENSDOC: CREDIT CARD DILEMMA (*CONTINUED*)

business." (Caswell 2000). Contrary to popular belief, in credit card fraud it is the merchant that loses, not the consumer. By law, consumer liability is limited to $50. If a consumer spots an instance of fraud on their credit card bill, the charge is removed from the merchant's account, credited to the customer's account, and a chargeback fee of $15 per instance is assessed. MasterCard is in the process of assessing additional fees if chargebacks are 1 percent or

more of a company's total sales transactions. This will force merchants to implement more stringent protections than those currently used to secure approval from the credit card company.

For the moment, LensDoc has implemented special handling procedures for authorizing credit card purchases. They manually process credit card orders and ask customers to fax a form that includes the cardholder's address as well as the shipping address. Obviously, the assumption is

that if the card is stolen, then the perpetrator is unlikely to know the cardholder's address.

LensDoc has investigated a number of alternative e-payment methods, including cash cards, special card-swiping peripherals, credit card processing services, and the like. Each has its advantages and disadvantages. To date, the disadvantages seem to outweigh the advantages, or at least none seems more advantageous than credit cards.

14.2   ELECTRONIC PAYMENTS: AN OVERVIEW

In the off-line world, consumers use cash, checks, or credit cards to make purchases. At a fast food restaurant, we usually pay with cash. If we purchase an appliance at a discount store, we're likely to use a credit card. When we pay our bills, most of us use checks. A couple of years ago, Americans spent over $4 trillion on consumer goods. Approximately 60 percent of these expenditures were paid by checks, 20 percent by cash, and 20 percent by payment cards.

The same isn't true in the online world. A few years ago, it was generally believed that consumers would be extremely reluctant to use their credit card numbers on the Web. The assumption was that special forms of electronic or digital cash were required for B2C and other forms of EC to survive and thrive. Today, EC is thriving, and, as noted, the overwhelming majority of Web purchases are made with credit cards. Yet, there are other statistics that indicate that the picture may change in the near future. First, two-thirds of the people that will be on the Internet in 2003 haven't even had their first Web experience. Many of the users will come from countries outside the United States, where the use of credit cards is not as prevalent. Many of these users are also likely to be younger and have less access to credit and debit cards. Many of the purchases they make will involve currency values that are too small for credit cards (e.g., purchasing a single song or playing an online game). Second, and more importantly, about 85 percent of the transactions that occur on the Web are B2B rather than B2C. Rarely are credit cards used in these transactions. Instead, more traditional methods of payment are used. In the future, a sizeable percentage of these payments will be electronic. However, these electronic payments are more likely to involve electronic funds transfers or electronic checks.

Besides credit cards and funds transfers, electronic payments (e-payments) take a variety of forms, such as smart cards, digital cash and script, digital checks, and electronic billing to name just a few. What these diverse e-payment methods share in common is the ability to transfer a payment from one person or party to another person or party over a network without face-to-face interaction. With each method, there are usually four parties involved:

- **Issuer.** Banks or nonbanking institutions that issue the e-payment instrument used to make the purchase.
- **Customer/payer/buyer.** Party making the e-payment in exchange for goods or services.
- **Merchant/payee/seller.** Party receiving the e-payment in exchange for goods and services.
- **Regulator.** Usually a government agency whose regulations control the e-payment process.

Although they are usually behind the scenes, issuers play a key role in any online purchase because customers must first obtain their e-payment accounts from an issuer and second they are usually involved in authenticating a transaction and approving the amount involved (often in real-time).

APPLICATION CASE 14.1

Online Credit Card Fraud: Serious Problem

A recent survey of 132 online merchants by transactions solution vendor Cybersource and research company Mindwave Research revealed that 83% say fraud is a serious problem. The percentage is slightly up from the 75% who reported it as a problem a year ago. Although online purchases only account for 5% of all credit card transactions, they account for 50% of fraud involving credit cards.

When asked who was responsible for the losses, 25% said they didn't know or indicated that it was the bank or credit card company. This figure is down from 41% a year ago. Actually, it's the merchant who is responsible. Online credit card purchases are treated as "card-not-present" transactions. This means that the merchant absorbs the loss. They also incur a "charge-back" fee of $25–$100 as well as the initial transaction fee of 2% levied by the credit card company.

Source: Duvall, 2000.

In the off-line world, where payments are often made face-to-face or through various physical instruments (such as a check), it is widely believed that it is much more difficult to perpetrate a fraud than it is in the online world. If someone hands you cash, issues of trust rarely arise (although the money could be counterfeit). If someone pays with credit card, you can check his or her signature against the signature on the back of the card (although the signature could still be a forgery). Because online buyers and sellers are not in the same place and cannot exchange payments and products at the same time, issues of trust come to the surface. The acronym PAIN (privacy, authentication, integrity, and nonrepudiation) has been devised to represent the key issues of trust that must be addressed by any method of e-payment (Cornwell 2000):

- **Privacy.** The parties must be assured that the details of the transaction are kept confidential, and that they are not used for purposes other than those agreed to by the parties.
- **Authentication and authorization.** Buyers, sellers, and any intermediaries (e.g., credit card issuer) must be assured that that the participants are who they claim to be and that each is acting within his or her authority when offering, transferring, or accepting payment.
- **Integrity.** The parties involved must be assured that the e-payments—the data and documents representing the e-payments—cannot be altered without detection.
- **Nonrepudiation.** The parties must be assured that e-payment binds the participants to the transaction and that no party can deny or illegally back out of the transaction.

Trust is not the only characteristic that determines whether a method of e-payment has a chance of acceptance. Consider, for example, the weak market position of digital cash in B2C commerce. Various forms of digital cash, which will be discussed later in the chapter, have come and gone over the past few years. Their demise can be attributed to any number of factors, although one comes immediately to mind. Digital cash requires a consumer to set up a specialized account with an issuer and to download specialized software in order to obtain the digital cash and spend it. Often, the cash is purchased with a credit card. Why would a consumer go through the inconvenience? Few merchants have accepted digital cash (and still don't), and it has been much easier to purchase an item with a credit card. To date, the obvious answer is that most consumers haven't gone through the inconvenience. There are a number factors that have and will come into play in determining whether a particular method of e-payment achieves widespread acceptance. Some of the crucial factors include:

- **Independence.** Some forms of e-payment require specialized software or hardware to make the payment. Almost all forms of e-payment require the seller or merchant to install specialized software to receive and authorize a payment. Those methods that require the payer or buyer to install specialized components are less likely to succeed.
- **Interoperability and portability.** All forms of EC run on specialized systems that are also interlinked with other enterprise systems and applications. An e-payment method must mesh with these existing systems and applications and be supported by standard computing platforms.
- **Security.** How safe is the transfer and what are the consequences of the transfer being compromised? Again, if the risk is higher for the payer or buyer than the payee or seller, then the method is not likely to be accepted.
- **Anonymity.** This is closely related to the issue of privacy. Unlike credit cards and checks, if a buyer uses cash, there's no way to trace the cash back to the buyer. Some buyers want their identities and purchase patterns to remain anonymous. To succeed, any e-cash or digital cash system has to maintain anonymity. In the future, other e-payment methods, including credit card purchases, may be required to minimize the e-paper trail from the buyer to the seller.
- **Divisibility.** Most sellers only accept credit cards for purchases within a minimum and maximum range. If the cost of the item is too small—say

you're purchasing a single article from a magazine that only costs a few dollars—a credit card won't do. On the other hand, if an item or set of items costs too much—say you're an airline company purchasing a new airplane—then a credit card won't work here either. Any method that can address the lower or higher end of the price continuum or can span one of the extremes and the middle has a chance being widely accepted.

- **Ease of use.** On the B2C side of e-payments, credit cards are the standard for ease of use. To make a Web purchase with a credit card, all a consumer has to do is select the type of card, enter the number and expiration date, then hit the submit button. If it's much more difficult than that, then it's simply going to fall prey to credit cards. On the B2B side, it's a different story. With B2B, the real question is whether the online e-payment methods can supplant the existing off-line methods of procurement.

- **Transaction fees.** When a credit card is used for payment, the merchant pays a transaction fee of up to 3 percent of the item's purchase price. Approximately 33 percent of that fee goes to the merchant's bank, about 4 percent to the credit card association (e.g., Visa), and the remainder to the issuer of the credit card. These fees make it prohibitive to support smaller purchases with credit cards and leave room for alternative forms of payment.

To date, the acceptance of various e-payment methods, outside of credit cards for consumer purchases, has been slow. There are some areas—online billing and online procurement—where e-payments are likely to make significant inroads in the near future. There are several key business drivers behind the growth of these alternatives. One of these is cost reduction. E-payments save processing costs while simultaneously reducing the cost of paper. In the United States, for instance, it costs firms over $1 on average to produce and handle paper bills. The same billing handled online costs around 25 to 30 cents. Another is speed. If you pay a bill by check, for example, it takes time to mail the bill, time to mail the check, and time to deposit and process the check. The whole process takes at least a week. If the bill is presented and paid on line, it takes a couple of days at most. E-payments also make it possible to conduct business across geographical and political boundaries, greatly enhancing the possibilities for international deals and transactions. The bottom line is that e-payments are what make EC possible.

In this chapter we consider various forms of e-payments for B2C, B2B, and C2C commerce, including e-cards, e-checks, e-cash, and e-billing. For each method of e-payment we look at the stages and systems involved, as well as the benefits and disadvantages. The discussion of the various forms is preceded by a discussion of the key technologies for securing online payments.

14.3   SECURITY FOR E-PAYMENTS

When you use a credit card to make a purchase on the Internet, how can you be sure that someone won't intercept the card number as it traverses the network and use it for their own purposes? If you contact an EC site with the intention of making a purchase, how can you be sure that it's a legitimate site? If one company sends a bill to another company over the Internet, how can the recipient be sure that the bill hasn't been changed? If a customer sends your company an e-check and later denies that he or she sent it, how can you refute the denial? These questions are illustrative of the issues of trust or "PAIN" that arise with e-payment systems. A well-devised online security system provides the answer to many, but not all, of these and similar questions. Internet security is a very complex issue that was addressed in Chapter 13. The security of e-payments is the focus of this section.

Public Key Infrastructure

One element that has emerged as the cornerstone for secure e-payments is **Public Key Infrastructure (PKI)**. PKI is also the foundation of a number of network applications, including supply chain management, virtual private networks, secure e-mail, and intranet applications. Basically, PKI refers to the technical components, infrastructure, and practices needed to enable the use of public-key encryption, digital signatures, and digital certificates with a network application.

At the heart of PKI is public-key encryption. Encryption or cryptography ensures the confidentiality and privacy of a message as it moves across a network by scrambling or encrypting it in such a way that it is difficult, expensive, or time consuming for an unauthorized person to unscramble or decrypt it. In the case of e-payments, the message could be credit card information entered in a form or contractual terms between two companies. While cryptography dates to the ancient Greeks, today's systems rely on sophisticated mathematical formulas and computer algorithms. Regardless of the level of sophistication, all **cryptography** has four basic parts:

1. **Plaintext.** The original message in human-readable form.
2. **Ciphertext.** The plaintext message after it has been encrypted into unreadable form.
3. **Encryption algorithm.** The mathematical formula used to encrypt the plaintext into ciphertext and vice versa.
4. **Key.** The secret key used to encrypt and decrypt a message. Different keys produce different ciphertext when used with the same algorithm.

There are two major classes of encryption systems: symmetric, or private key systems, and asymmetric, or public key systems. In a **symmetric key system** the same key is used to encrypt and decrypt the plaintext (see Figure 14-2). The key is called a **private key** and must be shared by the sender and receiver of the text. Several algorithms may be used to encrypt a message, including Data Encryption Standard (DES), triple-DES, IDEA, RC2, RC4, and RC5.

Figure 14-2	Private Key Encryption

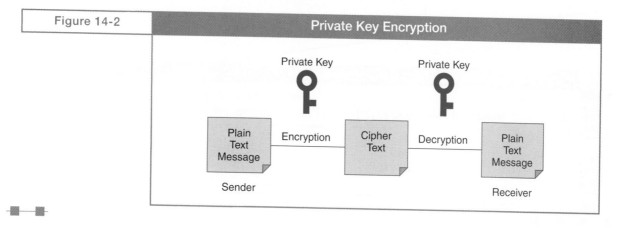

Even if the algorithm is known, the message is still secure as long as the key is unknown. It is possible to guess a key simply by having a computer try all the possibilities until the message is decrypted. High-speed and parallel processing computers can try millions of guesses in a second. This is why the length of the key (in bits) is the main factor in securing a message. If a key were 4 bits long (e.g., 1011), then there would only be 16 possibilities (i.e., 2^4). You wouldn't need a computer. Now, consider the figures shown in Table 14-1.

From Table 14-1 it's easy to see that 40-bit keys can be broken in seconds and 56-bit keys in a matter of days or faster depending on the power of the computer being used. A number of vendors of encryption systems have conducted contests in which they encrypt a message with a private key and ask the Internet community to decipher the message. *Distributed.net* is one group that has successfully used thousands of small computers to determine a number of the keys through exhaustive searches (*distributed.net*).

Imagine trying to use symmetric encryption to buy something offered on a particular Web server. If the server's private key were distributed to thousands of buyers, then the key wouldn't remain secret for long. This is where public key encryption comes into play. **Public key encryption** uses a pair of keys—a **public key** to encrypt the message and a private key to decrypt the message (see Figure 14-3). The most common public key encryption algorithm is **RSA**, named for its inventors Ronald Rivest, Adi Shamier, and Leonard Adelman. RSA uses keys ranging in length from 512 bits to 1024 bits. The advantage of public key encryption is that one half of the key pair can be made public. Now, if a Web site sends out its public key to a large group of prospective buyers, it doesn't matter because the only way to decrypt a message created with that public key is with the matching private key that only the Web site has.

The main problem with public key encryption is its speed. It can't be used to encrypt and decrypt large amounts of data. As Table 14-2 indicates, symmetrical algorithms are qualitatively faster than public key algorithms because they require shorter keys.

In practice, a combination of symmetric and public key encryption is used to encrypt messages. The combination is called a **digital envelope**. Here, the sender of a message first creates a symmetric key (also called a session key), encrypts it with the recipient's public key, and sends it to the recipient. The recipient decrypts the encrypted session key with his or her private key. Now, both the sender and recipient know the session key. Next, the sender uses the session key to encrypt the larger message and sends it to the recipient. The recipient uses the same session key to decrypt the larger message.

TABLE 14-1

Key Sizes and Time to Try All Possible Keys			
Key Size	Number of Possible Keys (2ˣ)	Time to Check All Keys (at 1.6 million keys per second)	Time to Check All Keys (at 10 million keys per second)
40	1,099,511,627,776	8 days	109 seconds
56	72,057,594,037,927,900	1,427 years	83 days
64	18,446,744,073,709,600,000	365,338 years	58.5 years
128	3.40282E + 38	6.73931E + 24 years	1.07829# + 21 years

Source: Howard (2000).

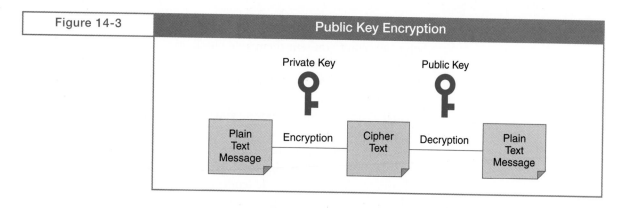

Figure 14-3 — Public Key Encryption

	Time (in msecs) to Encrypt 128-Byte Block	
Key Size in Bits	**Private Key Operation (msecs)**	**Public Key Operation (msecs)**
512	4	39.9
1024	12.8	255.8
2048	46.8	1796.0

TABLE 14-2

APPLICATION CASE 14.2

A New Encryption Algorithm for the U.S. Government

The National Institute of Standards and Technology (NIST; *nist.gov*) has been working with industry and the cryptographic community to develop an Advanced Encryption Standard (AES).

The overall goal has been to develop a Federal Information Processing Standard (FIPS) that specifies an encryption algorithm(s) capable of protecting sensitive government information well into the next century. The algorithm(s) will be used by the U.S. Government and, on a voluntary basis, by the private sector.

After a three-year search, the NIST announced on October 2, 2000, that a Belgium-born algorithm, **Rijndael**, had been selected. The algorithm replaces the 20-year old Data Encryption Algorithm (DEA) specified in the Data Encryption Standard (DES). During the three-year test, various candidates were considered. Rijndael proved to be the smallest and fastest and virtually "uncrackable" with security equivalent to a 128-bit key. Because of its size and speed it will be able to support new devices such as wireless phones, while at the same time handling the volume of traffic experienced by busy Web sites.

Chase Manhattan has already adopted the algorithm. This means that the algorithm meets the standard set by current banking security laws. Entrust Technologies (*entrust.com*), a major supplier of security technologies, has already announced support for the algorithm.

Source: Ovenstein (2000).

Digital Signatures: Authenticity and Nondenial

Someone claims you sent them an e-check; you deny it. Someone claims you sent him or her an e-check, you agree, but you don't agree on the amount. Someone claims you sent him or her an e-check, you agree, but you disagree on the time and date the e-check was sent. In the online world, how can you be sure that a message is actually coming from the person you think sent it? Similarly, how can you be sure that a person has no way of denying they sent a particular message? One part of the answer is a **digital signature**—the electronic equivalent of a personal signature that cannot be forged. Digital signatures are based on public keys. They can be used to authenticate the identity of the sender of a message or document. They can also be used to ensure that the original content of an electronic message or document is unchanged. Digital signatures have additional benefits in the online world. They are portable, cannot be easily repudiated or imitated, and can be time stamped.

Here is how a digital signature works (see Figure 14-4). Suppose you want to send the draft of a financial contract (as an e-mail message) to a company with whom you plan to do business. You want to assure the company that the content of the draft hasn't been changed enroute and that you really are the sender.

STEP 1: You create the e-mail message with the contract in it.

STEP 2: Using special software you "hash" the message. This is a special, compacted summary of the message.

STEP 3: Now, you use your private key to encrypt the hash. This is your digital signature.

STEP 4: You e-mail the message (assume that it's not encrypted to simplify the explanation) and the encrypted hash to the company.

STEP 5: Upon receipt, the company uses the same special software to hash the message they received.

STEP 6: Finally, the company uses your public key to decrypt the message hash that you sent. If their hash matches the decrypted hash, then the message is valid.

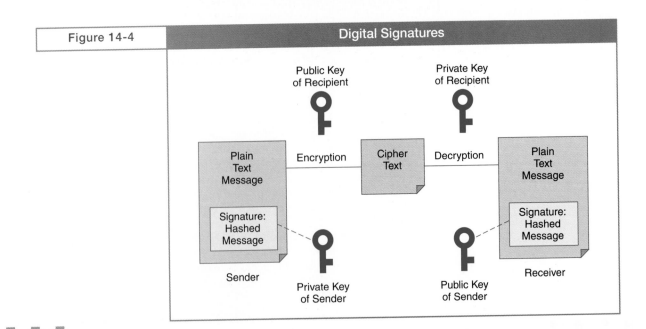

Figure 14-4	Digital Signatures

In this scenario, the company has evidence that it was really you that sent the e-mail because (theoretically) you're the only one with access to your private key. They know that the message wasn't tampered with because if it had been, then the two hashes wouldn't have matched.

Digital signatures don't address the issue of time stamping a message. Time stamping usually requires a third party to review, stamp, and archive the message. The details of the procedure are beyond this discussion. For those who are interested, see *surety.com* (especially the technical documents).

According to the Electronic Signatures in Global and National Commerce Act that went into effect on October 1, 2000, digital signatures in the United States now have the same legal standing as a signature written in ink on paper (Charles 2000). While PKI will certainly be the foundation of digital signatures, the act does not specify that any particular technology needs to be used. Several third-party companies are now exploring other methods to verify a person's legal identity, including the use of personal smart cards, PDA encryption devices, and biometric verifications (fingerprint, voice, or iris scans). Included among those companies are Illumin (*illumin.com*), which provides "digital handshaking" technology; SignOnLine (*signonline.com*), whose technology combines digital signatures (see following discussion) with e-documents; Litronic (*litronic.com*), the makers of smart cards and "eye" readers; and Interlink Electronics (*interlinkelectronics.com*), which manufactures an ePad device for digitally capturing written signatures. Because many businesses lack confidence in current security and verification procedures, the routine use of digital signatures won't occur in the near future.

Digital Certificates and Certificate Authorities (CAs)

If you have to know someone's public key to send him or her a message, where does it come from and how can you be sure of their actual identity? **Digital certificates** verify that the holder of a public and private key is who they claim to be. Third parties called **certificate authorities (CA)** issue digital certificates. Most certificates adhere to the Internet Engineering Task Force's (IETF) X.509 certificate standard. Under version 3.0 of this standard, a certificate contains things such as the subject's name (owner of the private key), validity period, subject's public key information, and a signed hash of the certificate data (i.e., hashed contents of the certificate signed with the CA's private key).

Individuals or companies apply for digital certificates by sending a CA their public key and identifying information. The CA verifies the information and the legitimacy of the application and creates a certificate that contains the applicant's public key along with identifying information. When someone wants to send the applicant a message, they first request the recipient to send their signed certificate. The sender uses the CA's public key to decrypt the certificate. In this way the sender can be more confident of the true identity of the recipient. After decrypting the certificate, the sender uses the embedded public key to encrypt the message. In this way, the only public key that the sender really has to know ahead of time is the CA's public key.

Certificates are used to authenticate Web sites (site certificates), individuals (personal certificates), and software companies (software publisher certificates). There is also a growing number of third-party CAs. VeriSign (*verisign.com*) is the best known of the CAs. VeriSign issues three classes of certificates. Class 1 verifies that an e-mail actually comes from the user's address; Class 2 checks the user's identity against a commercial credit database; and Class 3 requires notarized documents. Companies like Microsoft offer systems that enable companies to issue their own private, in-house certificates (see Howard, 2000, for a detailed discussion of the certification capabilities of Windows 2000). These can be used to identify users on their own networks.

Secure Socket Layer/Transport Layer Security

If the average user had to figure out how to use encryption, digital certificates, digital signatures, and the like, there would be few secure transactions and, in turn, few purchases made on the Web. Fortunately, all of these issues are handled in a transparent fashion by Web browsers and Web servers. This is done primarily through a special protocol called **secure socket layer (SSL)** that utilizes X.509 certificates for authentication and data encryption to ensure privacy or confidentiality. SSL was invented by Netscape and became a de facto standard adopted by the browsers and servers provided by Microsoft and Netscape. In 1996, the IETF standardized SSL and renamed it the **Transport Layer Security (TLS)**.

SSL operates at the TCP/IP layer—the base communication layer for the Internet. This means that any application that relies on TCP/IP—such as the Web, Usenet newsgroups, and e-mail—can be secured by SSL. SSL supports a variety of encryption algorithms and authentication methods. The combination of algorithms and methods is called a cipher suite. When a client contacts a server, the two negotiate a cipher suite, selecting the strongest suite the two have in common. For Web pages, the negotiation process is initiated when the user clicks on a link whose Web address (URL) begins with "https" rather than "http." For instance, *Amazon.com* allows a user to review their 1-Click shopping settings. These settings contain sensitive information about the user. The user accesses the settings by entering their e-mail address and password and then clicking the "Sign in using our secure server" button (see Figure 14-5). This takes the user to a page on *Amazon.com* whose address begins with "*https://amazon.com/* . . . " (see Figure 14-6). The "https" indicates that the communications are now being encrypted by SSL. This fact is also noted in the browser by the presence of an icon indicating that the page is "secured." In the case of Microsoft's Internet Explorer, a padlock icon is displayed at the bottom of the page.

Another low-level protocol that can be used to secure communications across the Internet is **IPSec**, a secure version of the IP protocol (from TCP/IP). IPSec is relatively new. There are important differences between SSL and IPSec. IPSec secures all the traffic between two computers using TCP/IP for communications, whereas SSL secures specific traffic such as Web communications. With IPSec everything is secure whether you want it to be or not. With SSL you can selectively secure specific communications. This requires less computer and network resources. IPSec can only be used to secure servers, whereas SSL can authenticate clients and servers. Finally, the major Web browsers and Web servers handle SSL automatically. The bottom line is that SSL is widely deployed and IPSec is not.

Secure Electronic Transactions

SSL makes it possible to encrypt credit card numbers that are sent from a consumer's browser to a merchant's Web site. However, there is more to making a purchase on the Web than simply passing a credit card number to a merchant. The

Figure 14-5	*InformIT.com* Online Bookstore

Source: informit.com.

number must be checked for validity, the consumer's bank must authorize the card, and the purchase must be processed. SSL is not designed to handle any of the steps beyond the transmission of the card number. A cryptographic protocol that is designed to handle the complete transaction is the **secure electronic transaction (SET)** protocol. Visa and MasterCard were instrumental in developing SET. Today, they manage the specifications for SET through a joint venture—SET Secure Electronic Transaction LLC (*setco.org*).

In a SET transaction there are three entities: the customer, the merchant, and the payment processing company. SET utilizes SET digital certificates for each of these entities to ensure mutual authentication. When a customer is ready to make a purchase, he or she uses an electronic wallet. An e-wallet is a helper application used to store information about the customer's credit cards and the SET digital certificates for each of the cards. The e-wallet sends both the order information and the payment. The former is encrypted with the merchant's public key and the latter with the payment processing company's public key. In this way, the payment processing company can't see the order information and the merchant can't see the

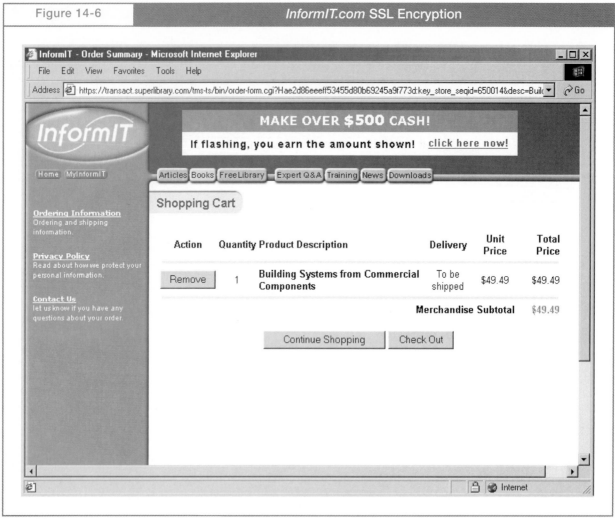

Figure 14-6 — *InformIT.com* SSL Encryption

Source: informit.com.

payment information. In addition to securing orders and payments, SET also supports the following features (Stein 1998):

- Cardholder registration
- Merchant registration
- Purchase requests
- Payment authorizations
- Payment capture
- Chargebacks
- Credits
- Credit reversal
- Debit card transactions

Acceptance of SET has been extremely slow. The main problems are that SET requires specialized software for both the client and the server, is slower than regular SSL, and has higher associated transaction costs.

14.4   E-CARDS

If you're an American, you're likely to have at least one payment card. In the United States there are over 700 million payment cards. They can be used at over 4 million merchants in the United States and another 11 million merchants around the world. Over the last few years Americans paid for over $850 billion worth of purchases with their payment cards. There are about 12 billion payment card transactions per year. These are amazing statistics given the relatively short history of payment cards (Evans 2000).

In the United States the major brands of payment cards are American Express, Discover, MasterCard, and Visa. American Express was started in 1958, Discover in 1985, and MasterCard and Visa in 1966. In thinking about new forms of e-payment, it is important to remember two things. First, in the early years, most of the large banks that issued payment cards lost substantial amounts of money. It wasn't until after 1982 that payment card usage enjoyed substantial growth. Second, this growth was fueled by a variety of factors, including some favorable court cases that enabled the banks to charge high interest rates, an improvement in the overall economy, and a great deal of mass marketing including mailing free, unsolicited payment cards. Taken together, these factors solved the "chicken-and-egg" problem. That is, consumers can only use payment cards if they are accepted by merchants, but merchants will only accept them if a number of their customers use them. Today, the payment card industry and its associated electronic infrastructure are ubiquitous. This is why payment cards have come to rule the online world—everyone has them and the electronic infrastructure for handling the cards was basically in place when EC came along on the Internet.

Not all payment cards are created equal. There are three common types of payment cards and another one on the way. The common types include:

- **Credit cards.** A credit card provides the holder with credit to make purchases up to a limit fixed by the card issuer. With a credit card there is rarely an annual fee. Instead, holders are charged interest—the annual percentage rate—on their unpaid balances. The interest rate is usually very high, and if the holder is tardy in making a payment the rates can exceed 20 percent. Visa and MasterCard are the predominant credit cards. Among all types of cards, Visa and MasterCard credit cards account for approximately 50 percent and 30 percent of the global payment card purchase volume.

- **Charge cards.** The balance on a charge card is supposed to be paid in full upon receipt of the monthly statement. Technically, the holder of a charge card receives a loan for 30 to 45 days equal to the balance of their statement. There are usually annual fees with charge cards. American Express's Green Card is the leading charge card, followed by the Discover card.

- **Debit cards.** With a debit card, the cost of a purchased item comes directly out of the holder's checking account (called a demand-deposit account). The transfer of funds from your account to the merchant's takes place within 1 to 2 days. MasterCard and Visa are the predominant debit cards worldwide, although in Europe it's the combined MasterCard/Europay (formerly Eurocard) that leads the pack.

There are interesting differences in the use of payment cards from one country to the next. In the United States, credit cards are used for most payment card purchases, although the use of debit cards has increased over the past few years. In the United Kingdom and France, payment card usage is high. In Germany it's low. In the United Kingdom, about 70 percent of payment card purchases are made with debit cards; in France the figure is 100 percent; in Germany it's better than 80 percent.

As noted, credit cards are the most popular payment method for B2C commerce on the Internet. Some B2C sites accept charge cards (such as American Express and Discover), but the vast majority of purchases are made with Visa and MasterCard credit cards.

The process of using a credit card off-line or online involves a number of participants. They are:

- **Cardholder.** Consumer or corporate purchaser who uses a credit card to pay for a purchase.
- **Merchant.** The entity that accepts credit cards and offers goods or services in exchange for payments.
- **Card issuer.** Financial institution (usually a bank) that establishes an account for the cardholder and issues credit.
- **Acquirer.** Financial institution (usually a bank) that establishes an account for a merchant and acquires the vouchers or authorized sales slips.
- **Card association.** Association of issuers and acquirers (such as Visa and MasterCard), which is created to protect and advertise the card brand, establish and enforce the rules for use and acceptance of their members' bank cards, and provide networks to connect the involved financial institutions. The brand authorizes the credit-based transaction and guarantees the payment to merchants.
- **Third-party processors.** Outsourcers who perform some of the same duties formerly provided by the issuers, acquirers, and card associations, including signing up merchants, selling and servicing card-reading terminals, and performing the preprocessing needed to send the customer a bill.

Among the largest card issuers in the world are Citibank, MBNA America, and First Chicago NBD. The 10 largest card issuers usually account for better than 60 percent of the charge volume. The largest third-party processor is First Data Corporation. First Data is not only the largest processor, handling more than 8 billion card transactions per year, but it is also the largest merchant acquirer. The processor in the second spot is Total System Services.

Whether a credit card payment is processed off-line or online, the processes involved are essentially the same (Figure 14-7). For example, suppose you want to buy some CDs from a Web site with your credit card. You add the CDs to your shopping cart and go to the checkout page. On the checkout page you select a method of shipping and enter your credit card information. The checkout page is usually secured, so that the credit card and other information is protected by SSL encryption. When you hit submit, the page is transmitted to the merchant. From there the information, along with the merchant's identification number, is passed on to the merchant's acquirer (or third-party

Figure 14-7	Online Credit Card Processing

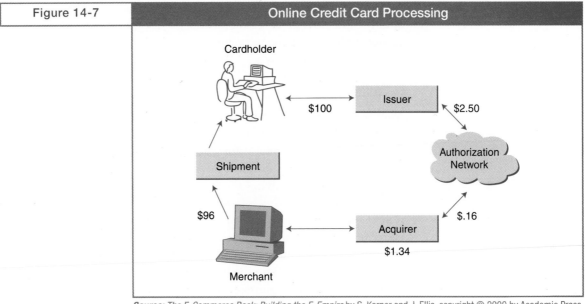

Source: *The E-Commerce Book: Building the E-Empire* by S. Korper and J. Ellis, copyright © 2000 by Academic Press, reproduced by permission of the publisher.

processor). The acquirer sends the information on to the customer's issuing bank for approval. The issuer sends its response (approve or disapprove) back to the acquirer where it is passed on to the merchant. Finally, the customer is notified. The entire set of processes takes place in seconds. After the transaction is complete, the issuer settles the transaction. For a $100 purchase, the merchant receives $96, the acquirer $1.34, the association $.16, and the issuer $2.50 (Korper and Ellis 2000).

It takes time, skill, money, software, and hardware to establish an online connection between the merchant's EC systems and the merchant's acquirer or third-party processor. Recognizing the difficulties associated with this task, several vendors now offer **credit card gateways** that tie the merchant's systems to the back-end credit card processing systems. Essentially, the gateway is a software component run on the same server as the merchant's storefront software. When an order is received, the gateway passes the payment information to an off-site server run by the gateway company. This latter server handles the request for authorization from the merchant's financial institution. A list of some of these vendors offering gateway software is provided below (Carr 2000):

- Authorize.net (*authorizenet.com*)
- Cybercash (*cybercash.com*)
- Cybersource (*cybersource.com*)
- First Data (*firstdata.com*)
- Fiserv (*fiserv.com*)
- Fullecom (*fullecom.com*)
- Paycom.net (*paycom.net*)
- SurePay (*surepay.com*)
- Total System Services (*totalsystem.com*)
- VeriSign (*verisign.com*)

Three of these vendors—First Data, Fiserv, and Total System Services—are already third-party credit card processors. They simply expanded their outsourcing services to handle online payments.

E-Wallets

Most of the time when you make a purchase on the Web you're required to fill out a form with your name, shipping address, billing address, credit card information, etc. Doing this a few times is fine, but having to do it every time you shop on the Web is an annoyance. Some merchants solve the problem by having you fill out a form once and then saving the information on their servers for later use. For instance, this is what *Amazon.com* has done with their "One-Click" shopping. It utilizes information you entered at their site on an earlier date. Of course, even if every merchant provided "one-click" shopping, you would still have to set up an account with every merchant. This would also increase the possibility that the information might fall into the hands of a merchant who wanted to use this information for some other purpose.

One way to avoid the problem of having to repeatedly fill out purchase information, while at the same time eliminating the need to store the information on a merchant's server, is to use an **electronic wallet (e-wallet)**. An e-wallet is a software component that a user downloads to their desktop and in which the user stores credit card numbers and other personal information. When a user shops at a merchant who accepts the e-wallet, the e-wallet allows the user to perform one-click-like shopping with the e-wallet automatically filling in the necessary information.

Credit card companies such as Visa (*usa.visa.com/personal/shopping/ewallets. html*) and MasterCard (*mastercard.com*) offer e-wallets. So do Yahoo!, AOL (Quick Checkout), and Microsoft (Passport). Of these, Yahoo! has the largest number of merchant participants, with over 10,000. Although e-wallets can make the transactions faster, they still face the same dilemma as any other form of specialized payment—creating a critical mass among merchants.

Security Risks with Credit Cards

Even though SSL can be used to secure the transaction between the Web browser and Web server, there are still risks with credit card payments. For the most part, the merchant bears the responsibility for these risks.

- **Stolen cards.** If someone steals a card and the valid cardholder contests any charges made by the thief, the issuer will credit the cardholder's account and "chargeback" the merchant. The merchant will bear the loss.
- **Reneging by the customer.** A customer can authorize a payment and later deny it. If the denial is creditable to the issuer, the merchant will bear the loss. This can be avoided by showing evidence the cardholder confirmed the order and received the goods. It can also be handled with a digital signature; however, most online credit card transactions do not require the customer to provide a digital signature.

- **Theft of card details stored on the merchant's computer.** There have been cases where hackers have electronically broken into a merchant's computer where credit card details were stored. The key to protecting this information is to isolate the computer storing this information so that it cannot be accessed directly from the Internet.

APPLICATION CASE   14.3

Virtual Credit Cards

For those users who are still leery of using their credit cards online, American Express has a new service called Private Payment. Private Payment works like a **virtual credit card**. Users download and install a special software component on their desktop. Now, when a user shops online and wants to use their American Express card for a payment, he or she either activates the software component or the check-out page will do it automatically. The first thing to be entered is a user name and password. This logs the user into a special site run by American Express. Next, the user selects the particular American Express card to be used for the purchase. At this point, American Express will generate a limited-life transaction number. Now, instead of the user entering his or her American Express number, he or she enters the transaction number. The transaction number is tied to the specific card and is good anywhere from 30 to 67 days. The merchant who receives the transaction number will pass this on to American Express in order to receive an authorization for the purchase. It operates just like a real credit card, however it's only good for one purchase and if it's stolen or intercepted it will do little harm since it can only be used once.

Source: American Express Press Release (2000).

Purchase Cards

While credit cards are the instrument of choice for B2C payments, they aren't for the B2B marketplace. Traditionally, payments between companies have been handled by check, electronic data transfer (EDI), or electronic funds transfer (EFT). For smaller purchases, checks have been the norm. The problem is that this is a costly process. Today, the major credit card players—Visa, MasterCard, and American Express—are trying to convince companies to utilize purchasing cards in order to reengineer the purchasing process for high-volume, low-cost purchases. According to the American Express Purchasing Process and Automation Study conducted by Ernst & Young in 1999, moving from checks to purchasing cards can lower average cost per transaction from 90 cents to 22 cents. The transaction cost involves the buying costs (sourcing/ordering), reconciliation and paying costs, and data integration costs.

Purchase cards are special-purpose, non-revolving payment cards issued to employees solely for the purpose of purchasing and paying for nonstrategic materials and services (e.g., stationery, office supplies, computer supplies, repair and maintenance services, courier services, and temporary labor services).

The following excerpt from Virginia Tech University's Purchase Card Policies document is a good example of the reasons for and the types of purchases made with a corporate purchasing card (*purch.vt.edu/html.docs/amex.html*).

In order to streamline the procurement process for small purchases, the American Express (AMEX) Purchasing Card (P-Card) is available. This is an alternative to the use of Speed Purchase Order (SPOs). The P-Card shifts paper processing of transactions to AMEX. This reduces Virginia Tech's administrative costs associated with Departmental and Accounts Payable documentation as well as invoice and payment processing. Use of the P-Card not only benefits the university by shifting paper processing to AMEX, it also benefits the vendor/suppliers by providing them payments within as few as 3 business days. Cardholders may directly contact vendors that accept AMEX to purchase goods and services with a maximum limit of $2,000 per transaction. The $2,000 transaction ceiling shall not be circumvented by "splitting" orders (i.e., placing more than one order in an attempt to purchase goods or services valued over $2,000). For security and/or fund management reasons, Departments may request lower transactions and monthly limits when applying for a card. The average card expenditure is between $100 and $200. An analysis of monthly departmental expenditures should be performed to determine the proper card limit.

Purchasing cards operate in essentially the same fashion as any other credit card.

- The cardholder of a corporation places an order for goods or services with the supplier either by mail, phone, fax, in person, or through online preferred supplier catalogs or other public catalogs at the Internet Web site.
- The supplier will process the transaction by requesting a network purchase authorization from the respective card issuer or third-party provider.
- The purchasing card issuer or third-party provider verifies that the purchase is within the cardholder's authorized spending limits, industry limit, etc. Within seconds, the supplier receives either an approval or a decline.
- At the end of a billing cycle, the corporation receives a central invoice from the card issuer for the corporation cardholder's transactions. The corporation can send a consolidated payment to the card issuer. The corporation may use an electronic payment solution to pay the card provider.
- Each cardholder receives his or her respective purchasing monthly memo statement at the end of the billing cycle to review for accuracy as the cardholder holds all invoices from every purchase they make. This statement can be reconciled and approved by the corporation's management. Any discrepancies are taken up with the supplier or card provider by the cardholder.
- The card issuer/provider can analyze the purchasing card transaction and produce a variety of standard and ad hoc reports to the corporation's management team (i.e., cost center managers so that they can look for exceptions to the corporation's policies).
- The card issuer/provider can create an electronic file with purchasing card charges to upload directly to corporation's general ledger system.

Besides the obvious cost savings associated with purchasing cards, several other benefits accrue from their use (Jilovec 1999):

- **Productivity gains.** Purchasing departments are freed from day-to-day procurement activities and can focus on developing and managing relationships with suppliers.

- **Bill consolidation.** Small purchases from many cardholders can be consolidated into a single invoice that can also be paid electronically through EDI or EFT.
- **Payment reconciliation.** Data from the card vendors can be more easily integrated with a corporation's general ledger system, making the process of payment reconciliation simpler, more efficient, and more accurate.
- **Preferred pricing.** Traditionally, suppliers have had to wait at least 30 days for payment. With purchasing cards, settlement occurs in a few days or less. This enables companies to negotiate with their suppliers for more favorable prices since suppliers have better control over their cash flow.
- **Management reports.** The financial institutions issuing the cards supply detailed reports of purchasing activities. This makes it easier for a company to analyze their spending behavior and monitor supplier compliance with agreed upon prices.

The key players in the purchasing card market are the credit card companies— Visa, MasterCard, and American Express. Both Visa and MasterCard have partnered with Ariba (*ariba.com*), an EC vendor of "operating resource management" B2B applications. Ariba's applications are designed to replace paper-based systems for acquiring operating resources—goods and services required to operate the company— from suppliers. The combination of Ariba's software with purchasing cards, enables an enterprise to automate the buying, payment, reconciliation, and data integration processes.

Smart Cards

The newest entrant in the e-card or payment card arena is the smart card. A **smart card** looks like any plastic payment card but it is distinguished by the presence of an embedded microchip (see Figure 14-8). The embedded chip can either be a microprocessor and a memory chip combined or only a memory chip with non-programmable logic. The microprocessor card can add, delete, and otherwise manipulate information on the card, whereas a memory-chip card can only

Figure 14-8	Smart Card Image

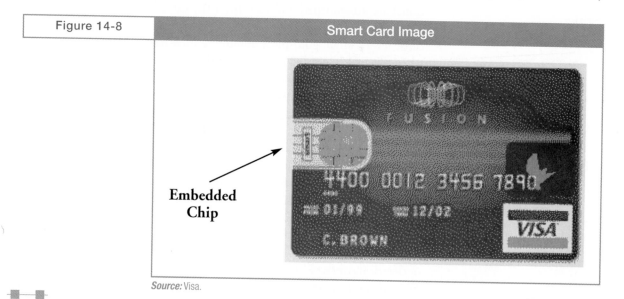

Embedded Chip

Source: Visa.

undertake a predefined operation. Although the microprocessor is capable of running programs like a computer, it is not a stand-alone computer. The programs and data must be downloaded from some other device (such as a card reader or an ATM machine).

Smart cards can be categorized in two ways. First, smart cards can be categorized by the presence or absence of a microprocessor (*java.sun.com/products/javacard/ smartcards.html*). Under this scheme there are three types of cards:

- **Integrated circuit (IC) microprocessor cards.** The current generation of microprocessor cards has an 8-bit processor, up to 32KB of read-only memory, and 512 bytes of random-access memory. This gives them the equivalent processing power of the original IBM-XT computer, albeit with slightly less memory capacity. These are used for a variety of applications, especially those requiring greater security and manipulation of large numbers. Some examples include: cards that hold money (stored-value cards); cards that hold money equivalents (affinity cards); and cards providing secure access to computers and cellular phones.
- **Integrated circuit (IC) memory cards.** IC memory cards can hold up to 1 to 4 KB of data, but have no processor on the card with which to manipulate that data. Thus, they are dependent on the card reader (also known as the card-accepting device) for their processing and are suitable for uses where the card performs a fixed operation. Memory cards represent the bulk of the cards sold over the past few years. Most have been disposable, prepaid phone cards.
- **Optical memory cards.** Optical memory cards look like a card with a piece of a CD glued on top. Optical memory cards can store up to 4 MB of data. Once written, the data cannot be changed or removed. This type of card is ideal for keeping records like medical files and driving records. These cards require expensive card readers. At the moment they have no processors, although this may change in the near future.

A second way to categorize smart cards is by the way in which data (and applications) are downloaded and read from the card. Under this scheme there are two types. The first type is a **contact card** that is inserted in a smart card reader. These cards have a small gold plate about 1/2 inch in diameter on the front such that when the card is inserted in the reader the plate makes contact and data is passed to and from the chip. The second type is the **contactless card**. Besides the chip, a contactless card has an embedded antenna. In this case, data (and applications) are passed to and from the card through the card's antenna to another antenna attached to a coupler or reader unit. Contactless cards are used for those applications where the data must be processed very quickly (e.g., mass-transit applications).

All smart cards must be designed for high levels of data security and must work under a variety of physical conditions including extremes of heat and cold, power fluctuations, and harsh handling. The production of smart cards is governed by a set of voluntary standards issued by the International Standards Organization (ISO). The size of the card is determined by the ISO 7810 standard, whereas the physical characteristics of the card (e.g., type of plastic, temperature range, position of electrical contacts, communications, etc.) are defined by the ISO 7816 standard. As it turns out, two companies—Gemplus (*gemplus.com*) and Schlumberger

(*1.slb.com/smartcards/*)—control about 85 percent of the smart card production market. They buy smart card chips from semiconductor vendors and then produce custom cards for other vendors (e.g., Visa).

Smart cards house or provide access to either valuable assets (e.g., e-cash) or to sensitive information (e.g., medical records). For this reason they must be secured against theft, fraud, or misuse. In general, smart cards are more secure than conventional payment cards. If someone steals a payment card, the number of the card is clearly visible and so is the owner's signature. Although it may be hard to forge the signature, there are many situations where only the number is required to make a purchase (e.g., mail order or phone purchases). The only protection the cardholder has is that there are usually limits on how much he or she will be held liable (e.g. in the United States it is $50). If someone steals a prepaid, stored value card (a phone card), you're out of luck. On the other hand, if they steal a microprocessor card, they're out of luck. Microprocessor cards don't have visible account numbers. Before they can be used, the holder must enter a PIN (personal identification number) that is stored on the card. Theoretically, it is possible to "hack" into a card. Most cards, however, can now store the information in encrypted form. The same cards can also encrypt and decrypt data that is downloaded or read from the card. Because of these factors, the possibility of hacking into a card is classified as a "class 3" attack. That is, the cost of doing so far exceeds the value of doing so.

Just like any other computer device, a smart card chip needs an operating system to run applications and a programming language in which to write those applications. Historically, smart cards have been based on proprietary systems with the operating system and applications tightly intertwined. Each card has been relegated to a single application. These applications have been developed by a handful of specialized companies. For companies issuing the cards (say a bank) this meant that they had to commit to a specific application developer, operating system, and chip for each service they wished to provide. Similarly, cardholders were forced to carry different cards for different services. More recently, multipurpose smart cards have been developed along with a number of new operating systems that open the world of smart cards to a much larger population of application developers. Among these new operating systems are:

- **MultOS.** Developed by a consortium of companies (e.g., MasterCard, Discover Card, American Express, Motorola, KeyCorp, Fujitsu, and others), MultOS (*multos.com*) is a secure, multiapplication operating system supporting the dynamic loading and deletion of applications over the life of a smart card. Programmers can use C or Java as the programming language for creating applications.
- **JavaCard.** The JavaCard (*java.sun.com/products/javacard/#about*) specifications enable Java applets to run on smart cards and other devices with limited memory. The JavaCard API allows applications written for one smart card platform enabled with JavaCard technology to run on any other such platform. This version of Java is only a subset of the larger programming language.
- **Microsoft windows for smart cards.** The Microsoft Windows Smart Card (*microsoft.com/windowsce/smartcard*) is an 8-bit multiapplication operating system for smart cards with 8KB of ROM (read only memory). It is designed to run applications written in Microsoft Visual Basic or C++.

According to a study made by Dataquest, the number of smart cards is estimated to grow from approximately 500 million in 1995 to 3 billion in 2001. Of these figures, the number of microprocessor-based cards is expected to grow from 85 million in 1995 to 1.2 billion in 2001.

The expected growth in smart card usage is being driven by applications. Today, the vast majority of cards are being issued in Europe, South America, and Asia. Over the next few years, the United States and Canada will account for about 15 percent of the total number of cards in use. While disposable, prepaid phone cards are the most widely used smart cards, there are a number of applications where smart cards have made and will make significant inroads. A thorough discussion of these applications can be found at the Smart Card Industry Association Web site (*scia.org/knowledgebase/default.htm*). The following summarizes some of the more important applications.

- **Loyalty.** Retailers are using smart cards to identify their loyal customers and reward them. The Boots project (*boots.co.uk/cgi-bin/enter.jsp*) and the Shell project are the largest in the world with millions of cards deployed. Both allow customers to collect points that can be redeemed for rewards in a number of ways. In the United States, the Rite Aid and SouthPark shopping mall are using smart-card-based reward systems.
- **Financial.** Financial institutions, payment associations, and card companies (Europay, MasterCard, Visa, American Express, and Discover) are using smart cards to extend traditional card payment services. Multiple applications such as loyalty programs, digital identification, and electronic money will be securely offered in the near future. In fact, in many countries, there are tens of millions of smart bankcards.
- **Information technology.** It won't be long before many PCs will contain smart card readers. All issuers will utilize the underlying security of the smart card to extend relationships from the physical world to the virtual world. Smart cards will allow individuals to protect their privacy while card issuers will be able to ensure only valid customers access services.
- **Health and social welfare.** Many countries with national health care systems are evaluating or deploying smart card technology to reduce the costs associated with delivering government services. The largest deployed system is one in Germany with over 80 million cards. The program was introduced in 1993 with the primary purposes of identification, eligibility verification, and electronic claims processing. In a similar vein, France, Italy, and the United Kingdom implemented a card-based system, Adicarte, which local authorities use to monitor and distribute social services in home care programs, eliminating the fraud and misuse of funds that previously plagued such programs.
- **Transportation.** The availability of low-cost single-chip contactless card technology with the emergence of combination smart card technology has many mass transit agencies evaluating the technology, especially for collecting fares. One of the first projects to mass deploy contactless card technology was the Seoul Bus Association, which won the SCIA 1998 Outstanding Smart Card Application award.

- **Identification.** Smart cards are a natural fit in the ID market and are being used in applications such as college campus IDs, driver's licenses, and immigration cards. In the United States, close to 1,000,000 Smart Cards will be used in the college market alone. This represents approximately 1 in 17 students.

14.5   E-CASH AND PAYMENT CARD ALTERNATIVES

It's the mid-1990s. EC was just beginning. As noted earlier, most pundits and analysts were suggesting that consumers would be unwilling to use their credit cards on the Internet. Other digital money schemes would be needed. Up stepped DigiCash. DigiCash offered a product called eCash—the digital equivalent of paper currency and coins. During its short life, DigiCash was only able to convince one U.S. bank, Mark Twain Bank in St. Louis, to participate. A few months later DigiCash ran out of money and filed for bankruptcy. A similar fate befell other early electronic payment and e-cash schemes. Early on, Cybercash launched a payment service called CyberCoins. The service died a quiet, but quick, death. CyberCash is now one of the leading providers of online credit card processing.

Conceptually, **e-cash** makes a lot of sense. It's secure, it's anonymous, and it can be used to support micropayments that can't be economically supported with payment cards. From a practical standpoint, the inconvenience of opening an account and downloading software or installing special EC systems and the difficulty of obtaining a critical mass of users seem to have outweighed the benefits of e-cash. However, in spite of these hurdles, new e-cash schemes or at least alternatives to payment cards, appear with some regularity. These schemes can be grouped into a series of categories including: e-cash and credit card alternatives, stored-value cards, e-loyalty and rewards programs, and person-to-person (P2P) payments.

E-Cash and Credit Card Alternatives

Consider the following online purchasing scenarios:

- You go to an online music store and purchase a single CD that costs $8.95.
- You go to a leading newspaper or news journal (such as *Forbes* or *Business Week*) and purchase a copy of an archived news article for $1.50.
- You go to an online gaming company, select a game, and play for 30 minutes. You owe them $3.00.
- You go to a site selling digital images and clip art. You purchase a couple of images at a cost of $.80.

These are all examples of **micropayments**, or payments that are under $10. The problem is that credit cards do not work well for micropayments. The typical credit card minimum transaction fee for vendors ranges from 25 cents to 35 cents, plus 2 to 3 percent of the purchase price. These fees are relatively insignificant for credit card purchases above $10, but are prohibitive for smaller transactions. And when the purchase amount is small, consumers are unwilling to type in credit card numbers or wait for a standard credit card authorization. This is one area where e-cash and other micropayment schemes come into play.

Ecoins, run by *eCoin.net* (*ecoin.net*), is typical of many e-cash systems. The system consists of three participants. The first participant is the user. The user opens an account with *eCoin.net* and downloads a special e-wallet to his or her desktop. The user then purchases some eCoins with a credit card. An eCoin is a digital string that is 15 bytes long and is worth 5 cents. Each string is unique so that it can be easily identified. The eCoins are downloaded into the e-wallet. The second participant is the merchant. To use eCoins, the merchant simply has to embed a special eCoin icon in their payment page. The final participant is the *Ecoin.net* server. The eCoin server operates as a broker that keeps customer and merchant accounts, accepts payment requests from the customer's e-wallet, and computes embedded invoices for the merchant.

Making an eCoin purchase consists of the following steps:

STEP 1: The user downloads eCoins from his or her online account to the e-wallet.

STEP 2: The merchant contacts the broker to get an embedded invoice tag.

STEP 3: The merchant inserts the invoice tag into the HTML page and sends it to the customer's browser.

STEP 4: The e-Wallet Manager plug-in interprets the embedded invoice.

STEP 5: The customer clicks on an embedded invoice displayed by the Wallet Manager.

STEP 6: The plug-in sends the invoice data and eCoins to the broker.

STEP 7: The broker decodes the invoice and verifies the eCoins.

STEP 8: The broker transfers the eCoins to the merchant account.

E-Coin. In an eCoin purchase, the identity of the user is hidden from the merchant. Only *eCoin.net* is aware of the user's identity. The communications between the user, the merchant, and *eCoin.net* are all secured with SSL. *Ecoin.net* also addresses the issue of double spending. Because eCoins are just collections of bytes and bits, they could be forged or duplicated. To prevent this, the eCoin server has a database of all the tokens that have been issued. When an eCoin is spent, the copy on the server is deleted. The next time someone tries to use the same eCoin, they will be refused.

ECoin is easier to use than some of the earlier e-cash systems. However, it suffers some of the same problems, requiring users and merchants to download specialized software and to go through a series of steps in order to make a purchase. Additionally, they have to repeat these steps with every purchase no matter how small the purchase price. Like its predecessors, the adoption rate of eCoin has been slow, and at the moment *eCoin.net* is no longer issuing U.S. dollar-based coins. ECoin is likely to have the same fate as its predecessors.

QPass. One micropayment system that avoids some of the problems and has enjoyed some success is Qpass (*qpass.com*). Qpass is used primarily to purchase content from participating news services and periodicals such as the *New York Times, Wall Street Journal*, and *Forbes*. With Qpass, the user sets up a Qpass account, creating a user name and password and specifying a credit card against which purchases will be charged. Now, when a purchase is made at a participating site, he or she simply enters his or her Qpass user name and password and confirms the purchase. Instead of immediately billing the user's credit card account, the charges are aggregated into a single monthly transaction and that transaction is billed to the user's credit card.

Although it's not a micropayment system, eCount's PrivateBuy (*privatebuy.com*) system also provides a secure, anonymous alternative to using credit cards for online purchases. Again, a user establishes an account and adds money to it with any credit card (see Figure 14-9) Upon completion, the user is assigned a 16-digit user number and an anonymous address. Now, when the user purchases something, he or she chooses MasterCard as the payment method, then enters the 16-digit user number in place of the credit card, "Private Buyer" for the name, and the anonymous address in the address field. The amount of cash in the user's account is reduced by the purchase price. This system hides the user's name and card number of the merchant site. It also eliminates the need for the merchant to install any specialized software. The system simply relies on the credit card system that is already in place.

Echarge is another credit card alternative that enables users to establish accounts, receive a user ID and password, and use this ID and password instead of their credit card numbers at participating merchants. Purchases are billed to the user's credit card, to a prepaid account, or to their phone bill. Unlike PrivateBuy, Echarge requires merchants to establish this as an alternative payment option.

To date, few merchants are participating.

Figure 14-9	PrivateBuy Anonymous Shopping

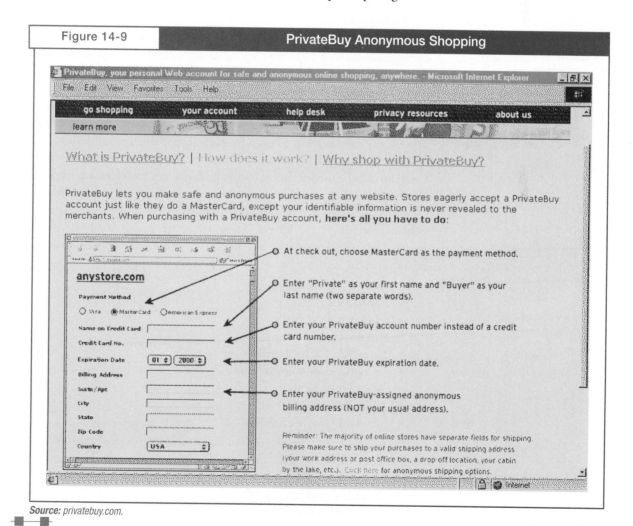

Source: privatebuy.com.

Stored-Value Cards

One of the primary uses of smart cards is to store cash downloaded from a bank or credit card account. The cards can then be used in place of cash to purchase items whose values range from a few cents to hundreds of dollars. The following list indicates some of the types of vendors worldwide where **stored-value cards** can be used:

- Fast-food restaurants
- Convenience stores
- Vending machines
- Gas stations
- Transportation
- Sundries stores
- Cinemas
- Parking garages
- Grocery stores
- Department stores
- Taxis
- Parking meters
- Cafeterias
- Video stores

Visa Cash is a relatively new stored-value card designed to handle small purchases or micropayments. **Visa Cash** is a chip-based card that can be used in the real world or on the Internet. There are two types of Visa Cash: disposable and reloadable. Disposable cards are loaded with a predetermined value. These cards typically come in denominations of local currency, such as $10. When the value of the card is used, the card is discarded and a new card may be purchased. Reloadable cards come without a predefined value. Cash value is reloaded onto the card at specialized terminals and at Automated Teller Machines (ATMs). When the value is used up, you can load the card again. Visa Cash can only be used at special terminals displaying the Visa Cash logo. When a purchase is made, the cost of the purchase is deducted from the cash loaded on the card.

Visa Cash cards can be obtained from financial institutions, special card dispensing machines, and kiosks. These cards are widely used outside the United States. They were introduced in Hong Kong in 1996 and can be obtained at a variety of financial institutions:

- Bank of China Group
- Bank of East Asia
- Chekiang First Bank
- Citibank
- Hong Kong Chinese Bank
- Shanghai Commercial Bank
- Wing Hang Bank
- Wing Lung Bank
- Standard Chartered Bank

They can be used at more than 1,500 merchants and reloaded at over 300 ATMs. For PCs with a Visa Cash card reader, it is also possible to make payments across the Internet.

The **Mondex** microchip card is the MasterCard equivalent of Visa Cash. It is administered and developed by Mondex International, a subsidiary of MasterCard.

Cash is downloaded onto the card through cash dispensers, pay phones, and home phones. Payments can be made wherever the Mondex sign is displayed. Using a Mondex Wallet, two cardholders can also transfer cash between their cards. A Mondex telephone can also be used to transfer cash from one party to the next. Unlike Visa Cash, a Mondex card can store up to five currencies at the same time. Mondex is currently on trial in the United Kingdom, Canada, United States, and New Zealand, and has also been launched at two sites in Hong Kong. It has been estimated there are about 150,000 Mondex cards in use.

APPLICATION CASE 14.4

Electronic Purses

If you make a purchase at a supermarket and pay with a credit or debit card, the same card reader is used to verify and authorize the payment. The same isn't true for stored-value cards. The hardware and cards are not interoperable. These stored-value cards are also known as **electronic purses**.

Recently a major step was taken in achieving worldwide interoperability of electronic purse programs with the publication of the Common Electronic Purse Specifications (CEPS), jointly developed by Europay International, SERMEPA, Visa International and ZKA (Zentraler Kreditausschuss, Germany).

CEPS defines the requirements needed by an organization to implement a globally interoperable electronic purse program. It requires compatibility with the EMV specifications for chip cards and defines the card application, the card-to-terminal interface, the terminal application for point-of-sale and local transactions, data element, and recommended message formats for transaction processing. It also provides functional requirements for the various electronic purse scheme participants and uses public key cryptography for enhanced security.

Organizations from 30 countries representing more than 100 million electronic purse cards have already agreed to adopt the specifications, creating a de facto, global electronic purse standard. It means that more than 90 per cent of the world's electronic purse cards will become interoperable, including GeltKarts, Proton-based cards, and Visa Cash cards. Additionally, some 200 technology vendors have agreed to work on developing CEPS-compliant products. The first implementations of CEPS are planned for early 2001 and will take place in Europe.

Source: cepsco.com

E-Loyalty and Rewards Programs

Some B2C sites spend hundreds of dollars acquiring new customers. Yet, the payback only comes after a customer has made several purchases. These repeat customers are also more likely to refer other customers to a site. In the off-line retail world, companies often use loyalty programs to generate repeat business. In the United Kingdom, for example, the Airmiles program is one of the best-known rewards programs. Airmiles can be earned at over 10,000 locations worldwide and exchanged for airline tickets and other merchandise (Cassy 2000). Today, loyalty programs are appearing online. *goldpoints.com*, MyPoints-CyberGold, and RocketCash are three of the better-known loyalty programs.

A **goldpoint** is a form of **electronic script**. *Goldpoints.com* sells a quantity of beenz to a Web site. See Figure 14-10. A consumer earns beenz by visiting, registering, or

Figure 14-10	Beenz Homepage

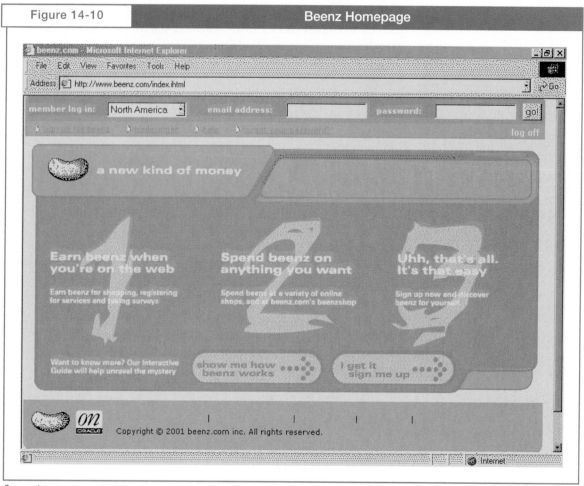

Source: beenz.com.

making purchases at participating sites. The beenz are deposited into a private account maintained by *Goldpoints.com*. Later, a consumer can redeem his or her beenz for products at the same sites. It is estimated that *Goldpoints.com* now has 300 participating sites and 3.5 million accounts.

Recently, *Goldpoints.com* partnered with MasterCard to offer rewardzcard, a stored-value card that can be used in the United States and Canada to make purchases wherever MasterCard is accepted. The rewardzcard is a way to transfer beenz that you earn on the Web into money you can spend on the Web, for mail or phone orders, and at physical store locations. The conversion rate is about 200 beenz to the dollar.

MyPoints-CyberGold (*mypoints.com*) is the result of the merger of two separate loyalty programs—MyPoints and CyberGold. Unlike beenz, customers earn cash by visiting, registering, or making purchases at affiliated MyPoints-CyberGold merchants. The cash can be used to make purchases at participating sites or transferred to a credit card or bank account.

RocketCash combines an online cash account with a rewards program. A user opens a RocketCash account and adds funds to the account with a money order, a credit card, beenz, or CyberGold. This cash account can then be used to make purchases at participating merchants. Purchases earn RocketCash rewards that can also be redeemed for merchandise.

Person-to-Person (P2P) Payments and Gifts

Person-to-person (P2P) payments are one of the newest and fastest growing payment schemes. They enable the transfer of funds between two individuals for a variety of purposes, such as repaying money borrowed from a friend, paying for an item purchased at an online auction, sending money to students at college, or sending a gift to a family member. One of the first companies to offer this service was PayPal (*paypal.com*). PayPal claims to have 4.5 million customer accounts and that it handles 25 percent of all transactions on eBay and funnels $2 billion in payments annually through its servers (Crockett 2000). Although PayPal is not profitable, this kind of activity has drawn the attention of a number of other companies who are trying to get in on the action. Citibank C2IT (*c2it.com*); AOL QuickCash (*aol.com*), which is a private-branded version of c2it; Bank1 eMoneyMail; Yahoo! PayDirect; and WebCertificate (*Webcertificate.com*) are all PayPal competitors.

Virtually all of these services work in exactly the same way. Assume you want to send money to someone over the Internet. First, you select a service and open up an account with the service. Basically, this entails creating a user name and a password, giving them your e-mail address, and providing the service with a payment card or bank account number. Next, you add funds to your account with your payment card or bank account. Once the account has been funded, you're ready to send money. You access the account with your user name and password. Now you specify the e-mail address of the person to receive the money along with the dollar amount that you want to send. An e-mail is sent to the specified e-mail address (see Figure 14-11).

Figure 14-11	Sending Money with PayPal

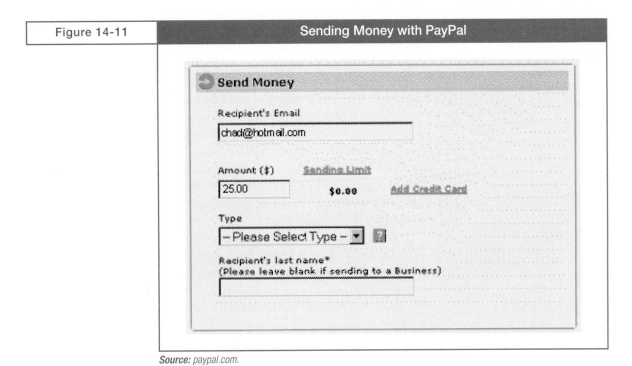

Source: paypal.com.

The e-mail will contain a link back to the service's Web site. When the recipient clicks on the link, they will be taken to the service. The recipient will be asked to set up an account to which the money that was sent will be credited. The recipient can then transfer the money from their account to his or her credit card or bank account.

While the various services all work in similar ways, there are differences. For example, c2it charges $2 per transaction, offers no insurance against fraud, and requires paperwork sent by snail mail if the money is being moved into a bank account. On the other hand, PayPal charges no fees, offers insurance against fraud, and doesn't require any paperwork for bank transfers.

14.6 E-CHECKING

Although there is some historical evidence that the Romans invented checks around 352 B.C., it wasn't until the 1500s in Holland that they experienced widespread usage. People who accumulated cash deposited it with "cashiers." These cashiers eventually began to pay the depositor's debts based on a written order or note. In the mid to late 1700s, the concept of writing and depositing checks as a method of payment spread to England and the United States. As they became more widely used, bankers were confronted with a problem—how to move the paper to collect money from many other banks. At first messengers were used, but this was too unwieldy and insecure. **Clearinghouses**, paper networks of banks that exchange checks with each other, arose to solve the problem.

In addition to being able to exchange checks directly, today banks in the United States can present checks to the Federal Reserve System or private clearinghouses for regional and national check collection. During the check-clearing process, checks pass through large sorting equipment that reads the **magnetic ink characters (MIC)** at the bottom of the check and places the check in sorting "pockets." The MICR (recognition) standard, developed in the United States by a consensus group of banks and technology in the 1950s, provided tremendous improvements to the check payment process by enabling the automation of many check handling procedures. The MICR contains information such as the routing number identifying the drawee bank, the payment amount, and the customer account number of the payor. The payee's bank is then credited for the payment amount, and it transfers these funds to the payee's account. The check is then physically transported to the drawee's bank by car, truck, or airplane, and presented to the drawee's bank by the clearing institution where the payment amount is debited from the payor's bank associated with the customer account number. The payor then receives the canceled physical check from the bank in the next statement.

Over 70 percent of all noncash payments in the United States are made by check. Today, U.S. consumers, businesses, and government entities write about 70 billion checks annually. It costs about 1 percent of the U.S. Gross Domestic Product (GDP) to process these checks. This doesn't count the costs associated with check fraud, which is estimated to be $53 billion annually, with banks absorbing about $1.34 billion in losses and retailers and other payees about $52 billion.

Figure 14-12	MICR Check Characters

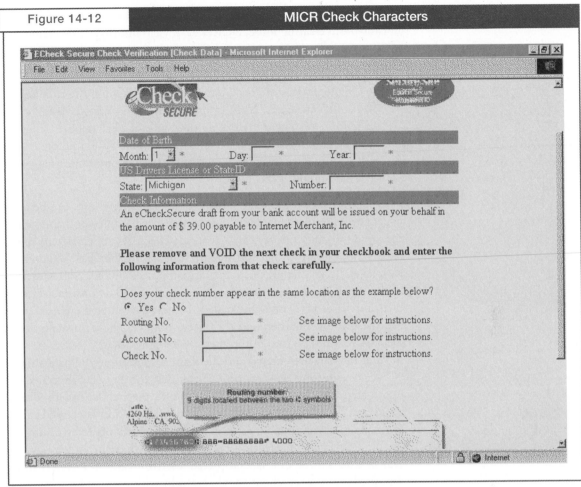

Source: echecksecure.com.

These costs are one of the driving forces behind the move to electronic checks (e-check). An **e-check** is the electronic version or representation of a paper check. Overall, e-checks (*echeck.org*):

- Leverage the check payment system, a core competency of the banking industry.
- Fit within current business practices, eliminating the need for expensive process reengineering.
- Work like a paper check does, but in pure electronic form, with fewer manual steps.
- Are designed to meet the needs of businesses and consumers in the twenty-first century, using state of the art security techniques.
- Can be used by all bank customers who have checking accounts, including small and mid-size businesses that currently have little access to electronic payment systems.
- Enhance existing bank accounts with new EC features.

According to the Electronic Check Clearing House Organization (*eccho.org*), a not-for-profit clearinghouse, e-checks can yield industry-wide savings and benefits of $2 to $3 billion per year including:

- Online check collection process—annual value $850 million
- Online notices of check returns (e.g., shortening the time to recognize an insufficient funds (NSF) or bad check)—annual value $450 million
- Truncating paper checks at the bank of first deposit (i.e., eliminating unnecessary processing steps)—annual value $600 million
- Creating new cash management product opportunities—annual value $700 million

E-checks contain the same information as a paper check, can be used wherever paper checks are used, are based on the same legal framework, and work essentially the same way that a paper check works. eCheck Secure (*troygroup.com*) is a third-party vendor that provides software that enables the purchase of goods and services with an e-check. The processes that are supported by their software are illustrative of the way e-checks work at most B2C sites. When a consumer elects to pay for their purchases with an e-check, they are asked to enter the check's routing number, the account number, and the check number. These numbers are taken from the MICR at the bottom of the check (see Figure 14-12).

After the data are entered and the form is submitted, the data are converted by eCheck Secure into an electronic check that can be securely transmitted to the Automated Clearing House (ACH) network, the standard method used by most banks and financial institutions. Once the information is verified through one of the many risk management services available, merchants receive authorization and customers receive an electronic confirmation that the order has been placed. Transaction settlement is completed electronically via ACH and funds are deposited into the merchant's bank, typically within 2 to 4 business days. The various processes and parties that are involved in the transaction are summarized in Figure 14-13.

eCheck Secure guarantees the checks that it handles. When you transmit the check information during a transaction, it is instantaneously sent to Equifax, the world's leading consumer information management company. Utilizing Equifax's extensive database, the information is verified and the amount of the check is guaranteed. The guarantee covers fraudulent, dishonored, and NSF transactions, meaning that if a check is returned, it is warranted and funds will be deposited into the merchant's account. eCheck Secure and Equifax will then attempt to collect funds from the customer.

Systems such as eCheck Secure are aimed at B2C merchants where the purchase prices are likely to be small relative to B2B or government purchases. In these latter cases where the dollar values can be in the hundreds of thousands of dollars, more secure transaction procedures are required. For the last 3 years, the eCheck Project Consortium (*echeck.org*), a team of over 15 banks, government agencies, technology vendors, and industry associations, has worked to develop e-check standards, worldwide interoperability, technology, and business models supporting B2B and government payments. There are two technologies that are key to this e-check initiative. The first of these is the Financial Services Markup Language (FSML). **FSML** is a special markup language that uses tags much like HTML (the

Figure 14-13	E-Check Processing by eCheck Secure

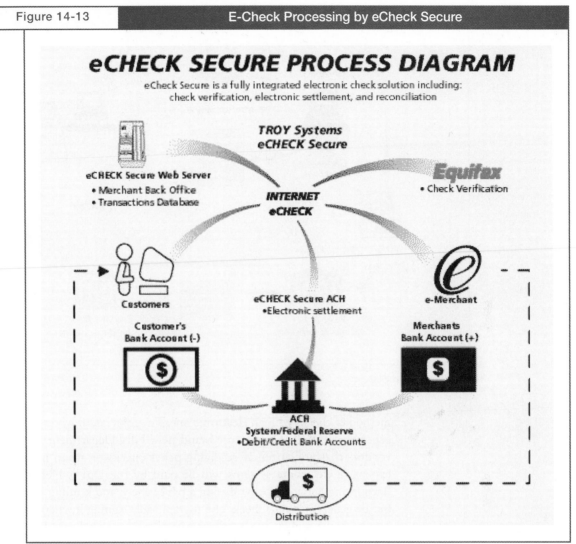

Source: *troygroup.com/financial/echecksecure/products/makingitwork.asp.*

language of the Web). The tags are used to create electronic payment messages that include the specifics of electronic checks, ACH payment authorizations, ATM network transaction authorizations, and variations of a check, such as a postal money order or gift certificate. The second key technology is digital signatures (described in detail earlier). In this instance, the consortium has extended digital signatures to apply to blocks of the FSML messages rather than to the whole message, and to support signatures of varying types, including basic signing, cosigning, and countersigning or notarizing. Figure 14-14 illustrates the role that digital signatures play in a consortium's payment architecture.

A pilot project has been underway at the U.S. Treasury Department. Each year, the U.S. Department of the Treasury's Financial Management Service (FMS) bureau issues approximately 857 million payments (494 million by Electronic Funds Transfer and 363 million by paper check) on behalf of non-defense government agencies, such as the Social Security Administration and the Department of Veterans Affairs. The Treasury eCheck pilot project is simply replacing the paper

Figure 14-14	Role of Digital Signatures in E-Check Processing

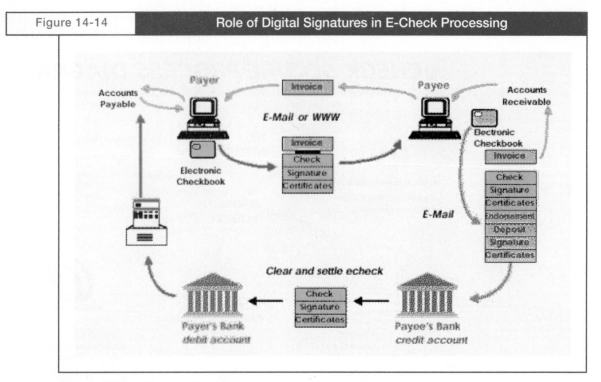

Source: Anderson (1998).

method of checks with an electronic one. The roles and flow stay the same, but the generation and distribution are brand new. Fifty Department of Defense (DoD) vendors that are currently receiving paper checks or are in need of converting expensive electronic systems will be paid by the DoD's Defense Finance and Accounting Service, not by issuing a paper check and sending it to their vendors, but by generating an eCheck, cryptographically signing it, encrypting it, and then sending it via e-mail. In the pilot project, e-checks are limited to a maximum of $50,000; later the limit will be raised to $100,000. In addition to the reduction in processing expenses, the Treasury Department expects e-checks to:

- Enhance security through the use of public key cryptography, X.509 certificates, and digital signatures allowing the eCheck to be private (unreadable except to the person with the correct private key), authenticated (verify who the sender is), and tamper-proof (identify if the eCheck has been modified or not).
- "Push" a payment to the payee, and not "pull" funds (i.e., direct debit) from the general account of the United States.
- Leverage the Internet for its strength as a ubiquitous communication vehicle, widely accessible for data exchange between parties of all types.
- Increase payment choices for U.S. Treasury payees.

14.7 E-BILLING

For a number of years, banks and companies like Intuit (*intuit.com*) have made it possible for customers to pay their bills online. Yet, better than 90 percent of all bills are still paid the traditional way. That is, on a regular basis a billing company calculates, prints, and mails the customer a paper bill. In turn, the customer sends back a paper check that is processed by the billing company in order to receive funds. It can take a week or more to complete the whole process.

Slowly, but surely, electronic billing (e-billing) is making some headway against traditional billing. By 2005 e-billing will represent 34 percent of all billing (Borths and Young 2000). E-billing is also called "electronic bill presentment and payment" (EBPP). **E-billing** enables the presentment, payment, and posting of bills on the Internet. Presentment involves taking the information that is typically printed on the bill and hosting it on a bill presentment Web server (see Figure 14-15 for an example). Once the bill is available on a Web server, a customer can access the bill with a browser, review it, and pay it electronically. After the payment is received and secured it must be posted against the biller's accounts receivable system.

In e-billing, the customers can either be individuals or companies. E-bills can be presented in a variety of ways. Two models are common—**biller direct** and **third-party consolidators**. With biller direct, the customer is presented with a bill from a single billing merchant. For example, a customer could access the Web site of a utility company in order to pay his or her bill. In contrast, a third-party consolidator

Figure 14-15	E-Bill Presentment

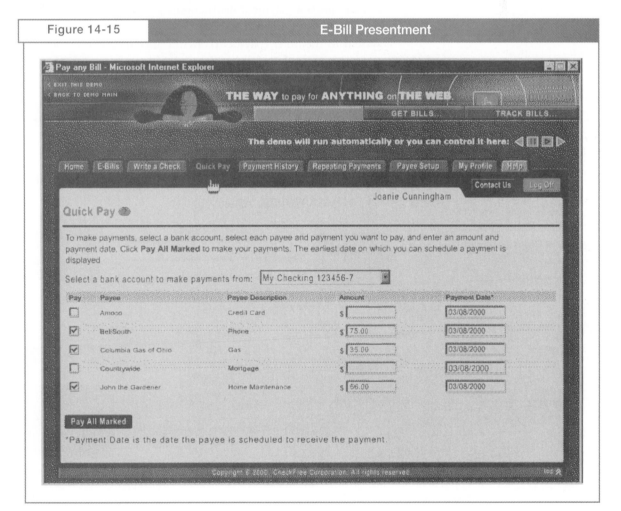

presents bills from multiple merchants. The steps involved with each model are essentially the same and are presented below:

- **Individual biller.** The customer signs up to receive and pay bills via the biller's Web site (service initiation). The biller makes the billing information available to the customer (presentment) on their Web site or the site of a (billing) hosting service. Once the customer views the bill, they authorize and initiate payment at the site (payment). The payment can be made with a credit/debit card or an ACH debit. The biller then initiates a payment transaction that moves funds through the payment system (payment). The biller updates its accounts receivable A/R system (posting).
- **Billing consolidator.** The customer enrolls to receive and pay bills for multiple billers (service initiation). Customer's enrollment information is forwarded to every biller the customer wishes to activate (service initiation). For each billing cycle, the biller sends a bill summary and/or bill detail to the consolidator (presentment). The bill summary, which links to the bill detail stored with the biller or consolidator, is forwarded to the aggregator and made available to the customer (presentment). The customer views the bill and initiates payment instructions (payment). The CSP/aggregator initiates a credit payment transaction that moves funds through the payment system to the biller (payment). Remittance data is provided to the biller, who posts this information to its own A/R system (posting).

Figure 14-16	E-Billing Process for Single Biller

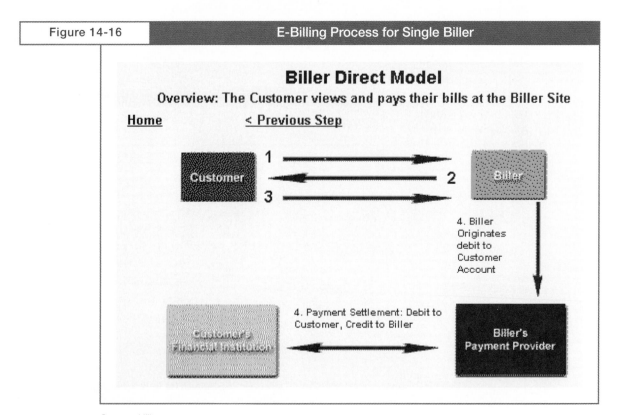

Source: ebilling.org.

| Figure 14-17 | E-Billing Processes for Bill Consolidator |

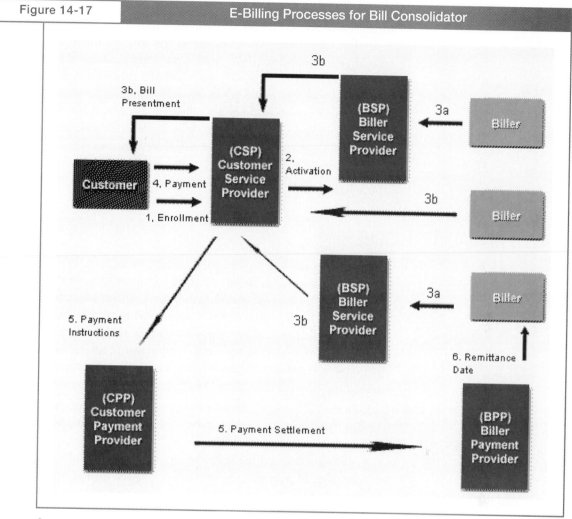

Source: ebilling.org.

From the perspective of the billing firm, e-billing has several advantages. The most obvious benefit is the reduction in expenses related to billing and processing payments. The estimate is that paper bills cost between $0.75 and $2.70 per bill. E-billing costs between $0.25 and $0.30 per bill. A paper bill can include advertising and marketing inserts. Usually, every customer gets the same ads or materials. With e-billing the electronic inserts can be customized to the individual customer. If a customer responds to the insert, then it is much easier to trace which ads or materials are successful. Finally, e-billing enables better customer service. Not only can customer service representatives see the same presentment that the customer is seeing, but the presentment can also provide access to frequently asked questions and help boxes.

There are also advantages from the customer's perspective. It reduces the customer's expenses by eliminating the cost of checks, postage, and envelopes. E-billing simplifies and centralizes payment processing and provides better record keeping.

Bills can be reviewed and payments made at virtually any time. In this way the customer has direct control over the timing and amount of the payment.

By far, Checkfree (*checkfree.com*) is the leading third-party e-billing vendor. Checkfree was founded in 1981 and is currently headquartered in Atlanta, Georgia. Checkfree is a consolidator, aggregating all of a customer's bills into a single presentment. They can also set up payments with companies who do not offer electronic billing. Checkfree serves about 3.5 million consumers, 1,000 businesses, and 350 financial institutions. In addition to these services, Checkfree also provides portfolio management, reconciliation products and services, and for years has been a leading processor of ACH (automated clearing house) payments. Today, more than two-thirds of the nation's 6 billion ACH payments are processed by Checkfree.

14.8 MANAGERIAL ISSUES

The following issues are germane to management:

In the online world, by far the most common form of e-payment is the credit card. In the B2C world, earlier attempts to initiate other forms of e-payment—e-cash, e-checks, electronic script—have failed miserably. In the B2B world, businesses have relied on traditional paper payment methods or EDI and EFT. Yet there are situations where alternative forms of payment can reap substantial cost savings or open new channels of business. Management needs to have an understanding of some of the alternatives and the hurdles and benefits associated with each.

1. **In the B2C world, understand your customers and products.** The vast majority of online merchants take credit cards. This implies that their customers have credit cards, that they are willing to use them, and that the associated transaction costs are not too onerous. But, using only credit cards rules out a number of potential markets and it is costly for many merchants. Teenagers, non-U.S. customers, and customers who don't want to use credit cards online are examples of market segments where credit cards are of little use. Here, e-cash, stored-value cards, and virtual credit cards are possibilities. When the purchase price is less than $10, credit cards are not often accepted. Again, e-cash and stored-value cards are possibilities. In the off-line world, small businesses often find it too costly to accept credit cards. The same is true in the online world. In some instances the seller is not a business but is instead an individual who cannot accept credit card payments. In these cases, third-party companies such as PayPal can handle the transactions via secure e-mail. In this way there is no requirement for the seller to open a credit card account with an acquirer. In all of these cases, merchants and other sellers need to be aware of the volatility of the alternatives they are adopting and their true costs. Because the various alternatives don't enjoy widespread use, there is always the possibility that they won't exist tomorrow.

2. **In the B2B world, keep an open mind about online alternatives.** When it comes to paying suppliers or accepting payments from partners, most businesses have opted to stick with the tried-and-true methods of EDI and EFT. Compared to traditional EDI, Internet-based e-payment schemes are viewed as too risky. Yet, there are a number of areas where the cost savings generated by new methods substantially outweigh the risks. One of these areas is purchasing

cards. Purchasing cards are special-purpose nonrevolving payment cards issued to employees solely for the purpose of purchasing and paying for nonstrategic materials and services. The use of these cards not only produces cost savings through bill consolidation, but makes it easier to analyze overall purchase patterns to see where special supplier deals can be negotiated and where other costs savings can be achieved. The use of e-checks is another area where costs savings can accrue. E-checks work just like their paper counterparts, but they truncate many of the manual tasks associated with sending, receiving, and processing checks. In all of these cases a key element is determining what is required and how these alternative methods work with existing A/R and GL systems.

3. **In-house or outsource.** It takes time, skill, money, software, and hardware to integrate the systems of all the parties involved in processing any sort of e-payment. For this reason, even a business that runs its own EC site should consider outsourcing the e-payment component. There are many third-party vendors who provide payment gateways designed to handle the interactions among the various financial institutions that operate in the background of an e-payment system. Many of these vendors—such as First Data—already handle payment processing in the off-line world. This is simply an extension of their existing business.

4. **Security continues to be a major issue.** A few years ago, consumers questioned the safety of using their credit card numbers online. Given the rapid rise in online credit card purchases, it no longer seems to be a big concern for a sizeable percentage of the online population. Now it's the merchants who have to be leery. Credit card fraud has turned out to be a big issue. In spite of all assurances, security is one of the major issues in making and accepting e-payments of all kinds. While PKI has gone a long way towards securing e-payments, any e-payment method has to interact with the off-line world. If someone steals a credit card or a checkbook and uses the number to place an online order, it doesn't matter whether the transmission is secure or not. On the other hand, if more stringent measures are put in place to ensure people's identities, then it may inhibit and discourage legitimate users. The measures that are employed to ensure the security of e-payments have to be part of a broader security scheme that weighs risks against issues like ease of use and that fit within the overall business context.

Summary

In this chapter, you learned about the following EC issues as they relate to the learning objectives:

1. **Crucial factors determining the success of a method of e-payment.** A crucial element in the success of a method of e-payment is the "chicken-and-egg" problem. How do you get sellers to adopt a method when there are few buyers using it? And, how do you get buyers to adopt a method when there are few sellers using it? At a minimum, overcoming this hurdle requires that the e-payment method requires little specialized hardware or software (independence), integrates well with existing EC and legacy systems (interoperability and portability), is secure, maintains the anonymity of the buyer (and

seller), supports products and services with varying prices (divisibility), is easy to use, and costs little for both the buyer and seller to use.

2. **Key elements in securing an e-payment.** In B2C, B2B, and C2C EC, issues of trust are paramount. These issues are summarized by the acronym PAIN—privacy, authenticity, integrity, and nonrepudiation. Public Key Infrastructure (PKI) is the base of secure e-payments. PKI utilizes encryption (through a combination of private and public encryption keys) to ensure privacy and integrity, and digital signatures to ensure authenticity and nonrepudiation. Digital signatures are themselves authenticated through a system of digital certificates issued by certificate authorities (CA). For the average consumer and merchant, the security of e-payments is simplified because it is built into Web browsers and Web servers. Here, the security comes about because they can rely on the secure socket layer/transport layer (SSL/TSL) in communicating with each other.

3. **Online credit card players and processes.** Unlike the off-line world, credit cards dominate the online world. The players in online credit cards are the same as they are in the off-line world: cardholder, merchant, card issuer (establishing the cardholder's account), acquirer (e.g., financial institution establishing the merchant's account), card association of issuers and acquirers (e.g., Visa), third-party processors to whom the handling of the card payments have been outsourced. Similarly, the processes are basically the same. When a consumer accesses the merchant's checkout page, selects a method of payment, and clicks submit, the information on the page is secured by SSL encryption and transmitted to the merchant's Web site. From there the information, along with the merchant's identification number, is passed on to the merchant's acquirer (or third-party processor). The acquirer sends the information on to the customer's issuing bank for approval. The issuer sends its response (approve or disapprove) back to the acquirer where it is passed on to the merchant. Finally, the customer is notified. The entire set of processes takes place in seconds.

4. **The uses and benefits of purchase cards.** Businesses spend billions of dollars purchasing low-cost goods and services (e.g., office supplies). Purchase cards are special-purpose, nonrevolving credit or payment cards issued to employees solely for purchasing these nonstrategic goods and services. Purchases with payment cards are controlled by establishing strict rules and dollar limits on their use. At the end of the month, a business receives a single billing statement from the card issuer (e.g., American Express). This substantially reduces the paperwork associated with these purchases. Besides this bill consolidation, purchase cards also free purchasing departments from day-to-day procurement activities, make it easier to reconcile purchases with the general ledger system, offer the possibility of getting preferential pricing from suppliers because it shortens the payment cycle, and make it easier for a company to track and analyze purchases.

5. **Categories, methods of programming, and potential uses of smart cards.** Smart cards look like credit cards but contain embedded chips. They can be categorized or distinguished by their underlying technologies. For some cards (microprocessor), the chips can be programmed to handle a wide variety of tasks. For others (memory), the chips are simply memory cards to which data

can be written and from which data can be read. Most of these memory cards are disposable, but others—optical memory cards—can hold large stores of data. Besides the type of chip, smart cards can also be distinguished by how the data are read from and written to the card. Some cards require the chip to come in contact with the reader/writer device. Others are contactless and transmit data through a built-in antenna. The manner in which microprocessor smart cards are programmed depends on the chip's operating system. Today, the major choices are: MultOS, supporting assembly language; C; and Java. The JavaCard supports Java, and Microsoft Windows for Smart Cards supports Microsoft Visual Basic and C++. The vast majority of smart cards have been issued in Europe, South America, and Asia. Although the majority of these cards have been prepaid, disposable phone cards and smart cards have been and will be used for a number of purposes, including generating loyalty among shoppers (loyalty cards), holding e-cash, ensuring secure payment card usage with digital signatures and certificates, maintaining health and social welfare records, paying for mass transit services, and identifying the cardholder (e.g., holding drivers licenses and immigration status).

6. **Online alternatives to credit card payments.** Although credit cards are the dominant B2C e-payment method, there are situations where credit cards are too costly to use, are perceived as being too insecure to use, or are simply unavailable to either the buyer or the seller. When the item or service being sold costs less than $10 (i.e., it's a micropayment), credit cards are too costly. Here, the 2 percent or more transaction fee charged by the credit card companies makes it unprofitable for merchants to rely on credit cards. This is a situation where e-cash loaded on special desktop software called e-wallets, or stored-value cards (smart cards with e-cash), or specialized electronic script like beenz or e-rewards such as MyPoints/CyberGold can come into play. These alternatives can also serve certain market segments (e.g., teenagers) that don't have their own credit cards but still want to make online purchases. Some buyers simply don't trust using their credit cards online. In this instance, systems like PrivateBuy allow a consumer to set up accounts that assign a special name and number that can be used in place of the consumer's own credit card number. Finally, there are cases where the seller can't really obtain a merchant account with an acquirer. For instance, in an online auction many of the sellers are individuals, not businesses. A number of alternatives like PayPal have been established to handle these C2C transactions through secure e-mail.

7. **E-check players and processes.** E-checks are the electronic equivalent of paper checks. E-checks are being employed in situations where consumers don't want to use their credit cards and in B2B EC and where the payments are too large for credit cards. E-checks are handled in much the same way as paper checks. When an e-payment is made by e-check, the numbers represented by the magnetic ink characters at the bottom of a check are entered on the payment page and submitted to the merchant's EC server or the server of a third-party outsourcing company handling the e-check. From there, the data are converted into an electronic check representation that can be securely transmitted to the Automated Clearing House (ACH) network, the standard method used by most banks and financial institutions. Once the information is verified through one of the many risk management services available,

merchants receive authorization and customers receive an electronic confirmation that the order has been placed. Transaction settlement is completed electronically via ACH and funds are deposited into the merchant's bank, typically within 2 to 4 business days. When e-checks are used by a business to pay suppliers, more stringent security is required because of the size of the payments and the sensitivity of the information. The eCheck Consortium has been working on establishing standards for these larger payments. The standards are currently being tested by the U.S. Treasury.

8. **Operation and benefits of e-billing.** E-billing, as opposed to traditional paper billing methods, enables the electronic presentment, payment, and posting of bills on the Internet. Checkfree is the undisputed leader in the e-billing arena. There are two types of e-billing models. In the first, the customer receives bills from individual billers. In the other, a billing consolidator enables a customer to pay bills from a number of billers. In either case the customer establishes an account with the biller or consolidator. The account is paid with a credit card or an ACH debit. After a customer views a bill and authorizes payment, the biller or consolidator initiates the credit or debit transaction and moves the funds in the same way that online credit card or e-check transactions are handled. The major benefit of e-billing is the savings in transaction costs for both the biller and customer. Paper bills cost $.75 to $2.70 to handle; it's $.25 to $.30 for e-bills. E-bills also offer the opportunity for billers to advertise other goods or services and to enhance overall customer service. For the customer, e-billing simplifies payment, enables better control of the time and amount of payments, and can improve record keeping.

Key Terms

Acquirer	Digital certificates
Anonymity	Digital envelope
Authentication	Digital signature
Authorization	Divisibility
Automated Clearing House (ACH)	E-billing
Beenz	E-cash
Bill consolidator	E-check
Biller direct	Electronic purses
Card association	Electronic script
Card issuer	Encryption algorithm
Cardholder	E-wallet
Certificate authority (CA)	Financial Services Markup Language (FSML)
Charge cards	IC memory card
Ciphertext	IC microprocessor card
Clearinghouse	Integrity
Contact card	IPSec
Contactless card	JavaCard
Credit card gateway	Key
Credit cards	Magnetic ink character recognition (MICR)
Cryptography	Micropayment
Debit cards	Microsoft Windows For Smart Cards

Mondex	Purchase card
MultOS	Rijndael algorithm
Nonrepudiation	RSA algorithm
Optical memory card	Secure electronic transaction (SET)
Payment cards	Secure socket layer (SSL)
Person-to-person payment (P2P)	Smart card
Plaintext	Stored-value card
Privacy	Third-party card processor
Private key	Third-party consolidators
Public key	Transport Layer Security (TLS)
Public key encryption	Virtual credit card
Public Key Infrastructure (PKI)	Visa Cash

Questions for Review

1. List the major parties in an e-payment.
2. What does the acronym PAIN stand for?
3. What are the major factors affecting the success of an e-payment method?
4. Who is responsible for a fraudulent credit card payment?
5. What is PKI?
6. List the basic parts of encryption.
7. What is a symmetric key? Public key?
8. What determines the strength of an encryption key?
9. How does a digital signature work?
10. What government act ensures that digital signatures have the legal standing of written signatures?
11. How do you get a digital certificate?
12. What is SSL/TSL? How does it differ from IPSec?
13. List some differences between credit, charge, and debit cards.
14. Who are the major participants in processing a credit card payment?
15. What are some of the security risks associated with credit card payments online?
16. List some of the benefits of a purchase card.
17. Describe the basic types of smart card technologies.
18. List the major operating systems for smart cards and the programming languages they support.
19. Describe some of the major applications of smart cards.
20. What is a micropayment? Where are micropayments likely to be used and by whom?
21. Describe some of the major barriers to e-cash acceptance and use.
22. What are some alternatives to online credit card purchases such as PrivateBuy?
23. What is a stored-value card and where are they being used?
24. How do P2P payment systems such as PayPal work?
25. What is MICR?
26. How does an e-check work in B2C commerce?
27. What are some of the benefits of using e-checks in B2B commerce?
28. What is FSML?
29. Why is the U.S. Treasury interested in e-checks?
30. How does e-billing work and what are the benefits for billers and customers?

Questions for Discussion

1. Online credit cards were able to overcome the "chicken-and-egg" problem. To date, various e-cash methods have failed. What are some of the reasons for the failure? What does an e-cash company need to do to break the barrier?

2. A small business owner wants to sell handcrafted jewelry to teenagers on the Web. What methods of e-payment would you recommend and why?

3. Recently, a merchant who accepts online credit card payments has experienced a wave of fraudulent charges. What sorts of security measures can the merchant impose without hindering legitimate customers?

4. You receive an online e-check. What security methods can be used to ensure the identity of the sender so that he or she can't claim that they didn't send the check?

5. You invite a group of friends to lunch. At the end of lunch, you pick up the check but your friends agree to pay you later. How could they pay you online?

6. Sears recently formed a partnership with CheckFree to do online billing. What measures can Sears take to ensure that the program will be adopted by a large number of customers?

7. Smart cards have taken off in Europe and Asia but not in the United States. Why hasn't the success been as great in the United States and what can be done to encourage their use?

8. The local transit authority decides to allow smart cards to be used to pay for bus rides. What types of smart card should be used (i.e., microprocessor, contactless, etc.)? Why?

9. A business wants to gain better control of its office supply purchases. What sort of e-payment could it use to solve this problem? What types of control would the method afford?

10. An online vendor of health care products has noticed that there is little repeat business. Recommend a method of e-payment that would encourage repeat business.

11. A business that purchases millions of dollars in goods and services from its suppliers would like to substitute an Internet-based e-payment system for its older EDI system. A consultant has recommended that it use e-checks. How would this work and what sorts of security issues would arise?

Exercises

1. Visit the VeriSign Web site. Take the guided tour of VeriSign's e-payment processing solutions (*verisign.com/payment/tour/tour0.html*). While at VeriSign sign-up for a digital ID that can be used with e-mail (*verisign.com/products/secureEmail.html*). Use the ID to encrypt and e-mail the message.

2. In 2000, the federal government announced the adoption of a new encryption algorithm to be used with nonsensitive information. Use the information provided at *nist.gov/public_affairs/releases/aesq&a.htm* to answer the following questions:
   a. What algorithm was selected?
   b. Who invented the algorithm?

c. What other algorithms were tested?

d. Why was this particular algorithm selected?

e. How long would it take someone to break the algorithm?

3. Go to the CheckFree Web site (*checkfree.com*). Run their e-billing demo. What features and functions does CheckFree provide?

4. Run the online merchant demo at eCheck Secure (*demo.echecksecure.net/ merchant/*). What specific information is needed to pay with an e-check? How does eCheck Secure guarantee online checks?

5. Visit *emvco.com*. What do the EMV specifications have to do with smart cards?

6. Go to the RocketCash site. What is RocketCash? What is RocketFuel? Approximately how many stores accept RocketCash? What types of stores are they and who do they cater to?

7. ECheque is a program modeled after the U.S. Treasury Department's eCheck pilot project. In what country is the program taking place? Who is the target audience? What equipment and technologies do they need in order to make ECheque payments? Are these requirements a barrier to the use of ECheques?

Team Assignments and Role Playing

1. Select a series of B2C sites that cater to teens and a series of sites that cater to older consumers. Have team members visit the sites. What types of e-payment methods do they support? Are there any differences among the methods used on different types of sites? What other types of e-payment would you recommend for the various sites and why?

2. A series of sites now support P2P or C2C payments. Locate as many of these sites as you can. What other types of services do they provide? Not all of these sites will be successful in the long run. Which of the sites do you think will be long-term players? Why?

3. NetCraft conducts surveys of secure servers and the types of security software and certificates being used on these servers. They provide a facility (at *netcraft.com/sslwhats/*) for determining the type of servers and certificates used at a site. Using this facility, inventory the servers and certificates being used at a large number (say, 30) well-known sites (e.g., *amazon.com*). Which servers and certificates predominate?

REAL-WORLD CASE: InternetCash—Solving the Chicken-and-Egg Problem in the Teenage Market

Harris Interactive and Nickelodeon Online estimate that 68 percent of all 13- to 18-year-olds in the United States are now online. About 50 percent spend an average of 8.5 hours a week on the Internet. What are they doing there? The primary reason for going online is e-mail. Other reasons include researching information, playing games, using chat rooms, and downloading music or videos. It's the same picture in the United Kingdom. Surveys indicate that over 75 percent of 13- to 16-year-olds in the United Kingdom are now online. Like their U.S. counterparts, teenagers in the United Kingdom are doing homework, sending and receiving e-mail, and playing games. In either case, what they aren't doing is shopping. They spend time researching potential purchases, but they don't spend money online. In the United States, teenagers spent somewhere between $110 to $140 billion dollars last year. Of this, less than 1 percent was spent online. When they did spend money, they were likely to purchase CDs, clothing, books, software, and toys in that order. This isn't much different than the pattern for adults where the top five purchases were books, CDs, software, toys, and clothing in that order.

Teenagers cite a number of reasons why they don't shop online—they can't touch the products, it's hard to return items purchased on the Web, they don't have the money, and it's insecure. The number one reason, however, is that their parents won't let them. Or, more specifically, their parents won't let them use their credit cards online. Just like their parents, when teens purchase something online they use credit cards. Because only 10 percent of U.S. teenagers have their own credit cards, this means that they have to use their parents' credit cards even if they have the cash to make a purchase. The fact that teenage consumers aren't financially independent creates challenges for online merchants. It also creates opportunities for firms who can come up with creative ways for teenagers to make purchases without relying on credit cards.

One firm that is addressing this opportunity is InternetCash. InternetCash is a New York-based start-up founded by a former steelworker, Charles Doherty. InternetCash offers prepaid stored-value cards sold in amounts of $10, $20, $50, and $100 at retail outlets. Like prepaid phone cards, they must be activated to work. This is a two-step process. First the merchant swipes the card through a specially programmed POS machine. Next, the user logs on to the InternetCash Web site (*InternetCash.com*), enters a 20-digit code from the back of the card, and creates a personal identification number (PIN). That gives the user shopping privileges at designated stores, which carry an InternetCash icon. Purchases are automatically deducted from the value of the card. When the value is used up, consumers throw it away, or link an amount not used to another card. As with cash, InternetCash's transactions are anonymous.

InternetCash has a number of competitors including *IcanBuy.com*, *Doughnet.com*, and *Rocketcash.com* who have already signed some major retailers such as CDNow, *Amazon.com*, and *BarnesandNoble.com*. Even if they didn't have any competitors, InternetCash would still be facing enormous obstacles. It's the old "chicken-and-egg" problem. First, they have to find retailers to distribute the cards. InternetCash is aiming for 30,000 outlets. The bait for the retailers is that it costs the retailers nothing to handle the cards. Instead, they receive 6 percent of the value of the card sold. Until recently, the cards were only distributed by a handful of retailers. In October 2000, they signed a partnership agreement with PaySmart America who will distribute the cards in over 5,000 PaySmart locations in 11 states. PaySmart is part of TSI Communications, the largest independent distributor of prepaid calling cards in the United States.

The second obstacle they face is trying to persuade merchants to accept the card for online purchases. This is a harder task since InternetCash charges commissions of 2.25 percent to 10 percent of sales. At last count, InternetCash had signed 150 merchants. The bulk of these were smaller businesses. In June they formed an alliance with *JustWebIt.com*, a supplier of EC software for small businesses. Through the deal, *JustWebit.com* was to set up its merchant clients to accept InternetCash's cards for purchases on their sites. The results have been mixed since *JustWebIt.com* has experienced an economic downturn since the alliance was formed.

Other InternetCash ventures in the works include U.S.-to-Mexico money transfers through the Internet using plastic cards with transferable balances, and a partnership for kiosk-based EC and money transfer using convenience store and check cashing outlet locations as a base.

Charles Doherty, the CEO, expects the company to break even by the middle of 2001 with revenues near $19 million. That means InternetCash will have to sell $100 million worth of cards in 2001 or somewhere between 100,000 to 1,000,000 cards. It's a daunting task. InternetCash and other vendors of e-cash products could also face some serious legal issues. For the moment they exist in a gray area regulated by individual state laws where the cards are used. The Federal Reserve is looking into treating these companies more like banks, which would open them up to a whole series of banking and depository institution regulations.

Questions for the case

1. What are the biggest obstacles that InternetCash needs to overcome in order to succeed? Given the history of various e-cash companies, is success likely? Why or why not?

2. What, if anything, is InternetCash doing to attract teenagers to use their stored-value cards? Is their anything else they should be doing to increase the popularity of their cards?

3. Is InternetCash's strategy of trying to sign up small businesses likely to entice teenagers to use their cards? Use some specific online merchants to support your argument.

4. Are there other demographic segments that are likely to use a stored-value card for online shopping?

5. Compare InternetCash's stored-value card with the offerings from RocketCash. Is there anything that distinguishes one offering from the other?

REFERENCES AND BIBLIOGRAPHY

American Express. "American Express Announces Expansion of Online Corporate Purchasing Through New Alliances and New Solution Set," Press Release. (*home3.americanexpress.com/corporateservices/news/press/article.asp?item_id=959*) (May 2000).

American Express. "American Express Continues 150-Year Tradition of Protecting Customers with New Suite of Online Privacy and Security Products," press release. (*home3.americanexpress.com/corp/latestnews/payments.asp*) (September 2000).

Anderson, M. "The Electronic Check Architecture." Financial Services Technology Consortium (1998).

Berst, J. "Sign of Trouble: The Problem with E-Signatures," *ZDNet AnchorDesk* (*zdnet.com/anchordesk/stories/story/0,10738,2604099,00.html*) (July 2000).

Borths, R. and D. Young. "E-Billing, Today and Beyond," *Information Strategy: The Executive's Journal* (Winter 2000).

Carr, J. "The Problem with Plastic," *eCommerce Business* (December 2000).

Cassy, J. "No Just Rewards in E-Heaven," *Business 2.0* (November 2000).

Caswell, S. "Credit Card Fraud Crippling Online Merchants," *E-Commerce Times* (March 2000).

Charles, D. "Clinton Signs Digital Signature Bill," *ZDNet News* (*zdnet.com/zdnn/stories/news/0,4586,2597132,00.html*) (June 2000).

Cornwell, A. "Commerce Service Providers and Future Internet Payment Methods," *World Market Series Business Briefings* (*wmrc.com*) (2000).

Crockett, R. "No Plastic? No Problem," *BusinessWeek* (October 2000).

Deitel, H., P. Deitel, and T. Nieto. *E-Business and E-Commerce: How-to Program.* Upper Saddle River, New Jersey: Prentice Hall, 2001.

Denison, D. "What's a Penny Worth on the Web? Maybe a Lot." *Boston.com* (December 2000).

Duvall, M. "Retailers Predict Increased Credit Card Theft," *Interactive Week* (November 2000).

E-Commerce Times Staff. "Credit Card Fraud Crippling Online Merchants," *E-Commerce Times* (*ecommercetimes.com/news/articles2000/000320-2.shtml*) (March 2000).

Enos, L. "Study: Teen E-Shoppers Face Barriers," *E-Commerce Times* (*localbusiness.com/Story/0,1118, NOCITY_209566,00.html*) (June 2000).

Evans, D. and R. Schmalensee. *Playing with Plastic: The Digital Revolution in Buying and Borrowing.* Cambridge, Massachusetts: MIT Press, 2000.

Fisher, S. "Card Game," *Supply Management* (September 1999).

Gaskin, J. "Electronic Billing Revs Up," *Interactive Week* (*zdnet.com/intweek/stories/news/0,4164,2522422,00.html*) (April 2000).

Gutzman, A. "An Overview of E-Payment Solutions," *Office.com* (*office.com*) (July 2000).

Harbrecht, D. "What Do E-Signatures Mean for You?" *Business Week Online* (*businessweek.com/bwdaily/dnflash/june2000/nf006 20f.htm?scriptFramed?scriptFramed*) (June 2000).

Higgins, K. "Take on a New E-Dentity," *InternetWeek* (December 1999).

Howard, M. *Designing Secure Web-based Applications.* Redmond, Washington: Microsoft Press, 2000.

Jilovec, N. *E-Business: Thriving in the Electronic Marketplace.* Loveland, Colorado: 29th Street Press, 1999.

Karpinski, R. "Web Merchants Try Debit Cards and Gift Certificates to Spur Sales," *InternetWeek* (October 2000).

Komp, L. and K. Walstrom. "Perceptions About Electronic Money: Form and Function," *Journal of Computer Information Systems* (Winter 1998–1999).

Korper, S. and J. Ellis. *The E-Commerce Book: Building the E-Empire.* New York: Academic Press, 2000.

Lawrence, S. "Study Peers into World Wide Wallet," *The Standard* (April 2000).

Lee, J. and H. Yoon. "An Intelligent Agents-Base Virtually Defaultless Check System: The SafeCheck System," *International Journal of Electronic Commerce* (Spring 2000).

Lemos, R. "E-Signatures Bill: Fraud Made Easy?" *ZDNet News* (*zdnet.com/zdnn/stories/news/0,4586,2589436,00.html?chkpt=zdnnrla*) (June 2000).

MasterCard. "SET Secure Electronic Transaction Setting the Stage for Safe Internet Shopping," (*mastercard.com/shoponline/set*) (2000).

Menasce, D. and V. Almeida. *Scaling for E-Business.* Upper Saddle River, New Jersey: Prentice Hall, 2000.

Microsoft. "The Smart Card Market Opportunity," (*microsoft.com/windowsce/smartcard/start/background.asp*) (February 2000)

Newing, R. "Time to Wise Up—But Banks Count the Cost," *FT.com* (*ft.com/ftsurveys/q6a0e.htm*) (March 2000).

Ovenstein, D. "The Feds' New Encryption Standard is a Lightweight Suit of Armor for Critical Data," *Business 2.0* (December 26, 2000).

Patel, B. J. and J. Fenner. "Handling Electronic Bill Payments," *Planet IT* (*PlanetIT.com/docs/PIT20000920S0015*) (September 2000).

Perry, G. and J. Perry. *Electronic Commerce.* Cambridge, Massachusetts: Thomson Learning, 2000.

Powell, E. "Banks, IBM Plan E-Check System," *Excite News* (*news.excite.com/news/ap/001101/15/banks-check-imaging.htm*) (November 2000).

Raik-Allen, G. "DoughNet Hooks Up Teenagers and Online Merchants," *Redherring.com* (June 1999).

Stein, L. *Web Security: A Step-by-Step Reference Guide.* (Reading, Massachusetts: Addison-Wesley, 1998).

Steinert-Threlkeld, T. "Show Me the E-Money," *Interactive Week* (*zdnet.com/intweek/stories/columns/0,4164,2631284,00.html*) (September 2000).

Thiessen, F. "Electronic Money: Some Reasons for the Failure of Internet Payment Systems," *World Market Business Briefings* (December 1999).

Visa. "Visa Cash" (*visa.com/nt/visacash/main.html*) (2000).

Weinberg, N. "Digital Dough Fails to Rise," *Network World* (*nwfusion.com.news/1999/0412dough.html*) (1999).

15

Order Fulfillment, Logistics, and Supply Chain Management

LEARNING OBJECTIVES

Upon completion of this chapter, the reader will be able to:

- Understand the role of order fulfillment and back-office operations in EC.

- Describe the order fulfillment process.

- Understand the concept of the supply chain, its importance, and management.

- Describe the problems of managing the supply chain and the use of innovative solutions to do so.

- Describe the need for integrating the information systems of the front and back offices.

- Trace the evolution of software that supports activities along and management of the supply chain.

- Understand the relationships among ERP, SCM, and EC.

15.1 THE TOY ORDER FULFILLMENT Y2K PROBLEM

While the entire world watched the transition into the third millennium happen without any major Y2K problems, the EC B2C industry in general, and the e-toys retailers in particular, experienced their own transition problem at the end of 1999.

According to many newspapers, TV, and EC research companies' reports, (e.g., see *Fortune*, January 24, 2000, p. 2), overall satisfaction with online shopping declined significantly in December 1999 and January 2000, driven by consumer frustration with late deliveries and with poor customer service before, during, and after purchases. In general, e-tailers struggled to meet the demands of last-minute shoppers. It became clear during the period of peak demand that the order fulfillment infrastructure of most e-tailers was pretty weak.

The situation was especially critical in the toy business. In fall 1999, a fierce competition developed among the online toy retailers. Many toy e-tailers promised to pay delivery charges and even gave $20 discount coupons. *Toysrus.com* averaged 1.75 million unique customers a day and eToys (assets purchased by *kbkids.com*) was flooded with 1.9 million unique customers a day. The number of orders far exceeded the projections. On December 1999, *Toysrus.com* notified customers that only orders made prior to December 14 would arrive in time for the holidays. After that, the customers would have to pay a premium for priority shipping. A few days prior to Christmas, *Toysrus.com* notified some customers that they would probably not get the toys they ordered by the holiday, offering them $100 coupons as compensation. eToys and other e-tailers experienced similar problems. *Amazon.com* was forced to ship orders for several products in several shipments instead of one, substantially increasing its expenses.

15.2 ORDER FULFILLMENT AND LOGISTICS—AN OVERVIEW

Introduction

The opening vignette illustrates that taking orders over the Internet could well be the easy part of B2C EC. Fulfillment and delivery to customers' doors is the sticky part. As a matter of fact, many e-tailers have experienced fulfillment problems since they started EC. *Amazon.com*, for example, which initially operated as a totally virtual company, added physical warehouses in order to expedite deliveries and reduce order fulfillment costs. Woolworths of Australia, a large supermarket that added online services, had serious difficulties with order fulfillment and delivery of fresh foods and had to completely reengineer its delivery system (see Application Case 15.1).

Several factors may be responsible for the delays in deliveries. They range from an inability to accurately forecast demand to ineffective e-tail supply chains. These will be discussed in Section 15.4. Several such problems exist also in off-line businesses. One factor that is typical for EC is that EC is based on the concept of "pull" operations that begin with an *order*, frequently a customized one. This is in contrast with traditional retailing that begins with a production to *inventory*, which is then pushed to customers (see Figure 15-1). In the pull case it is more difficult to forecast demand due to lack of experience. Another factor is that in a B2C pull model, the goods need to be delivered to the customer's door, whereas in brick-and-mortar retailing, the customers come to stores. Before we analyze the order fulfillment problems and describe solutions, we need to introduce some basic concepts.

APPLICATION CASE 15.1

Grocery Supermarket Keeps It Fresh: Woolworths of Australia

Dealing with early movers of pure e-tailing is a major problem for established retailing. How is a well-established major supermarket to respond? With huge investments in brick-and-mortar stores, Woolworths of Australia found itself dealing with just this question. The grocery market in Australia is dominated by three major players: Coles Myers, Woolworths, and Franklins. Between them they control some 80 percent of the marketplace. Franklins, which is owned by a company in Hong Kong, takes a low-cost, minimum-service approach. The others, both Australian-based, provide a full range of products, including fresh foods and prepared meals.

Woolworths' initial approach was to set up a standard Web site offering a limited range of goods, but excluding perishable items. The delivery service was initially available only in areas near the company's major supermarkets. They felt they had to respond to the newly emerging approaches from online entrepreneurs. If those organizations were allowed to take over a sizeable segment of the market, it could be difficult to recover it.

It was not long before management realized that this was not an effective approach. Woolworths' staff had to walk the aisles, fill the baskets, pack the goods, and deliver them. For an organization that had optimized its supply chain in order to cut costs, here was a sudden explosion in costs. When gross margins are only 10 percent, and net margins around 4 percent, it is very easy to become unprofitable.

Furthermore, Woolworths has established its place in public perception as "the fresh food people," with fruits and vegetables, freshly baked breads, meats, and prepared meals being promoted heavily. If home shopping ignores these, Woolworths is avoiding its strengths.

Woolworths' Homeshop, the second generation home shopping site (*woolworths.com.au*), was designed with freshness in mind, and all the fresh foods are available for delivery. Deliveries are arranged from major regional supermarkets, rather than from every local store. There is a AU$50 minimum order, 7.5 percent surcharge for home delivery, as well as a AU$6 delivery charge. This helps in recovering the additional costs, but an average order, around AU$200, still returns little profit.

New users can register only if deliveries are possible to their postal address. On first use of the system, the customer is guided to find the products that they want with suggestions from the list of best-selling items. Alternatively, the customer can browse for items by category or search by keyword. Items are accumulated in the "shopping trolley" (cart). The first order is entered into a master list for future orders, as are subsequent orders.

When the customer has selected the required items, they select "checkout"; at that point the total value is computed and the customer confirms the shopping list. Payment is made only at time of delivery using a mobile (cellular) electronic funds transfer (EFTPOS) terminal, and either a credit card or a debit card, In this way, precise charges can be made based on weight of meat or fish, as well as allowing for out-of-stock items.

The customer has to set the delivery time and day, and will bear an additional charge if they are not at home to accept the delivery.

Additional services that are available include dietary advice, recipes, and recording of preferred food items.

Sources: Written by Professor Ernest Jordan, Macquarie Graduate School of Management, Australia, August 2000.

Figure 15-1	Push vs. Pull Supply Chains

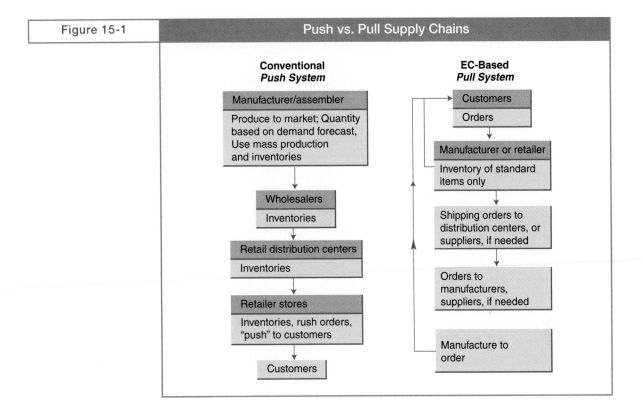

Major Concepts

ORDER FULFILLMENT

Order fulfillment refers not only to providing customers with what they ordered and doing it on time, but also to providing all related customer services. For example, the customer must receive assembly and operation instructions with a new appliance. This can be done by including a paper document with the product or by providing the instructions on the Web. (A nice example is available at *livemanuals.com*.) In addition, if the customer is not happy with a product, an exchange or return must be arranged. Thus, while order fulfillment is basically a part of the **back-office operations**, it is strongly related to the **front-office operation** as well.

LOGISTICS

There are several definitions of **logistics**. Here are some:

- The definition of logistics adopted by the Council of Logistics Management in the United States (*clm1.org*) is: "the process of planning, implementing, and controlling the efficient and effective flow and storage of goods, services, and related information from point of origin to point of consumption for the purpose of conforming to customer requirements." Note that this definition includes inbound, outbound, internal, and external movements, and return of materials and goods. It also includes *order fulfillment*. However, the distinction between logistics and order fulfillment is not always clear, and the terms are sometimes used interchangeably.

Other definitions are:

- The aspect of military science dealing with the procurement, maintenance, and transportation (of military material, facilities, and personnel).
- The management of the details of an operation.
- All activities involved in the management of product movement, that is, delivering the right product to the right place at the right time for the right price.

The Process of Order Fulfillment in EC

In order to understand why there are problems in order fulfillment, it is beneficial to first look at a typical *fulfillment process* of EC, which is shown in Figure 15-2. The process starts on the left when an order is received. Several activities take place, some of which can be done simultaneously, while others must be done in sequence. These activities include the following.

1. **Making sure the customer will pay.** Depending of the payment method and prior arrangements, an investigation must be made regarding the validity of the payment. This activity may be done by the company's finance department and/or a financial institution (i.e., bank, credit card brand such as Visa). Thus, the required payment information needs to be transferred to the checking mechanism and sometimes to an outsider. Then, a feedback to finance, accounting, and to the customer follows. The interfaces between the involved parties and the lines of communication must be both effective and efficient. Any delay may cause a shipment delay, resulting in a loss of goodwill or, more important, a customer.

2. **Checking for in-stock availability.** Regardless of whether the vendor is a manufacturer or a retailer, an inquiry needs to be made regarding stock availability. Several scenarios are possible here, involving both the material management and production departments, as well as outside suppliers. Here again, the order information needs to be connected to the information about in-stock availability. Furthermore, if an item has been promised for a delivery it should be deducted automatically from the in-stock inventory.

3. **Arranging shipments.** If the product is available, it can be shipped to the customer (otherwise go to Step #5). Products can be digital or physical. If the item is physical and it is readily available, packaging and shipment arrangements need to be made. Both the shipping (packaging) department and internal shippers or outside transporters may be involved. Digital items are usually available since their "inventory" is not depleted. However, a digital product, such as software, may be under revision, and thus unavailable for delivery at certain times. In either case, information needs to flow among several partners.

4. **Insurance.** Sometimes insurance for the shipment is needed. Both the finance department and an insurance company could be involved, and again, information needs to flow frequently not only inside the company, but also to and from the customers and insurance agents.

5. **Production.** Customized orders will always trigger a need for some manufacturing or assembly operation. Similarly, if standard items are out of stock they need to be procured. Production can be done in-house or by contractors. In-house production needs to be planned. Production planning involves people, machines, financial resources, and possibly suppliers and subcontractors. Manufacturing involves the acquisition of materials and components. The

Figure 15-2	Order Fulfillment and Logistics System

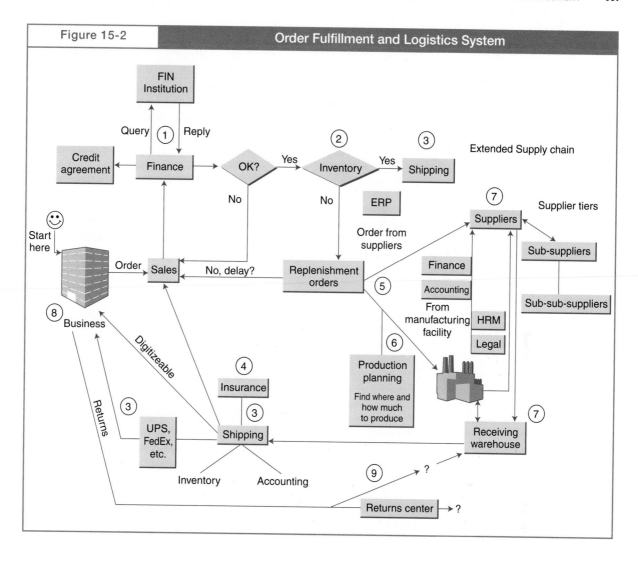

suppliers may have their own suppliers, frequently in several tiers. The actual production facilities may be in a different country from where the company's headquarters or the retailers are. This may further complicate the flow of information and communication.

6. **Plant services.** In the case of assembly and/or manufacturing, several plant services may be needed, including possible collaboration with business partners. Services may include scheduling of people and equipment, shifting other products' plans, or working with engineering on modifications.

7. **Purchasing and warehousing.** If the seller is a retailer, such as in the case of *Amazon.com* or *Walmart.com*, purchasing from manufacturers is needed. Several scenarios may exist. Purchased items can be stocked in warehouses, which is what *Amazon.com* does with its best-selling books. But *Amazon.com* does not stock books for which only a few orders are received. In such a case, special deliveries from the publishers or other sources must be made. Not only is an effective information flow needed, but also appropriate receiving and quality assurance of incoming materials and products must be done. Once purchasing and production is completed, shipments (Step #3) are arranged.

8. **Contacts with customers.** The salespeople need to keep in constant touch with customers, starting with notification of orders received and ending with notification of a shipment or changes in delivery dates. These contacts are usually done via e-mail, frequently generated automatically.

9. **Returns.** In some cases, customers want to exchange or return items. Such returns can be a major problem since up to 30 percent of all items purchased are returned to a vendor (in the United States). The movement of returns from customers to vendors is called **reverse logistics**.

Two other activities are related to the order fulfillment process:

1. Demand forecast. In the case of noncustomized items, such as toys, a demand forecast must be done in order to determine appropriate inventories at various points in the supply chain. Such a forecast is difficult in the fast growing field of EC. In the case of customized products, it is necessary to forecast the demand for the components and materials required for fulfilling customized orders. Demand forecasting must be done frequently with business partners along the supply chain, as will be discussed later on.

2. Accounting. In many cases the accounting department is involved in generating invoices and/or receipts, auditing internal transactions and inventories, monitoring payments, and updating the books. Tax and customs issues are also handled by the accounting department. Therefore, information flow and communications must be done for every transaction.

3. Reverse Logistics. The described process makes it clear that order fulfillment involves both the flow of goods (physical or digital) and a substantial flow of information among several units inside and outside the EC vendor. Therefore, the process needs to be connected not only to existing internal information systems (such as the legacy system), but also to the information systems of the suppliers, customers, and other business partners.

Order fulfillment processes may vary, depending on the product and the vendor. There are also differences between B2B and B2C activities, as well as between the delivery of goods and of services and between small-size and large-size products. Furthermore, additional steps may be required in certain circumstances such as in the case of ordering tropical fish (see Application Case 15.2), where a wholesaler is involved.

APPLICATION CASE 15.2

Can Tropical Fish Survive Online Logistics?

Petstore.com (Emeryville, California) now part of *Petsmart.com*, offers more than 1,000 types of rare tropical fish and other exotic sea life, to be ordered online and delivered to customers' doors in several countries.

Here is how the system works:

STEP 1: An order is placed on the Web from anywhere in the United States, Canada, or other countries where the company delivers. A payment by credit card is required. (Just click on the shopping cart.)

(continued)

STEP 2: Using B2C order-fulfillment software from Yantra Corp. (Acton, Massachusetts; *yantra.com*), the order is transferred to Petmart's warehouse. There, the order is checked to see if the fish is in stock in the company's high-tech, filtered ocean water aquarium. If the fish is not in stock, a special order is made electronically, using a wholesaler in Long Beach, California.

STEP 3: The wholesaler places the order electronically with a supplier on the South Pacific island of Fiji, usually with other orders.

STEP 4: The supplier finds the desired fish in Fiji, places it in a bag with filtered ocean water mixed with oxygen that protects the fish from temperature changes, and sends it on the next commercial airplane to the wholesaler.

STEP 5: The wholesaler sends the fish to Petmart's warehouse, where the fish is carefully repacked.

STEP 6: FedEx overnights the fish to the customer. The customer receives a confirmation of the shipment and a copy of the credit card payment transaction.

STEP 7: The customer receives the order with a guarantee of free replacement if the fish dies within 5 days of arrival.

There are some additional notes of interest:

- Fish cannot survive more than 48 hours in transit. If they die, it is *Pets.com*'s loss.
- The average fish costs $20 to $25 (some cost $1,500), plus there is a $25 to $30 delivery charge per order.
- As a comparison, orders placed with your neighborhood pet store will take 5 to 15 days to fill, will cost you more, and may even be refused.
- Customers usually order several fish to save on delivery charges.

Source: Compiled from *pets.com* and from *petstore.com* before they were closed.

15.3   THE SUPPLY CHAIN AND ITS MANAGEMENT

The basics of supply chains were presented in the appendix to Chapter 1. Our attention here is given to supply chain management (SCM).

Definitions

According to the SCM Forum at The Ohio State University, **supply chain management (SCM)** is the "integration of business processes from the end user through original suppliers, that provide products, services, and information that add values for customers." It includes many activities, such as purchasing, materials handling, production planning and control, logistics and warehousing, inventory control, and distribution and delivery.

The function of SCM is to plan, organize, and coordinate all the supply chain's activities. Today the concept of SCM indicates a holistic approach to managing the entire supply chain. For an overview of SCM see Handfield and Nichols Jr. (1999) and Poirier (2001).

The efficiency and effectiveness of supply chains in most organizations are critical for the success of EC and are greatly dependent upon the supporting information systems, as will be described soon.

In the appendix to Chapter 1 we showed a simple linear supply chain. However, supply chains come in all shapes and sizes and may be fairly complex as shown in Figure 15-3. As can be seen in Figure 15-3, the supply chain for a car manufacturer includes hundreds of suppliers, dozens of manufacturing plants (parts) and assembly plants (cars), dealers, direct business customers (fleets), wholesalers (some of which are virtual), customers, and support functions such as product engineering and purchasing.

Notice that in this case, the chain is not strictly linear. Here, we see some loops in the process. Sometimes the flow of information and even goods can be bidirectional. For example, not shown in this figure is the *return* of cars to the dealers, in cases of defects or recalls by the manufacturer.

Benefits of SCM

The goals of modern SCM are to reduce uncertainty and risks along the supply chain, thereby positively affecting inventory levels, cycle time, processes, and customer service. All of these contribute to increased profitability and competitiveness.

The benefits of SCM were long recognized not only in business, but also in the military. Clerchus of Sparta said, as early as 401 B.C., that the survival of the Greek army depended not only on its discipline, training, and morale, but also on its supply chain. The same idea was echoed later by famous generals such as Napoleon and Eisenhower, and by entrepreneurs such as Henry Ford, who purchased rubber plantations to ensure a supply of tires for the cars he manufactured (a vertical integration strategy).

The flow of goods, services, information, and other such products is usually designed not only to effectively transform raw items to finished products and services, but also to do it in an efficient manner. Specifically, the flow must be followed by an *increase in value*. One of the major goals of SCM is to maximize this value, and this is where information technology enters the picture as will be shown later in Sections 15.6, 15.11, and 15.12. Let us now pay attention to a special supply chain, where two or more countries are involved in the order fulfillment process.

Global Supply Chains

Supply chains that involve suppliers and/or customers in other countries are referred to as global supply chains. The introduction of EC made it much easier to find suppliers in other countries (e.g., by using electronic bidding for RFQs, see Chapter 6). Plus, it is much easier and cheaper to find customers in other countries.

Global supply chains are longer and may be very complex. Therefore, information needs to flow, sometimes in different languages and subject to different regulations. Information technologies are found to be extremely useful in supporting global supply chains. For example, TradeNet in Singapore connects exporters, importers, shippers, ships, and government agencies via EDI. A similar network called TradeLink operates in Hong Kong, using both EDI and EDI/Internet to connect about 70,000 trading partners. Some of the issues that may create delays

Figure 15-3	An Automotive Supply Chain

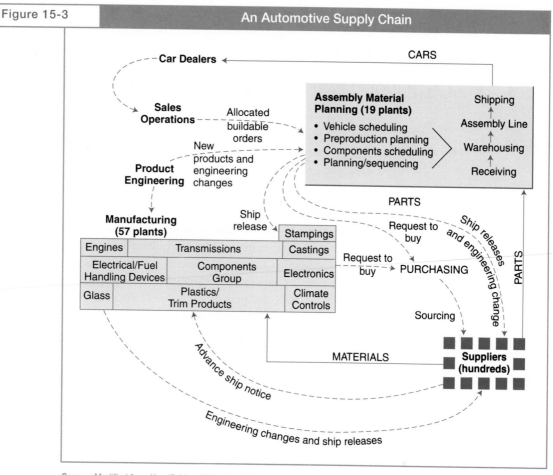

Source: Modified from Handfield and Nichols (1999), p. 3.

in global order fulfillment are legal issues, tariffs, customs fees and other taxes, language and cultural differences, fast changes in currencies' exchange rates, and political instabilities. (See Chapter 18 for a discussion.)

IT facilitates global SCM not only by providing EDI and other communication options, but also by providing expertise online in sometimes difficult and quickly changing regulations. IT also can be instrumental in helping to find trade partners (via electronic directories and search engines, e.g., see *alibaba.com*). Finally, IT facilitates outsourcing of products and services to countries with a plentiful and less expensive labor supply.

Companies are going global not only to find buyers or suppliers, but also to establish their manufacturing plants. The major reasons why companies are going global are: lower prices of material, products, and labor; availability of products that are unavailable domestically; firms' global operations and attitudes; advanced technology available in other countries; high-quality products available; intensification of global competition, which drives companies to cut costs; the need to develop a foreign presence; and fulfillment of countertrade. For these cases, collaborative commerce can be very helpful. For further discussion and details see Chase et al. (1998).

Now that you are familiar with the concepts of supply chain and order fulfillment, we can return to analyze the Y2K e-toys problem and other EC order fulfillment problems.

15.4 TYPICAL PROBLEMS ALONG THE SUPPLY CHAIN

As shown earlier, supply chains can be very long, involving many internal and external partners located in different places. Both materials and information flow among several entities, and this transfer, especially when manually handled, can be slow and error prone.

Overview

Supply chain problems have been recognized both in the military and in business operations for generations. These problems have caused some armies to lose wars and companies to go out of business. The problems are most apparent in complex or long supply chains and in cases where many business partners are involved.

The Y2K toys problem is not an isolated case. In the off-line world there are many examples of companies that were unable to meet demands for certain products while having too large and expensive inventories of other products. Several other corporate problems are related to deficiencies in the supply chain (e.g., see Chase et al., 1998 and Handfield and Nichols 1999). Some companies grapple with high inventory costs, quality problems due to misunderstandings, shipments of wrong materials and parts, and the high cost of expediting operations or shipments. On the other hand, some of the world-class companies such as Wal-Mart, FedEx, and Dell Computers have superb supply chains with innovative applications, some of which will be described later.

In EC there is a larger chance that supply chain problems will occur due to the lack of appropriate infrastructure and experience, as in the Y2K toys case, as well as due to the special characteristics of EC. For example, warehouses of conventional retailers are designed to ship large quantities to stores; they cannot optimally pack and ship many small packages to customers' doors.

Typical Problems

The problems along the EC supply chain of toy retailers and other companies stem mainly from *uncertainties,* and from the need to coordinate several activities and/or internal units and business partners.

The major source of the uncertainties in EC is the demand forecast, which may be influenced by several factors such as consumer behavior, economic conditions, competition, prices, weather conditions, technological developments, customers' confidence, and more. As we will show soon, companies attempt to achieve accurate demand by using methods such as IT-supported forecasts, which are done in collaboration with business partners. Other uncertainties exist in *delivery times,* which depend on many factors ranging from machine failures to road conditions. Quality problems of materials and parts may also create production time delays, and a labor strike may interfere with shipments.

Several other possible factors may create supply chain problems (see Ayers, 2000 for details). A major symptom of poor SCM is poor customer service—people do not get the product or service when and where needed, or they get it in poor quality. Other symptoms are high inventory costs, interferences with production or operation, loss of revenues, and extra costs for special and expedited shipments.

Pure EC companies are likely to have more problems because they do not have a logistics infrastructure and are forced to use external logistics services. This can be expensive, plus it requires more coordination and dependence on outsiders who may not be reliable. For this reason, large virtual retailers such as *Amazon.com* are developing physical warehouses and logistics systems. Other virtual retailers are creating strategic alliances with logistics companies or with brick-and-mortar companies that have their own logistics systems.

15.5   THE BULLWHIP EFFECT AND INFORMATION SHARING

By definition, a supply chain includes the flow of information to and from all participating entities. The information can be supportive of physical shipments or the shipment of digitized products (services). Many, if not most, of the supply chain problems are the result of poor flow of information, inaccurate information, untimely information, etc. Information must be managed properly in each supply chain segment.

Information systems are the *links* that enable communication and collaboration along the supply chain. They represent "one of the fundamental elements that link the organizations of the supply chain into a unified and coordinated system. In the current competitive climate, little doubt remains about the importance of information and information technology to the ultimate success, and perhaps even the survival, of any SCM initiative" (Handfield and Nichols 1999).

Case studies of some world-class companies such as Wal-Mart, Dell Computers, and FedEx, indicate that these companies created very sophisticated information systems, exploiting the latest technological developments and creating innovative solutions. Representative IT solutions are shown, together with the problems they solve, in Table 15-1.

One of the most important topics related to IT and SCM is information sharing along the supply chain.

Information Sharing Between Retailers and Their Suppliers

Information sharing among business partners, as well as among the various units inside each organization, is necessary for the success of SCM. Information systems must be designed so that sharing becomes easy. One of the most notable examples of information sharing is between Procter & Gamble (P&G) and Wal-Mart. Wal-Mart provides P&G access to sale information on every item P&G makes for Wal-Mart. The information is collected by P&G on a daily basis from every Wal-Mart store. Then, P&G is able to manage the inventory replenishment for Wal-Mart. By monitoring the inventory level of each P&G item in every store, P&G knows when the inventories fall below the threshold that triggers a shipment. All this is done automatically. The benefit for P&G is accurate demand information. P&G has similar agreements with other major retailers. Thus, P&G can plan production more accurately, avoiding the "bullwhip effect."

The **bullwhip effect** refers to erratic shifts in orders up and down the supply chain (See Lee et al., 1997). This effect was initially observed by P&G with their

IT Solutions to Supply Chain Problems

TABLE 15-1

Supply Chain Problem	IT Solution
Linear sequence of processing is too slow.	Parallel processing, using workflow software.
Waiting times between chain segments are excessive.	Identify reason (DSS software) and expedite communication and collaboration (Intranets, groupware).
Existence of non-value-added activities.	Value analysis (SCM software), simulation software.
Slow delivery of paper documents.	Electronic documents and communication system (e.g., EDI, e-mail).
Repeat process activities due to wrong shipments, poor quality, etc.	Electronic verifications (software agents), automation; eliminating human errors, electronic control systems.
Batching; accumulate work orders between supply chain processes to get economies of scale (e.g., save on delivery).	SCM software analysis, digitize documents for online delivery.
Learn about delays after they occur, or learn too late.	Tracking systems, anticipate delays, trend analysis, early detection (intelligent systems).
Excessive administrative controls such as approvals (signatures). Approvers are in different locations.	Parallel approvals (workflow), electronic approval system. Analysis of need.
Lack of information or too slow a flow of information.	Internet/intranet, software agents for monitoring and alerts. Bar codes, direct flow from POS terminals.
Lack of synchronization of moving materials.	Workflow and tracking systems. Synchronization by software agents.
Poor coordination, cooperation, and communication.	Groupware products, constant monitoring, alerts, collaboration tools.
Delays in shipments from warehouses.	Use robots in warehouses, use warehouse management software.
Redundancies in the supply chain: too many purchase orders, too much handling and packaging.	Information sharing via the Web creating teams of collaborative partners supported by IT (see Epner 1999).
Obsolescence of parts and components that stay too long in storage.	Reducing inventory levels by information sharing internally and externally, using intranets and groupware.

disposable diapers product (Pampers). While actual sales in stores were fairly stable and predictable, orders from distributors had wild swings, creating production and inventory problems for P&G. An investigation revealed that distributors' orders were fluctuating because of poor demand forecasts, price fluctuations, order batching, and rationing within the supply chain. All this resulted in unnecessary inventories in various areas along the supply chain, fluctuations of P&G orders to their suppliers, and the flow of inaccurate information. Distorted information can lead to tremendous inefficiencies, excessive inventories, poor customer service, lost revenues, ineffective shipments, and missed production schedules (Lee et al. 1997).

According to Handfield and Nichols (1999), the bullwhip effect is not unique to P&G. Firms from Hewlett-Packard in the computer industry to Bristol-Myers Squibb in the pharmaceutical field have experienced a similar phenomenon. Basically, even slight demand uncertainties and variabilities become magnified when viewed through the eyes of managers at each link in the supply chain. If each distinct entity makes ordering and inventory decisions with an eye to its own interest above those of the chain, stockpiling may be simultaneously occurring at as many as seven or eight places across the supply chain, leading in some cases to as many as 100 days of inventory—waiting "just in case." A 1998 industry study by the American Agricultural Economic Association (*aaea.org*) projected that $30 billion in savings could materialize, in the grocery industry supply chains alone, by sharing information. Thus, companies may avoid the "sting of the bullwhip." Such sharing is facilitated by EDI, extranets, and groupware technologies and is part of interorganizational EC and collaborative commerce.

15.6   SOLUTIONS TO SUPPLY CHAIN PROBLEMS

Supply chain problems have existed in military organizations for thousands of years and in industrial organizations since the beginning of the industrial revolution. Solutions to these problems have existed for generations. However, with the arrival of the information and Internet revolutions, new and very effective solutions had to be developed.

Preliminaries

The solutions to supply chain problems, regardless of whether they are online or off-line, involve a combination of tools and techniques, some of which are manual whereas others are IT supported.

The theory and practice of supply chain problem resolution is beyond the scope of this book. The interested reader should refer to Handfield and Nichols (1999), Ross (1998), Chase et al. (1998), and Gattorma (1998). In this chapter we will present only a few interesting EC-related solutions.

However, before we present these solutions, it is worthwhile to list some generic activities that must precede IT or EC solutions, or must be done concurrently with them.

- Most organizations are simultaneously members of multiple supply chains. Changes made in any chain may impact others. So it is necessary to look at all the major chains simultaneously.
- Understanding of each major chain is a must. Using flow charts and process maps (software is available) is recommended.
- Both internal and external portions of the chains must be studied.
- The performance of existing supply chains needs to be measured and compared in order to identify problems (opportunities). Benchmarking is recommended.
- Supply chain performance is measured in several areas including: customer service and satisfaction, cycle times, delivery, responsiveness, costs, quality, products (services) offered, and asset utilization.
- The supply chain may require business process reengineering (BPR) before a software solution is attempted. (See Chapter 3 in Handfield and Nichols 1999.)
- It is essential to develop and maintain relationships with business partners and with key employees in these organizations (See Chapter 4 in Handfield and Nichols 1999.)

Opportunities for SCM improvements exist in several places along the supply chain. Potential candidates include: manufacturing processes, warehousing operations, packaging and delivery, material inspection/receiving, inbound and outbound transportation, reverse logistics (returns), in-plant material handling, vendor management programs, customer order processing, invoicing, auditing and other accounting activities, collaboration procedures with partners, employee training and deployment, labor scheduling, use of teams and empowerment of employees, automation of processes, use of software for facilitating all of these, and inventory management and control.

Let's examine inventory management in more detail.

Using Inventories to Solve Supply Chain Shortages

A most common solution in the off-line world is *building inventories* as an "insurance" against uncertainties. This way products and parts flow smoothly. The main problem with this approach is that it is very difficult to correctly determine inventory levels, which must be done for each product and part. Furthermore, if the finished products are *customized,* as in some EC situations (e.g., Dell computers), one cannot have an inventory of finished goods; only components can be stocked. In general, if inventory levels are set too high, the cost of keeping the inventory will be very large. If the inventory is too low, there is no sufficient protection against high demand or slow delivery times, and consequently revenues (and customers) may be lost. In either event, the total cost, including opportunities and reputation lost, can be very high. Thus, major attempts are made to properly control inventories using information technologies, as shown in Application Case 15.3.

Proper SCM and inventory management requires coordination of all different activities and "links" of the supply chain so that goods can move smoothly and on time from suppliers to customers. This keeps inventories low and cost down. The

APPLICATION CASE 15.3

How Littlewoods Stores Improved Its SCM

Littlewoods Stores is one of Britain's largest retailers of high-quality clothing, with 136 stores around the United Kingdom and Northern Ireland. The retail clothing business is very competitive, so the company embarked, in the late 1990s, on an IT-supported initiative to improve its supply chain efficiency. A serious SCM problem was overstocking.

In order to get a better SCM, the company introduced a Web-based performance reporting system. The system analyzes, on a daily basis, marketing and financial data, space planning, merchandizing, and purchasing data. For example, the marketing department can now perform sophisticated sales, stock, and supplier analyses to make key operational decisions on pricing and inventory.

Using the Web, analysts can view sales and stock data in any grouping of levels and categories, even at stock keeping unit (SKU) and daily levels. Furthermore, users can easily drill down to detailed sales and other data.

The system uses a data warehouse, DSS, and other end-user-oriented software to make better decisions. Here are some of the results:

- Reduced back-up inventory expenses by about $4 million a year. For example, due to quick replenishment, stock went down by 80 percent.
- The ability to strategically price merchandise differently in different stores saved $1.2 million in 1997 alone.
- Reducing the need for stock liquidations saved $1.4 million a year.
- Marketing distribution expenses were cut by $7 million a year.
- Reduction of the logistics staff from 84 to 49 people resulted in a savings of about $1 million annually.
- Within a year, the number of Web-based users grew to 600.

In early 2000, the company integrated its internal supply chain with its online selling efforts (Home Shopping Channel).

Sources: Condensed from *microstrategy.com* (January 2000, Customers Success Stories) and from *littlewoods.co.uk* (November 2000)

coordination is needed because supply chain partners depend on each other but don't always work together toward the same goal.

To properly control the uncertainties mentioned earlier, it is necessary to identify and understand the causes of the uncertainties, determining how uncertainties will affect other activities up and down the supply chain, and then to formulate ways to reduce or eliminate the uncertainties. Combined with this is the need for effective and efficient communication among all business partners. To do the above effectively and efficiently, we can use information technologies in general and EC in particular as the major enabler. Let's see how it is done.

15.7   EC SOLUTIONS ALONG THE SUPPLY CHAIN

EC as a technology provides solutions along the supply chain as has been shown throughout this book. Such solutions are beneficial both to brick-and-mortar operations, as well as to online companies. Here is a summary of the major solutions provided by the EC approach and technologies:

- Order taking can be done on EDI, EDI/Internet, or an extranet and it may be fully automated. For example, in B2B, orders are generated and transmitted automatically to suppliers when inventory levels fall below certain levels. The result is a fast, inexpensive, and more accurate (no need to rekey data) order-taking process. In B2C, Web-based ordering using electronic forms expedites the processes, makes it more accurate (intelligent agents can check the input data and provide instant feedback), and reduces the processing cost of sellers.
- Electronic payments can expedite both the order fulfillment cycle, as well as the payment delivery period. Payment processing can be significantly less expensive and fraud can be better controlled.
- Inventories can be minimized both by introducing a make-to-order (pull) production process, as well as by providing fast and accurate information to suppliers. By allowing business partners to electronically track and monitor orders and production activities, inventory management can be improved and inventory levels, as well as administrative expenses of inventory management, can be minimized.
- Order fulfillment can become instant if the products can be digitized (e.g., software). In other cases, EC order taking interfaces with the company's back-office system (see Section 15.12). Such an interface, or even integration, shortens cycle time and eliminates errors.
- Collaborative commerce among members of the supply chain can be done in many areas ranging from product design to demand forecasting. The results are shorter cycle times, minimal delays and work interruptions, lower inventories, and less administrative cost.

15.8   INNOVATIVE SOLUTIONS TO THE ORDER FULFILLMENT PROBLEM

During the last few years, companies have developed interesting solutions to B2C and B2B order fulfillment issues. Here are some examples:

- Many companies allow customers to view goods in real-time. Live video is designed to allow traditional brick-and-mortar retailers to enhance online shopping. For example, *galleryfurniture.com* used 48 cameras, called **Webcam,** to demonstrate its stock on the Web. The innovation allowed the company to move inventory 70 times a year on the average, instead of five times a year in conventional stores, resulting in a huge inventory reduction (the company folded due to a shortage of funds in 2001). FAO Schwartz, the large toy store, uses cameras to demonstrate their world famous Manhattan store in New York.

- A joint venture of MailBoxes Etc., with a fulfillment services company, Innotrac Corp., and with a logistics firm, *Return.com*, developed a comprehensive logistics system that includes software that connects e-tailers and order management systems to *Return.com*'s intelligent system. The system determines whether a customer is entitled to a return and refund. Customers have the option of making returns at kiosks in MailBoxes Etc.'s physical franchises.

- 7-Eleven and other retailers, who have stores in many locations, can become distribution centers for the pick up of delivered goods and a drop-off center for returned goods. For example, any of the 8,000 7-Eleven stores in Japan is an order-placing station. Customers there use the stores' special multimedia computers (kiosks) to order products that can later be delivered to any 7-Eleven store or to the buyer's residence at an extra charge. This solves the problem of not finding customers at home and it reduces delivery costs, especially if several orders can be combined and directed to one store at a time. Furthermore, 7-Eleven of Japan collects cash or credit card payments for goods ordered from its kiosks, solving the problem of payment for those customers who do not have a credit card or do not want to give a credit card number over the Internet.

- A marketplace that helps companies with goods to find "forwarders"—the intermediary that prepares goods for shipping—is managed by *Relysoftware.com*. The company also helps forwarders find the best prices on air carriers and helps the carriers fill up empty cargo space by bidding it up.

Same Day, Even Same Hour Delivery

In 1973, a tiny company initiated the concept of "next day delivery." It was a revolution in door-to-door logistics. Today, this company, FedEx, is moving over 3 million packages a day, using several hundred airplanes and several thousand vans, all over the globe. Incidentally, according to *Business 2.0* (January 2000), 70 percent of these packages are the result of EC. FedEx introduced the "next morning delivery" service a few years later.

In the digital age, next morning is not fast enough. Today we talk about *same day delivery,* and even delivery within an hour. Deliveries of urgent material to and from hospitals is an example of such a service. One of the newcomers to this area is *sameday.com*, which created a network for rapid distribution of products, mostly EC related. A U.S. national distribution system is done in collaboration with FedEx and UPS. The company provides other logistics services. Delivering groceries is another area where speed is important, as discussed in Chapter 3 and in this section. Quick pizza deliveries have been available for a long time (e.g.,

Domino's Pizza). Pizza orders in many places are accepted today online. Many restaurants deliver food to online customers, which is a service called "dine online." Examples are *food.com*, *gourmetdinnerservice.com.au*, and *anniesdinners.com*. Some companies even offer aggregating services, processing orders for several restaurants (e.g., *dialadinner.com.hk* in Hong Kong) and making deliveries. Here is how it works:

STEP 1: Customers click on the dishes they want, then submit their request by e-mail.

STEP 2: The order is received by order processors at computer terminals.

STEP 3: For first-time customers, staff members phone to check delivery details and to make sure that the order is genuine.

STEP 4: The orders are forwarded electronically to the participating restaurants.

STEP 5: Delivery staff receive an e-mail on their mobile phones telling them which restaurant to go to. There they are handed the food and delivery details.

STEP 6: Customers receive their meal.

SUPERMARKET DELIVERIES

Supermarket deliveries are difficult, especially when fresh food is to be transported as discussed in Chapter 3. Buyers need to be home at certain times. Therefore, the distribution systems are critical. A delivery design of one is shown in Figure 15-4.

Order Fulfillment in B2B

Order fulfillment in B2B is different from that of B2C, due to the larger quantities delivered to businesses. Some representative B2B fulfillment players and challenges are listed in Table 15-2.

For more discussion on how fulfillment is done in B2B see Chapter 8, *fedex.com*, and *ups.com*.

E-Marketplaces and Exchanges

In Chapter 7 we introduced a variety of e-marketplaces and exchanges. One of the major objectives of these is to improve the operation of the supply chain. Let's see how this works with different business models.

- One business model is that of a procurement system controlled by one major corporation, as described in Application Case 15.4. In this case, the entire system is controlled by one buyer and the suppliers adjust their activities and information systems to fit the information system of the buyer. Such a system is especially suitable for a multinational corporation or a government that deals with many suppliers.
- A company-centric marketplace can solve several SCM problems. For example, CSX Technology developed an extranet for tracking cross-country train shipments as part of their SCM initiative, and was able to effectively identify bottlenecks and forecast demand.
- Citus Belgium (*citus.be*) (now an EDS company), a large wholesaler, facilitates the trade of MROs and other nonproductive materials. Citus hosts the

Figure 15-4	The Proposed Order Fulfillment for Groceryworks

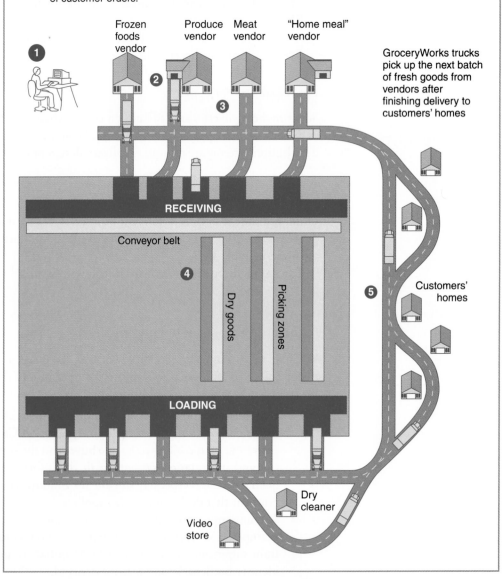

1. Each customer order is placed 6.5 to 9 hours ahead of delivery time.

2. Suppliers pick goods off their own shelves and package them for pickup, with orders sorted by customer and placed in coded bags.

3. GroceryWorks vans pick up the goods from suppliers.

4. Fresh goods from suppliers are sent along a conveyor belt; dry goods are picked from GroceryWorks warehouse shelves.

5. GroceryWorks vans head to customers' homes, stopping by suppliers on their return trip to the local warehouse to pick up the next round of customer orders.

Frozen foods vendor

Produce vendor

Meat vendor

"Home meal" vendor

GroceryWorks trucks pick up the next batch of fresh goods from vendors after finishing delivery to customers' homes

RECEIVING

Conveyor belt

Dry goods

Picking zones

Customers' homes

LOADING

Dry cleaner

Video store

Source: Steinert-Threlkeld (January 31, 2000). Originally published in *Interactive Week, www.xplane.com*

TABLE 15-2   B2B Fulfillment Players and Challenges

Players	Challenges
Shippers (sellers)	Mix of channels, choice of logistics partners, solo or go with aggregation, what to outsource, integration of strategic/tactical/operational decisions
Receivers (buyers)	Solo and/or consortia buy sites, supply chain collaboration, total delivered costs, when to buy
Carriers	Self-service Web sites, links to verticals and transportation marketplaces, institutional drag
Third-Party Logistics Providers	Cooperation from carriers, breadth of modes/services, IT resources, customer acquisition
Warehouse Companies	Location, operational intensity, capital investment, mode of automation, choice of builders
Vertical E-Marketplaces	Where's the "ship-it" button? Who's behind it? What services are offered?
Transportation E-Marketplaces	Moving beyond spot transactions to ASPs and value-added services, neutrality versus alignment, market mechanisms (e.g., bidding)
Logistics Software Application Vendors	Comprehensive solutions, e-marketplace involvement, strategic partnerships, integration with existing software.

APPLICATION CASE 15.4

Getting Your Suppliers Online: The Case of Caltex Corp.

As of spring 2000, companies that want to supply Caltex Corp., a multinational seller of gasoline and other oil products, must go online on one of the most advanced SCMs in the world.

Developed by Ariba (*ariba.com*), this electronic procurement, payment, and logistics system, initially introduced in the United States, is now deployed worldwide (see *caltex.com*). The online system requires suppliers to build electronic catalogs with Ariba's software. These catalogs are aggregated on Caltex's server so they can be used by any Caltex purchasing agent. Here are some of the system's benefits:

- Reduction in the number of suppliers from 7,000 to 800 due to the ability to interact easily with remote suppliers.
- Control over all content of all catalogs.
- Presentation of the negotiated prices to all Caltex buyers in comparison tables.
- Reduction of emergency, unplanned, expensive buying at local offices.
- Ability to automatically handle international trade issues: customs documentation, duties, language translation, and currencies conversion.
- Overcoming the lack of transparency in the supplier selection process.
- Overcoming the lack of coordination in spending across Caltex's geographical boundaries.
- Smooth integration with back office transactions, by tying the system with both the ERP and the EDI.
- Ability to drive down costs via bidding and RFQs.
- Reducing the need for third-party intermediaries for sourcing.

The system is especially useful in Asia, Africa, and the Middle East. It enables Caltex to more effectively handle complex business environments, such as multiple currencies, multiple tax regimes, the movement of goods across borders, dealing with poor electronic infrastructure, and unavailability of door-to-door delivery systems in some countries.

catalogs of all participating sellers and provides infrastructure for order entry and processing, as well as payments. For a complete story see Timmers (1999).

- Using an extranet, Toshiba America connects electronically with its dealers, who buy replacement parts for Toshiba's products, to smooth the supply chain and deliver superb customer service.
- Another model is a vertical exchange, such as that of *Covisint.com* in the automotive industry, which has thousands of suppliers. Hundreds of vertical exchanges exist all over the world; many of them deal with both buying and selling. The direct contact between buyers and sellers in e-marketplaces reduces communication and search problems in the supply chain.
- General Motors created a large marketplace called TradeXchange (now integrated with Covisint). Preliminary results indicate that the marketplace drives the supply chain to harmonization, shortens the customer order-to-delivery time, and reduces the combined administrative cost per order of GM and its suppliers by 90 percent (see Chapter 6 opening case for details).

Automated Warehouses

EC fulfillment of large volume requires automated warehouses. Regular warehouses are built to deliver large quantities to a small number of stores and plants. In B2C EC, you need to send small quantities to large numbers of individuals. Automated warehouses may include robots and other devices that expedite the pick up of products. An example of a company that built such a warehouse is *Amazon.com* (see Cone 1999). One of the largest warehouses in the United States is operated by a mail-order company, Fingerhut (*fingerhut.com*). This company handles the logistics of mail orders (including online orders) for Wal-Mart, Macy's, KbKids, and many others. The process used at the warehouse involves eight steps:

STEP 1: Retailers contract Fingerhut to stock products and deliver orders received on the Web.

STEP 2: Retailers' merchandise is stored by SKU at the warehouse.

STEP 3: Orders that arrive by e-mail, fax, phone, etc. are transferred to Fingerhut's mainframe computer.

STEP 4: To optimize the work of pickers, a special computer program consolidates the orders from all vendors (including Fingerhut itself) and organizes them into "picking waves." This way pickers aren't running from one end of the warehouse to another.

STEP 5: The picked items are moved by conveyors to the packing area. The computer configures the size and type of box (envelope) needed for packaging, and types special packaging and delivery instructions.

STEP 6: Packages pass on a conveyor belt through a scanning station where they are weighted (actual weight must match the SKU projected weight).

STEP 7: From the bar code scanner a destination is identified, and at an appropriate time each package is pushed onto one of 26 destination conveyer belts that brings the package directly to a waiting truck.

STEP 8: Once trucks are full they depart for local postal offices in 26 major cities, dramatically cutting shipping costs.

For details see Duvall 1999 and *Internet Week*, June 28, 1998.

Other companies provide similar services (e.g., *submitorder.com*). The key is *speed* and *efficiency*.

Dealing with Returns

Returning unwanted merchandise and exchanges of merchandise are necessary for maintaining customers' trust and loyalty. The Boston Consulting Group found that the "absence of a good return mechanism" was the second biggest reason shoppers cited for refusing to buy on the Web frequently. A major problem merchants face is how to deal with returns. Several options exist (e.g., see Trager 2000).

- Return an item to the place where it was purchased. This is easy to do in a brick-and-mortar store, but not in a virtual one. To do it in a virtual store you need to get authorization, then pack everything up, pay to ship it back, insure it, and wait up to two billing cycles for a credit to show up on your statement. The buyer is not happy, nor is the seller, who must unpack, check the paperwork, and resell the item, usually at a loss. This solution is good if the number of returns is small.
- Separate the logistics of returns from the logistics of delivery. Returns are shipped to an independent unit and handled separately inside the company. This solution may be more efficient from the seller's point of view, but the buyer is still unhappy.
- Allow the customer to physically drop the returned items at collection stations (such as at convenience stores or at MailBoxes Etc.). The same place that is used for returns can be used for collection as well. In Asia and Australia, returns are accepted in many 7-Eleven stores, and at gas stations. For example, BP Australia Ltd. teamed up with *wishlist.com.au*, and Caltex Australia is using its convenience stores. The accepting stores may offer in-store computers for ordering and payment options as is done in 7-Eleven of Japan stores.
- Completely outsource returns; several outsourcers provide such services, including UPS. The services deal not only with shipments, but with the entire logistics process.

15.9   OUTSOURCING LOGISTICS: THE UPS STRATEGY

The problem of returns, which reaches 30 percent of all deliveries in some cases, can be eased if customers can find a real person in a physical store to whom items can be handed. Research indicates that such an arrangement may increase customer trust in e-tailing because customers feel that there is less risk if they can have a place they can go to if something goes wrong. As a matter of fact, pure e-tailers, such as *Egghead.com*, plan warehouses and physical collection points for returns as their customer base increases, because renting warehouses operated by UPS, FedEx, and the U.S. Post Office may be too expensive. Let's examine how such delivery companies operate.

Many companies use the delivery services of FedEx, DHL, UPS, the U.S. Post Office, and others. However, some Internet companies, as well as some brick-and-mortar companies, are willing to outsource not only the shipment function, but the entire logistics, outsourcing order taking, warehousing, and packaging.

FedEx not only operates regular warehouses, but also assembles and tests products and makes arrangements for international deliveries. Through a process of strategic acquisition (e.g., RPS, a carrier of small packages, Caliber Systems Inc., a provider of just-in-time delivery and transportation management solutions), other companies are competing with FedEx in logistics services. Major efforts are being made by UPS (Application Case 15.5).

Now that you are familiar with order fulfillment and supply chain operations, as well as with problems and their resolution, we can examine the use of software support in solving supply chain problems.

APPLICATION CASE 15.5

UPS Provides Broad EC Services

UPS is not only the leading transporter of goods sold on the Internet, but is also a provider of several other EC-support services, ranging from SCM activities (inventory management) to electronic bill payment. UPS has, or is building, a massive infrastructure to support these efforts. For example, it has an over 120 terabyte (10^{12} byte) database containing customer information and shipping records.

Here are some of its EC initiatives:

- Electronic tracking of packages.
- Electronic supply chain services for corporate customers by industry. This includes a portal page with industry-related information and statistics.
- Calculators for computing shipping fees.
- Help speeding the supply chain by helping customers manage their electronic supply chains (e.g., expediting billing and speeding up accounts receivable).
- Improved inventory management, warehousing, and delivery. The first major corporate client was Ford Motor Co.
- A shipping management system that integrates tracking systems, address validation, service selection, and time-in transit tools with Oracle's ERP application suite (similar integration with SAP and PeopleSoft exists).
- Notification of customers by e-mail about the status and expected arrival time of incoming packages.

Representative Tools

UPS's line of online tools—a set of seven transportation and logistics applications—lets customers do everything from tracking packages to analyzing shipping history using customized criteria to calculate exact time-in-transit for shipments between any two postal codes in the continental United States.

The tools, which customers can download to their Web sites, let customers query UPS systems to get proof that specific packages were delivered on schedule. For example, if a company is buying supplies online and wants them delivered on a certain day, a UPS customer can use an optimal-routing feature to ensure delivery on that day, as well as to automatically record proof of the delivery into its accounting system.

APPLICATION CASE   15.5

(continued)

UPS is offering logistics services tailored for certain industries. For example, UPS Logistics Group provides supply-chain reengineering, transportation network management, and service parts logistics to vehicle manufacturers, suppliers, and parts distributors in the auto industry worldwide.

UPS Autogistics improves automakers' vehicle delivery networks. It improves the delivery network for Ford, Lincoln, and Mercury vehicles. Ford reduced the time to deliver vehicles from plants to dealers in North America from an average of 14 days to about 6. UPS Logistics Group plans on offering similar supply chain and delivery tracking services to other kinds of manufacturers.

UPS is also expanding into another area important to e-business—delivery of digital documents. The company was the first conventional package shipper to enter this market in 1998 when it launched UPS Document Exchange, which provides companies with total control over digitally delivered documents. The program monitors delivery and provides instant receipt notification, encryption, and password-only access. Finally documents can be resent or printed quickly.

Many other services exist. These include the ability to enter the UPS system from wireless devices, helping customers configure and customize services, and providing for electronic bill presentation and payment (for B2B), electronic funds transfer, and processing of COD payments.

Sources: Compiled from Violino (2000) and from *ups.com* (press releases 2000, 2001).

15.10   SOFTWARE SUPPORT AND INTEGRATION ALONG THE SUPPLY CHAIN

Implementing EC solutions to solve supply chain problems frequently requires interfaces with so-called back-end systems (such as inventory, billing). To do this properly it is necessary to integrate applications, databases etc., across the enterprise and with business partners. Let's see how this is done.

Software Support

Software support for the various activities along the supply chain has been provided for several decades. Software packages were initially designed to support individual *segments* of the supply chain. There are software applications for upstream supply chain operations, such as placing an order with suppliers. Many applications deal with activities of the internal supply chain, such as production scheduling, inventory control, and costing. Finally, software exists to support downstream activities, such as sales, delivery scheduling, and customers' billing (For details see Turban et al. 2002 and Chapter 7). Examples of such software are provided in Table 15-3.

A large number of vendors and products is available in each category. For example, Siebel is a leading CRM software provider, Manugistics, HP, and i2 provide software for production management, Oracle provides customer database management systems and many SCM applications, and Computer Associates provides dozens of packages to several of the supply chain segments.

Such software automates the work of a single person, a team, a single activity, or a business process. Some activities are fully automated, such as order issuing when

TABLE 15-3	Software Products for Supply Chain Segments	
	SCM Activities	**Type of Software**
	Upstream Activities	Suppliers' management, ordering systems, order tracking systems
	Internal Supply Chain Activities	• Inventory management, production planning and scheduling, engineering and product configuration, cost management, quality control
		• Purchasing and order management, distribution, warehousing, shipping, tracking
		• Budgeting, cost control, billing, asset management, general ledger, payable and receivable
		• Human resources information systems, recruitment, benefits, personnel management
	Downstream Activities	Salesperson productivity tools, online telemarketing, advertisement management, marketing management, salesforce compensation management, CRM, market research, customers' database, data mining, help desk, call centers

an inventory falls below a designated level, others are tools designed to increase productivity and/or quality of work, but not to completely automate an activity.

These software products were developed over the years independently of each other, mostly along functional lines: accounting, finance, marketing, manufacturing, human resource management, and engineering.

When these systems matured, it became clear that it was necessary to integrate them.

Why Integration

Creating the twenty-first-century enterprise cannot be done effectively with twentieth-century information technology, which is functionally oriented and unintegrated. Functional systems may not let different departments communicate with each other in the same language. Worse yet, crucial sales, inventory, and production data often have to be painstakingly entered manually into separate computer systems every time a manager needs ad hoc information, especially when this information is found in two or more sources. In many cases, employees simply do not get the information they need or they get it when it is too late.

According to Sandoe et al. (2001), supply chain software integration has the following benefits (listed in descending order of importance).

Tangible benefits. The tangible benefits are inventory reduction, personnel reduction, productivity improvement, order management improvement, financial cycle improvements, IT cost reduction, procurement cost reduction, cash management improvements, revenue/profit increases, transportation logistics cost reduction, maintenance reduction, and on-time delivery improvement.

Intangible benefits. The intangible benefits are information visibility, new/improved processes, customer responsiveness, standardization, flexibility, globalization, and business performance.

Notice that in both types of benefits many items are directly related to supply chain activities. For further discussion on the improvements integration provides to SCM see "Competition's New Battleground: The Integrated Value Chain," at *ctp.com* (2000).

According to Selland (1999), EC requires a new business model, one that lets companies gather the intelligence necessary to understand customer needs, and one that proactively allocates resources to fulfill customers' requirements in real-time. By combining the two, companies can gain a unique and powerful differentiation point—creating products and services designed to appeal to the mass market and the market of one at the same time. Such an approach can be done by integrating front-office applications, including CRM, and back-office activities, which are supported by ERP, the integration enabler of supply chains.

Integrating the Supply Chain's Activities

For decades, companies managed the various links of the supply chain and their supporting information systems independently of each other. However, since the 1960s, companies started to integrate the links. The integration was driven by the need to streamline operations in order to meet customers' demands in the areas of product and service costs, quality, on-time delivery, technology, and cycle time brought by increased global competition. Furthermore, the new forms of organizational relationships, such as virtual corporations, and the information revolution, especially the Internet and EC, brought SCM to the forefront of top management attention. This attention created a willingness to invest money in hardware and software that were needed for a seamless integration, as shown in the case of Warner Lambert Corp. (Application Case 15.6).

APPLICATION CASE   15.6

How Warner Lambert (WL) Applies an Integrated Supply Chain

It all begins on eucalyptus farms in Australia, where these fast growing trees produce some of the materials used in one of Warner Lambert's (WL) major products—Listerine antiseptic mouthwash. The materials collected from eucalyptus trees are shipped to the WL manufacturing plant in New Jersey. The major problem there is to determine how much Listerine to produce. Listerine is purchased by thousands of retail stores, some of which are giants such as Wal-Mart. The problem that the manufacturing plant is faced with is forecasting the overall demand. A wrong forecast will result either in high inventories at WL or in delivery shortages. Inventories are expensive to keep, and shortages may result in loss of business and reputation.

WL forecasts demand with the help of Manugistics Inc.'s Demand Planning information system. (Manugistics is a vendor of IT software for SCM, *manugistics.com*). Used with other products in Manugistics' Supply Chain Planning suite, the system analyzes manufacturing, distribution, and sales data against expected demand and business climate information to help WL decide how much Listerine (and other products) to make and distribute and how much of each raw ingredient is needed. For example, the model can anticipate the impact of advertisements or of a production line being down. The sales and marketing groups of WL meet monthly with WL employees in finance, procurement, and other departments. The groups enter the projected demand for Listerine into a Marcam Corp. Prism Capacity Planning system, which schedules the production of Listerine in the amounts needed, and generates electronic purchase orders for WL's suppliers. WL's supply chain excellence stems from its innovative Collaborative Planning, Forecasting, and Replenishment (CPFR) program. WL launched CPFR a few

APPLICATION CASE 15.6

(continued)

years ago when it started sharing strategic plans, performance data, and market insight with Wal-Mart, Inc. over private networks. The company realized that it could benefit from Wal-Mart's market knowledge, just as Wal-Mart could benefit from WL's product knowledge. During the CPFR pilot, WL increased its products' shelf-fill rate—the extent to which a store's shelves are fully stocked—from 87 to 98 percent, earning the company about $8 million a year in additional sales—the equivalent of a new product launch. WL is now using the Internet to expand the CPFR program to all its major suppliers and retail partners.

WL is a major player in other collaborative retail industry projects. One is the Collaborative Forecasting and Replenishment Project (CFAR). In CFAR, trading partners collaborate on *demand forecasting* using EC technology. The project includes major SCM and ERP vendors such as SAP and Manugistics. The other project is Supply Chain Operations Reference (SCOR), an initiative of the Supply Chain Council in the United States. SCOR, which decomposes supply-chain operations, gives manufacturers, suppliers, distributors, and retailers a framework to evaluate the effectiveness of their processes along the same supply chains.

Sources: Compiled from *Logistics Management and Distribution Report* (October 1998; November 1999), *stores.org* (1998), and Bresnahan (1998).

Areas of Integration

Here are some examples of areas of integration:

- Order taking must be integrated with product inventory levels.
- Payment information in B2C must be transferred automatically to Visa, MasterCard, etc., for authorization.
- Orders in B2B must interface both with pricing, to calculate the value of an order, and with finance, to assure sufficient credit line.
- Low inventory levels (at a designated level) must trigger automatic ordering.
- Orders to manufacturing must generate a list of the needed resources and their availability.
- Changes in an order must be transmitted automatically to suppliers and their suppliers. Changes may involve delivery dates, quantities, or changes in quality standards.
- Tracking systems must be available to customers so they can check the status of their orders. Such systems are connected to databases, usually via extranets.

Integrating software may not be a simple task, especially when different partners are involved. Let's see how such integration is being accomplished.

15.11   INTEGRATED SOFTWARE SOLUTIONS: FROM MRP TO ERP

The concept of SCM integration is interrelated with the computerization of supply chain activities, which has been evolving over the last 40 years.

The Evolution of Computerized Aids for SCM

Historically, many of the supply chain activities were managed manually, which can be a very inefficient and ineffective process. Therefore, since the early use of computers in business, attention was given to the automation of processes along the supply chain. The first software programs appeared in the 1950s and the early 1960s. They supported short segments along the supply chain. For example, programs that facilitated inventory management of single items, departmental work scheduling, payroll, and billing. The major objective was to reduce cost, expedite processing, and reduce errors. Such applications were developed in the functional areas, independent of each other. However, in a short time it became clear that interdependencies exist among some of the supply chain activities. One of the earliest realizations was that the production schedule is related to inventory management and purchasing plans. As early as the 1960s, the **material resource planning (MRP)** model was devised. Then it became clear that in order to use this model, which may require daily updating, one needs computer support. This resulted in commercial MRP software packages.

MRP packages were useful in many cases, helping to drive inventory levels down and streamline portions of the supply chain. However, they did not work in all cases. One of the major reasons for this was the fact that schedule-inventory-purchasing operations are closely related to both financial and labor planning resources, and cannot be managed, in many cases, without them. This realization resulted in an enhanced MRP methodology and software called manufacturing resource planning, or MRP II.

Note that during this evolution there was more and more integration of information systems. This evolution continued, leading to the Enterprise Resource Planning (ERP) concept, which concentrated on *integrating* all internal enterprise transaction processing activities. ERP was extended later to include internal suppliers and customers, and then was extended further to include external suppliers and customers in what is known as *extended ERP* software.

The latest move in this evolution is the inclusion of markets and communities. Such conceptualization is reflected in SAP's Internet-based initiative, known as mySAP (SAP is the world's largest ERP vendor) (see Application Case 15.7). Notice that with the passage of time, SAP products have been changed to include interenterprise cooperation with business partners and customers. Such cooperation includes EC, CRM, and business intelligence. The company also changed its business model to include application hosting (ASP). Other ERP vendors such as PeopleSoft and Oracle use a similar strategy.

Throughout this evolution there were more and more integrations along several dimensions (more functional areas, combining TPS and decision support, inclusion of business partners). Therefore, ERP software is characterized by a high degree of integration. Let's examine the essentials of ERP.

Enterprise Resource Planning (ERP)

With the advance of enterprise-wide client-server computing comes a new challenge: how to control all major business processes with a single software architecture in real-time. The integrated solution, known as **enterprise resource planning (ERP)**, promises benefits from increased efficiency to improved quality, productivity,

mySAP.com

As complements to existing SAP products (i.e., R/3, New Dimension prod-ucts, and Knowledge Management), *SAP.com* offers four building blocks, including the following:

- Workplace—A personalized interface
- Marketplace—One stop destination for business professionals to collaborate
- Business Scenarios—Products for the Internet and intranet
- Application-hosting—Hosting Web applications for SMEs

Together, these building blocks create a strategy that extends the reach of the Internet to empower employees and improve competitive advantage by participating in the EC marketplace. As part of Web-enabled applications, they can break down functional and geographic barriers while encouraging a high level of individual and collaborative performance.

Workplace

The Workplace is a role-based *enterprise portal* solution. Via an easy-to-use, personalized Web-browser-based front end, users are presented with all of the information, applications, and services they need to get their job done.

Targeted information is presented to users immediately when they log on. This can help alleviate information overflow. The Workplace comes with approximately 150 role templates that customers are free to use, modify, or define on their own.

Marketplace

The Marketplace is a one-stop destination for business and industry profes-sionals. It enables SAP collaborative business scenarios, allowing many buy-ers and sellers to come together and do business. It is an integration site for enterprises and business professionals to collaborate, conduct commerce, access personalized content, and interact in professional communities (see *sap.com/services/infrastructure*).

The Marketplace provides:

- The complete infrastructure, security, commerce-enabling applications, value-added services, and interoperability required to enable one-stop busi-ness anytime, anywhere, with anyone.
- A cross-industry horizontal marketplace as the basis for collaborative com-merce for business professionals in general.
- A number of vertical and regional marketplaces for specialized commerce among groups of users with similar interests, such as the oil and gas industry.

Business Scenarios

Business Scenarios offer the specific knowledge, functions, and services that one or more users may need to succeed in their business tasks. *SAP.com* provides a host of e-business-enabled solutions, including purchasing, col-laborative planning, employee self-service, direct customer servicing, and interbusiness knowledge management.

The major areas covered by SAP's Business Scenarios are:

- Effective B2B buying and selling with multiple buyers and sellers.
- Core CRM functions, including Internet sales and service, field sales and ser-vice, collaborative bidding, and Web-enabled customer service applications.

APPLICATION CASE 15.7

(continued)

mySAP.com supports catalog maintenance and ordering, and both integrating seamlessly with back-end systems. The CRM components of *mySAP.com* integrate customer news, background information, and vendor data.
- *mySAP.com* provides supply chain management (SCM) solutions, including scenarios in collaborative forecasting and planning.

Application Hosting

mySAP.com strategy is to target small and mid-size companies with Web-based application hosting services, which offer a more cost-effective and faster approach for companies to leverage SAP business scenarios and engage in the Internet collaborative market.

and profitability (see Sandoe et al., 2001 for details). The name ERP is misleading; the software does not concentrate on either *planning* or on *resources*. ERP's initial major objective was to *integrate* all departments and functions across a company into a single computer system that can serve all the enterprise's needs. For example, when an order is received, the software allows immediate access to inventory, product data, customer credit history, and prior order information. This raises productivity and increases customer satisfaction. However, ERP systems are very difficult to construct. How can a company build one?

One alternative is to self-develop an integrated system by using existing functional packages or by programming a system from scratch. This alternative was used by a few large corporations. Its major advantage is that it enables the use of "best of breed" components, providing a perfect fit for the users' needs. But it is expensive to build and maintain. Software for conducting SCM integration is available from several vendors including IBM and General Electronic Corp.

Another option is to use commercially available integrated software. The leading software for ERP is SAP R/3 from SAP. J. D. Edwards, Computer Associates, PeopleSoft, and Oracle make similar products. These products include Web modules.

Companies have been successful in integrating several hundred functional applications using ERP software, saving millions of dollars and significantly increasing customer satisfaction. For example, Mobil Oil Corp. consolidated 300 different information systems by implementing SAP R/3 in their U.S. petrochemical operations alone. ERP forces discipline and organization around business processes, making the alignment of IT and business goals more likely. Also, by installing and using ERP, a company may discover all the "dusty corners" of its business.

An ERP suite provides a single interface for managing all the routine activities performed in manufacturing—from entering sales orders to coordinating shipping and after-sales customer service. More recently, ERP systems have begun to incorporate functionality for customer interaction and managing relationships with suppliers and vendors.

ERP has also played a critical role in getting small and medium-sized manufacturers to focus, facilitating business process changes across the enterprise. By tying multiple plants and distribution facilities together, ERP solutions have facilitated a change in thinking that has its ultimate expression in the extended enterprise and better supply chain management. (For a comprehensive treatment of ERP, its cost, implementation problems, and payback see Koch et al., 1999.) Since ERP covers most back-office activities of an enterprise, it is obvious that it must interface with EC applications.

But, ERP was not designed to fully support EC supply chains. ERP solutions are transaction-centric. As such, they do not provide the computerized models needed to respond rapidly to real-time changes in supply, demand, labor, or capacity, which are typical in the EC environment. This deficiency could be overcome by the second generation of ERP and its interface with EC.

Post-ERP (Second-Generation ERP)

The first-generation ERP projects have saved companies millions of dollars. A 1998 report by Merrill Lynch & Co. noted that nearly 40 percent of all companies in the United States with more than $1 billion in annual revenues have implemented ERP systems. However, by the late 1990s, the major benefits of ERP were fully exploited. A second, more powerful generation of ERP development started with the objective of leveraging existing systems to increase efficiency in handling transactions, improving decision making, supporting EC and CRM, and further transforming ways of doing business. As a matter of fact, integration of EC with ERP systems is becoming a necessity. Let's explain.

First-generation ERP basically supported routine transactional activities. In other words, what ERP has traditionally excelled at is automating transaction management, that is, the ability to manage administrative activities like payroll, financials, inventory, and order processing. For example, an ERP system had the functionality of electronic ordering or the best way to bill the customer.

The reports generated by ERP systems gave planners statistics about what happened in the company in areas such as cost and financial performance. However, the planning systems with ERP were rudimentary. Reports from ERP systems provided a snapshot of time, but they did not support the continuous planning exercise that is central to supply chain planning, one that continues to refine and enhance the plans as changes and events are occurring, up to the very last minute before executing the plan.

This created the need for *decision making-oriented systems,* and this is what the independent SCM software vendors were providing. As an illustration, we look at ERP and SCM approaches to a planning scenario. There is a fundamental difference—the question in SCM becomes "Should I take your order?" instead of an ERP approach of "How can I best take or fulfill your order?" An EC computerized support system must be able to answer *both* questions.

Thus, SCM software systems have emerged as a *complement* to ERP software systems to provide intelligent decision support capabilities and support EC. An SCM system can be designed to overlay existing ERP systems and pull data from every step of the supply chain, providing a clear, global picture of where the enterprise is heading. Creating a plan from an SCM system allows companies to quickly assess the impact of their actions on the entire supply chain, including customer demand. Therefore, it makes sense to integrate ERP and SCM. How can such integration be accomplished?

One approach is to work with different software programs from different vendors, for example, using SAP as an ERP and adding Manugistics' manufacturing-oriented software, as shown earlier in the WL case. Such an approach requires integrating different software programs from several vendors, which may be a complex undertaking, unless special interfaces exist. Several vendors provide software for this kind of integration. For example, Tradelink from Hitachi Computer (*hitachi.com/worldwide/index.html*), is offered to U.S. companies. The software includes catalog management, payment gateway, mass customization capabilities, order management, connections to legacy databases and to ERP, and more. Tibco Inc. (*tibco.com*) provides connectivity for organizations with business partners, both internally and externally.

The second approach is for the ERP vendors to add some decision support and business intelligence capabilities to their software. This packaged approach solves the integration problem. But as in the integration of DBMS and spreadsheets in Excel, you get a product with some not-so-strong functionalities. Nevertheless, most ERP vendors are adding such functionalities for another reason—it is cheaper for the customers.

The added functionalities, which create the second-generation of ERP, include not only decision support, but also CRM, some EC tasks and interfaces, and even data mining.

The third option is to rent applications rather than to build systems. In renting applications, the ERP vendor takes care of the functionalities and the integration problems. This approach is known as the "ASP alternative."

ASPs and ERP Outsourcing

An **application service provider (ASP)** describes a software vendor who allows organizations to lease information systems applications. The basic concept is the same as the old-fashioned time-share. The outsourcers set up the systems and run them for you. ASP is considered a product risk prevention management strategy, and it best fits small to mid-size companies. The concept is becoming popular with ERP applications.

The ASP concept is especially useful in ERP projects, which are expensive to install and take a long time to implement and for which staffing is a major problem. However, ASP offerings are also evident in ERP-added functions such as EC, CRM, datamarts, desktop productivity, human resources information systems, (HRIS), and other supply-chain-related applications.

The use of ASP has some downsides. First, ERP vendors want a 5-year commitment. In 5 years ERP may look completely different and be simple to install and inexpensive to buy. Second, you lose flexibility. Rented systems are fairly standard and may not fit your needs. For a discussion of ASPs see *Datamation,* July 1999 (several papers). ASPs are especially beneficial to small companies such as online start-ups. For further discussion on ASPs and order fulfillment, see Rigney (2000).

15.12   MANAGERIAL ISSUES

The following issues are germane to management:

1. **Planning.** Planning for order fulfillment is a critical task, especially for virtual EC vendors. But even if you are a brick-and-mortar retailer with physical warehouses, delivery to the customers' door may be a problem. The problem is not just physical shipment, but the efficient execution of the entire order fulfillment process, which may be complex, along a long supply chain.

2. **Returns.** Dealing with returns can be a complex issue. The percentage of returns should be estimated and the process of receiving and handling them must be designed and planned. Some companies completely separate the logistics of returns from that of order fulfillment.

3. **Alliances.** Partnerships and alliances can improve logistics and alleviate supply chain problems. Many possibilities and models exist. Some are along the supply chain, whereas others are not related to it.

4. **Software Selection.** Many software products are available to improve SCM and logistics. The problem is to determine which one to use (see Chapter 12).

5. **Connectivity.** EC must be tightly connected with back-office operations. Otherwise, considerable problems may develop. In large organizations with existing ERP, it is necessary to integrate it with the EC front-office operations.

6. **EC Applications.** One should think not only about how to create logistical systems for EC, but also how to use EC applications to improve the supply chain.

7. **Integration.** Software integration may require considerable time and money. Several solutions are available ranging from packaged middleware and enterprise application integration (EAI) products from vendors such as GE (Integration Broker), IBM (MQ series), Active Software, and NEON to XML-based integration packages aimed at business partners, from vendors such as ViewLogic, Extricity, and WebMethods. The selection of a vendor can be complex. In any event, remember that integration is the enabler, not the goal. For details of EAI see *gegxs.com/geiscom/downloads/EAI_wp.pdf*, a white paper entitled, "Extending and Integrating the Enterprise" (2000).

Summary

In this chapter, you learned about the following EC issues as they relate to the learning objectives:

1. **The role of order fulfillment and back-office operations in EC.** Taking orders is necessary, but not sufficient in EC. Delivery to customers on time may be a difficult task, especially in B2C. Fulfilling an order requires several activities ranging from credit and inventory checks to shipments. Most of these activities are called back-office operations and they are related to logistics.

2. **The process of order fulfillment.** Order fulfillment steps differ, depending on the business and product, from business to business. Generally speaking, however, the following 11 steps are recognized: payment verification, inventory checking, shipping arrangement, insurance, production (or assembly) plant services, purchasing, demand forecasting, accounting, customer contacts, and return of products.

3. **The supply chain and its management.** The flow of materials, information, and services from sources to places where they are processed into products (services) and then distributed to customers is called the supply chain, which is composed of three major parts: upstream, internal, and downstream. The process may be complex, requiring the coordination of several business partners. Therefore, the supply chain process needs to be planned and managed properly.

4. **Problems in managing supply chains.** It is difficult to manage supply chains due to uncertainties in demand and potential delays in supply and

deliveries. To overcome supply chain problems companies use inventories. Inventories can be expensive. Several other innovative solutions exist, most of which are supported by software that facilitates correct inventories, coordination along the supply chain, and appropriate planning and decision making.

5. **The need for integration.** The different processes and activities along the supply chain must be coordinated to minimize delays. Coordination is best done in integrated systems. In addition to supporting coordination and communication, integrated systems expedite cycle time and reduce errors by automating activities and providing monitoring, checking, and controls.

6. **The evolution of software support to SCM.** Initially software was developed for isolated activities along the various segments of the supply chain in different functional areas. Beginning in the 1960s, integration began to take place, initially with MRP. Adding more activities resulted in MRP II, and then ERP was created by the addition of more integration. Now, an extended ERP that covers most routine activities along the supply chain, including suppliers and customers, is used. The latest development is the integration of decision-making tools and CRM capabilities with ERP.

7. **The relationships of EC, ERP, and SCM.** EC is related to the supply chain and its supportive software in two ways. First, EC can support various activities along the supply chain such as order taking, order tracking, and communication. Second, EC implies taking an order and fulfilling it. To do so, it is necessary to quickly and easily interface with inventory, scheduling, billing, and other systems. These back-office operations are managed, especially in large or medium-sized companies, with ERP. The SCM software helps in making decisions about how much to produce, how much inventory to stock, and how to best schedule shipments. Therefore, the current trend is to integrate the software support of ERP, SCM, and EC.

Key Terms

Application service provider (ASP)	Logistics
Back-office operations	Material resource planning (MRP)
Bullwhip effect	Order fulfillment
Customer Relationship Management (CRM)	Reverse logistics
Enterprise resource planning (ERP)	Supply chain
Front-office operations	Supply chain management (SCM)
Fulfillment	

Questions for Review

1. Define order fulfillment.
2. Define logistics and reverse logistics.
3. List the 11 steps of the order fulfillment process.
4. Define supply chain management.
5. List the major benefits of SCM.
6. Describe ERP.
7. Define reverse logistics.
8. Define ASP.

Questions for Discussion

1. Explain the need for integrating the back- and front-office operations in EC.
2. Discuss the problems of reverse logistics in EC. What kind of companies may suffer the most?
3. Discuss the extension of the supply chain beyond the corporation and in going global.
4. Discuss the need for integration along the supply chain and explain how it can minimize problems such as the Y2K toys problem.
5. Discuss how exchanges such as *ChemConnect.com* or a wholesaler like *bigboxx.com* can solve supply chain problems.
6. Explain why UPS defines itself as a "technology company with trucks," rather than a "trucking company with technology."
7. Distinguish between SCM and ERP software.
8. It is said that supply chains are essentially "a series of linked suppliers and customers; every customer is in turn a supplier to the next downstream organization, until the ultimate end user." Explain this statement (use of a diagram is recommended).
9. Explain the bullwhip effect. In which type of EC business is it most likely to occur? How can the effect be removed?
10. Examine Application Case 15.2, the tropical fish fulfillment case study.
    - Draw the supply chain from Fiji to a customer's home in Toronto, Canada. Identify the 11 steps of order fulfillment.
    - Examine the various parts of the supply chain. Which parts are supported by EC?
11. Chart the supply chain portion of returns to a virtual store. Check with *Amazon.com* and see how they handle returns. Check with *ups.com* for the details of their service. Prepare a report based on your findings.
12. Review the Listerine fulfillment scenario (Application Case 15.6).
    - Draw the supply chain
    - Surf the Internet to find more information on WL initiatives for SCM.
    - Why is demand forecasting so difficult?

Internet Exercises

1. Visit the following Web sites: *toysrus.com*, *KbKids.com*, *amazon.com*, *lego.com* and *dogtoys.com*. Find out what delivery options are offered by each company. Then examine delivery options offered by *starbucks.com* and *carsdirect.com*. Prepare a report based on your findings.
2. Enter *mysap.com/mysap*. Examine the mysap concept and identify the features related to EC. Write a report on the services provided along the supply chain.
3. The U.S Postal Service is entering the EC logistics field. Examine their services and tracking systems at *usps.com/shipping*. What are the potential advantages for EC shippers?
4. Enter *rawmart.com* and find what information they provide that supports logistics. Also find what shipment services they provide online.
5. Visit *manugistics.com* and find their logistics services. How do they act as a clearinghouse for freight shipments between customers and carriers?

6. Enter *brio.com* and identify their solution to SCM integration as it relates to decision making for EC. View the demo.

7. Visit *kewill.com*. Examine their various products that relate to SCM and logistics.

8. Enter *supply-chain.org* and find information about SCOR. What are the contributions of SCOR to EC?

9. Visit *UPS.com* and find their recent EC initiatives. Compare them with those of *fedex.com*.

10. Enter *coca-colastore.com* and check their delivery and return options.

11. Enter *relysoftware.com/index.jsp* and one or two other online freight companies. Compare the features offered by these companies.

12. Enter *giftcertificates.com* and learn about the company. Read stories about their order fulfillment process (e.g., in *Internet World*, February 1, 2000). Describe and evaluate their fulfillment process.

13. Enter *sameday.com*. Review their products. How do they organize the network? How are they related to companies such as FedEX? How do they make money?

Team Assignments and Role Playing

1. Each team (or team member) should investigate the order fulfillment process of an e-tailer, such as *Amazon.com*, *evineyard.com*, or *landsend.com*. Contact the company, if necessary, and examine business partnerships if they exist. Based on the content of this chapter, prepare a report with suggestions for how the company or companies can improve their order fulfillment process. All the groups' findings will be aggregated and compared in class. Based on the class's findings, draw some conclusions about how order fulfillment can be improved.

2. FedEx, UPS, the U.S. Postal Service, and others are competing in the EC logistics market. Each team should examine one such company. Investigate the services they provide. Contact the company, if necessary, and aggregate the findings into a report that will convince the reader that the company in question is the best. (What are the best features?)

REAL-WORLD CASE: Quantum Corporation Streamlined Its Supply Chain

Quantum Corporation (*quantum.com*) is a major U.S. manufacturer of hard disk drives and other high-technology storage components.

The Problems

Quantum faced two key challenges in its manufacturing process. The first was streamlining its component supply process to lower on-hand inventory. Quantum's traditional ordering process was labor intensive, involving numerous phone calls and manual inventory checks. To ensure that production would not be interrupted, the process required high levels of on-hand inventory. Quantum needed a solution that would automate the ordering process to increase accuracy and efficiency, reduce on-hand inventory to 3 days, and provide the company's purchasing agents with more time for non-transactional tasks.

Quantum's second challenge was to improve the quality of the component data in their Material Requirements Planning (MRP) system. Incomplete and inaccurate data caused delays in production. Quantum's solution of manually reviewing reports to identify errors was labor intensive and occurred too late, since problems in production were experienced before the reports were even reviewed. Quantum needed a technology solution that would enable it to operate *proactively* to catch problems before they caused production delays.

The Solution

To automate its component supply process, in 1999 Quantum initiated an enterprise system to automatically e-mail reorders to suppliers using an innovative event detection and notification solution from Categoric Software (*categoric.com*). The system scans Quantum's databases twice daily, assessing material requirements from one application module against inventory levels tracked in another. Orders are automatically initiated and sent to suppliers as needed, allowing suppliers to make regular deliveries that match Quantum's production schedule. The system not only notifies suppliers of the quantity of components required in the immediate orders, but also gives the supplier a valuable window into the amount of inventory on hand and future weekly requirements. The system also enabled Quantum to tap into multiple data sources to identify critical business events. To elevate data quality, Quantum implemented Categoric Alerts to proactively catch any data errors or omissions in its MRP database. The systems' notifications are now sent whenever any critical MRP data falls outside the existing operational parameters.

Results

The estimated value of the improved ordering process using the new system is millions of dollars in inventory reductions. The buyers have reduced transaction tasks and costs and both sides get a lot more information with a lot less work. Before the implementation of Categoric Alerts, the analysts would search massive reports for MRP data errors. Now that the new system is implemented, exceptions are identified as they occur. This new process has freed analysts from the drudgery of scanning reports and has greatly increased employee satisfaction.

Data integrity of the MRP increased from 10 percent to almost 100 percent, and Quantum is now able to quickly respond to changing customer demand. The system paid for itself in the first year.

Sources: Compiled from an advertising supplement in *CIO Magazine* (October 1, 1999) and from *categoric.com* (May 2000).

Questions for the case

1. Identify the internal and external parts of the supply chain that were enhanced by the enterprise system.

2. Enter *categoric.com* and find information about Categoric Alerts. Describe the capabilities of the product.

3. Explain how purchasing was improved by this system.

4. Describe how the customers are being better served since the implementation of the system.

5. Identify the EC solutions used in this case.

REAL-WORLD CASE: How Dell Computer Provides Superb Customer Service

One of Dell Computer's success factors (see Chapter 2) is its superb logistics and order fulfillment systems. Customer orders, which are received mostly online, are automatically transferred to the production area where configuration is done to determine which components and parts are needed to create the customized computer that the customer wants. Once that is done, the problem becomes how to get all the needed components so that a computer can be ready for shipment the next day. As part of the solution, Dell created a network of dedicated suppliers for just-in-time deliveries, as well as a sophisticated computerized global network of components and parts inventories. As indicated earlier, EC is not just selling. It is also order fulfillment and customer service throughout the product life cycle. Therefore, the global network is also used for product services: repairs per warranty commitments, upgrades, demanufacturing, etc.

Let's see how Dell provides service after the product is in the customer's possession. Dell is trying to achieve the next-day shipment target that is in place for new computers with repairs, upgrades, and other services. To do so, Dell is using an intelligent inventory optimization system from LPA software (*xelus.com*). The system can reconcile the numerous sources of demand with the myriad options (e.g., repair, upgrade, transfer, or demanufacture). For example, the system allows Dell to factor in the yield on reusable parts into Dell's supply projection. This allows Dell to use repairable parts to compress time

and reduce costs, enabling a team of about 10 employees to successfully process more than 6,000 service orders every day.

The system generates timely information about demand forecast, cost of needed inventory, and "days of supply of inventory." It compares actual to forecasted demand. This enables Dell to communicate critical information to external and internal customers, reducing SCM delays.

Part chaining through component substitution, upgrades, and engineering change orders must be effective in order to compete. All this is done in order to maintain high service levels at a low inventory cost. The system also provides a standard body of knowledge about parts and planning strategies.

Some of the system's capabilities are:

- Forecast multiple lead times (e.g., for old parts, new parts)

- Chain parts together

- Optimize service level and inventory levels

- Control of computers returned for repairs

- Assemble parts together in a kit format

- Flag problem conditions such as parts out of stock

- Flag order changes and cancellations in real-time

- Flag discrepancies between forecasted and actual demand as they occur

- Evaluate trade-offs between service levels and inventory cost

Sources: Compiled from advertisement supplement in *CIO* magazine (October 1, 1999), from *xelus.com* (June 2000), and from *dell.com* (November 2000).

Case Questions

1. Identify the parts of the supply chain that were improved in this case.

2. Enter *xelus.com* and find information about their inventory optimization and other SCM-related products. List the major capabilities of the products they offer.

3. Enter *dell.com* and find information about how Dell conducts repair (warranty) customer service.

4. Relate this case to the discussion about "returns" in this chapter.

5. What competitive advantage is provided by the Dell system?

REFERENCES AND BIBLIOGRAPHY

Ayers, J. "A Primer on Supply Chain Management," *Information Strategy: The Executive's Journal* (Winter 2000).

Bowersox, D. J. *Logistical Management: The Integrated Supply Chain Process.* New York: McGraw-Hill, 1996.

Bresnahan, J. "The Incredible Journey," *CIO Magazine* (August 15, 1998).

Bussiek, T. "The Internet-Based Supply Chain—New Forms of T. P. Procurement Utilizing Standard Business Software," *Electronic Markets*, vol. 9, no. 3 (1999).

Caldwell, B. and T. Stein. "Beyond ERP: New IT Agenda," *Information Week* (November 30, 1998).

Chase, R. B., et al. *Production and Operations Management*, 8th ed. Chicago, Illinois: R. D. Irwin, 1998.

Christopher, M. *Logistics and SCM: Strategies for Reducing Cost and Improving Service*, London: Pitman, 1998.

Clark, T. H. K., et al. "Performance, Interdependence, and Coordination in B2B Electronic Commerce and Supply Chain Management," *Information Technology and Management* (January 2000).

Cone, E. "E-Com Meets Logistical Web," *Interactive Week* (July 26, 1999).

Duvall, M. "Santa's Helpers Get Their Feet Webbed," *Interactive Week* (September 13, 1999).

Epner, S. "The Search for a Supply Team," *Industrial Distribution* (December 1999).

Frook, J. E. "Webifying the Channel," *Internet Week* (October 26, 1998).

Gattorma, J., editor. *Strategic Supply Chain Alignment: Best Practices in Supply Chain Management.* New York: Gower Pub. Co., 1998.

Handfield, R. B. and E. L. Nichols, Jr. *Introduction to Supply Chain Management.* Upper Saddle River, New Jersey: Prentice Hall, 1999.

Jacobs, R. R. and D. C. Whybark. *Why ERP.* Boston: McGraw-Hill, 2000.

Johnston, R. B., et al. "An Emerging Vision of Internet-Enabled Supply-Chain Electronic Commerce," *International Journal of Electronic Commerce* (Summer 2000).

Koch, C., et. al. "The ABCs of ERP," *CIO Magazine* (*cio.com*) (December 22, 1999).

Koloszyc, G. "Retailers, Suppliers Push Joint Sales Forecasting," *stores.org/archives/jun98edch.html* (June 1998).

Laios, L. and S. Moschuris. "An Empirical Investigation of Outsourcing Decisions," *Journal of Supply Chain Management* (Winter 1999).

Lee, L. H., et al. "The Bullwhip Effect in Supply Chains," *Sloan Management Review* (Spring 1997).

Lewis, I. and A. Talalayevsky. "Logistics and Information Technology: A Coordination Perspective," *Journal of Business Logistics*, no. 1 (1997).

Lin, F. R. and M. J. Shaw. "Reengineering the Order Fulfillment Process in Supply Chain Networks," *International Journal of Flexible Manufacturing* (March 1998).

Poirier, C. *Advanced Supply Chain Management.* San Francisco, California: Berrett-Koehler, 1999.

Poirier, C. C. and M. J. Bauer, *E-Supply Chain: Using the Internet to Revolutionize Your Business*, San Francisco, California: Berrett-Koehler, December 2000.

Rainer, A., et al. "Business Networking in the Swatch Group," *Electronic Markets* vol. 9, no. 3 (1999).

Rao, B., et al. "Building a World-Class Logistics, Distribution and Electronic Commerce Infrastructure," *Electronic Markets*, vol. 9, no. 3 (1999).

Rigney, P. "Eliminate Fulfillment Problems," *e-Business Advisor* (March 2000).

Ross, D. F. *Competing Through SCM*. New York: Chapman and Hall, 1998.

Sandoe, K. et al. *Enterprise Integration*. New York: John Wiley & Sons, 2001.

Schwartz, B. "E-Business: New Distribution Models Coming to a Site Near You," *Transportation and Distribution* (February 2000).

Selland, C. "Extending the E-Business to ERP," *e-Business Advisor* (January 1999).

Sellman, C. S. *Extending E-Business to ERP*. San Diego, California: Advisor Media, Inc., 1999.

Sellman, C. S. "The Key to E-Business: Integrating the Enterprise," *e-Business Advisor* (October 1999).

Steinert-Threlkeld, T. "GroceryWorks: The Low-Touch Alternative," *Interactive Week* (January 31, 2000).

Stricker, C., et al. "Market-based Workflow Management for Supply Chains of Services," Proceedings, 33rd HICSS, Hawaii (2000).

"Supply Chain Integration: The Name of the Game Is Collaboration." Special Advertising Supplement. *CIO Magazine* (*cio.com*) (November 1, 1999).

Timmers, P. *Electronic Commerce: Strategies and Models for B2B Trading*. Chichester, United Kingdom: John Wiley & Sons, 1999.

Trager, L. "Not So Many Happy Returns," *Interactive Week* (March 20, 2000).

Turban, E., et al. *Information Technology for Management*, 3rd ed. New York: John Wiley & Sons, 2002.

Violino, B. Supply Chain Management and E-Commerce," *Internet Week* (May 4, 2000).

Wicke, G. A. "Electronic Markets—A Key to Mobility," *Electronic Markets*, vol. 9, no. 3 (1999).

16

EC Strategy and Implementation

LEARNING OBJECTIVES

Upon completion of this chapter, the reader will be able to:

- Describe the importance and essentials of business and EC strategies.

- Describe the strategy planning process for EC.

- Understand the strategy formulation process.

- Understand how EC applications are discovered and prioritized.

- Describe the role of CSFs and justification of EC.

- Describe strategy implementation.

- Understand how to reassess EC strategy.

- Describe the role of metrics in EC.

- Understand EC failures and lessons for success.

CONTENT

16.1 IBM's E-Business Strategy

IBM's declared strategy is to transform itself into an e-business in order to provide business value to the corporation and its shareholders. IBM views e-business as being much broader than EC because it serves a broader constituency and a variety of Web-based processes and transactions. To assure successful implementation, IBM formed an independent division, called Enterprise Web Management, that has the following four goals:

1. To lead IBM's strategy to transform itself into an e-business and to act as a catalyst to help facilitate that transformation.
2. To help IBM's business units become more effective in their use of the Internet, both internally and with their customers.
3. To establish a strategy for the corporate Internet site. This includes a definition of how it should look, feel, and be navigated— in short, to create an online environment most conducive to customers doing business with IBM.
4. To leverage the wealth of e-business transformational accumulated case studies to highlight the potential of e-business to customers.

Like many other companies, IBM started to use the Internet as a static digital brochure—or a publication model—basically posting information. Now, however, it is moving toward a comprehensive e-business, namely carrying out transactions of all kinds over the Internet, intranets, and extranets between IBM and its suppliers, among members of its Business Partner network, among its employees, and so on. IBM wants to become truly e-business-oriented and to focus on how it can use this powerful networking technology to fulfill the diverse needs of its customers.

One of the major issues in moving to e-business was the redesign of many of its core business processes on the Internet—including commerce, procurement, customer care, and knowledge management. The company is developing consistent company-wide business strategies that leverage the size and scale of IBM's Web presence and investments. In addition, it is creating an Internet model that is both unified and user-centric. This involves the setting of site hosting and production standards related to design, functionality, and navigation.

The company targeted for redesign those areas in which IBM can make the biggest return on investment and which are most practical to address. IBM focused its activities around seven key initiatives:

1. Selling more goods over the Web—EC.
2. Providing all kinds of customer support online, from technical support to marketing backup— e-care for customers.
3. Support for IBM's business partners over the Web—e-care for business partners.
4. Dedicated services providing faster, better information for IT analysts and consultants, financial analysts, media, and stakeholders—e-care for influencers.
5. Improving the effectiveness of IBMers by making the right information and services available to them—e-care for employees.
6. Working closely with customers and suppliers to improve the tendering process and to better administer the huge number of transactions involved— e-procurement.
7. Using the Internet to better communicate IBM's marketing stance—e-marketing communications.

Some of these initiatives have already borne fruit. For example, IBM has implemented an e-procurement initiative that spans IBM globally, saving almost $5 billion in 3 years. It also helps IBM in its consultant services. However, there is more to e-business than just how many dollars per day IBM sells or saves on the Web. In the procurement area, for example, IBM is invoicing electronically to reduce the millions of paper invoices it sends out and to enable fast, competitive tendering from its suppliers. IBM has evaluated every step of the procurement process to determine where the use of the Web can add value. This has resulted in the identification of more than 20 initiatives—including collaboration with suppliers, online purchasing, and knowledge-management-based applications— in which the company can reduce cost and improve purchasing.

The major goal that IBM has set is to become the premier e-business. That means being the leader in each of the business-process areas outlined above. Leadership in these areas will improve customer satisfaction and will allow IBM to grow more profitably. As the recognized leader in e-business, IBM also adds tremendous credibility to its e-business marketing campaign.

Sources: ibm.com/procurement; ibm.com/ e-business and Bonnett (2000).

16.2   THE NEED FOR A STRATEGY

The opening vignette raises some interesting issues related to strategic planning for EC. First, IBM had a mission, to become a premier e-business. Second, it identified over 20 initiatives or applications to peruse. Third, IBM created an independent EC division; fourth, it introduced EC as a corporate culture; fifth, IBM leveraged its existing strengths; sixth, IBM tied EC with the reengineering of its processes; seventh, the company began with only seven out of the 20 EC initiatives; eighth, IBM decided to be an EC leader; and finally, it employed return on investment (ROI) as a criteria for selecting EC projects. These activities are typical activities taken by companies embarking on EC or e-business. Like any other significant project, and in EC too, it is necessary to have an EC corporate strategy. How to conduct an EC strategy is the subject of this chapter.

We distinguish several cases of **EC strategy** (or **e-strategy**)

- **Click-and-mortar companies that use several EC applications.** IBM and Qantas Airways are examples of companies that use this strategy. These large companies may consider a strategy that uses as many applications as possible, and they usually use a comprehensive strategy that determines the portfolio of applications, the priorities, and more.
- **Click-and-mortar companies that use only one or two EC applications.** In the late 1990s, many companies started EC by using it as an additional selling channel or for intrabusiness purposes. Over time, they may or may not add more applications. Companies such as Qantas Airways started this way, and only after a few years did they employ a comprehensive EC strategy as described in Chapter 1. In this case, the major strategic issue is when to add more applications and in what order.
- **Click-and-mortar companies that use one EC application that fundamentally changes all their business.** Examples are Schwab, which decided to sell online (Application Case 16.1), and Rosenbluth (see Chapter 2). In this case, the major strategic issue is basically "go or no go."
- **Pure-Play EC.** Companies that use this strategy include *Amazon.com* (Chapter 3), eVineyard (Chapter 12), and E*TRADE (Chapter 10). In such a case, the major strategy issue is how to survive.

APPLICATION CASE   16.1

Charles Schwab's EC Strategy

Charles Schwab is the world's largest discount stockbroker. On January 15, 1998, after conducting an opportunity analysis, Schwab launched *Schwab.com*, making the company one of the first click-and-mortar stockbrokers. The company decided to significantly drop its commission to $29.95 per transaction. This changed the company pricing structure radically, but the company decided to take a short-term revenue loss of $125 million to $150 million in order to gain a long-term strategic gain. The strategy paid off, and within a year Schwab handled over $81 billion on the Internet. This increased revenues by over $100 million a year and allowed for the 1,500 staff members and the technology required for the

APPLICATION CASE **16.1**

(continued)

project. The EC strategy fit well with the company's overall strategy that emphasizes a one-to-one relationship with its customers. Now Schwab can convey personalized information in real-time.

When Schwab embarked on EC, its competitors were offering significantly lower prices (Ameritrade, $8/transaction; E*TRADE, $15/transaction). But Schwab had the first mover advantage in securing key partnerships. Schwab maintained a competitive advantage by focusing on technology and innovation. For example, in November 2000, Schwab and Nextel agreed to build an infrastructure that will let customers perform investment functions through Web-enabled mobile phones or wireless handheld devices.

Schwab used a **value proposition** in its model as follows:

- **Target segments.** Existing off-line customers, trading customers with incomes over $150,000 a year, and those customers that buy and hold.
- **Key benefits.** Innovative products, superior service, low fees.
- **Supportive rationale.** Cutting-edge technology can be beneficial.

Schwab then moved to *products and services,* offering a large number of financial services online (e.g., life insurance, tax strategies, retirement planning, bill payments, after-hours trading, and even a college planner). In addition, all community services, from chat rooms to personalized services, are provided. To provide these services, Schwab partnered with content providers and with technology companies. It also planned a support resource system.

To assure financial viability, Schwab developed a financial model composed of three parts:

- **Revenue model.** Transaction fees, interest on margin loans to customers, etc.
- **Value model.** Schwab is known as a superb provider of the best information online, including personalized stock analysis, diversified stock analysis, and other services.
- **Growth model.** Schwab will create an online investment bank, online educational activities, and more. These are mostly provided by business partners.

Sources: Compiled from Pottruck and Pearce (2001) and *Schwab.com*

Several other cases and variations exist (e.g., see Plant, 2000, Kalakota and Robinson, 1999, and Deise et al., 2000).

It can be seen from the opening vignette that the executives of successful EC companies (IBM considers itself an e-business) seem to be *strategic thinkers* focusing on customers, markets, and competitive positioning, as well as on internal operations. Determination of a suitable EC strategy begins with identification of the opportunities and risks. The task of tracking changing environments, understanding customer groups, and devising methods of meeting the needs of customer groups, requires formulating strategies and planning their implementation.

Why Does a Company Need an E-Strategy?

EC initiatives are critical to the success or even the survival of many organizations. However, implementing EC initiatives can be a complex proposition. Therefore, a sound strategy, especially for large-scale or critical EC initiatives is needed.

Is an e-strategy always needed? Formal strategy in general is not always needed. Even some large companies can do without a strategy (e.g., see Semler, 2000). For SMEs, formal strategic planning can be too expensive, and it also may inhibit a quick adaptation to changing environments. However, in EC it may be too risky not to have some e-strategy. Many of the EC failures in the 2000–2001 period can be at least partially attributed to lack of strategy (Section 16.16). The fast changes in the business and technological environment are so vigorous that both the opportunities and the threats can change any minute. Therefore, any company considering EC must have at least some EC strategy that includes a contingency plan.

16.3   ESSENTIALS OF A BUSINESS STRATEGY

In order to understand how EC strategy is practiced, we will briefly review the essentials of generic business strategy.

Strategy Defined

A **strategy** is a broad-based formula for how a business is going to compete, what its goals should be, and what plans and policies will be needed to carry out those goals. *Strategy means a search for revolutionary actions that will significantly change the current position of a company, shaping its future.*

There are many ways to view strategies. For example, Porter (1996) views strategy as the creation of fit among a company's activities. Here are other definitions:

- Strategy is about finding the position in the marketplace that best fits a firm's skills. If there is no fit among activities, there is no distinctive strategy and little sustainability.
- A company's choice of a new position that must be driven by its ability to find new trade-offs and leverage a new system of complementary activities into a sustainable advantage.

Levels of Strategy

Strategy exists at various levels of an organization. In this chapter we will discuss issues related to the following levels:

- **Corporate (or organizational) strategy.** This is the strategy for the entire organization.
- **IT strategy.** This is the organizational strategy regarding IT.
- **EC strategy.** This is the corporate strategy regarding EC or e-business.
- **EC functional strategies.** These are strategies for each of the functional areas regarding EC, for example, a strategy regarding EC in marketing (e-marketing strategy).

The relationships among these strategies are displayed in Figure 16-1. The figure also shows typical output of the EC strategy.

Types of Strategy

Turban et al. (2002) view the following three types (dimensions) of strategy:

- **Strategic planning.** The major thrust here is preparing for the distant future, which means long-term planning.

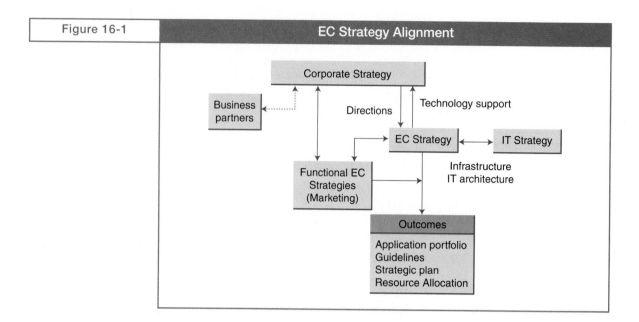

Figure 16-1

EC Strategy Alignment

- **Strategic response.** In today's turbulent environment it is often necessary to make strategic decisions in response to changes in the environment. Such changes can be a competitor's action, a technological innovation, a political development, or other event. This includes a contingency plan of "what if."
- **Strategic innovation.** Instead of waiting for some event that triggers a strategic response, an organization can be proactive and introduce an innovative strategy at any time that it finds an opportunity to do so.

The Elements of a Strategy

Strategy involves several elements or activities. Some of the most important ones are:

- **Forecasting.** Forecasting of the business, technological, political, economic, and other relevant environments.
- **Resource allocation.** Organizational resources are those owned, available to, and controlled by a company. They can be human, financial, technological, managerial, or knowledge. Resources need to be allocated so that the strategy is successful.
- **Core competency.** Core competency refers to the unique combination of the resources and experiences of a particular firm. It takes time to build these core competencies, and they are difficult to imitate. For example, a core competency of *Amazon.com* is to sell books online.
- **Strategy formulation.** Strategy formulation refers to the plan of how to get from the current position to the one desired by the strategy.
- **Environmental analysis.** Environmental analysis involves scanning the environment and collecting and interpreting relevant information. It is usually confined to the industry where the business belongs and is referred to as industry analysis.
- **Company analysis.** This analysis includes the business strategy, the capabilities, the constraints, and the strength and weaknesses.

Strategic Planning

Strategic planning is a formal process designed to interpret the organization's environment for the purpose of identifying its adaptive challenges and guiding its responses so as to optimize longer term competitive advantage. The strategic planning process involves the execution of activities such as the creation of a *mission statement,* development of goals, issuance of policies, and more.

The Strategy Landscape

Because there are so many types of strategies, levels, methodologies, and even definitions, it is difficult to have a single coherent view of the field. However, there are some major activities that are found in many formal strategic plans. These activities are organized here into four major phases and are shown in Figure 16-2. The major phases are:

- **Strategy initiation.** Here one prepares information about the organization's vision, mission, purpose, and the contribution of EC. It also includes environmental and company analyses, and it attempts to clarify the need for a formal strategy. Major goals are determined.
- **Strategy formulation.** This includes all the activities necessary to formulate a strategy, notably, identification of EC applications, cost-benefit analysis, risk analysis, and more. In the end, a list of candidate EC applications is created.
- **Strategy implementation.** Here the organization's resources are analyzed and a plan is developed for attaining the goals of the strategy. Options are

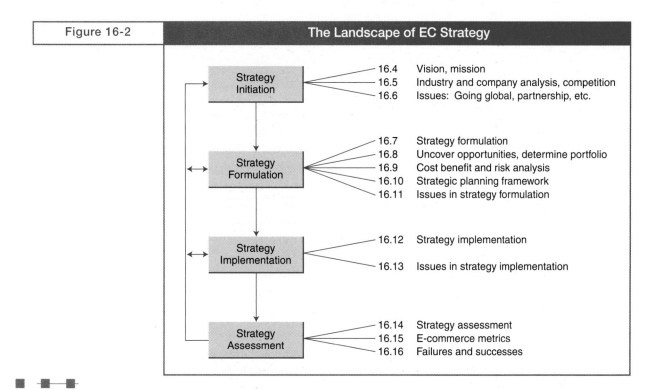

Figure 16-2	The Landscape of EC Strategy

Strategy Initiation
- 16.4 Vision, mission
- 16.5 Industry and company analysis, competition
- 16.6 Issues: Going global, partnership, etc.

Strategy Formulation
- 16.7 Strategy formulation
- 16.8 Uncover opportunities, determine portfolio
- 16.9 Cost benefit and risk analysis
- 16.10 Strategic planning framework
- 16.11 Issues in strategy formulation

Strategy Implementation
- 16.12 Strategy implementation
- 16.13 Issues in strategy implementation

Strategy Assessment
- 16.14 Strategy assessment
- 16.15 E-commerce metrics
- 16.16 Failures and successes

evaluated and specific milestones are established. Budget and other resources are planned for.

- **Strategy assessment.** Periodically, the progress toward the strategy's goals is assessed. Based on the results, actions are taken and the strategy is reformulated if needed. This phase involves the development of EC metrics (Section 16.15).

Note that Figure 16-2 provides a visual outline of this chapter, including specific section numbers. Methodologies and tools are available to support these phases. Some are described in this chapter.

Information Technology (IT) Strategy

EC strategy is either a subset of IT strategy (see Turban et al., 2002) or it is strongly correlated with it. Several reasons account for this situation:

- IT provides much of the infrastructure for EC. This infrastructure (e.g., databases, networks) is shared with non-EC applications.
- EC applications must be integrated with IT applications such as ERP, inventory control, and sales management.
- EC applications may replace or improve existing IT applications.
- EC organization may report to the CIO.
- Employees in the IS department work on EC applications.
- EC and IT may compete for the same organizational resources (e.g., budget).
- Some EC applications are designed to support the attainment of both business and IT goals.

Therefore, as shown in Figure 16-1, it is necessary to align both strategies.

E-Commerce Strategy

EC strategy can be very simple, or it can cover many topics. In Application Case 16.1 we provided an example of an EC strategy for Charles Schwab. A comprehensive EC strategy is also provided in the Real-World Case regarding Skymall, Inc., at the end of this chapter. Details of e-strategy in the private sector are usually considered propriety information and are not disclosed. In contrast, public organizations disclose their EC strategies. An interesting EC strategy of Malaysia is available at *malaysia.cnet.com/ ebusiness/ecommerce/* and that of the United Kingdom is at *e-envoy.gov.uk*.

COMPUTERIZED PLANNING OF E-STRATEGY

Several companies sell software that can help a company plan and write an e-strategy. One example is Web Strategy Pro from *paloalto.com*. It is a self-guided software program that allows a company to write its e-strategy as a business plan.

The details of EC strategy are the subject of the remaining sections of this chapter.

16.4   STRATEGY INITIATION

The first step in any strategy initiation is to review the organization's business and IT vision and mission. From there one can generate the vision and mission for EC. For example, for IBM (opening case), part of the EC mission is: "IBM plans to transform itself into an e-business in order to provide business value to the corporation and its shareholders." Although vision and mission statements are usually very vague, they do provide a springboard for generating more specific goals and objectives that are needed to initiate the strategy process. Examples of EC mission statements are given in Application Case 16.2.

Strategy initiation usually begin with an industry and competitive analysis.

APPLICATION CASE   16.2

A Sampler of EC Mission Statements

Here is a sampler of a variety of companies and their EC mission statements:

eBay.com

We help people trade practically anything on earth. eBay was founded with the belief that people are basically good. We believe that each of our customers, whether a buyer or a seller, is an individual who deserves to be treated with respect.

We will continue to enhance the online trading experiences of all— collectors, hobbyists, dealers, small business, unique item seekers, bargain hunters, opportunistic sellers, and browsers. The growth of the eBay community comes from meeting and exceeding the expectations these special people.

iopencommerce.com

We believe in providing you with the proper tools to overcome the complexities of the Internet. We achieve this by providing solutions that are based on open Internet standards that promote flexibility and compatibility with 100 percent of your potential online customers.

We believe that the Internet should not force your company to practice unprofitable business procedures. There must be a symbiotic (mutually beneficial) relationship between your on-line and off-line commerce.

We believe that you and your customers should experience a "user friendly environment that promotes simplicity and integrity."

Skymall, Inc.

Skymall is an integrated e-commerce specialty retailer committed to fostering a high-quality, one-to-one customer experience that exceeds expectations and engages customers in long-term relationships. We provide high-quality customer service and a vast selection of specialty products and services through unique channels and partnerships.

16.5   INDUSTRY, COMPANY, AND COMPETITIVE ANALYSIS

The purpose of this step is to analyze the position of the company in its industry and with respect to the competition. This is required for assessing the changes that the EC project may introduce and the chance for success. There are several methodologies for conducting such an analysis (e.g., see David, 1998; Shapiro and Varian, 1998; and

Kaplan and Norton, 2000a). A common way is to divide the analysis into three parts: industry assessment, company assessment, and competitiveness assessment.

Industry Assessment

Here one can conduct a diagnosis of items such as:

- What industry is the EC initiative is related to?
- Who are the customers (today and tomorrow)?
- What are the current practices of selling and buying?
- Who are the major competitors? How intense is the competition?
- What e-strategies are used and by whom?
- How is value added throughout the value chain?
- What are the major opportunities and threats?
- Are there any metrics or best practices in place?
- What are existing and potential partnerships for EC?
- Who are the major EC vendors in the industry?

As indicated earlier, one may use software for conducting this and other steps of the analysis. For further details and examples see Hackbarth and Kettinger (2000) and Plant (2000).

Company Assessment

In assessment, company analysis an investigation is made regarding the company's business strategy, performance, customers, partners, and so on. Examples of the activities in this area is provided in Figure 16-3.

Competitive Assessment

Information collected on the industry and company assessments are combined for evaluation. This can be done with methodologies such as SWOT.

SWOT ANALYSIS

SWOT is an acronym used to describe particular Strengths, Weaknesses, Opportunities, and Threats. The external environment consists of *opportunities* and *threats* that are outside the organization and are not typically within the short-run control of top management. These can be related to the corporate *strengths* and *weaknesses* in a four-cell matrix, as shown in Figure 16-4 (p. 684). This matrix is referred to as the SWOT matrix.

The elements of SWOT are the following:

- In the Opportunities (O) block, the external current and future opportunities available to the company are examined.
- In the Threats (T) block, the external threats facing the company now and in the future are analyzed.
- In the Strengths (S) block, the specific areas of current and future strengths for the company are described.
- In the Weaknesses (W) block, the specific areas of current and future weakness for the company are stated.

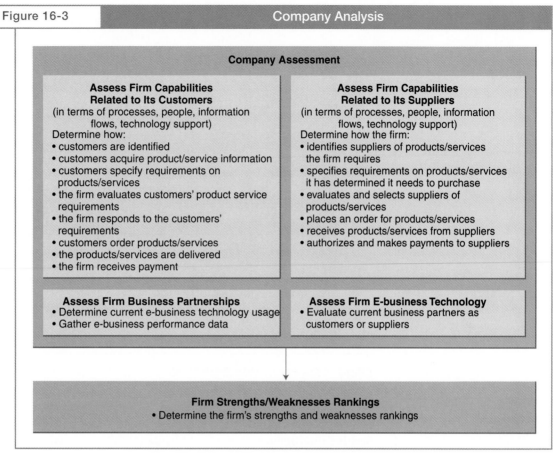

Figure 16-3   Company Analysis

Source: Hackbarth and Kettinger (2000), p. 85. Reprinted with permission of William J. Kettinger.

Thus, there are four cells in the matrix:

1. The opportunities as they relate to the company's strengths (OS)
2. The opportunities as they relate to the company's weaknesses (OW)
3. The threats as they relate to the company's strengths (TS)
4. The threats as they relate to the company's weaknesses (TW)

For example, the study may discover an opportunity to sell the company products online directly to consumers. The threat may come from the existing distributors or from spreading some corporate resources too thin. A strength can also be the ability of the company's programmers to build the application quickly, whereas a weakness may be a lack of experience in database integration. The SWOT analysis supports environmental scanning and interpretation, which can be facilitated by using the Internet. (For an example how this can be done in EC see Hackbarth and Kettinger, 2000).

In conducting the industry analysis, it is useful to employ some kind of competitive intelligence. This can be facilitated by using the Internet.

COMPETITIVE INTELLIGENCE ON THE INTERNET

Competitive intelligence is an integral part of strategic planning and can be conducted by conventional methods and by using the Internet.

Figure 16-4	SWOT Diagram

Internal Factors / External Factors	Strengths (S)	Weaknesses (W)
Opportunities (O)	**SO Strategies** Generate strategies here that use strengths to take advantage of opportunities	**WO Strategies** Generate strategies here that take advantage of opportunities by overcoming weaknesses
Threats (T)	**ST Strategies** Generate strategies here that use strengths to avoid threats	**WT Strategies** Generate strategies here that minimize weaknesses and avoid threats

Source: Strategic Management and Business Policy: Entering 21st Century Global 7e by Wheelen and Hunger © 1996. Reprinted with permission of Pearson Education Inc., Upper Saddle River, NJ.

The Internet can play a major role as a source of competitive information (competitive intelligence), and plays an increasingly important role in supporting **competitive intelligence**. Power and Sharda (1997) proposed a framework in which Internet capabilities are shown to provide information for strategic decisions. According to the framework, the external information required and the methods of acquiring such information can be supported by the Internet and the strategic planning process. The following Internet tools are available for competitive analysis:

- **Review competitors' Web sites.** Such visits can reveal information about new products or projects, potential alliances, trends in budgeting, advertising strategies used, financial strength, and much more.
- **Analyze related newsgroups.** Internet newsgroups help you find out what people think about a company and its products. For example, newsgroup participants state what they like or dislike about products provided by you and your competitors. You can also examine people's reactions to a new idea by posting a question.
- **Examine publicly available financial documents.** This can be accomplished by entering a number of databases. While some databases charge nominal fees, others are free. The most notable is the Securities and Exchange Commission EDGAR database (*gov/edgarhp.htm*).
- **Ask the customers.** You can give prizes to those visitors of your and your competitor's Web site who best describe the strengths and weaknesses of your competitor's products.
- **Information delivery services.** Use an information delivery service (such as Info Wizard, My Yahoo!, or Webcast) to find out what is published on

the Internet, including newsgroup correspondence, about your competitors and their products. Known as push technologies, these services provide any desired information including news, some in real-time, for free or for a nominal fee.

- **Corporate research companies.** Companies such as Dun & Bradstreet and Standard and Poor's provide information ranging from risk analysis to stock market analysts' reports about your competitors, for a fee. These are available electronically.
- **Chat Rooms.** Solicit opinions in chat rooms concerning your company, your competitors, or some other related communities.

Note that overreliance on such information can be dangerous. The problem is that by searching the overwhelming amount of data, one assumes that everything that could be learned has been found. Using publicly available search engines is free, but may produce lots of irrelevant information. Even advanced search engines such as *google.com* and the use of an indexing approach (such as Yahoo!) may not be sufficient or effective. Therefore, the use of specialty-built agents may be needed, as was done in the forest industry in Finland (Application Case 16.3).

APPLICATION CASE   16.3

Intelligent Agents in the Forest Industry

The pulp and paper industry includes major competitors from paper producing countries, small numbers of high-volume products, several industry and trade associations, suppliers of machines, energy, wood, etc. Both government agencies and environmentalists are watching the industry, closely imposing constraints on the business. To improve decision making in the industry, several intelligent agents were developed at the Institute for Advanced Management Systems Research at Abo Akademi University, Finland. One of these agents is monitoring, while another one is doing the interpretation (Liu et al., 2000). The scanning agent goes to predetermined databases and news services and finds information, such as pricing data. Pricing managers can find details via hyperlinks. The first-generation agents developed in the late 1990s worked with keywords and were basically specialized search engines that were programmed to find information within given parameters. The information was organized in a personalized "newspaper" for each manager.

The second-generation agents deal with interpretation of information and identification of events that bring meaning out of observations, assess the impacts, discover plausible relationships and structures, and assemble a conceptual scheme. The interpretation tasks include:

- Identify events and trends in data
- Determine the probability of an occurrence and the likely time of all major relevant events
- Assess the impact of major events
- Propose action/reaction strategies

Agents of this kind are not as accurate as humans are, but they are much faster and cheaper.

Source: Compiled from Liu et al. (2000).

CUSTOMIZED COMPETITIVE INTELLIGENCE

Current information about companies can be found in their press releases and information they publish on their Web sites. Several vendors offer free push technology services (Chapter 5) to inform users of the latest news on many companies. For example, Yahoo! provides a free service called "netcenter" that delivers up-to-date news on companies and topics selected by users. Also, online databases are a good source of information, especially for background research. However, they may not be the best source for fresh information. In response to the pressure of competition, commercial databases are beginning to incorporate push technology into their offerings. For example, Dialog Web (*dialogweb.com*) allows users to request updates of topics and have the latest records automatically delivered to users' e-mail addresses. Market research firms provide customized competitive intelligence for a fee.

However, for competitive intelligence professionals, Internet-based searches may not replace in-depth background research, but rather keep one up-to-date on current events within the search parameters. Despite the promise to reduce information overload, customized push technology has its downside. Users still tend to be overwhelmed by the delivered content, of which 90 percent may be irrelevant. This may be controlled by carefully monitoring the information specifications and continually editing and refining the search parameters.

In addition to push technology, business intelligence companies offer packaged competitive analysis. For example, *companysleuth.com* provides a wide variety of economic and legal information about companies, and *IDC.com* provides a rich set of market data and insight for competitive intelligence. Companies such as Fuld (*fuld.com*) or IDC, specializing in competitive intelligence, can be timely and effective sources of information for strategic decision making.

Once the preliminary analysis is completed, one can move to strategy formulation. However, before we do that, let's look at representative strategic issues that need to be clarified at this stage.

16.6   ISSUES IN STRATEGY INITIATION

Companies considering or using EC may have several strategic initiation issues. The major representative ones are discussed here.

To Be a First Mover or a Follower?

Is there a real advantage to being the first mover? In EC the answer is "maybe." Several first movers succeeded, but many failed (see Chapter 3 and Section 16.16). Pioneering companies such as Point Casting, eToy, and Chemdex went bankrupt or changed their operations. On the other hand, Ariba, eBay, VeriSign, and others are doing extremely well. Other pioneering companies such as *Amazon.com* may go either way. In addition to new Internet companies, established companies may assume leadership roles, as shown in Application Case 16.4.

The major advantages of being a first mover are:

- Chance to capture large market share
- Establishing a brand name
- Establishing exclusive strategic alliances

APPLICATION CASE 16.4

Examples of Market Leaders

Market leaders do not need to establish themselves in large markets to have a significant presence on the Internet, as we show in Chapter 18. An example of a market leader in a niche market is Virtual Vineyards (*evineyard.com*), the online seller of premium and specialty wines and foods. Another type of market leader is one that retains its off-line establishments, but intends to be a major player online, utilizing its off-line retail power on the Internet. Schwab, Land's End, Home Depot, Staples, and Tower Records are good examples of such leadership. Though *CDNow.com* was first on the Net, Tower quickly established a sizable presence and captured a large portion of the market share. Staples, Tower, Wal-Mart, Toys R Us, and others remain major players in the physical retail establishment arena but have broadened their business scope by retailing on the Internet. *Rowe.com* (Chapter 10) is another market leader with intentions of keeping its off-line facilities. The company markets a periodical and journal purchasing service to libraries, offering both on- and off-line technologies to facilitate intermediary activities between libraries and magazine publishers. *Rowe.com* has a competitive advantage in that they have had no significant off-line competition; now, any competitor establishing an online presence must sell both its name and the magazines at the same time, which is quite a formidable task. A similar case is Skymall (see Real-World Case 16.2). Finally Barnes & Noble created a powerful separate online business that in 1999 recaptured market share from *Amazon.com*.

The major disadvantages are:

- The cost of developing the EC initiative is usually very high
- The chance of failure is high
- The system may be obsolete as compared to the second wave of arrivals
- No support services are available at the beginning

A comparison between leader and follower strategies is provided in Table 16-1.

Large companies such as IBM, Oracle, Intel, and SAP are more likely to be first movers, but they may lack the flexibility and the innovation of start-ups.

What Do You Need an EC for?

A strategy is based on the organization's mission that states the purpose for the organization's existence. The mission may tell you what the company is providing through EC. Based on its EC mission, a company will formulate the objectives of each EC project. An EC objective is the measurable goal that the company wants to achieve with EC. First, a business should think about what it intends to accomplish by establishing EC. Determining the purpose of the site provides the initial framework for a company's EC strategy. In the strategy initiation the expectations need to be spelled out. Major EC contributions can be:

- Enhancing the sell channel by advertisement and sales
- Enhancing the buy (procurement channel)
- Enhancing the customer service channel
- Facilitating value-chain integration

TABLE 16-1

Comparing a Follower vs. a Leader Position in EC

	Be a Follower	Be a Leader
Customer Service	• Significant capability to increase customer service/intimacy	• New dimension in customer care
Price	• Reduced by cost efficiencies passed through to the customer	• Significant decrease • Source of competitive advantage for entire value chain
Quality	• Somewhat of an increase due to customer self-service	• Increased through standardized customer interface and automated processes
Fulfillment Time	• Decreased due to internal process theoretical minimum	• Drastically increased • Source of customer loyalty
Agility	• Increased through standardization of data formats and interoperability	• New strategies enabled
Time to Market	• Decreased through knowledge management and extended access to information throughout the company	• Greatly enhanced • Long-term advantages gained in the short term
Market Reach	• Increased • Defense of current reach likely	• Rapid geographic increase • Incremental penetration of "markets of one" served by competitors as market segments

Source: Compiled from Raisch (2000), pp. 202 and 203.

- Providing for new products and services
- Going into highly specialized markets (e.g., *dogtoys.com*)
- Going into mass customization (e.g., *Jaguar.com*, *dell.com*)

At this early stage, it is critical to clarify what the purpose of EC is.

Going Global

Going global on a large scale is a strategic issue. For example, Lego of Denmark elected to go global selectively (a few countries, a few products). The issues involved in deciding whether or not to go global are presented in Chapter 18. The strategy regarding going global is important enough to be a part of the strategy initiation.

Should You Have a Separate Online Company or Not?

When the volume of e-business is large, the temptation to create a separate company increases, especially if you can take it to an IPO. Barnes and Noble did just that. The advantages of creating a separate company are:

- Reducing or eliminating internal conflicts
- Providing more freedom for the online company's management in pricing, advertising, and other decisions
- You may create a new brand quickly
- You may take the e-business to an IPO, and if successful, make a fortune

The disadvantages of creating an independent division are:

- It may be very costly and risky
- Collaboration with the off-line business may be difficult
- You lose the expertise of the business functions (marketing, finance, distribution), unless you get superb collaboration

Several spin-offs, such as *barnesandnoble.com*, are not doing well, and *Grainger.com* has merged back into its parent company. Very few spin-off online companies have succeeded thus far.

Should You Merge?

An alternative to a joint venture is a complete merger. This strategy was pursued aggressively during the EC consolidation period in 2000 and 2001.

Once the preliminary analysis using SWOT or other methodologies is completed and the EC venture looks promising, we can proceed to strategy formulation.

16.7   STRATEGY FORMULATION

Based on the results of the analysis of the industry and competition, an EC strategy plan can be developed. Strategy formulation is the development of long-range and strategic plans for the effective management of environmental opportunities and threats, in light of corporate strengths and weaknesses. It includes examining or redefining the EC mission by specifying achievable objectives, developing strategies, and setting implementation guidelines for EC. It should be noted that "going EC" can be done in many ways, as demonstrated throughout this book. Strategy formulation is relevant both for going EC in general and for individual EC projects.

A strategy is a plan designed to help a company meet its goals. For example, a strategy might be to utilize a Web-based call center to enhance customer service. *Amazon.com*'s product diversification is an example of better utilization of IBM's resources, done as part of its overall strategy.

In strategy formulation, we need to provide answers to questions such as: Does your business have a product or a process that is a good candidate for EC? The usual examples of good candidates to sell are commodities—a commodity is a product that the buyer knows, such as books, CDs, stock purchasing, and travel tickets. If your particular product can be shipped easily or transmitted electronically, it targets knowledgeable buyers, and its price falls within a certain range, then it is also a good candidate for EC.

Unfortunately, many companies approach EC with no clear idea of where they are going. Often, they view the industry leaders' accomplishments superficially and try to imitate the front-runners. Such a shortsighted view may well be a waste of resources. What they fail to consider is the level of commitment to organizational redefinition that must occur behind the scenes. Attributing the success of an EC strategy to skillful marketing and wishful thinking is an illusion. Unless companies plan and redesign their organizations appropriately, EC implementation may not be followed by sales or cost reductions.

Strategy formulation includes several topics, and as a result is cumbersome. To help in focusing on the essentials, one can use a methodology such as that of the critical success factors (CSF), described next.

Critical Success Factors for EC

Critical success factors are the indispensable business, technology, and human factors that help an organization achieve its desired goals. Ghosh (1998) suggested a set of questions a company can ask that consider how EC can benefit its customers.

For example, the following are questions to consider when cost reduction and service enhancement are considered.

- How can I use the information I have about individual customers to make it easier for them to do business with me?
- How much does it cost me to provide services that customers could get by themselves over the Internet?
- What help can I give customers by using the experience of other customers or the expertise of my employees?
- Will I be at a significant disadvantage if my competitors provide these capabilities to customers before I do?

The answers to such questions can help plan for EC better and identify EC opportunities.

Several CSFs may be relevant to EC projects. For example, in addition to organization, customer, and supplier aspects, issues such as technology and information availability and human resources should not be underestimated as potential CSFs.

Several CSFs can be identified for specific circumstances. Some major CSFs for EC are:

- Specific products or services traded
- Top management support
- Project team reflecting various functional areas
- Technical infrastructure
- Customer acceptance
- User-friendly Web interface
- Integration with corporate legacy systems
- Security and control of the EC system
- Competition and market situation
- Pilot project and corporate knowledge
- Promotion and internal communication
- Cost of the EC project
- Level of trust between buyers and sellers

16.8   DISCOVERING EC OPPORTUNITIES AND DECIDING ON A PORTFOLIO

Finding appropriate EC opportunities may not be an easy task. There are dozens of possible initiatives, and companies must decide on which ones to adopt and in what order.

It is well known that only a few business investments are 100 percent safe, and in the digital economy the uncertainty level is high, so even the most robust traditional planning tools may not work. As a result, companies often make one of the following three mistakes in allocating their EC investment (per Tjan, 2001):

1. **Let a thousand flowers bloom.** Meaning, fund many projects indiscriminately. Experiment with many, hoping that the majority will succeed. This seldom happens.
2. **Bet it all.** Put everything on a single high-stake initiative. This is very risky. If you wager it all, you may lose it all.
3. **Trend-surf.** Follow the crowd toward the next "big thing," the most fashionable one. Then, too much capital ends up pursuing too few opportunities, or too much competition is created.

These mistakes can be very costly. Therefore, companies use a systematic approach in which they discover opportunities, as described in this section, and then evaluate them and prioritize them (next section).

Generally speaking, companies use one of the following approaches, which are shown in Figure 16-5, to find individual EC initiatives:

Problem-driven. In this case, organizations have a problem such as excess inventory or delays in deliveries. In such a case, an EC application may be attempted in order to solve the problem. An example is the GM case in Chapter 6. GM had a problem disposing of old equipment—the solution was found in forward e-auctions. They also had a problem in conducting RFQs manually—they were too slow and didn't bring enough bidders. The solution to this was reverse auctions.

Technology-driven. In this case, technology exists and the company is trying to use it. In doing so, the company may find problems that no one knew existed. An example of this is shown in the IBM opening case. IBM had the technology on hand. The strategy was to find as many areas to apply it to as possible. This approach is usually used by first movers and industry leaders.

Market-driven. In this case, the company is waiting to see what the competitors in the industry are doing. When one or more competitors start to use EC, and it seems that they are doing well, it is time to follow suit. Toys R Us followed eToys, Barnes and Noble followed *Amazon.com*, banks followed the virtual banks, and Merrill Lynch followed E*TRADE and Ameritrade.

Fear- or greed-driven. Here, companies are either so scared that they are afraid that if they do not practice EC they will be big losers, or they think that they can make lots of money by going EC. In such a case, they are afraid to "miss the boat," jumping to inappropriate ventures frequently.

Finding the right initiatives is very critical. Between 1997 and 2000 many companies dumped large amounts of money into ill-fated EC initiatives.

Two interrelated strategic issues are involved here. One is finding potential opportunities. The second one is deciding upon an appropriate **portfolio strategy**, namely, which initiatives to pursue and when.

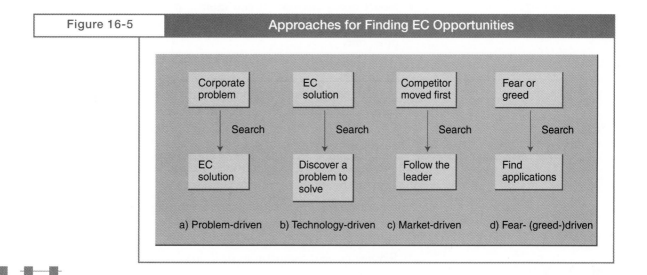

| Figure 16-5 | Approaches for Finding EC Opportunities |

a) Problem-driven   b) Technology-driven   c) Market-driven   d) Fear- (greed-)driven

A company may use any of the approaches listed earlier or similar ones. To implement EC, the company can create a special team, use brainstorming sessions, or hire a consultant. Creativity, knowledge of the market and the technology, discussions with vendors, use of analogies from other industries—all can be used. Actually, the process is similar to finding any other business opportunities. Let's look at this topic more closely.

Uncovering Specific EC Opportunities and Applications

Many companies are eager to know what the right opportunities are and what applications they should develop. The answers to such questions are not simple. It requires an understanding of how digital markets operate, how Internet customers behave, how competition is created, what infrastructure is needed, what the dynamics of EC are, and much more. Once a company has this understanding, it can begin mapping opportunities that match current competencies and markets.

It is interesting to note that in addition to just selling existing products/services on the Internet, there are many opportunities to create new products and services, some of which are unrelated to an existing business. For example, Fruit of the Loom developed Web sites for their wholesalers. Then they created a special organization that develops Web sites for any company that wants to develop one for its own wholesalers. In other words, they created a software and Web development business. One can organize the market and/or the sellers and/or the buyers. Opportunities have been pointed out by several researchers and consultants. For example, Mougayar (1998) suggests the following:

- **Matchmaking.** Matching buyers' needs with products and services from sellers, without former knowledge of either one.
- **Aggregation of services.** Combines several existing services to create a new service or category that didn't exist before.
- **Bid/ask engine.** Creates a demand/supply floating pricing system in which buyers and sellers bid and/or ask for prices (e.g., *Priceline.com*).
- **Notification service.** Tells you when the service becomes available, when it becomes cheaper, or when it goes on sale in your neighborhood.
- **Smart needs adviser.** "If you want it at this price, you have to wait until September; if you want this service, you may also want to consider this other one."
- **Negotiation.** Price, quantity, or features are negotiated according to a set of parameters.
- **Up-sell.** Suggests an additional product or service, so that if you buy both, you get a combined discount or an additional benefit.
- **Consultative adviser.** "Here's a tip on this new service you're about to purchase."

The process of finding EC applications is similar to the process of finding any IT applications. Some approaches to consider are:

- Brainstorming by a group of employees using a variety of methods, including electronic group support systems.
- Soliciting the help of experts, such as consultants.
- Reviewing what competitors are doing.

- Asking vendors to provide you with suggestions.
- Reading the literature to find out what's going on.
- Using analogies from similar industries or business processes.
- Using a conventional requirement analysis approach.

Determining an Appropriate EC Application Portfolio

For years companies were attempting to find the most appropriate portfolio of projects among which an organization should share its limited resources. The classical portfolio strategy attempted to balance investments with different characteristics, combining for example, long-term speculative investments in new potentially high-growth businesses with short-term investments in existing, profit-making businesses. The most well known framework of this strategy is Boston Consulting Group's matrix with its *cash cows, starts, questionable projects,* and *dogs.* A similar approach for EC was developed by Tjan.

TJAN'S PORTFOLIO STRATEGY

Tjan (2001) adopted the Boston Consulting Group's approach to create an Internet portfolio. However, instead of trading off industry growth and market position, here the strategy is based on *company fit,* which can be either low or high, and the project's *viability,* which can also be low or high. Together these create an *Internet portfolio map.*

Viability can be assessed by four criteria: market value potential, time to positive cash flow, personal requirements, and funding requirements. EC initiatives such as B2B procurement sites, B2C stores, portals for kids, etc., can be evaluated on a scale of 1–100, based on their ranking on each criteria. Then, an average score per criteria is computed (simple average). For **fit**, the following criteria are used: alignment with core capabilities, alignment with other company initiatives, fit with organizational structure, fit with company's culture and values, and ease of technical implementation. Again, each EC initiative is assessed on a scale of 1–100 (or on a qualitative scale of high, medium, low), and an average is computed. The various initiatives are then mapped on the Internet portfolio matrix, based on the two average scores. The Internet matrix is divided into four cells as shown in Figure 16-6. If both viability and fit are low, the project is *killed.* If both are high, then the project is *adopted.* If fit is high, but viability is low, the project is sent to *redesign.* Finally, if the fit is low but the viability is high, the project is to be sold to someone, or *spun off.* Figure 16-6 shows how several applications were rated for an e-marketplace for toys.

This method introduces a systematic approach to EC project selection. The assessment of the points per criteria can be done by several experts to assure quality. Cases where there is more agreement can be considered with more confidence. Organizations can add their own criteria to the methodology. Also, one can place important weights on the criteria, calculating a weighted rather than a simple average.

OTHER APPROACHES

Another model that can be used to determine the fate of an EC application was suggested by McFarlan (1984). According to this model, applications are sorted into four possible cells: *strategic, high potential, key operational,* and *support.*

Figure 16-6 Application Portfolio Map in Hypothetical Toy Manufacturer

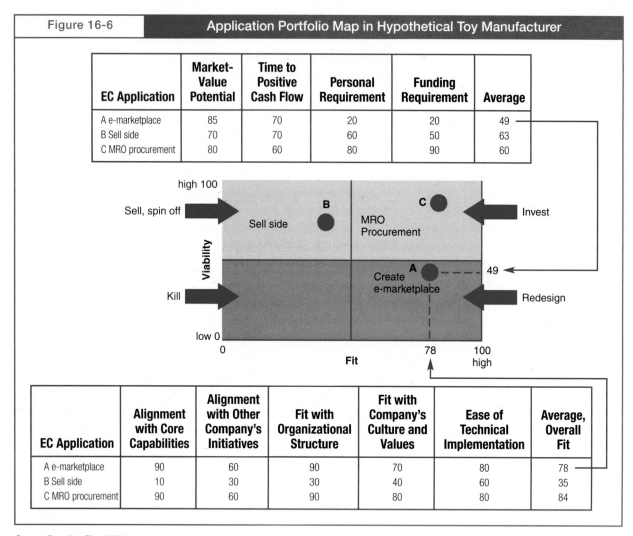

EC Application	Market-Value Potential	Time to Positive Cash Flow	Personal Requirement	Funding Requirement	Average
A e-marketplace	85	70	20	20	49
B Sell side	70	70	60	50	63
C MRO procurement	80	60	80	90	60

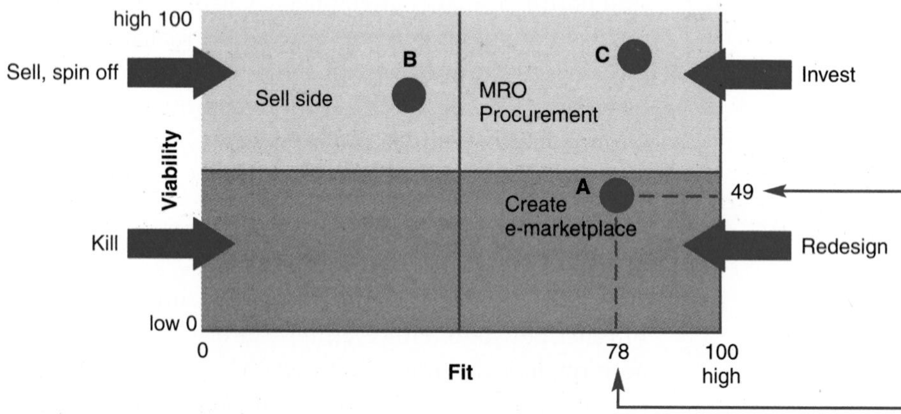

EC Application	Alignment with Core Capabilities	Alignment with Other Company's Initiatives	Fit with Organizational Structure	Fit with Company's Culture and Values	Ease of Technical Implementation	Average, Overall Fit
A e-marketplace	90	60	90	70	80	78
B Sell side	10	30	30	40	60	35
C MRO procurement	90	60	90	80	80	84

Source: Based on Tjan (2001).

Which Business Model to Use?

The issue of uncovering opportunities is related to the issue of which EC business model(s) to use. EC implementation can be done in several ways. A typical choice is that of Schubb Corp., which is shown in Application Case 16.5.

APPLICATION CASE 16.5

Strategic Directions at Schubb Corp.

Schubb Corp., a 115-year-old property and casualty insurance company, reviewed three EC strategies:

1. Create a new business model with EC as a major driver.
2. Spawn a secondary business model around EC; go directly to consumers.
3. Use EC as a tool within the existing business model.

APPLICATION CASE   16.5

(continued)

The first option was quickly discarded; the company had a successful business model with products matching distribution systems. The company sells differentiated products that require some degree of explanation and a deep understanding of customers' needs. Therefore, there is no logic in discontinuing a successful model.

The second model looked promising, but management did not want to disrupt the excellent relationship they had with their agents and brokers. It also required building an infrastructure: a call center staffed around the clock, technologies for processing tasks that agents and brokers traditionally did, and more.

The company opted for the third alternative. This EC initiative helped Schubb to further differentiate its products and services, basically by providing superb customer service over the Internet. Schubb opened several Web sites, one for each special interest group (e.g., for wine collectors).

Customers can view the status of their claims, and commercial clients can view their policies in full. Also, commercial customers are permitted into the data warehouse to view and use analytical tools to examine their policy-usage records.

The Web enabled superb communication with agents and business partners and allowed business expansion into 20 countries. Services include form creation, certification, validation, and more. A special value was the service to multinational corporations, which must be insured in several countries where different insurance regulations exist.

Source: Condensed from special supplement in *itol.com* (May 1, 1999).

USE OF METRICS

The strategic, tactical, and operational decisions about EC can often be facilitated by comparisons to industry standards. The standards against which a company can compare its EC strategy as well as its performance are called **metrics**. This topic is discussed in Section 16.15.

16.9   COST-BENEFIT AND RISK ANALYSIS

Executives need to be sure that EC initiatives can truly enhance their company's ability to generate revenues and reduce cost, thereby increasing competitiveness and profits. The process of doing so is referred to as the **business case** for EC.

The Business Case for EC

Managers use a business case approach for garnering funding for projects by providing *justification* for investments. The business case provides the bridge between the EC plan (or blueprint) and the execution. A good business case provides the foundation for tactical decision making and technology risk management. The business case helps to clarify how the organization will use its resources in the best way to accomplish the e-strategy.

THE CONTENT OF AN E-BUSINESS CASE

The content of an e-business case includes assessment of the project feasibility, the preliminary scope of the project, and the justification. It should show that EC investment is consistent with the overall business strategy. It should also show that the initiative will be managed efficiently. Kalakota and Robinson (1999) suggested the following four interrelated dimensions for an e-business case:

1. **Strategic justification—"where are we going?"** Capabilities, competitive landscape, market gap, and more. (What is the idea, how will customers be selected, and what is the value proposition?)
2. **Generational justification—"how will we get there?"** What will be done and how improvements will be made (channel and partner selection).
3. **Technical justification—"when will we get there?"** How EC will support the organization's technology strategy (technology and project selection).
4. **Financial justification—"why will we win?"** What are the costs and benefits, what measurements and metrics are used, and how is our business different?

HOW TO CONDUCT AN E-BUSINESS CASE

Per Kalakota and Robinson (1999), the following steps may be considered in preparing an e-business case:

- Develop a goal statement
- Set measurable goals
- Set objectives
- Develop short- and long-term action plans
- Gain approval and support

For additional discussion see Plant (2000).

REVENUE MODEL

One of the most critical success factors is to properly plan the revenue model. Many of the EC failures in 2000 and 2001 can be attributed to an incorrect revenue model. For example, many portals expected large revenues to come from advertisement. This was not the case. Revenues from sales depend on customer acquisition costs and on advertisement. Have you figured it into your analysis?

Cost-Benefit and Risk Analysis

Like any other investment, investment in EC, either as an EC start-up or an e-procurement application in a click-and-mortar company, must go through the scrutiny of cost-benefit analysis and justification.

It is difficult to justify EC investment due to the many intangible variables. The following methods were proposed by Turban et al. (2002):

- Value analysis and proposition
- Rate of return on investment (ROI) and/or discounted cash flow
- Real options valuation and analysis
- Management by maxim
- Information economics

Let's look at the first three methods.

VALUE ANALYSIS AND PROPOSITION

Value proposition refers to the benefit a company can derive from using EC, usually by increasing its competitiveness and by providing a better service to its customers. When customers use the Internet to conduct business, a new value for the selling company is created, and if the customers move from a competitor, this competitor may suffer a loss. One approach that can be used to assess the desirability of EC is to employ a **value chain analysis** (Porter, 1985). A **value chain** represents a series of activities a company performs to achieve its goal(s) at various stages of the production process, from resource acquisition to product delivery (see the discussion in Chapter 2). The added value of these activities contributes to profit and enhances the asset value as well as the competitive position of the company in the market. To examine the implications of an EC project on the value chain of the products and services the company offers, one may answer value chain questions such as those proposed by Ghosh (1998).

Representative Questions for Clarifying Value Chain Statements

- Can I realize significant margins by consolidating parts of the value chain (such as inventory control) for my customers?
- Can I create significant value for customers by reducing the number of entities they have to deal with in the value chain?
- What additional skills do I need to develop in order to take over the functions of others in my value chain?
- Will I be at a competitive disadvantage if someone else moves first to consolidate the value chain?

Representative Questions for Creating New Values

- Can I offer additional information regarding transaction services to my existing customer base?
- Can I address the needs of new customer segments by repackaging my current information assets or by creating new business propositions using the Internet?
- Can I use my ability to attract customers to generate new sources of revenue, such as advertising or sales of complementary products?
- Will my current business be significantly harmed by other companies providing some of the value I currently offer on an à la carte basis?

Another factor to consider is the relative position of the company in its industry's competitive market. One way for an EC vendor to achieve a more advantageous position is to differentiate itself by providing superior service at every point of contact with customers.

While the foregoing discussion emphasizes customer contact in the value chain, interaction with suppliers in the earlier stages of the chain can also significantly improve the efficiency of operation. Furthermore, such efficiency may be achieved by cost and time reduction, but it often requires changes in the company's organizational infrastructure as well as business procedures. Looking at value added activities provides only one aspect of EC justification.

THE RETURN ON INVESTMENT (ROI)

The **return on investment (ROI)** is a ratio of the cost of resources required to the benefits generated by the EC project. It includes both quantifiable and nonquantifiable (intangible) benefits. Although the cost of resources, such as hardware, software, and human resources for an EC project is relatively easy to quantify, the returns (benefits) are difficult to measure, as seen in many other information technology projects. Primary **intangible benefits** include an effective marketing channel, increased sales, and superior customer service. Even profit, which is easier to measure, may be difficult to forecast in EC due to lack of experience and fast-changing conditions. As an example of the difficulties in computing the ROI, let us look at the case of collaborative commerce at Lockheed Martin (Application Case 16.6).

APPLICATION CASE 16.6

Lockheed Martin Uses Collaborative Commerce to Compete

To win a tactical fighter prototype contract from the Department of Defense (DOD) against Boeing, Lockheed Martin had to stay within the DOD's $28 million to $35 million per aircraft budget. To reduce the cost of collaborating with its subcontractors, Robert Stephens, Lockheed's IS manager, turned to a collaborative EC solution using an extranet. The secured Web site he deployed let managers at Lockheed's headquarters in Fort Worth, Texas, share project management updates with design teams at British Aerospace Ltd. in the United Kingdom and Northrop Grumman Corp. in Southern California.

In order to win future contracts, Stephens has to document all productivity gains attributable to EC. As collaborative projects grow in scope and expense, he faces increased pressure to show bottom-line returns on the investment in EC. While business partners/subcontractors are happy, it is not exactly clear how many new orders this happiness will generate. Also, it is not clear how many dollars an EC solution can shave off the cost of doing business. If the investment in EC has been money well spent, Stephens wants his superiors and customers to know about it.

Measuring EC payoff is tricky; benefits are spread across functional units inside the company, and synergy with suppliers may generate benefits, too. The speed that the latter accrues depends on how quickly outsiders are willing to change the way they do business. Stephens also found major savings in intrabusiness EC, such as travel and training. "We're bringing in expertise when we need it, where we need it, without having to fly someone here to work side by side with us." For example, when a multicompany team writes a specification for a new part of a plane, the extranet serves as a common workplace, storing the input of everyone involved. When Lockheed engineers are on the road, they have instant access to relevant project data without the need to have a special hookup to Lockheed's private network. Even training courses, which used to be held offsite, are now available over the extranet.

Overall, Lockheed Martin management believes that the benefits of EC are enormous and the collaborative commerce strategy was right and inevitable for survival.

Sources: Misc. press releases at *lockheedmartin.com* (1998–2001).

The toughest part about calculating ROI for collaborative commerce, for example, is assessing the EC impact on business processes internally and across organizational boundaries. How do you measure the gains in such a case? Is it possible to quantify the benefits? Although ROI projections play a critical role in investment decision making, many of the critical benefits may not be easily converted to numbers. Measuring benefits and figuring ROI is difficult but essential for launching EC projects (e.g., Folz, 1999, and Whipple, 1999).

OPTIONS VALUATION

Of special interest is the adaptation of option valuation and analysis to emerging growth companies by Rayport and Jaworski (2001). The concept of option valuation is well known in stocks, commodities, and other markets. People are willing to pay a premium today for a stock they believe will increase in value in the future. To determine the option pricing, Rayport and Jaworski used a four-step process, shown in Figure 16-7, for assessing the value of an Internet company that requested $600 million from a suitor. The discounted cash value indicated that the company's value was $69 million. However, using the option approach, the value was computed at $443 million.

OTHER METHODS

One attempt to address the cost-benefit issue in IT in general was made by Parker (1996), who classified generic IT values and risks into (a) values: *financial, strategic,* and *stakeholder;* and (b) risks: *competitive strategy, organizational strategy risks,* and *uncertainty.*

Most *financial* values are measurable to some degree. *Strategic* values include competitive advantage in the market and benefits generated by streamlining back-end

Figure 16-7	Real Option Analysis			
Steps	Compute Base Case Present Value (PV) without Flexibility, Using DCF Valuation Model	Model the Uncertainty, Using Event Trees	Identify and Incorporate Managerial Flexibilities by Creating a Decision Tree	Calculate Real-Option Present Value (ROA)
Objectives	• Compute base case present value without flexibility	• Identify major uncertanities in each stage • Understand how those uncertainties affect the PV	• Analyze the event tree to identify and incorporate managerial flexibility to respond to new information	• Value the total project using a simple algebraic methodology
Comments		• Still no flexibility; this value should equal the value from Step 1 • Explicitly estimate uncertainty	• Incorporating flexibility transforms event trees, which transforms them into decision trees • The flexibility continuously alters the risk characteristics of the project, and hence the cost of capital	• ROA includes the base case present value without flexibility plus the option (flexibility) value • Under high uncertainty and managerial flexibility, option value will be substantial
Output	• Project's PV without flexibility	• Detailed event tree capturing the possible present values of the project	• A detailed decision tree combining possible events and management responses	• ROA of the project and optimal action plan for the available real options

Source: Rayport and Jaworski (2001); Exhibit 8-8; pg. 304.

or front-end business procedures. They are not easy to measure or quantify. *Stakeholder* values are reflections of organizational redesign, organizational learning, empowerment, and information-technology architecture, which are unique to each company. On the risk side, *competitive strategy* risks are external due to competitors' actions, joint venture alliances, or demographic changes, among others. Finally, *organizational strategy risks* and *uncertainty* are factors internal to the company. They cover short-term risks inherent in business reorganization and risks due to technical uncertainty as well as implementation risks. All these values and risks need to be examined in order to help formulate a desirable EC strategy.

Risk Analysis

It is extremely important to conduct risk analysis as part of an e-strategy. The first chance to deal with risk is when a SWOT analysis is done and the threats are diagnosed. When the strategy is formulated and specific initiatives are identified, a conventional risk analysis can be conducted. There are several methods to conduct risk analysis (e.g., see Porter, 1996; Wheelen and Hunger, 1998; and Kaplan and Norton, 2000a).

In a risk analysis program one should:

- Identify all potential risks
- Assess the potential damage if they occur
- Evaluate the possibility of protection (e.g., buying insurance)
- Evaluate the cost of protection versus the benefits

A comprehensive discussion of risk in EC is provided by Deise et al. (2000), who identified the following e-business risks (and several added by the authors):

- **Strategic risks.** These include competitive environment, wrong strategic direction, dependence on others (suppliers, buyers), wrong corporate culture, lack of reputation, regulatory changes, and governance.
- **Financial risks.** These include currency management and changes, unclear tax situations, and cash flow.
- **Operational risks.** These include technological changes and the use of poor technology; security; poor project management; business process controls; poor operations management; problems with employees, including a lack of skilled people.

An example of shareholder value that is more important than financial value is provided in Application Case 16.7.

One method that can be used to support risk analysis is scenario planning.

EC Scenarios

Scenario planning is a methodology used in planning situations that involve much uncertainty, like that of EC. With this approach, several different scenarios are created. Then a team compiles as many future events as possible that may influence the outcome of each scenario. This is kind of "what-if" analysis.

The analysis can be done as a workshop with the participation of all major decision makers (see Levinson, 1999/2000). Teams analyze a future that might be 3 to 5 years ahead. Finally, a consensus is attempted on the best strategy to pursue. It makes sense to use this approach in evaluating major EC initiatives.

APPLICATION CASE 16.7

> ### Marriott's Analysis Emphasizes Shareholders' Values
>
> Courtyard by Marriott used to fax stacks of marketing reports to its various hotels, including 16 operating manuals, one of which is over 500 pages long. In 1998, the hotel started to operate the Source, an information system where employees from more than 380 Courtyard-owned and franchised hotels can find all the information from new and old manuals and reports on the Web. "We used to spend $50 to $100 to print each manual, so that's a big savings," says Craig Lambert, a senior executive of the company. In addition, online employment forms have cut about an hour off the time it takes hotel managers to bring a new hire on board. It sounds like a simple thing, but multiply that by several hundred hotels and 50 employees per year and it becomes a lot of man-hours. According to Lambert, ROI projections played a major role in Courtyard's investment decision, but were not the most important factor. "What was driving the EC project was the knowledge management part of it, not the ROI part of it. We wanted to have a source for our people to get answers that lets them do their jobs more productively."
>
> *Sources:* Press releases at *marriott.com* (1998–2001).

Hutchinson (1997) described four EC scenarios that can be used to accomplish EC strategy. The first is the open, *global commerce scenario,* where removal of intermediaries is a powerful force that flattens the value chain. The *members-only subnet* scenario applies mostly to B2B EC. The *electronic middlemen* scenario shows that suppliers in both business and consumer markets can make their products and services available through independent third-party distribution channels. Finally, in the new *consumer marketing channels* scenario, traditional broadcasting, advertising, and consumer telephony collapse into a unified consumer-centric EC medium on the Internet. Although EC proliferation would certainly allow any combination or variation of such scenarios, each company has to select the most appropriate model for its needs. The use of this model can help EC planners to determine the EC initiative that best fits their organization.

16.10   STRATEGIC PLANNING FRAMEWORK

In this section we present some strategic planning frameworks.

EC Levels

EC implementation usually occurs at different levels. Companies start with a presence on the Internet and move to more complex applications. In Chapter 11 we introduced a six-level process for e-government. The GartnerGroup suggests the following four EC levels.

- **Level 1—Basic presence.** Here the company uses the Internet to feature company information and provide brochures.
- **Level 2—Prospecting.** Many features are added to the EC initiative, such as a search engine, extensive product information, links to services, and the ability to interact with the company. Basic customer service is provided.

- **Level 3—Business integration.** More features are added, primarily EC transaction capabilities, customization and personalization services, and tools fostering the creation of a community.
- **Level 4—Business transformation.** At this stage, supplier and customer integration is added. Also, multichannel integration, advanced customization and configuration, and superb customer service are achieved.

According to Hackbarth and Kettinger (2000), e-business strategies pass through three similar stages, as shown in Figure 16-8.

Generic Competitive Strategy Versus Cooperative Strategy

Business strategies in general, as well as in EC, can be competitive and/or cooperative. A **competitive strategy** assumes fighting against all competitors for the purpose of survival and to winning, whereas a **cooperative strategy** plans for working together with specific competitors to gain an advantage against other competitors. The following discussion covers both strategies.

COMPETITIVE STRATEGIES

A competitive strategy can be either offensive or defensive. An **offensive strategy** usually takes place in an established competitor's market location. Two common offensive strategies are:

- **Frontal assault.** The attacking firm goes head-to-head with its competitor. It matches the competitor in most of the categories, from price to promo-

Figure 16-8	Three Levels of E-Commerce		
	Level I	**Level II**	**Level III**
	Experimentation	**Integration**	**Transformation**
E-business Strategy	No E-business strategy	E-business strategy supports current (as is) corporate strategy	E-business strategy supports breakout (to be) corporate strategy
Corporate Strategy	E-business strategy not linked to corporate strategy	E-business strategy subservient to corporate strategy	E-business strategy is a driver of corporate strategy
Scope	Departmental/functional orientation	Cross-functional participation	Cross enterprise involvement (interconnected customers, suppliers, and partners)
Payoffs	Unclear	Cost reduction, business support and enhancement of existing business practices, revenue enhancement	New revenue streams, new business lines, drastic improvements in customer service and customer satisfaction
Levers	Technological Infrastructure and software applications	Business processes	People, intellectual capital and relationships, cooperation
Role of Information	Secondary to technology	Supports process efficiency and effectiveness	Information asymmetries used to create business opportunities
			Breakout Strategy
© 2000 CRC PRESS LLC	INFORMATION SYSTEMS MANAGEMENT SUMMER 2000		

Source: Kettinger and Hackbarth (2000). Reprinted with permission of William J. Kettinger.

tion to distribution channel. An example is Barnes & Noble, which has reacted to the swift entrance of *Amazon.com* into the online bookselling business. This can be an expensive strategy.

- **Flanking maneuver.** Here, a firm attacks a part of the market where the competitor is weak. To be successful, the flanker must have a relatively undefended market niche. For example, Barnes and Noble entered the B2B book market. Several other companies entered the online educational book market, where they have an advantage over Amazon.

The second type of competitive strategy is a defensive strategy. A defensive strategy usually takes place in the firm's own current market position as a defense against possible attacks by a rival(s). According to Porter (1985), **defensive strategies** aim to lower the probability of successful attack, divert attacks to less threatening avenues, or lessen the intensity of an attack. Two common defensive strategies are:

- **Raise structural barriers.** Entry barriers act to block a challenger's logical avenues of attack. For example, offering a full line of products in every profitable market segment to close off any entry points; increase buyer switching costs by offering low-cost training to users; increase the cost of gaining trial users by keeping prices low on items new users are most likely to purchase; or increasing scale economies to reduce unit costs. Examples of businesses that use this strategy are Cisco Online, Dell Computers, and eBay in their comprehensive offerings.
- **Lower the inducement for attack.** Another type of defensive strategy is to reduce a challenger's expectations of future profits in the industry. An example is *buycomp.com* with their "lowest price on earth" strategy.

COOPERATIVE STRATEGIES

Cooperative strategies are used to gain a competitive advantage within an industry by working with other firms. A typical cooperative strategy involves a **strategic alliance** through a joint venture or value-chain partnership. This may be done through consortia e-marketplaces, as shown in Chapter 7. A strategic alliance is a partnership of multiple corporations formed to achieve competitive advantages that are mutually beneficial. Companies may form a strategic alliance for a number of reasons, including: (1) to obtain technology and/or manufacturing capabilities, (2) to obtain access to specific markets, (3) to reduce financial risk, (4) to reduce political risk, (5) to achieve or ensure competitive advantage, (6) to utilize unused capacity, and (7) to combine areas of excellences. Chapters 2, 11, and 15 present several examples of strategic alliances. The major types of strategic alliance used in EC are:

- **Joint venture.** A joint venture is a cooperative business activity formed by two or more separate organizations for strategic purposes that creates an independent business entity and allocates ownership, operational responsibilities, and financial risks and rewards to each member, while preserving their separate identity/autonomy. Disadvantages of joint ventures include loss of control, lower profits, probability of conflicts with partners, and the likely transfer of technological advantage to the partner. An example in the United Kingdom is retailer W. H. Smith, which together with British Telecom and Microsoft Network, developed and operates an Internet portal that provides a variety of entertainment and educational services. Softbank (Japan), which is teaming up with Microsoft and Yahoo! in a joint venture to advertise and sell cars over the Internet, is another example.

- **Value-chain partnership.** A value-chain partnership is a strong, close alliance in which a company forms a long-term arrangement with a key supplier or distributor for mutual advantage. Value-chain partnerships are becoming popular as more companies outsource activities that were previously done within the company. Examples of such partnerships are Dell Computers and 7-Eleven stores, whose exclusive suppliers are located near their plants or stores. UPS and FedEx perform online-supported logistics activities, such as managing inventories and shipments, for many companies.

Sviokla's Strategy

Companies moving to EC are faced with four major issues according to consultant John Sviokla of Diamond Technology Partners (*diamtech.com*):

1. What's the company's *digital business strategy?* What's the right value proposition for its new business model? EC ventures don't usually fit neatly into established business categories. Traditional strategies probably won't fly either.

2. What's the right *organizational structure?* "Most of the time, existing companies' structures are designed to sustain the existing marketplace model," Sviokla says. "But it's like any other machine: You can't get a trench digger to be a lawnmower." Companies usually need to realign their structures to break functional "silos" and to meet very different e-business needs.

3. What's the best *capital structure?* With all the hot Internet stock activity, capital markets tend to reward innovative capital structures rather than traditional ones. They're buying the future and not the past, which can be very risky due to overvaluation.

4. What's the correct *technology platform?* Companies succeed online only with IT designed for a digital economy. And the EC technology must integrate seamlessly with call center, billing, and shipping systems.

Mougayar's Approach: Questions that a Strategic Plan Should Answer

Mougayar (1998) presented an e-strategy framework that guides the planner so that at the end of the strategic planning process a company can answer questions such as these:

- How is EC going to change our business?
- How do we uncover new types of business opportunities?
- How can we take advantage of new electronic linkages with customers and trading partners?
- Do we become intermediaries ourselves?
- How do we bring more buyers together electronically, and keep them there?
- How do we change the nature of our products and services?
- Why is the Internet affecting other companies more than ours?
- How do we manage and measure the evolution of our strategy?

Ware et al.'s Seven-Step Model E-Strategy

An alternative approach was suggested by Ware et al. (1998) who proposed a seven-step strategy for developing EC. It focuses on the following basic questions:

- Where are you along the continuum of possible EC applications?
- Where do you want to go?
- How are you going to get there?

There are crucial questions to address if you want to take a strategic approach to the application of EC technologies. For example, how do companies increase their ability to exploit digital economy opportunities for a sustainable value? Having the proper framework is the key to building capabilities of identifying and capitalizing on the opportunities. Ware et al. have developed an assessment and planning methodology and an approach for clarifying goals and expectations. The methodology includes the following seven steps:

STEP 1: Create a map of scenarios for aligning business strategy and Internet initiatives in the future.

STEP 2: Communicate a vision from top management to drive Internet initiatives.

STEP 3: Identify and transform key value constellations, specifically, what business core practices and processes could Internet technologies affect most? This step identifies possible opportunities, as shown in the IBM opening vignette.

STEP 4: Develop the portfolio of EC initiatives your company wants to pursue. (See the IBM opening case.)

STEP 5: Develop year-by-year objectives and plans for the chosen initiatives, including measures of effectiveness and their effect on the business.

STEP 6: Implement the change. The project participants must undergo the changes in attitudes and behavior required by such a system.

STEP 7: Monitor the overall plan, learn lessons, adjust, and improve. (One area that supports such strategies is competitive intelligence).

The Strategic E-Breakout Methodology of Kettinger and Hackbarth

To assist companies in their e-strategies Kettinger and Hackbarth (1999) and Hackbarth and Kettinger (2000), developed a four-stage methodology that is shown in Figure 16-9. The four stages are:

Initiate, diagnose, e-breakout, and transition. The *initiate* stage envisions potential strategic change, confirms top management support, and determines a project schedule. The *diagnose* stage gathers information about the strengths and weaknesses of the company as well as opportunities and threats present within the company's industry. This stage assesses company and industry processes. Finally, this stage benchmarks e-business technologies and scans across industries for best practices and e-business technologies. The *e-breakout* stage formulates an e-business strategy with the objective of breaking out of the box by using e-business technology to transform processes and people to better compete in a dynamic global marketplace. The *transition* stage recognizes the reality that the e-breakout strategy may not be immediately obtainable because of a company's unwillingness to change, lack of available resources, or shortage of qualified people. The transition strategy

Figure 16-9		The Strategic E-Breakout Method			
Major Stages	**Initiate** Kick-Off Project	**Diagnose** Assess Current Environment		**E-Breakout** Establish Strategic Target	**Transition** Plot Migration Path
		Industry	**Company**		
Strategic e-breakout Method Activities	• Outline project scope • Identify project stakeholders • Determine project schedule	• Conduct industry competitive assessment • Benchmark e-business technology • Assess industry business partnerships	• Identify current business strategies • Assess customer relationships • Assess supplier relationships • Assess e-business technology and architecture • Assess business partnerships • Current business strategies rankings	• Match current business strategies with industry opportunities and threats and company strengths and weaknesses • SWOT matrix • Brainstorm alternative e-business breakout strategies	• Analyze gap difference between e-breakout and current strategy • Factor in change readiness assessment and cost/benefit/risk analysis • Consider potential industry responses • Plot e-business transition strategy milestones
Outputs	Project work plan	Opportunities and threats rankings	Strengths and weaknesses rankings	E-business breakout strategy	E-business transition strategy

Source: Hackbarth and Kettinger (2000), Exhibit 3. Reprinted with permission of William J. Kettinger.

serves as a gap strategy that involves the company in incremental steps toward the e-breakout strategy.

The strategic e-breakout method involves four stages as shown in Figure 16-9. The complete methodology is available online at *brint.com/members/online/200603/ebizstrategy/ebizstrategy.html*.

16.11   ISSUES IN STRATEGY FORMULATION

A variety of issues exist in strategy formulation depending on the company, industry, nature of applications, etc. Some common issues are presented next.

EC Strategies in Small Businesses

Formulating strategies in small businesses is usually much less sophisticated than it is in large corporations. Senior managers tend to know the whole spectrum of the business and possess the knowledge and authority to control the destiny of the new EC venture. A fundamental reason for differences in strategy formulation between large and small companies lies in the relationship between owners and managers. The CEO of a large corporation has to consider and balance the diverse needs of the corporation's many stakeholders. The CEO of a small business, however, is very likely to be the owner (or one of the owners). For further discussion on EC in small companies see Chapter 18.

How to Handle the Channel Conflicts

Several options were cited throughout the book. These include:

- Let the established old-economy-type dealers handle e-business fulfillment, as the auto industry is doing, even for customized cars. The ordering can be done online, or directions to dealers can be provided.
- Sell some products only online, such as *lego.com* is doing. Other products are advertised online, but sold off-line.
- Help your intermediaries (e.g., by building portals for them as *fruit.com* did, but do not sell online).
- Sell online and off-line, such as the airlines are doing. Provide services to the intermediaries and encourage them to reintermediate themselves.
- Do not sell online.

Note that Schwab was experimenting with different prices when they started e-Schwab. However, in 1997 they merged their online services with the offline, resulting in one price for all Web trades (Pottruck and Pearce, 2000).

How to Handle the Conflict between the Off-Line and Online Businesses in a Click-and-Mortar Situation

The allocation of resources between off-line an online activities can be very difficult. In some organizations the two are viewed as competitors (in sell-side projects). Therefore, they may behave as competitors and not help each other. This may cause problems when the off-line side needs to handle the logistics of the online side and when prices need to be determined. Corporate culture, ability of top management to introduce the change properly, and the use of innovative processes that support collaboration will all determine the degree of collaboration. Clear support of top management and a clear strategy of "what and how" are essential. Some companies handle the situation by creating an independent division or subsidiary.

Pricing Strategy

Pricing products and services online may be a difficult decision for any click-and-mortar company (Choi and Whinston, 2000). Setting prices lower than the off-line business may lead to internal conflict, whereas setting at the same level will hurt competitiveness. Another strategic decision is how to price customized products and services. Dewan et al. (2000) and Prasad and Harker (2000) have developed quantitative economic models for making pricing decisions.

Where to Compete

The Web opens several new alternatives for competition. In addition to competing in your current business, you may go either backward or forward in the supply chain or move horizontally to new businesses.

Also, you may play different roles, such as an infomediary, content provider, aggregator, community creator, or portal builder.

Should You Get Financing from Big Venture Capital Firms?

When EC first started, it was very easy to get capital from a venture capital (VC) firm (see Chapter 8). Now, because of the many recent failures, it has become increasingly difficult. In either case a strategic issue is: Should an entrepreneur get VC financing and lose control over the idea and the business, or try to get funding from other sources? One benefit of VC funding is access to various VC experts who can be very useful due to their managerial experience.

Should You Join an Exchange? Which One?

One of the important strategic decisions is whether or not to join an exchange. And if you do decide to join one, which one should you choose? Joining an exchange has several benefits (Chapter 7), but many costs and limitations as well. An early decision is important, because you may not need a sell-side or a buy-side infrastructure if you join an exchange. One of the risks here is that the exchange may go out of business.

16.12 STRATEGY IMPLEMENTATION AND PROJECT MANAGEMENT

Before starting to implement the strategy, it is necessary to build an implementation plan that will outline the steps to follow during implementation. Then one needs to get organized, usually starting with establishing a Web team. Only then can one continue with the execution of the plan. In this section we deal only with some issues related to this process.

Creating a Web Team and Assigning Functional Skills to Subprojects

In creating a Web team, the roles and responsibilities of the team leader, user management, Webmaster, and technical staff should be defined. The project leader often has the strategic challenge of being a "visionary" regarding the tasks of aligning business and technology goals and implementing a sound enterprise EC plan. Such a plan is best arrived at by negotiation with those knowledgeable about particular data and information and how they should be structured and presented in an online, hypermedia environment. The details need to be developed through the joint efforts of different functional areas: IS, marketing, customer relations, purchasing, accounting, finance, human resources, security, and other operations. Usually the corporate IT or EC steering committee will provide such guidance.

If a mechanism is put in place that brings together all relevant technical people, the rules concerning security, authentication, link management, markup language standards, and so on can be properly developed, updated on a regular basis, and satisfactorily applied toward drafting and interpreting an enterprise-wide Internet policy. Such a mechanism is beneficial to the policy process in that it is more likely to produce a policy consistent with the enterprise's business goals and strategies.

A Pilot Project

Often, implementing EC requires significant investments in infrastructure. Therefore, a good way to start this is to undertake one or a few small EC pilot projects. Since pilot projects help discover problems early, the pilot project can be considered a part of planning. Modifications in the plan after the pilot is completed are likely. General Motors Corporation's pilot program (GM BuyPower) is an example of the successful use of a pilot project. On its Web site, *gmbuypower.com*, shoppers can choose car options, check local dealer inventory, schedule test drives, and get best-price quotes by e-mail or telephone. This pilot project has been in existence since 1997, starting in four western U.S. states and expanding to all states in 1999. Meanwhile, Chrysler also went nationwide with its pilot Get-a-Quote program, and Ford's Build Your Own program is also operational. Home Depot decided to go online in 2000. The company started in six stores on Las Vegas, then moved to four other cities in the western United States.

Planning for Resources

In strategy formulation a decision has been made on specific initiatives. The exact required resources depend on the information requirements and the capabilities of each project, as described in Chapter 12. However, the infrastructure that is shared by many applications, such as databases, the intranet, and possibly an extranet, needs to be evaluated at this time. Some of the required resources are in place, others are not. Obviously, the analysis of required resources is related to the strategy regarding outsourcing (Section 16.13). All relevant resources need to be planned for, primarily people and money. Other resources may be a physical space for the EC unit, a physical warehouse for storage and packaging (see Chapter 15), and specific hardware and software (and their trends!). Standard system design tools can help in executing the resource requirement plan.

Project Management

In addition to planning the EC team, it is necessary to develop an evaluation plan, identify tasks, and establish a methodology for project progress and monitoring, including milestones. Several generic project management software tools can be easily adapted to EC use.

Other Implementation Issues

Introducing EC applications creates a major change in most organizations, and therefore it is necessary to plan for an effective change management program. One important issue is that many EC applications involve business partners with different organizational cultures.

16.13   ISSUES IN STRATEGY IMPLEMENTATION

There are many strategy implementation issues, depending on the circumstances. Here we describe some common ones.

Evaluating Outsourcing

Implementing EC requires access to the Web, building the site, and connecting it to the existing corporate information systems (front-end for order taking, back-end for order processing), as described in Chapter 12. At this point the company is faced with the strategic outsourcing decision, which may be very complex: Should you build your own EC infrastructure in-house, purchase a commercial EC software package or EC suite, or use a Web hosting company? (A combination of these is also possible.) Building your own Web site, portal, or e-marketplace may be a complex and expensive solution compared with using a commercial software product or suite of products, which is usually quicker and less expensive, but your proprietary trade secrets may be in jeopardy. An example of comprehensive outsourcing services in given in Application Case 16.8. Further discussion is provided in Chapters 8 and 12.

APPLICATION CASE **16.8**

AT&T's Cyberspace Solution Helps Businesses Conduct Commerce on the Internet

Businesses large and small can now quickly and easily establish a full-featured e-business on the Internet, thanks to a turnkey solution introduced by AT&T. AT&T's Web Marketing Solution integrates all the critical elements necessary for a successful Internet-based business: access, hosting, advertising, and one-stop customer care.

Outsourcing addresses the major challenges companies face in launching a Web-based business: building the site, attracting existing and potential customers, growing the market, and managing the operation. This is a powerful way for companies to unlock the potential of the Internet. They can expand their reach, get closer to their customers, and dramatically reduce their costs—with confidence that AT&T will provide a total solution for Web success. Dan Schulman, AT&T vice president for marketing for business services, said that Web Marketing Solution's customized Internet access software gives businesses "an unparalleled opportunity to attract existing customers to their Web site."

Building Web Sites

AT&T provides many Web-related services (see *att.com*; AT&T business). They provide all the technical Web site infrastructure and management needed to host a reliable Web application including Web hosting and wireless. The service eliminates many of the complex and extensive steps required to establish, manage, and monitor a Web site, thereby allowing businesses to publish information on the Internet without having to own their servers.

Businesses can depend on AT&T to take care of connectivity issues, bandwidth requirements, server capacity, interface to the secure transaction platform, support for custom applications, state-of-the-art computers, network security, integrated site development tools, and Web site management services. In addition, AT&T's CRM and PRM programs link

APPLICATION CASE `16.8`

(continued)

clients with skilled, professional Web site creation and design services. For do-it-yourselfers, AT&T offers a 2-day, in-depth class on Web site design and development.

Attracting Customers with Commerce-Driven Programs

With AT&T's PRM services, clients can provide their existing and potential customers or suppliers with customized software to bring them onto the Internet.

Client Web sites may include AT&T's icon, which allows Internet surfers to click on the icon to initiate an immediate telephone conversation with a customer service agent. The agent can send images to a customer's screen to illustrate products or services being discussed. The phone conversation is provided over the AT&T network while images are simultaneously transmitted through the Internet.

Managing the Operation

AT&T assigns a project manager to oversee the creation and installation of a client's Web business and to ensure it goes online as scheduled. A specialized customer care center and a small business center serve as points of contact for the client's entire application. Additionally, as of November 1998, AT&T's secure services make it possible to conduct secure online transactions, including order processing and credit card verification. The cost to the client depends on the services used.

Sources: Compiled from *att.com* (June, 2001).

Partners' Strategy

Related to outsourcing is the issue of partners' strategy. There are many potential partners. For example, companies that make B2B e-marketplaces may consider logistics, technology, and e-payment partners. Partner selection and management issues are discussed in Chapters 8 and 12.

How to Coordinate B2B and B2C

Many companies are conducting both B2B and B2C. One example is *lego.com*. When you start selling direct you are creating a B2C business. The coordination between the two can be done in different ways. A strategic decision on how to do it is important.

16.14 STRATEGY AND PROJECT ASSESSMENT

The last phase of e-strategy is assessment, which is done periodically after the EC application is up and running.

Need for Assessment

Like any other project, Web projects need to be assessed during and after deployment, as does the overall EC strategy. Several objectives exist for strategic reassessment. The most important ones are:

- Find out if the EC project (and strategy) delivers what it was supposed to deliver.
- Determine if the EC project (and strategy) is still viable in an ever-changing environment.
- Reassess the initial strategy in order to learn from mistakes and improve future planning.
- Identify failing projects as soon as possible and determine the reasons for failures to avoid the same problems on subsequent systems.

EC performance results are monitored and assessed so that corrective actions, problem resolutions, or expansion plans can take place as needed. Assessing EC is not simple because of the many configuration and impact variables. Web applications grow in unexpected ways, often expanding beyond their initial plan. For example, Genentec Inc., a biotechnology giant, wanted merely to replace a home-grown bulletin board system. Genentec started with a small budget only to report that the internal Web had grown rapidly and become very popular, in a short span of time, encompassing many applications. Another example is Lockheed Martin, which initially planned to put its corporate phone directory and information on training programs on the intranet; in a short time, many of its human resources documents were placed on the intranet as well. Soon after, the use of the Web for internal information expanded from administrative purposes to collaborative commerce and PRM applications.

Measuring Results

Each company measures success or failure by different sets of standards. Some companies may find that their goals were unrealistic, that their Web server was inadequate to handle demand, or that expected cost savings were not realized. On the other hand, some may have to respond to exploding application requests from various functional areas in the company. A review of the requirements and design documents should help answer many of the questions raised during the assessment. It is important that the Web team develop a thorough checklist to address both the evaluation of project performance and the assessment of a changing environment. Table 16-2 summarizes a set of pertinent questions in evaluating EC projects.

To assess the impact of an EC project on the company's mission and formulate a new set of strategies, it is useful to pose a set of questions such as those shown in Table 16-2 to both internal management and to customers. Other information may be relevant as well.

Finalization and Adjustments

With the gathered data, the actual ROI can be computed and compared to the projected one. Also, if any part of the sales expectations were not met, a review of your marketing efforts is in order. Were the right prospects targeted? Were they

TABLE 16-2

Questions to Evaluate an EC Project

What were the goals? Were they met?
What were the expectations? Were they realistic?
What products and services did your company want to offer? Can the system deliver them?
Did unanticipated problems occur? If so, how were those handled?
What costs did you hope to reduce? Were you successful in doing so?
Did other costs increase unexpectedly? If yes, why?
What were the sales objectives? Were they realistic?
Did you intend to reduce distribution costs?
Did you intend to reduce travel expenses for corporate staff? Were you successful?
Did Web and Internet communications reduce traditional communications costs, such as long distance and fax?
Did you improve customer relations? If you did not, what went wrong?
How can those errors be corrected?
Was your project finished on time and on budget? If not, what went wrong?
Are recurring costs within the budget? If not, can contracts be renegotiated?
Was the budget realistic to begin with?
Should the budget be revised for the next stage or budget cycle?
Were additional people hired as expected?
What do customers want that you are not providing? What will the additional services cost?
What impact will the fulfillment of customers' needs have on the infrastructure, from bandwidth to software?
What specific changes have taken place among your competitors that might affect what you are trying to accomplish?
Have your suppliers provided adequate service?
Has training of employees been adequate?
What new internal needs have arisen that need to be addressed?
Did you learn some things in the process that were valuable?

Source: Compiled from Schulman and Smith (1997) pp. 277–78.

likely Internet or Web users? Was the Web site registered with the appropriate lists and search engines to ensure that prospects were likely to find your company? However, it is often difficult to distinguish the effect of online marketing and traditional off-line effort in correctly identifying the Web impact.

Web assessment can be done in different ways. Most major consultants can help with their own proprietary procedures. A theoretical model has been offered by Selz and Schubert (1997).

Based on the collected information, corrective steps might be required, from product offerings to pricing strategy or from Web promotion to a review of your software vendors. Once this is done an improved strategy can be formulated. A most common approach to measure EC performance is the use of metrics, as discussed in Section 16.15.

16.15   EC METRICS

One way to measure an organization's performance is to use **metrics**, which include benchmarks in different areas related to EC implementation and strategy. Metrics can produce very positive results in organizations by driving behavior in a number of ways. According to Rayport and Jaworski (2001) metrics can:

- Help define and refine business models by specifying concrete goals with precise measurement. For example, large buyers at Dell get personalized pages at "Dell Online Premier," where they can buy, track activities, and view historical activities.

- Help communicate strategy by specifying performance measures using participative management.
- Help track performance by collecting usability and other site data based on pageviews, etc. (see Chapter 12).
- Help increase accountability by linking metrics to performance appraisal programs.
- Help align objectives of individuals, departments, and organizations.

An example of metrics for CRM can be found in Voss (2000), where the following metrics are suggested:

- Response time to customers' enquiries (e.g., 24-hour limit)
- Response quality (making customers happy with the responses 95 percent of the time)
- Security/trust level (how confident the customers are)
- Navigability of site
- Download time, especially of important material
- Timeliness and quality of fulfillment (promises, promises, promises)
- Up-to-date information on products, prices, services, etc.
- Availability; customer should have what they want, when they want it, and where they want it
- Site effectiveness, content, ease of use, flexibility and usefulness
- Metrics can be set as a strategy ("we respond in 12 hours while the industry standard is 24")

Related to the above are usability metrics, some of which are described in Chapter 12 and in Plant (2000).

The Balanced Scorecard

An interesting proposal was made by Kaplan and Norton (1996) to use metrics to measure the health of organizations. In what they call the **balanced scorecard**, they advocate that managers focus not only on short-term financial results, but on four other areas for which metrics are available. These areas are:

- Finance—including both short- and long-term measures
- Customer—how the customers view companies
- Internal business process—finding areas in which to excel
- Learning and growth—sustain ability to change and expand

A SCORECARD APPROACH TO EC

An implementation of the scorecard approach in EC was proposed by Plant (2000). He offered seven sets of metrics. These cover the following areas: financial, markets, service, brand, competitive leadership, technology, and Internet site. For each of these, one can devise a set of metrics and then compare actual results with goals and industry best practices. An example of the service set is shown in Figure 16-10. The scorecard can then be used to compute an overall score in each set of metrics that can be tracked over time and related to strategies and modifications in strategies.

The use of metrics is especially popular in e-marketing due to the ease with which Web site measurements can be made (see Plant, 2000).

| Figure 16-10 | | | Metrics in the Service Area | | | |

Brand	Metric	Forecast Initial Goal	Actual Results	Industry Best Practice	Effectiveness Rating
By adding information surrounding the product to the site, did we effectively add value to the branding strategy?					
Has brand reinforcement been an effective intermediate strategy prior to offering online sales and services?					
Is brand reinforcement an effective strategy where we are prevented from selling online?					
Is continuous and innovative change of the information surrounding the products and the organization effective in adding value to the brand?					
Is mass customization as an approach to Internet branding an effective strategy for the organization?					
Is the Internet an effective mechanism for facilitating low-cost global branding?					
As an organization that has not created a brand position on the Internet, is it necessary to create an effective strategy as quickly and effectively as possible, and are we achieving this?					
					$\Sigma ER/8 =$

Source: Metrics for EC; a brand example from Plant, E-Commerce: Formulation of Strategy© 2000, p.212. Reprint by permission of Pearson Education, Inc., Upper Saddle River, NJ.

THE PERFORMANCE DASHCARD

The balanced-scorecard approach has some limitations when applied to EC. Therefore, Rayport and Jaworski (2001) propose a more suitable model, called the **performance dashboard**. The model is divided into five desired outcomes and five corresponding metrics (see Figure 16-11). Then metrics are mapped with leading and lagging indicators of performance, leading to calculated targets. Once performance measures are done, strategies can be evaluated and reformulated.

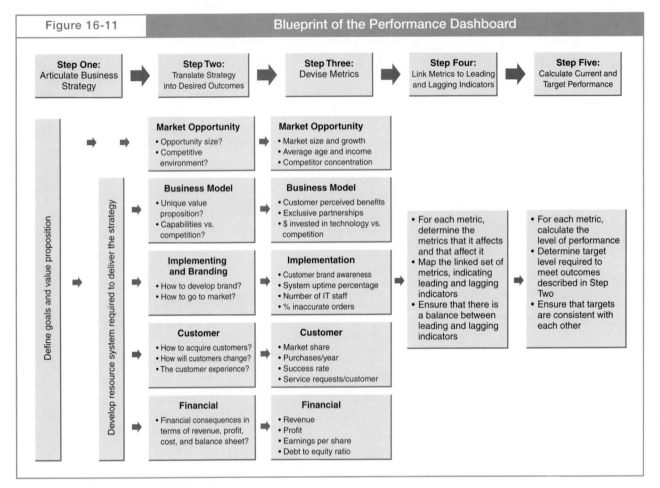

Figure 16-11	Blueprint of the Performance Dashboard

Step One: Articulate Business Strategy

Step Two: Translate Strategy into Desired Outcomes

Step Three: Devise Metrics

Step Four: Link Metrics to Leading and Lagging Indicators

Step Five: Calculate Current and Target Performance

Define goals and value proposition

Develop resource system required to deliver the strategy

Market Opportunity
- Opportunity size?
- Competitive environment?

Market Opportunity
- Market size and growth
- Average age and income
- Competitor concentration

Business Model
- Unique value proposition?
- Capabilities vs. competition?

Business Model
- Customer perceived benefits
- Exclusive partnerships
- $ invested in technology vs. competition

Implementing and Branding
- How to develop brand?
- How to go to market?

Implementation
- Customer brand awareness
- System uptime percentage
- Number of IT staff
- % inaccurate orders

Customer
- How to acquire customers?
- How will customers change?
- The customer experience?

Customer
- Market share
- Purchases/year
- Success rate
- Service requests/customer

Financial
- Financial consequences in terms of revenue, profit, cost, and balance sheet?

Financial
- Revenue
- Profit
- Earnings per share
- Debt to equity ratio

- For each metric, determine the metrics that it affects and that affect it
- Map the linked set of metrics, indicating leading and lagging indicators
- Ensure that there is a balance between leading and lagging indicators

- For each metric, calculate the level of performance
- Determine target level required to meet outcomes described in Step Two
- Ensure that targets are consistent with each other

Source: Rayport and Jaworski (2001), Exhibit 7-4, pg. 270.

16.16   EC FAILURES AND LESSONS LEARNED

EC initiatives and EC companies are likely to fail. The reasons why they fail vary and depend on the circumstances. In this section we will look at some failures and attempt to identify the common reasons. Then we will try to derive lessons for avoiding such failures. This section is divided into four categories: Failures of e-tailing, failing exchanges, failing individual EC initiatives, and other EC failures.

E-Tailing Failures

This is the most publicized area of failure. During 2000 and 2001, several hundred e-tailers and related companies went out of business or were struggling, trying to prevent failure (e.g., visit *startupfailures.com* and *disobey.com/ghostsites/index*). We discussed this topic in Chapter 3. One area with considerable failures is the retail toy industry. Not only did a large number of companies fail (e.g., eToys), but even efforts by click-and-mortar companies such as Toys R Us sustained heavy losses. Incidentally, the solution employed by Toys R Us, moving e-tailing to a joint venture with *Amazon.com* (see Chapter 3 for details), is a promising but not a guaranteed strategy. E-tailing failures were recorded in many countries and industries, especially in commodity products such as toys, CDs, or books. Some of the reasons were provided in Chapter 3; others are:

- **Lack of funding.** It takes a few years to acquire a large enough customer base. Most companies burned all the cash they had before they had enough customers. Additional funding became very difficult to obtain. Investors in 2000 and 2001 were not willing to wait a long time for profits, figuring that the risk was too high. Typical examples of companies that run out of funds are *boo.com*, *Garden.com*, *living.com*, and *eToys.com*.
- **Incorrect revenue model.** In the late 1990s, many companies used a business model where you spent as much as you could on customer acquisition. The idea was that if you had millions of hits and visitors per month, advertisers would rush to your site. This model was proven to be incorrect; the advertisement money did not come. With little revenue and big expenses you reach bankruptcy quickly.

The amount of advertisement money on the Internet, which had been growing at a rate of over 100 percent a year in the late 1990s, stopped growing, and declined in late 2000, due to a slowing economy and the disappearance of dotcom companies. Also, the competition for advertising money grew rapidly, since hundreds of companies were trying to get some portion of it.

Exchange Failures

In late 2000, the EC community was shocked to learn that *chemdex.com* had closed down. Chemdex was the "granddaddy" of the third-party exchanges, attracting lots of publicity and venture capital. The reasons provided by *ventro.com*, its parent company, were that the revenue growth was too slow and they wanted to move to a new business model.

It is predicted that as many as 90 percent of all exchanges will collapse. Some of the reasons for such failures are discussed in Chapter 7.

EC Initiative Failures

While failing companies, especially those publicly listed, are well advertised, failing EC initiatives within companies, especially private ones are less known. However, the news about some failing EC initiatives reached the media and are well advertised. Here are some examples.

- Levi's stopped online direct sales after its major distributors and retailers put pressure on the company. Furthermore, the site itself was poorly organized and managed.
- A joint venture between Intel and SAP, two world-class companies, which was designed to develop low-cost solutions for SMEs, collapsed in August 2000.

Other Failures

With dotcom failures, support companies and consultants that worked for dotcom companies suffered losses, or even failed. (Glater, 2000). For example, comparison sites are struggling (Tedeschi, 2000), even *Deja.com*, now *groups.google.com/googlegroups/ deja_announcement.html*), a well-known portal and community site was sold to *google.com*.

In early 2001, Walt Disney & Co. decided to close their *go.com* company. This was a service company that intended to manage and operate all Disney's e-projects (such as *espn.com*). The reason provided by Disney for the failure was that the business model was not working.

Are EC and the Internet Doomed?

The previous discussion and the fall of the technology stocks in 2000/2001 might suggest that EC is doomed (e.g., Mandel, 2000).

We do not believe that this is the case. We view the failures as a normal consolidation of an industry that was over optimistic and driven by greed between 1996 and 2000. History is simply repeating itself: Between 1904 and 1908 more than 240 companies entered the then new automobile business in the United States. In 1910 there was a shakeout, and today, there are only three domestic automakers. But the size of the auto industry has grown by several hundredfold since then. It is our belief that EC will go through a similar process. So, let's look at some success stories.

Success Stories and Recommendations for the Future

There are hundreds of success stories, primarily in specialty and niche markets. One example is *webrx.com*, a successful beauty and health product store. Another one is *campusfood.com*, which serves students at many universities. *Monster.com* in the job finding business is doing very well and so is the airline Southwest Airlines Online (*iflyswa.com*). *Alloy.com* is successful as a young adult shopping and entertainment portal. For some CSFs see Table 16-3. Here are some of the reasons these and other companies do so well and some suggestions from EC experts on how to succeed.

- As of late 2000, more companies were pursuing mergers and acquisitions (e.g., *ivillage.com* with *women.com*). This seems to be a growing trend (see Bodow, 2000).
- Thousands of brick-and-mortar companies are adding online channels, slowly, and with great success. Examples are *uniglobe.com, staples.com, homedepot.com, clearCommerce.com,* 1-800 FLOWERS, and Southwest Airlines.
- Peter Drucker, the management guru, provides the following advice: "Analyze the opportunities, go out to look, keep it focused, start small (one thing at a time), and aim at market leadership" (Daly, 2000).
- A group of Asian CEOs recommend the following: select robust business models, understand the dotcom future, foster e-innovation, carefully evaluate a spin-off strategy, co-brand, employ ex-dotcom staff, and focus on the e-generation (e.g., *alloy.com* and *bolt.com*). See Phillips, 2000.

TABLE 16-3

Critical Success Factors for EC	
CSFs in the Old Economy	**CSFs for EC Success**
Vertically Integrate or Do It Yourself	Create new partnerships and alliances, stay with core competency
Deliver High-Value Products	Deliver high-value service offerings that encompass products
Build Share to Establish Economies of Scale	Optimize natural scale and scope of business, look at mass customization
Analyze Carefully to Avoid Missteps	Approach with urgency to avoid being locked out; use proactive strategies
Leverage Physical Assets	Leverage intangible assets, capabilities, and relationships—unleash dormant assets
Compete to Sell Product	Compete to control access and relationships with customers; compete with Web sites

- PriceWaterhouseCoopers suggests avoiding technology malfunctions that erode consumer trust. They also recommend effective project and risk management, and finally, they suggest that companies view risk as an opportunity.
- Many experts recommend contingency planning and preparing for disasters.
- Agrawal and others at The McKinsey Co. (2001) suggest that companies should match value proposition with customer segmentations, control extensions of product lines and business models, and avoid expensive technology.

Useem (2000) uncovered 12 truths about how the Internet really works, by analyzing the dotcom crash. The truths are:

1. **The Internet is not as disruptive to business as we thought.** While some companies changed drastically their industries (e.g., e-brokerages, Napster, eBay, electronic ticketing), most other impacts are gradual.
2. **If it doesn't make cents, it doesn't make sense.** It is astounding to see how few pure dotcom e-tailers had even a grasp of their gross margin. Many EC companies and projects will never be profitable, or it will take many years to reach profitability. Thus, the investment is not justifiable (Section 16.9).
3. **Time favors incumbents.** The Internet is viewed as an enabler, and more and more click-and-mortar companies are doing well. The threat of channel conflict has been vastly overstated. The new catch phrase is *"channel confluence."*
4. **Making a market is harder than it looks.** As indicated in Chapter 7, B2B exchanges need CSFs to survive. In some areas there is too much competition among exchanges, in others there is a liquidity problem.
5. **There is no such thing as "Internet time."** Moving very fast is not possible in most EC initiatives. Few companies have succeeded as quickly as eBay has. For most EC ventures, a long time is needed to reach success.
6. **"Branding" is not a strategy.** Every company wants to have brand recognition, but very few can. Unfortunately, companies build their strategies on the assumption that they will get quick recognition by customers, funding agencies, etc. Usually, it does not work this way.
7. **Entrepreneurship cannot be systematized.** Not everyone with an Internet idea can be an entrepreneur. An example is the creation of more than 350 Internet incubators (Chapter 8), which now are described as "incinerators of money."
8. **Investors are not your customers.** It looks like many companies' advertisements were directed to investors instead of to customers. People created companies with the major objective of getting them to the stock market as IPOs. In the process they neglected the business side of e-business.
9. **The Internet still changes everything.** While the mood may be that B2C is dead, it is really not. Slowly but surely, Internet sales are increasing, and in some countries and with certain products, growth is progressing extremely rapidly. The current downturn is a period of consolidation due to the major changes introduced by EC.
10. **The Internet changes your job.** Disintermediation does occur in some industries, as does reintermediation. Many jobs will be eliminated or changed. Intermediaries will have to provide value-added services or risk going out of business.

11. **The distinction between Internet companies and non-Internet companies is fading fast.** Online companies such as *Amazon.com* are building physical facilities and off-line companies are moving to a click-and-mortar posture. We may be moving to what Andy Grove, Intel's chairman said, "Within several years there won't be any Internet companies. All companies will be Internet companies, or they will be dead."

12. **The real wealth creation is yet to come.** As with our example of the auto industry, in the end, we will witness a large and profitable EC industry. It will take time, patience, and the correct strategy, but no one can stop it. The survivors will be the great winners.

Mougayar (1998) recommends assessing the following 10 steps and perfecting the outcomes of each one:

STEP 1: Conduct necessary education and training
STEP 2: Review current distribution and supply chain models
STEP 3: Understand what your customers and partners expect from the Web
STEP 4: Reevaluate the nature of your products and services
STEP 5: Give a new role to your human resources department
STEP 6: Extend your current systems to the outside
STEP 7: Track new competitors and market shares
STEP 8: Develop a Web-centric marketing strategy
STEP 9: Participate in the creation and development of virtual marketplaces
STEP 10: Install an EC management style

CONCLUSION

The suggestions on how to succeed can be summarized as follows: E-business has two sides, one of which is business. Any EC strategy and application must involve the basics, a sound business approach including strategy is a must.

16.17   MANAGERIAL ISSUES

The following issues are germane to management:

1. **Considering the strategic value of EC.** Internet technology offers an unprecedented opportunity for EC. Management has to understand how EC can improve marketing and promotions, customer service, and sales. Furthermore, new business opportunities can be found through EC. To capitalize on the potential of EC, management needs to view EC from a strategic perspective, not merely as a technological advancement.

2. **Considering the benefits and risks.** Strategic moves have to be carefully weighed against potential risks. Identifying CSFs for EC and analyzing cost-benefit as well as ROI should not be neglected. Benefits are often hard to quantify, especially when they are more strategic than operational cost savings. In such an analysis, risks should be addressed with contingency planning (deciding what to do if problems arise).

3. **Integration.** EC may lead to the realignment of current business procedures and departmental units to maximize the long-term benefits for the company; integrating existing databases and legacy applications with Web-based new applications is not a trivial task (Chapter 12). Because of such technical

sophistication, as well the potential impact of the integration on functional areas, senior management involvement is critical.

4. **Metrics.** The use of metrics is very popular. The problem with metrics is that you must compare "apples with apples." Therefore, one needs to be very careful in using metrics and in deriving conclusions whenever gaps between the metrics and actual performance are evidenced.

5. **Pilot projects.** When a company decides to go for a pilot project, creating a Web team representing all functional areas of the company is an important part of the implementation plan. After the pilot project is completed, it is necessary to reexamine the EC project strategies to assess the EC strategic planning effort and its results.

6. **Integrating policies and strategies.** It is necessary to integrate the market, technology, and policy opportunities in e-business strategy (see Jarvenpaa and Tiller, 1999).

Summary

In this chapter, you learned about the following EC issues as they relate to the learning objectives:

1. **Importance of strategic planning for EC.** Strategic planning clarifies what an EC project should do or focus on with respect to the company's mission and the given business environment. Because of the comprehensiveness of EC, conducting formal strategic planning is a must in many cases.

2. **The strategy planning process.** It is composed of four major phases: initiation, formulation, implementation, and assessment. A variety of tools are available to execute this process.

3. **EC strategy formulation.** The strategy formulation process involves understanding the industry and competition, as well as analyzing cost-benefit and ROI. It further gives guidance on whether to compete against others or to cooperate, such as forming an alliance in the market.

4. **Application discovery and portfolio building.** Uncovering EC applications can be done in several ways, such as finding solutions to problems or finding problems for proven solutions. Building the correct portfolio can be facilitated by special methodologies.

5. **CSFs and EC justification.** Identifying the CSFs and relating them to the EC project is a critical step in strategic planning. Without such factors, an EC project is likely to fail.

6. **EC strategy implementation.** Creating a Web team representing various functional areas and planning for resources are important parts of an implementation plan. A major implementation issue is whether or not to outsource.

7. **Strategy assessment.** A strategy must be monitored and assessed periodically. Corrective actions and strategy reformulation must follow.

8. **The role of metrics.** Metrics serve as guidelines to the various EC areas, from e-marketing strategy to e-budgeting.

9. **Understanding failures and learning from them.** Many EC initiatives and companies failed in 2000/2001. The major reasons were lack of appropriate planning and neglect of the business side of the e-business.

Key Terms

Balanced scorecard	Return on investment (ROI)
Business case	Scenario planning
Company analysis	Strategic alliance
Competitive intelligence	Strategic planning
Competitive strategy	Strategy
Cooperative strategy	Strategy assessment
Critical success factors (CSF)	Strategy formulation
Defensive strategy	Strategy implementation
EC strategy (e-strategy)	Strategy initiation
Fit	Strengths, Weaknesses, Opportunities, and Threats (SWOT)
Implementation plan	Value chain
Industry and competition analysis	Value chain analysis
Intangible benefits	Value-chain partnership
Joint venture	Value proposition
Metrics	Viability
Offensive strategy	Web team
Performance dashboard	
Portfolio strategy	

Questions for Review

1. Describe the objectives of strategic planning.
2. List the stages of strategic planning.
3. Describe what SWOT is.
4. Define the meaning and purpose of critical success factors in EC.
5. Describe what the value chain is in EC.
6. Explain what ROI is. Why is it important for EC?
7. Explain the concept of competitive strategies.
8. Explain the concept of cooperative strategies.
9. Define competitive intelligence.
10. Describe the procedures for implementing EC.
11. Explain the nature of EC project assessment.
12. Describe the reasons for EC infrastructure outsourcing.
13. Define metrics.
14. What is an application portfolio?

Questions for Discussion

1. How would you start an industry analysis by a small business that wants to launch an EC project?
2. What are some typical difficulties you may encounter during an environmental scanning process?
3. How would you apply the SWOT approach to a small, local bank evaluating its e-banking services?
4. What are the organizational-level CSFs for a small, local bank that is considering e-banking?

5. What would be typical values EC can add to the product distribution channels of a major toy manufacturer?
6. What might be typical competitive strategies for a company trying to launch a bookselling business online?
7. What might be typical cooperative strategies for a company trying to launch a bookselling business?
8. What would you tell an executive officer of a real estate company about the competitive intelligence capabilities in the real estate business as a justification for launching a new Web-based real estate business?
9. Explain the logic of Tjan's application portfolio approach.
10. How would you organize a Web team for a large retailer trying to launch a direct-selling business on the Internet?
11. *Amazon.com* decided not to open physical stores, while First Network Security Bank (FNSB) opened its first physical bank in 1999. Compare and discuss the two strategies.

Internet Exercises

1. Survey several online travel agencies (e.g., *Travelocity.com*, *cheaptickets.com*, *priceline.com*, *expedia.com*, and so on) on the Web and compare their business strategies for customers. Especially focus on how they compete against physical travel agencies.
2. Enter *digitalenterprise.org* and find Web metrics. Read the material on metrics and the use of metrics for advertisement.
3. Go to Nissan Motor Corporation's Web site (*nissan.com*). Discuss how Nissan complements its promotion and sales program with its Web presence. What are the business values added by its Web site?
4. Visit *companysleuth.com* and discuss the types of competitive information the site offers. The information is offered free to anyone. Why? The same vendor offers the Electronic Library (*elibrary.com*) for a fee. How are these two services related? Why is the first one offered free?
5. Check the music CD companies on the Internet (e.g., *CDNow.com*) and find out if any focus on specialized niche markets as a primary strategy.
6. Enter *ibm.com/procurement* and go to the e-procurement section. Read IBM's e-procurement strategy and the "Consultant's Report—Best Practices." Prepare a report on the best lessons you learned.
7. American Greetings is the world's largest greeting card company. Until the early 1980s, cards were sold mainly in specialty card stores (about 65 percent). However, by 1999 over 65 percent were sold at discount stores (e.g., Wal-Mart). Because of this fact and the strong competition in the greeting card industry, American Greetings profits declined sharply in 1999. Your job as a strategy consultant is to assess the potential impact of EC on American Greetings' business. Use a SWOT approach and prepare a report. Use stock market and financial information available for free on the Internet.
8. Enter *bolt.com* and *upoc.com* and compare their marketing strategies.
9. Enter *bluelight.com* and find out why it has succeeded where Kmart failed.

Team Assignments and Role Playing

1. Have three teams represent the following units of one click-and-mortar company: (a) an off-line division, (b) an online division, (c) top management. Each team member represents a different functional (or other) role within the division. The teams will develop a strategy in a specific industry (each three teams will represent a company in one industry). Teams will present their strategies.

2. The relationship between manufacturers and their distributors regarding sales on the Web can be very strained. Direct sales may cut into the distributors' business. Review some of the strategies available to handle such channel conflicts. Each team member is assigned to a company in a different industry. Study the strategies, compare and contrast them, and derive a proposed generic strategy.

3. Investigate how a beauty shop/hair salon can take advantage of a Web presence. Each team member should visit a local beauty shop. What types of services can be on the Web? Discuss any possibilities in the area of marketing, customer service, and sales. Are there any EC activities in which the various vendors can collaborate? As a team, prepare a report based on your findings.

4. Review the story of Cisco Online (Chapter 6) and read the latest news releases about Cisco's EC activities. Have each team member research one aspect of Cisco's EC activities. Then have the team propose answers to the following:
   a. Assume you are conducting strategic planning for Cisco. Create a table listing the costs and benefits of such planning. List both quantifiable and non-quantifiable items.
   b. Check the Cisco Web site. Assume you were in charge of forming a Web team. Identify expertise/human resources you need from different functional areas, as well as the different types of tasks to be accomplished.
   c. If you were asked to develop strategic planning for a new competitor of Cisco, what types of strategies would you choose? Check the networking equipment industry status from a competitive intelligence perspective and discuss the alternatives for the competing company.
   d. Cisco started its EC efforts in mid-1996 and slowly expanded them. In contrast, Intel Corp. moved to EC only in late 1998, but did it very rapidly. Comment on the two strategies.

REAL-WORLD CASE: Skymall's EC Strategy

Skymall, an Internet and airline retailer (printed catalogs), unveiled its first EC strategy on April 12, 1999. "Our strategy is designed to capitalize on the exclusive relationships developed by our in-flight catalog business and last year's strong performance of our *skymall.com* site," said Robert Worsley, chairman and CEO. "We are convinced that consumers are not going to navigate and bookmark numerous sites to cover all their needs. Our ultimate goal is to build a comprehensive one-stop site that provides consumers with a broad selection of best-selling merchandise and travel-related services and content that is easy to navigate and provides unique and entertaining consumer experiences." The company's mission is shown in Application Case 16.2. The EC strategy has several components.

Infrastructure Strategy

"A key component of our e-commerce strategy is to apply the knowledge we have developed from our existing business to further develop the infrastructure necessary to support our Web efforts. Specifically, we plan to upgrade the speed, performance and functionality of the company's existing *skymall.com* site to ensure that by the fourth quarter the consumer experience at *skymall.com* meets or exceeds that of other major e-commerce sites.

Content Strategy

"Merchandising plans call for Skymall to increase the variety and selection of merchandise offered on the Web by two primary means. First, Skymall plans to further leverage its relationships with its existing base of over 100 catalog vendors by adding more of their products to Skymall's database, in addition to the best-selling items already available in the in-flight catalog. Skymall has already made progress in this area in 1999, and has increased the number of products available through its Internet site to approximately three times the print catalog offering.

"The company's second merchandising strategy is to secure product content in new categories that have not been traditionally covered by the catalog industry by securing relationships directly with the manufacturers and other major distributors of products.

"To date, Skymall has secured relationships with numerous manufacturers and other distributors in categories that include electronics, health-related products, and home furnishings. In connection with the second phase of the planned infrastructure upgrades, Skymall anticipates that the products from many of these manufacturers will be available on its site."

Travel Strategy

"Leveraging its relationships with its airline and other travel partners, Skymall expects to launch a travel site in the third quarter of 1999. Through its airline and other relationships, the company expects to be able to secure travel content and to provide various value-added services to travelers. Initial plans call for links between *Skymall.com*'s travel and shopping sites in order to increase awareness of both sites. Ultimately, the company plans to incorporate shopping and travel into one comprehensive site." This site was launched in July 1999 and targets frequent flyers.

Marketing Alliance Strategy

"*Skymall.com*'s e-commerce strategy is to implement marketing programs designed to improve brand awareness, drive traffic to its site and increase consumer spending. Skymall believes the key to Skymall's success in its in-flight catalog business has been to successfully secure and manage numerous partner relationships with major airlines and merchants.

"Skymall plans to use its partnership relationship experience to form additional strategic partnership alliances with third parties, such as financial service providers and media companies. By bringing Skymall's product content to third parties to enable them to conduct EC on a cobranded site, Skymall believes it can also secure additional on- and off-line channels for promotions to the customer bases of these third parties at little or no cost to Skymall.

"In turn, through these proposed alliances, Skymall plans to give its partners access to some of the most demographically appealing consumers in the country through its existing in-flight catalog and hotel channels." Since 1999 the company have had an affiliate program which allow customers to move from other Web sites to Sky Hall's."

Broad-Band Technologies

"Experts believe that the convergence of television and the Web will occur in the foreseeable future, creating the opportunity to provide a richer content experience to consumers via broad band technologies.

"The Company believes that broad-band technologies will allow it to expand its reach, customer base, and enhance brand awareness, while offering much needed support to potential broad-band partners."

Workplace Web Initiative

"Given the increasing use of Internet in the workplace, as well as the significant number of dual-income households, Skymall believes that the corporate workplace is an ideal channel for further distribution of its products and services. The company plans to implement workplace marketing initiatives on Web-based intranet systems that deliver logo merchandise as well as other product content to consumers at work."

Investment Spending

"Skymall plans to invest significantly in its e-commerce strategy, and the investment is expected to cause Skymall to experience a loss for 1999 ranging between $1.00 and $1.20 per share.

"Skymall plans to invest the $20 million of expense and $7 million of capital expenditures in four major areas: $5 million to staff the Internet development and support team and to operate the recently opened New York office, $10 million for sales and marketing of the new sites, $5 million for infrastructure and the management team to lead the Company's growth initiatives, and $7 million of capital expenditures for computer equipment and software development.

"The Company expects to fund the e-commerce investment through catalog operations cash flow and its current cash position of approximately $4 million, as well as by re-negotiating its line of credit to increase its borrowing capacity. While these funds are expected to be sufficient to meet *Skymall.com*'s expansion objectives for 1999, the Company is continuing to explore other financing options."

Summary

"Research shows that consumers are quickly accepting the Internet as a new shopping medium, with about half of the households in the United States that had Internet access making at least one purchase online in the last six months," stated Bob Worsley. "We believe the fourth quarter of 1999 will present us with important opportunities in this new era of Internet shopping and we plan to capitalize on these opportunities by executing the strategies we have discussed today."

Questions for the case

1. A major objective of the strategy is to "drive traffic to the site." Explain why the company is expecting more visitors as a result of this strategy.

2. Can you make a few suggestions to the company about how to increase site traffic even further?

3. The company is talking about "leveraging its relationship with its travel partners." What do they mean by that and how is it reflected in the strategy?

4. Visit *Skymall.com* and identify all EC activities not cited here. Relate the various new applications to the types of EC.

5. What kind of infrastructure does Skymall need? (Think about customers, business partners, products.)

Note: In 2001 Skymall was acquired by Gemstar-TV Guide International

Sources: Adopted from several press releases 1999–2001 regarding the corporate strategy at *skymall.com*.

REFERENCES AND BIBLIOGRAPHY

Agrawal, V., et al. "E-Performance: The Path to Rational Exuberance," *The McKinsey Quarterly*, vol. 1 (2001).

Applegate, L. *Creating E-Business Models*. Boston, Massachusetts: Harvard Business School Publishing, 2000.

Baker, W., et al. "Price Smarter on the Net," *Harvard Business Review* (February 2001).

Barash, J., et al. "How E-Tailing Can Rise from the Ashes," *The McKinsey Quarterly*, vol. 3 (2000).

Bichler, M. and C. Loebbeke. "Pricing Strategies and Technologies for Online Delivered Content," *Journal of End User Computing* (April/June 2000).

Bodow, S. "Getting Hitched," *Business 2.0* (November 28, 2000).

Bonnett, K. R. *An IBM Guide to Doing Business on the Internet*. New York: McGraw-Hill, 2000.

Carpenter, P. *eBrands*. Boston: Harvard Business School Publishing, 2000.

Choi, S. Y. and A. B. Whinston, *The Internet Economy: Technology and Practice*, Austin, Texas: Smartcom, 2000.

Cohan, P. S. *Net Profit*. New York: Jossey-Bass, 1999.

CommerceNet Survey. *Barriers to Electronic Commerce*. Palo Alto, California: CommerceNet, 2000.

Copeland, T. E., et al. *Valuation: Measuring and Managing the Value of Companies*, 3rd ed. New York: Wiley, 2000.

Cunningham, M. J. *B2B: How to Build a Profitable E-Commerce Strategy*. Cambridge, Massachusetts: Peruses, 2000.

Daly, J. "Sage Advice," *Business 2.0* (August 22, 2000).

David, F. *Strategic Management: Concepts and Cases*, 7th ed. Upper Saddle River, New Jersey: Prentice Hall, 1998.

Deise, M. V., et al. *Executive's Guide to E-Business— From Tactics to Strategy*. New York: Wiley, 2000.

Dewan, R., et al. "Adoption of Internet-Based Product Customization and Pricing Strategies," Proceedings, 33rd HICSS, Hawaii (January 2000).

Downs, L. and M. Chunka. *Unleashing the Killer App: Digital Strategies for Market Dominance*. Boston, Massachusetts: Harvard Business School Press, 1998.

Earle, N. and P. Keen. *From .com to Profit*. New York: Jossey-Bass, 2000.

Ezor, J. I. *Clicking Through: A Survival Guide for Bringing Your Company Online*. New York: Bloomberg Press, 1999.

Falla, J. "Launch a Successful E-Commerce Site," *e-business Advisor* (February 1999).

Folz, R. J. "Build an E-Commerce Site with True ROI," *e-Business Advisor* (February 1999).

Ghosh, S. "Making Business Sense of the Internet," *Harvard Business Review* (March/April 1998).

Glater, J. D. "A High-Tech Domino Effect: As Dot-com's Go, So Go the E-Commerce Consultants," *New York Times* (December 6, 2000).

Guimaraes, T. and C. Armstrong. "Exploring the Relations Between Competitive Intelligence, IS Support, and Business Change," *Competitive Intelligence Review*, vol. 9, no. 3 (1997).

Gulati, R. and J. Garino. "Get the Right Mix of Bricks and Clicks," *Harvard Business Review* (May/June 2000).

Hackbarth, G. and W. J. Kettinger. "Building an e-Business Strategy," *Information Resource Management* (Summer 2000).

Hagel, J. and A. Armstrong. *Net Gain*. Boston, Massachusetts: Harvard Business School Press, 1997.

Hamel, G. "Why . . . It's Better to Question Answers Than Answer Questions," *Across The Board* (November/December 2000).

Hutchinson, A. "E-Commerce: Building a Model," *Communications Week* (March 17, 1997).

Jarvenpaa, S. L. and E. H. Tiller. "Integrating Market, Technology, and Policy Opportunities in E-Business Strategy," *Journal of Strategic Information Systems* (November 1999).

Jutla, D., et al. "A Methodology for Creating E-Business Strategy," Proceedings, 34th HICSS, Hawaii (January 2001).

Kalakota, R. and M. Robinson. *E-Business 2.0—Roadmap for Success*. Reading, Massachusetts: Addison Wesley, 2001.

Kalin, S. "Title Search," *CIO Web Business Magazine* (February 1, 1999).

Kaplan, R. S. and D. Norton. *The Balanced Scoreboard*. Boston, Massachusetts: Harvard Business School Press, 1996.

Kaplan, R. S. and D. P. Norton. "Having Trouble with Your Strategy? Then Map It," *Harvard Business Review* (September/October 2000a).

Kaplan, R. S. and D. P. Norton. *The Strategy-Focused Organization*. Boston, Massachusetts: Harvard Business School Publishing, 2000b.

Kare-Silver, M. D. *E-Shock: The Electronic Shopping Revolution: Strategies for Retailers and Manufacturers*. New York: AMACOM, 1999.

Kettinger, W. J. and G. Hackbarth. *Reading the Next Level of E-Commerce, Financial Times* (March 15, 1999).

Levinson, M. "Don't Stop Thinking About Tomorrow," *CIO Magazine* (December 1999/January 2000).

Liu, S. et al., "Software Agents for Environmental Scanning in Electronic Commerce," *Information Systems Frontiers*, vol. 2, no. 1 (2000).

Maitra, A. K. *Building a Corporate Internet Strategy*. New York: van Nostrand Reinhold, 1996.

Mandel, M. J. *The Coming Internet Depression*. New York: Basic Book, 2000.

McFarlan, F. W. "Information Technology Changes the Way You Compete," *Harvard Business Review* (May/June 1984).

McWilliam, G. "Building Stronger Brands Through Online Communities," *Sloan Management Review* (Spring 2000).

Mougayar, W. *Opening Digital Markets*, 2nd ed. New York: McGraw-Hill, 1998.

Otto, J. R. and Q. B. Chung. "A Framework for Cyber-Enhanced Retailing: Integrating E-Commerce Retailing with Brick-and-Mortar Retailing," *Electronic Markets*, vol. 10, no. 3 (2000).

Parker, M. *Strategic Transformation and Information Technology*. Upper Saddle River, New Jersey: Prentice Hall, 1996.

Patel, K. *Digital Transformation: The Essentials of E-Business Leadership*. New York: McGraw-Hill (2000).

Pffafenberger, B. *Building a Strategic Internet*. Foster City, California: IDG Books, 1998.

Phillips, M. "7 Steps to Your New E-Business," *Business Online* (August 2000).

Pickering, C. *E-Business Success Strategies: Achieving Business and IT Alignment*. Charleston, South Carolina: Computer Technology Research Corp., 2000.

Plant, R. T. *E-Commerce: Formulation of Strategy*. Upper Saddle River, New Jersey: Prentice Hall, 2000.

Porter, M. *Competition in Global Industries*. Boston, Massachusetts: Harvard Business School Press, 1996.

Porter, M. E. *Competitive Advantage: Creating and Sustaining Superior Performance*. New York: Free Press, 1985.

Pottruck, D. and T. Pearce. *Clicks-and-Mortar*. New York: John Wiley & Sons, 2001.

Power, B. C. and R. Sharda. "Obtaining Business Intelligence on the Internet," *Long Range Planning* (April 1997).

Prasad, B. and P. Harker. "Pricing Online Banking Services Amid Network Extranalities," Proceedings, 33rd HICSS, Hawaii (January 2000).

Raisch, W. *The eMarketplace Strategies for Succeeding in B2B*. New York: McGraw-Hill, 2000.

Raskin, A. "The ROIght Stuff," *CIO Web Business Magazine* (February 1999).

Rayport, J. and B. J. Jaworski. *E-Commerce*. New York: McGraw-Hill, 2001.

Rosenoer, J., et al. *The Clickable Corporation: Successful Strategies for Capturing the Internet Advantage*. New York: Free Press, 1999.

Schulman, M. and R. Smith. *The Internet Strategic Plan*. New York: John Wiley & Sons, 1997.

Selz, D. and P. Schubert. "Web Assessment—A Model for the Evaluation and Assessment of Successful Electronic Commerce Applications," *Electronic Markets*, vol. 7, no. 3 (1997).

Semler, R. "How We Went Digital Without a Strategy," *Harvard Business Review* (September/October 2000).

Seybold, P., *Customers.com Handbook—An Executive Guide and Technology Roadmap,* Boston, Massachusetts: Patricia Seybold Group, Inc., 1998.

Shapiro, C. and H. Varian. *Competitive Strategy for the Information Age*, Boston, Massachusetts: Harvard Business School Press, 1998.

Shaw, J. and J. Sperry. *eCommerce as a Business Strategy: An Overview*. Marietta, Georgia: E-Commerce Strategies, 2000.

Stuart, A. "Hired Guns," *CIO Web Business Magazine* (November 1, 1999).

Tedeschi, B. "Lessons from Online Rubble," *New York Times* (December 11, 2000).

Tennant, H. R. *Effective E-Strategies: The Themes and Strategies at Work on the Web*. Dallas, Texas: Stanbury Press, 2000.

Timmers, P. *Electronic Commerce—Strategies and Models for Business-to-Business Trading*. Chichester, U.K.: Wiley, 1999.

Tjan, A. K. "Finally, A Way to Put Your Internet Portfolio in Order," *Harvard Business Review* (February 2001).

Turban, E., et al. *Information Technology for Management*, 3rd ed. New York: John Wiley & Sons, 2002.

Useem, J. "Dot-Coms: What Have We Learned," *Fortune* (October 2000).

Venkatraman, N. "Five Steps to a Dot-Com Strategy: How to Find Your Footing on the Web," *Sloan Management Review* (Spring 2000).

Voss, C. "Developing an eService Strategy," *Business Strategy Review* (Spring 2000).

Ward, J. and P. Griffiths. *Strategic Planning for Information Systems*, 2nd ed. Chichester, U.K.: Wiley and Sons, 1996.

Ware, J., et al. *The Search for Digital Excellence*. New York: McGraw-Hill, 1998.

Wheelen, T. and J. Hunger. *Strategic Management and Business Policy*, 6th ed. Reading, Massachusetts: Addison-Wesley, 1998.

Whipple, L. C. "The Web's Return on Investment," *e-Business Advisor* (January 1999)

Whitaker, B. "A Buyer's Market: The Dot-Com Liquidation Sale," *New York Times* (February 4, 2001).

Windham, L. "Overcome E-Business Barriers," *e-Business Advisor* (January 2000).

Yoffie, D. and M. Cusumano. "Judo Strategy: The Competitive Dynamics of Internet Time," *Harvard Business Review* (January/February 1999).

Young, D., et al. "Strategic Implications of Electronic Linkages," *Information Systems Management* (Winter 1999).

17

The Regulatory Environment of Electronic Commerce*

LEARNING OBJECTIVES

Upon completion of this chapter, the reader will be able to:

- List and describe the major legal issues related to EC.

- Understand the difficulties of protecting privacy and describe the measures taken by companies and individuals to protect it.

- Describe the intellectual property issues in EC and the measures provided for its protection.

- Describe some of the ethical issues in EC and the measures organizations take to improve ethics.

- Understand the conflict between Internet indecency and free speech and the attempts to resolve the conflict.

- Describe the issues involved in imposing sales tax on the Internet.

- Differentiate between contracts online and off-line.

- Discuss some legal issues of computer crimes.

- Describe the measures available to protect buyers and sellers on the Internet.

---

* This chapter was updated by Matthew K. O. Lee, City University of Hong Kong.

CONTRACTUAL ISSUES IN EC

ProCD sold a database program called SelectPhone containing information from 3,000 telephone directories. The company sold the same program to both commercial users and individual retail consumers, with a discount offered to the noncommercial consumers. The discount was based, in part, on an agreement, or license, that restricted the use of the program to noncommercial purposes. Mr. Zeidenberg bought a retail version of the program and proceeded to resell it over the Internet, a blatant violation of the agreement. When sued by ProCD, Zeidenberg argued that the contract was not enforceable since he was unable to examine it until after he had purchased and opened the package (the agreement is shrink-wrapped with the software). The court responded by explaining that Zeidenberg bound himself to the terms by using the program when he had the opportunity to return it. The Supreme Court held (in the 1990s) that "Shrink-wrap licenses are enforceable unless their terms are objectionable on grounds applicable to contracts in general."

The Court reasoned that placing the terms on the outside of the box would require such fine print that the function of the information would be diminished. Conversely, if the post-sale terms are additional to an already formed contract, then those terms are probably not enforceable as part of the agreement. The Court also recognized that an increasing number of software sales are performed by wire where the opportunity to review conditions may not occur until the "package" is in the possession of the consumer. As a result of these forward-looking facts and supposition of the direction of online software sales, the Court established a precedent that addressed a small portion of electronic contract law that paves the way for enhanced EC.

COPYRIGHT INFRINGEMENT ON THE WEB

David LaMacchia was a student at MIT who ran a computer bulletin board system that was accessible over the Internet. On this bulletin board he offered free copies of such copyrighted software as Word, Excel, and WordPerfect, among others. He was distributing the copyright-protected software without charge. When he was sued (*United States vs. LaMacchia*), he was found not guilty since he did not benefit financially from the sales. The applicable law, the Copyright Infringement Act, stated that "the defendant must have willfully infringed the copyright and gained financially." Although he had definitely infringed the copyright, he could not be held liable for damages since there was no financial gain on his part. This was a loophole in the Copyright Infringement Act, and it was fixed after LaMacchia's trial.

EMUSIC SUES *MP3.COM* OVER COPYRIGHTS

EMusic.com, Inc., an online music provider, filed a copyright infringement lawsuit in December 2000 against *MP3.com*, Inc. and its *My.MP3.com* streaming media service.

The suit alleges that *MP3.com* is infringing on the copyright of some albums for which *EMusic.com* owns the digital rights.

MP3.com has faced a number of copyright infringement suits during 2000. The Recording Industry Association of America (RIAA) targeted the company because of its *My.MP3.com* service, which, in its initial configuration, allowed users to listen to their CDs from any computer with an Internet connection.

Warner Brothers Music Group, Inc., EMI Group PLC, BMG Entertainment, and Sony Music Entertainment, Inc. settled their lawsuits against *MP3.com* for an estimated $20 million each.

My.MP3.com had been suspended since April 2000 because of the pending lawsuits. In December 2000, *My.MP3.com* began running again as a subscription-based music service.

JULIA ROBERTS DOMAIN NAME

The United Nation's World Intellectual Property Organization (WIPO) ruled in summer 2000 that movie star Julia Roberts owns her own domain name (although she is not using it at the moment). The Organization's Complaint and Arbitration Center, which coordinates international patents, copyrights, and trademarks, upheld the actress's claim against a U.S. dealer in celebrity names, asserting that he had no rights to *juliaroberts.com*. Conversely, New Jersey dealer Russell Boyd claims that Ms. Roberts has no common law trademark rights in her name. The WIPO ruled that Mr. Boyd had no rights or legitimate interest in the domain name and had registered it in bad faith. In November 1998, Mr.

Boyd put *juliaroberts.com* up for auction on the eBay site and turned down a $4,480 bid; at the same time

Mr. Boyd registered and auctioned approximately 50 other sites including *alpacino.com*.

17.2   ETHICS IN EC

The recent explosion of EC has provided businesses with enormous new opportunities undreamt of before. New industries are emerging and new business models are being invented constantly. An entirely new spectrum of business and commerce has emerged. The entire business environment is changing, and so are the regulatory regimes governing it. Law and ethics are the key regulatory components of any business environment. The new business environment includes new legal and ethical problems that businesspeople in the digital economy must be acquainted with in order to handle them properly and operate effectively.

There are three main groups of EC users in any country. They include businesses, private citizens, and government and law enforcement agencies. Regulating EC transactions among these groups of users is a difficult task, as they may want to pursue very different interests. Complicating the matter further is the global dimension of EC. Thus, regulating the relationships among these different groups of users across different countries poses an even greater challenge to laws and ethics.

The opening vignettes illustrate several legal issues related to EC. The first one deals with the validity of contracts related to software purchase and distribution. This issue is especially important because software is a digitized product and its sales online are growing rapidly. In addition to contract validity, this vignette is related to the issue of intellectual property and software piracy. The second vignette deals with the issue of unethical (now illegal) distribution of software, which is related to intellectual property and software piracy. The third vignette points to distribution of music, with possible violation of copyright. The last vignette deals with a domain name dispute.

EC is so new that the legal, ethical, and other public policy issues that are necessary for EC's existence are still evolving. The second vignette illustrates a legal loophole that was fixed only after the incident occurred. Yet, such issues are extremely important to the success of EC as they encompass one of the major pillars that support EC applications (see Figure 1-2 in Chapter 1). As a matter of fact, most of the surveys that attempt to find the inhibitors of EC consistently place legal and related public policy issues at the top of the list.

Legal and Ethical Issues: An Overview

The implementation of EC involves many legal issues. These can be classified in several ways. We have segregated the EC-related legal issues in this chapter into the following categories:

- **Privacy.** This issue is the most important issue for consumers in many countries. And indeed, privacy statements can be found today in most large EC-related Web sites. Compliance with the Privacy Act of 1974 (U.S.) and its extensions are not simple, since the line between legal definitions and ethics is not always clear, as we show later.
- **Intellectual property.** Protecting intellectual property on the Web is very difficult since it is easy and inexpensive to copy and disseminate digitized information. Furthermore, it is very difficult to monitor who is using others' intellectual property and how. Copyright, patents, trademarks, and other intellectual property issues are governed by both government legislations and the common law.
- **Free speech.** The Internet provides the largest opportunity for free speech that has ever existed. Yet, this freedom may offend some people and may collide with the United States' or other countries' indecency acts. Again, the line is not always clear between what is illegal and what is unethical.
- **Taxation.** At the present time, it is illegal to impose new sales taxes on Internet business. A possible collision between federal and state legislation is possible, as well as between tax laws of different countries.
- **Computer crimes.** Computers are an integral part of all EC processes. Therefore, crimes involving computers assume added significance in EC. Computer crime usually refers to computer fraud and computer abuse. Software piracy belongs to intellectual property infringement and is usually not classified as computer crime. This topic is further discussed in Chapter 13.
- **Consumer protection.** Many legal issues that deal with consumer protection, ranging from misrepresentation to different kinds of fraud, are related to electronic trade.
- **Other legal issues.** Several other EC legal issues exist, including topics such as validity of contracts, legality of public key encryption (PKI) infrastructures, jurisdiction over trades, encryption policies, Internet gambling, and legal liability of ISPs.

LEGAL ISSUES VS. ETHICS

In theory, one can distinguish between legal issues and ethical issues. If you do something that is illegal, you are breaking the law. If you do something unethical, you may not be breaking the law. Obviously, many illegal acts are unethical as well. The problem is that, in information technology (IT), it is not always clear what is illegal, and ethical issues may be debatable. In many cases, legislation is evolved from ethics (see Figure 17-1). The rest of this chapter deals with several topics that, under most circumstances, can be both illegal and unethical. Before we explore these issues, let us examine the meaning of ethics.

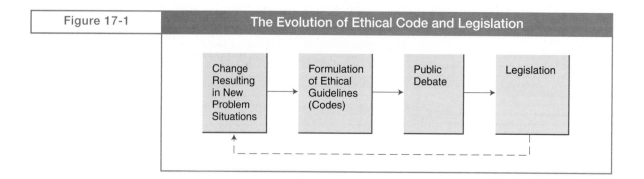

Figure 17-1 | The Evolution of Ethical Code and Legislation

Ethical Issues

There are some fundamental concepts that must be understood in order to make sense of the various issues in question. There is often confusion between legal and ethical issues. Indeed, they are very much related. But they are not the same.

Laws are enacted by governments and developed through case precedents (to form the body of common law). Laws are strict legal rules governing the acts of all citizens within their jurisdictions. **Ethics** is a branch of philosophy that deals with what is considered to be right and wrong. Over the years, philosophers have proposed many ethical guidelines, yet what is unethical is not necessarily illegal. Thus, in many instances, an individual faced with an ethical decision is not considering whether or not to break the law. In today's complex environment, the definitions of right and wrong are not always clear. Ethics has assumed a new dimension of importance as EC opens up a new spectrum of unregulated activities. Many of these activities fall into "gray" areas. Businesspeople need guidelines as to what behaviors are reasonable under any given set of circumstances. Consider the following scenarios:

- A company developed profiles of potential customers from information collected with cookies and questionnaires and sold the list to advertisers. Some of the profiles were inaccurate; consequently, people received numerous pieces of inappropriate e-mail.
- Management allowed employees to use the Web for limited personal use, then monitored usage without employees' knowledge.
- The president of a software development company marketed tax advice online, knowing it had bugs. As a result, some users filed incorrect tax returns and were penalized by the IRS.

Whether these actions are considered unethical depends on the organization, country, cultures, value systems, the ethical theories one subscribes to, and the specific circumstances surrounding the scenarios.

The spread of EC has created many new ethical situations. For example, the issue of a company monitoring e-mail is very controversial (47 percent of the readers of *Information Week,* May 10, 1999, believe companies have the right to do so, 53 percent disagree). Obviously, there are major differences among companies and individuals with respect to what is right and wrong.

There are also differences regarding ethics among different countries. What is unethical in one culture may be perfectly acceptable in another. Many Western countries, for example, have a much higher concern for individuals and their rights to privacy than some Asian countries. In Asia, more emphasis is, in general, placed on the benefits to society rather than on the rights of individuals. Some countries, such as Sweden and Canada, have very strict privacy laws; others have none. This situation may obstruct the flow of information among countries. And indeed, the European Community Commission issued guidelines in 1998 to all its member countries regarding the rights of individuals to access information about themselves and to correct errors.

The diversity of EC applications and the increased use of technology have created new ethical issues, as illustrated throughout this text. An attempt to organize IT ethical issues into a framework was undertaken by Mason (1986) and Mason et al. (1995), who categorized ethical issues into privacy, accuracy, property, and accessibility.

- **Privacy.** Collection, storage, and dissemination of information about individuals.
- **Accuracy.** Authenticity, fidelity, and accuracy of information collected and processed.
- **Property.** Ownership and value of information and intellectual property.
- **Accessibility.** Right to access information and payment of fees to access it.

Representative questions and issues in each category are listed in Table 17-1.

Mason et al. (1995) also developed a model for ethical reasoning that shows the process that leads to ethical judgment when an individual is faced with an ethical issue.

In an attempt to improve the ethical climate, companies and professional organizations develop their own codes of ethics, a collection of principles intended as a guide for its members (Oz, 1994). For a discussion of the code of the Association for Computing Machinery (ACM), see Anderson et al. (1993). Legal and ethical issues are important for the success of EC. Several organizations that are active in

TABLE 17-1

A Framework for Ethical Issues

Privacy	Accuracy
• What information about oneself should an individual be required to reveal to others? • What kind of surveillance can an employer use on its employees? • What things can people keep to themselves and not be forced to reveal to others? • What information about individuals should be kept in databases, and how secure is the information there?	• Who is responsible for the authenticity, fidelity, and accuracy of information collected? • How can we ensure that information will be processed properly and presented accurately to users? • How can we ensure that errors in databases, data transmissions, and data processing are accidental and not intentional? • Who is to be held accountable for errors in information, and how is the injured party compensated?

Property	Accessibility
• Who owns the information? • What are the just and fair prices for its exchange? • Who owns the channels of information? • How should one handle software piracy (copying copyrighted software)? • Under what circumstances can one use proprietary databases? • Can corporate computers be used for private purposes? • How should experts who contribute their knowledge to create knowledge bases be compensated? • How should access to information channels be allocated?	• Who is allowed to access information? • How much should be charged for permitting accessibility to information? • How can accessibility to computers be provided for employees with disabilities? • Who will be provided with equipment needed for accessing information? • What information does a person or an organization have a right or a privilege to obtain—under what conditions and with what safeguards

Sources: Compiled from Mason (1986) and Mason et al. (1995).

this area are the Organization for Economic Cooperation and Development (*oecd.org*), CommerceNet (*commerce.net*), and the Information Technology Association of America (*itaa.org*). For an overview see Creco (2001).

17.3   PROTECTING PRIVACY

Privacy means different things to different people. In general, **privacy** is the *right to be left alone and the right to be free of unreasonable personal intrusions.* A definition of **information privacy**, according to Agranoff (1993), is the "claim of individuals, groups, or institutions to determine for themselves when, and to what extent, information about them is communicated to others."

Privacy has long been a legal and social issue in the United States and many other countries. The right to privacy is recognized today in virtually all U.S. states and by the federal government, either by statute or common law. The definition of privacy can be interpreted quite broadly; however, the following two rules have been followed fairly closely in past court decisions: (1) The right of privacy is not absolute. Privacy must be balanced against the needs of society. (2) The public's right to know is superior to the individual's right of privacy. These two rules show why it is difficult, in some cases, to determine and enforce privacy regulations. Federal privacy legislation related to EC is listed in Table 17-2.

The complexity of collecting, sorting, filing, and accessing information manually from several different agencies was, in many cases, a built-in protection against misuse of private information. It was simply too expensive, cumbersome, and complex to invade privacy. However, personal computers, powerful software, large databases, and the Internet have created an entirely new dimension of accessing and using data. The inherent power in systems that can access vast amounts of data can be used for the good of society. For example, by matching records with the aid of a computer, it is possible to eliminate or reduce fraud, government mismanagement, tax evasion, welfare cheats, family support filchers, employment of illegal

TABLE 17-2 | **Representative U.S. Federal Privacy Legislation**

Legislation	Content
Privacy Act of 1974	Prohibits the government from collecting information secretly. Information collected must be used only for a specific purpose.
Privacy Protection Act of 1980	Provides privacy protection in computerized and other documents.
Electronic Communications Privacy Act of 1986	Prohibits private citizens from intercepting data communication without authorization.
Computer Security Act of 1987	Requires security of information regarding individuals.
Computer Matching and Privacy Act of 1988	Regulates the matching of computer files by state and federal agencies.
Video Privacy Protection Act of 1988	Protects privacy in transmission of pictures.
Fair Health Information Practices Act of 1997	Provides a code of fair information.
Consumer Internet Privacy Protection Act of 1997	Requires prior written consent before a computer service can disclose subscribers' information.
Federal Internet Privacy Protection Act of 1997 (H.R. 1367)	Prohibits federal agencies from disclosing personal records over the Internet.
Communications Privacy and Consumer Empowerment Act of 1997 (H. R. 1964)	Protects privacy rights in online commerce.
Data Privacy Act of 1997 (H. R. 2368)	Limits the use of personally identifiable information and regulates spamming.
Computer Security Enhancement Act of 2000	Policy on digital signature.
Financial Services Modernization Act of 1999	Bans dissemination of consumer information without consumer consent.

aliens, and so on. The question is: What price must every individual pay in terms of loss of privacy so that the government can better apprehend criminals?

One of the most difficult issues related to information privacy is "who owns information?" The information in large databases has been compiled by many people at different times. A comprehensive discussion of this issue is provided by Wells-Branscomb (1994). With the widespread use of the Internet and EC, the issue of privacy becomes more critical. A special organization called the Electronic Privacy Information Center (*epic.org*) is trying to protect privacy. Also see Cavoukian and Tapscott (1997); Schneier and Banisar (1997); and Wang, Lee, and Wang (1998) for comprehensive coverage. Some issues of privacy are discussed next.

Privacy Issues

Online businesses constantly gather and use demographic information from users who are afraid that their personal data, including credit card numbers or their behavior on the Internet, may be sold, used, or revealed in an inappropriate manner. Such fears keep many consumers from shopping online. Among the 77 percent of Internet users who have never purchased products online, 86 percent say that they have been holding back out of fear that others might use their credit card number or other private information without their consent. Obviously, this is a significant hindrance to the growth of EC.

There are several issues related to privacy, which we discuss here. One issue, spamming, we will discuss in Section 17.5.

How Is Private Information Collected?

Here are examples of the ways someone can collect private information through the Internet (Rainone et al. 1998):

- Reading your newsgroup postings.
- Finding you in the Internet directory.
- Making your browser record information about you.
- Recording what your browsers say about you.
- Reading your e-mail.

Web site self-registration and the use of cookies are two of the major sources of information for companies seeking to collect personal data.

WEB SITE SELF-REGISTRATION

Web sites can gather customer information through filled-out registration questionnaires. In a registration process, customers type in their private information, such as name, address, phone, e-mail address, or even interests and hobbies, in order to receive a password to participate in a lottery, to receive information, or to play a game. This information may be collected for planning the business, sold to a third party (sometimes an unknown party), and used in an inappropriate manner. Consequently, users have concerns over privacy information, although self-registration creates fewer concerns than cookies.

It is interesting to note that the Eighth User Survey by GVU (1998) found that 40 percent of all users have falsified information when registering online. Of all U.S. and European respondents, 66.49 percent reported that they don't register because they don't know how the information is going to be used. In addition, 62.78 percent don't feel that registration is worthwhile considering the content of the sites, and 57.57 percent stated that they don't trust the sites collecting this information from them. These reasons, along with others (lack of time, as well as unwillingness to report one's address, name, or e-mail), clearly illustrate why only 6.01 percent of all respondents always register when requested.

COOKIES

A **cookie** is a piece of information that allows a Web site to record one's comings and goings. Cookies help Web sites maintain user status. This means that Web sites can "remember" information about users and respond to their preferences on a particular site, process transparent user passwords, and so on.

A cookie can be viewed as a temporary identity. Each time a person goes to a Web site, it is as though they are visiting it for the very first time. Cookies allow Web sites to maintain information on a particular user across HTTP connections.

More specifically, cookies allow Web sites (servers) to deliver simple data to a client (user); request that the client store the information; and, in certain circumstances, return the information to the Web site. Most leading browsers, including Netscape Navigator and Microsoft Internet Explorer, support cookies.

Web sites use cookies for various reasons. Sites such as Yahoo! or Excite use cookies to personalize information. Some sites, such as *Amazon.com* or Microsoft, use cookies to improve online sales/services, while others, such as AltaVista or DoubleClick, attempt to simplify the way popular links or demographics are tracked. In addition, Web site designers can keep sites fresh and relevant to the user's interests by using cookies. For instance, an online newspaper may want to enable subscribers to log in without having to enter a password at every visit. An airline may want to keep track of a customer's seating preferences, so that it does not have to ask whether a window or aisle seat is desired each time a reservation is made. Cookies can be very handy for users, too. Some users do not mind having cookies used to make their Web browsing more convenient; they find it cumbersome to enter a password or fill out a form over and over again.

However, cookies have brought about more concerns over privacy than self-registration because cookies allow Web sites to collect private information such as users' preferences, interests, and surfing patterns on the Web sites users visit. Furthermore, personal profiles created by cookies are more accurate than self-registration because, as indicated earlier, almost half of users falsify information when registering. Therefore, cookie features have been very attractive for Internet marketers. The demand for cookies is unlikely to decline, and concerns such as user privacy and legal enforcement have grown. The potential for abuse also exists. For example, if a user often visits Web sites associated with racial issues and his or her surfing pattern is revealed by an opposing party, his or her rights might be abused. In a legal example, some perpetrators engaging in pornography have been arrested by tracking their behavior online. Although these cases were considered a success, anxiety remains. What if the government or police track behavior on the Internet without notice, consent, or just cause?

Protection Against Cookies. There are some solutions to cookies. First, users can delete cookie files stored in their computers. However, deleting cookie files entirely will cause users to start from scratch with every Web site they usually visit. It may, therefore, be preferable to open the cookies.txt file (in the case of Netscape) and remove only the entries users do not like, or go to the cookies folder (in the case of Microsoft Explorer) and delete the unwanted files from the servers.

The second solution is the use of anticookie software. Pretty Good Privacy's Cookie Cutter is free and uses filters to either block or allow cookies at a user's command. Luckman's Anonymous Cookie is also free for Windows users and instantly disables all cookies in a user's cookie directory or cookie file allowing users to browse the World Wide Web anonymously. Cookie Crusher is free as well and automatically accepts or rejects cookies from user-selected sites. Cookie Monster is free for Macintosh users.

After the FTC hearing of June 1997 regarding privacy concerns online, among other topics, Netscape and Microsoft introduced options in their browsers that allows users to refuse all cookies without having to click through the warnings. In addition, Netscape Communicator has an option for a user who wants to accept only the cookie that is going to be returned to the domain on which the user is logged. This option is aimed at stopping third-party cookies used by advertisers.

Privacy Protection Issues

How organizations collect and use personal information, together with their privacy protection practices, can be summarized in five principles, which provide guidelines for the collection and dissemination of personal information and which are shared by European countries, Canada, some other countries, and the United States. These five basic principles are:

1. **Notice/awareness.** Consumers must be given notice of an entity's information practices prior to collection of personal information. Consumers must be able to make informed decisions about the type and extent of their disclosures based on the intentions of the party collecting the information.
2. **Choice/consent.** Consumers must be made aware of their options as to how their personal information may be used as well as any potential secondary uses of the information. Consent may be granted through opt-out clauses requiring steps to prevent collection of information; in other words, no action equals consent. Consumers may grant consent through opt-in clauses, requiring steps to allow the collection of information.
3. **Access/participation.** Consumers must be able to access their personal information and challenge the validity of the data.
4. **Integrity/security.** Consumers must be assured that the data is secure and accurate. It is necessary for those collecting the data to take whatever precautions are required to ensure that data is protected from loss, unauthorized access, destruction, fraudulent use, and to take reasonable steps to gain information from reputable and reliable sources.
5. **Enforcement/redress.** There must always be a method of enforcement and remedy, otherwise there is no real deterrent or enforceability for privacy issues. The alternatives are government intervention, legislation for private remedies, or self-regulation.

The implementation of these principles may not be simple as is illustrated in Application Case 17.1.

APPLICATION CASE   17.1

The Case of Microsoft and GeoCities Privacy Policies

Microsoft

Microsoft's Web site posts privacy policies explaining why Microsoft asks customers about themselves, what cookies are used for, and so forth. Among other things, it says that customers are in charge of deciding what Microsoft knows about them and that Microsoft uses customers' information to improve its site and refine its services. Moreover, it says that although Microsoft may share customer information with its partner companies, it will not do so without the customer's consent. Also, customers can update and edit their information at the Personal Information Center, a service that should be obligatory rather than optional.

GeoCities

GeoCities has several million members, and industry reports have identified it as the third most frequently visited site on the Web. In August 1998, GeoCities agreed to settle Federal Trade Commission (FTC) charges that it misrepresented the purposes for which it was collecting personal identifying information. GeoCities misled its customers, both children and adults, by not telling the truth about how it was using their personal information. In order to become a member of GeoCities, individuals must complete an online application form that requests certain personal identifying information. Through this registration process, GeoCities created a database that held e-mail and postal addresses, member interest areas, and demographics, including income, education, gender, marital status, and occupation. The personal "mandatory" information was supposed to be used only in cases where members were provided with specific advertising offers and products or services they requested, and the "optional" information (education level, income, marital status, occupation, and interests) was not supposed to be released to anyone without the member's permission. In fact, this information was disclosed to third parties who used it to target members for solicitations beyond those agreed to by the member.

This is the first FTC case involving Internet privacy. Under the settlement, GeoCities agreed to post a clear and prominent privacy notice on its site telling consumers what information is being collected and for what purpose, to whom it will be disclosed, and how consumers can access and remove the information. GeoCities also must obtain parental consent before collecting information from children 12 and under. This provision conforms to current industry self-regulatory guidelines. This case is a wake-up call to all Internet marketers, because their information collection practices must be accurate and complete. The FTC will continue to monitor these Internet sites and bring enforcement actions when it is appropriate.

Source: Bowman (March 2000).

Protecting Your Privacy

Here are nine suggestions about how you can protect your privacy:

1. Think before you give out personal information on a site.
2. Track the use of your name.
3. Keep your newsgroup posts out of archives.

4. Use the Anonymizer when browsing.
5. Live without cookies.
6. Use anonymous remailers.
7. Use encryption.
8. Reroute your mail away from your office.
9. Ask your ISP or employer about a privacy policy.

ANONYMIZERS

One way to increase privacy is to surf the Web anonymously. A number of tools can be used to do so (Cranor, 1999). This is done with the help of intelligent agents, which can work along with regulatory and self-regulatory frameworks to provide online privacy protection (See Figure 17-2).

LEGISLATION

Legislation of private remedies has included the proposal of such acts as the U.S. Consumer Internet Privacy Act, which seeks to regulate the use of personal information by prohibiting third-party disclosure and expanding online subscriber rights. The Federal Internet Privacy Protection Act prohibits federal agencies from disclosing personal records or making identifying records about an individual's medical, financial, or employment history. The Communications Privacy and

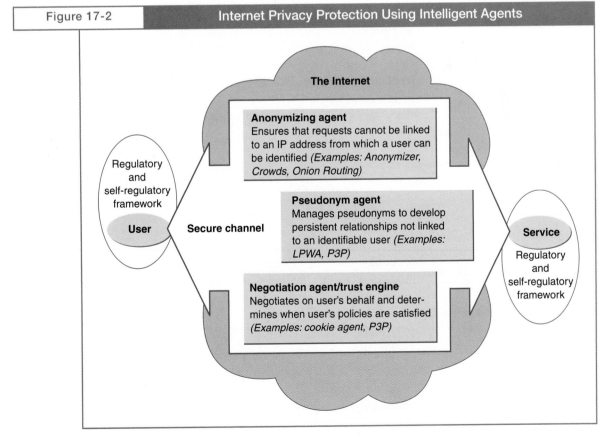

Figure 17-2   Internet Privacy Protection Using Intelligent Agents

The Internet

Anonymizing agent
Ensures that requests cannot be linked to an IP address from which a user can be identified *(Examples: Anonymizer, Crowds, Onion Routing)*

Pseudonym agent
Manages pseudonyms to develop persistent relationships not linked to an identifiable user *(Examples: LPWA, P3P)*

Negotiation agent/trust engine
Negotiates on user's behalf and determines when user's policies are satisfied *(Examples: cookie agent, P3P)*

Regulatory and self-regulatory framework

User   Secure channel

Service

Regulatory and self-regulatory framework

Source: Cranor (1999) pg. 30.

Consumer Empowerment Act is perhaps the most broad in scope and attempts to protect privacy rights in EC through a variety of measures. This act requires the FTC to report online privacy rights in EC including the collection and use of personal data. It also expands previous laws to include the facilitation and development of improved safety measures in online commerce and requires access providers to offer blocking software. Finally, it obligates the Federal Communications Commission to establish procedures to ensure consideration of the needs of ISPs and their customers for efficient interconnection for packet-switched networks.

The Data Privacy Act is another piece of legislation that seeks not only to limit the use of personal information, but also to regulate the dissemination of spam. This act calls for an industry committee that would establish voluntary guidelines to limit the use and collection of personal information for commercial marketing purposes. Another committee would develop a registration system for spammers and devise a process for consumer complaints.

The role of government in the protection of privacy is ambiguous. Societal regulation and authority has proven to be a necessity, but not at the expense of individual freedoms and civil liberties. Ultimately, self-regulation and discretion may be the best alternatives to reliance on outside oversight. Consumers must feel confident that policies, procedures, and avenues for redress of grievances are available before EC can reach its full potential.

FEDERAL TRADE COMMISSION (FTC) AUDIT

The FTC audited 1,400 U.S. commercial Web sites in March 1998 in order to measure the effectiveness of self-regulation; that is, whether Web sites are addressing consumers' privacy concerns through self-regulatory measures. The FTC surveyed Web sites that were likely to be of interest to consumers, including health, retail, and financial sites, and the most popular commercial sites. Specific practices examined were:

- Notice by the site of its information-gathering and dissemination policies.
- An opportunity for users to exercise choice over how their personal information is used.
- User control over personal information.
- Verification and oversight of claims made by the site.
- Recourse for resolving users' complaints.

As a result of the survey, the FTC found that privacy protection on the Internet is very poor. In its June 1998 "Report to Congress on Privacy Online," the FTC concluded that the "industry's efforts to encourage voluntary adoption of the most basic fair information practices have fallen short of what is needed to protect consumers."

MOVEMENT OF ADVOCATE GROUPS AND INDUSTRY

As the FTC survey shows, the private sector is apathetic in the public movement toward information protection. Many businesses seem to prioritize business profits by collecting private information without disclosure rather than change their business strategy to reduce consumers' privacy concerns. The passive mood in the private sector has prompted some groups to advocate self-regulation in their attempts to facilitate EC.

ELECTRONIC PRIVACY INFORMATION CENTER (EPIC)

The Electronic Privacy Information Center (EPIC), a public-interest research center in Washington, D.C., was established in 1994 to focus public attention on emerging civil liberties issues and to protect privacy, the First Amendment, and constitutional values. In February 1997, EPIC proposed a regulation that restricts the use of cookies. In the regulation, a user should be able to reject all cookies, know when cookies are being used, and manage cookies based on their origin or domain.

ELECTRONIC SURVEILLANCE

According to the American Civil Liberties Union (ACLU), monitoring computer users—**electronic surveillance**—is a widespread problem. The ACLU estimates that tens of millions of computer users are being monitored, many without their knowledge. Even though surveillance is one of the most extensively debated privacy issues, the practice is widely used.

Employees have very limited protection against employers' surveillance. Although several legal challenges are now under way, the law appears to support employers' rights to read e-mail and other electronic documents. Legislation now before the U.S. Congress attempts, at least, to require employers to inform employees that their on-the-job activities might be monitored electronically.

PROTECTING INFORMATION IN DATABASES

Information about individuals is being kept in many databases. When you apply for a new telephone, for example, you may be asked to fill in a two-page questionnaire. The questionnaire is reviewed and then stored in a database. Perhaps the most visible locations of such records are credit-reporting agencies. Other places personal information might be stored are banks and financial institutions; cable television, telephone, and utilities companies; employers; residential rental agencies and equipment rental companies; hospitals; schools and universities; supermarkets, retail establishments, and mail-order houses; government agencies (IRS, Census Bureau, your municipality); libraries; insurance companies; and online vendors. Records of purchasing, paying bills, transferring funds, buying stocks online, and more are available in vendors' databases.

There are several concerns about the information you provide to these record keepers. Under what circumstances will personal data be released? Do you know where the records are? Are these records accurate? Can you change inaccurate data? How long will it take to make a change? How are the data used? To whom are they given or sold? How secure are the data against unauthorized people?

Having information stored in many places increases the chance that the information is inaccurate, not up-to-date, or not secured properly.

PRIVACY POLICY

One way to protect privacy is to develop **privacy policies**, or *codes,* which can help organizations avoid legal problems. In many organizations, senior management has begun to understand that with the ability to collect vast amounts of personal information on customers, clients, and employees comes an obligation to ensure that the information—and, therefore, the individual—is protected. A privacy code was issued on June 22, 1998, by most major Internet-related companies including IBM and Microsoft. Let us look at what a privacy policy looks like.

Privacy Policy Basics—A Sample.

Data Collection

- Data should be collected on individuals only to accomplish a legitimate business objective.
- Data should be adequate, relevant, and not excessive in relation to the business objective.
- Individuals must give their consent before data pertaining to them can be gathered. Such consent may be implied from the individual's actions (e.g., applications for credit, insurance, or employment).

Data Accuracy

- Sensitive data gathered on individuals should be verified before it is entered into the database.
- Data should be accurate and, where and when necessary, kept current.
- The file should be made available so the individual can ensure that the data is correct.
- If there is disagreement about the accuracy of the data, the individual's version should be noted and included with any disclosure of the file.

Data Confidentiality

- Computer security procedures should be implemented to provide reasonable assurance against unauthorized disclosure of data. They should include physical, technical, and administrative security measures.
- Third parties should not be given access to data without the individual's knowledge or permission, except as required by law.
- Disclosures of data, other than the most routine, should be noted and maintained for as long as the data is maintained.
- Data should not be disclosed for reasons incompatible with the business objective for which it is collected.

The Organization for Economic Cooperation and Development (OECD) in Europe has probably provided the best-known set of guidelines intended to protect individuals' privacy in the electronic age (O'Leary, 1995).

EUROPEAN UNION (EU) DIRECTIVE ON INTERNET PRIVACY

Addressing privacy concerns on the Internet, the EU passed a privacy directive in 1998 reaffirming the principles of personal data protection in the Internet age. Member countries are required to put this directive into effect through introducing new laws or modifying existing laws in their respective countries. The directive aims to regulate the activities of any person (including a legal person: i.e., a company) that controls the collecting, holding, processing, or use of personal data on the Internet. Such a person is called a *data user*. The scope of the directive covers any data relating directly or indirectly to a living individual, who is called a *data subject*.

In general, data subjects are given the right to:

- know whether their personal data is held;
- access, erase, or block access to their personal data;
- object to usage;
- oppose automated individual decision making; and
- obtain judicial remedy and compensation in case of privacy infringement.

Meanwhile, data users are required to ensure that personal data on the Internet is:

- collected fairly and lawfully with the consent of the data subject;
- used only for a specific, explicit legitimate purpose consented to by the data subjects;
- accurate, current, and secured; and
- retained no longer than necessary for fulfilling the original purpose of collection.

17.4   PROTECTING INTELLECTUAL PROPERTY AND DOMAIN NAMES

Intellectual property (IP) is associated with intangible property rights, which are created and protected by law. The owner of a piece of intellectual property has a range of exclusive rights in dealing with the property. The law forbids nonowners from engaging in any such dealings without the consent of the owner. The main types of IP in EC are as follows:

- Copyright
- Patents
- Trademarks

Domain Names—A Related Issue

IP rights are not absolute. They are perishable (e.g., with the passage of time). There are also legal exceptions in the public interest to limit the rights of an IP owner. For example, in the public interest, an IP owner may be forced by law to grant a compulsory license to the public for the use of his or her IP at a specified rate. IP laws also set out mechanisms for:

- Acquiring and transferring rights (e.g., registration and licensing)
- Remedies and enforcement (both in a civil and a criminal sense)

Copyrights

Copyrighting is the major intellectual property issue related to EC. A copyright protects the product of human creativity. However, a copyright serves to protect the expression of ideas, not ideas *per se*. Copyright laws do not provide monopolistic protection of ideas—one cannot copyright an idea! For example, similar concepts, functions, and general features (such as pull-down menus, colors, or icons) are not protected by copyright law.

Copyrights usually exist in the following works:

- Literary works (e.g., books and computer software)
- Musical works (e.g., compositions)
- Dramatic works (e.g., plays)
- Artistic works (e.g., drawings, paintings)
- Sound recordings, films, broadcasts, cable programs
- Published editions of literary and musical works

Copyright confers to the owner an essential exclusive right to: (1) copy the work (in whole or in part) and (2) distribute it to the public (in any form or manner, including the Internet). A copyright owner may seek a court injunction to prevent or stop any infringement and claim damages. Copyright does not last forever; it is good for a fixed number of years (e.g., 50 in the United Kingdom and 28 in the United States) after the death of its author in most cases. Afterward, the copyright of the work will revert to the public domain.

In the area of copyright, three main international conventions exist. They are the:

- Berne Convention
- Universal Copyright Convention (UCC)
- WTO–TRIPS agreement

Contrary to practices in some other regions (notably in the United States), no formalities are required to obtain copyright protection in Europe and British Commonwealth countries. In these jurisdictions, legally speaking, there is no need to put the copyright © sign on the work to declare the existence of copyright.

If a copyright is infringed in certain ways, it will attract criminal liability in addition to civil liability. Infringements attracting criminal liabilities includes:

- Commercial production of infringing works
- Selling or dealing with infringing works
- Possessing infringing works for trade or business
- Manufacturing and selling technology for defeating copyright protection systems

The parallel importation of copyright works is a controversial issue. Even if a copyright work is legally purchased in some countries, it may be illegal to export it to another country. In general, the owner has an exclusive importation right to import the copyright work to another country.

Generally, contents of Web sites are protected by copyright. However, there are practical problems in doing so, for example:

- Identifying the real owner since a Web site typically involves numerous parties directly and indirectly in its creation
- Determining the threshold amount of "copying" that results in infringement. Is the copying of one text sentence from a hypertext page sufficient to amount to infringement?
- Including links to other sites—to what extent this is legal or not is still not very clear

HOW IS COPYRIGHT VIOLATED?: MP3, NAPSTER, AND AUCTIONS

One of the hottest Internet legal issues in 2000 and 2001 was the violation of copyright in the C2C environment. Such violation can be done in several ways. Here are three examples:

- *MP3.com* has been sued by several music distributors in 2000. The company allows users to listen to CDs from any computer with an Internet connection without paying any royalties.
- Napster has been sued by several music distributors for allowing people to share files that include music, games, and other digitizable information using a peer-to-peer technology (Chapter 11). Millions of people are doing just that without paying any royalties.
- A survey conducted by the Software Information Industry Association (SIIA), formed in April 2000, found that more than 90 percent of the software auctioned on auction sites were pirated products. Similar situations exist with auctions of CDs, games, videos, etc. (see Beato, 2000).

While *MP3.com* and Napster are moving to a subscription model in which users will have to pay fees for service, the control of what is being auctioned in hundreds of auction sites is much more difficult.

UNIQUENESS OF THE INTERNET

Copyright laws need to be changed to reflect the uniqueness of the Internet. Initially, there were no laws governing computer software protection rights. To provide some protection, current copyright laws were used to safeguard software business. Problems arise because copyright laws were written for physical products and not for digitized software. Companies argue that cyberspace soon will be little more than a vast copying machine for pirated software, CDs, and movies, destroying thousands of jobs and millions in revenue. Opponents fear that unbridled copyright power will threaten something equally important: the right to listen, read, and research without having to pay a toll any time a private citizen wants to gather information for his or her own use. A bill is required that will both protect intellectual property and afford the kind of access to it that is protected under the Copyright Act.

The most common intellectual property violation related to IT is software pirating. However, there are several other potential violations of intellectual property, as shown in Application Case 17.2.

APPLICATION CASE 17.2

Copyright Protection vs. Free Speech on the Internet

Gil Trevizo is a 25-year-old student who loves the television science-fiction series Millennium. He was able to get a bootlegged video of the first episode and other information and images regarding the show. He dedicated his Web site at the University of Texas to the show even before its big 1996 network premier. The show belongs to Twentieth Century-Fox, which has its own Web site dedicated to the show. The university switched off Trevizo's Internet account after Fox alerted them to the apparent piracy of its copyrighted material. Gil removed the material from his Web site.

Millennium's Internet fans were unhappy with the situation. The "First Unofficial Millennium WWW Site" went up before the second episode. Several dozen other fans activated protest sites before the third show aired on November 8, 1996. A university did not control these fans, so their sites remained open. "They [Fox] are shutting us down," the protest sites proclaim, playing on a line instantly recognizable to fans of the X-Files series—"Free speech is out there."

Although Gil does not receive any economic benefits, Fox could have been hurt by his site. Fox spent over $100,000 on its Millennium Web site and wants the fans to visit this site where promotional material is sold. If fans go to Gil's or similar sites, fewer visitors will come to the official site.

The problem is not unique to Fox. Thousands of Web sites are using unauthorized material, and it is unclear whether what is going on in cyberspace is governed by predigital copyright law.

Source: Based on A. Harmon, "Web Wars: Companies Get Tough on Rogues," *Los Angeles Times*, (November 12, 1996). Reprinted by permission.

COPYRIGHT PROTECTION TECHNIQUES

Besides providing laws to assist in both sides of this debate, there are a few methods of prevention a business can take to protect its intellectual property. These methods are personalized products, frequent updating, making the window of possibility narrow, and offering freeware.

Using Technology for Copyright Protection

It is possible today to codify copyrights in cyberspace. This technology could prevent circumvention of digital products. Software, movie, and record companies could, with a few lines of code, make it impossible to sample from larger works. For the user to do it would mean going around copy-protection schemes, which is illegal.

Some Practical Methods

Several methods are available to protect digitized material, such as music, from being copied. One such method is by the use of watermarks. **Digital watermarks** are embedded invisible marks that can be represented by bits in digital content. The watermarks are hidden in the source data, becoming inseparable from such data. Solana Corporation's system is being integrated into tools, developed by Liquid Audio Corp., that convert audio files into a format that can be delivered over the Internet. While the watermarks cannot prevent the duplication of music, the product can help, for example, identify who is passing around pirated versions of songs downloaded from the Internet. For details see Yeung (1998).

Legislation is currently being considered that bans *digital watermarks* and *validation codes*. Some feel that these tools violate the freedom of speech rights on the Internet. These tools are crucial in preventing online counterfeiting and could set back the growth of Internet business (Yeung, 1998).

LEGAL PERSPECTIVES OF COPYRIGHTS

Signed into law in December 1997, one of the most important legal developments (to date) in the protection of intellectual property in cyberspace is the No Electronic Theft (NET) Act. After the software industry lost $13.2 billion to pirates in 1997, this legislation imposed criminal liability for individuals who reproduce or distribute copies of copyrighted works. The language clarifies that reproduction or distribution can be accomplished by electronic means and that even if copyrighted products are distributed without charge, financial harm is experienced by the author of the software, as described in the second vignette at the beginning of this chapter.

The Software Publishers Association is the principal industry trade organization working to prevent piracy. Other concerned groups are the Electronic Frontier Foundation and the World Intellectual Property Organization; both are striving to implement methods of securing copyrights while allowing an acceptable level of public access.

Internet access providers are anxious to know how far the liability issue extends for violations of digital copyright law; under the current law there is no liability for a pirate who links his or her site to a party from which to download software. One answer is the Online Copyright Liability Limitation Act, which seeks to protect Internet access providers from liability for direct and vicarious violation under specific circumstances in which they have no control or knowledge of infringement.

This act also limits the remedy for contributory infringement to injunctive relief for such providers; however, it does provide civil liability for knowing misrepresentation of material. Internet access providers must act responsibly and make efforts to police piracy; not necessarily because of threats of litigation but because it is in their best long-term interest to do so.

The Digital Millennium Copyright Act (1998) (see Oliva and Prabanker, 1999) codifies how copyright applies in cyberspace. The bill:

- Reasserts copyrights in cyberspace.
- Makes illegal most attempts to defeat anticopying technology.
- Requires the National Telecommunications and Information Administration to review the effect the bill would have on the free flow of information and make recommendations for any changes 2 years after it is signed into law.
- Lets companies and common citizens circumvent anticopying technology when necessary to make software or hardware compatible with other products, to conduct encryption research, or to keep personal information from being spread by Internet cookies or other copy-protection tools.
- Forbids excessive copying of databases, even when those databases contain information already in the public domain.

INTERNATIONAL ASPECTS OF COPYRIGHTS

Copyright laws in the digital age are being challenged, and international agreements are needed. In 1996, WIPO began to discuss the need for copyright protection of intellectual property delivered on the Internet. More than 60 member countries were trying to bridge cultural and political differences and come up with an international treaty. Part of an agreement readied in 1998 is called the "database treaty," and its aim is to protect the investment of firms that collect and arrange information. This organization is continuously working on the many still-unresolved issues. For other international aspects see WIPO (*wipo.int/eng/main.htm*).

Patents

A patent is a document that grants the holder exclusive rights on an invention for a fixed number of years (e.g., 17 years in the United States and 20 years in the United Kingdom). Thousands of patents related to IT have been granted over the years. Examples of EC patents given to Open Market Corp. are Internet Server Access Control and Monitoring (5708780), Network Sales Systems (5715314), and Digital Active Advertising (5724424). Juno Online Services received an interactive ad patent (5809242). IBM has several patents, including 5870717, a system for ordering from electronic catalogs, and 5926798, using intelligent agents for performing online commerce. Patents are a very potent form of protection. They confer monopoly rights, not only in a particular embodiment of a creative idea (e.g., in copyright), but they also grant exclusivity in an idea or an invention, regardless of how it may be expressed. An invention may be in the form of a physical device or a method or process for making a physical device.

Patents serve to protect tangible technological inventions, especially in traditional industrial areas. However, patents are not designed to protect artistic or literary creativity—for this, copyright is more appropriate. In particular, it is diffi-cult to obtain a patent on the following things:

- discoveries, scientific theories, or mathematical principles
- literary, dramatic, musical or artistic work or any other *aesthetic creation*
- scheme, rule, or method for performing a mental act, playing a game, or doing business, or *a program for a computer* (unless it is an integral part of a device)
- the mere presentation of information
- methods of treating the human body by surgery or therapy or by diagnostic aids

However, developments in the United States are deviating from established practices in Europe in the treatment of what kind of invention may be considered for patents. For example, *Amazon.com* has successfully obtained a U.S. patent on its 1-Click book ordering procedure. Using this patent, *Amazon.com* sued Barnes and Noble, in 1999 and in 2000, alleging its rival has copied its patented technology. Similarly, *Priceline.com* filed a suit alleging that *Expedia.com* is using its patented model. *Priceline.com* has obtained a U.S. patent on its reverse-auction business process. Therefore, it seems that in the United States patents may be obtained for EC business models, although the legal validity of these patents are still expected to face tough challenges in the courts in future litigations (e.g., see Merges, 1999). This is not the current practice in Europe. It is almost impossible to obtain European patents on business methods or computer programs on their own. For example, Merrill Lynch's application for a UK patent on its computerized system for automated trading in securities was unsuccessful (Merrill Lynch Application [1989] RPC 561 CA).

To be eligible for a patent, the innovation must satisfy the following legal criteria:

- Novel (i.e., it is new and did not already exist as a part of the "state of the art" in the public domain)
- Involves a sufficiently "inventive step" (i.e., not trivial or obvious)
- Capable of industrial application (i.e., the idea must be able to be put to practical use, for example resulting in manufactured goods)

Various international treaties exist to facilitate such registrations. The Paris Union, the International Patent Corporation Union, and the European Patent Convention are the best known of these treaties. In spring 2000, IBM Corp. announced the creation of the global patent exchange, which provides a global market space for the trading of technology related patents.

Trademarks

Trademarks form an important type of intellectual property. Well-known trademarks are very valuable assets to a business. In a nutshell, a trademark is a graphical sign used by businesses to identify their goods and services. The sign can be composed of words, designs, letters, numbers, shapes, or a combination of colors, or other such identifiers. Trademarks need to be registered in a country in order to attract statutory protection in that country. To be eligible for registration, a trademark must be distinctive, original, and not deceptive. Domain names of Web sites can also be registered as trademarks if they fulfill the registration criteria.

The statutory law protects registered trademarks. Unregistered trademarks are protected by the common law of passing-off, which protects the reputation of a trader established through the use of a distinctive name, logo, and so on. Essentially, the law of passing-off prevents the selling of products or services by one trader representing those products or services as those of a competitor.

Contrary to registered trademarks, to take legal action, the owner of an unregistered trademark must first prove that the mark has an established reputation and that damage has been done to the owner due to an infringement. Therefore, it is much more difficult to enforce an unregistered trademark (see Sargert, 2000 for details).

The owner of a registered trademark has exclusive rights to:

- Use the trademark on his or her goods and services for which the trademark is registered.
- Take legal action to prevent anyone from using his or her trademark without consent on (identical or similar) goods and services for which the trademark is registered.

The term "use" has a wide interpretation. It includes the use of the trademark in advertising. Once registered, a trademark lasts forever, as long as a periodic registration fee is paid (e.g., once every 10 years in some jurisdictions).

Companies can rely on trademark laws (such as the Lanham Act in the United States) to help prosecute counterfeiters in the country where the trademark is valid. The problem is how to enforce it on the Internet where fake brand name products are sold or auctioned from anywhere. In many countries, but not all, the police can seize and destroy counterfeited goods. In 1998, Playboy was able to shut down an adult Web site that was using the Playboy trademark. Several trade associations help to protect trademarks (e.g., see *siia.net*). There are criminal liabilities for trademark infringement. In particular, it is criminal for anyone:

- to fraudulently use a registered trademark, including the selling and importing of goods bearing an infringing trademark.
- to use or possess equipment for forging registered trademarks.

There are a number of interesting and novel recent trademark litigation developments in the area of EC. One case in point is the assignment of keywords within search engines to enable users to search for intended Web sites more effectively. Estee Lauder has sued Excite, alleging that the unauthorized entry of its trademarked name in the keyword file of the search engine in the Excite Shopping Channel infringes its registered trademark and will direct users to unlicensed dealers' Web sites. Similar suits were filed by Playboy Enterprises against Excite and Netscape.

Domain Names

A **domain name** refers to the upper category of on Internet address (URL), such as *Prenhall.com*, or *oecd.org*.

There are two controversies concerning domain names. One is whether top-level domain names (similar to *.com*, *.org*, and *.gov*) should be added; the other is the use (as domain names) of trademarked names that belong to other companies. In November 2000, the Internet's governing body on Web site names approved the following top-level names: .biz, .info, .name, .pro, .museum, .aeor, and .coop.

NETWORK SOLUTIONS, INC.

At the heart of all the controversy is Network Solutions, Inc. (NSI), a subsidiary of Verisign Corp., which has been contracted by the U.S. government to assign domain addresses. Until 1998, NSI exclusively assigned domain names for several top levels: *.com*, *.net*, *.gov*, *.edu*, and *.org*. The United States, as well as the rest of the world, is subject to NSI for domain names. European critics are ready to relieve the United States of that responsibility. Europe is weary of the United States assuming the right to direct Internet governance and effectively subjecting the Internet to U.S. law. On June 1, 1998, the monopoly of NSI over domain names ended. Instead, the company created a registration system that it shares with several other competing companies. The new registration system is handled by an international nonprofit corporation called "Internet Corporation for Assigned Names and Numbers" (ICANN). This caused the registration price to drop.

The Council of Registrars (CORE), a European private sector group, and the Global Internet Project, a U.S. private sector group, want to increase the number of top-level names. One of the objectives is to create an adult-only top-level name that will prevent pornographic material from getting into the hands of children.

Both CORE and the Global Internet Project want to repair the trade name disputes over domain names. Companies are using trade names of other companies as their domain address to help attract traffic to their Web site. For example, DC Comics is suing Brainiac Services, Inc. for using one of their comic book names, Brainiac. Private sector groups will have to resolve this issue in the future before more lawsuits begin to surface. Major disputes are international in scope, because the same corporate name may be used in different countries by different corporations. A guide to domain names by the U.S. Patent and Trademark Office is available at *uspto.gov/Web/offices*.

DOMAIN NAME DISPUTES AND RESOLUTIONS

In order to avoid legal battles, the Internet community created a speedy way to resolve domain name disputes using arbitration. A new domain name dispute resolution procedure was adopted on January 1, 2000, for domain name addresses ending in *.com*, *.net*, and *.org*. Three arbitration organizations have been given the authority to make determinations regarding domain name disputes. They are as follows:

- *Disputes.org* Consortium
- The National Arbitration Forum
- WIPO

If one of these organizations makes a determination regarding a domain name dispute, NSI/ICANN will respect the decision and will transfer the registration of the disputed domain name in accordance with the arbitration determination. A core set of policies, rules, and procedures for dispute resolution under the three organizations are set forth in a document entitled "Rules for Uniform Domain Name Dispute Resolution Policy," which can be found at *domainmagistrate.com/publish/policy.html*.

Here are two interesting arbitration rulings:

- The World Wrestling Federation won the first ever ruling, against a California resident who filed for the name *worldwreslingfederation.com*
- Penguin Books was denied the name *penguin.org*. The name was given to a person who was known by the nickname Mr. Penguin (Not now in use).

In addition to the resolution of disputes by its submission to arbitration, a legal action can also be initiated in various jurisdictions. Legal action provides a more potent protection, because in addition to winning the right to use a certain domain name, courts can also grant monetary damages and enforce specific anti-cybersquatting legislation (e.g., against the trafficking of domain names).

For more on domain names and resolutions, visit *verisign.com*.

17.5   FREE SPEECH, INTERNET INDECENCY, SPAMMING, AND CENSORSHIP

The emergence of the Internet and EC generated one of the most heated debates of our times—free speech versus government censorship. This section will cover the highlights of this debate and the related issue of spamming.

Free Speech Versus Censorship Issues

Many surveys indicate that the issue of censorship is one of the most important issues of concern to Internet surfers, usually number one or number two in Europe and the United States. **Censorship** refers to government's attempt to control, in one way or another, the material broadcasted on the Internet. Here are some of the major elements of the debate regarding this issue.

DEFINING FREEDOM OF SPEECH (PER ABRAMS, 1998)

The First Amendment of the Bill of Rights in the Constitution of the United States reads as follows:

> *Congress shall make no law respecting an establishment of religion, or prohibiting the free exercise thereof; or abridging the freedom of speech, or of the press; or the right of the people peaceably to assemble, and to petition the government for a redress of grievances.*

The United Nations Universal Declaration of Human Rights in 1948 defined what constitutes human rights for the citizens of the world. Article 19 of that document addresses the right to freedom of expression:

> *Everyone has the right to freedom of opinion and expression; this right includes freedom to hold opinions without interference and to seek, receive, and impart information and ideas through any media and regardless of frontiers.*

Theoretically, free speech is guaranteed on the Internet to the world's people. If only it were so simple.

THE INTERNET: THE ULTIMATE MEDIUM FOR FREE SPEECH

"Free speech" has often been dictated by the voices of the few, the rich, and the powerful. The voices of the many, the not-quite-so-rich, and the not-nearly-as-powerful have heretofore not been given equal due. The Internet changes this tradition by allowing many voices, many cultures, and many opinions equal exposure. The Internet has opened doors to freedom of speech that have never been accessible before. The goal of free speech for all has only tacitly been achieved in the past.

The ultimate freedom of the Internet has been challenged by many parents and government officials. It resulted in the passage of the Communications Decency

Act (CDA), a bill that proposes restrictions on telecommunications in the United States, including the Internet. However, this bill was found *unconstitutional* since it contradicts the First Amendment cited earlier.

THE DEBATE ABOUT FREE SPEECH ON THE INTERNET

At a symposium on free speech in the information age, Parker Donham (1994) defined his own edict entitled "Donham's First Law of Censorship." This semi-serious precept states: "Most citizens are implacably opposed to censorship in any form—except censorship of whatever they personally happen to find offensive" (see *insight.mcmaster.ca/org/efc/pages/donham2.html*).

Nothing could more accurately describe the free speech debate than that quotation. Everyone is fundamentally for the right to free speech; the issue resides in the limits to free speech, what the boundaries are, and how we should enforce them.

On one side of the argument are governments protective of their role in society, parents concerned about exposing their children to inappropriate Web pages and chat rooms, and federal agencies attempting to deal with illegal actions like terrorism, gambling, and money laundering. On the other side are citizen action groups desiring to protect every ounce of their freedom to speak, individuals concerned about their right to information on the Internet, and organizations seeking to empower the citizens of the earth.

All groups want nothing except what is best from their position. The disagreements deal with the exact methods selected to achieve their goals. The debate can become very heated indeed when attempts are made to enact these methods into law. Generally, there are provisions in law for two cases that limit free speech: obscene material and a compelling government interest (Abrams, 1998).

All is relatively clear until the term "indecency" is thrown into the mix. The CDA, signed as part of a major telecommunications bill in the United States on February 1, 1996, defined indecency as: "any comment, request, suggestion, proposal, image, or other communication that, in context, depicts or describes, in terms patently offensive as measured by contemporary community standards, sexual or excretory activities or organs." This definition of indecency and its interpretation in the CDA has been found unconstitutional. Thus, with this rejection of censorship, the public argument on the true purpose and legal interpretation of indecency and the CDA commenced. The major arguments for and against the CDA are summarized in Table 17-3.

Protecting Children

One of the major points in the free speech versus censorship debate is the potential damage to children. Citizens are very concerned about children viewing inappropriate material, such as pornographic, offensive, hate, and other potentially dangerous material. Also, merchants solicit information from children about their parents and family. There are three approaches regarding the protection of children from inappropriate material on the Internet. The first view is that no information should be held back and parents should be responsible for monitoring their own children. The second is that only the government can truly protect children from this material, and the last approach is to hold the Internet providers responsible for all the material and information they provide. These approaches can be implemented for any surfer, not just children.

TABLE 17-3	Pro and Con Arguments on the CDA	
	Pro CDA	**Con CDA**
	The CDA is solely intended to protect children from "harmful" material on the Internet.	"Harmful" material is already restricted from children by the obscenity laws. And furthermore, there are clear judicial rulings on what is "harmful" to children as opposed to what is indecent. ("Harmful to children" terminology was removed from a draft version of the CDA and replaced with "indecency.")
	Courts should rule on what is included in the "indecency" clause and what is not. They argue the court rulings would limit the scope of the "indecency" clause to harmful material exposed to children.	The judges that ruled the CDA unconstitutional argued that the language of the CDA left open the possibility of restricting content that had artistic, educational, and political merit.
	The Internet is wide open to children who may unintentionally (or intentionally) come across indecent content.	The Internet is unlike broadcast media such as radio and television in that active use of the Internet must be made to encounter such indecent material.
	There will be legal restrictions applied to the Internet in some form if the CDA is ultimately proven unconstitutional by the Supreme Court, just as there have been restrictions applied to every other communication medium that has evolved in the past. Why resist restrictions that will only make the world safer and better for you and your children?	Unnecessary legislation imposed onto such a dynamic new medium could kill the very heart and soul of the medium itself. Protecting children from the indecent portions of the Internet can be achieved without hindering free speech with unnecessary laws. Why write new laws when proper ones already exist? What happened to the "least restrictive means possible?"

Source: Compiled from *World Wide Web: Beyond the Basics* by Abrams, Table 19-1, p. 349 © 1998. Reprinted by permission of Pearson Education, Inc. Upper Saddle River, NJ 07458.

PARENTS GOVERNING THEIR OWN CHILDREN

Some believe the parents need to take responsibility to monitor, teach, and control the material to which their children have access. They can simply advise children about what they can see and instruct them about merchants' questionnaires. Advocates of this approach do not want a government agency to interfere. They argue that government-mandated filters are too broad; an array of nonharmful speech—everything from the Quaker home page to the American Association of University Women—has been blocked by filtering programs. Information that can be checked out of the library cannot be accessed through the Internet in the same library. They further argue that there are already federal laws in place that give the Department of Justice power to arrest and charge those who deal in obscenity and child pornography.

GOVERNMENT PROTECTING CHILDREN

Those who want the government to control the material children view believe that the job can only be done through legislation. They want to see legislation that will force libraries and schools to use blocking filters. President Bill Clinton made a strong effort to prevent children from accessing offensive material on the Internet. Legislation is also being proposed that will make it illegal to put some information on the Internet, such as bomb-building procedures. More difficult to control is the information solicited by merchants about parents, their income level, and lifestyles.

RESPONSIBILITY FOR INTERNET PROVIDERS

America Online (AOL), in its attempts to take responsibility, is trying to build a medium that is friendly to consumers, safe for families, and affordable for everyone. They rely very much on their own members to police the system and bring to their attention things that violate the terms of service. Some of the material AOL's policy prohibits is hate speech or truly offensive speech. They have applied their policy in situations like a KKK site or a serial-killer Web site. Some believe that Internet providers, like AOL, should be held legally liable for all the material they allow to be accessed.

Forcing Internet Providers to be Accountable   In January 1998, a prosecutor in Munich, Germany, caused CompuServe, which provides its global subscribers with access to the Internet, to shut down 200 of the Net's sex-related newsgroups because they violated German law. Since the firm had no technical way to restrict Internet content only in Germany, it was obliged to impose the same restrictions on all of its 4 million subscribers worldwide. Some organizations are threatening to sue service providers for defamation or obscenity if they do not clean up their act. These watch groups believe that Internet providers can no longer be willfully blind; they are going to have to take responsibility for the services they provide.

LEGAL PERSPECTIVES IN THE UNITED STATES

When the CDA was declared unconstitutional, both sides of the debate agreed that controls are needed; but who has censorship responsibility or, in fact, authority will be disputed for years. Several bills are designed so they will not clash with the First Amendment yet provide protection. Here are some EC-related examples:

- The Child Online Protection Act (COPA) was enacted as part of the Internet Tax Freedom Act in July 1998. This law requires, among other things, that companies verify an adult's age before showing online material that is deemed "harmful to minors." Verification can be accomplished through a credit card number or access number. Included in the bill is a requirement for parental consent prior to collecting personal information from a minor. The language of the bill, however, is so restrictive that the "Starr Report" on President Clinton would probably be censored and access limited to only the most savvy senators. However, COPA was ruled as unconstitutional by the United States district court for the eastern district of Pennsylvania in February 1999, and a temporary injunction against COPA was granted preventing its enforcement. In June 2000, the U.S. Court of Appeals for the Third Circuit reaffirmed the injunction, rendering COPA unenforceable under current circumstances.
- Another piece of legislation is the Family Friendly Internet Access Act, which would require access providers to offer screening software at the time of sign-up that would enable customers to filter out material deemed inappropriate for children. Most Internet providers offer this feature now for competitive reasons rather than altruism.
- The Internet Protection Act seeks to limit state and federal regulation of the Internet and at the same time prohibit ISPs from providing accounts to sexually violent predators.
- The Internet School Filtering Act also attempts to limit access to inappropriate material by controlling federal funds and grants to schools and libraries. Schools must provide blocking software that restricts indecent and harmful material. Of course, the danger is that a lot of good information is blocked out along with the material considered unacceptable, and control is given to the government rather than the educators. Some of the filtering techniques include blacklists, which do not allow disapproved material; whitelists, which allow only approved sites; word blocking; and blocking entire areas that are deemed inappropriate.

RESPONSIBILITY OF EMPLOYERS

There are several legal implications regarding the use of e-mail in organizations. In many organizations, employees were found sending inappropriate or offensive material on company e-mails, usually among staffmembers. This may lead to sexual harassment allegations, with many employees suing their employers for the actions of their workmates. In fall 2000, 44 employees at a mobile phone company in the United Kingdom were dismissed for violating their company's policy. The reason is the employers are liable to protect their employees from harassment.

Controlling Spamming

Spamming refers to the practice of indiscriminate distribution of messages (for example, junk mail) without permission of the receiver and without consideration for the messages' appropriateness. One major piece of legislation addressing marketing practices in EC is the Electronic Mailbox Protection Act. The primary thrust of this law is that commercial speech is subject to government regulation, and secondly, that spamming, which causes significant harm, expense, and annoyance, should be controlled.

Spam comprised 30 percent of all mail sent on America Online in 1998. This volume significantly impairs an already limited bandwidth, slowing down the Internet in general and, in some cases, shutting ISPs down completely. This act requires those sending spam to identify it as advertising, to indicate the name of the sender prominently, and to include valid routing information. Recipients may waive the right to receive such information. Also, ISPs would be required to offer spam-blocking software, and recipients of spam would have the right to request termination of future spam from the same sender and to bring civil action if necessary. (Now spam is less than 10 percent and popular e-mail programs such as *Hotmail.com* provide blockers.)

A few other bills focused on similar objectives are the Unsolicited Commercial Electronic Mail Act, which requires all unsolicited e-mail to start with the word "advertisement" and include the name, address, and telephone number of the sender. The Netizens Protection Act seeks to expand the coverage of the Telephone Consumer Protection Act to include e-mail, unless there is a preexisting relationship between the sender and the receiver or the receiver requests the e-mail.

HOW TO CUT SPAMMING

Although companies are defenseless if spammers use their domain to falsify return addresses or transmit junk e-mail, there are a few things they (and "netizens") can do:

- Tell users not to validate their addresses by answering spam requests for replies if they want to be taken off mailing lists.
- Disable the relay feature on mail servers so mail cannot be bounced off the server.
- Delete spam and forget it—it is a fact of life and not worth wasting time over.
- Use blockers whenever possible.

Several software packages can help you to fight spamming. For example, message filters have been invented to put "a ban on spam." Web sites such as *junkbusters.com* provides free software that blocks unwanted banner ads and protects you from cookies and other threats. AOL, for example, is using an intelligent agent that resides on your PC and watches what you view and where. This way the agent "learns" you and will filter material that is pushed to you by content providers, keeping only the items that match material you have seen before.

NET ANONYMITY

Another controversial issue related to spamming is Internet anonymity. Using software, people can remain completely anonymous while sending e-mail, chatting, and visiting Web sites. This opens the door to criminals, sex offenders, and to fraud, and it compromises the ability of law enforcers to fight back (see Hancock, 2000b and Froomkin, 1999).

17.6   TAXATION

In this section we touch upon a controversial issue in EC—taxation. This issue is extremely important since it is related to global EC as well as to fairness in competition when EC competes with off-line marketing channels and conventional mail order where taxes are paid. It is also an important issue due to the large volume of trade forecasted for the next decade. Cities, states, and countries all want a piece of the pie.

The Taxation Exemption Debate

The Internet Tax Freedom Act passed the U.S. Senate on October 8, 1998, as bill S442. This act promotes EC through tax incentives by barring any new state or local sales taxes on Internet transactions until October 2001. Note: This law deals only with sales tax and not with federal or state income tax that Internet companies must pay. Similar acts exist in several other countries, such as Hong Kong. This act also carried an amendment known as the Children's Online Privacy Protection Act. This was added in an effort to prevent extension of tax benefits to pornographers.

The act also creates a special commission to study Internet taxation issues and recommends new policies to the president. This panel was required to submit an initial report by spring 2000. In the meantime, existing Internet taxes, taxes on mail-order goods, and other excise taxes already in place would remain unaffected. Basically, in the United States, a sales tax is paid only in the state where the vendor is located.

In April 2000, the special commission recommended the following to the U.S. Congress:

- Eliminate the 3 percent federal excise tax on telecommunications services.
- Extend the current moratorium on multiple or discriminatory taxation of EC through 2006.
- Prohibit taxation of digitized goods sold over the Internet.
- Make permanent the current moratorium on Internet access taxes.
- Establish nexus standards for U.S. businesses engaged in interstate commerce—rules that would spell out whether the use of a Web server in Indiana, for example, gives an Internet company based in New Jersey "nexus" in Indiana, where residents are subject to sales taxes.

- Place the burden on states to simplify their own telecommunications, sales, and use tax systems.
- Clarify state authority to use federal welfare money to give poor people more Internet access.
- Provide tax incentives and federal matching funds to states to encourage public–private partnerships to get low-income families online.
- Respect and protect consumer privacy.
- Continue to press for a moratorium on international tariffs on electronic transmissions over the Internet.

It's up to the U.S. Congress now to digest the contents of the report and hash out contentious tax issues. State and local governments, which depend on sales tax revenues, and traditional brick-and-mortar retailers that compete against e-tailers generally want to tax EC. Internet companies, antitax advocates and many politicians champion keeping the Internet tax-free.

EC transactions are multiplying at an exponential rate, and the $5–7 trillion forecasted for 2004 means lots of potential sales tax. The taxation issues that involve 30,000 state and local jurisdictions in the United States, in addition to the innumerable international jurisdictions, will add numerous volumes to an already complex tax code. Applying existing law to new mediums of exchange is far more difficult than ever imagined. The global nature of business today suggests that cyberspace be considered a distinct tax zone unto itself with unique rules and considerations befitting the stature of the environment. This is, in fact, what has occurred. The moratorium on taxation of Internet transactions is a fine temporary solution where no precedent exists; however, longer-range strategies must be developed quickly. There are some complicating factors to consider. Several tax jurisdictions may be involved in a single transaction, not only on a domestic level but internationally. The implications of such involvement are tremendous; the identity of the parties involved and transaction verification is frequently a problem.

Non-EC industries feel that Internet businesses must pay their fair share of the tax bill for the nation's social and physical infrastructure. They feel that the Internet industries are not pulling their own weight. These companies are screaming that the same situation exists in the mail-order business and that there are sufficient parallels to warrant similar legal considerations. In fact, in many states EC has already been treated the same as mail-order businesses. Others suggest using the established sales tax laws. "You've got a tax structure in place—it's called sales tax," said Bill McKiernan, chairman and CEO of *software.net*. "Just apply that to Internet transactions."

The probabilities for tax evasion are also potentially large. Tax havens and offshore banking facilities will become more accessible. Singapore has passed a law to establish itself as a legal and financial safe haven for the rest of the world for the EC industry, similar to Swiss banks' role in the financial industry.

There is debate about whether tax policies should promote businesses on the Information Superhighway or preserve those on Main Street. Many argue it is not the government's role to protect older industries that are threatened by emerging technologies. Laws were not enacted to protect blacksmiths when the automobile became popular.

Arguments exist concerning tax-free policies. Some say that tax-free policies give online businesses an unfair advantage. For instance, some argue that Internet phone services should be exempt from paying access charges to local telephone companies for use of their networks. In their effort to avoid sales taxes, Internet merchants like to point to the difficulty of tracking who should be paid what. The opposition argues that the same is true for telephone transactions, so existing laws should suffice. The same opposition asks, "Should EC business be allowed to operate without taxing consumers while regular telephone companies cannot?"

Proposed Taxation Solutions in the United States

The National Governors' Association, the National League of Cities, and the U.S. Conference of Mayors fought the Tax Free Bill for the Internet. The National Governors' Association estimates state governments are losing $3 billion to $4 billion a year on difficult-to-control, mail-order sales to out-of-state merchants and customers. They figure that more is lost through EC sales and are suggesting that the IRS might "come to the rescue" with a single and simplified national sales tax. That would reduce 30,000 different tax codes to "no more than 50." Net sales would be taxed at the same rate as mail-order or Main Street transactions. While states could set their one rate, each sale could be taxed only once. As stated, the details of Internet taxation would be settled by a panel of industry and government officials.

For services that compute sales tax see Chapter 8. To calculate international tax levies on European Union sales see *europa.eu.int*.

17.7   OTHER LEGAL ISSUES: CONTRACTS, ONLINE GAMBLING, AND MORE

Privacy, intellectual property, and censorship receive a great deal of publicity because consumers easily understand them. However, there are several other legal issues related to EC. Here are some examples:

- What are the rules of electronic contracting, and whose jurisdiction prevails when buyers, brokers, and sellers are in different states and/or countries?
- How can gambling be controlled on the Internet? Gambling is legal in Nevada and other states. How can the winner's taxes be collected?
- When are electronic documents admissible evidence in courts of law? What do you do if they are not?
- Time and place can carry different dates for buyers and sellers when they are across the ocean. For example, an electronic document signed in Japan on January 5 may have the date January 4 in Los Angeles; which date is legal?
- The use of multiple networks and trading partners makes the documentation of responsibility difficult. How is such a problem overcome?
- Liability for errors, malfunction of software, or theft and fraudulent use of data may be difficult to prove. How is such liability determined?
- What is considered misrepresentation? Where should you take legal action against misrepresentation?
- Much of the law hinges on the physical location of files and data. With distributed databases and replication of databases, it is difficult to say exactly where the data are stored at a given time. How is electronic storage related to existing legalities?

- Online corporate reports are difficult to audit since they can be changed frequently and auditors may not have sufficient time to perform with due diligence. There are no established auditing standards. How should such auditing be conducted and what legal value does it have?
- The legal aspects of electronic tendering and procurement are still evolving.
- Many issues are related to advertisement online, including liability of ISPs.
- How can money laundering be prevented when the value of the money is in the form of a smart card? (Japan limits the value of money on a smart card to about $5,000; other countries such as Singapore and Hong Kong set even lower limits.)
- Which government has jurisdiction over an EC transaction? (See Alberts, et al., 1998.)
- Can a company link into a Web site without permission? (See *Ticketmaster vs. Microsoft*, Application Case 17.3.)

Of the many issues presented, we will discuss only the first two here. For more information refer to Adam (1998).

APPLICATION CASE 17.3

Linking to Your Web Site

On April 28, 1998, Ticketmaster Corporation filed a suit against Microsoft charging that Microsoft's link to Ticketmaster's Web site infringes on its name and trademark by its mere presence on the Microsoft site. Meanwhile, Ticketmaster, claiming losses due to the linking, used a special computer code to block users from linking to its site from certain sites. Should Ticketmaster win, it may create a major problem for companies attempting to get permission to link (some Web sites have thousands of links) to other sites. Microsoft gave the service free to Ticketmaster.

Electronic Contracts

A legally binding contract requires a few basic elements: offer, acceptance, and consideration. However, these requirements are difficult to establish when the human element in the processing of the transaction is removed and the contracting is performed electronically. For example, Web site development agreements can be very complex.

The Uniform Electronic Transactions Act seeks to extend existing provisions for contract law to cyberlaw by establishing uniform and consistent definitions for electronic records, digital signatures, and other electronic communications. This act is a procedural act that provides the means to effectuate transactions accomplished through an electronic medium. The language purposefully refrains from addressing questions of substantive law, leaving this to the scope of the Uniform Commercial Code (UCC).

The UCC is a comprehensive law regarding business conduct. The proposed amendment to the UCC is Article 2B, which is also designed to build upon existing law by providing a government code that supports existing and future electronic technologies in the exchange of goods or services. This law was approved in 1999 and enacted in 2000. This law is one of the more significant EC legal developments.

Shrink-wrap agreements or box-top licenses appear in or on the package containing software. The user is bound to the license by opening the package even though he or she has not yet used the product or even read the agreement. This has been a point of contention for some time. The Court felt that providing information such as warranties or handling instructions inside the package would provide more benefit to the consumer given the limited space available on the exterior of the package. The *ProCD vs. Zeidenberg* case supported the validity of shrink-wrap agreements when the court ruled in favor of the plaintiff, ProCD.

Click-wrap contracts are an extension of this ruling and are contracts derived entirely over the Internet. The software vendor offers to sell or license the use of the software according to the terms accompanying the software. The buyer agrees to be bound by the terms based on certain conduct; usually that conduct is retaining the product for a sufficient time to review the terms and return the software if unacceptable.

INTELLIGENT AGENTS

Article 2B also makes clear that contracts can be formed even where no human involvement is present. It states:

> *(a) operations of one or more electronic agents which confirm the existence of a contract or indicate agreement, form a contract even if no individual was aware of or reviewed the actions or results. (b) In automated transactions, the following rules apply: (1) A contract may be formed by the interaction of electronic agents. A contract is formed if the interaction results in the electronic agents engaging in operations that confirm the existence of a contract or indicate agreement. The terms of the contract are determined under section 2B-209(b). (2) A contract may be formed by the interaction of an individual and an electronic agent.*

Article 2B also addresses language, timing, payments, forms, and other nuances particular to EC that are not currently covered in the existing UCC. Many solutions have not withstood the scrutiny of legal challenges in a court of law, but as common law has developed from case law, cyberlaw must be tested and validated as technology is introduced and applications challenged.

In fall 2000, the Electronic Signatures in Global and National Commerce Act was approved. It gives contracts signed online the same legal status as a contract signed with pen on paper. Similar law has been enacted in Europe and several Asian countries.

Gambling

Gaming commissions have had a tough time regulating gambling laws in Nevada, on Indian reservations, in offshore casinos, in sports bars, and other places where gambling is legal. Technology makes this effort all the more difficult to monitor and enforce since the individuals abusing the rules have at least the same level of sophistication available as the law enforcement officials; in many cases they are even better equipped. The ease and risk of online wagering is evidenced by many recent cases of individuals losing their life savings without understanding the implications of what they are doing with their home PC.

The Internet Gambling Prohibition Act of 1999 was established to make online wagering illegal except for minimal amounts. This act provides criminal and civil remedies against individuals making online bets or wagers and those in the business of offering online betting or wagering venues. Additionally, it gives U.S. district courts original and exclusive jurisdiction to prevent and restrain violations, and it subjects computer service providers to the duties of common carriers. The impact of this act is to make ISPs "somewhat" liable for illegal currency movements and reportable transactions requiring documentation by the carriers.

Online casinos have all of the inherent dangers of physical gaming houses with the added risk of accessibility by minors or individuals of diminished capacity who may financially injure themselves without the constraints otherwise found in a physical environment. As is the case with most issues in cyberspace, self-regulation may be the best policy. Methods of wagering can be found all over the Internet. For example, at the World Sports Exchange (*wsex.com*), they advertise: "If you can use a mouse, you can place a wager." Ostensibly located in Antigua where gaming is legal, not only have they shown the ease of wagering but they have made it their slogan. Here an account can be established by wiring or electronically transferring funds; even sending a check will establish an electronic gaming account. This account is used to fund a variety of available wagers on all types of sporting events that can be viewed and affected online. The issue is that anyone that travels physically to Nevada or Antigua can play there legally. But what about electronic travel from places where gambling is illegal? Related to the control of gambling is the tax on winners' profits. Because it is now illegal to tax Internet transactions, should taxes be paid on electronic winnings?

Blocking Online Gambling   According to the Australian Internet Industry Association (AIIA) (February 23, 2001), the Communication Ministry is looking favorably on imposing a total ban on interactive gambling using filtering technology. The attempt is to block Australian Internet users from accessing gaming sites. By the time this book was updating, there existed a moratorium on new interactive gaming only. While the AIIA campaigns against the ban, many politicians support it. Civil liberties groups in Australia, as in many other countries, oppose any Internet filtering.

17.8   COMPUTER CRIMES

Computer crimes usually refer to computer fraud and computer abuse. Software piracy belongs to intellectual property infringement and is usually not classified as computer crime. Computer frauds involve intentional dishonesty and personal gain and are simply frauds committed through the use of computers.

For example, computer frauds may be committed by means of:

- alteration of input
- alteration of computer data
- alteration/misuse of programs
- destruction/suppression/misappropriation of output

Computer abuse refers to several types of abusive misuse of computing resources, for example:

- misuse of company computer service/resources by performing unauthorized private work or playing games
- compromise of system integrity by altering company data/programs, introducing viruses into computer systems, or hacking (obtaining unauthorized access to a computer).

Unlike computer frauds, computer abusers do not always obtain personal gains from their abuses and in many cases they are not intentionally dishonest. However, computer abuses cause losses to many people because valuable computing resources are being abused and wasted, and people's confidence in the computer systems drops as a result of unpredictable abuses which affect the operations and performance of computer systems. For an overview see Nairm (1999).

The magnitude of damage due to computer crime is huge. An audit report has pointed out that in the United States 41 percent of firms have experienced "intrusion" or unauthorized use of computers in the span of only 1 year. In Britain, the estimated losses due to hacking alone were £5 to £10 billion in 1997. The newspaper *Australian* reported that in June 1996 a defense firm paid a £10 million ransom for removing "logic bombs," a kind of virus planted in computers. In Hong Kong, computer crime statistics indicate a rapid rise in the last couple of years, and the trend is upwards. The number of reported incidents has risen 10 times between 1998 and 1999. Internet shopping fraud has increased fourfold in the same period. The following are interesting characteristics about computer crime:

- Underreporting of abuse is chronic.
- Many firms do not introduce security until a major abuse has occurred.
- Organizational sizes are unrelated to severity of punishment.
- Serious abuses by trusted, high-level employees are less likely to be prosecuted.
- Programmers are the most difficult abusers to identify.
- Publicity discourages future abuses.
- Security efforts do deter abuse.

The following measures have been found effective in deterring computer crime:

- Make computer security visible, that is, make it known that the company has implemented strong security measures.
- Define and communicate to all staff regularly the company's policy on proper computer use.
- Let staff know the penalties (criminal and otherwise) for abuse of computers.
- Report cases to police.
- Publicize successful prosecution.
- Deploy security technologies extensively.

Legal Aspects

The legislation regarding computer crime is several years behind the criminals' actions, and their sophistication is growing rapidly. As a result, many computer criminals are not prosecuted. An example is the alleged creator of the I Love You bug in the Philippines, whose virus caused several billion dollars damage worldwide. He was released because the prosecutors were unable to find any law that he violated.

Hong Kong, for example, has enacted its own computer crime ordinance criminalizing the activity of hacking. According to this law, any person who, by using telecommunications, *knowingly* causes a computer to perform any function to obtain *unauthorized access* to a computer commits a hacking offense.

For example, the act of password guessing on a computer is a hacking offense, even if the person involved is unsuccessful in logging into the system. The maximum fine for hacking alone is HK$20,000 (about US$2,600). Under this law, the unlawful tampering of computers is also a criminal offense. In particular, it is an offense to do any of the following without express or implied consent:

- Cause a computer not to function normally
- Alter or erase any program or data
- Add any program or data to computer

This offense carries a maximum 10-year jail sentence. The maximum jail sentence increases to 12 years if the unlawful tampering is done with intent and when physical trespassing is involved.

Furthermore, regardless of whether access is authorized or not, accessing a computer with intent to commit either crimes or fraud or cause loss to someone is an offense. This offense carries a maximum 5-year jail sentence. Table 17-4 provides a comparison between computer crime legislation in Hong Kong and other countries.

Cooperation among different countries is desirable but not so easy to achieve (see Hancock, 2000a).

TABLE 17-4

Comparison of Computer Crime Legislation

Criminal Activities	Hong Kong	United States (Federal)	United Kingdom	Australia (Commonwealth)
Hacking				
Attempted Hacking (e.g., password guessing)	Yes	No	Yes	No
Successful Hacking (e.g., log-on is successful and access to data is obtained)	Yes	No	Yes	Yes
Successful Hacking Causing Some Damage	Yes	Yes	Yes	Yes
Hacking with Further Criminal Motives	Yes	Yes	Yes	Yes
Tampering				
Unauthorized Accessing and Tampering with Computer Data	Yes	Yes	Yes	Yes
Accessing Is Authorized but Tampering Is Unauthorized	Yes	No	No	Yes
Interference with and Impediment of Proper Computer Operations	Yes	Yes	No	Yes
Miscellaneous				
Trafficking with Password	No	Yes	No	No
Cross-Country Coverage	No	No	Yes	No
Covering All Computers	Yes	No	Yes	No
Maximum Jail Penalty				
Hacking	5 yrs.	20 yrs.	5 yrs.	2 yrs.
Tampering	12 yrs.	20 yrs.	5 yrs.	10 yrs.

17.9   CONSUMER AND SELLER PROTECTION IN EC

When buyers and sellers cannot see each other and may even be in different countries, there is a chance that dishonest people might commit all types of fraud and other crimes over the Internet. During the first few years of EC we witnessed many of these, ranging from the creation of a virtual bank that disappeared together with the investors' deposits to manipulating stocks on the Internet. This section is divided into the following parts: fraud, consumer protection, seller's protection, and automatic authentication.

Fraud on the Internet

Internet fraud and its sophistication have grown as much and even faster than the Internet itself, as we see in the following examples.

Online auction fraud. The majority (68 percent) of complaints registered at the National Consumers League (of Washington, D.C.) deal with auctions. Money is collected but the goods are not satisfactory or not even delivered.

Internet stocks fraud. In fall 1998, the Securities and Exchange Commission (SEC) brought charges against 44 companies and individuals who illegally promoted stocks on computer bulletin boards, online newsletters, and investment Web sites (details on both settled and pending cases are at *sec.gov*). In most cases, stock promoters falsely spread positive rumors about the prospects of the companies they touted. In other cases, the information provided might have been true, but the promoters did not disclose that they were paid to talk up the companies. Stock promoters specifically target small investors who are lured to the promise of fast profit.

Here is a typical example. In November 1996, a federal judge agreed to freeze the assets of the chairman of a little company called SEXI (Systems of Excellence) and the proprietors of an Internet electronic newsletter called SGA Goldstar. The latter illegally received SEXI stocks in exchange for promoting the stock to unwary investors. As a result, SEXI stock jumped from $0.25 to $4.75, at which time the proprietors dumped the shares (a "pump-and-dump" scheme). Cases like this, as well as ones involving nonregistered securities, are likely to increase because of the popularity of the Internet.

Other financial fraud. Stocks are only one of many areas where swindlers are active. Other areas include selling bogus investments, phantom business opportunities, and other schemes. Financial criminals have access to far more people, mainly due to the availability of e-mail. An example of a multibillion-dollar international fraud is provided in Application Case 17.4. In addition, foreign currency trading scams are increasing on the Internet because most online currency shops are not licensed (see *cftc.gov*).

Other fraud in EC. Many nonfinancial types of fraud exist on the Internet. For example, customers may receive poor-quality products and services, may not get products in time, may be asked to pay for things they assume will be paid for by sellers, and much more.

There are several ways buyers can be protected against EC fraud. The major methods are described next.

APPLICATION CASE   17.4

How David Lee Was Cheated by an International "Investment" Group

David Lee, a 41-year-old Hong Kong resident, replied to an advertisement in a respected business magazine that offered him free investment advice. When he replied, he received impressive brochures and a telephone sales speech. Then, he was directed to the Web site of Equity Mutual Trust (Equity) where he was able to track the impressive daily performance of a fund that listed offices in London, Switzerland, and Belize. From that Web site he was linked to sister funds and business partners. He monitored what he believed were independent Web sites that provided high ratings on the funds. Finally, he was directed to read about Equity and its funds in the respected *International Herald Tribune's* Internet edition items, which appeared as news items but were actually advertisements. Convinced that he would receive good short-term gains, he mailed US$16,000, instructing Equity to invest in the Grand Financial Fund. Soon he grew suspicious when letters from Equity came from different countries, telephone calls and e-mails were not answered on time, and the daily Internet listings dried up.

When David wanted to sell, he was advised to increase his investment and shift to a Canadian company, Mit-tec, allegedly a Y2K bug trouble-shooter. The Web site he was directed to looked fantastic. But David was careful. He contacted the financial authorities in the Turks and Caicos Islands—where Equity was based at that time—and was referred to the British police.

Soon he learned that chances were slim that he would ever see his money again. Furthermore, he learned that several thousand victims paid billions of dollars to Equity. Most of the victims live in Hong Kong, Singapore, and other Asian countries. Several said that the most convincing information came from the Web sites, including the "independent" Web site that rated Equity and its funds.

Source: Based on a story in the *South China Morning Post* (Hong Kong), May 21, 1999.

Consumer Protection

Buyer protection is critical to the success of any commerce, especially electronic, where buyers do not see sellers. Tips for safe electronic shopping include the following:

1. Look for reliable brand names at sites like Wal-Mart Online, Disney Online, and *Amazon.com*, and make sure that you enter the real Web site of these companies.
2. Search any unfamiliar site for an address and telephone and fax numbers. Call up and quiz a person about the sellers.
3. Check out the seller with the local chamber of commerce, Better Business Bureau (*bbbonline.org*), or TRUSTe, as described later.
4. Investigate how secure the seller's site is and how well it is organized.
5. Examine the money-back guarantees, warranties, and service agreements.
6. Compare prices to those in regular stores—too-low prices may be too good to be true.

7. Ask friends what they know. Find testimonials and endorsements.
8. Find out what you can do in case of a dispute.
9. Consult the National Fraud Information Center (*fraud.org*).
10. Check *consumerworld.org*. There you will find many useful resources.
11. Do not forget that you have shopper's rights (see Application Case 17.5).

For consumer protection in the European Union see McDonald (2000).

APPLICATION CASE   17.5

Internet Shopping Rights

Although the Web offers new ways to shop, you can still benefit from legal protections developed for shopping by telephone, mail, and other means. The two most important consumer protection laws for online shopping come from the U.S. government: the Mail/Telephone Order Rule and the Fair Credit Billing Act.

Mail/Telephone (E-Mail) Order Rule. Sellers must deliver your goods within certain time periods or they can face penalties from the FTC. If the seller advertises or tells you a delivery date before you purchase, it must deliver by that date.

If the seller does not give you a delivery date, it must deliver the item within 30 days after receiving your order. If the seller cannot deliver by the required date, it must give you notice before that date, so you can choose either to cancel your order and receive a full and prompt refund or to permit the seller to deliver at a later date. If delivery problems continue, look up the resources below for additional rights and how to make a complaint.

Fair Credit Billing Act. Using your credit card on the Web is like using it at a store. The Fair Credit Billing Act gives you certain rights if there is an error or dispute relating to your bill. If there is an error on your statement, you can withhold payment for the disputed amount while you notify the creditor.

You can withhold payment when your bill contains a charge for the wrong amount, for items you returned or did not accept, or for items not delivered as agreed. Notify the creditor of the error promptly, no later than 60 days after the first bill on which the error appeared. Put it in writing. Describe the error clearly and include your name, address, and credit card number. After you send the notice, the creditor must give written acknowledgment within 30 days and must resolve the error within 90 days.

New Payment Methods. A word of caution. While consumer protections for traditional credit cards are well established, the protections for those who use new forms of "digital payment," "digital cash," and the like are unclear. Some resemble credit cards; others resemble ATM cards; still others are brand-new forms of payment. Look up the resources below for the latest information on new regulations that may be developed to protect consumers using these payment methods.

Resources for Further Information

- Federal Trade Commission: *ftc.gov*; click on "complaint form"; Tel: (202) 382-4357
- Abusive e-mail: Forward the mail to *uce@fte.gov*

APPLICATION CASE 17.5

(continued)

- National Fraud Information Center: *fraud.org*
- Consumer Information Center: examine *pueblo.gsa.gov*; Tel: (729) 948-4000
- U.S. Department of Justice (*usdoj.gov*)
- Direct Market Association: call Tel: (202) 347-1222 for advice
- Internet Fraud Complaint Center: This is a new unit established at the FBI. It registers complaints online from consumers.

  Disclaimer: This is general information on certain consumer rights. It is not legal advice on how any particular individual should proceed. If you want legal advice, consult an attorney.

Source: Based on L. Rose, "Internet Shopping Rights," *Internet Shopper* (Spring 1997), p. 104.

THE FTC CONSUMER ALERTS

The FTC provides a list of 12 scams labeled the "dirty dozen" (the name of a famous movie) that are most likely to arrive by bulk e-mail (search for Internet fraud at *ftc.gov*). For more about the FTC and Internet scams see Teodoro (2001).

The EU and the United States are attempting to develop joint consumer protection policies. For details, see *tacd.org/about*.

Third-Party Services

Several public organizations as well as private companies attempt to protect consumers. Following are just a few examples.

TRUSTe'S "TRUSTMARK"

TRUSTe is a nonprofit group whose mission is to build user's trust and confidence in the Internet by promoting the policies of disclosure and informed consent. Through TRUSTe's program, members can add value and increase consumer confidence in online transactions by displaying the TRUSTe Advertising Affiliate Trustmark to identify sites that have agreed to comply with responsible information-gathering guidelines. Licensing fees of Trustmark range from $500 to $5,000 depending on the size of the online organization and the sensitivity of the information it is collecting. In addition, the TRUSTe Web site provides a "privacy policy wizard," which is aimed at helping companies create their own privacy policies.

The program is voluntary. By mid-1998, 130 prominent Web sites had signed on as TRUSTe participants, including AT&T, CyberCash, Excite, IBM, America Online, Buena Vista Internet Group, CNET, GeoCities, Infoseek, Lycos, Netscape, *The New York Times*, and Yahoo!. The number of members in the program has increased dramatically. However, there still seems to be fear that signing with TRUSTe could expose firms to litigation from third parties if they fail to live up to the letter of the TRUSTe pact, and it is most likely to deter some companies from signing. How well can TRUSTe and others protect your privacy? According to Rafter (2000), there are continuous violations of privacy by companies carrying the TRUSTe seal.

BETTER BUSINESS BUREAU (BBB)

The BBB, a private nonprofit organization supported largely by membership, provides reports on business firms that are helpful to consumers before making a purchase. The BBB responds to millions of such inquiries each year. They have a similar program to TRUSTe's Trustmark for EC. Companies that meet the BBBOnLine Standards exhibit a BBBOnLine seal on their Web sites. The seal indicates that they "care" about their customers. Consumers are able to click on the BBBOnLine seal and instantly get a BBB report on the participating company.

WHICHonline

WHICHonline is supported by the European Community and gives consumers protection by ensuring that online traders under its Which?Web Trader Scheme abide by a code of proactive guidelines that outline issues such as product information, advertising, ordering methods, prices, delivery of goods, consumer privacy, receipting, dispute resolution, and security (*which.net*).

WEB TRUST SEAL AND OTHERS

Web Trust seal is a program similar to that offered by TRUSTe. It is sponsored by the American Institute of Certified Public Accountants. *Gomez.com* monitors customer complaints and provides merchant certification.

ONLINE PRIVACY ALLIANCE

The Online Privacy Alliance is a diverse group of corporations and associations who lead and support self-regulatory initiatives that create an environment of trust and foster the protection of individuals' privacy online. They have guidelines for privacy policies, enforcement of self-regulation, and children's online activities. Major members are AT&T, Bell Atlantic, Compaq, Dell, IBM, Microsoft, NETCOM, Time Warner, and Yahoo!. The Online Privacy Alliance supports third-party enforcement programs, such as the TRUSTe and BBB programs. This is because these programs award an identifiable symbol to signifying to consumers that the owner or operator of a Web site, online service, or other online area has adopted a privacy policy that includes the elements articulated by the Online Privacy Alliance.

EVALUATION BY CONSUMERS

A large number of sites offer product and vendor evaluations offered by consumers. Notable are:

- **Deja.com.** Deja, now part of Google, is the home of many communities whose members trade comments about products at *groups.google.com/*.
- **epubliceye.com.** This site allows consumers to give feedback on reliability, privacy, and customer satisfaction. It makes available a company profile that measures a number of elements, including payment options.

Authentication and Biometric Controls

In cyberspace, buyers and sellers do not see each other. Even when videoconferencing is used, the authenticity of the person you are dealing with must be verified, unless you have dealt with the person before. If we can be assured of the identity of the person on the other end of the line, we can imagine improved and new EC applications:

- Students will be able to take exams online from any place, at any time, without the need for proctors.
- Fraud recipients of government entitlements and other payments will be reduced to a bare minimum.
- Buyers will be assured who the sellers are and sellers will know who the buyers are with a very high degree of confidence.
- Arrangements can be made that only authorized people in companies can place (or receive) purchasing orders.
- Interviews for employment and other matching applications will be accurate since it will be almost impossible for imposters to represent other people.
- Trust in your partners and in EC in general will increase significantly.

The solution for such authentication is provided by information technologies known as biometric controls. Biometric controls provide access procedures that match every valid user with a unique user identifier (UID). They also provide an authentication method to verify that users requesting access to the computer system are really who they claim to be. A UID can be accomplished in one or more of the following ways:

- Provide something only the user knows, such as a password.
- Present something only the user has, for example, a smart card or a token.
- Identify something only the user has, such as a signature, voice, fingerprint, or retinal (eye) scan. This is implemented by biometric controls.

A **biometric control** is defined as an "automated method of verifying the identity of a person, based on physiological or behavioral characteristics" (Forte, 1998). The most common biometrics are the following.

- **Photo of face.** The computer takes a picture of your face and matches it with a prestored picture. In 1998, this method was successful in correctly identifying users except in cases of identical twins.
- **Fingerprints (finger scan).** Each time a user wants access, matching a fingerprint against a template containing the authorized person's fingerprint identifies him or her.
- **Hand geometry.** Similar to fingerprints, except the verifier uses a television-like camera to take a picture of the user's hand. Certain characteristics of the hand (e.g., finger length and thickness) are electronically compared against the information stored in the computer.
- **Blood vessel pattern in the retina of a person's eye.** A match is attempted between the pattern of the blood vessels in the retina that is being scanned and a prestored picture of the retina.
- **Voice (voiceprint).** A match is attempted between the user's voice and the voice pattern stored on templates.
- **Signature.** Signatures are matched against the prestored authentic signature. This method can supplement a photo-card ID system.
- **Keystroke dynamics.** A match of the person's keyboard pressure and speed against prestored information.

- **Iris scan.** This technology uses the colored portion of the eye to identify individuals (see *iriscan.com*). It is a noninvasive system that takes a photo of the eye and analyzes it. It is a very accurate method.
- **Others.** Several other methods exist such as facial thermography or using a PIN.

These methods have different levels of advantages and disadvantages based on four characteristics (Figure 17-3). The closer you are to the center of the figure, the lower the value of the characteristic. Compare your favorite method against the ideal one. Note that an iris scan is both very accurate and inexpensive.

Seller's Protection

The Internet makes fraud by customers easier because of the ease of anonymity. Sellers must be protected against:

- Dealing with customers that deny that they placed an order. (See Application Case 17.6).
- Customers downloading copyrighted software and/or knowledge and selling it to others.

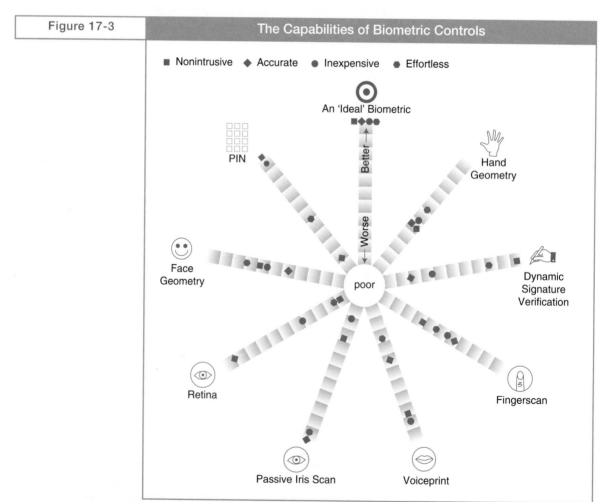

Figure 17-3 — The Capabilities of Biometric Controls

■ Nonintrusive ◆ Accurate ● Inexpensive ● Effortless

An 'Ideal' Biometric
PIN
Hand Geometry
Face Geometry
Dynamic Signature Verification
poor
Better → / Worse
Retina
Fingerscan
Passive Iris Scan
Voiceprint

Source: *InfoWorld* (June 29, 1998) pg. 88 and courtesy of International Biometric Group.

- Being properly paid for products and services provided.
- Use of their names by others.
- Use of their unique words and phrases, names and slogans, and their Web address (trademark protection).

APPLICATION CASE 17.6

Why Vendor Protection Is Needed

On April 2000, Amina Hadir visited the Web site of Victor Stein and ordered a $700 collector's edition of the *Billiard Encyclopedia*, which Mr. Stein co-authored. Ms. Hadir provided a Visa card number and address in Morocco. Once the transaction was authorized by Visa, Mr. Stein shipped the book.

But 2 months later, Mr. Stein found out the hard way that credit card fraud is a growing problem for Internet merchants. Ms. Hadir claimed to Visa a few weeks later that she hadn't ordered the book. She also disputed a number of other items on her bill that had been ordered from other Web sites, including *Amazon.com*. So at the request of Ms. Hadir's credit card issuer, Mr. Stein's bank took the money out of his account to reimburse the issuer for its payment to Mr. Stein.

Never mind that Visa had authorized the credit-card transaction or that Mr. Stein could prove that he had shipped the merchandise to Morocco via the U.S. Postal Service. He couldn't prove Ms. Hadir had ordered the book because he didn't have her signature on the sale or the delivery slip, and he hadn't shipped the book to her billing address.

It isn't clear who committed the fraud in this case. A third party may have used Ms. Hadir's credit card number to fraudulently obtain the book.

But in the world of Internet retailing, the customers are always right. As a result, whether customers are ripping off merchants or have been victimized themselves by credit card thieves, it is the merchants who almost always end up losing money.

The industry's name for a transaction that a customer disputes is a "chargeback," and the problem is growing rapidly.

What Can Vendors Do?

A Web site called *cardservicenow.com* is a database of credit card numbers that have charged back orders. Vendors can use it to decide whether to proceed with a sale. In the future, the credit card industry is planning to use biometrics to deal with electronic shoplifting. Also, using PKI and certificates, especially the SET protocol (see Chapter 14), can help vendors.

Other possible solutions are:

- Using intelligent software that signals questionable customers (or doing it manually in small companies). This involves comparing credit card billing and requested shipping addresses.
- Expedia.com wrote-off $4.1 million in May 2000, and as a result developed a list of warning signals for a possibly fraudulent transaction.
- Some retailers ask customers whose billing address is different from the shipping address to call their bank and ask the bank to have the alternate address added to their account. They ship the goods only if this is done.

For further discussion of the issue see Swisher (1998). Also, third-party escrow and trust companies help to prevent fraud against both buyers and sellers.

17.10   MANAGERIAL ISSUES

The following issues are germane to management:

Management attention must be directed to public policy issues such as privacy and legal and consumer protection surrounding EC. Here are some points to consider:

1. Multinational corporations face different cultures in the different countries in which they are doing business. What might be ethical in country A may be unethical in country B. Therefore, it is essential to develop a country-specific ethics code in addition to a corporate-wide one. Also, managers should realize that in some countries there is little legislation specifically concerned with computers and data.

2. Issues of privacy, ethics, and so on may seem tangential to running a business, but ignoring them may hinder the operation of many organizations. Privacy protection can cut into profits (Hildebrand, 1996).

3. The impacts of EC and the Internet can be so strong that the entire manner in which companies do business will be changed, with significant impacts on procedures, people, organizational structure, management, and business processes. (Read "The Economic and Social Impact of Electronic Commerce" at *oecd.org/subject/e_commerce/summary.html.*)

The following are typical points for an ethics policy or code concerning privacy and other issues:

- Decide whether you want to allow employees to set up their own Web pages on the company intranet. If you do, formulate a general idea of the role you want Web sites to play. This should guide you in developing a policy and providing employees with a rationale for that policy.
- Your policy should address offensive content and graphics, as well as proprietary information.
- Your policy should encourage employees to think about who should and who should not have access to information before they post it on the Web site.
- Make sure your Web content policy is consistent with other company policies.
- Don't be surprised if the policies you develop look a lot like simple rules of etiquette. They should.

The following are some useful Web warnings:

- Have attorneys review your Web content.
- Issue written policy guidelines about employee use of the Internet.
- Don't use copyrighted or trademarked material without permission.
- Post disclaimers concerning content, such as sample code, that your company does not support.
- Post disclaimers of responsibility concerning content of online forums and chat sessions.
- Make sure your Web content and activity comply with the laws in other countries, such as those governing contests.
- Appoint someone to monitor Internet legal and liability issues.

Summary

In this chapter, you learned about the following EC issues as they relate to the learning objectives:

1. **The major legal issues related to EC.** The legal framework for EC is just beginning to solidify. Major issues include privacy, protecting intellectual property, controlling Internet indecency, preventing fraud, establishing a tax framework, controlling gambling, determining jurisdiction, and protecting both sellers and buyers.

2. **The issue of privacy on the Net.** The implementation of EC requires considerable customer information, some of which can be acquired by tracking the customer's activities on the Internet. The major issues are how to protect privacy and whose responsibility it is to do so. While legal measures are being developed, it is basically up to the companies that collect such information to provide the necessary measures.

3. **The issue of intellectual property on the Net.** It is extremely easy and inexpensive to illegally copy intellectual work (e.g., music, knowledge) and resell it or sell it on the Internet without paying royalties to the owners. While the legal aspects are clear, monitoring and catching violators is difficult.

4. **Ethical issues in EC.** Lack of mature legal EC systems makes ethical issues very important. Therefore, ethics codes of companies and guidelines of various organizations help to fill the gap between the needed legal system and the existing one. The problem is that ethics are subjective and their implementation depends on the circumstances.

5. **The conflict between Internet indecency and free speech.** It is easy to distribute indecent material on the Internet, but it is very difficult to control it. The government attempts to control what is delivered on the Internet through censorship were found unconstitutional, contradicting the First Amendment. Other legislation is insufficient or not in place yet. Who will protect surfers, especially children, from indecent or offending material and how is still debatable.

6. **To tax or not to tax?** Although the federal government in the United States wants to have free trade without any tax or tariff on Internet transactions, almost every other local, state, or international government wants the opposite. The issue is the fairness to competitive traditional marketing systems, what kind of tax to impose, and how to allocate tax collected among several involved governments. In the meantime, there is a moratorium in the United States and several other countries on new sales taxes on Internet transactions.

7. **Online contracts vs. regular contracts.** You definitely need a lawyer to examine the differences. If you do not know the details, you may be heading for trouble.

8. **The legal aspects of computer crimes.** Computer crimes are spreading rapidly as the sophistication of the criminals is increasing. Computer crime legislation is slower in evolving, so many criminals are not punished or not punished properly. There are major differences regarding the speed of developing appropriate law in different countries.

9. **Protecting buyers and sellers online.** Protection is needed because there is no face-to-face contact, because there is a great possibility for conducting fraud, because there are no sufficient legal constraints, and because new issues

and scams appear constantly. Several organizations, private and public, attempt to provide protection that is needed to build the trust, which is essential for the success of widespread EC.

Key Terms

Biometric controls	Information privacy
Censorship	Intellectual property
Code of ethics	Privacy
Computer crimes	Privacy policies
Cookie	Software piracy
Domain name	Spamming
Electronic surveillance	Watermarks
Ethics	

Questions for Review

1. Define ethics and distinguish it from the legal aspects of activities.
2. What are the four categories of ethics as they apply to IT and EC?
3. Define cookies.
4. Why do the government and corporations use surveillance?
5. Why is there so much information about individuals in databases?
6. Explain the potential ethical issues involved in using electronic bulletin boards.
7. Describe the content of a code of ethics (for privacy).
8. Define intellectual property.
9. List the major legal issues of EC.
10. Define privacy.
11. Define how one can protect oneself against cookies.
12. List the five basic principles of privacy protection.
13. Define a domain name. What are its various levels?
14. Define spamming.
15. Describe the major kinds of computer crimes.
16. Describe biometric controls.

Questions for Discussion

1. There are three ways to alert employees that information in their computers is under observation: (1) notify all employees upon recruitment that they may be observed while working on their computers; (2) notify employees once a year that they may be under surveillance; or (3) alert employees by a light or visible message on the computer screen (each time the computer is turned on) that they may be under observation. Which alternative would you prefer and why?
2. The IRS buys demographic market research data from private companies. These data contain income statistics that could be compared to tax returns. Many U.S. citizens feel that their rights within the realm of the Privacy Act are being violated; others say that this is unethical behavior on the part of the government. Discuss.

3. Clerks at 7-Eleven stores enter data regarding customers (sex, approximate age, and so on) into the computer. These data are then processed for improved decision making. Customers are not informed about this, nor are they being asked for permission. (Names are not keyed in.) Are the clerks' actions ethical? Compare this with the case of cookies.

4. Many hospitals, health maintenance organizations, and federal agencies are converting, or plan to convert, all patient medical records from paper to electronic storage (using imaging technology). Once completed, electronic storage will enable quick access to most records. However, the availability of these records in a database and on networks or smart cards may allow people, some of whom are unauthorized, to view one's private data. To protect privacy fully may cost too much money and/or considerably slow accessibility to the records. What policies could health-care administrators use in such situations? Discuss.

5. Explain why there are such diverse opinions regarding specific ethical issues even within the same company.

6. It is said that EC has raised many new privacy issues. Why is this so?

7. Discuss the various aspects of relationships between IT and e-mail surveillance.

8. Several examples in this chapter illustrate how information about individuals can help companies improve their businesses. Summarize all the examples provided in this chapter, and explain why they may result in invasion of privacy.

9. Why do many companies and professional organizations develop their own codes of ethics?

10. What are the two major rules of privacy? Why do these two rules make it difficult to enforce privacy regulations?

11. The Kennedy Center Web site (*Kennedy-center.org*) is being visited by millions of people who enjoy different forms of art. The Center had a plan to offer snippets of classical concerts, plays, and so forth so that the public could view some of its programs. Artists and their unions objected. They wanted royalties from the snippets, which the Center was unable to pay. The unions of the Center's employees are also complaining. They do not like the online ticketing introduced by the Center. Discuss the ethical (and possible legal) issues of these incidents.

12. Cyber Promotions Inc. attempted to use the First Amendment right in their flooding of AOL subscribers with junk e-mail. AOL tried to block the junk mail. A federal judge agreed with AOL that unsolicited mail that is annoying, a costly waste of Internet time, and often inappropriate should not be sent. Discuss some of the issues involved, such as freedom of speech, how to distinguish between junk and nonjunk mail, and the analogy with regular mail.

13. Legal and ethical issues may differ. Why? When do they coincide?

14. Provide two privacy examples in EC where the situation is legal but not ethical.

15. What are some specific privacy issues related to EC?

16. Distinguish between self-registration and cookies in EC. Why are cookies a larger concern to individuals?

17. Compare and contrast mail orders (by paper catalogs) to Internet shopping. Why should one pay tax when one buys from a paper catalog but not when buying from an electronic one? (see *itaa.org* for latest developments).

18. Relate the control of offensive material on the Internet to the First Amendment.

19. Why is the copyright issue on the Internet so unique?

20. Why are companies willing to pay millions of dollars for domain names? (For example, Digital Equipment paid over $3 million for the AltaVista name.)
21. Why was the Communication Decency Act considered unconstitutional?
22. Why is the Internet considered the ultimate medium for free speech?
23. Why does the government warn customers to be careful with their payments for EC products and services?
24. Some say that it is much easier to commit a fraud online than off-line. Why?

Exercises and Debates

1. In late 2000, news leaked out that the White House drug control office was secretly placing digital bugs on the computers of people who visited one of its Web sites. The news caused an uproar and the practice was stopped. The technology used to monitor traffic was dropping "cookies" on the visitors' hard drives.

   The cookies were being slipped without notice on computers to monitor the effectiveness of an online anti-drug campaign. The ad campaign worked in much the same way as other advertising linked to Web search engines. When Web users typed in certain key words relating to drugs, a banner ad would pop up on the screen inviting them to click on *freevible.com*, an anti-drug site run by the drug control office. When people clicked on the site, a cookie was dropped onto their hard drives. The cookie's code allowed the advertiser to see how the user entered the site and what pages the user then entered.

   The use of cookies without notice or permission is a controversial but still commonplace practice in the private sector. The Federal Trade Commission has sought greater authority to set and enforce privacy standards.

   The White House press secretary, Joe Lockhart, said the drug control office has not tracked visitors by name or otherwise identified them.

   The drug control office's use of cookies was discovered by privacy advocate Richard Smith, who said he had found it while doing research on privacy practices of health-related Web sites.

   Mr. Smith said none of his research had proved that DoubleClick, a leading Internet advertising company, or the drug policy office had been spying on Americans, only that the technology would allow them to do so.

   As a class or in small groups, debate the following issue: Should the government be allowed to place cookies on individuals' computers to fight illegal drug distribution?
2. There is a major debate regarding taxes on the Internet. Investigate the status of the Internet Tax Freedom Act. Summarize the reasons for its initiation and the arguments against it.
3. Prepare a list of EC activities that are impacted by the First Amendment versus censorship debate.
4. Investigate the issue of sellers' protection from dishonest buyers. Prepare a report.
5. Many companies that provide their employees with Internet access are experiencing problems with employees spending too much time on the Web for personal reasons. As a result, employers are monitoring Web usage. Debate the pros and cons of such an approach.

6. California is one of the few states that publishes data about doctors on the Internet (*medbd.ca.gov*). For example, the Web site can reveal disciplinary actions by hospitals (recommended by fellow doctors) as well as court and private judgments against physicians. Consumer groups are delighted. The doctors claim an invasion of their privacy. Who is right? You may want to find out more information about this topic on the Web.

7. A 27-year-old science teacher was peddling cyanide pills to suicidal Japanese. Nawaki Hashimoto used his credentials as a pharmacist to buy enough cyanide to kill 3,000 people. Then he opened a home page with a consultation room encouraging people to kill themselves. Hashimoto had a good business. He paid $25 for the cyanide and collected $2,600 from the first eight people, one of whom died before the police intervened. The Internet cyanide case alarmed people all over the world and reheated the debate over whether potentially harmful information, such as the proliferating sites on how to commit suicide, should be kept in check. The government in Japan is seriously considering closely monitoring the Internet. On the other side are those that say that the same crime can be committed by telephone or newspaper—but few people would dream of imposing stricter controls on them. What should the government do? Why? As a class or in small groups debate these issues.

8. Should business models be patented? Find material on the topic and debate it.

Internet Exercises

1. Your mission is to identify additional ethical issues related to EC. Surf the Internet, join newsgroups, and read articles from the Internet.
2. Two interesting terms in Internet terminology are *flaming* and *spamming*. Surf the Internet to find out more about these terms. How are they related?
3. Enter *google.com*.
    a. Get a listing of industry organizations with privacy initiatives.
    b. Check out W3C's Privacy Preferences Project.
   Also, enter *privacyrights.org* to learn about privacy concerns.
4. Enter *nolo.com*.
    a. Click on free law centers. Try to find information about the legal issues of EC. Find information about international EC issues.
    b. Click on *lawstreet.com*. Try to find information about international legal aspects of EC.
    c. Support the above with a visit to *google.com* or a search on Yahoo!.
5. Find the status of the latest copyright legislation. Try *fairuse.stanford.edu*. Is there anything regarding the international aspects of copyright legislation?
6. Enter *ftc.gov* and identify some of the typical types of fraud and scams on the Internet.
7. Enter the Internet Service Providers' Web site (*ispc.org*) and find the various initiatives they take regarding topics discussed in this chapter.
8. Check the latest on domain names by visiting sites such as *netidentity.com*. Prepare a report.
9. Place an ad on the Internet and in some newsgroups saying that you want to buy something unique, such as the Brooklyn Bridge or the ship Queen Mary. Collect the responses and try to identify the type of fraud.

10. In order to confirm what you can and cannot place on your Web site without breaking the copyright law, consult *cyberlaw.com* and similar sites. Prepare a report.
11. Private companies such as *thepubliceye.com* and *investigator.com* act as third-party investigators of the honesty of your business. What do these companies do and why are the services of TRUSTe and BBBOnLine insufficient, making the services of these companies necessary?
12. Visit *consumerworld.org*. What protection can this group give that is not provided by BBBOnLine?
13. Visit *consumerworld.org*. What unique services are provided on this site?
14. Find the status of fingerprint identification systems. Try *onin.com*, *bergdata.com* and *morpho.com*.
15. Download freeware from *junkbuster.com* and learn how to prohibit unsolicited e-mail. Describe how your privacy is protected.
16. Enter *scambusters.com* and identify their anti-fraud and anti-scam activities.
17. Enter *nccusl.org* and find information regarding UCITA legislation. Write a report.

Team Assignments and Role Playing

1. Increasing numbers of legal suits filed in the United States and in other countries are related to EC. Have each team member search for specific cases (contracts, liability, and so forth.). Each team should prepare a list of about 12 cases from the past year.
   a. How are these cases related to the topics in this chapter?
   b. What is the likelihood of the court decision in each case? Why?
2. Search the Internet and newspapers for stories regarding Internet fraud. Specifically, assign group members to find stories that match the 12 scams (the "dirty dozen") that the FTC warns about. Also read Teodoro (2001). Each team should prepare a report suggesting how to improve the warning statements against such scams.
3. Enter *epic.org*. Each team is assigned to test privacy protection tools in one or two categories. Concentrate on privacy, encryption, cookies, and anonymity. Present a report.

REAL-WORLD CASE: Gnutella Programs and Intellectual Property Payment

Gnutella is an open, decentralized, peer-to-peer search system that is mainly used to find and exchange files over the Internet. Gnutella is neither a company nor a particular application. It is also not a Web site. However, several Web sites deliver news and information about Gnutella (e.g., *gnutella.wego.com*, *gnutella.co.uk*, and *gnutellanews.com*. Gnutella is a name for a technology, like the terms "e-mail" and "Web."

The original Gnutella client was developed by Justin Frankel and Tom Pepper at Nullsoft. AOL quickly closed the site down, but not before thousands of people had downloaded it.

The original version was a good starting point, but buggy. It's come a long way, and now many different companies, individuals, and groups develop software based on the ever-evolving Gnutella protocol.

What Makes Gnutella So Special?

Gnutella is decentralized—this means that there is no central company that the network relies on for its existence. If one company goes down, Gnutella keeps working. Gnutella users connect to each other, and not to a central server. To do this, they must find another user, either by connecting to a friend, to an index of other users (a host cache), or using Internet Relay Chat (IRC).

Advantages of Using Gnutella

- Share any file you want!

- Decentralized—Fully distributed search system provides a useful searching capability without requiring a centralized search database.

- Firewall-friendly transfers when one client is behind a firewall.

- Documented protocol (see *dss.clip2.com*)

- Free software, also any open source clients.

- Bandwidth shaping on many clients limits total and per-connect upload rates to keep your lines from oversaturating.

- Not anonymous—Ability to see what other people are searching for on the network. However, queries to certain URLs are anonymous.

- Ability to change port—difficult to block/restrict access to.

- Ability to define your own internal network with a single exit point to the rest of the Internet makes it difficult to block access to GnutellaNet.

Disadvantages of Using Gnutella

Some may consider certain of the advantages above as disadvantages. Here are some more:

- Can be slower, especially on dial up, since bandwidth is used to maintain connection to GnutellaNet. This problem is being solved. See Gomez (2001).

- Some IT experts say that using Gnutella may create a security problem for users.

- Lack of central coordination had been viewed as posing a limit on the Gnutella network's growth. But due to the work of a loosely affiliated group of software developers, the network's technical limitations are slowly being overcome. Gnutella was able to reach, in June 2001, tens of thousands of users at once, 20 times more than in December 2000.

- The program may cause a continuing headache for copyright holders.

Newer Gnutella programs are creating a large and increasingly vigorous network. Web site Download.com reported in June 2001 that nearly one million people a week are downloading Bear-Share and LimeWire, another of the new breed of Gnutella programs.

Some people believe peer-to-peer systems like Gnutella have other uses besides trading music files, such as searching for the sorts of information found on Web sites like *Yahoo.com*. With work on Gnutella continuing, the company behind LimeWire was offering cash prizes in summer 2001 for the best research papers on Gnutella—the Gnutella network appears to be on its way to becoming a permanent, standardized software system like others on the Internet.

A thriving Gnutella network is bad news for the entertainment industry, which assumed it had little to fear from Gnutella because technical problems would keep the network from growing too large. However, the explosion of usage in 2001 resulted in several test legal actions that have been taken against individual Gnutella users for copyright infringement. But Gnutella software developers aren't believed to be at legal risk, because their programs can be used for many things, and because, unlike Napster, they don't maintain any sort of database of copyrighted material.

Questions for the case

1. Identify all the differences between Napster and Gnutella.

2. Some believe that the legal actions against individual Gnutella users will fail. Why? Find more information about such actions (try the Web sites cited earlier and *google.com*).

3. Explore the issue of anonymity. Why are only some inquiries anonymous? Also, explore anonymity when downloading.

4. Some believe that any restrictions or royalty payments on Gnutella will violate the freedom of speech on the Internet. Explain.

REFERENCES AND BIBLIOGRAPHY

Abrams, M., ed. *World Wide Web: Beyond the Basics.* Upper Saddle River, New Jersey: Prentice Hall, 1998.

Adam, N. R., ed. *Electronic Commerce: Technical, Business, and Legal Issues.* Upper Saddle River, New Jersey: Prentice Hall, 1998.

Agranoff, M. H., "Controlling the Threat to Personal Privacy," *Journal of Information Systems Management* (Summer 1993).

Alberts, R. J., et al. "The Threat of Long-Arm Jurisdiction to Electronic Commerce," *Communications of the ACM* (December 1998).

Anderson, R. E., et al. "Using the New ACM Code of Ethics in Decision Making," *Communications of the ACM* (February 1993).

Bannan, R. "Net Tax Bill Sails by Committee to House Floor," *Interactive Week* (February 2, 1998).

Beato, G. "Online Piracy's Mother Ship," *Business 2.0* (December 12, 2000).

Berghel, H. "Identify Theft, Social Security Numbers, and the Web," *Communication of the ACM* (February 2000).

Bowman, L. "Is Microsoft's Privacy Plan an Improvement?," *CNETNews.com*, March 2000.

Cavoukian, A. and D. Tapscott. *Who Knows: Safeguarding Your Privacy in a Networked World.* New York: McGraw-Hill, 1997.

Cheeseman, H. R. *Business Law: The Legal, Ethical, and International E-Commerce Environment.* Upper Saddle River, New Jersey: Prentice Hall, 2000.

Clarkson, K. W., et al., ed. *West's Business Law: Text and Cases—Legal, Ethical, Regulatory, International, and E-Commerce Environment.* Cincinnati, Ohio: South-Western College Publishing, 2000.

Cozzoling, P. "Everyone Wants to Tax the Net," *Business Week* (April 13, 1998).

Cranor, L. F., "Internet Privacy," *Communications of the ACM*, Special issue (February 1999).

Creco, J. "Privacy—Whose Right Is It Anyhow?" *The Journal of Business Strategy* (January/February 2001).

Cross, F. B. and R. L. Miller. *West's Legal Environment of Business: Text and Cases—Ethical, Regulatory, International, and E-Commerce Issues*, Cincinnati, Ohio: South-Western College Publishing, 2000.

Denning, D. E. "To Tap or Not to Tap," *Communications of the ACM* (March 1993a).

Denning, D. E. *Information Warfare and Security.* Reading, Massachusetts: Addison Wesley, 1998.

Diffie, W. and S. Landau. *Privacy on the Line: The Politics of Wiretapping and Encryption.* Boston, Massachusetts: MIT Press, 1998.

Donham, P. "An Unshackled Internet: If Joe Howe Were Designing Cyberspace," *Proceedings of the Symposium on Free Speech and Privacy in the Information Age*, University of Waterloo, November 26, 1994.

Downing, D. "The Beat Goes On: Music Copyright on the Internet," *Managing Intellectual Property* (February 1999).

Electronic Privacy Information Center. "Internet Censorship," (*epic.org/free_speech/censorship/*) (August 4, 1998).

Federal Trade Commission, "Privacy Online: A Report to Congress," *ftc.gov/reports/privacy3*, June 1998.

Ferrera, G. R., et al. *Cyberlaw: Text and Cases.* Cincinnati, Ohio: South-Western College Publishing, 2000.

Forte, D. "Biometrics: Truths and Untruths," *Computer Fraud and Security* (November 1998).

Froomkin, A. U. "Legal Issues in Anonymity and Pseudonymity," *Information Society* (April–June 1999).

Gomez, L. "Gnutella May Become a Standard on the Web." *The Asian Wall Street Journal* (May 30, 2001).

GVU-Graphics, Visualization, and Usability Center at Georgia Tech University (*cc.gatech.edu/gv/user_surveys*), 1998.

Hancock, B. "U.S. and Europe Cybercrime Agreement Problems," *Computers & Security* (January 2000a).

Hancock, B. "'Anonymizing' Software Causes Law Enforcement Concerns," *Computers and Security* (January 2000b).

Harmon, A. "Web Wars: Companies Get Tough on Rogues," *Los Angeles Times* (November 12, 1996).

Harris, L. E. *Digital Property.* New York: McGraw-Hill, 1998.

Hawke, C. S. *Computer and Internet Use on Campus: A Legal Guide to Issues of Intellectual Property, Free Speech, and Privacy.* San Francisco: Jossey-Bass, 2000.

Herrington, T. K. *Controlling Voices: Intellectual Property, Humanistic Studies, and the Internet.* Carbondale, Illinois: Northern Illinois University Press, 2001.

Hildebrand, C. "Privacy vs. Profit," *CIO* (February 15, 1966).

Hinde, S. "Privacy and Security—The Drivers for Growth of E-Commerce," *Computers and Security*, vol. 17, no. 6 (1998).

Kaplan, C. S. "The Year Saw Many Milestones in Cyberlaw," *Cyberlaw Journal* (January 1, 1998).

Korzyk, A. "A Decision-Making Model for Security—Conducting Electronic Commerce," *NISSC* (1998).

Kravitz, P. M. and A. Pugliese. "Lawmakers Tackle Privacy," *Journal of Accountancy* (June 2000).

Kwok, S. H., et. al. "Watermark Design Pattern for Intellectual Property Protection in E-Commerce Applications," Proceedings, 34th HICSS, Hawaii (January 2001).

Mason, R. O. "Four Ethical Issues of the Information Age," *MIS Quarterly* (March 1986).

Mason, R. O., et al. *Ethics of Information Management.* Thousand Oaks, California: Sage Publishers, 1995.

McDonald, F. "Consumer Protection Policy in the European Union," *European Business Journal* (May 2000).

Merges, R. P. "Property Rights for Business Concepts and Patent System Reform," *Berkeley Technology Law Journal* (Spring 1999).

Miller, R. L. and F. B. Cross. *The Legal and E-Commerce Environment Today: Business in Its Ethical, Regulatory, and International Setting.* Eagan, Minnesota: West Publishing Company (Short Disc), 2001.

Mizell, L. R. *Invasion of Privacy.* Berkeley, California: Berkeley Publishing Group, 1998.

Morgan, J. P. and N. A. Wong. "Conduct a Legal Web Audit," *e-Business Advisor* (September 1999).

Nairm, G. "Increased Crime Is the Darker Side of E-Business," *Financial Times* (July 7, 1999).

Nadel, M. S. "Computer Code vs. Legal Code," *Federal Communication Law Journal* (May 2000).

National Research Council, ed. *The Digital Dilemma: Intellectual Property in the Information Age.* Washington D.C.: National Academy Press, 2000.

O'Leary, D. E. "Some Privacy Issues in Knowledge Discovery: The OECD Personal Privacy Guidelines," *IEEE Expert* (April 1995).

Oliva, R. A. and S. Prabankar. "Copyright Perils Can Lurk on Business Web," *Marketing Management* (Spring 1999).

Osen, J. "The Thorny Side of Jurisdiction and the Internet," *Network Security* (November 1998).

Owen, M. and R. Penfold. "Copyright Infringement in Online World," *Managing Intellectual Property* (January 2000).

Oz, E. *Ethics in the Information Age*. Dubuque, Iowa: Wm. C. Brown, 1994.

Page, T. "Digital Watermarks as a Form of Copyright Protection," *The Computer Law and Security Report* (November/December 1998).

Pink, S. W. *The Internet and E-Commerce Legal Handbook: A Clear and Concise Reference to Help You and Your Business*. Roseville, California: Prima Publishing, 2001.

Rafter, M. V. "Trust or Bust?" *The Standard* (March 6, 2000).

Rainone, S. H., et al. "Ethical Management of Employee E-Mail Privacy," *Information Strategy: The Executive Journal* (Spring 1998).

Reidenberg, J. R. "Restoring Americans' Privacy in E-Commerce," *Berkeley Technology Law Journal* (Spring 1999).

Sargert, J. L. "Cybersquatters and Invisible Ink: Challenges to Trademarks on the Internet," *Competitive Intelligence Review* (Third Quarter 2000).

Schneier, B. and D. Banisar. *The Electronic Privacy Paper*. New York: John Wiley & Sons, 1997.

Shim, J. P., et al. "Netlaw, a Tutorial," *Communications of the AIS* (September 2000).

Smith, G. V. and R. L. Parr. *Intellectual Property*. New York: John Wiley & Sons, 1998.

Smith, H. J., et al. "Information Privacy: Measuring Individuals' Concerns About Organizational Practices," *MIS Quarterly* (June 1996).

Smith, R. and R. H. Wientzen. "Privacy Sound Off: Regulation vs. Self-Regulation," *Internet Week* (September 21, 1998).

Stern, J. "The 10 Common Myths of Cookies," *Computer Fraud and Security* (July 1998).

Swisher, K. "Seller Beware," *Wall Street Journal* (December 7, 1998).

Tantum, M. "Legal Responsibility of Internet Service Providers," *The Computer Law and Security Report* (November/December 1998).

Teodoro, B. "Internet Scams 101: How You Can Protect Yourself," CNNFN (*cnnfn.com*), (June 6, 2001).

U.S. Department of Justice, "The Electronic Frontier: The Challenge of Unlawful Conduct Involving the Use of the Internet" (*usdoj.gov/criminal/ cybercrime/unlawful.htm*) (2000).

Wang, H., H. K. O. Lee, and C. Wang. "Consumer Privacy Concern About Internet Marketing," *Communications of the ACM* (March 1998).

Wells-Branscomb, A. *Who Owns Information? From Privacy to Public Access*. New York: Basic Books, 1994.

Yeung, M. M., ed. "Digital Watermarking," *Communications of the ACM* (Special Issue) (July 1998).

18

E-Communities, Global EC, and Other EC Issues

LEARNING OBJECTIVES

Upon completion of this chapter, the reader will be able to:

- Describe the role and impact of virtual communities.

- Evaluate the issues involved in global EC.

- Analyze the impact of EC on small businesses.

- Describe the relationship between EC and BPR, knowledge management, and virtual corporations.

- Understand the research opportunities in EC.

- Describe the future of EC.

CONTENT

Recreational fishing in Australia is popular both with residents as well as international visitors. Over 700,000 Australians are fishing regularly. The Australian Fishing Shop (AFS) (*ausfish.com.au*) is a small e-tailer, founded in 1994, initially as a hobby site carrying information for the recreational fisherperson. Over the last few years the site has featured a fishing portal that has created a devoted community behind it.

A visit to the site will show immediately that the site is not a regular storefront, but actually provides considerable information to the recreational fishing community. In addition to the sale of products (e.g., rods, reels, clothing, and boats and fishing-related books, software, and CD-ROMs) and services (e.g., fishing charters and holiday packages), the site provides the following information:

- Hints and tips for fishing.
- What's new?
- A photo gallery of visitors' prize catches.

- Chat boards—general and specialized.
- Directions from boat builders, tackle manufacturers, etc.
- Recipes for cooking fish.
- Information about newsgroups and mailing lists.
- Free giveaways and competitions
- Links to fishing-related government bodies, other fishing organizations (around the globe and in Australia), and daily weather maps and tides reports.
- General information site and FAQs.
- List of fishing sites around the globe.
- Contact details by phone, post, and e-mail.
- Free e-mail and Web page hosting.

In addition, there is an auction mechanism for fishing equipment and answers are provided for customer inquiries.

The company is fairly small (gross income of about AU$500,000 a year). How can such a small company survive? The answer can be found in its strategy of providing value-added services to the recreational fishing community. These services attract over

1.6 million visitors each month, from all over the world, of which about 1 percent make a purchase. Also, several advertisers sponsor the site. This is sufficient to survive. Another interesting strategy is to aim at the **global market.** Most of the total income is derived from customers in the United States and Canada who buy holiday and fishing packages.

The company acts basically as a referral service for vendors. Therefore, it does not have to carry an inventory. AFS does business with a small number of suppliers, thus they are able to aggregate orders from suppliers and then pack and send them to customers. Some orders are shipped directly from vendors to the customers.

This vignette demonstrates how a small e-tailer (Section 18.4) is surviving and making money. One of the reasons for the company's success is that it went global, a topic we discuss in Section 18.3. The other reason is the creation of a devoted, virtual Internet community, a topic we present next.

18.2 VIRTUAL COMMUNITIES

A **community** is a group of people who interact with one another. A **virtual community** is one where the interaction is done by using the Internet. Virtual communities parallel typical physical communities such as neighborhoods, clubs, or associations. Virtual communities offer several ways for members to interact, collaborate, and trade (see Table 18-1).

The Internet community described in the opening vignette has hundreds of thousands of members. Other communities may have millions. This is one major difference from physical communities, which are usually smaller. Internet communities could have significant effects on markets. Another difference is that off-line

TABLE 18-1

Elements of Interaction in a Community

Category	Element
Communication	Bulletin boards (discussion groups)
	Chat rooms/threaded discussions (string Q&A)
	E-mail and instant messaging
	Private mailboxes
	Newsletters, netzines (electronic magazines)
	Web postings
	Voting
Information	Directories and yellow pages
	Search engine
	Member generated content
	Links to information sources
	Expert advice
EC Element	Electronic catalogs and shopping carts
	Advertisements
	Auctions of all types
	Classified ads
	Bartering online

communities are frequently in geographical proximity, whereas only a few online communities are of this type. Many thousands of communities exist on the Internet. On many Web sites one can find services for community members. Several communities are independent and are growing rapidly. For instance, GeoCities (*geocities.com*) has grown to several million members in less than 2 years. Community members set up personal home pages on the site and advertisers buy ad space targeted to community members. In order to understand the economic impact of electronic communities, let us see what they really are. We start with some examples shown in Application Case 18.1.

APPLICATION CASE 18.1

Examples of Communities

The following are examples of online communities.

- **Associations.** Many associations have a Web presence. These range from PTAs (Parent-Teacher Associations) to professional associations. An example of this type of community is the Australian Record Industry Association (*aria.com.au*).
- **Ethnic communities.** Many communities are country-specific or language-specific. An example is *Elsitio.com* that provides content for the Spanish- and Portuguese-speaking audiences in Latin America and the United States. *China.com*, *sina.com*, and *sohu.com* cater to the world's large Chinese community.

APPLICATION CASE   **18.1**

(continued)

- **Gender communities.** *Women.com* and *ivillage.com*, the two largest female-oriented communities, merged in 2001 in an effort to cut losses and to become profitable.
- **Affinity portals.** These are communities organized by interest, such as hobbies, vocations, political parties, unions (*teamsters.workingfamilies.com*), and many, many more.
- **Catering to the young.** Many companies see unusual opportunities here. Three communities of particular interest are *Alloy.com*, *Bolt.com*, and *Blueskyfrog.com*. *Alloy.com* is based in the United Kingdom and claims to have over 10 million members. *Bolt.com* claims to have 4 million members and operates from the United States. Finally, *Blueskyfrog.com* operates from Australia on cell phones and claims to have more than 1 million devoted members.
- **Mega communities.** GeoCities is one example of a mega community, and it is divided into many subcommunities. It is by far the largest online community, and is owned by Yahoo!.
- **B2B online communities.** In Chapter 7 we introduced the "many-to-many" B2B exchanges. These are referred to by some (e.g., Raisch, 2001, and *CommerceOne.com*) as communities. These exchanges support community programs such as technical discussion forums, interactive Webcasts, user-created product reviews, virtual conferences and meetings, experts seminars, and user-managed profile pages. Classified ads can help members to find jobs or employers to find employees. Many also include industry news, directories, links to government and professional associations, and more. For example:
  - **a.** Altra Energy has discussion areas for members to discuss technical support issues and questions, as well as general discussion areas for each type of energy.
  - **b.** HoustonStreet's SquawkBox live discussion allows energy traders to discuss among themselves industry topics and questions they may have about the HoustonStreet marketplace.
  - **c.** PlasticsNet's 35,000 registered users generate thousands of classified advertisements every year. PlasticsNet also has searchable user profiles that allow users to submit contact information, Web links, and any personal or company information that they choose.

Internet Communities

Rheingold (1993) believes that the Web is being transformed into a social Web of communities. He thinks that every Web site should incorporate a place for people to chat. A community site should be an interesting place to visit, a kind of virtual community center. It is a place where discussions cover many controversial topics.

Electronic communities are closely related to EC. For example, Champy et al. (1996) describe online, consumer-driven markets where most of the consumers' needs, ranging from finding a mortgage to job hunting are arranged from home. Electronic communities will eventually have a massive impact on almost every company that produces consumer goods and services, as was shown in the opening case. The electronic communities will change the nature of corporate strategy and the manner in which business is done.

Electronic communities are spreading quickly over the Internet. Armstrong and Hagel (1996) and Hagel and Armstrong (1997) recognize the following four types of electronic communities.

COMMUNITIES OF TRANSACTIONS

Communities of transactions facilitate buying and selling. Community members include buyers, sellers, intermediaries, and so on. An example is Virtual Vineyards, (*evineyard.com*), which in addition to selling wines, provides expert information on wines and a place for wine lovers to chat with each other (see Chapter 12). The GE/TPN network created an infrastructure for communities of traders to conduct bids or simply buy and sell. Another example can be found in the opening vignette where a trading store acts also as a community center for the fisherperson.

COMMUNITIES OF INTEREST OR PURPOSE

In communities of interest or purpose people have the chance to interact with each other on a specific topic. For example, the Motley Fool (*fool.com*) is a forum for individual investors. Rugby365 attracts rugby fans and music lovers go to *mp3.com*. City411 provides comprehensive information about local physical communities and displays information on many topics, including entertainment, traffic, and weather reports.

GeoCities' (*geocities.com*) 40 million members are organized into dozens of communities such as MotorCity (car lovers) and Nashville (country music). Members have a marketplace for buying and selling goods and services.

COMMUNITIES OF RELATIONS (OR PRACTICE)

Communities of relations are organized around certain life experiences, situations, or vocations. For example, the cancer forum on CompuServe contains information and exchange of opinions regarding cancer. Parent Soup is a favorite gathering spot for parents, seniors like to visit "SeniorNet," and ivillage's Women's Wire is a well-known online community aimed at women that features regular celebrity chats and discussions.

Many communities are organized according to professional business interests. For example, *plasticsnet.com* is used by thousands of engineers in the plastics industry. A related extranet, *commerx.com*, provided a cybermarket for the industry. The company currently uses Vertical Net to connect industy-specific marketplaces. These communities offer opportunities for the translation of the community's interest into commerce revenue.

COMMUNITIES OF FANTASY

In communities of fantasy participants create imaginary environments. For example, AOL subscribers can pretend to be a medieval baron at the Red Dragon Inn. On ESPNet, participants can create competing teams and "play" with Michael Jordan. Related to this are the large numbers of games that thousands of people play simultaneously. In *4cweb.aliens.com* you can win only if you join a team for $10 a month, and Kingdom of Drakkar allows you to play various roles.

OTHER CLASSIFICATIONS

Another way to classify communities is by the nature or type of the members. One possibility is to classify members as traders, players, just friends, enthusiasts, or friends in need. A more complete classification is proposed by Schubert and Ginsburg (2000) and it is shown in Figure 18-1 on facing page.

Commercial Aspects

Interactive Week (May 11, 1998) provides the following suggestions on how to transform a community site into a commerce site:

- Understand a particular niche industry, its information needs, and the step-by-step process by which it does the research needed to do business.
- Build a site that provides that information, either through partnerships with existing publishers and information providers or by gathering it independently.
- Set up the site to mirror the steps a user goes through in the information-gathering and decision-making process, for example, how a chip designer whittles down the list of possible chips that will fit a particular product.
- Build a community that relies on the site for decision support.
- Start selling products and services, such as sample chips to engineers, that fit into the decision-support process.

Forrester Research conducted a survey in 1998 that found the following expected payback, for organizations that sponsor online communities, by order of importance:

- Customer loyalty increases
- Sales increases
- Customer participation and feedback increases
- Repeat traffic to site increases
- New traffic to site increases

Electronic communities can create value in several ways as summarized in Figure 18-2 (p. 792). Members input useful information to the community in the form of comments and feedback, elaborating on their attitudes and beliefs and information needs, that can then be retrieved and used by other members or by marketers. The community organizers may also supply their own content communities, as does America Online.

Another possibility for value creation in electronic communities arises from the fact that the community brings together consumers of specific demographics and interests. This presents opportunities for transacting business and for communicating messages about products and services, which marketers and advertisers value and are willing to pay for. Marketers actually offer various discounts to community members. In addition, electronic communities can attract advertising revenues from advertisers eager to communicate their messages to community members. (This may be a significant source of revenue for electronic communities.) Other opportunities arise from the marketing information that is generated within communities, which marketers and advertisers find valuable. Such information includes demographics and psychographics of members; their attitudes and beliefs about products, services, and issues; their behavior data with regard to business transactions within communities; and information on their interactions and

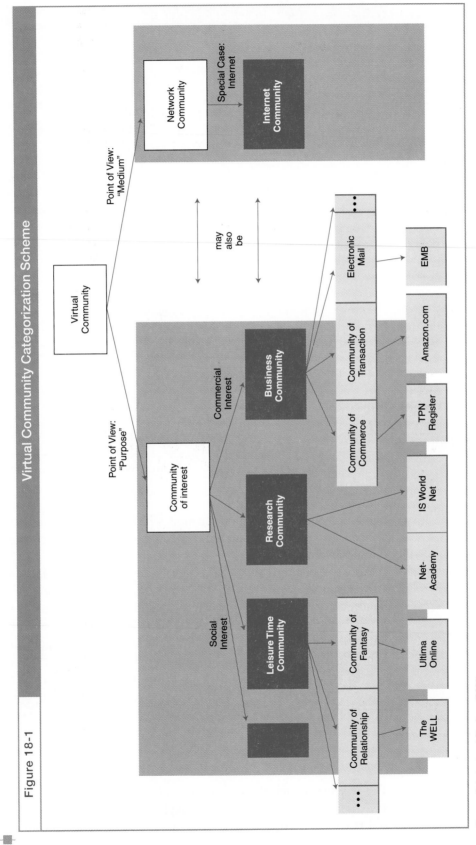

Figure 18-1

Virtual Community Categorization Scheme

Source: Schubert and Ginsburg (2000).

Figure 18-2	Value Creation in Electronic Communities

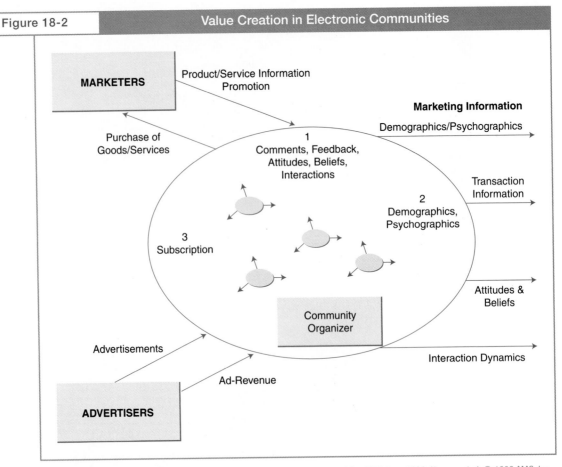

interaction dynamics. Such information, which is collected from chat rooms, questionnaires, or e-mail communications, could be sold to marketers and advertisers if the members do not object.

Also, some communities charge members content fees for downloading certain articles, music, or pictures. Finally, since community members create their own home pages, it is easy to learn about them and reach them with targeted advertisements and marketing. For a look at the ways companies can benefit by using communities to make connections with members and exploit opportunities, see the book *Net Gain* by Hagel and Armstrong (1997). Also see Preece (2000) and Bressler and Grantham (2000). A special report in *Business Week* (Hof et al. 1997) provides an overview of the field with coverage of the most interesting communities and their special terminology. Also see Kannan et al. (1998). For ways to manage communities see McWilliam (2000).

FINANCIAL VIABILITY OF COMMUNITIES

The revenue model of communities is basically based on sponsorship and on advertisement. The expenses are very high due to the need to provide fresh content and free services. In addition, most communities initially provide free membership. The objective is to have as many registered members as possible in order to attract advertisers. This model did not work too well. Several communities that were organized for profit, such as *ivillage.com* and *elsitio.com*, sustained heavy losses. Several communities ceased operations in 2000–2001 (e.g., *esociety.com*). Mergers and acquisitions started in 2001 are expected to improve the situation.

Key Strategies for Successful Online Communities

In early 2001, the losses of many online communities were growing rapidly. Some communities started to merge (e.g., *ivillage.com* and *women.com*), while others were talking about mergers (e.g., *china.com, sina.com, sohu.com*). Here are some suggestions for success based on Raisch (2001):

- Be member-centric from the start.
- Define the community's focus.
- Involve the community members.
- Weigh carefully internal staffing vs. outsourcing.
- Consider buying vs. building technologies.
- Minimize the need for the participants to go elsewhere for content, service, or trading.
- Provide personalization.
- Facilitate communication among members.
- Promote segmentation of the wider community into smaller, more focused areas.
- Keep an open door to the outside.
- Evaluate syndicated sources of content (Chapter 8).
- Build alliances and partnerships.

It is interesting to note that a major advocate of those suggestions, *esociety.com*, a community itself, ceased operation in late 2000.

Arthur Andersen, the consulting company, outlined the following eight principles of community success (see details in Duffy, 1999):

1. Increase traffic and participation in the community.
2. Focus on the needs of the members; use facilitators and coordinators.
3. Encourage free sharing of opinions and information—no controls.
4. Financial sponsorship is a must. Significant investment is required.
5. Consider the cultural environment.
6. Communities are not just discussion groups. Provide several tools and activities.
7. Community members must be involved in activities and recruiting.
8. Communities need to guide discussions, provoke controversy, and raise sticky issues.

Here are some interesting communities: *earthweb.com icollector.com, webMD.com, terra.es, angel/art-gallery.com, suretrade.com, icq.com, letsbuyit.com, Barclays.co.uk, parentsoup.com, radiolinja.fi,* and *realcall.com.*

18.3   GOING GLOBAL

A global electronic marketplace has become the mantra of the free market and free traders. It means access to larger markets, mobility (e.g., to minimize taxes), and flexibility to employ workers and manufacture products anywhere using a worldwide telecommuting workforce. The potential for a global economy is certainly here, while geographical borders are falling, artificial borders are being erected through local language preferences, local regulations, access limitations, and so on. However, going global may be complex due to a multiciplicity of issues, some of which are discussed in this chapter.

Overview

Global communities are springing up across geographical borders. These cybernations' interest or taste differences are as real as political boundaries. Online firms may gain access to these cybernations and to a specific segment of consumer groups on a worldwide scale.

Global electronic activities have existed for more than 25 years, mainly in support of B2B financial and other repetitive, standard transactions. Most well known are the EFT and EDI. However, these activities were supported by expensive and inflexible private telecommunications lines and, therefore, were limited to medium and large corporations, as well as by the nature of the transactions. The emergence of the Internet and extranets has resulted in an inexpensive and flexible infrastructure that can greatly facilitate global trade (Clinton and Gore, 1997). The major advantage of EC is the ability to do business anytime and from anywhere, and do it rapidly at a reasonable cost. Indeed, we have seen some incredible success stories in this area. For example:

- You can buy and sell stocks in several countries using E*TRADE as your broker.
- Exchanges such as e-Steel and ChemConnect have members in dozens of countries.
- *Amazon.com* sells books to individuals and organizations in over 190 countries.
- Small companies, such as *evineyard.com*, sell to hundreds of customers worldwide. Hothothot, for example, which has both a physical and online stores, reported its first international trade only after it went online. Within 2 years, Hothothot's global sales climbed from zero to 25 percent of the total sales after the storefront was opened.
- Major corporations, such as General Electric and Boeing Inc., reported an increasing number of out-of-the-country vendors participating in their electronic requests for quotes. These electronic bids resulted in a 10 percent to 15 percent cost reduction and an over 50 percent cycle time reduction.
- Many international corporations considerably increased their success in recruiting employees for foreign locations when online recruiting was utilized.

The Global Trading Exchange

Going global means not only selling or buying in a foreign country. It can be a joint venture or even a collaboration of B2B exchanges, as described in Application Case 18.2.

Barriers to Global EC

There are many barriers to global EC. Some are similar to barriers to any EC (Chapter 1). They are divided here into the following four categories:

APPLICATION CASE   18.2

The Global Trading Web

The Global Trading Web (GTW) exemplifies how technologies, business practices, governance, globalization, and localization can be executed in the context of e-marketplaces. The Global Trading Web, founded by Commerce One, is now the world's largest global online B2B trading community. It connects businesses via regional e-marketplaces located in the United States, Asia, Europe, the Middle East, and Africa. As of September 2000, the GTW comprised 80 global e-marketplaces. It enables companies to interact and conduct business with anyone, anytime, anywhere.

Linked together, the GTW e-marketplaces provide a common infrastructure that is similar to the Internet. As the number of users increases, so does its liquidity.

GTW provides global trading efficiencies through online aggregation. Each e-marketplace has access to the products, sources, and services of others, extending the market of buyers and suppliers bidirectionally. These ad hoc partnerships enable e-marketplaces to share economic advantages, such as access to trading partners and value-added services to eliminate redundant development efforts. They speed time-to-market and increase return on investment. Through the GTW, local markets in different parts of the world can be addressed in their native languages and according to their culture.

Some major players in the GTW are:

- **Asia:** Asia2B (China), NTT Marketsite (Japan), *Sesami.net* (Singapore)
- **Europe:** BT MarketSite (United Kingdom), D. T Marketplace (Germany), Opciona (Spain), PT Electronic (Portugal), Swisscom (Switzerland)
- **North America:** City Group, *CommerceOne.net*, Enporion, eScout, Exostar, Pantellos, (all from the United States); TD MarketSite (Canada), Artikos (Mexico)
- **Multiple countries:** Covisint, Concert, Metique, Trade Alliance Trade-Ranger

  For additional details see *commerceone.com*.

LEGAL ISSUES

The United States and other major international organizations such as the European Commission, the United Nations Commission on International Trade Law (UNCITRAL), the OECD (Chapter 17), and the World Trade Organization are presently engaged in discussions pertaining to the development of domestic and global legal frameworks that will facilitate EC worldwide. Among these organizations there seems to be a consensus only to the extent that uncoordinated actions must be avoided and that an international policy of cooperation should be encouraged. For example, for dealing with domain name issues see *1globalplace.com*.

The challenge of an international policy accord is essentially how to secure the legal framework that will facilitate EC throughout the world without infringing on the freedom of governments to pursue their own objectives. Some of the legal issues involved are jurisdiction issues, export/import regulations and compliance, intellectual property (enforcement), cryptography (encryption) and security, contracts, notarized documents, authentication procedures, privacy protection, cross-border transactions (data protection), content control, and consumer protection. Most of these issues are generic and were discussed in Chapter 17.

MARKET ACCESS ISSUES

Market access issues, if not addressed, could impede the growth of global EC. Building a telecommunications infrastructure capable of accommodating all users and all types of data is a necessity. Companies starting EC need to evaluate bandwidth needs by analyzing the data required, time constraints, access demands, and user technology limitations. Monitoring and complying with technical standards will also minimize, if not eliminate, the possibility of incompatible technologies between the company and the user. The key issue for any company thinking about engaging in global EC is to keep abreast of the changing standards and laws associated with the Internet. Other issues include technical standards and electronic transmissions standards.

FINANCIAL ISSUES

Financial issues encompassing global EC include customs, taxation, and electronic payment systems. It is difficult to administer tariffs for products ordered over the Internet and delivered electronically. Many countries may want to add tariffs to the products, increasing the price to the consumer or business. All products delivered the traditional way will need to go through customs, which will lengthen the amount of time it takes for the customer to receive the merchandise. The timely delivery of goods is a key factor in a consumer's decision to order products over the Internet. The biggest time savings are reached in digitized products. Thus far, such purchases are not subject to sales taxes and tariffs. This may have a large impact on the success of global EC. However, the tax freeze is on only for a few years, and its future is uncertain.

Pricing is another issue. The same products from the same vendors carry different prices in different countries. If a company has one Web site, what price will people pay in different countries? What currencies will be used?

Another financial issue to consider is money exchange. All electronic payment systems will need to be able to exchange currency at current rates. This is not the only currency-related issue. For example, with some currencies the decimal point is more important than in others when converting (Andrews, 1998). There are several other financial issues to consider when interacting in real-time with other countries, particularly when credit cards are not used. (Credit card purchases generally take care of the currency exchange for you.) For example, the imposition of sales tax and import/export charges. Also important is the integration of the EC transaction with the accounting/finance internal information system of the sellers. A major issue, at least in Europe, is the conversion to the Euro (see Barnea, 2000).

Finally, related to finance is the financial justification and the initial investment required to go global. An example is *Boo.com*, which expanded to 18 countries and folded as a result in 2000 (and revived in 2001).

OTHER ISSUES

Several other issues need to be considered in global EC, some of which are generic, whereas others are unique. Representative issues are:

- Authentication of buyers and sellers (see Chapter 14)
- Trust
- Order fulfillment and delivery (see Chapter 15)

- Security (e.g., viruses)
- International agreements
- Domain names (see Chapter 17)
- Language and translation
- Purchasing in different currencies
- Role and policy of government
- Localization
- Cultural diversity

Due to space limitations, we deal here only briefly with the last five issues.

Language and Translation

The language barrier between countries and regions presents an interesting and complicated challenge. (See discussion at *tradecompass.com* and Application Case 18.3). Although English is widely accepted as the primary language of the Internet, in some cases an effective Web site may need to be specifically designed and targeted to the country that it is trying to reach. The primary problems with this level of language customization are cost and speed. It currently takes a human translator about a week to translate a medium-size Web site into just one language. For larger

APPLICATION CASE **18.3**

Attracting Japanese Customers to Your Site

Japanese love to shop online but most of them do not read English. For example, when William Hunt tried to market his earthquake kit in Japan's largest department stores, he had very few buyers. So his wife, a native of Hiroshima, helped him develop a Web site in Japanese. Now the Hunts have moved into a new business. They help small companies market online to Japan, in Japanese.

The company, Global Strategies (*now ajpr.com*), helps clients avoid the mistakes entrepreneurs often make when they try to sell to the Japanese. Forget about scoring big with an English-only Web site. "You wouldn't market a car in Japan using an English ad campaign," the Hunts say. Also, they note, people too often overlook Japanese-only Web search engines, and it's not hard to see why those listings are critical. For example, the Hunts encourage clients to state their return policies on their Web site. The Japanese are understandably leery of overseas companies, and an explicit return policy seems to ease their worries. The company's translators are quick to alert companies when their logos or themes are likely to strike a sour chord with Japanese sensibilities. Finally, the Hunts may well suggest that clients have mascots. Japanese audiences, it seems, respond positively to the use of symbols or characters.

The Hunts caution that if your product is not one that will fly with Japanese males in their twenties and thirties, there probably isn't much the Web can do for you. What are the hottest Web-marketed products in Japan? Outdoor sporting goods, computer software, popular music CDs, and gourmet-cooking items.

The company also provides help to Japanese companies who want an English version of their site. It provides localization advice as well. In 2001, services were available in other languages as well.

Sources: Compiled from news items at *Interactive Week* (February 2000) and from *ajpr.com*.

sites the cost ranges from $10,000 to $500,000, depending on the complexity of the site and languages of translation. WorldPoint (*worldpoint.com*) presents a creative solution to these issues with their WorldPoint Passport multilingual software tool. The WorldPoint Passport solution allows Web developers to create a Web site in one language and deploy it in several other languages. Cost of translation using the software is estimated at 24 to 26 cents per word. In a 1999 demonstration of the software's power, WorldPoint translated Japan's primary telephone company's (NTT) Web site into 10 different Asian languages in only 3 days. Automatic translation can be inaccurate. Therefore, many experts advocate manual translation with the help of the computer as a productivity booster. However, as time passes, automatic translation becomes better.

Purchasing in Different Currencies

A potential barrier to global commerce is the different currencies whose exchange rates may change every minute. A solution was provided in 1998 by the WorldPay System. The WorldPay software lets online sellers offer products in 126 different currencies and receive settlement payments in 16. Based on the SET protocol, the system provides real-time exchange rate information so buyers get the price of the products in their own currency. The concept is revolutionary. Today, many credit card issuers provide their customers with automatic currency exchange services for multiple currencies. However, buyers do not know how much they really paid until they receive a monthly statement, and many banks add steep service charges for such transactions. (For further details see *Internet World*, October 6, 1997.)

The U.S. Policy Regarding Global EC

The U.S. policy on global EC per Clinton and Gore (1997) includes the following five principles:

1. The private sector should lead. The Internet should develop as a market-driven arena, not a regulated industry. Even where collective action is necessary, governments should encourage industry self-regulation and private sector leadership where possible.
2. Governments should avoid undue restrictions on EC. In general, parties should be able to enter into legitimate agreements to buy and sell products and services across the Internet with minimal government involvement or intervention. Governments should refrain from imposing new and unnecessary regulations, bureaucratic procedures, or new taxes and tariffs on commercial activities that take place over the Internet.
3. Where government involvement is needed, its aim should be to support and enforce a predictable minimalist, consistent, and simple legal environment for commerce. Where government intervention is necessary, its role should be to ensure competition, protect intellectual property and privacy, prevent fraud, foster transparency, and facilitate dispute resolution, not to regulate.
4. Governments should recognize the unique qualities of the Internet. The genius and explosive success of the Internet can be attributed in part to its decentralized nature and to its traditions of bottom-up governance. We should not assume that the regulatory frameworks established over the past 60 years for

telecommunications, radio, and television fit the Internet. Existing laws and regulations that may hinder EC should be reviewed and revised or eliminated to reflect the needs of the new electronic age.

5. Electronic commerce on the Internet should be facilitated on a global basis. The Internet is a global marketplace. The legal framework supporting commercial transactions should be consistent and predictable regardless of the jurisdiction in which a particular buyer and seller reside.

Another interesting issue in global EC is the opportunity for even the smallest businesses to go global with unprecedented low costs (see Application Case 18.4). The global marketspace erases national borders and gives even the smallest companies worldwide reach. For example, Schwartz (1997) reported that a small company in Gilbert, Arizona, generated half of its international trade on the Web during its first year, and that its international trade was growing at a rate of 50 percent per year.

APPLICATION CASE 18.4

Small Businesses and Global Trade

Cardiac Science (Irvine, California) has been trying to break into the international market for years. Today, 85 percent of the company's revenue is international and much of this is executed over a Web site (*cardiacscience.com*). The company makes cardiac medical devices, and in 1997, it shipped to 46 countries. The company answers inquiries within 24 hours, sending out product information to promising sales leads.

One of the issues to consider is that small businesses need a great deal of advice regarding doing global business. Here are some useful Web sites used by Cardiac:

- Universal Business Exchange (*unibex.com*) offers trade leads with the added capability of matching buyers and sellers automatically.
- Several government agencies provide online information for nominal fees (e.g., National Trade Data Bank, Economic Bulletin Board, and Globus; all are at *stat-usa.gov*).

The Web business is not as simple as it sounds. Cardiac's CEO said that "crafting a solid export strategy takes a lot more commitment than putting up a snazzy Web site and waiting for the world to show up at our door. It's all about building relationships." The Internet is important for introductions, but you must follow it up properly.

Localization

In Chapter 5 we introduced the concept of **localization** as it relates to advertisement. Companies are realizing that just translating Web content from one language to another is woefully inadequate. In response, some Web sites are opting to localize content, including adapting local business practices for employees, partners, suppliers, and customers within the target country or ethnic group. This factor is particularly important as more users worldwide begin utilizing Web browsers, cell phones, pagers, PDAs (personal digital assistants), and wireless systems to access an enterprise's Web site. For example, marketing and sales messages must be adapted to appeal to specific audiences, and purchasing data (e.g., product prices calculated in local currencies and terms and conditions based on local laws) must be made available. And because no successful online enterprise remains static, companies must keep their multiple international sites synchronized as content changes.

Many companies offer different sites in other countries. For example, there is an eBay and a Yahoo! in the United Kingdom. *China.com* and *Sina.com* ask users on the main menu to select a country. For further details see Fessenden and Dwyer (2000) and *tradecompass.com*.

Globalization and Joint Ventures
Many companies create joint ventures when going global, for example, E*TRADE, LG Securities of Korea, and Japan's Softbank (provider of venture capital). Hundreds of similar joint ventures exist all over the world.

Joining Marketplaces
One strategy companies should consider, especially small ones, is to join global e-marketplaces. In Chapter 6 we introduced *alibaba.com* and cited a few other companies (see *globalsources.com*, and *meetworld.com*). Another player is *pecld.com/global_online* or *teenstation.com/globalonline.com*.

Culture

Increasingly, the Internet is becoming a multifaceted marketplace made up of users from multiple cultures. These multiple cultures warrant different marketing approaches—something marketers may overlook. To tap the potential of the various cultures shopping on the Internet, marketers must adapt their efforts to the ways different groups of people make online purchase decisions. Even the way different groups access the Internet plays a significant role in deciding how to target them. Whether they access from home, work, or Internet cafes is often linked to the GDP and availability of the Internet in a specific country. The culture also has an impact on how consumers prefer to do business and pay for it.

Although credit cards are widely used in the United States, many European and Asian customers complete online transactions with off-line payments. Even within the category of off-line payments, companies must offer different options depending on the country. For example, French consumers prefer to pay with a check, Swiss consumers expect an invoice by mail, and Germans commonly pay for products upon delivery, whereas Swedes are accustomed to paying online with debit cards.

Frequently, small things that seem unimportant can make a large difference. Changes in colors, symbols, fonts, formatting, and navigation are just a few examples that produce a high-quality user experience. If the Web site does not appeal to people's cultural motivators, ethnicity, language, point of view, values, and so on, they will simply click elsewhere. A good example is the degree of formality expected by different customers. In the Netherlands, firms typically address business customers by title, first and middle initials, and last name—in contrast to the first-name familiarity of the United States. For further discussion see DePalma (2000b) who introduces the concept of **cultural** or **ethnic marketing**, a strategy for meeting the needs of a culturally diverse population.

Breaking Down the Global EC Barriers

Experts from Idiom Inc. (*idiomtech.com*) made the following suggestions on how to break down the barriers cited earlier (Cheng, 1999, and DePalma, 2000a). Some of their suggestions are:

- **Value the human touch.** Always trust the translation of your Web site content only to human translators, not automatic translation programs or machine translation tools. Although machine translation and translation memory software can be used as an aid, you want to trust the handling of your messaging, brand, and product descriptions to humans, not computers.
- **Be strategic.** Identify your starting point and lay out a globalization strategy. Remember that Web globalization is a business building process. Consider what languages and countries it makes sense for you to target, and how you will need to support the site for each target audience. Then evaluate the capacity of your resources and plan accordingly. Go to one country at a time, and do not forget what happened to *Boo.com* (trying to come back from the ashes).
- **Know your audience.** Carefully consider who it is you want to reach. Straight translations won't speak effectively and sell your products to a particular audience. Be fully informed of the cultural preferences, conventional differences, and legal issues that matter to your customers in a particular part of the world.
- **Be a perfectionist.** Involve several language and technical editors in your quality assurance process. One slight mistranslation or one out of place graphic will turn off your customers.
- **Remember, it's the Web.** One of the many things people have come to expect from the Internet is up-to-date information. This means that any Web site—especially global Web sites—should be kept current.
- **Integrate properly.** Web globalization should integrate seamlessly into the existing Web development architecture. Globalization works best when it's used to complement and enhance existing content management and workflow systems, not replace or change them.
- **Keep the site flexible and up-to-date.** A Web globalization solution needs to keep pace with ongoing change at every level. Flexibility is the key to successful globalization.
- **Synchronize content.** Global online businesses must synchronize the publication of content, product offerings, interactive applications, and other corporate information across their multiple international sites.
- **OECD.** A major report entitled "Dismantling the Barriers to Global Electronic Commerce" is available online at *oced.org*. It touches on all the issues discussed in this chapter and more.

Going global may be attractive, yet risky especially to small and medium-sized companies (see Hornby et al., 2000).

18.4   EC IN SMALL AND MEDIUM-SIZE ENTERPRISES

Some of the first companies to take advantage of EC on the Web were, in fact, small companies, some of which were start-ups. Prime examples are *evinyard.com*, *Hothothot.com*, and *HappyPuppy.com*. In this section we explore both the advantages and opportunities and the disadvantages and risks for small businesses in the Web economy.

The following are the major advantages:

- Inexpensive source of information
- Inexpensive way of advertising
- Inexpensive way of conducting market research
- Inexpensive way to build (or rent) a storefront
- Lower transaction costs
- Niche market; specialty products (cigars, wines, sauces) are the best
- Image and public recognition can be accumulated fast
- Inexpensive way of providing catalogs
- Inexpensive way and opportunity to reach worldwide customers

The following is a list of disadvantages and risks for small businesses:

- Inability to use the expensive EDI, unless it is EDI/Internet
- Lack of resources to fully exploit the Web
- Lack of expertise in legal issues, advertisement, etc.
- Less risk tolerance than a large company
- Disadvantage when a commodity is the product (e.g., CDs)
- No personal contact with customers, which is a strong point of a small business
- No advantage of being in a local community

There are basically two contradictory opinions regarding small companies. The first one is that EC is a blessing (e.g., see O'Connor and O'Keefe, 1997) for arguments and success stories). The second is that small companies will not be able to benefit from EC or even survive in the digital economy. Here are some of the arguments.

One attempt to explain the contradicting opinions was rendered by King and Blanning (1997), who developed a matrix that classifies online companies into two categories: convivial niche and virtual storehouse. **Convivial niches** are mainly small companies (such as *hothothot.com* or *dogtoys.com*) with low volumes of business (Table 18-2). The **virtual storehouse** is characterized by large-volume, commodity-type products (e.g., *Amazon.com*).

Market Models		
Feature	**Convivial Niche**	**Virtual Storehouse**
Focus	Select variety Shopping experience	Extensive listings Convenience
Buyers	Upscale	High-tech
Price	Not an issue	Discounted, adaptable
Information	In-depth reviews Customer education	Comparisons Configuration Third-party reviews
Promotions	Samplers, Gifts Featured product testimonials	Time-based specials Off-line ads
Feedback	Advice, forums	Customer support Demographic data
Size	Small	Large

TABLE 18-2

Source: Based on King and Blanning (1997).

Critical Success Factors

Small businesses have had online success mainly by selling specific product/ services such as:

- Niche products, such as those with a low volume that are not carried by regular retail stores (e.g., *dogtoys.com*).
- Specialty books (for example, old, technical).
- International products that are not easily available off-line to consumers.
- Information. This category has a wide spectrum. GartnerGroup provides access to online research material that users can subscribe to. Smaller companies may choose to provide specialized information such as home and gardening pages. Revenue sources could include home and garden retailers who place advertisements on the small business's Web page.
- Localized markets (e.g., *ausfush.com.au*).

Many of the small businesses that have succeeded on the Internet either as click-and-mortar or as virtual businesses have the following strategies in common:

- Capital investment must be small to keep the companies' overhead and risk low.
- Inventory should be minimal or nonexistent.
- Electronic payments must be transmitted using secure means to reassure customers. Small businesses can work with vendors to provide this service.
- Payment methods must be flexible to accommodate different levels of users. Some prefer to mail or fax in a form or talk to a live agent as opposed to transmitting a credit card number over the Internet.
- Logistical services must be quick and reliable. Small businesses have successfully subcontracted out their logistical services to FedEx, which is an expert in the field.
- The Web site should be submitted to directory-based search engine services like Yahoo!
- Membership must be made in an online service or mall, such as AOL or ViaWeb's Viamall.
- A Web site must be designed that is functional and provides all needed services to consumers. In addition, Web sites should look professional enough to compete with larger competitors and be updated on a continual basis to maintain consumer interest.

The following are suggestions made by Diane Gerrod from *workz.com*:

- Make sure your Web site design follows basic principles (see Chapter 4)
- Market properly (Chapters 4 and 5)
- Understand your customers and their buying habits (Chapter 4)
- Price your product or service correctly (Chapter 2)
- Anticipate cash flow needed (Chapter 16)
- Monitor your competition, technology, and marketplace changes. (Chapters 4, 8, 16)
- Keep growth slow and steady (Chapter 16)
- Delegate
- Develop good internal communication

For a comprehensive theoretical discussion of EC and SMEs, including global aspects, see Fariselli et al. (1999).

Although there are many risks associated with EC, overall, the level of risk would be less for a small business when compared to opening brick-and-mortar businesses that require much more capital. In addition, many businesses that could not have survived outside of the Internet have been able to thrive due to the lower cost of entry (e.g., *cattoys.com* or *ausfish.com.au*). Finally, small businesses can combine forces, for example, by developing a storefront jointly. They may also share the use of EC applications through group purchasing as described in Chapter 7.

Supporting Small Businesses

There are many ways in which support is provided to small businesses. For example, technical support is provided by IBM's services ($25 per month) (see *ibm.com. businesscenter*); Digital's virtual stores; and Microsoft's PWS. Even a government can provide support to small business EC, as shown in Application Case 18.5.

The U.S. government is encouraging small businesses to take advantage of EC opportunities (see *ecommerce.gov*).

Starting an online business involves two major issues. The first one is how to start a business, which is a generic issue. The second one is how to open a business online. For tutorials on both topics see *latimes.com*.

18.5   BPR FOR EC, VIRTUAL CORPORATIONS, AND ORGANIZATIONAL TRANSFORMATIONS

As the reader may recall from the IBM case in Chapter 12, it is sometimes necessary to restructure business processes before installing EC applications. Furthermore, as the Yoshida case will show (Real-World Case, end of this chapter), the introduction of EC may significantly change not only the organizational climate, but also the manner in which the entire organization operates, in other words, old-economy organizations are changing to meet the new economy. This change may be drastic and may be referred to as an **organizational transformation**, which is interrelated with the concept of organizational learning (see discussion in Chapter 2). Finally, organizations may transform themselves to virtual corporations. These three interrelated topics are the subject of this section.

Redesign of the Enterprise Processes and Business Process Reengineering (BPR)

Some people believe that it is necessary to conduct a complete BPR before introducing EC. This is rarely the case. However, like in many other IT projects, it is frequently necessary to restructure individual processes (e.g., see Turban et al. 2002). The restructuring or BPR may be needed for the following reasons:

- It does not make sense to automate poorly designed processes.
- It may be necessary to change processes so they will fit commercially available software.
- A fit is required between systems and processes of different companies.

Korean Government Helps Online Business

Most domestic software companies in Korea, especially small ones, do not have distribution channels of their own. Therefore, they pay almost a 40 percent commission to distributors pushing their products to end users. This is a major competitive disadvantage. To solve the problem, the government established a software cybermall. The Internet shopping mall, which opened in 1998, provides demonstration products and the ability to buy and pay electronically. The mall is connected to the sites of many vendors. The process of buying in the mall is shown in Figure 18-3. Note that the software is downloaded rather than delivered physically.

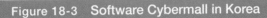

Figure 18-3   Software Cybermall in Korea

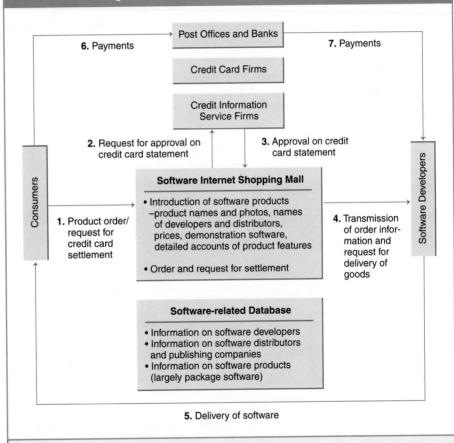

Source: Publicly distributed governmental documents in Korea.

- It is necessary to change processes to fit the procedures and standards of public e-marketplaces.
- It is necessary to adjust procedures and processes so they will be aligned with e-services such as logistics, payments, or security.
- It is necessary to make changes to assure flexibility and scalability.

Such restructuring may be very complex when many business partners are involved in one exchange.

For further discussion and methodology see El Sawy (2001). A major technology used in conjunction with redesign is workflow.

Workflow Technologies

Workflow is the automation of business processes, managing the movement of information as it flows through the sequence of steps that make up the work procedure by maintaining a record of changes in status and the state of the document or transaction. A workflow application defines all the steps in a process from start to finish, including all exception conditions, usually based on established business rules. The key to workflow management is the tracking of process-related information and the status of each instance of the process as it moves through an organization.

Workflow applications fall into two categories:

- **Collaborative workflow.** This type of workflow refers to those products that address project-oriented and collaborative types of processes. They are administered centrally, yet they are capable of being accessed and used by knowledge workers from different departments and even from different physical locations. The focus of an enterprise solution is on allowing workers to communicate and collaborate within a unified environment. Some leading vendors are Lotus, JetForm, FileNet, and Action Technologies.
- **Production workflow.** Production workflow tools address mission-critical, transaction-oriented processes and are often deployed only in a single department or to a certain set of users within a department. Often, these applications include document image storage and retrieval capabilities. They also can include the use of intelligent forms, database access, and ad hoc capabilities. In this type of application, the process being automated via workflow is typically central to the business itself, rather than merely supporting the business. Most of the systems in this category include a workflow management engine that controls the flow of information through the processing of each case or transaction. This engine interfaces with a database—usually a commercial relational database management system—in which the transaction-specific information is maintained. The leading vendors are FileNet and Staffware.

A major area for EC applications is the aggregation of sellers or buyers as described in Chapter 7. When large suppliers or buyers are involved, a workflow system is needed for both the collaborative efforts and for supply chain and production improvements.

Virtual Corporations: Networking Between Business Partners

One of the most interesting EC-related organizational structures is the virtual corporation (VC). There are several types of virtual corporations as well as several definitions. Some define a virtual corporation as a pure-play EC company such as

E*TRADE, *Amazon.com*, or AOL. In the conventional economy, a **virtual corporation** is defined as an organization composed of several business partners sharing costs and resources for the purchasing or production of a product or service. The partners can come to one physical place or they may be in different locations. Some can be pure-play EC players. It is common to distinguish between permanent virtual corporations, which are designed to create or assemble productive resources rapidly, frequently, concurrently, or to create or assemble a broad range of productive resources, and a temporary VC, which is created for a specific purpose and exists only for a short time.

Virtual corporations are not necessarily organized along the supply chain. For example, a business partnership may include several partners, each creating a portion of products or service in an area in which they have special advantage, such as expertise or low cost. So the modern VC can be viewed as a network of creative people, resources, and ideas connected by online services and/or the Internet.

The major attributes of VCs are:

- **Excellence.** Each partner brings its core competence, so an all-star winning team is created.
- **Utilization.** Resources of the business partners are frequently underutilized. A VC can utilize them more profitably.
- **Opportunism.** A VC can find and meet market opportunity better than an individual company.
- **Lack of borders.** It is difficult to identify the boundaries of a virtual corporation—it redefines traditional boundaries.
- **Trust.** Business partners in a VC must be far more reliant on each other and require more trust than ever before.
- **Adaptability to change.** The virtual corporation can adapt quickly to the environmental changes because its structure is relatively simple.
- **Technology.** Information technology makes the virtual corporation possible. A networked information system is a must.

The previous discussion relates to the definition of a VC being a partnership. If this is the case, then the role of EC is to provide the framework for collaborative commerce, which is discussed in Chapter 6. One of the major strengths of a VC is the knowledge it possesses.

Knowledge Management

The term knowledge management (KM) is frequently mentioned in a discussion of EC. Why is this so? To answer this question one needs to understand first what KM is. Knowledge is recognized as the most important asset in any organization, therefore, it is important to capture and apply it. This is one of the major purposes of **knowledge management**, which has several definitions and meanings. In our view, KM refers to the process of capturing or creating knowledge, storing and protecting it, updating it constantly, and using it whenever necessary. Knowledge is collected from both external and internal sources. Then it is examined, interpreted, refined, and stored in what is called a **knowledge base**, the repository place for the enterprise's knowledge.

A knowledge base is a database that contains knowledge, or the organization's know-how. The major purpose of an organizational knowledge base is to allow for **knowledge sharing**. Knowledge sharing among employees, with customers, and with business partners has a huge potential payoff in improved customer service, shorter delivery cycle times, and increased collaboration within the company and with business partners as well. Furthermore, some knowledge can be sold to others or traded for other knowledge.

Knowledge management promotes an integrated approach to the process of identifying; capturing, retrieving, sharing, and evaluating an enterprise's information assets, both those that are documented and the tacit expertise stored in individuals' heads. The integration of information sources is at the heart of KM.

EC implementation involves a considerable amount of information and knowledge about customers, suppliers, logistics, procurement, markets, and technology. The integration of the above is required for successful EC applications. These applications are aimed at increasing organizational competitiveness.

Knowledge management programs are frequently integrated with EC applications in enterprise computing. The two are also combined to offer a virtual workspace for collaborative communications, collaboration, and workflow. For further discussion see Raisch (2001).

18.6   RESEARCH IN EC

The multidisciplinary nature of EC opens the door to a wide range of research, some of which can be done jointly by two or more disciplines. A simple way to classify EC research is to divide it into three categories: behavioral, technical, and managerial. Suggested representative research topics in each category are provided.

Suggested Behavioral Topics

- Observing consumer behavior: cognitive processes, overcoming the limitations of remote control, and identifying impacts on people.
- Building consumers' behavioral profiles and identifying ways to utilize them.
- Evaluating consumers' attitudes towards e-books.
- Analyzing sellers' behavior and motivation: resistance to change and how to overcome it.
- Why is there a slow adaptation of some applications in some countries and rapid adaptation in others?
- How will people accept/adjust to EFT of government benefits?
- Examine Internet usage patterns and willingness to buy.
- Mental model of consumer product search process, comparison process, and negotiation.
- How to build trust in the marketspace (see Lee and Turban, 2001).

- What consumers want to have in m-commerce (by product or service).
- How to convince consumers to use m-commerce.

Suggested Technical Topics

- Developing methodologies and strategies for EC applications
- Methods that help customers find what they want and compare products/ services (such as using intelligent agents)
- Models for extranet design and management
- Natural language processing and automatic Web page translation
- Using multiple intelligent agents
- Matching smart-card technology with payment mechanisms
- Supply chain complementary technology
- Integrating EC with existing corporate information systems, databases, and so on
- Retrieval of information from industry directories
- Establishing standards for international trade
- Building a mobile Internet distribution and command system
- Integrating B2B exchanges with supply chains of traders
- Building networks of exchanges

Suggested Managerial and Other Research Topics

- Identification of business models and where to use them
- Organizing B2C warehouses and delivery systems
- Advertisement: measuring the effectiveness, integration, and coordination with conventional advertisement
- Applications: creating a methodology for finding EC business applications, analyzing the success or failure of applications (CSF), and configuring and distributing knowledge on the Internet
- Overcoming barriers for international trade
- Strategy: defending strategic advantage (attack, defense) strategy for EC; initiating "where to market" strategy; finding ways to integrate EC into organizations; developing methods of how to conduct "business intelligence"; and developing a methodology for conducting EC cost-benefit analysis
- The changing nature of competition and pricing strategies
- Impacts: identifying appropriate organizational structure and organizational culture
- Implementation: developing a framework for EC implementation activities like outsourcing, redesigning the role of intermediaries in EC, and developing methodologies for conducting consumer research
- The creation and use of EC matrices
- Others: building a framework for EC auditing, finding a methodology for pricing of online products/services, identifying solutions for distribution channel conflict management, and studying the relationship between EC and BPR and EC and supply chain management

The ISWorld Survey

In early 2000, the IS community's ISWorld portal conducted a survey on "Electronic Commerce Top Research Questions." The ISWorld Survey solicited 140 issues from 42 researchers, and organized them into the following categories:

- Strategic issues
- Assessment valuation
- Organizational transformation and societal issues
- Adoption issues
- Theory and methodology
- Marketing and CRM issues
- Technical issues
- Security and legal issues
- Logistics/operations
- Miscellaneous

In each category, there are about 10 subcategories. Details are available at *isds.bus.lsu.edu/cvoc/isworld/ecomtop.xls* or *commerce.uq.edu.au/isworld/research* under the title "Electronic Commerce Top Research Questions."

Kimbrough and Lee (1997) raised the following questions regarding EC research:

- What is possible and desirable with EC?
- What are the operational and functional requirements for the applications of EC?
- What does widespread realization of the possibilities for EC mean?

They also surveyed and summarized research issues, many of which related to EDI. Some of their suggested topic areas are open EC; electronic trade procedures; audit controls; automated trade procedures; protocols and contracts for intelligent negotiation agents; supporting management and decision making; optimizing using interface, interaction, and customization; and multilingual electronic documents.

A framework for B2C EC research is shown in Figure 18-4. The outcomes are basically consumers' buying attitudes and real purchasing. The influencing process variables are listed in the middle, and possible influential contextual variables are shown on the left. Many hypotheses can be formulated with this model and then tested empirically (journals such as the *International Journal of Electronic Commerce* and the *International Journal of Electronic Markets* publish such research results).

18.7 THE FUTURE OF EC

Generally speaking, there is a consensus regarding the future of EC—it is bright. Differences exist as to the anticipated growth rate and the identification of industry segments that will grow the fastest. Such optimism about the future of EC is based on the following trends and observations.

Internet usage. The number of Internet users is increasing exponentially. With the integration of computers and television, cheaper PCs, Internet access via

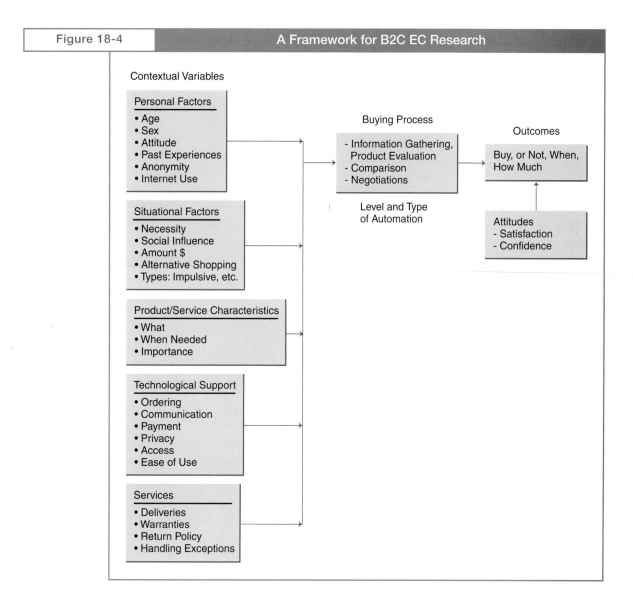

Figure 18-4   A Framework for B2C EC Research

mobile devices, increased availability of access kiosks, and increased publicity, there will be more and more Internet surfers. As younger people grow older, the usage will grow even further. There is no question that sooner or later there will be a billion people who surf the Internet. By 2001, the number of worldwide Internet users was estimated to be over 400 million.

Opportunities for buying. The number of products and services available online is increasing rapidly with improved trading mechanisms, intermediary services, presentations in multiple languages, and sellers' willingness to give it a try. It is logical to expect significantly more purchasing opportunities. Several Web sites are reporting 50 to 60 percent annual sales increases.

M-commerce. With over 1 billion people using cell phones (2001), the ease with which one can connect from them to the Internet, and the forthcoming 3G capabilities, it is clear that m-commerce will play a major role in EC. The fact that you do not need a computer will bring more and more people to the Web.

M-commerce, as will be seen in Chapter 19, has special capabilities that will result in new applications as well as in more people using traditional applications.

Purchasing incentives. The buyers' advantages described in Chapter 1 are likely to increase. Prices will go down, and the purchasing process will be streamlined. Many innovative options will be available, and electronic shopping may even become a social trend. For organizations, e-procurement is becoming the most attractive EC initiative.

Increased security and trust. One of the major inhibitors of B2C growth is the perception of poor security and privacy and a lack of trust. As time passes, we expect significant improvements in all these areas.

Efficient information handling. More information will become accessible from anywhere, in real-time. Using data warehouses and intelligent agents, companies can constantly learn about their customers, steering marketing and service activities accordingly. The notion of real-time marketing might not be so far away. This will facilitate the use of EC.

Innovative organizations. Organizations are being restructured and reengineered with the help of IT (Turban et al., 2002; Hammer and Stanton, 1995). Using different types of empowered teams, some of which are virtual, organizations become innovative, flexible, and responsive. The trend for process reengineering is increasing and so is the organizational creativity. Innovative organizations will probably be more inclined to use EC.

Virtual communities. Virtual communities of all kinds are spreading rapidly, with some already reaching several million members. As seen in the opening vignette, virtual communities can enhance commercial activities online. Also, some communities are organized around professional areas of interest and can facilitate B2B commerce.

Payment systems. The ability to use e-cash and make micropayments online is getting close to reality; when implemented on a large scale, many EC activities will flourish. As international standards become the norm, electronic payments will extend globally, facilitating global EC.

B2B EC. Figures about the growth of B2B are being revised frequently. In some cases, industry-type extranets are almost forcing everyone to participate. B2B will continue to dominate the EC field (in terms of volume traded) for the intermediate future. There will be more sellers, more buyers, more services; the rapid growth will continue. The success of B2B (as well as B2C) will depend upon the success of integrating EC technology with business processes and with conventional information systems.

B2B exchanges. In 2000, the number of B2B exchanges exploded, creating new opportunities for tens of thousands of companies to conduct EC. These exchanges will consolidate, many will collapse, and a few will mature in 3 to 5 years, providing the infrastructure for $3 to $5 trillion of B2B trade by 2005. However, company-centric marketplaces will account for the majority of the B2B trade.

Auctions. The popularity of auctions and reverse auctions is increasing rapidly in B2B, B2C, G2B, and C2C. This is an effective and efficient business model.

Going global. One of the most appealing benefits of EC is the ability to go global. However, many barriers exist. These are expected to be reduced with time, but at a fairly slow pace.

E-government. Starting in 1999, many governments launched comprehensive G2C, G2B, G2G, and G2E projects (see Chapter 11).

Intrabusiness EC. Many companies are starting to discover many opportunities for using EC in-house, particularly in improving the internal supply chain.

Technology Trends

The trend in EC technologies generally points toward significant cost reduction coupled with improvements in capabilities, ease of use, increased availability of software, ease of site development, and improved security and accessibility. Some specifics follow.

Clients. PCs of all types are getting cheaper, smaller, and more capable. The concept of a network computer (NC), also known as a thin client, which moves processing and storage off the desktop and onto centrally located servers running Java-based software on UNIX (Windows on Microsoft's version), could bring the price of a PC to that of a television.

Embedded clients. Another major trend is the movement toward embedded clients. A client, in such a case, can be a car or a washing machine with an embedded microchip. In many cases, an expert system is embedded with rules that make the client "smarter" or more responsive to changes in the environment.

Servers. A major trend is to use Windows NT as the enterprise operating system. Among NT's capabilities is clustering. Clustering servers can add processing power in much smaller increments than was previously possible. Clustering servers is very economical, resulting in cost reductions.

Networks. The use of EC frequently requires rich multimedia (such as color catalogs or providing samples of movies or music). A large bandwidth is required to accomplish this. Several broadband technologies (such as XDSL) will increase bandwidth manyfold. This could help in replacing expensive WANs or VANs with the inexpensive Internet. Security on the Internet can be enhanced by the use of VPNs.

Wireless communications. For countries without fiber-optic cables, wireless communication can save considerable installation time and money. In 1998, wireless access reached T1 speed (about 1.5 mbps), with cost savings of over 80 percent. However, wireless networks may be too slow for some digitized products (see Chapter 19).

EC software and services. The availability of all types of EC software will make it easier to establish stores on the Internet and to conduct all types of trades. Already, hundreds of sites offer pages for inexpensive rent for a variety of activities ranging from conducting your own auctions and bids to selling in a foreign language. Other support services, such as escrow companies that support auctions and multiple types of certifications, are developing rapidly. Also, a large number of consultants are being trained to assist in specialty areas.

Search engines. Search engines are getting smarter and better. This will enable consumers and organizational buyers to find and compare products and services easier and faster.

EC Knowledge. Being a new phenomenon, EC includes many uncertain and unknown aspects. However, as time passes the quantity and quality of related knowledge is increasing rapidly. The more we know about EC, the more we can facilitate its expansion, which, in our opinion, is grossly underestimated.

Peer-to-peer. This technology is developing rapidly and is expected to have a major impact on knowledge sharing, communication, and collaboration by making them better, faster, and more convenient.

Integration. The forthcoming integration of the computer and the TV, and the computer and the telephone, including Wireless One Inc., will increase accessibility of the Internet (e.g., see Silberman, 1999).

Digital Divide

Since the inception of technology in general and e-commerce in particular, we have witnessed a gap between those that have and those who do not have the ability to use technology. This gap is referred to as the **digital divide**. The gap exists between and within countries. The U.S. government is attempting to close this gap (see *ecommerce.gov*). The gap among countries, however, may be widening rather than narrowing. Many government and international organizations are trying to close the digital divide.

Integrating the Marketplace and Marketspace

Throughout this book we commented on the relationship between the physical marketplace and the marketspace. We pointed to conflicts in certain areas, as well as to successful applications and cooperation. The fact is that from the point of view of the consumer, as well as most organizations, these two entities exist, and will continue to exist, together.

Probably the most noticeable integration of the two concepts is in the **click-and-mortar** organization. The click-and-mortar organization will be the most prevalent model in the future (e.g., see Otto and Chung, 2000) and will take different shapes and formats. Some organizations will use EC as just another selling channel, as most large retailers do today. Others will use EC for only some products and services, while their other products will be sold the conventional way (e.g., *lego.com*). As experience is gained on how to excel in such a strategy, more and more organizations, private and public, will move to this mode of operation.

A major problem in the click-and-mortar approach is how to cooperate in planning, advertising, logistics, resource allocation, and so on and how to align the strategic plan of the marketspace and marketplace. We discussed some of the options in Chapter 16. Another major issue is the conflict with existing distribution channels (i.e., wholesalers, retailers).

Another area of coexistence is in many B2C ordering systems where customers have the option to order the new way or the old way. For example, you can do your banking both online and off-line. You can trade stocks via the computer, by placing a call to your broker, or just by walking into a brokerage firm and talking to a trader. Although in the B2B and G2B area this option may not continue to be available for a long time (some organizations may discontinue the old-economy option as the number of its users will decline below a certain threshold), in most B2C activities the options will remain, at least for the foreseeable future.

In conclusion, many people believe (e.g., Clinton and Gore, 1997) that the impact of EC on our lives will be as much as, and possibly more than, that of the Industrial Revolution. No other phenomenon since the Industrial Revolution has been classified in this category. It is our hope that this book will help you and your organization move successfully into this exciting and challenging digital revolution.

18.8   MANAGERIAL ISSUES

The following issues are germane to management:

1. **Finding a community.** Although sponsoring a community may sound like a good idea, it may not be simple to execute. Community members need services and these cost money. The most difficult task is to find a community that matches your business, or to start one.

2. **Going global.** This is a very appealing proposition, but may be difficult to do, especially on a large scale. In B2B one may create collaborative projects with partners in other countries, which will last for a long time. Once such partners are discovered, exchanges and third party marketplaces that promote global trade may lose business.

3. **Small can be beautiful.** This may be true, but it may be ugly too. Competing on commodities with the big guys is very difficult, even more so in cyberspace. Finding a niche market is advisable, but it will usually be limited in scope. Opportunity exists more in providing specialized support services than in trading.

4. **Restructuring.** Frequently it may be necessary to restructure business processes to assure the success of EC. This may be a long and expensive proposition. But, as IBM found out, if you do it properly, the reward could be enormous.

5. **The future of EC.** Despite the failures of companies and initiatives, the growth of EC is impressive and unstoppable. Doing it right is the secret. This book aims at teaching you to do just that.

Summary

In this chapter, you learned about the following EC issues as they relate to the learning objectives:

1. **The role and impact of virtual communities.** Virtual communities create new types of business opportunities—people with similar interests that are congregated in one Web site are a natural target for advertisers and marketers. Using chat rooms, members can exchange opinions about certain products and services. Of special interest are communities of transactions, whose interest is the promotion of commercial buying and selling. The communities help to foster customer loyalty, increase sales of related vendors, and increase customers' feedback for improved service and business.

2. **Issues in global EC.** Going global with EC can be done quickly and with a relatively small investment. However, businesses must deal with a number of different issues. These include legal issues such as jurisdiction and contracts, intellectual property, government regulations regarding export/import, tariffs and taxation, payment mechanisms, Web site presentation, language translation, and currency conversions. The U.S. government policy is to make global trade free from restrictions, simple, and without sales tax. There is little international agreement on such a policy as well as on the necessary payments and other standards.

3. **Small businesses and EC.** Depending on the circumstances, innovative small companies have a tremendous opportunity to enter EC with little cost and to expand rapidly; others may be eliminated by larger online competitors. Being in a niche market provides the best chance for small businesses. Going after high-volume, commodity-type products (such as CDs, books, or computers) can be too risky for a small company.

4. **Restructuring, knowledge management, and virtual organizations.** When implementing EC applications it is frequently necessary to redesign processes or even to perform a BPR. This may require the use of workflow tools. In addition, EC systems may interface with knowledge management systems. Finally, EC applications are frequently supporting virtual corporations.

5. **Research opportunities in EC.** There are hundreds of research topics in this new discipline. They can be categorized as behavioral (mainly concerning consumers), technological, and managerial.

6. **The future of EC.** EC will continue to expand fairly rapidly. There are a number of reasons for this. To begin with, its infrastructure is becoming better and less expensive with time. Second, consumers will be more experienced and will try different products and services and tell their friends about them. Security, privacy protection, and trust will be much higher, and more support services will simplify the transaction process. Legal issues will be clarified, and more and more products and services will be online at reduced prices. Nevertheless, the progress of B2C will be slow due to the shakeout and elimination of many companies and slow organizational learning and transformation. The fastest growing area is B2B EC, and company-centric systems (especially e-procurement) and auctions will spread rapidly. The development of exchanges and other many-to-many e-marketplaces will be much slower.

Key Terms

Business process reengineering (BPR)	Internet (virtual) community
Community	Knowledge base
Convivial niche	Knowledge management (KM)
Cultural (ethnic) marketing	Knowledge sharing
Digital divide	Localization
Global electronic commerce	M-commerce

Organizational transformation
Virtual corporations

Virtual storehouse
Workflow systems

Questions for Review

1. List the major barriers businesses face in going global.
2. List the five global EC principles of the U.S. government.
3. Define electronic communities.
4. List the major types of electronic communities.
5. List the major topics of behavioral research in EC.
6. List the major drivers of global EC.
7. List the potential benefits and limitations for small businesses online.
8. List the major factors that could facilitate EC in the future.
9. List some of the opportunities for SMEs doing EC.
10. Define the digital divide.

Questions for Discussion

1. Below are six statements regarding conditions that are necessary for success of an electronic market. For each, explain why you agree or disagree:
   a. The market should be fragmented on both the buying and selling side, with many vendors and many buyers and no overly dominant player on either side.
   b. The market should be technologically sophisticated and have an Internet-savvy customer base.
   c. The online service should be able to fully describe products on the Web so that buyers receive enough information to make purchases.
   d. The products being offered on the Web should not be a pure commodities; for a lively marketplace, vendors should be able to distinguish their offerings.
   e. If a certain market is already efficient, there is no sense moving it online.
   f. Trading stocks online turns stocks into commodities.
2. Discuss the relationship between virtual communities and doing business on the Internet.
3. How does behavioral EC research differ from behavioral IT research in general?
4. Discuss the pros and cons of going global with a physical product.
5. Find some success stories of SMEs and identify the common elements in them.
6. Discuss how cultural differences may impact what people buy on the Internet.
7. Discuss the issue of the digital divide and how to deal with the problem (see *ecommerce.gov*, *google.com*).

Internet Exercises

1. Compare the following industry associations: *aria.com.au* (Australia), *bpi.co.uk* (United Kingdom), *riaa.com* (United States). Consider the services offered, functionality of the site, use of multimedia, search capabilities, timeliness, range, links, customization (languages), product information, EC activities, etc.

2. Research the economic viability of different types of communities. Examine ethnic communities, gender communities, third-party communities (e.g., *ausfish.com*), and mega communities (e.g., GeoCities).

3. One of the most globalized companies is *Amazon.com*. Find stories about its global strategies and activities. What are the most important lessons you learned?

4. Visit *abcsmallbiz.com* and find some of the EC opportunities available for small businesses. Also, visit the Web site of your local SBA (Small Business Administration) office in your area. Finally, check *cnn.money.com* on Saturdays and look for Applegate's column on small businesses.

5. Enter *alloy.com* and *bolt.com* and compare the sites on functionality, ease of use, message boards, home page layout, etc.

6. Identify the CSFs in the opening case.

7. Find out how Web sites such as *tradecard.com* facilitate the conduct of international trade over the Internet.

8. Use a currency conversion table (e.g., *xe.com/ucc/*) to find out the exchange rate of $100 (U.S.) with the currencies of Brazil, Canada, China, India, Sweden, and South Africa.

9. Enter the Web site of an Internet community (*tripod.com*, or *geocities.com*). Build a home page free of charge. You can add a chat room and a message board using the free tools provided.

10. Several profession-oriented communities are active on the Internet. For example, *plasticsnet.com* caters to plastics-related industries. Explore the site and identify the benefits to members.

11. Investigate the community services provided by Yahoo! to its members (*clubs.yahoo.com*). List all the services available and assess their potential commercial benefits to Yahoo!.

12. Conduct research on small businesses and their use of the Internet for EC. Visit sites such as *success.com*, *Webcom.com*, and *uschamber.org*.

13. Enter *summerset.com*. Examine the community services offered. Read Caggiano (2000) to find the CSF of this business.

14. Enter *Google.com* and type "small businesses and electronic commerce." Use your findings to write a report on current issues.

15. Enter *internet.com* and identify discussions related to the latest trends of EC.

16. Enter *globalsources.com* and examine the services they offer, including auctions. Compare this site with *alibaba.com*. What are the major differences between the sites?

Team Assignments and Role Playing

1. Each team must find the latest information on one type of global EC issues (e.g., legal, financial, and so on). Create a report based on your findings.

2. Compare the AFS (opening vignette) against other Australian fishing-related sites (e.g., *navtronics.com.au*, *luresonline.com.au*, *fujitackle.com.au*) and

against similar sites in other countries (e.g., *fishingtackleonline.co.nz* and *daytickets.co.uk*).

3. Survey *google.com*, *electronicmarkets.org*, and *isworld.com* to find out about EC efforts in different countries. Assign a country to each member. Relate the developments to each country's level of economic development and to its culture.

REAL-WORLD CASE: Yoshida Original Inc. of Japan

Yoshida Original Inc. is a manufacturer of women's luxury bags. The company's strategy is to serve its customers during every stage in the life of its bags. The company sells its original design "warm, all-natural, hand-made bags" in various styles and in small lots with a lifetime guarantee. The company offers customers a variety of substantial sales services. These include product information, a free IBIZA Magazine, and even an annual letter signed by the company's CEO. The company has almost 800,000 devoted customers in Japan.

Over the years, the company has tried to build close relationships with its customers and salespeople. Unfortunately, using telephone, fax, e-mail, and groupware have not been effective. So, the company created a VAN-based *community net* to connect the company with its dealers, using video conferencing and phones. The idea was to expand the multimedia-rich system to employees and customers. The community net has two broad objectives: (1) winning more orders by sending product information on newly created products to dealers without delay and (2) taking orders and checking inventory quickly and accurately. This method replaced the old method of using exhibitions, private viewings, and semiannual private catalogs, together with lots of travel. Furthermore, the system allows one-to-one interaction.

Another application of the network is product repair and maintenance. Now repair staff can observe images of a bag that needs repairs when the bag is brought to any company outlet, check the work, and respond to customer inquiries. The network also reduces misunderstandings between customers and company employees. In addition, company employees can give direct product demonstrations to customers at the dealer's office, including production demonstrations, leading to more new orders. Thus, the company created a community management with virtual, real-time contact between the company and its customers, increasing trust and customer value.

The communication and collaboration is done via a high-speed, fiber-optic private network. This allows superb viewing of products. Sometime in the not so remote future, the system will expand to the Internet and eventually to mobile telephone viewing, collaborating, and ordering.

The system enables not only viewing, but also community members' participation in new product design and in idea generation and problem solving.

The system allows superb communication and collaboration in the community between its sales, design, development, and manufacturing departments, which are scattered all over Japan. Managers at headquarters can look at store's layout and product display, so guidelines for improvements can be given in real-time.

All this enables Yoshida to respond quickly and accurately to rapidly changing market needs and customer demands. The company's profits are increasing 20 percent each year as a result of the IT-based *community net* strategy.

Sources: Compiled from Kodama (1999) and from *IBIZA*.

Questions for the case

1. Using the community categories presented in this chapter, what kind of community is this?

2. Why is the system not an Internet-based system (as of 2000)?

3. The company brand name, IBIZA, comes from the Spanish island of IBIZA. Why do you think they selected this name?

4. Speculate on how the Internet can help this company go global (they currently sell mostly in Japan).

5. The company was awarded the 1998 Japan Quality Award, which recognizes excellence of management quality. How is community net related to quality?

6. Speculate on how community net can go on the Internet (extranet). What will be the derived benefits?

7. Why is the company contemplating going wireless?

REFERENCES AND BIBLIOGRAPHY

Andrews, W. "Global Commerce Forces Web Merchants to Find Ways to Handle Many Currencies," *Internet World* (February 23, 1998).

Armstrong, A. G. and J. Hagel. "The Real Value of Online Communities," *Harvard Business Review* (May/June 1996).

Barnea, A. "IT Strategies for Migrating to the Euro," *Information Systems Management* (Winter 2000).

Bishop, M. *How to Build a Successful International Website.* New York: Coriolis Group Books, 1998.

Botkin, J. W. and J. Botkin. *Smart Business: How Knowledge Communities Can Revolutionize Your Company.* New York: Free Press, 1999.

Bressler, S. E. and C. E. Grantham. *Communities of Commerce.* New York: McGraw-Hill, 2000.

Caggiano, C. "Cruising for Profits," *Inc. Tech.*, no. 4 (2000).

Champy, J., et al. "The Rise of the Electronic Community," *InformationWeek* (June 10, 1996).

Cheng, S. "Globalize Your Web Site," *E-Business Advisor* (October 1999).

Choi, S. Y. and A. B. Whinston. *The Internet Economy: Technology and Practice.* Austin, Texas: SmartEcon Pub., 2000.

Clinton, W. and A. Gore. *"A Framework for Global Electronic Commerce,"* (*iitf.nist.gov/eleccomm/ecomm.htm*, also in *ecommerce.gov*) (November 1997).

Cole, M. and R. M. O'Keefe. "The Dynamic of Globalization and Culture in EC," *Journal of Global Information Technology Management*, vol. 3, no. 1 (2000).

Cornet, P., et al. "From E-Commerce to Euro-Commerce," *The McKinsey Quarterly*, no. 2 (2000).

DePalma, D. "International E-commerce," *E-Business Advisor* (October 2000a).

DePalma, D. "Meet Your Customers' Need Through Cultural Marketing," *e-Business Advisor* (August 2000b).

Dickerson, M. "Going Global by Going Online," *Los Angeles Times* (February 11, 1998).

Duffy, D. "It Takes an E-Village," *CIO* (October 25, 1999).

El Sawy, O. *Redesigning Enterprise Processes for E-Business.* New York: McGraw-Hill, 2001.

Fariselli, P., et al. "E-Commerce and the Future for SMEs in a Global Market-Places," *Small Business Economics*, vol. 19 (1999).

Fessenden, K. and T. Dwyer. "Going Global with E-Business,"*Aberdeen.com.* (September 2000).

Goransan, H. T. *The Agile Virtual Enterprise: Cases, Matrices, Tools.* Westport, Connecticut: Quorum Books, 1999.

Hagel, J. and A. G. Armstrong. *Net Gain.* Boston: Harvard Business School Press, 1997.

Hammer, M. and S. A. Stanton. *The Reengineering Revolution: A Handbook.* New York: HarperCollins, 1995.

Hof, R. D., et al., "Electronic Communities," special report, *Business Week*, May 5, 1997.

Hornby, G., et al. "Export Through E-Business: Cultural Issues Faced by SME's," Proceedings, PACIS 2000, Hong Kong (May 2000).

Igbaria, M. "The Driving Forces in the Virtual Society," *Communications of the ACM* (December 1999).

Kannan, P. K., et al. "Marketing Information on the I-Way," *Communications of the ACM* (March 1998).

Kimbrough, S. D. and D. M. Lee. "Formal Aspects of Electronic Commerce: Research Issues and Challenges," *International Journal of Electronic Commerce* (Summer 1997).

King, D. and R. Blanning, "Electronic Commerce—A Tutorial," presented at *HICSS*, Hawaii (January, 1997).

Kodama, M. "Customer Value Creation Through Community-Based Information Networks," *International Journal of Information Management* (December 1999).

Lee, M. K. O. and E. Turban. "A Trust Model for Consumer Internet Shopping," *International Journal of Electronic Commerce* (Fall 2001).

Lotus Development Corp. "Knowledge Management Product Road Map," white paper, Lotus Development Corp. (*lotus.com* several related publications are in the site) (December 1999).

McWilliam, G. "Building Stronger Brands Through Online Communities," *Sloan Management Review* (Spring 2000).

O'Connor, G. C. and B. O'Keefe. "Viewing the Web as a Marketplace: The Case of Small Companies," *Decision Support Systems*, vol. 21 (1997).

Otto, J. R. and O. B. Chung. "A Framework for Cyber-Enhanced Retailing: Integrating EC Retailing with Brick-and-Mortar Retailing," *Electronic Markets*, vol. 10, no. 3 (2000).

Poon, S. and P. M. C. Swatman. "An Exploratory Study of Small Business Internet Commerce Issues," *Information and Management*, no. 35 (1999).

Pottruck, D. and T. Pearce. *Clicks and Mortar*. San Francisco, California: Jossey-Bass, 2000.

Preece, J. *Online Communities*. Chichester, U.K.: Wiley and Sons, 2000.

Preston, H. H. and U. Flohr. "Internationalizing Code from the Start Minimizes and Leads to Big Payoffs," *Byte* (March 1997).

Raisch, W. D. *The E-Marketplace*. New York: McGraw-Hill, 2001.

Rayport, J. F. and J. J. Sviokla. "Managing in the Marketspace," *Harvard Business Review* (November/December 1994).

Rheingold, H. *The Virtual Community: Homesteading on the Electronic Frontier*. Reading, Massachusetts: Addison-Wesley Publishing Co., 1993.

Schubert, P. and M. Ginsburg. "Virtual Communities of Transaction: The Role of Personalization in E-Commerce," *Electronic Markets*, vol. 10, no. 1 (2000).

Schwartz, M. "How Big Can a Community Get?" *Computerworld* (April 10, 2000).

Silberman, S. "Just Say Nokia Wired," (*wired.com/wired/archive/7.09/nokia_pr.html*) (September 1999).

Turban, E. et al. *Information Technology for Management*, 3rd ed. New York: Wiley & Sons, 2002.

Upton, D. and A. McAfee. "The Virtual Factory," *Harvard Business Review* (July/August 1996).

Walker, J. S. "The Future of E-commerce: Five Years Forward," *Interactive Week* (October 25, 1999.

Wang, H., et al. "Consumer Privacy About Internet Marketing," *Communications of the ACM* (March 1998).

Ware, J., et al. *The Search for Digital Excellence*. New York: McGraw-Hill (with CommerceNet Press), 1998.

19

Mobile Commerce

LEARNING OBJECTIVES

Upon completion of this chapter, the reader will be able to:

- Describe the characteristics and attributes of m-commerce.

- Describe the drivers of m-commerce.

- Understand the supportive technologies and their capabilities.

- Describe the wireless standards and transmission networks.

- Describe applications of m-commerce in finance, marketing, and customer service.

- Describe the intra-enterprise applications of m-commerce.

- Describe B2B and supply chain applications of m-commerce.

- Describe consumer and personal applications of m-commerce.

- Describe some non-Internet m-commerce applications.

- Describe location-based commerce (L-commerce).

- Describe the major limitations and implementation issues of m-commerce.

Let's look at several m-commerce applications.

NEXTBUS

San Francisco bus riders carrying an Internet-enabled wireless device, such as a cell phone or Palm VII, can instantly find out when a bus is due to arrive at a particular bus stop. They can find not only the scheduled arrival time, but also the actual one, at any given time. The system tracks public transportation buses in real-time. Knowing where each bus is and factoring in traffic patterns and weather reports, NextBus calculates the estimated arrival time of the bus to each bus stop on the route. While this is currently an ad-free customer service, in the near future you may receive advertisement information when you use this service. Since the system also knows exactly where you are and how much time you need to wait for the bus, it may send you to the nearest Starbucks for a cup of coffee, giving you an electronic $1 discount coupon. The system is used in several other cities around the United States. The arrival times are also transmitted on the Internet. This is an example of **location-based e-commerce,** or **l-commerce,** which is a major part of mobile commerce (m-commerce).

DINE ONE ONE

Dine One One delivers restaurant food to several hundred customers every day in the San Francisco Bay area. The food is delivered by 100 drivers. Food must be delivered on time and hot, so every minute is important. Unsatisfied customers may not order again, and in the best case the drivers will lose a tip. The old way was to try to call drivers on their cell phones and find out who is going to pick up from a restaurant and deliver an order. Four dispatchers were busy chasing drivers. Late delivery occurred frequently, and drivers' productivity and tips were not very high.

SOLUTION

Dine One One equipped its San-Francisco-Bay-area drivers with AT&T's PocketNet service, which includes portable smartphones that work over a wireless IP network. The phones were integrated with Dine One One's existing customized dispatching software and vehicle location system.

When an order comes into the company's dispatching center, Dine One One's computer system locates a driver, notifies him or her of when and where to pick up the order, and then e-mails or faxes the customer's order to the restaurant. The system automatically selects the driver based on his or her current location (using a GPS, as will be explained later) and driving habits, as well as how long it takes the restaurant to prepare the food. Drivers use their PocketNet phones to signal their arrival at the restaurant and notify the dispatcher once the food has been delivered.

The system allows for better service (and better tips for the drivers). Also, drivers' productivity increased significantly, so fewer drivers are needed. The system automatically does 99 percent of the drivers' assignments, thus reducing the number of dispatchers from four to one. Finally, similar IP systems exist in more than 70 metropolitan areas in the United States; therefore, Dine One One can easily extend its services to other cities across the country.

CELL PHONE SERVICES

Smart Search is a service provided to cell phone subscribers by PCCW of Hong Kong. Similar services are provided by DoCoMo's i-Mode in Japan, which we described in Chapter 2, and by many other companies worldwide. Here are some Smart Search's services:

- **Shopping guide.** Addresses and telephone numbers of the favorite shops in the major shopping malls in Hong Kong are provided with a supporting search engine.
- **Maps and transportation.** Digital maps show detailed guides of local routes and stops of the major public transportation systems.
- **Ticketing.** Movie tickets can be ordered online from wherever the subscribers are.
- **News & reports.** Fast access to global news, local updated traffic conditions, the air pollution index, and weather reports are provided continuously.
- **Gambling.** You can legally gamble on horse racing in Hong Kong from any location.
- **Personalized movie service.** Updates on the latest movies with related information including movie category, casting, and show times. Also, subscribers can search for their own favorite movies by entering the name of the movie or the name of the movie theater.

- **Entertainment.** Up-to-date person-alized entertainment, such as favorite games, can be searched easily and online "chatting" is also provided.
- **Dining and reservations.** Using a digital map, the exact location of a

selected participating restaurant is shown. The subscriber can also find a restaurant that provides a meal in a particular price range. Then a booking can be made online.

- **Additional services.** Additional services such as banking, stock trading, telephone directory searches, dictionary services, and a horoscope are available and more services are being added.

19.2   THE BENEFITS AND DRIVERS

The vignettes presented in Section 19.1 are three different applications of one of the most talked about areas of EC, mobile commerce. More applications will be presented later (also see *mobileinfo.com/case_study/ups.htm*).

Definitions

There are several definitions of **mobile commerce**, also known as **m-commerce, m-business**, and **pervasive computing**. Here are just a few:

- Any transaction with a monetary value that is conducted via a mobile telecommunication network (Durlacher, 2000).
- Any e-commerce done in a wireless environment.

Like regular applications of e-commerce, m-commerce can be done via the Internet (mostly), private communication lines, smart cards, or other infrastructures.

The pervasive m-commerce market is not merely a variation on existing Internet services. It's a natural extension of e-business. Pervasive devices create an opportunity to deliver new services to your existing customers and to attract new ones. The applications of m-commerce were classified by Varshney and Vetter (2001) into 12 categories, as shown in Table 19-1. This classification covers most of the applications that existed in 2001. A classification by industry is provided at *mobile.commerce.net*.

Terminology and Generations

Before proceeding to describe the benefits and drivers of m-commerce, it will be useful to define some of the terminology of the field. Here we present only of the most common terms used. They will be discussed later with additional terms, as they relate to specific topics. The terms are:

- **1G.** The wireless technology in existence from 1979–1992 (analog-based).
- **2G.** This digital technology is in existence today. This technology accommodates mainly text, it is based on digital radio technology.

Classes of M-Commerce Applications	
Class of Applications	**Examples**
Mobile Financial Applications (B2C, B2B)	Banking, brokerage, and payments for mobile users
Mobile Advertising (B2C)	Sending user-specific and location-sensitive advertisements to users
Mobile Inventory Management (B2C, B2B)	Location tracking of goods, boxes, troops, and people
Proactive Service Management (B2C, B2B)	Transmission of information related to distributing components to vendors
Product Locating and Shopping (B2C, B2B)	Locating/ordering certain items from a mobile device
Wireless Reengineering (B2C, B2B)	Improvement of business services
Mobile Auction or Reverse Auction (B2C)	Services for customers to buy or sell certain items
Mobile Entertainment Services (B2C)	Video-on-demand and other services to a mobile user
Mobile Office (B2C)	Working from traffic jams, airport, and conferences
Mobile Distance Education (B2C)	Taking a class using streaming audio & video
Wireless Data Center (B2C, B2B)	Information can be downloaded by mobile users/vendors
Mobile Music/Music-on-demand (B2C)	Downloading and playing music using a mobile device

TABLE 19-1

Source: U. Varshney and R. Vetter, January 2001. "A Framework for the Emerging M-Commerce Applications," *Proceedings 34th HICSS,* Hawaii © 2001 IEEE.

Two competing signal digitizations exist: TDMA and CDMA (see Section 19.4).

- **2.5G.** An interim technology based on GPRS and EDGE, which can accommodate graphics (see Section 19.4).
- **3G.** The third generation of mobile computing that started in 2001 in Japan and in 2002 in Europe, it is expected to reach the United States in 2003. Its technology is a non-IP-based air interface, using W-CMDA and UMTS standards (Section 19.4). This technology will support rich media such as video clips.
- **4G.** The next generation after 3G; fully end-to-end IP networks, expected in 2006–2010.
- **GPRS.** General Packet Radio Services, which will replace today's circuit switching technology.
- **GPS.** A satellite-based Global Positioning System, which enables the determination of a location where the GPS device is located.
- **GSM.** Global System of Mobile Communication, which is the wireless communication specification in existence since 1992. It is based on TDMA.
- **PDA.** Personal Digital Assistant, which is a small portable computer, such as a Palm VII.
- **SMS.** Short Message Service is a facility for sending short text messages (up to 160 characters as of 2001) on GSM cell phones. In existence since 1991, data is borne by the signaling radio resources reserved in cellular networks for locating mobile devices and connecting calls. SMS messages can be sent or received concurrently, even during a voice or data call. It is used by hundreds of millions of users and is known as the e-mail of m-commerce.
- **EMS.** Enhanced Messaging Service is an extension of SMS that is capable of simple animation, tiny pictures, and short melodies.
- **MMS.** Multimedia Messaging Service is the next generation of wireless messaging that will be able to deliver rich media.
- **UMTS.** This is the Universal Mobile Telecommunications System for 3G mobile standard.

- **WAP.** The Wireless Application Protocol offers Internet browsing from wireless devices (see Section 19.4).
- **Smartphones.** These are Internet-enabled cell phones with attached applications (phones with a "brain"). **Smartphones** are becoming standard devices. They include WAP microprocessors for Internet access.

The Benefits and Attributes of Mobile Communication

Generally speaking, many of the EC applications described in Chapters 1–18 can be done in m-commerce. For example, e-shopping, e-banking, e-stock trading, and e-gambling are gaining popularity in wireless B2C. Auctioning is just beginning to take place on cell phones, and wireless collaborative commerce in B2B is emerging. Wireless, non-Internet intrabusiness applications have been in use since the early 1990s. However, in addition to conducting regular EC in a wireless environment, there are several new applications that are possible only in the mobile environment. To understand why this is so, let's review the major attributes of m-commerce.

THE ATTRIBUTES OF M-COMMERCE AND ITS ECONOMIC ADVANTAGES

The interest in m-commerce is not only because of the prospect of a large number of users and the possibility of inexpensive Internet access, but also due to the characteristics shown in Figure 19-1 together with their derived attributes and values.

The characteristics of m-commerce are:

- **Mobility.** M-commerce is based on the fact that users carry a cell phone or other mobile device everywhere they go. So, users can initiate a contact with commercial and other systems anytime they feel a need to do so.
- **Broad reachability.** People can be reached at any time. Of course, you can block certain hours or certain messages, but when you carry an open mobile device, you can be reached instantly.

These two characteristics break the geographic and time barriers, resulting in the following value-added attributes:

- **Ubiquity.** Availability of a mobile terminal in the form of a smartphone or a PDA can fulfill the need both for real-time information and for communication anywhere, independent of the user's location. It creates easier information access in a real-time environment.

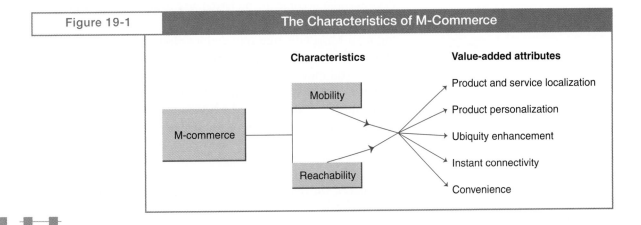

Figure 19-1   The Characteristics of M-Commerce

- **Convenience.** Convenience is an attribute that characterizes a mobile terminal. Devices that store data are always at hand, and are increasingly easy to use. Also, you can connect to the Internet, intranets, and databases.
- **Localization of products and services.** Knowing where the user is physically located, at any particular moment, is a key to offering relevant services that could drive users towards transacting on the network; this is known as location-based e-commerce or l-commerce. Precise location information is known when a GPS is attached to the wireless device. The cost of GPS is declining rapidly, and so is the cost of using it. GPS may be a standard feature in many mobile devices by 2004. When the mobile operator knows where the user is physically located, he can arrange for localization of services. For instance, a businessperson arriving on a plane in Tokyo can expect to receive a message asking whether she needs a hotel for the night, and if you stroll in your favorite shopping center you may receive a message regarding a special sale in that mall.

Mobile location-based services provide end users with Internet access to information that is relevant to their location, such as nearby businesses, routing directions, and personalized marketing offers. Location-based services offer advantages both for telecommunications equipment vendors and carriers and convenience for end user customers:

- Vendors and carriers can differentiate themselves in the competitive marketplace by offering new, exciting, and useful services, helping them attract and keep customers and grow their revenues.
- End users can now use their Web-enabled mobile phone or PDA to access information and services that are relevant to their geographical location. Location-based services include the ability to find the nearest location (restaurant, hotel, hospital, ATM, etc.); locate others; get directions to the next sales or service call; access roadside emergency assistance; and receive marketing offers from nearby business establishments.
- Instant connectivity to the Internet from a mobile device is becoming a reality. Today, even with WAP or any microbrowser over GSM, a call to the Internet still has to be made before applications can be used. Soon, using GPRS, it will be easier and faster to access information on the Web without booting up a PC or placing a call via a modem. Thus, the new wireless devices could become the preferred way to access information.
- Personalization is available today, but it is limited. However, the emerging need for conducting transactions electronically, combined with availability of personalized information and transaction feasibility via mobile portals, will move personalization to new levels, leading ultimately to the mobile device becoming a major EC tool. For example, by responding "Yes" to the question "do you need a hotel room?," the network will advise the arriving traveler what rooms are available by location and price range, and will match any other variables they may have input through their personalization tool.

These benefits will facilitate the use of m-commerce as will the following drivers.

OTHER DRIVERS OF M-COMMERCE

In addition to the benefits resulting from the above attributes, m-commerce is driven by the following factors:

- **Widespread availability of devices.** The number of cell phones exceeded 1 billion in spring 2001; that number is growing rapidly, and is expected to reach 1.3 to 1.4 billion by 2004 (according to Intex Management Services). It is estimated that about 70 percent of cell phones will have Internet access within a few years. Thus, a potential mass market is available for conducting m-commerce. Cell phones are spreading quickly in developing countries such as China, since there is no need for cables. In 2001, there were significantly more cell phone users than Internet users in most countries of the world. In some countries (Finland, Hong Kong), 80 percent of the population carries a cell phone.

- **No need for a PC.** Using a cell phone or other Internet-enabled wireless device, there is no need for a PC to access the Internet. Even though the cost of a PC that is used primarily for Internet access can be as low as $500 or even less, it is still a major expense for the vast majority of people in the world. Furthermore, one needs to learn to operate a PC, service it, and replace it every few years.

- **The handset is becoming a culture.** The widespread use of cell phones is becoming a social phenomenon, especially among the 15-to-25-year-old age group. These users are growing up and will constitute a major force of online buyers once they begin to make and spend money. For instance, the use of Short Message Service (SMS) has been spreading like wildfire in several European and Asian countries. An example is the Philippines, where SMS use is a national phenomenon in the youth market.

- **Vendors' push.** Both mobile communication network operators and manufacturers of mobile devices are advertising the many potential applications of m-commerce so that they can push new technologies to buyers.

- **Declining prices.** With the passage of time, the price of wireless devices is declining, and the per-minute pricing of mobile services is expected to decline by 80 percent before 2005. At the same time, functionalities are increasing.

- **Improvement of bandwidth.** To properly conduct m-commerce, it is necessary to have sufficient bandwidth for transmitting text, but also voice, video, and multimedia. The 3G technology is expected to do just that, at a data rate of up to 2 Mbps. This enables information to move seven times faster than when 56K modems are used.

- **The explosion of EC in general.** Despite the failure of many Internet start-ups, the use of EC is growing rapidly, especially in B2B, some parts of B2C, e-government, and C2C. Therefore, more applications and opportunities are available online. The more EC is conducted, the more opportunities for m-commerce exist.

- **The digital divide.** In Chapter 18 we discussed the issue of the digital divide. According to UN and ITU reports, more than 90 percent of all Internet hosts are in developed countries where only 15 percent of the world's population resides. In 2001, the city of New York, for example, had more Internet hosts than the whole continent of Africa. Cell phones can change this situation. It is projected that by 2005 there will be more

Internet users in China than in the United States. (In 2001 there were about 600 percent more Internet users in the United States.) Of course, being on the Internet does not mean having the ability to shop. However, the income level of people in developing countries is rising, so the cell phone is clearly helping to close the digital divide in EC.

19.3 MOBILE COMPUTING INFRASTRUCTURE

Mobile computing requires hardware, software, and networks. The major components of each are described in this section.

Hardware

To conduct m-commerce, one needs devices for data entry and access to the Internet, applications, and other equipment.

Several mobile computing devices are used in m-commerce. The major ones are:

- **Cellular (mobile) phones.** All major cell phone manufacturers are making or plan to make Internet-enabled cell phones. These cell phones are improving with time, adding more features, a larger screen, a keyboard, and more. You can even play games and download music files. An example (as of 2001) is the Nokia 9110 Communicator. A newer model 9290 arrived in May 2001 (see Figure 19-2). It has a size of $158 \times 56 \times 27$ mm (about 6 in. $\times$ 2 in. $\times$ 1 in.) and a weight of 253g (about 0.6 lb.). The Nokia 9290 includes Internet access and fax capabilities, SMS, regular e-mail, digital camera connectivity, scheduling features, games, and more (see demo at *nokia.com*). Notice that even phones without screen displays can be used to retrieve voice information from the Web (see *tellme.com* and *portableinternet.com*).
- **Attachable keyboard.** Transactions can be executed with the regular telephone entry keys, but it is fairly time consuming to do so. An alternative is to use a larger cell phone such as the Nokia 9290 that contains a small-scale keyboard. Yet another solution is to plug an attachable keyboard to the cell phone (attachable keyboards are also available for other wireless devices).
- **PDAs.** PDAs with Internet access are now available from several vendors, and their capabilities are increasing. One example of a PDA is the Palm VIIx Handheld (see Figure 19-3 and *palm.com/products/palmviix*). Using special software, one can connect the PDA to the Internet via a wireless modem.
- **Interactive pagers.** Some two-way pagers can be used to conduct limited m-commerce activities on the Internet (mainly sending and receiving text messages, such as stock market orders).
- **Screenphones.** A telephone equipped with a color screen, possibly a keyboard, e-mail, and Internet capabilities is referred to as a **screenphone**. Initially, these were **wirelined** (regular phones connected by wires to a network), but as of 2000, wireless screenphones are available. Some are portable and are used mainly for e-mail.
- **E-mail solutions.** To enhance wireless e-mail capabilities one can use devices such as the BlackBerry Handheld (*blackberry.net*). This device includes a keypad, making it easy to type messages. It is an integrated package, so there is no need to dial into an Internet provider for access. There are

Figure 19-2	Nokia 9290 Communicator

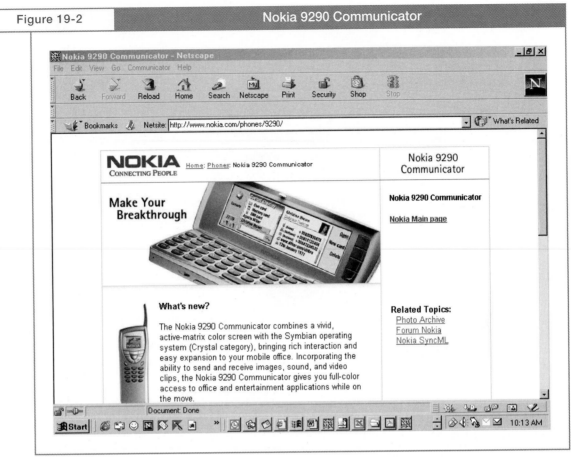

Source: www.nokia.com.

a variety of services for data communication, so you can receive and send messages from anywhere. A product demo is available at *blackberry.net*. Enterprise and home/personal solutions are available.

- **Other devices.** Notebooks, hand-held computers, and other mobile computers can be used in m-commerce. Access from portable PCs to the Internet has been available since the early 1990s.
- **Convergence.** There is a clear trend for the convergence of PDAs and cell phones. In 2001, Palm Corp. added a telephony attachment device that enables Palm V to function like a cell phone. At the same time Nokia, NEC, and other cell phone manufacturers are adding PDA functionalities. For example, Nokia's 9110 includes a calendar. The border between mobile devices, including intelligent home appliances, is beginning to blur. For example, phones with an integrated MP3 player and/or video player are coming to market. For the state of the art see the QCP smart phone at *kyocera-wireless.com* (check the demos).

In addition to the mobile computing devices described here, m-commerce has other hardware needs.

- A suitably configured wireline or wireless WAN modem, wireless LAN adapter, or wireless MAN (metro-area network) adapter.
- A Web server with wireless support, WAP gateway, a communications server and/or MCSS (mobile communications server switch)—this device

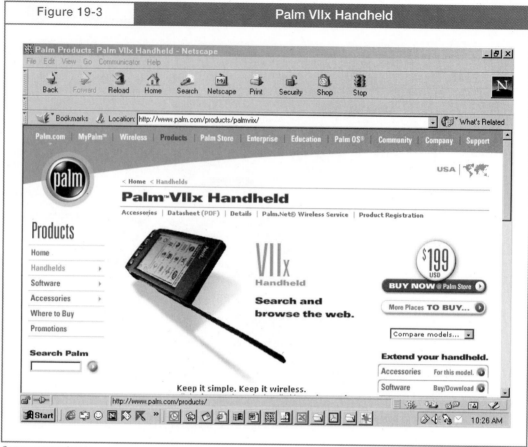

Figure 19-3 — **Palm VIIx Handheld**

provides communications functionality to allow the handheld device to communicate with the Internet or intranet infrastructure.

- An application or database server with application logic and business application database.
- A large enterprise application server.
- A Global Positioning System (GPS) that is used to determine the location of the person carrying the mobile computing device. This is the basis for location-based applications, as described in Section 19.11. The GPS can be attached or inserted into a mobile device.

Software

Developing software for wireless devices is challenging since there is no widely acceptable standard for applications (as of 2001). Therefore, applications need to use customized software for each type of device with which the application may communicate. Here are the major required software products:

- **Microbrowser.** Software product used to view online WML-created content.
- **Mobile client operating system (OS).** Operating system software that resides in the mobile device—it may be Windows 2000/2001/NT, PalmOS, Win CE (or Pocket PC), EPOC, a specialized OS such as BlackBerry, or a Web browser.

- **Mobile application user interface.** The application logic in a handheld PDA, smart phone, Palm, or Wintel notebook. In the Internet world, it is often under the control of a browser or microbrowser.
- **Back-end legacy application software.** Legacy software that resides on large Unix servers (from vendors such as Sun, IBM, and HP) or on mainframes, is a major part of m-commerce software.
- **Application middleware.** Middleware is a piece of software that communicates with back-end legacy systems and Web-based application servers. IBM's WebSphere is one such example.
- **Wireless middleware.** Middleware that links multiple wireless networks to application servers.

Networks and Access

A wireless network may be either a private network that police agencies and emergency health services use or a public shared network that is provided by network providers, such as Motient, Cingular (formerly Bell South Wireless Data), Verizon, Sprint, Metricom, Nextel, Bell Mobility (Canada), Roger's AT&T (Canada), BT in United Kingdom, Deutsche Telecom, France Telecom, Vodafone, SK Telecom, NTT DoCoMo (Japan), etc. Wireless networks provide true mobility. Mobile users may use a wireless network for occasional connections from hotels or airport VIP lounges. Access to the Internet is provided by these companies or by specialized wireless ISPs.

WIRELESS TRANSMISSION MEDIA

The following are the major wireless transmission media.

Microwave   Microwave systems are widely used for high-volume, long-distance, point-to-point communication. These systems were first used extensively to transmit very high-frequency radio signals in a line-of-sight path between relay stations spaced approximately 30 miles apart (due to the Earth's curvature). To minimize line-of-sight problems, microwave antennas are usually placed on top of buildings, towers, and mountain peaks. Long-distance telephone carriers adopted microwave systems because they generally provide about 10 times the data-carrying capacity of a wire. Compared to 30 miles of wire, microwave communication segments can be set up much more quickly (sometimes within a day) and at a much lower cost.

The fact that microwave requires line-of-sight transmission severely limits its usefulness as a practical large-scale solution to data communication needs, especially over very long distances. Additionally, microwave transmissions are susceptible to environmental interference during severe weather such as heavy rain or snowstorms. Although still fairly widely used, long distance microwave data communications systems have been replaced largely by satellite communications systems.

Satellites   Although the radio frequencies used by satellite-data communication transponders are also line-of-sight, the enormous "footprint" of a satellite's coverage area from high altitudes overcomes the limitations of microwave data relay stations. For example, a network of just three evenly spaced communications satellites in stationary "geosynchronous" orbit 22,300 miles above the equator is sufficient to provide global coverage.

Currently, there are three types of orbits in which satellites are placed: geostationary earth orbit (GEO), medium earth orbit (MEO), and low earth orbit (LEO).

Radio Radio electromagnetic data communications do not have to depend on microwave or satellite links, especially for short ranges such as within an office setting. Radio is being used increasingly to connect computers and peripheral equipment or computers and local area networks. The greatest advantage radio has for data communications is that no metallic wires are needed. Radio waves tend to propagate easily through normal office walls. The devices are fairly inexpensive and easy to install.

However, radio media can create reciprocal electrical interference problems—with other office electrical equipment and from that equipment to the radio communication devices. Also, radio transmissions are susceptible to snooping by anyone similarly equipped and on the same frequency.

Infrared Infrared light is red light, which is not commonly visible to human eyes, that can be modulated or pulsed for conveying information. The most common application of infrared light is with television or videocassette recorder remote control units. With computers, infrared transmitters and receivers (or "transceivers") are being used for short-distance connections between computers and peripheral equipment or between computers and local area networks.

Advantages of infrared light include: no need for metallic wires, equipment is highly mobile, no electrical interference problems, no Federal Communications Commission (FCC) permission is required to operate an infrared transmitter, no certification is needed before selling an infrared device, and fairly inexpensive devices exist that have very high data rates. Disadvantages of infrared media include susceptibility to fog, smog, smoke, dust, rain, and air temperature fluctuations.

Cellular Radio Technology Telephone users of data communications are increasingly employing cellular radio technology. The basic concept is relatively simple. The FCC has defined geographic cellular service areas; each area is subdivided into hexagonal cells that fit together like a honeycomb to form the backbone of that area's cellular radio system. Located at the center of each cell is a radio transceiver and a computerized cell-site controller that handles all cell-site control functions. All the cell sites are connected to a mobile telephone switching office that provides the connections from the cellular system to a wired telephone network and transfers calls from one cell to another as a user travels out of the cell serving one area and into another.

The cellular telephone infrastructure has initially been used for voice transmission, but the development of a transmission standard called Cellular Digital Packet Data (CDPD) has made it possible for the infrastructure to support two-way digital transmissions.

WIRELESS SYSTEMS

The above components need to be integrated into one system. Such integration may be done with a platform such as IBM's WebSphere software that integrates diverse data, applications, and processes. An example of such an application used by Delta Airlines is shown in Figure 19-4. In the application, Delta Airline's cus-

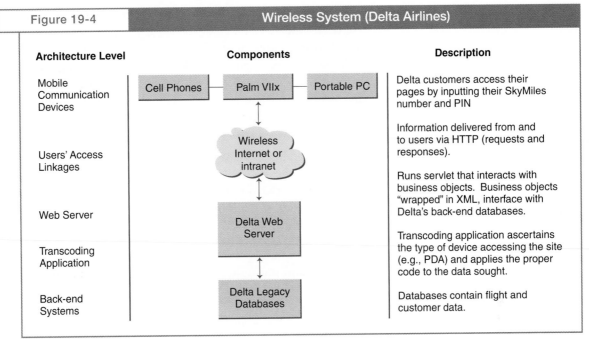

Figure 19-4   Wireless System (Delta Airlines)

Source: ibm.com/software, and delta.com (2000).

tomers can access their mileage account, flight information, and much more. For further details see *ibm.com/software*.

Wireless systems connect wireless devices to applications, networks, databases, etc. (e.g., see *idini.com*.) For such connectivity one needs standards.

19.4   WIRELESS TECHNOLOGY, STANDARDS, AND SECURITY

M-commerce is supported by Internet infrastructure (when done on the Internet) and by other technologies, standards, security, and voice systems. The important items are described here briefly.

Technology

The following technologies are required for wireless communications.

- **Microbrowsers.** These browsers are designed with limited bandwidth and limited memory requirements. They can access the Web via the wireless Internet.
- **Bluetooth.** Bluetooth (named after a famous Danish King), is a chip technology that enables voice and data communications between many digital devices (e.g., between a digital camera and a PC) through low-power, short-range, digital two-way radio frequency (RF). Bluetooth is a Wireless Personal Area Network (WPAN) standard backed by most major corporations in the world (e.g., see *bluetooth.com*). It is deployed by placing a radio chip and special software into the devices that you want to communicate with each other. As of 2001, it is effective up to 30 meters. The

technology enhances ubiquitous connectivity and enables easy data transfer. For details see *Bluetooth.com*.

- **Wireless local area networks (WLANs).** A major application of wireless technology is the creation of WLANs. This can be done with one or more support technologies such as RF, infrared, and Bluetooth. WLANs are easy and fast to install and to change. This allows organizations to quickly relocate or return to normal in case of a disaster.

Standards

Several standards are related to m-commerce. They are developed by several organizations worldwide. A leading organization is ETSI (the European Telecommunications Standards Institute), which aims to create global wireless. The most important standards and technologies are:

- **Time-division multiple access (TMDA).** This technology has been in use since 1992, mainly in Europe. Its capacity is limited to 9.6 to 14.4 Kbps.
- **Code division multiple access (CDMA).** The CDMA allows reuse of scarce radio resources in adjacent areas.
- **CDMA one.** This is an interim standard available commercially since October 2000 (first used in Korea). Considered as 2.75G, it is more advanced than 2.5G.
- **W-CDMA.** Wideband-CDMA and CDMA 2000 are technologies for 3G with up to 2Mbps capacity. The capabilities of CDMA as envisioned by NTT of Japan, are shown in Figure 19-5.
- **Wireless application protocol (WAP).** WAP is a set of communication protocols designed to enable different kinds of wireless devices (e.g., mobile phones, PDAs, pagers, etc.) to talk to a server installed on a mobile network, so users can access the Internet. It standardizes developments across different wireless technologies worldwide. It was designed especially for small screens and limited bandwidth. It enables the deployment of a microbrowser into mobile devices (see Redman, May 2000). WAP is being challenged by several competing standards, including Java-based applications (the J2ME platform), which offer better graphics and security (see *wapforum.org*).
- **Subscriber identification module (SIM).** This is a smart card that holds a user's identity and includes it in a telephone directory.
- **Wireless markup language (WML).** WML is the scripting language used for creating content in the wireless Web environment. It is based on XML and it removes unnecessary content, such as animation. This increases speed. WML works with WAP to deliver content. WML does not require a keyboard or a mouse.
- **Voice XML (VXML).** This is an extension of XML designed to accommodate voice.
- **Enhanced data rates for global evaluation (EDGE).** This is an extension to GSM that leverages TDMA and GPRS infrastructures.
- **Universal mobile telecommunications system (UMTS).** This is the 3G mobile standard. It allows different mobile systems to talk to each other across international borders.

Figure 19-5

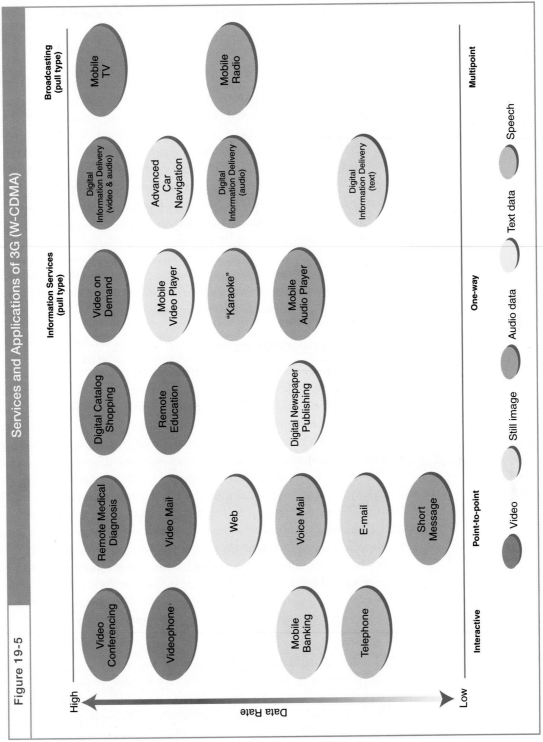

Services and Applications of 3G (W-CDMA)

Source: NTT DoCoMo publicity

Security Issues

A number of security issues affects wireless communications and m-commerce.

VIRUSES

Computer viruses have begun the migration to mobile devices as such terminals gain more processing power and intelligence. The GartnerGroup predicts a proliferation of viruses afflicting hand-held computers by late 2001 and mobile phones by mid-2002. This presents a significant security risk to mobile users.

The first computer virus that targeted mobile phones was identified in mid-2000. The virus was spread as an e-mail enclosure on conventional computers but was also designed to send prank SMS text messages to randomly selected mobile phone numbers on a particular cellular network in Spain. Had the outbreak not been contained early, the flood of messages could potentially have crippled Spain's wireless network. Few mobile phones today handle e-mail attachments, but subsequent generations of better-equipped Internet-enabled devices that will receive attachments will be more vulnerable. Antivirus vendors have already begun shipping antivirus programs for hand-held computers.

SMART CARD SECURITY SOLUTIONS

Many of the generic EC security issues discussed in Chapter 13 are applicable to m-commerce; in addition, there are issues related mainly to m-commerce. For example, problems may result from the ease with which wireless voice communication can be intercepted by hackers. According to Baltimore Technologies (2000), it is more difficult to assure confidentiality (privacy), authentication, integrity, and nonrepudiation in m-commerce than in e-commerce.

One practical solution is to use smart card technologies embedded in cell phones. Smart cards, with a biometric add-on feature (*mbusiness-insight* 2000), can enhance the security level. The success of smart card/biometric applications on mobile phones for improved security depends on the existence of a standardized multiapplication card, which allows the incorporation of a number of different applications, including GSM-SIM, and security applications such as PKI, all on the same card. This may be implemented in 2003 or 2004.

BACK-END SECURITY SOLUTIONS—PUBLIC KEY INFRASTRUCTURE (PKI) AND M-CERT

A PKI system (Chapter 14) can be adapted to m-commerce. A PKI solution can be integrated with other security measures or applications in providing a comprehensive security framework. For example, PKI on a SIM card can be attached to a GSM phone (Durlacher, 2000). Alternatively, PKI solutions can be connected to WTLS (Baltimore Technologies, 2000). The wireless version of the industrial standard of Transport Layer Security (TLS), which is equivalent to SSL, is called Wireless Transport Layer Security (WTLS). TLS provides a secure network connection session between a client and a server. It is most commonly adopted between a Web browser and a Web server. Such security measures tightly bind digital identities to content providers and wireless customers, making their associated transactions more secure.

In fall 2000, a common security standard called "m-cert" was launched on all local PKI-based mobile EC services in Hong Kong. This m-cert standard is used to ensure authentication, integrity, nonrepudiation, and confidentiality of electronic transactions (*South China Morning Post*, April 26, 2000). This enables customers to conduct PKI-based services and applications such as paying utility bills, making credit card payments, purchasing movie and air tickets, and conducting stock trading and banking services securely from mobile devices.

Security products and services are offered by companies such as VeriSign. Products include: wireless personal trust agent (PTA), a transparent microclient code that can be embedded in handheld devices to enable the use of private keys, digital certificates, and digital signatures; short-lived wireless server certificates, "mini-digital certificates," which provide authentication and real-time certificate validation; and gateway-assisted SSL, which enables network service providers to substitute wireless certificates for existing SSL certificates.

New wireless services include: subscriber trust services, which allow for secure messaging and transactions via wireless handhelds; server/gateway trust services to deliver secure applications over wireless networks; developer trust services to digitally protect downloadable content; enterprise trust services to provide wireless services such as e-banking, e-brokerage, e-healthcare, and e-messaging; and service provider platforms to offer a range of VeriSign-based wireless trust services.

For a comparative study of Europe, Japan, and the United States, see Macklin (2001).

Voice Systems for M-Commerce

The most natural mode of communication is voice. When people need to communicate with each other from a distance, they use the telephone more frequently than any other communication device. Voice communication can now be done on the computer using a microphone and a sound card.

Voice and data can work together to create useful applications. For example, operators of PBXs are letting callers give simple computer commands using interactive voice response. The number and type of voice technology applications is growing.

Voice technologies have the following advantages:

- Hands-free and eyes-free operations increase the productivity, safety, and effectiveness of operators ranging from forklift drivers to military pilots.
- Disabled people can use voice data to command a computer to perform various tasks.
- Voice terminals are designed for portability. Users do not have to go to the computer.
- Voice terminals are more rugged than keyboards, so they can operate better in dirty or moving environments.
- It is about two-and-a-half times faster to talk than to type.
- In most circumstances, fewer errors in voice data entry are made compared with keyboard data entry, assuming a reliable voice recognition system is used.

Until the late 1990s, voice communication was done via regular phones and 2G cell phones. Now there is a move to the Web. But first let's examine one of the most popular conventional voice applications, the IVR.

Interactive Voice Response (IVR) systems enable users to interact with a computerized system to request and receive information and enter and change data. These systems have been in use since the 1980s. The communication is conducted through regular telephone lines or through 1G cell phones. Examples of this include: patients can schedule hospital and doctors' appointments; users can request a pick-up from FedEx and others; employees can find information about fringe benefits, select benefits, or make changes to their benefits package; and electric companies respond to customers who are calling to report power outages. The systems try to diagnose the problem and route it to the proper department. Customers may be prompted to answer some questions and are instructed what to do.

Originally, IVR was conducted from a regular telephone and the receiving system was hosted inside the application (e.g., a call center) inside an organization. Now these systems are moving to the Web where they are incorporated into voice portals.

VOICE PORTALS

A **voice portal** is a Web site with audio interface. Voice portals are not really Web sites in the normal sense because they're designed to be accessed through a standard or a cell telephone. Several of these new sites are in operation. Sites like *Tellme.com* and *BeVocal.com* allow callers to request information about weather, local restaurants, current traffic, and other handy information.

In addition to retrieving information, some sites provide true interaction. *iPing.com* is a reminder and notification service that allows you to enter information via the Web and receive reminder calls. In addition, *iPing.com* can call a group of people to notify them of a meeting or conference call.

The real value for Internet marketers is that these voice portals can help find new customers. Several of these sites are ad supported; thus, the customer profile data they have available can deliver very precisely targeted advertising. For instance, a department-store chain with an existing brand image can use short audio commercials on these sites to deliver a message related to the topic of the call, as will be described in Section 19.7.

19.5   M-COMMERCE APPLICATIONS: AN OVERVIEW

The number of m-commerce applications is growing rapidly. Applications are derived from the following sources:

- Wireless access provided to existing B2C applications. This includes e-banking, e-stock trading, e-shopping, etc. The advantage here is that the user can do it from anywhere, and there is no need for a PC.
- Existing wireless intrabusiness and CRM applications enhanced by adding Internet/intranet access, smartphones, and other devices. In such cases, connectivity to legacy systems and ERP is important.
- Location-based applications. These applications are either stand-alone (e.g., NextBus described earlier) or they are integrated with other EC applications.
- SMS-based applications which may be location-base related.

M-commerce applications are divided here into the following categories:

- Financial applications (Section 19.6)
- Marketing, advertisement, and customer service (Section 19.7)
- Enterprise (intrabusiness) applications (Section 19.8)
- B2B and supply chain (Section 19.9)
- Individual consumers (Section 19.10)
- Location-based applications (Section 19.11)
- Non-Internet applications (Section 19.12)

19.6   MOBILE FINANCIAL APPLICATIONS

Mobile financial applications are likely to be one of the most important components of m-commerce. These include **mobile banking** and **m-brokerage services,** including mobile money transfers and mobile micropayments. These services could turn a mobile device into a business tool, replacing banks, ATMs, and credit cards by letting a user conduct financial transactions with a mobile device.

Examples of Financial Applications

The following are examples of m-commerce financial applications.

- The Swedish Postal Bank (Postbanken) and Telia's Mobile Smart service allow consumers to make Giro payments from their handsets. Merita-Nordbanken's customers in Sweden can check their balance and transaction logs from their mobile phones and conduct some types of transactions.
- Dagens Industri, Europe's fourth-largest business daily, allows subscribers to receive financial data and trade on the Stockholm Exchange.
- Citibank has a diversified mobile banking service. Consumers can use their mobile handsets to access their account balance, pay bills, and transfer funds using SMS.
- Many banks in Japan allow for all banking transactions to be done from cell phones. An online bank (Japan Net Bank) allows customers to pay for goods and services from their cell phones, debiting their purchases from their accounts.
- Hoover's wireless (*hoovers.com*) can be accessed from mobile devices. Investors can get stock information, news, quotes, and more.
- ASB Bank (New Zealand) provides customers with a personalized service that alerts them with an SMS to their cell phone when a specific stock breaks a personally defined price threshold. The customer is then linked to his ASB account for possible trading.
- Charles Schwab, E*TRADE (see *omnisky.com*), and other online brokers offer mobile Internet stock trading applications, including diversified information and execution. Mobile stock trading is extremely popular in Korea and Japan.
- Customers at SEB in Sweden can do all their banking transactions from anywhere at any time using cell phones. Many other banks in Europe, Asia, and North America offer similar services.

- Vendors selling from portable carts at Boston's Fanual Hall Marketplace did not have dedicated telephone lines. This meant that they were unable to get real-time authorization for credit cards. Vendors lost about 15 percent of their annual sales due to fraud because they were only able to check credit card purchases after they went home for the day. Installing wireless point-of-sale terminals, the vendors can now process cards in 3 to 5 seconds, resulting in increased sales and decreased fraud.

WIRELESS ELECTRONIC PAYMENT SYSTEMS

Wireless payment systems transform mobile phones into secure, self-contained purchasing tools capable of instantly authorizing payments over the cellular network for goods and services consumed. For example, in Finland, SMS messages sent from GSM handsets are already being used to pay for food and drinks at some outlets. Users can also initiate automatic car washes and trigger vending machines into dispensing goods, all by simply dialing special phone numbers posted for those purposes.

MICROPAYMENTS

Micropayments, as discussed in Chapter 14, are used for small purchase amounts. A mobile device can communicate with a vending machine using a local wireless network, and items can be purchased. Micropayments can be implemented in a variety of ways. One way is that the user could make a call to a certain number where per-minute charges equal the cost of the vending item. This approach has been used by Sonera, a Finnish wireless provider, in their famous Coke (and now Pepsi) machine service (see Muller-Veerse, 2000). In effect, it transfers money from the user's telephone bill to the vending provider's account. Another way to perform micropayments is by using prepaid cards purchased from a service provider, bank, or credit card company. Attaching a smart card with prepaid money on it to a mobile device is another option.

An Israeli firm, TeleVend, Inc. (*televend.com*), has pioneered a secure platform that allows subscribers to make payments using mobile phones of any type on any cellular infrastructure. A customer places a mobile phone call to a number stipulated by the merchant to authorize a vending device to dispense the service. Connecting to a TeleVend server, the user selects the appropriate transaction option to authorize payment. Billing can be made to the customer's bank or credit card account or to the mobile phone bill. This technology has wide-ranging applications, such as payment collection at parking garages, restaurant tabs, grocery bills, and public utility tariffs. Such an application depends on the transaction costs. The transaction costs will be small only if there is a large volume of transactions.

WIRELESS WEB WALLET

In Chapter 14 we described the concept of an e-wallet. *NextCard.com* developed a wireless wallet that enables cardholders to make purchases with a single click from their wireless devices. Called **m-wallet**, the service is offered by other companies as well. It is basically a single-click checkout. For details see *verifone.com*.

Shoppers in certain Swedish stores can pay for their purchases with a virtual credit card (from Eurocard) that is stored in their Ericsson or Nokia handsets. Using Bluetooth technology, the handset interacts with the in-store payment terminal.

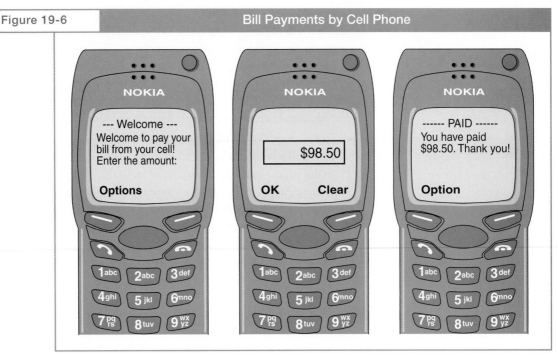

Figure 19-6 — Bill Payments by Cell Phone

Source: Courtesy of Nokia, at nokia.com.

BILL PAYMENTS

In addition to bill payments via banks, one can pay bills directly from a cell phone. This can be done via a bank, a credit card, or a prepaid arrangement. An example of how this is done is shown in Figure 19-6.

Here are some examples of bill payment m-commerce applications.

- Over 50 percent of Portuguese mobile phone customers are anonymous prepaid subscribers. They use ATM bill payment facilities to "reload" their mobile phones for more talk time.
- Motorists in Scandinavia use their mobile phones to pay for unattended car parking, soft drinks in vending machines, and car washes. The goods and services are charged through the telecom operators and show up on the consumers' bills.
- McDonald's customers in some cities in the United States can use their Mobile Speedpass Transportation devices to pay for their meals.

19.7   MOBILE MARKETING, ADVERTISEMENT, AND CUSTOMER SERVICE

M-commerce applications in B2C are expected to be mainly in three areas: shopping online, advertisement (possibly targeted), and providing personalized customer services.

Shopping from Wireless Devices

Many vendors allow customers to shop from wireless devices. For example, AT&T customers that use an Internet-ready phone can shop at certain sites such as *buy.com*. Customers can perform quick searches, compare prices, order, and view the status of their order. A start-up, *smartshop-inc.com*, allows users to use their mobile device to check prices while shopping. Shoppers are supported by services similar to those available for wireline shoppers. For example, at *verifone.com* users have access to a shopping cart, as well as product search and price comparison tools. The wireless shopping process is shown in Figure 19-7. The relationship to customer service, which is discussed later, is also shown in the figure.

Here are some other examples of wireless shopping:

- *Amazon.com*'s CEO believes that in 5 to 10 years most business will be wireless. Today you can buy books or check online auctions at *Amazon.com*, and many more features will be added in 2002.
- Online stores will become showrooms. Handheld devices with bar code scanners will let users purchase products and even customize products. The merchandise will be delivered directly to the home, eliminating the need for store inventories.

USING VOICE PORTALS IN MARKETING AND CUSTOMER SERVICE

Voice portal technology can be connected to legacy systems to provide enhanced customer service or to improve access to data for employees, as shown in the following examples:

- Customers who are away from the office could use a vendor's voice portal to check on the status of deliveries to a job site.
- Service technicians could be provided with diagnostic information.
- Salespeople could check on inventory status during a meeting to help close a sale.

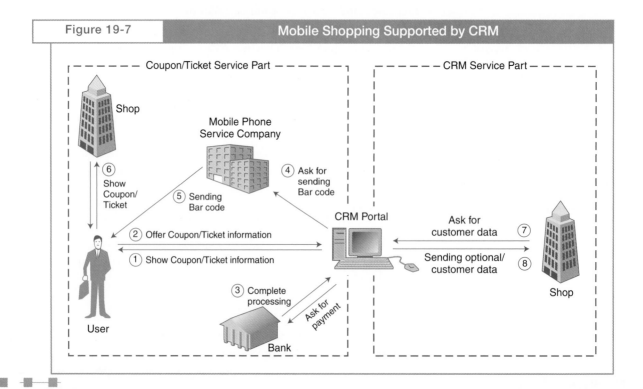

Figure 19-7   **Mobile Shopping Supported by CRM**

There is a wide variety of customer-relationship management applications for voice portal technology. The challenge is in learning how to create the navigation and other aspects of interaction that makes customers feel comfortable with voice-access technology.

Targeted Advertisement

Using demographic information collected by wireless services, *barnesandnoble.com*, which launched wireless services for mobile devices in 1999, now provides more personalization of services and an enhanced user interface for its wireless Web page. In one improvement, the company added music clips to its wireless Web page so that customers can download and listen to the clips on their cell phones. "Wireless is a very small piece of our overall revenues right now," says Carl Rosendorf, a senior vice president for *barnesandnoble.com* in New York. "But we're at the first phase of a massive growth. Mobile commerce is going to be the ultimate personal shopping experience."

Knowing the current location of mobile users (using GPS) and their preferences or surfing habits, advertisement messages can be very user-specific based on methods described in Chapters 4 and 5. The advertisements sent to a user can also be location-sensitive, informing a user about various ongoing special sales (shops, malls, and restaurants) in areas close to where a potential buyer is. This type of advertising can be performed using SMS to a cell phone or by using short paging messages to pager users. The basic method used is customer profiling that can be done by collaborative filtering (Chapter 5). One company that capitalized on this approach is C5, as described in Application Case 19.1.

APPLICATION CASE 19.1

Cases of Wireless Advertisement

The following are a few examples of wireless advertisement in action.

Vindigo.com

Vindigo.com has a large database of customers (over 300,000 in early 2001) willing to accept promotions. This is known as permission marketing, and the users download a special software on their PDAs. These users use *Vindigo.com* to help them decide where they will eat, shop, and play. They trust *vindigo.com* because the company delivers timely, accurate information about places to go and things to do in their area. Along with every listing, the company can deliver a customized message to the users at a time and place where it's of most interest to them and they are most likely to act on it.

The company targets ads based on city (New York, San Francisco, Los Angeles, etc.) and channel (Eat, Shop, or Play). *Vindigo.com* tracks which ads a user sees (and taps on), enables advertisers to offer promotions and discounts, and even allows a user to request information from an advertiser via e-mail.

Vindigo.com finds a user's location through GPS or by asking the user which neighborhoods they want to be matched with.

(continued)

The following are some examples of how *vindigo.com* works:

• Let's say you own a men's clothing store and are looking to announce the opening of a new location. Through *vindigo.com*, you can deliver your message regarding the opening to men searching for things to do or places to shop in that specific neighborhood.

• Let's say you own an Italian restaurant chain. You can use *vindigo.com* to send a message to anyone looking for Italian food within a few blocks of one of your locations. You can give them directions to that restaurant and even offer them the list of specials on the menu.

C5solutions.com

C5Solutions.com is a Hong Kong-based company that provides a marketing infrastructure platform that offers the mobile carrier an opportunity to provide value-added marketing content to subscribers. Information such as special restaurant promotions and sales promotions can be delivered to the subscriber's handset relevant to their personal tastes and location. Mobile carriers can provide marketers with a channel to interact on a true one-to-one basis with subscribers.

Capabilities provided include:

• Ability to deliver location-specific, personalized, and relevant marketing messages to subscribers.

• Reporting capabilities that allow the mobile carriers to learn about trends and patterns.

• Enterprise-ready scaleable architecture.

GeePS.com (not available)

In a reverse of the push for bricks-and-mortar businesses to create virtual malls for online shoppers, location-based start-up GeePS is delivering coupons to the cell phones of shoppers at the Palisades Center Mall near New York City and mobile customers in upscale Summit, New Jersey.

Mobile customers, after finding coupons at the wireless version of New Jersey Online (*nj.com*), show store employees the digital coupon and claim their discounts.

GeePS plans on offering its location-based ads throughout Maryland, Ohio, Pennsylvania, and West Virginia. What's next for GeePS? Location-based radio commercials when 3G becomes widespread.

Go2Online.com

Hoping to become the king of location-based Web domains, *go2online.com* can help mobile travelers find everything from lodging (choose go2hotels) to Jiffy Lube stations (choose go2oilchanges). Partnering with Sprint, NexTel, Verizon, and BellSouth, go2 services are available on every Web-enabled phone, Palm Pilot, and BlackBerry RIM pager in America. Entering "JiffyLube" or hundreds of other brands into the go2 system will bring up the nearest location.

Source: Compiled from *vindigo.com*, *c5solutions.com*, *geeps.com*, and *go2online.com*.

As more wireless bandwidth becomes available, content-rich advertising involving audio, pictures, and video clips will be generated for individual users with specific needs, interests, and inclinations. Also, depending on the interests and personality types of individual mobile users, the network provider may consider using "push" or "pull" methods of mobile advertising on a per user basis or to a class of users (segmentation). The number of ads pushed to an individual customer should be limited, to avoid overwhelming the user with too much information, and also to avoid the possibility of congestion over the wireless networks. Wireless network managers may consider advertising to a lower priority traffic if network traffic crosses certain thresholds. Finally, since ad pushers need to know the current location information about a user, a third-party vendor may be used to provide location services. This requires a sharing of revenues with a location service provider.

GET PAID TO LISTEN TO ADVERTISEMENTS

Would you be willing to listen to a 10-second ad when you dial your cell phone if you were paid 2 minutes of free long-distance time? It depends in which country you are. In the United States this service was a flop and was discontinued in 2000. In Singapore it works very well. Within a few months more than 100,000 people subscribed to the free minutes for listening to ad service offered by SingTel Mobile.

SingTel operates its program in partnership with Spotcast. In exchange for Spotcast's software platform, SingTel paid the Maryland-based company $600,000 and will continue to pay ongoing maintenance fees. Spotcast's technology enables SingTel to build increasingly accurate profiles of subscribers and target ads to them. SingTel recouped its initial investment from ad revenues in about a year. By Spring 2001, about 100 advertisers had signed up, but their ads are getting 10 times the response rate of an average Internet banner ad. Subscribers to SingTel's service fill out a personal questionnaire when they sign up. This information is fed into the Spotcast database and encrypted to shield subscribers' identities—Spotcast can't match phone numbers to names. To collect their free minutes—1 minute per call, up to 100 minutes a month—subscribers dial a four-digit code, then the phone number of the person they want to talk to. The code prompts SingTel to forward the call to Spotscast and, in an instant, Spotcast's software finds the best ad to send to the subscriber based on the subscriber's profile.

ADVERTISEMENT STRATEGIES AND GUIDELINES

On one hand there are hundreds of millions of people with mobile devices. On the other hand there is a lack of experience. The Wireless Ad Industry Association (*waaglobal.org*) is trying to establish wireless ad guidelines. Issues such as spamming and unethical strategies need to be addressed too.

Supporting Customers and Business Partners (Consumer Services)

Supporting customers and business partners is the essence of the CRM and PRM programs described earlier in this text. The wireless solutions complement the wireline solutions, as shown in Figure 19-8. As can be seen in the figure, the customer is at the center and is surrounded by the various applications.

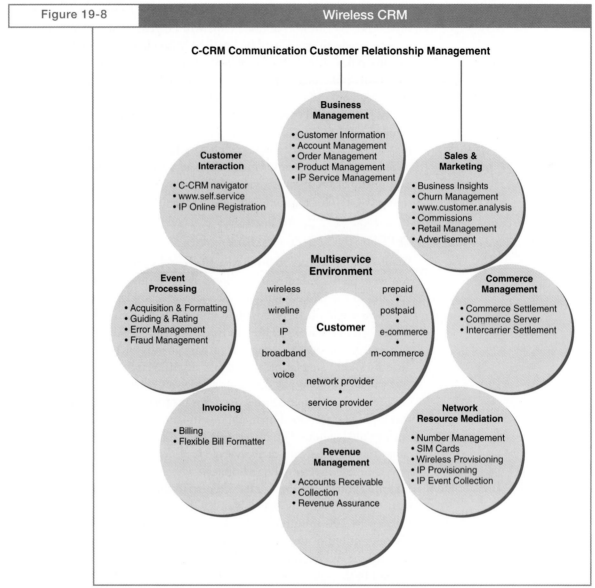

| Figure 19-8 | Wireless CRM |

C-CRM Communication Customer Relationship Management

Business Management
- Customer Information
- Account Management
- Order Management
- Product Management
- IP Service Management

Customer Interaction
- C-CRM navigator
- www.self.service
- IP Online Registration

Sales & Marketing
- Business Insights
- Churn Management
- www.customer.analysis
- Commissions
- Retail Management
- Advertisement

Event Processing
- Acquisition & Formatting
- Guiding & Rating
- Error Management
- Fraud Management

Multiservice Environment
- wireless
- wireline
- IP
- broadband
- voice
- prepaid
- postpaid
- e-commerce
- m-commerce

Customer

network provider
service provider

Commerce Management
- Commerce Settlement
- Commerce Server
- Intercarrier Settlement

Invoicing
- Billing
- Flexible Bill Formatter

Revenue Management
- Accounts Receivable
- Collection
- Revenue Assurance

Network Resource Mediation
- Number Management
- SIM Cards
- Wireless Provisioning
- IP Provisioning
- IP Event Collection

Source: Publicly distributed information from Amdocs Corp. St. Louis, MO (Dec. 2000).

19.8   MOBILE APPLICATIONS IN THE ENTERPRISE

Although B2C m-commerce is getting considerable publicity, most of today's applications are done inside organizations. As a matter of fact, wireless applications from several devices have been popular since the early 1990s. Let's look at some.

Supporting Mobile Employees (Enterprise Solutions)

GartnerGroup predicted in 2000 that by 2002 over 25 percent of all workers could be mobile workers. These mobile employees need the same corporate data they use at their desks. Using wireline devices may be inconvenient or even impossible when people are out of their offices.

The solution is a myriad of smaller, simple wireless devices—the smartphones and handheld companions carried by mobile workers; the in-vehicle information systems installed in cars; the Internet screenphones and the set-top boxes in homes.

None of these will replace the PC. Rather, they broaden the total e-marketplace for the delivery of information. They answer the demand for universal access to information the mobile employee needs. Examples of mobile employees are: sales people in the field, traveling executives, telecommuters, people working in corporate yards and warehouses, and repair or installation employees who work at customers' sites or on utility lines. The last type of employees, especially those who work on buildings and electrical poles and other difficult to climb places, are equipped with several wireless devices, including:

- **Cameras.** Without using their hands, workers can take digital photos and videos and transmit them to the company. The camera is mounted on the safety hat.
- **Screen.** Also mounted on the safety hat, in front of the eyes, is a computer screen that displays information to the worker.
- **Keyboard.** A wrist-mounted keyboard enables typing by the other hand. It is an alternative to voice recognition systems, which are also wireless. The keyboard can be used for intranet use with the screen.
- **Touch-panel display.** Also attached to the hand is a flat-panel screen that responds to the taps of a finger or stylus.

For examples of using wireless to support mobile employees see Application Case 19.2 and *ericsson.com/enterprise/products*.

APPLICATION CASE 19.2

Mobile Workplace Applications in *mySAP.com* Environment

The following are two scenarios of wireless applications for mobile employees.

Sales Support Scenario

Linda is a member of the field sales team at Theru Tools (a fictitious company name). Each day she drives out to her customers with a van stocked with products. For each sale she has to note the customer, the number and type of products sold, and any special discounts made. This used to be done manually, and many errors were made, leading to customer complaints and lost sales.

There had been reluctance to invest in laptops for such a limited application, but Linda wanted the speed and reliability of automation. With the help of SAP, Theru was able to implement a system using low-cost but powerful handheld wireless devices.

Using Mobile Sales (an application for handhelds), accessed via the *mySAP.com* Mobile Workplace, Linda and her coworkers in the field now have information at their fingertips, including updates on new tools and special promotions. She can place orders without delay and get immediate feedback on availability and delivery times. What's more, the system at

APPLICATION CASE 19.2

(continued)

headquarters can prompt Linda and make plausibility checks, eliminating many of the errors associated with the manual process. It can also check if she is giving the right discounts to the right customer, and immediately trigger the invoicing process or print out a receipt on the spot.

Customer Service Support Scenario

Michael works for Euroblast Inc. (a fictitious company name) as a service engineer. It's his job to provide time-critical maintenance and support for the company's customers' electromechanical control systems. To do so, he needs to know immediately when a customers' system is faltering, what is malfunctioning, and what type of service contract is in effect for billing purposes.

Using Mobile Service, Michael does not need to carry all of this information in his head, but instead has it in the palm of his hand. With only a few taps of the stylus, Michael accesses the *mySAP.com* Mobile Workplace for all the data he requires, including the name and address of the next customer he should visit, equipment specifications, parts inventory data, and so forth.

Once he has completed the job, he can report back on the time and materials he used, and this data can be employed for timely billing and service quality analysis. In addition, his company is able to keep track of his progress and monitor any escalations. As a result, both Michael and his supervisors are better informed and better able to serve the customer.

Source: Compiled from *CRM* and the *mySAP.com: Mobile Workplace*, SAP AG Corp., 2000 (a publicly available brochure).

Non-Internet Applications

Wireless applications in the non-Internet enterprise environment have been around since the early 1990s. Examples of such services are:

- Wireless networking is used for inventory picking in warehouses with PCs mounted on forklifts, other vehicles, or carried by employees.
- Delivery and order status updates on PCs inside distribution trucks.
- Online dispatching, online diagnosis support from remote locations, and parts ordering/inventory queries from service people in the field.
- Mobile shop-floor quality control systems. These include voice reports by inspectors, data collection from facilities, and its transmission to a central processor.
- Salespeople connect their PCs to the corporate networks, reporting sales, competitors' inventories in stores, orders from customers' sites, and charging customers' credit cards.
- Remote database queries regarding order status or product availability.

The variety of possible wireless applications is shown in Figure 19-9. Some of these are amenable to Web technologies. For details see *mdsi-advantex.com*.

The advantages of intrabusiness wireless can be seen in the example of workflow applications, as summarized in Table 19-2. Some of these are done on the Web.

Figure 19-9	Automated Workflow Applications

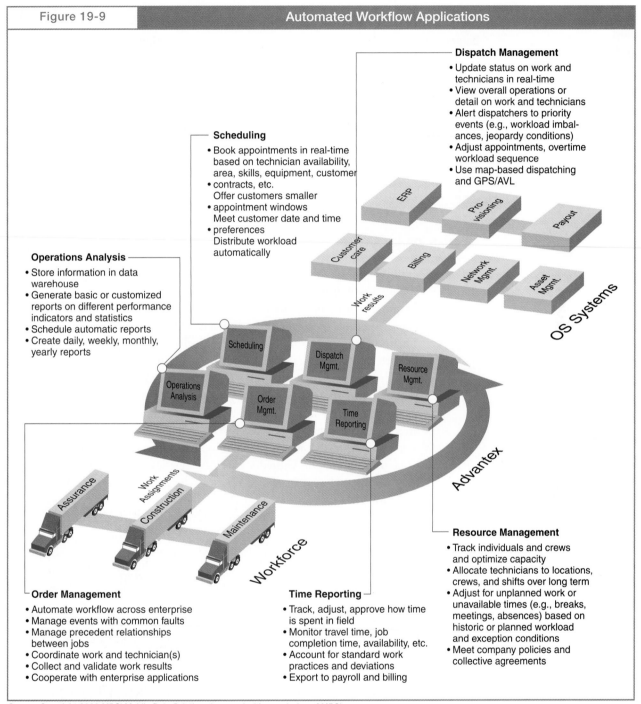

Dispatch Management
- Update status on work and technicians in real-time
- View overall operations or detail on work and technicians
- Alert dispatchers to priority events (e.g., workload imbalances, jeopardy conditions)
- Adjust appointments, overtime workload sequence
- Use map-based dispatching and GPS/AVL

Scheduling
- Book appointments in real-time based on technician availability, area, skills, equipment, customer
- contracts, etc. Offer customers smaller
- appointment windows Meet customer date and time
- preferences Distribute workload automatically

Operations Analysis
- Store information in data warehouse
- Generate basic or customized reports on different performance indicators and statistics
- Schedule automatic reports
- Create daily, weekly, monthly, yearly reports

Order Management
- Automate workflow across enterprise
- Manage events with common faults
- Manage precedent relationships between jobs
- Coordinate work and technician(s)
- Collect and validate work results
- Cooperate with enterprise applications

Time Reporting
- Track, adjust, approve how time is spent in field
- Monitor travel time, job completion time, availability, etc.
- Account for standard work practices and deviations
- Export to payroll and billing

Resource Management
- Track individuals and crews and optimize capacity
- Allocate technicians to locations, crews, and shifts over long term
- Adjust for unplanned work or unavailable times (e.g., breaks, meetings, absences) based on historic or planned workload and exception conditions
- Meet company policies and collective agreements

Intrabusiness Workflow

TABLE 19-2

Before	After
Work orders are manually assigned by multiple supervisors and dispatchers.	Work orders are automatically assigned and routed for maximum efficiency in minutes.
Field service technicians commute to dispatch center to pick up paper work orders.	Home-based field service technicians receive first work order via mobile terminal and proceed directly to first assignment.
Manual record keeping of time, work completed and billing information.	Automated productivity tracking, record keeping, and billing updates.
Field service technicians call in for new assignments and often wait because of radio traffic or unavailable dispatcher.	Electronic transmittal of additional work orders with no waiting time.
Complete work orders dropped off at dispatch center at the end of the day for manual entry into the billing or tracking system. Uncompleted orders are manually distributed to available technicians. Overtime charges often result.	Technicians close completed work orders from the mobile terminals as they are completed. At the end of the shift, the technicians sign off and go home.

Sources: From publicly distributed information of Smith Advanced Technology, Inc.

Web-Based Applications (Intrabusiness M-Commerce)

A large number of wireless applications have been implemented inside enterprises. Here are some examples.

- Employees at companies such as Sonera (Finland) must get their monthly pay slips either by regular e-mail or via SMS sent to their mobile phone. The money itself is transferred electronically to a designated bank account. In both cases, it is much cheaper for Sonera and it results in less paperwork.
- At Chicago's United Center—home of the NBA's Bulls and NHL's Blackhawks—manual inventory systems were replaced with procedures that take advantage of mobile computing. In November 1999, the concessionaire, Bismarck Enterprises, deployed 25 handheld devices from Symbol Technologies Inc. that run the Palm operating system and custom applications throughout the United Center. Bismarck employees now can inventory a full warehouse in about 3 hours. The company used to hand-count everything once a month, and it would take between 48 and 72 hours to do inventory. Now the employees can do reconciliation right on the spot. The system saves the company about $100,000 a year in labor.
- Businesses such as FedEx and UPS have been employing handheld wireless devices for several years, but the units were usually connected to a private network and generally were designed to serve one vertical industry and transfer a specific type of data, say, the location of a package on the road. New wireless devices that access the Web using cellular or other wireless networks give employees access to the Web, e-mail, databases, and intranets or extranets (see Redmann, March 2000 for details).
- Bertelsmann AG of Germany gives junior-level executives wireless access to a company portal, JuniorNet, from almost anywhere. When a manager is about to give a presentation and he or she wants to pull up a profile on one of the company's employees or any other information, she can contact JuniorNet with a cell phone and get the information instantly. Bertelsmann's wireless feature integrates WAP with mobile phones and other wireless appliances so that users can access company intranets from Internet-enabled mobile phones and Palm VIIs.
- Kemper Insurance Company, which is based in Kentucky, has piloted an application that lets property adjusters report from the scene of an accident.

Kemper attached a wireless digital imaging system to a camera that lets property adjusters take pictures in the field and transmit them to a processing center. The cameras are linked to Motorola's StarTac data-enabled cellular, which sends the information to database. There is a strong business case for this application, especially the elimination of delays and film processing that exist with conventional methods.

- The U.S. Internal Revenue Service ("the taxman") is equipping 15,000 of its mobile employees with mobile devices that can connect them to the agency's secured intranet. This way audits can be conducted anywhere, anytime.

JOB DISPATCH

Mobile devices are increasingly becoming an integral part of groupware and work-flow applications. For example, non-voice mobile services can be used to assign new jobs to a mobile employee, together with detailed information about the task. If the employee is a service technician, he or she can be notified about the customer's problem and provide quick service.

The target application areas for mobile delivery and dispatch services are:

- Transportation (delivery of food, oil, newspapers, cargo, courier services, towing trucks)
- Taxis in Korea and Singapore
- Utilities (gas, electricity, phone, water)
- Field service (computer, office equipment, handymen)
- Health care (visiting nurses, doctors, social services)
- Security (patrols, alarm installation)

A dispatching solution allows improved response with reduced resources, real-time work order tracking, increased dispatcher efficiency, and reduction in administrative work. An interesting solution is delivered by *eDispatch.com*. With a Web-based dispatching solution using smartphones, it is possible to save about 30 percent of communication costs and workforce efficiency can increase by about 25 percent.

MOBILE SALES FORCE AUTOMATION

The current sales force automation (SFA) tools (e.g., those from *Microsoft.com/mobile*) integrate software that is aimed for m-commerce applications. The sales force on the road is equipped with smartphones in order to have easy access to customer data at the central office. Key data that can be retrieved include contact management information, order entry, product and spare part availability, and deal tracking. Using SFA tools, a traveling salesperson is able to check the latest status of a customer just before the salesperson is going to a customer's office, and she is able to report a successful contract immediately after signing it. Sales forecasting and opportunity tracking could be done as well. For how SFA is done on wireless see *salesnet.com* and *iconverse.com*

INTELLIGENT OFFICES

Wireless LANs are introduced in many offices where all communications services are being integrated, as shown in Figure 19-10. This arrangement improves productivity and quality of office operations.

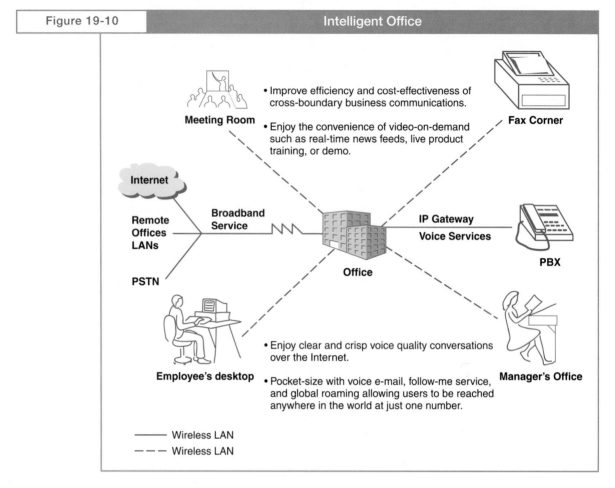

Figure 19-10   **Intelligent Office**

- Improve efficiency and cost-effectiveness of cross-boundary business communications.
- Enjoy the convenience of video-on-demand such as real-time news feeds, live product training, or demo.

Meeting Room   Fax Corner

Internet

Remote Offices LANs   Broadband Service   Office   IP Gateway Voice Services   PBX

PSTN

Employee's desktop

- Enjoy clear and crisp voice quality conversations over the Internet.
- Pocket-size with voice e-mail, follow-me service, and global roaming allowing users to be reached anywhere in the world at just one number.

Manager's Office

——— Wireless LAN
– – – Wireless LAN

19.9   SUPPORTING B2B AND THE SUPPLY CHAIN

With the increased interest in collaborative commerce comes the opportunity to use wireless communication and to do collaboration along the supply chain. For this, integration is needed.

Mobile Supply Chain Integration

Integration of business processes along the supply chain is a key issue in wireline B2B EC. As these become increasingly time sensitive and participants become more mobile, mobile devices will be integrated into information exchanges as one possible distribution path. The integration of mobile is taking place on the buy-side as well as on the sell-side of Enterprise Resource Planning (ERP).

Unified messaging is at the center of those communications, making the user's choice of information access device and technology less of an issue. Moreover, it is possible to make mobile reservations of goods, order a particular product from the manufacturing department, or provide security access to obtain confidential financial data from a management information system.

By integrating the mobile terminal into the supply chain, it is possible, for example, for a pharmaceuticals sales representative to check from the road or the customer's premises whether a particular item is available in the warehouse.

3Com and Aether Technologies created OpenSky, a service that gives smartphones and communicators mobile access to database applications. OpenSky provides remote wireless access via PDAs to establish secure connections to applications, such as Lotus Notes, Microsoft Exchange, ERP, and CRM.

- **Collaboration.** Collaboration among members of the supply chain can be facilitated by mobile devices. There is no need anymore to call the partner company and ask someone to find certain employees that work with your company. A special organization, Global Commerce Forum (*gmcforum.com*) is an international cross-industry group that facilitates the use of m-commerce for collaboration.
- **Telemetry.** Wireless telemetry, which is described in Section 19.11, can drive supply chain efficiency and productivity through large-scale automation of data capture, improved billing timeliness and accuracy, reduced overhead associated with the manual alternative, and increased customer satisfaction through service responsiveness. For example, vending machines can be kept replenished and in reliable operation by wirelessly polling inventory and service status continually to avert costly machine downtime.

19.10   SUPPORTING CONSUMER AND PERSONAL SERVICES

A large number of applications exist that support consumers and provide personal services. As an example, let's look at a person going to the airport. Table 19-3 lists 12 problem areas that can be solved by mobile devices.

Mobile Games

By the end of 2000, there were virtually no wireless multiplayer games for use over the mobile network on the market. With GSM phones, only very simplistic single-player games were available, such as *Snake* (on Nokia 6110), *Mobiletrivia, Navystrike,* and *Stockmarket* (all on Nokia 7110).

Nokia has also developed a mobile entertainment solution that allows users of a 7110 terminal to play interactive games that are located on a server, such as traditional board and adventure games. More advanced games are available for the Nokia 9290.

Mobile games are being developed for PDAs, such as Handspring's Visor, which is equipped with a slot for an external Flash RAM (Random Access Memory). Nintendo's Game Boy Advance, Sony's PocketStation, or Sega's portable device, which connects with the Dreamcast controller, also plan links to wireless networks by 2002. Nintendo Game Boy users, for example, can exchange game data with other users and send e-mails from the device.

Mobile Music

The availability of portable MP3 players has lead to the development of music devices integrated with mobile phones. Samsung Corp. has already developed an MP3-phone. Music titles are stored locally on the mobile device. Korean consumer electronics company HanGo sells a portable MP3 player that can hold 4.86 GB or up to 81 hours of music. It is now possible to download streaming audio files from radio stations, record companies, and Web sites onto mobile devices. Streaming

TABLE 19-3

Traditional vs. Mobile Support at an Airport

Problem	Traditional	Enabled by the Local Mobile Network
Find a cart for your luggage.	You have to search for a cart and sooner or later you will find one.	Your PDA/cell will inform you where you are and where to find the closest available cart.
Find the right check-in desk.	Review all check-in desks and sooner or later you will find the right check-in desk. You could also find a monitor and hopefully there is one close to where you are.	Your PDA/cell will, as soon as you have entered the departure hall, show you the way to the right check-in desk, and inform you of the estimated check-in time.
Line-up and wait your turn at the check-in desk.	Try to find the quickest line.	Your PDA/cell has already shown you which check-in desk to go to.
Find the way to customs.	Check the signs that will lead you to customs.	Your PDA/cell will inform you of the way to customs.
Find the duty-free products you are looking for.	Review the duty-free stores and find the products you are looking for. Hopefully you'll get a good price.	When getting close to the shopping area, your PDA/cell will inform you where to find the products you already pre-programmed to buy on the way to the airport. You will also be informed about the price and "today's offering" for the product groups you are interested in.
Find a place to eat.	Review the different restaurants and their menus.	You just type in what you want to eat and are informed by the PDA/cell where to find the food. The PDA/cell may also present alternative restaurants, their menu, prices, seat availability, and order time.
Find the closest washroom.	Walk around and try to find signs with directions.	Your PDA/cell will show you the closest washroom.
Find out if there are any delays and when you have to board the aircraft.	Find a monitor, which informs you of any delays, and which gate to go to.	Your PDA/cell will beep and tell you when you have to go to the gate depending on where you are in the airport building.
Find where to get your luggage.	Find a monitor, which informs you of the baggage claim location.	Your PDA/cell will inform you of the baggage claim location to pick up your luggage.
While waiting for the luggage at the baggage claim, you want to use the time to make taxi and hotel reservations.	There are no options. You have to wait until you are in the arrival hall.	The local airport portal provides a number of services. While waiting for your luggage you can, from your PDA/cell, make taxi and hotel reservations and other arrangements.
You are waiting for your luggage, but it never shows up.	You have to find a place to report the missing luggage and make a loss report.	The luggage will be automatically identified when leaving the cargo space and you will be informed that the luggage has arrived and its estimated time to the baggage claim area. If the luggage is missing, you will be informed and a loss report automatically generated.
You have a connecting flight and you want information about where to catch this flight.	Find a monitor, which informs you about connecting flights.	Your PDA/cell will, after you have left the aircraft, directly inform you where to go.

Source: From publicly available brochure of AXIS Communications (*axis.com*)

media enables the real-time playback of audio or video clips as they are being retrieved, without waiting for the entire file to be downloaded.

It could be possible that the user has a set of music licenses stored in his device, which permits users to download more titles. With the arrival of GPRS and new billing mechanisms, it will be possible to pay for titles rather than for a minute of downloading time.

Conventional radio broadcasters have the opportunity to tap into the vast wireless subscriber base, and music vendors can offer instant delivery of songs from their music libraries for online purchase. Location-based services can even be integrated to target subscribers with location-sensitive streaming content such as audio jingles promoting offers at retail outlets in the vicinity or movie trailer previews for films showing at the nearest theater.

Mobile Video

Packet Video Corporation of the United States pioneered real-time streaming video (see *packetvideo.com*) via wireless networks. Up to five frames per second can be delivered over the existing CDMA network. A new standard, MPEG-4, is emerging for video decoding.

Store and replay technology from Replay Networks and TiVo allow customers to download videos overnight or at preset times and play them from their phone-video player whenever they want.

Mobile Electronic Pets

Yazimi, the first WAP electronic pet cat, originated in Hong Kong and has all the features of the Japanese electronic pet or I-Mode. However, although the traditional electronic pet still has a physical body (e.g., the robotic pets), Yazimi is stored in the server and you can raise it from anywhere with your mobile. It is 100 percent electronic!

Users can interact with Yazimi in many different ways. Users can feed Yazimi, play with it, bathe it, give medicine to it, and make it sleep. Every interaction affects the status of Yazimi in some way, including its health, hunger, and cleanliness. The facial expressions of Yazimi change according to its status. If it is healthy and full, it will smile. Otherwise, it will show an unhappy face.

Mobile Betting and Gambling

Mobile betting could become a very interesting application for m-commerce because it is time-critical and may involve a lot of money. In Germany, the first online lotto company, *fluxx.com*, has announced that they intend to offer their service via mobile terminals, and in Hong Kong, betting on horse races via cell phones is popular.

More interesting perhaps are the opportunities that will emerge for spread betting, for instance the odds on how many corners David Beckham might take in a particular soccer match of United (UK), or how many he might take in the last 15 minutes of the match, or if the match has already begun, how many he might make in the next 5 minutes. The type of bets offered over the network would correspond to the profile submitted by the mobile betting service provider.

Auctions

As indicated in Chapter 9, eBay offers wireless services, and car dealers in the United Kingdom can bid on used cars from anywhere. Services available include sending SMS to users when the items they want to buy are being auctioned somewhere, or if they are in the middle of a bid, the message tells people when the bidding price reaches a certain level. The bidder can then change the bid or quit.

Tracking Athletes

Real-time tracking of marathon runners has been done with iPAQ PocketPC since 2001. Initially the system worked as a smartphone, but in 2001, a GPS was added.

Hotels

Guests in hotels equipped with Bluetooth-enabled mobile devices are instantly recognized when they enter the hotel. After confirming that the guest is properly registered, the guest can use a password on the device to open his (her) room's door, so safety is increased. The system can also be used for checkout, buying from the hotel's vending machines, any other hotel shopping, and paying the bill and getting loyalty points (see *tesalocks.com*). For a list of other m-commerce hotel services see Table 19-4.

Intelligent Homes and Appliances

Intelligent homes include many appliances and devices and they can reside on a wireless LAN. This way you do not need all the cables and the wires, and your home security devices cannot be tampered with. An intelligent home is shown in Figure 19-11.

Intelligent home appliances will popularize Internet services, particularly in countries where PC prices and complexity have been a barrier to the widespread of Internet use.

Of special interest are kitchen appliances. These appliances can be controlled from cell phones. Smart appliances are coming from Sharp and Sunbeam. These appliances can "talk" to each other, coordinate tasks, and deliver convenience and safety. For details see *electronichouse.com* and Norman (1998).

TABLE 19-4 **Traditional vs. Mobile Support at a Hotel**

Problem	Traditional	Enabled by the Local Mobile Network
Arrive at the hotel for a check-in.	Line up at the check-in desk and sign in, hand over your credit card and receive the room key.	You send your personal information, preferences, and credit card details to the hotel system via your PDA/cell. The hotel system sends back the designated room number and the PIN-code to the room door.
Arriving at the room, you want to know what restaurants and facilities exist at the hotel.	Look in the hotel binder, call the reception, or find the info on the hotel TV broadcast.	Hotel information, e.g., what facilities are available and different restaurants with menus, are automatically transferred to your PDA/cell upon arrival.
Review and order food from the room service.	Look in the hotel binder and call the room service telephone number to order.	The room service menu is downloaded to your PDA/cell and you may directly order the food of your choice. Next day's breakfast selection can also be ordered at the same time.
Access the Internet and the corporate Internet with a high-speed connection from hotel room, lobby and conference facilities.	Find the analog telephone plug, connect your laptop through a wire and make a remote dial-up. At some hotels, a specific device is required to be connected to the telephone.	As you enter the room, you will have instant broadband access available on your laptop and your PDA/cell will automatically synchronize the latest information, latest news headlines and your private e-mail and calendar information.
Make work-related telephone calls and call home from abroad.	Make the call on the available hotel phones and pay the local premium rates or use your mobile phone.	Specific discount telephony rates are offered by the hotel through VoIP over your mobile phone with Bluetooth wireless technology.
You need to book a rental car the next day.	Ask the concierge or call the rental car companies directly.	Information is available on your PDA/cell. You may book a car directly with a simple click and send over the required personal information at the same time.
Order transportation to the office or to the airport.	Ask the concierge or reception to book taxi or bus transportation.	A selection of transportation means is presented on your PDA/cell. You may book and pay your preference directly with your hand phone or PDA/cell.

Source: From publicly available brochure of AXIS Communications (*axis.com*)

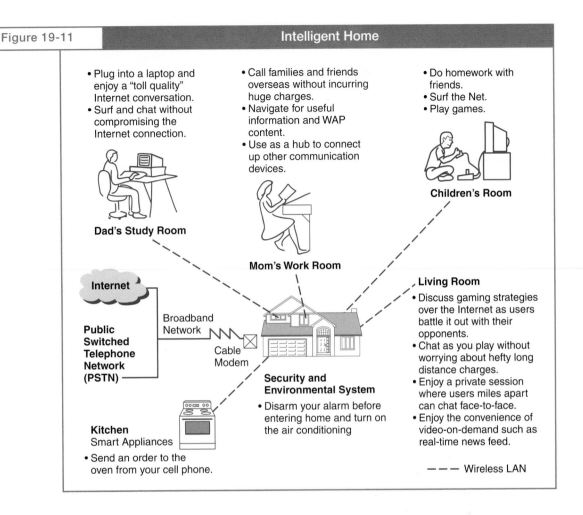

Figure 19-11 — Intelligent Home

Dad's Study Room
- Plug into a laptop and enjoy a "toll quality" Internet conversation.
- Surf and chat without compromising the Internet connection.

Mom's Work Room
- Call families and friends overseas without incurring huge charges.
- Navigate for useful information and WAP content.
- Use as a hub to connect up other communication devices.

Children's Room
- Do homework with friends.
- Surf the Net.
- Play games.

Internet

Public Switched Telephone Network (PSTN)

Broadband Network

Cable Modem

Kitchen
Smart Appliances
- Send an order to the oven from your cell phone.

Security and Environmental System
- Disarm your alarm before entering home and turn on the air conditioning

Living Room
- Discuss gaming strategies over the Internet as users battle it out with their opponents.
- Chat as you play without worrying about hefty long distance charges.
- Enjoy a private session where users miles apart can chat face-to-face.
- Enjoy the convenience of video-on-demand such as real-time news feed.

– – – Wireless LAN

Wireless Telemedicine

Wireless telemedicine refers to the use of mobile telecommunications infrastructures and multimedia technologies to provide medical information and deliver health care services remotely. It facilitates the continuous monitoring of a patient's vital signs and condition by a hospital physician (see *micromed.com.au*). This would allow, for example, a medical situation to be managed by a physician when a patient is attended to by a paramedic en route to a hospital in an ambulance fitted with a wireless transmission system. Research experiments have demonstrated the feasibility of simple implementations over 2G infrastructure.

Teleconsultations have traditionally been conducted between doctors and patients in distant, rural areas over ISDN networks. With the impending introduction of broadband 3G mobile systems, the concept of mobile medical clinics on wheels may become commercially viable, leveraging 3G multimedia capabilities, potentially reducing costs and improving delivery of quality health care in remote regions.

Other Services for Consumers

Many other services exist for consumers. Some are summarized in Table 19-5. For others see *mobileinfo.com* (case studies).

Consumer-Oriented Services	
General News	**Education** (*continued*)
• What's happening today	• Online library
• Events	• Online language labs
• Weather reports	• Training
• Attractions	• Museums (location, hours)
Specialized News	**Communication Services**
• Sports	Person-to-person services such as:
• Financial (stocks, etc)	• Video telephony
• Currency converter	• Videoconferencing
• TV and radio information	• Voice response and recognition
	• Personal location
Information	
Public information services such as:	**Entertainment**
• Browsing the WWW	• Audio on demand (as an alternative to CDs, tapes, or radio)
• Interactive shopping	• Horoscopes
• Online equivalents of printed media	• Games on demand
• Online translations	• Lotto, bingo results
• Location-based broadcasting services	• Video clips
• Intelligent search and filtering facilities	• Virtual sightseeing
• Directory of services	
	Road Transport Telematics
Travel Information	• Special services
• Public transportation	• Telemedicine
• Parking	• Security monitoring services
• Hotels	• Instant help line expertise on tap
• Taxi	• Personal administration
Education	**Community Services**
• Virtual school	• Emergency services
• Online science labs	• Government procedures

TABLE 19-5

19.11 LOCATION-BASED COMMERCE (L-COMMERCE)

Location-based commerce (L-commerce) refers to localization of products and services as defined in Section 19.2. It means that the applications are specific to a user's location. L-commerce provides for additional services that EC cannot provide, and therefore has been touted as the "next big thing." However, by 2001, there were only a few commercial applications. On the other hand, in the United States, Emergency 911 is moving rapidly to wireless technology, as will be described later. Two main factors are holding back l-commerce, the accuracy of the location technology and the bandwidth of GSM networks. Let's first examine l-commerce technologies.

Global positioning systems. A global positioning system (GPS) is a wireless system that uses satellites to enable users to determine their position anywhere on the earth. GPS equipment has been used extensively for navigation by commercial airlines and ships and for locating trucks. GPS is supported by 24 U.S. government satellites that are shared worldwide. Each satellite orbits the earth once every 12 hours on a precise path at an altitude of 10,900 miles. At any point in time, the exact position of each satellite is known, because the satellite broadcasts its position and a time signal from its onboard atomic clock, accurate to one-billionth of a second. Receivers also have accurate clocks that are synchronized with those of the satellites. Knowing the speed of signals (186,272 miles per second), it is possible to find the location of any receiving station (latitude and longitude) within an accuracy of 50 feet by triangulation, using the distance of the three satellites for the computation. GPS software computes the latitude and longitude and can convert it to an electronic map. For an online tutorial on GPS see *trimble.com/gps*.

Geographical information systems (GIS) and GPS. The location provided by GPS is in terms of latitudes and longitudes. Therefore, it is necessary in many cases to relate it to a certain place or address. This is done by inserting the latitudes and longitudes on electronic maps (see Steede-Terry, 2000 for how this is done). Companies such as *mapinfo.com* provide the GIS core spatial technology, maps, and other data content to power location-based GIS/GPS services, as shown in Figure 19-12.

An interesting application is now available from several car manufacturers (e.g., Toyota) and car rental companies (e.g., Avis). Some cars have a navigation system that indicates how far away the driver is from gas stations, and so on.

GPS handsets. GPS handsets can be stand-alone units for applications such as tracking buses (NextBus case), tracking trucks on the roads, or finding your location in outdoor activities. They can also be plugged into a mobile device or completely embedded in it. The cost of GPS is declining to the $50 level. The manner in which the GPS device is connected to an l-commerce system is shown in Figure 19-13.

GPS provides a location that is accurate up to 15 meters. Less accurate technologies can be used instead to find an approximate location (within about 500 meters).

E-911 Emergency Cell Phone Calls

The U.S. Federal Communication Commission's e-911 directive effective October 1, 2001, seeks to improve the reliability of wireless 911 services. Among its requirements is that U.S wireless carriers must provide a feature that allows carriers to identify the telephone number and location of a cell phone caller to 911 within 100 meters at least 67 percent of the time. (More than 50 million emergency calls were received on cell phones in the United States in 2000.) The FCC also requires that emergency calls be forwarded immediately by carriers to the appropriate public safety department. It is expected that many other countries will follow the example of the United States.

In the future, cars will have a device called automatic crash notification (ACN), which will automatically notify the police of an accident involving an ACN-equipped car and its location.

Telematics

Telematics (or **telemetry**) refers to the integration of wireless communications, vehicle monitoring systems, and vehicle location devices. MobileAria (*mobilearia.com*) is a proposed standards-based telematics platform designed to bring multimedia services and m-commerce to automobiles. A cellular phone, a hand-held computer like a PDA, and other appropriate hardware are integrated to provide personal information management, mobile Internet services, and entertainment right on the vehicle dashboard. Sophisticated text-to-speech and voice recognition capabilities

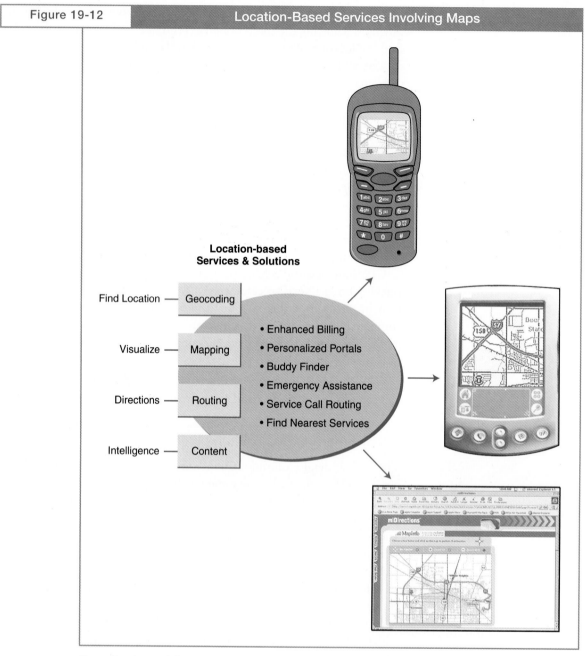

Figure 19-12   Location-Based Services Involving Maps

Source: Based on *mapinfo.com*

minimize driver distraction during use. For example, a user can compose and send e-mail by dictation and have news read aloud to them.

Telemetry offers diverse applications for cars, for example, as a remote vehicle diagnostics tool. Field trials have been conducted by DaimlerChrysler and Volvo to install GSM chip sets in cars to monitor performance and to provide an early warning system, which sends a message to the manufacturer indicating what problem is occurring (e.g., high temperature in the engine, brake problems, or "out of oil" alarm). The manufacturer's system is able to analyze the various data and pro-

Figure 19-13	GPS System

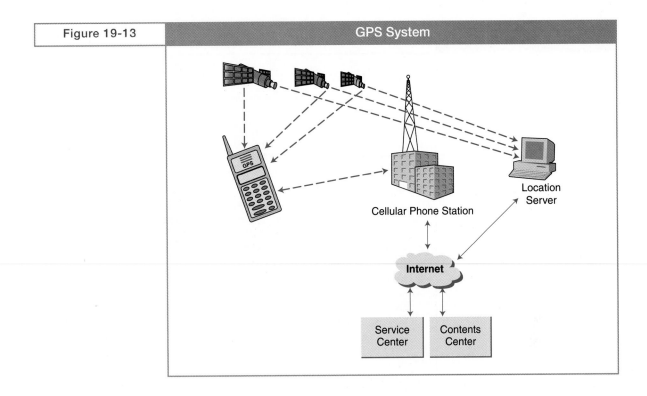

vide a fix (via a software tool) to be sent to the car or by asking the vehicle owner to go to a service station. Thus, developing faults can be found early and the continuous operation of the car can be ensured.

Nokia has set up a business unit focusing solely on telematics, called Smart Traffic Products. They believe that every vehicle will be equipped with at least one IP address in the year 2010. The following applications are included within telematics: self-diagnostic service checks for trucks and cars before breakdowns occur, breakdown service when the vehicle has an immediate fault, emergency calls when the car breaks down in a deserted area and, of course, positioning information about the exact location of the car. Similar services are already offered via a satellite network for high-end Chrysler customers in the United States.

19.12   NON-INTERNET APPLICATIONS

Non-Internet EC applications, mainly those using smart cards, have existed since the early 1990s. Active use of the cards is reported in transportation where millions of contactless (proximity) cards are used to pay bus and subway fares and road tolls. Amplified remote-sensing cards that have an RF of up to 30 meters are used in several countries for toll collection (see Application Case 19.3).

19.13   LIMITATIONS OF M-COMMERCE

Several limitations slow down the spread of m-commerce. The major ones are covered in the following discussion.

The Highway 91 Project

Route 91 is a major eight-lane, east-west highway east of Los Angeles. Traffic is especially heavy during rush hours. California Private Transportation Company (CPT) built six express toll lanes along a 10-mile stretch in the median of the existing Highway 91. The express lane system has only one entrance and one exit, and it is totally operated with EC technologies. Here is how the system works:

Step 1: Only prepaid subscribers can drive the road. They receive an automatic vehicle identification (AVI) device that is placed on the rearview mirror of the car. The device, about the size of a thick credit card, includes a microchip, an antenna, and a battery.

Step 2: A large sign over the tollway tells drivers the current fee for cruising the express lanes. In 2000 it varied from $0.50 in slow traffic hours to $3.25 during rush hours.

Step 3: Sensors in the pavement let the tollway computer know that a car has entered; the car does not need to slow or stop.

Step 4: The AVI makes radio contact with a transceiver installed above the lane.

Step 5: The transceiver relays the car's identity through fiber-optic lines to the control center, where a computer deducts the fee from the driver's prepaid account.

Step 6: Surveillance cameras record the license numbers of cars without AVIs. These cars can be stopped by police at the exit or fined by mail.

Step 7: Video cameras along the tollway enable managers to keep tabs on traffic, for example, sending a tow truck to help a stranded car. Also, through knowledge of the traffic volume, pricing decisions can be made. Raising the price ensures the tollway will not be jammed.

Step 8: The system accesses the driver's account and the fare is automatically debited. A monthly statement is sent to the subscriber's home.

The system saves commuters between 40 and 90 minutes each day, so it is in high demand. An interesting extension of the system is the use of the same AVIs for other purposes. For example, they can be used in paid parking lots. And one day you may be recognized when you enter the drive-through lane of McDonalds and a voice asks you, "Mr. Smart, do you want your usual meal today?" Proximity cards that are used in Hong Kong for paying for public transportation are also used to pay for products in vending machines.

The Usability Problem

Mobile visitors to a Web site are typically paying premium rates for connections and are focused on a specific goal (e.g., conducting a stock trade). Therefore, if customers want to find exactly what they are looking for, easily and quickly, they need more than text-only devices with small screens.

Most of the 2001 WAP applications were text-based and had only simple black and white graphics. As for mobile shopping, all the transactions performed are essentially non-catalog-based, i.e., mobile users cannot "browse" an online catalog. This situation is expected to improve with 3G.

There are three dimensions to usability, namely *effectiveness, efficiency,* and *satisfaction.* When mobile Internet visitors successfully come to mobile Internet sites, usability is critical to attract attention and retain user *stickiness.* But the current mobile devices are ineffective, particularly with respect to restricted keyboards and pocket-size screens. In addition, there is a lack of efficient computing resources for downloading large files on smartphones and PDAs due to their limited storage capacity and information access speed.

Lack of Standardized Security Protocol

In 2001, there was no consensus or standardization on the security methodologies that must be incorporated in all mobile-enabled Web sites. In this connection, customer confidence in utilizing their mobile phones or PDAs to make payments, for example, is low and needs to be raised.

Insufficient Bandwidth

A shortage of bandwidth, that will exist until the global introduction of 3G, limits the extent to which mobility can be viewed as a commodity.

For 3G technology to perform up to expectations, the availability of chipsets is vital (cdg.org, 2001). However, these chipsets were still in development in 2001 and the special terminal for 3G was introduced only in late 2001 for UMTS. This resulted in delays of 3G network operations in some countries.

3G Licenses

3G licenses are auctioned by governments. During the late 1990s, many licenses were sold at very high prices. But starting in 2000, investors were unwilling to support such purchases, and in many countries, 3G licenses were not sold, or only very few, by 2001. This means that certain countries or areas within countries cannot be served by 3G devices.

Transmission Limitations

Depending on the media used, one may experience multipath interference, weather and terrain problems, and distance-limited connections. In addition, reception in tunnels and certain buildings may be poor. For example, GPS may be inaccurate if the device is in a city with tall buildings.

Power Consumption

As bandwidth increases, power consumption increases. In a mobile device, this reduces battery life.

Limitations of the 2001 WAP Applications

In 2001, WAP was still unable to meet the following expectations of the mobile phone industry:

- Connections to WAP sites were too slow.
- It took too long for a WAP site to build a screen. As Internet experience shows, Web sites that take too long to load are abandoned almost instantly by many users.

- High fees for mobile phone users.
- A WAP phone is only able to access sites that are written in WML.

There were only 24,000 WAP-accessible sites worldwide by the end of 2000 (*mobileinfo.com*, 2001) compared to many millions of HTML-written sites.

Wireless and Health Hazards

The issue of cellular RF emissions and the fear that radiation from wireless mobile devices may induce cancer has been debated for several years. So far there is no conclusive evidence that links radiation from wireless devices with cancer. However, there are more traffic accidents when mobile telephones are in use, even when people are using hands-free kits. Also, the use of cell phones may interfere with sensitive medical devices, such as pacemakers. Researchers are examining these topics. Results are expected in 2003–2005. However, lawsuits have already been filed against major vendors (see Borland, 2000). In the meantime, the public is advised to adopt a more precautionary approach in using mobile phones (e.g., use an earphone device that keeps the phone's antenna away from your head).

Disappointed Users

While many companies worldwide are experimenting with m-commerce, the existing limitations disappoint many customers. For example, getting the location of establishments may be inaccurate, and is subject to priorities set by the companies, some of which are based on how much the advertisers pay for ads. Disappointed customers may not come back. Such stories are publicized making users skeptical.

19.14   IMPLEMENTING M-COMMERCE

The limitations of m-commerce described earlier are slowing its spread. However, their impact is expected to lessen with time. Other issues need to be considered in implementing m-commerce. Here are some of them.

Revenue Models

Devising innovative m-commerce applications is one thing, but collecting revenues from them is something else altogether. In theory there are seven places (see Figure 19-14) in which revenue can be generated; these are:

A   Basic (fixed) fee and traffic fees by users
B   Point-of-traffic fees
C   Transaction fees
D   Content and service charges
E   Payment clearing
F   Hosting fees
G   Certification (PKI) fees

Although cell phone customers do not necessarily assume that services are free, like on the wireline Internet, there is a limit to how much they may be willing to pay. Also, collecting fees is not simple, especially micropayments from consumers.

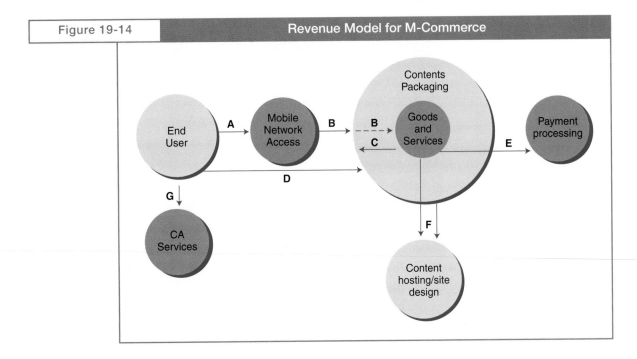

| Figure 19-14 | Revenue Model for M-Commerce |

Consumer Confidence and Trust

As in EC, here too, consumer confidence and trust is a CSF. Consumers love free services and are willing to pay a small amount of money for SMSs and other services like those offered by i-Mode, but they will not spend large amounts of money until they trust the wireless system and its security. Confidence is expected to increase with reliable payment mechanisms. Several companies and research institutions around the globe are conducting research regarding consumer adoption of m-commerce. Until we see the results of these studies and statistics about actual adoption, we will not know how widespread B2C m-commerce is.

TABLE 19-6 — M-Commerce Value Chain

Value Chain Member		Role
Technology Platform Vendors	↓	Delivering operating systems and microbrowsers
Infrastructure and Equipment Vendors	↓	Developing both the network infrastructure equipment and new technologies (WAP, GPRS, UYMTS)
Application Platform Vendors	↓	Providing middleware infrastructure such as WAP gateways; contributing to standards
Application Developers	↓	Applications are developed on Windows CE, PalmOS and Symbian's EPOC32. Applications are for SMS, SIM, WAP, and more.
Content Providers	↓	Internet content providers (e.g., Reuters) prepare content for m-commerce as well. Major issue: how to charge.
Content Aggregators	↓	Repackaging available data for distribution to wireless devices, providing value added. See *digitallook.com* and *Olympic-worldlink.co.uk*
Mobile Portal Providers	↓	Mobile portals are created by aggregating applications and content. Yahoo! mobile and MSN wireless are examples.
Mobile Network Operators	↓	Mobile network operators (Orange, Vodafone, Sprint) can provide m-commerce services. They try to become ISPs.
Mobile Service Providers	↓	Mobile service providers sell services of others to customers under their name. Large telecoms offer such services.
Handset Vendors	↓	Here are the manufacturers of the mobile devices. They are closest to the customers and they create values.
Customers ☺ ☺ ☺	⟵	Mostly, 15–25 youth market or 25–36 business market: sales, service, logistics. They buy and they pay.

M-Commerce Value Chain

The implementation of m-commerce involves many business partners, as shown in Table 19-6. The success of the implementation depends on coordination among all the participants and on sufficient compensation to all. While some implementations involve only some of the members listed; other applications involve most or all. This brings us back to the issue of using ASPs to deliver m-commerce. ASPs can deliver end-to-end solutions. Alternatively, some large vendors such as IBM or Microsoft contract other vendors that complement their services, offering customers comprehensive wireless systems.

19.15   MANAGERIAL ISSUES

The following m-commerce issues are germane to management:

1. **Timing.** Large-scale m-commerce applications are not expected in the near future. Exceptions are some applications in e-banking, e-stock trading, e-gambling, emergency services, and some B2B tasks. This means that companies have time to carefully craft an m-commerce strategy. This will reduce failing initiatives and bankrupted companies.

2. **Which applications first?** Finding and prioritizing applications is a part of e-strategy (see Chapter 16 for methods). While location-based advertisement is logically attractive, its effectiveness may not be known for several years. Therefore, one should be very careful in committing resources to m-commerce. On the other hand, "missing the boat" can be as risky.

3. **Which system to use?** The multiplicity of standards, devices, and supporting hardware and software can confuse a company planning to implement m-commerce. An unbiased consultant can be of great help. Checking the vendors and products carefully and who is using them is also critical. This issue is related to the issue of using an ASP for m-commerce or not.

Summary

In this chapter, you learned about the following EC issues as they relate to the learning objectives:

1. **Characteristics and attributes.** M-commerce is based on mobility and reachability of users. These characteristics provide convenience, instant connectivity, l-commerce, ubiquity enhancement, and personalization.

2. **Drivers of m-commerce.** The major drivers are large numbers of users of mobile devices, especially cell phones; no need for a PC; using a cell phone is becoming a culture in some places; vendors are pushing it; prices are declining; bandwidth is increasing; and EC is growing rapidly. In addition, it is driven by its characteristics and attributes.

3. **Supporting technologies.** M-commerce requires mobile devices (e.g., PDAs, cell phones) and other hardware, different types of software, and wireless networks. Commercial services and applications are still emerging. These

technologies allow users to access the Internet any time, from anywhere. For l-commerce a GPS is needed.

4. **Wireless standards and technologies.** Several standards are being developed by several organizations in different countries, creating some competing systems. It is expected that with time some of these will converge. Transmission media include microwave, satellites, infrared, and radio, and cellular radio.

5. **Finance and marketing applications.** Many EC applications in the service industries (e.g., banking, travel, stocks, etc., see Chapter 10) can be conducted with wireless devices. Also, shopping can be done from mobile devices. Location-based advertisement and advertisement via SMSs on a very large scale is expected.

6. **Intrabusiness applications.** Large numbers of intrabusiness applications, including inventory management, sales force automation, wireless voice, job dispatching, wireless office, and more are evident already inside organizations.

7. **B2B applications.** These emerging applications are done along the supply chain and between business partners.

8. **Consumer targeted applications.** M-commerce is used to provide entertainment, personalized information in emergency services, auctions, and delivery of education and medical services. Many other applications for individual consumers are planned for, especially targeted advertisement.

9. **Non-Internet applications.** Most non-Internet applications involve various types of smart cards. They are used mainly in transportation, security, and shopping from vending machines and gas pumps.

10. **L-commerce.** Location-based commerce, or l-commerce, is emerging in emergency services. In the future, it will be used to target advertisements to an individual based on his or her location. Using the system to calculate arrival time of buses is spreading rapidly. Other innovative applications are expected.

11. **Limitations of m-commerce.** The major limitations are: small screens, limited bandwidth, high cost, lack of (or small) keyboard, transmission interferences, unproven security, and possibility of health hazards. Most limitations are expected to diminish over time.

Key Terms

2G	Mobile commerce
3G	Personal Digital Assistant (PDA)
Automatic crash notification (ACN)	Pervasive computing
Bluetooth	Permission marketing
E-911	Smartphone
Interactive voice response (IVR)	Screenphones (wireless)
Location-based commerce	Telematics
L-commerce	Telemetry
M-business	Voice portal
M-cert	WAP
M-commerce	Wireless
M-wallet	Wireline

Questions for Review

1. Define m-commerce.
2. List the major attributes of m-commerce.
3. Define 3G.
4. List the m-commerce access devices.
5. Define a PDA.
6. Define l-commerce.
7. Describe m-wallet.
8. Describe e-911.
9. Define Bluetooth.
10. Describe localization in m-commerce.
11. Define a smartphone.
12. Describe a voice portal.
13. Describe WAP and its importance.

Questions for Discussion

1. Discuss how m-commerce can solve some of the problems of the digital divide described in Chapter 18. (See the 1999 report "Challenges to the Network" at *itu.int.*)
2. Discuss how m-commerce can expand the reach of EC.
3. Discuss the issue of content aggregation for m-commerce (see *digitallook.com* and *olympic-worldlink.co.uk*).
4. Explain the role of protocols in m-commerce.
5. Discuss the impact of e-911 on m-commerce.
6. Relate smartphones to screenphones.
7. Discuss the relationship of GIS and GPS.
8. List all the advantages of wireless commerce presented in this chapter.
9. Using location-based tools can help you find your car. But, some see location-based tools as an invasion of privacy. Discuss.
10. Discuss how wireless devices can help disabled people.
11. Discuss the relationship of voice to data in wireless systems.
12. Discuss the benefits of telemetry-based systems.
13. Describe m-commerce applications supported by smart cards.
14. Which of the current m-commerce limitations will be minimized within 5 years? Which ones will not?
15. Describe some m-commerce B2B applications along the supply chain.

Internet Exercises

1. Learn about PDAs by visiting vendors' sites such as at Palm, Handspring, HP, IBM, Phillips, NEC, Hitachi, Compaq, Casio, Brother, Texas Instruments, and others. Start with a visit to *4pads.4anything.com.*
2. Access *Progressive.com*, an insurance company, from your cell phone (use the Go to. . . . feature). If you have a Sprint PCS wireless phone, do it via the Finance menu. Then try *pda.progressive.com* from any wireless PDA. If you

have a Palm VII Handheld you can download the Web-clipping application from Progressive. Report on the capabilities.

3. Research the status of 3G and the future 4G by visiting *itu.org* and *wapforum.org*.
4. Explore what AT&T, MCI, and other telecommunications companies are doing in the area of mobile communications.
5. Enter *Nokia.com/corporate/wap/sdk.html* and download (for free) the WAP Developer Toolkit. What can you do with this tool kit?
6. Enter *kyocera-wireless.com*. Take the smart tour and view the demos. What is a smartphone? What are its capabilities? How does it differ from a regular cell phone?
7. Enter *ibm.com/software* and click on the case studies. Read the two wireless-related stories and a story in an industry you are familiar with. Prepare a summary of the systems' capabilities.
8. Building m-commerce systems can be complex. Enter *ibm.com* and find the capabilities of their WebSphere Suite.
9. Enter *alcatel.com*, *siemens.com*, and *nortelnetworks.com* and find all their products and services related to m-commerce.
10. Enter *ericsson.com* and review all the available demos. Also play the stock trading game.
11. Enter *mapinfo.com* and look for their location-based services demos. Try all the demos. Find all of the wireless services. Summarize your findings.
12. Enter *ordersup.com*, *astrology.com*, *vicinity.com*, and similar sites that capitalize on l-commerce. What is common to all of them?
13. Enter *packetvideo.com* and *microsoft.com/mobile/pocketpc* and examine their demos and products.
14. Learn about intelligent home appliances by visiting *x-home.com* and *sunbeam.com*.
15. Enter *mdsi-advantex.com* and review their wireless products for the enterprise. Summarize the advantages of the different products.

Team Assignments and Role Playing

1. Each team should examine a major vendor of mobile devices (Nokia, Kyocera, Motorola, Palm, BlackBerry, etc.). Each team will research the capabilities and prices of the devices and then make a class presentation, the objective of which is to convince the rest of the class why one should buy that company's products.
2. Each team should explore the commercial applications of m-commerce in one of the following areas: financial services, including banking, stocks, and insurance; marketing and advertising; manufacturing; travel and transportation; HRM, public services, and health care. Present a report to the class based on your findings.
3. Each team will investigate a global organization involved in m-commerce, such as *gmcforum.com*, *wapforum.com*, etc. Each team will investigate the membership and the current projects the organization is working on. As a team, present your findings to the class.
4. Each team will investigate a standard setting organization and its procedures and progress for wireless applications. Start with the following: *atis.org*, *etsi.org*, and *tiaonline.org*.

REAL-WORLD CASE: BlueSkyFrog

The Australian Mobile Phone Market

Australia has a mobile phone penetration rate of about 60 percent. There are currently (2001) about 11 million mobile phones in total, but only 15,000 are WAP-enabled. The majority are GSM-compatible, and practically all can send and receive SMS messages except the very early models. The CDMA network is the primary technology used.

Company Background

BlueSkyFrog.com (*blueskyfrog.com*) was founded in Australia in December 1999 with about 100 users, initially to enable SMS interconnectability among the three major mobile phone networks. Users grew to 1,000 within a week by word of mouth, proving the popularity of SMS services even then. By April 2000, the telecommunications networks announced interconnectability of their services and predicted the demise of SMS-based companies such as BlueSkyFrog (BSF). However, BSF membership had grown to almost 50,000 in a few weeks, and the unique SMS functionalities it offered increased the user base to over 1.3 million by April 2001. The rapid growth was, in part, a result of active promotion, viral marketing, and publicity by the local mobile network operators attempting to emulate European SMS success.

BlueSkyFrog also has a corporate division responsible for marketing SMS and other wireless solutions to businesses (*business.blueskyfrog.com*). These include enabling SMS message broadcasting from corporate Internet Web sites or intranets and providing the technology to develop m-commerce applications and mobile Web portals.

Demographics, Facts, and Figures

BlueSkyFrog is among the most popular telecommunications Web portals in Australia and is regularly featured as one of the most visited consumer Web sites in the country as ranked by *top100.comx.au*. About 15 percent of all Australians between the ages of 18 and 25 were BSF members in spring 2001. The phenomenon of higher overall SMS use by youths could stem from their lower technology aversion—the so-called "Nintendo-generation" having grown up playing computer video games and the like. The lower cost of SMS messaging compared to voice calls is yet another draw.

About 75 percent of all BSF members are under 25 years old, making the portal a very attractive advertising channel for retailers targeting the "Generation-Y" market. Since each user is authenticated to his or her mobile telephone number, potential advertisers are assured of an audience made up of unique phone owners and mobile service subscribers. However, 35 percent of users are under age 18, posing an issue with credit card payment administration. The acceptance of the Internet currency beenz as payment has partly overcome this problem, making BSF one of the most popular online destinations for beenz credit redemption.

Mobile Services

As of this writing (April 2001), *BlueSkyFrog.com* provides the following value-added SMS services:

- Mobile information services on news, finance, sports, and entertainment.

- Personalization services, which include composing and downloading phone ring tones, designing and downloading phone display logos and icons.

- Users may schedule information services for automatic delivery of SMS messages.

- Personal assistant and alerts. Short memos, to-do lists, reminders, time sheets.

- Games.

- Web-based e-mail with integrated SMS alerts.

- SMS-to-Web messaging.

- SMS-to-Web chat.

- User response to online surveys is rewarded with bugz. An actual survey conducted for a local mobile network reseller registered 16,000 responses to a questionnaire within an hour of its online posting.

- Targeted marketing channel. Corporations may target specific segments of the BSF user base for direct marketing by sponsoring e-mail or SMS messages to those interested in receiving them. For example, members can subscribe to an assortment of SMS information services, one of which is live surf reporting provided by Coastalwatch Technology (*coastalwatch.com*).

- Sale of bugz to users.

Mobile Commerce and the BlueSkyFrog Consumer Portal

New users are initially given a set number of message credits called "bugz." More credits may be obtained as follows:

- Purchase credits on the Web.

- Earn credits by participating in online surveys and questionnaires.

- Earn credits by visiting sponsored beenz sites and converting credited beenz to bugz.

- Earn credits by direct BSF membership referrals to friends and acquaintances.

The consumer portal also generates revenue from the following sources:

- Web banner advertisements

- Sponsored SMS message transmissions. A sponsor message is appended to BSF originated messages.

The Future for BlueSkyFrog

BlueSkyFrog intends to maintain the popularity of its mobile portal through technological superiority. Its WAP site, *WAPMeBaby.com* (*wapmebaby.com*), hosts a large number of WAP sites for its members. The BSF WAP gateway provides users the facility to go beyond the "garden wall" that some mobile network operators have erected to restrict subscribers from accessing nonaffiliated sites. WAPMeBaby has garnered about a 50 percent market share of all WAP phone owners in Australia. BlueSkyFrog is poised to migrate the majority of its SMS users to WAP once the latter technology becomes more popular with the introduction of faster bandwidth technology such as GPRS.

BlueSkyFrog has patents pending on a filtering tool called FeedMeBaby that allows a user to select text or image content on any Web site and customize it for delivery to their mobile phone via SMS or WAP. Other products in development include SMS Secure and SMS Access. The former enables secure transactions on mobile phones via SMS without any hardware modification. It is a purely software driven solution that verifies message receipt and authenticates the message sender to achieve nonrepudiation in m-commerce transactions. SMS Access is a proprietary technology that enables conventional Web applications by providing online access to BlueSkyFrog's virtual SMS gateway via Microsoft SOAP (Simple Object Access Protocol) and COM (Component Object Model).

Questions for the case

1. Enter *blueskyfrog.com* and review the services provided.

2. Enter *business.blueskyfrog.com* and review the services offered.

3. What is, in your opinion, the CSF of BSF?

4. What are the major threats to BSF?

5. Explain the role of viral marketing in this type of company.

Source: Provided by Clarence Tan, Bond University, Australia.

REFERENCES AND BIBLIOGRAPHY

Adam, J. "Internet Everywhere," *Technology Review* (September/October 2000).

Baltimore Technologies PLC. "Wireless e-Security" Telepathy WST Whitepaper, (*baltimore.com*) (2000).

Barnett, N., et al. "M-Commerce," *The McKinsey Quarterly*, no. 3 (2000).

Barney, D. "Wireless: On the Verge of Greatness," *Network World* (September 18, 2000).

Bergeron, B. *The Wireless Web: How to Develop and Execute a Winning Wireless Strategy*. New York: McGraw-Hill, 2001.

Berry, N. "Get Ready for the Wireless Web," *e-Business Advisor* (September 2000).

Borland, J., "Technology Tussle Underlies Wireless Web," *CNET News.com* (April 19, 2000).

Boyd, J. "The Web Goes Wireless," *Internet Week* (September 11, 2000).

Buckman, R. "Microsoft, Advertisers Target the Wireless Web," *The Wall Street Journal* (July 24, 2000).

cdg.org. "Kyocera Wireless Corp. Provides Prototype cdma2000 1X Handsets to Lucent Technologies for 3G Demonstration at CTIA," *cdg.org/hot_news/index.asp?hnYY=2001&hnMM= 03#032001_ven_n.html*, March 20, 2001.

Champy, J. "Wireless Dreams," *Computerworld* (May 22, 2000).

de-Chernatony, L., et al. "Added Value: Its Nature, Roles, and Sustainability," *European Journal of Marketing* nos. 1 and 2 (2000).

Clearly, S. "Location Services Enter the Mobile-Phone Game," *The Wall Street Journal* (September 11, 2000).

Datamonitor "The Race for M Commerce" (*datamonitor.com/tc/mcommercebrief.asp*) (2000).

Dodd, A. *The Essential Guide to Telecommunication*, 2nd ed. Upper Saddle River, New Jersey: Prentice Hall, 2000.

Durlacher Research. "Mobile Commerce Report," (*durlacher.com*) (2000). (See also Muller-Veerse.)

Durlacher Research. "UMAT Research Report" (*durlacher.com*) (2001).

Gantz, J. "Wireless Protocol Is Coming. Are You Ready?" *Computerworld* (April 17, 2000).

Goldman Sachs. "Wireless Data II: The Data Wave Unplugged" (*goldmansachs.com*) (2000).

Hamblen, M. "Wireless Insecurity," *Computerworld* (September 4, 2000a).

Hamblen, M. "Wireless Meets Web," *Computerworld* (February 28, 2000b).

Hicks, M. "Wireless Intranets: Proceed With Caution," *PC Week* (March 20, 2000).

Intex Management Services, "One billion cellular handsets are to be shipped yearly by 2004," (*gsmbox.co.uk*), February 23, 2001.

Joshi, J. B. D., et al. "Security Models for Web-based Applications," *Communications of the ACM* (February 2001).

Kannan, P. K. "Wireless Commerce: Marketing Issues and Possibilities," Proceedings, 34th HICSS, Hawaii (January 2001).

Lewis, P. "Heading North to the Wireless Future," *The New York Times* (June 1, 2000).

Macklin, B. "The Global Wireless Market— Benchmarking Europe with Japan and the U.S.," (*emarketer.com/analysis/wireless*) (April 17, 2001).

May, P. *Mobile Commerce, Cambridge,* U.K.: Cambridge University Press, 2001.

McVicker, D. "So Where Is the Wireless Web?" *Upside* (April 2000).

Muller-Veerse, F. "Mobile Commerce Report." (*durlacher.com*) (2000).

Neil, S. "Walking the Wireless Web," *PC Week* (March 20, 2000).

Norman, D. A. *The Invisible Computer.* Boston, Massachusetts: MIT Press, 1998.

Phillips, M. "Making Money Out of Thin Air," *BusinessOnline* (November 2000).

Rash, W. "The Future Is Now for Wireless E-Commerce" *Internet Week* (February 14, 2000).

Redman, P. "Mobile E-Commerce Evolves," *e-Business Advisor* (July 1999).

Redman, P. "Access Corporate Data on Your Wireless Phone," *e-Business Advisor* (March 2000).

Redman, P. "Tap WAP for Enterprise Mobile Solutions," *e-Business Advisor* (May 2000).

Smith, M. "M-Commerce: What's Missing," *e-Business Advisor* (February 2001).

Steede-Terry, K. *Integrating GIS and the Global Positioning System.* Redlands, California: Environmental Systems Research Institute, 2000.

Tiller, E. "Make Small Devices a Corporate Asset," *e-Business Advisor* (March 2000).

Varshney, U. "Recent Advances in Wireless Networking," *IEEE Computer* (June 2000).

Varshney, U. and R. Vetter. "A Framework for the Emerging M-Commerce Applications," Proceedings, 34th HICSS, Hawaii (January 2001).

Vetter, R. "The Wireless Web," *Communications of the ACM* (February 2000).

Walters, D. and G. Lancaster. "Implementing Value Strategy Through the Value Chain," *Management Decision*, no. 3 (2000).

Walters, D. and G. Lancaster. "Value and Information—Concepts and Issues for Management," *Management Decision*, no. 8 (2000).

"Wireless Application Protocol—WAP: Future Outlook for WAP" (*www.mobileinfo.com/WAP/future_outlook.htm*) (2001).

Glossary

2G. Second-generation digital wireless devices that feature text-based applications.

3G. Third-generation digital wireless devices, first seen in Japan in 2001, that allow for limited media.

access log file. Text file consisting of entries recording each instance a Web server is accessed. Access log contents adhere to common log file format standards.

acquirer. Financial institution (usually a bank) that establishes a credit card account for a merchant and processes authorized sales slips.

ad server. A Web-based server that delivers banner ads to the requesting Web pages. For companies that sell their own ads, the ad server may be in-house or offsite at an ISP or it may be owned by an Internet advertising company.

ad server networks. Service that inserts ads (usually banner ads) onto Web pages when the pages are accessed by a user. The Web page and the ad may be served (i.e., delivered) by entirely different companies using geographically separated servers.

ad views. The number of times an advertisement is seen by users. Measures exposure of an ad.

advertisement. Dissemination of information to potential buyers to influence a purchase.

advertorial. An ad that appears as an editorial or unbiased article.

advocacy marketing. *See* viral marketing.

affiliate program. Promotion where companies pay a very small commission to other sites for "driving traffic" to their Web site. The target site uses its affiliate program to help acquire customers. The members of the affiliate program earn a commission every time a customer "clicks through" their site to the target site. Oftentimes payment is made only if the customer completes a purchase.

analytical buyers. Consumers who perform substantial research before making a decision to purchase products or services.

application-level proxy firewall. A firewall consisting of a special server called a bastion gateway that runs special programs called proxies that pass repackaged packets from outside a protected network to inside the network.

application servers. Provide integration across services, such as transaction processing.

application service provider (ASP). A service that provides business applications (standard or customized) to users over the Internet for a per-use or monthly fee. It is a form of outsourcing.

architecture. *See* EC architecture.

asset. Anything of value that is worth securing.

associated ad display strategy. *See* text link.

asymmetrical key encryption. *See* public key encryption.

attack. A cyberthreat that has actually occurred.

auction aggregation. Identification of where specific auctions are conducted by sending software agents to auction sites and aggregating their findings.

auction vortals. *See* vertical auctions.

auctions. Model that involves selling (forward auctions) or buying (reverse auctions) goods and services to the highest or lowest bidder. Various auction mechanisms exist.

auditing. The collection of detailed information about any attempt to access a computer network.

authentication. The process by which one entity verifies that another entity is who they claim to be.

authenticity. One of the cornerstones of secure Internet communications, it is the idea that the sender (either client or server) of a message is who they claim to be.

authorization. Process ensuring that the participants in an e-payment transaction are who they claim to be and that each is acting within his or her authority when offering, transferring, or accepting payment.

Automated Clearing House (ACH). A banking network that handles the processing and settlement of checks.

availability. An online site is available if a person or program can gain access to the pages, data, or services provided by the site when they are needed.

avatar. Animated computer character reflecting the chosen identity of an individual.

B2B exchange. *See* exchange.

B2B portals. Portals that support B2B activities.

B2X networks. Business-to-exchange networks that link a company to a variety of online B2B services or to marketplace exchanges (buyers and/or sellers).

back end operations. *See* back office operations.

back office operations. The activities that support the fulfillment of online sales (e.g., accounting, accounts receivable, logistics, databases, and other services).

balanced scorecard. A structured methodology for measuring performance in organizations. It translates an organization's objectives into a set of performance indicators in four areas: financial, customer, internal business process, and learning and growth.

bandwidth. The speed at which content can be delivered across a network.

banner. A graphic display on a Web page advertising a service or product. The banner ad is linked to the advertiser's Web page.

banner exchange. A market where companies can trade or exchange placement of banner ads on each other's Web sites.

barter exchange. A marketplace in which companies receive "trade credits" for goods and services they want to sell. They can then use the trade credits to buy what they need.

bartering. Exchange of goods and services.

bastion gateway. A special type of server that connects a private internal network to the outside Internet for networks using a dual-homed gateway firewall.

beenz. A special form of electronic script offered by *Beenz.com* that can be redeemed for products or services.

bill consolidator. An outside company that consolidates small credit card purchases made by the employees of a business into a single invoice that can be paid electronically through EDI or EFT.

Biller Direct. An e-billing system in which merchants send individual bills to a buyers.

biometric controls. Security controls that use unique physical or behavioral characteristics of an individual (e.g., fingerprints, retinal scans).

Bluetooth. A chip technology that allows wireless devices to communicate with each other up to 30 meters apart (both data and voice). It is a global wireless standard.

brand recognition. Consumer knowledge of a product name or organization (e.g., Coca Cola, IBM, *Amazon.com*).

brick-and-mortar organizations. Old-economy-style organizations that perform most of their business off-line in real storefronts.

buffer. A temporary region of a specific size in computer memory that is used by a computer program to hold data or instructions.

buffer overflow. Problem that occurs when the amount of data written by a program to a memory buffer exceeds the amount of space set aside for the buffer.

build-to-order. A manufacturing strategy according to which production is made only once an order is received.

bullwhip effect. Large fluctuations in inventories along the supply chain that result from small fluctuations in demand for finished products.

bundle trading. Trading several related products and/or services together.

business case. Preparation of the economic justification of a project.

business drivers. The factors in the business environment that drive the use of EC.

business model. The method by which a company generates revenue to sustain itself.

business process reengineering (BPR). A methodology for introducing a fundamental change to the way a company does business, for example, a complete corporate restructuring.

business-to-business (B2B) e-commerce. EC model where both the buyers and the sellers are organizations.

business-to-consumer (B2C) e-commerce. EC model where a business sells to individual consumers.

business-to-employees (B2E) e-commerce. EC model where an organization delivers products and/or services to its employees.

business-to-government (B2G) e-commerce. EC model in which governments purchase products from vendors, usually via reverse auctions.

buy-side marketplace. Online venue where one buyer buys from many sellers, frequently through reverse auctions.

call center. An integrated help desk where customers can communicate with customer service staff by telephone, fax, or e-mail.

card association. Association of issuers and acquirers (e.g., Visa and MasterCard) that protect and advertise the card brand, establish and enforce rules for use and acceptance of their bank cards, and provide networks to connect the involved financial institutions.

card issuer. Financial institution (usually a bank) that establishes an account for a credit cardholder and issues credit.

cardholder. Consumer or corporate purchaser who uses a credit card to pay for a purchase.

censorship. Control by the government on what can and cannot be published over the Internet.

certificate. A document that is issued by a trusted third party, usually a certificate authority, to identify the holder.

certificate authority (CA). A third party that issues digital certificates.

certifying authorities. Trusted third-party companies that issue digital certificates. Individuals use these certificates to verify their identity and to distribute their public keys.

channel conflict. Conflict between existing distribution channels and the new channel of selling directly to customers. Bypassing traditional distribution partners can strain existing channel relationships.

charge cards. A payment card where the outstanding balance must be paid in full upon receipt of a monthly statement.

chat group. A real-time online forum for discussing issues of public and personal interest.

ciphertext. A plaintext message that has been encrypted so that it is unreadable.

clearinghouse. A network of organizations that perform regional and national check collection activities.

click. Each time a visitor clicks on an advertising banner to access the advertiser's Web site, it is counted as a "click" or "click through."

click-and-mortar organizations. Organizations use both off-line and online sales strategies, rather than going 100 percent online. This is the most common business model.

click-and-mortar strategy. Strategy that combines the benefits of a physical presence ("brick and mortar") with the benefits of an online presence ("click") to maximize the value proposition for the customer. Also known as the "click-and-brick strategy."

click ratio. The ratio between the number of clicks on a banner and the number of times it is seen by viewers.

click through (or ad click). The action of clicking on a banner ad that results in the transfer of the user to the home page (or other page) of the advertiser.

clickstream data. Data collected on user activity on a Web site. (e.g., where they come from, what pages they look at, etc.) These data are captured by various methods, including cookies, and are mined by advertisers.

code of ethics. A set of rules for ethical behavior developed by an organization or professional society.

collaborative e-commerce (c-commerce). (1) Electronic collaboration between buyers and sellers, usually along the supply chain. (2) Activities that take place between partners in an exchange.

collaborative filtering. The process of using customer data to infer what other consumers may enjoy. This is a major personalization method.

Common Electronic Purse Specifications (CEPS). An e-wallet standard.

Common Vulnerability and Exposure Board. A public board of security-related organizations whose aim is to develop a standardized list of computer security vulnerabilities and exposures.

company analysis. An e-strategy step where strengths and weaknesses of a company are investigated.

company-centric B2B electronic commerce. B2B EC conducted on a company's server where there is either one seller and many buyers (sell side), or one buyer and many sellers (sell side).

component-based development. A strategy for developing IT (and EC) applications by assembling and integrating existing components.

components. Self-contained preprogrammed segments of an EC application such as a search engine or order taking, inventory tracking, or e-payment application.

competitive intelligence. Information about competitors and their actions that is useful when analyzing a company's strategic position within an industry.

competitive strategy. Strategy aimed at increasing a company's competitiveness. The strategy can be offensive or defensive.

computer crimes. Crimes performed against computers and crimes performed with the aid of computers.

Computer Emergency Response Team (CERT). Organization at Carnegie-Mellon University that collects and analyzes information on computer attacks and incidents.

Computer Security Institute (CSI). A nonprofit organization that conducts an annual survey (in conjunction with the FBI) of computer attacks against major enterprises.

confidentiality. Ensuring that private or sensitive information is not disclosed to unauthorized individuals, entities, or computer software processes.

consortium trading exchange (CTE). An exchange owned and operated by either a group of very large buyers or a group of very large sellers.

consumer behavior. The process by which consumers make decisions to purchase goods and services.

consumer decision making. Process by which consumers decide what to buy and when and where to buy it.

consumer-to-business (B2C) model. Consumers place a bid for a service or product and suppliers complete to get the job. The bid can be at a certain price, or it can be a competitive bid.

consumer-to-consumer e-commerce (C2C). Online transactions where both the buyer and the seller are individuals.

consumer-to-consumer payments. Electronic payment systems (e.g., PayPal) that enable consumers to carry out financial transactions with other individual consumers.

contactless card. A type of smart card in which data are passed to and from the card through an embedded antenna.

content management. The management of the content of a Web site. Content can be created in-house and/or purchased from a third-party source.

cookie. A small application placed onto an individual's hard drive by a Web server that collects information about a user's activities at a particular site. The information stored will surface when the user's browser crosses a specific server. The cookie is frequently placed without disclosure or the user's consent.

cooperative strategy. A strategic alliance or joint venture between competitors in an industry.

corporate portal. An online gateway for entering a corporate Web site. The portal is usually a home page that provides information and allows for communication, collaboration, and access to company information. Companies may have separate portals for outsiders and for employees.

CPM (cost-per-thousand impressions). The cost of delivering an impression to 1,000 viewers.

credit card gateway. A software component that runs on a server and ties a merchant's e-commerce system to a backend credit card processing system.

critical success factors (CSF). The indispensable business, technology, and human factors necessary to achieve an organization's goal.

cryptography. The use of encryption algorithms and secret keys to ensure the confidentiality and privacy of messages.

customer loyalty. A customer's tendency to stay with a specific vendor or brand.

customer profile. Information about the customer and his or her preferences (e.g., amount of money spent, types of items purchased).

Customer Relationship Management (CRM). The entire process of maximizing the value proposition to the customer through every interaction—online and traditional—the customer has with a company. Effective CRM occurs when a vendor provides extensive and useful online help, product information, and tools to customers regardless of the type of interaction method—Web, telephone, wireless device, or personal contact. CRM promotes one-to-one relationships, participation of customers in related business decisions, and more.

customer service. Activities designed to enhance the level of customer satisfaction before, during, and after a purchase.

customer value. The difference between the benefits a customer receives from an acquired product and service and the effort and cost that the customer has to invest to get the product or service. Also known as the customer value proposition.

customization. Creation of a product or service according to the buyer's specifications. Same as personalization.

cyberbanking (electronic banking). Banking using online resources. May include the ability to use the Internet to pay bills, secure a loan, or transfer funds between accounts.

cybermediation. Electronic mediation of negotiations between buyers and sellers by third-party auction sites or e-marketplaces.

cycle time reduction. Expediting activities to reduce the amount of time needed to complete an entire process.

Data Encryption Standard (DES). The most acceptable standard for encryption in EC payment systems.

data mining. The process of searching for unknown relationships in large amounts of data using various algorithms (e.g., neural computing).

debit cards. A payment card that debits the cost of a purchase directly from the cardholder's checking account.

decryption. The process of restoring encrypted messages.

dedicated server. A server dedicated to one purpose, such as a customer.

defensive strategy. An e-strategy that aims to lower the probability of a successful attack by a competitor.

demilitarized zone (DMZ). Area just outside a bastion gateway server that permits open access to Web servers, mail servers, and so on.

denial-of-service (DOS) attack. An attack on a Web site where a hacker brings the operation of a site to a halt by flooding it with so many requests that all the bandwidth at the site is consumed or by issuing specific requests that consume all of the computing resources of a site.

deterrence-based trust. Trust that is related to the threat of punishment.

digital certificates. A certificate that is issued by a trusted third party to verify that the holder of a public encryption key is who he or she claims to be.

digital divide. The gap within a country or between countries with respect to their citizens' ability to access the Internet.

digital envelope. A sender key is encrypted by a receiver's public key and sent to the recipient. The recipient opens the secret key and uses it to read the message enclosed in the digital envelope. Use of digital envelopes increases the transmission speed of large documents.

digital products (services). Products that are transformed to information that can be expressed digitally. Music, software, movies, and magazines can be digitized and delivered electronically to buyers.

digital signature. A phrase (like John J. Jones) that is encrypted with a sender's private key and attached like a signature to an encrypted message to ensure that the sender is who he or she claims to be. The recipient uses the sender's public key to decrypt the signature.

direct marketing. Marketing without intermediaries between sellers and buyers.

direct materials. Materials used in the production of an item (e.g., steel and aluminum in cars and grapes in wine).

disintermediation. Elimination of intermediaries; removal of the layers of intermediaries between sellers and buyers.

distance learning. Formal education that takes place off campus, usually through online resources.

distributed denial-of-service (DOS) attacks. A denial-of-service attack perpetrated by gaining unauthorized administrative access to a large number of computers distributed throughout the Internet and then using them to send repetitive messages to the site under attack.

divisibility. A feature of an electronic payment system that enables it to support a wide range of purchase prices, especially those for very small amounts.

DNS spoofing. Attack where a hacker modifies a domain name server (DNS) address table or router maps in order to reroute communications in such a way that the recipient is fooled into believing that they have come from a legitimate address.

domain name. The name used to reference a Web page on the Internet (e.g., *abc.com*). The name is divided into segments with the top-level domain on the right, the designation of the specific computer on the left, and the subdomain between the two.

double auction. Auctions with multiple sellers also acting as buyers, such as in the stock market.

dual-homed gateway. A basic type of firewall in which a bastion gateway server is used to connect a private internal network to the outside networks. The gateway has two network cards so that communications reaching one card are not directly relayed to the other. The communications between the networks are controlled by special software programs called proxies.

Dutch auction. An auction of several identical items (e.g., flowers) where prices start high and then are reduced quickly. A buyer stops the price decline and purchases the quantity of the item they want. The winner is the buyer that places the first bid.

dynamic content. Web site content that changes frequently, such as stock prices, news headlines, or commodity prices.

dynamic pricing. Prices that change based on supply and demand relationships at any given time (e.g., pricing in auctions or stock markets).

dynamic trading. Mechanisms that provide for dynamic pricing such as auctions or exchanges that match supply and demand.

E-911. A wireless-based emergency communication system.

eB2B. Electronic B2B. Same as B2B EC.

e-bartering. Online negotiation of the exchange of goods or services among companies. Transactions can take place directly between two partners, but are usually performed via a bartering exchange.

e-billing. The presentment, payment, and posting of bills on the Internet.

e-business. The broadest definition of e-commerce, including intrabusiness, IOS, and c-commerce. Many use the term interchangeably with e-commerce (EC).

e-cash. The electronic equivalent of paper money or coins that enables the secure, anonymous purchase of low-priced items over the Internet.

e-check. The electronic version or representation of a paper check.

e-government. The use of electronic commerce to improve the internal operations of the government as well as its communication and collaboration with citizens and businesses.

e-loyalty. Customer loyalty to e-tailers and brand names in cyberspace.

e-marketplace. An electronic marketspace where buyers and sellers do business online.

e-markets. *See* electronic markets.

e-mercial. A Web page (or part of it) that pops up on the computer screen in order to capture the user's attention for a short period of time. Also known as an interstitial or splash screen.

e-procurement. Electronic acquisition of goods or services.

e-service. (1) Online customer service. (2) Services provided to online business. (3) Service provided online.

e-strategy. Corporate strategy for e-commerce or e-business.

e-tailers. Retailers that sell goods or services through an online storefront..

e-tailing. Online retailing. Can be pure (all sales are online sales) (e.g., *Amazon.com*) or

e-wallet. Software that stores information about the buyer (credit card number, address, etc.) so that the buyer does not have to reenter the information for every online purchase they make.

EC architecture. A conceptual framework for the organization of EC infrastructure.

economics of electronic commerce. *See* Webonomics.

edutainment. The combination of education and entertainment.

electronic auctions. Auctions that are conducted online.

electronic banking (e-banking). Banking done via the Internet or over private lines. Customers perform all banking activities from their home or other location.

electronic books (e-books). Presentation of books in a digital form on a CD-ROM or other storage device. Users read the books from a PC, a handheld device, or a special e-book reader. Many e-books have search engines and other tools.

electronic cash (e-cash). A form of digital money stored on a smart card or a hard drive.

electronic catalog. The online presentation of information about products that traditionally was displayed in paper catalogs. Unlike paper catalogs, online catalogs can include multimedia, such as voice and video clips.

electronic check. *See* e-check.

electronic commerce (EC). Business transactions that take place over telecommunications networks. A process of buying and selling products, services, and information over computer networks.

electronic communities. Internet communities of people who share an interest and gather to exchange information, chat, and collaborate online.

Electronic Data Interchange (EDI). Standard for computer-to-computer direct transfer of business documents (e.g., purchase orders).

electronic exchanges. *See* exchanges.

Electronic Fund Transfer (EFT). Electronic transfer of money from one account to another.

electronic intermediary. An intermediary who fulfills online orders as a wholesaler or retailer.

electronic marketplaces. *See* electronic markets.

electronic markets. An online marketplace where buyers and sellers negotiate, submit bids, agree on orders, and, if appropriate, complete transactions.

electronic purses. *See* e-wallet.

electronic script. A specialized form of electronic money issued by a third party that can be used by consumers to make purchases at participating electronic stores.

electronic shopping cart. A virtual shopping cart that enables consumers to collect items as they browse an online store until they are ready to purchase the items.

electronic shopping mall (e-mall). A set of independent electronic storefronts who share an electronic marketing environment, using the same servers, software, and payment system.

electronic surveillance. The tracking of users' online activities (e.g., monitoring e-mail or Web visits).

electronic (digital) wallet. *See* e-wallet.

empowerment. Sharing of the decision-making process with employees.

encryption. Process of making messages indecipherable for security purposes. Messages can only be read by those who have an authorized decryption key.

encryption algorithm. The mathematical formula used to convert a plaintext message into an unreadable ciphertext message and vice versa.

end-to-end service providers. Full-service companies that provide its customers with all the Internet-related services they may require. Some service providers even manage inventory and process orders (order fulfillment) on their clients' behalf. *See also* B2X and Hypermediation.

English auction. An auction of a single item with escalating bidding prices.

Enterprise Application Integration (EAI). The integration of an existing application with another application.

enterprise portal. *See* corporate portals.

enterprise resource planning (ERP). An integrated process of planning and managing all resources and their use in the entire enterprise. It includes contacts with business partners.

ethics. A branch of philosophy that deals with what is considered to be right or wrong.

exchange. An exchange is a many-to-many e-marketplace. Some say an exchange must exhibit dynamic pricing (e.g., auctions).

exchange-to-exchange (E2E) e-commerce. Transaction and/or flow of information among exchanges. E2E is conducted at *commerceone.com*.

eXtensible Markup Language. *See* XML.

extranet. A network that uses a virtual private network (VPN) to link the intranets of business partners over the Internet.

fare tracking. Monitoring, usually by a software agent, of a price of a service or product and automatic notification of the customer when the price (e.g., that of an airline ticket to a certain destination) reaches a desired level.

filtering process. The process of blocking the viewing of certain Web sites (e.g., those with offensive content).

Financial Services Markup Language (FSML). A special markup language used to create electronic payment documents such as electronic checks, etc.

firewall. A network node consisting of both hardware and software that isolates a private network from public networks. There are two basic types of firewalls: dual-homed gateways and screen-host gateways.

forward auction. Auction where the sellers entertain bids from buyers.

free-fall auction. A Dutch auction in which one item is sold at a time.

front-office operations. The portion of the business process visible to customers, such as advertising, e-catalogues, and order taking.

global e-commerce. Electronic commerce where the buyer is in a different country than the seller. The buyer imports the product (or service) from another country.

government-to-business (G2B) e-commerce. An e-commerce relationship in which the government sells to businesses or provides them with services.

government-to-citizens (G2C) e-commerce. An e-commerce relationship in which the government provides services to citizens electronically (e.g., forms and information, payments, etc.).

government-to-government (G2G) e-commerce. E-commerce activities within government units or between governments.

group purchasing. Aggregation of purchase orders from many buyers so that a volume discount can be obtained.

handset. Cellular phone or other handheld device that allows for wireless communication.

hit. Web speak for any request for data from a Web page or file.

horizontal exchange. *See* horizontal marketplace.

horizontal marketplace. A marketplace that deals with products and/or services that are used in several different industries such as office supplies or MROs (maintenance, repairs, and operations items).

host-based intrusion detection system. An intrusion detection system that is run from a host computer.

host search. TBA

Hypermediation. Extensive use of intermediaries to provide assistance for all processes of managing an e-commerce venture. By using intermediaries a firm can outsource ad serving, customer acquisition (to affiliate sites), content sourcing (syndicators), content delivery maximization, and many other functions to trusted third-party providers.

Hypertext Transport Protocol (HTTP). A lightweight, stateless protocol that Web browsers and Web servers use to communicate with one another.

IC memory card. A smart card with a memory chip that allows the storage of data.

IC microprocessor card. A smart card with a microprocessor chip that enables the storage and execution of software programs.

identification-based trust. Trust based on empathy and shared values.

implementation plan. The strategy for implementing an e-strategy.

impressions. *See* ad views.

impulsive buyer. Consumer who purchases products quickly and without analysis or much thought.

incident response team. A company team that responds to both successful and unsuccessful attacks against an organization's computer networks.

indirect materials. *See* MRO.

industry and competitive analysis. Monitoring, evaluating, and disseminating information from the external and internal corporate environments.

influencer. A person whose advice or views carry some weight in the consumer purchase decision-making process.

infomediary (infomediaries). Service provider(s) that provide information-related services to e-businesses.

For example, an infomediary may collect customers' information, repackage it and sell it.

information brokers. Agents that aggregate consumers' information and negotiate with vendors on behalf of the consumers. An information intermediary.

information privacy. Maintaining the confidentiality of personal and corporate information from parties that would seek to exploit it.

Information Protection Assessment Kit (IPAK). A list of generic computer security controls developed by the Computer Security Institute.

input validation attack. An attack that occurs when a hacker discovers that a Web form does not check the validity of input data and that the invalid data can be used to gain unauthorized control of a network or server.

integrity. One of the cornerstones of secure Internet communications, this refers to the fact that the contents of a message are not modified (intentionally or accidentally) during its transmission.

intellectual property. The right of an individual or organization to receive royalties for copyrighted or patented original work.

intelligent agent. Software agent that includes an intelligent system (such as an expert system) that can be used to perform routine tasks that require intelligence.

interactive advertisement. Any advertisement that requires or allows the viewer/consumer to take some action.

interactive marketing. Marketing that allows the consumer to interact with an online seller (e.g., requesting information, sending e-mail, clicking on a link, answering a questionnaire).

Interactive Voice Response (IVR). A computer voice system that converses with customers by telephone. In most cases, the computer system instructs the customer to provide information or ask a question (by voice of by using the telephone keypad) and the computer provides the appropriate voice response.

intermediary. A third party between sellers and buyers (e.g., retailers or distributors).

Internet. A self-regulated network connecting millions of computer networks around the globe.

Internet 2. *See* next generation Internet.

Internet-based EDI. The EDI that runs on the Internet. *See also* Electronic Data Interchange (EDI).

Internet community. A group of people with similar interests who use a Web site to chat, collaborate, and share information.

Internet ecosystem. The system that provides the economic foundation of EC. It includes e-markets, digital products, infomediaries, support services, buyers and sellers, and electronic infrastructure.

Internet exchanges. *See* exchanges.

Internet incubator. Firms that provide startup assistance, including funding and management services, to new Internet ventures. The incubator also provides management services, business partners, legal assistance, and other synergies to the companies they assist.

Internet mall. *See* electronic shopping mall.

Internet portal. A public portal (such as Yahoo!) that is used as a gateway for finding information, communicating, shopping, collaborating, and more.

Internet Protocol (IP). In order for one computer to send a request or a response to another computer on the Internet, the request or response must be divided into packets that are labeled with the addresses of the sending and receiving computers. The Internet Protocol formats the packets and assigns addresses.

Internet radio. A Web site (e.g., *Live365.com*) that provides music, talk shows, and other entertainment from a variety of radio stations. Can have stored as well as live programs.

Internet service provider (ISP). Companies supplying individuals and businesses with local and regional connections to the Internet for a fee.

Internet telephony. A system that enables people to talk to each other in voice via the Internet. By 2001 the service was free of charge and its quality was improving.

interorganizational information system (IOS). A communications system that allows information flow between two (or more) business partners.

intrabusiness e-commerce. Application of EC methods within an organization, usually on its intranet, with the goal of creating a paperless environment. Activities range from providing internal customer service to selling products to employees.

intranet. A corporate LAN or WAN that functions with Internet technologies behind the company's firewall.

intrusion detection system (IDS). A special category of software located on a network or host system that can monitor activity across a network or on a host computer, watch for suspicious activity, and take automated action based on what it sees.

IP fragmentation. A cyberattack perpetrated by sending communications packets with incorrect header information, causing some computers to hang, crash, or perform slowly.

IPSec (IP Security Protocol). A low-level communication protocol that ensures the security of all TCP/IP traffic between two computers.

IP Security Protocol. A popular tunneling protocol developed by the Internet Engineering Task Force.

Javacard. A computer specification that enables Java applets to run on smart cards and other devices with limited computer memory.

joint application development (JAD). A collaborative methodology for determining information requirements for an IT (EC) application.

just-in-time delivery. Delivery of ordered items at a designated time. This is needed by business buyers who perform just-in-time manufacturing.

keyword banners. Banners that appear on a Web page when a predetermined word is queried from a search engine.

knowledge-based trust. Trust that is grounded in the knowledge of the other trading partner.

knowledge curve. A curve that describes the process of learning over time (the pace of learning).

l-commerce. This is a form of EC that delivers information about product/services based on where the customer is at a specific time.

latency. Time that is wasted in a system (e.g., when one component is waiting for another).

Layer 2 Tunneling Protocol (L2TP). TBA.

learning agent. Software agents with that have a high level of intelligence and are able to learn.

liquidity. Having a sufficient number of paying customers or market participants. The faster a company reaches liquidity, the better.

localization. The process of adapting media products to a local situation, for example, translating to another language. It considers local culture, language, and other factors.

location-based e-commerce (l-commerce). Providing e-commerce to customers based on where they are at any given time.

logistics. Handling of operations. Involves the acquisition of material, labor, and other services to accomplish a mission.

M-cert. A PKI-based standard for mobile security that involves certification.

m-commerce. *See* mobile commerce.

m-wallet. A wireless e-wallet that enables consumers to pay for purchase with a single click.

macro virus. A type of computer virus that propagates within a system when a macro (program) in an application (e.g., spreadsheet, Word document, etc.) is opened or executed.

macro worm. A type of computer worm that is propagated across a network when a macro (program) in an application (e.g., spreadsheet, Word document, etc.) is opened or executed.

Magnetic Ink Character Recognition (MICR). The characters at the bottom of a check that specify the routing number identifying the payor's bank, customer account number, and the payment amount.

maintenance, repairs, and operations (MRO). These are indirect materials, such as light bulbs or office supplies, used by most businesses in relatively small quantities.

malicious code. Also known as malware, this is malicious software used to attack computers and computer networks that falls into one of several categories including viruses, worms, macro viruses, macro worms, and Trojan horses.

malicious mobile code. ActiveX components or Java applets that are used by hackers to perpetrate attacks against desktop computers.

management service provider (MSP). A company that delivers IT infrastructure management services, such as back-office services or order fulfillment, over a network to subscribers. It delivers system management services to clients who usually manage their own technology assets. Some ASPs are also MSPs.

market maker. A company that operates an e-marketplace. It can be a third party if the market is public, or a large company(ies) if the market is private.

market research. Company efforts to locate useful information that describes the relationship between consumers, products, marketing methods, and marketers through experiments, information research, and data processing.

market segmentation. The process of dividing a consumer market into a logical group for market research, advertisement, and sales activities.

marketspace. *See* electronic marketplace.

mass customization. Production of large quantities of customized items.

material resource planning (MRP II). A system, usually computerized, that integrates production planning, inventory management, labor, and financial resources in an enterprise.

maverick buying. These are unplanned purchases of items that are needed quickly. Usually the buyers pay a premium because these purchases are not planned.

maximum bid. The highest price that a bidder is willing to place (delegated to a proxy bidder).

merchant server. Packaged software system designed to help companies establish and run an electronic storefront on a single server (computer). The software usually provides templates for creating an electronic product catalog, setting up electronic shopping carts, handling secure payments, and processing customer orders.

metatag. A metatag is a tag embedded in the code of a Web page that gives a search engine specific information about the Web site, such as keywords or site summaries.

metrics. Quantitative or qualitative measures of performance.

micropayment. An electronic payment of less than $10 that cannot be handled by a credit card. Payments may be as small as $0.10.

Microsoft Windows for Smart Cards. An 8-bit multiapplication operating system for smart cards with 8KB of ROM (read only memory) that is designed to run applications written in Microsoft Visual Basic or C++.

mobile commerce. E-commerce conducted in a wireless environment.

Mondex. A smart card that was developed and administered by Mondex International, a subsidiary of Mastercard.

Multiprotocol networking. Collection of protocols that are used for communications within local area networks (LANs).

Multipurpose Internet Mail Extension (MIME). A header found at the top of all documents returned by a Web server that describes the contents of the document (e.g., a Web page, a multimedia object, or a document produced by an external program).

Multos. Developed by a consortium of companies (MasterCard, Discover Card, American Express, Motorola, KeyCorp, Fujitsu, and others), Multos is a secure, multiapplication operating system supporting the dynamic loading and deletion of applications over the life of a smart card.

"name-your-own-price." Business model where a buyer specifies the price (and other terms) he or she is willing to pay to any willing and able seller.

negotiation online. Electronic negotiation done by software or intelligent agents.

network access point (NAP). An intermediate network exchange point that connects Internet service providers (ISPs) to the Internet backbone.

network-based intrusion detection system (IDS). An intrusion detection system that is run from a network.

network service provider (NSP). A company that maintains and services the Internet's high-speed backbones (e.g., MCI, Sprint, UUNET/MIS, PSINet, and BBN Planet).

next generation Internet. An initiative of the U.S. government supporting the creation of a high-speed network connecting various research facilities across the country.

nonrepudiation. Refers to the fact that the senders of a message cannot deny that they actually sent the message; ability to limit parties from refuting that a legitimate transaction has taken place.

nontechnical attack. In this type of cyberattack, a perpetrator uses chicanery or other forms of persuasion to trick people into revealing sensitive information. Hackers then use that information to perform actions that can be used to compromise the security of a network. Also called social engineering.

offensive strategy. Various direct-attack strategies on competitors such as frontal assault or flanking maneuvers.

one-to-one marketing relationship. Marketing that treats each customer in a unique way to fit the customer's need and other characteristics.

online banking. *See* cyberbanking.

online catalogs. *See* electronic catalogs.

online customer service. Web-based help desks, frequently asked questions (FAQ), and other assistance for customers.

online intermediary. A third party that facilitates trades (or other activities) between business partners. It can be an auction house, exchange, or a broker. The intermediation process is performed online and is usually automated.

online market research. Market research that utilizes the Internet, may include online surveys or feedback forms.

online publishing. Dissemination of newspapers, magazines, and other publishable material on the Internet (or intranets). Also includes the dissemination of material specially prepared for the Web.

online stock trading. Buying and selling stocks online.

optical memory card. A special smart card that can store up to 4 megabytes of data and prohibits the editing or deleting of data once it has been written to the card.

order fulfillment. All the activities needed to deliver a product (or service) to a customer after an order has been taken.

order taking. The act of taking an electronic order from a customer.

organizational buyer. Buyers who purchase products and services for organizations.

organizational transformation. The process of transforming an entire organization to a new mode of operation, such as to the digital economy. It follows a BPR or complete restructuring.

packet. In order for one computer to communicate with another over the Internet, the communications or message must be broken down into smaller units called packets. Each packet contains both data and a header specifying the addressees of the sending and receiving computers.

packet filter. Rules used by a firewall to accept or reject incoming (network communication) packets based on source and destination IP addresses, source and destination port numbers, and packet type. These rules can also be used to reject any packet from the outside that claims to come from an address inside the network.

packet-filtering router firewall. A firewall that uses packet filtering rules to control communications across a network.

pageviews. All files that either have a text file suffix (.txt, .doc) or which are directory files.

partner relationship management (PRM). A strategy that focuses on providing quality service for business partners by facilitating communication and collaboration and addressing problems quickly and effectively while at the same time monitoring service levels provided by the partners.

peer networks. See peer-to-peer e-commerce.

peer-to-peer (P2P) technology. Technology that connects client computers directly with other client computers. It enables sharing and exchanging of information (Napster uses P2P technology).

People-to-People (P2P) e-commerce. E-commerce activities where both the buyer and the seller are individuals. Most common P2P EC activities are auction trading, classified ad sales, and personal services. Basically the same as C2C.

People-to-People (P2P) publishing model. People can swap files that include digital information, such as music. Napster is a prime example.

permission advertisement (marketing). Advertisement and marketing that is done only after customers give their consent to receive it.

personal digital assistant (PDA). A handheld wireless device that contains several different applications (e.g., calendars, e-mail, address books).

personal firewall. Firewalls used to protect desktop computers in homes or small businesses that have "always-on" connections via cable or DSL modems.

Personalization. The preparation of advertisements or information for specific consumers. A one-to-one matching of services and products.

ping of death. An attacker perpetrates this type of attack by sending a large ping command to a computer that is ill-equipped to handle a command of that size.

plaintext. The readable form of a message before it is encrypted.

pointcasting. The delivery of customized information using push technology (in contrast to information broadcast to everyone).

point-to-point tunneling (PTP). This VPN tunneling protocol is an extension of the PTP protocol used by internet service providers (ISPs) to provide dial-up Internet access. It supports client-to-LAN connections instead of LAN-to-LAN connections.

port. Computers are connected to the Internet via ports that have different numbers to represent different services (e.g., Web communications are usually carried out via port 80).

portals. Gateways to the World Wide Web. They can be public (Yahoo!) or private (corporate portals).

price discovery. The ability to find the lowest prices of an item through auctions, bids, and other Internet-based searches.

price discrimination. Charging different buyers different prices for the same product or service.

privacy. The right to be left alone and free of unreasonable personal intrusions.

privacy policies (codes). Organizational policies and rules designed to protect the privacy of employees and customers.

privacy protection. Ensures that the privacy of a consumer, such his or her name, price paid, etc., are kept confidential and not used for purposes other than those agreed to by the parties to the transaction.

private e-marketplace. A marketplace where one seller operates a sell-side e-marketplace or one buyer operates a buy-side e-marketplace.

private exchanges. E-marketplaces which are owned and operated by one or few large companies. Private exchanges can be operated as trading rooms in public exchanges.

private key. A key in PKI that is

procurement management. The management of the acquisition of goods or services.

product brokering. Recommendation of products to people by software agents.

product lifecycle. All activities related to the acquisition of a product, its use, and disposal.

promiscuous mode. An operating mode that enables a computer to monitor all communications on a network regardless of whether the communications were addressed to that computer or not.

protocol. A set of rules that determines how two computers communicate with one another over a network.

protocol tunneling. Technique allowing secure communications across the Internet to an enterprise's internal LAN. With tunneling, the data packets are first encrypted and then encapsulated into IP packets that can be transmitted across the Internet. The IP packets are decrypted by a special host or router at the destination address.

proxy. A special software program that runs on a firewall gateway server, intercepts the communications sent across the Internet, and repackages it so that it can be sent to a secure internal network.

proxy bidding. A system that places bids on behalf of bidders.

psychographic segmentation. Market segmentation based on customers' life styles and preferences.

public e-marketplace. A third-party e-marketplace that is open to all. In contrast, private marketplaces conduct business only with invited partners.

public key. The key that is open to all authorized senders for secure encryption of messages to be sent to the receiver who holds the counterpart private key.

public key encryption. Also known as an asymmetrical key encryption. With this type of encryption, a pair of encryption keys are used—a public key and a private key. The public key is made available to anyone who wants to send an encrypted message to the holder of the private key. The only way to decrypt the message is with the private key.

Public Key Infrastructure (PKI). A security based on public key encryption that is used to secure e-payments. It also enables digital signatures and certificates.

pull (passive) strategy. An advertising strategy on one's Web site only.

purchasing card. A special type of credit card provided by an organization to their employees, usually for unplanned (maverick) purchasing. The purchase card has a preset limit set by the organization.

purchasing channel. The different ways products and services are delivered to consumers (also known as the marketing channel).

pure cybermarketing. A strategy of selling products and services only through the Internet.

push technology. Automatic delivery of information to a viewer who specifies the types of information they wish to receive. Push technology aggregates information from several sources and pushes it to the user. This is in contrast to pull technology where the user actively searches for information (e.g., by using a search engine).

quality uncertainty. Buyer uncertainty about product quality or service that occurs when a buyer makes a purchase from an unknown vendor or buys an unknown brand or product

quantitative risk analysis. An equation used to assign a numerical value to a risk so risks can be prioritized and safeguarded accordingly.

random banners. Banners that appear at random, not as a result of the viewer's action.

reach. The number of people or households that are exposed to an advertisement at least once over a specified period of time.

reintermediation. (1) Redefining the role of traditional intermediaries that provide value-added services that cannot be provided online; (2) Establishing new electronic intermediaries in place of disintermediated traditional intermediaries.

relationship marketing. The overt attempt of trading partners to build a long-term relationship and association for marketing purposes.

request for quote (RFQ). A tendering (bidding) system where a buyer places items to be purchased on a reverse auction for suppliers to bid on.

reserve price auction. An auction where the seller sets the lowest price he or she is will accept for an item.

return on investment (ROI). A ratio of resources required versus benefits generated. It measures the success of an investment.

reverse auction. An e-procurement mechanism in which sellers are invited to bid on the fulfillment of an order to produce a product or provide a service. In this type of auction bids decline and the lowest bidder wins.

reverse logistics. The steps involved in the return of products from customers. The items flow in a reverse direction, from the buyer back to the seller.

reverse syndication. Customers (such as in B2B exchanges) that aggregate information for syndicators.

rich media. Advanced multimedia, including video, audio, 3D technologies, and virtual reality.

Rijndael algorithm. A new encryption algorithm selected by the U.S. government to secure nonsensitive information.

risk management. Assessing and controlling the threats to and vulnerabilities of a computer network.

ROI. *See* return on investment (ROI).

router. Special computers whose primary task is to guide the transmission of data packets across the Internet. Routers have updateable maps of the networks on the Internet that enables the routers to determine the paths for the data packets.

scenario planning. A methodology of dealing with uncertain environment by comparing several potential future scenarios.

screened-host firewall. A firewall in which a packet-filtering router firewall is used to control access to the bastion gateway.

screened-host gateway. A special firewall architecture with a network router that controls access to a bastion gateway server and ensures that all inbound Internet traffic must pass through the bastion gateway.

screened-subnet gateway. A variant of a screened-host gateway in which a bastion gateway offers access to a small segment of the internal network that is known as the demilitarized zone (DMZ).

screenphones. Telephones with a visual screen.

secret key. The key that is used to send a message in a digital envelope.

secure electronic transaction (SET). A set of cryptographic protocols jointly developed by Visa, Mastercard, Netscape, Microsoft, and others that was designed to provide comprehensive, secure Web credit card transactions for both consumers and merchants.

Secure Socket Layer (SSL). A special communication protocol used by Web browsers and servers to encrypt all online communications. This protocol makes secure Web transmissions transparent to end users and provides for privacy and confidentiality.

segmentation. Division of the consumer market into segments by age, location, gender, etc. The market segments can then be targeted for advertisements.

sell-side marketing. An e-marketplace with one seller and many buyers.

sell-side marketplace. A e-marketplace with one seller and many buyers (one-to-many).

Service Level Agreement (SLAs). Contracts between end users and providers of services, that specify what, when, and how work is to be performed.

session key. *See* secret key.

shopbots (agents). Tools used to search the Web for product information, most commonly the vendor that offers the product at the lowest price. Assists the consumer in identifying the best place to purchase a product.

shopping portal (customer portal). A site that has organized links to e-tailers, often with comparisons, reviews, or shopping tools for consumers. Many shopping portals are targeted toward a specific market niche (e.g., investment information, stereo information, etc.).

single key. Also called a symmetric key, the same key is shared by the sender and receiver of a message and used to encrypt and decrypt the message, respectively.

smart card. A plastic payment card with an embedded computer chip that can store data and, in some instances, store and execute computer programs.

smartphone. A cellular phone with Internet access and intelligent capabilities such as searching, faxing, and messaging.

smurf attack. A spoof attack in which a hacker sends a broadcast ping command supposedly from a particular computer to a range of computers on a network. The responses from the pinged computers overwhelm the computer sending the broadcast ping.

sniffer. A program used by hackers to eavesdrop on communications traversing a network.

sniping. Entering a last-minute bid in an effort to win an auction that has a time limit.

social engineering. *See* nontechnical attack.

software agent. *See* intelligent agent.

software piracy. The illegal copying of software without paying for it or getting permission from the owner.

spamming. Sending an unwanted advertisement to users. Analogous to "junk mail."

splash screen. A multimedia effect designed to capture the user's attention for a short time. *See also* e-mercial.

spoofing. Providing false information about one's identity in order to obtain unauthorized access to a network.

spot buying (purchasing). Buying products and services as they are needed. Purchases are usually those that cannot be planned for. With this type of purchasing, buyers and sellers do not have a long-term relationship and frequently do not know each other.

stateful packet inspection firewall. A firewall that looks at the contents of a communication packet (not just the packet header) in order to determine whether the packet should be allowed across the firewall.

stateless. A property of the Web's Hypertext Transport Protocol (HTTP) that refers to the fact that every request made by a Web browser for a particular Web document opens a new connection on a Web server that is immediately closed after the document is returned.

stickiness. Customer loyalty to a Web site demonstrated by customers who shop a site frequently and do not switch to a competitor.

stored-value card. A smart card that stores electronic cash that can be used to purchase items or services.

storefront. The Web site or corporate portal of a single company from which it sells its products or services. *See also* sell-side marketplace.

strategic alliance. A partnership among multiple corporations to achieve strategically significant objectives that are beneficial to all parties.

strategic planning. Set of managerial decisions and actions that determine the long-term performance of an organization.

strategic sourcing. Purchases between parties seeking long-term relationships. Negotiations and long-terms contracts are established.

strategy formulation. Development of long-range plans to effectively manage environmental opportunities and threats in light of corporate strengths and weaknesses.

strategy implementation. The execution of the e-strategy plan.

strategy initiation. The initial phase of e-strategy in which industry and company analysis is done to determine the feasibility and business case for e-commerce applications.

strategy reassessment. Review and monitoring of a strategy after its implementation to evaluate its effectiveness and to decide whether any changes are needed for the future.

supply chain. All the activities related to the acceptance of an order to its fulfillment. The movement of material from the suppliers to the manufacturer, in the factory, and the finished product to the end customer. Also includes flow payments and other types of information.

supply chain management. Management of all the activities along the supply chain; from suppliers to internal logistics within a company to distribution to customers. Includes ordering, monitoring, billing, and so on.

SWOT (strengths, weaknesses, opportunities, and threats). A methodology for strategic position assessment.

syndication. The process of aggregating, integrating, packaging, and delivering digital content and processes to the end user. Sometimes occurs through intermediaries. Syndicators gather digital content from various sources, reformat it, and repackage it according to the buyer's needs. The buyers are often B2C sites that display content to consumers.

SYNFlood. A cyberattack perpetrated by sending multiple ACK messages from a fictitious computer to another computer in such a way that when the computer responds to the fictitious computer, it will eventually run out of resources waiting for a return responses from the fictitious computer.

systematic purchasing. *See* strategic sourcing.

technical attack. Cyberattacks perpetrated solely with computers.

technical standards. Standards (frequently global) that are used in e-commerce technologies (networks, transmission, security).

telematics. An integrated wireless communication system involving various types of motor vehicles.

telematry. *See* telematics.

teleweb. A call center that uses Web channels and portal-like self-service.

tendering systems. Auctions that are conducted by the government with a public call for bidders. Can be used to buy from suppliers (reverse auctions) or to sell surpluses in forward auctions.

text links. An advertisement approach by which a related banner ad appears when a user searches for a term in a search engine (e.g., ad for a book on the subject).

third-party card processor. Third parties that perform some of the duties formerly provided by credit card issuers, acquirers, and card associations, including signing up merchants, selling and servicing card-reading terminals, preprocessing transactions, and sending customer bills.

throughput. The amount of material or information that can pass through a system during a specific time period.

time stamp. An unforgeable digital attestation that a document was in existence at a particular time.

trading community. *See* trading exchange.

trading exchange. An e-marketplace with many sellers and buyers (many-to-many).

Transmission Control Protocol (TCP). A part of the combined TCP/IP protocol, TCP ensures that two computers can communicate with one another in a reliable fashion. Each TCP communication must be acknowledged as received.

Transport Layer Security (TSL). Another name for the Secure Socket Layer (SSL) protocol.

Trojan horse. A program that appears to have a useful function but also contains a hidden function that presents a security risk.

trust. The psychological status of involved partners who are willing to pursue further interactions to achieve a planned goal.

tunneling protocol. A protocol for secured data transmission across the Internet by authenticating and encrypting all IP packets. *See also* protocol tunneling.

ubiquity. Existence everywhere, all the time. Refers to the real-time reach of mobile devices.

Uniform Resource Locator (URL). The addressing scheme used to locate documents on the Web. The complete syntax for a Web address is "access-method://servername[:port]/directory/file". An example of a complete address is "*http://mycompany.com:80/default.htm*." A shortened address relying on default settings might be "*mycompany.com*."

usability. Usefulness of a Web site for a user as measured by a set of metrics.

user profile. The particular requirements, preferences, behavior, and demographics traits of a user.

utilitarian consumer. Consumer who carries out a shopping activity to achieve a goal or complete a task.

value-added networks (VANs). Networks that add communication services to existing common carriers.

value chain. A series of activities a company performs to achieve its goal by adding additional values when each activity proceeds from one stage to the next one.

value-chain partnership. A strong and close alliance in which a company forms a long-term arrangement with a key supplier or distributor for a mutual advantage.

value proposition. The measurable value and return to a company, customers, etc. Value added through technology. The business case of a venture.

venture capital (VC). A source of financial assets (funding) for new ventures (business startups). VC firms often target specific business startups, such as Internet-related companies.

vertical auctions. Auctions for one industry or one commodity (e.g., flowers, cars, or cattle).

vertical exchange. An exchange whose members and activities are in one industry or segment of it (e.g., steel, rubber, or banking).

vertical marketplace. *See* vertical exchange.

viral marketing. Word-of-mouth advertisement in which customers promote a product or service without cost (or minimal cost) to the company. (or minimal cost).

virtual community. *See* Internet community.

virtual corporation. A partnership of two or more companies that create a new organization whose partners are in different locations. The corporation can be temporary or permanent.

virtual credit card. An e-payment system where companies issue 16-bit numbers that can be used in place of credit card numbers to make online purchases at participating merchants.

virtual malls. Electronic shopping malls.

virtual private network (VPN). A network that combines encryption, authentication, and protocol tunneling technologies to provide secure transport of private communications over the public Internet. Most enterprises rely on third-party companies to host their VPNs.

virtual universities. Also known as open universities or universities without walls. Students take classes from home or other off-site location via the Internet.

virus. A piece of code that inserts itself into a host, including the operating systems, in order to propagate itself. It cannot run independently. It requires that its host program be run to activate it. The virus may act maliciously and disrupt the operations of a computer or network.

Visa Cash. A new stored-value smart card issued by VISA designed to handle small purchases or micropayments.

visit. A sequence of requests made by one user to enter a site. Once a visitor stops making requests from a site for a given period of time, called a time-out, the next hit by this visitor is considered a new visit.

voice portal. A device that enables access to the Internet by voice, by making a telephone call.

vortal (vertical portals). A portal in a vertical (one industry) market.

vulnerability. A weakness in a security safeguard.

watermarks. Invisible unobstructive marks embedded in source data that can be traced to discover illegal copying of digital material.

Web content design. The process of planning what to include on a Web site.

Web hosting. The placement and maintenance of a Web site on a server.

Web hosting company. A company that hosts Web sites.

Web team. A group of people recruited from different functional areas to accomplish a Web project.

Webcasting. Internet-based broadcasting of audio and video content. Differs from standard Web content delivery as it provides a constant stream of information. May be presented live or on-demand. Offers the potential for two-way communications between the broadcaster and the listener/viewer.

Webonomics. The Web economy. The economic environment and rules of electronic commerce.

wireless. Electronic transmissions conducted without physical cables.

wireline. Electronic transmissions conducted over physical cables (e.g., copper or fiber optic cables).

workflow systems. Software programs that manage the flow of information in organizations (e.g., route orders to departments or monitor progress).

worm. A program that can run independently and consume the resources of its host from within in order to maintain itself. It can propagate a complete working version of itself onto another machine.

XML (eXtensible Markup Language). An open standard for defining data elements on a Web page and business-to-business documents. It uses a similar tag structure as HTML; however, whereas HTML defines how elements are displayed, XML defines what those elements contain. XML is expected to become the dominant format for B2B including electronic data interchange (*See* EDI) and extranets.

Yankee auctions. Auctions of multiple items where the bids are for a specific quantity and increase over time.

zombie. A computer on which a hacker loads special software in order to conduct a distributed denial-of-service (DOS) attack.

Index

Forward auctions
  B2B, 225–226
  B2C and C2C, 216
  General Motor's implementation of, 216
Fragmented markets, 274–275
Frankel, J., 781
Fraud
  financial, 766
  online credit card, 584
  protection agents, 159
  types of EC, 766
fraud.org, 768, 769
Free-fall (declining price) auctions, 357–358
FreeFlow technology, 337
FreeMarkets.com (*freemarkets.com*), 237, 388–389
Free Samples, 55
Free speech
  CDA (Communications Decency Act) and, 753–754, 755*t*
  censorship issues and, 753
  copyright law vs., 747
  defining freedom of, 753
  Internet as ultimate medium for, 753
  protecting children and, 754–755
Free Trade Zone (FTZ, *freetradezone.com*), 331–332
Frost, S., 494
FSML (Financial Services Markup Language), 614–615
FTC (Federal Trade Commission) consumer alters, 769
FTC (Federal Trade Commission) Web site audit (1998), 742
FTC.gov, 769
FT (Financial Times) Electronic Publishing, 440
Fujitsu targeted advertising, 195
Fuld (*fuld.com*), 686
FXall.com, 412–413

G

G2B (government-to-business), 453–454, 458
G2C (government-to-citizens)
  as EC classification, 14
  major categories of applications of, 452–455
  overview of, 451–452
G2E (government-to-employees), 455
G2G (government-to-government), 455
Gambling
  issues of online, 762–763
  mobile, 857

Gannon, P., 198
GAO (Government Accounting Office) survey (1998), 571
Garden.com, 110, 717
GartnerGroup (*gartnergroup.com*), 30, 483, 848
Gattorma, J., 645
Geeps.com, 846
Gegxs.com, 7, 238, 258, 664
Gehrke, D., 187
geis.com, 66
Gemplus (*gemplus.com*), 602
General Electric (GE), 7, 72, 223, 237–239
General Motors (GM), 20, 71, 216, 306
General Motor's Tradexchange Web site, 473–475, 474*f*
General purpose e-tailers, 98
General Services Administration auction site (*GSAAuction.gov*), 453
GeoCities (*geocities.com*), 740, 787, 789
Gerrod, D., 803
Gerstner, L., 5
GE's TPN (Trading Process Network) Post, 237–239
GetThere.com, 7
Ghosh, S., 697
Giaglis, G. M., 425
Ginsburg, M., 790
GIS (geographical information systems), 861
Global auctions, 380
Global business communities, 340
Global commerce scenario, 701
Global EC market
  access to, 796
  barriers to, 794–797
  breaking down barriers to, 801
  cultural differences and, 800
  different currencies and, 798
  financial issues of, 796
  future of, 812
  language and translation issues of, 797–798
  legal issues of, 795
  localization and, 799–800
  managerial issues of, 815
  overview of, 794
  small businesses and, 799
  strategy regarding, 786
  trading exchanges in, 794, 795
  U.S. policy regarding, 798–799
  See also Markets
Global stock exchanges, 409–410
Global Strategies (*ajpr.com*), 797
Global supply chains, 640–641

GM BuyPower, 709
Gnutella programs, 462, 781–782
Go2online.com, 846
Go.com, 718
Goldman and Sachs, 277
Gomez Advisors (*gomez.com*), 91, 770
Google.com, 338
Gore, A., 798
Gosling, P., 411
GPS (Global System of Mobile Communication), 826, 828, 832, 860–861, 863*f*
GPS handsets, 861
Grading services, 376
Grainer (*Grainger.com*), 130
Grantham, C. E., 792
Greenbaum, T., 148
Greenfield Online, 148–149
Grocery online services, 99–100, 649, 650*f*
GroceryWorks, 650*f*
Gronbach, B., 124
Group filtering, 134
Group purchasing business model, 7, 240–241, 242*f*
groups.google.com/googlegroups, 717
Groups Plus, 148
GSD (interactive government services director), 569
GTW (Global Trading Web), 795
Gurus (*guru.com*), 422
GVU (Graphic, Visualization, and Usability) Center [Georgia Tech University], 123
GVU Survey (1998), 149

H

Hackbarth, G., 682, 702, 705
Hackers
  computer attacks by, 542*f*–544, 550*t*, 554
  reason for attacks by, 544
  See also Computer attacks
Hadir, A., 773
Hagel, J., 789, 792
hamaracd.com, 138
Handfield, R. B., 219, 639, 644, 645
Hand geometry, 771
Harker, P., 707
Harris Interaction, 89
Harvard Business Review, 143
Hasan, H., 122
Hazari, S., 564
Health care services, 422
Health and social welfare applications, 604

Kaplan, S., 266
Kasbah (*Kasbah.com*), 56, 157, 158
Kauffman, R., 426
KCPL (Kansas City Power & Light), 167–168
Keen, P., 132
Keiretsuu (permanent business alliance), 20
Kelly Blue Book (*kbb.com*), 97
Kettinger, W. J., 682, 702, 705
Keys, 587–589*f*
Keystroke synamics, 771
Keyword banners, 181
King, D., 802
King, S., 419
KIST (Korean Institute of Science and Technology), 240
Klakota, R., 696
Klein, S., 353
KM (knowledge management), 807–808
Knowledge dissemination services, 420–422, 424
Knox Box (*theknox.com*), 174
Knox Escrow Service, 462
Koontz, C., 481
Korean government EC policies, 805
Kounadis, T., 445, 448

L

L2PT (layer 2 tunneling protocol), 569
LaMacchia, D., 731
Lambert, C., 701
Lands' End, 95
LAN (local area network), 290, 291, 438–41
Lazar, J., 150
L-commerce (location-based commerce), 860–863
LCs (Letter of Credit), 321–322
Learning agents, 160
Learning-agent technology, 133
Leasing EC technology
  advantages of, 484–485, 489
  outsourcing benefits to leasing companies, 489
  for spot advertisements, 184
  types of vendors for, 485
Lederer, A., 44
Lee, D., 767
Lee, H.K.O., 737
Lee, J. K., 283
Lee, M.K.O., 126, 132, 730
Legacy systems, 503–505
Legal advice, 422
Legal issues
  additional Internet, 760–761
  for B2B consortia, 277–278

categories listed, 733
of computer crimes and abuse, 763–765*t*
consumer and seller protection, 766–774
copyrights examined as, 748–749
electronic contracts, 761–762
ethical vs., 733–734*f*
free speech on the Internet, 747, 753–755
of global EC market, 795
linking Web sites as, 761
managerial issues of, 774
patent protection, 749–750
of protecting privacy, 736–745
recent incidents regarding, 731–732
representative U.S. privacy legislation, 736*t*, 741–742
trademark protection, 750–751
U.S. perspectives on Internet, 756
See also Copyright protection
LensDoc (*lensdoc.com*), 582–583, 582*f*
Levi Strauss, 124
Lewicki, R. J., 131
Lewis, B., 487
LG Securities, 800
Lim, G. G., 283
Lim, S., 410
Linking Web sites, 761
Lipper (*Lipperweb.com*), 409
Liquid Audio Corp., 748
Liquidity
  described, 55
  early, 55, 288
  third-party exchanges to increase, 273
Li, S. T., 316
Litronic (*litronic.com*), 591
Littlewoods Stores, 646
Living.com, 85, 110
Localization process
  global EC market and, 799–800
  internationalization guidelines for, 204
  using Internet radio for, 205
  L-commerce and, 860–863
Lockheed Martin, 698, 712
The Los Angeles Times, 417
lotus.com, 822
Loyalty
  customer, 129–130
  rewards programs and, 609–611
  smart card, 604
Luckman's Anonymous Cookie, 739

M

McCuley, M., 323
McEachern, T., 126
McFarland, F. W., 693

McKeown, P. G., 135
McKiernan, B., 759
The McKinsey Co., 719
McNealy, S., 489
Macro viruses, 560–561
Macro worms, 560–561
McWilliam, G., 792
Maes, P., 154
"Mafiaboy," 540
MailBoxes Etc., 648
Mailing list, 183
Mail/Telephone (E-mail) Order Rule, 768
MainView, 513
malaysia.cnet.com, 680
Malicious codes, 546, 560–561
Malicious mobile code, 562
Management consulting, 421–422
Management. *See* EC management
Managing B2B exchanges, 284–287
Manheim Auctions, 359
Manheim Market Report, 359
Manufacturing
  build-to-order, 72
  EC impact on, 71–72
Many-to-many marketplaces, 220
Market functions, 46, 47*t*
Marketing
  advocacy, 189–190
  B2B services in, 328–329
  EC and, 15
  KCPL (Kansas City Power & Power) real-world case of, 167–168
  management, 90–91, 161–163
  mobile, 843–847
  The New Marketing Cycle of Relationship Building (The GartnerGroup) strategy, 128–129*f*
  one-to-one, 127–129
  P2P application to, 463
  segmentation, 145–147, 146*f*, 171–172
  storefront, 514
  viral, 133, 188–190
  See also E-marketplaces
Marketing channels
  EC business strategy for handling, 707
  e-tailing, 104, 106–107
  managing exchange conflict in, 290
Marketing management, 90–91, 161–163
Market leaders, 687
Market maker
  described, 266
  matching by, 280
  trading information flow and, 267*f*
Market pressures, 18*t*